MMD =
EL = e
t = tim
T = ter
T_p = Tr
S_p = Sh
A = Je
EPS =
$P(x)$ =
p_i = ma
v = dis
Cc = c
Pp = p
k = ex   k-adjusted
   co
h = he
x_i = w
gr = g
ar = a
g = gr
λ = la
b = be
e = ep
m = m

Investments:
Analysis and
Management

Archer and Kerr: *Readings and Cases in Corporate Finance*
Brealey and Myers: *Principles of Corporate Finance*
Doherty: *Corporate Risk Management: A Financial Exposition*
Edmister: *Financial Institutions: Markets and Management*
Francis: *Investments: Analysis and Management*
Francis: *Management of Investments*
Fuller and Farrell: *Modern Investments and Security Analysis*
Garbade: *Securities Markets*
Johnson and Slottje: *Case Studies in Finance Using Microsoft Excel*
Lang: *Strategy for Personal Finance*
Levi: *International Finance: The Markets and Financial Management of Multinational Business*
Maness: *Introduction to Corporate Finance*
Martin, Petty, and Klock: *Personal Financial Management*
Schall and Haley: *Introduction to Financial Management*
Sharpe: *Portfolio Theory and Capital Markets*
Smith: *Case Problems and Readings: A Supplement for Investments and Portfolio Management*
Smith: *The Modern Theory of Corporate Finance*
Stevenson: *Fundamentals of Finance*

Also Available from McGraw-Hill

Schaum's Outline Series in Accounting, Business & Economics

Most outlines include basic theory, definitions, and hundreds of solved problems and supplementary problems with answers. Titles on the current list include:

Accounting I, 3d edition
Accounting II, 3d edition
Advanced Accounting
Advanced Business Law
Advertising
Bookkeeping & Accounting
Introduction to Business
Business Law
Business Mathematics
Introduction to Business Organization &
    Management
Business Statistics, 2d edition
College Business Law
Contemporary Mathematics of Finance
Cost Accounting I, 2d edition
Cost Accounting II, 2d edition
Development Economics
Financial Accounting

Intermediate Accounting I, 2d edition
International Economics, 3d edition
Macroeconomic Theory, 2d edition
Managerial Accounting
Managerial Economics
Managerial Finance
Marketing
Mathematics for Economists
Mathematics of Finance
Microeconomic Theory, 2d edition
Money and Banking
Operations Management
Personal Finance & Consumer
    Economics
Principles of Economics
Quantitative Methods in Management
Statistics and Econometrics
Tax Accounting

Available at your college bookstore. A complete listing of Schaum titles may be obtained by writing to: Schaum Division, McGraw-Hill, Inc., Princeton Road, S-1, Hightstown, NJ 08520.

Investments:
Analysis and
Management

Fifth Edition

Jack Clark Francis

Bernard M. Baruch College
City University of New York

McGraw-Hill, Inc.

New York   St. Louis   San Francisco   Auckland   Bogotá
Caracas   Hamburg   Lisbon   London   Madrid   Mexico
Milan   Montreal   New Delhi   Paris   San Juan
São Paulo   Singapore   Sydney   Tokyo   Toronto

Investments: Analysis and Management

2 3 4 5 6 7 8 9 0 DOC DOC 9 5 4 3 2 1

ISBN 0-07-021814-5

This book was set in Times Roman by General Graphic Services, Inc.
The editors were Ken MacLeod and Ira Roberts;
the designer was Robin Hessel;
the production supervisor was Friederich W. Schulte.
New drawings were done by J&R Services, Inc.
R. R. Donnelley & Sons Company was printer and binder.

Library of Congress Cataloging-in-Publication Data

Francis, Jack Clark.
    Investments: Analysis and management / Jack Clark Francis.—
    5th ed.
        p.   cm.—(McGraw-Hill series in finance)
    Includes bibliographical references.
    ISBN 0-07-021814-5
    1. Investments.   2. Securities.   3. Financial futures.
4. Arbitrage.   I. Title.   II. Series.
HG4521.F685   1991
332.6—dc20   90-33289

About
the Author

Jack Clark Francis was born in Indianapolis, Indiana, received his Bachelors and M.B.A. degrees from Indiana University, and served as a Lieutenant in the U.S. Army where he was a Paratrooper and a Company Commander. He later obtained his Ph.D. from the University of Washington in Seattle. Francis then joined the finance faculty of the Wharton School of Finance, University of Pennsylvania, for four years. He also served as a Federal Reserve Economist for two years. Since leaving his position at the Federal Reserve, Dr. Francis has been a tenured Professor of Economics and Finance at Bernard M. Baruch College in New York City.

Dr. Francis has written several books. This is the fifth edition of *Investments: Analysis and Management*. He co-authored a Canadian edition of *Investments: Analysis and Management* published by McGraw-Hill Ryerson Limited; co-authored three editions of *Portfolio Analysis* published by Prentice-Hall; authored two editions of *Management of Investments* published by McGraw-Hill; and co-edited *Readings in Investments* published by McGraw-Hill. Dr. Francis has also published papers in various scholarly journals, including the *Journal of Finance, Journal of Financial and Quantitative Analysis, Financial Review, Financial Management, Journal of Economics and Business, Journal of Business Research, Quarterly Review of Economics and Business, Journal of Futures Markets, Journal of Monetary Economics, Journal of Portfolio Management,* and the *Review of Business*. In addition to writing articles for these journals, Dr. Francis has served on the editorial boards of several of them.

Dr. Francis has been a consultant for various banks, investment advisers, brokerage houses, manufacturing corporations, federal and international governmental agencies, computer time sharing companies, software firms, publishing companies, and other clients.

To Harry M. Markowitz—

He received his Ph.D. from the University of Chicago in 1954 and, early in his career, he laid the foundation for modern financial theory when he published *Portfolio Selection.*

During the 1950s and 1960s he did research for the Rand Corporation and the General Electric Corporation.

In the early 1960s he designed and helped develop the computer simulation language SIMSCRIPT.

He served as President of the Arbitrage Management Company from 1969– 1972.

During the 1970s and 1980s he worked at the IBM Corporation's T.J. Watson Research Center.

He was recipient of the 1989 John Von Neumann Theory Prize awarded by ORSA/TIMS.

I first became acquainted with Markowitz as a graduate student during the late 1960s when I studied his portfolio theory and SIMSCRIPT.

In the early 1970s I had the privilege of becoming his faculty colleague at the Wharton School.

During the 1980s I had the privilege of being a faculty colleague of his again—at Baruch College.

In 1989 I was a Student in his Measure Theory seminar for doctoral students at Baruch College.

I was again his student in a Stochastic Calculus seminar for doctoral students at Baruch College in 1990.

Over the years I have known him, he has been an outstanding scholar, a fine teacher, and a charming person.

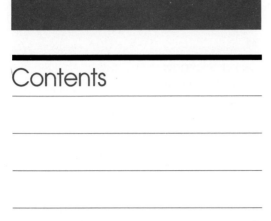

Contents

Preface

Writing five editions of a textbook that attempts to survey all aspects of investments management gives one some perspective. The experience has led me to conclude that the rate of change in the level of sophistication and the number of new products in investments is increasing. As you review the changes I have felt obliged to make in the fifth edition simply to keep the book current, the basis for my conclusion will become clear.

CHANGES IN THIS FIFTH EDITION

This fifth edition has been more substantially changed than any previous revision of *Investments: Analysis and Management*. These changes take several forms. *The most important and far-reaching change is the incorporation of arbitrage concepts into more chapters.* In addition to a whole chapter entitled Arbitrage Pricing Theory (APT), the *law of one price,* which forms the basis for arbitrage, is invoked in discussing bonds, stocks, options, futures, and international investing. The implications of APT are omnipresent.

The October 1987 stock market crash is another topic that pops up throughout the fifth edition. This historic event is a classic example of undiversifiable market risk discussed in the chapters on law, stock valuation, technical analysis, options (used to create portfolio insurance), futures, and international markets.

The global nature of investing also appears in a number of chapters. Figure 1-1 starts the coverage by illustrating the *international* scope of the October 1987 stock market crash. The divergent nature of the stock markets in 23 different countries is summarized in Table 3-9 after being discussed in the chapter about securities markets. Global mutual funds are described in the chapter about investment performance evaluation. In addition, there is an entire chapter entitled "International Investing."

The market development that I find particularly striking is *the large number of new investment products*. Portfolio insurance, exotic new kinds of options that have been embedded into various securities, stock index arbitrage, dedicated pension funds, procedures to alter the convexity of a fixed income portfolio, financial futures, options on futures, numerous synthetic positions that can be created in different ways, asset-backed securities that have different tranches, junk bonds, indexed portfolios—none of these was in existence when the first three editions of this book were written. These new products create complicated and exciting new investing opportunities and new job openings for students of investing. For the authors of investments textbooks, they create added work—and a refreshing sense of excitement.

The fifth edition also delves deeper into option theory than previous editions. An improved presentation of binomial option pricing, the mechanics of creating a protective put in order to establish portfolio insurance, and an explanation of how to value common stock by treating it as a call option on a leveraged company are among the examples of new option theory material.

ORGANIZATIONAL CHANGES

As in previous editions, most parts of the early chapters of the book (Chapters 2 through 7) may be skipped by those who present an advanced, theory-oriented course. I have endeavored to make the different sections and chapters of this book stand independently. This permits instructors to choose and reorder the chapters and thus tailor-make a course. I have substantially reorganized other aspects of this edition as well. Unlike the previous editions, Chapter 1 has been written so that even the most advanced readers should benefit from it. Furthermore, the theoretical backbone of the book is introduced earlier than in previous editions—Chapters 8 through 11 inclusive introduce hedging, arbitrage, portfolio theory, the capital asset pricing model, and APT. This sets the stage for all of the new material that is introduced in the later chapters.

TEACHING AIDS

I have created several kinds of new teaching aids for those who use the fifth edition. Every chapter now has a number of new end-of-chapter essay questions and/or problems. An average of 10 nontrivial numerical problems at the end of each chapter were added to give students practice in solving such problems. The *Instructor's Manual* contains detailed solutions to all of these problems.

In addition, students can find the answers to the numerical problems following Chapter 25 of this book. The *Instructor's Manual* also contains a bank of test questions—at least 10 true-false and 10 to 20 multiple-choice questions for every chapter. Some chapters also contain cases or other teaching aids. Attractive illustrations that can be used to create photocopies to hand out in class or transparencies for an overhead slide projector are also included in the *Instructor's Manual*.

Hand-held calculators have become more powerful and cheaper. As a result, each year more professors tell me they are teaching their investments students how to use these handy devices. In response to the growing demands of these folks, Professor Richard Taylor and I have created end-of-the-book Appendix E, entitled "Investment Analysis with Hand-Held Calculators."

USING COMPUTERS

This book does not call for the use of a computer; it is not tied to computers in any way. But, for those who want to use computers, McGraw-Hill provides an incredible amount of valuable data and software. These computer supplies are available free of charge to adopters of *Investments: Analysis and Management,* 5 ed. This software is easy to use; none of it is copy-protected. It is all menu-driven, so no computer experience is required. An end-of-book appendix describes the different kinds of data and software available.

ACKNOWLEDGMENTS

Many people have assisted me in preparing the fifth edition. All of my colleagues at Baruch College helped in some way or another. But, in particular, Professors Harry Markowitz, Doug McCann, Avner Wolf, Robert Ariel, Jae Won Lee, Giora Harpaz, Damodar Gujarati, Joel Segall, Hanan Eytan, and Joel Rentzler made special contributions that were above and beyond the call of collegial duty.

Academics at other colleges also helped me in numerous ways. Professors Jonathan E. Ingersoll of Yale University and David F. Babbel of Wharton School allowed me to reproduce a teaching note they wrote as Appendix B to Chapter 12. Professors Frank J. Fabozzi at MIT, Cheng few Lee at Rutgers University, Ronald W. Anderson at the City University of New York Graduate Center, Carl McGowan of Michigan State University, Richard Taylor at Arkansas State University, Wi Saeng Kim of Rutgers University, Gunter Dufey at the University of Michigan, Susan Jarzombek at Sacred Heart University, and James Morris at the University of Colorado are all friends who help me personally as well as intellectually. Professors W. Brian Barrett of the University of Miami, Diana R. Harrington at the University of Virginia, Raymond M. Leuthold at the University of Illinois, Gregory R. Niehaus of the University of Michigan, Raj Aggarwal at John Carroll University, K. C. John Wei at Indiana University, and C. Thomas Howard at the University of Denver all provided valuable assistance. The following reviewers provided many helpful comments and suggestions for this edition: Raj Aggarwal, John Carroll University; James S. Ang, Florida State University; Scott Besley, University of South Florida; Gerald O. Bierwag, University of Arizona; Stephen J. Brown, New York University; Eric Chang, University of Maryland; Ronald Christner, Loyola University; Prabin Datta, University of Arizona; Samuel A. Dyckman, Baruch College; David H. Goldenberg, Rensselaer Polytechnic Institute; Joseph Golec, Clark University; Kendall P. Hall, University of Alabama; Gloria Harpaz, Baruch College; C. Thomas Howard, University of Denver; Eric Kirzner, University of Toronto; Dorothy E. Koehl, University of Puget Sound, Washington; Jaroslav Komarynsky, Northern Illinois University; Brian Langemeir, Louisiana State University; Steven P. Lilien, Baruch College; Edward M. Miller, University of New Orleans; Robert J. Shiller, Yale University; Gary L. Tidwell, College of Charleston; James M. Tipton, Baylor University; and Kathleen Weiss, University of Michigan.

A number of gracious folks who are investment managers also aided me. I am especially indebted to Richard Bookstaber, an exprofessor of finance who is now at Morgan-Stanley; Russell Cornelius of Morgan-Stanley; Sam Eisenstadt, Senior Vice President, Value Line; Deborah Susan Francis, C.P.A., Senior Trust Auditor at Seattle First National Bank; Edward Mader, Senior Vice President, Prudential-Bache; Gary Gastineau, Vice President, Salomon Brothers; Richard O. Michaud, Vice President, Merrill Lynch; Bruce I. Jacobs, a private consultant; and Ken Hackel and Jason Wallach, who run Cash Flow Investors, Inc.

Although some of them have never met each other, numerous members of the huge McGraw-Hill family provided valuable aid in a gracious manner. It was a pleasure to work with Kenneth W. Lutz, Publisher, Trendline Services, who provided valuable artwork and computer software; Barbara Munder, Vice President at *Business Week* and creator of the Mutual Fund Scoreboard; Scott Stratford, Suzanne BeDell, Catherine Woods, and Ken MacLeod, my successive sponsoring editors; Sheila Gillams, a punctilious editing supervisor who was unfortunately transferred away from me; Ira Roberts, another highly professional editing supervisor who was a pleasure to work with; San Rao, a creative marketing manager; John Aliano, a senior editor in the Schaum's Division who was very helpful; Allan Forsyth, a McGraw-Hill alumnus and a peerless development editor; and Terry Pace, an instructor's manual editor who adds value to each of my books.

All of these folks made significant contributions to the fifth edition. I am indebted to every one of them. Whatever errors remain are clearly of my own making.

Jack Clark Francis

Investments:
Analysis and
Management

Chapter 1

Expected Return

and Risk

An **investment** is a commitment of money that is expected to generate additional money. Every investment entails some degree of risk; it requires a *present certain* sacrifice for a *future uncertain* benefit. This book describes various ways to select the investments that will provide the maximum future return at an acceptable level of risk. It examines such marketable financial instruments as common stocks, preferred stocks, bonds, put options, call options, combination options, futures contracts on the traditional commodities, financial futures, and other investments, as well as the risks associated with each. It analyzes these assets, the markets in which they are traded, the laws governing the trading, the valuation of the assets, the construction of a diversified portfolio, and other important investment management techniques. If you prefer to have *more wealth* instead of less and you are *risk-averse*—that is, you dislike risk—this book is appropriate for you.

1-1   **THE SINGLE-PERIOD RATE OF RETURN**

The single-period rate of return is the *basic random variable* in investments analysis. This **rate of return** concept is important because it measures the speed at which the investor's wealth increases—or decreases. An investment's single-period rate of return, denoted r, is simply the total return an investor would receive during the **investment period** or **holding period** stated as a percent of the investment's price at the start of the holding period.

$$r = \frac{\text{ending wealth } - \text{ beginning wealth}}{\text{beginning wealth (or, purchase price)}} \qquad (1\text{-}1)$$

An investor can obtain two kinds of income from an investment in a share of stock or a bond:

1. Income from price appreciation (or losses from price depreciation), sometimes called capital gains (or losses). This quantity is denoted $p_t - p_{t-1}$.
2. Cashflow income from cash dividend or coupon interest payments, represented by the convention c_t.

The sum of these two sources of income (or loss) equals the change in the invested wealth during any given holding period. The rate-of-return formula can be restated in a form appropriate for almost any investment.

$$r_t = \frac{\text{price change} + \text{cashflow (if any)}}{\text{price at beginning of the period}} = \frac{(p_t - p_{t-1}) + c_t}{p_{t-1}} \qquad (1\text{-}2)$$

where p_t = market price at end of period t
p_{t-1} = price at end of period $t-1$
c_t = cashflow income received during the tth period

Let us use Equation (1-2) to calculate the returns for the investments listed in Table 1-1.

Last year's *historical* rate of return from the stock in Table 1-1 was 10 percent.

$$r_t = \frac{(p_t - p_{t-1}) + c_t}{p_{t-1}} = \frac{\$2.50 + \$3.90}{\$64.00} = \frac{\$6.40}{\$64.00} = 0.1 \times 100 = 10\%$$

Last year's *historical* rate of return from the bond was 2.04 percent.

$$r_t = \frac{(p_t - p_{t-1}) + c_t}{p_{t-1}} = \frac{-\$40.00 + \$60.00}{\$980.00} = \frac{\$20.00}{\$980.00}$$

$$= 0.0204 \times 100 = 2.04\%$$

Table 1-1
PAST AND FUTURE YEARS' DATA FOR A STOCK AND A BOND

Data	Description	Stock	Bond	Time
p_0	Last year's closing price	$64.00	$980.00	$t = 0$
p_1	Current year's closing price	$66.50	$940.00	$t = 1$
c_1	Current year's cashflow income	$3.90*	$60.00†	$t = 1$
$E(p_2)$	Next year's expected closing price	$70.50	$1005.00	$t = 2$
$E(c_2)$	Next year's expected cashflow	$4.10*	$60.00†	$t = 2$

*Cash dividend per share.
†Coupon interest per bond per period.

The investor's *expected* rate of return for next year from the stock is 12.18 percent.

$$r_t = \frac{[E(p_t) - p_{t-1}] + E(c_t)}{p_{t-1}} = \frac{\$4.00 + \$4.10}{\$66.50} = \frac{\$8.10}{\$66.50}$$

$$= 0.1218 \times 100 = 12.18\%$$

The investor's *expected* rate of return for next year from the bond is 13.3 percent.

$$r_t = \frac{[E(p_t) - p_{t-1}] + E(c_t)}{p_{t-1}} = \frac{\$65.00 + \$60.00}{\$940.00} = \frac{\$125.00}{\$940.00}$$

$$= 0.133 \times 100 = 13.3\%$$

1-2   SOURCES OF INVESTMENT UNCERTAINTY

Every investment involves uncertainties that make future investment returns risky. Consider some of the sources of uncertainty that contribute to investment risk.

Interest Rate Risk   **Interest rate risk** is defined as the potential variability of return caused by changes in the market interest rates. Interest rate risk can be demonstrated if we reconsider the single-period rate-of-return formula for a bond or a stock, Equation (1-2). This rate-of-return formula can be rearranged to obtain these different but equivalent rate-of-return equations.

$$r_t = \frac{p_t}{p_{t-1}} - \frac{p_{t-1}}{p_{t-1}} + \frac{c_t}{p_{t-1}} = \frac{p_t}{p_{t-1}} + \frac{c_t}{p_{t-1}} - 1.0$$

$$1.0 + r = \frac{p_t + c_t}{p_{t-1}} \tag{1-2a}$$

Equation (1-2a) can be restated as the *present value* equation (1-3).

$$p_{t-1} = \frac{p_t + c_t}{1.0 + r} \tag{1-3}$$

Equation (1-3) defines the present value p_{t-1} of a stock or a bond that pays cashflows of c_t during the next period and is then sold for p_t dollars at the end of that period. The equation also indicates how changes in market interest rates affect an investment's value. Equation (1-3) says, in words, that if market interest rates, represented by r, rise (fall), then the investment's present value p_{t-1} will fall (rise). More succinctly, *present value moves inversely with changes in the market rate of interest.*

In more general terms, if market interest rates rise, then investments' values and market prices will fall, and vice versa. The variability of return that results is interest rate risk. This interest rate risk affects the prices of bonds, stocks, real estate, gold, puts, calls, futures contracts, and other investments as well.

Purchasing Power Risk

Purchasing power risk is the variability of return an investor suffers because of inflation. Economists measure the rate of inflation by using a price index. The consumer price index (CPI) is a popular price index in the United States. The percentage change in the CPI is a widely followed measure of the **rate of inflation.**

$$\frac{\text{CPI}_t - \text{CPI}_{t-1}}{\text{CPI}_{t-1}} = q_t = \text{rate of inflation in the CPI in period } t$$

When a savings account pays a certain rate of return, that rate is called a "nominal rate of return." **Nominal rates of return** contain no adjustment to eliminate the effects of inflation. Equation (1-4) defines the **real rate of return,** *rr,* which is adjusted for the effects of inflation.

$$1.0 + rr = \frac{1.0 + r}{1.0 + q} \tag{1-4}$$

Equation (1-4) can be restated as Equation (1-4a).

$$rr = \frac{1.0 + r}{1.0 + q} - 1.0 \tag{1-4a}$$

For instance, if a savings account yields a 10 percent nominal rate of return, $r = 0.1 \times 100 = 10\%$, in a year when the inflation rate is 5 percent, $q = 0.05 \times 100 = 5.0\%$, then its real rate of return is slightly less than 5 percent.

$$1.0 + rr = \frac{1.10}{1.05} = 1.0476 \times 100 = 100\% + 4.76\%$$

In other words, the investment resulted in a 4.76 percent increase in real purchasing power. The only portion of an investment's nominal rate of return that results in increased consumption opportunities for an investor is the *real* rate of return. The rest of the investment's nominal rate of return simply compensates for purchasing power lost to inflation.

Bull-Bear Market Risk

As its name suggests, **bull-bear market risk** arises from the variability in market returns resulting from alternating bull and bear market forces.

When a security index rises fairly consistently from a low point, called a **trough,** for a period of time, this upward trend is called a **bull market.** The bull market ends when the market index reaches a **peak** and starts a downward trend. The period during which the market declines to the next trough is called a **bear market.** Figure 1-1 illustrates the sudden bearish downturn that buffeted security markets around the world in October 1987.[1]

In recent decades bear markets have lasted from one month to over 3 years, with an average duration of about 1 year. Stock market indexes like the S&P 500 have fallen as little as 8 percent or as much as 85 percent, with an average decline of about 25 percent during these bearish declines.

During a small bear market, only about half the stocks listed on the New York Stock Exchange (NYSE) wind up with lower prices than they had at the beginning of the decline, but at other times as many as 99 percent of the stocks fall before the bearish period ends. About 85 percent of stocks finish the average bear market with lower prices. Luckily, bear markets are followed by bull markets that usually rise more than enough to compensate for the bear market losses. But, the alternating bull and bear market forces create a perennial source of investment risk.

Management Risk Though many top executives earn princely salaries, occupy luxurious offices, and wield enormous power within their organizations, they are mortal and capable of making a mistake or a poor decision. Furthermore, errors made by business managers can harm those who invested in their firms. Forecasting management errors is difficult work that may not be worth the effort and, as a result, imparts a needlessly skeptical outlook. *Agency theory* provides investors with an opportunity to replace skepticism with informed insight as they endeavor to analyze subjective management risks.

An **agent-principal relationship** exists whenever decision-making authority must be delegated. Corporations are an example of a common principal-agent relationship—a corporation's shareholder-owners delegate the day-to-day decision-making authority to managers who are hired employees rather than substantial owners. Jensen and Meckling argued that corporate managers who have little or no ownership interest in the corporation that employs them have more incentive to consume certain nonpecuniary benefits than they would if they were substantial owners of the firm.[2] These nonpecuniary benefits include nonsalary benefits like limousines, liberal expense accounts, corporate jets, and other executive ego-boosters. Stated differently, agency theory suggests

---

[1]The October 1987 crash will be discussed further in this book. The findings of the Brady Commission's investigation into the collapse, the effects of portfolio insurance and program trading, the implications of the Arrow-Debreu market theory, the components of market liquidity, and the efficient markets theory are all reviewed. For details about the crash, see Richard Roll, ''The International Crash of 1987,'' *Financial Analysts Journal,* Sept.–Oct. 1988, pp. 19–35.

[2]Michael C. Jensen and William H. Meckling, ''Theory of the Firm: Managerial Behavior, Agency Costs and Ownership Structure,'' *Journal of Financial Economics,* 1976, vol. 3, pp. 305–360.

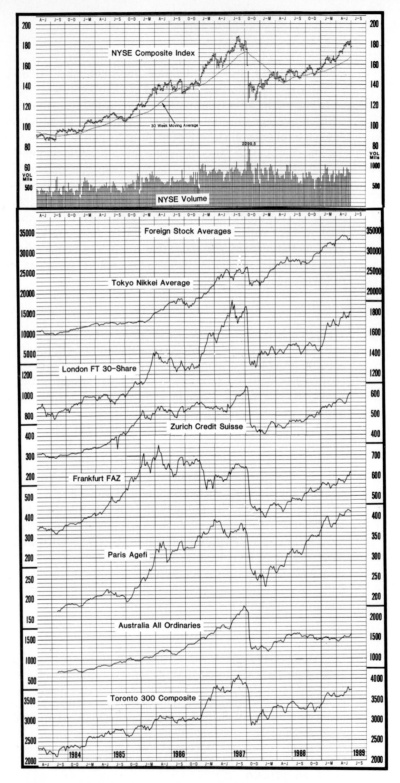

Figure 1-1 International stock market crash—October 1987. (*Source:* Daily Action Stock Charts, June 16, 1989, published by Trendline, A Division of Standard & Poor's Corporation.)

that owners will work harder to maximize the value of the company than employees will.

The Jensen-Meckling discussion of agency theory assumes that securities markets efficiently process information about the principal-agent conflict that exists within many corporations. Research by Kim, Lee, and Francis (KLF) suggests that security markets do not process this information efficiently, and, as a result, owner-managed corporations are better investments than employee-managed firms.[3] Securities markets appear to ignore valuable public information about agency costs. KLF reported that over the sample of corporations they studied, there was a statistically significant tendency for investors' equity returns to increase directly with the proportion of the outstanding shares that were owned by executives in the firm. This finding implies that investors can reduce their losses to difficult-to-analyze management errors by buying shares in those corporations in which the executives have significant equity investments.

Default Risk

Default risk is that portion of an investment's total risk that results from changes in the financial integrity of the investment. For example, when a company that issues securities moves either further away from bankruptcy or closer to it, these changes in the firm's financial integrity will be reflected in the market price of its securities. The variability of return that investors experience as a result of changes in the creditworthiness of a firm in which they invested is their default risk.[4]

Almost all the losses suffered by investors as a result of default risk are not the result of actual defaults and/or bankruptcies. Investor losses from default risk usually result from security prices falling as the financial integrity of a firm weakens—the losses are *anticipatory losses.* By the time an actual bankruptcy occurs, the market prices of the troubled firm's securities will already have declined to near zero. Thus, the bankruptcy losses would be only a small part of the total losses resulting from the process of financial deterioration.

Liquidity Risk

Liquidity risk is that portion of an asset's total variability of return which results from price discounts given or sales commissions paid in order to sell the asset without delay.

Perfectly liquid assets are highly marketable and suffer no liquidation costs. Illiquid assets are not readily marketable—either price discounts must be given

---

[3]Wi Saeng Kim, Jae Won Lee, and J. C. Francis, "Investment Performance of Common Stocks in Relation to Insider Ownership," *Financial Review,* Feb. 1988, vol. 23, no. 1, pp. 53–64.
[4]Default risk may be further divided into two components. The two parts of a security's default risk might be called *business risk* (from the assets on the issuing firm's balance sheet) and *financial risk* (from the liabilities on the issuing firm's balance sheet).

or sales commissions must be paid, or both of these costs must be incurred by the seller, in order to find a new investor for an illiquid asset. The more illiquid an asset is, the larger the price discounts and/or commissions which must be given up by the seller in order to effect a quick sale.

Callability Risk   Some bonds and preferred stocks are issued with a provision that allows the issuer to call them in for repurchase. Issuers like the call provision because it allows them to buy back outstanding preferred stocks and/or bonds with the funds from a newer issue if market interest rates drop below the level being paid on the outstanding securities. But, whatever the issuing company gains by calling in an issue is gained at the expense of the investors who have their securities called. Investors should view the call provision as a threat that may deprive them of a good investment at a time when their funds can only be reinvested at a lower yield.

That portion of a security's total variability of return that derives from the possibility that the issue may be called is the **callability risk.** Callability risk commands a risk premium that comes in the form of a slightly higher average rate of return. This additional return should increase as the risk that the issue will be called increases.

Convertibility Risk   Callability risk and convertibility risk are similar in two respects. First, both are contractual stipulations that are included in the terms of the original security issue. Second, both of these provisions alter the variability of return (that is, the risk) from the affected security. **Convertibility risk** is that portion of the total variability of return from a convertible bond or a convertible preferred stock that reflects the possibility that the investment may be converted into the issuer's common stock at a time or under terms harmful to the investor's best interests.

Political Risk   **Political risk** arises from the exploitation of a politically weak group for the benefit of a politically strong group, with the efforts of various groups to improve their relative positions increasing the variability of return from the affected assets. Regardless of whether the changes that cause political risk are sought by political or by economic interests, the resulting variability of return is called political risk if it is accomplished through legislative, judicial, or administrative branches of the government.

International Political Risk   International investors face political risk in the form of expropriation of nonresidents' assets, foreign exchange controls that won't let foreign investors withdraw their funds, disadvantageous tax and tariff treatments, requirements that nonresident investors give partial ownership to local residents, and unreimbursed destruction of foreign-owned assets by hostile residents of the foreign country. Foreign investors deal with *international political risk* by requiring higher expected rates of return from foreign investments than from domestic investments, by obtaining written guarantees from high-level government officials, and by using nonrecourse financing provided by the foreign country before undertaking any foreign investing.

Domestic Political Risk Domestic political risk arises from changes in environmental regulations, zoning requirements, fees, licenses, and, most frequently, taxes. The taxes may be property taxes, sales taxes, income taxes, or employment taxes. The tax and the transfer of the wealth are accomplished through the jurisdiction of some governmental unit that can be manipulated politically.[5]

Some types of securities and certain categories of investors enjoy a privileged tax status. Legislators' penchant for writing new tax laws, however, creates continual political risk for those investors affected by the tax laws.[6]

Industry Risk

An *industry* may be viewed as a group of companies that compete with each other to market a homogeneous product. **Industry risk** is that portion of an investment's total variability of return caused by events that affect the products and firms that make up an industry. The stage of the industry's life cycle, international tariffs and/or quotas on the products produced by an industry, product- or industry-related taxes, industrywide labor union problems, environmental restrictions, raw material availability, and similar factors interact and affect all the firms in an industry simultaneously. As a result of these commonalities, the prices of the securities issued by competing firms tend to rise and fall together.

Risk Factors Sum Up to Total Risk

The uncertainties discussed above are the major sources of investment risk, but by no means do they make up an exhaustive list. If all the uncertainties could be listed, they would add up to total risk, or total variability of return. Table 1-2 suggests the additive nature of the sources of risk.

The dictionary defines *risk* as "the chance of injury, damage, or loss." This is an intuitively pleasing definition. However, verbal definitions can be interpreted in different ways by different people. They can be made clearer only

[5]Tamir Agmon and M. Chapman Findlay, "Domestic Political Risk and Stock Valuation," *Financial Analysts Journal,* Nov.–Dec. 1982, pp. 3–6.
[6]The *major federal tax acts* passed in the United States in recent years include The Tax Reform Act of 1976, The Revenue Act of 1978, The Economic Recovery Tax Act of 1981, The Tax Equity and Fiscal Responsibility Act of 1982, The Tax Reform Act of 1984, and The Tax Reform Act of 1986. Such frequent changes keep investors confused. Tax law is the topic of Chapter 5.

Table 1-2
SOME RISK FACTORS THAT MAY AFFECT AN ASSET

	(a) Interest rate risk (if present)
plus:	(b) Purchasing power risk (if present)
plus:	(c) Bull-bear market risk (if present)
plus:	(d) Management risk (if present)
plus:	(e) Default risk (if present)
plus:	(f) Liquidity risk (if present)
plus:	(g) Callability risk (if present)
plus:	(h) Convertibility risk (if present)
plus:	(i) Taxability risk (if present)
plus:	(j) Political risk (if present)
plus:	(k) Industry risk (if present)
plus:	(l) The first additional risk (if present)
plus:	(m) Other additional risk factors (if present)
equals:	Total risk, Var(*r*)

by means of other verbal definitions or by examples which are not always entirely appropriate and are rarely concise. Moreover, verbal definitions do not yield to measurement. The dictionary definition of risk, for example, is not sufficiently precise to allow risky objects to be unambiguously ranked in terms of their riskiness. Thus, it is desirable to develop a *quantitative surrogate* for the dictionary definition of risk.

The rate of return is the single most important outcome from an investment, and, as a result, most quantitative risk surrogates focus on it. In an uncertain world, investors cannot tell exactly what rate of return an investment will yield. However, they can formulate a *probability distribution of the possible rates of return*. A quantitative risk surrogate is suggested below that can be measured from the investment's probability distribution of rates of return. It indirectly measures "the chance of injury, damage, or loss" so that it may be used synonymously with the word "risk."

1-3   THE PROBABILITY DISTRIBUTION OF RETURNS

Investment risk is usually analyzed by writing down the various possible rates of return and attaching probabilities to each one. Table 1-3 contains a **probability distribution of returns** for an investment with three possible outcomes. Figure 1-2 illustrates the probability distribution.

Some probability distributions are *objective;* they are based on *ex post* (after-the-fact) returns. These are called *relative frequency distributions*. Other probability distributions are *subjective;* they are based on a financial analyst's best guesses about the future returns and their probabilities. Either way, the prob-

Table 1-3
PROBABILITY DISTRIBUTION OF RETURNS FOR A $100 STOCK

State of nature	Event's probability	Stock's ending price	Cash dividend	Single-period rate of return
Booming economy	.3 × 100 = 30%	$130.00	0	0.3 × 100 = 30%
Slow growth	.4 × 100 = 40%	$110.00	0	0.1 × 100 = 10%
Recession	.3 × 100 = 30%	$ 90.00	0	−0.1 × 100 = − 10%
	1.0 × 100 = 100%			

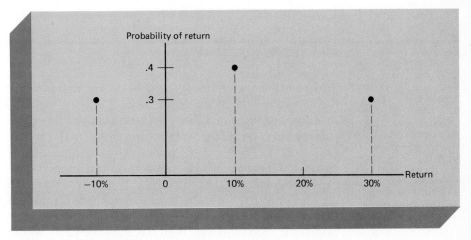

Figure 1-2 Finite probability distribution of returns for a $100 stock with three possible outcomes.

ability distribution is the foundation on which quantitative investments analysis rests.

1-4   **THE EXPECTED RATE OF RETURN, $E(r)$**

Investment decisions are based on expectations about the future. The **expected rate of return** for any asset is the weighted average rate of return, using the probability of each rate of return as the weight. The expected rate of return is calculated by summing the products of the rates of return and their respective probabilities.

$$E(r) = \sum_{t=1}^{T} P_t r_t \tag{1-5}$$

$$= P_1 r_1 + P_2 r_2 + \cdots + P_T r_T$$

The subscripts in the formula for the expected return are event counters that are appended to each possible rate of return and the probability (denoted P) for that event. T different events are perceived as possibilities. Calculating the expected rate of return for the probability distribution shown in Table 1-3 and Figure 1-2, we find:

$$\begin{aligned} E(r) &= P_1 r_1 + P_2 r_2 + P_3 r_3 \\ &= (.3)(-0.10) + (.4)(0.10) + (.3)(0.30) \\ &= -0.03 + 0.04 + 0.09 = 0.1 \times 100 = 10\% \end{aligned} \qquad (1\text{-}5a)$$

The investment analyst expects the stock with the $100 starting price to yield a 10 percent rate of return, $E(r) = 10\%$.

1-5   **STATISTICAL RISK ANALYSIS**

When analyzing investments, analysts define **risk** as *variability of return*. Thus, the wider the probability distribution of returns, the riskier the investment.

According to the dictionary definition of risk ("the chance of loss or injury"), it might seem more logical to measure risk by the area in a probability distribution that lies *below* the expected return. However, this procedure is unnecessary if the probability distribution is *symmetric*.

Figure 1-4 shows several probability distributions of returns; notice that they are all symmetric.[7] Assets' *total* variability of return will be twice as large as their variability below the expected return if their probability distributions are symmetric. Nevertheless, both risk measurements will result in the same risk rankings.[8] Thus, the choice of which quantitative risk surrogate to use can be based solely on convenience.

Financial analysts and statisticians prefer to use a quantitative risk surrogate called the *variance of returns,* denoted **Var(r).** The **variance** is well known

---

[7]Empirical studies of historical probability distributions of returns indicate they are symmetric. See L. Fisher and J. H. Lorie, "Some Studies of Variability of Returns on Investments in Common Stocks," *Journal of Business,* April 1970, pp. 99–134. Also see J. C. Francis and S. H. Archer, *Portfolio Analysis,* 2d ed. (Englewood Cliffs, N.J.: Prentice-Hall, 1979); see Tables 14-2 and 14-3.

[8]For a detailed discussion comparing different quantitative risk surrogates when the probability distributions are symmetric, see Harry Markowitz, *Portfolio Selection* (New York: Wiley, 1959), Chap. 9. Markowitz recommends use of the variance instead of his semivariance (SVR), which measures variability below the expected return.

$$\text{SVR} = \sum_{t=1}^{T} P_t [\text{BER}_t - E(r)]^2$$

where BER_t is the tth below the expected rate of return.

Table 1-4
CALCULATION OF VARIANCE AND
STANDARD DEVIATION

$$(P_1)[r_1 - E(r)]^2 = .3[0.3 - 0.1]^2 = 0.012$$

$$(P_2)[r_2 - E(r)]^2 = .4[0.1 - 0.1]^2 = 0$$

$$(P_3)[r_3 - E(r)]^2 = .3[-0.1 - 0.1]^2 = 0.012$$

$$\text{Total} = \text{Var}(r) = 0.024$$

$$\sigma = \sqrt{\text{Var}(r)} = \sqrt{0.024} = 0.155 \times 100 = 15.5\%$$

among statisticians; several hand calculators and computers are programmed to calculate it. The variance of an asset's rates of return equals the sum of the products of the squared deviations of each possible rate of return from the expected rate of return multiplied by the probability that the rate of return occurs.

$$\text{Var}(r) = \sum_{t=1}^{T} P_t[r_t - E(r)]^2 \tag{1-6}$$

$$= P_1[r_1 - E(r)]^2 + P_2[r_2 - E(r)]^2 + \cdots + P_T[r_T - E(r)]^2$$

The square root of the variance of the rates of return is called the **standard deviation** σ of the rates of return.

$$\sigma = \sqrt{\text{Var}(r)} \tag{1-7}$$

The standard deviation and the variance are equally acceptable and conceptually equivalent quantitative measures of an asset's **total risk.**

Equations (1-6) and (1-7) can be used to calculate the variance and standard deviation of an investment's rates of return. The rate-of-return data are taken from Table 1-3 and used in Table 1-4 to calculate the risk statistics for the stock with a purchase price of $100.

Equations (1-6) and (1-7) can be used to calculate variability of return for an individual asset, such as a stock or a bond, a portfolio of diversified assets, or many other investments. Investment decisions can then be made using the risk and return statistics.

1-6　　　　　　　**MAKING INVESTMENT DECISIONS BASED ON *E(r)* AND RISK STATISTICS**

Dominant assets have the maximum expected rate of return at any selected level of risk or, conversely, the minimum risk of all assets with a given expected rate of return. Table 1-5 presents an example involving six hypothetical assets to illustrate how the *dominance principle* works. Figure 1-3 shows a graph of

Table 1-5
RISK AND RETURN STATISTICS FOR SIX INVESTMENTS

Asset	Expected rate of return	Risk, σ	Dominated?
M	$0.1 \times 100 = 10\%$	.1	No
B	$0.05 \times 100 = 5\%$	.1	Yes, by T and M
C	$0.05 \times 100 = 5\%$	.2	Yes, by T, B, and A
A	$0.15 \times 100 = 15\%$	.2	No
E	$0.15 \times 100 = 15\%$	.3	Yes, by A
T	$0.05 \times 100 = 5\%$	.05	No

these six assets in risk-return space.[9] Any vertical line drawn in Figure 1-3 delineates a **risk class.**

According to the dominance principle, assets T and A dominate assets B, C, and E, respectively, because they have less risk for their given levels of expected return. Similarly, assets M and A dominate assets B and C, respectively, because they have the largest expected rates of return in their risk classes. Thus, a wealth-seeking risk-averse investor would prefer investing in asset T, M, or A rather than in asset B, C, or E.

Which of the dominant assets the investor prefers depends on personal investment preferences. A *timid* investor who is highly risk-averse would prefer dominant investment T, whereas an *aggressive* investor who is less risk-averse

Figure 1-3 Six assets graphed in risk-return space.

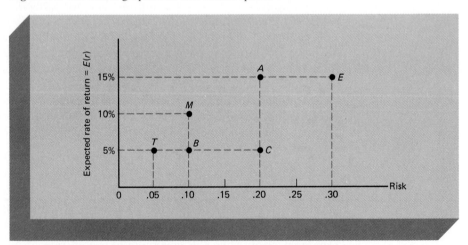

[9]Diversification is examined in detail in Chapter 9. Chapter 9 explains why the individual assets graphed in Figure 1-3 will always be dominated by portfolios because of the risk-reducing effects of diversification.

would prefer dominant investment *A*. A "*medium* investor," halfway between timidity and aggressiveness, will prefer asset *M*, but the dominance principle assumes that no rational investor would prefer asset *B*, *C*, or *E*.

Next, consider the economic implications of a straight line-of-best-fit that was drawn through the points representing dominant assets *T*, *M*, and *A* in Figure 1-3. Do points *T*, *M*, and *A* trace out a meaningful risk-return relationship?

1-7   **EMPIRICAL EVIDENCE ABOUT THE RISK-RETURN RELATIONSHIP**

Table 1-6 displays risk and average return statistics measured over hundreds of different assets and averaged over a sample period that covers decades. Figure 1-4 shows some continuous probability distributions that are represen-

Figure 1-4 Several representative continuous probability distributions of returns. (*a*) Common stocks; (*b*) long-term corporate bonds; (*c*) long-term government bonds; (*d*) U.S. Treasury bills. (*Source: Stocks, Bonds, Bills and Inflation (SBBI): 1982 Edition*, by R. G. Ibbotson and Rex A. Sinquefield, updated in *SBBI 1988 Yearbook*, Ibbotson Associates Inc.)

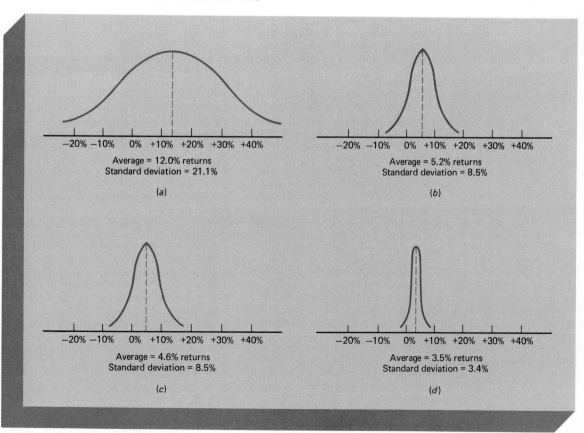

Table 1-6
RISK AND AVERAGE RETURN STATISTICS FOR DIFFERENT CATEGORIES OF INVESTMENTS, 1960–1984

Asset category	Geometric mean return,* %	Arithmetic mean return, %	Standard deviation of returns, %
Common stocks			
United States			
NYSE	8.71	9.99	16.30
AMEX	7.28	9.95	23.49
OTC	11.47	13.88	22.42
U.S. total	8.81	10.20	16.89
Foreign stocks			
Europe	7.83	8.94	15.58
Asia	15.14	18.42	30.74
Other	8.14	10.21	20.88
Foreign total	9.84	11.02	16.07
Common stock total	9.08	10.21	15.28
Bonds			
Corporate			
Intermediate-term	6.37	6.80	7.15
Long-term	5.03	5.58	11.26
Corporate total†	5.35	5.75	9.63
Government			
Treasury notes	6.32	6.44	5.27
Treasury bonds	4.70	5.11	9.70
U.S. agencies	6.88	7.04	6.15
Government total	5.91	6.10	6.43
U.S. total	5.70	5.93	7.16
Foreign bonds			
Corporate domestic	8.35	8.58	7.26
Government domestic	5.79	6.04	7.41
Crossborder	7.51	7.66	5.76
Foreign total	6.80	7.01	6.88
Bonds total	6.36	6.50	5.56
Cash equivalents			
United States			
Treasury bills	6.25	6.29	3.10
Commercial paper	7.03	7.08	3.20
U.S. cash equivalents total	6.49	6.54	3.22
Foreign	6.00	6.23	7.10
Cash total	6.38	6.42	2.92
Real estate‡			
Business	8.49	8.57	4.16
Residential	8.86	8.93	3.77
Farm	11.86	12.13	7.88
Real estate total	9.44	9.49	3.45

Table 1-6
**RISK AND AVERAGE RETURN STATISTICS FOR DIFFERENT CATEGORIES OF INVESTMENTS,
1960–1984 (Continued)**

Asset category	Geometric mean return,* %	Arithmetic mean return, %	Standard deviation of returns, %
Metals			
Gold	9.08	12.62	29.87
Silver	9.14	20.51	75.34
Metals total	9.11	12.63	29.69
U.S. total wealth portfolio	8.63	8.74	5.06
Foreign total wealth	7.76	8.09	8.48
World wealth portfolio			
Excluding metals	8.34	8.47	5.24
Including metals	8.39	8.54	5.80
U.S. inflation rate	5.24	5.30	3.60

*The geometric mean rate of return is explained in the Appendix at the end of this chapter.
†Including preferred stock.
‡United States only. Real estate risk statistics are typically downward biased because appraised values fluctuate less than actual sales prices.
Source: Roger G. Ibbotson, Laurence Siegel, and Kathryn S. Love, "World Wealth: Market Values and Returns," *Journal of Portfolio Management,* Fall 1985, table 4, p. 17.

tative of a few major categories of investment securities. The risk and average rate-of-return statistics in Table 1-6 and Figure 1-4 were estimated over enough different assets and a sufficient number of bull and bear market periods to average over highly abnormal rates of return.

Any individual investment may differ substantially from the average risk and return statistics. That is why it is prudent to investigate any asset before investing. However, the average risk and rate-of-return statistics in Table 1-6 and Figure 1-4 provide valuable investment guidelines.[10]

1-8   **THE POSITIVE TRADEOFF BETWEEN RISK AND RETURN**

Note that a *positive relationship* between expected rate of return and risk can be discerned from Table 1-6 and Figure 1-4. This means that an investment manager can usually attain more return by selecting dominant assets that involve more risk. While it is not always true that a riskier asset will pay a higher average rate of return, it is *usually* true. The reason is that investors are *risk-*

[10]Those who wish to see additional information about security market indexes are invited to see Chapter 7.

averse. As a result, high-risk assets must offer investors high returns to induce them to make the riskier investments. We can see this relationship between risk and return by comparing investment securities. For example, consider the typical U.S. Treasury bills, corporate bonds, and common stock investments shown in Table 1-6 and Figure 1-4.

Treasury bills are short-term bonds issued by the U.S. Treasury. When you purchase such a bond, you are lending the government money to be paid back with interest. There is virtually no chance that any U.S. Treasury bill will default because the wealth of a mighty nation backs these bonds. In fact, Treasury bills are probably the safest bond in the world. Their short time to maturity and default-free status make Treasury bills the least risky investment, as indicated by the fact that they have the least variability of return. This small variability of return attracts highly risk-averse investors to buy Treasury bills even though the average returns are small. See Figure 1-4*d*.

Treasury bills have earned an average rate of return about equal to the inflation rate—a lackluster performance. Risk-averse investors are nevertheless happy to buy Treasury bills because they expose the investor to zero default risk, zero management risk, zero liquidity risk, zero convertibility risk, zero political risk, and zero industry risk and because many of the issues are not callable. Treasury bills only expose the investor to income taxes that are fairly predictable, a little interest rate risk, and a modest amount of purchasing power risk.

Corporate bonds represent investors' loans to corporations which must be paid back with interest. Corporate bond investments are riskier than Treasury bills because, unlike the U.S. Treasury, a corporation can go bankrupt. In addition to default risk, corporate bond investors must also bear interest rate risk and purchasing power risk. Furthermore, they must also assume management risk, political risk, industry risk, and, perhaps, other risks (such as convertibility). This greater risk exposure causes a greater variability of return that can be seen by comparing the width of the probability distributions in Figure 1-4. Since corporate bonds, on average, experience more variability of return than Treasury bills, corporate bonds must pay a higher average rate of return in order to entice investors to place their funds at risk.

If the bankruptcy courts declare a corporation bankrupt, its assets are auctioned off to get cash to pay the firm's outstanding bills. Certain classes of creditors must be completely paid off before more junior classes of creditors can receive any repayment from the proceeds of the bankruptcy auction. More specifically, all bills must be paid, all bondholders must be repaid, and all preferred stockholders must be repaid before the common stockholders of a bankrupt firm are eligible to be repaid for their investment. Since common stock has the last legal claim on the proceeds from a corporate bankruptcy auction, the common stockholders usually do not receive anything from the proceeds of bankruptcy auctions, because there is nothing left. This default risk makes common stock far more risky than default-free Treasury bills—and riskier than bonds issued by the same corporation.[11] These facts are reflected in the common stock's high variability of return (see Table 1-6) and in its wide probability distribution of returns (see Figure 1-4). This high level of risk explains why common stock tends to have the largest average rate of return.

1-9   **THE CAPITAL MARKET LINE (CML)**

Figure 1-5 depicts a formal risk-return relationship that is called the **capital market line** (CML). The dots that lie below the CML represent *individual* stocks, bonds, commodity futures, puts, calls, and other investments. The dots labeled CS, CB, and TB represent the average common stock (CS), corporate bond (CB), and Treasury bill (TB) investments that were shown in Figure 1-4. Table 1-6 contains empirical statistics documenting the positive relationship

Figure 1-5 The capital market line (CML) and other investment opportunities.

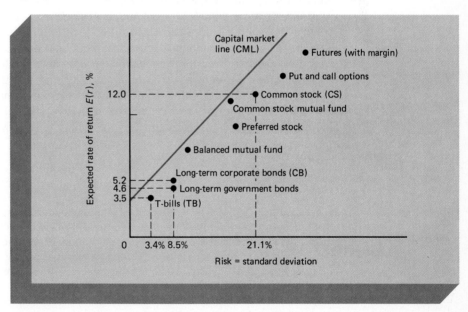

[11]A caveat is appropriate here. The common stock of a blue-chip public utility like AT&T, for instance, is less risky than "junk bonds." **Junk bonds** are low-quality bonds issued by corporations that have a significant probability of going bankrupt. The point is that common stock is not universally riskier than corporate bonds. However, the common stock of *any given corporation* is always riskier than bonds issued by that same corporation—because of the priority of claims mandated by the bankruptcy laws.

between risk and average return illustrated by the CML. The CML will always be positively sloped because investors are risk-averse. Investors are risk-averse because they dislike sleepless nights, professional investment managers fear losing their jobs if they make imprudent investments, and investors are scared by the occasional suicides that are reported after some unfortunate investor suffers traumatic losses.[12]

The CML traces out what is called the "efficient frontier." The **efficient frontier** is the locus of investments graphed in risk-return space which have (1) the maximum expected rate of return in their risk class or (2) the minimum risk at whatever rate of return is selected. Any vertical line drawn in Figure 1-5 delineates a *risk class*. The efficient investments are called **efficient portfolios** because individual assets are dominated and will not be able to attain the efficient frontier.

Note that the CML dominates every individual asset in Figure 1-5. The risk-reducing power of diversification is needed to reach a position in risk-return space that is on or near the CML. Only efficiently diversified portfolios can attain the CML. Chapter 21 shows that no mutual funds are sufficiently well managed to attain the CML, for example. The CML is the locus of the most desirable, or most dominant, investment portfolios.

Even the simplest approaches to diversification can contribute to risk reduction. However, some approaches to diversification are more effective than others. **Markowitz diversification** is a mathematical procedure that can analyze any number of different assets simultaneously and tell the portfolio analyst precisely how to combine the single assets to form dominant portfolios. Markowitz diversification is the best approach to diversification; it is explained in Chapter 9. Chapter 9 also explains how to delineate the CML and how to form

---

[12]It is worthwhile to bear in mind the distinction among gambling, speculating, and investing. A *gamble* involves the purchase of an opportunity to win some game of chance that will typically be completed in a few seconds. The results of a gamble are quickly resolved by the roll of the dice or a turn of a card—it is over with much more quickly than a speculation or an investment. Rational, risk-averse people undertake gambles as a form of entertainment. Casino gambling typically involves transactions that have a negative expected value for the gambler—thus, gambling is not a rational way to earn one's lifetime income.

Speculations last longer than gambles, but have shorter durations than investments. *Speculation* involves the purchase of a marketable asset in hopes of making a profit from an increase in price that is expected to occur within a few weeks or months. Speculators can expect to gain by exploiting research insights. Speculating is examined in Chapters 17, 18, 22, 23, and 24.

Investing occurs when someone buys an asset and holds it in order to earn income and, typically, to benefit from long-term price appreciation. Financial analysts are employed to research investments with the best potential long-run rewards. The capital market line (CML) is a long-run investment relationship that is more relevant to investors than it is to speculators or gamblers.

a portfolio that is efficient enough to lie on the CML. Throughout the rest of this book we will be learning how to select investments that are efficient.

1-10   **SUMMARY AND CONCLUSIONS**

The single-period rate of return is the most important outcome from an investment; it measures the investor's rate of wealth accumulation (or decrease) per period.

The primary risk factors that create investment uncertainties are interest rate risk, purchasing power risk, bull-bear market risk, management risk, default risk, liquidity risk, callability risk, convertibility risk, political risk, and industry risk. However, there are an infinite number of other factors that can contribute to risk.

Investment analysts can represent assets as probability distributions of single-period returns that subsume every fact about the asset (see Figures 1-2 and 1-4). These probability distributions form the basis for further analysis. The analyst can calculate the variance, Equation (1-6), and expected return, Equation (1-5), statistics for each asset from the raw return data in the probability distribution. The variance (or standard deviation) is a quantitative risk surrogate that measures variability of return.

The standard deviation (or variance) and expected return statistics from different investment candidates can be analyzed in risk-return space. Empirical risk-return statistics from a diversified sample of investments (like those in Table 1-6) will reveal a positive relationship between the variance (or standard deviation) and average rate of return when measured over at least one complete business cycle. This positive risk-return relationship is always present in portfolio analysis. In fact, the most dominant investment opportunities will always be the diversified portfolios that form the capital market line (CML) in risk-return space (see Figure 1-5).

The tradeoff between risk and return that was documented in Table 1-6 and illustrated in Figure 1-5 will change with the passage of time but will always be positive because investors are risk-averse. Investors require higher expected rates of return to induce them to place their funds in riskier assets.

Essay Questions

1-1 "The rate of return is the most important outcome from an investment." Is the statement true, uncertain, or false? Explain.

1-2 How would you define the rate of inflation in terms of the Producers' Price Index (PPI)?

1-3   What economic event separates a bull market from a bear market? . . . a bear market from a bull market?

1-4   (*a*) Over the long run (over at least one complete business cycle), do bear markets predominate over bull markets in the U.S. stock markets? Or, do bull markets predominate over bear markets? Or, do the effects of bull and bear markets tend to cancel each other in the long run? (*b*) What sort of investment strategy is suggested by your conclusion?

1-5   (*a*) Which asset is more liquid—a family's investment in NYSE-listed stocks, the family's late model American car, or the family's single-family residence? Assume all of these assets are in good condition. Which category of assets is the least liquid? (*b*) Do you think liquidity should be a major or minor consideration in selecting investments?

1-6   A dormant volcano inside of Mount Rapture exploded. As a result the Mount Rapture Ski Resort (MRSR) went bankrupt. Should the investors who owned MRSR stock sue the president of their resort company for malpractice?

1-7   You are a financial analyst who has to choose between using two quantitative risk surrogates: (i) the range between the largest and the smallest returns, or (ii) the variance (or, equivalently, the standard deviation) of returns. Which risk measure would you choose? Defend your choice.

1-8   Ponder the risk-return relationship documented in Table 1-6 and Figure 1-5. Can you discern any other significant risk-return or risk-income relationships in your life? Feel free to suggest relationships that are unrelated to investments.

Problems

1-9   You purchased a share of stock on January 15, 19X8 for $40 and sold it on January 15, 19X9 for $42 after collecting a $2 per share cash dividend. What was your single-period rate of return for this 1-year investment?

1-10 You purchased a share of stock on January 15, 19X8 for $40 and sold it on July 15, 19X8 for $42 after collecting a $2 per share cash dividend. (*a*) What was your single-period rate of return for that half-year investment? (*b*) What was your single-period rate of return over the half-year investment period, stated at an *annualized* rate?

1-11 Calculate five annual rates of return for the Consolidated Business (CB) Corporation from the raw data in Table 1-7.

1-12 Draw a historical finite probability distribution of returns for the six rates of return that you calculated in Problem 1-11 for the Consolidated Business (CB) Corporation's stock. Label all parts of the graph.

1-13 Calculate the average (or expected) rate of return and the variance of returns for

Table 1-7

STOCK PRICE AND CASH DIVIDEND DATA FOR THE CONSOLIDATED BUSINESS (CB) CORPORATION

Year	Years' closing prices*	Annual cash dividends	Annual rates of return, Equation (1-2)
19X0	$60.00	$3.00	Insufficient data to calculate
19X1	69.00	3.00	$[(\$9.00 + \$3.00)/\$60] \times 100 = 20\%$
19X2	100.50	3.00	
19X3	47.25	3.00	
19X4	39.525	3.00	
19X5	72.0975	3.00	
19X6	82.517	4.00	

*Stock prices are usually quoted in increments of one-eighth of $1 (that is, the three decimal place quantity $0.125 is the minimum price change). Slightly unrealistic stock prices that run to four decimal place accuracy are used in Table 1-7 so that the computed annual rates of return will all work out to tenths of a percentage point exactly.

the Consolidated Business (CB) Corporation using the objective historical data from Table 1-7 and the five annual rates of return you calculated for Problem 1-11 plus the one return that was given to you. Assume all six rates of return are equally likely, so they all have probabilities of occurring of $\frac{1}{6} = .166666$.

1-14 Susan Ling is trying to decide which of the following common stocks to purchase. What would you recommend?

Name of issuer	Expected return, $E(r)$	Standard deviation, σ
Able Corporation (A)	7.0%	3.7%
Baker Inc. (B)	7.7%	4.9%
Charles & Company, Ltd. (C)	15.0%	15.0%
Diamond Corporation (D)	3.0%	3.7%
Energy Design, Inc. (E)	7.7%	12.0%

1-15 Benjamin Karl deposited $2000 in a federally insured savings account to earn 7 percent interest for 1 year. During the year that the money was deposited in the savings account, the rate of inflation was 5 percent. (*a*) What was Benjamin's nominal rate of return from his 1-year savings deposit? (*b*) What was his real rate of return from the 1-year savings deposit? (*c*) How many dollars of additional purchasing power did he earn from the 1-year deposit?

1-16 Maureen Carey could earn 10 percent interest on a AAA-grade corporation bond or 8 percent interest on a AAA-grade municipal bond. If both bonds have the same amount of risk and Maureen is in the 30 percent income tax bracket, which bond should she buy? Show your calculations.

1-17 (*a*) According to the bankruptcy law, which of the following classes of creditors has the most junior (that is, last) claim on the cash proceeds from a corporation's liquidation auction?

a. Preferred stockholders

b. Bond investors

c. Unpaid wages

d. Lawyer's fees

e. Any utility bills

f. Common stockholders

g. Unpaid taxes

(*b*) Does the legal priority of claims in bankruptcy have any implications for the risk that common stockholders experience? (*c*) Does the legal priority of claims in bankruptcy have any implications for the rate of return that common stockholders should expect?

1-18 Steve Garabaldi is a stockbroker whose boss just asked him to help sell out quickly a block of municipal bonds in which the firm just took a large position. Steve, a new broker with little experience, was given a list of people to "cold call" on the phone and try to sell some of the municipal bonds. After each name on the list, there is a symbol that indicates each individual's income category, whether they own their home or rent it, and how many automobiles are registered in their name. Can you give Steve any hints about which category of people he should call to be the most productive? Explain your choice.

Appendix 1A

Geometric Mean
Return

When you are dealing with several *successive* rates of return, the distinction between the *arithmetic average* rate of return and the *geometric mean* return should be recognized.

The Misleading Arithmetic Multiperiod Average Return

Asset A is purchased at $40 at time $t = 0$, and its price rises to $60 at the end of the first period, $t = 1$, for a 50 percent gain during the first period. Then the price of A falls back to $40 at the end of the second period, $t = 2$, and the asset is sold at that price for a 33 percent drop during period 2. The *arithmetic average* rate of return of 50 percent and -33.3 percent is 8.35 percent.

$$\frac{50\% + (-33.3\%)}{2} = 8.35\% = \text{arithmetic average return on A}$$

Asset B also has a purchase price of $40 at time $t = 0$, but asset B's price falls to $20 at the end of period 1, $t = 1$. Then it rises back to $40 at the end of period 2, $t = 2$. The arithmetic average rate of return for asset B is the average of -50 and 100 percent, which is 25 percent.

$$\frac{-50\% + 100\%}{2} = 25\% = \text{arithmetic average return for B}$$

The behavior of the prices of assets A and B over the two periods is summarized graphically in Figure 1A-1.

An asset purchased for $40 and sold for $40 two periods later did not return 8.35 percent or 25 percent; it earned nothing. The two numerical examples above point to the fact that *the arithmetic average of successive one-period returns is not the true average rate of return over multiple periods.*

Internal Rate of Return In classes about capital budgeting (or capital expenditures or corporation finance, as it is variously called), the rate of return from a multiperiod

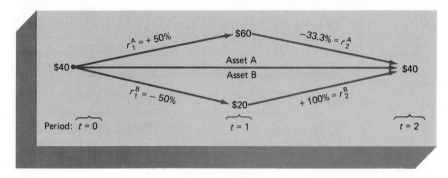

Figure 1A-1 The movements of the prices of assets A and B over two periods.

investment is defined to be the discount rate which equates the present value of all cashflows c_t to the cost of the investment c_0, as shown below.

$$c_0 = \sum_{t=1}^{T} \frac{c_t}{(1 + r)^t} \qquad (1A\text{-}1a)$$

The multiperiod rate of return in Equation (1A-1a) is sometimes called the *dollar-weighted rate of return*, or the **internal rate of return.**

For a one-period investment we set $T = 1$ in Equation (1A-1a) to obtain:

$$c_0 = \frac{c_1}{1 + r} \qquad (1A\text{-}1b)$$

In cases that only span one period, the *internal rate of return* is equivalent to the one-period rate of return shown in Equation (1A-2).

$$r = \frac{c_1 - c_0}{c_0} \qquad (1A\text{-}2)$$

The quantity $c_1 - c_0$ equals capital gains or losses plus cash dividends from stock (or coupon interest from bonds).

One-Inflow-and-One-Outflow Multiperiod Model For *multiperiod investments involving only one cash inflow,* if the cost (or outflow) of the asset is c_0 and the cash inflow is c_t, the internal rate of return yields the same solution as the geometric mean rate of return. For example, for asset A the cashflows were $c_0 = \$40$ and $c_2 = \$40$, which yields $r = 0$ over $T = 2$ periods, as shown in Equation (1A-1c).

$$\$40 = \frac{\$40}{(1 + r)^2} \qquad \text{if and only if } r = 0 \qquad (1A\text{-}1c)$$

The internal rate of return is different from the (average compounded or) geometric mean rate of return for multiperiod investments that involve *multiple cash inflows* or outflows, however.

The internal rate of return is also called the dollar-weighted rate of return because it is influenced by how many total dollars are invested in a multiperiod investment.

Thus, the dollar-weighted rate of return is not useful for comparing the rates of return for, say, two mutual funds that have different amounts of total assets. The *time-weighted rate of return* is the true (average compounded or geometric mean) rate of return, which is useful for such comparisons because it is not affected by the dollar amount invested.

Formulas for Geometric Mean Return

The true rate of return over T periods is called the **compounded rate of return** or **geometric mean return** (gr) and is defined in Equation (1A-3a).

$$(1 + gr)^T = \frac{p_1}{p_0} \frac{p_2}{p_1} \cdots \frac{p_T}{p_{T-1}} \qquad (1A\text{-}3a)$$

Letting $p_t/p_{t-1} = 1 + r_t$ yields Equation (1A-3b).

$$(1 + gr)^T = (1 + r_1)(1 + r_2) \cdots (1 + r_T) \qquad (1A\text{-}3b)$$

The arithmetic average of successive one-period rates of return is defined in Equation (1A-4).

$$\bar{r} = \frac{1}{T} \sum_t^T r_t \qquad (1A\text{-}4)$$

The arithmetic average return $\bar{r}$ is an approximation of the true multiperiod rate of return. As the variance of the r_t's grows smaller, this approximation becomes better. Equation (1A-5) shows the nature of this approximation.

$$\bar{r} = [gr^2 + \text{Var}(r)]^{1/2} \qquad (1A\text{-}5)$$

Maximizing the Geometric Mean Return as a Goal

Dr. Henry A. Latane has suggested that maximizing the geometric return is a good investment goal.[13] This suggestion is well taken, since maximizing gr involves maximizing the r_t's each period while minimizing $\text{Var}(r)$—that is, risk—at the same time. To see this more clearly, solve Equation (1A-5) for the geometric mean return.[14]

$$gr = [\bar{r}^2 - \text{Var}(r)]^{1/2} \qquad (1A\text{-}6)$$

Equation (1A-6) shows that minimizing risk $\text{Var}(r)$ and maximizing the arithmetic average return $\bar{r}$ will tend to maximize the geometric mean return. Such a policy is equivalent to maximizing *terminal wealth* because the ratio of terminal wealth, denoted w_T, to beginning wealth, denoted w_0, equals the Tth root of $1 + gr$.

$$(1 + gr)^T = \frac{w_T}{w_0} \qquad (1A\text{-}7)$$

Equation (1A-7) shows that maximizing the geometric mean return is equivalent to maximizing terminal wealth.

[13]H. A. Latane, ''Criteria for Choice among Risky Ventures,'' *The Journal of Political Economy,* April 1959, pp. 144–155.

[14]William E. Young and Robert H. Trent, ''Geometric Mean Approximations of Individual Security and Portfolio Performance,'' *Journal of Financial and Quantitative Analysis,* June 1969, pp. 179–199.

Some financial economists have suggested that maximizing the terminal wealth or geometric mean return of a portfolio is an investment objective that may be preferable to maximizing the portfolio's expected return in a selected risk class each period. Although this suggestion may be true for some investors, it is not true for all of them. The portfolio that maximizes the geometric mean return or terminal wealth is just one portfolio on or near the efficient frontier.[15]

[15]Nils H. Hakansson, "Capital Growth and the Mean-Variance Approach to Portfolio Selection," *Journal of Financial and Quantitative Analysis,* Jan. 1971, pp. 517–557; Jan Mossin, "Optional Multi-Period Portfolio Policies," *Journal of Business,* April 1968, pp. 215–229; E. F. Fama, "Multi-Period Consumption-Investment Decisions," *American Economic Review,* March 1970, pp. 163–174; Harry M. Markowitz, "Investment for the Long-Run: New Evidence for an Old Rule," *Journal of Finance,* Dec. 1976, vol. 31, pp. 1273–1286.

Part 1

The Setting

Chapter 2

Securities

Securities represent specific claims on a stream of income and/or particular assets. Bonds and mortgages are typical debt securities. Ownership securities include common stocks. Preferred stock is a hybrid security that entails a mixture of both ownership and creditorship privileges. Table 2-1 lists the common types of securities and their general characteristics. The table compares Treasury bonds and different securities that might be issued by a hypothetical corporation.[1] The securities in Table 2-1 will be defined, additional securities will be introduced, and other characteristics will be enunciated in this chapter and the chapters that follow.

This chapter's discussion of securities begins with money market securities because they are the simplest kind of security. Both companies and governments issue money market securities.

2-1　　　　　**MONEY MARKET SECURITIES**

Something that is **liquid** will flow freely from one place to another without being reduced or expanded in the process. U.S. dollars, for example, are a *perfectly liquid asset.*

[1]Tax laws that exempt intercorporate cash dividend payments from income taxes under certain circumstances, the tax-free coupons on municipal bonds, the existence of certain tax-exempt investors, the existence of different classes of common stock issued by the same corporation, and other complications make Table 2-1 less than totally descriptive. The table should be viewed as an introductory framework for comparing the securities issued by a single corporation and Treasury bonds. Securities issued by different corporations are not described by Table 2-1 because, for instance, some junk bonds are riskier and pay a higher return than the common stock issued by some blue-chip corporations. More comprehensive risk-return relationships are topics for later chapters.

Table 2-1
SECURITIES AND THEIR CHARACTERISTICS

Types of security	Risk	Average return	Investors' control	Liquidity
XYZ Corporation's common stock	Most, 1	Most, 1	Most, 1	2
XYZ Corporation's preferred stock	2	2	2	3
XYZ Corporation's bond	3	3	3	Least, 4
U.S. Treasury bond	Least, 4	Least, 4	Least, 4	Most, 1

Highly liquid debt securities that have short terms until they mature and involve little or no risk of default are called **money market securities.** All money market securities are debts that mature within 270 days or less. A federal law (enforced by the Securities and Exchange Commission) requires that all securities with maturities in excess of 270 days go through a costly *registration process* (described in Chapters 3 and 4); money market securities are frequently issued instead of longer-term debt securities in order to avoid this costly administrative process. Money market securities pay continuously fluctuating rates of interest that exceed the rate of inflation only slightly.

Money market securities typically pay interest to their investors by selling at a **discount** from their face (or maturity) values. United States **Treasury bills,** for instance, are offered in *denominations* of $10,000, $15,000, $50,000, $100,000, $500,000, and $1 million. A 90-day T-bill with a $100,000 face value might sell for $98,000 when issued by the U.S. Treasury Department. The buyer can either hold the security for 90 days or sell it in the active secondary market before it matures. Upon maturity, whoever owns the T-bill can redeem it for its face value of $100,000. The $2000 difference between the discounted purchase price of $98,000 and the maturity value of $100,000 is the interest paid to the T-bill's investor (or series of investors).[2]

Negotiable certificates of deposit (CDs) were originated by Citibank of New York in 1961. A negotiable CD is a receipt from a commercial bank for a deposit

---

[2]Money market securities adhere to the unrealistic convention that there are 360 days in the year for interest rate calculations. Using the conventional discount pricing method, the 90-day T-bill in the example would be discounted and priced as shown below.

$$\begin{array}{l} \text{Dollar} \\ \text{discount} \\ \text{from face} \end{array} = \begin{array}{l} \text{face} \\ \text{value} \end{array} \times \begin{array}{l} \text{discount rate} \\ \text{at an annual} \\ \text{rate} \end{array} \times \frac{\text{days to maturity}}{360 \text{ days}}$$

$$= (\$100,000)(0.08)\frac{(90 \text{ days})}{(360 \text{ days})} = \$2000$$

$$\text{Price} = \text{face value} - \text{dollar discount}$$

$$= \$100,000 - \$2000 = \$98,000$$

(continues)

of $100,000 or more, with certain provisions attached. One of the provisions is that the deposit will not be withdrawn from the bank before a specific maturity date. If the bank's deposits are insured by the Federal Deposit Insurance Corporation (FDIC), the CD is a safe investment. Negotiable CDs can therefore be easily traded in active secondary markets. CDs with denominations as small as $500 are sold by some banks, but these CDs are not negotiable.

Banker's acceptances are securities that are written when a bank inserts itself between the borrower and the investor and accepts the responsibility for paying the loan; this shields the investor from the risk of default. Banker's acceptances are often preceded by a written promise from the lending bank that it will make the loan—such letters are called *letters of credit*. The lending bank does not actually ''accept'' the banker's acceptance until the borrower takes down the loan. Later, if the lending bank wants to withdraw the money it has invested in the loan before the loan expires, the bank can sell the banker's acceptance to another investor. Banker's acceptances may be resold to any number of other investors before the loan is repaid; there is an active secondary market in these debts. Any investor who buys a banker's acceptance can collect the loan on the date it is scheduled to be repaid.

Banker's acceptances are one of the oldest money market securities. They are typically used to expedite foreign trade by financing account receivables between a buyer and seller from different countries. For a fee plus the interest on the loan, large international banks create banker's acceptances.

Commercial paper refers to the short-term promissory notes issued by ''blue-chip'' corporations—large, old, safe, well-known, national companies like IBM, Exxon, and GM. The maturities vary from 5 to 270 days, and the denominations are for $100,000 or more—usually more. These notes are backed only by the high credit rating of the issuing corporation.

Commercial paper issuers typically maintain open lines of bank credit sufficient to pay back all of their outstanding commercial paper. They issue commercial paper only because that type of credit is quicker and easier to obtain than bank loans. The credit ratings of most commercial paper issuers are so high that the so-called prime (that is, highest-quality credit rating) commercial paper interest rate is essentially a riskless rate of interest matching the yields on negotiable CDs and banker's acceptances.

Overnight loans between commercial banks are called ''federal funds loans'' or, more commonly, **fed funds.** Fed funds arise when a bank holds reserves in excess of those that the Federal Reserve System requires the bank to hold to meet its reserve requirement. Federal funds are thus simply bank reserves

---

(continued)
The annualized rate of return from this 90-day T-bill is actually $1.0854 - 1.0 = 0.0854 \times 100 = 8.54$ percent for the 365-day year, as shown below.

$$\left(\frac{\text{Face}}{\text{Price}}\right)^{\left(\frac{365 \text{ days}}{\text{days to maturity}}\right)} = \left(\frac{\$100,000}{\$98,000}\right)^{\left(\frac{365}{90}\right)} = 1.0854$$

loaned from banks with excess reserves to banks with insufficient reserves. The interest rate on these 1-day bank loans is called the *federal funds rate*. The fed funds rate is probably the interest rate most studied by money market economists in business, finance, and government policy-making agencies. It fluctuates quickly over a wide range and is considered one of the best indicators of the U.S. monetary authority's (namely, the Federal Reserve System's) current confidential credit-tightening or credit-easing actions. Bankers obtain or sell federal funds simply by calling other bankers.

Eurodollar loans are large, short-term loans denominated in U.S. dollars. The loans are usually arranged by banks with large international operations such as Citibank in New York City or the Bank of America in San Francisco. Large banks around the world arrange Eurodollar loans; the market is global.

Eurodollar loans are typically made to borrowers in countries with sound national economies and higher current interest rates. International bankers arrange Eurodollar loans for their banks' customers, and banks frequently borrow or lend Eurodollars for themselves. An intermediary's fee of one-tenth of 1 percent, or a yield spread of the same size, presents ample profit opportunity for a banker arranging a multimillion Eurodollar loan for a client.

Repurchase agreements, or *repos,* are instruments used by securities dealers to help finance part of their multimillion-dollar inventories of marketable securities for one or a few days. For instance, if a securities dealer ends a day of trading with an increase of $40 million in its inventory of marketable securities, a repo may be sold to finance the $40 million inventory overnight. The securities dealer pays a repo broker a finder's fee (or broker's commission) to find an investor with $40 million of unused cash that needs to be invested overnight, while agreeing to repurchase these securities the next day at a slightly higher price. This slightly higher price represents the interest income for the overnight investor who purchased the repo. The investor is essentially making a short-term loan to the securities dealer with the securities dealer's inventory serving as collateral.

Repos that last longer than overnight, called *term repos,* can span 30 days or even longer. Term repos are marketable securities, actively traded between the money market trading desks of large banks and brokerage houses.

Securities issued by the U.S. government are traded by calls between Treasury bond dealers, the Treasury bond trading desks of large banks, and the Treasury bond trading desks of brokerage houses, just as money market securities are traded.

2-2   **U.S. GOVERNMENT SECURITIES**

Demand for increased government services has led to continual increases in the debt issues of the U.S. government in recent decades. These debt issues have been increasing in absolute amounts and on a per capita basis.

Government securities represent the indebtedness of U.S. governmental bodies. The owners of the securities are creditors; the governmental bodies are debtors. We will discuss the debt of the federal government in this section and the debt of state and local governments in the next section.

United States government securities are of such high quality that their yield is often used as an example of a **riskless,** or **default-free, interest rate.**

Nonmarketable Issues

Approximately 30 percent of the U.S. public debt consists of nonmarketable issues. They cannot be traded in the securities market; they are not transferable or negotiable; they cannot be used as collateral for a loan; they can be purchased only from the Treasury; and they can be redeemed only by the Treasury. By far the major portion of these nonmarketable securities are **U.S. savings bonds.**

The Series EE government savings bonds that are currently being issued pay interest rates that fluctuate; their rates are set to equal 85 percent of the current market yield on 5-year Treasury securities issued on the same date. Moreover, the EE savings bonds guarantee a minimum yield of 7.5 percent, no matter how low market interest rates may fall. The redemption prices and yields of these bonds, if held to any point in time, are printed on the bond. The buyers of savings bonds are discouraged from redeeming them before their maturity dates by being forced to accept the penalty of a lower rate of interest for early redemptions.

Marketable Issues

Marketable issues make up about 70 percent of the federal debt of the United States. Most investors purchase these issues from a bank or a securities dealer or broker. The holder of marketable government securities gains not only from the interest paid on these bonds but also from price appreciation. Bid and asked prices for these marketable issues are published daily in many newspapers. The prices are quoted in thirty-seconds of 1 percent of par (face value); fractions are written as though they were decimals. For example, 70.16 means $70\frac{16}{32}$ or 70.5 percent of par. Treasury bills are the most *liquid* marketable security issued by the U.S. Treasury because they have the shortest term to maturity.

Treasury bills were introduced above; they are short-term notes that mature in 13, 26, or 52 weeks from date of issue. The Treasury offers new T-bills every week, selling them on a *book entry basis*—the buyer never receives the security, only a receipt. Treasury bills are issued at a discount, which is the source of the investor's interest income. For example, a $10,000 Treasury bill maturing in 13 weeks—bond traders call it a 90-day T-bill—could be purchased for $9750 if it were to yield $250 of appreciation income. At the end of the 90 days, the buyer or current holder is repaid $10,000 by the U.S. Treasury.[3]

---

[3]The effective quarterly rate of return is $250/$9750 = 0.0256 × 100 = 2.56%; it is annualized as follows:

$$(1.0 + qr)^4 = (1.0256)^4 = (1.0 + ar) = 1.106399$$

where *qr* denotes the quarterly rate and *ar* denotes the annual rate of interest. Subtracting 1 from both sides of the equation gives 0.106399, or 10.6399%, or approximately 10.64 percent, compounded at an annual rate.

Certificates of indebtedness are issued at par (or face) value. Once issued, certificates are traded at fluctuating market prices. Certificates bear a fixed interest rate that is printed on the certificate and never varies—the coupon rate. The **coupon rate** tells what percent of the certificate's face value will be paid out as semiannual coupon interest payments. Certificates usually mature about a year from the date of issue, but the Treasury may set the period at any length of time up to 1 year. The U.S. Treasury does not issue certificates very frequently.

Treasury notes are like certificates of indebtedness but with longer maturities. Treasury notes are bonds that typically have maturities from 1 to 10 years. They are marketable debt securities that pay coupon interest semiannually, just like the certificates. The Treasury issues T-notes periodically, and the issues are traded actively.

Treasury bonds constitute about 10 percent of the federal debt. Treasury bonds have the longest maturities, ranging from 10 to 30 years from date of issue. Some issues of T-bonds are *callable* prior to their maturity date.[4] If the bonds are selling in the market above par, their *yield-to-maturity* is calculated to the nearest call date. If they are selling at a discount, the yield-to-maturity is calculated on the basis of their maturity date. The yield-to-maturity is a compound average rate of return calculated over the bond's entire life (it is explained in Chapters 12 and 13). A bond's one-period rate of return is calculated over a shorter period—as we saw in Table 1-1.

Agency Securities   The Federal Land Banks, the Federal Home Loan Banks, the Central Bank for Cooperatives, the Federal National Mortgage Association (called Fannie Mae), the Government National Mortgage Association (called Ginnie Mae), the Postal Service, and the Federal Intermediate Credit Bank are all U.S. government agencies allowed to issue their own debt obligations. Their bonds similar to other government bonds, but the federal government makes no guarantee that the interest and principal of these bonds will be paid. Therefore, they must pay slightly higher yields than federal bonds. However, it would be poor political and economic policy for the government to allow any of its agencies to default—and in several instances the Treasury has provided the funds needed to prevent such embarrassment. The debt of two agencies is *officially* guaranteed by the Treasury: the outstanding debt of the District of Columbia Armory Board and some Federal Housing Administration (FHA) bonds. The income from **federal agency bonds,** like all federal government bonds, is taxable.

Price Quotations in Newspapers   Figure 2-1 shows how market prices for U.S. government bonds are listed in the newspapers. If the securities are

---

[4]The Treasury bond issue maturing in November 2014 with a 11.75 percent coupon, for instance, is callable any time after 2009. The issue is listed in the newspapers as the 11¾'s of 2009–2014. Section 23-7 of Chapter 23 explains how to assess the value of the *call option* embedded in a callable bond.

TREASURY BONDS, NOTES & BILLS

Representative Over-the-Counter quotations based on transactions of $1 million or more as of 4 p.m. Eastern time.

Hyphens in bid-and-asked and bid changes represent 32nds; 101-01 means 101 1/32. a-Plus 1/64. b-Yield to call date. d-Minus 1/64. k-Nonresident aliens exempt from withholding taxes. n-Treasury notes. p-Treasury note; nonresident aliens exempt from withholding taxes.

TREASURY BONDS AND NOTES

Rate	Mat.	Date	Bid	Asked	Bid Chg.	Yld.
7 1/8	1989	Apr p	99-25	99-28	....	9.35
14 3/8	1989	Apr n	99-30	100-01	....	9.88
6 7/8	1989	May p	99-22	99-25	- 01	9.04
9 1/4	1989	May n	99-29	100-01	....	8.58
8	1989	May p	99-24	99-27	....	8.91
11 3/4	1989	May n	100-04	100-07	....	8.90
7 3/8	1989	Jun p	99-17	99-20	+ 01	8.94
9 5/8	1989	Jun p	100	100-03	....	8.94
7 5/8	1989	Jul p	99-13	99-16	....	9.18
14 1/2	1989	Jul n	101-05	101-08	....	9.25
7 3/4	1989	Aug p	99-10	99-13	+ 01	9.27
6 5/8	1989	Aug p	99	99-04	+ 01	9.15
13 7/8	1989	Aug n	101-13	101-17	....	9.11
8 1/2	1989	Sep k	99-13	99-17	....	9.52
9 3/8	1989	Sep p	99-25	99-29	....	9.56
11 7/8	1989	Oct n	101-03	101-06	....	9.42
7 7/8	1989	Oct p	99	99-04	....	9.53
6 3/8	1989	Nov p	98-04	98-08	+ 02	9.47
10 3/4	1989	Nov n	100-18	100-22	....	9.49
12 3/4	1989	Nov p	101-26	101-30	....	9.27
7 3/4	1989	Nov p	98-25	98-29	+ 01	9.54
7 7/8	1989	Dec p	98-21	98-25	+ 01	9.64
8 3/8	1989	Dec p	99	99-04	....	9.63
8 5/8	1995	Oct p	96-03	96-07	+ 02	9.41
9 1/2	1995	Nov p	100-07	100-11	+ 01	9.43
11 1/2	1995	Nov	109-30	110-02	+ 01	9.41
9 1/4	1996	Jan	99-07	99-11	+ 01	9.38
8 7/8	1996	Feb p	97-06	97-10	- 01	9.41
7 3/8	1996	May p	89-15	89-19	....	9.42
7 1/4	1996	Nov p	88-12	88-16	+ 01	9.40
8 5/8	1997	Aug k	95-17	95-21	- 01	9.38
8 1/2	1997	May k	94-29	95-01	....	9.39
8 7/8	1997	Nov p	96-31	97-03	- 01	9.37
8 1/8	1998	Feb p	92-21	92-25	+ 01	9.34
9	1998	May p	98-01	98-05	+ 01	9.30
9 1/4	1998	Aug p	99-15	99-19	-- 01	9.31
7	1993-98	May	86-04	86-08	+ 01	9.27
3 1/2	1998	Nov	94-27	95-13	+ 01	4.08
8 7/8	1998	Nov p	97-06	97-10	+ 03	9.30
8 7/8	1999	Feb p	97-11	97-15	+ 01	9.27
8 1/2	1994-99	May	94-09	94-13	+ 01	9.37
7 7/8	1995-00	Feb	90	90-04	+ 02	9.34
8 3/8	1995-00	Aug	93-07	93-11	+ 02	9.34
11 3/4	2001	Feb	117-01	117-07	....	9.32
13 1/8	2001	May	127-06	127-12	- 01	9.30
8	1996-01	Aug	90-30	91-04	- 01	9.22
13 3/8	2001	Aug	129-04	129-10	+ 04	9.32
15 3/4	2001	Nov	147-27	148-01	- 01	9.22
14 1/4	2002	Feb	136-17	136-23	- 09	9.29
11 5/8	2002	Nov	117-14	117-20	- 01	9.31
10 3/4	2003	Feb	110-29	111-03	- 01	9.31
10 3/4	2003	May	111	111-06	- 01	9.31
11 1/8	2003	Aug	114	114-06	- 01	9.31
11 7/8	2003	Nov	120-01	120-07	- 01	9.31
12 3/8	2004	May	124-15	124-21	- 01	9.30
13 3/4	2004	Aug	135-29	136-03	- 01	9.29
11 5/8	2004	Nov k	118-22	118-28	- 01	9.30
8 1/4	2000-05	May	91-10	91-16	+ 02	9.28
12	2005	May k	122-09	122-15	- 01	9.28
10 3/4	2005	Aug k	112-04	112-10	+ 02	9.27
10 5/8	2015	Aug k	114-01	114-07	....	9.18
9 7/8	2015	Nov k	106-23	106-29	+ 01	9.18
9 1/4	2016	Feb k	100-21	100-27	- 01	9.16
7 1/4	2016	May k	80-29	81-01	....	9.15
7 1/2	2016	Nov k	83-10	83-14	- 02	9.16
8 3/4	2017	May k	95-28	96	- 01	9.15
8 7/8	2017	Aug k	97-05	97-09	....	9.14
9 1/8	2018	May k	99-25	99-29	....	9.13
9	2018	Nov k	98-21	98-25	+ 01	9.12
8 7/8	2019	Feb k	97-19	97-23	+ 01	9.10

U.S. TREASURY BILLS

Mat. date	Bid (Discount)	Asked (Discount)	Yield
-1989-			
4-13	8.26	8.14	8.25
4-20	9.59	9.55	9.70
4-27	8.39	8.32	8.46
5- 4	8.66	8.59	8.76
5-11	8.69	8.63	8.81
5-18	8.50	8.43	8.62
5-25	8.54	8.48	8.69
6- 1	8.59	8.55	8.77
6- 8	8.70	8.66	8.90
6-15	8.59	8.56	8.81
6-22	8.68	8.65	8.92
6-29	8.61	8.58	8.86
7- 6	8.73	8.69	9.00
7-13	8.68	8.64	8.96
7-20	8.64	8.60	8.93
7-27	8.64	8.57	8.91
8- 3	8.74	8.70	9.07
8-10	8.72	8.65	9.03
8-17	8.73	8.67	9.07
8-24	8.71	8.67	9.08
8-31	8.77	8.73	9.16
9- 7	8.77	8.73	9.18
9-14	8.79	8.75	9.22
9-21	8.79	8.76	9.25
9-28	8.80	8.76	9.26
10- 5	8.77	8.74	9.26
10-26	8.78	8.74	9.27
11-24	8.80	8.76	9.32
12-21	8.78	8.74	9.32
-1990-			
1-18	8.72	8.68	9.29
2-15	8.77	8.73	9.39
3-15	8.77	8.74	9.45
4-12	8.75	8.72	9.47

Figure 2-1 Newspaper excerpt showing the day's prices for federal bonds.

coupon-paying bonds, the left-hand column gives the coupon rate. The next-to-the-left-hand column gives the maturity date of the issue; the lower-case letter "n" signifies Treasury notes. Treasury bills have no coupon rates since they pay interest as price appreciation rather than by coupon payments. The bid and asked prices are in the next two columns of Figure 2-1. For coupon-paying bonds, the bid and asked prices are stated as percentages of the bond's face value. For T-bills the bid and asked values are the annualized percentage discounts from face value which the investor will earn if the T-bills are purchased at their respective bid or asked prices. The **bid price** is the highest price (stated as a percentage of face value) that any potential investor is willing to pay. The **asked price** is the lowest price that any potential seller is willing to take.[5] The column headed "Chg." shows the difference between the previous day's closing price and the current day's closing price. The right-hand column headed "Yield" contains the yield-to-maturity the investor will earn if the security is purchased at the current market price and held to the maturity date.

Zeros Many investors cannot buy U.S. government securities because the *denominations* are so large. The smallest Treasury bill denomination, for ex-

[5]For money market securities, the bid and asked prices are stated as interest rates instead of percentages of face value in some newspapers. The bid and asked prices stated as interest rates are simply the yield-to-maturity an investor would earn if the T-bill were purchased at the current bid and asked dollar prices, respectively.

ample, is $10,000. As a result, in 1982 two security brokerages started regularly purchasing multimillion-dollar blocks of Treasury bonds, **stripping** the coupons from the principal (or corpus) of the bonds, and selling certificates that were essentially small-denomination shares in the pool of default-free Treasury securities. The brokerages profited from selling the certificates at a slightly higher price than they paid and, in so doing, created convenient denominations that small investors could afford. **Zeros** also eliminated the semiannual problem about where to invest the coupons. Merrill Lynch, Pierce, Fenner & Smith called their certificates Treasury Investment Growth Receipts (TIGRs). Salomon Brothers called their similar product Certificates of Accrual on Treasury Securities (CATS).

TIGR and CATs investors got their certificates at a deep discount from maturity value—the price gain was the investor's interest income. But, the investor would *receive nothing* until the selected maturity date arrived—months, years, or decades later. The further away the maturity date, the deeper the discount (and resulting price gain) to the investor. Under this process one 20-year T-bond can be converted into 41 different zeros that mature on 40 different dates that are all 6 months apart. The pool of underlying T-bonds is held in trust until the last zero matures and the pool is liquidated to repay it.

To buy a zero coupon bond that will mature in the year 2012 with a face value of $14,000, an investor need only spend about $1000 in 1990 to buy the certificate. This will yield an average annual rate of return of slightly over 7 percent per year over the 22 years, if the zero is held to maturity. The disadvantage of investing in zero coupon bonds is that taxable investors must pay income taxes on the *implicit* interest income each year—even though they do not receive any coupons or other cash inflows of any kind. Zero coupon bonds cannot be used to delay income tax payments—only the previously taxed income is postponed.

After private enterprise created CATS and TIGRs in 1982, the U.S. Treasury announced in 1985 the introduction of Separate Trading of Registered Interest and Principal of Securities (STRIPS). Under the STRIPS program, Treasury bonds are eligible to have their coupons and corpus (the underlying bonds) registered separately in a book-entry system at the Federal Reserve to facilitate transfers between investors. Essentially, the Treasury decided not to issue zero coupon bonds but to make the zeros market that the brokerages operate more efficient. Since 1985 Merrill Lynch, Salomon, and other brokerages have been selling STRIPS instead of TIGRs, CATS, and other zero coupon securities.

2-3   **MUNICIPAL BONDS**

Bonds issued by states, counties, parishes, cities, towns, townships, boroughs, villages, and special tax districts of municipal corporations (such as toll bridge authorities, college dormitory authorities, sewer districts, *ad infinitum*) are all called **municipals.** With such a wide assortment of issuing entities, there is naturally just as wide a variety of agreements with "muni" bond investors.

Federal laws provide that the *coupon income* from obligations of political subdivisions is exempted from federal income taxes.[6] This tax exemption does not apply to any capital gains that may be earned. Because of their tax exemption, munis are frequently held by individuals and partnerships in high income tax brackets.

The interest on **registered bonds** is paid by a check that is written in favor of the bond's registered owner. Bonds that do not have their owners' names registered are called bearer bonds. **Bearer bond** investors cash in the coupons that are attached to their bond as each coupon comes due. Investors who own municipal bonds that are bearer bonds do not have to periodically report to the federal government that they own the bonds because the coupon income from municipals is exempt from federal income taxes. *Tax evaders* loved the bearer bonds because when they sold munis or gave them away, it was easy to avoid paying the capital gains or gift tax, respectively, because there was no registered list of owners that reflected coupon income payments or changes in ownership. To reduce the opportunities for tax evasion the federal government curtailed the issue of new bearer bonds by municipalities after 1981 by removing their tax-exempt status, unless the issue was registered. However, bearer bonds issued before 1981 can still be traded.

The disadvantage of owning bearer bonds is that thieves find them easy to sell since the owner's name is not registered. In contrast, owners of **registered bonds** are protected because all registered owners must notify the trustee of the bond issue of any change in ownership. This registration procedure makes stolen bonds difficult to transfer and also makes it easier for tax collectors to track down tax evaders. Municipal bonds' tax-exemption advantage also works to the benefit of the issuers. Municipal bonds can usually be sold at lower market interest rates than taxable bonds with equal quality ratings.

General Obligation (GO) Bonds

Municipal bonds fall into one of two categories—general obligation (GO) bonds and limited obligation bonds. **General obligation bonds** are often called *full faith and credit bonds* because of the strength of their pledge. GO bonds are issued by muncipalities that have unlimited power to tax property to meet their obligations and promise to pay them without any limitations.

Limited Obligation Bonds

The term **limited obligation bonds** is applied when the issuer is in some way restricted in raising revenues to pay its debts. **Revenue bonds** are the most significant form of limited obligation. Such bonds are only entitled to the rev-

---

[6]The federal tax exemption on coupons paid by municipal bonds does not apply to all munis. *Industrial development bonds* and certain other categories of municipal bonds are not exempt from federal income taxes.

enue generated by the specific property that is providing service. These bonds are widely used to finance municipally owned businesses like water works, electricity, gas, and sewage disposal systems.

Insured Municipal Bonds

Though tax-exempt income from a municipal bond attracts some investors, they may still shy away from such bonds if there is any risk that the issue might not be able to repay its obligations. This understandable risk aversion makes it difficult for municipalities whose bonds do not receive the highest quality ratings to issue bonds. In the 1970s two firms began to insure bonds issued by municipalities that did not merit the highest quality credit ratings. The two firms are the American Municipal Bond Insurance Association (AMBAC) and the Municipal Bond Insurance Association (MBIA). Insuring municipal bond issues proved to be such a profitable business that several similar firms were started in the 1980s.

Standard & Poor's and some other bond-rating agencies have agreed to give municipal bond issues insured by the best **muni bond insurance** companies the highest quality bond ratings. Thus, if a muni bond insurer agrees to insure a municipality's bond issue, the issue will get a top credit rating, which it would never have been able to obtain otherwise. This makes it much easier for small and/or risky municipalities to sell their bond issues—and to sell them at lower interest rates.

2-4   **BONDS ISSUED BY CORPORATIONS**

A **bond** is a marketable legal contract that promises to pay its investor a stated rate of interest and to repay the principal at the maturity date. Bonds differ according to their provisions for repayment, security pledged, and other technical aspects. Bonds are the **senior securities** of a firm; the law requires bankrupt firms to pay off their bondholders before their stock investors.

The Indenture Contract

The **indenture,** or deed of trust, is the legal agreement between the corporation and the bondholders. Every bond issued under one indenture has the same rights and protection. However, bonds of the same issue may mature at different dates and have different interest rates.

The indenture is a complicated legal instrument containing restrictions, pledges, and promises. The **trustee,** usually a large bank, ensures that the issuing firm keeps its promises and obeys the restrictions of the contract. The trustee also takes any appropriate legal action to see that the terms of the contract are kept and the rights of the bondholders are upheld. Because individual bondholders cannot make sure that the company does not violate its agreements and cannot take substantial legal action if the firm does violate them, the trustee assumes these responsibilities. Essentially, the trustee is the "watchdog" for the bondholders.

Varying Features of Bonds

Interest Payments   Bond interest is usually paid semiannually, though annual payments are also popular. The method of payment depends on whether the bond is a registered or coupon bond. The interest on *registered bonds* is paid to the holder by check. **Coupon bonds** have a series of attached coupons that are clipped off at the appropriate times and sent to a bank for collection of the interest.

Bearer Bonds   If the coupon interest may be paid to whoever has the bond, the bonds are called *bearer bonds*. Unlike registered bonds, the ownership of bearer bonds may be transferred simply by handing them over, like cash.

Coupon Rate   The **coupon rate** is the stipulated interest rate to be paid on the face value of a bond. It represents a fixed annual dollar amount that is paid as long as the debtor is solvent. (Corporations' income bonds or adjustment bonds are the only exceptions.) The coupon rate is fixed after the issuing corporation's investment banker has weighed the risk of default, the credit standing of the issuer, the convertibility options, the investment position of the industry, the security backing of the bond, and the appropriate market rate of interest for the firm's industry, size, and risk class. The goal is to pick a coupon rate that is just high enough to attract investors.

Money market securities, zero coupon bonds, and certain other debt instruments pay no coupons, as we have seen.

Yield-to-Maturity   Riskier bonds must pay higher **yields-to-maturity** (YTM) to attract investors.[7] The YTM is more significant than the coupon rate to bond investors. If the bond is selling at a *discount,* its market price is below its face value. In this case the bond's YTM exceeds its coupon rate. If it is selling at a *premium,* the market price of the bond is above its face value and the coupon rate is higher than the YTM.

Maturities   Maturities vary widely. Bonds are sometimes grouped by the length of time until maturity that existed on the date the bond was first issued. *Money market securities* mature in 270 days or less. *Short-term bonds* are any bonds maturing within about 1 to 5 years. They are common in industrial financing and may be secured or unsecured. *Medium-term bonds* mature in 5 to about 10 years. If a bond is originally issued as a medium-term bond, it is usually secured by a real estate or equipment mortgage or it may be backed by another

[7]The phrases *yield-to-maturity* and *average rate of return compounded annually to maturity* both refer to the effective rate of return to the owner if the bond is held to maturity. Bond yields are discussed in detail in Chapters 12 and 13.

security. *Long-term bonds* have lives of 20 or more years. Capital-intensive industries with long expectations of equipment life, such as railroads and utilities, are the greatest users of long-term bonds.

Call Provision   A call provision may be included in the indenture. This provision allows the debtor to call or redeem (or call in) the bonds at a specified amount (above par) before the maturity date.[8]

Sinking Fund   Sinking fund bonds are not special types of bonds. This is just a name given to describe the method of repayment. Any bond issue can have a sinking fund by merely providing for it in the indenture. **Sinking funds** arise when the issuer decides to retire its bond issue systematically by setting aside a certain amount each year for that purpose. The payment is made to the sinking fund agent, who is usually the trustee. This third party uses the money to call the bonds annually at some call premium or to purchase them on the open market if they are selling at a price that is below the call price. Sinking funds are used in risky financings because such debt issues can be made more attractive to investors by adding a provision that assures the debt's repayment.[9]

Secured Bonds

The most important criterion for classifying corporate bonds is whether they are secured or unsecured. The question is what **collateral**, if any, has been pledged to help pay investors if the company should default?

If the indenture provides for a **lien** on designated property, the bond is a secured bond. A lien is a legal right given to the bondholders, through the trustee, to sell the pledged property so as to obtain the money to satisfy the unpaid portion of interest or principal. Pledged security makes bonds more attractive to investors because it makes repayment more likely. In reality, the collateral is seldom sold if the issue defaults. The company is usually reorganized with more junior securities (such as unsecured bonds or preferred stock) issued to replace the secured bonds that defaulted. The presence of a lien on the property strongly supports the bondholders' interests in the reorganization, however.

Mortgage Bonds   A bond issue secured with a lien on real property or buildings is a **mortgage bond**.[10] If all the assets of the firm are collateral under the terms of the indenture, it is called a *blanket mortgage*. The total assets need not be

---

[8]The effect of call provisions on bond pricing is analyzed in Chapter 23 by treating the callable security as a noncallable bond with an embedded call option attached.

[9]The effects that a sinking fund and/or the provision of collateral has on the pricing of a bond issue are analyzed in Chapter 14.

[10]*Mortgage bonds* are different from *home mortgages* in several important respects. (1) A home mortgage is a loan that a potential home buyer obtains from a single mortgage investor (such as a commercial bank) in order to buy a house. The typical home mortgage

(continues)

pledged; only some of the land or buildings of the company may be mortgaged. It can be a first mortgage, second mortgage, or subsequent mortgage, each with its respective claim on the assets of the firm in case of default. A first mortgage is the most secure because it enjoys first claim to assets. A mortgage bond may be *open-end, limited open-end,* or *closed-end,* or it may contain an *after-acquired property* clause.

An *open-end mortgage* means that more bonds can be issued on the same mortgage contract. The creditors are usually protected by restrictions limiting such additional borrowing. The open-end mortgage will normally contain an *after-acquired property* clause, which provides that all property acquired after the first mortgage was issued be added to the property already pledged as security by the contract. A *limited open-end mortgage* allows the firm to issue additional bonds up to a specified maximum (for example, up to 50 percent of the original cost of the pledged property). A *closed-end mortgage* allows no additional borrowing on that mortgage. This, with an after-acquired property clause, guarantees an increasing security base for the creditors. These various collateral provisions all affect the risk and return of a mortgage bond issue.

Collateral Trust Bonds   When the collateral deposited with the trustee of a bond issue consists of the stocks and bonds of other companies, these secured bonds are called **collateral trust bonds.** Since the assets of holding companies are usually largely in the form of stocks and bonds of their subsidiaries, holding companies are the main issuers of collateral trust bonds.

Unsecured Bonds   **Debenture bonds** are unsecured bonds. Debentures are issued with no lien against specific property provided in the indenture. They are considered a claim on earnings, not assets. This is not to say that the bondholders are unprotected in case of default but rather that they are general creditors. All assets not specifically pledged and any balance remaining after payment of secured debts from assets previously pledged are available to pay the legal claims of **general creditors.** Debenture indentures usually take this added riskiness into account and contain specific protecting provisions. The indentures may restrict any further issuing of debentures unless earnings over a certain number of years are 2 or 3 times what is needed to cover the original debenture interest. Another

---

(continued)
is worth less than $100,000, and a home mortgage as large as $1 million is rare. An issue of mortgage bonds usually involves much larger amounts. (2) An issue of mortgage bonds might be made up of hundreds or thousands of bonds that each have a face value of $100 or $1000, for instance. (3) The issuer of mortgage bonds usually sells the whole issue to one investment banker, who, in turn, distributes the individual bonds to the investing public through a series of transactions having an aggregate value in the millions of dollars. In contrast, the home mortgage lender owns the entire home mortgage. (4) Many home mortgages are not readily marketable or transferable to another investor, but mortgage bonds are marketable securities.

common clause says that if any secured debt is issued, the debentures will be secured by an equal amount. Sometimes working capital (that is, current assets minus current liabilities) must be maintained at a certain ratio to the principal amount of the debenture or the issuing corporation is not allowed to pay dividends on its common stock.

Subordinate debentures are explicitly subordinate to all other general creditors holding claims on the issuer's assets. These other general creditors are usually raw material suppliers who sell to the firm on credit and/or financial institutions that have granted loans to the firm. Debentures with this junior position among the issuer's creditors must pay high rates of interest to attract investors.

Bonds with Special Characteristics

Several types of debt instruments have the general characteristics of bonds but, because they have some special distinguishing characteristic, are given special names. For example, if a mortgage bond is secured so that it covers only part of the property of the firm or only a specific section of a railroad, it is called a *divisional bond*. It is the first mortgage on that operating division of the firm.

Direct Lien Bonds   These are special bonds secured by one piece of property, such as a railroad terminal or bridge. Such a bond might then be referred to as a *terminal bond* or a *bridge bond*. If two or more companies own the property that is securing the bond, such as a railroad bridge, it is called a *joint bond*.

Prior Lien Bonds   These are bonds that have been placed ahead of the first mortgage, usually during the reorganization of a bankrupt firm. Only with the permission of the first mortgage bondholders can prior lien bonds be issued, taking over the first mortgage's previous first claim on assets.

Junior Mortgage Bonds   These bonds have a claim to assets and earnings that is secondary to senior mortgage bonds. Because it is poor public relations for an issue to bear the title *second mortgage,* these issues typically have names such as *refunding mortgage* or *consolidated mortgage.*

Convertible Bonds   **Convertible debentures** have all the characteristics of debenture bonds, but under certain conditions they may be converted into a specified number of shares of preferred or common stock. This conversion privilege is a ''sweetener'' to make the unsecured debt more attractive.

Assumed or Guaranteed Bonds   When a large firm takes over a small one in a merger or consolidation, the bonds of the small company must be recognized. If the small company is dissolved by the merger, the new entity assumes the liability represented by the bonds. These bonds are then covered not only by the specific property pledged in the indenture but also by the large firm's promise-to-pay clause.

If the merged company continues to operate as a unique division within the large company, its bonds will be guaranteed by the larger firm. Depending upon the willingness of the parent company to continue the guarantee through endorsement of the bonds, rental of its property, or some other legal agreement between the two companies, these bonds may be solid or very weak.

Participating Bonds **Participating bonds** share in the earnings of the firm. They have a guaranteed rate of interest but may also participate in earnings up to an additional specified percentage. Because they pay increased interest with increased earnings, they are unpopular with the common stockholders of the company, who prefer to keep all earnings for themselves. For this reason, participating bonds may be issued by companies that have such poor credit positions that they could not raise the funds needed to survive by any other means.

Zeros As explained above, *zero coupon bonds* are sold at discounts from their face (or maturity) value so that the investor's price gain is the interest income.

Put Bonds In 1974 Citibank issued the first **put bonds** in the United States. However, they had been issued in Canada for years and are called either *extendables* or *retractables* there. These bonds all have an early redemption option that allows the bond's investor to put (or sell) the bond back to the issuer before the bond's maturity date at a price called the strike price (or contract price or exercise price). Investors benefit from this early redemption option because it essentially puts a floor under the bond's market price so that it cannot fall below the strike price.[11]

Asset-backed securities are another category of special bonds. However, these securities constitute such a large and rapidly growing part of the outstanding debt in the United States that they are the topic of the next section.

2-5 ASSET-BACKED SECURITIES AND SECURITIZATION

Asset-backed securities are a relatively new category of marketable securities that are collateralized by financial assets like accounts receivable—most commonly, mortgages, leases, or installment loan contracts. "Financial-asset-backed securities" would be a more descriptive name than asset-backed securities. Asset-backed financing involves a process called *securitizing*.

---

[11]Put options and the exercise price of a put option are examined more deeply in Chapter 23. For a particularly rich discussion of fixed-income option valuation see Robert W. Kopprash, "Contingent Take-Down Options on Fixed Income Securities," in *The Handbook of Fixed Income Securities,* Frank J. Fabozzi and I. M. Pollack, eds. (Homewood, Ill.: Dow Jones–Irwin, 1983), chap. 23.

Securitization is a disintermediating process in which the credit from commercial banks and other lenders is replaced by marketable debt securities that can be issued at a lower cost. Securitization involves forming a pool of financial assets so that debt securities can be sold to external investors to finance the pool.

Chronological Development of Securitization

Asset-backed securities, in chronological order of their date of inception, include the following types.

1. *Repurchase agreements (repos)* are money market securities that date back to the 1950s; they were discussed in Section 2-1. Repos are the oldest asset-backed security.
2. *Mortgage pass through securities (MPTS)* are certificates backed by a pool of insured mortgages. They were first sold in 1970 by the Government National Mortgage Association (GNMA), nicknamed Ginnie Mae.
3. *Mortgage-backed bonds (MBB)* are debt securities that have had their credit enhanced by being overcollateralized and by the purchase of credit insurance.
4. *Collateralized mortgage obligations (CMO),* issued by the Federal Home Loan Mortgage Corporation (FHLMC), called Freddie Mac, are multiclass debt securities used to finance a pool of insured mortgages.
5. *Student loans* were first pooled and sold by the Student Loan Marketing Association (SLMA), called Sallie Mae, in 1973.

Categories 2 through 5 were assisted by U.S. federal government agencies that insured the pools of financial assets against default. The profitability of these government-subsidized financing plans set the stage for the following private securitization programs.

6. *Trade-credit-receivable-backed bonds* were first issued by AMAX in 1982.
7. *Equipment-leasing-backed bonds* were first issued by Comdisco in 1984.
8. *Certificates of automobile receivable securities (CARS)* were first issued by Salomon Brothers in 1985.
9. *Small Business Administration* loans were pooled and issued as equity shares by the First National Bank of Wisconsin in 1985.
10. *Collateralized lease equipment obligations (CLEOs)* include the computer-lease-backed bonds issued by First Boston in 1985.
11. *Certificates amortizing revolving debts (CARDS)* were pools of credit card receivables that were first issued by Salomon Brothers in 1986.

12. *Policyholder loan bonds (PHL bonds)* were underwritten by Morgan Stanley in 1988 to securitize a pool of loans from Prudential Life Insurance Company's whole life insurance policyholders who had borrowed against the cash value of their policies.

During the 1980s these financial-asset-backed securitization plans became a multibillion-dollar business, increasing faster than any other type of financing. Securitization is a growing trend that will reshape the investment banking industry and, most especially, the commercial banking industry in the years ahead.

Costs Involved in Securitizing Assets

The costs involved in securitizing financial assets include the costs of administration (such as investment bankers' fees), of providing information to the public and the credit-rating agencies, and, in most instances, of providing the insurance and/or guarantees needed to enhance the credit ratings of the underlying loans. Some form of credit enhancement is needed to raise the quality rating of the pool of financial assets high enough to make them marketable to investors.

Various Forms of Credit Enhancement

Securitization usually involves the creation of debt securities. As a result, the default risk that is traditionally borne by equity investors must be assumed by some other method. **Credit enhancement** is typically accomplished via the following procedures. First, the assets to be financed are placed in trust with some third party, such as a bank, as collateral. The next challenge is to provide for AAA-, or at least AA-, grade ratings by the major credit-rating agencies like Moody's or Standard & Poor's for the collateral. If the proper credit enhancement arrangements are not made, investors' fears of default will keep them from buying the new debtlike securities. There are several methods of obtaining high credit ratings for securitized assets.

1. If the seller of the financial assets has a bond rating of AAA and that seller will grant the investors recourse in case the assets default, then the rating agencies will usually give the asset-backed securities the same AAA rating as the AAA-grade corporation that stands behind them.

    For example, a AAA-grade commercial bank could finance its inventory of home mortgages by selling CMOs. However, the bank would have to show the mortgages as both an asset and a liability on its balance sheet, since the CMO investors have recourse on the bank in case the mortgage pool defaults.

2. Credit enhancement can be obtained through a letter of credit from a highly rated bank or insurance company. If the financial assets that might default are guaranteed by a company with a AAA rating, the

credit-rating agencies will usually assign the insurer's AAA grade to the insured securities.

3. Credit enhancement can be obtained from a surety bond that is purchased from a AAA-rated bank or insurance company. The pool of financial assets that might default gain a AAA rating because the insurance indemnifies investors against potential losses.

4. The seller of the financial assets can **overcollateralize** the pool; posting collateral valued at 125 percent of the value of the financial assets in the pool is customary. Thus, if 25 percent of the collateral assets default, there are still enough sound assets left to provide full collateral for the remaining assets in the pool.

    MBBs, for instance, are overcollateralized. The disadvantage to the issuer of MBBs is that the excess of the collateral over the market value of the MBBs is, in effect, an equity investment in the pool that the issuer must retain until the pool of MBBs is liquidated.

5. Insurance can be purchased from an insurance company (or other AAA-grade-rated third party) on a pool of financial assets that involve some default risks. The insured collateral can usually obtain AAA ratings if the insurer has a AAA-grade rating.

6. A pool of assets that are highly diversified geographically, by debtor, by collateral, or in other ways can be created; this is a venerable method of reducing risk. Securities issued against the lower-risk pool can obtain higher credit ratings than the individual assets in the pool.

Benefits Derived from Securitization

The benefits obtained from securitization vary with the form of the issue. Typical benefits are (1) the seller of the financial assets can avoid the interest rate risk and the default risk associated with carrying the assets in inventory, (2) *prepayment risks* borne by the seller of the financial assets may be transferred to the investors, (3) diversification opportunities are increased for both the seller of the financial assets and those who invest in them, (4) lower-cost financing for inventories of financial assets may be available, and (5) funds flow more efficiently from investors to borrowers. Finally, as a result of the preceding benefits, the seller of the financial assets gains liquidity. Stated differently, assets that may be illiquid individually (such as mortgages) are repackaged and turned into liquid financial securities.[12] Attainment of liquidity is one of the primary goals of securitization.

[12]See Christine A. Pavel, *Securitization* (Chicago, Ill.: Probus, 1989). This nonmathematical text examines the development of the loan-based asset-backed securities markets. The nature of securitization, its benefits and drawbacks, accounting for the transactions, regulatory issues, and implications for the future are discussed. Also see *Journal of Applied Corporate Finance,* Fall 1988, vol. 1, no. 5; the entire issue is devoted to securitization.

Different Types of Mortgage-Backed Securities

Mortgage-backed securities are the oldest and largest of the asset-backed financing plans; they have evolved into several forms that furnish blueprints for other forms of asset-backed securities.

1. *Mortgage pass through securities (MPTS),* as their name implies, immediately pass all cashflows to those who invest in the pool. As a result, MPTS investors suffer with the uncertainties of mortgage prepayments. Even mortgage defaults result in prepayments because the mortgages in the pool are insured against default. MPTS are popular in spite of their prepayment uncertainty because the MPTS issuers get to remove the mortgage assets and all associated liabilities from their balance sheets.

2. *Mortgage-backed bonds (MBB)* modify the uncertain mortgage payments flowing into the pool and transform them into cashflows that are like fixed coupons for the MBB investors. The MBB issuer must over-collateralize the pool to enhance its credit rating and make the MBBs easier to sell. In so doing, the MBB issuer, in effect, takes a residual risk position in the pool, which detracts from the issuer's balance sheet.

3. *Collateralized mortgage obligations (CMO)* allow their issuers to repackage the uncertain mortgage payments flowing into the pool and use them to service several different classes of debt securities called **tranches.** If two tranches are used, say, a fast-pay tranch and a slow-pay tranch, the slow-pay tranch would presumably be the class of securities with the higher risk. The disadvantages of CMOs are that the issuer must retain the lowest class of CMOs (which is like an equity investment in the pool) until the entire pool is liquidated, and the issuer must show the pool's assets and liabilities on its balance sheet.

4. *The real estate mortgage conduit (REMIC)* is a promising new instrument created by subtitle H of the Tax Reform Act of 1986. A REMIC is a separate legal entity into which mortgage originators can sell mortgage assets and thus simplify their balance sheet (as with the MPTS). In addition, REMICs can use the cashflows from their mortgages to service multiple classes of debt securities (like a CMO's tranches).[13]

5. *Shared appreciation mortgages (SAMs)* are arrangements in which a real estate buyer who is seeking a mortgage at a lower interest rate gives a cooperating lender an **equity kicker.** This equity kicker comes in the form of a share of the property appreciation when the property is sold.

[13]For more details about mortgage-backed securities see Frank Fabozzi, *The Handbook of Mortgage-Backed Securities* (Chicago, Ill.: Probus, 1985). See also Frank Fabozzi, *Mortgage-Backed Securities* (Chicago, Ill.: Probus, 1987) and Jess Lederman, *Secondary Mortgage Market* (Chicago, Ill.: Probus, 1987).

Most asset-backed securities are liquid because the investment banking firm that securitized the assets agrees to maintain a liquid secondary market in the securities.

COMMON STOCK

Common stock is the first security of a corporation to be issued and, in the event of bankruptcy, the last to be retired. Common stock represents an ownership share in the firm; it has the lowest-priority claim on earnings and assets of all securities issued. The chance of a common stockholder getting anything back from a bankrupt firm is minimal. But, common stock has an unlimited potential for dividend payments and price appreciation. In contrast, bonds and preferred stock have a contract for fixed interest or dividend payments that common stock does not have. As Table 2-1 shows, the investor's risk is higher with common stock than with any other security a firm might issue. As a result of this risk, investors refuse to invest in common stocks unless they offer a rate of return sufficiently high to induce the investors to assume the possible losses.

When investors buy common stock, they can obtain certificates as proof of their part as owners of the firm if they so desire. A stock certificate states the number of shares purchased, their par value (if any), and usually the transfer agent. When stock is purchased, the new owner and the number of shares bought are noted in the stock record book of the *transfer agent*. As a result, there is little reason for most investors to have stock certificates prepared. The *registrar* checks to verify that the transfer agent made no errors.

Common Stockholders' Voting Rights

Common stockholders elect the board of directors and vote on major issues that affect the corporation because they are the owners of the corporation. But most stockholders are not interested in the voting power they possess and simply sign and return the proxies mailed to them by the company. A **proxy** allows a named person, usually a member of corporate management, to vote the shares of the proxy signer at the stockholders' meeting. The use of proxies usually allows management, which seldom owns a majority of votes, to vote its decisions into effect.

Many corporate charters allow for **cumulative voting.** This permits a stockholder to have as many votes as he or she has shares of stock times the number of directors being elected. The stock owner may cast all these cumulative votes for only one director or divide them among several. This provision allows stockholders with a significant minority of shares to gain representation on the board of directors.

The **preemptive right** allows existing stockholders the right to subscribe to any new issue of stock so that they can maintain their previous fraction of total outstanding shares. The preemptive right, if exercised, prevents dilution of ownership control inherent in additional stock issues. Not all issues of stock have the preemptive right.

Par Value

Par value is the face value of a share of stock. It was introduced to guarantee that the corporation would receive a fair price for the value of the firm, as represented by a share of stock. However, the concept was undermined during the early 1900s when dishonest dealers sold stock for less than its par value—this is sometimes called ''watering the stock.'' In 1912, New York became the first state to allow stock to be issued with no par value. Such stock can be issued at any price because it has no par to dictate a minimum value. However, since no-par stock's peak of popularity in the 1920s, corporations have largely given it up in favor of low-par shares. Today most companies set a par value on their stock at a level below the price the shares will command on the market; $1 per share is common.[14] The par value of a stock today tells us little or nothing about the value of the shares.

Book Value

The **book value** per share is calculated by adding total liabilities and preferred stock (if any), which are obtained from the balance sheet, subtracting that sum from total assets, and then dividing the difference (which equals total common equity) by the number of shares of common stock outstanding. Book value gives some indication of the net assets per common share, but it has no substantial effect on stock prices. During the Depression of the early 1930s and again in recent years, many companies found their stock was selling far below book value. Book and market values might be equal on the day the stock in a new corporation is issued, but after that, it appears that only coincidence will ever make them equal at any given moment. Table 2-2 shows how book value and par value compare with the actual market price of the stock for a few randomly selected corporations. The variations in the three values for each corporation are wide.

Stock Price Quotations

Figure 2-2 shows two different newspaper excerpts listing the previous day's closing stock prices. Figure 2-2a provides New York Stock Exchange (NYSE) prices. The two columns on the left side of Figure 2-2a present the highest and lowest prices on record for each stock during the previous 365 days. The name of the issuing corporation in abbreviated form and the most recent cash dividend

---

[14]**Master limited partnerships** are an alternative to the corporate form of business organization. Those who invest in a master limited partnership can enjoy many of the benefits of common stock investment without suffering the burden of double taxation. For details about this form of investment see J. M. Collins and R. P. Bey. ''The Master Limited Partnership: An Alternative to the Corporation,'' *Financial Management,* Winter 1986, vol. 15, pp. 5–14.

Table 2-2

COMPARISON OF 1988 PAR, BOOK, AND MARKET VALUES FOR SHARES OF RANDOMLY SELECTED CORPORATIONS

Corporation	Par per share	Cash div. per share	Number of common shares (000)	Book value per share	Range of market price
ATT	$1	$1.20	1,075,000	$10.68	$24–$30
COMPAQ Computer	$0.01	$ 0	4,300	$21.13	$42–$66
Firestone Tire	None	$0.95	35,000	$33.72	$23–$50
General Motors	$1.66	$2.50	610,200	$57.81	$30–$44
Goodyear Tire	None	$1.70	57,400	$35.30	$47–$68
IBM	$1.25	$4.40	590,800	$66.99	$104–$130

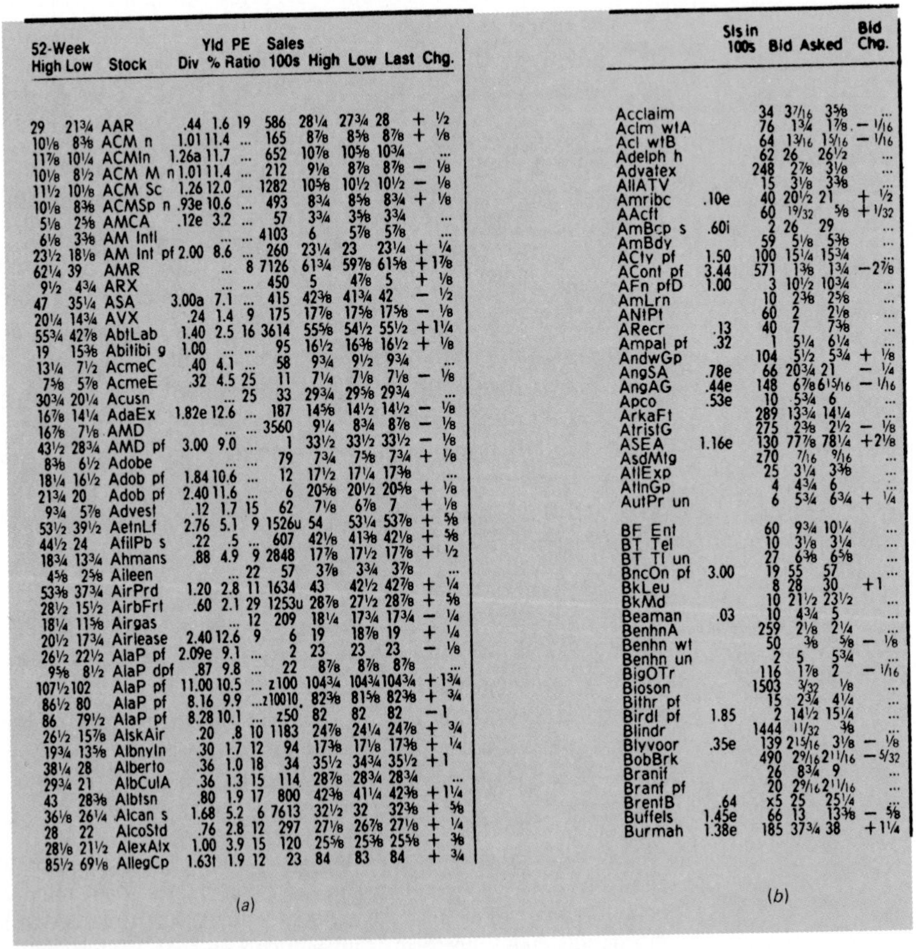

52-Week High	52-Week Low	Stock	Div	Yld %	PE Ratio	Sales 100s	High	Low	Last	Chg.
29	21 3/4	AAR	.44	1.6	19	586	28 1/4	27 3/4	28	+ 1/2
10 1/8	8 3/8	ACM n	1.01	11.4	...	165	8 7/8	8 5/8	8 7/8	+ 1/8
11 7/8	10 1/4	ACMIn	1.26a	11.7	...	652	10 7/8	10 5/8	10 3/4	...
10 1/8	8 1/2	ACM M n	1.01	11.4	...	212	9 1/8	8 7/8	8 7/8	− 1/8
11 1/2	10 1/8	ACM Sc	1.26	12.0	...	1282	10 5/8	10 1/2	10 1/2	− 1/8
10 1/8	8 3/8	ACMSp n	.93e	10.6	...	493	8 3/4	8 5/8	8 3/4	+ 1/8
5 1/8	2 5/8	AMCA	.12e	3.2	...	57	3 3/4	3 5/8	3 3/4	...
6 1/8	3 3/8	AM Intl		...	...	4103	6	5 7/8	5 7/8	...
23 1/2	18 1/8	AM Int pf	2.00	8.6	...	260	23 1/4	23	23 1/4	+ 1/4
62 1/4	39	AMR		...	8	7126	61 3/4	59 7/8	61 5/8	+ 1 7/8
9 1/2	4 3/4	ARX		...	...	450	5	4 7/8	5	+ 1/8
47	35 1/4	ASA	3.00a	7.1	...	415	42 3/8	41 3/4	42	− 1/2
20 1/4	14 3/4	AVX	.24	1.4	9	175	17 7/8	17 5/8	17 5/8	− 1/8
55 3/4	42 7/8	AbtLab	1.40	2.5	16	3614	55 5/8	54 1/2	55 1/2	+ 1 1/4
19	15 3/8	Abitibi g	1.00	...	...	95	16 1/2	16 3/8	16 1/2	+ 1/8
13 1/4	7 1/2	AcmeC	.40	4.1	...	58	9 3/4	9 1/2	9 3/4	...
7 5/8	5 7/8	AcmeE	.32	4.5	25	11	7 1/4	7 1/8	7 1/8	− 1/8
30 3/4	20 1/4	Acusn		...	25	33	29 3/4	29 5/8	29 3/4	...
16 7/8	14 1/4	AdaEx	1.82e	12.6	...	187	14 5/8	14 1/2	14 1/2	− 1/8
16 7/8	7 1/8	AMD		...	...	3560	9 1/4	8 3/4	8 7/8	− 1/8
43 1/2	28 3/4	AMD pf	3.00	9.0	...	1	33 1/2	33 1/2	33 1/2	− 1/8
8 3/8	6 1/2	Adobe		...	...	79	7 3/4	7 5/8	7 3/4	+ 1/8
18 1/4	16 1/2	Adob pf	1.84	10.6	...	12	17 1/2	17 1/4	17 3/8	...
21 3/4	20	Adob pf	2.40	11.6	...	6	20 5/8	20 1/2	20 5/8	+ 1/8
9 3/4	5 7/8	Advest	.12	1.7	15	62	7 1/8	6 7/8	7	+ 1/8
53 1/2	39 1/2	AetnLf	2.76	5.1	9	1526u	54	53 1/4	53 7/8	+ 5/8
44 1/2	24	AfilPb s	.22	.5	...	607	42 1/8	41 3/8	42 1/8	+ 5/8
18 3/4	13 3/4	Ahmans	.88	4.9	9	2848	17 7/8	17 1/2	17 7/8	+ 1/2
4 5/8	2 5/8	Aileen		...	22	57	3 7/8	3 3/4	3 7/8	...
53 3/8	37 3/4	AirPrd	1.20	2.8	11	1634	43	42 1/2	42 7/8	+ 1/4
28 1/2	15 1/2	AirbFrt	.60	2.1	29	1253u	28 7/8	27 1/2	28 7/8	+ 5/8
18 1/4	11 5/8	Airgas		...	12	209	18 1/4	17 3/4	17 3/4	− 1/4
20 1/2	17 3/4	Airlease	2.40	12.6	9	6	19	18 7/8	19	+ 1/4
26 1/2	22 1/2	AlaP pf	2.09e	9.1	...	2	23	23	23	− 1/8
9 5/8	8 1/2	AlaP dpf	.87	9.8	...	22	8 7/8	8 7/8	8 7/8	...
107 1/2	102	AlaP pf	11.00	10.5	...	z100	104 3/4	104 3/4	104 3/4	+ 1 3/4
86 1/2	80	AlaP pf	8.16	9.9	...	z10010	82 3/8	81 5/8	82 3/8	+ 3/4
86	79 1/2	AlaP pf	8.28	10.1	...	z50	82	82	82	− 1
26 1/2	15 7/8	AlskAir	.20	.8	10	1183	24 7/8	24 1/4	24 7/8	+ 3/4
19 3/4	13 5/8	Albnyln	.30	1.7	12	94	17 3/8	17 1/8	17 3/8	+ 1/4
38 1/4	28	Alberto	.36	1.0	18	34	35 1/2	34 3/4	35 1/2	+ 1
29 3/4	21	AlbCulA	.36	1.3	15	114	28 7/8	28 3/4	28 3/4	...
43	28 3/8	Albtsn	.80	1.9	17	800	42 3/8	41 1/4	42 3/8	+ 1 1/4
36 1/8	26 1/4	Alcan s	1.68	5.2	6	7613	32 1/2	32	32 3/8	+ 5/8
28	22	AlcoStd	.76	2.8	12	297	27 1/8	26 7/8	27 1/8	+ 1/4
28 1/8	21 1/2	AlexAlx	1.00	3.9	15	120	25 5/8	25 3/8	25 5/8	+ 3/8
85 1/2	69 1/8	AllegCp	1.63t	1.9	12	23	84	83	84	+ 3/4

(a)

Stock	Div	Sls in 100s	Bid	Asked	Bid Chg.
Acclaim		34	3 7/16	3 5/8	...
Aclm wtA		76	1 3/4	1 7/8	− 1/16
Acl wtB		64	1 3/16	1 5/16	− 1/16
Adelph h		62	26	26 1/2	...
Advatex		248	2 7/8	3 1/8	...
AllATV		15	3 1/8	3 3/8	...
Amribc	.10e	40	20 1/2	21	+ 1/2
AAcft		60	19/32	5/8	+ 1/32
AmBcp s	.60i	2	26	29	...
AmBdy		59	5 1/8	5 3/8	...
ACty pf	1.50	100	15 1/4	15 3/4	...
ACont pf	3.44	571	1 3/8	1 3/4	− 2 7/8
AFn pfD	1.00	3	10 1/2	10 3/4	...
AmLrn		10	2 3/8	2 5/8	...
ANtPt		60	2	2 1/8	...
ARecr	.13	40	7	7 3/8	...
Ampal pf	.32	1	5 1/4	6 1/4	...
AndwGp		104	5 1/2	5 3/4	+ 1/8
AngSA	.78e	66	20 3/4	21	− 1/4
AngAG	.44e	148	6 7/8	6 15/16	− 1/16
Apco	.53e	10	5 3/4	6	...
ArkaFt		289	13 3/4	14 1/4	...
AtristG		275	2 3/8	2 1/2	− 1/8
ASEA	1.16e	130	77 7/8	78 1/4	+ 2 1/8
AsdMtg		z70	7/16	9/16	...
AtlExp		25	3 1/4	3 3/8	...
AtlnGp		4	4 3/4	6	...
AutPr un		6	5 3/4	6 3/4	+ 1/4
BF Ent		60	9 3/4	10 1/4	...
BT Tel		10	3 1/8	3 1/4	...
BT Tl un		27	6 3/8	6 5/8	...
BncOn pf	3.00	19	55	57	...
BkLeu		8	28	30	+ 1
BkMd		10	21 1/2	23 1/2	...
Beaman	.03	10	4 3/4	5	...
BenhnA		259	2 1/8	2 1/4	...
Benhn wt		50	3/8	5/8	− 1/8
Benhn un		2	5	5 3/4	...
BigOTr		116	1 7/8	2	− 1/16
Bioson		1503	3/32	1/8	...
Bithr pf		15	2 3/4	4 1/4	...
Birdl pf	1.85	2	14 1/2	15 1/4	...
Blindr		1444	11/32	3/8	...
Blyvoor	.35e	139	2 15/16	3 1/8	− 1/8
BobBrk		490	2 9/16	2 11/16	− 5/32
Branif		26	8 3/4	9	...
Branf pf		20	2 9/16	2 11/16	...
BrentB	.64	x5	25	25 1/4	...
Buffels	1.45e	66	13	13 3/8	− 5/8
Burmah	1.38e	185	37 3/4	38	+ 1 1/4

(b)

Figure 2-2 Newspaper excerpts of stock price quotations: (*a*) New York Stock Exchange and (*b*) NASDAQ National List of OTC stocks.

per share (if one was paid) are in the third and fourth columns. The lower-case letters refer to footnotes that provide details (for example, "pf" indicates an issue of preferred stock). Columns 5 and 6 contain each stock's cash dividend yield and price-earnings ratio. The volume of shares traded (in hundreds) during the last trading day is in column 7. Columns 8, 9, and 10 contain the previous high, low, and closing prices from the most recent day of trading, respectively. The change in the closing price between the last two trading days is in the right-hand column of Figure 2-2a.

Figure 2-2b contains the prices of over-the-counter (OTC) stocks that were obtained from the National Association of Security Dealers Automated Quotations (NASDAQ). The two left-hand columns in Figure 2-2b list the abbreviated name of the issuing corporation and the latest cash dividend per share (if any). Column 3 tells how many hundreds of shares traded during the previous trading day. The bid and asked prices for each stock are in columns 4 and 5, respectively.[15] And the right-hand column of Figure 2-2b shows how much the price of each stock changed (if at all) between the two most recent trading days' closing prices.

Classified Common Stock

Occasionally an investor will come across **classified common stock.** Traditionally the stock referred to as class A was nonvoting, dividend-paying stock issued to the public. Class B stock was voting stock held by management, which therefore had control of the firm. Class B paid no dividends; however, the owners did enjoy the residual benefits of a growing company.[16]

Issuing classified common stock is one way for the management of a corporation to try to stop so-called *corporate raiders* from tendering an unwanted offer to buy a controlling interest in their corporation. "Outside investors" are sold a class of stock that receives cash dividends but has little or no voting power. Members of the corporation's management get a different class of common stock that receives no cash dividends but has voting power. This arrangement inhibits corporate takeovers that are unfriendly to management.[17]

[15]Although Figure 2-2a shows only one price for each stock, the NYSE actually continuously uses separate bid and asked prices for every stock it trades. The NYSE apparently prefers to publicize only one price for public relations reasons.
[16]Important investigations into classified common stock include H. DeAngelo and L. DeAngelo, "Managerial Ownership of Voting Rights: A Study of Public Corporations with Dual Classes of Common Stock," *Journal of Financial Economics,* 1985, vol. 14, pp. 33–69; and M. Partch, "The Creation of a Class of Limited Voting Common Stock and Shareholders' Wealth," *Journal of Financial Economics,* June 1987, vol. 18, no. 2, pp. 313–340.
[17]In 1924, the New York Stock Exchange stopped listing issues of nonvoting, classified stock. In total disregard of the NYSE's rule, General Motors Corporation issued what it called its class E stock when it acquired the Electronic Data Systems (EDS) Corporation in 1984. The prospect of not being able to trade GM shares would deny the NYSE so much brokerage income that the Exchange immediately reevaluated its ad-

(*continues*)

Cash Dividends   Fast-growing corporations tend to pay little or no cash dividends to their stock-holders in order to retain as much capital as possible for internal financing. Some firms (such as Teledyne, Tosco, Data General, Penn Central, and Memorex) even have a corporate policy against cash dividend payouts. In contrast, some established firms tend to pay out a larger portion of their earnings in dividends. Most public utilities take pride in their regular, substantial cash dividend payments, for example.

At one time it was thought that the market price of a corporation's shares tended to increase when the firm maintained stable cash dividend payments; that idea is less prevalent today. Now, most companies determine their cash dividend policy according to their need for financing and investor expectations about growth. Cash dividends may or may not be important to the investor. The investors who prefer regular income from large cash dividends can buy dividend-paying stock. Investors more concerned about price appreciation can look for growth stocks that retain their earnings to finance expansion rather than pay cash dividends.

Stock Dividends   **Stock dividends** are dividends paid in shares of the issuing corporation's stock instead of cash. When a stock dividend is paid, the stock account is increased and the capital surplus account is decreased within the net worth section of the balance sheet. Except for these accounting entries, stock dividends and stock splits are identical. For this reason, the New York Stock Exchange has adopted a rule calling all distributions of stock under 25 percent per share *stock dividends* and distributions over 25 percent *stock splits* even if the corporation involved calls its action something different.

Stock Splits   When a company divides its shares, it is said to have had a **stock split.** If a corporation had 2 million shares outstanding and split then 2 for 1, it would then have 4 million shares outstanding. In a stock split, the firm must correspondingly reduce the par value of the common stock, but it does not change its capital stock and paid-in surplus accounts. If the firm's stock had a par of $1 before the split, then the 2-for-1 split would give it a par of 50 cents.

A common reason for a corporation to split its stock is to reduce the stock's market value. The split divides the market price per share in proportion to the

---

(continued)
mirable policy of delisting corporations that issued classified stock. However, generating commission income seemed to be more important than maintaining the "one share, one vote" principle that is the basis for what the U.S. State Department calls "shareholders' democracy." A year later the NYSE forbid new listings (which typically trade in low volume) from having classified stock while permitting the large, old firms like GM to continue trading their classified stock. Officers of the Securities and Exchange Commission (SEC) made public statements in favor of the "one share, one vote" principle, but the SEC did not mandate a national policy on the matter.

split. For example, a $100 per share stock will sell at $50 after a 2-for-1 split, just as a $100 per share stock will sell at $50 after a 100 percent stock dividend. In both cases there will be twice as many shares outstanding so that *the total market value of the firm is unchanged by such changes in the unit of account.* In other words, stock splits and stock dividends do not affect the value of the firm or the shareholder's returns.[18]

| 2-7 | **PREFERRED STOCK** |

Preferred stockholders have legal priority (or seniority) over common stockholders with respect to earnings and also with respect to assets in the event of liquidation. But, preferred stockholders are in a more risky (or junior) position relative to the corporate bondholders. Preferred stockholders generally receive a greater rate of return on their investment than bondholders in compensation for the greater risk they bear. However, they generally receive a lesser rate of return than the common stockholder because they assume less risk. Unlike common, preferred is limited (except for an issue of participating preferred) in the amount of dividends it can receive. If the firm is prosperous, the preferred receives only its stipulated dividend; all the residual earnings go to the firm's common stockholders. In terms of control, the preferred stockholder usually is in a better position than the bondholder—assuming that the preferred stockholder has voting rights. Common stockholders have the most control since they are almost always given full voting rights.

Voting

Prior to 1930, preferred stockholders had few, if any, voting rights. The theory was that as long as holders of this class of stock received their dividends, they should have no voice in the company. Currently, however, there is a pronounced trend to give preferred shares full voting rights. Moreover, nonvoting preferred may become voting stock if preferred dividend payments are missed for a stated length of time. This is consistent with the idea that as long as dividends are paid, preferred stock should have no voice in management. Nonvoting preferred may be given voting rights under special circumstances, such as authorization of a new bond or stock issue or the merger of the company.

Preferred's Par Value

Most preferred stock has a par value. When it does, the dividend rights and call prices are usually stated in terms of par value. However, these rights are

[18]The economic effect of stock dividends and splits is analyzed in Chapter 18. That chapter reviews the classic study by E. Fama, L. Fisher, M. Jensen, and R. Roll, "The Adjustment of Stock Prices to New Information," *International Economic Review,* Feb. 1969, vol. 20, no. 2, pp. 1–21.

specified directly if the preferred has no par value. It seems, therefore, as with common stock, that preferred with a par value has no real advantage over preferred that has no par value.

Cash Dividend Payments

Dividends are the most significant aspect of preferred stock, since preferred stockholders stand to gain more from dividends than from capital appreciation. The dividend paid is usually a stipulated percentage of par value, or for a stock with no par, a stated dollar amount per year.

Most of the preferred issues outstanding today have a **cumulative cash dividend** clause. This means that the preferred stockholder is entitled to a dividend regardless of whether the firm earns it. If the corporation omits a preferred dividend payment, or any part of it, the omitted dividend is not lost but must be made up in a later year before any dividend can be paid to the common stockholders.

Not all preferred stock is cumulative. **Noncumulative preferred stock** is entitled to its promised rate of cash dividends only if the issuing corporation earns enough to pay it. If the firm's earnings are insufficient some year, the preferred stockholders will not get a cash dividend that year. In order to protect noncumulative preferred investors from being exploited by common stockholders who want to keep all the corporation's earnings for their common stock dividends, some state laws say that a corporation cannot legally pay dividends to its common stockholders if it has missed a preferred dividend during that dividend period.

Call Feature

Considering the various cash dividend guarantees and other inducements needed to make a preferred stock issue attractive, the issuing companies want to be in a position to *call in* their preferred shares if they become financially able. A *redemption clause* gives the company the right to call in the issue. As in a bond redemption, a preferred stock redemption is allowed after the public announcement of such action, and a *call premium* is paid above the par value of the stock and its regular dividend. These call premiums run from 5 to 20 percent of par.

Call features are usually disadvantageous to those who invested in the callable securities. However, this is a desirable provision for the firm since it allows a prospering corporation to end relatively high fixed charges, namely, preferred dividends. The call price has the effect of setting a ceiling that limits the price rise for the callable security.

Participating Preferred Stock

Participating preferred stock, like a participating bond, is uncommon. Both are entitled to a stated rate of dividends (or coupon interest) and then a share of the earnings available to be paid to the common stock. Since participating preferred stock is not popular with common shareholders, only weak firms will use such a provision to help sell this type of preferred stock. Because preferred stock is basically a fixed-income investment like a bond but has few, if any, of the legal guarantees and recourses as to payment of interest that are inherent in a bond, the issuer may add protective clauses to the contract in order to make the stock safer and more salable.

Adjustable Rate Preferred Stock

Issues of preferred stock that had adjustable rather than fixed rates of cash dividend payments were marketed in the United States for the first time in 1982. These innovative new issues had their dividend rates tied to the market interest rates on Treasury bonds and were adjustable quarterly. Most of the new issues allowed their rate of cash dividend payments to fall no lower than 7.5 percent and rise no higher than 15.5 percent. Corporate investors bought most of these preferred stocks because the tax law says that 85 percent of intercorporate cash dividends are tax-exempt.[19]

Money Market Preferred Stock (MMPS)

Money market preferred stock (MMPS) is a type of preferred stock that is reissued with a new cash dividend rate so frequently that it is like an adjustable rate preferred. The MMPS typically has a brief life—some issues have lives of only 7 weeks.[20] MMPS are typically offered in large denominations, such as $100,000, because they are targeted at large corporate investors. These issues are sold at a **Dutch auction** in which potential buyers bid for the stock by offering to accept a certain rate of cash dividends for the short life of the MMPS. The entire issue is sold at the lowest dividend rate bid that fills all the bids that were submitted.[21]

[19]Details about sophisticated investment strategies employing adjustable rate preferred stock have been published by Bernard J. Winger, Carl R. Chen, John D. Martin, J. William Petty, and Steven C. Hayden, ''Adjustable Rate Preferred Stock,'' *Financial Management,* Spring 1986, vol. 15, no. 1, pp. 48–57.

[20]Federal income tax laws allow corporate investors that hold a preferred stock investment 46 days or more to be exempt from federal income tax on 85 percent of the cash dividends received. This intercorporate tax exemption explains why some corporations invest in preferred stock—and, in particular, the short-term MMPS. For an empirical analysis of so-called dividend-stripping (or cash-dividend-capture) investment strategies see Theoharry Grammatikos, ''Dividend Stripping, Risk Exposure, and the Effect of the 1984 Tax Reform Act on the Ex-Dividend Day Behavior,'' *Journal of Business,* April 1989, vol. 62, no. 2, pp. 157–173.

[21]Those wishing to learn more about auction-type market processes should consult Michael J. Alderson, Keith C. Brown, and Scott L. Lummer, ''Dutch Auction Rate Preferred Stock,'' *Financial Management,* 1987, vol. 16, no. 2, pp. 68–73; and Paul R. Milgrom and Robert J. Weber, ''The Theory of Auctions and Competitive Bidding,'' *Econometrica,* September 1982, vol. 50. See also R. Engelbrecht-Wiggans, M. Shubik, and R. Stark, eds., *Auctions, Bidding, and Contracting: Uses and Theory* (New York: New York University Press, 1983).

Conclusions About Preferred Stock

Preferred stock is a hybrid security made from elements of both debt and equity.[22] Although it is technically a form of equity investment, it has many of the characteristics of debt, such as fixed income and call provisions. Its one-period rate of return is calculated like common stock returns.

2-8   **CONVERTIBLE SECURITIES**

A **convertible security** can be converted by its owner into another security that has different rights and privileges. A convertible security is usually a preferred stock or a bond that can be converted into common stock. Once converted into stock, it cannot be changed back. If it is a bond, the convertible security provides the investor with a fixed interest payment, and if it is a preferred stock, with a stipulated dividend. Since the convertible security investor gets the option to convert the instrument into common stock, convertibles have the speculative aspects of equity ownership.[23] The conversion option allows investors to participate in the residual earnings of the firm that are reflected in rises in the stock price. Convertibles allow their investors to earn their guaranteed fixed return until they are assured of a capital gain and to then convert to get the common stock's price appreciation.

Many convertibles have a specific period in which the issue may be converted. They may stipulate that conversion cannot take place until 2 or 3 years after the issue. This stipulation allows the money obtained through such financing to be utilized by the corporation for investment and growth that will show up in higher common stock prices only after a period of time. A limited issue will also place a time limit on when the conversion can take place, typically 10 to 15 years. Convertible preferred stocks usually allow unlimited time for conversion. An unlimited bond is eligible for conversion for the entire time it is outstanding.

As a rule, convertible securities are callable. The purpose of the call provision is not to redeem the convertible bonds or preferred stock but to force

---

[22]For detailed studies of preferred stock see J. S. Bildersee, "Some Aspects of the Performance of Preferred Stock," *Journal of Finance,* Dec. 1973, pp. 1187–1201. Also D. B. Smith, "A Framework for Analyzing Nonconvertible Preferred Stock," *Journal of Financial Research,* Summer 1983, pp. 127–139. See also D. Emanuel, "A Theoretical Model for Valuing Preferred Stock," *Journal of Finance,* Sept. 1983, pp. 1133–1155. Also see E. H. Sorensen and C. A. Hawkins, "On the Pricing of Preferred," *Journal of Financial and Quantitative Analysis,* Nov. 1981, pp. 515–528.

[23]Valuing the option portion of a convertible has been investigated by M. H. Brennan and E. S. Schwartz, "Convertible Bonds: Valuation and Optimal Strategies for Call and Conversion," *Journal of Finance,* Dec. 1977, pp. 1699–1715. Also see J. E. Ingersol Jr., "A Contingent Claims Valuation of Convertible Securities," *Journal of Finance,* May 1977, pp. 463–478.

conversion of the issue when the conversion value of the security is well above the call price. In practice, few convertibles are ever redeemed.

Conversion Ratio

The **conversion ratio** is the ratio of exchange between the common stock and the convertible security. For example, a $1000 convertible bond may provide for a conversion to 10 shares of common stock. The *conversion price* is then simply the bond's $1000 face value divided by the conversion ratio ($1000/10 = $100 per share conversion price). In this case the ratio may be stated as 10 shares of stock for each bond.

The conversion price is not constant over time in every issue of convertibles. The conversion price might change with the length of time outstanding or with the proportion of the issue converted. A bond might have a conversion price of $100 per share the first 5 years, $105 per share for the next 5 years, $110 for the third 5 years, and so on. Under a provision stipulating an increasing price with the amount of outstanding securities that have been redeemed, a bond might have a conversion price of $100 per share for the first 25 percent of the shares converted, $105 for the second 25 percent, $110 for the third, and $115 per share for the final 25 percent converted. Such provisions for increasing conversion prices give the issuer some power to force investors to convert their issues quickly when the market price has substantially exceeded the conversion price.

Changes in the Terms of Conversion

Changes in the issuer's unit of account caused by stock splits and/or stock dividends affect the terms of conversion. If the issuer splits its stock or declares a stock dividend, the conversion value of the convertible instrument is lowered appropriately. For example, if the conversion price of a bond were $100 per share and the conversion ratio were 10 shares of common stock per bond, a 2-for-1 stock split would change the conversion ratio from 10 to 20 (just as the number of shares would be doubled) and the conversion price from $100 to $50 (just as the market price of the common stock would be halved).

Conversion Diminishes the Preexisting Stockholders' Positions

The preexisting common stock investors in a corporation fear having the value of their holdings and their control of the corporation diminished by a conversion. This dilution is well recognized, and as a result, at the announcement of a convertible issue, the market price of the issuer's common stock usually declines. If a conversion occurs, the value of the preexisting common stock investors' positions is diminished because the increased number of outstanding common shares after the conversion causes dilution of the corporation's earnings per share. Likewise, the preexisting common stock investors' control of their corporation is diluted because the shares they own will represent a smaller proportion of the voting stock outstanding after a conversion occurs.

To maintain the current stockholders' position, the company issuing the convertible security can include a preemptive rights provision. Under this provision, the convertible securities must be offered to the existing stockholders before they can be sold to the general public. Dilution of the preexisting stockholders' positions is not a significant problem for large companies with millions of different stockholders, but it can be a very real consideration for a small firm or one just going public.

An Overhanging Issue

When a company is unable to force the conversion of an issue because the market price of the common stock has not risen to a point that will induce investors to convert, the issue is said to be an *overhanging issue*. Ordinarily a company will plan for the issue to be converted within a certain period of time. A growth company may expect conversion as soon as 18 months after its issue. The failure of the market price of the stock to rise sufficiently for conversion to occur might indicate a failure of the company to perform as expected. Such an overhanging issue can cause serious problems, since the company would find it difficult to gain market acceptance for another convertible issue or even for nonconvertible financing.[24]

2-9   **OTHER INVESTMENTS**

This chapter has introduced the primary securities. More complicated investment instruments will be examined in later chapters. The investments listed below provide a partial menu of some of the topics covered in more detail in the later chapters.

Investment Companies

Investment companies take in funds from people who want to have their wealth invested and managed for them by professional money managers. Investment companies typically charge a management fee of about 1 percent of the value of the assets managed per year. The investment managers pool investors' funds to buy a diversified list of securities selected to achieve some stated investment objective.

   Mutual fund is a synonym for **open-end investment company.** A mutual fund is a popular kind of investment company that is allowed, by law, to sell shares as long as it can find investors—the company is open-ended. Examples of the investment objectives pursued by various mutual funds include (1) maximization of capital gains through aggressive common stock investing; (2) conservation of principal by investing only in high-grade bonds and high-quality

---

[24]The conversion option embedded within convertible securities is analyzed further in Section 23-6 of Chapter 23, where call options are analyzed.

preferred stock; (3) generation of federal tax-exempt interest income by investing in municipal bonds; (4) generation of high levels of coupon interest income by investing in a diversified portfolio of *junk bonds*;[25] and (5) attainment of the same rate of return as some stock or bond market index that is selected—such portfolios are called *index funds*. There are also other investment goals pursued by mutual funds.

Closed-end investment companies are like **open-end investment companies** in some ways and different in others. Both categories of investment companies sell shares for cash, commingle the funds, and seek investments that conform to some prestated investment objective. Some closed-end funds pursue the same investment objectives as the open-end investment companies, but many of them seek riskier goals than the mutual funds. One big difference between the open-end and the closed-end investment companies is that the law forbids the closed-end portfolios from ever selling more shares after their initial public offering is completed. Another difference is that the law requires mutual funds to sell and redeem shares at their net asset value per share. In contrast, the shares in closed-end investment companies can only be bought and sold in a secondary market where their prices are determined by supply and demand (and usually deviate from their net asset value per share). Investment companies are examined in more detail in Chapter 21.

Put and Call Options

Options are financial instruments that give their owners the right but not the obligation to buy or sell a stated number of shares (usually 100) of a particular security at a fixed price within a predetermined time period. There are two basic types of options—the put option and the call option.

A **call** is an option to ''call in'' shares for purchase. It is a negotiable contract giving the owner the option to buy 100 shares of a security within a fixed period at a predetermined price. Warrants and rights are special types of call options.

A **put** is an option that gives its owner the legal right to *put* shares to someone else. It is a negotiable contract giving the owner the option to sell 100 shares of a security at any time within a fixed period at a predetermined price.

Options are the topic of Chapters 22 and 23.

Commodity Futures Contracts

A **futures contract** is a legal agreement between a potential buyer and a potential seller of a commodity. The futures contract stipulates that the seller will deliver to a designated location a specified quantity of a particular commodity for the buyer of the futures contract to accept at a prearranged price at some specific time in the future. For example, seller A agrees to deliver to buyer B at a

---

[25]Speculative-grade bonds that Standard & Poor's rates BB or below and/or Moody's rates Ba or lower are called *junk bonds* or *high-yield bonds*. For an introduction to junk bonds see Jane Tripp Howe, *Junk Bonds: Analysis and Portfolio Strategies* (Chicago, Ill.: Probus, 1988). Junk bonds are discussed further in Chapter 14.

warehouse in Chicago 1000 bushels of wheat at 174 cents per bushel in December of next year, and buyer B agrees to accept the wheat and pay cash on delivery. Such a future contract would be called a "December contract for Chicago wheat." Commodity futures contracts are negotiable financial instruments that can be bought and sold for a profit or loss. Chapter 24 delves into commodity futures contracts.

Financial Futures

Although commodity futures contracts have been traded successfully in large organized exchanges for over a century, the volume of commodity futures contracts traded has been exceeded in recent years by the volume of financial futures contracts. Financial futures contracts are a new kind of instrument that did not exist 20 years ago; these intriguing contracts are referred to as simply **financial futures.** Financial futures contracts are not futures contracts that promise the delivery of physical commodities. Financial futures contracts apply to Treasury bonds, stock market indexes, and esoteric financial quantities. In fact, in many cases financial futures call for a *cash settlement* that is based on some market-determined outcome instead of the delivery of a commodity or security. Financial futures are examined in Chapter 24.

American Depository Receipts (ADRs)

American depository receipts (ADRs) are certificates used by international investors. ADRs represent shares of a foreign common stock and can be purchased instead of the stock itself by Americans who want to make dollar investments in a foreign stock that is not dollar-denominated. The ADRs are legal claims on the equity shares in the foreign corporation. To create ADRs, an American investment bank or brokerage firm purchases the foreign shares and has them held in trust at a commercial bank. The trustee bank issues the ADRs to acknowledge that it holds the underlying shares of stock. For a small fee the trustee bank collects cash dividends in the foreign currency, converts them to U.S. dollars, makes dollar-denominated dividend payments to the investors, and performs the necessary bookkeeping. International investing is the topic of Chapter 25, and ADRs are discussed there.

Menu of Investment Opportunities

The menu of investment opportunities is large, exotic, and tantalizing. Short sales, spreads, options on futures contracts, hedging, arbitrage, and other sophisticated delicacies will be investigated in the later chapters.[26]

---

[26]The complexity of some of the financial instruments and the large and rapidly growing number of different financial instruments is explained by Nobel laureate Kenneth Arrow and Gerard Debreu; their theory of financial markets is presented in the appendix to Chapter 3. The theory suggests that a large number of diverse securities are needed in order to achieve what they define as *complete markets*.

2-10 **SUMMARY AND CONCLUSIONS**

Debt securities come in many forms. The debt securities traded in the money markets all mature in less than 1 year and involve virtually no risk of default. The securities issued by the U.S. government and its agencies are free from default risk; their maturities vary from 3 months to 30 years. Unlike federal government bonds, tax-exempt municipal bonds include default risk. Corporate bonds are another category of bonds that involve default risk. However, protective provisions in the indenture contract that governs the terms of a corporate bond issue can furnish some protection to investors if the issuer becomes bankrupt. Investors in mortgages and securities that are backed by other assets (namely, securitized financial assets) can avert default risk by investing in securities that are either insured or backed by substantial guarantees.

The common stockholder has the right to receive a certificate to evidence share ownership, to receive dividends, and to vote at the stockholders' meetings, and, in many states, the preemptive right to maintain a proportionate share in the corporation's assets, earnings, and voting control. But, in return for these advantages the common shareholders are forced to accept (1) only a residual claim on the corporation's earnings after all other bills have been paid and (2) the last claim on the assets if the corporation goes bankrupt. If the corporation prospers, however, these last two residual rights can become lucrative privileges.

Unlike common stockholders, preferred stockholders participate in the corporation's earnings to only a limited extent. Preferred stock promises a cash dividend that has a prior claim on corporate earnings over the common stock dividends. It also promises a fixed rate of cash dividends. If the preferred issue is cumulative, any missed cash dividend payments may be collected eventually, unless the issuer goes bankrupt. And, some issues of preferred stock allow their owners to vote at the stockholders' meeting if the preferred dividends are in arrears. Some issues of preferred are also backed by a sinking fund. High-grade preferred stock thus offers good security and a stable income if the issuing corporation flourishes.

Convertible preferred stocks combine all of the features of ordinary preferred stock with the added benefit of being convertible into common stock in the event that the common appreciates nicely. Convertible preferred thus offers both safety features not found in common stock and the opportunity to participate in the price appreciation of the common stock.

Essay Questions

2-1   Differentiate between a bond's coupon rate and its one-period rate of return. Which of these two rate-of-return measures varies the most? Why?

2-2   Is a call provision in the indenture helpful or detrimental to bond investors? Explain.

2-3   Why are participating bonds not issued more frequently?

2-4   List four characteristics that all money market securities have in common.

2-5   What are the differences between U.S. government marketable and nonmarketable securities? Give examples of each.

2-6   What characteristics of municipal bonds are unique and important to the potential investor?

2-7   Define the striking price of a put bond. When would an investor utilize the striking price of a put bond?

2-8   What do the acronyms AMBAC and MBIA stand for? What functions are performed by AMBAC and MBIA?

2-9   Do you expect the market price of a corporation's common stock to fluctuate the same way as the price of its preferred stock? Explain.

2-10 What are the advantages of investing in the common stock rather than the bonds of a corporation? What are the relative disadvantages of common stock investing?

2-11 "Stock dividends and stock splits have no effect on the value of a company." True, false, or uncertain? Discuss.

Problems

2-12 Sally Stein is an investment officer at a life insurance company that is in the 25 percent marginal corporate income-tax bracket. Which of the following two securities will provide the corporation's portfolio with the highest yield-to-maturity if neither defaults? (a) A new issue of AAA-grade corporate bonds selling at par with a coupon rate of 10 percent. (b) An issue of AAA-grade preferred stock with an 8 percent cash dividend rate. *Hint: Consider the tax rate on intercorporate cash dividends.*

2-13 Assume that the United Motors Corporation (UMC) issues $50 million of 7 percent convertible debentures at a conversion price of $25 per share. Upon conversion the total number of additional shares would be $50 million/$25 = 2 million new shares. UMC had 4 million shares outstanding originally and no other debt. It expects earnings of $20 million in 3 years; the income tax rate is 50 percent. (a) Will UMC's earnings per share be diluted if the conversion takes place? (b) What effect will the conversion probably have on UMC's common stock price?

2-14 A $10,000 T-bill can currently be purchased for $9600. What rate of return (or percentage gain) will an investor earn from holding the T-bill until it matures in 65 days?

2-15 A 10-year zero coupon bond with a face value of $1,000 can be purchased for $285. What before-tax rate of return will an investor earn if the bond is held to maturity?

2-16 John Stone is considering the purchase of one of the following bonds: (*a*) a 7 percent annual coupon municipal bond and (*b*) a 12 percent annual coupon corporate bond. Mr. Stone is in the 33 percent tax bracket. If both bonds are selling at par, have similar maturities, and are equally risky, which bond should he purchase?

2-17 A bond of the XYZ Company sold for $980 on January 1, 1989 and $910 on January 1 of the preceding year. If this bond paid $70 in interest during the year, what was its 1-year rate of return?

2-18 What would be the 1-year rate of return for the bond in Problem 17 if the XYZ bond sold for $800 on January 1, 1989?

2-19 The common stock of the Biddle Corporation has had the following end-of-year prices and dividend record for three consecutive years.

Year	Price	Dividend
t + 1	$50	$2
t + 2	30	1
t + 3	45	1.50

(*a*) Calculate the rate of return for Biddle for years 2 and 3. (*b*) Recalculate the rate of return for Biddle for the same 2 years if a 2-for-1 stock split took place during year 2.

2-20 The convertible bond of the GGG Corporation has a conversion ratio of 20. If the common stock of the GGG Corporation is currently selling for $40 per share, what is the conversion value of the bond?

2-21 If the convertible bond of the GGG Corporation in Problem 2-20 has a current market price of $950, determine its conversion premium.

2-22 J. J. Evans recently sold 200 shares of BGO stock for $40 per share. (*a*) If she purchased the stock 1 year ago for $30 per share and during the year received a $2 dividend per share, what return did she earn? (*b*) Assume Ms. Evans is in a 33 percent tax bracket. What return did she earn on an after-tax basis?

2-23 For the T-bill in Problem 2-14, annualize the rate of return to find the equivalent bond yield from the investment. *Note: It is always assumed that there are only 360 days in the year when working with T-bills.*

2-24 An investor purchased a 90-day T-bill for $9600. Thirty days later, the investor sold the T-bill for $9700. What was the annualized rate of return on this investment? *Note: It is always assumed that there are only 360 days in the year when working with T-bills.*[27]

---

[27]For an explanation of the rate quotations and yields on Treasury bills see John H. Wood and Norma L. Wood, *Financial Markets* (New York: Harcourt Brace Jovanovich, 1985), chap. 6, pp. 123–138. Alternatively, see Marcia Stigum, *Money Market Calculations: Yields, Break-Evens, and Arbitrage* (Homewood, Ill.: Dow Jones–Irwin, 1981), chaps. 4 and 5. For a shorter discussion see Marcia Stigum, *The Money Market*, rev. ed. (Homewood, Ill.: Dow Jones–Irwin, 1983), pp. 45–49.

Selected References

Cottle, Sidney, R. F. Murray, and F. E. Block, *Security Analysis,* 5th ed. (New York: McGraw-Hill, 1988).

This nonmathematical book about fundamental analysis explores many facets of common stock, preferred stock, and bond securities.

Fabozzi, Frank J., *Mortgage-Backed Securities* (Chicago, Ill.: Probus, 1987).

This nonmathematical book explores investing in mortgage-backed securities. Tables and graphs of empirical data are analyzed. The book presumes the reader knows the definition of the word ''mortgage'' and understands present values.

Fabozzi, Frank J., *The Handbook of Treasury Securities* (Chicago, Ill.: Probus, 1988).

This nonmathematical book contains voluminous detail about the securities issued by the U.S. Treasury and the markets where they are traded.

Fabozzi, Frank J., and Irving M. Pollack, eds., *The Handbook of Fixed Income Securities,* 2d ed. (Homewood, Ill.: Dow Jones–Irwin, 1987).

A collection of informative essays written by experts in the field of fixed-income (that is, debt and preferred stock) securities. Some algebra is used in describing the different securities.

Feldstein, Sylvan G., Frank J. Fabozzi, Irving M. Pollack, and Frank G. Zarb, *The Municipal Bond Handbook,* Vols. I and II (Homewood, Ill.: Dow Jones–Irwin, 1983).

These two thick volumes are comprehensive in their discussion of municipal bond topics. No mathematics is used in this collection of readings by experts in every phase of municipal bond analysis.

Schall, Lawrence D., and Charles W. Haley, *Introduction to Financial Management,* 6th ed. (New York: McGraw-Hill, 1991).

Chapters 20, 21, and 22 provide an easy-to-read and informative discussion of common stock, long-term debt, preferred stock, convertible securities, and warrants.

Stigum, Marcia, *The Money Market,* 3d ed. (Homewood, Ill.: Dow Jones–Irwin, 1990).

A detailed, nonmathematical explanation of money market securities and the markets where they are traded. This volume presents the historical development and additional details of the money market securities introduced above in Section 2-1.

Stigum, Marcia, *Money Market Calculations: Yields, Break-Evens, and Arbitrage* (Homewood, Ill.: Dow Jones–Irwin, 1981).

As the title implies, this book explains the vocabulary, presents the formulas, and shows how to perform the calculations to determine the price quotations and yields for various kinds of debt securities in a manner that conforms to the accepted financial conventions.

Wiesenberger Services, Inc., *Investment Companies* (New York), published annually.

This large reference book explains investment companies, summarizes relevant laws, and gives raw financial data for many open-end and closed-end funds.

Wood, John H., and Norma L. Wood, *Financial Markets* (New York: Harcourt Brace Jovanovich, 1985).

Chapter 6 contains an explanation of interest rate quotations and the yields on Treasury bills, notes, and bonds and includes a number of illustrations and numerical examples.

Chapter 3

Securities Markets

New York, London, and Tokyo contain the largest securities markets in the world—all are about equal in size. There are other important markets too. Trading goes on 24 hours a day someplace in the world. Each market conducts trading differently. However, telecommunications networks transmit up-to-the-minute price quotations around the world, so that these different securities markets should be viewed as components of a *global market*.

This chapter focuses primarily on the common stock trading in the United States. American methods are contrasted with procedures and institutions used in other markets around the world. The discussion begins with an explanation of how new securities are brought into existence. New securities are usually issued by corporations and governmental bodies in what is called the *primary market*. After the securities have been issued, they are traded in the *secondary market*.

3-1   **INVESTMENT BANKERS MAKE THE PRIMARY MARKETS**

The people responsible for finding investors for the **initial public offerings** (IPOs) of securities sold in the primary market are called *investment bankers*. **Investment bankers** are also called **underwriters;** they purchase new issues from security issuers and arrange for their resale to the investing public.

The firms listed in Table 3-1 do most of the underwriting for the United States. In addition to investment banking, some of these firms perform brokerage services. Merrill Lynch, Pierce, Fenner & Smith, for example, controls some of the largest brokerage operations in each of the following markets: government securities, securities issued by governmental agencies, commodity

Table 3-1
THE LARGEST INVESTMENT BANKING FIRMS
IN THE UNITED STATES

Shearson Lehman Hutton*
Salomon Brothers Holding Company
Merrill Lynch, Pierce, Fenner & Smith*
Goldman Sachs & Company
Dean Witter Reynolds*
Paine Webber Group*
Bear Stearns & Company
Prudential-Bache Securities*
First Boston Corporation
Morgan Stanley & Company

*These firms are full-service brokerage houses; some are more active in providing a diversified line of brokerage services than in investment banking.

futures, options, corporate bonds, preferred stocks, common stocks, and bonds. Also, through its subsidiaries, Merrill Lynch provides real estate financing and investment advisory services. Merrill Lynch employs over 12,000 brokers. Thus, investment banking is only a small part of the Merrill Lynch operation. In contrast, firms like Salomon and Goldman Sachs each employ less than 2000 brokers—they are investment banking firms that limit their retail brokerage activities.

Functions of the Investment Banker

Investment bankers advise their clients, handle the administrative tasks, underwrite the issue, and distribute the securities as follows.

The Advisory Role   In the first few meetings with a potential security issuer, the investment banker typically serves as an advisor. The underwriter helps the issuing firm analyze its financing needs and suggests various ways to raise the needed funds. The underwriter may also function as an advisor in mergers, acquisitions, and refinancing operations.

If the issuer and investment banker agree to proceed with a primary issue, further investigations must be conducted by accountants, engineers, and attorneys. After these experts give their assessments of the situation, the investment banking firm draws up a tentative underwriting agreement with the issuer that specifies all terms of the issue except the specific price that will be set for the new security.

The investment banking firm that first reaches an agreement with the issuer is called the **originator.** The originator ultimately manages the flotation and coordinates two temporary groups called the "underwriting syndicate" and the "selling group." The members of the **underwriting syndicate** share the under-

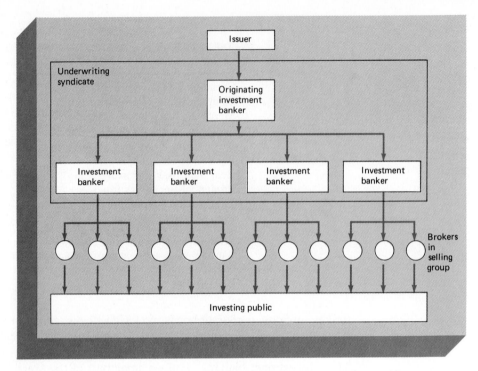

Figure 3-1 Flowchart of a primary offering made through a syndicate of investment bankers and brokers.

writing risk; syndicates are composed of from 5 to 200 investment banking houses, depending on the total dollar value of the issue. The **selling group** is made up of brokerage firms that have agreed to sell the primary offering to investors. Figure 3-1 illustrates the relationships between the originator, the underwriting syndicate, and the selling group that is formed to carry out a typical underwriting.

The Administrative Function   The investment banker shares with the issuer the responsibility of seeing that everything is done in accordance with the relevant securities laws. The Securities and Exchange Commission (SEC) requires that most primary issues be accompanied by a registration statement.[1] The **registration statement** must disclose information that will allow an investor to judge the investment quality of the new issue (see Table 3-2). Once the SEC registration statement is filed, there is usually only a brief delay until the new issue may be offered for sale. During this period, the SEC analyzes the reg-

[1]The SEC is the federal agency that regulates securities markets in the United States. The SEC and securities markets regulation will be discussed in Chapter 4.

Table 3-2

INFORMATION REQUIRED IN AN SEC REGISTRATION STATEMENT

1. A copy of the issuer's articles of incorporation
2. Purpose for which the proceeds of the issue will be spent
3. Offering price to the public
4. Offering price for special groups, if any
5. Fees promised to developers and/or promoters
6. Underwriter's fees
7. Net proceeds to the issuer
8. Information on the issuer's products, history, and location
9. Copies of any indentures affecting the new issue
10. Names and remuneration of any officers receiving over $25,000 per year
11. Details about any unusual contracts, such as a managerial profit-sharing plan
12. A detailed statement of capitalization
13. Detailed balance sheet
14. Detailed income and expense statements for three preceding years
15. Names and addresses of the issuer's officers and directors and the underwriters
16. Names and addresses of any investors owning more than 10% of any class of stock
17. Details about any pending litigation
18. A copy of the underwriting agreement
19. Copies of legal opinions on matters related to the issue

istration statement to determine if it provides all the information that the securities law requires. The SEC may delay approval by requesting that additional information be supplied, in which case the waiting period may last for weeks.

The **prospectus** is a portion of the registration statement. After approval and after the price has been set, the prospectus is reproduced in quantity and delivered to potential investors. The law provides that all investors must have a prospectus before they can invest. According to the Securities Act of 1933, every prospectus must disclose all relevant facts that a potential investor needs to evaluate the new offering. Approval of the registration statement and the prospectus within is not an endorsement by the SEC of the investment value of the securities offered. SEC approval implies only that adequate information has been revealed so that investors can make their own judgments about the value of the security offer.

Not all issues must be registered with the SEC. Security issues made by governmental bodies and some companies that are regulated by governmental agencies are exempt from the registration process. The latter must apply for exemption, however. Other issues that are likely to be exempt include intrastate offerings, issues that are offered to only a few investors, and issues of less than $1.5 million, the most frequently exempted group (under Rule 254). Exemption does not make the issuer and underwriters immune from legal action if fraud is involved in the flotation; it merely simplifies the administrative work.

Underwriting   **Underwriting** refers to the guarantee by the investment banker that the issuer of the new securities will receive a fixed amount of cash. The brief period between the time the investment banking houses purchase an issue from the issuer and the time they sell it to the public is *risky*. Because of unforeseen changes in market conditions, the underwriters may not be able to sell the entire issue, or they may have to sell it at less than the price they paid for it.

Perhaps the most difficult decision in a flotation is setting the "right" price. The right price is not too low; this would be unnecessarily costly to the issuer. It also cannot be too high; this might cause losses for the underwriters. To minimize risk, the price generally is set at the end of the registration period.[2] If the syndicate waits to set the final price until the issue is ready for marketing, it will have the most up-to-date information on the market situation. When the price is right, market conditions are good, and the issuer and underwriters are reputable, the flotation will "go out the window"—it will be sold in one or a few days. When one or more of these conditions is lacking, it may become a *sticky issue,* taking a week, month, or even more to sell, and it may result in multimillion-dollar losses for the underwriting syndicate if it is a big deal.

Not all new security issues are underwritten. If the investment banker finds one buyer for an entire new issue and arranges for a direct sale from the issuer to this large investor, a **private placement** is said to have occurred. In a private placement, the investment banker is compensated for bringing buyer and seller together, for helping to determine a fair price, and for executing the transaction. Table 3-3 contains empirical statistics that indicate that bond issuers, especially

Table 3-3
DEBT PLACEMENT COSTS ARE LESS FOR PRIVATE PLACEMENTS THAN FOR PUBLIC OFFERINGS

Issue size, millions of dollars	Private placements			Public issues		
	Underwriting expenses, %	Other expenses, %	Total, %	Underwriting expenses, %	Other expenses, %	Total, %
Under 0.50	1.7	1.1	2.8	7.3	2.9	10.9
0.50–0.99	1.4	0.9	2.3	5.5	3.2	8.7
1.00–2.99	0.9	0.5	1.4	3.5	2.1	5.6
3.00–4.99	0.6	0.4	1.0	1.4	1.3	2.7
5.00–9.99	0.6	0.3	0.9	0.9	1.0	1.9
10.00–24.99	0.3	0.3	0.6	1.0	0.7	1.7
25.00 and above	0.2	0.2	0.4	0.7	0.4	1.1

Source: A. B. Cohan, *Yields on Corporate Debt Directly Placed* (Washington, D.C.: National Bureau of Economic Research, 1967), p. 127.

[2]"Shelf registration" is an expeditious new procedure for registering primary offerings. Shelf registration is discussed in Chapter 4.

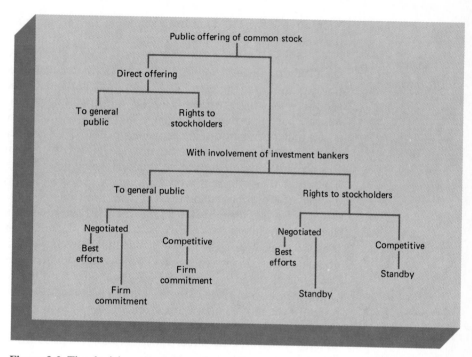

Figure 3-2 The decision alternatives for a primary issue. (*Source:* Adapted from Sanjai Bhagat, "Wealth Effects of Preemptive Rights Removal," *Journal of Financial Economics,* Nov. 1983, p. 290.)

small issuers, get their bond issues sold more cheaply by using direct placement rather than public offerings.[3]

In some IPOs the investment banker may not assume the role of underwriter. Instead the investment banker may agree to use certain facilities and services in distributing new shares on a **best efforts basis,** that is, while assuming no financial responsibility if all the securities cannot be sold. The investment banker's charges for best efforts offerings are typically more than for a direct placement but less than for a fully underwritten public offering.[4] Best efforts offerings are an uncommon kind of IPO. Figure 3-2 illustrates the decision

---

[3]For more information about private placements and public issues see G. D. Hawkins, "Essays on Non-Publicly Issued Debt: Revolving Credit Agreements and the Pricing of Privately Placed Debt," unpublished Ph.D. dissertation, M.I.T., 1982. Also see Louis H. Ederington, "Uncertainty, Competition, and Costs in Corporate Bond Underwriting," *Journal of Financial Economics,* March 1975, pp. 71–94. Alternatively, see Burton Zwick, "Yields on Privately Placed Corporate Bonds," *Journal of Finance,* March 1980, pp. 23–29.

[4]For more details about best efforts offerings see Jay R. Ritter, "The Costs of Going Public," *Journal of Financial Economics,* Dec. 1987, pp. 269–282.

alternatives that the security issuer and the investment banker must work through as they plan a primary issue.

Distribution   Investment bankers can distribute securities to investors in different ways. The investment banker may buy the issue and then sell the securities—an underwriting. Or, the investment banker may simply act as an intermediary in bringing together issuer and investors in a private placement.

An underwriting firm occasionally must stabilize the price of an IPO during the distribution period in order to prevent it from drifting downward. To achieve this objective, the underwriting syndicate's manager "pegs" the price by placing orders to buy the newly issued security at a specified price in the secondary market where the outstanding securities are trading. Although this procedure might seem like illegal price-fixing, the SEC approves it as long as full, prior disclosure of intent to stabilize is made. It is defended on the grounds that if price-pegging were not allowed, the underwriting syndicate's risk would be greater and the underwriting cost to the issuer would increase correspondingly. Price-pegging usually continues for about 30 days after the IPO.

If the issue has been badly priced, the pegging operation cannot support the price. In the most extreme occurrence, the managing underwriter would start buying back every share that had been sold in an effort to keep the price up. In such a case, all the underwriters in the syndicate would experience severe losses.[5]

Costs of Issuing Securities

Investment bankers make a profit by selling an IPO at a higher price than what they paid for it. The difference is called the *spread*. Four percentage points is a normal spread for a bond issue, for example. These percentage points are stated as a percent of the bond issue's face value. The four-percentage-point spread is typically divided as follows:

1. The managing underwriter keeps one-half of one point of the four-point spread for originating and managing the syndicate.
2. The entire underwriting group earns about one and one-half percentage points.
3. The members of the selling group earn the remaining two percentage points.

[5]For more details about investment banking see Ernest Bloch, *Inside Investment Banking* (Homewood, Ill.: Dow Jones–Irwin, 1986). Also see C. W. Smith, "Investment Banking and the Capital Acquisition Process," *Journal of Financial Economics,* Jan.–Feb. 1986, vol. 15, pp. 3–29. See also D. P. Baron, "A Model of the Demand for Investment Bank Advising and Distribution Services for New Issues," *Journal of Finance,* Sept. 1982, vol. 37, pp. 955–976.

If the managing underwriters sell to an ultimate buyer, they receive the full four-percentage-point spread.

Tables 3-4 and 3-5 show the results from surveys of investment bankers' charges. The tables indicate that, first, it is considerably more expensive to issue common stock than to issue the same amount of fixed-income securities. Second, a large part of the investment banking costs is a fixed cost that does not vary with the size of the issue. As a result, considerable economies of scale exist in investment banking. Third, Table 3-5 shows that a *preemptive rights offering* can be used to reduce issuing costs.

Rights Offerings
As suggested in Chapter 2, an IPO of common stock or preferred stock with voting rights can either be underwritten and sold to the investing public for cash or be sold to the company's existing investors through a **preemptive rights offering.** Most issues of common stock sold outside the United States are sold by preemptive rights offerings to reduce the costs of underwriting the shares and to eliminate the possibility that an IPO would be priced so low that wealth is transferred from the existing shareholders to the new investors. For reasons not yet discerned, these **privileged subscriptions,** as they are also called, are infrequent in the United States.

The process of registering a rights offering with the SEC proceeds the same way as registering a nonrights issue. However, as illustrated in Figure 3-2, the issuer must decide how to distribute the shares. If a rights offering is chosen, it is common in the United States to grant the shareholders one ''warrant'' for each share owned. The terms of the **warrants** granted in each rights offering are different. A typical issue of warrants might entitle its recipients to use 10 warrants to buy 1 share of the new stock at a price of $40 per share anytime within 25 days after the IPO.[6] These warrants may be exercised, sold, or thrown away.

Many of the warrants granted in rights offerings are sold in an active market that emerges and lasts until the warrants expire. The warrants will be worthless if the price of the optioned stock is below the $40 exercise price of the warrant and/or after their exercise period is past. It is easy for the issuer to reduce the probability that its warrants become worthless before they expire by setting their exercise price substantially (say, 20 percent) below the price of the stock. However, issuers usually want to *totally preclude* the possibility that their warrants become worthless and are not exercised because, if that happened, the issuer would not get from the rights issue the proceeds needed for expansion. In order to completely eliminate this possibility, an investment banker can be

---

[6]Each right in the example above is a *call option* on one-tenth of a new share that has an exercise price of $40 per share and expires in 25 days. Warrants and call options are examined in Chapters 22 and 23.

Table 3-4

AVERAGE UNDERWRITING AND ADMINISTRATIVE COSTS AS A PERCENTAGE OF THE PROCEEDS FROM IPOs

Size of issue, $ millions	Bonds			Preferred stock			Common stock		
	Underwriting commissions, %	Administrative expenses, %	Total costs, %	Underwriting commissions, %	Administrative expenses, %	Total costs, %	Underwriting commissions, %	Administrative expenses, %	Total costs, %
Under 1.0	9.8	4.0	13.8	11.1*	5.3*	16.4*	12.7	9.1	21.8
1.0–1.99	8.0	2.9	10.9	9.5*	3.9*	13.4*	10.9	5.8	16.7
2.0–4.99	4.1	2.0	6.1	5.7*	2.9*	8.6*	8.5	3.9	12.4
5.0–9.99	2.4	0.9	3.3	2.1	0.7	2.8	6.4	2.9	9.3
10.0–19.99	1.3	0.8	2.1	1.5	0.5	2.0	5.1	1.0	6.1
20.0–49.99	1.0	0.5	1.5	1.4	0.4	1.8	4.2	0.5	4.7
50 and over	0.9	0.3	1.2	1.3	0.2	1.5	3.2	0.2	3.4

*Lack of information necessitated considerable interpolation to estimate the preferred stock small issues costs.

Sources: See R. Hillstrom and R. King, eds., "1960–69: A Decade of Corporate and International Finance," *Investment Dealers Digest*, New York, p. 18. Also see R. Beatty and J. Ritter, "Investment Banking, Reputation, and the Underpricing of Initial Public Offerings," *Journal of Financial Economics*, March 1986, vol. 15, pp. 213–232. See also A. J. Chalk, and J. W. Peavy, III, "Initial Public Offerings: Daily Returns, Offering Types, and the Price Effect," *Financial Analysts Journal*, 1987, vol. 43, no. 5, pp. 65–69. In addition, see R. Rock, "Why New Issues Are Underpriced," *Journal of Financial Economics*, Jan.–Feb. 1986, vol. 15, pp. 187–212.

Table 3-5

COMMON STOCK ISSUE COSTS STATED AS A PERCENTAGE OF THE PROCEEDS FOR RIGHTS AND NONRIGHTS ISSUES

Size of issue	General underwritten cash offers			Underwritten rights issues			Nonunderwritten rights issues
	Underwriters'	Other	Total	Underwriters'	Other	Total	Total
Under 0.50	—	—	—	—	—	—	9.0
0.50–0.99	7.0	6.8	13.7	3.4	4.8	8.2	4.6
1.00–1.99	10.4	4.9	15.3	6.4	4.2	10.5	4.9
2.00–4.99	6.6	2.9	9.5	5.2	2.9	8.1	2.9
5.00–9.99	5.5	1.5	7.0	3.9	2.2	6.1	1.4
10.00–19.99	4.8	0.7	5.6	4.1	1.2	5.4	0.7
20.00–49.99	4.3	0.4	4.7	3.8	0.9	4.7	0.5
50.00–99.99	4.0	0.2	4.2	4.0	0.7	4.7	0.2
100.00–500.00	3.8	0.1	4.0	3.5	0.5	4.0	0.1
Average	5.0	1.2	6.2	4.3	1.7	6.1	2.5

Source: C. W. Smith, "Alternative Methods for Raising Capital: Rights versus Underwritten Offering," *Journal of Financial Economics,* Dec. 1977, vol. 5, pp. 273–307, table 1, p. 277.

retained on a **standby basis.** A standby underwriting agreement is a contract in which the issuer pays an investment banker to stand by and be ready to support the price of its stock at a level above the exercise price of the warrant. Stated differently, in case the price of the stock falls, the investment banker is paid an insurancelike fee to buy any unsubscribed rights and exercise them.

Issuers Can Seek Competitive Bids for Their IPO

To keep down the underwriting costs of a new issue, some potential issuers of new securities solicit bids from competing investment banking firms. The underwriter that offers to pay the highest net cash proceeds for the issue gets the deal. The law requires that public utility holding companies seek competitive bids for all their IPOs rather than simply negotiate a fee structure with one underwriter. Research to determine the advantage of seeking competitive bids instead of negotiating with only one investment banker suggests that the issuer gets about the same price for the issue either way.[7] Potential issuers who do

[7]For more details see Dennis E. Logue and R. A. Jarrow, "Negotiation versus Competitive Bidding in the Sale of Securities by Public Utilities," *Financial Management,* Autumn 1978, pp. 31–39. Or see Sanjai Bhagat and Peter A. Frost, "Issuing Costs to Existing Shareholders in Competitive and Negotiated Underwritten Equity Offerings," *Journal of Financial Economics,* Jan.–Feb. 1986, pp. 233–259; and Seha M. Tinic, "Anatomy of Initial Public Offering of Common Stock," *Journal of Finance,* Sept. 1988, vol. 43, no. 4, pp. 789–822.

not solicit competing bids surely "shop around" for a good deal before selecting an underwriter.

ORGANIZED SECURITIES EXCHANGES

Investors usually purchase securities in the secondary market by calling a securities brokerage firm. After an account has been opened, the broker relays the investor's order to a dealer that handles that security.

Brokerage houses typically utilize the services of security dealers at either the organized exchanges or the over-the-counter (OTC) markets. In these secondary markets the investors buy and sell securities between themselves; the issuer never gets any cashflow from the trades. Our discussion of the secondary markets begins with the organized stock exchanges; one of the best known is the New York Stock Exchange (NYSE). Table 3-6 shows that the NYSE handles about half of the volume of shares traded in the United States.

The American Stock Exchange (AMEX), with only 3.6 percent of total share volume, follows far behind the NYSE. The other organized exchanges listed in Table 3-6 are called the **regional exchanges;** their volume makes up the balance of the trading in exchange-listed stocks. These smaller exchanges provide a

Table 3-6
VOLUME OF EQUITY TRADING ON NYSE, AMEX, REGIONAL EXCHANGES, AND OTC MARKETS IN THE UNITED STATES, 1987

	Number of shares		Dollar volume	
	Millions of shares	% of total	Billions of dollars	% of total
NYSE	47,801	49.0	$1874	69.0
NASDAQ OTC trading	37,890	38.9	500	18.4
American Stock Exchange	3,506	3.6	52	1.9
OTC's third market	1,170	1.2	43	1.6
Regional markets				
Midwest Stock Exchange*				
Pacific Stock Exchange*				
Philadelphia Stock Exchange*				
Boston Stock Exchange*				
Cincinnati Stock Exchange*				
Regionals' subtotal:	7,156	7.3	248	9.1
Totals	97,523	100.0	$2717	100.0

*For details about these exchanges see R. J. Tewles and E. S. Bradley, *The Stock Market* (New York: Wiley, 1982), chap. 11.
Source: NASDAQ Fact Book 1988, p. 8.

valuable market-making service for local businesses and for the issuers of municipal bonds. In addition, approximately 90 percent of the trading volume on the regional exchanges is in stocks that have **dual listings** on the NYSE and the regional exchanges. Stated differently, most stocks listed on the NYSE can also be bought and sold at one or more of the regional exchanges and/or in the over-the-counter (OTC) market. The regional exchanges provide market-making competition for the NYSE, which helps keep brokerage commissions low.

Functions Performed by Securities Markets

One of the most valuable services performed by a securities market is to *maintain active trading* so investors can buy or sell securities immediately at a price that varies little from the previous selling price. A continuous market increases the liquidity of the assets traded there.

The existence of markets also facilitates the *price discovery process*. Price is determined by buy and sell orders that flow from investors' demand and supply preferences. In addition, when securities markets publicly disseminate their prices, this information helps the nation allocate its financial resources more efficiently.

Securities markets indirectly *aid new financing*. If it is easy for investors to trade securities in a liquid secondary market, they are more willing to invest in IPOs, which finance economic growth.

To a certain extent, all securities markets in the United States are *self-regulating organizations*. The markets monitor the integrity of their members and employees, the firms listed on the exchanges, and the people who trade there. Through continuous internal audits they guard against unfair trading practices. The market makers (see Section 3-3 entitled Liquidity) willingly pay the costs of performance reviews and expel dishonest members because they realize that the survival of their market depends on its good reputation. The OTC market is also self-regulating, but, as will be discussed below, it operates under a somewhat different legal framework than the organized exchanges.[8]

Listing Requirements

All firms whose stock is traded on an organized exchange must have filed an application for listing. Many NYSE-listed firms are listed on more than one exchange. But, the NYSE has the most stringent listing requirements of all the exchanges. In addition to meeting the listing requirements in Table 3-7, a firm must pay a listing fee.

---

[8]In addition to the internal auditing activities of the individual securities markets, the SEC oversees all securities trading and supplements the markets' self-regulating activities. Securities law is the topic of Chapter 4. As explained there, the OTC market operates under the jurisdiction of the Maloney Act of 1936, which was passed at the request of the participants in the OTC market.

Table 3-7
NEW YORK STOCK EXCHANGE LISTING REQUIREMENTS

1. Earnings before taxes of at least $2.5 million in the most recent year
2. Earnings before taxes of at least $2.0 million during the two preceding years
3. Net tangible assets of at least $16.0 million
4. Total market value of common stock of at least $16.0 million
5. Publicly held shares of at least $1.0 million
6. More than 2000 holders of 100 shares or more

Once a company has met the requirements for listing, it must meet certain additional requirements established by the exchange and the SEC in order for its securities to be traded. For example, the listed firm must publish quarterly earnings reports; fully disclose financial information annually; obtain approval by the SEC of proxy forms before they can be sent to stockholders; and, among other things, insiders of the firm are prohibited from short selling.[9]

Considering the strict listing requirements and other provisos after membership, one wonders why firms would rather be listed on organized exchanges rather than be traded OTC. One answer is that the listed firm may benefit from the publicity it gains from being listed on an organized exchange and having its trading data reported in the daily news. It is possible that this exposure may have a favorable effect on the sale of the issuer's products. Supporters of exchange listing also claim that listing enhances the prestige of the listed corporation. However, research has cast doubts on the NYSE's claims that securities listed there sell at higher prices than securities that are not listed on the NYSE.

Organization of a Securities Exchange

Since the NYSE is the major securities market in the United States, the discussion will initially focus on its form of organization. The other organized exchanges in the United States tend to follow the pattern of the NYSE. The initial discussion of the NYSE is not meant to imply that its form of organization is superior to any other market. Each of these markets has unique organizational strengths and weaknesses and are discussed in this chapter.

The NYSE is a *voluntary association* that endeavors to maintain a smoothly operating marketplace. The NYSE Corporation is directed by a board of directors elected by its members. The NYSE board, representing both member firms and the public, is the chief policy-making body of the exchange. It approves or rejects applications of new members; accepts or rejects budget proposals; disciplines members through fines, suspension, or expulsion; accepts or rejects proposals for new security listings; submits requests to the SEC for changes; assigns securities to the various posts on the trading floor; and administers the other affairs of the exchange.

[9]Short selling is discussed in Section 8-3.

The main trading floor of the NYSE is about the size of a football field. There is an annex in which bonds and less actively traded stocks are bought and sold. Around the edges of both rooms are telephone booths, used primarily to transmit orders and sales confirmations between the brokers' offices and the exchange floor. On the floor are 18 U-shaped counters, each with a number of assigned **trading posts.** Every one of the approximately 1550 corporations listed on the NYSE (the number changes constantly) is assigned to be traded at one of these trading posts.

Members of the NYSE

There are 1366 members of the NYSE; this number has remained constant since 1953. Memberships are frequently referred to as *seats,* although trading is conducted without the benefit of chairs. In 1969, seats sold at a record high of $515,000, but by 1977 they were down to only $35,000. More recently, seat prices have risen above $1 million. In most years there are over 100 transfers of exchange memberships. Exchange members perform one of several specialized functions, as follows.

Commission Brokers   Several hundred seats on the NYSE are owned by **commission brokers,** who are agents on the exchange floor who buy and sell securities for clients of brokerage houses. They may also act as dealers for their own position. Commission brokers communicate via telephone with brokerages; they receive transactions from the brokerages that employ their services, and they send back confirmation messages.

The NYSE requires that all seats be owned by individuals. The NYSE does not allow institutions (such as brokerages, banks, and mutual funds) to own seats because they are the biggest customers of the NYSE. However, institutional investors can exert considerable indirect control over the seat owner's voice in the management of the NYSE. For example, a large brokerage like Merrill Lynch, Pierce, Fenner & Smith (MLPFS) can influence the actions of several seat owners. MLPFS may have extended loans that enabled the seat owner to buy the seat. Moreover, MLPFS sends thousands of transactions to the NYSE every day and can direct its trades to whichever commission broker it chooses. The commission income from MLPFS alone may be millions of dollars per year for each commission broker chosen by MLPFS. With all of this clout, MLPFS can easily find several commission brokers who will be eager to work for MLPFS's interests.

Other categories of NYSE members include floor brokers, floor traders, and specialists.

Floor Brokers   Floor brokers are sometimes called *two-dollar brokers* because for a commission (which once was $2 per order) they execute orders for commission brokers who have more orders than they can handle. Floor brokers are ordinarily free-lance members of the exchange. They serve to prevent backlogs of orders and allow many firms to operate with fewer exchange memberships than would be needed without their services.

Floor Traders   Floor traders, sometimes called *registered traders,* differ from floor brokers because they trade primarily for their own account. Floor traders are speculators who search the exchange floor for profitable buying and selling opportunities. They trade free of commission, since they own their own seats and deal for their own account. As a result, floor traders sometimes buy and sell the same stock on the same day, an activity that is called **day trading,** in order to profit from small price moves.

When trading accelerates, floor traders sometimes act as floor brokers and may even assist the specialists. However, NYSE rules forbid floor traders from acting as both agent (or broker) and principal (or dealer) for the same stock on the same day. In recent years, floor trading has declined.

Specialists   Several hundred seats on the NYSE are owned by people called specialists. **Specialists** are assigned to posts on the trading floor where they **make a market** in one or more stocks that are assigned to them by the NYSE. NYSE specialists are monopolistic market makers in one or more stocks. They may act as broker or dealer in a transaction. As **brokers,** the specialists execute orders for other brokers for a commission; no risk is involved. As **dealers,** the specialists buy and sell for their own accounts shares of the stock in which they are specializing, thereby putting their own capital at risk.

The specialists make more money on average than any other category of NYSE member. However, *specialists must earn the right to be a specialist by accepting the obligation to make a "fair and orderly market" for their assigned stocks.* To keep the market in a stock fair and orderly when there are more buy orders than sell orders, specialists must either raise the market price of the security they control or sell shares out of their inventory to meet the excess demand. And, when there are more sell orders than buy orders, specialists must either lower the price of the stock or buy it for their own account in order to equalize supply and demand. Within the limits set by their desire to trade profitably from shifts in supply and demand, specialists set the market prices for their assigned securities.

Specialists earn profits from two market activities. They take the bid–asked spread from every share that passes through their post, and they try to manage their inventory so that they can buy stocks at a price that is below the selling price.

A specialist is supposed to help achieve an orderly, continuous market, in which only small price changes occur from trade to trade; otherwise the NYSE Board of Directors would remove the specialists from their position. To become a specialist requires experience, ability as a dealer, a seat on the exchange, selection by the Board of Directors, and a minimum capital requirement. All

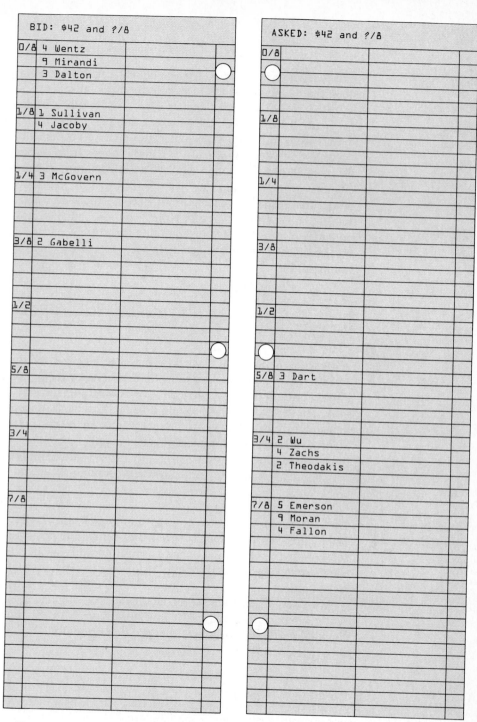

Figure 3-3 Computer printout from a specialist's book for a stock with a bid of $42-3/8 and $42-5/8 asked.

specialists are required to have adequate capital to own a position of at least 4000 shares of each stock in which they specialize.[10]

Every NYSE specialist keeps a separate **specialist's book,** or **limit-order book,** for each stock in which they make a market. These books are administrative diaries used to record unexecuted buy and sell orders that come in from the specialist's customers. Figure 3-3 shows pages from a specialist's book which list 1 day's orders for one stock. The information includes the names of the customers, the quantity they want to buy or sell, and the limit on the price at which they want the specialist to execute their transaction. The specialists' books are kept secret because they contain valuable information; the list of potential trades in the book outlines the supply and demand pressures that determine the price of the security. This information aids specialists in earning trading profits.

3-3	**LIQUIDITY**

A **securities market** is a place where people buy and sell financial instruments. A **dealer** is an individual or a firm that puts its own capital at risk by investing in a security in order to carry an inventory of the security and make a market in it. Those dealers that provide other parties with immediacy of supply and demand by trading the security they inventory at posted prices are called **market makers. Brokers** are commission sales people who need not invest their own funds in the securities they sell. Many brokers are employed by dealers. Dealers, market makers, and brokers work together to create markets that are *liquid.*

Liquidity of Individual Assets

Perfectly liquid assets are *perfectly marketable;* they suffer no price shrinkage if they are liquidated hastily. Cash and demand deposits are examples of perfectly liquid assets. Real estate is not a liquid asset because sellers typically must grant large price discounts below the asset's equilibrium value in order to sell quickly.

Most securities have more "moneyness" than real estate but are not perfectly liquid assets like cash. Investors pay a slightly higher price, called a **liquidity premium,** for assets that are more liquid.[11]

---

[10]Most specialists join other specialists to form *specialist firms,* so as to help each other obtain operating capital and achieve economies of scale in processing their administrative paperwork. As a result, most specialists on the floor of the NYSE are members of one of approximately ninety specialist firms.

[11]See Y. Amihud and H. Mendelson, "Liquidity and Asset Prices: Financial Management Implications," *Financial Management,* Spring 1988, vol. 17, no. 1, pp. 5–15. Also see Y. Amihud and H. Mendelson, "Dealership Market: Market-Making with Inventory," *Journal of Financial Economics,* May–June 1980, vol. 8, no. 1, pp. 31–53.

**Liquidity of a
Market**

Liquid markets possess the qualities of depth, breadth, and resiliency, in varying degrees.

1. A market has **depth** if buy and sell orders exist (or can be easily uncovered) both above and below the price at which the security is transacting. A market that lacks depth is said to be **shallow.**

2. *Breadth* is related to depth. A market has **breadth** if buy and sell orders exist in volume. Markets that lack the volume of orders needed to provide liquidity are called **thin markets.**

3. A market has **resiliency** if new orders pour in immediately in response to price changes caused by temporary order imbalances. A speedy price discovery process is an essential precondition for a resilient market.

Table 3-8 illustrates the implications of breadth, depth, or the lack thereof for the bid page of a market maker's limit-order book (for instance, a specialist's book). Table 3-8 illustrates four different sets of bid orders for a security that has $50 as the highest bid.

**Illiquidity and
Execution Costs**

Illiquid assets cannot be sold quickly unless the seller incurs significant execution costs. **Execution costs** are defined as the total of the following factors:[12]

1. **Transaction size effects,** or *market impact effects,* occur when the total dollar size of a transaction influences the price at which the trade is transacted. Market impact effects vary inversely with the breadth of the market.

2. **Inaccurate price discovery** can occur when a market lacks the resiliency needed to quickly correct disequilibrium prices as they occur. Buy and sell orders should emerge quickly enough to prevent a transaction price from deviating from its equilibrium value.

3. **Brokerage commissions** tend to vary inversely with two factors: the operational efficiency of the security brokerage firms and the amount of price competition between the brokerage firms.

4. The **bid–asked spread** is the difference between the lowest asked (or offered) price and the highest bid price. The bid–asked spread is like a commission that a dealer earns on each share trade for making a market in a security. The market is said to lack depth when the bid–asked

[12]This section draws from J. Hasbrouck and R. Schwartz, "Liquidity and Execution Costs in Equity Markets," *Journal of Portfolio Management,* 1988. Also see Robert A. Schwartz, *Equity Markets* (New York: Harper and Row, 1988), pp. 36–37 and chap. 11.

Table 3-8

FOUR EXAMPLES OF THE BID PAGE FROM A MARKET MAKER'S LIMIT-ORDER BOOK

Bid price	Number of shares ordered at each bid price			
$50	100	100	500	500
$49⅞	200	200	500	500
$49¾	0	300	0	700
$49⅝	0	300	0	900
$49½	0	300	0	1500
Condition of the market:	Thin and shallow	Thin and deep	Broad and shallow	Broad and deep

Source: Adapted from Kenneth Garbade, *Securities Markets* (New York: McGraw-Hill, 1982), table 20-1, p. 421.

spread is wide. *The bid–asked spread is an inverse measure of liquidity.*[13] Figures 2-2*b* and 3-3 show examples of some bid–asked spreads.

3-4   **OVER-THE-COUNTER (OTC) MARKETS**

The phrase "over-the-counter" originated in the days when securities were traded over the counters of various dealers. Today, the OTC market is more a way to do business than a place. The OTC market competes with investment bankers and the organized exchanges because OTC dealers can operate in both the primary and the secondary markets.

The broker-dealers who trade OTC securities are linked by an international network of telephone lines and computer systems through which they deal

---

[13]For details about the determinants of the bid–asked spread see Seha Tinic, "The Economics of Liquidity Services," *Quarterly Journal of Economics,* February 1972. For the classic study see Harold Demsetz, "The Cost of Transacting," *Quarterly Journal of Economics,* Oct. 1968, fig. 1, p. 36. Also see K. Cohen, S. Maier, R. Schwartz, and D. Whitcomb, "Transactions Costs, Order Placement Strategy, and Existence of a Bid–Asked Spread," *Journal of Political Economy,* April 1981. See also George J. Benston and Robert L. Hagerman, "The Determinants of Bid–Asked Spreads in the Over-the-Counter Market," *Journal of Financial Economics,* Dec. 1974, vol. 1. Also see Lawrence R. Glosten and Lawrence E. Harris, "Estimating the Components of the Bid–Asked Spread," *Journal of Financial Economics,* May 1988, vol. 21, no. 1, pp. 123–142. For a study of the bid–asked spreads on CBOE options see J. Y. Choi, Dan Salandro, and Kuldeep Shastri, "On the Estimation of Bid–Asked Spreads: Theory and Evidence," *Journal of Financial and Quantitative Analysis,* June 1988, vol. 23, no. 2, pp. 219–230.

directly with one another and with their clients. This elaborate communications system allows investors to select among competing market makers instead of being forced to trade through one monopolistic market maker (such as NYSE specialists). Although the competing market makers all probably sell any given stock at the same price, they compete by offering to execute transactions faster and/or for smaller commissions.

Securities Traded in the OTC

The securities traded over-the-counter range from risk-free U.S. government bonds to the most speculative common stocks. Historically, the OTC markets have been more important as bond markets than as stock markets. Currently, virtually all U.S. government, corporate, and municipal obligations are traded OTC, although U.S. government bonds and many corporation bonds are also traded at organized exchanges. More than 90 percent of corporate bonds are traded OTC, although many of them are also listed on organized exchanges. The organized exchanges prefer to trade stocks rather than bonds because common stock commission rates are higher.

The OTC stock market is not quite as large as the OTC bond market. About a third of stock trading in the United States is conducted OTC—over 30,000 different common stock issues are traded there. But, many of these issues generate virtually no trading activity because they are shares in small, local corporations that are closely held by the founder's family. Many bank, insurance, and investment company shares are traded OTC because in the past the OTC markets required less financial disclosure. However, the 1964 Amendments to the Securities Exchange Act of 1934 mandated that OTC securities disclose essentially the same information as the exchange-listed securities. Many preferred stock issues are traded OTC, and practically all the securities listed on the NYSE are also being traded OTC via the "third market," which is discussed below.

OTC Broker-Dealers

Some of the OTC broker-dealers registered with the SEC are organized as sole proprietorships, some as partnerships, and many as corporations. Many of them have memberships in more than one stock exchange. Some are wholesalers (who buy from and sell to other dealers), some are retailers selling mostly to the public, and some serve both functions. Dealers who regularly buy and sell a particular security are said to *make a market* in that security, much like the specialists on the NYSE. Broker-dealer firms can be categorized according to their specialties. An *OTC house* specializes in OTC issues and rarely belongs to an exchange; an *investment banking house* that specializes in the underwriting of new security issues may diversify by acting as dealer in both listed and OTC securities. A *commercial bank* or a *trust company* may make a market in U.S. government, state, and local obligations. A *stock exchange member house* may have a separate department specifically formed to carry on trading in OTC markets; some *bond houses* deal almost exclusively in municipal issues or federal government bond issues. Every OTC broker-dealer operates differently.

National Association of Securities Dealers (NASD)

The **National Association of Securities Dealers** (NASD) is a voluntary organization of security dealers that performs a self-regulating function for the OTC markets, similar to that which the NYSE performs for its members. To qualify as a **registered representative,** or *securities broker,* the candidate must file an application with the NASD. In addition, the applicant must be recommended by a partner, officer, or employee of an NASD broker-dealer firm and pass a written qualifying examination prepared by the NASD. Once a member, any individual or firm that violates the *Rules of Fair Practice* outlined by the NASD is subject to censure, fine, suspension, or expulsion.

The NASD also serves as an advocate for its members. It lobbies in Congress, negotiates with the SEC, and deals with the public in an effort to represent favorably the interests of its membership and create a favorable public image for the OTC market.

OTC Stock Price Quotations

Competitively negotiated bid and asked prices are determined by approximately 500 OTC market makers. A computerized communications network called NASDAQ serves the OTC market. **NASDAQ** (pronounced Naz′ dak) is an acronym for the initials NASD and AQ, which stands for *automated quotations*. NASDAQ provides instantaneous bid and asked prices for thousands of securities; all it takes is pressing a few keys on a computer terminal.

When an NASD broker or dealer makes an inquiry, the NASDAQ computer and telecommunications system instantly flashes prices on the screen of any computer terminal linked to NASDAQ's central computer. This allows OTC-registered representatives to easily obtain the bid–asked quotations of all dealers making a market in the security they wish to trade. The OTC broker then contacts the dealer offering the best price plus commission cost and executes a trade. The advantage to investors using this system of competing market makers is the assurance that, although they are usually obtaining about the same security price from the competing market makers, they can select the trade with the lowest commission cost (which is approximately equal to the bid–asked spread).

NASDAQ is designed to handle up to 20,000 stocks but currently lists only about 2500 (which is still considerably more than are listed on the NYSE). Not all OTC stocks are listed in NASDAQ because some are not traded actively enough to be included within the system. NASDAQ's excess capacity may eventually be put to use by including stocks listed on the exchanges. It would be advantageous for investors to have all exchange-listed and OTC securities reported through NASDAQ. Investors could easily compare the prices from competing market makers, and increased competition should minimize the costs of buying and selling securities.

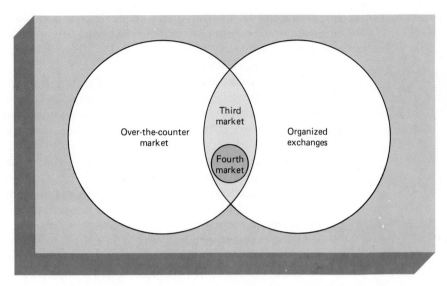

Figure 3-4 Venn diagram of the organized exchanges, the OTC market, and the third and fourth markets.

The thousands of stock prices quoted in NASDAQ are not all published in daily financial newspapers. To be included in NASDAQ's widely publicized **national daily list,** a stock must have at least three market makers, a minimum of 1500 stockholders distributed throughout the country, and command what is called "investor interest."[14]

For OTC stocks not included in the national daily list, a more comprehensive quotation service is provided by the National Quotation Bureau (NQB), whose subscribers are primarily security dealers. The NQB quotes prices of over 8000 securities on its daily "pink sheets." Its information is derived chiefly from OTC dealer firms.

The Third Market   The **third market** is an OTC market in NYSE-listed stocks. Figure 3-4 illustrates the relationship between the organized exchanges, the OTC market, and the third market. Dealers in the third market provide only execution and record-keeping services for their clients. These dealers compete with NYSE member firms; they pass on the cost savings they achieve by providing minimal client services in the form of lower commissions.

[14]To measure *investor interest,* NASDAQ officials calculate the market value of trading in every issue at 6-month intervals. They multiply the average weekly volume of shares traded in each issue by the price per share to estimate the market value of a security's trading activity. The top 1400 stocks are placed on the "most active list," and the next 950 stocks are placed on the "supplementary list." Then the news media publish whatever they wish from these lists.

The Fourth Market   Direct investor-to-investor trades occur in what is called the **fourth market**—a communications network between block traders. (A **block** is a single transaction that involves 10,000 or more shares.) Fourth-market participants completely bypass normal dealer services.

The fourth market organizer collects only a small commission or an annual retainer for helping to arrange block transactions. Thus, the costs of trading blocks is very small. Traders operating in the fourth market also expect to obtain a better price through direct negotiation, more rapid execution, and protection of anonymity.

There are several privately owned fourth-market organizations; each one operates somewhat differently. Most use telephones to communicate with their institutional customers, whereas others use computers. For example, a fourth-market firm named **Instinet** uses a computer network to connect geographically dispersed terminals.

An Instinet subscriber who wants to buy or sell begins by asking the Instinet computer for current market prices. To trade, the subscriber enters the name of the stock, its bid or asked price, and the desired number of shares into Instinet's computer network, plus a personal code number. This entry is an offer to buy or sell which prints out on the computer terminals of other Instinet subscribers around the world. Another subscriber who wants to trade may contact the first subscriber and negotiate via the computer. If they agree on the price and size of a trade, Instinet's computer prints out confirmation slips for both subscribers. The deal is completed without the services of a market maker (such as a specialist), who would charge a standard commission. The buying and selling subscribers never even learn each others' identities; this anonymity is valued by some fourth-market clients.[15]

May Day—The End of Fixed Minimum Schedules in the United States   The efficiency of the NYSE was improved by competition from the third and fourth markets and by a law which took effect on May 1, 1975, a day called **May Day** on Wall Street. Before May Day, all the NYSE member firms charged a substantial brokerage commission on every trade. The NYSE enforced this fixed minimum commission schedule because its members thought it would maximize their profits. As a result, prior to May Day the NYSE was a system of monopolistic market makers because the NYSE specialists never compete with each other. The NYSE was also a price-fixing cartel because its commission rates were not negotiable.

The Securities and Exchange Commission decreed that the NYSE must replace its fixed commissions with negotiated commissions on May 1, 1975. Lower commission rates offered by the third market dealers also pressed the

---

[15]Instinet is a registered trademark of the Institutional Networks Corporation. It is a subsidiary of Reuters, a large international financial news and quotation service. Telerate, owned by Dow Jones, is the largest of several competitors that Reuters faces in its drive to automate the world's securities markets.

NYSE to cut its commissions charges. These pressures to lower commission rates forced rapid improvements in the NYSE's operational efficiency. The commission rate that NYSE brokerages charged dropped approximately 25 percent soon after May Day.[16] This improved operational efficiency also increased the market's liquidity.

Block Positioners   Because multiple buyers must usually be lined up to purchase a block of securities, a special type of broker called a **block positioner** has developed. Block positioners routinely process block transactions and rarely cause the market price of the issue to change significantly. Most block positioners are employees of brokerage firms that have seats on the NYSE—these large firms have both the capital to carry a block in inventory and the connections to distribute it. Block positioners also operate in the third and fourth markets. Some say block positioners operate in the **upstairs market,** meaning an office that trades NYSE-listed stocks but is removed from the floor of the NYSE.

The commission rates charged by block positioners are low; one-fourth of 1 percent is not unusual. In contrast, odd lots typically incur commission rates of 2 to 6 percent because economies of scale are not possible in the small transactions. The low commission rates offered by block positioners are another source of competitive pressure that helps maintain low brokerage commissions.

3-5   **TRADING ARRANGEMENTS**

Before a buy or sell order can be executed, the security broker must have explicit trading orders from the customer. The orders that clients can give to their brokers are executed similarly around the world.

Types of Orders   There are several ways to execute buy and sell orders.

[16]In hindsight it is clear that the high, fixed minimum commissions the NYSE supported before May Day restricted the exchange's volume of shares traded and diminished the members' profits. After May Day, lower negotiated commissions were initiated and the NYSE's trading volume and member profits soared to new highs year after year.

To learn more about the commission rates, see R. O. Edmister, "Commission Cost Structure: Shifts and Scale Economies," *Journal of Finance,* May 1978, vol. 33, no. 2, pp. 477–486. Or see J. L. Hamilton, "Competition, Scale Economies, and Transaction Costs in the Stock Market," *Journal of Financial and Quantitative Analysis,* 1976, vol. 11, pp. 779–802. Also see J. L. Hamilton, "Marketplace Fragmentation, Competition, and the Efficiency of the Stock Exchange," *Journal of Finance,* March 1979, vol. 34, no. 1, pp. 171–187. For more information see Hans Stoll, "The Pricing of Security Dealer Services: An Empirical Study of NASDAQ Stocks," *Journal of Finance,* 1978, vol. 33, pp. 1153–1172.

Market Orders   **Market orders** are the most common, fastest, and most easily executed kind of order. With a market order the customer is instructing the broker to buy or sell the specified securities at the best possible price as soon as the order reaches the trading floor of the exchange. Market orders are usually executed immediately. Market orders sent to NYSE specialists when the exchange is closed are recorded in the appropriate specialist's book (see Figure 3-3 and Table 3-8) to be executed at the opening market price.

Limit Orders   There are two types of limit orders; both set price limits. A **limit buy order** stipulates the maximum price that the investor is willing to pay for some quantity of a given security. A **limit sell order** specifies the minimum price at which the investor is willing to sell some quantity of a security. If the limit price cannot be obtained, the limit order is recorded in the market maker's **limit-order book** (or specialist's book) and held for future execution, if and when the limit condition is attained. If an expiration time is affixed to the order, it may pass before the order gets executed. Limit orders can be combined with other requirements to create orders with more complicated terms.

Stop Orders   **Stop orders,** often called *stop-loss orders,* are designed to either protect a customer's existing profit or limit potential losses. For example, if an investor bought a stock for $50 and its current market price is $75, the investor has a *paper profit* of $25 per share. If the investor fears a drop in the current market price, a stop order to sell at, say, $70, could be issued. This stop order would in effect become a market order if the security falls to $70 and would be executed as soon as possible. The $70 liquidating price is not guaranteed. The stock might be down to $69 or $68 or even lower by the time the sale could be executed. However, the investor's profit position is protected to a large extent. The danger of using stop-loss orders is that the investor runs the risk of being **whip-sawed**—selling a security with a future of long-run price appreciation in a temporary decline.

Specialists on the NYSE must keep a record of stop orders. They are executed in order of priority, as are all limit orders. That is, the first stop order received at a given price is the first order executed. An accumulation of stop orders at a certain price can cause a sharp break in the market price of the issue involved. In such an event, the NYSE may suspend the stop orders just when the traders most need the protection. The value of a stop order is undermined by the possibility of these occurrences.

Stop-Limit Orders   These orders specify both the stop price and the limit price at which the customer is willing to buy or sell. The customer must be willing to run the risk that the security will not reach the limit price, resulting in no trade. If the trade cannot be executed by the broker when the order reaches the trading floor, the broker will turn the order over to the specialist, who will execute the order if the limit price or better is reached. An example will clarify this complicated order.

Mr. Morgan owns 2000 shares of a stock that is currently selling at $40, but Morgan fears the price may drop. To allay his fears, Morgan places an order: "Sell 2000 shares at $39 stop, $38 limit." If the price of the stock falls to $39, the broker will immediately try to execute the stop portion of the stop-limit order. If the stop order cannot be executed at $39, it may be executed at the $38 limit price or better. But, the stock will not be sold at a price below $38.

A stop-limit order to buy is the reverse of a stop-limit order to sell. As soon as the stock's price reaches the stop level, the stop order to buy is executed at the limit level or better—that is, below the limit price, if possible. Unfortunately, prices may jump so fast in a fast-moving market that even a well-placed stop-limit order gets passed over without being exercised.

Good-Till-Canceled (GTC) Order A GTC order is also called an *open order*. A **GTC order** remains in effect indefinitely. In contrast, a **day order** remains in effect only for the day that it is brought to the exchange floor. The vast majority of orders are day orders. However, customers may prefer a GTC order, particularly for limit orders, when they are willing to wait until the price is right for trading. GTC orders must be confirmed at various intervals to remain in effect.

Margin Trading

A new client opening an account at a securities brokerage must choose between a cash account and a margin account. Investors applying for a **cash account** need only furnish their name, address, and social security number because they pay cash for any securities they buy. **Margin account** investors must furnish more information because they are applying to the brokerage for permission to buy securities on credit.[17]

When investors buy securities on margin, they buy some shares with cash and borrow from their brokerage to pay for additional shares, using the paid shares as collateral. The shares paid for with the investor's money are like the equity or down payment on an installment purchase agreement. The Federal Reserve Board of Governors controls the amount that may be borrowed. If the Federal Reserve Board stipulates a 55 percent margin requirement, for instance, the investor must pay cash for at least 55 percent of the value of the securities purchased. The Federal Reserve's margin requirements have varied from a low of 25 percent in the 1930s to a high of 100 percent in the 1940s.[18]

To see how margins work, let us assume the margin requirement is 55 percent

---

[17]Investors who open a margin account are required by the NYSE to make a minimum initial deposit of $2000; this is enough for Merrill Lynch, for example. In contrast, Salomon Brothers and Goldman Sachs require $1 million to open an account—a few places require even more.

[18]Margin trading includes both margin buying and margin short selling. However, only a small portion of total trading on the margin is short selling. Short selling is discussed in detail in Chapter 8.

and an investor wishes to purchase 100 shares of a $100 stock. To pay for this total investment of $10,000, the investor puts up only $5500 cash for 55 shares and uses the shares as collateral for a loan to pay for 45 additional shares. Consider the investor's position after investing $100 per share (1) if the share price doubles to $200 and, in contrast, (2) if the share price drops to $50.

Good News for the Investor   If the investor's shares double in value from $100 to $200, the total profit will be $100 profit per share times 100 shares, or $10,000 before interest, commissions, and taxes. Compare this $10,000 gross gain with $100 profit per share times 55 shares, or a $5500 gross profit, if the shares had not been bought on margin. The investor's gains were larger because the shares were bought on margin—as shown in the following account.

Assets	Liabilities and net worth
Market value $20,000	$4,500 debit balance (the loan)
	$15,500 equity
	$20,000 total

The investor's gross gain of $10,000 equals a 181.8 percent return on the $5500 margin investment. Favorable financial leverage magnified the 100 percent gain in the stock's price to a 181.8 percent return on equity.

Bad News for the Investor   What if the investor's shares decreased in price from $100 to $50 per share? In this case, the current market value of the investment has dropped from $10,000 to $5000, resulting in a $5000 loss. If the shares had not been bought on margin, that is, if only 55 shares had been bought for cash, the loss would have been $50 per share times 55 shares, or $2750. By buying stock on 55 percent margin, the investor nearly doubled the loss. The investor's final position is summarized in the following T-account.

Assets	Liabilities and net worth
Market value $5000	$4500 debit balance (the loan)
	$500 equity
	$5000 total

The investor's total loss of $5000 equals 91 percent of the $5500 cash investment. Adverse financial leverage magnified the 50 percent price drop into a 91 percent decline in equity.

The Worst News for the Investor—A Margin Call   If a margined stock decreases in value sufficiently, the investor will receive a **margin call** from the broker (brokers also call it a *maintenance call*). The broker informs the client that it is necessary to put up more margin money. If the investor cannot come up with the additional cash within a day or two, the broker must liquidate enough of the investor's securities to bring the equity in the account up to the legally required minimum level. Liquidating the margined client's shares is easy, as margin customers must keep their securities on deposit at the brokerage house as collateral for their loan. If anything is left in the margin account after the margin call, forced sale, and loan repayment, the investor receives the balance. By how much must the stock decrease in value before there is a margin call? The New York Stock Exchange has answered this question by stipulating a maintenance margin requirement.

According to the NYSE's *maintenance margin requirement,* a margin call must occur when the equity in the account is less than 25 percent of the market value of the account. For our investor, a margin call would be required when the market value of the $10,000 margined purchase of common stock falls below $6000. Stated differently, the loan cannot be more than 75 percent of the account's market value. The investor's $4500 loan is *fixed* at 75 percent of a market value of $6000. In practice, most brokers set higher margin requirements than the 25 percent minimum set by the NYSE.

The Federal Reserve Board's Regulation T, called the **initial margin requirement,** is effective only when the stock is sold short or on an initial margin purchase. After the initial purchase margin requirement has been met, the Federal Reserve has no maintenance margin requirements.

The reason for buying on margin is that it allows investors to magnify their gross profits by the reciprocal of the margin requirement (that is, 2 times if the margin requirement is one-half, 3 times if it is one-third, and so forth). The major risk is that it causes magnified losses of the same reciprocal if stock prices decline. There is the added disadvantage of fixed interest payments whether stock prices advance or decline. In sum, margin trading increases the investor's potential profits and potential losses.

When an investor buys on margin, the one-period rate of return is defined in Equation (3-1).

$$r_t = \frac{p_{t+1} - p_t + d_t - i(1 - m)p_t}{mp_t} \tag{3-1}$$

The margin percentage is denoted by m. The denominator mp_t is the dollar amount of the margin buyer's equity investment, ignoring commissions. The margin buyer borrowed $(1 - m)p_t$ dollars at an interest rate of i, so the dollar amount of the interest expense, $i(1 - m)p_t$, is deducted from the numerator to obtain the net income return on equity.[19]

[19]For details about margin requirements see Robert P. Rittereiser and John P. Geelen, *Margin Requirements and Practices,* 2d ed. (New York: New York Institute of Finance, 1983).

Discount Brokers   **Discount brokerages** seek to attract clients by offering lower brokerage commissions than the full-service brokerages. Merrill Lynch, Pierce, Fenner & Smith; Shearson Lehman Hutton; and, Prudential-Bache are examples of **full-service brokerages:** they typically require their brokers to be college graduates. They also provide free investment research advice for their clients, free safe-keeping of the client's securities, monthly statements and year-end tax summaries, and other customer services that are paid for by high commission rates. Discount brokers do not provide these amenities—they just do the paperwork that every brokerage must do and charge minimal commission rates for their austere service. Charles Schwab & Company, Rose & Company, and Quick & Reilly are large discount brokerage firms.[20]

Clients of brokerage firms offering the full line of services pay brokerage commission rates (stated as a percent of the market value of the total transaction) roughly equal to those illustrated in Figure 3-5. Clients of discount brokerages enjoy fewer services but pay only a fraction of the commissions charged by a full-service broker.

Figure 3-5 Typical common stock commission rates for full-service brokerage house.

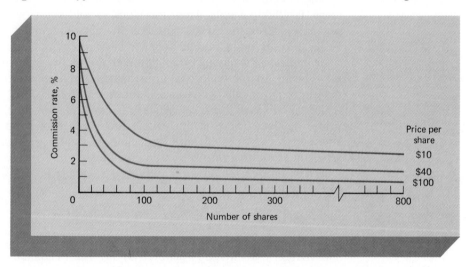

[20]Charles Schwab & Company was acquired by the BankAmerica bank holding company in 1983. The Federal Reserve Board allowed this merger because Schwab was only a brokerage—the firm did no investment banking. The Fed's ruling was widely interpreted as a significant limitation on the provisions of the Glass-Steagall Act (which requires the separation of commercial banking and investment banking). BankAmerica later sold Schwab, but the legal precedent stood. In the same vein, in 1983 Chase Manhattan Bank acquired a discount brokerage firm named Rose & Company. Since then dozens of banks have either acquired a discount broker subsidiary or started one of their own.

3-6   **CHARACTERISTICS OF DIFFERENT SECONDARY MARKETS**

Differences between secondary markets around the world exceed those between the organized stock exchanges and the OTC market in the United States. Each market's organization bestows certain advantages and limitations that deserve consideration.

Intertemporal Consolidation of Trades

Call markets accumulate clients' trading orders, which arrive over a period of time, into batches that are executed simultaneously. Simultaneous execution is accomplished by crossing all buy and sell orders for the same financial instrument at one price; if that price is outside of the limits stipulated on some orders, then those trades do not get exercised at that call. Traders whose orders are unfilled may resubmit them at the next call. It is common to have trading calls once or twice per trading day at the same time every day. Each financial instrument traded in the market is called sequentially until the batches of trades for all financial instruments have been cleared. Call markets are most useful in markets where the volume of trading is not large—Austria and Norway, for instance.

The stock exchanges in Canada, Britain, and the United States have **continuous markets** that allow trades to be executed anytime during the trading day. In contrast, the stock exchanges in Sweden, Switzerland, Denmark, and France have **mixed markets,** in which one group of stocks is traded continuously for, say, 10 minutes, then a different group of stocks is traded continuously for the next 10 minutes, and this pattern continues throughout the day until all groups of stocks have been traded.

Spatial Consolidation of Trades

The NYSE and AMEX are **geographically consolidated markets** that bring together trades from all over the world to be executed on the floor of the exchange. In contrast, NASDAQ is a **geographically fragmented market** because the market makers competing to make a market in any given financial instrument operate from different geographic locations. NASDAQ's geographic fragmentation does not diminish its ability to make liquid markets, however, because the bid and asked quotes from the geographically separated market makers are all brought together in the NASDAQ computer to create one electronically centralized market.

Maximum Daily Price Change Limitations

Most stock exchanges in the world and all stock exchanges in the United States allow the prices of the securities traded there to fluctuate freely. However, the stock exchanges in Italy, Spain, Switzerland, Austria, France, and some other countries impose maximum daily price change limitations. If the price of any stock changes more than that exchange's maximum daily limit, trading is stopped—usually for the rest of that day. These maximum daily limitations range from 4 percent to as much as 20 percent. Such price fluctuation limitations have been used for decades in commodity exchanges in the United States and around the world; they can limit destabilizing price swings.[21] If more stock exchanges around the world enforced maximum daily price change limitations, perhaps the October 1987 international stock market crash might have been diminished.

Margin Requirements Are a Mixed Bag

Federal Reserve regulations require investors in the United States to submit to a complex array of margin requirements. These requirements range from tiny down payments for investments in Treasury securities to initial margins of over 50 percent for purchases of common stocks. Britain, Australia, Switzerland, and many other foreign security markets are not subject to margin requirements. At the other extreme, margin requirements are 100 percent in Ireland, Italy, and Austria.

Margin requirements are supposed to restrain speculative excesses, but their administration has been called into question. In 1985 the U.S. Treasury and the Federal Reserve both asked Congress to transfer the responsibility for setting margin requirements from the Federal Reserve to the securities exchanges. Congress has not responded to that request.

Should We Have Crowds in a Pit or CLOBs or Specialists?

Members of the commodity exchanges in the United States that wish to trade a particular commodity go to the designated floor space, called the **pit,** where the commodity exchange requires all trading in that commodity to be conducted. Once in the appropriate pit the traders publicly indicate their desires to buy or sell via public outcry and/or hand signals. Members of the **crowd** in the pit with compatible desires consummate trades, and clerks immediately communicate the price and quantity of every transaction around the world via telecommunications. Thus, a crowd of traders with similar interests, which meets at a designated place, provides a way to make a market that is a good alternative to having a monopolistic market maker like a NYSE specialist standing ready to transact at an assigned post. Using a CLOB is another viable way of making markets.

CLOB stands for **consolidated limit-order book.** A CLOB should contain *all limit orders* from all exchanges in a publicly accessible form so that all traders from all markets could freely transact trades through the CLOB. The CLOB could be maintained either by administrative assistants (they are called the *Saitori* at the Japanese CLOB) or by telecommunications links to a central computer (like NASDAQ, or something different). The primary advantages of

[21]For a theoretical analysis of price limit moves, see Michael J. Brennan, "A Theory of Price Limits in Futures Markets," *Journal of Financial Economics,* June 1986, vol. 16, no. 2, pp. 213–234.

Table 3-9

COMPARISON OF INSTITUTIONAL ARRANGEMENTS IN STOCK MARKETS AROUND THE WORLD

Country	Type of auction	Official specialists	Forward trading on exchange	Automated quotations	Program trading	Options/ futures trading	Price limits	Transaction tax (round trip)	Margin requirements	Trading off exchange
Australia	Continuous	No	No	Yes	No	Yes	None	0.6%	None	Infrequent
Austria	Call	Yes	No	No	No	No	5%	0.3%	100%	Frequent
Belgium	Mixed	No	Yes	No	No	No[a]	10%/none[b]	0.375%/0.195%	100%/25%[b]	Occasional
Canada	Continuous	Yes	No	Yes	Yes	Yes	None[c]	0	50%[d]	Prohibited
Denmark	Mixed	No	No	No	No	No	None	1%	None	Frequent
France	Mixed	Yes	Yes	Yes	Yes	Yes	4%/7%[e]	0.3%	100/20%[f]	Prohibited
Germany	Continuous	Yes	No	No	No	Options	None	0.5%	None	Frequent
Hong Kong	Continuous	No	No	Yes	No	Futures	None[g]	0.6%+	None	Infrequent
Ireland	Continuous	No	No	Yes	No	No	None	1%	None	Frequent
Italy	Mixed	No	Yes	No	No	No	10–20%[h]	0.3%	100%	Frequent
Japan	Continuous	Yes	No	Yes	Yes	No[i]	−10%	0.55%	70%[j]	Prohibited
Malaysia	Continuous	No	No	Yes	No	No	None	0.03%	None	Occasional
Mexico	Continuous	No	Yes	No	No	No	10%[k]	0	None	Occasional
Netherlands	Continuous	Yes	No	No	No	Options	Variable[l]	2.4%[m]	None	Prohibited
New Zealand	Continuous	No	No	No	No	Futures	None	0	None	Occasional
Norway	Call	No	No	No	No	No[n]	None	1%	100%	Frequent
Singapore	Continuous	No	No	Yes	No	No[n]	None	0.5%	71%	Occasional
South Africa	Continuous	No	No	Yes	No	Options	None	1.5%	100%	Prohibited
Spain	Mixed[o]	No	No	No	No	No	10%[p]	0.11%	50%[p]	Frequent
Sweden	Mixed	No	Yes	Yes	No	Yes	None	2%	40%	Frequent
Switzerland	Mixed	No	No	Yes	No	Yes	5%[q]	0.9%	None	Infrequent
United Kingdom	Continuous	No	No	Yes	Yes	Yes	None	0.5%	None	Occasional
United States	Continuous	Yes	No	Yes	Yes	Yes	None	0	Yes	Occasional

[a] Calls only on just five stocks.
[b] Cash/forward.
[c] None on stocks; 3–5% on index futures.
[d] 10% (5%) for uncovered (covered) futures.
[e] Cash/forward; 40% if forward collateral is stock rather than cash.
[g] "Four spread rule": offers not permitted more than four ticks from current bids and asks.
[h] Hitting limit suspends auction; auction then tried a second time at end of day.
[i] Futures on the Nikkei Index are traded in Singapore.
[j] Decreased to 50% on October 21, 1987 "to encourage buyers."
[k] Trading suspended for successive periods, 15 and then 30 minutes; effective limit: 30–40%.
[l] Authorities have discretion. In October, 2% limits every 15 minutes used frequently.
[m] For nondealer transactions only.
[n] Only for Nikkei Index (Japan).
[o] Groups of stocks are traded continuously for 10 minutes each.
[p] Limits raised to 20% and margin to 50% on October 27, 1987.
[q] Hitting limit causes 15-minute trading suspension. Limits raised to 10–15% in October 1987.

Source: Richard Roll, "The International Crash of October 1987," Financial Analysts Journal, Sept.–Oct. 1988, p. 29, Table III.

using a CLOB are (1) all orders would be fully exposed to the market so that no orders got sidetracked and executed at less than the most advantageous price and (2) the rules of trading priority would never be violated. The **rules of trading priority** are that the highest bidder should always get the trade, and if more than one trader submits the highest bid, then the first party to submit that bid gets the trade.

Specialists oppose both trading crowds that operate without the aid of a specialist and CLOBs because they do not want to share their lucrative business.[22] NYSE specialists try to justify their monopolistic market-making positions by saying they maintain *fair and orderly markets*. However, NASDAQ uses competition between independent market makers to maintain fair and orderly markets. Many commodity exchanges use maximum price change limit rules that temporarily stop trading anytime the price of a futures contract moves too fast. Furthermore, organized stock exchanges abroad, which are as large as the NYSE, have market-making systems that function effectively without specialists. Some of these systems appear to be more cost-effective than an expensive specialist system. Table 3-9 summarizes some characteristics of stock markets around the world that are worthy of further consideration.

3-7   **SUMMARY AND CONCLUSIONS**

Primary securities markets are made by investment bankers who originate new issues of stocks and bonds. After the investment bankers' distribution is completed, the securities are traded in secondary markets. There are several types of secondary markets in the United States—organized exchanges like the NYSE and the OTC market. Brokers that work the secondary markets range from austere discount brokerages that supply only bare bones services (like Charles Schwab & Company) to the more costly full-service brokerages (like Merrill Lynch).

When an investor makes a trade, instructions must be given to the broker about whether the transaction is for cash or on margin. The client must also decide what type of order to give—market orders are the most common and the most likely to be executed.

One of the most important modifications in the securities industry in recent decades went into effect on May 1, 1975. On that date, the SEC abolished the fixed minimum commissions that had given organized exchanges like the NYSE market-making powers that subsidized their profits at the expense of investors. This change was caused by economic pressures from competing market makers, and investors have benefited from negotiated commission rates ever since.

---

[22]Even though they oppose a centralized market-making computer, more specialists each year are keeping their stock's book in a personal computer instead of on paper, as illustrated in Figure 3-3.

Merchant banks are financial enterprises that are involved in investment banking, securities brokering, and commercial banking. Merchant banks do not exist within the United States because the Glass-Steagall Act of 1933 forbids investment banks from doing commercial banking, and vice versa.[23] This law puts investment bankers and commercial bankers that are chartered in the United States at a competitive disadvantage relative to merchant bankers from foreign countries. Americans are legally forbidden from offering the full line of financial services that the merchant banks provide.[24]

Essay Questions

3-1 Compare and contrast how stock prices are determined (*a*) in the OTC market and (*b*) on organized exchanges like the NYSE.

3-2 "Price-pegging assures the investment banking syndicate that no losses will be incurred." Is the preceding statement true, false, or uncertain? Explain.

3-3 Do you see any conflict of interest between a stockbroker's roles as (*a*) sales representative working to maximize commission income and (*b*) investment advisor trying to give clients advice to maximize their wealth? Explain.

3-4 What does it mean to give a broker a "market order"?

3-5 Who are the people called "floor brokers" within an organized exchange and what do they do?

Problems

3-6 If the initial margin requirement is 60 percent and an investor purchases 500 shares of a $40 per share stock, what is the minimum initial margin that is required for this transaction?

3-7 Reconsider Problem 3-6. If the initial margin requirement were 75 percent, what minimum margin would be required?

3-8 If the margin requirement is 65 percent and an investor intends to purchase 100 shares of $50 per share stock, what is the minimum down payment required? Show your calculations.

---

[23]The Glass-Steagall Act of 1933 is officially called the Banking Act of 1933; it is discussed in Chapter 4. The Glass-Steagall Act of 1933 should not be confused with the Glass-Steagall Act of 1932; they deal with different issues.
[24]Economic theory suggests that the complex patchwork of different markets that operate with dissimilar regulations contributes toward a concept called **market completeness** and a Pareto optimal resource allocation. The appendix to this chapter reviews the theory of financial markets.

3-9   An investor purchased a $100 stock on 55 percent margin and then its price doubled to $200. The brokerage firm charged 10 percent interest for the loan on the margined investment. No cash dividends were received while the investor held the stock. What was the investor's one-period rate of return on this transaction, net of all costs? Show your calculations.

3-10   John Jones recently opened a margin account with the ESQ Investment Company, which currently has a 65 percent initial margin requirement and a 35 percent maintenance margin. Mr. Jones initially purchased 300 shares of YXZ stock at $50 per share. How much can the price of YXZ stock decline before a margin call is required?

3-11   If the price of YXZ from the preceding problem falls to $15, how much must Mr. Jones deposit in his brokerage account to maintain the minimum margin requirement?

3-12   If the price of YXZ stock of Problem 3-10 rises to $75 per share, what is Mr. Jones' one-period return? Ignore commission cost, but assume that the interest rate was 12 percent and no cash dividends were received.

3-13   What would be Mr. Jones' 1-year return if he had not purchased the stock in Problem 3-12 on margin? Ignore commission cost.

3-14   In Problem 3-12, if a $4 dividend was earned on YXZ stock for the year, what would be the annual rate of return?

3-15   Consider the four hypothetical numerical examples from a NYSE specialist's book that are listed below. The numbers in the body of the table refer to the number of shares available at each bid price. The highest bid price is $68 per share.

Bid price	Column 1	Column 2	Column 3	Column 4
$68	100	100	600	500
$67	100	100	600	600
$66	0	200	0	700
$65	0	300	0	1000
$64	0	300	0	1400

Describe the four columns above in terms of the breadth and depth of each market situation (or, the lack of these qualities, called thinness and shallowness).

3-16   (a) Define the bid–asked spread. (b) List the primary factors that determine the size of the bid–asked spread. *Hint: This requires outside research. For example, see Seha Tinic, "The Economics of Liquidity Services," Quarterly Journal of Economics, Feb. 1972, pp. 79–93.*

3-17   Why does the theory of financial markets suggest that trading many different securities in many different markets might be desirable? *Hint: Read the appendix to this chapter.*

Selected References

Bloch, Ernest, *Inside Investment Banking,* 2d ed. (Homewood, Ill.: Dow Jones–Irwin, 1989).

This nonmathematical book provides rich detail about investment banking.

Cohen, Kalman J., Steven F. Maier, Robert A. Schwartz, and David K. Whitcomb, *The Microstructure of Securities Markets* (Englewood Cliffs, N.J.: Prentice-Hall, 1986).

This economic study analyzes the workings of securities markets and uses statistics to examine various behavioral hypotheses.

Lowenstein, Louis, *What's Wrong with Wall Street* (Reading, Mass., Addison-Wesley, 1988).

Lowenstein, a professor of finance and law, proposes some insightful and penetrating reforms to improve the equity markets in the United States. No mathematics is used.

National Association of Securities Dealers, *The NASDAQ Handbook* (Chicago, Ill.: Probus, 1987).

This book describes the OTC market and the NASDAQ system and provides a wealth of descriptive statistics.

Schwartz, Robert A. *Equity Markets* (New York: Harper and Row, 1988).

This book provides a detailed economic analysis of the markets where stocks are traded. Some mathematical statistics is used.

Smith, C. W., "Investment Banking and the Capital Acquisition Process," *Journal of Financial Economics,* Jan.–Feb. 1986, vol. 15, pp. 3–29.

This economic study uses statistics to analyze the way investment bankers raise capital in the primary markets.

Tewles, Richard J., and Edward S. Bradley, *The Stock Market* (New York: Wiley, 1982).

This book goes into detail, explaining the institutions and practices which make up the securities markets in the United States. No mathematics is used.

Appendix 3A

Theory of Financial Markets

Arrow and Debreu established a state-preference framework within which the theory of financial markets has developed.[25] It is possible to extend the state-preference theory so that it becomes a time–state-preference theory that encompasses multiple periods. But, here we will consider only two periods: "now" (or $t = 0$) and "later" (denoted $t = 1$).

The **state-preference model** is a systematic method of handling uncertainty about the future which has a list of events called *states of nature* at its foundation. Each *asset* is defined in terms of a set of payoffs that is defined over all possible states of nature. Thus, when investors buy assets, they are purchasing a list (or vector) of **state contingent claims** that enumerates payoffs to be made when the state of nature is revealed.

Assumptions Underlying the Theory

State-preference theory assumes that:

1. Everyone agrees about all possible states of nature that may occur, but each person may assign different probabilities to their occurrence.

2. Only one state can exist at a time.

3. Everyone agrees about what the set of dollar payoffs will be for *any particular asset* across all possible states of nature. (Hopefully, however, every asset will have a different set of payoffs.)

4. Investors have preferences that remain unchanged across different states of nature. Stated differently, a state-independent utility function is assumed.

[25]See Kenneth Arrow, "The Role of Securities in the Optimal Allocation of Risk Bearing," *Review of Economic Studies*, 1964, pp. 91–96. For an extension of Arrow's model to choices over time see Gerard Debreu, *The Theory of Value* (New York: Wiley, 1959). For a literature review, see Jacques H. Dreze, "Market Allocation under Uncertainty," *European Economic Review*, Winter 1970–1971, pp. 133–165.

**The Securities-
States Tableau**

In its most elegant form, state-preference theory deals with different commodities. However, for expediency's sake the theory of financial markets focuses on only J different assets, denoted $j = 1, 2, \ldots, J$. These assets can include various stocks, bonds, options, and other instruments. These securities are left unspecified and simply called **contingent claims.** An exhaustive list of S mutually exclusive **states of nature** is assumed to fully describe every feature of the environment; these are denoted by the convention $s = 1, 2, \ldots, S$. These market opportunities are summarized by the $J \times S$ matrix A. Each element a_{js} in matrix A represents the gross dollar **payoffs** of security j in state s.[26]

States: $s = 1 \quad s = 2 \qquad s = S$

$$A = \begin{bmatrix} a_{11} & a_{12} & \cdots & a_{1S} \\ a_{21} & a_{22} & \cdots & a_{2S} \\ \vdots & \vdots & & \\ a_{J1} & a_{J2} & \cdots & a_{JS} \end{bmatrix} = \begin{bmatrix} a_1 \\ a_2 \\ \vdots \\ a_J \end{bmatrix} \quad J \text{ assets} \qquad (3A\text{-}1)$$

The $J \times S$ matrix in Equation (3A-1) is referred to as the *market structure*, the *payoff matrix*, the **securities-states tableau,** and/or simply "the markets."

Consider the column vector in Equation (3A-1) above. Every a_j in that column vector stands for a row vector. Each one of these J different row vectors is a payoff vector that lists some asset's payoff under each state of nature, as shown below.

$$a_j = (a_{j1}\ a_{j2} \cdots a_{jS})$$

This column vector is a shorthand representation of matrix A.

Investor's Budget Constraint   The row vector $z = (z_1, z_2, \ldots, z_J)$ is called an **investment plan.** The vector z stands for a list of the number of units of each asset in the investor's portfolio.

The theory of financial markets assumes that the investor is operating in perfect markets. Thus an infinite number of units of any asset can be purchased at a price of p_j per unit without affecting the market prices and without paying any transaction costs. Thus, the portfolio's total cost is $z \times p$, where $p = (p_1, p_2, \ldots, p_J)$ stands for a column vector of prices.

$$z \times p = \sum_{j=1}^{J} z_j p_j = \text{total cost}$$

It is said that the plan z has a total initial cost of $z \times p$ at time $t = 0$.

At time $t = 0$ the investor's initial (or endowed) wealth equals $w_0 = z \times p$ dollars, no more and no less. This initial wealth represents the investor's *budget constraint.*[27]

---

[26]If the model assumes the investor has *limited liability*, as represented by the inequality $a_{js} > 0$ for all j and all s, more implications can be drawn from the analysis than if the assets are allowed to default and accumulate liabilities against their owner.

[27]The investor's total asset holdings may exceed w_0 if short sales are permitted. **Short sales** are represented by negative values for z_j if asset j is sold short.

Valuing the Investor's Portfolio

Using the vector z enables us to say that if state s prevails, the investor will have w_s dollars available to spend at time $t = 1$, as shown below.

$$w_s = \sum_{j=1}^{J} z_j a_{js}$$

Spanning the Security-State Space

In matrix algebra terms, it is possible to premultiply the $1 \times J$ row vector z by the compatible securities-states tableau of dimension $J \times S$ and obtain the $1 \times S$ row vector denoted w, as shown below.

$$w = zA = (w_1, w_2, \ldots, w_S)$$

The vector of payoffs denoted w must be attainable in the **span** of the securities-states tableau A; otherwise, the analysis lacks meaningful economic content.

Investor's Preferences

In order to make investment decisions, we explicitly bring the investor's personality into the model by using a **utility of wealth function,** denoted $U = f(W)$. Think of the investor's utility as being measured in units called "utils." Utils are units of happiness such that as someone gets more utils, they get happier (or have a higher level of utility).

We assume two things about the investor's personality. First, we assume that the investor prefers having more wealth to having less wealth, or, equivalently, $dU/dW = f'(W) > 0$. This is called having *positive marginal utility of wealth.* Second, we assume that the investor also has *diminishing marginal utility of wealth;* or, equivalently, $d^2U/dW^2 = f''(W) < 0$. Stated differently, the investor is risk-averse.

Figure 19-6 illustrates the type of monotonically increasing but strictly concave utility function we are attributing to the investor. Your attitudes toward investing are probably nicely described by this utility function.[28]

The Standard Problem

The investor is presumed to have the following vector of probability beliefs defined over the states of nature:

$$P = (P_1, P_2, \ldots, P_S) \quad \text{where } \sum_{s=1}^{S} P_s = 1.0, \quad P_s > 0$$

where P represents probabilities. Combining the investor's probability beliefs, preferences, and budget constraint with the available market opportunities leads to the following mathematical problem: maximize the investor's expected utility of wealth.

$$\text{Max}_z \sum_{s=1}^{S} P_s U(W_s)$$

subject to the two constraints,

---

[28]In order to be able to obtain interesting conclusions, we must assume that investors have utility functions that are state-independent, that is, invariant across the different states of nature. Utility theory is studied in more detail in Chapter 19.

$$w_0 = z \times p$$

$$w_s = \sum_{j=1}^{J} z_j a_{js}$$

within the market structure represented by the $J \times S$ matrix A.

The No-Arbitrage Condition

Arbitrage is a way to earn guaranteed profits without investing any money. To see how arbitrage works, consider a two-asset model in which both assets have identical payoffs but different prices. Arbitrage opportunities violate the "law of one price." The **law of one price** says the same good cannot sell at two different prices because people will buy the good at the cheap price and sell it at the higher price, and continue to do so repeatedly until the two different prices are driven together by supply and demand. The 2×2 matrix A' below provides a numerical example of what happens when the law of one price is violated.

$$A' = \begin{bmatrix} a_{11} & a_{12} \\ a_{21} & a_{22} \end{bmatrix} = \begin{bmatrix} 2 & 1 \\ 2 & 1 \end{bmatrix} \qquad \begin{array}{l} \text{asset 1 has } p_1 = \$3 \\ \text{asset 2 has } p_2 = \$2 \end{array}$$

Assume that even though the two assets in matrix A' have identical payoffs, asset 1 sells at a higher price than asset 2, $p_1 = \$3$ and $p_2 = \$2$. This situation cannot possibly be sustained as an equilibrium solution for three reasons: (1) an economic reason, (2) a geometric reason, and (3) an algebraic reason. All three reasons are explained below.

The Economic Reason In the situation hypothesized above, riskless arbitrage will be profitable until $p_1 = p_2$ and the profit disappears. More specifically, it will be profitable to buy asset 2 ($z_2 > 0$) and simultaneously sell asset 1 ($z_1 < 0$) in large quantities so that a riskless profit of $z_2(p_1 - p_2)$ can be earned. For instance, if $z_2 = 100$ shares, then the profit would be $100.

$$z_2(p_1 - p_2) = (100 \text{ shares})(\$3 - \$2) = \$100$$

If the arbitrager wants to earn a \$1 million riskless profit, then all that need be done is to buy $z_2 = 1$ million shares of asset 2 and simultaneously sell them at the higher price. Such situations will not last long because buying and selling by greedy arbitragers will drive the two prices together.

Geometric Reason In terms of geometry, the profitable arbitrage situation above can be represented by two parallel lines that never intersect. Two lines that do not intersect cannot possibly yield a simultaneous solution. Stated differently, no graphical solution is possible.

Algebraic Reason Algebraically, the two linear equations below are linearly dependent so they cannot be solved simultaneously.

$$(a_{11} \times p_1) + (a_{12} \times p_1) = (\$2 \times \$3) + (\$1 \times \$3) = \$9$$

$$(a_{12} \times p_2) + (a_{22} \times p_2) = (\$2 \times \$2) + (\$1 + \$2) = \$6$$

In order to avoid such situations, which cannot possibly yield solutions or insights, we must impose the condition that no profitable arbitrage exists in our model of financial markets. As a matter of fact, this assumption is realistic.

**Market
Completeness**

Complete markets are said to exist when investors can construct portfolios with any desired pattern of payoffs. In complete markets any type of payoffs across the different states of nature can be constructed by combining existing securities without the aid of any new securities or any options.[29] Intuitively, complete markets have enough unique assets so that portfolios can be created which have whatever payoff pattern may be desired but do not have redundant assets that would encumber the portfolio formation process without adding any new payoff opportunities. Complete markets are desirable because they contribute toward the maximization of social welfare and help achieve what is called "Pareto optimality."[30] We say a market is complete when the existing securities *span* all possible states.

An **Arrow-Debreu security** is defined as an asset that pays $1 in one particular state of nature and zero in all other states. Arrow-Debreu securities are also called *pure securities, state securities,* and/or *primitive securities.*

An alternative way to define complete markets is to say that if the securities-states tableau A in Equation (3A-1) is composed of (or can be reduced to) S unique Arrow-Debreu securities, then it represents a special case of complete markets.[31]

If the market contains fewer unique securities than states of nature, it will be impossible to create as many Arrow-Debreu securities as there are states of nature. In this case, **incomplete markets** exist.

The addition of new securities to incomplete markets may allow payoff opportunities to be created in ways that were not previously possible. Sometimes the cheapest way to create new securities is to create put and/or call options on existing securities.[32] The addition of enough unique new securities may allow incomplete markets to achieve completeness.[33]

Uniqueness is the key to achieving complete markets; adding new assets that replicate the payoff patterns of the existing assets will not enable incomplete markets to achieve completeness. However, unique options on existing assets or options on new economic variables (such as security market indexes, interest rates, the inflation rate, and basic

---

[29]In matrix algebra terms, completeness requires that the securities-states tableau A must have S linearly independent equations. Stated differently, the securities-states tableau A must have rank S. Thus, there must be at least as many securities as states of nature, $J \geq S$.

The securities-states tableau A may have more assets than states of nature, $J > S$, and still represent complete markets if $(J - S)$ of the assets are linearly dependent and can be eliminated. See Fred Arditti and K. John, "Spanning the State Space with Options," *Journal of Financial and Quantitative Analysis,* March 1980, vol. 15, pp. 1–9.

[30]In classic welfare economics, Pareto optimality is sometimes called economic efficiency or Pareto efficiency. **Pareto optimality** is defined as the resource allocation that is superior to all other resource allocations because any of the others would result in a reduction of happiness for at least one person.

[31]If the securities-states tableau A happens to be an *identity matrix,* then it is a special case of complete markets. That is, if $A = I$, then A represents a special case of complete markets that is exquisitely simple.

[32]Put and call options are financial instruments and are discussed in Chapter 22.

[33]Sanford J. Grossman shows that a **redundant security** that can be synthesized from previously existing opportunities may still advance the Pareto optimality because it makes valuable information available. See S. J. Grossman, "An Analysis of the Implications for Stock and Futures Price Volatility of Program Trading and Dynamic Hedging Strategies," *Journal of Business,* vol. 61, no. 3, pp. 275–298.

commodities like petroleum), new types of bonds (like zero coupon bonds and securities used in asset-backed financing), and new types of stocks (such as adjustable-rate preferred stock) can create beneficial new securities. These new securities would be beneficial if they provided new hedging opportunities that traders could use to limit their risk exposure, helped span the state space, moved security markets closer to completeness, helped society attain a higher level of social welfare, and/or contributed to a Pareto optimality allocation of resources.

Ross's Theorem About Index Options

Ross pointed out that if all the payoff patterns present in a securities-states tableau like matrix A can be taken together and used to establish different payoff patterns for each state of nature, then market completeness can be achieved by trading put and/or call options written on a single portfolio.[34] Although this portfolio need not be unique, it must have different payoffs for every state of nature. The 2×4 securities-states tableau A'' below furnishes an example of the property Ross requires.

$$A'' = \begin{bmatrix} a_{11} & a_{12} & a_{13} & a_{14} \\ a_{21} & a_{22} & a_{23} & a_{24} \end{bmatrix} = \begin{bmatrix} 5 & 4 & 4 & 5 \\ 4 & 4 & 5 & 5 \end{bmatrix}$$

Since each of the four columns of the securities-states tableau A'' represents a unique payoff pattern for a different state of nature, the precondition for Ross's theorem exists.

The Standard & Poor's and/or the Dow Jones stock market averages, for instance, might be portfolios that provide a unique payoff pattern for every state of nature. Thus, Ross's theorem suggests that the put and/or call options that are traded on market indexes like the Standard and Poor's and/or the Dow Jones stock market averages might represent a cheap and easy way to move security markets closer to completeness, a higher level of social welfare, and Pareto optimality.

Pricing Arrow-Debreu Securities in Complete Markets

When markets are complete, it is possible to determine the prices of all the pure state-contingent securities. The 3×3 securities-states tableau A''' below provides a numerical example of complete markets.[35]

$$A''' = \begin{bmatrix} a_{11} & a_{12} & a_{13} \\ a_{21} & a_{22} & a_{23} \\ a_{31} & a_{32} & a_{33} \end{bmatrix} = \begin{bmatrix} 2 & 1 & 3 \\ 4 & 5 & 6 \\ 7 & 8 & 9 \end{bmatrix} \begin{matrix} \text{asset 1} \\ \text{asset 2} \\ \text{asset 3} \end{matrix}$$

In order to create an Arrow-Debreu security that has a \$1 payout in the third state of nature we must select numbers of units of the three assets, z_1, z_2, and z_3, such that the payoff vector a_3 below is obtained.

$$a_3 = (a_{31}\ a_{32}\ a_{33}) = (0\ 0\ 1)$$

[34]Steven Ross, "Options and Efficiency," *Quarterly Journal of Economics,* Feb. 1976, vol. 90, pp. 75–89.

A caveat has been suggested by Oliver D. Hart, "On the Optimality of Equilibrium when the Market Structure Is Incomplete," *Journal of Economic Theory,* Dec. 1975, vol. 11, pp. 418–443. Hart shows that adding nonredundant assets is not always beneficial. He shows that adding new markets when the structure is incomplete might make everyone worse off.

[35]Speaking mathematically, matrix A''' has a nonsingular determinant, $|A'''| = -9$. Therefore, the rows and columns of A''' are linearly independent and its inverse exists.

Uses for the State-Preference Theory

The securities-states tableau provides a precise array of all possible outcomes. State-preference theory implies no financial theory but, depending on the additional assumptions that are made, can be used to analyze any financial theory. Complete specification of all possible outcomes may not be possible. However, a complicated problem may be formulated in a more manageable fashion by grouping different states (into categories such as peace or war, for instance).

Further Implications of the Theory of Financial Markets

Considerable research has been done in an effort to discern the kinds of financial markets and related conditions that are needed to raise the level of social welfare. Essentially, the theory suggests that the development of more unique securities and more markets will tend to raise the level of social welfare by providing investors with more opportunities to reduce their risks by hedging, more ways to correct mispriced assets via arbitrage, more instruments with which to span the state space, more opportunities with which to make security markets complete, and/or more pathways on which to move closer to a Pareto optimal allocation of resources.[36]

Selected Appendix References

Arditti, F., and K. John, "Spanning the State Space with Options," *Journal of Financial and Quantitative Analysis,* March 1980, vol. 15, pp. 1–9.

Arrow, K. "The Role of Securities in the Optimal Allocation of Risk Bearing," *Review of Economic Studies,* 1964, pp. 91–96.

Breeden, D., and R. Litzenberger, "Prices of State-Contingent Claims Implicit in Option Prices," *Journal of Business,* Oct. 1978, vol. 51, pp. 621–651.

Brennan, M. "The Pricing of Contingent Claims in Discrete Time Models," *Journal of Finance,* March 1979, vol. 34, pp. 53–68.

Cox, J., and S. Ross, "The Valuation of Options for Alternative Stochastic Processes," *Journal of Financial Economics,* Jan.–March 1976, vol. 3, pp. 145–166.

Debreu, Gerard, *The Theory of Value* (New York: Wiley, 1959).

Dreze, Jacques H., "Market Allocation under Uncertainty," *European Economic Review,* Winter 1970–1971, pp. 133–165.

[36]For details about what the theory of financial markets says about Pareto optimal market structures, see James Ohlson, *The Theory of Financial Markets and Information* (New York: North-Holland, 1987), chap. 3. Or, see Chi-fu Huang and R. H. Litzenberger, *Foundations of Financial Economics* (New York: North-Holland, 1988), chap. 5.

A caveat furnishes an appropriate note on which to close this appendix. The theoretical analysis reviewed above assumes away market imperfections (like brokerage commissions and taxes) in order to obtain simple models that are easy to manipulate and interpret. As a result of these simplifications the models that are developed may suggest too many new developments. Stated differently, if the costs of creating new securities and new markets were considered, there is little doubt that not all of the theoretical changes would be considered worthwhile. The theory is useful, however, in pointing directions for possible change.

Huang, Chi-fu, and R. H. Litzenberger, *Foundations of Financial Economics* (New York: North-Holland, 1988), chap. 5.

Ingersoll, Jonathan E., *Theory of Financial Decision Making* (Totawa, N.J.: Rowman and Littlefield, 1987), chap. 2.

John, K. "Efficient Funds in Financial Markets with Options: A New Irrelevance Proposition," *Journal of Finance,* June 1981, vol. 37, pp. 685–695.

John, K. "Market Resolution and Valuation in Incomplete Markets," *Journal of Financial and Quantitative Analysis,* March 1984, vol. 19, pp. 29–44.

Myers, Stewart C., "A Time-State-Preference Model of Security Valuation," *Journal of Financial and Quantitative Analysis,* March 1968, vol. 3.

Ohlson, James A., *The Theory of Financial Markets and Information* (New York: North-Holland, 1987), chaps. 2–3.

Ross, Stephen, "Options and Efficiency," *Quarterly Journal of Economics,* Feb. 1976, vol. 90, pp. 75–89.

Ross, Stephen, "Mutual Fund Separation in Economic Theory: The Separating Distributions," *Journal of Economic Theory,* vol. 17, pp. 274–286.

Chapter 4

Securities Law

One reason the United States has been able to develop a successful economy is that the country has good capital markets. United States capital markets channel billions of dollars from savers who invest to businesses that need money to finance their advancement. Without having these investment funds to finance business growth, the U.S. economy would stagnate, unemployment would rise, and the gross national product (called GNP or national income) would fall.

The U.S. government has established various legal procedures to ensure that securities markets are fair and honest places. Laws have been passed forbidding fraud and price-manipulation schemes, and federal agencies have been established to enforce these laws. Furthermore, some of the professional associations for investments executives (such as the Financial Analysts Federation and the National Association of Securities Dealers) have established guidelines that their members are bound to uphold. This chapter describes the various laws and legal agencies that govern capital markets and the investment industry in the United States. First, however, let us consider the problems that led to federal regulation of securities markets.

SECURITIES TRADING ABUSES

Before the United States established any federal securities regulations, financial abuses were rampant. Some states had passed securities laws. But these state laws became known as *blue sky laws,* because some were so naive that they declared it illegal for someone to sell another person part of ''the blue sky.''[1]

[1]Justice McKenna in *Hall v. Geiger-Jones Company,* 242 U.S. 539, 550, in 1917, used the phrase ''speculative schemes which have no more basis than so many feet of blue sky.''

Furthermore, when a state threatened to prosecute, the criminals simply left the state. Such laws made securities crime easy; federal laws were needed to prohibit the abuses listed below and to monitor the securities markets.

Fraud

Fraud means deliberate deception performed in order to obtain unfair or illegal gain. Insider trading, wash sales, matched orders, price manipulation schemes, cornering the market, misrepresentation of any individual, misrepresentation or concealment of any relevant investment-related facts, and churning are all examples of fraudulent activities.

Unauthorized Trading

Unauthorized trading occurs when a client's account shows securities trades that were not authorized verbally and/or in writing by the client before the transaction occurred. (Today NYSE and NASD rules require written client authorization. During the early 1900s such authorizations were not required—producing, at times, horrible results.)

Unauthorized Securities Exchange

An **unauthorized exchange** is an established securities exchange that operates without first obtaining from the SEC written approval or written exemption from registration.

Illegal Solicitation

Illegal solicitation occurs when a broker or dealer tries to sell an issue without first giving the investor the issuer's prospectus, which reveals all the relevant facts.

Unsuitability

Unsuitability occurs when the client is sold an investment inappropriate to his or her wealth, health, age, risk-taking abilities, and/or other circumstances.

Unregistered Securities

Unregistered securities are any securities that are traded on a registered exchange but have not been properly registered with the SEC. Alternatively, unregistered securities are any securities issued by a corporation that has more than a few shareholders, is significant in size, and sells the securities across a state line without having its registration statement approved by the SEC in advance of the offering. Any securities that were registered with the SEC may become unregistered securities if the SEC issues a *cease and desist order* withdrawing its approval of the registration.

Unqualified Salesperson

An **unqualified salesperson** is any broker or dealer who solicits trades without first passing the appropriate examination and/or without being registered with the National Association of Securities Dealers (NASD).

Due Diligence Violation	A **due diligence violation** occurs whenever a dealer, managing director, or partner fails to learn every essential fact about every underwriting that falls within that person's area of responsibility and/or fails to ensure that these facts are made available to investors.
Inadequate Disclosure	**Inadequate disclosure** is defined as the failure to deliver an SEC-approved prospectus prior to or during the time that a broker or dealer solicits a trade. Failure to register an issue with the SEC before the securities are sold is another form of inadequate disclosure (unless the issue is explicitly exempted from the registration process by some SEC regulation, such as the "Regulation A" issues).
Wash Sale	A **wash sale** is a deceptive transaction in which a seller of securities repurchases the same or identical securities almost immediately. The purpose of a wash sale is to create a record of a sale. This record is used to establish the appearance of a loss for income tax purposes or to deceive someone into believing that a market price has changed.
Matched Orders	**Matched orders** involve illusory transactions in which two individuals act in concert to "paint the tape." The co-conspirators create a record of a trade and give the impression that delivery was made without a true change in ownership occurring. As with a **wash sale,** the record is needed to establish the appearance of a tax loss, deceive someone into believing that a market price has changed, or make it appear that someone else has purchased the securities.
Cornering the Market	A **market is cornered** when some schemer buys all the securities or all of a commodity available for sale. This nefarious person then owns the total supply and can exert control over the price. Price manipulators who corner a market typically liquidate their position at a high price for a gain. Or a manipulating speculator may corner a market in hope of trapping, or "squeezing," short sellers.[2]

Example 4-1	### Cornering the Market in the Good Old Days
	Commodore Cornelius Vanderbilt obtained a spectacular market corner in 1862. Vanderbilt started buying stock in the Harlem Railroad in New York City for $8 per share. He continued buying until the price was driven up to $100 per share

[2]**Short sellers** are speculators who contract to sell an asset they do not own. Short sellers expect the price of that asset to fall, enabling them to purchase the asset at a lower price later and then deliver it at the higher price at which they had previously arranged to sell it. Thus, short sellers profit from price declines. Short selling is discussed in Chapter 8.

and he had control of the railroad. Then Vanderbilt invested more money in the railroad to extend its lines into Manhattan. Daniel Drew, a ruthless price manipulator, had also purchased shares in the railroad as the price rose. However, Drew wanted more profit, so he conspired to sell his shares to drive the price down and simultaneously took a short position in the stock to profit from its decline in price. The unscrupulous Mr. Drew influenced Boss Tweed and other dishonest New York City politicians to repeal the railroad's legal franchise to operate in New York City. Since the railroad was unable to operate legally, it was worthless. Then Drew sold all his holdings and also sold short 137,000 shares he did not own with the expectation that the price would fall rapidly from $100. The price fell to $72—but Vanderbilt used his great wealth to purchase every available share. Vanderbilt then raised the price of his shares to $179, and Drew was thrown for a loss on his short sales of 137,000 shares. There were only 27,000 shares of stock outstanding! Drew was forced to settle with the buyers of the 137,000 shares that he had contracted to deliver at prices well below $100, while Vanderbilt held the price at $179. Since Vanderbilt had cornered the market, Drew's losses became Vanderbilt's gains.

Churning

Churning involves an abuse of the customer's confidence by a securities broker through numerous transactions that are disproportionate to the size and nature of the client's account in order to generate commission income for the broker. The practice is called churning because it involves "turning over" the client's account to generate sales commissions.

Example 4-2

A True Case of Churning

Bertha, a poor young immigrant when she arrived in the United States, worked most of her life as a $125 per month housekeeper for a Mr. Hecht. Later in life her fortunes improved; Bertha became Mrs. Hecht. In 1939, before her marriage, Bertha had opened a brokerage account with $2000 of her hard-earned money. She opened this account near her home with a securities broker named Asa Wilder.[3]

From 1939 to 1955 Bertha's account grew from $2000 to $65,000 as a result of additional deposits, dividend income, and capital gains. During those 16 years Bertha's account showed a total of 32 sales and 41 purchases; it was traded infrequently. Over those years Asa Wilder and Bertha became friendly even though Wilder had moved to a brokerage firm different from the one where Bertha's account was maintained.

In 1955 Mr. Hecht died and left his 62-year-old widow an estate with a net value of $502,532. (That amount has the purchasing power of about $2 million 1989 dollars.) After Hecht's death, Bertha and Asa Wilder started a close business and social relationship. She transferred $42,000 of her personal account and the

---

[3]Since churning occurs continuously, it would be possible to find a more current example. This decades-old case was selected for review, however, because it involves more "color" than the average churning case.

proceeds from Mr. Hecht's estate to Hooker and Fay Co., where Wilder was then employed. In 1957, when Wilder left Hooker and Fay to become a broker at Harris, Upham and Co., the Hecht account of $533,161 was transferred to Harris, Upham and Co. under Wilder's guidance.

Bertha Hecht dealt with Asa Wilder through Harris, Upham and Co. and saw him socially for several years after her husband died. But, in 1964 Mrs. Hecht's tax accountant advised the perky 71-year-old widow that her account at Harris, Upham and Co. was way down to $251,161.

Bertha Hecht brought suit against Asa Wilder and Harris, Upham and Co. for recovery of $1,109,000. This suit claimed damages for three reasons: (1) The Hecht account had been converted from a blue-chip investment account to an inappropriate low-grade, speculative account by Wilder. (2) Wilder traded excessively in the account for the purpose of generating commissions. (3) Wilder had defrauded Bertha Hecht by trading between their accounts in such a manner that he profited from her losses in two different securities transactions.

The court found that, if it were still intact, Mrs. Hecht's original Harris, Upham & Co. account would have had a value of $1,026,775. Dividend and bond interest would have amounted to $194,135 instead of the $124,237 earned under Wilder's guidance. The court also learned that during the 6 years and 10 months that Wilder handled Hecht's account at Harris, Upham and Co., he entertained his client socially. During this time Mrs. Hecht had paid $91,000 in commissions and mark-ups on securities, $98,000 in commissions on commodity trades, and $13,000 in interest on loans advanced to her margin account. These charges covered 1300 transactions in 200 different corporate stocks and 9000 commodity transactions— very active trading.

In assessing the role of Wilder's employer in allowing Bertha's account to be depleted, the court pointed out that, although the account amounted to only one-tenth of 1 percent of the total of all accounts in the firm's San Francisco office, the Hecht account had supplied, in commissions and interest, at least 4.7 percent of the office's total income. Furthermore, the charges against the Hecht account, stated as a percent of the value of the account, were about 50 times the average. If the brokerage firm had monitored its accounts properly, these unusual statistics would have pinpointed what Asa Wilder was doing with the Hecht account so that the problem could have been resolved.

In defending his actions, Wilder claimed that as he was paid on salary rather than on straight commission, he had no incentive to churn Mrs. Hecht's account. The court pointed out, however, that Wilder had received bonuses and pay increases that corresponded chronologically with the periods when he was depleting the Hecht account most actively. Furthermore, 3 months after Wilder lost the Hecht account, his salary was reduced from $1250 per month to $850 per month. Thus, it appeared that his income was related to the brokerage's income from the Hecht account.

The court concluded that Mrs. Hecht had not monitored her account and therefore could not rightfully assert that it was wrongfully or unwillingly converted to a speculative account. On the issue of excessive trading (or churning), the court ruled that Mrs. Hecht should receive $143,000 in damages, which equaled the full amount of commissions she had paid to Harris, Upham and Co. On the issue of the two fraudulent self-dealing securities transactions perpetrated by Wilder on Hecht, the court granted Hecht $232,000 in damages.

Illegal Pools

An illegal **pool** is an association of two or more persons which has the objective of manipulating prices and profiting therefrom. When this objective is attained, the pool is dissolved. Pool members may provide capital or inside information; some may manage the pool's operations. During the early 1890s there were two kinds of pools that have since been made illegal. A **trading pool** purchased the target securities in the open market. An **option pool** acquired all or most of its securities at advantageous prices under *option contracts*.

Example 4-3

The Sinclair Option Pool of 1929

The Sinclair Consolidated Oil option pool of 1929 was highly profitable. While Sinclair stock was selling in the $28 to $32 range, a contract was obtained from Sinclair granting the pool an option to buy 1,130,000 shares at $30 per share. The pool then purchased 634,000 shares in the open market to bid up prices. Next, the pool exercised its options to buy at $30, and then liquidated its holdings while the stock was selling in the $40 range. The pool also sold 200,000 shares short as the price fell. The pool's total profit was approximately $12.5 million from the following sources: $10 million profit from optioned shares purchased at $30 per share, $500,000 profit from shares purchased in the market, and $2 million profit from the short sales.[4]

Insider Trading

Insider trading occurs when *securities transactions are made based on material nonpublic information that was obtained in breach of a fiduciary trust*. Inside information may be procured by **insiders**, such as corporate directors, owners of 10 percent or more of the equity shares, and executives who have access to material nonpublic information about their corporation. In addition, auditors, consultants, financial analysts, bank lenders, printers, photocopiers, and typists can be **temporary insiders** if they are exposed to material nonpublic information. Even *temporary insiders* will be guilty of breach of a fiduciary trust if they profit from information to which they had temporary access.[5]

[4] "Stock Exchange Practices," Senate Report 1455, Seventy-third Congress, 2d session, p. 63.

[5] Insider trading has been defined by case law instead of legislated law and, as such, the definition continues to evolve. See *Chiarella v. United States,* 445 U.S. 222.245 (1980). Also see *Dirks v. Securities and Exchange Commission,* 463 U.S. 646.662 (1983). See also *United States v. R. Foster Winans, K. P. Felis, and D. J. Carpenter,* 84 Cr. 605 (CES) (S.D.N.Y. 1984). For more discussion of insider trading see Gary L. Tidwell, "Here's a Tip—Know the Rules of Insider Trading," *Sloan Management Review,* Summer 1987, pp. 93–97.

Example 4-4

Even Bigshots Go to Jail
_____

In 1985 a federal judge sentenced Paul Thayer to 4 years in prison and a $5000 fine for passing inside information to two of his friends, who traded on it: a Dallas stockbroker named Billy Bob Harris and a close personal friend named Sandra K. Rayno. Ms. Rayno cooperated with the SEC, telling investigators that Thayer supported her financially and gave her inside information about the LTV Corporation, on which she traded profitably, while Thayer was chairman of LTV's board. The stockbroker and Thayer pleaded guilty to lying to the SEC in earlier hearings in an effort to cover up their insider trading. The remarkable thing about this case is the position that Thayer held and the length of his jail sentence.

Thayer, a distinguished-looking 65-year-old when he was sentenced in 1985, had served as a Deputy Director of Defense. A married man with a daughter and a wealthy business executive who had worked his way up to become chairman of the vast LTV Corporation, Thayer was also a highly decorated U.S. Navy pilot from World War II. Thayer had received no profits himself from the insider trading he facilitated by passing along the inside information to his friends. And he had already voluntarily paid over $1.5 million in restitution for his wrongdoing. A number of lawyers and high-ranking government officials asked the sentencing judge to be lenient. Thayer was nevertheless given a 4-year sentence out of a maximum possible of 5 years.[6]

Pyramiding of Debt

Pyramiding of debt begins when speculators purchase securities with small cash margins (say, 5 percent of the purchase price) and borrow the rest (in this example, 95 percent of the cost of the position). If the securities rise in price, some aggressive lenders will treat these unrealized paper gains as if they were additions to new equity. These aggressive lenders then advance the borrower even more money, based on the speculator's "additional margin." This pyramiding of debt on top of unrealized paper profits is disastrous when the securities prices decline significantly (more than 5 percent, in this case).[7] Margin requirements legislated in 1934 controlled speculators' ability to pyramid debt.

_____

[6]*The New York Times,* May 9, 1985, p. 1.

[7]Securities price declines equal to speculators' down payments may bankrupt imprudent speculators who have overextended themselves by pyramiding debt on top of unrealized paper profits. When the aggressive lenders then try to sell the securities held as collateral, they may find that the securities' declining market value is not sufficient to cover the debt. To avoid further capital losses, lenders who hold securities as collateral hurriedly dump the shares on the market, accelerating the price decline and further aggravating their financial decline.

4-2   **EVENTS SET THE STAGE FOR CHANGE DURING THE EARLY 1930s**

The rampant securities frauds and abuses outlined above were not illegal during the early 1900s. It took some painful lessons during the early 1930s to motivate Congress to take some action.

The Great Stock Market Crash

The Great Crash began late in September of 1929. As always happens in business downturns, many stock market investors foresaw the depression and liquidated their positions several months before it began. As a result, the Great Crash preceded the Depression by a few months even though the Depression caused the Crash.

The Dow Jones Industrial Average (DJIA) closed at a peak of 381 on September 3. On October 2 the DJIA fell 49 points and dropped another 43 points the next day. By October 23 the DJIA had slipped to 306—a decline of nearly 20 percent in less than 2 months—and it continued to drop. The worst market collapse in the history of the United States had begun. The ensuing market decline continued for over 3 years, until 1932. On July 8, 1932, the DJIA closed at 41—less than 11 percent of its peak in 1929!

The Depression

The Depression was a period of agonizing economic decline that grasped the United States (and much of the world) during the 1930s. The demand for goods and services decreased as pessimism prevailed. The purchases of millions of unemployed consumers dropped to subsistence levels and many people survived on handouts. As unemployment rose, demand for goods continued to drop and prices fell. Between 1929 and 1931 the price of a dozen eggs dropped from 30 to 18 cents and corn sank from 80 to 32 cents per bushel. Unemployment spread, reaching a peak of 24.9 percent in 1933. Numerous businesses went bankrupt because of lack of sales. Creditors fell behind on their repayments. Lacking liquid assets, many commercial banks defaulted when depositors tried to withdraw their deposits. A banking panic resulted, causing even some of the most soundly managed banks to become temporarily insolvent. Between 1930 and 1932 over 5000 commercial banks went bankrupt.

4-3   **FEDERAL SECURITIES REGULATION BEGINS**

The first federal securities laws were passed following the Great Crash and the ensuing Depression. The federal laws that were passed are discussed in chronological order, to show how legislative thinking about securities laws evolved after the economic disasters of the early 1930s. These laws increased the stability of U.S. securities markets.

Glass-Steagall Act of 1933

The Banking Act of 1933, called the Glass-Steagall Act:

a. Prohibits commercial banks from doing investment banking.
b. Establishes the Federal Deposit Insurance Corporation (FDIC), which insures bank deposits.
c. Forbids commercial banks from paying interest on demand deposits.

In 1933, the United States was mired in the Depression. To alleviate their nation's pain, Representative Steagall and Senator Glass pushed a law through Congress that was designed to decentralize financial power. Though the law applied primarily to the commercial banking industry, it also affected the investments industry.

The part of the Glass-Steagall Act that most affects the investments industry is the section that forbids commercial banks from underwriting primary issues of corporate stocks and bonds. To give just one example: This section of the Glass-Steagall Act split the venerable House of Morgan into what is today known as the Morgan Guaranty Trust (America's fifth-largest, most profitable, and most prestigious commercial bank) and the Morgan Stanley investment banking firm (a large and equally prestigious investment banking firm).

The Glass-Steagall Act mandated separation of commercial banking and investment banking, and is increasingly considered to be against the better interests of the United States. In the 1980s, the Federal Reserve allowed commercial banks to acquire brokerage houses that handled secondary trades (but not corporate primary issues), thereby weakening this separation.[8]

Securities Act of 1933

The Securities Act of 1933:

a. Requires full disclosure of all relevant information about new issues of corporate securities.
b. Mandates that almost all new securities issues made by large corporations be registered with the federal government.
c. Requires that registration statements contain financial statements au-

---

[8]Another part of Glass-Steagall forbids commercial banks from paying interest on checking account deposits. This second part of the law was largely overcome with the development of NOW accounts (that is, personal checking accounts that are allowed to pay interest) and cancellation of the Federal Reserve's interest rate ceilings in the 1980s.

Establishing the FDIC was the only part of the Glass-Steagall Act to gain wide approval. This deposit insurance has stabilized the U.S. banking system.

dited by an independent accountant and other information relevant for potential investors.

d. Forbids fraud and deception.

The Securities Act of 1933 governs primary issues of securities. This act, also known as the *truth-in-securities law,* requires securities issuers to fully disclose all information that may affect the value of their securities; it also prohibits certain types of fraud. Let us consider some details.

Registration of IPOs   The main objective of the Securities Act is to provide potential investors in initial public offerings (IPOs) the facts they need to make informed investment decisions. To achieve this objective, the Securities Act of 1933 specifies that the issuing firm and the investment banker must register the issue, unless an applicable exemption applies. **Registration** involves filing with the federal government audited financial statements, information about the underwriting agreement, and other information about the firm. Table 3-2 outlines the information that must be disclosed.

After a firm registers the required information about an IPO with the Securities and Exchange Commission (SEC), it usually must wait a few weeks before issuing the securities. During the waiting period the SEC investigates the information to ensure that everything necessary has been disclosed. The **prospectus** contains most of the information in the registration statement and is prepared for public distribution. Every investor who buys the new securities must be provided with one. If the prospectus is distributed before the end of the waiting period, it must have a note in red ink on its cover stating that it has not yet received SEC approval for issuance as a final prospectus—it is called a **red herring.**

SEC approval, when it is granted, does not imply that the securities are a good investment. It merely indicates that the legally required information has been properly disclosed for investors to analyze if they wish.

In 1982, the SEC modified the registration process slightly in order to reduce the red tape. **Rule 415** was temporarily adopted to allow large corporations to file with the SEC **shelf registration** statements that give details about the firm's long-run financing plans. Thereafter, the corporation that filed the shelf registration can quickly float new issues of stocks or bonds without filing a separate registration statement for each individual issue.[9]

[9]For more information about Rule 415 see David S. Kidwell, M. Wayne Marr, and G. Rodney Thompson, "SEC Rule 415: The Ultimate Competitive Bid," *Journal of Financial and Quantitative Analysis,* June 1984, vol. 19, no. 2, pp. 183–196; Robert J. Rogowski and Eric H. Sorenson, "Deregulation in Investment Banking: Shelf Registrations, Structure, and Performance," *Financial Management,* Spring 1985, vol. 14, no. 1, pp. 5–15; and Sanjai Bhagat, M. Wayne Marr, and G. Rodney Thompson, "The Rule 415 Experiment: Equity Markets," *Journal of Finance,* Dec. 1985, vol. 40, no. 5, pp. 1385–1402.

Exemptions   The following types of securities offerings are exempted from the full registration requirements of the Securities Act of 1933:

Small issues: Small issues are those offered by firms issuing less than $1,500,000 of new securities per year.

Secondary trading: Secondary trades are trades between previous investors; the issuer receives no money. (Although they are exempt under the Securities Act of 1933, secondary sales are regulated by the Securities Exchange Act of 1934.)

Private offerings: Private offerings are stock issues offered to small groups of private investors who are experienced or informed enough not to require disclosure statements for their own protection. Such purchases must be for investment purposes and not for resale to the public; they are sometimes called **letter stocks** because the investors must sign a letter promising not to sell the shares too soon. The investors must keep the shares for at least 2 years to prove their investment motives.

Antifraud Provisions   In addition to the requirements for full disclosure of information, the Securities Act of 1933 contains antifraud provisions. It provides remedies against securities salespersons or others who disseminate untrue or misleading information about securities. Courts finding fraudulent statements being made about securities can issue injunctions to stop such action and require other civil law remedies, such as reimbursement for damages.

The Securities Act limits the techniques that can be used to sell securities. It provides the basis for a later legal ruling that all public securities dealers imply, by offering their services to the public, that they will deal fairly. This ruling provides a basis for prosecuting securities salespersons who issue misleading advice or perpetrate frauds.

Securities Exchange Act (SEA) of 1934

The Securities Exchange Act of 1934:

a. Establishes the Securities and Exchange Commission (SEC).

b. Requires the SEC to approve all commission rate changes proposed by the securities exchanges.

c. Empowers the SEC to change rules at the securities exchanges, to formulate additional regulations, and to prohibit stock price manipulation.

d. Extends disclosure requirements established by the 1933 Act to include secondary markets.

e. Empowers the SEC to regulate the business conduct of broker-dealer members of an exchange.

f. Supports self-regulation by assigning disciplinary power over its members to the exchanges.

g. Empowers the Federal Reserve Board to set minimum initial margin requirements.

h. Prohibits fraud and price manipulation.

After the Securities Act of 1933 was passed, its limitations were quickly recognized. Congress quickly extended its provisions by enacting the Securities Exchange Act of 1934 to cover the secondary markets and established the Securities and Exchange Commission (SEC) to enforce the 1933 Act.

Establishment of the SEC   The Securities Exchange Act of 1934 created the SEC and charged it with the responsibility for regulating securities markets.

The SEC has offices in New York City, Boston, Atlanta, Miami, Chicago, Detroit, Houston, Fort Worth, Los Angeles, San Francisco, Seattle, and Philadelphia. Investors can write to the SEC about allegations of fraud and wrongdoing and the SEC lawyers will consider taking action to rectify wrongdoing—at the government's expense.

The SEC may take action to require conformance with the securities laws. The SEC is granted the right to suspend trading in particular securities, to withdraw approval of the registration of a securities exchange, to expel officers or members of an exchange who operate illegally, and to suggest changes in an exchange's rules and bylaws and require their implementation. The SEC also has the right to collect financial statements and records, to conduct investigations and hearings as needed to enforce the law, to obtain injunctions requiring the cessation of activities violating the securities laws, and to obtain writs requiring violators to comply with the law.

Disclosure Requirements for Secondary Securities   To ensure full disclosure of information about securities traded in secondary markets, the 1934 Act requires that annual reports and other periodic reports be filed for public inspection at the SEC offices before the listing of securities for trading on an organized exchange. The **Securities Acts Amendments of 1964** extended these registration requirements to securities traded OTC and established other requirements. Companies must provide the SEC with the following reports about their operations:

1. The audited annual **10K Report** contains four parts: Part I—description of operations, Part II—financial statements, Part III—information about executive personnel, and Part IV—additional financial details about assets.

2. The quarterly **10Q Report** may or may not be audited. It contains condensed quarterly financial statements.

3. The event-oriented **8K Report** is required within 15 days after a merger, acquisition, resignation of a director, change in certifying accountant, or other events.

These SEC reports (and others) are available to the public.

Registration of Organized Exchanges The Securities Exchange Act of 1934 grants the SEC considerable authority over organized exchanges. It requires that all exchanges register with the SEC, comply with the law, adopt rules for disciplining members who do not conduct their business in a legal and ethical manner, and furnish the SEC with copies of its rules and bylaws. Within these guidelines the exchanges are free to regulate themselves. However, the SEC can intervene in the operations of an exchange and alter penalties, expel members of the exchange, or even close the exchange. In fact, the SEC rarely intervenes.

Credit Regulation When Congress wrote the Securities Exchange Act of 1934, it wanted to prohibit debt pyramiding. Since the Federal Reserve Board is charged with controlling the money supply and credit conditions, Congress gave it the authority to set margin requirements for credit purchases of securities.[10] The Fed then wrote Federal Reserve Regulations T and U to cover *initial margin requirements*. The initial margin is the percentage of the purchase price that investors must pay with their own equity funds. Regulations T and U allow the Board of Governors of the Federal Reserve to set the margin requirements for loans made to securities buyers. In recent years the initial margin requirement has varied between 50 and 80 percent for common stocks. (See Chapter 3 for calculation of reserve requirements.)

The Securities Exchange Act of 1934 also limited securities dealers' total indebtedness to 20 times their owners' equity capital.

Proxy Solicitation The Securities Exchange Act of 1934 requires that the SEC establish rules to govern solicitations by registered issuers of stock to obtain their shareholders' voting rights, called **proxies,** on matters to come before the shareholders meeting. In response to this statute, the SEC requires that all proxy solicitations contain some information about the issues to be voted upon, a proxy card for the shareholder to express approval or disapproval of each issue, and a complete list of candidates if the proxy solicitation is for the election of directors.

Exemptions Securities of federal, state, and local governments, securities that are not traded across state lines, and any other securities specified by the SEC are exempt from registering with the SEC. Certain organized exchanges may also be exempted from registering if the SEC chooses. As a matter of practice, certain small local exchanges have been exempted from SEC registration (namely,

---

[10]The Board of Governors also controls banks' reserve requirements and Federal Reserve open-market operations, and it sets the discount rate at which banks may borrow from the Federal Reserve system. The Treasury and the Federal Reserve publicly suggested in 1984 that the securities exchanges be allowed to take over setting the margin requirements for themselves. Congress has not yet responded to this suggestion.

the exchanges in Honolulu and in Wheeling, West Virginia). Many of the provisions of the SEA do not apply to exempted securities and exchanges.

Insider Activities Recent common law cases have established policies that extend the prohibition against insider trading beyond the insiders explicitly mentioned in the 1934 Act. The latest view is that both part-time and full-time employees of a corporation at all levels have a **fiduciary responsibility** to the shareholders of the corporation. Stated differently, anyone who has access to material nonpublic information about the firm can be considered an **insider.** Insiders are forbidden by the Securities Exchange Act of 1934 from earning speculative gains by trading in the firm's securities. To help enforce this prohibition, Section 16(a) of the SEA requires that those most likely to possess material nonpublic information (namely, every officer, director, and owner of more than 10 percent of a listed corporation's shares) must file a statement, called an **insider report,** of their holdings of that firm's securities in every month in which a change in those holdings occurs. These insider reports are public information. Section 16(b) requires that insiders' profits from investments that were held for less than 6 months be returned to the issuing corporation. Section 16(c) forbids insiders from making short sales in the firm's shares. Section 32, as amended in 1975, provides for penalties in the form of fines and/or up to 10 years imprisonment.[11]

Price Manipulation The Securities Exchange Act of 1934 forbids price manipulation schemes such as wash sales, pools, circulation of manipulative information, and false and misleading statements about securities.

---

[11]Arguments can be made in support of insider trading as a way to increase market efficiency. See Harold Demsetz, "Corporate Control, Insider Trading and Rates of Return," *American Economic Review,* May 1986, vol. 76, no. 2, pp. 313–316. Also see Joseph E. Finnerty, "Insiders and Market Efficiency," *Journal of Finance,* Sept. 1976, vol. 31, pp. 1141–1148; Henry Manne, "In Defense of Insider Trading," *Harvard Business Review,* Nov.–Dec. 1966; George Benston, "Required Disclosure and the Stock Market: An Evaluation of the Securities Exchange Act of 1934," *American Economic Review,* March 1973, pp. 132–155. Try to read Henry G. Manne et al., *Wall Street in Transition: The Emerging System and Its Impact on the Economy* (New York: New York University Press, 1974). Also see George J. Stigler, "Public Regulation of the Securities Markets," *Journal of Business,* April 1964, vol. XXXVII, no. 2, pp. 117–142. See Harold Demsetz and Kenneth Lehn, "The Structure of Corporate Ownership: Causes and Consequences," *Journal of Political Economy,* Dec. 1985, vol. 93, pp. 1155–1177.

On the difficulties of enforcing the insider trading rule, see Nils H. Hakansson, "On the Politics of Accounting Disclosure and Measurement," *Journal of Accounting Research,* vol. 19, suppl. 1981, pp. 1–34.

For a rigorous explanation of how insider trading is harmful to society, see Norman S. Douglas, "Insider Trading: The Case Against the 'Victimless Crime' Hypothesis," *The Financial Review,* May 1988, vol. 23, no. 2, pp. 127–142.

Public Utility Holding Company Act of 1935

The Public Utility Holding Company Act of 1935:

a. Mandates that all public utility holding companies register with the SEC.

b. Empowers the SEC to break up public utility holding companies that exploit consumers.

c. Forbids exploitation of operating units by holding companies, but empowers the SEC to oversee the integration of utilities where improved efficiencies are attainable.

In 1928 the Federal Trade Commission (FTC) discovered a system of huge utility empires that were organized to provide profit for the owners of the utility holding companies rather than serve public needs. Congress enacted the Public Utility Holding Company Act of 1935 to halt such exploitation. Section 11(a) of the 1935 Act gave the SEC the responsibility and the authority "to determine the extent to which the corporate structure . . . may be simplified, unnecessary complexities thereby eliminated, voting power fairly and equitably distributed . . . and the properties and business thereof confined to those necessary and appropriate to the operations of an integrated public utility system." The 1935 Utility Holding Company Act also gave the SEC the power to regulate the terms and form of securities issued by utility companies, regulate the accounting systems used, approve all acquisitions and dispositions of assets and securities, and regulate intercompany transactions, such as the payment of cash dividends and the making of loans. Profiteering by public utility holding companies has ceased to take the form of major rip-offs. The kind of problems occurring today are more subtle (such as overcharging consumers for management errors in the construction of nuclear power plants).

Maloney Act of 1938

The Maloney Act of 1938:

a. Brings the over-the-counter (OTC) market under the supervision of the SEC.

b. Encourages the over-the-counter market to establish private trade associations for self-regulation but gives the SEC authority to oversee and to change the rules of these private associations.

The Maloney Act is an extension of the Securities Exchange Act of 1934, adopted at the request of OTC securities dealers to provide for their self-regulation. The act stipulates that one or more associations of OTC brokers and dealers may apply for registration with the SEC, that these groups may regulate themselves within the guidelines laid down by the SEC, and that the groups may grant discounts on securities traded among their members. OTC dealers who are not members of an association deal with members of an association by paying full retail prices for any securities they purchase. The price concessions provide a strong incentive for all OTC dealers to belong to an association.

National Association of Securities Dealers (NASD)   To date, only one association of OTC dealers has registered with the SEC under the provisions of the Maloney Act—the **National Association of Securities Dealers** (NASD). The **NASD** has about 7000 member firms that operate over 20,000 branch offices and employ approximately 500,000 registered representatives who sell securities in the OTC market. The NASD has established a test that must be passed by any individual wishing to join; a set of rules forbidding fraud, manipulation, and excessive profit-taking; a uniform-practices code standardizing and expediting routine transactions, such as payments and deliveries; and a procedure for disciplining members who engage in illegal or unethical conduct.

Penalties involving suspensions and fines may be levied by the NASD. Expulsion from the NASD is the severest penalty, since nonmembers cannot obtain the purchase discounts they need to survive. All decisions may be appealed to the NASD's board of governors, the SEC, or the courts.

The SEC possesses direct power over the NASD. It must be given copies of all rules adopted by the NASD (or any other association of OTC dealers that may be formed). It may suspend or revoke an association's registration for failure to follow its guidelines. And the SEC may review and alter the verdict in any judicial proceedings of the association.

The Federal Bankruptcy Act of 1938, as Amended in 1978

The Federal Bankruptcy Act of 1938, as amended in 1978:

a. Requires that court-appointed trustees oversee the affairs of firms against which bankruptcy charges have been filed.

b. Chapter X of the Act provides for *liquidation* of hopelessly troubled firms.

c. Chapter X also provides for *reorganization* of troubled firms that might be able to survive.

d. Chapter XI provides for *arrangements* to govern moderately troubled firms that should be able to survive.

e. Chapter XIII provides for *repayment plans* to govern moderately troubled firms that might be able to survive.

Bankruptcy law is of interest to those who invest in junk bonds and special situations.[12] It is the foundation upon which *default risk* is defined. The actions of the bankruptcy courts can have dramatic effects on the prices of securities

[12]For a financial analyst's view of bankruptcy, see Edward I. Altman, *Corporate Financial Distress* (New York: Wiley, 1983).

issued by financially distressed firms. Interestingly, the prices of securities that are affected by the bankruptcy laws *do not react directly* to court declarations of bankruptcy, reorganization, or other such financial traumas. Security analysts anticipate these events and, as a result, *securities prices typically react to such changes months before they actually occur.* Default risk is discussed in Chapter 14 of this book.

Trust Indenture Act of 1939

The Trust Indenture Act of 1939:

a. Mandates that every bond issue be governed by an indenture contract between the issuer and the bond investors.

b. Requires the appointment of an objective third party to be **trustee** and enforce the provisions of the indenture contract.

c. Requires that the bond investors and, most particularly, the trustee be provided with full disclosure of relevant information about the issuer's condition.

An **indenture** is a contract written by a firm that issues bonds, stipulating certain promises the firm makes to its bond investors. A common provision of an indenture is that the issuing corporation can pay no dividends on common stock if interest payments on its bonds are past due. The Trust Indenture Act of 1939 requires that a *trustee* (for example, a bank) be appointed to act as a ''watchdog'' for the bondholders to make certain that their protective provisions in the indenture are not violated. If a provision is violated, the trustee should sue the issuing corporation on behalf of the bond investors.

4-4   **SECURITIES REGULATIONS PASSED IN 1940 AND THEREAFTER**

The series of laws discussed above represent the foundation of U.S. securities law. The laws passed more recently are also important, but they are narrower in scope.

Investment Company Act of 1940

The Investment Company Act of 1940, and its 1970 Amendments:

a. Requires all open-end and closed-end investment companies to register with the SEC.

b. Requires all open-end and closed-end investment companies to make prospectuses available to potential investors before shares can be sold.

c. Mandates publicly available statements outlining each investment company's investment goals.

    d. Requires that outsiders be on every board of directors.

    e. Forbids fraud and requires that uniform accounting practices be used.

    f. Requires shareholder approval of changes in the management agreement.

The Investment Company Act of 1940 is the main piece of legislation governing the management of investment companies. An **investment company** takes in money from various investors, commingles these funds, and then invests the money in a large, diversified portfolio of marketable securities that it manages for a fee. The investment company keeps track of every investor's fractional ownership of the portfolio of diversified investments. There are two types of investment companies. The most popular type is the open-end investment company, commonly called a **mutual fund.** Mutual funds can keep growing as long as investors keep on sending in money to be managed—that is, the portfolio is open-ended. The other type of investment company is less popular; it is called a **closed-end investment company** because such a company cannot accept more investments after its initial offering. Thus, closed-end funds cannot grow by selling additional shares.

The Investment Company Act of 1940 requires that investment companies avoid fraudulent practices, fully disclose their financial statements, and give their prospectuses to potential investors. The Investment Company Act of 1940 also requires that investment companies limit the issuance of debt, not employ persons convicted of securities frauds as officers, and operate the fund for the benefit of shareholders rather than for the benefit of its managers.[13]

Investment Advisers Act of 1940

The Investment Advisers Act of 1940:

    a. Requires any individual who sells investment advice to 15 or more interstate clients to register with the SEC.

    b. Requires all registered investment advisers to file information about their education and background with the SEC.

    c. Forbids investment advisers from assigning investment advisory contracts without the client's consent.

    d. Forbids investment advisers from entering into profit-sharing agreements with their clients.

    e. Prohibits investment advisers from using selected testimonials in their advertising.

Essentially, the Investment Advisers Act requires that investment advisers register with the SEC and disclose the required information about their back-

---

[13]The financial performance of mutual funds is analyzed in Chapter 21.

ground. It is not the intent of the Act to deny an applicant the right to sell investment advice even if that person is obviously incompetent. As with all securities laws, the law expects the investor to evaluate the information required by the law and then make informed judgments.

Securities Investor Protection Corporation Act of 1970

The Securities Investor Protection Corporation (SIPC) Act:

a. Mandates the establishment of SIPC to insure clients' accounts at brokerage firms that fail.

b. Requires that all registered securities brokerages pay SIPC dues annually to support it.

The Securities Investor Protection Corporation, or **SIPC** (pronounced "sip-ic"), was established to indemnify the clients of bankrupt brokerage firms. The act requires that all registered securities brokers and dealers and all firms that are members of national securities exchanges join SIPC and pay dues equal to approximately one percent of the firm's gross income—just as banks pay FDIC dues.

SIPC dues are placed in a fund that is used to repay clients of a bankrupt brokerage firm if the firm loses the client's securities and/or does not have the capital to repay client losses arising from the brokerage's failure. SIPC was formed to free investors from worry about selecting a brokerage by providing insurance to protect investors in case their brokerage firm fails.

The Employee Retirement Income Security Act (ERISA) of 1974

The Employee Retirement Income Security Act:

a. Requires employers that promised pension benefits to employees to set aside the funds needed to pay for these pension payment liabilities.

b. Requires employers providing defined-benefit pension plans to make good any shortfall in the pension monies available to meet the promised pension benefits.

c. Requires employers to provide employees *vesting rights* in their pension fund.

d. Prohibits employers from investing substantial amounts of their pension funds in their firm's own securities.

e. Establishes the Pension Benefit Guarantee Corporation to insure pensioners against losing their pensions if their employer goes bankrupt and leaves an underfunded pension plan.

The rapid growth of pension funds since 1940 has led to a similar growth in the number of abuses by pension fund managers, resulting in the loss of pension benefits to employees. To safeguard pension funds, Congress passed the Employee Retirement Income Security Act of 1974, called **ERISA.** Among ERISA's provisions is a novel application of the "prudent man rule" of law.

ERISA stipulates that the managers of pension funds are liable for the preservation of the fund's principal and also for sufficient growth through "prudent investment" to enable the fund to pay retirement benefits when they come due. What is novel is that ERISA refers to the *overall investment portfolio* rather than to each individual asset in the portfolio, which is the way the prudent man rule is applied in most applications of the law. Thus, it appears that junk bonds or options or other investments that might ordinarily be judged to be imprudent when viewed in isolation are acceptable pension assets under ERISA, as long as these assets are appropriate within the pension portfolio's overall strategy.

ERISA also requires that pension funds explicitly define the eligibility of employees and the way employees' benefits are funded. The act also resolved certain inherent conflicts of interest—for example, a pension fund cannot invest in the employer's securities. This latter provision helps ensure that the pensioners will not be affected if their former employer goes bankrupt.

Commodity Futures Trading Commission (CFTC) Act of 1974

The Commodity Futures Trading Commission (CFTC) Act:

a. Mandates the establishment of an independent federal agency, named the CFTC, to take over the duties and responsibilities of the Commodity Exchange Authority. Thus, the CFTC has sole authority to approve futures contracts to be traded and to oversee the trading of futures contracts.

b. Gives the CFTC authority to stop trading in futures contracts.

c. Gives the CFTC authority over all futures contracts in the world when they are traded in the United States.

Commodity futures contracts are marketable financial instruments that have a long legislative history. Starting in 1884, there was a new bill about trading futures contracts introduced in Congress almost every year. Most of these proposed bills sought to ban trading in futures contracts. In those early days of finance, many believed that trading in futures contracts destabilized market prices or was just another form of gambling.[14]

The Commodity Exchange Authority (CEA) Act of 1936 established the CEA

---

[14]For evidence about how speculators help make markets more liquid and decrease rather than increase price fluctuations see William L. Silber, "Marketmaker Behavior in an Auction Market: An Analysis of Scalpers in Futures Markets," *Journal of Finance,* Sept. 1984, vol. 39, no. 4, pp. 937–953. Also see Robert Forsythe, Thomas R. Palfrey, and Charles R. Plott, "Futures Markets and Informational Efficiency: A Laboratory Examination," *Journal of Finance,* Sept. 1984, vol. 39, no. 4, pp. 954–981.

to regulate trading in domestic agricultural commodities. The CEA granted approval for new futures contracts to be publicly traded, policed the registration of the commodity futures commission merchants, investigated charges of cheating and fraud in commodity trading, and prevented price manipulation in U.S. commodity trading. Commodity futures trading started growing rapidly in the 1960s, and the tiny CEA proved inadequate to handle the larger work responsibilities. Therefore, the Commodity Futures Trading Commission Act of 1974 passed all of the CEA's regulatory authority on to a new, larger independent regulatory agency, the Commodity Futures Trading Commission, or **CFTC.**

The CFTC is an independent federal regulatory agency overseen by five commissioners appointed by the President of the United States. The CFTC also has a staff of economists and other regulatory officials who research the commodity markets in an effort to discern what rules and regulations about commodity futures trading will best promote the public welfare.

In addition to establishing the CFTC and giving it the powers that had previously been assigned to the CEA, the 1974 Act also gave the CFTC authority to sue any person or organization that violated the CFTC Act; take charge of a commodity market in an "emergency" situation and direct whatever actions it deemed necessary to restore an orderly market; and issue "cease and desist" orders, backed up with criminal or civil sanctions and fines. One of the most sweeping changes brought about by the CFTC Act was to grant the CFTC authority over all commodities from all over the world when they are traded in the United States.

The Securities Exchange Act of 1934 authorized the SEC to supervise trading in put and call options. But in 1981 the SEC and the CFTC announced an administrative pact between the two governmental agencies which clarified their jurisdiction over recently developed financial futures and option products. The SEC agreed to oversee almost all options trading, while the CFTC now regulates almost all futures contracts and options on futures.

The Securities Acts Amendments of 1975

The Securities Acts Amendments of 1975:

a. Require the SEC to develop a national market system (NMS).

b. Amend the Securities Exchange Act of 1934 by obligating the SEC to nullify exchange rules that are anticompetitive.

c. Prohibit the use of fixed commission rate schedules.

d. Clarify the jurisdiction of the courts and the process of judicial review in securities law.

e. Call for fair competition among brokers, dealers, and securities markets.

f. Call for wide public availability of information on securities price quotations and transactions.

g. Require provision of opportunities for investors' orders to be executed without the participation of a dealer (like the NYSE specialists).[15]

The Securities Acts Amendments (SAA) directed the SEC to oversee the development of a vaguely defined national securities market. Section 3-4 describes some of the new securities market developments that are emerging under this legislation.[16]

4-5   **SUMMARY AND CONCLUSIONS**

The Securities Act of 1933 and the Securities Exchange Act of 1934 are the backbone of federal securities law. The 1933 Act established the concept of providing investors with full disclosure of relevant investment information, and made fraud and price manipulation illegal. The Securities Exchange Act of 1934 established the SEC to enforce the federal securities laws; suggested self-regulation of the securities industry, which was to be overseen by the SEC; and extended the 1933 Act's provisions for the primary markets to include the secondary markets.

Securities legislation after 1934 was aimed at overcoming problems with public utility holding companies, the OTC markets, bankruptcy, bond issue indentures, investment companies, investment advisers, bankrupt brokerage firms, pension management, commodity futures trading, and the development of a more competitive national market system.

---

[15]For financial economic analysis of the Securities Acts Amendments of 1975 see Kalman J. Cohen, Steven F. Maier, Robert A. Schwartz, and David K. Whitcomb, *The Microstructure of Securities Markets* (Englewood Cliffs, N.J.: Prentice-Hall, 1986), pp. 152–154. Also see Robert A. Schwartz, *Equity Markets* (New York: Harper and Row, 1988), pp. 137–154.

[16]During the 1980s, securities brokerage firms began asking their clients to sign a form stating that any misunderstandings that might arise between the client and the brokerage firm would be submitted to **binding arbitration** rather than being adjudicated via court proceedings. The U.S. Supreme Court declared such agreements legal in 1989. Conceptually, arbitration is a sound way to control prohibitive legal expenses. But, arbitration can be biased in favor of the brokerage firms; many of the *arbitrators* are securities brokers. The brokerage firms argue that it is appropriate for brokers to be arbitrators because they know the brokerage business. However, bias in the arbitrating brokers could be reflected in a low rate of arbitrated judgments in favor of the clients. As a result, if a broker requests it, clients are well advised to refuse to sign the arbitration agreement and threaten to go to another brokerage firm that does not require advance written agreement to go to binding arbitration.

Essay Questions

4-1   What harm can come to a national economy if some investors occasionally corner a market or operate pools?

4-2   Compare and contrast the Securities Act of 1933 and the SEA of 1934 with respect to the registration of securities issues. Which federal agency does each act specify for the required registration? What act provides for the registration of IPOs and for previously issued securities traded in secondary markets?

4-3   What is a prospectus? What is its purpose? To whom should prospectuses be provided and at what time? When the SEC releases a prospectus for public dissemination, what is the implication of this release?

4-4   What is the SEC? How did it develop? What functions does it perform?

4-5   How is the credit used to purchase securities on margin regulated?

4-6   What is the NASD? How did it develop? What are its functions? What powers does it have to enforce the law?

4-7   What is an indenture? Who is an indenture contract supposed to protect? What precautions discourage violation of an indenture?

4-8   Is it legal to trade securities on the basis of a so-called ''hot tip'' from someone who has access to inside information about the issuing company?

Matching Questions

4-9   Match the definitions listed below to the appropriate undesirable activity.

Illegal activities	Description of illegal activities
1. Churning	A. A phony transaction carried out to create the illusion that a significant transaction occurred
2. Cornering the market	B. The Dow Jones Industrial Average fell drastically from a high reached in 1929
3. The Depression	C. The common practice of brokers to generate commissions from their clients by fruitless securities trading
4. Insider	D. An executive, owner of shares, or either an internal or external employee having access to information that may affect the firm's securities prices
5. Pool	E. Buying almost all the supply of a good which is available

6. Wash sale

F. Several years in the early 1930s when unemployment was high and bankruptcies were rampant

7. The Great Crash

G. An association of people formed to profit from manipulating securities prices

4-10 Match the following 12 brief descriptions of securities laws to the title of the appropriate law.

Acts	**Brief descriptions of securities laws**
1. Glass-Steagall Act	A. The contracts governing bond issues must clearly specify the rights of bond owners. Trustees must not allow anything to impair their willingness or legal right to sue the issuer.
2. Securities Act	B. Mutual funds and closed-end investment companies were brought under federal control.
3. Securities Exchange Act	C. Sellers of investment advice are required to register with the SEC.
4. Public Utility Holding Company Act	D. The federal insurance program to reimburse clients for losses resulting from bankrupt brokerage firms was established.
5. Maloney Act	E. Pension fund management was brought under federal control.
6. Trust Indenture Act	F. The law establishing a federal agency to oversee futures markets.
7. Investment Company Act	G. The SEC was directed to establish a new national market system (NMS) with negotiated commission rates.
8. Investment Advisors Act	H. Forbids commercial banks from engaging in investment banking.
9. Securities Investor Protection Corporation (SIPC) Act	I. Firms issuing securities must register new issues with federal authorities. Registration information is made available to the public in the form of a prospectus.
10. Employee Retirement Income Security Act (ERISA)	J. The SEC was set up to regulate the securities industry. All securities exchanges must register with the SEC. The SEC must regulate proxy voting. Regulations of earlier laws were extended to cover secondary sales.

11. Commodity Futures Trading Act

K. Empowered the SEC to oversee the finances, accounting, organization, and activities of public utilities to ensure that the public welfare is served.

12. Securities Acts Amendments

L. Associates of qualified over-the-counter brokers and dealers can register with the SEC and regulate themselves within SEC guidelines.

Problems

4-11 The Securities Acts Amendments legislation is best described by which one of the following statements?

    a. It is a law passed in 1975.

    b. It requires the SEC to establish a national market system (NMS).

    c. The law is vague and leaves much of the implementation to the discretion of the SEC.

    d. Brokerage commission rates should be competitively determined by competing market makers.

    e. All of the above are true.

4-12 The NASD is best described by which of the following statements?

    a. A trade association of securities dealers.

    b. The organization that oversees and regulates the over-the-counter market.

    c. The provider of a computerized clearinghouse for a geographically fragmented market.

    d. All of the above.

    e. Nonactive Securities Dealers (NASD) are limited partners who have no voice in the management of the firm.

4-13 Investors are insured against loss if their brokerage firm goes bankrupt by which of the following bodies?

    a. SIPC

    b. FDIC

    c. SEC

    d. Federal Reserve

4-14 The Securities Exchange Act of 1934 forbids insiders from participating in which of the following activities?

    a. Passing inside information to other investors

    b. Short selling their company's stock

    c. Taking profits from price appreciation of their firm's stock if they owned it for less than 6 months

    d. All of the above

4-15 Which of the following categories of people are *insiders*?

    a. Members of the board of directors

    b. Investment bankers, external accountants conducting a periodic audit, and consultants

    c. The president and vice presidents of a firm

    d. All of the above

4-16 Which of the following statements describes a wash sale?

    a. There is no sale at all.

    b. Transactions are performed merely to establish the record of a sale.

    c. It may be done to establish a tax loss.

    d. All of the above are true.

4-17 Insider activities are required to be reported under which of the following laws?

    a. Securities Act of 1933

    b. Securities Exchange Act of 1934

    c. Maloney Act of 1936

    d. Trust Indenture Act of 1939

4-18 The National Association of Securities Dealers registered with the SEC under the provision of which of the following laws?

    a. Securities Act of 1933

    b. Securities Exchange Act of 1934

    c. Maloney Act of 1936

    d. Trust Indenture Act of 1939

4-19 Which of the following does the CFTC regulate?

    a. Securities markets

    b. Trading in options

    c. Trading of futures contracts

    d. Options on futures contracts

    e. Both c and d

Selected References

Budd, Martin L., and Nicholas Wolfson, *Securities Regulation: Cases and Materials* (Charlottesville, Va.: The Michie Company, 1984).

An easy-to-read law school textbook, large sections of which can be read and understood by the layperson.

Hammer, Richard M., Gilbert Simonetti, Jr., and Charles T. Crawford, eds., *Investment Regulation Around the World* (Somerset, N.J.: Ronald Press, 1983).

A collection of readings about the investment regulations in foreign countries.

Jennings, Richard W., and Harold Marsh, Jr., *Securities Regulation: Cases & Materials,* 5th ed. (Mineola, N.Y.: Foundation Press, 1982).

This is a popular law-school textbook that is easy for nonlawyers to read.

Loll, L. M., and G. Buckley, *The Over-the-Counter Securities Markets,* 4th ed. (Englewood Cliffs, N.J.: Prentice-Hall, 1981).

This is an easy-to-read book about securities markets, securities trading, and securities law. The book is widely used by people studying to pass the NASD exam to become securities brokers.

Lowenstein, Louis, *What's Wrong with Wall Street?* (Reading, Mass.: Addison-Wesley, 1988).

Professor Lowenstein is a professor of law and finance. As such he offers some ingenious suggestions for making securities markets in the United States more efficient and less prone to speculative excesses.

Pessin, Allan H., *Securities Law Compliance* (Homewood, Ill.: Dow Jones–Irwin, 1990).

A Wall Street executive explains how to apply securities laws in practical situations.

Phillips, Susan M., and J. Richard Zecher, *The SEC and the Public Interest* (Cambridge, Mass.: The MIT Press, 1981).

This scholarly economic analysis and criticism of the SEC was written by two professors of finance who worked at the SEC. No mathematics is used.

Schwartz, Robert A., *Equity Markets* (New York: Harper and Row, 1988).

Chapter 5 of this financial economics book discusses securities law.

Securities and Exchange Commission, Securities Act of 1933, Release No. 4725; Securities Exchange Act of 1939, Release No. 7425.

The SEC provides these and numerous other releases to document and explain its legal activity in the securities industry.

Tewles, Richard J., and Edward S. Bradley, *The Stock Market,* 4th ed. (New York: Wiley, 1982).

Chapters 17 and 18 provide some good legal discussion for investors who are not lawyers.

Wiesenberger Investment Company Services, Inc., *Investment Companies* (New York, published annually).

The first few chapters discuss the law relating to investment companies, with special emphasis on recent developments in the area.

Chapter 5

Federal Taxes

The 1986 Tax Reform Act dramatically changed both the individual and the corporate income tax systems in the United States. Essentially, the 1986 Tax Act reduced the tax rate that most taxpayers pay and thus reduced the incentives for trying to avoid taxes. A reasonable understanding of the tax structure is nevertheless worthwhile. Most people find that their federal income tax still rivals their mortgage payments as their single largest expense, so legally minimizing this tax expense is worth some effort. Furthermore, substantial penalties can be invoked for noncompliance with the tax law, and ignorance is not an acceptable defense. This chapter will present both an overview of the federal tax structure and some legal and ethical ways to minimize, defer, and occasionally avoid taxation. Different categories of investors are considered. The individual investor is considered first.

5-1 **FEDERAL PERSONAL INCOME TAX**

This section outlines the steps needed to derive taxable income from gross income.

Deriving Taxable Income

Gross income is the starting point for computing taxable income. Gross income represents all income, with certain exclusions specified in the Internal Revenue Code. Some specific tax-exempt items include interest on most municipal bonds, gifts, a portion of social security benefits, and most life insurance proceeds, to name a few. Unless the Internal Revenue Code specifically excludes a source of income from taxation, *all income is subject to taxation.*

Adjusted gross income is gross income after adjustments are subtracted. Some IRA contributions, Keogh contributions, alimony payments, and penalties on early withdrawal of savings are examples of **adjustments** that can be deducted. Adjustments are especially valuable since they benefit both taxpayers who itemize deductions and those who use the standard deduction.[1]

The **taxable income** computation begins with adjusted gross income. Adjusted gross income is reduced by exemptions and the greater of the standard deduction or itemized deductions. Table 5-1 illustrates the computation of an individual taxpayer's taxable income. The remaining portion of this section describes in more detail the meaning of terms like "standard deduction," "itemized deductions," and "exemptions."

The Standard Deduction

Approximately 80 percent of taxpayers claim the standard deduction rather than itemize their deductions. The **standard deduction** is a flat deduction used by people whose itemized deductions are less than the standard. The standard deduction that is allowed depends on the taxpayer's filing (that is, family) status.

	Years' standard deductions		
Filing status	1988	1989	1990, etc.
Married, filing jointly	$5000	$5200	Continuing
Head of household	4400	4550	inflation-
Single	3000	3100	adjusted
Married, filing separately	2500	2600	amounts

In addition, the standard deduction is increased by $600 for each elderly (65 or over) or blind individual who is married (or $1200 for a married individual who is both blind and elderly). An additional standard deduction of $750 is allowed for an unmarried individual who is elderly or blind ($1500 if both). Both the basic standard deduction and the additional allowances for the blind and elderly are subject to inflation adjustments after 1988. The tax benefits for being elderly and/or blind apply to taxpayers using the standard deduction—but not to taxpayers who itemize.

Itemized Deductions

If itemized deductions exceed the standard deduction, the taxpayer will want to itemize. Allowable itemized deductions are explained below.

Medical Expenses   Medical expenses unreimbursed by insurance are deductible to the extent they exceed 7.5 percent of the taxpayer's adjusted gross

---

[1]The Tax Reform Act of 1986 recharacterized several pre-1986 adjustments as itemized deductions. Thus, moving expenses and unreimbursed employee business expenses are no longer available to taxpayers who claim the standard deduction.

Table 5-1
PROCEDURE FOR DERIVING TAXABLE INCOME

Gross income: Includes wages, salaries, net rents, etc., but excludes such things as interest on most municipal bonds, gifts, some social security benefits, and most life insurance proceeds.
less: Alimony payments, some IRA contributions, Keogh contributions, etc.
equals: Adjusted gross income
less: The greater of the standard deduction or itemized personal deductions. The latter include such items as:

1. Medical expenses in excess of 7.5% of adjusted gross income
2. State and local taxes, except sales taxes
3. Charitable contributions (with certain limitations)
4. Some but not all interest expenses
5. Casualty losses in excess of $100 per loss and 10% of adjusted gross income
6. Various miscellaneous deductions in excess of 2% of adjusted gross income

less: $2000 for each allowable exemption (the amount is adjusted for inflation annually)
equals: Taxable income

income. For example, a taxpayer with $100,000 of adjusted gross income will have a medical expense deduction limited to unreimbursed medical payments in excess of $7500. Few individuals qualify for this deduction.

State and Local Sales Taxes   State and local income taxes, real estate taxes, and personal property taxes qualify as itemized deductions. However, the 1986 Tax Reform Act excluded state and local sales taxes from itemized deductions.

Charitable Deductions   Charitable deductions are fully deductible for itemizing taxpayers only. Such taxpayers are limited to a deduction of no more than 50 percent of adjusted gross income for cash contributions to qualifying charities. Any excess deductions can be carried forward to the next five tax years, however. Donations of appreciated property are subject to stricter limitations.

Interest Expense   Prior to 1986, interest expense was always deductible (with one or two rare exceptions). But the 1986 Tax Reform Act phased out the deduction for interest on installment and credit card purchases; none of this interest will be deductible beginning in 1991. The implicit Congressional message: Save now and pay cash for your car, boat, stereo, TV, and other personal items. The government will no longer subsidize your credit purchases with interest deductions.

There is one loophole left. Interest on up to $100,000 of *home equity loans* is fully deductible, regardless of the purpose for which the funds are used. Therefore, home equity loans may be used to pay off other consumer loans in order to turn nondeductible interest into deductible interest. The wisdom of mortgaging one's home to pay for consumer purchases is dubious, but the tax law encourages such folly.

In the interest of fairness, some other types of interest expense were declared deductible, as follows:

1. Interest paid or accrued in connection with a trade or business is deductible.
2. Interest expense on loans incurred to finance investments is deductible to the extent of investment income; any excess can be carried forward to future years, when "unused" or "leftover" investment income may exist.
3. Mortgage interest is deductible, with restrictions (but the restrictions are liberal).
4. Passive activity interest is deductible, to the extent allowed by the passive activity rules (explained in a later section).

Possibly the only rule that has remained constant regarding interest deductions over the past few decades is the nondeductibility of interest on loans used to finance tax-exempt income, such as municipal bonds. Logically, the costs of generating tax-exempt income should not be granted a tax deduction.

Miscellaneous Deductions Miscellaneous deductions include personal expenses incurred to generate business or investment income and/or to preserve or protect income-producing assets. These types of expenses are deductible to the extent they exceed 2 percent of adjusted gross income. Examples of miscellaneous deductions include 80 percent of business meals and entertainment, 100 percent of other unreimbursed employee expenses, tax preparation fees, union dues, dues for professional organizations, subscription fees for business- and investment-related periodicals, and safety deposit box rentals. Certain moving expenses are also miscellaneous itemized deductions but are not subject to the 2 percent limitation. To illustrate the miscellaneous itemized deduction: a taxpayer who has an adjusted gross income of $20,000 and total qualifying miscellaneous deductions (not including moving expenses) of $1000 would be allowed an itemized miscellaneous deduction of $600, since only those items in excess of $400 (that is, 2 percent of $20,000) are deductible.

Casualty Losses A **casualty loss** may arise from fire, storm, shipwreck, or other events emanating from sudden, unexpected, or unusual causes. Casualty losses are deductible only to the extent that they exceed 10 percent of adjusted gross income plus $100 per loss. The amount of the loss is reduced by insurance awards in arriving at the proper deduction subject to the 10 percent plus $100 limitation.

Example 5-1

An Actual Court Case About a Dead Horse

Jimmy Silver was a jockey whose horse, Lightning, had a voracious appetite. Lightning swallowed the lining of Jimmy's hat and died 2 weeks later. Did the court allow Jimmy a casualty deduction for his horse? No, but only because Lightning's death could not be directly linked to the ill-fated hat. If death had unquestionably resulted from the hat lining, a tax-deductible casualty loss would have resulted. Thus, "suddenness" is a critical factor in determining whether a loss is a casualty.

Exemptions   **Exemptions** represent additional reductions of taxable income for qualifying individuals. Each taxpayer is allowed a personal exemption. Each taxpayer is also allowed an exemption for his or her spouse (if filing a joint return) as well as for each qualifying dependent. In the case of divorced parents, the custodial parent claims the dependent child exemption unless (1) a legal agreement was in effect prior to 1985 giving the noncustodial parent the exemption or (2) the custodial parent signs IRS Form 8332 giving the noncustodial parent the exemption (which the noncustodial parent attaches to his or her tax return). Each exemption claimed has a value: $2000 for each exemption in 1989, and after 1989 the amount is indexed to increase with the rate of inflation. For high-income taxpayers, however, the benefit of the exemption amounts is phased out. This is further explained in the next section.

Calculating a Person's Tax Liability

One of the most dramatic effects of the 1986 Tax Reform Act was the restructuring of tax rates. The progressive tax system was modified by a reduction from as many as 15 different tax rates down to 2. The 1988 rate structure is shown in Table 5-2.

Table 5-2 does not reveal the entire personal tax rate structure. Congress decided to deny the low 15 percent tax rate to people who had incomes large enough to qualify them for the upper-middle-income tax brackets. Congress accomplished this goal by imposing a 5 percent surcharge on taxable income between $71,950 and $149,250 for joint returns and between $43,150 and $89,560 for single returns. This 5 percent surcharge is indexed to increase directly with the rate of inflation after 1988. While the surcharge was meant to deny the benefits of the 15 percent tax rate to upper-middle-income taxpayers, it effec-

Table 5-2
1988 TAX RATES ON A PERSON'S TAXABLE INCOME

Tax rates	Joint returns	Single individuals
15% on incomes up to	$29,750	$17,850
28% on incomes over	29,750	17,850

tively placed them in a special 33 percent income tax bracket for a portion of their income.

In addition, Congress denied the upper-middle-income taxpayers the personal exemptions. These taxpayers' benefits from personal exemptions (worth $2000 apiece in 1989 and indexed to rise with inflation) are erased by extending the 5 percent surcharge to cover an additional $11,200 of taxable income for each exemption claimed by an upper-middle-income taxpayer.

The final effects of the 5 percent surcharge are threefold: (1) the top income tax rate is effectively 33 percent, (2) the income tax structure is regressive over the upper income levels, and (3) the upper cutoff point for taxpayers in the 33 percent tax bracket varies with each individual taxpayer's family situation (namely, marital status and number of exemptions). Example 5-2 provides an example of a person in the 33 percent tax bracket.

Example 5-2	**Computing a Single Person's Marginal Tax Rate**

A single person with a taxable income of $80,000 would calculate their 1988 tax as follows:

15% of first $17,850	$ 2,677.50
28% of balance ($80,000 − $17,850 = $62,150)	17,402.00
5% surcharge ($80,000 − $43,150 = $36,850)	1,842.50
Total tax	$21,922.00

or alternatively,

15% of first $17,850	$ 2,677.50
28% of next $25,300 ($43,150 − $17,850)	7,084.00
33% of next $36,850 ($80,000 − $43,150)	12,160.50
Total tax	$21,922.00

Therefore, this single person is paying tax at a *marginal rate* of 33 percent.

Marginal tax rate is the term used to describe the rate a taxpayer pays on the last dollar of income, or alternatively, the rate the taxpayer saves on the last dollar of deductions. The marginal rate, in this case 33 percent, is the appropriate rate to consider for investment decision-making purposes. The **average tax rate** (in this case, $21,922 divided by $80,000 equals 27.4 percent) has limited usefulness for decision-making purposes. The taxpayer is more interested in how decisions will affect tax liability at the margin—that is, the last dollars earned or last dollars saved through deductions. For example, if the single taxpayer in Example 5-2 is paid a $5000 year-end bonus, Uncle Sam will take 33 percent of the $5000—not 27.4 percent of it. Figure 5-1 illustrates some effective personal income tax brackets; the solid straight lines delineate the marginal tax brackets, and the dotted curve indicates the average tax rates.

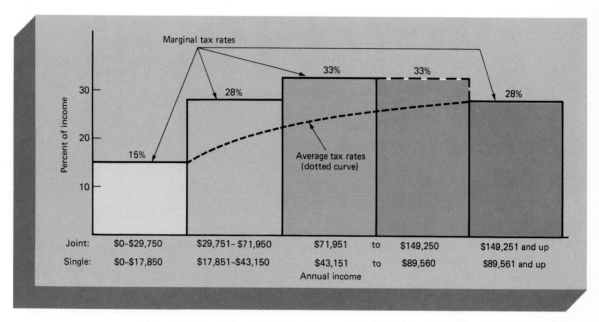

Figure 5-1 The 5% surcharge causes personal income tax brackets to be progressive-then-regressive.

The Marriage Penalty   Although it is probably unintentional, the tax system penalizes some married people while it benefits others. A **marriage penalty** exists for married couples with roughly equal incomes, as Example 5-3 shows.

Example 5-3

John and Mary's Marriage Penalty

Assume John and Mary each have adjusted gross income of $35,000 in 1988. Their tax liabilities are computed (A) for two singles and (B) for a married couple filing jointly according to Table 5-2.

A. John and Mary's taxes as singles

Adjusted gross income for John	$35,000
less: Standard deduction	3,000
less: Exemption	2,000
Taxable income for John	$30,000

Tax on $30,000

0.15 × $17,850	$ 2,677.50
0.28 × ($30,000 − $17,850 = $12,150)	3,402.00
John's total tax	$ 6,079.50
Mary's taxes as a single (calculated the same as John's)	6,079.50
Total taxes for John and Mary as singles	$12,159.00

B. John and Mary filing jointly

Adjusted gross income	$70,000
less: Standard deduction	5,000
less: Exemptions	4,000
Taxable income	$61,000

Tax on $61,000

$0.15 \times \$29,750$	$ 4,462.50
$0.28 \times (\$61,000 - \$29,750 = \$31,250)$	8,750.00
	$13,212.50

The marriage penalty for John and Mary is $13,212.50 − $12,159.00, or $1053.50.

A Tax Benefit from Marriage   A *marriage benefit* exists for the couple whose taxable income is all earned (or nearly all) by one of the two, as Example 5-4 reveals.

Example 5-4

Rhonda and Ray's Marriage Benefit

Assume Rhonda earns $60,000 per year and Ray earns nothing. If Rhonda were single, her tax liability would be:

$0.15 \times \$17,850$	$ 2,677.50
$0.28 \times (\$60,000 - \$17,850 = \$42,150)$	11,802.00
$0.05 \times (\$60,000 - \$43,150 = \$16,850)$	842.50
Rhonda's taxes when single	$15,322.00

As married taxpayers filing jointly, Rhonda and Ray's joint tax would be calculated as follows:

$0.15 \times \$29,750$	$ 4,462.50
$0.28 \times (\$60,000 - \$2000 - \$29,750 = \$28,250)$	7,910.00
Rhonda and Ray's taxes when married	$12,372.50

Rhonda and Ray's tax saving from being married is $15,322.00 − $12,372.50, or $2949.50.

As a result of the curious effects of marriage on tax liabilities, one may expect to see taxes discussed in marital planning.

Federal Income Tax Deductions— Past and Present

The 5 percent surcharge in effect creates the following schedule of tax rates: 15 percent, 28 percent, 33 percent, and 28 percent. Thus, a taxpayer's marginal income tax rate rises *progressively* to 33 percent as the taxpayer's income rises to the upper-middle level of income and then declines *regressively* from 33 to 28 percent for the largest income producers. This progressive-then-regressive phenomenon may soon vanish, given the U.S. government's penchant for passing tax legislation. The 1986 Tax Reform Act was the culmination of a decade of passing major tax legislation every year or two. Major tax acts in recent years include:

Tax Reform Act of 1976

Revenue Act of 1978

Economic Recovery Tax Act of 1981 (ERTA)

Tax Equity and Fiscal Responsibility Act of 1982 (TEFRA)

Tax Reform Act of 1984

Tax Reform Act of 1986

The 1986 tax law was the most dramatic change of all—and most financial and political commentators expect continuing tax changes. By the time you read this text, the rate structure reported here may well have been changed by new tax legislation. Therefore, while this chapter will provide you with a good understanding of the basic nature of the tax system, you should consult the IRS regulations (available in U.S. Post Offices) before you try to calculate any precise tax liabilities.

One of the messages Congress sent the public in 1986 was that the tax structure's primary objective is to raise revenue. Many proinvestment portions of the Internal Revenue Code were repealed or watered down. Investment credit was repealed, the capital gains exclusion was repealed, tax-sheltered investments were shut down, real estate investment lost many of its tax benefits, and Individual Retirement Account (IRA) benefits were lost to many taxpayers. The political forces molding 1986 tax policy seemed determined to focus on revenue raising and to deemphasize tax incentive systems.

Capital Gains and Losses   Capital gains and losses arise out of the purchase or sale of capital assets, which include such things as securities and real estate. The exchange of these capital assets can result in either a *long-term capital gain or loss* or a *short-term capital gain or loss,* depending upon the length of the holding period. If a capital asset had been held for more than 1 year, a gain is **long term.** If a capital asset is held 1 year or less, a gain is called **short term.** Prior to 1986, long-term gains were taxed at a lower rate than short-term gains. However, in 1987 differences in taxability between long-term gains and short-term gains were eliminated. All **capital gains** (both short term and long term) are taxed as though they were ordinary income taxed at ordinary income tax rates. A maximum of $3000 per year of net capital losses (that is, total capital losses in excess of total capital gains) can be used to offset ordinary income. Any excess above the $3000 may be carried forward to future years indefinitely, until the death of the taxpayer. This is just one more example of the fact that you really "can't take it with you"—neither you nor your estate.

The historic intent of a preferential capital gains tax rate was to foster and reward risk-taking investors. Theoretically, because some people are willing to risk money developing products and processes, our economy should be more competitive with foreigners, as well as generate a higher quality of life for its citizens. The repeal in 1986 of the preferential capital gains tax rate may well have been the largest capital gains tax rate increase since the advent of the income tax in 1913. Taxpayers with incomes under $30,000 per year saw an effective tripling of their long-term capital gains tax rates. Reinstating a preferential capital gains tax rate is more than a remote possibility. The well-documented economic benefits of such a preferential tax break are too great to be ignored by the political forces shaping tax law.

Wash Sales   The **wash sale** provisions prohibit deduction of losses on the sale or exchange of securities if substantially identical securities are acquired within 30 days before or after the sale or exchange. The wash sale rules apply whether the investor voluntarily sells the stock in order to register a loss for income tax purposes, is forced to sell, or sells in order to prevent a greater loss. The provisions also apply when the investor enters into a contract or option to acquire substantially similar stock or securities. Note, however, that the wash sale rules apply only to loss transactions, not transactions involving gains. And the loss is not lost forever; recognition of a wash sale loss is merely postponed until the replacement security is finally sold.

Home Ownership as a Tax-Favored Investment   Two provisions of the 1986 tax law affecting capital gains are helpful to homeowners: (1) the one-time exclusion of up to $125,000 of gain on the sale of a principal residence by a taxpayer who is 55 or older, and (2) the nonrecognition rule for gains on the sale of a principal residence when the proceeds from the old home are reinvested in a new residence within 2 years of sale and when the purchase price of the new residence equals or exceeds the selling price of the old residence. These two provisions, in addition to the mortgage interest deduction and real estate tax deduction, continue to make home ownership a tax-favored investment.

Taxation of Futures Contracts   Prior to 1987, futures contracts enjoyed favorable capital gains tax benefits; a portion of the gain was taxed as a long-term gain and the balance as a short-term gain. However, as with other capital assets, the distinction between short and long term has been eliminated—and with it, the tax-favored status once enjoyed by investors in futures contracts.

Although the 1986 law eliminated the lower tax rate for long-term capital gains from the Internal Revenue Code, all of the other capital gains provisions remain, although their relevance is questionable. The 1986 law was drafted in this way so that a favored long-term capital gains provision could be easily reinstated into the Internal Revenue Code by changing only one section. In other words, the lawmakers seemed to doubt that this change to the tax system would last long.

Tax-Exempt Municipal Bonds

Municipal bonds are bonds issued by municipalities (states, counties, townships, cities, and school districts) to finance local projects (see Section 2-3 for more details). The Internal Revenue Code specifies that the interest income from most municipal bonds is completely exempt from federal income taxes.[2] The purpose of this tax exemption is to make it easier for small municipalities to sell their bonds and thus obtain financing for projects to improve their community. Most municipalities need the tax exemption to attract investors.

Consider an investor in the 28 percent income tax bracket who is trying to decide between a municipal bond and a corporate bond of equivalent riskiness, both of which pay a 10 percent rate of interest. On an after-tax basis, the municipal bond will pay the full 10 percent interest, whereas the corporate bond will pay only 7.2 percent.

$$
\begin{bmatrix} \text{Pretax} \\ \text{interest rate,} \\ \text{e.g., } 10\% \end{bmatrix} \times \begin{bmatrix} 1.0 - \begin{array}{c} \text{Investor's} \\ \text{income tax rate,} \\ \text{e.g., } 28\% \end{array} \end{bmatrix} = \begin{array}{c} \text{After-tax} \\ \text{interest rate,} \\ \text{e.g., } 7.2\% \end{array}
$$

Since 72 percent of the 10 percent interest rate equals a 7.2 percent after-tax return, the investor will do better with the tax-exempt municipal bond.

The higher an investor's income tax bracket, the more incentive there is for the investor to seek tax-exempt bond interest. This fact is illustrated in Table 5-3, which shows the after-tax rates of return for investors in three income tax

[2]When a municipality issues *industrial development bonds* to finance business development, the income may be *alternative minimum taxable income* (AMTI) and may be subject to the AMTI tax (instead of ordinary income tax). The AMTI is too complicated and affects too few to concern most investors; it is, therefore, not discussed further in this chapter.

Table 5-3

AFTER-TAX RETURNS FOR INVESTORS IN THREE TAX BRACKETS

Various before-tax returns			
Three federal income tax brackets			After-tax returns
15%	28%	33%	
5.29%	6.25%	6.75%	4.50%
5.88	6.94	7.50	5.00
6.47	7.64	8.25	5.50
7.06	8.33	9.01	6.00
7.65	9.03	9.75	6.50
8.24	9.72	10.49	7.00
8.82	10.42	11.24	7.50
9.41	11.11	12.00	8.00

brackets. For instance, an investor in the 33 percent tax bracket must earn a before-tax rate of return of 12 percent in order to get an after-tax return of 8 percent. This 8 percent after-tax return is computed by multiplying the 12 percent before-tax return by 100 percent minus 33 percent, or 67 percent.

Rental Real Estate The 1986 Tax Reform Act states that losses from *passive* activities (as opposed to activities involving material participation by the investor) can be used only to offset other passive income (but not ordinary or portfolio income).[3] Included in such passive activities are real estate investments. Thus, even investors who actively participate in the management of rental real estate cannot offset excess real estate losses with ordinary income or portfolio income. There is one small exception: When an individual actively participates in rental real estate activities, up to $25,000 of losses from these activities may be taken in each year against ordinary and portfolio income.[4]

Tax-Sheltered Retirement Plans Tax shelters for individuals' contributions to their own retirement funds are provided because the federal government does not want elderly people to become wards of the state. In fact, several **tax-sheltered retirement plans** are in the federal tax laws. These plans are essentially savings plans, but they offer two tax incentives. First, the money saved from current income and put in these retirement plans may be deducted from gross income to determine taxable income. Second, the interest income, cash dividends, and any capital gains are not taxable until the taxpayer retires and actually receives the retirement funds. This tax deferment is advantageous because most people will be in a lower income tax bracket after they retire.

To see how tax-sheltered retirement plans work, consider Example 5-5.

Example 5-5

Saving for Retirement Cuts Income Taxes

An individual who has $20,700 taxable income and is subject to an average tax rate of 20 percent saves $1500 in a tax-sheltered retirement plan. This retirement saver enjoys an income tax savings of $300 by putting $1500 aside for retirement.

[3]The 1986 Tax Act eliminated virtually all of the traditional passive investments that were designed to generate tax losses in excess of income in order to reduce an individual's total tax liability. These **tax shelters** generally involved oil and gas, equipment leasing, and real estate.

[4]The $25,000 exception for rental loss write-offs is phased out ratably between $100,000 and $150,000 of adjusted gross income. The $25,000 rental real estate exception is available to each married couple filing a joint return; the $25,000 exception is also available to each single individual. This is one more marriage penalty in the tax law: two married people are allowed one $25,000 exemption, but two single people are allowed two $25,000 exemptions.

		Without retirement plan	With retirement plan
	Taxable income	$20,700	$20,700
less:	Contributions to retirement plan	0	1,500
	Taxable income	$20,700	$19,200
times:	Average tax rate	0.20	0.20
	Income taxes	$ 4,140	$ 3,840

The income tax savings from the plan is $4140 − $3840, or $300.

There are many types of tax-sheltered retirement plans, including pension plans, profit-sharing plans, 401K plans, IRAs, and Keogh plans, to name a few. Pension and profit-sharing plans typically are employer-paid benefits. Most large corporations provide one or more such plans. Employees included in these plans do not pay income taxes on these delayed and indirect forms of compensation until they retire and begin receiving their benefits.

Pension and Profit-Sharing Plans

The provisions of employer-provided pension and profit-sharing plans vary with each corporation. There are certain parameters within which each plan must stay, however. These parameters are defined by the Pension Reform Act of 1974, also known as the **Employee Retirement Income Security Act,** or simply **ERISA.** For example, vesting is one of many issues for which ERISA provides guidelines. **Vesting** occurs when an employee obtains a legally enforceable claim on pension benefits such that the benefits cannot be taken away even if that person resigns or is dismissed. There are many different vesting plans, but in general complete vesting must occur within a 3- to 7-year period. Each corporation's written pension plan must meet official government approval prior to adoption.[5]

401K Plans

A plan that has been gaining popularity in recent years is the 401K plan (named for Section 401 of the Internal Revenue Code, which created it). This plan differs from the others in that it provides for employee contributions in addition to employer contributions. The great advantage is that the employee contributions (in addition to the employer's contribution) are excluded from the employee's taxable income until withdrawals begin.

Contributions and all earnings thereon accumulate tax-free until withdrawn by the employee. Plans differ among companies, and Congress changes the guidelines frequently. The maximum contribution is the lesser of some stipulated percentage of wages (as provided for in the plan) or $7313 adjusted annually for inflation. The employee benefits of both (1) a retirement plan and (2)

[5]ERISA is discussed more fully in Chapter 4, entitled Securities Law.

a tax shelter on current income have caused a proliferation of such tax-deferred retirement plans.[6]

Keogh Plans

Keogh plans are sometimes referred to as *H.R. 10 plans* or *self-employed retirement plans*. In the past the rules governing Keogh plans were much more restrictive than for corporate profit-sharing plans. But recent legislation has established parity between corporate plans and self-employed (or Keogh) retirement plans. One effect of this new parity is that one major reason for incorporating a business (namely, the more favorable corporate retirement plan benefits) has been eliminated.

Self-employed individuals can invest up to 25 percent of their annual net income from their business into a tax-deferred Keogh plan. There is a $30,000 annual maximum allowable deduction. However, people who receive profit-sharing pension benefits from their employers are limited to a 15 percent maximum annual deduction from the income they receive from their employer. Employed individuals who receive profit-sharing pension benefits from their employers and also own a profitable business are allowed to use Keogh plan investing to supplement the 15 percent maximum on the profit-sharing pension plan provided by their employer.

Individual Retirement Accounts (IRA)

All taxpayers are allowed to contribute the lesser of $2000 per year or their total earned income to an IRA (or $2250 for spousal IRAs). But not all taxpayers are allowed to deduct their IRA contributions from their gross income in order to arrive at their taxable income. Only those individuals who are not active participants in employer-maintained retirement plans *and* who have *adjusted gross incomes* of not greater than $40,000 ($25,000 for single individuals) are allowed to fully deduct such contributions. For individuals who are active participants in an employer-maintained retirement plan with adjusted gross incomes over $40,000 ($25,000 for single individuals), the deductible portion of the contribution is reduced on the basis of adjusted gross income before reductions by deductible IRA contributions. Zero deduction is allowed for

[6]Employees of not-for-profit institutions (like college professors and hospital employees) may have tax-deferred annuities (such as the Supplemental Retirement Annuities under TIAA-CREF, for example) under Section 403b of the Internal Revenue Code. IRS regulations allow these employees to contribute up to almost 17 percent of their pretax gross salary, subject to a limitation based on their base retirement plan (which the employer provides, for example, the basic TIAA-CREF pension). Any withdrawals made before age 59.5 are subject to a 10 percent penalty plus the ordinary income tax on the total withdrawal. Up to $50,000 can be borrowed out of a 403b tax-deferred annuity without any penalty, however. These loans must be repaid systematically within 5 years unless the loan is used to finance the employee's primary residence.

Table 5-4
IRA DEDUCTIONS FOR JOINT FILERS

Adjusted gross income	Retirement plan	No retirement plan
0 to $40,000	Full IRA deduction	Full IRA deduction
$40,000 to $50,000	Partial deduction	Full deduction
$50,000 and up	No deduction	Full deduction

individuals with adjusted gross income of $50,000 or more ($35,000 or more for single individuals). These rules are summarized in Table 5-4. For married taxpayers, the phase-out and loss of deductions applies when either spouse is covered by an employer-provided retirement plan. That is, when one spouse is covered by an employer-provided retirement plan, *neither* spouse is allowed to have an IRA deduction—yet another *marriage penalty* built into the federal tax system.

Those individuals *not* qualifying for an IRA income tax deduction for their contributions must meet IRS bookkeeping requirements. Form 8606 is required to be filed with the individual's annual income tax return. Failure to file this nondeductible IRA contribution form subjects the taxpayer to a $50 penalty. The form must reflect the aggregate balance of all individual retirement plans as of the end of the calendar year in which the taxable year begins. Since the nondeductible IRA contribution achieves only tax deferral of the investment income earned by the IRA, some investors have decided that the additional bookkeeping costs are greater than the tax benefit and have therefore chosen other investment options.

People who establish IRAs must select investment vehicles for their retirement contributions. Popular IRA investment vehicles include common stocks, bonds, or a savings account. Most mutual funds, banks, and savings and loan associations actively solicit IRA contributions. Since 1987, taxpayers may also hold gold and silver coins issued by the United States in their IRAs.

An IRA participant can make contributions every year or only occasionally. To discourage people from using IRAs, 401K plans, and pension profit-sharing plans as savings pools to evade (or, at least, delay) income taxes, a penalty of 10 percent is levied on any withdrawals made before the contributor reaches the age of 59.5. In addition, the entire amount of the early withdrawal becomes immediately subject to ordinary income taxes. These fines make it unprofitable to use an IRA as a tax shelter for short-run savings.

Tax planning should not be discontinued after a taxpayer reaches retirement age. Estate taxes must be paid on the value of a deceased person's assets. Furthermore, gift taxes, which are imposed to stop people who are near death from giving away their wealth in order to avoid estate taxes, must be considered also.

5-2   ESTATE TAXES AND GIFT TAXES

Estate planning is something that affluent people should do in order to keep their wealth from being taken away by estate taxes. We will discuss estate taxes first, and then consider tax-exempt gifts as a legal way to reduce estate taxes.

Estate Taxes

Dead people do not pay taxes, but their estates do. Federal **estate taxes** (or death taxes) are progressive. The estate-tax schedule is shown in Table 5-5.

A deceased taxpayer's net taxable estate is less than the gross estate because of deductions allowed by the tax law. For married people, the most significant deduction is the **marital deduction,** which is unlimited. The marital deduction can eliminate estate taxes when the first spouse dies. However, the problem of estate tax minimization remains with the surviving spouse.

Gift Taxes

To maximize the portion of their estate that the heirs may inherit, some people make gifts to eliminate the appreciated value of the donated assets from their taxable estates. But not all gifts are tax free. Any time one person gives money

Table 5-5
UNIFIED FEDERAL ESTATE AND GIFT TAX RATES*

(1) Over	But not over	Tax on (1)	Tax rate on excess over (1)
$ 0	$ 10,000	$ 0	18%
10,000	20,000	1,800	20
20,000	40,000	3,800	22
40,000	60,000	8,200	24
60,000	80,000	13,000	26
80,000	100,000	18,200	28
100,000	150,000	23,800	30
150,000	250,000	38,800	32
250,000	500,000	70,800	34
500,000	750,000	155,800	37
750,000	1,000,000	248,300	39
1,000,000	1,250,000	345,800	41
1,250,000	1,500,000	448,300	43
1,500,000	2,000,000	555,800	45
2,000,000	2,500,000	780,800	49
2,500,000	3,000,000	1,025,800	53
3,000,000		1,290,800	55

*Lifetime transfers (gifts) and transfers at death are added together for the purpose of determining the applicable rate for transfers at death.

to another person without receiving goods or services of equal value in return, the IRS considers this transfer of wealth to be subject to the unified transfer tax shown in Table 5-5.[7] However, there is a generous tax credit applicable to the unified transfer tax, as we shall see next, and there are also other gift tax exemptions.

Up to $10,000 per year may be gifted to as many people as a taxpayer desires without incurring any tax. Unlimited amounts may be given to one's spouse tax free. When the gift-giver dies, the deceased person's total taxable gifts are added to the estate, and the unified estate and gift tax schedule shown in Table 5-5 is applicable.

The taxes shown in Table 5-5 apply to the total amount of taxable gifts given before the donor dies plus the taxable estate of the donor. Stated differently, the deceased person's taxable gifts are added to the deceased person's taxable estate and the total is taxed using Table 5-5. The first $600,000 of transfers are exempt from the unified transfer tax. This $600,000 exemption is equivalent to a tax credit of $192,800 subtracted from the estate and gift unified tax. The $192,800 credit is in addition to the $10,000 annual exclusions and the unlimited marital deductions.

Example 5-6

Mr. John White's Estate Taxes

John White, a widower, dies with a taxable estate of $800,000. Four years before his death John gave his son and his daughter gifts of $100,000 apiece. The net estate tax of the late Mr. White is calculated below.

John White's taxable estate	$800,000
plus: Two $100,000 gifts	200,000
less: Two annual gift tax exclusions	20,000
Adjusted taxable estate	$980,000
Estate tax from Table 5-5	$338,000
less: Unified credit	192,800
Net estate tax	$145,200

5-3

FEDERAL CORPORATE INCOME TAXES

Unlike people, corporations may live forever. Even if a corporation's life ends (for instance, in bankruptcy), it incurs no gift or estate taxes. However, corporations must pay taxes on income.

[7]Estate and gift taxes are also known as *unified transfer taxes;* both are subject to the same tax rates, as shown in Table 5-5.

Corporations are legal entities that exist to allow the ownership of a firm to be subdivided into shares that are readily transferable. Unlike a proprietorship or a partnership, both of which are considered to be extensions of their owners, corporations are treated by the law as separate entities. As a result, income earned by corporations is taxed twice. First, profitable corporations pay corporate income taxes of about one-third of every dollar of earnings. Second, the people who own the corporation's shares must also pay federal income taxes on whatever dividends and capital gains their shares yield. Many people believe **double taxation** weakens the incentive to make corporate investments that strengthen the U.S. economy. On the bright side, however, the corporate income tax structure is simple.

Corporate Tax Structure

A corporation must pay federal income tax according to three different tax rates, as shown in Table 5-6. For example, consider a corporation that earns $80,000 of taxable income. This corporation would pay a total federal income tax of $15,450, as shown in Example 5-7.

As Table 5-6 shows, **marginal tax rates** (or progressive tax rates) on corporate income vary from 15 to 34 percent. But Example 5-7 shows that the **average tax rate** is 19.3 percent. (That is, the total tax of $15,450 is 19.3 percent of the total income of $80,000.) The average corporate tax rate starts at the minimum marginal tax rate of 15 percent for incomes of $50,000 or less and rises toward the maximum marginal tax rate of 34 percent as corporate income increases. Most large corporations pay 34 percent taxes on almost their entire annual earnings in profitable years.

Table 5-6
FEDERAL CORPORATE INCOME TAX RATES*

For taxable income	The tax rate is
Not over $50,000	15%
Over $50,000 but not over $75,000	25%
Over $75,000	34%

*The benefit of the lower and progressive 15 and 25 percent corporate income tax brackets begins to be phased out when a corporation's taxable income reaches $100,000. This phase-out occurs via a *5 percent surcharge*. The benefit of graduated rates is fully phased out for corporations with more than $335,000 of taxable income. Stated differently, the corporate marginal income tax rate is effectively 39 percent for incomes between $100,000 and $335,000.

Example 5-7

Computation of Federal Income Tax on $80,000 of Corporation Income

Marginal tax rate	times	Portion of total income	equals	Portion of total tax
15%	×	$50,000	=	$ 7,500
25	×	25,000*	=	6,250
34	×	5,000†	=	1,700
	Totals	$80,000		$15,450‡

*The amount between the first $50,000 and $75,000.
†The amount over the first $75,000.
‡The corporation's **average tax rate** is 19.3 percent because the total tax of $15,450 is 19.3 percent of the total income of $80,000.

Interest Expense

Corporations are allowed to deduct interest they pay on borrowed funds from their gross income to arrive at their taxable income. The deductibility of interest encourages corporations to pay for purchases with borrowed money rather than to wait until they can save enough cash to pay for the purchase. One effect of this accelerated spending is to stimulate the U.S. economy by creating more sales of goods and thus more jobs. Another effect is the proliferation of leveraged companies.

Corporate Income Statements

Although the corporate income tax structure is simple, measuring a corporation's taxable income is complicated. Table 5-7 outlines the essentials of an accountant's income statement. Despite the seeming simplicity, many questions arise concerning definitions and measurements of the various items determining income. For answers to these questions, the accounting profession can turn to several sources.

Generally accepted accounting principles (GAAP) are followed by virtually all practicing accountants in the United States. But more than one procedure may be acceptable for reporting a business transaction. The American Institute of Certified Public Accountants (AICPA) hands down opinions on which practices are acceptable and which are not. Often these opinions eliminate the less desirable (that is, the extreme or the completely ambiguous) alternatives while still allowing several accounting choices. The result is a narrowing of practices but not the creation of uniform accounting. Thus, the same economic event can often be legitimately reported in more than one way.

The body of accounting practice has also been shaped by professional organizations, government agencies, and legislative acts. The most important institutions influencing accounting practices are the SEC, the AICPA, Financial Accounting Standards Board (FASB), and the IRS.

Table 5-7

FORMAT FOR CORPORATE INCOME STATEMENTS

Sales revenue
  less: Cost of goods sold

Gross operating margin
  less: Selling and administrative expenses and depreciation

Net operating income (earnings before interest and taxes)
  less: Interest expense

Taxable income
  less: Taxes

Net income
  less: Dividends on preferred stock

Net income for common equity
  less: Dividends to common equity

Retained earnings

Persons unfamiliar with the complexity of accounting procedures often assume that corporate income is a clearly defined quantity; the financial statements published in annual reports do not seem open to dispute. The following quotation from a widely used intermediate accounting textbook gives a truer picture.[8]

> The measurement of periodic income of a business enterprise is perhaps the foremost objective of the accounting process. The word *estimate* is appropriate because income is one of the most elusive concepts in the business world. The art of accounting probably never will progress to the point where "income" can be defined to everyone's satisfaction.

Some groups of investors are not so concerned about how their incomes are measured because they are exempt from income taxes, as we shall see next.

5-4   **TAX-EXEMPT INVESTORS**

To prevent double taxation and to encourage charitable giving, certain conduit-type investment organizations are allowed to operate either partially or totally free from income taxes. Some of these income tax exemptions are granted to the biggest investors in the world. As a result of these exemptions, some large

[8]A. N. Mosich and E. John Larsen, *Intermediate Accounting*, 5th ed. (New York: McGraw-Hill, 1982), p. 85.

investors do not buy tax-exempt municipal bonds or pursue other tax-avoidance strategies. The major categories of investors are discussed below.[9]

Pension Plans

Employee pensions, stock bonus plans, and profit-sharing plans can accumulate funds and earn tax-free income on those funds. However, the funds are taxable income to the retired employees of the sponsoring organization when they receive the benefits. Since pension funds are the largest investors in the United States, they represent a multibillion dollar pool of income tax-free investment money.

Investment Companies

Investment companies (which include mutual funds and closed-end funds) can choose to be taxed as **regulated investment companies.** To qualify for this income tax exemption, an investment company must invest in a diversified portfolio of securities and pay out all capital gains, cash dividends, and interest income in the same year that the income was realized. The purpose of this law's two stipulations is to stop investment companies from being used as holding companies for accumulating assets and thus building corporate empires, or as tax avoidance devices that accumulate tax-free income for investors. The income paid out by regulated investment companies becomes a taxable part of the shareholder's total income when it is realized by the shareholder. This realized income may be automatically reinvested in the same investment company immediately if the investor desires. However, taxes must be paid even though the realized income was reinvested.

Trusts

Individuals sometimes place monies into **trusts** for a variety of reasons—such as asset management, asset protection, estate planning, or charity funding. Lawyers call the contracts between the benefactor and the trust manager **fiduciary agreements.** If the trust fund distributes all of its income to the trust's beneficiaries, the receiving beneficiaries must pay income taxes on that income (unless they too are tax-exempt organizations)—the trust pays no income taxes if all income is distributed. However, if income is accumulated in the trust, the trust can be taxed.

Charities and Foundations

Nonprofit charities, religious groups, and educational foundations are allowed to invest their endowments and earn income that is free from income taxes if certain annual payments are made. There are different tax regulations for different types of charities and foundations. However, a minimum of 5 percent of the assets or all earned income, whichever is larger, must be paid out an-

[9]The income from subchapter S corporations is generally exempt from income taxes. However, most subchapter S corporations do not own a portfolio of investment securities.

nually. If a foundation performs the modest annual expenditures required by law, it need only pay an excise tax of 1 to 2 percent on its income.

5-5   **SUMMARY AND CONCLUSIONS**

Both private individuals and corporate entities are required by law to pay income taxes. Individual income tax rates are progressive for lower incomes, regressive for upper incomes, and proportional for the highest income levels. Progressive gift and estate taxes encourage careful estate planning in order to minimize the government's share of the wealth of the deceased.

One of the many objectives of the 1986 Tax Reform Act was to restore a perception of fairness to the federal income tax. Too many wealthy people had been paying very little tax via perfectly legal means. And too many taxpayers knew of people who did not declare their income to the government and thus evaded taxes.[10] For these reasons, the 1986 Tax Reform Act was a tax bill with teeth. Gone are tax shelters as we once knew them; gone is the low preferential tax rate on long-term capital gains; but perhaps most important, gone is much of the driving incentive to avoid taxation. The top tax rates tumbled from 1981's high of 70 percent to 1988's high of 28 to 33 percent. Perhaps these lower rates are the best tax shelter ever contrived.[11]

Essay Questions

5-1   Name three allowable deductions from adjusted gross income that can be used in arriving at a person's taxable income; do the same for a corporation's taxable income.

5-2   How is the corporate federal income tax rate structured?

5-3   What are the major benefits of investing in an IRA?

5-4   What are the disadvantages of investing in an IRA?

5-5   What is the difference between marginal and average tax rates?

[10]Peter M. Gutmann, "The Subterranean Economy," *Financial Analysts Journal*, Nov.–Dec. 1977; P. M. Gutmann, "Are the Unemployed, Unemployed?" *Financial Analysts Journal*, Sept.–Oct. 1978; P. M. Gutmann, "The Subterranean Economy Five Years Later," *Across the Board*, Feb. 1983, vol. xx, no. 2 (the Conference Board Magazine).
[11]This chapter presents only a thumbnail sketch of the federal tax laws. Many details were omitted, and state taxes were ignored completely. Therefore, do not think that this chapter can be used to train tax experts. There are college-level tax-accounting courses available for would-be tax experts.

5-6 Do you believe that the income tax system in the United States should be (*a*) graduated upward (also called progressive) or (*b*) graduated downward (also called regressive)? Explain your choice. *Hint: It would probably be a good idea to get a welfare economics textbook and read about progressive and regressive taxes.*

5-7 Is the personal income tax structure in the United States progressive, regressive, or what? Explain.

5-8 When and why did the United States enact income taxes? *Hint: Consult an economic history textbook.*

5-9 One way to define *capital assets* is in terms of the kind of income they produce. A capital asset produces *capital gains* income if its price appreciates. (*a*) Give a different definition of capital assets that does not refer to the income the capital asset produces. (*b*) Can the following four assets be correctly called capital assets? (1) General Motors' inventory of automobile engines. (2) GM's inventory of finished cars. (3) Ms. Jones' inventory of stocks and bonds. (4) Merrill Lynch, Pierce, Fenner & Smith's inventory of securities.

Problems

5-10 Assume the adjusted gross income (not including capital gains and losses) of Mr. and Mrs. Taylor, filing a joint return, is $20,000 in 1989. The Taylors, during the taxable year, also had $5000 in capital gains and $6000 in capital losses. Figure the Taylors' tax due, assuming no other deductions or inflation adjustment in 1991.

5-11 Jack Lind has a marginal tax rate of 33 percent and must choose between a tax-free municipal bond paying 6 percent and a taxable security paying 8 percent. Which security should he choose? Explain why.

5-12 After being happily married for many years, Mary Jones died in 1987. Her husband John passed away in 1988. The value of their estate was $1,800,000 at the time of Mary's death and $2,000,000 when John died. In 1983 John and Mary had given $500,000 to their only child. Based on these facts, what is Mary's taxable estate and estate tax due? What is John's taxable estate and estate tax due?

5-13 The one-period rate of return from an investment in common stock is calculated with the formula below if the investor purchases the stock at $50 per share, sells it at $58 per share, collects $2 per share cash dividend, and is tax-exempt.

$$\text{One-period rate of return} = \frac{\text{price change } + \text{ cash dividend, if any}}{\text{purchase price}}$$

The rate of return that is calculated with the formula above is 20 percent.

$$\frac{(\$58 - \$50) + \$2}{\$50} = \frac{\$8 + \$2}{\$50} = \frac{\$10}{\$50} = 0.2 \times 100 = 20 \text{ percent return}$$

(*a*) Calculate the after-tax one-period rate of return from this common stock investment if a tax rate of 28 percent is charged on both capital gains (that is, changes in the stock's price) and cash dividends. Show the formula you use (with all parts labeled) and your calculations. (*b*) How is the after-tax one-period rate of return calculated if the tax rate on capital gains is half the tax rate on ordinary income and the tax rate on ordinary income and cash dividends is 28 percent? Show the formula you use and your calculations.

References

Kess, Sidney, and Bertil Weslin, *Estate Planning Guide* (Chicago: Commerce Clearing House, 1986).

This book is a comprehensive analysis of estate planning for most types of situations.

Prentice-Hall, *Federal Tax Course* (Englewood Cliffs, N.J.: Prentice-Hall, annual).

A comprehensive text, revised annually, that explains the tax law with numerous examples.

U.S. Treasury Dept., Internal Revenue Service, *A Guide to Federal Estate and Gift Taxation,* Publication 448 (Washington, D.C.: Government Printing Office, annual).

This publication is a concise summary of federal estate and gift taxes. Examples are sparse; legal terms are plentiful. There is no mathematics.

U.S. Treasury Department, Internal Revenue Service, *Tax Guide for Small Business,* Publication 334 (Washington, D.C.: Government Printing Office, annual).

This publication explains the tax laws that apply to businesses, including sole proprietorships, partnerships, and corporations. There is no mathematics.

U.S. Treasury Department, Internal Revenue Service, *Your Federal Income Tax,* Publication 17 (Washington, D.C.: Government Printing Office, annual).

This publication explains many specific problems and gives examples. There is no mathematics.

Chapter 6

Sources of Financial Information

Investments analysis typically begins with an inquiry into world affairs, because wars and international tensions affect nations' economies and securities markets. After the world and national situations have been considered, the analyst can focus on specific industries. Labor negotiations, changes in legislation, sales, and competition within the industry are considered. After this background investigation has been completed, the financial analyst is ready to examine a particular firm.

The remainder of this chapter explores sources of information about world affairs, national economies, industries, and individual firms. Computer databases that provide economic financial data are also suggested. Security market indexes, another source of reference information that can be useful to investors, are the topic of Chapter 7.

6-1 EXAMPLES OF SOME POPULAR SOURCES OF INFORMATION

The services that provide economic and financial information make up a bustling industry. Each year more people develop an interest in investment news; therefore, demands on the industry are growing. Some of the information sources that are popular with many investors are discussed below.

World Affairs *The New York Times* and *The Wall Street Journal* are two useful newspapers. These papers carry current reports on political and economic conditions around the world.[1]

[1]The *Economist* and the *Financial Times* are international periodicals published in London that are useful to international investors; they are both expensive.

National Affairs   The price movements of most securities are, in large part, attributable to systematic movements that simultaneously affect all securities markets in the nation. These undiversifiable price movements reflect changes that many financial analysts anticipate in the national economy. As a result, forecasting the level and direction of the national economy is a useful way to predict bullish and bearish security price movements.[2]

The National Bureau of Economic Research (NBER) studies business cycles by using widely publicized **economic indicators.** Its findings are published by the Census Bureau. Each month *Business Conditions Digest* (BCD) charts the values of the NBER's economic indicators.[3] In the first part of the issue, 30 leading indicators, 15 coincidental indicators, 7 lagging indicators, and 7 international comparisons are given, along with other economic information. The final section of BCD examines trends, cyclical indicators, and other data. Figure 6-1 contains a sample of the graphs that are published in BCD. Note the darkened vertical strips in Figure 6-1; they delineate official NBER recessions.

The Research Department of the St. Louis Federal Reserve Bank publishes weekly and monthly economic newsletters that contain excellent monetary economic analyses.[4]

Investment Information Services   Syntheses of financial information about industries and individual firms are published by various investment information services. Such firms offer subscriptions to their daily, weekly, and monthly publications. The Internal Revenue Service allows the costs of subscribing to sources of investment information to be deducted from an investor's taxable income. Or, public libraries usually carry the publications of one or more of these services which may be consulted without charge. The leading investment information services are:

Standard & Poor's Corporation (owned by McGraw-Hill)
25 Broadway
New York, N.Y. 10004

Moody's Investor Services, Inc. (owned by Dun & Bradstreet)
99 Church Street
New York, N.Y. 10007

The Value Line, Inc. (majority owned by the family of the late Arnold
   Bernhard, founder of the firm).
711 Third Avenue
New York, N.Y. 10017

[2]Geoffrey H. Moore, *Business Cycles, Inflation, and Forecasting,* National Bureau of Economic Research Study Number 24 (Cambridge, Mass.: Ballinger, 1980), pp. 187–202.
[3]A 1-year subscription to BCD costs $44.00. To subscribe, write to Superintendent of Documents, U.S. Government Printing Office, Washington, D.C. 20402.
[4]For subscriptions, write to the Federal Reserve Bank of St. Louis, P.O. Box 442, St. Louis, Mo. 63166.

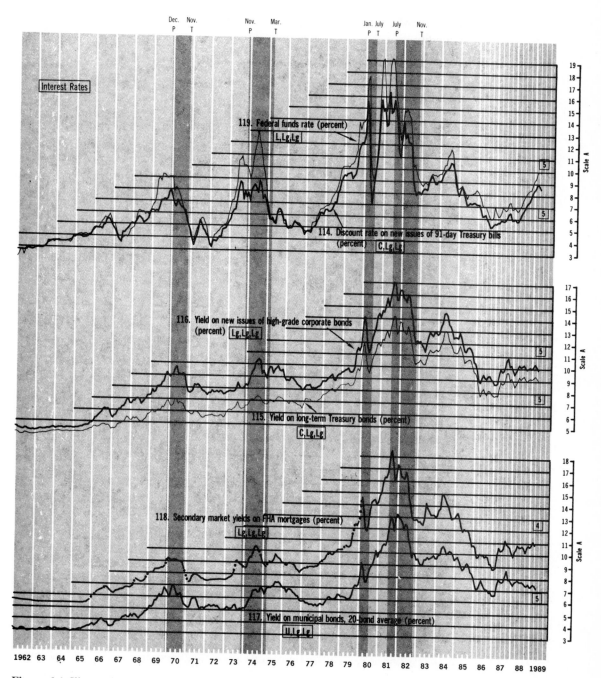

Figure 6-1 Illustrative page from *Business Conditions Digest*.

S&P's Outlook   A weekly publication of S&P named the *Outlook* surveys market conditions, recommends common stocks, discusses stocks that are in favor, reports on overall business conditions, and contains data on S&P's 90 different industry stock price indexes. Figure 7-1 shows some market indexes from the *Outlook*. The major Standard and Poor's stock price indexes are illustrated graphically in Figure 9-2. Moody's publishes the *Stock Survey*, which is similar to Standard & Poor's *Outlook*.

Stock Guide   S&P publishes the monthly pocket-sized pamphlet entitled *Stock Guide* and the similar *Bond Guide*. These two monthly booklets contain many salient financial statistics. Figure 6-2 shows two adjacent pages of the *Stock Guide*. It also lists the categories "stocks for potential appreciation," "recommended stocks primarily for appreciation," "candidates for dividend increases," "candidates for stock splits," and "25 of the best low-priced stocks." The back pages of the *Stock Guide* contain data about the hundreds of mutual funds. S&P's *Bond Guide* provides summary statistics for thousands of corporate bond issues in a form similar to that of the *Stock Guide*.

Moody's Handbook of Common Stocks   Four times a year *Moody's Handbook of Common Stocks* provides a brief summary of about 1000 firms. Figure 6-3 shows a sample page. For each firm the price is charted; the firm's background, current developments, and future prospects are summarized; and several years of financial statistics are reported. S&P's counterpart to *Moody's Handbook* is the *Stock Market Encyclopedia*.

Value Line Investment Survey   The *Value Line Investment Survey* differs from the Moody's and S&P publications. Value Line reports on 1400 stocks in 60 industries, covering each stock in detail once per quarter. Figure 6-4 shows one of Value Line's reports on a firm.

A unique feature of Value Line's service is its investment scoring system. Value Line rates every stock from 1 to 5 with respect to four factors: quality, performance in the next 12 months, appreciation potential in 3 to 5 years, and income from dividends. Value Line suggests that investors select securities with the highest weighted average rating. Investors select the weights to be assigned to each rated item to reflect their investment preferences.[5] Studies suggest that Value Line's recommendations are better than picking stocks randomly. Such favorable studies have not been published for other investment advisory services by unbiased outside researchers.

A Caveat About Timeliness   In viewing the exhibits discussed in this chapter, it is important to remember that these examples become invalid and, in some

[5]For analysis of Value Line's investment advice see T. E. Copeland and D. Mayers, "The Value Line Enigma (1965–1978): A Case Study of Performance Evaluation Issues," *Journal of Financial Economics*, Nov. 1982, vol. 10, no. 3. Also see the references cited in this article for similar studies.

118 INT-INT Standard & Poor's Corporation

¶S&P 500 •Options Index	Ticker Symbol	Name of Issue (Call Price of Pfd. Stocks)	Market	Com. Rank. & Pfd. Rating	Par Val.	Inst. Hold Cos	Inst. Hold Shs. (000)	Principal Business	Price Range 1971-87 High	1971-87 Low	1988 High	1988 Low	1989 High	1989 Low	Feb. Sales in 100s	February, 1989 Last Sale Or Bid High	Low	Last	%Div Yield	P-E Ratio
1	ILCO	Intercont'l Life	OTC	B−	2/3	2	9	Accident,health,life insur	17¼	5/16	14⅝	9	11⅛	9½	252	11	11	11B	...	10
2	IFSIA	Interface Inc'A'	OTC	A−	10¢	81	10880	Mfrs free lying carpet tile	16¼	3¼	16⅝	8⅜	16½	14⅞	12984	16½	15½	16B	1.3	14
3	INTF	Interface Systems	OTC	B+	10¢	20	666	Mfrs IBM compatible printers	11	⅝	7⅞	5	7¾	7⅛	1906	7⅝	7⅛	7¼B	...	10
4	IFSC	Interferon Sci's	OTC	NR	1¢	2	40	Research on interferon-devl	10⅞	2¼	6¼	2½	5⅝	3⅝	1117	5⅝	4¼	4¾B	...	d
¶5•[1]	INGR	Intergraph Corp	OTC	B+	10¢	216	34586	Computer graphics systems	40½	3⅞	32½	19¼	22¾	19½	80884	22¾	19½	20B	...	13
6	IHEIF	Interhome Energy	OTC,Mo,To	↓B+	No	47	1591	Longest NoAmer petrol pipeln	41⅞	9⅞	40½	32⅝	39¾	35⅝	40	39¾	37½	38B	♦4.4	15
7	INSY	Interim Systems	OTC	NR	1¢	50	12746	Temporary personnel service	2¼	1⅛	4	1⅜	3¼	2 7/16	7650	3	2½	2½B	...	15
¶8	IK	Interlake, Corp	NY,B,M,P	B+	1	123	5494	Diversified ind'l mfg co	55	6½	46¾	38⅝	45¼	41¾	4346	44¾	42½	43	3.5	11
9	LEAF	Interleaf Inc	OTC	NR	1¢	77	6725	Computer aids for publishing	24⅛	7½	21⅜	6⅜	9½	6⅝	24032	9⅜	6¾	8⅜B	...	36
10	INMA	Intermagnetics Gen'l	OTC	C	10¢	18	1025	Mfr superconductive mtls	23⅜	3⅛	6⅝	3⅞	7⅛	6	5384	7	6⅛	6½B	...	38
11	IMI	Intermark Inc	AS	B−	1	18	844	Broadly diversified holding co	16½	⅛	14⅞	8⅜	15	13	3653	15	13¾	14⅝	0.9	6
12	Pr	Ptc Pfd(NC)	AS	NR	1	3	82		14½	7⅛	12½	8⅜	11⅞	10¾	211	11⅞	11	11¼B	1.1	..
13	INTR	Intermec Corp	OTC	B	60¢	69	3441	Mfr printing/reading prdts	22¼	1/16	22½	12⅞	24	18⅝	23091	23⅝	20¾	20¾B	...	19
14	INMT	Intermet Corp	OTC	B	10¢	38	2515	Iron foundry-auto indus	19	4¾	14	8	11⅛	8⅝	12756	11⅛	9	10⅞B	1.8	14
15	IMET	Intermetrics Inc	OTC	B−	1¢	7	578	Computer software prod & svc	20¾	2¼	5½	2⅝	6	4¾	441	5¾	4¾	5½B	...	10
16	IAL	Int'l Aluminum	NY,B,M,P	B+	1	44	1870	Mfr & sale aluminum prod	24¾	1	29¾	18	27⅜	25½	595	27⅜	26½	27⅜	3.2	8
17	HOME	Int'l American Homes	OTC	NR	1¢	8	376	Home building/financing	8¼	1⅝	2 5/16	1¼	1⅞	1 7/16	3314	1⅞	1 9/16	1 11/16B	...	3
18	IBK	Int'l Banknote	AS,B,M,P,Ph	C	1	23	4228	Prints securities,currencies	10⅜	¼	4⅜	2⅝	4¼	3	13089	4⅛	3⅛	4	...	44
19	IBCA	Int'l Broadcasting	OTC	NR	.001	8	155	Promotes entrnmt attractions	18⅛	¾	14⅜	7⅝	12⅝	8½	4092	12⅝	9⅞	10B	...	d
¶20•[2]	IBM	Int'l Bus. Machines	[3]NY,B,C,M,P,Ph	A+	1¼	1772	289758	Lgst mfr business machines	175⅞	37⅝	129½	104¼	130⅞	120⅝	286975	130⅞	120⅝	121½	3.6	13
21	BZU	IBM,Americus(Unit)	AS,M	NR	No	12	3990	Unit Trust for IBM	166	113½	128¾	107	129½	126¼	15	129½	126¼	121B	3.6	..
22	BZS	Score	AS,M	NR	No	9	1572	capital appreciation	58	14⅛	24⅛	8⅛	13¼	9½	7115	13¼	10½	10¾	...	..
23	BZP	Prime	AS,M	NR	No	57	3271	divd income pay'g component	126½	88½	115⅜	92¾	117½	111	976	117½	111	111¼	3.9	..
24	ICSI	Int'l Container Sys	OTC	NR	1¢	6	219	Mfrs plastic beverage cases	15⅞	2½	7⅜	2⅞	8¾	6	2661	8¾	7¼	7¾B	...	14
25	INDQA	Int'l Dairy Queen[53]	OTC	B+	1¢	56	3055	Lmtd menu stores: franch'g	35¾	3/16	35½	22½	39¼	34¼	1487	39¼	36	37¼B	...	18
¶26•[4]	IFF	Int'l Flavors/Fragr	NY,B,C,M,P,Ph	A	12½¢	275	20338	Dev&mfr flavor&fragr prod	58	16⅝	54½	43⅛	52⅜	48½	15198	52⅜	48½	49	3.9	14
27	IGAM	Int'l Game Tech	OTC	B−	1¢	45	2964	Coin oper video/reel games	20	7⅛	27	8¼	23	19⅞	10143	22¾	20½	22¼B	...	16
28	ISLH	Int'l Hldg Capital	OTC	NR	1	3	16	Savings & loan,Hawaii	19½	6⅞	16¼	11¼	13½	12½	169	13½	12½	12¾B	3.9	4
29	IIP	Int'l Income Ppty	AS	NR	1¢	15	1695	Real estate investment trust	16¼	7	14⅞	11⅞	14¼	13⅛	665	14¼	13¼	14⅛	7.6	..
30	ILFC	Int'l Lease Finance	OTC	B+	10¢	63	6983	Leas'g/sale of jet aircraft	22¼	3⅜	18⅛	11½	21¼	15¾	54072	21¼	17¾	20⅝B	0.4	18
31	IMPX	Int'l Microelectronic Pr	OTC	NR	0.001	20	6355	Mfr integrated circuits	8¼	2 5/16	4½	1⅞	2½	1⅜	6201	2½	1⅝	1⅞B	...	12
¶32•[2]	IGL	Int'l Minerals/Chem	NY,B,C,M,P,Ph	B	5	194	17716	Phospate rock:chemicals	66½	6¾	51½	37¼	41¾	38	27456	41¾	38⅝	39½	2.5	15
33	Pr	4% cm Pfd (110) vtg	NY,M	BBB−	100	..	...	potash,hydro-carbons	54½	28½	47¼	39	42½	41½	18	42½	41½	41B	9.8	..
34	Pr A	$3.75cmCv[59]Ex A Pfd([60]53)	NY,M	BBB−	1	55	1903		67	45½	65	49½	53¾	51	1799	53½	51	52	7.2	..
35	Pr B	$3.25cmCv[62]Ex B Pfd([63]52.925)	NY	BBB−	1	28	1212		67¼	48⅛	66¾	51¼	55½	53	321	55½	53	53B	6.1	..
36	IMMC	Int'l Mobile Machs	OTC	NR	1¢	20	980	Develop ultraphone system	20⅝	2⅜	13⅛	6⅞	11⅜	8⅜	16044	11⅜	9¾	10⅛B	...	d
37	IMC	Int'l Multifoods	NY,M,P	A−	10¢	72	7496	Flours, durum prods, feeds	39¾	5⅝	33⅞	26	30½	27½	3487	30½	27⅞	28¼	4.2	11
¶38•[2]	IP	Int'l Paper	NY,B,C,M,P,Ph,Mo	B+	1	570	70540	World's largest paper maker	57⅞	14¼	49⅜	36½	51⅞	46	108876	51⅞	46⅛'	46¾	3.2	7
39	PWR	Int'l Pwr Machines	AS	C	10¢	7	339	Uninterruptible power sys	22½	3½	5⅛	3¾	4¼	4	46	4¼	4	4⅛	...	20
40	PRO	Int'l Proteins	AS	C	16⅔¢	8	263	Mfr & dstr fishmeal: shrimp	26⅞	1½	16⅜	10	14	13⅛	177	14	13⅜	14	...	12
41	INT	Int'l Recovery	AS	NR	1¢	4	84	Recycles used oil into fuel	14	1⅝	11¾	7⅜	10⅞	9⅝	466	10⅜	9⅝	9¾	...	17
42	IRF	Int'l Rectifier	NY,B,M,P	C	1	22	1750	Power semiconductors	17⅝	1	9½	4	4¾	3⅜	3423	4¼	3½	3¾	...	d
43	IRIS	Int'l Remote Imag'g	OTC	NR	No	10	413	Medic analysis image sys	10	7/16	1⅝	5/16	¾	⅜	2812	¾	7/16	½B	...	d
44	IRDV	Int'l Research & Dev	OTC	↑B+	50¢	21	1750	Safety evaluation,drugs,chem	10	¼	8¾	2⅞	10	6½	2489	10	8¾	9¼B	2.2	14
45	INSH	Int'l Shipholding	OTC	B−	1	25	904	Ocean shipping	13⅝	1⅞	20	9⅜	17¾	16	1077	17¾	16¼	17½B	1.1	8
46	ITX	Int'l Technology	NY,B,M,Ph	C	1	52	7885	Hazardous waste disposal svc	27⅜	3¾	5⅝	1⅞	7⅜	5⅛	28437	7⅜	6¼	6⅝	...	27

Uniform Footnote Explanations-See Page 1. Other: [1]ASE:Cycle 1. [2]CBOE:Cycle 1. [3]Mo,To [4]CBOE:Cycle 2. [51]®$1.15,'88. [52]Incl redemption of com stk pur rt. [53]Cl'A'. [54]Fiscal Dec'85 & prior. [55]12 Mo Sep'86. [56]®$1.13,'88. [57]$0.945 non-taxable,'88. [58]®$1.40,'87. [59]Co opt fr 6-30-89 exch for 7½%Cv2016. [60]Thru 6-29-89,scale to $50 in'96. [61]Com price equals 150%Cv price-20trad'g days. [62]Co opt fr 4-15-90 exch for $50amt6½%Cv2017. [63]Thru 4-14-89,scale to $50 in'97. [64]△$2.50,'87. [65]Accum on pfd.

(a)

Common and Preferred Stocks **INT-INT** 119

Splits ♦ Index	Cash Divs. Ea. Yr. Since	Dividends Latest Payment Period $	Date	Ex. Div.	Total $ So Far 1989	Ind. Rate	Paid 1988	Financial Position Mil-$ Cash& Equiv.	Curr. Assets	Curr. Liab.	Balance Sheet Date	Capitalization Lg Trm Debt Mil-$	Shs. 000 Pfd.	Com.	Earnings $ Per Shr. Years End	1984	1985	1986	1987	1988	Last 12 Mos.	Interim Earnings Period	$ per Shr. 1987	1988	Index
1	....	0.18	5-20-85	5-7	....	Nil	....	Equity per shr $15.24			12-31-87	★41.8	...	1481	Dc	□1.25	□1.13	△0.73	□2.18	....	1.05	9 Mo Sep	△1.29	□0.16	1
2♦	1977	Q0.05	3-13-89	2-23	0.05	0.20	0.15½	23.5	222	85.5	10-02-88	263	...	±17120	Dc	±0.35	±0.59	±0.68	±0.87	P±[51]1.18	1.18				2
3♦	....	None Since Public			....	Nil	....	4.11	18.2	4.75	6-30-88	1.04	...	4251	Sp	0.42	0.56	0.64	0.54	P△0.66	0.70	3 Mo Dec	△0.09	0.13	3
4	....	None Since Public			....	Nil	....	....	0.28	3.01	9-30-88	0.78	...	±4595	Dc	d0.33	d0.35	d0.49	d1.02	....	d0.76	9 Mo Sep	d0.88	d0.62	4
5♦	....	None Since Public			....	Nil	....	176	612	154	9-30-88	3.29	...	56565	Dc	1.22	1.25	1.26	1.23	P1.55	1.55				5
6	1952	gQ0.50	3-1-89	2-9	g0.50	2.00	g2.00	37.3	180	232	j9-30-88	1081	...	39577	Dc	3.47	3.71	3.36	3.09	P△2.60	j2.60				6
7	....	None Since Public			....	Nil	....	4.36	26.5	12.8	9-30-88	....		126532	Dc	0.08	0.11	0.12	0.13	P0.17	0.17				7
8♦	1941	Q0.37½	3-31-89	3-7	†[52]0.42½	e1.50	1.45	87.0	390	226	9-25-88	79.7	...	10392	Dc	3.34	2.53	2.85	4.69	P3.75	3.75				8
9	....	None Since Public			....	Nil	....	0.90	39.4	13.4	9-30-88	7.55	...	11454	Mr	d0.26	d0.29	d0.04	*0.47	....	0.23	9 Mo Dec	*0.27	0.03	9
10	....	None Since Public			....	Nil	....	0.50	29.7	9.85	11-27-88	7.51	...	6401	My	d0.78	d0.01	*0.14	d0.62	0.13	0.17	6 Mo Nov	0.09	0.13	10
11♦	1978	0.03	3-29-89	3-9	0.06	0.132	0.11¼	33.3	250	149	12-31-88	258	2471	5758	Mr	d0.27	d0.50	0.38	□1.71	....	2.51	12 Mo Dec	□0.35	2.51	11
12♦	1986	0.02¾	3-29-89	3-9	0.05½	0.121	0.10¼	....	...	...		....	2471	...	Mr	...	...	b1.37	b1.87	....	....				12
13	....	None Since Public			....	Nil	....	2.72	62.3	33.5	12-31-88	1.74	...	6611	Mr	0.80	0.28	0.65	0.85	....	1.08	9 Mo Dec	0.51	0.74	13
14♦	1985	Q0.05	3-6-89	2-13	0.05	0.20	0.20	14.1	94.6	47.5	9-25-88	44.2	...	18043	Dc	*0.70	0.71	0.90	1.00	P0.76	0.76				14
15	....	None Since Public			....	Nil	....	6.61	21.6	9.59	11-30-88	0.85	...	3492	Fb	0.20	d1.48	*0.10	*0.40	....	0.57	9 Mo Nov	*0.27	*0.44	15
16	1966	Q0.22	4-10-89	3-14	0.44	0.88	0.82	2.24	83.9	32.9	9-30-88	4.65	...	4518	Je	1.98	2.08	1.29	1.58	3.06	3.30	6 Mo Dec	1.34	1.58	16
17	....	None Since Public			....	Nil	....	Equity per shr $1.50			9-30-88	94.8	...	7947	Mr	...	*0.14	0.42	0.40	....	0.51	9 Mo Dec	0.30	0.41	17
18	....	0.02	6-15-84	6-4	....	Nil	....	21.8	51.1	13.2	9-30-88	27.5	247	18028	Dc	△d1.13	*0.02	*0.09	□d0.36	....	0.09	9 Mo Sep	□d0.38	0.07	18
19♦	....	None Paid			....	Nil	....	0.58	7.70	7.71	10-02-88	30.6	5000	2275	Sp	d0.35	d0.95	d0.83	△3.11	d0.03	d0.87	3 Mo Dec	d0.38	d1.22	19
20	1916	Q1.10	3-10-89	2-2	1.10	4.40	4.40	5491	29903	12975	9-30-88	5051	...	592127	Dc	10.77	10.67	7.81	8.72	P△9.27	9.27				20
21	1987	Q1.08¾	3-21-89	2-2	1.08¾	4.35	4.35	....	...	...		....	...	8191	Dc	...	...	...	§115.50	....	....	Expires 6-30-92			21
22	....	None Since Public			....	Nil	....	....	...	...		....	...	...	Dc	...	...	...	....	....	....				22
23	1987	Q1.08¾	3-21-89	2-2	1.08¾	4.35	4.35	Termination claim $210				....	...	...	Dc	...	...	...	....	....	....				23
24♦	....	None Since Public			....	Nil	....	2.81	5.66	1.73	9-30-88	....	...	2839	Mr	*0.10	*0.26	0.28	0.21	....	0.57	9 Mo Dec	0.06	0.42	24
25♦	....	None Since Public			....	Nil	....	7.65	33.8	26.1	11-30-88	27.0	...	±9477	Nv	0.72	±0.98	±1.25	±1.54	±2.09	2.09				25
26	1956	Q0.48	4-11-89	3-20	0.96	1.92	1.60	226	634	136	9-30-88	....	...	37908	Dc	1.89	1.89	2.29	2.83	P3.40	3.40				26
27	....	None Since Public			....	Nil	....	3.59	83.5	37.7	12-31-88	16.5	...	7197	Sp	1.36	[54]0.18	[55]d0.88	*0.13	△[56]1.21	1.36	3 Mo Dec	△0.21	0.36	27
28♦	1987	S0.25	9-30-88	9-2	....	0.50	0.50	Book Value $26.48			12-31-88	176	...	1115	Je	*1.19	△□1.55	□d2.10	5.66	4.02	3.11	6 Mo Dec	2.19	1.28	28
29	1979	Q0.27	3-1-89	2-17	0.27	1.08	[57]1.05	Equity per shr $6.62			9-30-88	125	...	15539	Dc	0.37	0.19	□d0.05	d0.23	P0.14	0.14				29
30♦	1988	0.02	1-18-89	12-8	0.02	0.08	0.06	Equity per shr $7.23			8-31-88	1158		132425	Nv	0.51	0.70	1.02	△[58]1.41	P1.14	1.14				30
31	....	None Since Public			....	Nil	....	18.9	44.4	9.58	9-25-88	6.17	...	25520	Mr	d0.17	d0.44	*0.07	*0.16	....	0.16	6 Mo Sep	*0.09	*0.09	31
32	1971	Q0.25	3-31-89	3-13	0.25	1.00	1.00	591	1013	280	12-31-88	729	4035	p21900	Je	■3.04	4.39	d8.04	□0.49	*3.11	2.72	6 Mo Dec	△2.25	1.86	32
33	1942	Q1.00	3-31-89	3-13	1.00	4.00	4.00	....	...	...		....	98	...	Je	b4.61	b5.20	bd0.25	b1.02	b1.93	....				33
34	1986	Q0.93¾	3-31-89	3-13	0.93¾	3.75	3.75	Cv into 1.218com,$41.05				....	2538	...	Je	...	...	...	b1.02	b1.93	....	Call rest to 6-30-89[61]			34
35	1987	Q0.81¼	4-15-89	3-13	1.62½	3.25	3.25	Cv into 1.2658 com,$39.50				....	1398	...	Je	...	...	...	....	b1.93	....	Call restr to 4-15-90[61]			35
36	....	None Since Public			....	Nil	....	3.23	14.9	6.84	9-30-88	7.89	1221	13037	Dc	d0.75	d0.96	d0.95	d1.06	....	d1.58	9 Mo Sep	d0.53	d1.05	36
37♦	1923	Q0.29½	1-15-89	12-21	0.29½	1.18	1.18	58.1	507	343	11-30-88	148	41	12812	Fb	1.77	2.04	△[64]1.14	2.26	E2.55	2.46	9 Mo Nov	1.73	1.93	37
38♦	1946	Q0.37	3-15-89	2-17	0.37	1.48	1.27½	137	2194	1220	9-30-88	1775	20	111054	Dc	0.94	△1.06	2.89	3.68	P6.57	6.57				38
39	....	0.04	9-17-84	8-29	....	[65]Nil	....	0.16	20.1	15.0	9-30-88	0.10	400	4264	Dc	0.01	d1.42	□d0.49	d0.30	....	0.21	9 Mo Sep	d0.33	0.18	39
40	....	0.05	12-15-80	11-21	....	Nil	....	1.96	51.2	24.6	9-30-88	35.8	...	3351	Dc	△d2.35	*0.22	*0.49	d1.67	P1.15	1.15				40
41	....	None Since Public			....	Nil	....	2.42	8.59	3.57	9-30-88	3.23	...	3450	Mr	...	0.10	0.06	0.30	....	0.57	9 Mo Dec	0.18	0.45	41
42♦	....	0.107	10-1-81	9-4	....	Nil	....	3.25	91.7	55.2	9-30-88	138	...	11108	Je	*0.59	△d0.05	△d0.05	d1.55	d1.09	d1.00	6 Mo Dec	d0.85	d0.76	42
43	....	None Since Public			....	Nil	....	2.56	5.86	0.89	9-30-88	....	...	19321	Dc	d0.24	d0.14	d0.15	d0.07	....	d0.10	9 Mo Sep	d0.03	d0.06	43
44♦	1973	Q0.05	2-24-89	2-6	0.05	0.20	0.19	13.1	16.7	12.1	9-30-88	1.45	...	5549	Dc	0.42	0.21	0.07	0.35	P0.65	0.65				44
45♦	1988	Q0.05	3-30-89	3-10	0.05	0.20	0.10	27.1	57.7	52.8	9-30-88	★145	85	4058	Dc	1.03	1.33	0.80	1.43	P△2.15	2.15				45
46♦	....	None Since Public			....	Nil	....	n/a	86.7	48.5	12-31-88	88.9	...	31712	Mr	0.32	0.58	0.28	d3.80	E0.25	0.14	9 Mo Dec	d5.76	0.18	46

♦**Stock Splits & Divs By Line Reference Index** [2]2-for-1,'87. [3]15%,'85:5-for-4,'86:10%,'87. [5]2-for-1,'85. [8]2-for-1,'86. [11]Vote 10% stk div,ex Mar 13. [12]Vote 10% stk div,ex Mar 13. [14]3-for-2,'86. [19]1-for-25 REVERSE,'87. [24]3-for-2,'86. [25]5-for-1(3 in Cl'A' & 2 in Cl'B'),'86. [28]10%,'85. [30]3-for-2,'85,'87. [37]3-for-2,'86. [38]2-for-1,'87. [42]3-for-2,'84. [44]2-for-1,'88. [45]3-for-1,'86:5-for-4,'88. [46]3-for-2,'85:2-for-1,'86.

(b)

Figure 6-2 Sample pages from S&P's *Stock Guide*.

INTERNATIONAL BUSINESS MACHINES CORPORATION

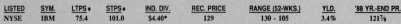

LISTED	SYM.	LTPS♦	STPS♦	IND. DIV.	REC. PRICE	RANGE (52-WKS.)	YLD.	'88 YR.-END PR.
NYSE	IBM	75.4	101.0	$4.40*	129	130 - 105	3.4%	121⅞

HIGH GRADE. AGGRESSIVE RESEARCH AND STRONG MARKETING COUPLED WITH AN EXTENSIVE COST REDUCTION PROGRAM SHOULD HELP GROWTH CONTINUE OVER THE LONG TERM.

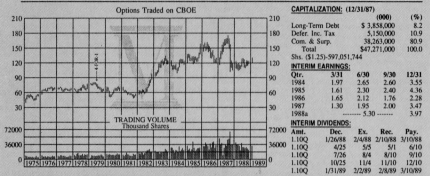

CAPITALIZATION: (12/31/87)

	(000)	(%)
Long-Term Debt	$ 3,858,000	8.2
Defer. Inc. Tax	5,150,000	10.9
Com. & Surp.	38,263,000	80.9
Total	$47,271,000	100.0

Shs. ($1.25)-597,051,744

INTERIM EARNINGS:

Qtr.	3/31	6/30	9/30	12/31
1984	1.97	2.65	2.60	3.55
1985	1.61	2.30	2.40	4.36
1986	1.65	2.12	1.76	2.28
1987	1.30	1.95	2.00	3.47
1988a	-------- 5.30 -------			3.97

INTERIM DIVIDENDS:

Amt.	Dec.	Ex.	Rec.	Pay.
1.10Q	1/26/88	2/4/88	2/10/88	3/10/88
1.10Q	4/25	5/5	5/1	6/10
1.10Q	7/26	8/4	8/10	9/10
1.10Q	10/25	11/4	11/10	12/10
1.10Q	1/31/89	2/2/89	2/8/89	3/10/89

BACKGROUND:

IBM's operations are mainly in the field of information handling systems, equipment and services. Products include information processing products and sytems, program products, communications systems, workstations, typewriters, copiers, educational and testing materials, and related supplies and services. Most products are both leased and sold through IBM's worldwide marketing organizations. Selected products are distributed through authorized dealers and remarketers.The 1987 revenue breakdown was as follows: sales, 67%; maintenance services, 14.2%; program products, 12.6%; rentals and other services, 6.2%.

RECENT DEVELOPMENTS:

In January, IBM brought a 25% stake in PCO Inc., a maker of fiber-optics. For the year ended 12/31/88, income from continuing operations advanced 4.4% to $5.49 billion from $5.26 billion last year. Income excludes a $315.0 million credit from an accounting adjustment. Revenues, which reflect a change in method of accounting to include finance subsidiaries on a consolidated basis, were $59.68 billion, up 8%. Software sales increased 16% while rentals and financing dropped 7%. Per share earnings before accounting adjustment jumped 6.3% to $9.27 on 10,600,000 fewer average shares outstanding.

PROSPECTS:

Near-term results are expected to improve benefiting from a recovery in domestic demand for computers. International sales should benefit from the lower dollar and the introduction of new products in high growth areas. New personal computer products should enhance profits aided by high margins and proprietary design. Profit margins are further enhanced by a retreat from the telecommunications market. Introduction of low end single-user PC machines should help regain simple program market. Steps taken to lower costs, such as workforce reductions, will help.

STATISTICS:

YEAR	GROSS REVS. ($mill.)	OPER. PROFIT MARGIN %	RET. ON EQUITY %	NET INCOME ($mill.)	WORK CAP. ($mill.)	SENIOR CAPITAL ($mill.)	SHARES (000)	EARN. PER SH.$	DIV. PER SH.$	DIV. PAY. %	PRICE RANGE	P/E RATIO	AVG. YIELD %
79	22,863	22.9	20.1	3,011	4,406	1,589	583,594	5.16	3.44	67	80½ - 61⅛	14.1	5.0
80	26,213	21.9	21.6	3,562	3,399	2,099	583,807	6.10	3.44	56	72¾ - 50⅜	10.1	5.6
81	29,070	20.7	18.2	3,308	2,983	2,669	592,294	5.63	3.44	61	71½ - 48⅜	10.7	6.0
82	34,364	23.4	22.1	4,409	4,805	2,851	602,406	7.39	3.44	47	98 - 55⅝	10.4	4.5
83	40,180	23.9	23.6	5,485	7,763	2,674	610,725	9.04	3.71	41	134¼ - 92¼	12.5	3.3
84	45,937	24.5	24.8	6,582	10,735	3,269	612,686	10.77	4.10	38	128½ - 99	10.6	3.6
85	50,056	22.4	20.5	6,555	14,637	3,955	615,418	10.67	4.40	41	158½ - 117⅜	12.9	3.2
86	51,250	15.3	13.9	4,789	15,006	4,169	605,923	7.81	4.40	56	161⅞ - 119¼	18.0	3.1
87	54,217	14.3	13.7	5,258	17,643	3,858	597,052	8.72	4.40	50	175⅞ - 102	15.9	3.2
p88	**59,681**			**a5,491**				**a9.27**	**4.40**	**47**	**129½ - 104½**	**12.6**	**3.8**

♦Long-Term Price Score — Short-Term Price Score; See page 4a. STATISTICS ARE AS ORIGINALLY REPORTED. Adjusted for 4-for-1 stock split, 5/79. a-Excludes $315 million ($0.53 per share) credit for an accounting change.

INCORPORATED:
June 16, 1911 — NY

PRINCIPAL OFFICE:
Armonk, NY 10504
Tel.: (914) 765-1900

ANNUAL MEETING:
Last Monday in April

NUMBER OF STOCKHOLDERS:
787,988

TRANSFER AGENT(S):
Company Office, New York, NY
Trust General du Canada
Morgan Shareholder Services Trust Co., NY

REGISTRAR(S):
Morgan Shareholder Services Trust Co., NY
Montreal Trust Co.

INSTITUTIONAL HOLDINGS:
No. of Institutions: 1,755
Shares Held: 288,231,488

OFFICERS:
Chairman
J. F. Akers
Vice Chairmen
K. V. Cassani
J. D. Kuehler
V.P. & Controller
J. P. Cunningham
Treasurer
D. A. Finley
Secretary
W.W.K. Rich

Figure 6-3 A sample page from *Moody's Handbook of Widely Held Common Stocks*.

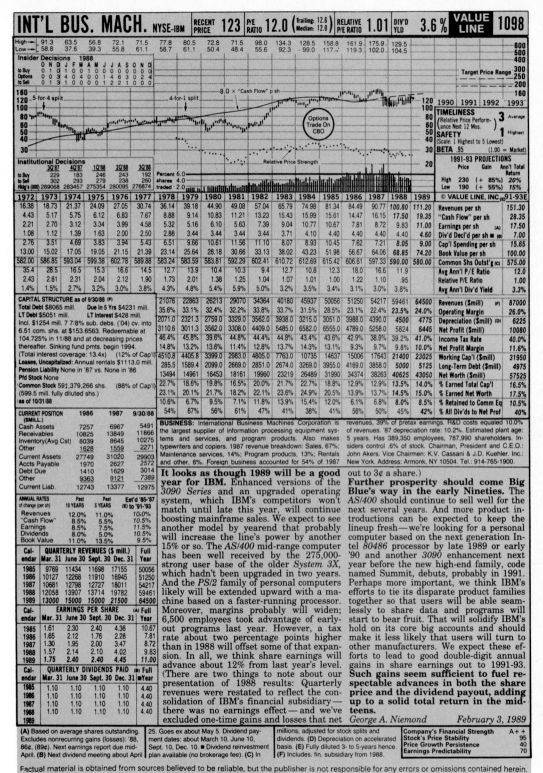

Figure 6-4 A sample page from the *Value Line Investment Survey*.

cases, might even suggest counterproductive investment recommendations after they become out-of-date. When making investment decisions, it is always wise to have the most recent and complete information available.

Brokerage Houses   To promote their sales efforts, brokerage offices usually carry one or more of the leading investment surveys for their customers' use. In addition, large brokerages maintain their own research departments that generate investment information for their clients. These research departments usually disseminate their publications, in the form of market newsletters, on request at no charge.

The Issuers of Securities   One of the best sources of financial information is the firm that issued the securities. The filing, registration, and other statements required by the organized securities exchanges, the SEC, the government agencies in charge of regulating various industries (such as the Civil Aeronautics Board, the Interstate Commerce Commission, and the Federal Communications Commission), and other institutions provide detailed information that usually is not published in companies' annual and quarterly reports.

Investors may also obtain information about a firm by reading its annual report or interviewing its executives. However, both these sources are usually biased—management is reluctant to publicize its errors.

Professionally Managed Portfolios   Information about mutual funds (that is, open-end investment companies) and closed-end investment companies is published by several sources. The investment companies themselves, especially the mutual funds, are always eager to mail out copies of their prospectuses and other free promotional literature. There are also firms that, for a fee, provide information about investment companies. Two of the more prominent firms in this field are Arthur Wiesenberger Services, Inc., which reports on all mutual funds, and Donoghue's Moneyletter, Inc., which focuses on money market mutual funds.

6-2   **A CATALOG OF SOURCES OF INVESTMENT INFORMATION**

There are many investment information organizations that investors can consult for information. The following outline lists sources for various categories of investment information.

I. ADVICE ABOUT INVESTMENT SECURITIES
   A. Stock and Bond Ratings
      1. Moody's Manuals
         a. *Moody's Bank & Finance Manual*
         b. *Moody's Industrial Manual*
         c. *Moody's International Manual*

       d. *Moody's OTC Industrial Manual*
       e. *Moody's Public Utility Manual*
       f. *Moody's Transportation Manual*
       g. *Moody's OTC Unlisted Manual*
    2. *Moody's Bond Record*
    3. Salomon Brothers, *Preferred Stock Guide*
    4. Standard & Poor's *Bond Guide*
    5. Standard & Poor's *Commercial Paper Ratings Guide*
    6. *Value Line Investment Survey*
  B. Beta Systematic Risk Measurements
    1. Goldman, Sachs & Co., *Risk, Return and Equity Evaluation*
    2. Merrill Lynch, Pierce, Fenner & Smith, Inc., *Quantitative Analysis*
    3. *Value Line Investment Survey*
  C. Outlook for Securities Markets
    1. *Moody's Bond Survey*
    2. *Moody's Stock Survey*
    3. Standard & Poor's *Outlook*
    4. United Business Service, *United & Babson Investment Report*
  D. Recommendations and Security Analysis
    1. Kidder Peabody & Co., *Research Department Service*
    2. *Moody's Bond Survey*
    3. *Moody's Stock Survey*
    4. Standard & Poor's *CreditWeek*
    5. Standard & Poor's *Outlook*
    6. United Business Service, *United & Babson Investment Report*
    7. *Value Line Investment Survey*
  E. Put and Call Information
    1. Standard & Poor's *Options Handbook*
    2. *Value Line Convertibles*
    3. *Value Line Options*

II. FINANCIAL AND ECONOMIC NEWSPAPERS
  A. Daily Business Newspapers
    1. *American Banker*
    2. *Daily Commerce*
    3. *Financial Times*—from London
    4. *The Journal of Commerce*
    5. *The New York Times*
    6. *The Wall Street Journal*
    7. *Washington Post*
  B. Weekly Business Newspapers
    1. *Barron's National Business*
    2. *Commercial and Financial Chronicle*
    3. *Financial Post*—from Canada
    4. *Market Chronicle*

      5. *Vie Francais l'Opinion*
      6. *Wall Street Transcript*
      7. *Weekly Bond Buyer*
  C. Weekly Business Periodicals
      1. *Business Week*
      2. *Financial World*
      3. *Investment Dealers' Digest*
      4. *Japan Stock Journal*
      5. *United States Banker*
      6. *World Business Weekly*
  D. Biweekly Business Periodicals
      1. Chase Manhattan Bank, *International Finance*
      2. *Forbes*
  E. Monthly Economic Periodicals
      1. *Across the Board*
      2. Bank letters issued by various banks, namely, Federal Reserve Bank of St. Louis, Morgan Guaranty Trust, Chase Manhattan, and others
      3. *Business Conditions Digest*
      4. *Conference Board Statistical Bulletins*
      5. Donoghues *Money Fund Report*
      6. *Dun's Business Ranking*
      7. *Economic Indicators*
      8. *Federal Reserve Bulletin*
      9. *Federal Reserve Chart Book*
     10. *Financial Executive*
     11. *Fortune*
     12. *Going Public*
     13. *Institutional Investor*
     14. *OTC Review*
     15. *Stock Market Magazine*
     16. *Survey of Current Business*
     17. *Venture Capital Journal*
  F. Bimonthly Business Periodical
      1. *Financial Planning*
  G. Quarterly Business Periodicals
      1. *Business Starts*
      2. *Mergers and Acquisitions*
  H. Annual Economic Reviews
      1. U.S. Bureau of Domestic Commerce, *U.S. Industrial Outlook*
      2. U.S. Office of Business Economics, *Business Statistics*
      3. U.S. President, *Presidential Economic Report*
III. ACADEMIC RESEARCH PUBLICATIONS
      1. *Financial Analysts Journal*
      2. *Journal of Banking and Finance*
      3. *International Review of Financial Analysis*

4. *Journal of Business*
5. *Journal of Finance*
6. *Journal of Financial Economics*
7. *Journal of Financial Education*
8. *Journal of Financial Research*
9. *Journal of Financial and Quantitative Analysis*
10. *Journal of International Finance*
11. *Journal of Money, Credit, and Banking*
12. *Journal of Portfolio Management*
13. *The Review of Financial Studies*
14. *The Financial Review*
15. *Review of Quantitative Finance and Accounting*

IV. INDUSTRY INFORMATION
  A. U.S. Government Publications
    1. Annual reports of regulatory commissions, such as the FPC, FTC, ICC, and SEC
    2. *Survey of Current Business* (monthly)
    3. *Treasury Bulletin* (monthly)
    4. U.S. Census Bureau, *Census of Manufacturers*
    5. U.S. Census Bureau, *Annual Survey of Manufacturers*
    6. U.S. Census Bureau, *Census of Retail Trade*
    7. U.S. Census Bureau, *Census of Service Industries*
    8. U.S. Census Bureau, *Census of Wholesale Trade*
    9. U.S. Census Bureau, *Current Industrial Reports*
    10. U.S. Census Bureau, *Statistical Abstracts of the U.S.*
    11. U.S. Industry & Trade Administration, *U.S. Industrial Outlook*
    12. U.S. Office of Business Economics, *Business Statistics*
  B. Reports from Investment Services
    1. Value Line, Inc.
      a. *Value Line Investment Survey*
      b. *Value Line Convertibles*
      c. *Value Line Options*
      d. *Value Line OTC Special Situations Service*
    2. Howard & Company, *Going Public*
    3. Kidder Peabody & Co., *Research Service*
    4. Moody's
      a. Manuals
      b. *Moody's Industry Review*
      c. *Moody's Bond Survey*
      d. *Moody's International Bond Review*
    5. Smith Barney Harris Upham & Co., *Research Service*
    6. Standard & Poor's
      a. *Industry Survey*
      b. *Outlook*
      c. *Statistical Service, Current Statistics*

C. Special Bibliographies (indexes to periodicals)
   1. *Business Periodicals Index*
   2. Public Affairs and Information Service, *Bulletin*
   3. *The Wall Street Journal Index*
D. Mergers and Acquisitions
   1. *Announcements of Mergers and Acquisitions* (monthly publication by The Conference Board)
   2. Financial Stock Guide Service, *Directory of Obsolete Securities*
   3. Predicasts, *F&S Index of Corporate Change*. Quarterly
E. Reports and Brochures of Brokerage and Banking Firms
   1. Bank of America
      a. Daily Quotation Sheets: *U.S. Government Securities, Federal Agencies and Other Securities*
      b. *Small Business Reporter*
      c. *Weekly Monetary Summary*
   2. Bankers Trust, *Current Business Picture*
   3. Goldman, Sachs & Co., *Risk, Return and Equity Valuation*
   4. Kidder Peabody & Co.
      a. *Current Investment Policy and Strategy Implementation*
      b. *Emerging Growth Stocks*
      c. *Money and Capital Markets*
      d. *Monthly Earnings Summary*
      e. *Monthly Valuation Information*
      f. *Portfolio Manager's Review*
   5. Merrill Lynch, Pierce, Fenner & Smith, *Quantitative Analysis*
   6. Siegel Trading Company, *Weekly Market Letter*
   7. Salomon Brothers
      a. *Analytical Record of Yields and Yield Spreads*
      b. *Bond Market Roundup*
      c. *Bond Portfolio Analysis*
      d. *Comments on Credit*
      e. *Monthly Stock Review*
      f. *Preferred Stock Guide*
      g. *Prospects for Financial Markets*
      h. *Strategy Systems*
      i. *Total Rate-of-return Indexes*
   8. Smith Barney Harris Upham & Co., *Analysts Roundtable*
   9. *Wall Street Transcript* (weekly newspaper; most of the contents are reprints of brokerage house reports)
   10. *Dow Jones Investor's Handbook*

V. COMPANY INFORMATION
   A. Reports from the Securities Issuers

1. Annual reports to shareholders
2. Financial Stock Guide Service, *Directory of Obsolete Securities*
3. Prospectuses

B. Publications of Brokerage Firms—issued ad hoc
C. Manuals from Financial Information Services
1. Moody's Manuals (*Banks & Finance; Industrial; International; Municipals and Governments; OTC Industrials; Public Utility; Transportation*)
2. Standard & Poor's *Standard Corporation Descriptions*
3. Standard & Poor's *Stock Reports* (American Stock Exchange; New York Stock Exchange; Over-the-Counter and Regional Exchanges)
4. Value Line, Inc.
    a. *Value Line Investment Survey*
    b. *Value Line Convertibles*
    c. *Value Line Options*
    d. *Value Line OTC Special Situations Service*
5. Moody's
    a. *Moody's Bond Record*
    b. *Moody's Bond Survey*
    c. *Moody's Dividend Record*
    d. *Moody's Handbook of Common Stocks*
    e. *Moody's Industry Review*
    f. *Moody's International Bond Review*
    g. Manuals (note especially the semiweekly supplements and the sections in the center of the volumes)
    h. *Moody's Stock Survey*
6. Standard & Poor's
    a. *Analysts Handbook* (annual, with monthly supplements)
    b. *Bond Guide*
    c. *Called Bond Record*
    d. *Commercial Paper Rating Guide*
    e. *Corporation Records*
    f. *CreditWeek*
    g. *Dividend Record*
    h. *Earnings Forecaster*
    i. *Industry Surveys*
    j. *Outlook*
    k. *Standard Corporation Descriptions* (note especially the daily supplements)
    l. Statistical Service, *Current Statistics*
    m. *Stock Guide*
    n. *Stock Reports* (NYSE, ASE, OTC)

7. United Business Service, *United Investment Report*
8. *Vickers Guide to Investment Company Portfolios*

VI. PRINTED SECURITY PRICE QUOTATIONS
  A. Daily Range and Closing Prices
    1. *Commercial and Financial Chronicle* (Monday issue contains high and low for each day of the preceding week)
    2. *The New York Times*
    3. *Investor's Daily*
    4. Standard & Poor's *Daily Stock Price Record*
    5. *The Wall Street Journal*
  B. Weekly Range and Close
    1. *Barron's*
    2. *Financial Post*—from Canada
  C. Monthly Range
    1. *Bank and Quotation Record*
    2. *Capital International Perspective*
    3. Standard & Poor's *Daily Stock Price Record* (ASE, NYSE, and OTC)
  D. Annual Range
    1. *Bank and Quotation Record* (January issue has range for preceding year)
    2. *Barron's National Business* (first issue in January has range for preceding year)
    3. *Commercial and Financial Chronicle* (see the Monday issue)
    4. Dow Jones *Investor's Handbook* (annual)
    5. Standard & Poor's
      a. *Bond Guide*
      b. *Standard Corporation Descriptions*
      c. *Stock Guide*
      d. *Stock Reports* (ASE, NYSE, OTC, and regional exchanges)
  E. Other Sources of Price Quotations
    1. *Daily Stock Price Record* (ASE, NYSE, and OTC)
    2. National Quotation Bureau, *Monthly Bond Summary*
    3. National Quotation Bureau, *Monthly Stock Summary*

VII. SECURITY PRICE AVERAGES AND INDEXES
  A. Financial newspapers—see VI.A, VI.B, and VI.C
  B. Periodicals
    1. *Barron's*
    2. *Commercial and Financial Chronicle* (Monday issue)
    3. *CPI Detailed Index*
    4. *Federal Reserve Bulletin*
    5. *Producer Prices and Price Index*
    6. *Survey of Current Business*

C. Financial Information Services
1. Standard & Poor's
   a. *Outlook*
   b. Statistical Service. *Current Statistics*
   c. *Daily Stock Price Index*
2. Moody's
   a. *Manuals* (blue section)
   b. *Bond Survey*
   c. *Stock Survey*
D. Other Price Indexes and Averages
1. *Capital International Perspective*
2. *Dow Jones Averages 1885–1980* (averages for each day since the series began)
3. L. Fisher and J. H. Lorie, *A Half Century of Returns on Stocks and Bonds*
4. Ibbotson Associates, *Stocks, Bonds, Bills and Inflation: 1989 Yearbook,* Chicago

VIII. MONEY MARKET DATA
A. *Weekly Bond Buyer*
B. Salomon Brothers
1. *Analytical Record of Yields and Yield Spreads*
2. *Bond Market Roundup* (weekly)
3. *Bond Portfolio Analysis*
4. *Comments on Credit*
5. *Prospects for Financial Markets* (annual)
6. *Total Rate-of-Return Indices*
C. *Euromoney* (monthly)

IX. MUTUAL FUND DATA
A. Computer Directions Advisors
1. *Spectrum 1: Investment Company Stock Holdings Survey*
2. *Spectrum 2: Investment Company Portfolios*
B. *Donoghue's Money Fund Directory*
C. *Donoghue's Money Fund Report*
D. *Institutional Investor* (monthly periodical)
E. Investment Company Institute, *Mutual Fund Fact Book*
F. Investment Dealers' Digest, *Mutual Fund Forum*
G. *Johnson's Investment Co. Charts*
H. *Lipper Mutual Fund Performance Analysis*
I. Morningstar Inc., Chicago
J. *Mutual Funds Almanac*
K. N-SAR reports (annual reports of mutual funds to SEC)
L. United Business Service, *United Mutual Fund Selector*
M. Vickers Stock Research Corp, *Guide to Investment Company Portfolios*

7. The Reuter Monitor, Reuters, Ltd., New York
8. Value Line Data Base II, New York
9. Quotron, Quotron Systems, Inc., Los Angeles
10. Merrill Lynch Research Service, Merrill Lynch Inc., Securities Research Division, New York
11. Microquote, The Gregg Corporation, Waltham, Mass.
12. Munifacts, The Bond Buyer, New York
13. Extat, Extel Statistical Services, Ltd., London
14. Ford Data Base, Ford Investor Services, San Diego
15. IBES, Lynch, Jones & Ryan, New York
16. Analytics, Chase Econometrics/Interactive Data Corp., Waltham, Mass.
17. Commodities, Data Resources, Inc., Lexington, Mass.
18. Market Decision System 7, Bunker Ramo Information Systems, Trumbull, Conn.
19. Markets Advisory, Racine, Wisc.
20. Media General Data Base, Media General Financial Services, Inc., Richmond, Va.
21. Mergers and Acquisitions, Securities Data Company, Inc., New York
22. Berkeley Options Data Base, University of California at Berkeley
23. Dow Jones News Retrieval Service
24. Center for Research and Security Prices (CRSP), University of Chicago
25. Chicago Board of Trade
26. Ibbotson Associates, Chicago
27. FactSet, New York

6-3   SUMMARY AND CONCLUSIONS

The old adage "investigate before you invest" is advice well taken. This chapter suggested sources of investment information that investors may consult. Some of these information sources charge high fees for their information, but some of the best are cheap (for instance, *Business Conditions Digest* and material from the research department of the St. Louis Federal Reserve Bank).

Computers and telecommunications are revolutionizing the way financial analysis is done. Massive amounts of financial data may be amassed and processed with lightning speed. It is usually too expensive for amateur investors to use electronic data bases. Students should exploit any opportunity their college makes available to them to use such resources at a low cost so they can familiarize themselves with these modern research tools.

Essay Questions

6-1 The financial newspapers contain analytical studies aimed at determining the cause-and-effect relationships between various economic variables. Is this true, false, or uncertain? Explain.

6-2 What is a 10K report? Where does one obtain this investment information? What information is contained in the 10K report? *Hint: See Chapter 4 for additional information.*

6-3 Select a publicly traded security and compare the reports on it found in Standard & Poor's *Stock Market Encyclopedia*, in *Moody's Handbook of Widely Held Common Stocks*, and in the *Value Line Survey*. Write a page about the significant differences among these three sources. (This assignment will require outside research.)

6-4 Write a short essay contrasting Moody's Aa bond rating with Standard & Poor's AA bond rating. *Hint: See Table 14-2.*

6-5 Where could an investor interested in buying shares in a mutual fund find information that would help in choosing a fund?

6-6 If you had to prepare a graph of AAA-grade corporate bond yields showing the path of the interest rates monthly for the last 10 years, where could you find the raw data quickly, easily, and inexpensively?

The Thaddeus Smith Case

Thaddeus Smith is a 31-year-old assistant vice president at the First State Bank of Omaha (FSBO) in Omaha, Nebraska. Smith received his bachelor's degree in business finance from the University of Nebraska 9 years ago, and after working for a large Minneapolis bank's trust department for 2 years, he returned to his home town of Omaha to take a position at the FSBO as a junior officer. Smith works hard at the FSBO and in addition takes night-school courses toward an MBA in finance. He was promoted to assistant vice president 4 years ago. Since then, the young executive has impressed the FSBO's senior management so much that this middle-sized bank has offered to promote him to vice president and put him in charge of starting a trust department.

The FSBO's executive committee has offered Smith the promotion and the trust department assignment with certain guidelines. A few days after Smith was offered this opportunity at FSBO by his boss, Fred Hannah, executive vice president in charge of commercial loans, he was summoned to the bank's executive conference room. At that time various members of the bank's executive committee cordially explained to Smith that even though usually only large banks started trust departments, they had nevertheless decided to offer Smith the chance to start one in their medium-sized bank. The FSBO had total deposits of $316 million and net income of $21 million last year. The bank has six branches in and around Omaha, and while it is a major bank in Omaha, it has no significant impact outside the Omaha area. In spite of the moderate size and influence of the FSBO, its executive committee had decided that it was desirable for the bank to start a trust department to hold and attract depositors in the Omaha area. No other bank in or around Omaha had a trust department, and top management felt that FSBO would be able to attract wealthy depositors by offering them the unique local service of a bank trust department to manage their investments. The executive committee told Smith that the trust department should charge 1 percent per year of the value of the assets managed and that the new department could spend all fees collected. That is, the bank expected no profits from the trust department's fees. It was felt that the trust department's customers would sooner or later bring their personal and business checking accounts to FSBO and that the bank would thereby profit from the trust department's activities indirectly. Thus, the trust department was visualized as a public-relations and marketing service to attract deposits from the wealthy people in the area. The members of the executive committee explained that for the first few years, at least, they did not envision the new trust department as consisting of more than the following:

One full-time vice president, tentatively, Thaddeus Smith

One full-time secretary-receptionist, who would work for both Smith and another vice president

Assistance as needed from the FSBO's bookkeeping department to account for the clients' funds and send out periodic statements and bills for the trust service

Assistance from the FSBO's legal counsel, Larry Miller, in drawing up the legal fiduciary agreements specifying how the clients want their trusts administered

Smith is a polished young man who feels confident that with the contacts the other bank officers at FSBO can give him, he can surely bring new trust business into the bank. He already knows of two large corporate pension funds he can solicit, and the FSBO's corporate loan customers can be approached as well. Furthermore, one of the FSBO's senior vice presidents, Tom Hensley, is also membership-committee chairman at a prestigious Omaha country club. Hensley has offered to share confidentially all of the country club's membership applications with Smith and thus help Smith find wealthy local people who may be in need of the services of a trust department. The recruitment of clients will require much personal salesmanship, but Smith is willing to tackle it.

The rank of vice president and the opportunity to have a private office greatly appeal to Smith. The promotion would also entail a pay raise. But Smith has some reservations about the new job; he has never managed an investment portfolio by himself (other than his family's modest portfolio of $31,000). He is uncertain how to apply the investment management principles he learned in college to the management of millions of dollars of other people's money. Smith is trying to deal with his fears by writing down specific questions that concern him. He reasons that if he can find answers to these anticipated problems, then he will feel more capable of tackling the new responsibilities. Can you offer suggestions to help Smith deal with his new trust management position? Smith's questions are listed below.

1. Where could I get quality ratings to enable me to make safe bond and stock investment decisions? Would such quality ratings cost more than the fee FSBO will

charge to manage the funds? Would these quality ratings be in a form such that I could show them to my clients and to senior management at the bank to justify my investment decisions?

2. Where will I get economic forecasts about booms and recessions, the level of interest rates, and the profitability of various sectors of the economy? How much would such forecasts cost? Are good opinions on which to base my decisions available?

3. Should I count on my close friend Bob Daley, who is an experienced stockbroker, to help me select investments? If I give Bob the brokerage commissions, he should be willing to help me manage the clients' accounts, shouldn't he?

4. Where can I get accurate financial analyses of every corporation in which I may consider investing? Can I get these analyses quickly when I need them? Will they be too expensive for the bank?

5. If I get a $20 million or $30 million pension-fund client, how will I invest all that money quickly? Is there a professional money-management service I can use that is not too expensive? Will it reflect unfavorably on me if I use such a service? That is, how could I justify the use of such a service except by pleading personal incompetence?

Chapter 7

Market Indexes

Securities market indexes have been constructed to give a quick answer to the question: What is the market doing? The Dow Jones Industrial Average (DJIA) is probably the best-known stock market average among the dozens in use worldwide.

Technically speaking, the DJIA is an average, not an index. A **stock market average** is a weighted or unweighted average stock price for a specified group of stocks. In contrast, an index is a series of pure index numbers.

Index numbers are devoid of dollar values or other units of measure. Stock market indexes are "pure numbers" used for making comparisons between different index numbers in the same series or other index numbers. An index is usually a ratio tabulated from averages of different securities. Typically, a time-series of index numbers is constructed from the same **base date** and **base value** (usually set at 100, 10, or 1) to make them directly comparable. Some past year is selected as the *base year* from which the index's base value is calculated in order to impart time perspective to the index.

7-1　　　**MANY DIFFERENT SECURITIES MARKET INDICATORS EXIST**

Numerous securities market indexes and averages are published to measure many distinct phenomena. Among the most popular stock exchange indexes are:

The Dow Jones Composite Average

The Dow Jones Industrial Average (DJIA)

The Dow Jones Transportation Average

The Dow Jones Utility Average

TSE 300 Composite Index (from Toronto Stock Exchange)

Moody's Industrial Average

Moody's Railroad Stock Average

Moody's Utility Stock Average

Standard & Poor's Stock Averages from 90 different industrial categories

Standard & Poor's 400 Industrial Stocks Average (S&P 400)

Standard & Poor's 20 Transportation Stocks Average

Standard & Poor's 40 Utility Stocks Average

Standard & Poor's Financial Stocks Average

Standard & Poor's 500 Stocks Composite Average

The New York Times Index

Value Line Average

Wilshire 5000 Equity Index

"footsie," or FT-SE, or Financial Times–Stock Exchange Index (from London)

New York Stock Exchange Composite Index (NYSE average)

New York Stock Exchange Industrial Index

New York Stock Exchange Utilities Index

New York Stock Exchange Transportation Index

New York Stock Exchange Financial Index

Nikkei Stock Market Index (from Tokyo)

Center for Research on Securities Prices (CRSP) Index

    Equally weighted (CRSPEQ)

    Value weighted (CRSPVW)

National Quotation Board Index of Over-the-Counter Stocks (OTC Comprehensive)

American Stock Exchange (ASE) Index

Barron's 50 Stock Average

Well-known bond indexes include:

Dow Jones 20 Bonds Index

Dow Jones Public Utility Bond Index

Dow Jones Industrial Bond Index

Salomon Brothers Corporate Bond Index

Standard & Poor's Municipal Bond Index

Standard & Poor's U.S. Government Bond Index

Hundreds of other bond indexes[1]

Commodity indexes are also available, including Commodity Research Bureau Futures Index, Dow Jones Spot Commodity Index, Dow Jones Futures Commodity Index, and Reuters' United Kingdom Commodity Index.

These securities market indicators are published in financial newspapers and business periodicals, used in various research studies, and employed as a basis for investment strategies.[2]

The averages and indexes listed above are indicators of various trends. Someone searching for a growth industry in which to invest, for instance, would be more interested in Standard & Poor's indexes of stocks from 90 different industrial categories than in the Standard & Poor's Composite Index of 500 stocks from all industries. Figure 7-1 shows values for 90 different Standard & Poor's industry stock price indexes, which are published weekly, along with other information, in Standard & Poor's publication, *The Outlook*.

Market indexes furnish a handy summary of historical price levels in their specific markets, especially when they are presented in graphical form, as shown in Figure 1-1. This type of information has several uses. First, investors who own several securities in a given market or industry can quickly get an indication of how market movements have affected the value of their portfolio.

---

[1]See Frank Fabozzi and Irving Pollack, *The Handbook of Fixed Income Securities,* 2d ed. (Homewood, Ill., Dow Jones–Irwin, 1987), appendix entitled ''Fixed Income Indexes'' by Arthur Williams and Noreen M. Conwell, pp. 1288–1342. The appendix lists details of approximately 400 different indexes for corporate bonds and government bonds; U.S. government, U.S. government agencies, and corporate bonds; municipal bonds; Yankee bonds; Eurodollar bonds; foreign bonds; zero coupon bonds; and high-yield bonds. Salomon Brothers has 45, Standard & Poor's has 15, Shearson Lehman has 36, Moody's has 19, and Merrill Lynch has 95 bond indexes which they maintain and publish.

[2]A type of mutual fund called an *index fund* became popular during the 1980s. The stated objective of the index funds was to invest in the same stocks used to compute some broad stock market index (like the S&P 500 index) in order to earn the same return as the market average. Construction of an index fund is discussed by K. P. Ambachtsheer and J. L. Farrell, ''Can Active Management Add Value?'' *Financial Analysts Journal,* Nov.–Dec. 1975, pp. 39–48.

S&P Indexes of the Securities Markets

†Monthly stock price indexes

	Mar. Month End	% Change from Prev. Month	†Mar. Avg.	Apr. 5	1989 Range High	1989 Range Low
500 Composite	294.87	+ 2.1	292.71	296.24	299.63	275.31
Industrials	339.42	+ 1.8	337.74	340.97	346.41	318.66
Transportation	244.20	- 1.7	245.69	246.18	255.19	226.42
Utilities	117.60	+ 2.1	116.65	117.80	118.56	111.15
Financial	27.83	+ 6.0	26.96	28.06	28.06	24.30
OTC 250	261.45	+ 1.3	260.46	262.98	265.26	245.95
Capital Goods	258.64	- 2.5	262.31	258.76	277.89	257.02
Consumer goods	358.66	+ 3.6	352.18	360.63	360.63	334.31
Energy Composite	290.89	+ 4.4	288.85	293.42	295.97	270.63
High Tech Composite	179.39	- 5.0	183.59	178.43	197.62	177.00
High Grade	219.09	+ 3.2	216.00	218.91	220.63	205.51
Low Priced	645.52	- 0.1	644.16	648.76	678.56	603.26

INDUSTRIALS

	Mar. Month End	% Change from Prev. Month	†Mar. Avg.	Apr. 5	1989 Range High	1989 Range Low
Aerospace/Defense	342.06	+ 4.8	333.74	342.61	342.61	313.83
Aluminum	257.70	- 3.3	259.57	256.82	287.84	249.35
Automobile	175.77	- 4.4	179.25	170.08	200.68	170.08
Excl. General Motors	120.28	- 5.4	123.13	117.09	138.81	117.09
Auto Parts: After Mkt.	34.25	+ 0.8	34.09	33.72	36.11	33.50
Heavy Duty Trucks & Parts	73.39	+ 1.9	73.00	73.68	74.34	69.75
Beverages: Alcoholic	241.10	+ 4.6	235.69	244.41	244.41	216.51
Soft Drinks	466.49	+ 8.3	451.97	476.34	476.34	408.89
Broadcast Media	3991.42	+ 6.4	3875.66	4062.03	4062.03	3592.72
Building Materials	227.35	+ 0.4	225.69	227.37	234.75	216.33
Chemicals	160.26	+ 2.4	159.25	161.81	164.76	146.63
Chemicals: Diversified	410.69	+ 8.3	384.97	422.73	422.73	363.14
Coal	317.31	- 3.2	324.61	318.19	336.78	309.63
Commercial Services	28.91	- 3.6	29.40	29.28	30.55	28.73
Communication—Equip./Mfrs.	65.74	- 2.5	66.81	64.69	71.63	64.69
Computer Software & Serv.	185.36	- 9.5	194.61	182.65	217.08	182.65
Computer Systems	407.31	- 8.6	425.02	400.71	466.21	399.24
Excl. I.B.M.	54.91	+ 5.1	53.71	55.46	55.46	51.00
Conglomerates	209.63	+ 5.4	202.50	206.40	212.61	193.00
Containers: Metal & Glass	1050.29	- 0.8	1056.86	1041.21	1134.92	996.17
Paper	105.80	+ 0.4	104.68	106.68	106.68	100.39
Cosmetics	691.72	- 2.5	699.92	695.96	747.19	690.14
Electrical Equipment	115.41	+ 0.7	115.27	118.68	118.68	109.35
Electronics: Defense	84.71	- 6.6	88.02	86.20	100.77	83.77
Electronics: Instrumentation	48.29	- 1.1	47.42	47.96	51.86	45.32
Electronics: Semiconductors	97.36	+ 0.0	98.25	96.54	103.98	96.12
Engineering & Construction	957.21	+ 7.5	941.77	971.14	971.14	807.14
Entertainment	457.20	+ 4.7	443.38	466.05	466.05	435.09
Foods	263.82	+ 3.4	257.82	265.11	265.11	250.43
Food Wholesalers	34.38	+ 7.0	33.78	35.74	35.74	31.28
*Gaming Cos.	177.03	- 6.4	180.76	172.66	187.00	157.66
Gold Mining	19.22	- 4.6	20.00	19.50	20.79	19.07
Hardware & Tools	45.09	+ 4.3	44.55	46.09	46.15	42.76
Homebuilding	117.85	+ 4.8	115.08	119.11	119.11	108.02
‡ Health Care: Composite	210.19	+ 4.2	204.68	209.74	209.74	193.26
Diversified	81.57	- 5.8	84.93	81.45	87.87	73.62
Miscellaneous	735.98	+ 5.3	718.02	751.51	751.51	669.26
Drugs	66.72	+ 7.6	64.50	66.92	66.92	56.48
Hospital Management	118.80	+ 1.4	117.81	120.14	124.21	114.16
Medical Prod. & Sup.	213.67	+ 2.7	208.19	214.28	217.79	206.43
Hotel-Motel	458.39	+ 2.2	447.55	453.93	463.10	426.05
Household Furnish. & Appliances	474.02	+ 2.9	465.60	474.76	474.76	447.52
Household Products	234.52	+ 6.0	223.50	236.35	236.35	212.23
Insurance Brokers						

	Mar. Month End	% Change from Prev. Month	†Mar. Avg.	Apr. 5	1989 Range High	1989 Range Low
Leisure Time	238.94	+ 6.4	226.02	240.45	240.45	197.80
Machine Tools	129.92	+ 2.2	130.11	127.30	141.30	127.30
Machinery: Diversified	231.06	+ 0.9	230.56	233.12	244.50	228.28
Manufactured Housing	159.27	+11.1	154.31	157.69	159.80	135.89
Manufacturing: Div. Industrials	210.66	- 2.3	213.04	212.60	224.98	209.08
Metals: Miscellaneous	211.17	- 1.1	213.77	208.79	226.34	201.44
Miscellaneous	86.26	+ 2.3	85.86	86.75	87.94	80.98
Office Equipment & Supplies	200.08	- 1.0	201.32	201.93	212.38	194.70
Offshore Drilling	49.95	+11.8	47.81	49.42	50.16	42.47
Oil: Composite	563.96	+ 4.1	580.70	569.55	574.65	528.17
Domestic Integrated	585.18	+ 5.1	578.03	596.50	596.50	528.88
Int'l Integrated	263.88	+ 3.6	263.28	265.16	270.81	251.80
Oil Well Equip. & Service	1278.87	+ 7.5	1260.35	1268.98	1294.22	1104.06
Paper & Forest Products	636.76	- 0.3	637.48	635.46	669.43	628.47
Pollution Control	229.49	+ 5.7	222.37	235.34	235.34	213.31
Publishing	1679.76	+ 1.5	1667.40	1698.56	1763.29	1644.28
Publishing: Newspapers	108.48	+ 2.7	105.87	109.43	110.12	102.33
Restaurants	148.85	+ 0.8	147.19	149.83	150.73	135.18
Retail: Composite	325.97	+ 2.7	321.81	326.84	329.60	307.66
Department Stores	809.73	+ 5.8	788.40	818.15	818.15	736.02
Drug Stores	96.39	- 0.2	96.21	98.52	100.21	89.76
Food Chains	327.81	+ 4.9	316.40	325.92	325.92	303.91
Gen. Merchandise Chains	24.95	+ 3.3	24.61	25.17	25.46	23.59
Specialty	441.99	- 0.6	443.61	435.64	454.04	428.01
Shoes	247.86	+ 8.5	238.95	251.87	251.87	209.46
Steel	53.94	- 3.3	54.34	53.41	60.02	52.12
Textiles: Apparel Mfrs.	171.41	+ 5.4	167.10	170.08	174.04	153.19
Tobacco	584.80	+ 9.9	563.87	585.36	585.36	499.40
Toys	22.61	+ 9.7	22.09	22.49	23.12	19.33

UTILITIES

	Mar. Month End	% Change from Prev. Month	†Mar. Avg.	Apr. 5	1989 Range High	1989 Range Low
Electric Companies	53.48	+ 0.2	53.21	53.75	55.04	52.93
Natural Gas	353.69	+ 0.4	353.87	358.43	363.63	332.51
Telephone	219.86	+ 3.8	216.49	219.19	219.19	201.60

TRANSPORTATION

	Mar. Month End	% Change from Prev. Month	†Mar. Avg.	Apr. 5	1989 Range High	1989 Range Low
Airlines	297.68	+ 8.2	278.06	298.30	298.30	244.25
Railroads	179.19	- 5.2	185.35	180.75	190.42	174.36
Truckers	254.04	- 5.4	261.17	261.17	295.21	253.26

FINANCIAL

	Mar. Month End	% Change from Prev. Month	†Mar. Avg.	Apr. 5	1989 Range High	1989 Range Low
Bank Composite	161.90	+ 8.4	152.77	161.08	161.08	141.94
Money Center Banks	115.59	+14.8	104.67	113.57	113.57	97.55
Major Regional Banks	111.46	+ 2.6	109.29	112.04	112.04	102.65
Other Major Banks	123.74	+ 9.6	116.52	123.69	123.69	104.05
Life Insurance	737.79	+ 5.1	711.81	749.69	749.69	669.64
Multi-Line Insurance	46.30	+ 5.4	45.35	46.94	46.94	41.90
Property-Casualty Insurance	302.13	+ 4.6	295.79	307.42	307.42	267.36
Savings & Loan Holding Cos.	43.16	- 0.1	43.08	45.19	46.08	40.84
Personal Loans	222.14	+ 4.0	219.60	224.89	224.89	204.39
Financial Miscellaneous	28.03	+ 3.0	27.60	28.69	28.69	25.06
Brokerage Firms	56.00	- 1.9	57.09	56.20	60.21	50.32
Real Estate Investment Trusts	3.63	- 1.4	3.69	3.67	3.76	3.58
* Investment Cos.	55.66	- 1.4	56.41	56.07	57.30	54.97
* Investment Cos.: Bond Funds	8.93	- 1.3	8.96	8.84	9.20	8.84

*Not included in composite indexes.
†Figures for 500 Composite, Industrials, Transportation, Utilities and Financial based on daily indexes. All others based on weekly indexes. ‡Group established in January 1987.

Figure 7-1 Industry index values published in *The Outlook*. (*Source: The Outlook,* Standard & Poor's Corporation, April 12, 1989, p. 848.)

Second, indexes are useful for historical analysis. By analyzing market indexes and other economic indicators, an analyst may detect some consistent relationships between different indexes and the fortunes of sectors of the economy. Such relationships are useful in forecasting and analysis.

7-2   CONSTRUCTION OF AN INDEX

Each index is constructed differently. A well-constructed market index will give an unbiased indication of the prices of the population under consideration. A poorly constructed index will indicate only what an unrepresentative sample of the population is doing. (If a population is homogeneous, however, even a poorly constructed index will give a good indication of its movement.) The following factors should be considered when selecting or designing an index:

1. *Sample size:* The **sample** should be a statistically significant fraction of the *population* studied. Larger samples give clearer indications about what the underlying population is doing. But, if the sample is too large and diverse, it will be uneconomical to compile and would be uninteresting to specialized investors.

2. *Representativeness:* The sample should be **representative** of all sections of the population; a broad sample of securities should not contain only large firms or firms which are all in the same industry.

3. *Weighting:* The various elements in the sample should be assigned **weights.** A security's weight in an index should be proportional to the fraction of total market value represented by the firm's currently outstanding shares. *Value-weighted* systems reflect the investment opportunities actually available in the market. When *equal weights* are used in an index, they represent the probability of selecting any given security at random.

4. *Convenient units:* An index should be stated in **convenient units** that are easy to understand and that facilitate answering relevant questions.

7-3   CONTRASTING STOCK MARKET INDICATORS

It is instructive to compare and contrast one of the most useful stock market indicators with one of the vaguest. Therefore, we will compare the popular and highly publicized Dow Jones Industrial Average (DJIA hereafter) with the equally well-known Standard & Poor's 500 Stocks Composite Average (S&P 500 hereafter), using the criteria listed in Section 7-2.

The S&P 500 index is sold commercially to anyone who subscribes to it through the Standard & Poor's Corporation. The DJIA is published daily by the Dow Jones Company, owner of *The Wall Street Journal* and *Barron's* newspapers.

Sample Size   The S&P 500 index's 500 common stocks represent about one-third of the population of NYSE-listed stocks. The DJIA is an average of 30 securities listed on the NYSE. Thus, the DJIA samples only 2 percent of the population of about 1500 stocks listed on the NYSE and only 6 percent of the stocks in the S&P 500 index.

Using a small sample size has both advantages and disadvantages. The main advantage of a small sample size is that it is cheap and quick to tabulate. The main disadvantage of small samples of any kind is that they are subject to larger **sampling errors** than larger samples.

Representativeness   The DJIA contains only securities of *large, old, blue-chip NYSE-listed firms*. The DJIA does not contain small or new firms. In contrast, the S&P 500 includes a representative sample of stocks of large and small, new and old, profitable and unprofitable, NYSE-listed and over-the-counter, service and manufacturing corporations. The DJIA became popular decades ago when large samples such as the S&P 500 index were prohibitively costly. Such costs are not a problem today, however, because the clerical work has been computerized.

Weighting   The S&P 500 weights each security in proportion to the market value of all outstanding shares. These *market value weights* correspond to the investment opportunities that each issue of stock provides in the market. This value-weighting scheme is rational. The DJIA's weighting system is not as well planned.

In 1928, when the DJIA was expanded to 30 stocks, the 30 market prices were simply summed up and divided by 30 to obtain the DJIA.

$$\text{DJIA}_t = \sum_{i=1}^{30} p_{i,t} \bigg/ \text{divisor}_t \qquad \text{where} \begin{cases} \text{divisor} = 30 \text{ in } 1928 \\ \text{divisor} = 0.70 \text{ in } 1989 \end{cases}$$

Thus, equal weights of $\frac{1}{30}$ were assigned to the 30 securities used in 1928. Over the years, many of the 30 securities underwent stock splits and paid stock dividends, so the weights had to be changed frequently. A simplified numerical example in Table 7-1 demonstrates how the weights of a market average like the DJIA are changed to reflect stock dividends and splits.[3]

Convenient Units   The DJIA ranged between 500 and 2700 "points" in the 1980s. The Dow Jones Company said that each of these points equaled about a 7-cent change in the market value of an "average share of stock." Seen objectively, the so-called DJIA points are practically void of meaning.

---

[3]Split shares usually increase in value, but this is due to retained earnings or growth in earnings and is unrelated to the stock split. The effects of stock splits and stock dividends, analyzed in Chapter 18, are seen to be nil, on average. See H. L. Butler, Jr., and R. F. DeMong, "The Changing Dow Jones Industrial Average," *Financial Analysts Journal*, July–Aug. 1986, pp. 59–62.

Table 7-1

CALCULATING THE DIVISOR FOR A THREE-STOCK AVERAGE, CALCULATED LIKE THE DJIA, WHEN ONE STOCK IS SPLIT

Three stocks	Prices before stock X is split 2-for-1 at 9 a.m. on split day	Prices after stock X is split 2-for-1 at 9:05 a.m. on split day
X	$40	$20
Y	30	30
Z	20	20
Totals:	$90/3 = 30	$70/divisor = 30
Divisors:	3	2.333

Unlike the DJIA, the S&P 500 is an index. This index is calculated from a 1941–1943 base value, as follows:

$$\text{S\&P 500} = \frac{\sum_{i=1}^{500} p_{i,t}N_{i,t}}{\sum_{i=1}^{500} p_{i,B}N_{i,B}} \times 10$$

$$= \frac{p_{1,t}N_{1,t} + p_{2,t}N_{2,t} + \cdots + p_{500,t}N_{500,t}}{p_{1,B}N_{1,B} + p_{2,B}N_{2,B} + \cdots + p_{500,B}N_{500,B}} \times 10$$

where p_{it} and N_{it} represent the market price per share and the number of shares outstanding for the ith stock during period t; the index is calculated over $i = 1, 2, \ldots, 500$ issues; and p_{iB} and N_{iB} denote the market price per share and number of shares of the ith stock used in the computations during the 1941–1943 base (B) period. The resulting index value has a starting value of 1 sometime during the 1941–1943 base period. But, this index number is multiplied by 10. The resulting market index is useful for gauging the performance of the market's prices in a perspective that facilitates comparisons.

7-4   MAINTENANCE PROBLEMS

Compelling situations arise periodically that necessitate the revision of a securities market index. The three main problems that cause an existing index to need revision are (1) making adjustments for stock dividends and stock splits, (2) changing the number of stocks in the sampled list, and (3) making substitutions to replace unsatisfactory securities. The way these three problems affect the DJIA and the S&P 500 index are considered next.

Stock Splits

The strange way that stock splits are reflected in the divisor of the DJIA was explained in Table 7-1. As a result of the Dow Jones procedure, the relative importance of stocks that split decreases and the importance of nonsplit stocks increases. There is no economic or statistical logic behind these shifts in the relative weights of the stocks in the DJIA.[4]

In contrast to the DJIA, the S&P 500 index handles stock splits logically. The S&P 500 index is constructed from presplit and postsplit market prices to nullify any changes in the units of account. Changes caused by stock dividends and/or splits do not distort the index because each security's market price is multiplied by the number of shares outstanding, as shown in the S&P 500 index formula above. Every market-value-weighted security in the S&P 500 index is unaffected by stock splits since the total value of the corporation is unaffected by changes in the unit of account.[5]

Size of the Sample

The DJIA sample size of 30 stocks was adopted in 1928. The total market value of these 30 blue-chip stocks equals about 25 percent of the aggregate value of all NYSE-listed stocks. The S&P 500 sample size of 500 stocks has been used since 1957. The 500-stock sample is 16.6 times larger than the DJIA sample of 30. The total market value of all the NYSE and over-the-counter stocks that comprise the S&P 500 equals approximately 75 percent of the total value of all NYSE-listed stocks.

Substitutions

Substitutions can be a recurrent and troublesome problem for an index, like the DJIA, computed from a small sample. There have been many substitutions in the DJIA over the decades that it has been popular.

One of the more interesting substitutions involved IBM's stock. IBM was *added* to the DJIA in 1932 and then *deleted* in 1939 in order to make room for American Telephone and Telegraph (AT&T). The logic behind this substitution was murky since AT&T is not an industrial stock, as the name DJIA would suggest. In 1979, IBM was once again *added* to the DJIA, along with Merck & Co., and Chrysler and Esmark were deleted. Sources from Dow Jones explained this change by saying that the two new stocks were more "blue-chip" than the two which were eliminated.

[4]H. L. Butler and J. D. Allen, "Dow Jones Industrial Average Re-examined," *Financial Analysts Journal,* Nov.–Dec., 1979, pp. 23–32. Butler and Allen discuss the effect of stock splits and substitutions on the DJIA. For a statistical analysis of the DJIA see Andrew T. Rudd, "The Revised Dow Jones Industrial Average," *Financial Analysts Journal,* Nov.–Dec. 1979, pp. 57–63. Also see Harold Bierman, Jr., "The Dow Jones Industrials. Do You Get What You See?," *Journal of Portfolio Management,* Fall 1988, vol. 15, pp. 58–60.

[5]Stock dividends and splits are analyzed in Chapter 18, where it is shown that the total value of the corporation is unaffected.

Substitutions in the S&P 500 are more logical and are also of only minor importance because of the small weight given to each individual stock. Essentially, stocks are added or deleted from the S&P 500 index only when they are listed or delisted from the NYSE or disappear because of mergers or acquisitions.

7-5 CORRELATIONS BETWEEN MARKET INDICATORS

The DJIA comes away from our comparison of the DJIA and the S&P 500 stock market indicators seeming very inadequate. Surprisingly, the two indicators are highly positively correlated with each other in spite of their statistical differences. In fact, nearly all the stock market indicators for markets in the United States are highly positively correlated with each other. Table 7-2 shows nine stock market indicators and their correlation coefficients.

Note that the American Stock Exchange (ASE), which has the lowest correlations with the other U.S. stock markets, nevertheless has a robust .67 as its lowest correlation coefficient. This is a highly significant positive correlation, and the other U.S. stock market indicators are even more highly correlated.[6]

[6]Levels of significance are highly dependent on the size of the underlying sample. When using the normal distribution (that is, for sample sizes in excess of 30) a simple correlation coefficient in excess of .35 is significantly different from zero. For large samples .20 is a statistically significant correlation.

Table 7-2
CORRELATION COEFFICIENTS OF DIFFERENT STOCK MARKET INDICATORS*

	DJIA	S&P 400	S&P 500	NYSEAVG	ASEAVG	OTCIND	OTCCOMP	CRSPEQ	CRSPVW
DJIA	1.0								
S&P 400	.951	1.0							
S&P 500	.967	.980	1.0						
NYSEAVG	.941	.984	.988	1.0					
ASEAVG	.676	.791	.790	.840	1.0				
OTCIND	.773	.805	.811	.839	.702	1.0			
OTCCOMP	.795	.826	.856	.842	.761	.824	1.0		
CRSPEQ	.935	.943	.942	.944	.857	.742	.810	1.0	
CRSPVW	.944	.943	.953	.953	.853	.768	.811	.925	1.0

*Monthly returns from 1977 to 1988 inclusive. The nine averages are: (1) Dow Jones Industrial Average (DJIA), (2) Standard & Poor's 400 Industrial Stocks Average (S&P 400), (3) Standard & Poor's 500 Composite Stocks Average (S&P 500), (4) New York Stock Exchange Average (NYSEAVG), (5) American Stock Exchange Average (ASEAVG), (6) Over-the-Counter Industrial Stocks Average (OTCIND), (7) OTC Composite Stocks Average (OTCCOMP), (8) CRSP Equally Weighted Stocks Index (CRSPEQ), (9) CRSP Value Weighted Stocks Index (CRSPVW).

Table 7-3
S&P 500 AVERAGE COMMON STOCK RATES OF RETURNS, 1926–1987

To the end of	From the beginning of 1926	1927	1928	1929	1930	1931	1932	1933	1934	1935	1936	1937	1938	1939	1940	1941	1942	1943	1944	1945	1946
1926	11.6																				
1927	23.9	37.5																			
1928	30.1	40.5	43.6																		
1929	19.2	21.8	14.7	-8.4																	
1930	8.7	8.0	-0.4	-17.1	-24.9																
1931	-2.5	-5.1	-13.5	-27.0	-34.8	-43.3															
1932	-3.3	-5.6	-12.5	-22.7	-26.9	-27.9	-8.2														
1933	2.5	1.2	-3.8	-11.2	-11.9	-7.1	18.9	54.0													
1934	2.0	0.9	-3.5	-9.7	-9.9	-5.7	11.7	23.2	-1.4												
1935	5.9	5.2	1.8	-3.1	-2.2	3.1	19.8	30.9	20.6	47.7											
1936	8.1	7.8	4.9	0.9	2.3	7.7	22.5	31.6	24.9	40.6	33.9										
1937	3.7	3.0	0.0	-3.9	-3.3	0.2	10.2	14.3	6.1	8.7	-6.7	-35.0									
1938	5.5	5.1	2.5	-0.9	-0.0	3.6	13.0	16.9	10.7	13.9	4.5	-7.7	31.1								
1939	5.1	4.6	2.3	-0.8	-0.1	3.2	11.2	14.3	8.7	10.9	3.2	-5.3	14.3	-0.4							
1940	4.0	3.5	1.3	-1.6	-1.0	1.8	8.6	11.0	5.9	7.2	0.5	-6.5	5.6	-5.2	-9.8						
1941	3.0	2.4	0.3	-2.4	-1.9	0.5	6.4	8.2	3.5	4.3	-1.6	-7.5	1.0	-7.4	-10.7	-11.6					
1942	3.9	3.5	1.5	-1.0	-0.4	2.0	7.6	9.3	5.3	6.1	1.2	-3.4	4.6	-1.1	-1.4	3.1	20.3				
1943	5.0	4.7	2.9	0.6	1.3	3.7	9.0	10.8	7.2	8.2	4.0	0.4	7.9	3.8	4.8	10.2	23.1	25.9			
1944	5.8	5.5	3.8	1.7	2.5	4.8	9.8	11.5	8.3	9.3	5.7	2.6	9.5	6.3	7.7	12.5	22.0	22.8	19.8		
1945	7.1	6.9	5.4	3.5	4.3	6.6	11.5	13.2	10.4	11.5	8.4	5.9	12.6	10.1	12.0	17.0	25.4	27.2	27.8	36.4	
1946	6.4	6.1	4.7	2.8	3.5	5.6	10.1	11.6	8.8	9.7	6.8	4.4	10.1	7.7	8.9	12.4	17.9	17.3	14.5	12.0	-8.1
1947	6.3	6.1	4.7	3.0	3.7	5.6	9.8	11.2	8.6	9.4	6.7	4.5	9.6	7.5	8.5	11.4	15.8	14.9	12.3	9.9	-1.4
1948	6.3	6.1	4.7	3.1	3.8	5.6	9.6	10.8	8.4	9.1	6.6	4.6	9.2	7.3	8.1	10.6	14.2	13.2	10.9	8.8	0.8
1949	6.8	6.6	5.3	3.8	4.5	6.3	10.1	11.2	9.0	9.7	7.4	5.6	10.0	8.3	9.2	11.5	14.8	14.0	12.2	10.7	5.1
1950	7.7	7.5	6.4	4.9	5.6	7.4	11.1	12.3	10.2	11.0	8.9	7.3	11.5	10.0	11.0	13.4	16.6	16.1	14.8	13.9	9.9
1951	8.3	8.1	7.1	5.7	6.4	8.2	11.7	12.9	11.0	11.7	9.8	8.4	12.4	11.1	12.1	14.3	17.3	16.9	15.9	15.3	12.1
1952	8.6	8.5	7.5	6.2	6.9	8.6	12.0	13.2	11.3	12.1	10.3	9.0	12.8	11.6	12.5	14.6	17.4	17.1	16.1	15.7	13.0
1953	8.3	8.1	7.2	5.9	6.5	8.2	11.4	12.4	10.7	11.4	9.6	8.3	11.9	10.7	11.5	13.4	15.7	15.3	14.3	13.7	11.2
1954	9.6	9.5	8.6	7.4	8.1	9.7	12.9	14.0	12.4	13.1	11.6	10.4	13.9	12.9	13.9	15.8	18.2	18.0	17.4	17.1	15.1
1955	10.2	10.2	9.3	8.2	8.9	10.5	13.7	14.7	13.2	13.9	12.5	11.4	14.8	13.9	14.9	16.8	19.1	19.0	18.5	18.4	16.7
1956	10.1	10.1	9.2	8.2	8.8	10.4	13.4	14.4	12.9	13.6	12.2	11.2	14.4	13.5	14.4	16.1	18.2	18.1	17.5	17.3	15.7
1957	9.4	9.3	8.5	7.4	8.1	9.5	12.3	13.2	11.8	12.4	11.0	10.0	13.0	12.1	12.8	14.3	16.2	15.9	15.2	14.9	13.2
1958	10.3	10.2	9.5	8.5	9.1	10.6	13.3	14.3	12.9	13.6	11.6	11.4	14.3	13.5	14.3	15.8	17.6	17.5	16.9	16.7	15.3
1959	10.3	10.3	9.5	8.6	9.2	10.6	13.3	14.2	12.9	13.5	12.3	11.4	14.2	13.4	14.1	15.6	17.3	17.1	16.6	16.4	15.1
1960	10.0	10.0	9.3	8.3	8.9	10.3	12.8	13.7	12.4	13.0	11.8	10.9	13.5	12.8	13.5	14.8	16.4	16.1	15.6	15.3	14.0
1961	10.5	10.4	9.7	8.8	9.4	10.8	13.3	14.1	12.9	13.4	12.3	11.5	14.1	13.4	14.0	15.3	16.9	16.7	16.2	16.0	14.8
1962	9.9	9.9	9.2	8.3	8.8	10.1	12.5	13.2	12.1	12.6	11.4	10.7	13.0	12.3	12.9	14.1	15.5	15.3	14.7	14.4	13.3
1963	10.2	10.2	9.5	8.7	9.2	10.5	12.8	13.5	12.4	12.9	11.8	11.1	13.4	12.7	13.3	14.5	15.8	15.6	15.1	14.9	13.8
1964	10.4	10.4	9.7	8.9	9.4	10.6	12.9	13.6	12.5	13.0	12.0	11.3	13.5	12.9	13.5	14.5	15.7	15.5	15.2	14.9	13.9
1965	10.4	10.4	9.8	9.0	9.5	10.7	12.9	13.6	12.5	13.0	12.0	11.3	13.5	12.9	13.4	14.5	15.7	15.5	15.0	14.8	13.8
1966	9.9	9.8	9.2	8.4	8.9	10.1	12.2	12.8	11.8	12.2	11.2	10.5	12.6	12.0	12.4	13.4	14.5	14.3	13.8	13.6	12.6
1967	10.2	10.2	9.6	8.8	9.3	10.4	12.5	13.1	12.1	12.5	11.6	10.9	12.9	12.4	12.8	13.8	14.9	14.7	14.2	14.0	13.1
1968	10.2	10.2	9.6	8.9	9.3	10.4	12.4	13.1	12.1	12.5	11.6	10.9	12.9	12.3	12.8	13.7	14.7	14.5	14.1	13.9	13.0
1969	9.8	9.7	9.1	8.4	8.9	9.9	11.8	12.4	11.4	11.8	10.9	10.3	12.1	11.6	12.0	12.8	13.8	13.6	13.1	12.9	12.0
1970	9.6	9.6	9.0	8.3	8.7	9.7	11.6	12.2	11.2	11.6	10.7	10.1	11.9	11.3	11.7	12.5	13.5	13.2	12.8	12.5	11.7
1971	9.7	9.7	9.1	8.4	8.9	9.9	11.7	12.2	11.3	11.7	10.8	10.2	11.9	11.4	11.8	12.6	13.5	13.3	12.8	12.6	11.8

Table 7-3 (continued)

From the beginning of	1947	1948	1949	1950	1951	1952	1953	1954	1955	1956	1957	1958	1959	1960	1961	1962	1963	1964	1965	1966	1967
1972	9.9	9.9	9.3	8.7	9.1	10.1	11.9	12.4	11.5	11.9	11.0	10.5	12.1	11.6	12.0	12.8	13.7	13.5	13.0	12.8	12.0
1973	9.3	9.3	8.7	8.1	8.5	9.4	11.1	11.7	10.8	11.1	10.3	9.7	11.3	10.8	11.1	11.8	12.7	12.4	12.0	11.7	10.9
1974	8.5	8.4	7.8	7.2	7.5	8.4	10.1	10.6	9.7	10.0	9.1	8.5	10.1	9.5	9.8	10.5	11.2	10.9	10.5	10.2	9.4
1975	9.0	8.9	8.4	7.7	8.1	9.0	10.6	11.1	10.2	10.6	9.8	9.2	10.7	10.2	10.5	11.1	11.9	11.6	11.2	11.0	10.2
1976	9.2	9.2	8.7	8.0	8.4	9.3	10.9	11.4	10.5	10.9	10.1	9.5	11.0	10.5	10.8	11.5	12.2	12.0	11.6	11.3	10.6
1977	8.9	8.8	8.3	7.7	8.1	8.9	10.5	10.9	10.1	10.4	9.6	9.1	10.5	10.0	10.3	10.9	11.6	11.4	11.0	10.7	10.0
1978	8.9	8.8	8.3	7.7	8.0	8.9	10.4	10.8	10.0	10.3	9.6	9.0	10.4	9.9	10.2	10.8	11.5	11.3	10.9	10.6	10.0
1979	9.0	9.0	8.5	7.9	8.2	9.1	10.6	11.0	10.2	10.5	9.8	9.2	10.6	10.1	10.4	11.0	11.7	11.4	11.1	10.8	10.2
1980	9.4	9.4	8.9	8.3	8.7	9.5	11.0	11.4	10.6	10.9	10.2	9.7	11.1	10.6	10.9	11.5	12.2	11.9	11.6	11.4	10.7
1981	9.1	9.1	8.6	8.1	8.4	9.2	10.6	11.0	10.3	10.6	9.9	9.4	10.7	10.2	10.5	11.1	11.7	11.5	11.1	10.9	10.3
1982	9.3	9.3	8.8	8.3	8.6	9.4	10.8	11.2	10.5	10.8	10.1	9.6	10.9	10.5	10.8	11.3	11.9	11.7	11.4	11.2	10.6
1983	9.6	9.5	9.1	8.5	8.9	9.6	11.0	11.5	10.7	11.0	10.3	9.9	11.1	10.7	11.0	11.5	12.2	12.0	11.6	11.4	10.9
1984	9.5	9.5	9.0	8.5	8.8	9.6	10.9	11.3	10.6	11.0	10.3	9.8	11.0	10.6	10.9	11.4	12.0	11.8	11.5	11.3	10.7
1985	9.8	9.8	9.4	8.9	9.2	9.9	11.3	11.7	11.0	11.3	10.7	10.2	11.4	11.1	11.3	11.8	12.4	12.3	12.0	11.8	11.2
1986	10.0	9.9	9.5	9.0	9.4	10.1	11.4	11.8	11.2	11.4	10.8	10.4	11.6	11.2	11.5	12.0	12.6	12.4	12.1	11.9	11.4
1987	9.9	9.9	9.5	9.0	9.3	10.0	11.3	11.7	11.0	11.3	10.7	10.3	11.5	11.1	11.3	11.8	12.4	12.2	11.9	11.8	11.2

To the end of	From the beginning of																				
	1947	1948	1949	1950	1951	1952	1953	1954	1955	1956	1957	1958	1959	1960	1961	1962	1963	1964	1965	1966	1967
1947	5.7																				
1948	5.6	5.5																			
1949	9.8	11.9	18.8																		
1950	14.9	18.2	25.1	31.7																	
1951	16.7	19.6	24.7	27.8	24.0																
1952	17.0	19.4	23.1	24.6	21.2	18.4															
1953	14.2	15.7	17.9	17.6	13.3	8.3	-1.0														
1954	18.4	20.4	23.9	23.9	22.0	21.4	22.9	52.6													
1955	19.8	21.7	24.2	25.2	23.9	23.9	25.7	41.7	31.6												
1956	18.4	19.9	21.9	22.3	20.8	20.2	20.6	28.9	18.4	6.6											
1957	15.4	16.4	17.7	17.6	15.7	14.4	13.6	17.5	7.7	-2.5	-10.8										
1958	17.5	18.7	20.1	20.2	18.8	18.1	18.1	22.3	15.7	10.9	13.1	43.4									
1959	17.1	18.1	19.3	19.4	18.1	17.3	17.2	20.5	15.0	11.1	12.7	26.7	12.0								
1960	15.8	16.6	17.6	17.5	16.2	15.3	14.9	17.4	12.4	8.9	9.5	17.3	6.1	0.5							
1961	16.5	17.3	18.3	18.3	17.1	16.4	16.2	18.6	14.4	11.7	12.8	19.6	12.6	12.9	26.9						
1962	14.8	15.4	16.1	15.9	14.7	13.9	13.4	15.2	11.2	8.5	8.9	13.3	6.8	5.2	7.6	-8.7					
1963	15.2	15.8	16.6	16.4	15.3	14.6	14.3	15.9	12.4	10.2	10.8	14.8	9.9	9.3	12.5	5.9	22.8				
1964	15.3	15.9	16.6	16.4	15.4	14.7	14.3	16.0	12.8	10.9	11.5	15.1	10.7	10.7	13.5	9.3	19.6	16.5			
1965	15.1	15.7	16.3	16.2	15.2	14.6	14.3	15.7	12.8	11.1	11.6	14.7	10.9	11.0	13.2	10.1	17.2	14.4	12.5		
1966	13.7	14.2	14.7	14.4	13.4	12.7	12.4	13.4	10.7	9.0	9.2	11.7	8.2	7.7	9.0	5.7	12.4	5.6	0.6	-10.1	
1967	14.2	14.6	15.1	14.9	14.0	13.4	13.1	14.2	11.6	10.1	10.5	12.8	9.9	9.6	11.0	8.6	12.2	9.9	7.8	5.6	24.0
1968	14.0	14.5	14.9	14.7	13.8	13.3	13.0	14.0	11.6	10.2	10.5	12.7	10.0	9.8	11.0	8.9	12.2	10.2	8.6	7.4	17.3
1969	13.0	13.3	13.7	13.4	12.5	11.9	11.6	12.4	10.1	8.7	8.9	10.7	8.2	7.8	8.7	6.6	9.0	6.8	5.0	3.2	8.0
1970	12.6	12.9	13.2	13.0	12.1	11.5	11.1	11.9	9.7	8.4	8.6	10.2	7.8	7.5	8.2	6.3	8.3	6.4	4.8	3.3	7.0
1971	12.6	12.9	13.3	13.0	12.2	11.6	11.3	12.0	10.0	8.8	8.9	10.5	8.3	8.0	8.7	7.1	9.0	7.4	6.1	5.1	8.4
1972	12.9	13.2	13.5	13.3	12.5	12.0	11.7	12.4	10.5	9.4	9.5	11.0	9.0	8.8	9.5	8.1	9.9	8.6	7.6	7.0	10.1
1973	11.7	11.9	12.2	11.9	11.2	10.6	10.3	10.8	9.0	7.9	7.9	9.2	7.3	6.9	7.5	6.0	7.4	6.0	4.9	4.0	6.2
1974	10.1	10.2	10.4	10.1	9.3	8.7	8.2	8.7	6.9	5.7	5.7	6.7	4.8	4.3	4.6	3.0	4.1	2.5	1.2	0.1	1.4
1975	10.9	11.1	11.3	11.0	10.3	9.7	9.4	9.9	8.2	7.1	7.1	8.2	6.4	6.1	6.5	5.2	6.3	5.1	4.1	3.3	4.9
1976	11.3	11.5	11.7	11.5	10.8	10.3	9.9	10.4	8.8	7.8	7.9	9.0	7.3	7.1	7.5	6.3	7.5	6.4	5.6	5.0	6.6

Table 7-3 (continued)

To the end of	From the beginning of																				
	1947	1948	1949	1950	1951	1952	1953	1954	1955	1956	1957	1958	1959	1960	1961	1962	1963	1964	1965	1966	1967
1977	10.7	10.8	11.0	10.7	10.0	9.5	9.2	9.6	8.1	7.1	7.1	8.1	6.5	6.2	6.6	5.4	6.4	5.4	4.6	3.9	5.3
1978	10.5	10.7	10.9	10.6	9.9	9.4	9.1	9.5	8.0	7.1	7.1	8.0	6.5	6.2	6.6	5.5	6.5	5.4	4.7	4.1	5.4
1979	10.8	10.9	11.1	10.8	10.2	9.7	9.4	9.8	8.4	7.5	7.6	8.5	7.1	6.8	7.2	6.2	7.1	6.2	5.6	5.1	6.3
1980	11.3	11.5	11.7	11.5	10.9	10.4	10.2	10.6	9.2	8.4	8.5	9.4	8.1	7.9	8.3	7.4	8.4	7.6	7.1	6.7	8.0
1981	10.8	11.0	11.2	10.9	10.3	9.9	9.6	10.0	8.7	7.9	7.9	8.8	7.5	7.3	7.6	6.8	7.6	6.9	6.3	5.9	7.1
1982	11.1	11.3	11.5	11.2	10.7	10.2	10.0	10.4	9.1	8.4	8.4	9.3	8.1	7.9	8.2	7.4	8.3	7.6	7.1	6.8	8.0
1983	11.4	11.6	11.8	11.6	11.0	10.6	10.4	10.8	9.6	8.8	8.9	9.8	8.6	8.5	8.8	8.1	8.9	8.3	7.9	7.6	8.8
1984	11.3	11.4	11.6	11.4	10.9	10.5	10.2	10.6	9.4	8.7	8.8	9.6	8.5	8.4	8.7	8.0	8.8	8.2	7.8	7.5	8.6
1985	11.8	11.9	12.1	11.9	11.4	11.1	10.8	11.2	10.1	9.5	9.6	10.4	9.3	9.2	9.6	8.9	9.7	9.2	8.8	8.7	9.7
1986	11.9	12.1	12.3	12.1	11.6	11.3	11.1	11.4	10.4	9.7	9.8	10.6	9.6	9.5	9.9	9.3	10.1	9.6	9.3	9.1	10.2
1987	11.8	11.9	12.1	11.9	11.4	11.1	10.9	11.3	10.2	9.6	9.7	10.4	9.5	9.4	9.7	9.1	9.9	9.4	9.1	8.9	9.9

To the end of	From the beginning of																			
	1968	1969	1970	1971	1972	1973	1974	1975	1976	1977	1978	1979	1980	1981	1982	1983	1984	1985	1986	1987
1968	11.1																			
1969	0.8	-8.5																		
1970	1.9	-2.4	4.0																	
1971	4.8	2.8	9.0	14.3																
1972	7.5	6.7	12.3	16.6	19.0															
1973	3.5	2.0	4.8	5.1	0.8	-14.7														
1974	-1.5	-3.4	-2.4	-3.9	-9.3	-20.8	-26.5													
1975	2.7	1.6	3.3	3.2	0.6	-4.9	0.4	37.2												
1976	4.9	4.1	6.0	6.4	4.9	1.6	7.7	30.4	23.8											
1977	3.6	2.8	4.3	4.3	2.8	-0.2	3.8	16.4	7.2	-7.2										
1978	3.9	3.2	4.5	4.6	3.3	0.9	4.3	13.9	7.0	-0.5	6.6									
1979	5.0	4.5	5.9	6.1	5.1	3.2	6.6	14.8	9.7	5.4	12.3	18.4								
1980	6.9	6.5	8.0	8.4	7.8	6.5	9.9	17.5	13.9	11.6	18.7	25.2	32.4							
1981	6.0	5.6	6.9	7.2	6.5	5.2	7.9	14.0	10.6	8.1	12.3	14.3	12.2	-4.9						
1982	7.0	6.7	7.9	8.3	7.7	6.7	9.4	14.9	12.1	10.2	14.0	16.0	15.2	7.4	21.4					
1983	7.9	7.7	8.9	9.3	8.9	8.0	10.6	15.7	13.3	11.9	15.4	17.3	17.0	12.3	22.0	22.5				
1984	7.8	7.6	8.7	9.1	8.7	7.9	10.2	14.8	12.5	11.2	14.1	15.4	14.8	10.7	16.5	14.1	6.3			
1985	9.0	8.9	10.1	10.5	10.2	9.6	11.9	16.2	14.3	13.3	16.2	17.6	17.5	14.7	20.2	19.8	18.5	32.2		
1986	9.5	9.4	10.6	11.0	10.8	10.2	12.4	16.4	14.7	13.8	16.4	17.7	17.6	15.3	19.9	19.5	18.5	25.1	18.5	
1987	9.3	9.2	10.3	10.6	10.4	9.9	11.9	15.5	13.9	13.0	15.3	16.3	16.0	13.8	17.3	16.5	15.0	18.1	11.7	5.2

Source: R. G. Ibbotson and Rex A. Sinquefield, *Stocks, Bonds, Bills and Inflation (SBBI): 1982 Ed.,* updated in *SBBI 1988 Yearbook* (Chicago, Ill.: Ibbotson Associates Inc.).

The Naive-Buy-and-Hold Strategy

One typical question in the minds of potential investors is: "What kind of return can I earn if I invest in common stocks?" The answer is shown in Table 7-3, which gives the annual rates of return from Standard & Poor's 500 Stocks Composite Average over every year and every combination of consecutive years from 1926 to 1987. These rates of return were calculated with Equation (7-1).

$$r_t = \frac{\text{S\&P } 500_t - \text{S\&P } 500_{t-1} + \text{S\&P } 500 \text{ cash dividends}_t}{\text{S\&P } 500_{t-1}} \tag{7-1}$$

where S&P 500_t denotes the market value of Standard & Poor's 500 Stocks Composite Index at the end of period t.

Table 7-3 shows what an investment in the S&P 500 would earn, assuming all cash dividends were reinvested and no income taxes or brokerage commissions were paid. The returns in Table 7-3 are described as the returns from a *naive buy-and-hold strategy*. These common stock returns convert to price indexes, like those illustrated in Figure 7-2.

Naive buy-and-hold strategy is a phrase used to describe various random and uninformed approaches to the management of investments. A portfolio of investments selected by an uninformed investor who picked a diversified list of assets randomly (by throwing an unaimed dart at the stock listings page in a newspaper, for instance) and then simply held this portfolio and ignored all new information would be called a naive buy-and-hold portfolio. These types of portfolios are constructed and used as standards of comparison against which more informed and aggressive investment strategies may be measured.

The S&P 500 is one well-known naive buy-and-hold portfolio; it is well constructed for gauging the performance of other common stock investment strategies. We saw the S&P 500 returns in Table 7-3. Table 7-4 shows the correlation coefficients between various naive buy-and-hold strategies.

Comparing Indicators from Different Markets

Hypothetical portfolios have been prepared to facilitate the comparison of investment returns from different categories of assets. A portfolio of common stocks, a portfolio of U.S. Treasury bills, a portfolio of U.S. Treasury bonds, and a portfolio of corporate bonds were prepared by randomly selecting a representative sample of each of these types of securities. The portfolios thus represent naive buy-and-hold investment performances.

Long-Term Bond Returns The one-period market rates of return for both long-term corporate and U.S. Treasury bonds were calculated from Equation (7-2).

$$r_t = \frac{p_t - p_{t-1} + c_t}{p_{t-1}} = \frac{\text{price change} + \text{coupon}}{\text{purchase price}} = \frac{\$3 + \$8}{\$94} = 11.7\% \tag{7-2}$$

Consider one hypothetical bond in the portfolio. Let $c_t = \$8$ denote the coupon interest payment in the tth period, $p_t = \$97$ represent the sales price

Table 7-4

CORRELATIONS BETWEEN DIFFERENT INVESTMENT RETURNS

	NYSE	AMEX	OTC	U.S. total equities	European equities	Asian equities	Other equities	Foreign total equities	World equities	U.S. Treasury notes	U.S. Treasury bonds	U.S. agencies	U.S. total government bonds
NYSE	1.000												
AMEX	0.851	1.000											
OTC	0.900	0.897	1.000										
U.S. equities	0.997	0.883	0.929	1.000									
European equities	0.618	0.689	0.651	0.640	1.000								
Asian equities	0.237	0.123	0.244	0.237	0.391	1.000							
Other equities	0.792	0.848	0.766	0.807	0.731	0.320	1.000						
Foreign equities	0.656	0.657	0.666	0.672	0.908	0.695	0.765	1.000					
World total equities	0.955	0.879	0.914	0.964	0.787	0.409	0.853	0.841	1.000				
U.S. Treasury notes	0.105	-0.102	-0.117	0.068	-0.159	-0.108	-0.252	-0.192	-0.037	1.000			
U.S. Treasury bonds	0.091	-0.153	-0.094	0.056	-0.130	-0.005	-0.266	-0.165	-0.041	0.904	1.000		
U.S. agencies	0.007	-0.201	-0.187	-0.030	-0.280	-0.178	-0.342	-0.327	-0.156	0.962	0.904	1.000	
U.S. total government bonds	0.033	-0.183	-0.189	-0.006	-0.201	-0.067	-0.296	-0.226	-0.105	0.972	0.950	0.964	1.000
U.S. intermediate-term corporate bonds	0.361	0.078	0.132	0.322	0.099	0.045	-0.028	0.072	0.242	0.900	0.865	0.848	0.887
U.S. long-term corporate bonds	0.341	0.058	0.110	0.302	0.095	0.022	-0.033	0.052	0.219	0.858	0.912	0.808	0.859
U.S. total corporate bonds	0.361	0.083	0.132	0.323	0.117	0.033	-0.019	0.075	0.243	0.865	0.902	0.809	0.863
U.S. total bonds	0.206	-0.047	-0.031	0.166	-0.045	-0.007	-0.160	-0.074	0.075	0.954	0.956	0.915	0.967
Foreign domestic corporate bonds	0.044	0.025	0.107	0.050	0.315	0.269	-0.028	0.314	0.156	0.035	0.172	-0.008	0.085
Foreign domestic government bonds	0.010	0.078	0.097	0.024	0.345	0.084	0.058	0.255	0.115	0.061	0.190	0.044	0.117
Foreign crossborder bonds	0.270	0.116	0.172	0.255	0.253	0.154	0.017	0.215	0.249	0.560	0.716	0.552	0.607
Foreign total bonds	0.042	0.067	0.052	0.052	0.343	0.153	0.028	0.281	0.144	0.097	0.239	0.072	0.153
World total bonds	0.136	0.035	0.069	0.124	0.248	0.122	-0.041	0.194	0.155	0.511	0.619	0.473	0.561
U.S. business real estate	0.159	0.227	0.138	0.164	0.268	0.218	0.243	0.332	0.233	0.262	0.036	0.179	0.206
U.S. residential real estate	0.123	0.213	0.090	0.125	0.207	-0.080	0.356	0.141	0.133	0.068	-0.039	0.095	0.066
U.S. farm real estate	-0.164	-0.093	-0.223	-0.171	-0.097	-0.003	-0.063	-0.065	-0.139	-0.315	-0.256	-0.273	-0.267
U.S. real estate total	0.054	0.166	0.006	0.054	0.156	-0.033	0.288	0.129	0.083	-0.051	-0.138	-0.024	-0.040
U.S. Treasury bills	-0.055	-0.063	-0.160	-0.070	-0.169	-0.157	-0.101	-0.153	-0.114	0.395	0.111	0.328	0.325
U.S. commercial paper	-0.112	-0.130	-0.210	-0.127	-0.211	-0.176	-0.150	-0.199	-0.174	0.394	0.115	0.348	0.330
U.S. total cash	-0.064	-0.080	-0.170	-0.079	-0.178	-0.159	-0.112	-0.162	-0.125	0.400	0.119	0.340	0.332
Foreign total cash	-0.393	-0.355	-0.289	-0.386	-0.127	0.009	-0.270	-0.107	-0.311	-0.203	-0.183	-0.154	-0.143
World total cash	-0.225	-0.240	-0.284	-0.238	-0.212	-0.115	-0.225	-0.180	-0.242	0.270	0.032	0.237	0.236
Gold	-0.094	-0.024	-0.067	-0.088	0.032	0.046	0.140	0.044	-0.058	-0.277	-0.252	-0.178	-0.206
Silver	0.093	0.374	0.142	0.116	0.052	-0.181	0.410	-0.020	0.070	-0.131	-0.140	-0.064	-0.109
World total metals	-0.093	-0.011	-0.064	-0.086	0.032	0.036	0.152	0.039	-0.058	-0.279	-0.253	-0.177	-0.207
U.S. market wealth portfolio	0.915	0.837	0.831	0.917	0.605	0.209	0.754	0.626	0.886	0.214	0.162	0.139	0.152
Foreign market wealth portfolio	0.493	0.498	0.544	0.510	0.823	0.602	0.556	0.865	0.678	-0.086	0.021	-0.201	-0.083
World market wealth portfolio (excl. metals)	0.853	0.799	0.814	0.861	0.782	0.406	0.765	0.815	0.914	0.109	0.119	0.007	0.066
World market wealth portfolio (incl. metals)	0.747	0.723	0.727	0.757	0.706	0.351	0.753	0.732	0.805	-0.010	0.016	-0.059	-0.023

Table 7-4 (continued)

	U.S. intermediate corporate bonds	U.S. long corporate bonds	U.S. total corporate bonds	U.S. total bonds	Foreign corporate bonds	Foreign government bonds	Cross-border bonds	Foreign total bonds	World total bonds	Business real estate	Residential structures	Farm real estate	Total U.S. real estate
U.S. intermediate-term corporate bonds	1.000												
U.S. long-term corporate bonds	0.941	1.000											
U.S. total corporate bonds	0.960	0.996	1.000										
U.S. total bonds	0.956	0.956	0.962	1.000									
Foreign domestic corporate bonds	0.211	0.263	0.264	0.180	1.000								
Foreign domestic government bonds	0.203	0.269	0.266	0.192	0.890	1.000							
Foreign crossborder bonds	0.741	0.814	0.807	0.721	0.626	0.628	1.000						
Foreign total bonds	0.260	0.326	0.323	0.242	0.950	0.985	0.689	1.000					
World total bonds	0.635	0.693	0.692	0.646	0.829	0.860	0.866	0.895	1.000				
U.S. business real estate	0.335	0.107	0.152	0.192	0.165	0.249	0.203	0.228	0.256	1.000			
U.S. residential real estate	0.085	-0.039	-0.030	0.017	0.091	0.293	0.108	0.225	0.191	0.493	1.000		
U.S. farm real estate	-0.252	-0.255	-0.273	-0.274	0.176	0.103	0.049	0.125	-0.013	0.016	0.214	1.000	
U.S. real estate total	-0.004	-0.129	-0.123	-0.082	0.164	0.303	0.123	0.256	0.172	0.518	0.916	0.570	1.000
U.S. Treasury bills	0.336	0.094	0.135	0.244	-0.269	-0.224	-0.060	-0.240	-0.091	0.685	0.428	-0.053	0.389
U.S. commercial paper	0.313	0.070	0.108	0.230	-0.289	-0.232	-0.078	-0.254	-0.108	0.655	0.462	-0.040	0.415
U.S. total cash	0.339	0.096	0.136	0.247	-0.265	-0.217	-0.054	-0.234	-0.085	0.681	0.447	-0.046	0.405
Foreign total cash	-0.191	-0.225	-0.225	-0.192	0.616	0.617	0.191	0.608	0.393	0.231	0.317	0.306	0.399
World total cash	0.222	-0.005	0.029	0.141	0.048	0.080	0.007	0.065	0.106	0.705	0.528	0.096	0.529
Gold	-0.235	-0.316	-0.323	-0.280	0.001	0.107	-0.046	0.062	-0.079	0.219	0.586	0.517	0.684
Silver	-0.150	-0.177	-0.187	-0.153	-0.286	-0.054	-0.076	-0.136	-0.177	0.188	0.532	0.351	0.580
World total metals	-0.239	-0.318	-0.326	-0.282	-0.011	0.104	-0.047	0.056	-0.085	0.220	0.596	0.526	0.696
U.S. market wealth portfolio	0.446	0.367	0.393	0.284	0.153	0.171	0.395	0.191	0.288	0.394	0.422	-0.019	0.371
Foreign market wealth portfolio	0.192	0.221	0.236	0.080	0.723	0.687	0.517	0.718	0.603	0.329	0.174	-0.008	0.177
World market wealth portfolio (excl. metals)	0.390	0.354	0.377	0.231	0.431	0.428	0.504	0.455	0.471	0.407	0.365	-0.014	0.332
World market wealth portfolio (incl. metals)	0.238	0.193	0.207	0.093	0.380	0.426	0.404	0.429	0.389	0.390	0.552	0.133	0.531

	U.S. Treasury bills	U.S. commercial paper	U.S. total cash	Foreign total cash	World total cash	Gold	Silver	World total metals	U.S. market wealth portfolio	Foreign market wealth portfolio	World market excl. metals	World market incl. metals
U.S. Treasury bills	1.000											
U.S. commercial paper	0.990	1.000										
U.S. total cash	0.999	0.995	1.000									
Foreign total cash	-0.008	0.033	0.010	1.000								
World total cash	0.881	0.895	0.891	0.460	1.000							
Gold	0.179	0.256	0.210	0.419	0.366	1.000						
Silver	0.125	0.127	0.123	-0.203	-0.014	0.438	1.000					
World total metals	0.177	0.253	0.207	0.401	0.355	0.999	0.477	1.000				
U.S. market wealth portfolio	0.133	0.088	0.130	-0.233	0.013	0.104	0.291	0.111	1.000			
Foreign market wealth portfolio	-0.254	-0.298	-0.258	0.218	-0.122	0.025	-0.110	0.018	0.533	1.000		
World market wealth portfolio (excl. metals)	-0.033	-0.083	-0.037	-0.059	-0.053	0.075	0.142	0.077	0.925	0.812	1.000	
World market wealth portfolio (incl. metals)	-0.014	-0.027	-0.004	0.105	0.046	0.427	0.283	0.427	0.873	0.727	0.924	1.000

Source: Roger G. Ibbotson, Laurence S. Siegel, and Kathryn S. Love, "World Wealth: Market Values and Returns," *Journal of Portfolio Management,* Fall 1985, table 5, pp. 19–20.

of the bond, $p_{t-1} = \$94$ represent the purchase price of the bond, and $r_t = 0.117 \times 100 = 11.7\%$ denote the rate of return during period t. The appropriately weighted arithmetic average of simultaneous returns from all bonds in the portfolio yields the index's return during period t.

Treasury Bill Returns   Equation (7-3) defines how the one-period rates of return were computed for a diversified portfolio of Treasury bills.

$$r_t = \frac{p_t + p_{t-1}}{p_{t-1}} \tag{7-3}$$

Table 7-4 shows the high, positive correlation coefficients between investment returns from many different markets. Table 7-4 also shows that the U.S. stock market returns are not highly correlated with the returns from most other U.S. assets. In fact, the stock market returns are slightly negatively correlated, on average, with the returns from several types of bonds and real estate investments listed in Table 7-4. Investment managers need to understand why the prices of each category of assets are affected differently by the underlying economic forces.

Table 1-6 contains summary statistics calculated from the different investment indexes. The correlation coefficients between these differing investment indexes are shown in Table 7-4. The geometric mean rate of return, the arithmetic average rate of return, and the standard deviations of the year-to-year rates of return for each different index are shown in Table 1-6.

Weighing the summary statistics in Table 1-6 and the correlation coefficients in Table 7-4 will give an investor insights into various investment possibilities.

Figure 7-2 illustrates for some of the different indexes shown in Tables 1-6, 7-3, and 7-4 how \$1 invested at the end of 1925 would have grown over several decades.[7]

| 7-6 | **SUMMARY AND CONCLUSIONS** |

The average and the index are the two major types of securities market indicators. Market indexes (like the S&P 500) are more scientific than market averages (like the DJIA) for three main reasons: (1) the indexes have base years to facilitate comparisons, (2) the indexes can employ some meaningful weighting system if it is appropriate, and (3) the index is usually given in more useful units of measure than an average is.

---

[7]For empirical risk and return statistics from various investments in foreign countries see Yasushi Hamao, "Japanese Stocks, Bonds, Bills and Inflation, 1973–1987," *Journal of Portfolio Management,* Winter 1989, pp. 20–26. Also see Daniel Wydler, "Swiss Stocks, Bonds and Inflation, 1926–1987," *Journal of Portfolio Management,* Winter 1989, pp. 27–32.

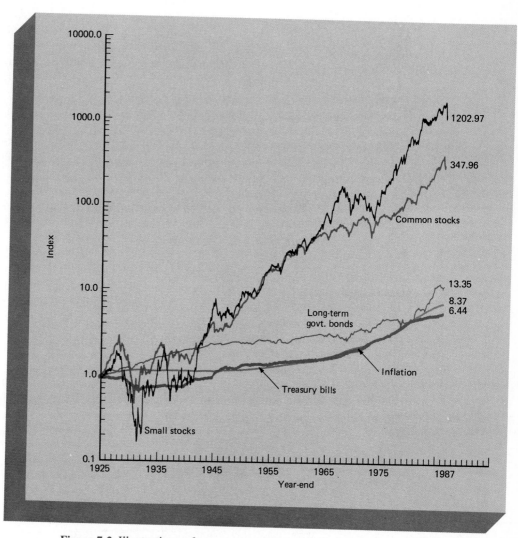

Figure 7-2 Illustrations of average wealth cumulations from $1 invested in different categories of assets, 1925–1987. (*Source:* R. G. Ibbotson and Rex A. Sinquefield, *Stocks, Bonds, Bills and Inflation (SBBI): 1982 Edition,* updated in *SBBI 1988 Yearbook,* Chicago, Ill.: Ibbotson Associates Inc.)

Hundreds of different securities market averages and indexes are tabulated and published in the United States every day. Stock market indicators for each different market and for various industrial categories within each stock market, bond market indexes for varied categories of bonds, price level measures for diverse groups of commodities, and foreign exchange indexes are all prepared daily. Numerous economic indexes, such as the consumer price index, which is used to measure the general level of prices and inflation, are also available. Each index is designed to give a meaningful indication of the level of the prices of some important collection of market assets. Each index should be scrutinized before you use it, however, because some are biased and unrepresentative.

A well-constructed index uses a statistically significant sample of the population being surveyed, and this sample should be representative of the population being studied. A good index also employs a weighting system grounded in economic logic—such as an equally weighted securities index—to show what an unskilled investor could expect. And, it is always better to use an index that is reported in convenient units rather than in numbers that lack intuitive interpretations.

After an index is established, it must be properly maintained. Securities market indexes must have adjustment mechanisms so that stock dividends and splits do not distort the index. Changes and substitutions in the list of assets being sampled should also be made judiciously.

In spite of the statistical sampling considerations that should be considered when constructing a scientific market index, it is nevertheless fairly simple to construct a satisfactory stock market index. To a large extent the prices of all common stocks in the United States are simultaneously affected by the same common economic factors. As a result of these common driving forces, different stock market indicators all move together systematically through the alternating bull and bear market periods. This is why a poorly constructed average like the DJIA is highly positively correlated with the more scientific S&P 500 index. Markets such as the commodity and bond markets, however, require the selection of separate market indexes because these markets respond to different economic forces.

Essay Questions

7-1   Compare and contrast (*a*) a stock market average and (*b*) a stock market index.

7-2   Compare and contrast the following two weighting systems which are frequently used in the construction of stock market indexes: (*a*) equal weights; (*b*) market value weighting. Define each. For what purpose are these different weighting systems used?

7-3   What is a "naive buy-and-hold strategy"? Have any stock market indicators been constructed to correspond to a naive buy-and-hold investment strategy? Would a serious investor ever follow a naive buy-and-hold strategy? If so, explain why.

7-4   (*a*) What is the arithmetic average rate of return from an investment measured over *T* periods? (*b*) What is the geometric mean rate of return from an investment measured over *T* periods? (*c*) What is the difference between these two measures? *Hint: See Appendix 1A at the end of Chapter 1.*

7-5   Table 7-4 shows that the correlation coefficients between the various common stock market indicators, commodity market indicators, bond market indicators, and the other categories of market indicators differ substantially. Why are the market indicators between these different markets so uncorrelated while the indicators shown in Table 7-2 are all so highly positively correlated?

7-6   Consider the 30 stocks that make up the Dow Jones Industrial Average. (You will have to go to the library and find a list of the 30 stocks.) Can you think of a new name that would be more appropriate for the DJIA? Why or why not?

7-7   The well-known Laspeyres (L) and Paasche (P) price index formulas are shown below in a modified form, using weights instead of physical quantities.

$$L = \Sigma p_2 w_1 / \Sigma p_1 w_1$$

$$P = \Sigma p_2 w_2 / \Sigma p_1 w_2$$

The subscripts refer to periods $t = 1$ and $t = 2$ when the prices (p) and the weights (w) of the stocks in the indexes were established. Which of these two indexes would be more appropriate for a stock market index? Explain why.

7-8   If you were searching for a stock market index to track a portfolio of small new growth stocks, would you be better off using a price-weighted or an equally weighted index? Explain why.

Problems

7-9   Form a stock price index from the three common stocks listed below. These three stocks issued no additional shares and had no stock dividends or splits. Ignore cash dividend payments when computing this price index.

Stock	Total shares outstanding on both dates	Base period market price July 1, 1960	More recent period market price July 1, 1987	Percentage price change
Middie	50,000	$40	$60	+50
Mite	10,000	20	70	+250
Maxum	100,000	60	80	+33

(a) If the new three-stock index is value-weighted, what will its value be on July 1, 1987? (b) If the new three-stock index is price-weighted, what will its value be on July 1, 1987? (c) If the new three-stock index is equally weighted, what will its value be on July 1, 1987? (d) Compare and contrast the price-weighted, the value-weighted, and the equally weighted index numbers you obtained from the same three stocks and explain why they differ.

7-10 Consider the effect of one 10 percent change in one stock's price on the computation of the following hypothetical three-stock portfolio.

	Prices at time	Prices at time $t = 1$	
Stocks	**$t = 0$**	**Low-price change**	**High-price change**
Ace	$80	$80	$80(1.1) = $88
Baker	50	50	50
Case	20	$20(1.1) = 22	20
Totals	$150	$152	$158
Divisor	3	3	3
Average	50	50.66	52.66
Percent change in the average		1.3%	5.3%

To what do you attribute the fact that the average rose 1.3 percent when the price of Case's stock rose 10 percent, but the same average rose 5.3 percent when the price of Ace went up 10 percent? What implications do your findings have for the DJIA?

7-11 The BEG Company's stock has had the following returns the past 10 years: 20, -5, 35, 5, 10, -10, 25, 2, 15, and 18 percent. Calculate BEG's standard deviation of returns, average return, and geometric mean return over the 10-year period. *Hint: See Chapter 1 and its appendix for the needed formulas.*

7-12 Calculate the standard deviation of IBM's stock returns with the data given below.

Year and quarter	IBM's quarterly return, %
1984-Q3	18.53
1984-Q4	−0.02
1985-Q1	4.04
1985-Q2	−1.69
1985-Q3	0.99
1985-Q4	26.42

7-13 Using the data in Problem 7-12, calculate IBM's geometric mean return.

7-14 Calculate the standard deviation of returns for Acorn Fund with the data given below.

Year and quarter	Acorn quarterly return, %
1985-Q1	13.95
1985-Q2	6.95
1985-Q3	−6.66
1985-Q4	3.62
1986-Q1	17.14
1986-Q2	2.9

7-15 Calculate the geometric mean return for Acorn Fund with the data given in Problem 7-14.

Selected References

Carleton, W. T., and J. Lakonishok, "Risk and Return on Equity: The Use and Misuse of Historical Estimates," *Financial Analysts Journal,* Jan.–Feb. 1985, pp. 38–47.

Empirical analysis is used to show that common stock returns can be highly sample dependent and vary substantially from industry to industry, for samples of firms of different size within the same industry, with the weighting system used, and with the averaging method used.

Fabozzi, Frank, and Gregory M. Kepnis, eds., *Handbook of Stock Index Futures and Options* (Homewood, Ill.: Dow Jones–Irwin, 1989).

Chapter 7, entitled "Stock Market Indicators," provides details of stock market index construction.

Ibbotson, R. G., R. C. Carr, and A. W. Robinson, "International Equity and Bond Returns," *Financial Analysts Journal,* July–Aug. 1982, fig. C, p. 66.

Empirical data about international investments in common stocks and bonds are compiled and analyzed to provide a helpful selection of international indexes. No mathematics is used in this easy-to-read article.

Ibbotson, Roger G., Laurence Siegel, and Kathryn S. Love, "World Wealth: Market Values and Returns," *Journal of Portfolio Management,* Fall 1985.

This easy-to-read article suggests how worldwide diversified investments in both real and monetary assets performed over the 1960–1984 sample period.

Ibbotson Associates, *Stocks, Bonds, Bills and Inflation: 1989 Yearbook* (Chicago, Ill.: Ibbotson Associates, 1989).

This annual book presents an easy-to-read explanation of how different securities market and economic indicators are constructed, with the aid of a little freshman college algebra. Graphs and tables of the summary statistics yield themselves to comparisons which will be insightful to astute investors. Data from 1926–1988 are presented.

Part 2

Introduction to Investments Theory

Chapter 8

Determinants of Securities Prices

If you studied all the newspaper stories about securities markets that have been published in the last decade, you would probably finish with many misapprehensions but very few clues about the economic process that actually determines securities prices. Newspapers publish sensational tales of insider trading scandals; warnings that something given the reprehensible label of "junk bond market" is tearing at the fabric of our society; scary hypotheses about the effects of "computer-driven program trading" on securities prices; and details about "leveraged buyouts" in which billions of dollars change hands overnight while senior executives, afraid of losing their jobs, bargain for "golden parachutes." These sensational stories leave many newspaper readers wondering if massive fraud and price manipulation are rampant in securities markets.

This chapter explains a security valuation process that quickly absorbs sensational events like those reported in newspapers. This *economic process generates rational securities prices.* Although the price fluctuations may appear to be chaotic, they are random fluctuations that result from the random arrival of new information. As we study this valuation process, we will see that when investors take long positions and short positions in hopes of earning gains for themselves, they become part of the economic force that moves securities prices toward their values. After delving into hedging and arbitrage, we will see that these activities also help align prices and values—they support what economists call the "law of one price." We will see that the decision to take many of these investment positions can be traced to security analysts' value estimates. *Value estimates provide the focal point toward which natural economic forces push securities prices.*

The present value model is one of the engines that powers this chapter's analysis of securities prices.

8-1   **THE VENERABLE PRESENT VALUE MODEL**

The process used to find the value of a security varies with the type of security. But the following present value formula is the basic economic model that can be employed to value any security (with varying degrees of success):

$$\text{Present value}_0 = \frac{\text{cashflow}_1}{(1 + k)^1} + \frac{\text{cashflow}_2}{(1 + k)^2} + \cdots + \frac{\text{cashflow}_T}{(1 + k)^T} \qquad (8\text{-}1)$$

The present value model shown in Equation (8-1) says that the present value at time $t = 0$ equals the discounted present value of all the investment's future cashflows at times $t = 1, 2, 3, \ldots, T$, where T is the *terminal* (or final) period in the investment's life. The convention k represents a risk-adjusted discount rate (or, synonymously, cost of capital, or capitalization rate, or equilibrium rate of return). The cashflows could be cash dividends from a common stock, coupon interest from a bond, rent from a piece of real estate, and/or the price at which the asset is finally sold.

Assume, for instance, that you are thinking of purchasing a share of stock you think should earn $k = 0.1 \times 100 = 10$ percent return to induce you to undertake the risks inherent in the investment. If you expect to sell the stock for $55 after you collect cash dividends of $3 per share at the end of each of the next 2 years, Equation (8-1a) suggests you should be willing to pay $50.66 for this investment opportunity.

$$\$50.66 = \frac{\$3.00}{(1.10)^1} + \frac{\$3.00 + \$55.00}{(1.10)^2} \qquad (8\text{-}1a)$$

Stated differently, you estimate the stock's *value* to be $50.66. If its *market price* happens to be less than your estimated value of $50.66, you would say the stock is a good investment because it is underpriced.

Equation (8-1) illustrates how a security's **value** (or, equivalently, **present value,** or **economic value,** or **intrinsic value**) is calculated. After the security's present value is determined, buy-sell decisions can be made by comparing the security's price to its value.

8-2   **THE BUY-SELL DECISION RULES**

A security's value determines its price. But, not all the millions of investors in the United States know that fact; they are the amateur investors who are most likely to misunderstand why securities prices change. The professional investors follow the more scientific procedure of forming estimates of a security's value before they make a decision to buy or sell the security. To see how these value estimates determine security prices, consider the following buy-sell decision rules.

The buy rule: If a security's price is below its value, it is **underpriced** and should be bought and held in order to profit from price gains that should occur in the future. More succinctly, if the actual market price of security i at the tth instant in time is p_{it} and its intrinsic economic value is v_{it}, then the buy rule says:

$$\text{If } p_{it} < v_{it}, \text{ buy}$$

The don't trade rule: If the ith asset's market price *equals* its economic value, then the price is in equilibrium and is not expected to change. The asset is **correctly priced** and there is no profit likely to be made from buying or selling it.

$$\text{If } p_{it} = v_{it}, \text{ don't trade}$$

The sell rule: If the ith security's market price is above the security's value, the security is **overpriced;** sell the security if it is owned in order to avoid losses when its price falls down to the level of its value. If the security is not owned, then it may be sold short in order to profit from the expected price decline.

$$\text{If } p_{it} > v_{it}, \text{ liquidate or sell short}$$

Profit-seekers using *the buy-sell decision rules provide the economic force that keeps securities prices moving in pursuit of their values.* Selling overpriced securities drives their prices down. Buying underpriced securities bids their prices higher. These economic forces are aiming at a moving target, however, because securities values keep changing as fresh news arrives.

The buy-sell rules are simple to understand but difficult to implement because it is hard to assess the *value* of most assets. Some securities analysts earn more than $100,000 per year merely for providing and explaining their value estimates for a few securities. For example, an expert automotive analyst might only be responsible for four stocks—Ford, Chrysler, General Motors, and Honda. An analyst who can correctly predict which direction the prices of these stocks will move most of the time will develop a track record for making good predictions and a *following of investors* will materialize. As a result, some stock brokerage firm can profit from employing this analyst because the analyst's following of investors will generate trading commissions for the brokerage firm in excess of the analyst's salary.

To gain a clearer picture of how an investor can hope to profit from buying underpriced securities and selling overpriced securities, we will examine long and short positions more closely in the next section.

8-3   **LONG AND SHORT POSITIONS**

Investors may assume either or both of two basic positions in a market asset. A **long position** means simply buying and holding the asset—this is the only position that many investors understand. The short position is more complicated.

The Short Position

A **short sale** occurs when one person sells a second person an asset borrowed from a third person. Short sales are routine transactions, but they require a little more sophistication than the buy-and-hold position.

Short sellers sell an asset (such as a stock or a bond) short because they expect its price to fall and they want to profit from the expected price fall. So a short seller sells a borrowed asset to a second party, who buys a long position in that asset. Buyers take the long position because they expect to profit from a price rise. Thus, a short sale requires a short seller who is bearish (that is, one who expects a price decline) and a long buyer who is bullish (that is, one who expects price appreciation) about the same asset at the same time; it is a case of opposites attracting each other in search of profit.

The short seller borrows the shares of stock (or whatever asset is involved) from a third party in order to make delivery on the short sale. Then the short seller waits for the asset's price to fall, intending to purchase it at a lower price. If the asset's price does fall, the short seller's profit equals the difference between the price paid for the asset used to repay the third party and the price paid for the asset by the long buyer. Aside from the commission costs, the short seller's profit equals the long buyer's loss—or vice versa, if the asset's price rises after the short sale. Short sellers can open their bearish positions at any price and hold the position open as long as their broker can find a third party to loan them the shares.

A second reason to take a short position is to create a counterbalance to an existing long position, in order to reduce risk in the resulting two-position portfolio. That is, a short position may be taken to establish a risk-reducing hedged portfolio composed of a long position and an offsetting short position.

Complicated Aspects of Short Positions

Short sales are even more complicated than they may seem initially, for several reasons. First, short sales of NYSE common stocks, for instance, can be made only on an "up-tick"—that is, after a trade in which the stock's price was bid up. This NYSE rule is designed to keep short sellers from accentuating a downturn in the price of a stock. Second, if a common stock that has been sold short pays a cash dividend while on loan to the short seller, the short seller must pay an equivalent amount to the third party who lent the shares. Third, the short seller may be required to put up margin money equaling as much as 100 percent of the value of the borrowed shares as collateral for the third party who lent the shares. Higher margins mean lower expected rates of return. Fourth, the short seller can get forced out of a short position at any time if the third party who lent the shares demands the securities back. For example, if the price of the security which was sold short goes up, the third party who lent the shares, wanting to sell and recognize a gain, can call for the shares to be returned immediately. This forces the short seller to cover the short position by buying the shares at a higher price. Such a disadvantageous purchase price could result in a loss for the short seller unless the shares can be borrowed elsewhere, which they usually can.

Gain-Loss Illustrations for Long and Short Positions

Figure 8-1 illustrates the gain-loss positions for the long and the short positions. The vertical axes in these two gain-loss graphs show the dollars of profit above the origin and the dollars of loss below the origin. The horizontal axis shows the market price of the asset.

The profit-loss graph for the long position in Figure 8-1*a* has a slope of positive unity, indicating that the person holding the long position makes a dollar of profit (loss) for each dollar increase (decrease) in the market price. In contrast, the profit-loss graph for the short position in Figure 8-1*b* has a slope of negative unity, indicating a dollar of loss (profit) for the short seller for each dollar increase (decrease) in the market price.

Short sales have been conducted on the floor of the New York Stock Exchange for decades. The volume of short sales is reported daily in the financial newspapers under the heading "Short Interest." The **short interest** is the total number of shares that brokers have listed in their accounts as being sold short. The short interest is usually below 5 percent of the total volume of shares traded, and the NYSE specialists do most of it.

Figure 8-1 Gain-loss illustrations for the long and short positions. (*a*) Long position; (*b*) short position.

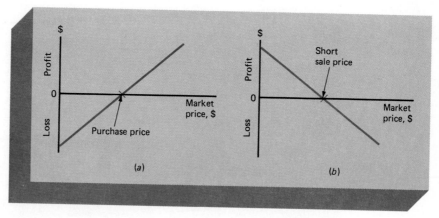

VALUATION AND INVESTMENT PROCEDURE

If you went to work as a securities analyst, you would find that the valuation process is actually more complex than suggested by Equation (8-1) and the buy-sell rules. One problem encountered in practice is determining how much confidence to give a securities analyst's value estimate. Value estimates are rarely in the form of a specific price; instead, the estimate includes a margin for error. For example, an expert analyst might estimate that XYZ stock is worth $30 per share plus or minus a $5 per share *margin for error*. This means the analyst estimates the equity share's value to be within the $25 to $35 range. Thus, the buy-sell rules are oversimplified because they are based on one specific value estimate.

Another practical problem is that a security's risk and return, and thus also its value, keeps changing. For example, selling a security puts downward pressure on its market price, and buying a security tends to bid up its price. With every change in its price level, the security's expected future price gains or losses must be revised; this can affect both its expected return and its risk.

Clearly, securities analysts must continually reevaluate the securities that they follow. The valuation process is more realistically represented by the dynamic interactions illustrated in Figure 8-2. The flowchart in Figure 8-2 is a never-ending loop of reconsidering the value, comparing the price and the value, and then reconsidering the buy-sell decision based on the latest value estimates. Every time a new piece of information about a security is obtained, that security's value may change. Since new information arrives continuously, the value estimates change continuously. And the buying and selling pressures in the marketplace keep market prices in continuous motion as they pursue the

Figure 8-2 Flowchart of the endless Valuation Process.

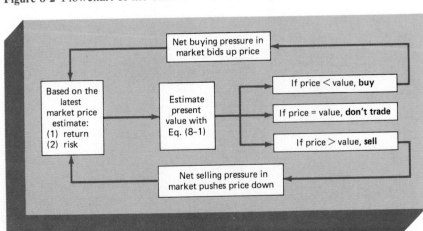

continuously changing values. This is what makes being a securities analyst a fast, exciting job that pays princely incomes to those who are proficient at it—and quickly wipes out those who are not.

| 8-5 | **A PRICE-VALUE INTERACTION MODEL** |

Securities prices can be viewed as a series of constrained *random fluctuations around their intrinsic value*. Let's consider two hypothetical groups of investors who influence securities prices. The first group can be referred to as the **liquidity traders**—that is, those who have access only to the public news media for their information and may not even know how to interpret that news. Some liquidity traders are impetuous speculators who trade on "hot tips." Others base their investment timing decisions upon the arrival of an income tax refund, an inheritance, lottery winnings, or other random good fortunes. Likewise, they might sell their investments when they need to pay a medical bill, buy a new furnace for their house, or finance a birth in the family. Liquidity traders seldom recognize divergences of prices from intrinsic values. Essentially, they buy and sell at random times without regard to the stage of the business cycle. Moreover, they often do not investigate before they invest.

The second group of investors is the **information traders,** those who have the resources to discover new information and revise their estimates of intrinsic value before most liquidity traders even get the news. As a result, the information traders will recognize significant deviations from intrinsic value and then buy and/or sell in a manner that tends to align the market price with the intrinsic value.

The erratic solid lines in Figure 8-3 illustrate how a security's price might fluctuate over time. The dashed line traces the path of the security's value. Note that the information traders' consensus estimate of the intrinsic value of the security illustrated in Figure 8-3b changes at times t and $t + 1$, while the value remains unchanged at $30 per share in Figure 8-3a.

Since trading by liquidity traders is seldom based on analysis of the news, these unsophisticated investors may buy securities whose market prices are above their intrinsic values. Such buying is illustrated in Figure 8-3a and b by the price fluctuating above the value in phase I. After this initial overoptimistic buying, the liquidity traders may sell the stock when its price falls below its value, as shown in phase II of Figure 8-3a and b. Unprofitable speculative trades by uninformed amateur investors, combined with the trades executed to meet liquidity needs, are responsible for the aimless price fluctuations that cause prices to diverge from values.

When a security's price does differ significantly from its intrinsic value, the information traders find it profitable to correct this disequilibrium. Small deviations will not be profitable to correct because the profits will not be sufficient to pay for the brokerage commissions. But when prices are significantly out of

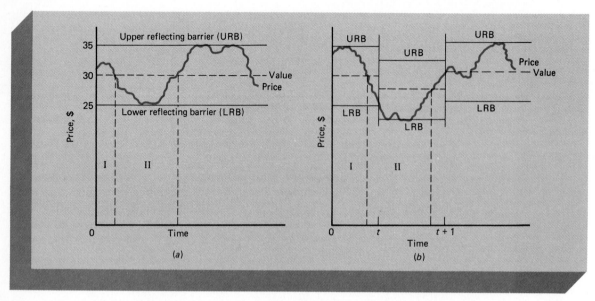

Figure 8-3 Random stock price fluctuations within reflecting barriers. (*a*) No change in intrinsic value; (*b*) intrinsic value changes at times *t* and *t* + 1.

line, the information traders will respond by bidding up the low prices and/or selling overpriced securities. In effect, the information traders erect **reflecting barriers** around the intrinsic value. These reflecting barriers are represented by the solid lines above and below the intrinsic value lines in Figure 8-3. The upper reflecting barrier is denoted URB and the lower reflecting barrier is labeled LRB. Prices will fluctuate freely within these reflecting barriers. But when prices reach the reflecting barriers, the information traders will move in and drive prices toward their intrinsic value. Such a market was named an **intrinsic-value random-walk market** by Professor Fama.[1] The process is called a *random walk within reflecting barriers* by mathematical statisticians.[2]

8-6   **SAMUELSON'S CONTINUOUS EQUILIBRIUM**

Economists who have studied the intrinsic-value random-walk model have accepted and/or modified it in varying degrees. The Nobel Prize–winning economist, Paul Samuelson, for example, has theorized about how securities prices

---

[1]Eugene Fama, ''The Behavior of Stock Market Prices,'' *Journal of Business,* Jan. 1955, p. 36.
[2]For a stochastic calculus formulation of the model, see Jonathon E. Ingersol, Jr., *Theory of Financial Decision Making* (Totowa, N.J.: Rowman and Littlefield, 1987), chap. 16.

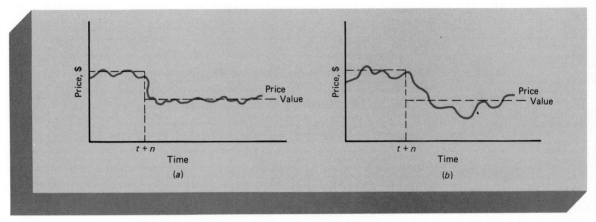

Figure 8-4 Varying degrees of pricing efficiency. (*a*) Strongly efficient price fluctuations; (*b*) weakly efficient price fluctuations.

would behave if securities markets were what economists call "perfectly competitive" or "perfectly efficient."

Samuelson supplemented the intrinsic-value random-walk model of Figure 8-3 by defining *perfectly efficient prices* to be market prices that reflect all information.[3] Samuelson suggests that a security with perfectly efficient prices would be in "continuous equilibrium." This **continuous equilibrium** will not be static through time, however. Every time a new piece of news is released, the security's intrinsic value will change and the security's market price will adjust toward the new value. It is the speed of this price adjustment process which gauges the efficiency of a price. *A perfectly efficient security price is in a continuous equilibrium such that the intrinsic value of the security vibrates randomly and the market price equals the fluctuating intrinsic value at every instant in time.* If any disequilibrium (of even a temporary nature) exists, then the security's price is less than perfectly efficient.[4] Of course, actual market prices are not perfectly efficient because different securities analysts typically assign different value estimates to any given security.

Actual market prices can only pursue a *consensus* estimate of any given security's intrinsic value since securities analysts' value estimates differ. If most securities analysts' value estimates happen to be similar at a point in time, then the **consensus value estimate** may only vary within a small range. In this case, the security's price will be almost perfectly efficient as it fluctuates in a narrow range around its changing equilibrium economic value, as shown in Figure 8-4*a*.

[3]Paul Samuelson, "Proof That Properly Discounted Present Values of Assets Vibrate Randomly," *Bell Journal of Economics and Management Science,* Autumn 1973, pp. 369–374.
[4]Eugene F. Fama, "Efficient Capital Markets: A Review of Theory and Empirical Work," *Journal of Finance,* May 1970, pp. 383–417.

Both panels of Figure 8-4 depict two different securities that have the same intrinsic values. Both securities' intrinsic values decline instantaneously at time period $t + n$ when some bad news about the security emerges. However, the security in Figure 8-4*b* "fell in disfavor," a Wall Street phrase meaning that few investors were interested in the security. Since fewer investors were studying and analyzing the security, large divergences between the security's price and its value could occur. As Figure 8-4*b* shows, the security's price declined more slowly but fluctuated far below its value because not enough investors were continuously estimating the security's value, comparing value and price, and making frequent rational buy-sell decisions about it.

Figure 8-4*a* describes an asset that is more efficiently priced than the asset in Figure 8-4*b* because the following inequality, which measures the pricing discrepancies, is true.

$$\text{Variance}(\text{price}_{at} - \text{value}_{at}) < \text{variance}(\text{price}_{bt} - \text{value}_{bt})$$

If securities prices reacted to new information *inefficiently*, as represented by Figure 8-4*b*, securities analysts should be able to make fortunes. They could reap large profits by finding underpriced securities, buying them, and holding them in long positions while their prices rise or by finding overpriced securities, selling them short, and holding them in short positions to profit from their falling prices. The profitability of doing good securities analysis will increase as securities prices become more inefficient, and so will the desirability of being an aggressive investment manager.

8-7   **PASSIVE VERSUS AGGRESSIVE INVESTMENT MANAGEMENT**

In spite of the evidence suggesting that securities markets in the United States are highly efficient,[5] few people would argue that prices have attained perfect efficiency. Quite the contrary, scientific evidence suggests that expert securities analysts can profit from finding undervalued and overvalued securities.[6] The existence of these lucrative opportunities encourages one to become an **aggressive investment manager** who buys and sells securities in order to maximize trading profits.

---

[5]Eugene F. Fama, "Efficient Capital Markets: A Review of Theory and Empirical Work," *Journal of Finance,* May 1970, pp. 383–417.
[6]See Sanjoy Basu, "The Investment Performance of Common Stocks Relative to Their Price-Earnings Ratios: A Test of the Efficient Markets," *Journal of Finance,* June 1977, vol. XXXII, no. 3, pp. 663–682. And see Robert J. Shiller, "Do Stock Prices Move Too Much to Be Justified by Subsequent Changes in Dividends?" *American Economic Review,* June 1981, vol. 71, pp. 421–436. Also see the more recent studies by Terry A. Marsh and Robert C. Merton, "Dividend Variability and Variance Bounds Tests for the Rationality of Stock Market Prices," *American Economic Review,* June 1986, vol.

(continues)

EXAMPLE 8-1

Estimating IBM Common Stock's Intrinsic Value per Share

A securities analyst's 1988 estimates of the earnings per share, cash dividend payout ratio, cash dividends per share, appropriate risk-adjusted discount rate,[7] and present value of all cashflows from purchasing a share of IBM common stock early in 1989 and selling it late in 1992 are shown below.

Part A: The present value of 4 years of cash dividends per share is $17.72.

Year	Estimated earnings per share (10% annual growth)	× Estimated cash dividends payout	= Estimated cash dividends per share	× 12% present value factor	= Present value of estimated cash dividend
Actual					
1988	$9.27	0.475	$4.40	0.893	$3.93
Forecast					
1989	$10.20	0.5	5.10	0.893	4.55
1990	$11.22	0.5	5.61	0.797	4.47
1991	$12.34	0.5	6.17	0.712	4.39
1992	$13.57	0.5	6.78	0.636	4.31

1988 present value of forecasted cash dividends $17.72

Part B: The present value of the estimated 1992 selling price is $94.94 for the share.

Year	Estimated earnings per share	× Price-earnings ratio	= Estimated value per share	× 12% present value factor	= E (present value per share)
1992	$13.57	11 times	$149.27	.636	$94.94

Part C: The 1988 estimate of the intrinsic value per share for IBM stock is $112.66.

(Part A: $17.72) + (part B: $94.94)

$$= \text{part C: } \$112.66 = E \text{ (present value per share)}$$

Equation (8-1) suggests the value of IBM was $112.66 in 1988. IBM's market price actually fluctuated between $106 and $130 in 1988.

(continued)

76, no. 3, pp. 483–498. In addition, see Robert J. Shiller, "The Marsh-Merton Model of Managers' Smoothing of Dividends," *American Economic Review,* June 1986, vol. 76, no. 3, pp. 499–503. See also Lawrence H. Summers, "Does the Stock Market Rationality Reflect Fundamental Values?" *Journal of Finance,* July 1986, vol. 41, no. 3, pp. 591–600; and Eugene F. Fama and Kenneth French, "Permanent and Temporary Components of Stock Prices," *Journal of Political Economy,* vol. 96, no. 21, pp. 246–273. Chapter 18 discusses these studies and other empirical evidence that documents significant market inefficiencies.

[7]Determining the appropriate risk-adjusted discount rate to use when finding the present value of an asset is the subject of Chapters 10 and 11. Essentially, either the capital asset pricing model (CAPM of Chapter 10) or the arbitrage pricing theory (APT model of Chapter 11) may be used.

Aggressive Investment Management

Securities analysis is at the heart of aggressive investment management. Example 8-1 shows how an analyst might estimate the intrinsic value per share of a common stock and presents a sample of the difficulties involved in making value estimates.

The scientific evidence supporting the efficiency in securities prices means that it will require a good education, a significant amount of experience, and some hard work to profit from aggressive investment management.

Passive Investment Management

Because of the scientific evidence suggesting that the prices of securities fluctuate in a random walk that approaches what Samuelson called a continuous equilibrium, **passive investment management** became popular during the 1980s. The passive investors reasoned that if many investors are highly informed and some degree of consensus exists about most securities' intrinsic values, then doing securities analysis and trading aggressively is too much trouble and involves too many risks. As a result, many of these investors invest in special portfolios called **index funds.** Index funds buy most of the same stocks that are in some securities market index they select. The Standard & Poor's 500 Stocks Composite Index is a popular index to emulate; the stated investment objective of such an index fund is to perform exactly like the S&P 500 index. Several of these funds now manage billions of dollars for passive investors.[8] The efficient markets research has made such passive investment management practices a respectable alternative to estimating values, comparing them to prices, and trading aggressively.

Do not be misled into thinking that aggressive and passive investment managers disagree fundamentally. Both types of investment managers agree that the buy-sell decision rules are rational, that the price fluctuation model of Figure 8-3 is realistic, and that the continuous flowchart shown in Figure 8-2 is a logical way to manage investments. Furthermore, statistical studies of securities prices reveal that securities price changes do tend to fluctuate randomly, as indicated in Figures 8-3 and 8-4.[9] Aggressive and passive investment managers believe in different approaches, not diametrically opposed or irreconcilable viewpoints.

The next section's discussion of hedging and arbitrage explores the kinds of securities pricing inefficiencies that professional investors love to discover because they can profit from correcting them.

---

[8]Wells Fargo Investment Advisors, a subsidiary of Wells Fargo Bank in San Francisco, Batterymarch Financial Management Corporation in Boston, and the Trust Department of the American National Bank and Trust Company in Chicago are examples of large index funds.

[9]Eugene F. Fama and others have given the name *efficient markets* to securities markets in which the prices fluctuate randomly around their intrinsic values in a narrow range. Chapter 18 delves into the efficient markets model and reviews many empirical studies about securities price fluctuations.

8-8	HEDGING AND ARBITRAGE

Although millions of amateur investors have no idea what the word "arbitrage" means, the relatively few professional investors who do arbitrage have a considerable impact on securities prices. An *arbitrage position* may be defined as an *imperfect hedge*—which means we must explore *perfect hedges* and imperfect hedges before delving into arbitrage.

Perfect Hedges

Hedging means arranging for two different positions, such that potential losses from one position will be more or less offset by profits from the other position. Alternatively, hedging can be defined as the establishment of offsetting long and short positions in order to diminish the risk that the portfolio could be hurt by an adverse price movement.

There are many different reasons to hedge. Some hedges are undertaken to reduce potential losses from adverse price movements. Other hedges are set up with the expectation of reaping profits. The easiest hedge of all to explain is the perfect hedge, from which no profits or losses can be earned. Figure 8-5 is a gain-loss graph that illustrates the position of an investor who is perfectly hedged.

Figure 8-5 combines the long position from Figure 8-1*a* and the short position from Figure 8-1*b* at the same purchase and sale prices. The hedger is **perfectly hedged** because the profits and the losses from these two positions sum up to zero at any value of the market price. Figure 8-5 might result, for instance, if an investor purchased a long position of 100 shares of a common stock at $64 per share and simultaneously sold 100 shares of the same security short at $64 per share to establish a perfect hedge. Figure 8-5*a* shows that if the market price of the hedged asset rises above the price of p_0 at which both the long position and the short position were opened, to the higher price of p_1 dollars, then the profit on the long position will be exactly offset by the loss on the short position. The hedger cannot earn either profits or losses at any price. Perfect hedges are used to eliminate risk while still maintaining a desired position.

Two conditions are essential for a hedge to be perfect: (1) equal dollar amounts must be held in both the long and the short positions, and (2) the purchase price for the long position must be identical to the sales price for the short sale.[10]

---

[10]The long and short positions do not always have to be of equal dollar magnitude to create a perfect hedge. For instance, an investment of half as many dollars in a negatively correlated offsetting position that had twice the price volatility could result in a perfect hedge.

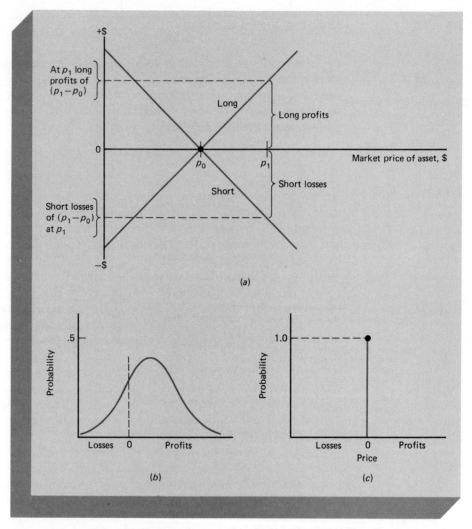

Figure 8-5 (*a*) Gain-loss diagram for a perfect hedge; (*b*) probability distribution of outcomes from an unhedged portfolio; (*c*) probability distribution of outcomes from a perfectly hedged portfolio.

Imperfect Hedges   A hedge will be imperfect if the dollar commitments to the long and the short positions are not perfectly balanced or if the short sale price is not equal to the purchase price for the long position.

Figure 8-6 illustrates two **imperfect hedges.** Since the size of the dollar commitments to the long and the short positions cannot be illustrated in a gain-loss figure, let us assume that these dollar commitments are equal. The two hedges are imperfect because their short sales price, denoted p_s, differs from the purchase price for the long position, designated p_p.

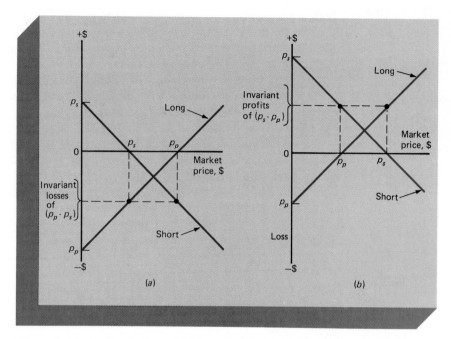

Figure 8-6 Imperfect hedges. (*a*) Unprofitable hedge; (*b*) profitable hedge.

The hedge in Figure 8-6*a* involves a purchase price for the long position that is above the sales price for the short position: $p_p > p_s$. The resulting hedge will yield an *invariant loss* at whatever value the market price may assume. This loss will equal the excess of the purchase price over the short sale price, $p_p - p_s$, a constant amount.

The hedge in Figure 8-6*b* is imperfect because its short sales price is above the purchase price for its long position. As a result the hedge will yield an *invariant profit* equal to the excess of the short sale price over the purchase price. It is impossible for the imperfect hedge in Figure 8-6*b* to do anything except yield a profit of $p_s - p_p$, regardless of how the market price of the hedged asset changes.[11]

Various Reasons for a Short Sale

As mentioned, short sales are used by bearish speculators in search of profits from an expected price decline. A second reason to use short sales is to create a risk-reducing hedge. For example, a hypothetical investor named Mr. Ford owns a substantial interest in a corporation and wishes to maintain continuous

[11]For additional discussion of hedging, see Frank J. Fabozzi and Gregory M. Kipnis, eds., *Handbook of Stock Index Futures and Options* (Homewood, Ill.: Dow Jones–Irwin, 1989).

control of it. If Mr. Ford expects the price of his stock to fall, he may hold his long position and sell short to establish a hedge that will minimize his anticipated loss. If the price then falls, the losses on Mr. Ford's long position are matched by gains on his short position. Thus, investor Ford has maintained control and hedged away his loss. Since Mr. Ford actually owned the shares that he sold short (presumably they were in his safe-deposit box), he did what is commonly referred to as **selling short against the box**.[12]

A third reason to use short sales is to sell short against the box in order to carry a taxable gain from a high-income year into a low-income year and thus decrease income taxes. For example, suppose that Ms. Gaynor is having a high-income year which puts her in the top tax bracket. If she has a $10,000 gain on December 15, she might not want to liquidate the shares and take the gain until the next year, when she expects to be in a lower tax bracket. However, if Ms. Gaynor fears the price of the securities she holds may decline before the new year, she can sell short against the box. This "locks in" her gain because the long and short positions' profits and losses cancel each other and any subsequent price decline does not diminish her $10,000 paper profit. After January 1 Ms. Gaynor can deliver her shares against the short sale to terminate both of her positions. Thus the $10,000 gain occurs and is taxable in the year when Ms. Gaynor anticipates a lower tax rate.

8-9   ARBITRAGE

A fourth reason to be short in a security is to carry on arbitrage. **Arbitrage** employs imperfect hedges to good advantage. Arbitrage involves simultaneously, or almost simultaneously, buying long and selling short the same assets, or different but related assets, in an effort to profit from unrealistic price differentials.

Law of One Price

Arbitrage may take place in the same or different markets. For an example of arbitrage between different markets, consider General Motors (GM) common stock. If GM stock is selling in the U.S. and London markets at different prices, arbitrage can be profitable. Profit-seeking arbitragers facilitate enforcement of the economic **law of one price** by buying the stock in the market where its price is lowest and selling in the market where the stock's price is higher. Arbitragers

[12]If the security involved in the short selling is required to be listed with the SEC (see Chap. 4), then the short sale against the box described above would be illegal because insiders are not allowed to sell short. Thus, if our Mr. Ford owned a substantial interest in Ford Motor Company, for instance, he would be legally prohibited from selling Ford stock short against the box.

will go on buying at the low price and selling at the higher price until the price of GM stock is the same in all free markets around the world. The price of GM stock may never be exactly identical in all markets because of transaction costs, such as broker's commissions, foreign exchange fees, governmental foreign exchange controls, long distance telephone costs, mail costs, and other "frictions," that slow up arbitrage and erode arbitrage profits. However, with the exception of these transaction costs (which are typically only a few cents per share), GM stock should cost the same no matter where in the world it is sold.

Arbitrage Profits
Some arbitrage is risky and some is riskless. In order to earn riskless trading profits, an arbitrager simultaneously sells the security short in the market where its price is high and buys an equal amount of the security long in the market where the price is low. Figure 8-6*b* illustrates a profitable hedge of the type that arbitragers strive to establish. Arbitragers keep buying the security in the market where it is cheapest until they bid up its low price. Simultaneously, these same arbitragers keep selling in the high-priced market everything they bought in the low-priced market until they drive down the high price. The short sale price and the long purchase price are thus driven together by the actions of profit-seeking arbitragers.

Stated differently, arbitragers enforce the law of one price as they pursue their profits. Furthermore, the arbitrage will be profitable regardless of what other price fluctuations occur. The powerful economic force of arbitrage makes securities prices around the world respond efficiently to new information. Greed motivates arbitragers to do a social good.[13]

As our examples show, short sales are not always undertaken in search of a speculative profit. Short sales may be used like insurance to hedge away risks. Or they may be used to maintain control, distribute income tax burdens to later years, or arbitrage differential prices into equilibrium. Thus, risk-averse investors and risk-taking speculators both use short selling.

8-10   **SUMMARY AND CONCLUSIONS**

The present value model shown in Equation (8-1) provides value estimates that could be used as the basis for rational, well-informed, wealth-maximizing investment decisions. The buy-sell investment decision rules are simple to use after the estimate of a security's value is obtained. Every time a piece of new

---

[13]Short selling is also used by hedgers and arbitragers in developing the arbitrage pricing theory (Chapter 11), in options markets (Chapters 22 to 23), in futures markets (Chapter 24), and in foreign exchange markets (Chapter 25).

information arrives, it may change the value estimates for one or more securities. As a result, the flowchart shown as Figure 8-2 illustrates the never-ending series of investment decisions that keep securities analysts busy.

The market prices of securities fluctuate in an unpredictable fashion because they are pursuing ever-changing intrinsic values. These changes in value estimates motivate investors to either buy and bid up or sell and push down the securities prices. Some investors pursue this aggressive investment management eagerly. At the same time many rational investors prefer to hire a passive investment management service or invest in an index fund in order to avoid the difficulties associated with aggressive investment management.

As informed professional investors buy and sell securities and profit by arbitraging the unjustified price differentials away to zero, market prices are continually adjusted to reflect the latest information that is available anywhere in the world. Efficiently priced securities are socially desirable because they help allocate resources to where society needs them the most.

Essay Questions

8-1 Why must a securities analyst have estimates of a security's risk and return before preparing estimates of the security's value? Explain your answer in terms of present value Equation (8-1).

8-2 Should the value of a security remain stable in equilibrium? What might change the value of a security? How often might such changes occur?

8-3 Define the phrase "efficient price." Give an example.

8-4 Suppose the Chairman of the Board of General Motors (GM) appeared on the late night news of every television station in the United States and announced that GM had discovered a sea of oil under one of its factories. Assuming the gentleman would not distort the truth, how would his announcement affect the market price of GM stock? Would the price of GM move upward in a trend as more and more investors learned of the GM discovery each day and then bid the stock's price up day after day as they reached their decisions to buy the stock after a learning lag? Explain how you think the market would react to such a public announcement.

8-5 Are short sellers primarily risk-taking speculators or risk-averse hedgers? Explain.

8-6 There are millions of part-time amateur investors in the United States. However, there are only 15,000 members of the Association for Investment Management and Research (AIMR). These AIMR members constitute a significant proportion of the full-time professional investment managers. Given that there are millions of unsophisticated amateur investors and, in contrast, only thousands of professional investors, which group do you think dominates the market? That is, do you think that securities prices fluctuate randomly because there are mostly part-time amateur investors in the market? How can the small number of professional investors have any impact on security prices?

8-7   Reconsider Example 8-1, which shows how to estimate the intrinsic value per share for IBM stock, in light of the more recent information that has become available since this estimate was prepared in 1988. (*a*) What do you currently estimate the value of a share of IBM stock will be 4 years in the future? Show the calculations used in preparing your estimate. *Hint: Chapter 6 gives sources of financial information where you can get up-to-date information about IBM.* (*b*) After you have finished preparing your estimate of IBM's value 4 years in the future, write a few sentences explaining whether you think you will be a passive or an aggressive investor in the future. Why did you choose to be passive or aggressive?

8-8   If you were managing a billion dollar pension fund portfolio, do you think it would be wiser for you (*a*) to pursue a passive investment policy of indexing the billion dollars so that you could earn 10 percent per annum over the long run or (*b*) to pursue an aggressive investment management program that requires you to spend many thousands of dollars annually on securities analysis and brokerage commissions in order to earn 12 percent per year rate of return over the long run? Explain your decision.

8-9   John Malone was bearish about the stock issued by American Telephone & Telegraph (AT&T). He expected the price of AT&T to fall significantly within the next 3 months. So, Malone sold 100 shares short. Malone's stockbroker arranged to loan Malone's account the 100 shares to deliver with the understanding that these shares would be replaced with other AT&T shares later. A month after Malone opened his short position, AT&T announced a cash dividend of $1.32 per share. How will this cash dividend affect people like Mr. Malone who have sold AT&T stock short?

Problems

8-10   After comparing their prices and values, decide whether buying, no action, or selling is appropriate for the following common stocks.

Corporation's name	Market price of stock	Estimated value per share	Buy, sell, or no action?
Acme Corp.	$87.75	$90	
Baker Inc.	$11.125	$13	
Crown Corp.	$31.75	$40	
Delta Inc.	$19.50	$25	
Evans Corp.	$44.25	$30	

8-11 Write out the formulas for the one-period rates of return for an investor who (*a*) buys a share of the Ace Corporation's common stock for $40, holds the stock in a long position for 6 months while collecting a $2 cash dividend, and sells it for $42 and (*b*) sells a share of Ace common stock short at $40 per share, holds the short position open for 6 months while Ace pays a $2 cash dividend, and covers the short position at $42 per share.

8-12 Edie Evans is considering purchasing a 20-year 10 percent annuity that pays $8000 at the end of each year. How much will she be required to pay for this annuity?

8-13 Joey L. Clay is considering investing in the common stock of the QED Company. Joey has estimated the following cashflows for a 5-year holding period:

Year	Cashflow
1	$2
2	3
3	4
4	4
5	2 + 73 = $75 = E(dividend + price)

(*a*) If Clay's projections are accurate and if the appropriate return over this period for the stock is 14 percent, what should he currently pay per share for QED? (*b*) If QED is currently selling for $52, what should Joey do?

8-14 The stock of the ABC Company is currently selling for $30. If the stock is held for 10 years, the following dividend payments are expected: years 1 to 5, $2, and years 6 to 10, $3. What must the stock's selling price be in 10 years for an investor to earn a 12 percent return before taxes?

8-15 Find the present value of the following cashflows. Assume a rate of return of 14 percent.

Year	Cashflow
1	$100
2	-50
3	200
4	400
5	-300

8-16 Elaine R. Fox has been offered an investment opportunity that currently will require an initial investment of $50,000. (*a*) In 5 years, she can liquidate the investment for $100,000. If Fox makes the investment, what annual rate of return will she earn on a before-tax basis? (*b*) If Fox is in a 33 percent tax bracket, what after-tax return will she earn?

8-17 An investment of $2000 today will return $4000 at the end of 8 years. What is the compounded effective rate of return for this investment?

Matching Questions

8-18 Match the following words and phrases with their correct definitions.

Word or Phrase	Definition or Description
1. Price per share	A. The value and price fluctuate randomly together.
2. Passive investment management	B. A quantity determined by market processes that can sometimes be irrational.
3. Intrinsic value per share	C. A buy and hold without trading strategy.
4. Continuous equilibrium	D. The appropriate decision when an underpriced security is discovered.
5. Buy a security	E. A quantity estimated by an informed analyst.

Selected References

Fabozzi, Frank, and Gregory M. Kipnis, eds., *The Handbook of Stock Index Futures and Options* (Homewood, Ill.: Dow Jones–Irwin, 1989).

Chapter 13 is about hedging. Chapters 14 and 15 deal with arbitrage. The book is easy to read; elementary algebra is used sparingly. Numerical examples enrich the discussion.

Figlewski, Stephen, *Hedging with Financial Futures for Institutional Investors* (Cambridge, Mass.: Ballinger, 1986).

A mathematical book about hedging that has numerical examples.

Kaufman, Perry J., *Handbook of Futures Markets* (New York: Wiley-Interscience, 1984).

Chapters 9 and 10 introduce hedging and arbitrage with a minimum of mathematical notation so that it is easy to read. Only very elementary algebra is used.

Welles, Chris, "Inside the Arbitrage Game," *Institutional Investor,* Aug. 1981, pp. 41–44.

This easy-to-read magazine article discusses **risk arbitrage,** a dubiously labeled form of trading that involves risky speculation in corporate reorganizations. Risk arbitrage is unrelated to the kind of arbitrage that economists have discussed for centuries.

Chapter 9

Diversification and Portfolio Analysis

Investment positions are undertaken with the goal of earning some expected rate of return. Investors seek to minimize inefficient deviations from this expected rate of return. Diversification is essential to the creation of an efficient investment because it can reduce the variability of returns around the expected return.

The portfolio manager seeking efficient investments works with two kinds of statistics—expected return statistics and risk statistics. The expected return and risk statistics for individual assets are the exogenously determined **input data** analyzed by the portfolio analyst. The **objective of portfolio analysis** is to develop a portfolio that has the maximum return at whatever level of risk the investor deems appropriate. All information available to the securities analyst is supposed to be summarized in the risk-return statistics describing the investment candidates.

Let's consider some different diversification techniques for reducing a portfolio's risk.

9-1   **SIMPLE DIVERSIFICATION**

Simple diversification can be defined as "not putting all the eggs in one basket," or "spreading the risks."

Benefits of Simple Diversification

Figure 9-1 shows how simple diversification works. The figure was prepared using empirical data on 470 common stocks from the NYSE. The figure shows that the average standard deviation of returns for all 470 stocks was 0.21. The

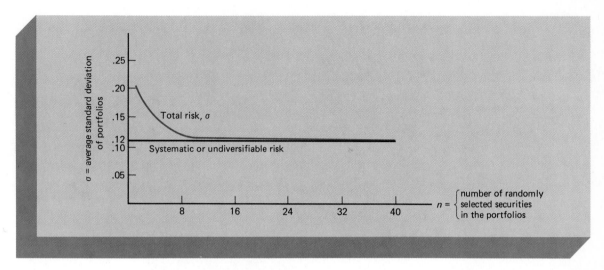

Figure 9-1 Simple diversification reduces a portfolio's total diversifiable risk to zero and only the undiversifiable risk remains (*Source:* J. Evans and S. H. Archer, "Diversification and the Reduction of Dispersion: An Empirical Analysis," *Journal of Finance,* Dec. 1968, pp. 761–767.)

level of undiversifiable risk in the market was estimated at 0.12 (that is, $\sigma_m = 12$ percent).

Sixty different portfolios of each size were assembled from *randomly selected* NYSE stocks and used to prepare Figure 9-1. That is, 60 one-security portfolios, 60 different two-security portfolios, 60 different three-security portfolios, and so on, up to 40-security portfolios were calculated by computer. These portfolios were constructed so that each randomly selected security was allocated an *equal weight* in its portfolio. Then the *average* standard deviation of returns was calculated for the 60 different portfolios of each size. Figure 9-1 shows the average standard deviations for each portfolio size. From the figure we can see that, on the average, randomly combining 10 to 15 stocks will reduce a portfolio's total risk to the *undiversifiable* level of variation found in the market averages. Spreading the portfolio's assets randomly over two or three times as many stocks cannot be expected to reduce risk any further.

Conclusions about Simple Diversification

Simple diversification was analyzed using random selections and equal weighting to simulate the techniques a naive investor might employ. Using these naive techniques to implement simple diversification does not nullify its ability to reduce risk in a diversified portfolio. Figure 9-1 shows that simple diversification over about 15 naively selected assets will almost halve risk, on average.

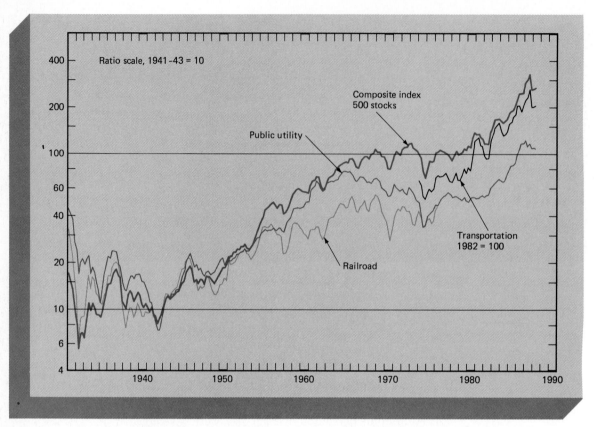

Figure 9-2 Standard & Poor's stock market indexes from different industries, 1931–1987.

Table 9-1
STATISTICS FROM VARIOUS DIVERSIFICATION TECHNIQUES

Stocks in portfolio	Technique used to diversify	Minimum rate of return	Maximum rate of return	Mean rate of return	Standard deviation of returns
8	Random	−47%	164%	13%	0.22
8	Across industries	−47	158	13	0.22
16	Random	−37	121	13	0.21
16	Across industries	−37	121	13	0.21
32	Random	−31	98	13	0.20
32	Across industries	−29	93	13	0.20
128	Random	−29	76	13	0.19

Source: L. Fisher and J. Lorie, "Some Studies of Variability of Returns on Investments in Common Stocks," *Journal of Business,* April 1970, p. 112, table 5.

9-2   **DIVERSIFICATION ACROSS INDUSTRIES**

Some investment counselors advocate selecting securities from different industries to achieve better diversification. It is certainly better to follow this
advice than to select all the securities in a portfolio from one industry. But,
empirical research has shown that diversifying across industries is not much
better than simply selecting securities randomly.

Studies of the rates of return from securities in many industries have shown
that nearly all industries are highly correlated with one another. The easiest
way to see the meager benefits of diversifying across various industries is to
examine the movement of Standard & Poor's indexes for transportation stocks,
utility stocks, and the Composite Index made up of 500 stocks from 90 different
industries. Figure 9-2 shows how these three different indexes move up and
down together month after month. The *undiversifiable variability* illustrated in
Figure 9-2 cannot be diversified away simply by selecting securities from different industries.

Professors Lorie and Fisher measured the effectiveness of diversifying across
different industries and of increasing the number of different assets in the
portfolio. Portfolios containing 8, 16, 32, and 128 NYSE-listed common stocks
were formed by two separate techniques. The first technique involved simple
random selection of assets. The second technique drew each asset in the portfolio from a different industry. Numerous portfolios were constructed in this
study, and statistics were tabulated about the portfolio's rates of return. Table
9-1 presents the findings of the study.

Table 9-1 suggests two conclusions: (1) diversifying across industries is not
better than simple diversification, and (2) increasing the number of different
assets held in the portfolio above eight does not significantly reduce the portfolio's risk.

9-3   **SUPERFLUOUS DIVERSIFICATION**

If 10 or 15 different assets are selected for a portfolio, the maximum risk-
reduction benefits from simple diversification have most likely been attained.
Further spreading of the portfolio's assets is **superfluous diversification** and
should be avoided. Superfluous diversification will usually result in the following portfolio management problems:

1. *Impossibility of good portfolio management:* If the portfolio contains
   dozens of different assets, the portfolio's management cannot consider
   the status of all of them simultaneously.

2. *Purchase of lackluster performers:* The search for numerous different
   assets to buy will ultimately lead to the ill-informed purchase of investments that will not yield an adequate rate of return for the risk they
   bear.

3. *High search costs:* As the number of candidate securities for a portfolio increases, it will be more costly to do the necessary security analysis.

4. *High transaction costs:* Frequent purchases of small quantities of shares will result in larger broker's commissions than will less frequent purchases of larger blocks of shares.

Although more money is spent to manage a superfluously diversified portfolio, there will most likely be no concurrent improvement in the portfolio's performance. Thus, superfluous diversification may lower the net return to the portfolio's owners after the portfolio's management expenses are deducted.

9-4   **SIMPLE DIVERSIFICATION ACROSS QUALITY RATING CATEGORIES**

Two investment analysts named Wagner and Lau analyzed the effects of simple diversification across stocks that have the same Standard & Poor's quality ratings. Quality ratings measure default risk—essentially, the risk of bankruptcy. Standard & Poor's quality ratings are explained in Table 14-2.

Statistics Describing Different Quality Rating Categories

Table 9-2 shows risk and return statistics for portfolios of stocks having different quality ratings. Each of the six simply diversified portfolios in Table 9-2 contains 20 equally weighted common stocks that all have *identical quality ratings*.

Economic theory suggests that risk-averse investors should require higher average rates of return in order to induce them to assume higher levels of risk. The empirical statistics shown in Table 9-2 support the theory.

Table 9-2

RISK AND RETURN STATISTICS FOR SIMPLY DIVERSIFIED PORTFOLIOS WITHIN HOMOGENEOUS QUALITY RATING CATEGORIES

Homogeneous quality rating	Average standard deviation	Monthly average return
A+	0.039	0.67
A	0.042	0.69
A−	0.045	0.78
B+	0.045	1.04
B	0.063	1.05
B− to C+	0.063	1.03

Source: W. H. Wagner and S. Lau, "The Effect of Diversification on Risk," *Financial Analysts Journal*, Nov.–Dec. 1971, p. 52.

Simple Diversification within Homogeneous Quality Categories

Wagner and Lau extended the methodology used to create Figure 9-1 to generate the risk statistics for portfolios that were *randomly diversified within homogeneous quality ratings*. The Wagner-Lau results are illustrated in Figure 9-3. Comparing Figures 9-1 and 9-3 reveals that simple diversification yields significant risk reductions within homogeneous quality rating categories, just as it did across the more heterogeneous sample used in Figure 9-1.

Figure 9-3 shows that the standard deviations of portfolios of different homogeneous quality rating attained different levels of risk. The highest-quality

Figure 9-3 Simple diversification reduces risk within categories of stocks that all have the same quality rating.

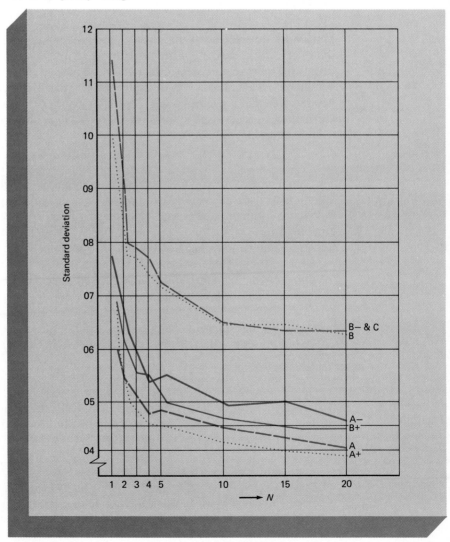

portfolio of randomly diversified stocks was able to achieve lower levels of risk than the simply diversified portfolios of lower-quality stocks. This result reflects the fact that default risk (as measured by the quality ratings) is part of total risk. The higher-quality portfolios in Figure 9-3 contain assets with less default risk. This finding suggests that portfolio managers can reduce portfolio risk to levels lower than those attainable with simple diversification by not diversifying across lower-quality assets.

The next section explains a more sophisticated method of diversification that simultaneously considers both the risk and the return of the portfolio.

9-5   MARKOWITZ DIVERSIFICATION

Markowitz diversification may be defined as combining assets which are less than perfectly positively correlated in order to reduce portfolio risk without sacrificing portfolio returns.[1] It can sometimes reduce risk below the undiversifiable level. Markowitz diversification is more analytical than simple diversification and considers assets' correlations (or covariances). The lower the correlation between assets, the more that Markowitz diversification will be able to reduce the portfolio's risk.

Numerical Example of Risk Reduction

The simplest way to see the benefits of combining securities with low correlations is to use a numerical example. Consider what happens when two hypothetical common stocks that have negatively correlated rates of return are combined into a portfolio. The symbol S denotes the stock in the Summer Resorts Corporation, and the symbol U stands for Umbrella Corporation of America's stock. Table 9-3 shows the results.

A portfolio made up of equal parts of asset S and asset U has zero variability of returns. This total elimination of risk was due to the perfect negative correlation of the rates of return of S and U. The returns from S and U move inversely, so that the gains on one stock exactly offset the losses on the other. This example shows that it is theoretically possible to *create riskless portfolios from risky assets*.

Calculating a Portfolio's Expected Return

It is a logical error to draw general conclusions from specific cases. Therefore, we will consider a more general analysis of Markowitz diversification which focuses on the correlation between assets.

[1] H. Markowitz, "Portfolio Selection," *Journal of Finance,* March 1952, p. 89. There is a natural trade-off between risk and return in the market. But, at any given level of expected return, Markowitz diversification can reduce risk more than simple diversification.

Table 9-3
NUMERICAL EXAMPLE OF DIVERSIFICATION WITH INVERSELY CORRELATED STOCKS

	Time and weather				
	$t = 1$ Sunny	$t = 2$ Rainy	$t = 3$ Rain and sun	$t = 4$ Rain and sun	Var(r), or risk
U's return	-10%	$+35\%$	$+20\%$	$+15\%$	0.2625
S's return	$+30\%$	-15%	0	$+5\%$	0.2625
Returns on portfolio	$\dfrac{-10\% + 30\%}{2} = 10\%$	$\dfrac{+35\% - 15\%}{2} = 10\%$	$\dfrac{+20\% + 0}{2} = 10\%$	$\dfrac{+15\% + 5\%}{2} = 10\%$	Zero, or riskless

Expected Return Formula for Portfolios   Equation (9-1) defines a **portfolio's expected rate of return,** denoted $E(r_p)$, for an n-asset portfolio.

$$E(r_p) = \sum_{i=1}^{n} x_i E(r_i) \tag{9-1}$$

The character x_i represents the fraction of the total value of the portfolio invested in the ith asset. The x_i's are called **weights** or **participation levels.** These weights are the **decision variables** upon which the portfolio manager is paid to decide. The symbol $E(r_i)$ denotes the expected rate of return from the ith asset; it is an *exogenously determined* value that was defined in Equation (1-5).

The Weights Sum to One   Portfolio analysis always assumes that the weights sum to 1 since it is pointless to account for more or less than 100 percent of the funds in the portfolio.

$$\sum_{i=1}^{n} x_i = 1.0 \tag{9-2}$$

Calculating a Two-Asset Portfolio's $E(r)$ Table 9-4 gives the risk and return of two ($n = 2$) hypothetical common stocks issued by the Abercrombie and Bean Corporations.

Suppose that two-thirds of the portfolio's funds are invested in asset Abercrombie and the other one-third in Bean. Symbolically, $x_A = \frac{2}{3}$ and $x_B = \frac{1}{3}$.

Table 9-4
STATISTICS FOR THE ABERCROMBIE AND BEAN CORPORATIONS

Stock issuer	Expected return $E(r)$	Risk σ, %
Abercrombie	5%	20%
Bean	15	40

The formula for the weighted average return from the portfolio is below.

$$E(r_p) = x_A E(r_A) + x_B E(r_B) \tag{9-1a}$$

The equation above can be equivalently rewritten in terms of one weight, since $x_B = 1.0 - x_A$.

$$E(r_p) = x_A E(r_A) + (1 - x_A)E(r_B) \tag{9-1b}$$

$$= x_A(5\%) + x_B(15\%) \tag{9-1c}$$

$$= \tfrac{2}{3}(5\%) + \tfrac{1}{3}(15\%)$$

$$= 0.666(0.05) + 0.333(0.15) = 0.083 \times 100 = 8.3\%$$

The portfolio with two-thirds of its funds invested in Abercrombie and the other one-third in Bean has an expected rate of return of 8.3 percent.

Objective of Portfolio Analysis

The portfolio manager's task is to select the investment weights that will result in dominant investments. Hereafter, dominant assets will be called "efficient portfolios" whether they contain one or many assets. An **efficient portfolio,** then, is any asset or combination of assets that has (1) the maximum expected return in its risk class, or conversely, (2) the minimum risk at its level of expected return.

The *objective of portfolio management* is to analyze different individual assets and delineate efficient portfolios. The group of all efficient portfolios will be called the **efficient set of portfolios.** The efficient set of portfolios comprises the "efficient frontier." The **efficient frontier** is the locus of points in risk-return space having the maximum return at each risk class. The efficient frontier dominates all other investments.

The portfolio manager starts with the risk and return statistics that were estimated by securities analysts. These input data are exogenous information that form the basis for portfolio analysis. The portfolio manager's job is to analyze the risk and return data describing each investment candidate and determine which assets to buy, what not to buy, and what to sell short. The portfolio risk formula plays an important role in developing an optimal portfolio.

Quadratic Risk Formula for a Portfolio

Total risk is measured by either the variance or its square root, the standard deviation, of returns. The variance of returns from a portfolio made up of n assets is defined by Equation (9-3).

$$\text{Var}(r_p) = \sum_{i=1}^{n} \sum_{j=1}^{n} x_i x_j \sigma_{ij} \tag{9-3}$$

Equation (9-3) defines the **variance-covariance matrix** for a portfolio of n assets.

Equation (9-3a) expands the formula to show how the variances and covariances of every asset determine the portfolio's risk.

$$\text{Var}(r_p) = \sum_{i=1}^{n} \sum_{j=1}^{n} x_i x_j \sigma_{ij} \tag{9-3a}$$

$$= \underbrace{x_1^2 \sigma_{11}^2}_{\text{1 asset}} + 2x_1 x_2 \sigma_{12} + 2x_1 x_3 \sigma_{13} + \cdots + 2x_1 x_n \sigma_{1n}$$

$$\underbrace{+ x_2^2 \sigma_{22}^2 + 2x_2 x_3 \sigma_{23} + \cdots + 2x_2 x_n \sigma_{2n}}_{\text{for 2 assets}}$$

$$\underbrace{+ x_3^2 \sigma_{33}^2 + \cdots + 2x_3 x_n \sigma_{3n}}_{\text{for a 3-asset portfolio}}$$

$$\vdots$$

$$\underbrace{\cdots + x_n^2 \sigma_{nn}^2}_{\text{for a portfolio of } n \text{ assets}}$$

where

σ_p = standard deviation of portfolio's rates of return

σ_i^2 and σ_{ii} = two equivalent conventions for variance of returns from ith asset

σ_{ij} and $\text{cov}(r_i, r_j)$ = equivalent representations for covariance of returns between assets i and j

Since $\sigma_{ij} = \sigma_{ji}$, each covariance in Equation (9-3a) is multiplied by 2 rather than repeat each term.

The **covariance** is related to the correlation coefficient as shown in Equation (9-4).

$$\sigma_{ij} = \sigma_i \sigma_j \rho_{ij} \tag{9-4}$$

where ρ_{ij} is the correlation coefficient between variables i and j. Note that the covariance of the random variable i with itself equals the variance, $\sigma_{ii} = \sigma_i \sigma_i \rho_{ii} = \text{Var}(r_i)$. Also observe that Equation (9-4) can be solved to obtain a definition of the correlation coefficient.

The covariance measures how two variables covary. If two assets are positively correlated, their covariance will also be positive. For example, most common stocks have a positive covariance with each other. If two variables are independent, their covariance is zero. For example, the covariance of stock market prices and sunspot activity is zero. If two variables vary inversely, their covariance is negative.

Equation (9-5) is a simple case of Equation (9-3); it defines the standard deviation of returns for a two-asset portfolio of common stocks issued by the Abercrombie and Bean Corporations.[2]

$$\sigma_p = \sqrt{x_A^2\sigma_A^2 + x_B^2\sigma_B^2 + 2x_Ax_B\sigma_{AB}} \qquad (9\text{-}5)$$

Substituting Equation (9-4) into Equation (9-5) yields Equation (9-6), which shows how the correlation between the returns from Abercrombie and Bean affects the portfolio's risk.

$$\sigma_p = \sqrt{x_A^2\sigma_A^2 + x_B^2\sigma_B^2 + 2x_Ax_B\sigma_A\sigma_B\rho_{AB}} \qquad (9\text{-}6)$$

Substituting in the risk statistics from Table 9-4 yields

$$\sigma_p = \sqrt{x_A^2(0.2)^2 + x_B^2(0.4)^2 + 2x_Ax_B(0.2)(0.4)\rho_{AB}} \qquad (9\text{-}6a)$$

$$= \sqrt{x_A^2(0.04) + x_B^2(0.16) + 0.16x_Ax_B\rho_{AB}} \qquad (9\text{-}6b)$$

Figure 9-4a, b, c, and d shows graphs in risk-return space of the two assets, Abercrombie and Bean, and the portfolios that can be formed from them at three different values for their correlation coefficient, $\rho_{AB} = -1, 0,$ and $+1$. This figure was prepared by plotting the risk and return of the various portfolios composed of Abercrombie and Bean stocks for all the positive weights that sum to unity (that is, $x_A + x_B = 1$) and for three different correlation coefficients, $\rho_{AB} = -1.0, 0,$ and $+1.0$.

In order to understand Figure 9-4, it is necessary to verify a few points in the figures by substituting some appropriate numbers into Equations (9-1c) and (9-6b) and calculating the portfolio's expected return and risk. For example, the portfolio which has $x_A = \frac{2}{3}$ and $x_B = \frac{1}{3}$ has an expected return of 8.3 percent, as shown in Equation (9-1c), regardless of the value assumed by the correlation coefficient. However, the risk for the portfolio with $x_A = \frac{2}{3}$ and $x_B = \frac{1}{3}$ varies directly with the correlation coefficient ρ_{AB}.

[2]The risk formula for a two-asset portfolio is derived below:

$$r_p = x_1r_1 + x_2r_2 \qquad \text{by definition}$$

$$E(r_p) = x_1E(r_1) + x_2E(r_2) \qquad (9\text{-}1)$$

These two equations are used in the following derivation.

$$\begin{aligned}
\text{Var}(r_p) &= E[r_p - E(r_p)]^2 \qquad \text{the definition of Var}(r_p)\\
&= E\{x_1r_1 + x_2r_2 - [x_1E(r_1) + x_2E(r_2)]\}^2 \qquad \text{by substitution for } r_p\\
&= E\{x_1[r_1 - E(r_1)] + x_2[r_2 - E(r_2)]\}^2 \qquad \text{collecting like terms}\\
&= E\{x_1^2[r_1 - E(r_1)]^2 + x_2^2[r_2 - E(r_2)]^2 + 2x_1x_2[r_1 - E(r_1)][r_2 - E(r_2)]\}\\
&= x_1^2E[r_1 - E(r_1)]^2 + x_2^2E[r_2 - E(r_2)]^2 + 2x_1x_2E\{[r_1 - E(r_1)][r_2 - E(r_2)]\}\\
&= x_1^2 \text{Var}(r_1) + x_2^2 \text{Var}(r_2) + 2x_1x_2 \text{Cov}(r_1, r_2) \qquad \text{restating definitions}
\end{aligned}$$

$$\sigma_p = \sqrt{x_A^2\sigma_A^2 + x_B^2\sigma_B^2 + 2x_Ax_B\sigma_A\sigma_B\rho_{AB}} \qquad (9\text{-}6)$$

$$= \sqrt{(\tfrac{2}{3})^2(0.2)^2 + (\tfrac{1}{3})^2(0.4)^2 + 2(\tfrac{2}{3})(\tfrac{1}{3})(0.2)(0.4)\rho_{AB}}$$

$$= 0.0175 + 0.0175 + 0.035\rho_{AB} \qquad (9\text{-}6b)$$

$$= 0.035 + 0.035\rho_{AB}$$

Figure 9-4 Portfolio analysis with two assets that are (a) perfectly positively correlated; (b) zero correlated; (c) perfectly negatively correlated; (d) assumed to have different correlations.

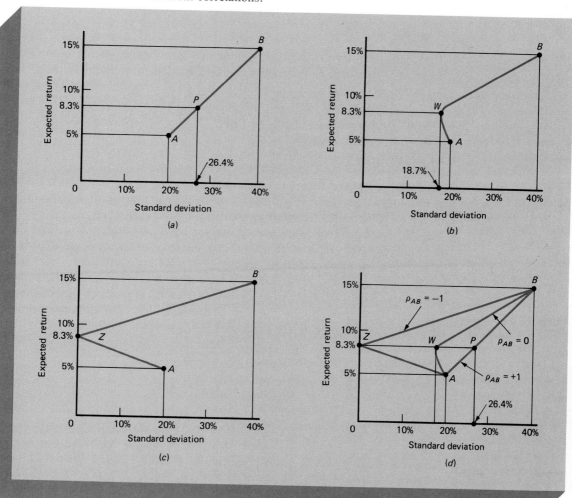

Perfectly Positively Correlated Returns, Figure 9-4a

Portfolio analysis of the two-asset portfolio illustrated in Figure 9-4a shows that when the correlation coefficient of the rates of return from the Abercrombie and Bean assets is at its maximum value of positive unity, the linear risk-return relationship in Figure 9-4a results. This straight line between assets A and B in risk-return space is derived by first setting ρ_{AB} to positive unity in Equation (9-6b). Next the values of the two assets' weights are varied from 0 to 1 (that is, $0.0 < x < +1.0$) inversely so that they always sum to positive unity (namely, $x_A + x_B = 1.0$). Finally, the infinite number of pairs of positive values for x_A and x_B that sum to 1 are substituted into the portfolio risk formula, Equation (9-6b), and the portfolio return formula, Equation (9-1c). The infinite number of risk and return statistics for the two-asset portfolio thus derived trace out the straight line in Figure 9-4a when $\rho_{AB} = +1.0$.

Uncorrelated Assets, Figure 9-4b

If the rates of return from Abercrombie and Bean stocks are zero-correlated, substantial risk reduction benefits can be obtained from diversifying between the two assets. This beneficial risk reduction can be seen analytically by noting what happens to the portfolio risk equation (9-6b) when $\rho_{AB} = 0$. The last quantity on the right-hand side of Equation (9-6b) becomes zero when $\rho_{AB} = 0$. This obviously reduces the portfolio's risk level below what it was when this correlation was larger (for example, when $\rho_{AB} = +1.0$).

The results of the uncorrelated returns are illustrated in Figure 9-4b. The portfolio's expected return is unaffected by changing the correlation between assets—this is because ρ_{AB} is not a variable in the portfolio return equation (9-1c). All differences between the portfolios generated when $\rho_{AB} = +1.0$ and when $\rho_{AB} = 0$ are risk differences stemming from Equation (9-6b). Figure 9-4b shows that the portfolios with $\rho_{AB} = 0$ have less risk at every level of expected return than the same portfolios with $\rho_{AB} = +1.0$ in Figure 9-4a.

The substantial risk reductions available by diversifying across uncorrelated assets are readily available to all investors. Empirical research has shown that common stock price indexes, bond price indexes, and commodity price indexes all tend to be uncorrelated.[3] Thus, any investor who diversifies across these different market assets can expect to benefit from the diversification between uncorrelated assets illustrated in Figure 9-4b.

[3]See R. G. Ibbotson and R. A. Sinquefield, *Stocks, Bonds, Bills, and Inflation: The Past (1926–1976) and the Future (1977–2000)* (Charlottesville, Va.: Financial Analysts Research Foundation, 1977), exhibit 7. See also K. Dusak, "Future Trading and Investor Returns: An Investigation of Commodity Risk Premiums," *Journal of Political Economy*, Dec. 1963, vol. 81, no. 6, pp. 1387–1406. Also see Zvi Bodie and Victor Rosansky, "Risk and Return in Commodity Futures," *Financial Analysts Journal*, May–June 1980, pp. 38–39.

Perfectly Negatively Correlated Returns, Figure 9-4c

The lowest possible value for a correlation coefficient is negative unity. When the correlation coefficient in the portfolio risk equation (9-6b) reaches negative unity, the last term on the right-hand side of the equation assumes its maximum negative value for any given pair of values for x_A and x_B. In fact, the portfolio's risk can be reduced to zero when $\rho_{AB} = -1.0$ for one particular set of portfolio weights. For example, for the portfolio made up of Bean and Abercrombie stocks, Figure 9-4c shows that when $x_A = \frac{2}{3}$, $x_B = \frac{1}{3}$, and $\rho_{AB} = -1.0$, the portfolio's risk vanishes. For all other weights the portfolio's risk is above zero, but portfolio risk is always at its lowest possible level over all possible sets of portfolio weights when $\rho_{AB} = -1.0$.

If it seems dubious that two perfectly negatively correlated *risky assets* like Abercrombie and Bean can be combined in just the correct proportions to form a *riskless portfolio* like the one at $x_A = \frac{2}{3}$ and $x_B = \frac{1}{3}$ in Figure 9-4c, reconsider the example in Table 9-3. This numerical example demonstrates that when two assets are perfectly negatively correlated, their prices and returns move inversely. As a result of these perfect inverse movements, whatever losses one asset has can be exactly offset by equal-sized gains from the other asset. That leaves the portfolio with zero variability or return—that is, a riskless portfolio has been created.

Portfolio Analysis Using Markowitz Diversification

Figure 9-4d summarizes the three illustrated examples from Figure 9-4a, b, and c. To summarize, it was shown in Figure 9-4a that at point P, $x_A = \frac{2}{3}$ and $x_B = \frac{1}{3}$, and for a correlation of $\rho_{AB} = +1$, the portfolio's total risk is $\sigma_p = \sqrt{0.07} \times 100 = 26.4$ percent. Figure 9-4b shows that if $\rho_{AB} = 0$, then $\sigma_p = \sqrt{0.035} \times 100 = 18.7$ percent at point W. And Figure 9-4c illustrates that if $\rho_{AB} = -1$, then $\sigma_p = \sqrt{0} = 0$ at point Z. Figure 9-4d was constructed by plotting all the points (like P, W, and Z, respectively) from Figure 9-4a, b, and c together.

Markowitz diversification can lower risk below the undiversifiable level if the securities analyst can find securities whose rates of return have low enough correlations. Unfortunately, there are only a precious few securities that have low correlations. Therefore, using Markowitz diversification requires a data bank of financial statistics for many securities, a computer, and some econometric analysis.

Applying Markowitz diversification to a collection of potential investment assets with a computer is called **Markowitz portfolio analysis.** It is a scientific way to manage a portfolio, and its results are quite interesting. Since Markowitz portfolio analysis considers both the risk and return of dozens, or hundreds, or thousands of different securities simultaneously (the number is limited only by the size of the computer and the number of securities for which the risk and return statistics are known), it is a more powerful method of analyzing a portfolio than using intuition or selecting investments by committee. A person's mind (even the mind of a genius) cannot simultaneously evaluate hundreds of different investment opportunities and balance the risks and returns of them

Table 9-5

**RETURN, RISK, AND CORRELATION STATISTICS FOR TWO CATEGORIES OF ASSETS,
1926–1987**

A. Expected rates of return	
Common stocks (s)	12.0%
Treasury bonds (b)	4.6%

B. Variance-covariance matrix		
	Common stocks (s)	**Treasury bonds (b)**
Common stocks (s)	$\sigma_s = 21.1\% = \sqrt{445.21}$	$\text{Cov}(s, b) = 19.7\%$
L-T Treasury bonds (b)		$\sigma_b = 8.5\% = \sqrt{72.25}$

C. Correlation matrix		
	Common stocks (s)	**Treasury bonds (b)**
Common stocks (s)	1.0	.11
Treasury bonds (b)		1.0

Source: R. G. Ibbotson and Rex A. Sinquefield, *Stocks, Bonds, Bills and Inflation (SBBI): 1982 Edition,* updated in *SBBI 1988 Yearbook,* exhibits 8 and 32 (Chicago, Ill.: Ibbotson Associates, Inc., 1988).

all to find efficient portfolios that dominate all other investment opportunities. Markowitz portfolio analysis is essentially a mathematics problem requiring that many different equations be solved simultaneously. This can be done on a large scale only by using a computer program which does what is called "quadratic programming." **Quadratic programming** minimizes the portfolio's risk (a quadratic equation) at each level of average return for the portfolio.[4]

The type of portfolio manager who is not sufficiently analytical to use quadratic programming is sometimes lightly referred to as a "financial interior decorator."

Financial Interior Decorating

Many investment counselors are **financial interior decorators,** meaning that they design portfolios of securities to match the investors' personalities. Thus, an elderly person who is naive about financial matters and depends on the

---

[4]Computer programs that perform portfolio analysis and other forms of investment analysis are publicly available. See William B. Riley, Jr., and Austin H. Montgomery, Jr., *Guide to Computer Assisted Investment Analysis* (New York: McGraw-Hill, 1982). Chapter 8 contains a simplified Markowitz portfolio analysis program that can be run on a personal computer. More sophisticated portfolio analysis programs are available from Richard Bookstaber, *The Complete Investment Book* (Glenview, Ill.: Scott, Foresman, 1985), chap. 9. Also, see the appendix about computer software at the end of this book.

income from a modest investment would be advised to invest in low-risk low-return assets, like bonds and utility stocks, on the assumption that this course would minimize risk. Little or no consideration would be given to the correlation between these low-risk assets by a financial interior decorator. On the other hand, a young professional person with a promising future would be advised to invest in high-risk high-return securities. A financial interior decorator would make this suggestion on the oversimplified assumption that the high-risk stocks must combine to make a portfolio with the highest long-run rate of return. Table 9-5 shows that this assumption is not necessarily true. In spite of the superficial intuitive appeal of the financial interior decorating approach to portfolio management, the portfolio analysis above reveals its fallacy.

| 9-6 | ASSET ALLOCATION |

Asset allocation decisions deal with attaining the optimal proportions of investments from different asset categories. Portfolio managers focus primarily on the stock-bond mix; the decision often boils down to trying to determine the best long-run stock-bond distribution.[5]

Individual securities are not analyzed when solving asset allocation problems. Risk and return statistics that are supposedly representative of different *asset categories* are analyzed. Table 9-5 shows statistics representing two types of assets that might be considered.

Delineating the Menu of Optimal Asset Allocations

Some portfolio managers choose to use equally weighted categories of assets, while others use their judgment and intuition to select an appropriate asset mix. Still others use Markowitz portfolio analysis to delineate the set of optimal asset mixes from which they can select. Table 9-6 lists the menu of alternatives delineated using the Markowitz method; Figure 9-5 illustrates these optimal alternatives.

Reasons Why Asset Allocation Should Precede Security Selection

Some portfolio managers prefer to make asset allocation decisions before selecting which securities to buy for two reasons. First, some believe that selecting the optimal asset mix is more important to the portfolio's performance than security selection and/or active asset management.[6] Second, **estimation risk** can be reduced by optimizing with asset categories before analyzing the individual securities. Estimation risk is related to statistical sampling errors.

---

[5]For further information see K. P. Ambachtsheer, ''Pension Fund Asset Allocation: In Defense of a 60/40 Equity/Debt Asset Mix,'' *Financial Analysts Journal,* Sept.–Oct. 1987, pp. 14–24. For a varied selection of readings on this topic see Robert D. Arnott and Frank J. Fabozzi, *Asset Allocation* (Chicago: Probus, 1988).

[6]See G. P. Brinson, J. J. Diermeier, and G. G. Schlarbaum, ''A Composite Portfolio Benchmark for Pension Plans,'' *Financial Analysts Journal,* March–April 1986, pp. 271–280. Also see Richard O. Michaud, ''Pension Policy and Benchmark Optimization,'' *Industrial Management Review,* March–April 1989, pp. 25–30.

Table 9-6
EFFICIENT FRONTIER OF OPTIMAL ASSET MIXES

Portfolio's expected return	Portfolio's standard deviation, σ_p	Weight in common stock, x	Weight in T-bonds, $(1 - x)$
12.0%	21.1%	100%	0
11.3	19.1	90	10
10.5	17.1	80	20
9.8	15.3	70	30
9.0	13.5	60	40
8.3	11.8	50	50
7.6	10.3	40	60
6.8	9.1	30	70
6.1	8.4	20	80
5.3	8.2	10	90
4.6	8.5	0	100

Performing Markowitz portfolio analysis on the risk and return statistics from securities representative of categories of homogeneous assets involves less sampling error than analyzing the individual securities that underlie these portfolios.[7]

Suppose the portfolio manager selects the 50-50 stock-bond mix at point P in Figure 9-5. A large and a small confidence region have been drawn around efficient portfolio P. The efficient frontier derived by optimizing the asset mixes results in a smaller confidence region than an identical efficient frontier delineated with individual assets whose statistics contained larger sampling errors. As a result, efficient portfolio P can be expected to perform within the smaller confidence region if its asset mix was determined before the individual assets were chosen.

9-7   **PORTFOLIO ANALYSIS WITH NEGATIVE WEIGHTS**

All the investment opportunities illustrated in Figures 9-4 and 9-6a were computed using nonnegative weights, $x > 0$. If negative weights are allowed to

---

[7]To learn more about estimation risk see G. J. Alexander and J. C. Francis, "Estimation Risk," in *Portfolio Analysis*, 3d ed. (Englewood Cliffs, N.J.: Prentice-Hall, 1986), chap. 6. For a less rigorous discussion see Richard O. Michaud, "The Markowitz Optimization Enigma: Is 'Optimized' Optimal?" *Financial Analysts Journal*, Jan.–Feb. 1989, pp. 31–42. Essentially, the *weak law of large numbers* tells us that the return and risk statistics from the S&P 500 Stocks Index will have smaller sampling errors, on average, than the return and risk statistics from the 500 individual stocks that make up the S&P 500 Index.

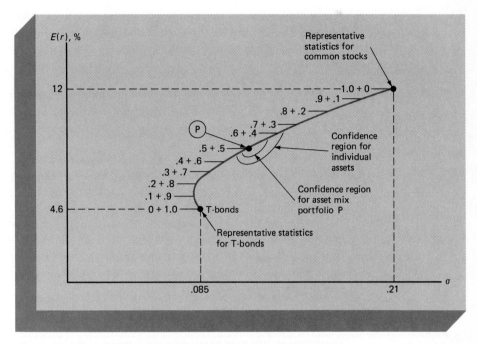

Figure 9-5 The efficient frontier derived from two categories of assets.

Figure 9-6 Portfolio analysis of opportunities from Abercrombie and Bean with (*a*) only nonnegative weights; (*b*) negative weights allowed.

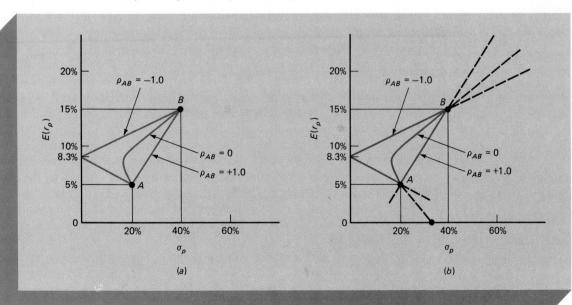

enter the analysis, the additional investment opportunities indicated by the dashed lines in Figure 9-6*b* are also available.

The dashed lines in Figure 9-6*b* represent portfolios that involve assets that have negative weights, $x < 0$. If an asset has a negative weight, two economic interpretations are possible. First, a negative weight can be used to represent a short sale. Second, a negative weight may indicate that the investor created a leveraged (or borrowed, or margined) portfolio by selling (or issuing) a security that has the same risk and return statistics as the asset with the negative weight.

Constraining portfolios to have nonnegative weights as shown in Figure 9-6*a* is realistic for some institutional investors. For instance, pension funds, mutual funds, and endowment funds are legally prohibited from borrowing or short selling. In contrast, negative weights are appropriate for most individual investors and for closed-end funds because there are no prohibitions forbidding them from borrowing or short selling. Comparing Figure 9-6*a* and *b* shows that portfolio analysis of any particular group of individual assets results in more, and sometimes better, investment opportunities when borrowing and short selling are permissible activities.

9-8   CONVEXITY OF THE EFFICIENT FRONTIER

The risk and return of all individual assets (such as stocks, bonds, options, oil paintings, commodity future contracts, gold, ad infinitum) can be plotted in risk-return space. They are represented by the dots in Figure 9-7, which represents the set of all investment opportunities available in the world.

The scalloped, quarter-moon-shaped opportunity set in Figure 9-7 contains individual assets represented by dots in the right-hand portion of the opportunity set. The efficient frontier is represented by the heavy dark curve from E to F. Only portfolios will lie along the efficient frontier. Portfolios will always dominate individual assets because of the risk-reducing benefits of diversification that only portfolios enjoy. Only the highest-return portfolio F in Figure 9-7 is likely to be a single-asset efficient portfolio.

The opportunity set is constructed from curves that are all *convex toward the E(r) axis*. This is because all assets have correlation coefficients between positive unity and negative unity. As shown in Figure 9-4, such correlations result in a locus of portfolios that trace a curve which is convex to the $E(r)$ axis in $[\sigma, E(r)]$ space. Only perfectly positively correlated (that is, $\rho = +1$) assets will generate linear combinations of risk and return, and under no circumstances will a portfolio possibility locus ever curve away from the $E(r)$ axis in $[\sigma, E(r)]$ space.

Not all portfolios will lie on the efficient frontier; some will dominate others. For example, Markowitz diversification will generate portfolios which are more efficient than simply diversified portfolios. If Markowitz diversification is ap-

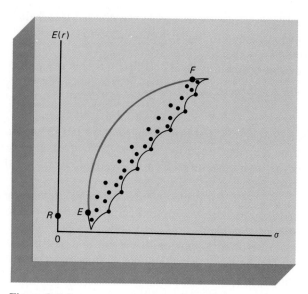

Figure 9-7 Investment opportunities have an efficient frontier that is convex toward the $E(r)$ axis.

plied to all marketable assets, the resulting portfolios would be the efficient set of portfolios that forms the efficient frontier in Figure 9-7.[8]

9-9

DYL'S PORTFOLIO THEORY WITH MARGINED SHORT SALES

An investor who buys a long position in a bond or stock earns the following one-period rate of return.

$$r_{Lt} = \frac{\text{price change } + \text{ cashflow (if any)}}{\text{purchase price}} = \frac{(p_t - p_{t-1}) + c_t}{p_{t-1}} \quad (1\text{-}2)$$

Section 8-3 explained short sales. Someone that sells a security short in a margined account earns the one-period rate of return defined in Equation (9-7), where M denotes the percentage margin requirement.

$$r_{St} = \frac{(p_{t-1} - p_t) - c_t}{Mp_{t-1}} = \frac{\begin{array}{c}\text{price change from}\\ \text{Eq. (1-2) reversed } - \text{ cashflow}\end{array}}{(\% \text{ margin})(\text{purchase price})} \quad (9\text{-}7)$$

---

[8]Appendix 9A shows how to perform mathematical portfolio analysis to find the efficient frontier.

The security's cashflow (such as a cash dividend) is deducted because the short seller must pay money equal to any cashflows accruing to the owner of the securities.[9]

Comparing Equations (1-2) and (9-7) reveals the following relationship:

$$r_{Lt} = \frac{(-1)r_{St}}{M} \tag{9-8}$$

Equation (9-8) shows that the one-period rates of return from a long and a short position in the same security are perfectly inversely correlated because the gains on the long position exactly offset the losses from the short position, or vice versa.

Dyl pointed out that if *margined short sales* are assumed to be possible for the n securities that are investment candidates for a portfolio, then the number of investment candidates doubles to become $2n$.[10] These n "new" negatively correlated investment opportunities result in a new efficient frontier that dominates the efficient frontier attainable without margined short sales.

The inclusion of margined short sales not only allows the creation of a new and more dominant efficient frontier, it also redefines the minimum variance portfolio on the efficient frontier at point E. Consider equally valued long and short positions in any asset. The result of combining these two offsetting positions can be seen by adding Equations (1-2) and (9-7); the sum is zero. Combining long and short positions of equal value in the same asset creates a perfect hedge that has zero expected return and zero risk. The zero-return and zero-risk position attained via the perfect hedge is equivalent to holding cash or, alternatively, to having no position at all. This investment position is plotted at the origin in risk-return space. Figure 9-8 shows that this zero-variance portfolio and the rest of the efficient frontier attainable with margined short sales totally dominates the efficient frontier attainable without margined short sales.

---

[9]Most short sellers do not get the use of the proceeds paid by the buyer. The short seller's brokerage house typically holds the proceeds from short sales and also requires the short seller to make an **initial margin deposit** equal to M percent of the market value of the short sale. When the short seller closes out the short position and returns the borrowed securities to make delivery on the short sale, the brokerage returns the short seller's margin money plus the proceeds from the short sale. The arrangements of each short sale vary with the short seller's position. *In contrast to nonprofessional investors, stock exchange specialists and brokerage houses that sell short can keep the proceeds from their short sales.*

[10]Edward A. Dyl, "Negative Betas: The Attractions of Short Selling," *Journal of Portfolio Management*, Spring 1975, pp. 74–76.

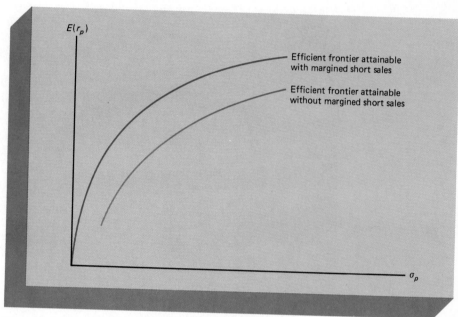

Figure 9-8 The efficient frontier attainable with margined short sales.

TOBIN'S RISKLESS ASSET IMPROVES THE EFFICIENT FRONTIER

Nobel laureate James Tobin extended the portfolio models shown in Figures 9-4 to 9-8 by including a riskless asset.[11] The riskless asset is represented by point R in Figure 9-9; by definition it has $Var(R) = 0$. A Treasury bill that is held to maturity or an FDIC-insured savings deposit are examples of riskless assets.

Linear Formulas for Both Return and Risk

Consider a two-asset portfolio that is constructed from the riskless asset R and risky asset m. This portfolio's expected return is defined in Equation (9-9).

$$E(r_p) = x_m E(r_m) + (1 - x_m)R \qquad (9\text{-}9)$$

The two-asset portfolio's risk can be simplified to Equation (9-10b), as follows:

$$Var(r_p) = x_m^2 \sigma_m^2 + x_R^2 \sigma_R^2 + 2 x_m x_R \sigma_{mR} \qquad (9\text{-}10)$$

$$= x_m^2 \sigma_m^2 + 0 + 0 \qquad \text{since } Var(R) = Cov(R, r) = 0 \quad (9\text{-}10a)$$

[11]James Tobin, "Liquidity Preference as Behavior Towards Risk," *The Review of Economic Studies,* Feb. 1958, vol. XXVI, no. 1, pp. 65–86.

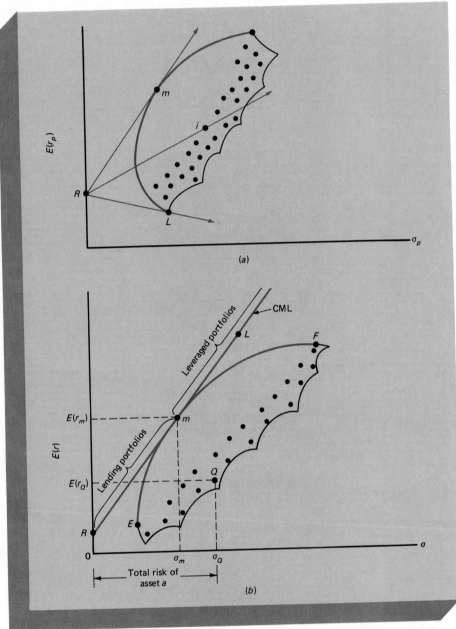

Figure 9-9 Tobin's portfolio theory includes a riskless rate of interest: (*a*) portfolio possibility lines; (*b*) borrowing and lending portfolios.

By taking the square root of Equation (9-10), we can see that the two-asset portfolio's risk formula is linear in the standard deviations.

$$\sigma_p = x_m \sigma_m$$

(9-10b)

Linear equations (9-9) and (9-10b) mean that *all portfolios made up of one risky asset and one riskless asset must form straight lines of investment opportunities in risk-return space,* as shown in Figure 9-9a.

Borrowing and Lending Portfolios Defined

The straight lines that originate from point R in Figure 9-9a are **portfolio possibility lines** that can be formed by combining one risky asset and one riskless asset. The return and risk of every portfolio on these portfolio possibility lines is defined by two linear formulas, like Equations (9-9) and (9-10b). When the weight in risky asset m is positive but less than 1, $0 < x_m < 1$, the remaining proportion, $(1 - x_m) = x_R$, of the portfolio's funds are invested in the riskless asset. Any portfolio that has some of its funds invested in asset R (symbolically, x_R) is called a **lending portfolio** because the investor has lent funds at the riskless rate of interest.

Assume that it is possible to lend and borrow at the riskless interest rate. That is, suppose it is possible to go to the bank and either deposit money to earn a rate R or borrow money and pay rate R. Borrowing at interest rate R is represented by negative values for the weight x_R. When x_R is negative, then x_m must be larger than 1 because portfolio analysis is based on the assumption that the weights always sum to 1, Equation (9-2). Portfolios that have negative values for x_R and values for x_m that exceed 1 are called **borrowing portfolios,** or **leveraged portfolios,** or **margined portfolios.** Figure 9-9b illustrates the borrowing and lending portfolios on one of the portfolio possibility lines.

Suppose portfolio L has $x_R = -1.0$ and $x_m = 2.0$. These values mean that the investor borrowed an amount of money equal to the portfolio's initial value and then used the borrowed funds to invest an amount equal to 200 percent of the portfolio's initial value in risky asset m. Stated differently, this situation can be interpreted to mean that either (a) some of asset m was purchased on margin or (b) a riskless bond that pays interest rate R was printed and sold and the proceeds from this bond issue were used to buy more of asset m. The resulting leveraged portfolio is at point L in Figure 9-9b.

Tobin's development of the portfolio possibility lines has important implications and is the basis for other important economic models.

9-11   **THE CAPITAL MARKET LINE (CML)**

The efficient frontier that can be constructed without borrowing or lending is convex toward the $E(r)$ axis in risk-return space. However, if borrowing and lending opportunities are included in the analysis, a linear set of investment opportunities called the capital market line (CML) emerges. Figure 9-9b depicts the CML.

Figure 9-9a illustrates the rationale for the CML of Figure 9-9b. The CML is simply the most dominant portfolio possibility line illustrated in Figure 9-9a; it is made up of both borrowing and lending portfolios. The risk and return of the portfolios on the CML can be calculated with Equations (9-9) and (9-10b). The CML is the locus of the portfolios that wealth-seeking risk-averse investors will find more desirable than any other portfolios.[12]

Numerical Example of a Leveraged Portfolio

Consider a numerical example of the leveraged portfolio at point L on the CML illustrated in Figure 9-9b. Suppose one share of portfolio m costs $1000 and offers a 50-50 chance of returning either $1000 or $1200. The calculations below show that the expected return for the holding period is 10 percent.

$$E(r_m) = \sum_{i=1}^{2} P_i r_i = P_1 r_1 + P_2 r_2$$

$$= .5 \left(\frac{1000 - 1000}{1000} \right) + .5 \left(\frac{1200 - 1000}{1000} \right)$$

$$= .5(0) + .5(20\%)$$

$$= 0 + 10\% = 10\%$$

The standard deviation of returns from portfolio m is 10 percent.

$$\sigma_M = \sqrt{\sum P_i [r_i - E(r)]^2}$$

$$= \sqrt{.5(0 - 0.1)^2 + .5(0.2 - 0.1)^2}$$

$$= \sqrt{.5(0.01) + .5(0.01)}$$

$$= \sqrt{0.01} = 0.1 \times 100 = 10\%$$

Consider buying portfolio m with borrowed money. If an investor borrows $1000 at $R = 5\%$ and buys a second share of m, $x_m = 2.0$ and $x_R = -1.0$. In this case the investor has a 50-50 chance of receiving $950 or receiving $1350 on the $1000 of original equity.

---

[12]See William F. Sharpe, "Capital Asset Prices: A Theory of Market Equilibrium under Conditions of Risk," *The Journal of Finance*, Sept. 1964, pp. 425–552.

	Two alternative outcomes	
	Bad	**Good**
Original equity	$1000	$1000
Principal amount borrowed at 5%	1000	1000
Total amount invested in m	$2000	$2000
Return on two shares of m	$2000	$2400
Repayment of loan principal	(1000)	(1000)
Payment of interest at 5%	(50)	(50)
Net return on original equity	$ 950	$1350
Probability of outcome	.5	.5

The expected return on asset m leveraged out to point L in Figure 9-9b is 15 percent.

$$E(r) = \sum_{i=1}^{2} P_i r_i = P_1 r_1 + P_2 r_2$$

$$= .5 \left(\frac{950 - 1000}{1000} \right) + .5 \left(\frac{1350 - 1000}{1000} \right)$$

$$= .5(-5\%) + .5(35\%)$$

$$= -2.5\% + 17.5\% = 15\%$$

The standard deviation of returns from leveraged portfolio L is 20 percent, as shown below.

$$\sigma_p = \sqrt{\sum P_i [r_i - E(r_i)]^2}$$

$$= \sqrt{.5(-5\% - 15\%)^2 + .5(35\% - 15\%)^2}$$

$$= \sqrt{.5(-20\%)^2 + .5(20\%)^2}$$

$$= \sqrt{.5(.04) + .5(.04)}$$

$$= \sqrt{.02 + .02}$$

$$= \sqrt{.04} = .2 = 20\%$$

The statistics above are illustrated in Figure 9-9b as portfolios m and L on the CML. The reliability of Equations (9-9) and (9-10b) may be checked by substituting the values from this example.

Market Portfolio   Imagine a capital market that is like the one in Figure 9-9b and that is at equilibrium. By definition, *at economic equilibrium supply and demand are equal.* So every security in the market must be held by some owner. Since all investors unanimously want m, it follows that, in equilibrium, m must be a huge portfolio containing all securities in the proportions x_i^* where

$$x_i^* = \frac{\text{total market value of the } i\text{th issue of securities}}{\text{total market value of all securities in the market}}$$

Portfolio m is called the market portfolio.[13] *The **market portfolio** is the unanimously desirable portfolio containing all securities in exactly the proportions in which they are supplied.* The return on the market portfolio is the weighted average return on all capital assets.

In reality it is possible to obtain only estimates of the market portfolio. However, the market portfolio is a useful theoretical construct since the return on m is the return estimated by the Dow Jones Averages, Standard & Poor's indexes, the NYSE index, and similar indexes.

Undiversifiable Risk and the CML

We saw in Figure 9-4a that when assets form a linear opportunity locus in risk-return space, they must be perfectly positively correlated. This means that the returns from portfolios on the CML must all *vary together systematically.* The portfolios along the CML have had their diversifiable risk reduced to zero. As a result, they contain only undiversifiable risk, which can be decreased by reducing the amount of leverage.

Individual assets, represented by dots like point Q in Figure 9-9b, are not efficient because their total risk includes both undiversifiable and diversifiable risk. These individual assets have not had their total risk reduced by diversification. The total risk of asset Q is equal to the distance from the origin to σ_Q along the horizontal axis of Figure 9-9b.

9-12   **EMPIRICAL TEST OF THE CML**

Models like the CML are simplified versions of reality. The CML was mathematically derived from the efficient frontier by unrealistically assuming that money could be freely borrowed or lent at the risk-free rate R. Of course, private citizens cannot borrow money at the low interest rate R. But, by making such assumptions, we keep the model simple and easy to manipulate. In spite of the simplifications used to derive the market model shown in Figure 9-9b, it is still realistic. Most portfolios' rates of return are highly positively correlated and lie along a curve like the efficient frontier EF in Figure 9-9b.

Table 9-7 lists the risk and return statistics of 34 mutual funds. These port-

---

[13]For the original discussion of the market portfolio, see Eugene Fama, "Risk, Return and Equilibrium: Some Clarifying Comments," *Journal of Finance,* March 1968, pp. 32–33. Chapter 7 explains some empirical estimates of the market portfolio.

Table 9-7
PERFORMANCE OF 34 MUTUAL FUNDS

	Average annual return, %	Std. dev. of annual return, σ, %
Affiliated Fund	14.6	15.3
American Business Shares	10.0	9.2
Axe-Houghton, Fund A	10.5	13.5
Axe-Houghton, Fund B	12.0	16.3
Axe-Houghton, Stock Fund	11.9	15.6
Boston Fund	12.4	12.1
Board Street Investing	14.8	16.8
Bullock Fund	15.7	19.3
Commonwealth Investment Company	10.9	13.7
Delaware Fund	14.4	21.4
Dividend Shares	14.4	15.9
Eaton and Howard, Balanced Fund	11.0	11.9
Eaton and Howard, Stock Fund	15.2	19.2
Equity Fund	14.6	18.7
Fidelity Fund	16.4	23.5
Financial Industrial Fund	14.5	23.0
Fundamental Investors	16.0	21.7
Group Securities, Common Stock Fund	15.1	19.1
Group Securities, Fully Administered Fund	11.4	14.1
Incorporated Investors	14.0	25.5
Investment Company of America	17.4	21.8
Investors Mutual	11.3	12.5
Loomis-Sales Mutual Fund	10.0	10.4
Massachusetts Investors Trust	16.2	20.8
Massachusetts Investors—Growth Stock	18.6	22.7
National Investors Corporation	18.3	19.9
National Securities—Income Series	12.4	17.8
New England Fund	10.4	10.2
Putnam Fund of Boston	13.1	16.0
Scudder, Stevens & Clark Balanced Fund	10.7	13.3
Selected American Shares	14.4	19.4
United Funds—Income Fund	16.1	20.9
Wellington Fund	11.3	12.0
Wisconsin Fund	13.8	16.9

Source: William F. Sharpe, ''Mutual Fund Performance,'' *Journal of Business,* Jan. 1966, suppl., p. 125. This classic study has been replicated by other researchers who obtained similar results using more recent data.

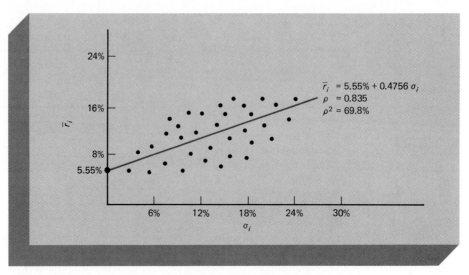

Figure 9-10 An empirical regression estimate of the CML.

folios' average rates of return were regressed onto their standard deviations. The results are shown in Figure 9-10. The correlation coefficient for the regression line shown in Figure 9-10 is high and positive. The empirical data indicate the nature of the trade-off of risk for return available in the market. The data also attest to the realism of the CML model in Figure 9-9*b*.

9-13   **SUMMARY AND CONCLUSIONS**

Simple diversification of even the most naive variety (for example, selecting securities randomly) will reduce risk. However, Markowitz diversification is the most effective way of reducing risk.

After deriving the efficient frontier in terms of Markowitz diversification without negative weights, we derived a more dominant efficient frontier by allowing negative weights to enter the solution. Then an even more dominant efficient frontier was introduced by considering margined short sales. Finally, we introduced borrowing and lending at the riskless interest rate and showed how the CML was derived. We found that the dominant assets were always diversified portfolios that involved lending and/or borrowing. Figure 9-11 compares and contrasts the efficient frontiers that can be attained under different kinds of investment constraints.

Portfolio analysis leads to the conclusion that *diversification is essential* for a rational, risk-averse wealth-seeking investor. Markowitz diversification helps the investor attain a higher level of expected utility (or happiness) than with

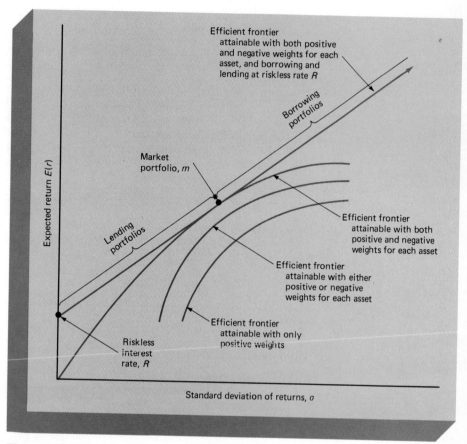

Figure 9-11 Different efficient frontiers are attainable under different constraints.

any other risk-reduction technique. Thus, rational investors will be concerned with the *correlation* between assets, in addition to the assets' expected returns and standard deviations.

After investors delineate their efficient frontier, they still must select a portfolio in which to invest their funds. After the efficient frontier is delineated scientifically, portfolio selection is a personal choice.

Essay Questions

9-1   (*a*) What does portfolio analysis assume about the weights of the assets in a portfolio? (*b*) Is this assumption necessary? Why or why not?

9-2   (*a*) Define simple diversification. (*b*) Will simple diversification reduce total risk? Explain. (*c*) Will simple diversification reduce diversifiable risk? Why or why not? (*d*) Will simple diversification reduce undiversifiable risk? Explain.

9-3   (a) Define superfluous diversification. (b) What problems frequently result from superfluous diversification?

9-4   Consider Figures 9-4 through 9-6. Why are all the curves drawn convex (rather than concave) to the expected return axis?

9-5   "Apart from negatively correlated stocks, all the gains from diversification come from 'averaging over' the independent components of the returns and risks of individual stocks. Among positively correlated stocks, there would be no gains from diversification if independent variations [or, diversifiable risk] were absent." Quotation from Professor John Lintner, "Security Prices, Risk, and Maximal Gains from Diversification," *Journal of Finance*, Dec. 1965, p. 589 (bracketed words added). Explain this statement.

9-6   What statistical inputs are required for a portfolio analysis of N different assets?

9-7   Mathematically expand the following formula for a portfolio's variance of returns for four assets into a form showing all four assets' variances and covariances.

$$\text{Var}(r_p) = \sum_{i=1}^{N} \sum_{j=1}^{N} x_i x_j \sigma_{ij} \qquad \text{for } N = 4$$

Problems

9-8   Below are the returns for two assets.

State of nature	r_1	r_2		Probability
Weak growth	15%	15%		$\frac{1}{3}$
Strong growth	30	12		$\frac{1}{3}$
Very strong growth	45	9		$\frac{1}{3}$
Expected returns	30	12	Total	1.0

Calculate the two variances and $\text{Cov}(r_1, r_2)$. If assets 1 and 2 are combined 50-50 into a portfolio, what is the variance of this portfolio? Show your calculations.

9-9   Calculate the correlation coefficients for the returns of the three stocks over the 7-year sample period.

Table 9A
Data for Problems 9-9 to 9-15

Year	Stock A returns	Stock B returns	Stock C returns
19X1	10%	6%	-5%
19X2	-5	10	15
19X3	-7	12	20
19X4	15	8	25
19X5	20	14	30
19X6	-30	7	-35
19X7	12	8	20

9-10 Calculate the standard deviations of the returns from the three stocks over the 7-year sample period.

9-11 What is the expected return from a portfolio made up of 20 percent asset A, 40 percent B, and 40 percent C? Assume the expected returns are the annual returns given in year 19X7.

9-12 Determine the standard deviation of a portfolio made up of 20 percent asset A, 40 percent B, and 40 percent C.

9-13 What is the expected return for a portfolio that is 50 percent invested in A and 50 percent in B? Use all 7 years of historical data from the table above.

9-14 Determine the standard deviation of the two-asset equally weighted portfolio suggested in Problem 9-13.

9-15 Determine the covariance of returns for stocks A and B over the 7-year sample. *Hint: The information from Problems 9-9 and 9-10 can be useful.*

9-16 If the correlation between D and G is .1, determine the minimum standard deviation portfolio for D and G. What is the expected return of that portfolio? *Hint: The following formula will determine the amount of D for a minimum standard deviation portfolio:*

$$x_D = \frac{\sigma_G^2 - \rho_{DG}\sigma_D\sigma_G}{\sigma_D^2 + \sigma_G^2 - 2\rho_{DG}\sigma_D\sigma_G}$$

Table 9B
Data for Problems 9-16 and 9-17

Stock	$E(r)$	Std. dev.
D	10%	15%
G	18	30

9-17 Using the information given in Problem 9-16, what would an investor's risk and return be if they (a) invested only in the risk-free asset, R = 8%, (b) invested one-half of the portfolio's funds in the risk-free asset and one-half in the market portfolio (m), and (c) borrowed 50 percent of their initial funds for an additional investment and then invested all the funds in the market portfolio?

9-18 If the market portfolio has an expected return of 15 percent and a standard deviation of 20 percent, and the risk-free rate of interest is 8 percent, what is the slope of the capital market line (CML)? What does this mean to an investor?

9-19 What is the optimal asset allocation between common stocks, long-term Treasury bonds, and money market securities like Treasury bills? Use the input statistics below.

A. Expected rates of return

Common stocks (s)	12.0%
Treasury bonds (b)	4.6%
Treasury bills (i)	3.5%

B. Variance-covariance matrix

	Common stocks (s)	Treasury bonds (b)	Treasury bills (i)
Common stocks (s)	$\sigma_s = 21.1\% = \sqrt{445.21}$	Cov(s, b) = 19.7%	Cov(s, i) = −5.02%
Treasury bonds (b)		$\sigma_b = 8.5\% = \sqrt{72.25}$	Cov(b, i) = 6.07%
Treasury bills (i)			$\sigma_i = 3.4\% = \sqrt{11.5}$

C. Correlation matrix

	Common stocks (s)	Treasury bonds (b)	Treasury bills (i)
Common stocks (s)	1.0	.11	−.07
Treasury bonds (b)		1.0	.21
Treasury bills (i)			1.0

Source: R. G. Ibbotson and Rex A. Sinquefield, *Stocks, Bonds, Bills and Inflation (SBBI): 1982 Edition,* updated in *SBBI 1988 Yearbook,* exhibits 8 and 32 (Chicago, Ill.: Ibbotson Associates, Inc., 1988).

Selected References

Francis, J. C., and Gordon Alexander, *Portfolio Analysis,* 3d ed. (Englewood Cliffs, N.J.: Prentice-Hall, 1986).

   The CML and other more sophisticated models are developed. Graphical utility analysis and elementary statistics are used in the chapters.

Markowitz, Harry M., *Portfolio Selection* (New York: Wiley, 1959).

   Chapters 1 through 5 present the foundations for portfolio analysis. Chapters 7 and 8 present different techniques for performing portfolio analysis. Algebra is used.

Markowitz, Harry M., *Mean-Variance Analysis in Portfolio Choice and Capital Markets* (New York: Basil Blackwell, 1987).

   The first six chapters present portfolio analysis. Chapters 7 through 13 explore mathematical implications and intricacies. A quadratic program is in the appendix.

Appendix 9A

Mathematical
Portfolio Analysis

Markowitz portfolio analysis performed graphically cannot handle more than four securities. The graphical analysis does serve well as an introduction to portfolio analysis and may permit a better understanding of the analysis and of the solution obtained.[14] However, a more efficient solution technique for portfolio analysis, which uses differential calculus and linear algebra, is explained in this appendix.

A Calculus Risk Minimization Solution: General Form

Calculus can be used to find the minimum risk portfolio for any given expected return E^*. Mathematically, the problem involves finding the minimum portfolio variance. That is,

$$\text{Minimize} \quad \text{Var}(r_p) = \sum_{i=1}^{n} \sum_{j=1}^{n} x_i x_j \sigma_{ij} \qquad \text{(A9-1)}$$

subject to two Lagrangian constraints. The first constraint requires that the desired expected return E^* be achieved. This is equivalent to requiring the following equation:

$$\sum_{i=1}^{n} x_i E(r_i) - E^* = 0 \qquad \text{(A9-2)}$$

The second constraint requires that the weights sum to unity. This constraint is equivalent to requiring the following equation:

$$\sum_{i=1}^{n} x_i - 1 = 0 \qquad \text{(A9-3)}$$

---

[14]Informative examples of Markowitz portfolio analysis performed graphically may be found in Harry Markowitz, *Portfolio Selection* (New York: Wiley, 1959), chap. 7 or J. C. Francis and S. H. Archer, *Portfolio Analysis*, 2d ed. (Englewood Cliffs, N.J.: Prentice-Hall, 1979). Or see J. C. Francis, *Investments: Analysis and Management*, 3d ed. (New York: McGraw-Hill, 1980), appendixes A and B to chap. 18; Appendix B contains a short FORTRAN computer program to plot the isovariance ellipses.

Combining these three quantities above yields the Lagrangian objective function of the risk minimization problem with a desired return constraint:

$$z = \sum_{i=1}^{n} \sum_{j=1}^{n} x_i x_j \sigma_{ij} + \lambda_1 \left(\sum_{i=1}^{n} x_i E(r_1) - E^* \right) + \lambda_2 \left(\sum_{i=1}^{n} x_i - 1 \right) \qquad \text{(A9-4)}$$

The minimum risk portfolio is found by setting $dz/dx_i = 0$ for $i = 1, \ldots, n$ and $dz/d\lambda_j = 0$ for $j = 1, 2$ and by solving the resulting system of equations for the x_i's. The number of assets analyzed n can be any positive integer. Martin solved this problem and has shown the relationship between the solution and the graphical critical line solution in a readable article, which the interested reader is invited to pursue.[15]

Calculus Minimization of Risk: A Three-Security Portfolio

For a three-security portfolio, the objective function to be minimized is shown below.

$$z = x_1^2 \sigma_{11} + x_2^2 \sigma_{22} + x_3^2 \sigma_{33} + 2x_1 x_2 \sigma_{12} + 2x_1 x_3 \sigma_{13} + 2x_2 x_3 \sigma_{23}$$
$$+ \lambda_1 (x_1 E_1 + x_2 E_2 + x_3 E_3 - E^*) + \lambda_2 (x_1 + x_2 + x_3 - 1) \qquad \text{(A9-4)}$$

Setting the partial derivatives of z with respect to all variables equal to zero yields Equation (A9-5).

$$\frac{dz}{dx_1} = 2x_1 \sigma_{11} + 2x_2 \sigma_{12} + 2x_3 \sigma_{13} + \lambda_1 E_1 + \lambda_2 = 0$$

$$\frac{dz}{dx_2} = 2x_2 \sigma_{22} + 2x_1 \sigma_{12} + 2x_3 \sigma_{23} + \lambda_1 E_2 + \lambda_2 = 0$$

$$\frac{dz}{dx_3} = 2x_3 \sigma_{33} + 2x_1 \sigma_{13} + 2x_2 \sigma_{23} + \lambda_1 E_3 + \lambda_2 = 0$$

$$\frac{dz}{d\lambda_1} = x_1 E_1 + x_2 E_2 + x_3 E_3 - E^* = 0$$

$$\frac{dz}{d\lambda_2} = x_1 + x_2 + x_3 - 1 = 0 \qquad \text{(A9-5)}$$

This system is linear, since the weights (x_i's) are the variables and they are all of degree one; thus the system may be solved as a system of linear equations. The matrix representation of this system of linear equations is shown below as Equation (A9-6).

$$\underset{C}{\begin{bmatrix} 2\sigma_{11} & 2\sigma_{12} & 2\sigma_{13} & E_1 & 1 \\ 2\sigma_{21} & 2\sigma_{22} & 2\sigma_{23} & E_2 & 1 \\ 2\sigma_{31} & 2\sigma_{32} & 2\sigma_{33} & E_3 & 1 \\ 1 & 1 & 1 & 0 & 0 \\ E_1 & E_2 & E_3 & 0 & 0 \end{bmatrix}} \underset{x}{\begin{bmatrix} x_1 \\ x_2 \\ x_3 \\ \lambda_2 \\ \lambda_1 \end{bmatrix}} = \underset{k}{\begin{bmatrix} 0 \\ 0 \\ 0 \\ 1 \\ E^* \end{bmatrix}} \qquad \text{(A9-6)}$$

This system may be solved in several different ways. With matrix notation, the inverse of the coefficient matrix, denoted C^{-1}, may be used to find the solution (weight) vector x as follows:

---

[15]A. D. Martin, Jr., "Mathematical Programming of Portfolio Selections," *Management Science*, Jan. 1955, pp. 152–166. Reprinted in E. B. Frederickson, *Frontiers of Investment Analysis* (Scranton, Pa.: International Textbook, 1965), pp. 367–381.

Table A9-1

Statistical Inputs for Portfolio Analysis of Three Common Stocks

Asset	$E(r_i)$	$\text{Var}(r_i) = \sigma_{ii}$	$\text{Cov}(r_i, r_j) = \sigma_{ij}$
Homestake Mining	$E(r_1) = 5\% = 0.05$	$\sigma_{11} = 0.1$	$\sigma_{12} = -0.1$
Kaiser Aluminum	$E(r_2) = 7\% = 0.07$	$\sigma_{22} = 0.4$	$\sigma_{13} = 0.0$
Texas Instruments	$E(r_3) = 30\% = 0.3$	$\sigma_{33} = 0.7$	$\sigma_{23} = 0.3$

$$Cx = k$$
$$C^{-1}Cx = C^{-1}k$$
$$Ix = C^{-1}k$$
$$x = C^{-1}k \tag{A9-7}$$

The solution will give the n (in this case, $n = 3$) weights in terms of E^*.

$$x_1 = a_1 + d_1 E^*$$
$$x_2 = a_2 + d_2 E^*$$
$$x_3 = a_3 + d_3 E^* \tag{A9-8}$$

where the a_i and d_i are constants. For any desired E^*, the equations give the weights of the minimum risk portfolio. These are the weights of a portfolio in the efficient frontier. By varying E^*, the weights may be generated for the entire efficient frontier. Then the risk $\text{Var}(V_p)$ of the efficient portfolios may be calculated, and the efficient frontier may be graphed.

As a numerical example, the data from the three-security portfolio problem indicated in Table A9-1 are solved to obtain the following coefficients matrix.

$$
\begin{bmatrix}
2\sigma_{11} & 2\sigma_{12} & 2\sigma_{13} & E_1 & 1 \\
2\sigma_{21} & 2\sigma_{22} & 2\sigma_{23} & E_2 & 1 \\
2\sigma_{31} & 2\sigma_{32} & 2\sigma_{33} & E_3 & 1 \\
1 & 1 & 1 & 0 & 0 \\
E_1 & E_2 & E_3 & 0 & 0
\end{bmatrix}
=
\begin{bmatrix}
2(.1) & 2(-.1) & 2(0) & .05 & 1 \\
2(-.1) & 2(.4) & 2(.3) & .07 & 1 \\
2(0) & 2(.3) & 2(.7) & .3 & 1 \\
1 & 1 & 1 & 0 & 0 \\
.05 & .07 & .3 & 0 & 0
\end{bmatrix}
$$

Multiplying the inverse of this coefficients matrix by the constants vector k yields the weights vector ($C^{-1}k = x$) as shown below.

$$
\overset{C^{-1}}{
\begin{bmatrix}
.677 & -.736 & .059 & .789 & -1.433 \\
-.736 & .800 & -.064 & .447 & -2.790 \\
.059 & -.064 & .005 & -.236 & 4.223 \\
-1.433 & -2.790 & 4.223 & .522 & -15.869 \\
.789 & .447 & -.236 & -.095 & .552
\end{bmatrix}}
\overset{k}{
\begin{bmatrix}
0 \\
0 \\
0 \\
1 \\
E^*
\end{bmatrix}}
\overset{= \quad W}{
\begin{bmatrix}
x_1 \\
x_2 \\
x_3 \\
\lambda_2 \\
\lambda_1
\end{bmatrix}}
$$

Evaluating the weights vector yields the system of equations below.

$$x_1 = .789 - 1.433E^*$$
$$x_2 = .447 - 2.790E^* \qquad x_1 + x_2 + x_3 = 1 \text{ for any given } E^*$$
$$x_3 = -.236 + 4.223E^*$$
$$\lambda_1 = .522 - 15.869E^*$$
$$\lambda_2 = -.095 + .522E^*$$

The weights in the three equations above sum to unity, are a linear function of E^*, and represent the weights of the three securities in the efficient portfolio at the point where $E(r_p) = E^*$. Varying E^* generates the weights of all the efficient portfolios.

Chapter 10

The Characteristic
Line and the CAPM

Chapter 1 defined an asset's **total risk** to be its *total variability of return.*[1] That chapter went on to show how to calculate two equivalent measures of total risk, called the variance and the standard deviation. This chapter extends Chapter 1 by showing that the total risk of an asset can be divided into two parts—diversifiable risk and undiversifiable risk.

$$
\begin{array}{r}
\text{Undiversifiable risk} \\
\text{Plus: } \underline{\text{Diversifiable risk}} \\
\text{Total risk}
\end{array}
$$

Partitioning total risk into these two segments yields an important insight called the capital asset pricing model (CAPM hereafter) or, synonymously, the security market line (SML).

10-1　　　　**DIVERSIFIABLE RISK AND UNDIVERSIFIABLE RISK**

This chapter's exploration of the asset pricing implications of risk begins with introductions to diversifiable risk and undiversifiable risk.

Diversifiable Risk Comes from Unsystematic Changes

Diversifiable risk is that portion of total risk which is unique to the firm that issued the securities. Events such as labor strikes, management errors, inventions, advertising campaigns, shifts in consumer taste, and lawsuits cause unsystematic variability in the value of a market asset. Since unsystematic changes

264　　　　[1]This chapter presumes a knowledge of Chapter 1.

affect one firm, or at most a few firms, they must be forecast separately for each firm and for each individual incident. Unsystematic security price movements are *statistically independent* from each other, and so they may be averaged to zero when different assets are combined to form a diversified portfolio. Therefore, *unsystematic risk* is also called diversifiable risk.

To be more concrete, the rate of return from the *i*th security in the *t*th period can be written as the sum of two components:

$$r_{i,t} \quad = \quad E(r_i) \quad + \quad e_{i,t} \qquad (10\text{-}1)$$

$$\begin{matrix} \text{Total rate} \\ \text{of return} \end{matrix} = \begin{matrix} \text{expected rate} \\ \text{of return} \end{matrix} + \begin{matrix} \text{diversifiable} \\ \text{return} \end{matrix}$$

The part of the *i*th asset's total return that fluctuates around its expected return is denoted $e_{i,t}$. The diversifiable return can make either a positive or a negative contribution to an asset's total return in any particular period; it has an expected value of zero, $E(e_{i,t}) = 0$. This portion of the asset's return is unique to asset *i* and may be diversified to zero in a portfolio of different securities.

Undiversifiable Risk Is Systematic Variability

Undiversifiable risk is that portion of total variability in return caused by market factors that *simultaneously* affect the prices of all securities.[2] The systematic nature of these price changes makes them immune to much of the risk reduction effects of diversification. Thus, *systematic risk* is also called undiversifiable risk.

Changes in the economic, political, and sociological environment that affect securities markets are sources of systematic risk. Systematic variability of return is found in nearly all securities to varying degrees because most securities tend to move together in a systematic manner. Figure 9-2 shows how averages of mutually exclusive samples of railroad stocks and utility stocks tend to vary in price together; this is systematic variability. The prices of nearly all individual common stocks also tend to move together in this manner; that is why nearly all stocks listed on the New York Stock Exchange (NYSE) are positively correlated with each other (see Table 7-2).

The systematic nature of the undiversifiable portion of a security's return is stated formally as follows:

$$E(r_i) = a_i + b_i E(r_m) \qquad (10\text{-}2)$$

[2]The simultaneity of systematic stock price movements was documented using monthly data; see J. C. Francis, "Intertemporal Differences in Systematic Stock Price Movements," *Journal of Financial and Quantitative Analysis,* June 1975, pp. 205–219. For a later study using daily data, see G. A. Hawawini and A. Vora, "Evidence of Intertemporal Systematic Risks in the Daily Price Movement of NYSE and AMEX Common Stocks," *Journal of Financial and Quantitative Analysis,* 1979. The Hawawini-Vora study suggests that sometimes there is a 1- or 2-day lead or lag in the speed with which some thinly traded stock prices react to systematic changes.

Equation (10-2) says that the ith asset's expected return is a simple linear function of $E(r_m)$, the expected return from a highly diversified *market portfolio*. The a_i term is a constant that is called the asset's *alpha;* the alpha has a value near zero for most assets. The b_i term is called *beta*. The betas of most assets have values near positive unity. The beta is an index of undiversifiable risk that gauges how much the ith asset's return typically reacts to a change in the market portfolio's return. These terms and concepts will be discussed in more detail later in this chapter when they are used to rationalize a body of knowledge called "portfolio theory."

Preview of
Portfolio Theory

During the 1950s and 1960s, Harry Markowitz, James Tobin, Jack Treynor, Bill Sharpe, and others showed that rational investors should ignore the investment characteristics of *individual assets* and focus instead on *diversified portfolios*.[3] They proved that portfolios are more desirable than individual assets because portfolios can benefit from the risk-reducing power of diversification that individual assets cannot obtain. Researchers went on to demonstrate that once portfolios are the investment of choice, the individual assets need only be analyzed to find out their expected rate of return and what risk they might contribute to a diversified portfolio. One eye-opening implication of this analysis is that *undiversifiable risk should not play a role in the determination of securities prices*. These *portfolio theory* ideas form the foundation for the capital asset pricing model (CAPM), which is a major component of modern financial theory.

10-2   **THE CHARACTERISTIC LINE**

Portfolio theory was developed mathematically without reference to the "characteristic line."[4] The "characteristic line" will nevertheless be investigated

---

[3]Portfolio theory was put forth by Harry Markowitz. See Harry Markowitz, *Portfolio Selection,* Cowles Foundation Monograph 16 (New York: Wiley, 1959). James Tobin extended the asset pricing and utility theory implications of portfolio theory. See James Tobin, "Liquidity Preference as Behavior towards Risk," *Review of Economic Studies,* Feb. 1958, vol. 26, no. 1, pp. 65–86. Jack L. Treynor showed how to use portfolio theory to analyze the prices of individual securities and portfolios. See Jack L. Treynor, "Toward a Theory of Market Value of Risky Assets," unpublished manuscript, 1961. And see Jack L. Treynor, "How to Rate Management of Investment Funds," *Harvard Business Review,* Jan.–Feb. 1965, pp. 63–75. Working independently of Treynor, William F. Sharpe published a model that used portfolio theory to trace out the pricing implications for stocks and bonds. See William F. Sharpe, "Capital Asset Prices: A Theory of Market Equilibrium under Conditions of Risk," *Journal of Finance,* Sept. 1964, pp. 425–552. Sharpe was Markowitz's Ph.D. student.

[4]The so-called characteristic line traces its roots back to Harry Markowitz, *Portfolio Selection,* Cowles Foundation Monograph 16 (New York: Wiley, 1959). The book's

(*continues*)

here because it provides an easy way to gain important insights into portfolio theory.

If we substitute Equation (10-2) into Equation (10-1), we obtain Equation (10-1a).

$$r_{i,t} = E(r_i) + e_{i,t} \tag{10-1}$$

$$r_{i,t} = a_i + b_i E(r_m) + e_{i,t} \tag{10-1a}$$

The expected value in Equation (10-1a) can be converted to a time-series variable by simply replacing the market's expected return $E(r_m)$ with the market's rate of return in the tth period $r_{m,t}$ to get Equation (10-3).

$$r_{i,t} = a_i + b_i r_{m,t} + e_{i,t} \tag{10-3}$$

Equation (10-3) is called the **characteristic line** for the ith asset.[5] Statistically speaking, a_i and b_i can be estimated as regression intercept and slope statistics, respectively, and $e_{i,t}$ is the regression model's unexplained residual return that occurs in period t. The characteristic line is used to measure statistically the undiversifiable risk and diversifiable risk of individual assets and portfolios.

Rearranging Equation (10-3) so that the undiversifiable and diversifiable sources of the assets' returns are grouped yields Equation (10-3a).

$$r_{i,t} \quad = \quad b_i r_{m,t} \quad + \quad a_i + e_{i,t} \tag{10-3a}$$

Total rate	undiversifiable	diversifiable
of return	= return in	+ return in
in period t	period t	period t

Figure 10-1 illustrates the characteristic line for three different assets with low, medium, and high levels of systematic risk. Statistically speaking, characteristic lines are ordinary least-squares regression lines of the form shown in Equation (10-3). Statistics books sometimes call the characteristic line a simple linear regression model or an ordinary least squares (OLS) model.

Market Returns: The Characteristic Line's Independent Variable

Exogenous forces generated in the market for capital assets are measured along the horizontal axes of Figures 10-1 and 10-2. These market rates of return from different periods, denoted $r_{m,t}$, are the *explanatory variable* in the characteristic line. Equation (10-4) shows how rates of change in the stock market are calculated using, for example, Standard & Poor's (S&P) market index.

$$r_{m,t} = \frac{\text{S\&P}_{t+1} - \text{S\&P}_t}{\text{S\&P}_t} \tag{10-4}$$

(continued)

footnote 1 on page 100 contains the first published characteristic line; Markowitz called it an index-model. Markowitz presented the characteristic line as a detail worthy of further consideration; it plays no essential role in the development of portfolio theory. Stated differently, the characteristic line and portfolio theory are independent models that point to similar conclusions.

[5]The term *characteristic line* was first used by Jack L. Treynor, "How to Rate Management of Investment Funds," *Harvard Business Review*, Jan.–Feb. 1965, pp. 63–75.

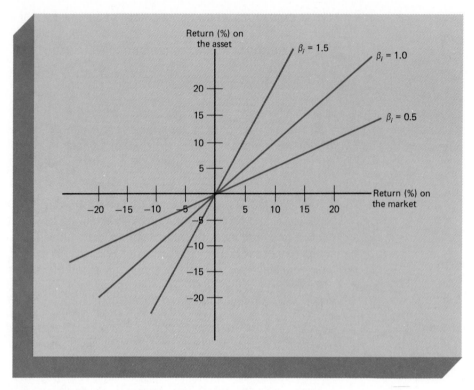

Figure 10-1 Characteristic lines for assets with high, medium, and low betas.

where S&P$_{t+1}$ is the dollar amount of the S&P index at the beginning of period $t + 1$ and S&P$_t$ is the value of the index at the beginning of period t. These period-by-period rates of change in the market index are downward-biased estimates of average returns available in the market because cash dividends are excluded. There is no reason that dividends should not be included in $r_{m,t}$ or that other market indexes should not be used in determining characteristic lines. However, once a market index is adopted, it should be used consistently in determining all the characteristic lines if they are all to be comparable.

Asset Returns: The Characteristic Line's Dependent Variable

Rates of return for which the characteristic line is being prepared are calculated by using Equation (1-2) for stocks or a different formula for other types of assets.

$$r_{i,t} = \frac{p_{t+1} - p_t + d_t}{p_t} \tag{1-2}$$

where d_t = cash dividend in period t from ith stock
p_t = market price of stock at beginning of tth period
p_{t+1} = price at end of period t (or, equivalently, at beginning of period $t + 1$)

Returns on the ith asset are the *dependent variable;* they are measured on the vertical axes of Figures 10-1 and 10-2. If the ith asset has any systematic risk, part of its variation in rates of return is dependent on the independent variable—the market. Daily, monthly, quarterly, yearly, or any other **differencing interval** may be used to calculate the returns used in estimating a characteristic line, as long as the interval is used consistently throughout the regression.[6]

Estimating a Characteristic Line

The characteristic line is a line of best fit. It may be estimated intuitively, or regression techniques may be used. If historical data are to be used, the first step in estimating the characteristic line for some asset is to calculate each period's return for the asset, for example, by using Equation (1-2) for stocks and Equation (10-4) for returns on the market. The periods used for calculating returns on the asset and the market must be *simultaneous* because the characteristic line model measures an investment asset's simultaneous reactions to market forces.

Table 10-1 shows the quarterly data used to fit the characteristic line for IBM's common stock. These data can be obtained from the sources of financial information discussed in Chapter 6. The analyst may need to make the appropriate adjustments for stock dividends and splits, if any occurred, so that these changes in the unit of account do not distort the returns.

The rates of return from the market and the asset may be plotted as shown in Figure 10-2. Point E in this figure, for example, is a point where the market return was 11 percent and IBM's return was 18 percent during the same period. Each dot represents the rate of return on the asset and the market during a given period. A line of best fit can be "eyeballed" through these points, or the dependent variable r_i can be regressed onto the independent variable r_m. Table 10-2 contains statistics that describe the IBM characteristic line in Figure 10-2.

Interpreting the Characteristic Line

Equations (10-2) and (10-2a) both represent the characteristic line for the ith asset. The symbol $E(r_i|r_m, a, b)$ is read as "the expected return of asset i given the returns on the market, alpha, and beta." Equations (10-2) and (10-2a) are similar to Equation (10-3) except that the residual return $e_{i,t}$ has been summed over all the observations to attain a total value of zero, and therefore, the $e_{i,t}$

---

[6]It is desirable to have at least 30 observations over a sample period of no longer than a decade when estimating the characteristic line. Thirty observations are suggested because that is where small-sample theory typically ends and large-sample sampling theory begins—for example, the t-distribution may be dropped and the normal distribution used in its place. The reason a decade is suggested as an upper limit for the sample period is that the asset's risk and return characteristics may change over longer sample periods.

Table 10-1
IBM COMMON STOCK DATA FOR CHARACTERISTIC LINE CALCULATIONS, 1979–1988

Year and quarter	Reported data		Adjusted data		Quarterly dividend yield	Quarterly price change	Quarterly rate of return
	Beginning market price	Cash dividend	Beginning market price	Cash dividend			
1979 Q1	$298.500	$2.880	$74.625	$0.720	0.965%	5.695%	6.660%
1979 Q2	315.500	3.440	78.875	0.860	1.090	−6.973	−5.883
	On June 11, 1979 a 4-for-1 stock split was declared						
1979 Q3	73.375	0.860	73.375	0.860	1.172	−7.666	−6.494
1979 Q4	67.750	0.860	67.750	0.860	1.269	−4.982	−3.712
1980 Q1	64.375	0.860	64.375	0.860	1.336	−13.398	−12.062
1980 Q2	55.750	0.860	55.750	0.860	1.543	5.381	6.924
1980 Q3	58.750	0.860	58.750	0.860	1.464	9.149	10.613
1980 Q4	64.125	0.860	64.125	0.860	1.341	5.848	7.189
1981 Q1	67.875	0.860	67.875	0.860	1.267	−8.103	−6.836
1981 Q2	62.375	0.860	62.375	0.860	1.379	−7.214	−5.836
1981 Q3	57.875	0.860	57.875	0.860	1.486	−6.479	−4.994
1981 Q4	54.125	0.860	54.125	0.860	1.589	5.081	6.670
1982 Q1	56.875	0.860	56.875	0.860	1.512	5.055	6.567
1982 Q2	59.750	0.860	59.750	0.860	1.439	1.464	2.904
1982 Q3	60.625	0.860	60.625	0.860	1.419	21.031	22.449
1982 Q4	73.375	0.860	73.375	0.860	1.172	31.175	32.348
1983 Q1	96.250	0.860	96.250	0.860	0.894	5.714	6.608
1983 Q2	101.750	0.860	101.750	0.860	0.845	18.182	19.027
1983 Q3	120.250	0.950	120.250	0.950	0.790	5.509	6.299
1983 Q4	126.875	0.950	126.875	0.950	0.749	−3.842	−3.094
1984 Q1	122.000	0.950	122.000	0.950	0.779	−6.557	−5.779
1984 Q2	114.000	0.950	114.000	0.950	0.833	−7.237	−6.404
1984 Q3	105.750	0.950	105.750	0.950	0.898	17.494	18.392
1984 Q4	124.250	1.100	124.250	1.100	0.885	−0.905	−0.020
1985 Q1	123.125	1.100	123.125	1.100	0.893	3.147	4.041
1985 Q2	127.000	1.100	127.000	1.100	0.866	−2.559	−1.693
1985 Q3	123.750	1.100	123.750	1.100	0.889	0.101	0.990
1985 Q4	123.875	1.100	123.875	1.100	0.888	25.530	26.418
1986 Q1	155.500	1.100	155.500	1.100	0.707	−2.572	−1.865
1986 Q2	151.500	1.100	151.500	1.100	0.726	−3.300	−2.574
1986 Q3	146.500	1.100	146.500	1.100	0.751	−8.191	−7.440
1986 Q4	134.500	1.100	134.500	1.100	0.818	−10.781	−9.963
1987 Q1	120.000	1.100	120.000	1.100	0.917	25.104	26.021
1987 Q2	150.125	1.100	150.125	1.100	0.733	8.243	8.976
1987 Q3	162.500	1.100	162.500	1.100	0.677	−7.231	−6.554
1987 Q4	150.750	1.100	150.750	1.100	0.730	−23.383	−22.653
1988 Q1	115.500	1.100	115.500	1.100	0.952		

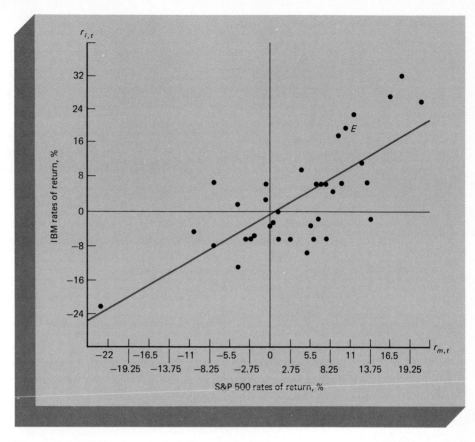

Figure 10-2 IBM's characteristic line, 1979–1987.

Table 10-2
RISK AND RETURN STATISTICS FROM IBM'S CHARACTERISTIC LINE REGRESSION

	IBM	Market portfolio
Expected return = $E(r)$ = mean	0.03108	0.04064
Total risk, or Var(r)	0.01389	0.00749
Total risk, or standard deviation	0.11785	0.08654
Two equivalent systematic risk measures:		
$b_i^2 \text{Var}(r_m) = \rho^2 \text{Var}(r_i)$	0.007802	NA*
Unsystematic risk measure:		
Residual variance = Var(e)	0.00609	NA*
Standard error = $\sqrt{\text{Var}(e)}$	0.07803	NA*
Beta = index of systematic risk	1.021	NA*
Alpha = intercept	−0.0104	NA*
Correlation with market = ρ	0.7495	NA*
Systematic risk percentage = ρ^2	0.56176	1.0

*NA means not applicable.

term disappears. The time subscripts in Equation (10-3) have also been deleted because Equations (10-2) and (10-2a) encompass different periods and different states of nature.

$$E(r_i|r_m, a, b) = a_i + b_i r_m \tag{10-2a}$$

Statisticians call Equation (10-2a) a **conditional expectation** because the ith asset's return is conditional on the alpha and beta statistics and on the market's returns.

Alpha In Equations (10-2) and (10-3) alpha is the intercept, where the characteristic line intercepts the vertical axis. Alpha is an estimate of the ith asset's rate of return when the market is stationary, $r_{m,t} = 0$. The alpha intercept statistic is defined in Equation (10-5).

$$a_i = \bar{r}_i - b_i \bar{r}_m = E(r_i) - b_i E(r_m) \tag{10-5}$$

$$-1.04\% = 3.108\% - (1.021)(4.064\%) \text{ for IBM}$$

Beta The b_i is the **beta coefficient**; it measures the slope of the characteristic line. The beta coefficient is defined by Equations (10-6) and (10-6a).

$$b_i = \frac{\text{Cov}(r_i, r_m)}{\text{Var}(r_m)} \tag{10-6}$$

$$= \frac{.007647}{.00749} = 1.021 = \text{IBM's beta}$$

$$b_i = \frac{\text{units of rise}}{\text{units of run}} = \text{slope of characteristic line} \tag{10-6a}$$

The term $\text{Var}(r_m)$ represents the variance of returns for the market portfolio, and $\text{Cov}(r_i, r_m)$ denotes the "covariance" of returns of the ith asset with the market.

Covariance The ex post **covariance of returns** of the ith asset with the market is defined in Equation (10-7). Equation (10-7a) gives the ex ante definition. Equation (10-7b) provides a more intuitive, but numerically identical, definition of the covariance.

$$\text{Cov}(r_i, r_m) = \left(\frac{1}{T}\right) \sum_{t=1}^{T} [r_{i,t} - E(r_i)][r_{m,t} - E(r_m)] \tag{10-7}$$

$$\text{Cov}(r_i, r_m) = E\{[r_{i,t} - E(r_i)][r_{m,t} - E(r_m)]\} \tag{10-7a}$$

$$\text{Cov}(r_i, r_m) = \rho_{i,m} \sigma_i \sigma_m \tag{10-7b}$$

$$.00764 = (.74951)(.11785)(.08654) \qquad \text{for IBM}$$

Beta Measurements   The beta coefficient is an *index of systematic risk.* Beta coefficients may be used for ranking the systematic risk of different assets. If the beta is larger than 1, $b > 1.0$, then the asset is more volatile than the market and is called an **aggressive asset.** If the beta is less than 1, $b < 1.0$, the asset is a **defensive asset;** its price fluctuations are less volatile than the market's. Figure 10-1 illustrates the characteristic lines for three different assets that have low, medium, and high levels of beta (or undiversifiable risk).

Figure 10-2 shows that IBM is a stock with an average amount of systematic risk. IBM's beta of 1.02 indicates that its return tends to increase 2 percent more than the return on the market average when the market is rising. When the market falls, IBM's return tends to fall 2 percent more than the market's. The characteristic line for IBM has an above average correlation coefficient of $\rho = .7495$, indicating that the returns on this security follow its particular characteristic line slightly more closely than those of the average stock.

Partitioning Risk

Total risk can be measured by the variance of returns, denoted Var(r). This measure of *total risk is partitioned into its systematic and unsystematic components in Equation (10-8).*[7]

$$\begin{aligned}
\text{Var}(r_i) &= \text{ total risk of } i\text{th asset}\\
&= \text{Var}(a_i + b_i r_{m,t} + e_{i,t})\\
&\quad \text{by substituting } (a_i + b_i r_{m,t} + e_{i,t}) \text{ for } r_{i,t}\\
&= 0 + \text{Var}(b_i r_{m,t}) + \text{Var}(e_{i,t})\\
&\quad \text{since } \text{Var}(a_i) = 0
\end{aligned} \tag{10-8}$$

$$\begin{aligned}
\text{Var}(r_i) &= b_i^2 \, \text{Var}(r_m) + \text{Var}(e) \quad \text{since } \text{Var}(b_i r_m) = b_i^2 \, \text{Var}(r_m)\\
&= \text{systematic} + \text{unsystematic risk}
\end{aligned} \tag{10-8a}$$

$$.01389 = .00780 + .00609 \quad \text{for IBM}$$

The unsystematic risk measure Var(e) is called in regression language the *residual variance* or, synonymously, the *standard error squared.*

Undiversifiable Proportion   The percentage of total risk that is systematic can be measured by the coefficient of determination ρ^2 (that is, the characteristic line's squared correlation coefficient).

---

[7]In this context, **partition** is a technical statistical term that means to divide the total variance into *mutually exclusive* and *exhaustive* pieces. This partition is only possible if the returns from the market are statistically independent from the residual error terms that occur simultaneously, $\text{Cov}(r_{m,t}, e_{i,t}) = 0$. The mathematics of regression analysis will orthogonalize the residuals and thus ensure that the needed statistical independence exists.

$$\frac{\text{Systematic risk}}{\text{Total risk}} = \frac{b_i^2 \, \text{Var}(r_m)}{\text{Var}(r_m)} = \rho^2 \qquad\qquad (10\text{-}9)$$

$$\frac{.007802}{.01389} = \frac{(1.021)^2 \, (.00749)}{.00749} = .5617 \times 100 = 56.17\% \qquad \text{for IBM}$$

Diversifiable Proportion   The percentage of unsystematic risk equals $(1.0 - \rho^2)$.

$$\frac{\text{Unsystematic risk}}{\text{Total risk}} = \frac{\text{Var}(e)}{\text{Var}(r_i)} = (1.0 - \rho^2)$$

$$\frac{.00609}{.01389} = (1.0 - .5617) = .438 \times 100 \qquad\qquad (10\text{-}10)$$

$$= 43.8\% \text{ unsystematic} \qquad \text{for IBM}$$

Studies of the characteristic lines of hundreds of stocks listed on the NYSE indicate that the average correlation coefficient is approximately $\rho = .5$.[8] This means that about $\rho^2 = 25$ percent of the total variability of return in most NYSE securities is explained by movements in the market.

	NYSE average	IBM
Systematic risk: ρ^2	.25	.5617
Unsystematic risk: $(1.0 - \rho^2)$	.75	.4383
Total risk: 100%	1.00	1.0000

As explained above, systematic changes are common to all stocks and are therefore undiversifiable.

A primary use of the characteristic line (or *market model*, or the *single-index model*, as it is also called) is to assess the risk characteristics of one asset.[9] The statistics in Table 10-2, for instance, indicate that IBM's common stock is slightly more risky than the average common stock in terms of total risk and

[8]The average ρ was found to be about .5, as reported in Marshall Blume, "On the Assessment of Risk," *Journal of Finance*, March 1971, p. 4. For similar estimates, see J. C. Francis, "Statistical Analysis of Risk Surrogates for NYSE Stocks," *Journal of Financial and Quantitative Analysis*, Dec. 1979.

[9]Professor Jensen reformulated the characteristic line in a risk-premium form. See M. C. Jensen, "The Performance of Mutual Funds in the Period 1945 through 1964," *Journal of Finance*, May 1968, pp. 389–416. See also M. C. Jensen, "Risk, the Pricing of Capital Assets, and the Evaluation of Investment Portfolios," *Journal of Business*, vol. XLII, 1969. Jensen interprets the alpha intercept term of the characteristic line, as he formulates it, as an investment performance measure. It has been suggested that Jensen's performance measure is biased. See Keith V. Smith and Dennis A. Tito, "Risk-Return Measures of Ex-Post Portfolio Performance," *Journal of Financial and Quantitative Analysis*, Dec. 1969, vol. IV, no. 4, p. 466.

systematic risk.[10] New risk measurements must be made periodically, however, because the risk and return of an asset may change with the passage of time.[11]

10-3   **CAPITAL ASSET PRICING MODEL (CAPM)**

An old axiom states "there is no such thing as a free lunch." This means that you cannot expect to get something for nothing—a rule that certainly applies to investment returns. Investors who want to earn high average rates of return must take high risks and endure the associated loss of sleep, the possibility of ulcers, and the chance of bankruptcy. The question to which we now turn is: Should investors worry about total risk, undiversifiable risk, diversifiable risk, or all three?

In Chapter 1 it was suggested that *investors should seek investments that have the maximum expected return in their risk class*. Their happiness from investing is presumed to be derived as indicated in the expected utility $E(U)$ function below.

$$E(U) = f[E(r), \sigma]$$

The investment preferences of wealth-seeking risk-averse investors represented by the function above cause them to maximize their expected utility (or, equivalently, happiness) by (1) maximizing their expected return in any given risk class, $\partial E(U)/\partial E(r) > 0$, or, conversely, (2) minimizing their total risk at any given rate of expected return, $\partial E(U)/\partial \sigma < 0$. However, in selecting individual assets, investors will not be particularly concerned with the asset's total risk σ. Figure 9-1 showed that the unsystematic portion of total risk can be easily diversified by holding a portfolio of different securities. But, systematic risk affects all stocks in the market because it is undiversifiable. Portfolio theory therefore suggests that only the undiversifiable (or systematic) risk is worth avoiding.[12]

[10]Statements about the relative degree of total risk are made in the context of a long-run horizon—that is, over at least one *complete business cycle*. Obviously, an accurate short-run forecast which says that some particular company will go bankrupt next quarter makes it more risky than IBM, although IBM may have had more historical variability of return.

[11]Empirical studies documenting the intertemporal instability of betas have been published. Marshall Blume, "Betas and Their Regression Tendencies," *Journal of Finance,* June 1975, pp. 785–795. See also J. C. Francis, "Statistical Analysis of Risk Coefficients for NYSE Stocks," *Journal of Financial and Quantitative Analysis,* Dec. 1979, vol. XIV, no. 5, pp. 981–997. An appendix at the end of this chapter reviews some evidence about shifting betas, standard deviations, and correlations.

[12]Both the systematic and unsystematic portions of total risk must be considered by **undiversified investors.** Entrepreneurs who have their entire net worth invested in one business, for example, can be bankrupted by a piece of bad luck that could be easily averaged away to zero in a diversified portfolio. Poorly diversified investors should not treat diversifiable risk lightly. Only well-diversified investors can afford to ignore diversifiable risk.

In the search for individual assets that will minimize their portfolio's risk exposure at a given level of expected return, investors tend to focus on each asset's *undiversifiable systematic risk*. They will bid up the prices of assets with low systematic risk (that is, low beta coefficients). In contrast, assets with high beta coefficients will experience low demand and market prices that are low relative to the assets' income. Stated differently, assets with high levels of systematic risk will tend to have high expected returns. This may be seen by noting in Equation (10-11) that the expected return is higher after the purchase price for the asset falls. Obviously, the expected return ratio, denoted $E(r)$ in Equation (10-11), will be larger after the denominator decreases, as indicated by the arrows in Equation (10-11).

$$\uparrow E(r) = \frac{E(p_{t+1} - p_t + d_t)}{\downarrow p_t} \qquad (10\text{-}11)$$

$$E(r) = \frac{\text{expected income}}{\text{purchase price}} \qquad (10\text{-}11a)$$

An asset with high systematic risk will experience price declines until the expected return it offers is high enough to induce investors to assume this undiversifiable risk. This price level is the equilibrium price, and the expected return is the equilibrium rate of return for that risk class.

Figure 10-3 shows the capital asset pricing model (CAPM), which graphically depicts the results of the price adjustments that should result from risk-averse trading. The CAPM is a relationship in which the expected rate of return of the ith asset is a linear function of that asset's systematic risk as represented by b_i. Symbolically, Equation (10-12) represents the CAPM.

Figure 10-3 The capital asset pricing model (CAPM).

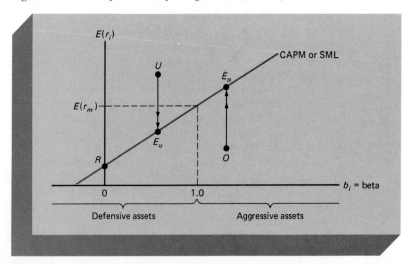

$$E(r_i) = R + \left(\frac{E(r_m) - R}{b_m}\right) b_i \qquad\qquad (10\text{-}12)$$

$$E(r_i) = R + [E(r_m) - R]b_i \qquad \text{since } b_m = 1.0 \qquad (10\text{-}12a)$$

where
b_i = independent variable representing systematic risk of ith asset; it determines the dependent variable $E(r_i)$, expected rate of return for asset i

R = vertical axis intercept, the riskless rate[13]

$[E(r_m) - R]$ = slope of CAPM

U.S. Treasury bill yields are a good approximation of R, as they are generally considered risk-free.

Any vertical line drawn on Figure 10-3 is a **risk class** for systematic risk. The CAPM relates an expected return to each level of systematic risk. These expected returns can be interpreted as the appropriate discount rates, as the cost of capital, or as equilibrium rates of return that investors expect for that amount of systematic risk.

Systematic or undiversifiable risk is the main factor risk-averse investors should consider in deciding whether a security yields enough rate of return to induce them to buy it. Other factors, such as the "glamour" of the stock and the company's financial ratios, are important only to the extent they affect the security's risk and return. The CAPM graphically represents the trade-off of systematic risk for return that investors expect and are entitled to receive. This implies that the CAPM has asset-pricing implications.

Assets' Price Adjustments

After an asset's average return and systematic risk have been estimated, they may be plotted in reference to the CAPM. In equilibrium every asset's $E(r)$ and beta systematic risk coefficient should plot as one point on the CAPM. To

[13]Dr. Fischer Black has suggested a model in which it is not necessary to assume the existence of a riskless rate; see Fischer Black, "Capital Market Equilibrium with Restricted Borrowing," *Journal of Business*, July 1972, pp. 444–454. In Black's model the riskless interest rate is replaced by a portfolio which has a beta equal to zero but still has some small amount of variance. The **zero-beta portfolio** is uncorrelated with the market portfolio, so that its total risk and its unsystematic risk are identical and both are positive quantities. The zero-beta portfolio is created by holding risky securities and leveraging and selling short. Some preliminary empirical estimates of the rates of return on the zero-beta portfolio have been published; see F. Black, M. C. Jensen, and M. Scholes, "The Capital Asset Pricing Model: Some Empirical Tests," in M. C. Jensen (ed.), *Studies in the Theory of Capital Markets* (New York: Praeger, 1972). Professor G. Alexander has shown an algorithm which could be used to obtain estimates of the returns from the zero-beta portfolio. Gordon Alexander, "An Algorithmic Approach to Deriving the Minimum Variance Zero-Beta Portfolio," *Journal of Financial Economics*, March 1977.

see why this is true, consider Figure 10-3, which shows two assets denoted O and U. Asset U is underpriced because its average rate of return is too high for the level of systematic risk it bears. Asset O is overpriced because its expected rate of return is too low to induce investors to accept its undiversifiable risk. These two assets should move to the CAPM as shown by the arrows to their equilibrium positions at the points marked E in Figure 10-3.

To see why assets O and U are incorrectly priced, reconsider Equation (10-11b), which defines the expected rate of return for a common stock.

$$E(r) = \frac{\text{expected capital gains or loss} + \text{expected cash dividends}}{\text{purchase price}} \qquad (10\text{-}11b)$$

To reach their equilibrium positions on the CAPM, assets O and U must go through a price readjustment. Assuming the assets' systematic risk remains unchanged, the expected return of U must fall to E_U and the expected return of O must rise to E_O in Figure 10-3. To accomplish this move to an equilibrium rate of return, the denominator of Equation (10-11b) must rise for asset U and fall for asset O. Assets O and U, or any marketable capital asset (such as a portfolio, stock, bond, or real estate), will be in disequilibrium unless its risk and return lie on the CAPM. Supply and demand will set to work as outlined above to correct any disequilibrium from the CAPM.

The economic process outlined above implies that, generally speaking, every asset that lies above the CAPM in Figure 10-3 is underpriced. Symmetric but opposite logic implies that every asset that lies below the CAPM in Figure 10-3 is underpriced.

Market Imperfections

The operation of the rational forces of supply and demand can be expected to move assets lying off the CAPM toward the CAPM, but because of market imperfections, an asset's risk-return characteristics never lie exactly on the CAPM. Some market imperfections that preclude attainment of a complete equilibrium include the following:

1. *Transaction costs:* The stockbroker's commissions and transfer taxes associated with each security transaction erode investors' profit-maximization incentive to correct minor deviations from the CAPM.

2. *Differential tax rates on capital gains:* Capital gains from price appreciation have been taxed differently from income from dividends and interest at various times in the history of the United States. When capital gains are taxed differently from income from dividends and interest, the after-tax rate of return (*atr*) defined in Equation (10-13) differs with the investor's tax bracket. Thus, each investor envisions a slightly different CAPM in terms of after-tax returns.

$$atr_t = \frac{d_t\,(1 - T_o) + (p_{t+1} - p_t)(1 - T_g)}{p_t} \qquad (10\text{-}13)$$

where T_o is the ordinary income tax rate and T_g is the capital gains tax rate.

3. *Heterogeneous expectations:* Different investors assess the systematic risk of any given asset differently and therefore perceive different equilibrium rates of return as being appropriate for any given asset.

4. *Imperfect information:* Some investors are irrational, some are uninformed, and some receive financial news later than others.

Because of these market imperfections, every asset cannot be expected to lie exactly on the CAPM. Thus, the CAPM is a band instead of a line. The width of this band varies directly with the imperfections in the market. As a result, the CAPM cannot be used to pinpoint an asset's equilibrium price precisely. It can only suggest a *conditional probability distribution* of possible prices.

10-4   **EMPIRICAL RISK-RETURN ESTIMATES**

The next logical question is: If stocks' betas and average returns are measured empirically over a representative sample period, will the high beta stocks really have higher rates of return? Or, put more crassly: Does the CAPM theory have any predictive power? Supportive empirical tests of the CAPM theory are described in the following paragraphs. Additional studies have extended the CAPM to embrace other variables and also reached conclusions that tend to support the CAPM (with some refinements).[14]

---

[14]Empirical tests of the CAPM include: M. Blume and I. Friend, "A New Look at the Capital Asset Pricing Model," *Journal of Finance,* March 1973, pp. 19–34; F. Black, M. C. Jensen, and M. Scholes, "The Capital Asset Pricing Model: Some Empirical Tests," in M. C. Jensen (ed.), *Studies in the Theory of Capital Markets* (New York: Praeger, 1972); M. Blume and F. Husic, "Price, Beta and Exchange Listing," *Journal of Finance,* May 1973, pp. 283–299; M. Miller and M. Scholes, "Rates of Return in Relation to Risk: A Re-Examination of Some Recent Findings," in M. C. Jensen (ed.), *Studies in the Theory of Capital Markets* (New York: Praeger, 1972), pp. 47–78; E. F. Fama and J. MacBeth, "Risk, Return and Equilibrium: Empirical Tests," *Journal of Political Economy,* May–June 1973, pp. 607–636; M. R. Reinganum, "Misspecification of Capital Asset Pricing: Empirical Anomalies Based on Earnings Yields and Market Values," *Journal of Financial Economics,* March 1981, pp. 19–46; R. Litzenberger and K. Ramaswamy, "The Effect of Personal Taxes and Dividends and Capital Asset Prices: Theory and Empirical Evidence," *Journal of Financial Economics,* June 1979, pp. 163–195; R. W. Banz, "The Relationship between Return and Market Value of Common Stocks," *Journal of Financial Economics,* March 1981, pp. 3–18. Deficiencies in the preceding empirical tests are pinpointed in Richard Roll, "A Critique of the Asset Pricing Theory's Tests," *Journal of Financial Economics,* March 1977, pp. 129–176. In addition, Chapter 18 reviews empirical studies that document anomalies in the CAPM.

The Sample and the Statistics

In a study by Sharpe and Cooper, monthly stock prices for hundreds of NYSE stocks from a sample period of over four decades provided the raw data. Monthly rates of return were first calculated by using Equation (1-2) for every stock and every month. Second, betas were calculated with Equation (10-6), using 5 years (or 60 monthly observations) of rates of return. Third, an annual rate of return was calculated for each stock. Fourth, the stocks were all grouped into *risk deciles* based on their beta coefficients. The risk classes were based on the 5 years preceding the year in which the annual return was calculated to simulate picking stocks for future investment based on 5 years of past data—a procedure that assumes betas are stable over time.

The procedure was replicated for hundreds of stocks every year over a sample period that spanned decades. Betas were calculated from 5 years of data, risk deciles formed from the betas, and annual returns measured during the sixth year; then the procedure was repeated for the next year. When the procedure had been repeated once for each (5 + 1 =) 6-year period, the 10 risk deciles from 37 years were averaged to obtain average risk deciles and average annual returns. Figure 10-4 shows the beta coefficients averaged over

Figure 10-4 Average beta values for each risk decile, 1931–1967. (*Source:* W. F. Sharpe and G. Cooper, "Risk-Return Classes of NYSE Common Stocks, 1931–1967," *Financial Analysts Journal,* March–April 1972.)

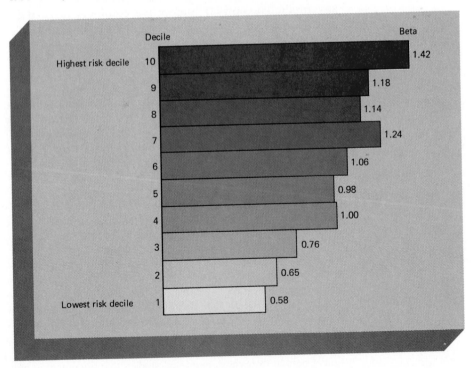

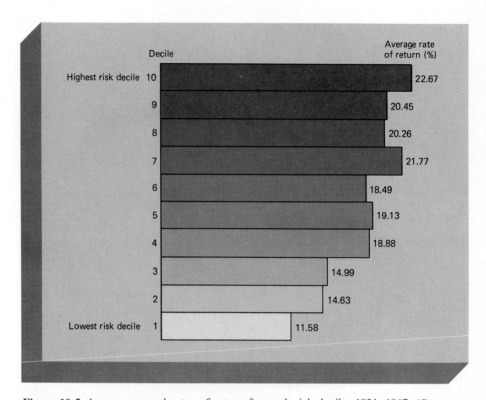

Figure 10-5 Average annual rates of return for each risk decile, 1931–1967. (*Source:* W. F. Sharpe and G. Cooper, "Risk-Return Classes of NYSE Common Stocks, 1931–1967," *Financial Analysts Journal,* March–April 1972.)

all stocks in all years for the 10 risk classes. The annual returns averaged over all stocks and all years in each risk decile are shown in Figure 10-5.

A simple linear regression of the form shown in Equation (10-14) was fitted through the 10 average betas from Figure 10-4 and their associated average annual returns, denoted $\bar{r}_i$, from Figure 10-5 for $i = 1, 2, \ldots, 10$ deciles. deciles.

$$\bar{r}_i = a + b(\text{average beta}_i) + u_i \qquad \text{for } E(u_i) = 0 \qquad (10\text{-}14)$$

Figure 10-6 shows a graph of the risk-return relationship estimated with Equation (10-14).

The Sharpe-Cooper investigation was constructed to minimize bias. Some sampling error exists in the study, as it does in every statistical study, but the statistics nevertheless furnish empirical support for the CAPM theory. The results suggest that, in the long run, buying stocks with high (or medium or low) degrees of systematic risk will yield portfolios with high (or medium or low) average future rates of return. On a single-stock basis, this may not occur because the issuer of the single stock selected may go bankrupt or the stock

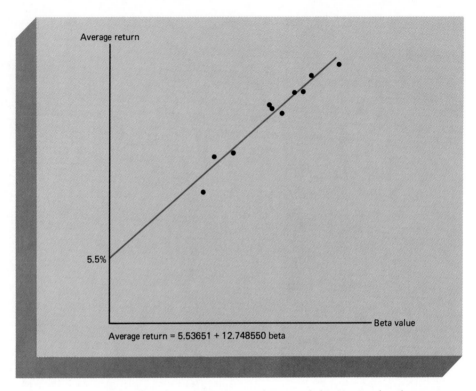

Average return = 5.53651 + 12.748550 beta

Figure 10-6 Regression line through 10 average betas and the 10 associated average returns. (*Source:* W. F. Sharpe and G. Cooper, "Risk-Return Classes of NYSE Common Stocks, 1931–1967," *Financial Analysts Journal,* March–April 1972.)

may experience a change in its systematic risk or undergo some other change which was not representative of most stocks. But by using hundreds of stocks and decades of data, such sampling problems were averaged to zero and the market's equilibrium tendencies could be discerned.

10-5   **EXTENDING THE CHARACTERISTIC LINE**

The characteristic line, Equation (10-3), is sometimes called a *single factor model* because it contains only one source of systematic risk, $r_{m,t}$. The simplicity of the equation might prompt you to ask: What about interest rate risk, default risk, and all those other risk factors that were introduced in Chapter 1?

The characteristic line can be decomposed into a *multifactor model* that includes interest rate risk, default risk, and other risk factors.

$$r_{i,t} = a_i + b_i r_{m,t} + e_{i,t} \tag{10-3}$$

$$r_{i,t} = a_i + b_{i1}F_{1,t} + b_{i2}F_{2,t} + b_{i3}F_{3,t} + \cdots + b_{ik}F_{k,t} + e_{i,t} \tag{10-15}$$

Equation (10-15) is called a *K-factor return generating function*. Stated differently, Equation (10-15) is like a characteristic line that contains K different risk factors to explain the ith asset's return. The random variables denoted $F_{k,t}$ represent K different **risk factors,** $F_{k,t}$ for $k = 1, 2, \ldots, K$, that were observed over T different periods, $t = 1, 2, \ldots, T$. The K regression coefficients represented by the symbols b_{ik} in Equation (10-15) measure the sensitivity of the ith asset's returns to the kth risk factor. b_{i1} might be the beta for the interest rate risk factor, and b_{i2} might be the default risk beta, for example.

Table 10-3 lists various risk factors that contribute to an asset's total risk. These risk factors may contribute to an asset's diversifiable risk, its undiversifiable risk, or both. The makeup of every asset's risk is unique. For instance, default risk may affect the total risk of common stock returns in a systematic manner which contributes to that asset's undiversifiable risk. Assets like U.S. Treasury bills have zero default risk, however.

Equation (10-15) suggests that risk factors like those in Table 10-3 might contribute to the single beta in the characteristic line of Equation (10-3). Essentially, b_i can be thought of as being a weighted average of K different b_{ik}'s. Chapter 11 introduces *arbitrage pricing theory (APT)* and goes on to trace the asset pricing implications of multiple risk factor models.

Table 10-3
CATEGORIES OF RISK FACTORS THAT MIGHT
CONTRIBUTE TO AN ASSET'S TOTAL RISK

1. Sources of Undiversifiable Risk
   a. Systematic interest rate risk (if present)
   b. Systematic purchasing power risk (if present)
   c. Systematic market risk (if present)
   d. Systematic management risk (if present)
   e. Systematic default risk (if present)
   f. Systematic marketability risk (if present)
   g. Systematic callability risk (if present)
   h. Systematic convertibility risk (if present)
   i. Other systematic risk factors (if present)
2. Sources of Diversifiable Risk
   a. Unsystematic interest rate risk (if present)
   b. Unsystematic purchasing power risk (if present)
   c. Unsystematic market risk (if present)
   d. Unsystematic management risk (if present)
   e. Unsystematic default risk (if present)
   f. Unsystematic marketability risk (if present)
   g. Unsystematic callability risk (if present)
   h. Unsystematic convertibility risk (if present)
   i. Other unsystematic risk factors (if present)

Aggregate: Total risk

10-6   **SUMMARY AND CONCLUSIONS**

The total risk of any asset can be assessed by measuring its variability of returns. Total risk can be partitioned into two main parts—systematic risk and unsystematic risk. Both can be estimated by using the characteristic regression line. The characteristic regression line of an asset explains the asset's systematic variability of return in terms of market forces that affect all assets simultaneously. The sources of systematic risk include changes in the purchasing power of money, fluctuations in interest rates, swings in the security market prices called bull and bear markets, and other factors that contribute to undiversifiable fluctuations.

The portion of total risk that is not explained by an asset's characteristic regression line is called unsystematic risk. Unsystematic variability is unique to each asset. Unsystematic fluctuations in a security's price are diversifiable because they occur in an idiosyncratic fashion that makes them statistically independent.

Since unsystematic variations are unique to each firm, they are easily diversified to zero by spreading the investment funds across the securities of firms that operate independently. Figure 9-1 illustrates how the simplest kind of diversification could eliminate unsystematic risk. Systematic risk, on the other hand, is more difficult to reduce through diversification because it is common to all assets in the market. Assets with high degrees of systematic risk must be priced to yield high rates of return in order to induce investors to accept high degrees of risk that are undiversifiable within that market. The CAPM illustrates the positive relation between assets' systematic risks and their expected rates of return. Empirical tests support the validity of the CAPM.

The characteristic line is a single-factor model that may be decomposed into a multifactor model, such as Equation (10-15), that shows how different systematic risk factors contribute to an asset's undiversifiable risk.

Essay Questions

10-1   (*a*) Write one-sentence verbal definitions for each of the following three types of risk: (1) total risk, (2) systematic risk, (3) unsystematic risk. (*b*) Write out the mathematical formula for each of the three risk measures. (*c*) Mathematically derive the relationship between the three risk measures for the *i*th asset. *Hint: Partition the variance.*

10-2   How do you expect the total risk of a highly diversified mutual fund to be divided between systematic and unsystematic risk? Explain.

10-3   Assume that a tire company named the Cyclical Rubber Corporation (CRC) acquired the Countercyclical Red Ink Corporation (CRIC), a firm that produces red ink. (*a*) Create diagrams of the characteristic lines for CRC and CRIC to illustrate what you want to assume about their risk and return characteristics. (*b*) Use a diagram of the CAPM to show the asset-pricing implications of this change in

CRC. (*c*) How would the CRC acquisition affect the value of a share of the merged rubber corporation's stock?

10-4   Could a security analyst expect to find any worthwhile information by studying the residual errors $e_{i,t}$ from the characteristic line regression? Explain.

10-5   Are the beta coefficients in the characteristic line stable through time? Explain. Is it worthwhile to study betas if they are intertemporally unstable? *Hint: See Appendix 10A concerning the intertemporal stability of betas.*

10-6   Do you believe that an asset's unsystematic risk should have no effect on its market price as the capital asset pricing model (CAPM) suggests? Explain why or why not.

Problems

10-7   (*a*) Gather quarterly data from 1979 1Q through 1988 1Q inclusive for Homestake Mining Corporation, a NYSE-listed common stock, and prepare a table of data analogous to Table 10-1. See Chapter 6 for suggestions of where to find the needed data. (*b*) After you have the data, use a computer program to do simple linear regression analysis. Estimate Homestake's characteristic line, Equation (10-3), like the one for IBM shown in Table 10-2 and Figure 10-2. (*c*) After you get the regression results, answer the following questions. Is Homestake a defensive or an aggressive asset? Does the characteristic line for the asset have much predictive power? Is Homestake stock good for diversification purposes?

10-8   (*a*) Gather quarterly data from 1979 1Q through 1988 1Q inclusive for the General Motors Corporation (GM) and prepare a table of data analogous to Table 10-1. See Chapter 6 for sources of the needed data. (*b*) After you have the data, use a computer program to do simple linear regression analysis. Estimate GM's characteristic line, Equation (10-3), like the one for IBM shown in Table 10-2 and Figure 10-2. (*c*) After you get the regression results, answer the following questions. Is GM a defensive or an aggressive asset? Does GM's characteristic line for the asset have much predictive power? Is GM stock good for diversification purposes?

10-9   Calculate the beta coefficient for IBM from the 12 quarters of data below.

Year and quarter	IBM quarterly return	S&P 500 quarterly return
1983 Q1	6.61%	10.02%
1983 Q2	19.12	11.10
1983 Q3	6.3	−0.10
1983 Q4	−3.09	0.40
1984 Q1	−5.78	−2.40
1984 Q2	−6.40	−2.61
1984 Q3	18.53	9.68
1984 Q4	−0.02	1.76
1985 Q1	4.04	9.18
1985 Q2	−1.69	7.34
1985 Q3	0.99	−4.10
1985 Q4	26.42	17.19

10-10 Calculate the variance of returns for IBM with the data given in Problem 10-9. Partition IBM's variance into its systematic and unsystematic risk components. Determine IBM's coefficient of determination with the S&P 500. What is the relationship between IBM's systematic risk and its coefficient of determination? Show the relationship mathematically. *Hint: Partition the variance.*

10-11 Calculate the beta coefficient for Twentieth Century Growth Fund from the 12 quarters of data below.

Year and quarter	Growth quarterly return	S&P 500 quarterly return
1983 Q1	13.92%	10.02%
1983 Q2	19.75	11.10
1983 Q3	−5.82	−0.10
1983 Q4	−3.16	0.40
1984 Q1	−10.68	−2.40
1984 Q2	−5.17	−2.61
1984 Q3	5.45	9.68
1984 Q4	0.58	1.76
1985 Q1	7.94	9.18
1985 Q2	9.48	7.34
1985 Q3	−6.57	−4.10
1985 Q4	21.25	17.19

10-12 Determine the variance of returns for the Twentieth Century Growth Fund from the data in Problem 10-11 above. Separate variance into its systematic and unsystematic risk components. Calculate Twentieth Century Growth's coefficient of determination with the S&P 500. Why does the coefficient of determination for Twentieth Century Growth differ as much as it does from the one calculated for IBM in Problem 10-10?

10-13 Compute the beta coefficient for stocks A and B with the information given below. (*a*) Which stock has the most total risk? (*b*) The most undiversifiable risk?

Stock	Correlation coefficient with market	Standard deviation, σ
A	.4	.5
B	.75	.6

The variance of market returns is .20.

10-14 Calculate the beta coefficient for the two stocks given below. Which stock is the most defensive?

Year/quarter	General Motors quarterly return	DuPont quarterly return	S&P 500 quarterly return
1983 Q1	−3.05%	17.70%	10.02%
1983 Q2	23.54	16.16	11.10
1983 Q3	2.03	9.90	−0.10

Year/quarter	General Motors quarterly return	DuPont quarterly return	S&P 500 quarterly return
1983 Q4	2.38%	1.59%	0.40%
1984 Q1	−11.26	−3.94	−2.40
1984 Q2	2.50	−5.94	−2.61
1984 Q3	19.89	10.41	9.68
1984 Q4	3.24	1.26	1.76
1985 Q1	−5.26	6.31	9.18
1985 Q2	0.34	13.49	7.34
1985 Q3	−5.21	0.00	−4.10
1985 Q4	6.90	19.61	17.19

10-15 Suppose the current expected return on the market is 16 percent and the risk-free rate is 10 percent. The expected return and betas for three stocks are listed below. Which is overpriced? Which is underpriced? Draw a graph and show how you reached your conclusion about which asset is over- or underpriced.

Stocks	Expected return	Beta
Franklin Corp.	16%	1.2
AZZ Corp.	19	1.3
BBB Corp.	13	.75

10-16 (a) If everything remained unchanged in Problem 10-15 except that the expected return from the market and the risk-free rate rose to 18 and 14 percent, respectively, which stocks would be underpriced? Overpriced? (b) What conclusions can you draw about the robustness of the CAPM model from your solution to this problem?

10-17 The covariance of returns between stocks X and Y is $\text{Cov}(r_X, r_Y) = +10$; stock X's variance of returns is 12, and Y's variance of returns is 8. What is the correlation between stocks X and Y?

10-18 Assume that for asset Q the standard deviation of returns is 5.3 percent and the residual standard deviation (or standard error) around asset Q's characteristic line is 1.89 percent. If the market standard deviation is 6.4 percent, what is stock Q's beta coefficient?

10-19 Assume that stock QZR has a beta of 1.25 and residual standard deviation (or standard error) of 3.2 percent. If the market portfolio's standard deviation is 8 percent, what is QZR's variance?

Selected References

Breeden, D. T., "An Intertemporal Asset Pricing Model with Stochastic Consumption and Investment Opportunities," *Journal of Financial Economics,* Sept. 1979, pp. 265–296.

Advanced calculus is employed to develop an extension of the capital asset pricing model (CAPM) which maximizes the investor's expected utility from consumption. Breeden's model maximizes the investor's lifetime utility from consumption over multiple periods and explains consumption-investment decisions. As a result, asset prices depend on their covariances with aggregate consumption rather than with any market index.

Sharpe, W. F., "Capital Asset Prices: A Theory of Market Equilibrium under Conditions of Risk," *The Journal of Finance,* Sept. 1964, pp. 425–552.

This classic article suggests the asset-pricing implications of systematic risk. Sharpe develops the risk-return relationship for portfolios (that is, the capital market line, or the CML) and for individual assets (namely, the CAPM). Calculus is used only in the footnotes. A knowledge of elementary statistics is assumed.

Appendix 10A

Stability of
Risk Statistics

The statistics from an asset's characteristic line contain much information about various aspects of its price movements. However, when the data points (for instance, the dots in Figure 10-2) do not fit closely around it, the characteristic line's predictive power diminishes accordingly. Since *the correlation coefficient ρ is a goodness-of-fit statistic* that measures how well the data points conform to the characteristic line, this statistic gives some indication of how much faith should be placed in the risk statistics associated with the regression.

Beta Stability

The characteristic line statistics shown at the bottom of Table A10-1, for example, imply a correlation coefficient of .10 for Homestake Mining during the sample period from January 1927 through June 1935. Homestake's coefficient of determination of 1 percent (that is, .01) for the 1927–1935 sample period tells what percent of the total variance in the stock's price is explained by the regression. The fact that Homestake's coefficient of determination for the 1927–1935 sample is not significantly different from zero suggests that the associated beta contains no meaningful economic information.[15]

Securities that have very low goodness-of-fit statistics for their characteristic lines (like the early Homestake data, for example) frequently have beta coefficients that are random coefficients. These *random coefficients* are essentially wild beta coefficients, which move up and down over a wide range in a spurious fashion as the characteristic line is empirically estimated again and again using data from different sample periods. (In statistical terms, the changes in the values of the beta from sample to sample are called **sampling errors**.) Furthermore, a firm's beta may change drastically if, for instance, it undertakes production of new products with a completely new management team. But year after year most firms' probability distributions of returns and betas are relatively stable through time; see Table A10-1. Considering that the data for these

---

[15]Equations (10-6) and (10-7*b*) tell us that a correlation coefficient that is inconsequential implies the beta will also have a numerical value near zero.

Table A10-1
BETA COEFFICIENTS CHANGE OVER TIME

Firm	Period, month/year	Beta	ρ^2
Union Oil of	1/27–6/35	.55	.58
California	7/35–12/43	.57	.49
	1/44–6/51	.97	.45
	7/51–12/60	.98	.32
IBM	1/27–6/35	.49	.49
	7/35–12/43	.25	.26
	1/44–6/51	.56	.29
	7/51–12/60	.86	.23
May Department	1/27–6/35	.83	.74
Stores	7/35–12/43	.64	.49
	1/44–6/51	.72	.35
	7/51–12/60	.82	.32
Atlantic Coast	1/27–6/35	1.2	.73
Line Railroad	7/35–12/43	1.26	.7
	1/44–6/51	1.7	.43
	7/51–12/60	1.63	.57
Homestake Mining	1/27–6/35	.042	.01
Corp.	7/35–12/43	.235	.07
	1/44–6/51	.333	.09
	7/51–12/60	.465	.11

ρ^2 = coefficient of determination for characteristic regression line
= correlation coefficient squared
= percent of variation explained

Source: Marshall E. Blume, "The Assessment of Portfolio Performance: An Application of Portfolio Theory," unpublished doctoral dissertation, University of Chicago, March 1968.

calculations span 33 years, the stability of the betas over time for May Department Stores, for instance, is impressive.

Betas Regress Toward the Mean

Blume developed a time-series regression model that takes betas from one 7-year period and predicts their values in the next 7-year period.[16]

$$\text{Beta in second} \atop \text{7-year period} = 0.343 + 0.677 \left(\text{beta in first} \atop \text{7-year period} \right) \qquad \text{(A10-1)}$$

Figure A10-1 illustrates Equation (A10-1). Essentially, Blume's model predicts that the betas regress toward their mean value of positive unity. Blume's model imparts a small

[16]Marshall Blume, "On the Assessment of Risk," *Journal of Finance,* March 1971, vol. VI, no. 1.

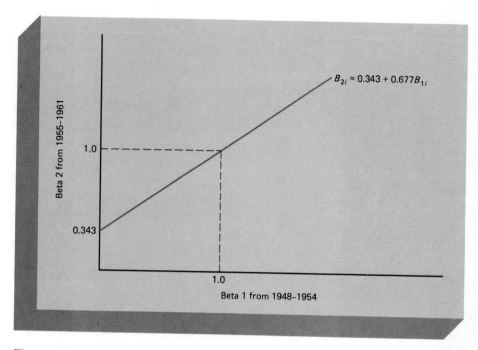

Figure A10-1 Illustration of how Blume's model predicts that betas regress toward their mean value of 1.

upward bias in its forecasts. To see this bias, consider that an asset had a beta of 1.0 in the first 7-year period. Inserting 1.0 into Equation (A10-1) produces a larger-than-average forecasted beta of 1.02 [= 0.343 + 0.677(1)]. Ignoring this tiny bias, Equation (A10-1) predicts that larger-than-average betas regress downward toward the average, and smaller-than-average betas tend to shift upward toward the mean.[17]

**Francis's
Transition Matrix**

It is important to ask whether the risk statistics for different investments are stable through time or whether they jump around randomly (like the Homestake Mining statistics shown at the bottom of Table A10-1, for instance). If the statistics gyrate wildly, they have little value to financial analysts because today's historical statistics are a poor predictor of the future riskiness of an investment.

Francis analyzed 750 NYSE stocks over a decade in order to assess the stability of three statistics which measure the riskiness of financial assets. The three statistics analyzed are (1) the beta coefficient from the characteristic line, (2) the correlation coefficient, which measures how closely the data points fit around the characteristic line, and (3) the standard deviation, which measures the asset's total risk.

Francis divided the decade he studied into two 60-month subsamples and measured

---

[17]Francis developed models that are useful in predicting betas, standard deviations, and correlations. See J. C. Francis, "Statistical Analysis of Risk Statistics for NYSE Stocks," *Journal of Financial and Quantitative Analysis,* Dec. 1979, vol. XIV, no. 5, pp. 981–998.

the three statistics for 750 different stocks. After calculating all of these statistics over the first 5 years (or 60 months) and also over the second 5 years, he *arrayed* the statistics with the largest values at the top of the list and the smallest statistics at the bottom of the list. Six arrays were thus constructed:

1. An array of 750 betas over the first 60 months
2. An array of 750 betas from the same stocks over the second 60 months
3. An array of 750 standard deviations over the first 60 months
4. An array of 750 standard deviations from the same stocks over the second 60 months
5. An array of 750 correlation coefficients over the first 60 months
6. An array of 750 correlation coefficients from the same stocks over the second 60 months

Then Francis divided each of the six arrays of 750 statistics into 10 equal-sized deciles with statistics from 75 stocks in each *decile*. He then arranged these six arrays of deciles of statistics into the transition matrix shown in Table A10-2 in order to see how stable the statistics were from one 5-year subsample until the next 5-year subsample. Table A10-2 is actually three different transition probability matrices—one for betas, one for standard deviations, and one for correlation coefficients—all in one matrix.

The transition probability matrix for betas in Table A10-2 shows, for example, that 0.4267 (or 42.67 percent) of the betas in the top decile in the first 5 years turned up in the top decile in the next 5-year period. Slightly over a quarter (25.33 percent, to be exact) of the betas from the same top decile declined in value enough to be in the second decile in the second 5-year period. Note that betas in the top decile in the first 60-month subsample dropped into every one of the deciles except the eighth decile in the following 60-month subsample. But, only 0.0133 (or 1.33 percent) fell clear from the first to the tenth decile in the next 5-year subsample. After studying the entire transition matrix, you can see that very few betas rose or fell more than two or three deciles during a 5-year period. Table A10-2 shows that the betas in the deciles around the median (that is, the fiftieth percentile) moved into the farthest deciles.[18]

Further study of Table A10-2 reveals that the standard deviations are the most stable of the three statistics analyzed. For example, 0.2267 (or 22.67 percent) of the standard deviations that started out in the fifth decile in the first 60-month subsample ended up in the same decile in the next 5-year subsample. This finding means that most common stocks' total risk are fairly stable through time.

The correlation coefficients were the least stable statistics. Only 0.0933 (or 9.33 percent) of the correlations that started in the fifth decile in the first subsample were still in the fifth decile 5 years later, for example. Findings like this indicate that simply because an asset's data points fit closely around that asset's characteristic line in one 5-year period does not mean that that asset will experience the same goodness-of-fit in the following 5-year period.

[18]The median betas probably changed deciles more than the extreme betas because the values of the statistics in the fourth, fifth, and sixth deciles were compressed into a narrow numerical range. In contrast, the highest and lowest deciles included a wider range of values so that larger numerical changes were needed to move out of these extreme deciles.

Table A10-2
TRANSITION MATRIX SHOWING THE RISK DECILE IN YEAR *t* VERSUS THE SAME STATISTIC'S RISK DECILE IN YEAR *t* + 5

Deciles	1	2	3	4	5	6	7	8	9	10
Beta1	0.4267	0.2533	0.0800	0.0400	0.0533	0.0400	0.0533	0.0000	0.0400	0.0133
StdD1	0.5067	0.1867	0.0800	0.0667	0.0667	0.0400	0.0267	0.0133	0.0133	0.0000
Corr1	0.1867	0.200	0.1067	0.1600	0.0667	0.0400	0.1067	0.0667	0.0533	0.0133
Beta2	0.1867	0.2933	0.1600	0.0933	0.0800	0.0267	0.0533	0.0533	0.0267	0.0267
StdD2	0.2267	0.2400	0.2133	0.1467	0.0800	0.0267	0.0267	0.0267	0.0000	0.0133
Corr2	0.2000	0.1600	0.1600	0.1600	0.0800	0.0133	0.0400	0.0400	0.1067	0.0400
Beta3	0.1733	0.1200	0.2000	0.1333	0.1067	0.1333	0.0667	0.0267	0.0133	0.0267
StdD3	0.1200	0.1867	0.2000	0.1867	0.0800	0.0800	0.0400	0.0667	0.0133	0.0267
Corr3	0.1200	0.1067	0.1200	0.0800	0.0400	0.1867	0.0933	0.1200	0.0800	0.0533
Beta4	0.0933	0.0667	0.1867	0.1733	0.1733	0.1067	0.0267	0.0667	0.0800	0.0267
StdD4	0.0800	0.1467	0.2267	0.0667	0.1200	0.1600	0.0933	0.0533	0.0533	0.0000
Corr4	0.0933	0.1467	0.1333	0.0267	0.1067	0.1467	0.0800	0.0933	0.0933	0.0800
Beta5	0.0667	0.1067	0.1067	0.1467	0.1200	0.1200	0.1067	0.0933	0.1067	0.0267
StdD5	0.0533	0.1333	0.0667	0.1467	0.2267	0.0800	0.1467	0.1067	0.0400	0.0000
Corr5	0.1200	0.1067	0.0933	0.0800	0.0933	0.0400	0.1333	0.1467	0.0667	0.1200
Beta6	0.0400	0.0667	0.0933	0.1067	0.0933	0.2000	0.1600	0.1467	0.0667	0.0267
StdD6	0.0000	0.0533	0.0800	0.2400	0.1600	0.1200	0.1600	0.0800	0.0667	0.0267
Corr6	0.0667	0.0800	0.1067	0.1333	0.0667	0.1867	0.0533	0.0933	0.1200	0.0933
Beta7	0.0000	0.0533	0.0533	0.1200	0.0933	0.0800	0.1600	0.2000	0.1600	0.0800
StdD7	0.1033	0.0267	0.0933	0.0933	0.1200	0.2000	0.1867	0.1333	0.0933	0.0400
Corr7	0.0667	0.0667	0.0667	0.0933	0.1200	0.0667	0.1600	0.0933	0.1333	0.1333
Beta8	0.0000	0.0267	0.0667	0.1067	0.1600	0.1733	0.1333	0.0800	0.0667	0.1867
StdD8	0.0000	0.0267	0.0400	0.0267	0.1067	0.1467	0.1733	0.1867	0.1333	0.1600
Corr8	0.0667	0.0533	0.0667	0.1200	0.1733	0.1467	0.1333	0.1333	0.0000	0.1067
Beta9	0.0133	0.0133	0.0400	0.0533	0.0667	0.0933	0.1467	0.2267	0.1600	0.1867
StdD9	0.0000	0.0000	0.0000	0.0267	0.0400	0.1067	0.0667	0.2133	0.2400	0.3067
Corr9	0.0400	0.0400	0.0933	0.0667	0.0933	0.1067	0.1067	0.1333	0.1867	0.1333
Beta10	0.0000	0.0000	0.0133	0.0267	0.0533	0.0267	0.0933	0.1067	0.2800	0.4000
StdD10	0.0000	0.0000	0.0000	0.0000	0.0000	0.0400	0.0800	0.1200	0.3333	0.4267
Corr10	0.0400	0.0400	0.0533	0.0800	0.1600	0.0667	0.0933	0.0800	0.1600	0.2267

Source: J. C. Francis, ''Statistical Analysis of Risk Statistics for NYSE Stocks,'' *Journal of Financial and Quantitative Analysis.* Dec. 1979, vol. XIV, no. 5, p. 992, table 4.

The three transition matrices in Table A10-2 suggest that betas, standard deviations, and correlations may not be as stable as financial analysts might desire. Nevertheless, these risk statistics do appear to exhibit sufficient intertemporal stability to make them worthy of financial analysis.

**Random
Coefficients**

The classic characteristic-line model, Equation (10-3), must be modified slightly to embrace the securities which experience changing betas. Equation (A10-2) is identical to Equation (10-3) in every respect except one—the beta in Equation (A10-2) has a time subscript, denoted t.[19]

$$r_{i,t} = a_i + b_{i,t}r_{m,t} + e_{i,t} \qquad \text{(A10-2)}$$

The time subscript on the beta indicates that the beta may assume a different value in each period—that is, $d[\text{Var}(b_{i,t})]/dt > 0$. Empirical research indicates[20] that the unstable characteristic-line model of Equation (A10-2) is appropriate for some of the stocks listed on the NYSE. Making continual adjustments for these changing betas creates additional work for the security analysts.[21]

[19]P. A. V. B. Swamy, *Statistical Inference in Random Coefficient Regression Models* (Berlin: Springer-Verlag, 1971); H. Theil, *Principles of Econometrics* (New York: Wiley, 1971), sec. 12-4.
[20]The following studies of intertemporal shifts in beta coefficients suggest that most, but not all, betas are fairly stable through time. F. J. Fabozzi and J. C. Francis, "Beta as a Random Coefficient," *Journal of Financial and Quantitative Analysis,* March 1978; F. J. Fabozzi and J. C. Francis, "Stability Tests for Alphas and Betas over Bull and Bear Market Conditions," *Journal of Finance,* Sept. 1977; F. Fabozzi and J. C. Francis, "The Effects of Changing Macroeconomic Conditions on Alphas, Betas, and the Single Index Model," *Journal of Financial and Quantitative Analysis,* June 1979; S. J. Kon and G. C. Jen, "Estimation of Time Varying Systematic Risk and Performance for Mutual Fund Portfolios: An Application of Switching Regression," *Journal of Finance,* May 1978; B. Rosenberg, "A Survey of Stochastic Regression Parameters," *Annals of Economic and Social Measurement,* 1973, vol. 2, no. 4, pp. 381–397; B. Rosenberg and J. Guy, "Beta and Investment Fundamentals," *Financial Analysts Journal,* May–June 1976.
[21]Practically all preceding empirical research with the characteristic line has been limited to a partial-equilibrium analysis in which the interactions of individual securities with some stock market index are measured. Professor Roll has suggested that a *general equilibrium analysis* would be a more appropriate context in which to test the risk-return capital market theory; Richard Roll, "A Critique of the Asset Pricing Theory's Tests; Part 1: On Past and Potential Testability of the Theory," *Journal of Financial Economics,* March 1977, vol. 4, no. 2, pp. 129–176. Roll would include commodities, bonds, art objects, real estate, investments in human capital, and all other capital assets in the market index. The validity of Roll's general equilibrium suggestion is acknowledged. However, at the present time no general market index of the scope Roll visualizes is available. For broad-based empirical estimates of the market portfolio see Ibbotson Associates, *Stocks, Bonds, Bills and Inflation: 1989 Yearbook* (Chicago, Ill.: Ibbotson Associates Inc., 1989).

Chapter 11

Arbitrage Pricing
Theory (APT)

Markowitz's portfolio theory was developed to minimize the risk of a portfolio at any level of return. The capital asset pricing model (CAPM), developed by Markowitz, Tobin, Sharpe, Treynor, and others, was introduced in Chapter 10. More recently, Stephen Ross proposed the arbitrage pricing theory (APT hereafter), an investments theory that both competes with Markowitz portfolio theory and complements it.[1] We introduce the APT in a simple two-asset context that is intuitive.

11-1   INTRODUCTION TO ARBITRAGE PRICING THEORY (APT)

The APT is based on the **law of one price,** which says that the same good cannot sell for two different prices. If the same good does sell for different prices, arbitragers will buy the good where it is cheap, thereby bidding up the low price, and simultaneously sell the good where its price is higher, thereby driving down the high price. Arbitragers will continue this activity until all prices for the good are equal.[2]

[1]See Stephen A. Ross, ''Return, Risk and Arbitrage,'' in I. Friend and J. Bicksler, eds., *Risk and Return in Finance* (Ballinger Press, Cambridge, Mass., 1976). Also see S. Ross, ''The Arbitrage Pricing Theory of Capital Asset Pricing,'' *Journal of Economic Theory,* Dec. 1976, pp. 334–360.

[2]Section 8-9 discusses the *law of one price* and *arbitrage* in more detail.

Two Identical Streams of Stochastic Cashflows

Consider the returns from assets 1 and 2. In Equations (11-1) and (11-2) the term $p_{i,t}$ denotes the price for asset i in period t.

$$r_{1,t} = E(r_1) + e_t = \frac{p_{1,t}}{p_{1,t-1}} - 1.0 \qquad (11\text{-}1)$$

$$r_{2,t} = E(r_2) + e_t = \frac{p_{2,t}}{p_{2,t-1}} - 1.0 \qquad (11\text{-}2)$$

The random variable e_t is identical for the two asets in Equations (11-1) and (11-2); it is assumed to have a mathematical expectation of zero, $E(e_t) = 0$. Equations (11-1) and (11-2) show that assets 1 and 2 have equally risky cashflows and equally risky rates of return. When trying to figure out the equilibrium prices of market assets, the *law of one price* is interpreted to mean that assets with identical risks are equivalent investments and therefore must have the same expected rates of return; in this case, $E(r_1) = E(r_2)$.

As long as the expected returns from assets 1 and 2 are equal, arbitrage between them will not be profitable. But, what happens if the two expected rates of return are not equal? Consider $E(r_1) > E(r_2)$. In this case an investor can create *arbitrage profits* by taking the proceeds of $p_{2,0}$ dollars from a short sale of asset 2 at time $t = 0$ and investing the funds in a long position in asset 1. More concisely, $|-p_{1,0}| = p_{2,0}$. This arbitrage portfolio requires *zero initial investment* since $-p_{1,0} + p_{2,0} = 0$. The portfolio is also perfectly hedged to *zero risk* because any gains on the long position will be exactly offset by the simultaneous losses on the short position of equal size, and vice versa. The arbitrager can nevertheless confidently expect to earn positive profits since $[E(r_1) - E(r_2)] > 0$. Arbitrage opportunities like this are disequilibrium situations that will quickly be corrected by the first arbitrager that discovers them and finds a way to trade on them.

Let us return to the equilibrium situation in which $E(r_1) = E(r_2)$ and continue to develop that model.

Undiversifiable Risk from a Common Factor

Assume that the one-period rates of return for all assets are generated by a *single risk factor* denoted F in accordance with the linear models of Equations (11-3) and (11-4).

$$r_{1,t} = a_1 + b_1 F_t \qquad (11\text{-}3)$$

$$r_{2,t} = a_2 + b_2 F_t \qquad (11\text{-}4)$$

Let F_t be a random variable with an expected value of zero, $E(F_t) = 0$. This variable might represent the unanticipated changes in GNP; concisely, $F_t = [GNP_t - E(GNP)]$. The b_i *slope coefficients* in Equations (11-3) and (11-4) are measures of undiversifiable risk—they indicate how sensitive the asset returns are to the common source of variations F. If you like, you can think of Equations

(11-3) and (11-4) as being simplified characteristic lines that have no unexplained residual error terms so that the total risk is undiversifiable systematic risk.

$$\text{Total risk} = \text{Var}(r_{i,t}) = \text{Var}(a_i + b_i F_t) = b_i^2 \, \text{Var}(F_t) = \text{systematic risk}$$

Since the independent variable F was constructed so that it averages to zero, $E(F) = 0$, it follows that Equations (11-3) and (11-4) should have $bE(F) = E(bF) = 0$. By taking this logic a step farther, we see that the two expected rates of return must also be equal to their intercept terms, as shown in Equations (11-5) and (11-6).

$$E(r_1) = a_1 \tag{11-5}$$

$$E(r_2) = a_2 \tag{11-6}$$

Equations (11-5) and (11-6) show that $E(r_i) = a_i$. In addition, the law of one price tells us that since assets 1 and 2 are equally risky, they should have identical expected rates of return, $E(r_1) = E(r_2)$. From these facts we can conclude that the two assets' expected rates of return and intercept terms should all be equal, $E(r_1) = a_1 = E(r_2) = a_2$.

Let x represent the weight or proportion of a two-asset portfolio's total wealth that is invested in asset one, $0 < x < +1.0$. Consider what would happen if an arbitrager set out to create a perfectly hedged portfolio by investing a fraction x of the portfolio's total wealth in asset 1 and the remainder $(1.0 - x)$ in asset 2. Equation (11-7) defines the weighted average rate of return for the portfolio.

$$r_{p,t} = xr_{1,t} + (1 - x)r_{2,t} \tag{11-7}$$

Substituting Equations (11-3) and (11-4) into Equation (11-7) produces Equation (11-7a).

$$r_{p,t} = x(a_1 + b_1 F_t) + (1 - x)(a_2 + b_2 F_t) \tag{11-7a}$$

$$r_{p,t} = x(a_1 - a_2) + a_2 + [x(b_1 - b_2) + b_2]F_t \tag{11-7b}$$

Let us select the proportion $x^* = [b_2/(b_2 - b_1)]$ that creates a perfectly hedged portfolio and then mathematically analyze the asset pricing implications of the resulting portfolio. The quantity x^* can be substituted into Equation (11-7b) in place of x to obtain, after some rearranging, Equation (11-8).

$$r_p = a_2 + \frac{b_2(a_1 - a_2)}{b_2 - b_1} \tag{11-8}$$

We can tell that Equation (11-8) represents a perfectly hedged riskless portfolio since the systematic risk factor F, which is the *only source of risk in this model, drops completely out of the equation.*

In equilibrium a riskless investment must yield the risk-free rate of return, denoted R. This allows us to say that $r_p = R$ and also permits us to substitute

R in place of r_p and to rewrite Equation (11-8) equivalently as Equation (11-9).

$$R = a_2 + \frac{b_2(a_1 - a_2)}{b_2 - b_1}$$ (11-9)

Multiplying both sides of Equation (11-9) by the quantity $(b_2 - b_1)$ and rearranging the terms results in Equation (11-10).

$$\frac{a_1 - R}{b_1} = \frac{a_2 - R}{b_2}$$ (11-10)

From Equations (11-5) and (11-6) we know that $E(r_i) = a_i$. Substituting for a_i allows Equation (11-10) to be restated as Equations (11-10a) and (11-10b).

$$\frac{a_i - R}{b_i} = \frac{E(r_i - R)}{b_i}$$ (11-10a)

$$\frac{a_i - R}{b_i} = \lambda = \frac{\text{risk premium}}{\text{risk measure}}$$ (11-10b)

Equations (11-10), (11-10a), and (11-10b) all define a constant term, denoted lambda λ, that represents a **factor risk premium.**

The Arbitrage Pricing Line

Equation (11-10a) can be equivalently rewritten as Equations (11-11) and (11-11a) to obtain the **arbitrage pricing line.** Combining Equations (11-5), (11-6), and (11-10a) results in Equation (11-11).

$$E(r_i) = R + b_i \frac{[E(r_i) - R]}{b_i}$$ (11-11)

$$E(r_i) = R + b_i\lambda$$ (11-11a)

Equation (11-11a) was derived by substituting from the definition of lambda in Equation (11-10b). Figure 11-1 illustrates the arbitrage pricing line of Equation (11-11).

The factor risk premium λ can be interpreted as the excess rate of return $[E(r_i) - R]$ for a risky asset with $b_i = 1.0$. Equation series (11-11) is the essence of the APT. Equations (11-11) and (11-11a) say that in the absence of profitable arbitrage opportunities, the expected rate of return from risky asset i equals the risk-free rate of return plus a risk premium that is proportional to the asset's sensitivity b_i to the common risk factor F. This sensitivity is measured by the **sensitivity coefficient,** or **factor loading,** or **factor beta,** denoted b_i, for the ith asset.

The **arbitrage pricing line** shown in Figure 11-1 is a risk-return relationship. Risk is proportional to the asset's sensitivity coefficient b_i and is measured along the horizontal axis. Assets' expected rates of return are measured along the vertical axis of Figure 11-1. The arbitrage pricing line intersects the vertical

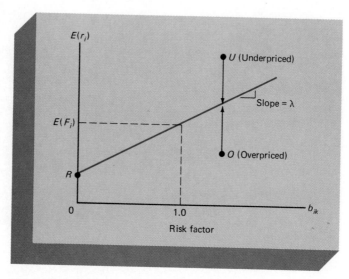

Figure 11-1 A simple APT model for one risk factor.

axis at point R, the riskless rate of interest. APT considers all assets that are in the same risk class to be perfect substitutes that should yield the same rate of return in equilibrium.

Overpriced and Underpriced Assets

Consider two assets in the same risk class, like the two assets at points U and O in Figure 11-1. Asset O is overpriced relative to its value; asset U is underpriced. Figure 11-2 illustrates the two return generating functions, represented by Equations (11-3) and (11-4), for these two disequilibrium priced assets. Assets U and O violate the law of one price because they are both in the same risk class, $b_1 = b_2$, but do not have the same expected rate of return. The supply and demand forces created by arbitragers will modify the prices of all assets until an equilibrium is attained in which all assets lie someplace on the arbitrage pricing line. The arbitrage process outlined next will tend to move all assets onto the arbitrage pricing line.

As investors investigate before they invest, some of them will discover that asset O in Figure 11-1 offers investors a lower rate of return than asset U, even though they both involve *equal amounts of risk.* Investors will sell asset O because it is a less desirable investment. The resulting excess supply for asset O will drive down its market price. As the price of asset O is driven down, the expected return from asset O will rise correspondingly; this price-adjustment process is indicated by the arrows in the following equation, which defines the expected return for a common stock.

$$\uparrow E(r) = \frac{E(p_{t+1} - p_t + d_t)}{\downarrow p_t} = \frac{\text{price change } + \text{ cash dividend, if any}}{\downarrow \text{ purchase price}}$$

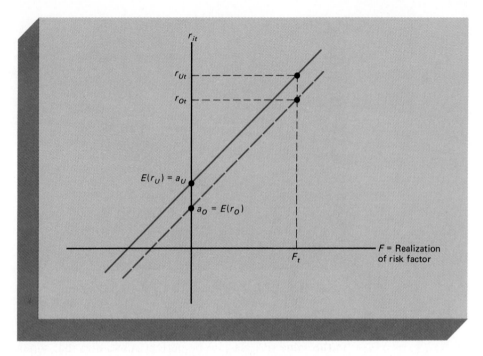

Figure 11-2 An arbitrage opportunity exists because two equally risky assets have different expected returns, $a_U > a_O$.

Investors will continue to sell asset O until its price is driven down and its expected rate of return rises up to a competitive level on the arbitrage pricing line in Figure 11-1. The upward pointing arrow in Figure 11-1 traces the path that $E(r_O)$ should follow until it reaches equilibrium on the arbitrage pricing line. These same equilibrium-seeking economic adjustments would push the return generating model for the overpriced asset, represented by the dashed line in Figure 11-2, upward until it coincides with the solid line, representing the other asset. When the two lines in Figure 11-2 are identical, the two assets will have identical rates of return and have equilibrium prices.

Smart investors will not only liquidate asset O if they own any of it, they will also sell asset O short and use the cash from the short sale to buy a long position in asset U. Investors will buy asset U in order to enjoy its high expected rate of return—which lies above the arbitrage pricing line in Figure 11-1 and also above the expected return from asset O. As these profit seekers buy asset U in order to obtain its high return, they bid up its price. And, as the price of asset U is bid higher, its expected rate of return comes down. This process can be traced by reversing the direction of the arrows in the common stock's expected return equation above.

Because most people prefer more wealth to less wealth, asset U will experience more buyers than sellers until its purchase price is bid so high that its expected rate of return falls onto the arbitrage pricing line in Figure 11-1, as indicated by the downward pointing arrow in that figure. When $E(r_U)$ is driven down onto the arbitrage pricing line, the asset's price will be in equilibrium. Similarly, the return generating model for the underpriced asset represented by the solid line in Figure 11-2 will equilibrate downward until it coincides with the dashed line representing the other asset. When the two lines in Figure 11-2 coincide, the two assets will have attained equilibrium prices.

The price adjustment process outlined above will work for all assets in all risk classes. This means that *every asset that plots above the arbitrage pricing line in Figure 11-1 is underpriced,* and its price will adjust upward in the same way that the price of asset U rose. Likewise, *every asset that plots below the arbitrage pricing line is overpriced,* and its price will be driven down by the same market mechanism that lowered the price of asset O in Figure 11-1.

The Arbitrage Portfolio Requires No Investment of Funds

To maximize the profits they can derive from their research finding, smart investors will sell asset O short and *simultaneously* buy a long position of equal dollar value in asset U. They will not have one cent of their own cash invested in their **arbitrage portfolio** made up of a short position in asset O combined with an equal long position in asset U, $p_{O,0} - p_{U,0} = 0$. They can use the cash from the short sale of asset O to buy a long position of equal value in asset U. Furthermore, these smart investors will not be exposed to any risk because their arbitrage portfolio is perfectly hedged, with long and short positions of equal value that offset each other's gains and losses, $\text{Var}(p_O - p_U) = 0$. And finally, the *arbitrage portfolio* will earn a riskless profit rate of $[E(r_U) - E(r_O)] > 0$. The arbitrage portfolio earns this profit by raising funds from the short sale on which the arbitrager must pay a rate of return of $E(r_O)$ and, simultaneously, investing these funds in the long position at a higher rate of return of $E(r_U)$.

Most private investors in the world will never even consider arbitrage. But, according to APT theorists, only a few aggressive professional traders running multimillion dollar arbitrage portfolios would be sufficient to generate the APT equilibrium condition illustrated in Figure 11-1.

Formal Definition of an Arbitrage Opportunity

APT defines an **arbitrage opportunity** to be a perfectly hedged portfolio that can be acquired at a cost of zero and that generates zero cash outflows or inflows at any time before the position is terminated, but will have a positive value with *certainty* at the end of the investment period. An arbitrage opportunity is expressed more formally in Equations (11-12), (11-13), and (11-14) below. These three equations are denominated in dollars.

$$\sum_{i=1}^{n} p_{i,0} = 0 \qquad \text{that is, zero money initially invested at } t = 0 \qquad (11\text{-}12)$$

$$\sum_{i=1}^{n} p_{i,T} > 0 \qquad \text{that is, positive profits at } t = T \qquad (11\text{-}13)$$

$$\sum_{i=1}^{n} \sum_{j=1}^{n} \sigma_{ij} = 0 \qquad \text{that is, zero risk} \qquad (11\text{-}14)$$

where $p_{i,0}$ = initial price of position in ith asset

$p_{i,T}$ = terminal value of position in asset i when arbitrage position is lifted, a random variable

σ_{ij} = covariance of *dollar* values of the positions in assets i and j

The dollar profits must be positive, as indicated in Equation (11-13), in order for arbitrage to occur.

No money was invested to create this profitable arbitrage portfolio because some securities were sold short to obtain cash inflow (that is, $p_{i,0} > 0$) while other securities cost money (that is, $p_{j,0} < 0$) when they were purchased to be held in a long position. Investors are assumed to receive the proceeds (that is, positive cash inflows) from their short sales to invest in their long positions (which result in negative cash outflows) so that Equation (11-12) is not violated. Equations (11-12), (11-13), and (11-14) define the type of arbitrage opportunity that forms the basis for APT.

Why Arbitrage Pricing Models Are Linear

Are you wondering if the arbitrage pricing line in Figure 11-1 might ever be nonlinear? The curve illustrated in Figure 11-3, for instance, contains five points labeled A, B, C, D, and E. You might ask: Is the curve $ABCDE$ any less plausible than straight line $RA_eBC_eDE_e$? The answer is yes; arbitrage makes any nonlinear risk-return arrangement unsustainable.

Consider what arbitragers would do if they discovered a set of five investment opportunities arrayed along the curve $ABCDE$ in Figure 11-3. They would sell overpriced assets to raise funds. Specifically, an arbitrager might sell G dollars worth of asset A short and also sell H dollars worth of asset E short to raise $G + H$ dollars to invest in an underpriced asset. Selling assets A and E short would drive their prices downward. If assets A and E were common stocks, this short selling would also tend to increase their expected rates of return as shown in the formula below.

$$\uparrow E(r) = \frac{E(p_{t+1} - p_t + d_t)}{\downarrow p_t} = \frac{\text{price change} + \text{cash dividend, if any}}{\downarrow \text{purchase price}}$$

Note that in Figure 11-3 the arrows starting from assets A and E point upward toward points A_e and E_e on the straight line $RA_eBC_eDE_e$. The short sales of assets A and E would tend to push their expected returns up toward points A_e and E_e.

After selling assets A and E short to raise $G + H$ dollars, the arbitrager will have created a portfolio we will call S. Portfolio S contains $G + H$ dollars and

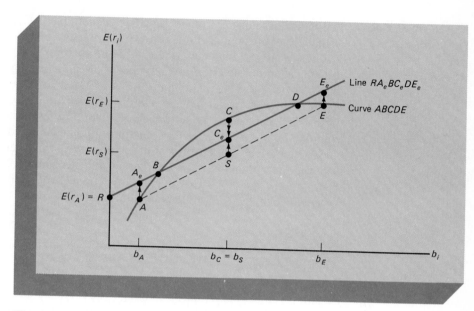

Figure 11-3 Why the arbitrage pricing line is linear.

lies on a straight line connecting points A and E. We know portfolio S lies on a straight line between points A and E because both the portfolio return formula, Equation (9-1), and the portfolio beta formula, Equation (11-17), are *linear* weighted average formulas. Furthermore, if we create portfolio S to be composed of equal parts of assets A and E (so $G = H$), the portfolio will lie halfway along the straight line connecting A and E.

Note that portfolio S is in the same risk class as asset C; the arbitrager constructed it this way for a reason. (Can you guess why?) In an effort to earn riskless arbitrage profits, the arbitrager will take the $G + H$ dollars in portfolio S and invest them in a long position in asset C. This purchase of asset C will bid up its price and tend to drive its expected return downward, as indicated by the arrows directed downward toward point C_e in Figure 11-3. (You might want to reverse the arrows in the common stock's expected return formula above to aid you in visualizing this price adjustment process.)

The arbitrager will essentially be obtaining funds at a weighted average cost of capital of $E(r_S)$ and investing the money to earn an expected return of $E(r_C)$. This riskless arbitrage will continue until the profit rate of $[E(r_C) - E(r_S)]$ is driven down to zero; at that point the following equilibrium condition will be attained: $E(r_C) = E(r_{Ce}) = E(r_S)$. In addition to bringing the return on asset C, $E(r_C)$, down to a level of $E(r_{Ce})$, this arbitrage will also raise the expected returns of assets A and E up to points A_e and E_e, respectively. In summary, the arbitrager profits from helping align curve $ABCDE$ in Figure 11-3 so that it coincides with straight line $RA_eBC_eDE_e$. Analogous arbitrage operations will ensure that all other arbitrage pricing relationships are linear.

Implications and Extensions of the APT

The capital asset pricing model (CAPM), Equation (10-12), happens to be mathematically equivalent to Equation (11-11), which defines the one-factor APT. It is reassuring to find that when only one factor exists in the whole world, that single factor must be the *market portfolio,* and the single-factor APT model turns out to be identical to the CAPM.[3] Stated differently, *two completely different theories about asset pricing lead to identical conclusions.*

The APT can be extended to include several different common factors. For example, F_1, F_2, F_3, or even more factors could be included as different sources of risk that affect market prices. Much empirical work remains to be done to discover the number of relevant factors that determine asset returns and the identity of these factors. However, before considering such empirical evidence, we will develop the APT more completely and more formally in the next section.

11-2   A MORE GENERAL DEVELOPMENT OF THE APT MODEL

Equation (11-15) below may be thought of as an extended characteristic line with k different economic factors as explanatory variables.[4] It is the return generating model for asset i that underlies APT.

$$r_{i,t} = a_i + b_{i1}F_{1,t} + b_{i2}F_{2,t} + \cdots + b_{ik}F_{k,t} + e_{i,t} \qquad (11\text{-}15)$$

where $r_{i,t}$ = one-period rate of return from ith asset in period t

$\qquad a_i$ = riskless rate of return equals expected rate of return for asset i if all risk factors have a value of zero, $F = 0$

$\qquad F_{j,t}$ = jth risk factor (or communality) that affects assets' returns, where $j = 1, 2, \ldots, k$ different risk factors exist. These risk factors all have mathematical expectation of zero, $E(F_{jt}) = 0$

$\qquad b_{ij}$ = sensitivity indicator[5] (or factor loading) that measures how responsive returns from asset i are to index j

$\qquad e_{i,t}$ = random error term for asset i in period t, which measures unexplained residual return, and which has an expected value of zero and a variance of Var(e)

---

[3]See Robert Jarrow and Andrew Rudd, ''A Comparison of the APT and CAPM,'' *Journal of Banking and Finance,* June 1983, vol. 7, no. 2, pp. 295–303.

[4]The characteristic regression line from Chapter 10, Equation (10-3), is reproduced below as an orientation for those who may already be familiar with it.

$$r_{i,t} = a_i + b_i r_{m,t} + e_{i,t} \qquad (10\text{-}3)$$

Although Equations (10-3) and (11-15) are different return generating functions, they have enough in common to make comparing and contrasting them insightful.

[5]The b_{ij} term is called a *factor loading* if it is estimated using factor analytic procedures; it is called a *regression slope coefficient* if it is estimated via regression analysis. Equation (10-6) provides a mathematical definition of beta.

Return Generating Function in Risk-Premium Form

Some people worry that limiting the factors to only those which have an expected value of zero, $E(F) = 0$, will severely restrict the number of factors that can be used in APT. But this is not a problem. Taking the expected value of Equation (11-15) and subtracting that expectation from Equation (11-15) results in the equivalent Equations (11-15a) and (11-15b).

$$r_{i,t} - E(r_i) = \sum_{j=1}^{k} b_{ij}[F_{j,t} - E(F_j)] + e_{i,t} \tag{11-15a}$$

$$r_{i,t} = E(r_i) + \sum_{j=1}^{k} b_{ij}[F_{j,t} - E(F_j)] + e_{i,t} \tag{11-15b}$$

The new factors we have created in Equations (11-15a) and (11-15b), $[F_{j,t} - E(F_j)]$, will obviously always have zero expected values, $E[F_{j,t} - E(F_j)] = 0$. These new factors are sometimes called *unanticipated changes in factor j*. Equation (11-15a) is called the *return generating function in risk-premium form*. Equations (11-15), (11-15a), and (11-15b) are equally useful.

Unsystematic Risk Vanishes

Three statistical conditions (or assumptions) must be true of the return generating equations (11-15), (11-15a), and (11-15b).

1. The unexplained residuals between all assets must be independent, $E(e_i e_j) = 0$, where $i \neq j$.
2. All factors must be independent (or orthogonal), $E[F_i F_j] = 0$ for all i and j.
3. All factors must be independent of the unexplained residual, $E\{e_i, [F_j - E(F_j)]\} = 0$ for all j.

The three assumptions above result in diversified portfolios that have desirable properties. Contemplate the returns from a diversified portfolio; they are simply the linear weighted average of the returns from the assets in that portfolio.

$$r_{p,t} = \sum_{i=1}^{n} x_i r_{i,t}$$

$$= \sum_{i=1}^{n} x_i[a_i + b_{i1}F_{1,t} + b_{i2}F_{2,t} + \cdots + b_{ik}F_{k,t} + e_{i,t}] \tag{11-16}$$

The portfolio's betas are simply the linear weighted average of the assets' betas.

$$b_{pj} = \sum_{i=1}^{n} x_i b_{ij} \qquad \text{for } j = 1, 2, \ldots, k \text{ risk factors} \tag{11-17}$$

Taking the variance of both sides of Equation (11-15) yields the risk partition shown in Equation (11-18).

$$\text{Var}(r_{p,t}) = b_{1p}^2 \text{Var}(F_1) + b_{2p}^2 \text{Var}(F_2) + \cdots + b_{kp}^2 \text{Var}(F_k) + \text{Var}(e_{p,t})$$
$$(11\text{-}18)$$

| Total portfolio variance | = | sum of k different systematic risks | + | portfolio's residual variance |

Equation (11-18) contains no covariance terms because the risk factors are statistically independent (assumption 2 above).

Consider the case in which all n assets in the portfolio are equally weighted so all weights are equal, $x_i = 1/n$. In this case the portfolio's residual variance $\text{Var}(e_{p,t})$ can be rewritten in the following equivalent ways:

$$\sum_{i=1}^{n} x_i^2 \text{Var}(e_i) = \sum_{i=1}^{n} \left|\frac{1}{n}\right|^2 \text{Var}(e_i) = \left|\frac{1}{n}\right| \sum_{i=1}^{n} \left|\frac{\text{Var}(e_i)}{n}\right| = \left|\frac{1}{n}\right| \overline{\text{Var}(e)} \qquad (11\text{-}19)$$

where $\overline{\text{Var}(e)}$ represents the *average residual variance*. Consider the fact that as n grows large, Equation (11-19) asymptotically approaches zero.

$$\lim_{n \to \infty} \left|\frac{1}{n}\right| \overline{\text{Var}(e)} = 0 \qquad (11\text{-}20)$$

The result shown in Equation (11-20) was illustrated in Figures 9-1 and 9-3. This result is formalized here because it is important in all portfolio theories. Equation (11-20) and Figures 9-1 and 9-3 show why unsystematic risk is presumed to have no role in the asset pricing models derived from portfolio theories; *unsystematic risk can easily be diversified to zero.* As a result, the elegant asset pricing models like the CAPM and APT are only functions of undiversifiable risk measures. The diversifiable unsystematic risk has no asset pricing implications in the CAPM or the APT.[6]

Next, let us derive the APT from a particular return generating process like Equation (11-15).

---

[6] For refinements in Ross's original APT model see Gary Chamberlain, "Funds, Factors, and Diversification in Arbitrage Pricing Models," *Econometrica,* Sept. 1983, vol. 51, no. 5, pp. 1305–1325. Also see Gary Chamberlain and Michael Rothschild, "Arbitrage, Factor Structure, and Mean-Variance Analysis on Large Asset Markets," *Econometrica,* Sept. 1983, vol. 51, no. 5, pp. 1281–1304. In addition, see Philip H. Dybvig, "An Explicit Bound on Individual Assets' Deviations from APT Pricing in a Finite Economy," *Journal of Financial Economics,* Dec. 1983, vol. 12, no. 4, pp. 483–496. See also Gur Huberman, "A Simple Approach to Arbitrage Pricing Theory," *Journal of Economic Theory,* Oct. 1982, vol. 28, no. 1, pp. 183–191. And, see Jonathan E. Ingersoll, Jr., "Some Results in the Theory of Arbitrage Pricing," *Journal of Finance,* Sept. 1984, vol. 39, no. 4, pp. 1021–1039. See also Robert F. Stambaugh, "Arbitrage Pricing with Information," *Journal of Financial Economics,* Nov. 1983, vol. 12, no. 3, pp. 357–369.

11-3   DERIVING A TWO-FACTOR APT MODEL

A linear additive return generating process like Equation (11-15) underlies all APT. We will derive an APT model from a return generating function like Equation (11-15) that has $k = 2$ indices:

$$r_{i,t} = a_i + b_{i1}F_{1,t} + b_{i2}F_{2,t} + e_{i,t} \qquad (11\text{-}21)$$

If you want a concrete example, think of the first risk factor in Equation (11-21) as being the unanticipated change in GNP, $F_{1,t} = [GNP_t - E(GNP)]$, and the second risk factor $F_{2,t}$ as being the unanticipated change in the cash dividend payout ratio. Both factors are observed simultaneously over $t = 1$, $2, \ldots, T$ periods. There is nothing sacrosanct about these suggestions. *APT gives us no clue as to what indices could be relevant*—unlike the capital market theory, which is based on a solitary risk factor called the *market portfolio.*

Three Highly Diversified Portfolios

Consider three risk-averse investors who form portfolios B, C, and D that each contain n assets. In order to solve APT problems mathematically, we must assume that the number of assets exceeds the number of indices, $n > k = 2$ in this example, and that n is some large number.

Reconsider Equation (11-20) and Figures 9-1 and 9-3, and you will see the desirability of having a large number of assets. The larger n is, the more certain you can be that diversifiable risk disappears.[7]

The return from a two-factor portfolio is defined in Equation (11-22). Equation (11-22) is simply Equation (11-16) when $k = 2$.

$$r_{p,t} = \sum_{i=1}^{n} x_i [a_i + b_{i1}F_{1,t} + b_{i2}F_{2,t} + e_{i,t}] \qquad (11\text{-}22)$$

Equation (11-23) is the balance sheet identity which cannot be violated if the investor's portfolio is to have any rational interpretation. Equation (11-23) requires that the weights add up to zero, which is simply another way of asserting that no money is invested.

---

[7] If n is a small number, we might obtain an APT model composed of rough lines and surfaces with finite thicknesses which has no unique solutions. For two articles that show that the APT models derived with small values of n are approximate rather than exact, see Philip H. Dybvig, "An Explicit Bound on Individual Assets' Deviations from APT Pricing in a Finite Economy," *Journal of Financial Economics*, Dec. 1983, vol. 12, no. 4, pp. 483–496. Also see Mark Grinblatt and Sheridan Titman, "Factor Pricing in a Finite Economy," *Journal of Financial Economics*, Dec. 1983, vol. 12, no. 4, pp. 497–507.

$$\sum_{i=1}^{n} x_i = 0 \tag{11-23}$$

In a widely diversified portfolio (which means n is large), the unsystematic residual risk diversifies to zero, as indicated above in Equations (11-19) and (11-20). As the result, Equation (11-22) will contain only the two *systematic risk factors* shown below:

$$b_{1p} = \sum_{i=1}^{n} x_i b_{i1} \tag{11-24}$$

$$b_{2p} = \sum_{i=1}^{n} x_i b_{i2} \tag{11-25}$$

Table 11-1 shows the risk and return statistics for widely diversified portfolios B, C, and D.

APT Model

Equation (11-26) shows the *general form* of the APT model that can be derived from the two-factor return generating function of Equation (11-21). The two sensitivity values, b_{i1} and b_{i2}, are the *explanatory variables* in Equation (11-26).

$$E(r_i) = \lambda_0 + \lambda_1 b_1 + \lambda_2 b_2 \tag{11-26}$$

$$E(r_1) = 5.629 + 7.777 b_{i1} + 3.703 b_{i2} \tag{11-26a}$$

Equation (11-26a) shows the specific APT model, which can be derived from the numerical values in Table 11-1. Deriving the values for λ_0, λ_1, and λ_2 is explained below.

Any three points like $E(r_p)$, b_{i1}, and b_{i2} define a geometric plane. Equation (11-26a) is the formula for a specific three-dimensional plane in $[E(r_p), b_{i1}, b_{i2}]$ space. More specifically, Equation (11-26a) is an asset pricing model for the three portfolios in Table 11-1. Figure 11-4 illustrates the APT plane of Equation (11-26a). Substituting the numerical value for any of the three portfolios in

Table 11-1

RISK AND RETURN STATISTICS FOR THREE PORTFOLIOS

Portfolio	Expected return	b_{p1}	b_{p2}
B	$E(r_B) = 16.0\%$	1.0	0.7
C	$E(r_C) = 14.0\%$	0.6	1.0
D	$E(r_D) = 11.0\%$	0.5	0.4

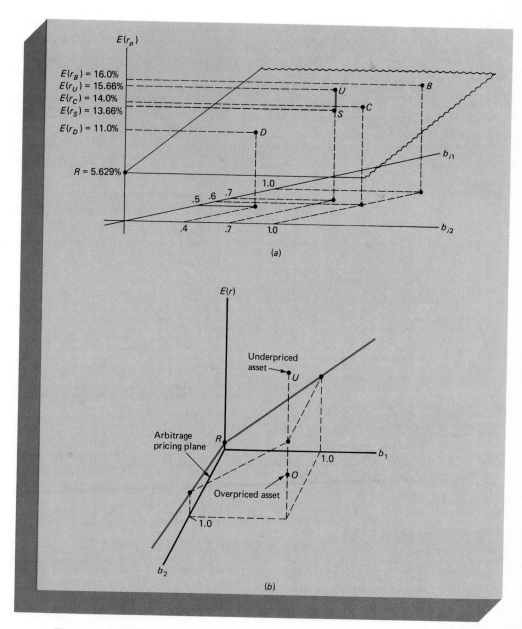

Figure 11-4 APT plane for two-factor model. (*a*) Illustration of the APT plane from Equation (11-26*a*); (*b*) an APT plane without any measurements.

Table 11-1 into Equation (11-26a) proves numerically that the three points all fit on this APT plane.[8]

Arbitrage Portfolio

In equilibrium, if a sufficiently large number of assets were to average the unsystematic risk to zero [as in Equations (11-19) and (11-20)] and if there were no transaction costs to impede the price revision process, the risks and return of every asset should conform to the APT model of Equation (11-26) and Figure 11-4. Consider a specific case where one asset is mispriced to see how the profit-seeking actions of arbitragers will realign prices.

Suppose that a wealth-seeking investor analyzes portfolio U in Table 11-2 and discovers that it is underpriced. To make this discovery, the investor had to analyze a portfolio with the same risks, like S. Portfolio S is made up of three equal investments of one-third each in portfolios B, C, and D from Table

[8]This footnote shows the mathematical derivation of Equation (11-26a) and the plane in Figure 11-4. The APT model of Equation (11-26) can be rewritten for the three portfolios in Table 11-1 as shown below.

$$E(r_i) = \lambda_0 + \lambda_1 b_{i1} + \lambda_2 b_{i2} \qquad (11\text{-}26)$$

$$16.0 = \lambda_0(1.0) + \lambda_1(1.0) + \lambda_2(0.7) \qquad (11\text{-}26b)$$

$$14.0 = \lambda_0(1.0) + \lambda_1(0.6) + \lambda_2(1.0) \qquad (11\text{-}26c)$$

$$11.0 = \lambda_0(1.0) + \lambda_1(0.5) + \lambda_2(0.4) \qquad (11\text{-}26d)$$

Equations (11-26b), (11-26c), and (11-26d) constitute three equations in three unknowns (namely, λ_0, λ_1, and λ_2), which are equivalently rewritten in matrix equations (11-27) and (11-27a) below.

$$\begin{bmatrix} 16.0 \\ 14.0 \\ 11.0 \end{bmatrix} = \begin{bmatrix} 1.0 & 1.0 & 0.7 \\ 1.0 & 0.6 & 1.0 \\ 1.0 & 0.5 & 0.4 \end{bmatrix} \begin{bmatrix} \lambda_0 \\ \lambda_1 \\ \lambda_2 \end{bmatrix} \qquad (11\text{-}27)$$

$$R \quad = \quad\quad C \quad\quad\quad \lambda \qquad (11\text{-}27a)$$

The vector of unknowns λ is evaluated by first finding the inverse of the coefficients matrix C. This inverse is denoted C^{-1}. The second step is to premultiply the inverse of matrix C by the return vector R, which yields the values of the vector of unknowns λ as shown below in Equations (11-28) and (11-28a).

$$\begin{bmatrix} -0.9629 & -0.1851 & 2.1481 \\ 2.2222 & -1.1111 & -1.1111 \\ -0.3703 & 1.8518 & -1.4814 \end{bmatrix} \begin{bmatrix} 16.0 \\ 14.0 \\ 11.0 \end{bmatrix} = \begin{bmatrix} 5.629 \\ 7.7777 \\ 3.7037 \end{bmatrix} = \begin{bmatrix} \lambda_0 \\ \lambda_1 \\ \lambda_2 \end{bmatrix} \qquad (11\text{-}28)$$

$$C^{-1} \quad\quad\quad\quad\quad R \quad = \quad \lambda \quad = \quad \lambda \qquad (11\text{-}28a)$$

The values for the lambdas in matrix equation (11-28) are used in APT Equation (11-26a).

Table 11-2

RISK-RETURN STATISTICS FOR TWO PORTFOLIOS

Portfolio	$E(r_p)$	b_{i1}	b_{i2}	Definition
S	13.66%	0.7	0.7	⅓B + ⅓C + ⅓D
U	15.66%	0.7	0.7	Underpriced

11-1. The two sensitivities and the expected return reported in Table 11-2 for portfolio S are calculated as follows:

$$E(r_S) = \tfrac{1}{3}E(r_B) + \tfrac{1}{3}E(r_C) + \tfrac{1}{3}E(r_D) \qquad (11\text{-}29)$$

$$13.66\% = \tfrac{1}{3}(16.0\%) + \tfrac{1}{3}(14.0\%) + \tfrac{1}{3}(11.0\%)$$

$$b_{S1} = \tfrac{1}{3}b_{B1} + \tfrac{1}{3}b_{C1} + \tfrac{1}{3}b_{D1} \qquad (11\text{-}30)$$

$$0.7 = \tfrac{1}{3}(1.0) + \tfrac{1}{3}(0.6) + \tfrac{1}{3}(0.5)$$

$$b_{S2} = \tfrac{1}{3}b_{B2} + \tfrac{1}{3}b_{C2} + \tfrac{1}{3}b_{D2} \qquad (11\text{-}31)$$

$$0.7 = \tfrac{1}{3}(0.7) + \tfrac{1}{3}(1.0) + \tfrac{1}{3}(0.4)$$

Portfolios S and U in Table 11-2 have identical risk statistics, but they have different expected rates of return. The *law of one price* says this should not happen. Since portfolios S and U have identical factor risks, they are perfect investment substitutes. Therefore, investors should buy portfolio U in order to get more return at the same risk as portfolio S.

In a theoretically ideal market, the smartest investors will use the law of one price to earn riskless arbitrage profits. By setting up an imperfect hedge with portfolios S and U, smart investors can create a profit without investing any money or taking any risks. Table 11-3 illustrates how a shrewd investor could sell $100 of portfolio S short, and then take the $100 from the short sale and buy a $100 long position in portfolio U. This no-money-invested charac-

Table 11-3

THE ARBITRAGE PORTFOLIO

Portfolio	Initial cashflow	Ending cashflow	b_{i1}	b_{i2}
S = short	+$100	−$113.66	−0.7	−0.7
U = underpriced (long)	−$100	$115.66	0.7	0.7
A = arbitrage (hedged)	0	+$2.00	0	0

teristic of the arbitrage portfolio (shown in the second column of Table 11-3) was formalized as Equation (11-12).[9]

Table 11-3 shows how the shrewd investor set up a riskless *arbitrage portfolio,* denoted A, which is made up of both long and short assets with identical risks. These identical long and short positions create a riskless hedge that can neither enjoy gains nor suffer losses from any price changes. Arbitrage portfolio A is riskless because any gains and losses from the long and short positions will exactly offset each other. The zero-systematic-risk-of-any-kind characteristic of the arbitrage portfolio is formalized in Equations (11-24) and (11-25).[10]

$$\sum_{p=1}^{p=2} x_p b_{p1} = 0 \qquad \text{no systematic risk of type one} \qquad (11\text{-}32)$$

$$\sum_{p=1}^{p=2} x_p b_{p2} = 0 \qquad \text{no systematic risk of type two} \qquad (11\text{-}33)$$

The third column of Table 11-3 shows that at the end of the arbitrage the closing cashflows sum up in favor of the arbitrager. In theory, this investor can sell portfolio U and collect the $100 investment plus the 15.66 percent return for a total of $115.66 cash inflow. At the same time, the investor must spend $113.66 to cover the $100 short position in portfolio S and pay the 13.66 percent interest (or cash dividend) that the person who bought $100 worth of S expected to receive for making this risky investment. After these cashflows, our theoretical investor will earn $2 profit without investing any money or taking any risk. In short, arbitragers will bid up the price of the underpriced portfolio U and thereby drive down its expected return, as indicated in Equation (11-34).

$$\downarrow E(r_U) = \frac{E(\$15.66 \text{ income per period})}{\uparrow \text{purchase price (bid upward)}} \qquad (11\text{-}34)$$

The arbitrage will continue until portfolio U is priced so that it lies on the APT plane at point *S* in Figure 11-4. In fact, arbitrage will cause the price of every asset to be revised until its expected return and risk statistics align with the APT model of Equation (11-26) and the associated APT plane illustrated in Figure 11-4.

[9]Note that Equation (11-12) is similar to, yet different from, Equation (11-23). They differ because Equation (11-12) is summing across the assets' prices. In contrast, Equation (11-23) is summing across portfolio weights. Conceptually, the two equations are identical; they both require that total inflows equal total outflows.
[10]Note that although they may appear similar at a glance, Equations (11-32) and (11-33) are different from Equations (11-30) and (11-31), because Equations (11-30) and (11-31) are averaging across B, C, and D while Equations (11-32) and (11-33) are summing across the objects in the arbitrage portfolio—namely, portfolios S and U.

The k-Dimensional APT Hyperplane

The k-factor return generating process of Equation (11-15) was abbreviated to Equation (11-21) for simplicity's sake. If this simplification were not employed, the k-factor APT model shown in Equation (11-35) would have been derived.

$$E(r_i) = \lambda_0 + \lambda_1 b_{i1} + \lambda_2 b_{i2} + \cdots + \lambda_k b_{ik} \qquad (11\text{-}35)$$

Equation (11-35) is the APT in a **k-dimensional hyperplane** that has all the implications suggested for the two-factor APT model.

11-4 COMPARING APT WITH THE CAPM

A moment's contemplation will reveal that the intercept term λ_0 in Equation (11-26) must equal the riskless rate of return for an asset with zero sensitivities to all the risk factors. Unlike the CAPM, the derivation of the APT does not depend on the existence of a riskless asset. However, if we define the return on a zero beta asset to be the riskless rate of return R, then if such an asset exists, it follows that $\lambda_0 = R$. By using this equality, we can rewrite the APT model of Equation (11-26) in the equivalent *risk-premium forms* shown as Equations (11-26.1) and (11-26.2).

$$E(r_i) - \lambda_0 = \lambda_1 b_{i1} + \lambda_2 b_{i2} \qquad (11\text{-}26.1)$$

$$E(r_i) - R = \lambda_1 b_{i1} + \lambda_2 b_{i2} \quad \text{since } \lambda_0 = R \qquad (11\text{-}26.2)$$

The lambda coefficient associated with the risk sensitivity to the jth index, denoted λ_j, measures the increase in the expected return required by investors to induce them to assume a one unit increase in b_{ij} risk. The λ_j coefficient thus measures the **market price of risk** for whatever risk is measured by b_{ij}.

The CAPM Is Equivalent to the One-Factor APT Model

When $b_{i1} = 1.0$ and $b_{i2} = 0$, then the APT Equation (11-26) reduces to Equations (11-26.3) and (11-26.4).

$$E(r_i) - R = \lambda_1 b_{i1} \qquad (11\text{-}26.3)$$

$$E(r_i) = R + \lambda_1 b_{i1} \qquad (11\text{-}26.4)$$

Equation (11-26.4) is equivalent to the capital asset pricing model (CAPM); λ_1 is defined in Equation (11-36). The b_i is the beta coefficient from the characteristic line of Equations (10-3) and (11-21).

$$\lambda_1 = E(r_m) - R \qquad \text{from Equation (11-26.4)} \qquad (11\text{-}36)$$

The mathematical equivalence of the APT one-factor model and the CAPM shows that the two models do not conflict. In fact, they complement each other—they use different economic logic to arrive at similar asset pricing implications.

The Characteristic Line Is Equivalent to the k-Factor Return Generating Function

The sensitivity coefficients from the k-factor return generating process [namely, the k different values of b_{ij} in Equation (11-15)] can each be multiplied by the covariance of their factor with the *market portfolio*, $\text{Cov}(F_j, r_m)$, and summed up to obtain the covariance between the return from the ith asset and the market portfolio.

$$\text{Cov}(r_i, r_m) = b_{i1} \text{Cov}(F_1, r_m) + b_{i2} \text{Cov}(F_2, r_m)$$
$$+ \cdots + b_{ik} \text{Cov}(F_k, r_m) + \text{Cov}(e_i, r_m)$$

where $\text{Cov}(e_i, r_m)$ is so small that omitting it will not introduce a substantial approximation. If, in actuality, there are more than k factors in the market portfolio, the equation above will result in an approximation. Omitting more factors will make the approximation worse. However, if the market portfolio contains k factors and they are all included in this equation, it will be exact.

Dividing both sides of the equation by the variance of the *market portfolio* results in the definition of the beta coefficient from the characteristic line, Equation (10-6), for asset i.

$$b_i = \frac{\text{Cov}(r_i, r_m)}{\text{Var}(r_m)} = \frac{b_{i1} \text{Cov}(F_1, r_m)}{\text{Var}(r_m)} + \cdots + \frac{b_{ik} \text{Cov}(F_k, r_m)}{\text{Var}(r_m)} + \frac{\text{Cov}(e_i, r_m)}{\text{Var}(r_m)}$$

This equation shows the precise relationship between the sensitivity coefficients in the k-factor return generating function and the beta coefficient for the same asset's characteristic line. Viewed in this context, the APT models simply refine the capital market theory models by decomposing them and restating them equivalently in terms of more basic risk factors. The algebraic equation above is another piece of evidence showing the similarity between the capital market theory of Chapter 10 and APT.

Burmeister and McElroy prepared empirical estimates of a linear factor model under various assumptions about the structure of the returns and the error terms.[11] Their insightful econometric work suggests that under reasonable assumptions the CAPM can be found nested inside of the APT. Wei analyzed the CAPM and APT models theoretically and showed that they are equivalent under plausible assumptions.[12] Wei went on to extend the CAPM and APT models and integrate them by including the CAPM's market portfolio within an APT model. Wei's extension provides the theoretical foundation for exciting new empirical research.

APT Employs Fewer Assumptions

All economic theories are based on one or more simplifying assumptions. Economic theories that are based on fewer and more realistic assumptions are easier to appreciate than more highly contrived theories because they are easier

[11]See Edwin Burmeister and Marjorie B. McElroy, "Joint Estimation of Factor Sensitivities and Risk Premia for the Arbitrage Pricing Theory," *Journal of Finance*, July 1988, pp. 721–733.
[12]See K. C. John Wei, "An Asset-Pricing Theory Unifying the CAPM and APT," *Journal of Finance*, Sept. 1988, pp. 881–892.

to learn, apply, and explain. APT and the capital market theory of Chapter 10 both employ simplifying assumptions. One of the arguments favoring APT over the capital market theory's CAPM is that the APT's greater generality is accomplished in spite of the fact that APT is based on fewer simplifying assumptions.

Like the capital market theory, APT assumes that investors prefer more wealth over less wealth. Both theories also assume that investors dislike risk. Stated in terms of the utility theory (explained in Chapter 19), both theories assume that all investors have positive but diminishing marginal utility and make investment decisions that will maximize their expected utility. These are realistic assumptions.

Other CAPM simplifying assumptions (explained in Chapters 10 and 20) that are shared by the APT are (1) capital markets are *perfect* and (2) investors have *homogeneous expectations*. Perfect markets is an assumption widely used by economists. By assuming that capital asset markets are perfect, economists exclude the possibility that prices are manipulated or distorted away from their equilibrium values.

Homogeneous expectations is a more heroic assumption. **Homogeneous expectations** implies that all investors share the same risk and return perceptions for any given asset. Both the CAPM and APT theories allow divergent statistical assessments for different assets. Assuming homogeneous expectations for any individual asset, however, simplifies the economic model by obviating the need for the model to explain the differences of opinion between investors' assessments of any one particular investment opportunity.

The CAPM is based on four assumptions: (1) rates of return conform to a normal probability distribution, (2) investors' utility of wealth functions exhibit positive but diminishing marginal utility, (3) a uniquely desirable investment called the *market portfolio* exists, and (4) riskless borrowing and lending is possible. Some supporters of the APT argue that it is superior to the CAPM because only the second assumption is needed to generate the APT.

Although the APT requires fewer assumptions than the more specific CAPM model, the APT does depend on one unique and fairly unrealistic assumption. The APT no-money-invested assumption, embodied in Equations (11-12) and (11-23), presumes that arbitraging short sellers are able to obtain 100 percent of the proceeds from their short sales to finance the purchase of their long positions.[13] Realistically, only a few large professional investors (such as bro-

---

[13]Federal Reserve Board margin requirements forbid amateur investors from taking positions with zero funds invested. Since amateur investors must meet margin requirements on both long and short positions with their own funds, they could not get their brokers to give them the cash proceeds from their short sale. Therefore, amateur investors will never comprise a powerful arbitrage force. However, specialist firms on the stock exchanges and brokerage houses obtain millions of dollars of proceeds from short sales in different securities every day. And only a few of these professionally managed multimillion-dollar arbitrage portfolios are needed to enforce the law of one price. See Edward M. Miller, ''A Problem in Textbook APT Examples,'' *Financial Management*, Summer 1989, vol. 18, no. 2, pp. 9–10.

kerage houses and specialist firms at stock exchanges) could possibly achieve anything approaching this utopian situation. Nevertheless, only a few well-funded arbitragers may be sufficient to support the law of one price, on which the APT is based.

11-5 EMPIRICAL TESTS

Empirical tests of the APT employ a procedure that is analogous to the procedure used to estimate the CAPM empirically.

Review of the Procedure for Estimating the CAPM Empirically

Getting empirical estimates of the CAPM is a two-step process. It is informative to recall how the CAPM is estimated in order to gain insights into how the APT tests proceed.

The CAPM's First-Pass Time-Series Regressions   Empirically testing the CAPM begins with a first-pass *time-series regression* for each different asset to estimate its characteristic line. Essentially, a list of one-period returns from the ith asset,

$$[r_{i,t}, r_{i,t+1}, r_{i,t+2}, r_{i,t+3}, \ldots, r_{i,t+T}]$$

are regressed onto a list of concurrent market returns.

$$[r_{m,t}, r_{m,t+1}, r_{m,t+2}, r_{m,t+3}, \ldots, r_{m,t+T}]$$

The market returns are the *independent (or explanatory) variable* that is used to explain the behavior of the ith asset's returns in the simple regression called the characteristic line, Equation (10-3).

$$r_{i,t} = a_i + b_i r_{m,t} + e_{i,t} \qquad (10\text{-}3)$$

CAPM's Second-Pass Cross-Sectional Regression   After regression Equation (10-3) is estimated for many different assets, a second-pass *cross-sectional regression* is used to measure the risk-return relationship between the average rates of return and the beta risk coefficients for the sampled assets. This, second-pass regression is another simple linear regression, as shown below.

$$\begin{pmatrix} \text{Average rate of} \\ \text{return for asset } i \end{pmatrix} = A + B \begin{pmatrix} \text{beta for} \\ \text{asset } i \end{pmatrix} + u_i \quad \text{for } E(u_i) = 0$$

where the u_i is the unexplained residual return for asset i. The cross-sectional regression above is an empirical estimate of the CAPM.

Two Different APT Empirical Estimation Procedures

Empirical estimates of an APT model can be obtained by using either factor analysis or regression analysis. Estimating the APT model with factor analysis is discussed before the regression analysis approach is considered.

APT's First-Pass Estimation Procedures Vary   Most computer algorithms that perform **factor analysis** accomplish two functions in their first-pass computation. The factor analysis algorithm analyzes time-series data over $T + 1$ periods' rates of return from n different assets and statistically *extracts* those risk factors that systematically affect the returns from the n assets in the sample. Stated differently, factor analysis *simultaneously analyzes* all the returns from n assets over $T + 1$ periods in its first-pass computation. The raw data matrix that is analyzed is below.

$$\begin{bmatrix} r_{1,t}, \ r_{1,t+1}, \ r_{1,t+2}, \ \dots, \ r_{1,t+T} \\ r_{2,t}, \ r_{2,t+1}, \ r_{2,t+2}, \ \dots, \ r_{2,t+T} \\ \cdot \\ \cdot \\ \cdot \\ r_{n,t}, \ r_{n,t+1}, \ r_{n,t+2}, \ \dots, \ r_{n,t+T} \end{bmatrix}$$

Factor analysis *extracts* its own explanatory variables called **factors** from the matrix of returns above. The purpose of factor analysis is to reduce the n by $T + 1$ data matrix of raw returns to a smaller k by $T + 1$ matrix of **factor scores** that explains all or most of the variation in the matrix of returns. The k factors extracted have factor scores like the $F_{i,t}$ value for the ith factor in period t, shown in the matrix of factor scores below.

$$\begin{bmatrix} F_{1,t}, \ F_{1,t+1}, \ F_{1,t+2}, \ \dots, \ F_{1,t+T} \\ F_{2,t}, \ F_{2,t+1}, \ F_{2,t+2}, \ \dots, \ F_{2,t+T} \\ \cdot \\ \cdot \\ \cdot \\ F_{k,t}, \ F_{k,t+1}, \ F_{k,t+2}, \ \dots, \ F_{k,t+T} \end{bmatrix}$$

When the factor analysis procedure is being used, the factor scores in the matrix above are used as the independent variables in the second phase of the first-pass APT computations.

The first-pass factor analysis computations accomplish more than the extraction of the factor scores. The second phase of the first-pass computation uses regression analysis to estimate the b_{ij} coefficients for the ith asset's sensitivity to the jth factor. These b_{ij} coefficients are called **factor loadings** or simply **factor betas**. Time-series regressions estimates of factor loadings for each asset are obtained by estimating Equation (11-15) for each of the n different assets.

More specifically, factor analysis yields factor scores in the first phase of its first-pass computation which are employed in the phase-two regression to get estimates of the factor loadings, denoted b_{ij}. Thus, the finished products from the first-pass factor analysis are factor loadings for each asset ($i = 1, 2, \dots, n$) and every risk factor ($j = 1, 2, \dots, k$). The APT factor betas are somewhat like the beta coefficients from the first-pass characteristic line estimates that are obtained when estimating the CAPM. The only difference is that the CAPM only considers the market portfolio instead of k different factors and, as a result, only requires one beta for each asset.

Estimates of the factor loadings (or betas) can also be obtained via multiple regression. Instead of using factor analysis to create the explanatory variables for Equation (11-15), some researchers use economic theory and their intuition to select empirical variables to use as the explanatory variables in multiple regressions. Then they use regression analysis to estimate Equation (11-15) for each of the n different assets they are investigating. Researchers who use regression analysis argue that it is superior to factor analysis because intellect is used to select the explanatory risk factors rather than a mysterious statistical extraction procedure that produces factors which the researchers are often unable to identify.

APT's Second-Pass Cross-Sectional Regression   Regardless of whether factor analysis or regression analysis was used to obtain the factor loadings in the first pass, the same second-pass regression is used to estimate the APT **factor risk premiums,** denoted λ_j. The cross-sectional model below is used to regress the assets' average returns $\bar{r}_i$ on their factor loadings b_{ij} and obtain estimates of the λ regression slope coefficients.

$$\bar{r}_i = \lambda_0 + \lambda_1 b_{i1} + \lambda_2 b_{i2} + \cdots + \lambda_k b_{ik} + u_i \quad \text{where } E(u_i) = 0$$

If the lambda risk premiums λ are significantly different from zero, the jth factor is said to be *priced* or *valued* by the market in the determination of market prices. The second-pass regression's goodness-of-fit statistics (such as the correlation coefficient) also indicate how well the factors explain the security's average returns.

A Study by Roll and Ross

Doctors Stephen Ross and Richard Roll (R&R hereafter) employed factor analytic techniques to analyze 1260 NYSE stocks that were divided into 42 groups of 30 stocks.[14] They analyzed daily stock price returns over a decade. In the first step of their study, R&R estimated the factor loadings. For their second step, they ran a separate cross-sectional multiple regression for each of the 42 groups of stocks. The cross-sectional regression coefficient λ_j for the jth factor loading is an empirical estimate of that factor's risk premium. One or more of these regression coefficients should be statistically significantly different from zero if the APT is to be substantiated.[15] The R&R study concluded that it was most likely that there were four or fewer important factors.[16]

[14]R. Roll and S. Ross, ''An Empirical Investigation of the Arbitrage Pricing Theory,'' *Journal of Finance,* Dec. 1980, vol. 35, pp. 1073–1103.
[15]R&R also tested to see if securities' variances had significant explanatory power over the stocks' average returns. Assets' variances should not be important if APT is valid because the diversifiable component of the returns can be diversified to zero. APT suggests that the only contribution to a portfolio's risk would be made by its factor loadings. R&R found that even though variances and average returns were highly correlated, the variance did not contribute to the explanatory power of an APT model.
[16]See Stephen J. Brown and Mark I. Weinstein, ''A New Approach to Testing Asset

(continues)

Four Factors Are Identified

Chen, Roll, and Ross (CRR) isolated four factors that significantly influenced securities returns.[17] These factors represented changes in the following four variables.

1. Unanticipated changes in the rate of inflation $[q - E(q)]$
2. Unanticipated changes in the index of industrial production $[\text{IIP} - E(\text{IIP})]$
3. Unanticipated changes in the yield spread between high-grade and low-grade corporate bonds $[\text{spread} - E(\text{spread})]$
4. Unanticipated changes in the slope of the term structure of interest rates, as measured by the difference between the yields on long-term government bonds and T-bills $[\text{slope} - E(\text{slope})]$

CRR's delineation of these factors corresponds with dividend discount models like Equation (15-2). The first two factors affect the numerator (that is, the income) and the last two factors affect the denominator (that is, the discount rate) of the present value of the future cash dividends model.

Chen's Tests

Professor Chen conducted a series of insightful empirical tests of APT.[18] He compared the empirical characteristics of APT and the CAPM using daily stock returns from 1963 to 1978. First, cross-sectional regressions of the historical average returns from the sampled stocks were related to the APT and CAPM models of Equations (11-37) and (11-38), respectively.

APT:

$$\bar{r}_i = \lambda_0 + \lambda_1 b_{i1} + \cdots + \lambda_k b_{ik} + e_i \qquad (11\text{-}37)$$

CAPM:

$$\bar{r}_i = \lambda_0 + \lambda_1 b_i + z_i \qquad (11\text{-}38)$$

where $b_{i1}, \ldots, b_{ik}$ = estimated factor sensitivities
b_i = estimated beta coefficient for stock i
e_i and z_i = unexplained residual returns

(continued)
Pricing Models: The Bilinear Paradigm," *Journal of Finance,* June 1983, vol. 38, no. 3, pp. 711–743. The B&W study suggests that common stock returns were consistent with the existence of three factors, but the existence of more than three factors was dubious.

[17]See Nai-Fu Chen, Richard Roll, and Stephen A. Ross, "Economic Forces and the Stock Market: Testing the APT and Alternative Asset Pricing Theories," *Journal of Business,* July 1986. Also see R. Roll and S. A. Ross, "The Arbitrage Pricing Theory Approach to Strategic Portfolio Planning," *Financial Analysts Journal,* May–June 1984, p. 14.

[18]Nai-Fu Chen, "Some Empirical Tests of the Theory of Arbitrage Pricing," *Journal of Finance,* Dec. 1983, vol. 38, no. 5, pp. 1393–1414.

The sensitivity measure on the first factor has the highest statistical significance. Therefore, it was noteworthy that the simple correlation coefficient between b_i and b_{i1} was found to be high and positive (in excess of .9) regardless of the market index used to estimate the betas b_i. This finding suggests that the first risk factor may somewhat resemble the *market portfolio*. In addition, the hypothesis that $\lambda_2 = \lambda_3 = \cdots = \lambda_k = 0$ in Equation (11-37) was rejected. This suggests that more than one risk factor should be considered.

Chen conducted a second test using cross-sectional regression equation (11-39).

$$\bar{r}_i = k\hat{r}_{i,\text{APT}} + (1 - k)\hat{r}_{i,\text{CAPM}} + e_i \tag{11-39}$$

Equation (11-39) relates the historical average return from the ith stock to a weighted average of the stock's average returns that are predicted by the right-hand sides of APT equation (11-37), $\hat{r}_{i,\text{APT}}$, and CAPM equation (11-38), $\hat{r}_{i,\text{CAPM}}$, respectively. Various estimates of Equation (11-39) all produced values of k that were in excess of 0.9; this finding implies that APT predicts average returns better than the CAPM.

Chen also formulated a third test that employed cross-sectional regression equations (11-40) and (11-41).

$$e_i = \lambda_0 + \lambda_1 b_i + w_i \tag{11-40}$$

$$z_i = \lambda_0 + \lambda_1 b_{i1} + \cdots + \lambda_k b_{ik} + u_i \tag{11-41}$$

where w_i and u_i are estimates of errors in the residual terms e_i and z_i from Equations (11-37) and (11-38), respectively, for the ith stock. This test was designed to detect unused information about stocks' expected returns that turned up as residue in the random error terms e_i and z_i. The tests were based on the idea that if a particular model was valid, its random error term should be *white noise*—the residuals should contain no additional information. Chen reported that the CAPM appeared to be econometrically misspecified in most cases. The APT model was able to explain some of the CAPM's unexplained residual returns. In contrast, the CAPM was unable to explain anything about the error terms from the APT model.

Chen formulated two additional tests based on empirical anomalies in the CAPM that can be interpreted as evidence against it. The tests were designed to see if (1) the total variance of a stock's returns or (2) the size of the issuing firm were cross-sectionally related to the stock's average return after removing that part of the return that was explained by the APT model. The results indicated that neither the firms' variances nor the firms' sizes had significant explanatory power over the unexplained residual return left by the APT. This is another shred of evidence in support of the APT.

There are criticisms of Chen's empirical tests, however; so, the empirical superiority of the APT is still dubious.[19]

[19]Professor Gehr appears to have published the first APT empirical study; see A. Gehr, "Some Tests of the Arbitrage Pricing Theory," *Journal of the Midwest Finance Association*, 1978. For criticisms of the APT empirical tests see Jay Shanken, "The APT: *(continues)*

11-6   SUMMARY AND CONCLUSIONS

The APT is a model that suggests how to price market assets. Prior to the APT, the capital asset pricing model (CAPM) was the most prominent financial theory to explain the prices of market assets. It is natural to compare and contrast these two important theories.

The APT requires fewer underlying assumptions and admits more different variables into the analysis than the CAPM. Therefore, the APT is a more general theory than the CAPM. However, the APT is mathematically equivalent to the CAPM when only one risk factor is considered. Other similarities also show that the two theories do not contradict each other. Moreover, the two theories are similar because both delineate *systematic communalities* that form the basis for risk premiums in market prices and returns.

Since APT has been in existence a relatively short time, it has not been tested extensively with empirical data. Results of the initial published tests are moderately favorable; they tend to suggest that the APT might have more empirical explanatory power than the CAPM.[20]

Essay Questions

11-1   The riskless rate of interest plays a key role in the APT. True, false, or uncertain? Explain.

11-2   Compare and contrast the role of the market portfolio in the CAPM with its role in the APT.

11-3   What does the APT tell us about the risk factors that should determine the size of the average (or expected) returns from market assets?

(continued)

Is It Testable?'' *Journal of Finance,* 1982, and Phoebus J. Dhrymes, Irwin Friend, and N. Bulent Gultekin, ''A Critical Re-examination of the Empirical Evidence on the Arbitrage Pricing Theory,'' *Journal of Finance,* June 1984, vol. 39, no. 2, pp. 323–346. For replies see Philip N. Dybvig and Stephen A. Ross, ''Yes, the APT Is Testable,'' *Journal of Finance,* Sept. 1985, vol. 40, no. 4, pp. 1173–1188; R. Roll and S. A. Ross, ''A Critical Re-examination of the Empirical Evidence on the Arbitrage Pricing Theory: A Reply,'' *Journal of Finance,* June 1984, vol. 39, no. 2, pp. 347–350; Jay Shanken ''Multi-Beta CAPM or Equilibrium APT?: A Reply,'' *Journal of Finance,* Sept. 1985, vol. 40, no. 4, pp. 1189–1196. And, see Phoebus J. Dhrymes, Irwin Friend, Mustafa N. Gultekin, and N. Bulent Gultekin, ''New Tests of the APT and Their Implications,'' *Journal of Finance,* July 1985, vol. 40, no. 3, pp. 659–674.

[20]For empirical tests favoring the APT over the CAPM see Nai-Fu Chen, ''Some Empirical Tests of the Theory of Arbitrage Pricing,'' *Journal of Finance,* Dec. 1983, vol. 38, no. 5, pp. 1393–1414. Also see Edwin Burmeister and Marjorie B. McElroy, ''Joint Estimation of Factor Sensitivities and Risk Premia for the Arbitrage Pricing Theory,'' *Journal of Finance,* July 1988, pp. 721–733.

11-4 Why is it claimed that the APT is a more general theory than the CAPM?

11-5 Empirical estimates of the riskless rate of interest obtained from estimates of the APT are far from realistic. True, false, or uncertain? Explain.

11-6 What problems cloud the results of empirical tests of the APT?

11-7 Compare and contrast the beta coefficient from the characteristic regression line with the sensitivity coefficient (or factor loading) in the APT.

11-8 The capital asset pricing model (CAPM) and the arbitrage pricing theory (APT) models are very similar. True, false, or uncertain? Explain.

Problems

11-9 Assume that a two-factor model is descriptive of reality, and determine the equation that describes the equilibrium returns for the following three portfolios:

Portfolio	$E(r_p)$	b_{i1}	b_{i2}
D	10%	1.2	0.8
E	12	2	0.5
G	14	2.1	1.2

Hint: You must solve three equations in three unknowns simultaneously; a computer program (like LOTUS 1-2-3, or some statistical software package) that does matrix inversion is the easiest way to solve the mathematics part of this problem.

11-10 Use the information in Problem 11-9 and assume that portfolio i exists and has the following characteristics:

$$E(r_i) = 14\% \qquad b_{i1} = 1.6 \qquad b_{i2} = 0.65$$

What arbitrage opportunities are present? *Hint: A portfolio that duplicates the risk factors of i can be created by investing appropriate amounts in portfolios D and E.*

11-11 Assume that a two-factor model is descriptive of reality, and determine the equation that describes the equilibrium returns for the following three portfolios:

Portfolio	$E(r_p)$	b_{i1}	b_{i2}
Q	11%	1	0.6
R	13	2	.1
Z	11	2	-0.6

11-12 Use the information in Problem 11-11, and assume the following portfolio called q exists:

$$E(r_q) = 15\% \qquad b_{q1} = 2 \qquad b_{q2} = -0.25$$

Arbitrage opportunities are present here; show how you can profit from them.

Hint: Create a portfolio with the same risk factors as q by investing in portfolios R and Z from Problem 11-11.

11-13 Assume that a single-factor model of the following form is descriptive of reality.

$$E(r_i) = 11\% + b_{i1}(5\%)$$

Also assume that the following two portfolios exist:

Portfolio	$E(r_p)$	b_{i1}
A	10.5%	0.5
B	15.5	1.5

An undervalued portfolio called Q exists that has a beta of 1.4 and an expected return of 18 percent. Show how an investor could take advantage of the arbitrage opportunities that exist here by constructing a new portfolio called Z that is composed of some to-be-determined proportions of portfolios A and B. If an investor purchases $1000 of portfolio Z and engages in arbitrage, what riskless gain will they earn? Assume the expected returns are all for 1 year.

11-14 The cash dividends per share of the OBC Company have been growing at an annual rate of 5.0 percent, and this growth rate is expected to continue unabated into the foreseeable future. OBC's current cash dividend is $2 per share. The following two-factor model is assumed to be appropriate for OBC:

$$E(r_{OBC}) = 10\% + b_{i1}(2\%) + b_{i2}(7\%)$$

The factor betas for OBC stock are:

$$b_{i1} = 1.5 \quad \text{and} \quad b_{i2} = 0.5$$

Use the information above and the present value model to value a share of OBC's stock. Use the dividend discount model for a stream of cash dividends that grows at a constant rate until infinity. *Hint: See Chapter 15 for the valuation model.*

11-15 Reconsider Problem 11-14 and assume that the betas for the two risk factors of OBC are changed to become:

$$1.25 = b_{i1} \quad \text{and} \quad -0.1 = b_{i2}$$

What will the value of OBC's common stock be if everything else stays the same?

11-16 The cash dividends of the TTT Corporation have been growing at a rate of 25 percent the last few years. Analysts expect this rate to continue for five more years and then fall to a more normal growth rate of 5 percent thereafter. The following three-factor model is assumed to be descriptive of stock market conditions.

$$E(r_i) = 9\% + b_{i1}(3\%) + b_{i2}(2\%) + b_{i3}(4\%)$$

The factor beta coefficients for TTT's stock are as follows:

$$b_{i1} = 1.5 \quad b_{i2} = -0.5 \quad b_{i3} = 0.5$$

If the TTT Corporation has a current cash dividend of 25 cents per share, what is the present value of one share of its common stock?

11-17 Reconsider Problem 11-16. If the factor betas for the three risk factors were changed to $1.2 = b_{i1}$, $1.0 = b_{i2}$, and $-0.75 = b_{i3}$, what would be the value of the TTT Corporation's common stock? Assume everything else except the risk factors stays the same as in Problem 11-16.

11-18 The General Enterprise Corporation (GEC) has a two-factor return generating function. GEC's stock is expected to earn a 4.0 percent rate of return if the economy is stagnant, $E(r_{GEC}) = a_{GEC} = 4.0\% = 0.04$. In addition, GEC has a beta on the rate of inflation of 0.9, and its beta on the percentage change in the gross national product (GNP) is 1.1. What rate of return do you expect GEC's stock to earn this year if the rate of inflation is 5.0 percent and the GNP rises 5.0 percent?

Selected References

Comrey, Andrew L., *A First Course in Factor Analysis* (New York: Academic, 1973).

   A mathematical statistics book that uses matrix algebra supplemented with easy-to-read examples to explain various approaches to factor analysis.

Dhrymes, Phoebus, "Arbitrage Pricing Theory," *Journal of Portfolio Management,* Summer 1984, pp. 35–44.

   An empirical study and critique of the APT that uses no rigorous mathematics.

Ross, Stephen A., "Return, Risk and Arbitrage," in I. Friend and J. Bicksler, eds., *Risk and Return in Finance* (Ballinger Press, Cambridge, Mass., 1976).

   Ross uses only algebra and statistics in this seminal presentation of the APT.

Wei, K. C. John, "An Asset-Pricing Theory Unifying the CAPM and APT," *Journal of Finance,* Sept. 1988, pp. 881–892.

   Mathematical statistics is used to show the conditions under which the CAPM and the APT are mathematically equivalent.

Part 3

Bond Valuation

Chapter 12

Market Interest Rates

Market interest rates change continuously (as shown in Figure 6-1). These fluctuations may be viewed as arising from two sources—sources that are *internal* and sources that are *external* to the bond issuer.

1. *Internal sources:* Most changes that occur within a bond issuer and that affect its bonds' prices and yields are caused by changes in the issuer's risk of default. Default risk is peculiar to corporate and municipal bonds and is the topic of Chapter 14.

2. *External sources:* Exogenous changes affect all issuers' bonds simultaneously. The supply of and demand for credit, the inflation rate, and other changes in the macroeconomic environment are external factors that affect all bonds' prices and yields. These external factors, which determine the level and structure of market interest rates, are the focus of this chapter.

The market interest rates analyzed in this chapter are also called the *appropriate discount rates* for finding a bond's present value, the *risk-adjusted cost of debt capital,* and/or the investor's *required rate of return.* But regardless of what you call these market rates of interest, calculating bond values is easy once the appropriate discount rates have been determined; just use the present value model of Equation (8-1).

12-1 **LEVEL OF INTEREST RATES**

This section deals with the *level,* not the *structure,* of interest rates. It considers such questions as why all interest rates are high, low, rising, or falling.

Fisher's Classic Theory about the Level of Interest Rates

In 1930 Irving Fisher articulated what many people consider to be the most logical explanation of what determines the level of all market interest rates.[1] Fisher suggested that nominal interest rates tend to rise and fall in a one-to-one correspondence with the rate of inflation.

Fisher's idea makes sense. Because interest rates and loans are stated in nominal money quantities rather than as real physical quantities, the nominal interest rate must contain an allowance for the rate of price change that is expected.[2] Otherwise, lenders' wealth would be eroded by inflation. For example, if a lender loans $100 for a year at 3 percent interest, the lender will be repaid $103. But, if an inflation rate of 10 percent exists, $E(\Delta P/P) = 10$ percent, this $103 will have the purchasing power of $1/1.1 = 90.9$ percent of $103, or $93.627, because of the inflation. Thus, the lender must charge 3 percent interest plus a 10 percent **inflation allowance,** or 13 percent per year, to allow for the inflation. In this case, the lender will be repaid $113 [=$100 times (100% + 3% + 10%)]. After 10 percent inflation, the $113 has a real purchasing power of $1/1.1 = 90.9$ percent of $113, or $102.72. The lender thus gains only a $2.72 increase, or 2.72 percent, in purchasing power by loaning money at 13 percent interest during a year in which inflation was 10 percent. This shows that lenders need to raise interest rates by at least the rate of inflation in order to maintain the real purchasing power of their wealth. This inflation adjustment is widely called the **Fisher effect.**

Fisher's theory is summarized formally by Equation (12-1).

$$\begin{matrix} \text{Nominal} \\ \text{interest} \\ \text{rate, } r_t \end{matrix} = \begin{matrix} \text{real} \\ \text{interest} \\ \text{rate, } rr_t \end{matrix} + E\begin{pmatrix} \text{rate} \\ \text{of} \\ \text{inflation, } q_t \end{pmatrix} \qquad (12\text{-}1)$$

Or, more concisely:

$$r_t = rr_t + E(q_t) \qquad \text{for } t = 1, 2, 3, \ldots$$

Theoretical equation (12-1) can be equivalently restated as Equation (12-1a) for empirical testing as a simple linear time-series regression.

$$r_t = a + bq_t + e_t \qquad \text{for } t = 1, 2, 3, \ldots, T \text{ periods} \qquad (12\text{-}1a)$$

The regression intercept term in Equation (12-1a) is an estimate of the real rate of return, $a = rr$. The unexplained regression residual has an expected value of zero, $E(e) = 0$, and b is the regression slope coefficient that estimates the

[1] Fisher first discussed the effects of inflation on market interest rates in Irving Fisher, *Appreciation and Interest* (New York: Macmillan, 1896), pp. 75–76. He expanded the ideas in Irving Fisher, *The Theory of Interest* (New York: Macmillan, 1930). These books are classics.

[2] The symbol E denotes the mathematical expectation and the Greek letter delta Δ means "finite change." If ΔP measures the change in the Consumer Price Index, this represents a change in the general level of prices. Therefore, $E(\Delta P/P)$ represents the rate of inflation expected by the consensus; it is represented by the convention q in this book.

impact that the rate of inflation has on the nominal interest rate in the simultaneous time period.

In Fisher's model the real rate of interest is assumed to be some positive constant, for instance, $rr = 0.03 \times 100 = 3$ percent. If the rate of inflation is expected to be, say, $E(q) = 0.10 \times 100 = 10$ percent, then that amount is added to the real rate to obtain an estimate of the nominal rate. In this example Fisher's interest rate theory would suggest that the nominal rate should be $r = rr + E(q) = 3\% + 10\% = 13\%$.

Fisher's suggestion that the real rate of interest should be a positive constant was too idealistic.[3] The real rate of interest can be determined empirically by observing nominal rates and the inflation rate.

$$r_t - q_t = rr_t = \text{realized real rate}$$

The real rate of interest that is realized is not constant. In fact, the real rate of return sometimes attains negative values. Unfortunately, Fisher's intuitively logical equation (12-1a) fails to describe reality as well as we might hope.[4]

Gibson's 1923 Findings Reconsidered

In 1923 A. H. Gibson published the two interest rate graphs shown in Figure 12-1.[5] When he suggested his interest rate theory in 1930, Fisher evidently overlooked Gibson's earlier interest rate graphs because Gibson's graphical findings contradict the interest rate theory Fisher set forth in Equation (12-1a).[6]

---

[3]Some respected financial economists have supported Fisher's view that the real rate of return should be a positive constant. For example, see E. F. Fama, "Short-Term Interest Rates as Predictors of Inflation," *American Economic Review,* June 1975, pp. 269–282. Also see C. R. Nelson and G. W. Schwert, "Short-Term Interest Rates as Predictors of Inflation: On Testing the Hypothesis That the Real Rate of Interest Is a Constant," *American Economic Review,* June 1977, pp. 478–486. Professor John Wood explains the flaws in the Fama and the Nelson-Schwert research; see J. Wood and N. Wood, *Financial Markets* (New York: Harcourt Brace Jovanovich, 1985), pp. 589–598.

For an empirical study of realized real rates (as contrasted with expected real rates) showing that (*a*) the real rate is not constant and (*b*) the real rate is sometimes negative, see Steven C. Leuthold, "Interest Rates, Inflation and Deflation," *Financial Analysts Journal,* Jan.–Feb. 1981, pp. 28–41. Also see Andrew K. Rose, "Is the Real Interest Rate Stable?," *Journal of Finance,* 1988, vol. 43, no. 5, pp. 1095–1112.

[4]Fisher's theory can be defended by saying Equation (12-1) refers to the *expected* rate of inflation rather than the *realized* rate of inflation. Unfortunately, it is difficult to measure expectations and test Fisher's theory in terms of expectations; the results of empirical tests have been sample dependent. In terms of empirically measured real returns, however, the evidence is unequivocal. Figure 7-2 illustrates real rates of return that are unstable and sometimes negative.

[5]A. H. Gibson, "The Future Course of High Class Investment Values," *Bankers Magazine* (London), Jan. 1923, pp. 15–43. A. H. Gibson's 1923 graph has been updated by adding the more recent data to obtain Figure 12-1.

[6]Keynes noted the contradiction between Gibson's graph and Irving Fisher's interest rate theory and called it the "Gibson Paradox." See J. M. Keynes, *A Treatise on Money* (New York: Macmillan, 1930).

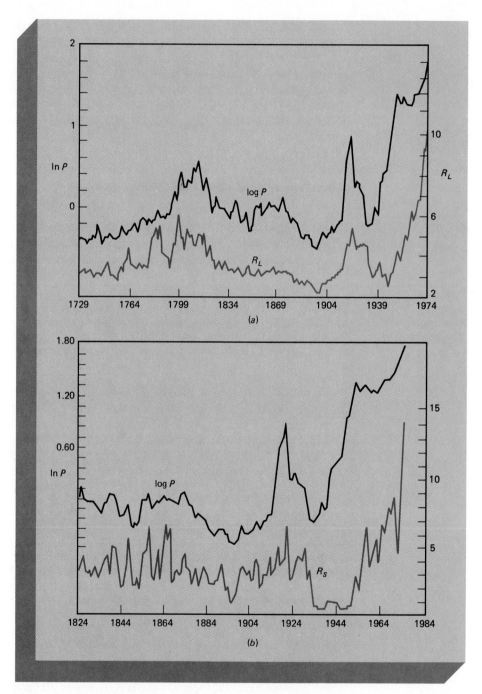

Figure 12-1 Natural logarithm of price index and (*a*) long-term interest rates and (*b*) short-term interest rates. *Source:* Robert J. Shiller and Jeremy J. Siegel, ''The Gibson Paradox and Historical Movements in Real Interest Rates,'' *Journal of Political Economy,* 1977, vol. 85, no. 5, pp. 892–893, figs. 1 and 2.

Figure 12-1a traces the paths of the market interest rate on long-term bonds and the logarithm of a price level index, denoted log(P), for 245 years. Figure 12-1b illustrates how the market interest rate on short-term bonds fluctuated with the same price level index data used in Figure 12-1b for 160 years. The long-term interest rates in Figure 12-1a are correlated .743 with log(P). In Figure 12-1b the short-term interest rates are correlated .421 with log(P).[7]

Figure 12-1a and b shows that both the nominal interest rates follow large movements in the price level, both upward and downward. Although the long-term interest rates in Figure 12-1a are more highly correlated with the price level index than are the short-term interest rates in Figure 12-1b, all three variables are positively correlated. In contrast, both of the nominal interest rates have very low correlations with the *rate of inflation*. The long-term interest rates in Figure 12-1a are correlated .045 with the rate of inflation; the short-term interest rates are zero correlated with the rate of inflation. These low correlations with the inflation rate mean that Fisher's theory and Equation (12-1a) cannot describe reality as well as the highly correlated relationships visible to the naked eye in Figure 12-1.[8]

Reformulating Fisher's Theory with Distributed Lags

Fisher knew that Equation (12-1a) might be too simple a model to obtain a good statistical fit. So, in his 1930 book he suggested, in addition to Equation (12-1a), a *distributed lag time-series regression model* like the one shown as Equation (12-1b).

$$r_t = a + b_0 q_t + b_1 q_{t-1} + b_2 q_{t-2} + \cdots + b_N q_{t-N} + e_t \qquad (12\text{-}1b)$$

The intercept term of multiple regression equation (12-1b) is an estimate of the real rate of return, $a = rr$, and the unexplained residual has an expected value of zero, $E(e) = 0$, as was also true in Equation (12-1a). The center portion of Equation (12-1b) is like the explanatory variable in Equation (12-1a) with N

---

[7]This section draws on the insightful paper by Robert J. Shiller and Jeremy J. Siegel, "The Gibson Paradox and Historical Movements in Real Interest Rates," *Journal of Political Economy,* 1977, vol. 85, no. 5, pp. 891–907.

Following A. H. Gibson, and Shiller and Siegel, the logarithm of the price index was used to compress the values of the price index so it would fit into Figure 12-1 with the small interest rate values. The high positive correlations between both market interest rates and the logarithm of the price index are still present if the logarithmic transformations are abandoned.

[8]Several economists have published empirical evidence to support Fisher's theory that nominal interest rates included an allowance for inflation. For example, see William E. Gibson, "Interest Rates and Inflationary Expectations: New Evidence," *American Economic Review,* Dec. 1972, pp. 854–865. The flaw in William Gibson's research is that if he had used sample data from a different sample period he would have gotten different results. For a critical analysis of Fisher's model and many empirical tests of it, see Robert J. Shiller and Jeremy J. Siegel, "The Gibson Paradox and Historical Movements in Real Interest Rates," *Journal of Political Economy,* 1977, vol. 85, no. 5, pp. 891–907.

previous periods' inflation rates added on and given the weights b_n over $n = 1, 2, \ldots, N$ past periods, respectively. Stated differently, Equation (12-2) suggests that expectations of inflation might be some weighted average of the inflation rates from N past periods, as follows:

$$E\left(\begin{array}{c}\text{rate of}\\ \text{inflation}\end{array}\right) = b_0 q_t + b_1 q_{t-1} + b_2 q_{t-2} + \cdots + b_N q_{t-N} \qquad (12\text{-}2)$$

Equation (12-1b) can be formulated in an infinitely large number of different ways. Each period's inflation rate can be assigned an equal weight of $b = 1/N$, or ascending or descending weighting schemes can be used, and N can be any positive integer. Over any given sample of data, if an econometrician tries enough different formulations of Equation (12-1b), one of them will eventually yield statistically significant explanatory power.

The most insightful thing about Fisher's distributed lag model is its similarity to Gibson's relationships exhibited in Figure 12-1. If N in Equation (12-1b) is increased to cover 5 or more years of past inflation rates and each period's inflation rate is given an approximately equal weight, Fisher's model will predict what we see in Figure 12-1!

Conclusions about the Level of Nominal Interest Rates

From the research of Irving Fisher and A. H. Gibson, we can draw some conclusions about what determines the *level* of nominal interest rates. A consensus of economists might agree on the following list.

1. The level of market interest rates *tends* to vary directly with large movements in the general price level. But, during a short-run period of several months (or even for 2 or 3 years) the level of market interest rates may vary inversely or not respond at all to movements in the general price level.

2. It is possible to find periods of years when Fisher's equation (12-1a) explains even the short-term movements in nominal interest rates very well. It is also easy to find periods of years when Fisher's equation has absolutely no ability to explain either the short-term or the long-term movements in nominal interest rates. In view of these results, Fisher's equation cannot be relied on for consistently predicting movements of nominal interest rates.

3. If Fisher's theory about the positive relationship between nominal interest rates and the inflation rate is reformulated with distributed lags, as in Equation (12-1b), it can be made to demonstrate statistically significant explanatory power. However, any econometric model that might be developed in this way will be very unstable from sample to sample.[9]

---

[9]To gauge the instability in various versions of Fisher's distributed lag models see Thomas F. Cargill and Robert A. Meyer, "Intertemporal Stability of the Relationship between Interest Rates and Price Changes," *Journal of Finance*, Sept. 1977, pp. 1001–1015.

4. The tendency of nominal interest rates to respond slowly and weakly to changes in the rate of inflation means the real interest rates realized from security investing tend to be negatively correlated with the inflation rate. This inverse correlation is most consistently observable over short-period returns, for example, monthly returns.

5. Even though Fisher's inflation allowance theory about nominal interest rates is difficult to formulate so that it can be used statistically, it is an intellectual tool that is useful. Stated differently, Equation (12-1) may only yield rough approximations, but it is nevertheless a useful way to think about the relationship between inflation and nominal interest rates.

6. Explanatory factors other than the rate of inflation, which are represented by the unexplained residual e_t in Equations (12-1a) and (12-1b), also influence the level of nominal interest rates.

Financial economists routinely study current events and the business cycle and make predictions about the level of interest rates. Some of the noninflation explanatory factors they study are discussed next.

Supply of and Demand for Credit

Figure 12-1a and b illustrates changes in the *level* of interest rates that are unrelated to the *rate of inflation*. These changes in the interest rate result from various changes in the supply of and demand for loanable funds, the ebb and flow of the business cycle, the Federal Reserve's monetary policies, risk premiums, and other factors.

The Business Cycle   The business cycle affects credit conditions by affecting the supply of and the demand for funds. Economists at banks, bond portfolio managers, and others who must forecast day-to-day changes in interest rates study *flow-of-funds* data that show where credit inflows (savings) and credit outflows (borrowings) originate in an effort to ascertain the effects of short-run changes in the supply of and demand for loanable funds.[10] During a period of economic expansion, the unemployment rate falls, business activity quickens, and businesses borrow money to build bigger plants and to finance more inventory. The resulting credit demands bid up interest rates. In contrast, during slow-downs and recessions, unemployment increases, manufacturing activity slows, demand for credit shrinks, and so interest rates fall, if all other factors are constant.

Treasury Borrowing and "Crowding Out"   President Ronald Reagan pushed income tax cuts through the Congress during his first term in the White House,

---

[10]See Rudolf Hauser, "Flow of Funds," in Frank J. Fabozzi and Harry I. Greenfield, eds., *The Handbook of Economic and Financial Measures* (Homewood, Ill.: Dow Jones–Irwin, 1984), chap. 12.

1980–1984. But Congress did not reduce the level of federal spending to reflect these reduced tax revenues. As a result, federal budget deficits of $150 to $200 billion per year occurred repetitively during the 1980s. The U.S. Treasury had to sell $150 to $200 billion of bonds per year to raise the money to pay for the government's deficit spending. These huge back-to-back deficits caused serious problems.

During the 1980s, businesses and the U.S. Treasury were competing to borrow whatever loanable funds were available. The resulting demand for credit exceeded the available supply of loanable funds and some businesses were *crowded out* of the credit markets by the massive borrowing demands of the U.S. Treasury. This borrowing competition between businesses and the federal government bid up market interest rates to levels above what they would have been if the government had balanced its budget.

Essentially, market interest rates may be viewed as being the "price" of credit. When the demand for credit exceeds the supply of loanable funds, market interest rates are bid upward by those seeking to borrow.

The Federal Reserve's Monetary Policies   The **Federal Reserve** is the part of the U.S. federal government that oversees the banking system and is charged with controlling the money supply, flow of credit, interest rates, and inflation rate. The Federal Reserve develops objectives for itself in terms of the dollar value of the nation's aggregate money supply and the level of selected interest rates. Then the "Fed" uses its ability to create and extinguish money to achieve its objectives.

The Federal Reserve has considerable power to influence the movements of market interest rates. As a result, large investment banking firms and the nation's largest commercial banks each have vice presidents, managing directors, and partners whose job title is "economist" and whose primary assignment is to study the Federal Reserve and try to anticipate its effects on market interest rates.[11] Furthermore, newspapers like *The Wall Street Journal* continually report rumors about the Fed's confidential actions because they can have immediate effects on market interest rates.

Inflationary expectations, the phase of the business cycle, the size of the federal deficit and how it is being financed, and the Federal Reserve's day-to-day actions are some of the main factors affecting interest rates. But various "yield spreads" that rise and fall can also have a significant effect on market interest rates.

---

[11]See William C. Melton, "Fedwatching and the Federal Funds Market," in Frank J. Fabozzi and Harry I. Greenfield, eds., *The Handbook of Economic and Financial Measures* (Homewood, Ill.: Dow Jones–Irwin, 1984), chap. 20.

Table 12-1
AVERAGE YIELDS AND A YIELD SPREAD AT PEAKS AND TROUGHS

Date	AAA	AA	A	BBB	I-T*	BBB less I-T*
August 1957 (peak)	4.13%	4.27%	4.39%	5.11%	3.84%	1.27%
April 1958 (trough)	3.63	3.82	4.03	4.82	2.58	2.24
April 1960 (peak)	4.44	4.56	4.75	5.34	4.13	1.21
February 1961 (trough)	4.28	4.40	4.66	5.22	3.74	1.48
December 1969 (peak)	7.65	7.83	8.10	8.67	7.47	1.20
November 1970 (trough)	7.79	8.31	8.69	9.38	6.52	2.86
November 1973 (peak)	7.76	7.95	8.17	8.67	6.83	1.84
March 1975 (trough)	8.63	8.86	9.08	9.66	6.92	2.74
January 1980 (peak)	10.98	11.36	11.59	12.12	10.70	1.42
July 1980 (trough)	10.63	10.96	11.25	12.10	9.72	2.38
July 1981 (peak)	14.11	14.54	14.79	15.74	14.11	1.63
November 1982 (trough)	10.95	11.33	11.88	13.19	10.09	3.10

*I-T stands for an average yield of *intermediate-term* U.S. Treasury bonds.
Source: Official National Bureau of Economics Research (NBER) Peaks and Troughs. Yields from Standard & Poor's *Security Price Index Record,* 1988.

12-2 YIELD SPREADS

Yield spreads are the differences between the yields of any pair of bonds— usually a default-free U.S. Treasury bond and another, more risky bond. Yield spreads are defined in Equation (12-3) for the tth instant in time.

$$(\text{Yield spread})_t = \left(\begin{array}{c} \text{Yield on} \\ \text{risky bond} \end{array} \right)_t - \left(\begin{array}{c} \text{U.S. Treasury} \\ \text{bond yield} \end{array} \right)_t \qquad (12\text{-}3)$$

Yield spreads like the one in Equation (12-3) are also called **risk premiums** because they measure the additional yield that risky bonds pay to induce investors to buy them rather than risk-free Treasury bonds.

Yield Spreads Move with the Business Cycle

The market interest rate data in Table 12-1 show that yield spreads vary with the business cycle.[12] The right-hand column of Table 12-1 shows, for example, how the average risk premiums on BBB-grade bonds varied over the business

[12]Roll and Ross report a statistically significant relationship between common stock returns and the (orthogonalized) market interest rate yield spreads (and several other economic variables too). See Richard Roll and Stephen Ross, "The Arbitrage Pricing Theory Approach to Strategic Portfolio Planning," *Financial Analysts Journal,* May–June 1984, pp. 14–29.

cycle. If other yield spreads were calculated from the data, they would show that all risk premiums tend to be larger at economic troughs than at the peaks in economic activity. This cyclical fluctuation can be forecast and used to establish profitable hedges and spreads between different bonds that are expected to have opening or closing yield spreads.

Risk Premiums Are Largest at Economic Troughs   Risk premiums are higher at economic troughs for two main reasons. First, unemployment, fear of job loss, and risk aversion are higher during recessions. Therefore, most investors demand larger risk premiums to induce them to buy risky bonds. Second, corporate bond issuers typically experience reductions in their sales and profits during recessions. Since the issuers are more subject to bankruptcy during recessions, investors require larger risk premiums.[13] These cyclical changes in the risk premiums are a second reason why market interest rates fluctuate. However, there are other noncyclical causes of changes in risk premiums.

12-3   **TERM STRUCTURE OF INTEREST RATES**

Figure 12-1 shows that varying inflationary expectations and changing credit conditions cause the *level* of market interest rates to vary over a wide range. The *level* of interest rates is different from the ''term structure of interest rates.'' For a given bond issuer, the *structure* of nominal interest rates for a set of bonds that differ only with respect to the length of time until they reach maturity is called the **term structure of interest rates.** The phrase **yield curve** is a synonym for the *term structure of interest rates.*

The yield curve for U.S. Treasury bonds that existed at a particular date is graphed in Figure 12-2—it is a line of best fit. All Treasury securities do not

---

[13]See Lawrence Fisher, ''Determinants of Risk Premiums on Corporate Bonds,'' *Journal of Political Economy,* June 1959, pp. 217–237. Also see W. Braddock Hickman, *Corporate Bond Quality and Investor Experience* (Princeton, N.J.: Princeton Univ. Press, 1958) and *Statistical Measures of Corporate Bond Financing since 1900* (Princeton, N.J.: Princeton Univ. Press, 1960). See also George E. Pinches and Kent A. Mingo, ''A Multivariate Analysis of Industrial Bond Ratings,'' *Journal of Finance,* March 1973, pp. 1–18. In addition to the risk premiums which investors demand and which *vary over the business cycle,* the current supply of and demand for loanable funds also affects yield spreads; see Ray C. Fair and Burton G. Malkiel, ''The Determination of Yield Differentials between Debt Instruments of the Same Maturity,'' *Journal of Money, Credit and Banking,* Nov. 1971, pp. 733–749.

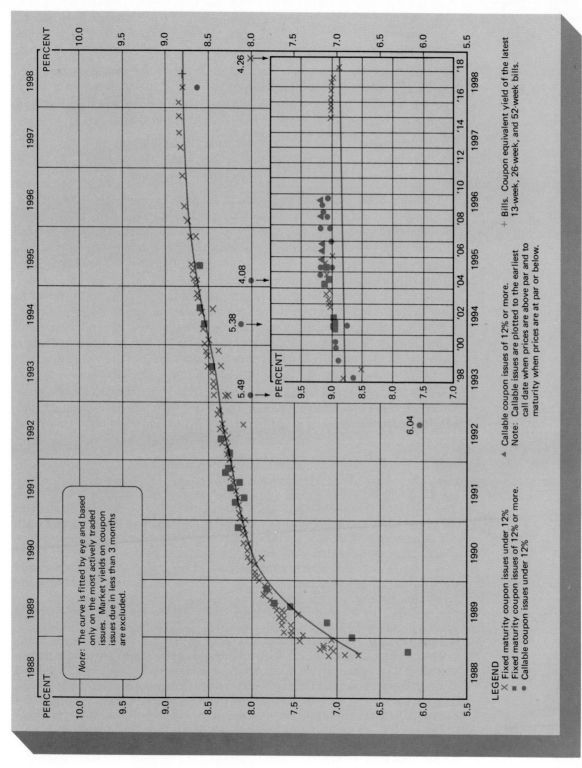

Figure 12-2 The Treasury yield curve of June 30, 1988 based on closing bid quotations. *Source: Treasury Bulletin,* Sept. 1988, p. 51, Office of the Secretary, Department of Treasury, Washington, D.C.

lie precisely on the yield curve because the issues differ with respect to their coupons,[14] callability,[15] and taxability.[16]

Since a bond's term to maturity affects its nominal interest rate, Equation (12-1) must be extended as shown below in Equation (12-4).

$$
\begin{matrix}
\text{Nominal} \\ \text{interest} \\ \text{rate, } r
\end{matrix}
=
\begin{matrix}
\text{real} \\ \text{interest} \\ \text{rate, } rr
\end{matrix}
+ E
\begin{pmatrix}
\text{rate} \\ \text{of} \\ \text{inflation}
\end{pmatrix}
+
\begin{matrix}
\text{default} \\ \text{risk} \\ \text{premium}
\end{matrix}
+
\begin{matrix}
\text{maturity} \\ \text{premium}
\end{matrix}
\qquad (12\text{-}4)
$$

Equation (12-4) differs from Equation (12-1) in two respects. The first difference is that **default risk premiums** were added to Equation (12-4). Figure 14-1 shows the structure of default risk premiums at several dates. A detailed discussion of default risk premiums is provided in Chapter 14. The second change is that a **maturity premium** is added into Equation (12-4) to reflect the effects of the term structure.

The *term structure of interest rates* changes a little every day, and in addition, there are different yield curves for each risk class of bonds. The yield curve for AAA corporate bonds, for example, is different from the yield curve for U.S. Treasury bonds on any given day. Figure 12-3 shows several hypothetical yield curves for bonds from different default risk classes. The yield curves for the riskier classes of bonds are at a higher level than the yield curves for less risky bonds as a result of the *default risk premiums*. We shall confine our attention to the yield curve for U.S. Treasury bonds (until we reach Chapter 14). By restricting discussion to marketable U.S. government bonds, we have,

---

[14]A yield curve created from only zero coupon bonds differs from a yield curve created from coupon-paying bonds. This difference has been called the **coupon bias** by Bierwag; see Gerald Bierwag, *Duration Analysis* (Cambridge, Mass.: Ballinger Press, 1987). Appendix 12B explains why *coupon bias* will preclude many bonds from being located on a yield curve that is constructed using yields-to-maturity (YTMs). Appendix 12B also suggests that by creating a yield curve from *spot rates,* which are defined below, coupon bias can be avoided.

[15]Some issues of Treasury securities are *callable* before their maturity date. Investors require a higher yield to be induced to assume the risk that the bonds might be called before they mature.

[16]**Flower bonds** are a subset of all Treasury bonds that the Internal Revenue Service will accept at their full face value for payment of federal inheritance taxes. To the extent that flower bonds can be bought at a discount from their face value and given to the IRS before they mature, they can provide some exemption from inheritance taxes. As a result of this tax exemption, flower bonds have lower yields than normally taxable T-bonds that are similar in all other respects. In fact, the amount of discount or premium from par included in any taxable bond's purchase price affects its after-tax yield and its price. These tax effects explain why some Treasury securities do not lie precisely on the yield curves created from coupon-paying bonds. To avoid **taxability bias** only bonds selling at their par values can be used to create a yield curve; the result is called the **par bond yield curve.**

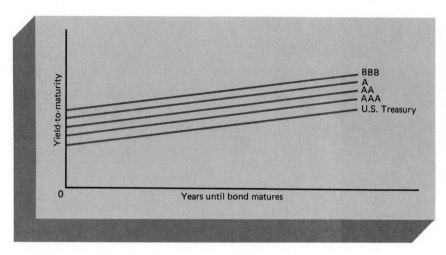

Figure 12-3 Yield curves for different default classes at a point in time.

in financial parlance, focused on the **Treasury yield curve.** Figure 12-4 shows graphs of historical yield curves; these yield curves illustrate how the term structure of interest rates has varied over several decades.

12-4   **THREE THEORIES ABOUT YIELD CURVES**

There are three main theories about how the shape of the yield curve is determined:

1. The **liquidity premium theory** asserts that, on average, the yields from long-term bonds should be a little higher than the yields from short-term bonds. This theory maintains that investors pay a price premium (resulting in lower yields) on short maturities to avoid the higher interest rate risk prevalent in the longer maturities. Thus, an upward sloping yield curve is considered ''normal.''

2. The **segmentation theory** asserts that the yield curve is composed of a series of somewhat independent maturity segments. For example, commercial banks predominantly purchase short maturities, savings and loan associations mainly demand intermediate maturities, and pension funds purchase long-term bonds. This oversimplified example suggests why yields on each segment of the yield curve are determined independently by the supply and demand conditions peculiar to that maturity segment.

3. The **expectations theory** asserts that long-term yields are the average of the short-term yields expected to prevail during the intervening period.

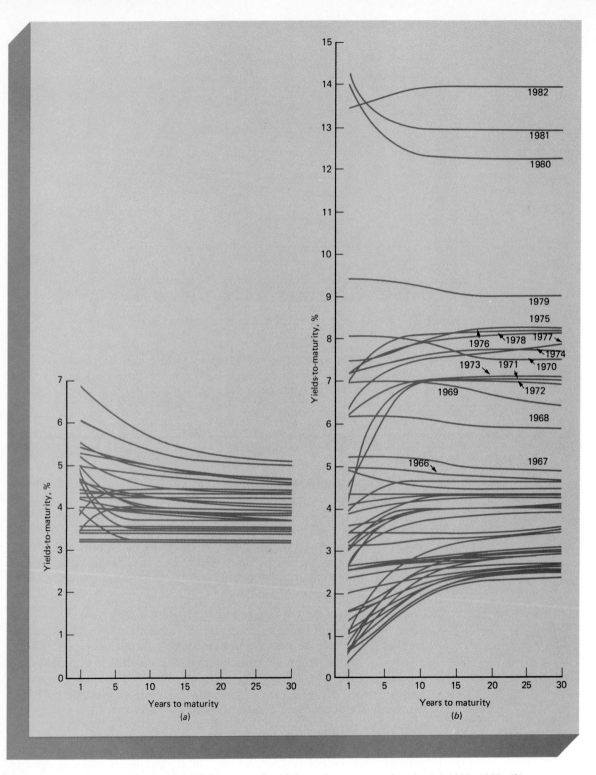

Figure 12-4 Yield curves for high-grade corporate bonds. (*a*) 1900–1929; (*b*) 1930–1982.

This implies that if all investors expect rates to rise, the yield curve will slope upward; if they expect rates to remain unchanged, the yield curve will be horizontal; if they expect rates to fall, the yield curve will slope downward.

We will consider each of the three theories about the term structure of interest rates separately. After the three theories have been explained, they will be integrated into one unified theory. Remember, however, that some people adhere to only one of these theories and believe that it alone explains the term structure of interest rates.

Liquidity Premium Hypothesis

Long-term bonds have more interest rate risk than short-term bonds because the prices of long-term bonds fluctuate more than the prices of shorter-term bonds (even though, as Figure 12-4 shows, long-term rates fluctuate less than short-term rates).[17] These large price fluctuations in the longer-term bonds provide the basis for the *liquidity premium hypothesis.*

> Liquidity preference produces asymmetry in the relationship between short-term and long-term rates at cycle peaks and troughs. It accounts for the failure of short-term rates to exceed long-term rates at peaks by as much as they fall below long-term rates at troughs.[18]

Advocates of the liquidity premium theory support their opinion by taking yield curves from each phase of several business cycles and showing that the average of short-term Treasury bond rates is less than the average of long-term Treasury bond rates. Graphically speaking, this means that, on average, the yield curve is upward sloping. Although this is usually true, it does not prove the validity of the liquidity premium theory.

Four reasons why the liquidity premium theory might be reversed (that is, why higher rates should be observed for short-term bonds) have been suggested.[19] First, with the passage of time, short-term rates fluctuate in an uncertain manner. Investors in short-term maturities must, therefore, face a series of reinvestments at risky and uncertain returns. Second, increased transaction

[17]J. B. Yawitz, G. H. Hempel, and W. J. Marshall, "The Use of Average Maturity as a Risk Proxy in Investment Portfolios," *Journal of Finance,* May 1975, vol. XXX, no. 2, tables 1 and 2.
[18]R. Kessel, *The Cyclical Behavior of the Term Structure of Interest Rates,* National Bureau of Economic Research, Occasional Paper No. 91, 1965.
[19]F. Modigliani and Richard Sutch, *Supplement to Journal of Political Economy,* August 1967, 569–589. Also see B. P. Malkiel, *The Term Structure of Interest Rates* (Princeton, N.J.: Princeton Univ. Press, 1966), for a discussion of the liquidity premium hypothesis.

and information costs required to refinance frequently in the short-term maturities (instead of in fewer, longer-term bond issues) reduce net returns from such investments. Third, investors in long-term bonds can reduce their risk by hedging (that is, by synchronizing their assets and liabilities to mature simultaneously). For instance, long-run funds requirements can be hedged by buying long-term bonds that mature when the investor expects the funds will be needed. Fourth, the yield curve could slope downward because investors expect lower inflation premiums, and consequently, lower interest rates, in the future than at present. Here, then, are four possible reasons why the long-term bonds might sell at higher prices and lower yields.

Despite these challenges to the liquidity premium theory, it contains some truth and most economists consider it in their thinking. Short-term bonds are more like money than long-term bonds, and investors are willing to pay higher prices (and accept lower yields) for that liquidity.

Segmentation Theory

The segmentation theory asserts that lenders and borrowers confine themselves to certain segments of the yield curve for the following reasons:

1. Regulations, called **legal lists,** limit the types of investments that banks, savings and loan associations, insurance companies, and other institutions are allowed to make.
2. The high cost of information leads investors to specialize in one market segment.
3. The fixed maturity structure of the liabilities that various bond investors tend to have tends to cause these investors to *hedge* their liabilities with assets of equivalent maturity.
4. Simple preferences that are not dependent on theories or plans.

Because of these considerations the rates on different maturities tend to be determined independently by the differing supply and demand conditions in the various market segments.

The segmentation theory is also referred to as the **hedging theory.** The implication of this name is that investors are typically obligated by some particular maturity pattern of liabilities. Given the maturity of their liabilities, investors can hedge against capital losses in the bond market by synchronizing the maturities of their assets and liabilities. Thus, investors are confined to some maturity segment which corresponds their liability maturities. For this reason the market segmentation theory is sometimes also called the **preferred habitat theory.** Figure 12-5 shows a grossly simplified conception of how the yield curve might be segmented.

Some profit-seeking arbitragers earn their living by smoothing out irregularities in the yield curve. Although these professional arbitragers may be few

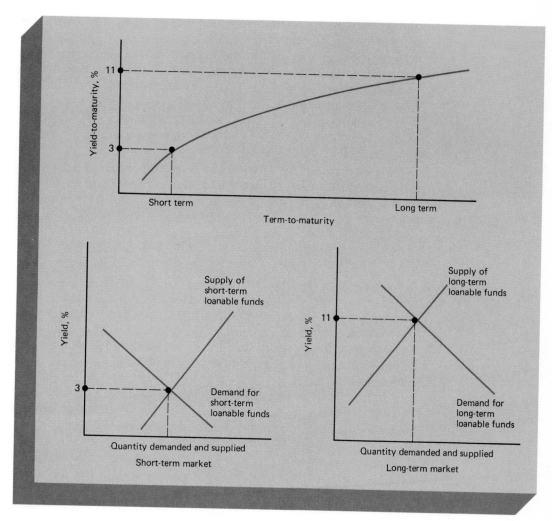

Figure 12-5 Illustration of segmented yield curve.

in number, their presence and effectiveness are attested to by the lack of profitable arbitrage opportunities existing in the yield curve of any date.[20]

[20]Yield curves are often estimated simply by "eyeballing" a line of best fit through data points representing bonds in a homogeneous default-risk class. However, scientific methods have also been developed to eliminate coupon bias and taxability bias. Some of the algorithms tend to generate smooth yield curves; see S. W. Dobson, "Estimating Term Structure Equations with Individual Bond Data," *Journal of Finance*, March 1978, pp. 75–92. Also see A. Vasicek and H. Gifford Fong, "The Tax Adjusted Yield Curve," *Journal of Finance*, June 1975, pp. 811–830. Some algorithms generate more disjointed estimates of the yield curve; see J. H. McCulloch, "Measuring the Term Structure of Interest Rates," *Journal of Business*, Jan. 1971, pp. 19–31.

**Expectations
Hypothesis**

The **expectations hypothesis** asserts that the long-term rates are the average (or, more precisely, the geometric mean) of the short-term rates expected to prevail between the current period and the maturity date of the bonds.[21] For example, using the simple arithmetic average, if 1-year rates are now 10 percent and 1-year rates are expected to be 12 percent next year, then rates on 2-year bonds today will be approximately 11 percent.

$$11\% = \frac{10\% + 12\%}{2 \text{ years}} = 2\text{-year average}$$

If we assume that the 1-year forward rate we expect to exist 3 years ahead is 14 percent, we can calculate the current (or spot) rate on a 3-year loan to be the average of the next three consecutive 1-year future rates, as shown below.

$$12\% = \frac{10\% + 12\% + 14\%}{3 \text{ years}} = 3\text{-year average}$$

In developing the expectations hypothesis, we will discuss two types of interest rates—the ''spot rate'' and the ''forward rate.'' **Forward rates,** denoted $_tF_{t+1}$, refer to the yields for bonds that are expected to *exist in the future.* More specifically, $_tF_{t+1}$ denotes the market interest rate that is currently expected to apply to some future 1-year bond that will exist during period t. **Spot rates,** denoted $_0S_t$, refer to the interest rates for bonds which *currently exist* and are being traded currently, at time $t = 0$. More specifically, $_0S_n$ denotes the market interest rate for a currently existing bond that matures n periods in the future. These conventions are used in making the rigorous statement of the expectations hypothesis shown as the system of equations numbered (12-5) in Table 12-2.[22]

The forward rates $_1F_2$, $_2F_3$, . . ., $_{n-1}F_n$ are implicit; that is, these interest rates on future bonds cannot be observed. In contrast, the spot rates $_0S_n$ can be observed—they are printed in the daily newspapers. This means that the implicit future rates must be determined for any future period or series of future years by solving the series of equations (12-5) for the appropriate value of $_nF_{n+1}$. This is not a statement of economic behavior, it is simply a mathematical fact. The implicit market interest rate for a one-period loan which is expected

[21]The appendix to Chapter 1 explains the *geometric mean rate of return.*
[22]Handling coupon interest payments can be perplexing when formulating a mathematical statement of the expectations hypothesis. The easiest way to deal with this problem is to assume all bonds are zero coupon bonds. This simplifying assumption will also avoid *coupon bias* in the yield curve.
For more information about zero coupon bonds and coupon bias see Miles Livingston and Deborah Wright Gregory, *The Stripping of U.S. Treasury Securities,* Salomon Brothers Center for the Study of Business, Monograph 1989-1. Also see Gerald O. Bierwag, *Duration Analysis* (Cambridge, Mass.: Ballinger Publishing Company, 1987).

Table 12-2

A FORMAL STATEMENT OF THE EXPECTATIONS HYPOTHESIS

The following conventions will be used:

$_0S_n$ = spot rate published in daily newspaper for a loan that starts immediately (at time $t = 0$) and is repaid n periods in the future.

Date the money is actually loaned—the left-hand subscript

Repayment date—the right-hand subscript

$_tF_{t+n}$ = forward rate for a loan that starts at time t and is to be repaid n periods later at time $t + n$; this interest rate is implicit and cannot be observed directly.

Using the mathematical conventions defined above, a rigorous statement of the expectations theory is given in equation series (12-5) below.

$$(1 + {}_0S_1) = (1 + {}_0F_1) \tag{12-5a}$$

$$(1 + {}_0S_2)^2 = (1 + {}_0F_1)(1 + {}_1F_2) \tag{12-5b}$$

$$(1 + {}_0S_3)^3 = (1 + {}_0F_1)(1 + {}_1F_2)(1 + {}_2F_3) \tag{12-5c}$$

$$\cdots$$

$$(1 + {}_0S_n)^n = (1 + {}_0F_1)(1 + {}_1F_2) \cdots (1 + {}_{n-1}F_n) \tag{12-5n}$$

---

to exist t periods in the future can be found by solving Equation (12-6) for $_tF_{t+1}$.

$$1 + {}_tF_{t+1} = \frac{(1 + {}_0S_{t+1})^{t+1}}{(1 + {}_0S_t)^t}$$

$$= \frac{(1 + {}_0S_1)(1 + {}_1F_2)(1 + {}_2F_3) \cdots (1 + {}_{t-1}F_t)(1 + {}_tF_{t+1})}{(1 + {}_0S_1)(1 + {}_1F_2)(1 + {}_2F_3) \cdots (1 + {}_{t-1}F_t)} \tag{12-6}$$

It is also possible to determine the implicit future rates for multiperiod bonds. For a bond with a life of n periods, which starts in period t and ends in period $t + n$, the yield over the life (that is, over the n periods) of this bond can be derived from Equation (12-7).

$$\left(\frac{(1 + {}_0S_{t+n})^{t+n}}{(1 + {}_0S_t)^t} \right)^{1/n} = \sqrt[n]{(1 + {}_tF_{t+1})(1 + {}_{t+1}F_{t+2}) \cdots (1 + {}_{t+n-1}F_{t+n})}$$

$$= 1 + {}_tF_{t+n} \tag{12-7}$$

where $_tF_{t+n}$ is the market yield for an n-period bond that starts in future period t and matures in the more distant future period $t + n$.

The relations suggested by the expectations hypothesis will not hold exactly in the "real world" because transactions costs (such as sales commissions and taxes) will inhibit trading. But, ignoring transactions costs, arbitrage ensures that Equation (12-5) will tend to hold if some of the bond traders are profit seekers. **Arbitrage** is a series of transactions that must yield a profit—no risk is involved. Arbitrage between maturities will tend to maintain the expectations theory as it is represented in Equation (12-5).[23]

Arbitrage Will Maintain the Expectations Model

Some investors will rearrange their bond portfolios and cause bond prices and yields to be revised according to Equation (12-5) because they expect to profit from it. For example, suppose inequality (12-8) occurs—this violates Equation (12-5).

$$(1 + {}_0S_T)^T > (1 + {}_0F_1)(1 + {}_1F_2) \cdots (1 + {}_{T-1}F_T) \tag{12-8}$$

Some profit-seeking investors with money to invest for T periods will buy the existing long-term bond yielding ${}_0S_T$. This will drive up its price and drive down its yield until Equation (12-8) becomes an equality that aligns with Equation (12-5n).

After profit-maximizing investors purchase the long-term bond yielding ${}_0S_T$, its price may later drop because of changing credit conditions and/or changing expectations. In this case, the investor must hold the long-term bond until it matures to attain the yield ${}_0S_T$. Since it is not always possible for profit-seeking investors to hold long-term bonds until they mature, they may sell them after their price has fallen and inequality (12-8) exists again. In this case, the sale will lower the bond's price and increase inequality (12-8). As a result of such disadvantageous sales (which even a profit-seeking speculator may sometimes be forced to make), the arbitrage process cannot be expected to maintain Equation (12-5) as an exact equality. However, the actions of these profit seekers will tend to make current yields (that is, ${}_0S_t$) a function of expected

[23]Cox, Ingersoll, and Ross (CIR) have shown different versions of the expectations theory that had traditionally been considered to be equivalent are inconsistent with each other when interest rates fluctuate randomly. Essentially, a combination of uncertainty and Jensen's inequality is used to drive a wedge between different risk-premium measures. CIR use stochastic calculus to show that in a continuous-time arbitrage pricing framework only one formulation of the expectations theory is compatible with equilibrium. See John C. Cox, Jonathan E. Ingersoll, and Stephen A. Ross, ''A Re-examination of Traditional Hypotheses About the Term Structure of Interest Rates,'' *Journal of Finance,* Sept. 1981, vol. 36, pp. 769–799.

   John Wood estimated that the problem CIR highlight is numerically small and probably not statistically significant to those doing empirical work. See J. H. Wood and N. L. Wood, *Financial Markets* (New York: Harcourt Brace Jovanovich, 1985), pp. 647–650.

   Campbell considered CIR's model and argued in support of the simpler term structure theory that is normally tested empirically. See John Y. Campbell, ''A Defense of Traditional Hypotheses About the Term Structure of Interest Rates,'' *Journal of Finance,* March 1986, vol. XLI, no. 1, pp. 183–193. For these and other reasons, the CIR model will not be discussed further.

future yields (that is, the $_tF_{t+1}$'s) as suggested by the expectations theory of Equation (12-5).[24]

One empirical test which supports the expectations theory of Equation (12-5) is simply to compare the interest rate forecasts inherent in the yield curve of some past date with the record of business activity after that date. Assuming professional investors have worthwhile ideas about the future level of business activity, and also assuming they believe the level of interest rates follows the level of business activity, it then follows directly from the definition of the expectations hypothesis that the yield curve should usually slope upward preceding economic expansions and slope downward preceding contractions. Without recognizing the implicit reasoning, a more common version of the expectations theory would be: "Declining business activity during the period of time presented by the yield pattern will result in a negatively sloped yield pattern," or vice versa for a period when business activity is accelerating.

The interest rates graphed in Figure 6-1 tend to bear out the expectations hypothesis. A yield curve constructed at nearly any of the cyclical peaks would slope downward, and a yield curve drawn at nearly any of the troughs would slope upward.[25] The yield curves existing at the economic troughs are the classic upward-sloping yield curves which forecast expectations of rising interest rates; they are seen more frequently than other shapes. This is usually attributed to the predominance of optimism over pessimism. However, it also supports the liquidity premium theory and is the "proof" frequently used to support that theory.

12-5   **RIDING THE YIELD CURVE**

Some bond portfolio managers attempt to increase their portfolio's yields by using a bond investment strategy called "riding the yield curve." This strategy may be undertaken when long-term rates are higher than the short-term rates.

Riding the yield curve is a buy-and-hold strategy in which the bond investor purchases an intermediate- or long-term bond when the yield curve is sloped

---

[24]Rigorous monetary economists make a distinction between spot rates and the yield-to-maturity (YTM) of a bond which explains why arbitrage will not maintain inequality (12-8) as an equation continuously and why some bonds will never lie exactly on the yield curve. The difference is that a bond's spot rate is a time-weighted (or geometric mean) rate of return, while the YTM is a dollar-weighted rate of return that differs from the time-weighted rate of return whenever the yield curve is not horizontal at the bond's YTM. The implicit reinvestment rate is the key to this difference. Appendix 1A explains the difference between the dollar-weighted and the time-weighted rates of return. Appendix 12B analyzes the economics.

[25]Peaks and troughs are official National Bureau of Economic Research (NBER) estimates.

upward and is expected to maintain the same level and slope. The purchased bond is then simply held in order to obtain the capital gains that occur as the years remaining until its maturity decrease and the bond moves along toward the lower end of the upward-sloping yield curve. That is, in addition to the bond's coupon interest, the bond investor earns capital gains resulting from the lower market interest rates encountered as the bond rides down the yield curve. The danger inherent in this strategy is that the level of interest rates may rise or that the short-term end of the yield curve may swing upward. Either development would cause the bond investor to suffer losses. Profit opportunities such as these lead professional bond investors to study monetary economics and work at forecasting the yield curve.

12-6   **CONCLUSIONS ABOUT THE TERM STRUCTURE**

There is an undeniable element of logic in each of the three theories about the term structure of interest rates, and each is supported to a certain extent by empirical data. In fact, a combination of all three theories probably furnishes the best description of what determines the term structure of interest rates.

In essence, expectations of forward rates determine a yield curve. However, the yield curve based on pure expectations is unobservable. Let us assume that the yield curve denoted *EE* in Figure 12-6 is such an invisible yield curve. The liquidity premium theory says that liquidity premiums which increase with the term to maturity are superimposed on the yields that are purely a function of expectations. Thus, a yield curve such as *YY* in Figure 12-6, which is observable, represents a combination determined by expectations of forward rates and liquidity premiums. The *liquidity premium* at any given time is equal to

Figure 12-6 Yield curve determined by expectations and liquidity premium.

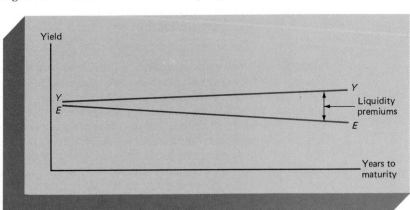

the vertical distance between *YY* and *EE*. This combination means that the liquidity premium theory is not invalidated by the occasional existence of a downward-sloping yield curve. The curve *EE* symbolizes the **pure expectations theory** and curve *YY* represents the **biased expectations theory.**

The long-term end of the yield curve is determined by investors' expectations and the liquidity premiums needed to induce investors to hold those bonds. In addition, the segmentation theory explains the frequent movements in the short-term end of the yield curve. The Federal Reserve's Open Market Committee endeavors to control the money supply and exert pressures on market interest rates by buying and selling millions of dollars of Treasury bills on a daily basis. Thus, the Fed's interactions with the liquidity needs of commercial banks provide the primary supply and demand forces at work on the short-term end of the yield curve. The wide and frequent swings in that portion of the yield curve with less than 1 year to maturity (illustrated in Figure 12-4) are largely attributed to changes in these supply and demand factors. The effects of these forces on the yield curve are segmented and therefore diminish rapidly in the intermediate and long-term maturities.

12-7   CONCLUSIONS ABOUT THE LEVEL OF MARKET INTEREST RATES

Figure 12-1 documents the fact that inflationary expectations are the primary determinant of the level of interest rates. In addition, shifts in the supply of and demand for credit can result in faster interest rate changes than shifting inflationary expectations alone would dictate. Variable risk premiums that occur as the phases of the business cycle change can also contribute to movements in the level of market interest rates.

Since bond prices are strongly affected by market interest rates, forecasting interest rates is an important task of a bond portfolio manager. Those who manage bond portfolios should be monetary economists as well as bond analysts if they hope to maximize profits.

Essay Questions

12-1   How should the inflationary concerns of 1-year bond investors differ from the inflationary concerns of investors in 20-year bonds? Does the distinction between the *level* and the *structure* of market interest rates become relevant?

12-2   (*a*) Give two reasons why the yield curve might be expected to slope upward most of the time. (*b*) Give two reasons why the yield curve might usually slope downward.

12-3   When U.S. Treasury bond yields for a given day are plotted against their years to maturity to draw a yield curve, why do the data points not all lie exactly on the yield curve if it is drawn to be smooth? Does the fact that not all of the data points lie on the yield curve diminish the value of theories about the term structure of interest rates? Explain. What variables can be held constant in the preparation of a yield curve? What variables cannot be held constant in the preparation of a yield curve?

12-4 Explain why the yields on short-term bonds fluctuate more than the yields on long-term bonds, but the prices of long-term bonds nevertheless fluctuate more than the prices of short-term bonds.

12-5 Bond dealers define a *bear hedge* as a transaction in which "a short sale of longs is hedged by going long shorts." This statement means that a short position of long-term bonds is hedged by taking a long position in short-term bonds. Why would a bond dealer enter such a bear hedge? (You can refer to Chapter 8 for an explanation of long and short positions.)

12-6 The following questions about market interest rates were used on the CFA (Chartered Financial Analysts) exam. (*a*) *Explain* what is meant by the term structure of interest rates. *Explain* the theoretical basis of an upward-sloping yield curve. (*b*) *Explain* the economic circumstances under which you would expect to see the inverted yield curve prevail. (*Note:* An inverted yield curve is downward-sloping.) (*c*) *Explain* "real" rate of interest. (*d*) *Explain* the characteristics of the market for U.S. Treasury securities. *Compare* it to the market for AAA-corporate bonds. *Discuss* the opportunities which may exist in bond markets that are less than efficient. (*e*) Over the past several years, fairly wide yield spreads between AAA-corporates and Treasuries have occasionally prevailed. *Discuss* the possible reasons why this occurred.

Problems

12-7 Assume 4-year bonds are currently yielding 7 percent and 3-year bonds are yielding 6 percent. What is the implied yield for 1-year bonds starting 3 years from now? Show your work. *Hint: Use the expectations theory.*

12-8 What is the yield-to-maturity (YTM) of a zero coupon bond with a face value of $1000 if it is selling for $880 and it has 5 years until it matures? *Hint: The YTM is identical to the internal rate of return (IRR) in Equation (1A-1a) in Appendix 1A. And, Equation (1A-1a) simplifies to be equivalent to Equation (1A-7) for a bond that pays no coupons. The YTM is also defined in Equation (13-3).*

12-9 What should be the price for a $10,000 face value bond with 7 years until it matures if it pays coupons of 9.0 percent annually and has a YTM of 8.0 percent?

Use the following data for Problems 12-10 through 12-13:

Bond	Maturity, years	YTM
W	1	8.0%
X	2	9.0
Y	3	10.5
Z	4	12.0

Hint: The yield-to-maturity (YTM) is identical to the internal rate of return (IRR) in Equation (1A-1a) in Appendix 1A. The YTM is also defined in Equation (13-3).

12-10 Calculate the implied 1-year forward rate starting in year 2.

12-11 Calculate the implied 1-year forward rate starting in year 3.

12-12 Calculate the implied rate for a 3-year bond starting in year 2.

12-13 Calculate the implied rate for a 2-year bond starting in year 3.

12-14 If a 15-year T-bond is yielding YTM = 12% and a 5-year T-bond is yielding YTM = 8%, what is the expected return on a 10-year bond starting at the end of year 5?

12-15 Assume the following zero coupon bonds with face values of $1,000 are available:

Bond price	Maturity, years
$935	1
870	2
800	3
750	4

(*a*) Determine the YTM for each bond. (*b*) Determine the 1-year forward rate at the beginning of year 3.

12-16 Using the information given in Problem 12-15, describe how an investor could lock-in the 1-year forward rate for year 3.

12-17 Using the information given in Problem 12-15, determine the YTM for a 3-year bond beginning in year 1.

12-18 If the real rate of return is 3 percent, *rr* = 0.03, what inflation forecast is implied by the yield curve given in Problem 12-15?

12-19 Using the information given in Problem 12-15, determine the 1-year forward rate beginning in year 2.

12-20 The YTM on a 10-year bond is 10.5 percent. If the YTM on a 9-year bond is 10.25 percent, what is the implied 1-year forward rate for year 10?

12-21 Suppose the YTM on a 11-year bond is 10.6 percent. If the YTM on the 9- and 10-year bonds is the same as in Problem 12-20, determine the forward rate on a 2-year bond starting in year 10.

Selected References

Culbertson, J. A., "The Term Structure of Interest Rates," *Quarterly Journal of Economics,* Nov. 1957, pp. 485–517; also, J. B. Michaelson, "Comment," *ibid.,* Feb. 1963, pp. 166–174, and J. A. Culbertson, "Reply," *ibid.,* Nov. 1963, pp. 691–696.

This series of nonmathematical articles articulates the viewpoint of classic advocates of the segmentation theory.

Fabozzi, Frank J., and T. Dessa Fabozzi, *Bond Markets, Analysis and Strategies* (Englewood Cliffs, N.J.: Prentice-Hall, 1989).

This college finance textbook describes bond markets and surveys modern interest rate theory. Algebra and a little differential calculus are used.

B. G. Malkiel, *The Term Structure of Interest Rates* (Princeton, N.J.: Princeton Univ. Press, 1966).

This book uses graphs and empirical data supplemented with algebra and differential calculus to analyze various theories about the shape of yield curve. The book also contains an informative review of the literature that existed up to 1965.

Meiselman, D., *The Term Structure of Interest Rates* (Englewood Cliffs, N.J.: Prentice-Hall, 1962).

This classic book explains the expectations hypothesis and supporting data using regression analysis and elementary difference equations.

Appendix 12A

Interest Rate Swaps
and Bond Swaps

Although their names sound similar, "interest rate swaps" and "bond swaps" are unrelated approaches to dealing with interest rate risk. Both tactics are examined in this appendix.

Interest Rate Swaps

Interest rate swaps are a new financial product that originated in the early 1980s. The annual volume of interest rate swaps has grown rapidly—to a value in excess of $1.5 trillion by the late 1980s. Swaps are used by borrowers seeking to reduce their borrowing costs or investors attempting to enhance asset yields. Interest rate swaps are off-balance-sheet transactions used to hedge or restructure the exposure of balance sheets to interest rate risk. More specifically, a **swap** is a contractual exchange of two different cashflows between two **counterparties**—the counterparties could be two corporations, two finance companies, two banks, or any two borrowers. The relative financing advantage of each counterparty in different financial markets can produce an opportunity for both to reduce their costs via an appropriate swap.[26]

The structure of a swap is determined when two borrowers agree to make a series

---

[26]See Susan M. Jarzombek, "Interest Rate Swaps Can Reduce Borrowing Costs," *The Financial Manager,* May–June 1989, pp. 70–74. Or, see Frank J. Fabozzi and Irving M. Pollack, eds., *The Handbook of Fixed Income Securities,* 2d ed. (Homewood, Ill.: Dow Jones–Irwin, 1987), chaps. 57 and 58. For more detail see Carl R. Beidleman, *Interest Rate Swaps* (Homewood, Ill.: Dow Jones–Irwin, 1991). Furthermore, see Carl R. Beidleman, *Cross-Currency Swaps* (Homewood, Ill.: Dow Jones–Irwin, 1991). See also James Bicksler and Andrew Chen, "An Economic Analysis of Interest Rate Swaps," *Journal of Finance,* July 1986. In addition, see Arvind Mahajan and Dileep Mehta, "Swaps, Expectations, and Exchange Rates," *Journal of Banking and Finance,* 1986, vol. 10, no. 1, pp. 7–20. And, see Clifford W. Smith, Jr., Charles W. Smithson, and Lee Macdonald Wakeman, "The Market for Interest Rate Swaps," *Financial Management,* 1988, vol. 17, no. 4, pp. 34–44. See also Stuart M. Turnbull, "Swaps: A Zero Sum Game?," *Financial Management,* 1987, vol. 16, no. 1, pp. 15–21. Furthermore, see John F. Marshall and Kenneth R. Kapner, *Understanding Swap Finance* (Cincinnati: South-Western Publishing Company, 1990).

353

of payments to each other on specified payment dates. One counterparty typically agrees to pay a *fixed* rate of interest to the second in return for a series of payments tied to some *fluctuating* market interest rate. The London Interbank Offered Rate, called LIBOR, is an example of a fluctuating market interest rate on which swap contracts might be based. Swaps usually involve no exchange of principal. The *face value* of the swap is therefore called the **notional principal amount.** The fixed rate, which determines the fixed-rate payer's payment, typically equals the yield of a specified U.S. Treasury security plus some number of basis points that is stipulated in the swap contract. The size of this **swap spread** varies—it reflects the prevailing supply of and demand for fixed-rate borrowings in that particular maturity.

Consider an example in which two companies reach a swap agreement. The management of the J. C. Bulling Corporation anticipates rising interest rates and therefore wants to obtain a loan for 4 years that has a fixed rate of interest. Bulling can raise money in the fixed-rate bond market at a total (called the "all-in") cost of 80 basis points over the yield on U.S. Treasury notes, which we will assume is currently at 9.0 percent. Alternatively, under its revolving bank loan Bulling can borrow short-term funds priced at LIBOR and roll the loan over at this fluctuating interest rate every 30 days for the next 4 years. The Bear Products Corporation's management is in a different situation; they have a forecast that is the opposite of Bulling's. Bear Products expects interest rates to decline and therefore wants to shorten its liabilities and roll them over at the progressively lower rates of interest that are foreseen. Bear Products Corporation is currently paying 9.5 percent interest on a 4-year bond. It can borrow in the short-term market at a rate equal to LIBOR plus 15/100 of 1 percent. However, Bear Products would still have to pay its original bondholders because it cannot prepay under the terms of its bond issue's indenture. Here is a case of opposites attracting each other.

The swaps department at a major bank arranges for the Bulling Corporation to swap interest rates with Bear Products. Bulling happily agrees to pay Bear Products the swap fixed rate of 9.60 percent annually at the end of each year for the next 4 years. In exchange, Bear Products eagerly agrees to pay Bulling a fluctuating interest rate pegged to the LIBOR. Figure 12A-1 illustrates the direction of the cashflows in this exchange. The computations assume Bulling Corporation borrows funds in the short-term bank market in lieu of the fixed-rate bond market.

Figure 12A-1 Cashflows for an interest rate swap between the J. C. Bulling Corporation and the Bear Products Corporation.

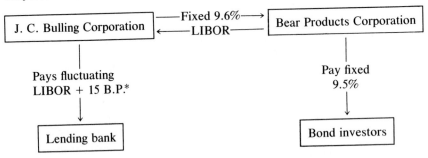

*B.P. = basis points.

Table 12A-1

CONTRASTING THE ALTERNATIVE BORROWING POSSIBILITIES AVAILABLE TO THE J. C. BULLING AND BEAR PRODUCTS CORPORATIONS

	Without swap	With swap	Net savings
Bulling Corporation	9.8%	9.6%	20 B.P.
Bear Products Corp.	LIBOR + 15 B.P.*	LIBOR	15 B.P.

*B.P. = basis points.

The savings enjoyed by each company as a result of the interest rate swap are compared with the two companies' traditional method of achieving their financing objectives in Table 12A-1. The executives at Bulling, for instance, believed their firm's interests were best served by borrowing in the fixed-rate market because they thought interest rates were headed up. Bear Products' management, expecting market interest rates to go down, thought it advantageous to borrow in the floating rate market. It does not matter which interest rate forecast was correct; the interest rate swap enables each company to borrow in the market in which it has a relative cost advantage and therefore to reduce its effective funding cost while still achieving its desired exposure to changes in interest rates. The Bear Products Corporation saves 15 basis points by not having to borrow short-term funds from a commercial bank. Bear also saves another 10 basis points because it receives a swap-related payment at a rate of 9.6 percent but pays its bondholders a rate of only 9.5 percent. Bulling saves 20 basis points since it pays Bear Products a swap rate of 9.6 percent instead of borrowing in the bond market at a fixed rate of 9.8 percent.

Each company has succeeded in reconfiguring its exposure to the interest rate change it believes lies ahead. Bulling has fixed its cost of funding for the next 4 years; if interest rates rise as its management expected, Bulling is protected from rising financing costs. At the same time, Bear Products Corporation was able to shorten its liabilities and thereby pay short-term interest rates that will be reset every 30 days. Note that both parties benefit from the exchange. Furthermore, neither company alters its balance sheet.

Interest rate swaps are not speculative—but some default risk is involved. Should one of the counterparties default, the remaining party's resulting loss can be no more than the difference between the rate that the remaining party was obligated to pay under the original swap contract and what it must now pay on a second swap contract. For example, assume Bear Products defaults on its obligation to pay the floating rate to Bulling with 2 years remaining until the swap agreement is completed; also assume market interest rates have risen. Bulling enters into a new swap with a new counterparty whereby it pays a fixed rate of 10.0 percent, 40 basis points more than its original fixed rate of 9.6 percent. The J. C. Bulling Corporation will probably sue to recoup the increased cost of 10% − 9.6%, or 40 basis points for each of the next 2 years from the defaulting Bear Products Corporation. However, even if Bulling is not able to gain any compensation for its loss, the loss should not be large enough to endanger the Bulling Corporation.

The documentation for most swaps is fairly uniform. Standardized contract terms are defined in a code published by the International Swap Dealers Association in New York, a global self-regulatory organization. After deciding on an interest rate swaps structure, any major bank can quote swap prices. The minimum notional principal amount for a swap is $5 million. The larger the amount above this standard minimum, the more negotiating power an aspiring swapper has in dealing with a swap bank.

The dollar amounts and maturity dates of swaps are easily customized to the swapper's needs. More important, there is a deep secondary market for swaps that facilitates liquidating or neutralizing the position. A swap can be wiped out by doing a *mirror swap* to offset the economic effect of the original swap.

As the volume of swaps increased, the opportunities to customize them multiplied. **Swap options** are an example of a new swap instrument. As explained in Chapter 22, an option gives its owner the right to enter into a swap of a specified maturity at a fixed rate that is set in advance of the option's exercise date. Swap options are attractive for a party that is unsure whether the need for a swap will materialize. For a fee paid by the option buyer, who would be the fixed-rate payer in the example above, protection against rising rates can be obtained while still allowing the option buyer to walk away if the transaction does not materialize.

Bond Swaps

Unlike interest rate swaps, bond swaps are usually speculative. A **bond swap** involves the purchase and sale of equal amounts of similar bonds undertaken in an effort to increase a bond portfolio's rate of return. The substitution swap is explained first because it is the simplest type of bond swap.[27] In the following bond swap discussion the bond which is *to be sold* (TBS) if the swap is consummated is called the **TBS-bond** and the bond which is *to be purchased* (TBP) is called the **TBP-bond.**

The Substitution Swap

The **substitution swap** involves bonds which are perfect substitutes (in theory, at least) in every respect except their prices (or equivalently, their yields-to-maturity). For two bonds to be perfect substitutes, the TBS-bond and the TBP-bond must have identical quality ratings, numbers of years to maturity, coupon interest payments, sinking fund provisions, call features, and be identical in every other aspect.

All bond swaps are based on the *law of one price,* which states that the same good cannot sell at different prices. If it temporarily emerges, a price disparity between homogeneous goods will not endure because arbitragers will buy the homogeneous good from the cheapest supplier and sell it to the highest bidder as long as it is profitable to do so. This arbitrage will continue until the cheapest seller's price is bid up and/or the highest buyer's price is driven down to the point where the highest bid price and the lowest asked price are equal.[28]

Consider an example of a substitution bond swap. Suppose that a bond swapper has a TBS-bond which has 30 years to maturity, yields 7 percent if held to maturity, and

---

[27]The four most common types of bond swaps are substitution swaps, intermarket spread swaps, rate anticipation swaps, and pure yield-pickup swaps. There are other types of bond swaps which are not discussed here because they are less common. They include tax swaps, multibond swaps, liquidity improvement swaps, quality improvement swaps, and price volatility control swaps.

[28]The highest bid and the lowest offering price will not always be equal because of intermediary charges, transportation costs to get the goods from the seller to the buyer, sales commissions, etc. These market imperfections inhibit the law of one price. *Arbitrage* was introduced in Section 8-9.

is currently priced at its par value so that its coupon rate equals its yield-to-maturity (YTM). The bond swapper's bond broker will be only too happy to find another bond issued by an equivalent corporation that has identical provisions to the TBS-bond.

Suppose that because of what economists call a temporary market imperfection (or because the bond swapper is unable to see that the TBS-bond is not really a perfect substitute for the TBP-bond) the TBP-bond is priced to yield 7.10 percent. The 10-basis-point yield-pickup opportunity between the two presumably identical bonds will motivate the swap. This arbitrage should continue profitably until the law of one price is satisfied.

Measuring the Gains from a Substitution Swap   Bond swaps are undertaken because some bond investor expects to profit in the future as the price of the TBP-bond is realigned to equal the price of the TBS-bond. The time that elapses while the prices of the two swapped bonds become realigned is called the ''workout time.'' The **workout time** can be as short as a few weeks if the bond swapper has detected a true market imperfection that is corrected quickly by a rush of profitable arbitrages. Or the workout time can be as long as the time until the bonds mature. Assuming that the bonds are identical substitutes and that neither of the swapped bonds defaults, they will mature with prices equal to their face values. Thus, in our hypothetical example of a substitute swap of 30-year bonds, the workout time might drag on for 30 years.

No one can know the workout time for a swap before the swap is completed. Therefore, some workout time assumption must be made in order to calculate the additional rate of return expected from any potential bond swap. Assume a 1-year workout time to enable us to analyze our substitution swap.

The substitution swap of two bonds with 7 percent coupon rates and 30 years to maturity was undertaken because the TBP-bond yielded a modest 10 basis points more than the presumably identical TBS-bond. The present value of the TBP-bond was thus $987.70. To construct a concrete example, we assume that the yields converge on 7 percent within a 1-year workout time. Thus, both the TBS-bond and the TBP-bond will be selling for their face values of $1000 at the end of the workout time. Of course, the TBS-bond will yield 7 percent throughout the workout year. However, the TBP-bond will experience price appreciation as its YTM falls from 7.1 to 7.0 percent, causing it to earn a compound yield of 8.29 percent during the 1-year workout time. In other words, this hypothetical swap yielded a 1.29 percent, or 129 basis points, *yield improvement* on a one-time basis during the workout year. The profitability calculations are shown in Table 12A-2.

Risks Inherent in Bond Swaps   The calculations in Table 12A-2 assume a 1-year workout time. If the workout takes longer, then the capital gains must be spread over more years. Table 12A-3 shows that the realized compound yield during the workout period varies inversely with the length of the workout time. Table 12A-3 lists different potential gains involving the substitution swap of two 30-year bonds if the yields are calculated as outlined in Table 12A-2.

The risks associated with a bond swap are too substantial to ignore. The swap should promise a sufficiently large gain in realized yield to (1) pay for the bond brokerage commissions generated by the swap and (2) also compensate the bond swapper for the risks incurred.

Table 12A-2
PROFITABILITY CALCULATIONS FOR A HYPOTHETICAL BOND SWAP

Assumptions:

1. The TBS-bond was a 30-year bond which continuously sold at its par value to yield its coupon rate of 7%.
2. The TBP-bond was purchased at $987.70 to yield 7.1% over its 30-year life, but its price rose to $1000 as its yield fell to 7.0% during the year after it was purchased.
3. The workout time was 1 year.
4. All cashflows were reinvested at 7%.

	TBS-bond	TBP-bond
Original bond investment	$1000.00	$987.70
Two $35 semiannual coupons	$70.00	$70.00
Interest at 7% for 6 months on first coupon	$1.23	$1.23
Bond's price at end of workout year	$1000.00	$1000.00
Total dollars at end of workout	$1071.23	$1071.23
Total dollar gain during workout	$71.23	$83.53
Gain per dollar of investment	0.07123	0.08458
Year's realized compound yield	7.0%	8.29%

Conclusion: The swap earned 129 basis points for 1 year.

Source: Sidney Homer and Martin L. Leibowitz, *Inside the Yield Book* (Englewood Cliffs, N.J.: Prentice-Hall, 1972), table 29.

Table 12A-3
THE RELATIONSHIP BETWEEN THE WORKOUT TIME AND THE REALIZED YIELD GAIN FOR THE HYPOTHETICAL BOND SWAP

Workout time, years	Realized compound yield gain, basis points per year
30	4.3
20	6.4
10	12.9
5	25.7
1	129.0
$\frac{1}{2}$	258.8
$\frac{1}{4}$	527.2

Source: Sidney Homer and Martin L. Leibowitz, *Inside the Yield Book* (Englewood Cliffs, N.J.: Prentice-Hall, 1972), table 30.

There are four types of risks involved in a bond swap:

1. The workout time may be longer than anticipated. This lowers the realized additional yield, as shown in Table 12A-3.

2. The yield spreads may move adversely. For example, if the yield spread in our substitution swap opened up to more than 10 basis points rather than closing toward zero as anticipated, the bond swapper would incur losses.

3. The overall level of interest rates may change adversely. As a result the bond swapper could suffer losses. Even if the yield spread narrowed to zero as hoped, a rise in interest rate levels could cause all 30-year bonds to fall in price. If interest rates are expected to rise, the portfolio manager should switch to cash holdings or bonds with shorter maturities to minimize losses.

4. The TBP-bond may not be a good substitute for the TBS-bond. To use the substitution swap for another example, if the TBP-bond was intrinsically more risky than the TBS-bond, then their yields could never be expected to converge and produce additional yield. Thus, the bond swapper should analyze the bonds carefully before entering into a swap. The intermarket spread swap explained next is particularly vulnerable to this type of risk.

Intermarket Spread Swap   A second major category of bond swaps is the **intermarket spread swaps.** These swaps involve a TBS-bond and a TBP-bond that differ in one significant respect. The swapped bonds may have different coupon rates but be issued by the same issuer and be similar in every other way.

For an example, consider swapping a 25-year TBS Treasury bond with a 7 percent coupon rate which is selling at par to yield 7 percent. The TBS-bond is to be swapped for another 25-year T-bond. The bonds differ because the TBP-T-bond has a 5 percent coupon rate and is selling at a discount from par to yield 6.60 percent if held to maturity. Assume that based on a study of historical yield spreads, the 40-basis-point spread appears to be unusually small to the holder of the TBS-T-bond. If the 7 percent TBS-T-bond is sold and replaced by the TBP-T-bond, there are three ways the yield spread could increase from 40 to 50 basis points:

1. The 7 percent TBS-bond's yield could rise from 7.0 to 7.10 percent.

2. The 5 percent TBP-bond's yield could drop from 6.60 to 6.50 percent.

3. Some combination of both (1) and (2) could occur. If the expected yield spread increase materializes from any of these possibilities, the swap is desirable.

To see the advisability of the hypothetical intermarket spread swap, let us evaluate each of the three possible outcomes listed in the preceding paragraph.

1. If the high-coupon 7 percent TBS-T-bond experiences a 10-basis-point increase in its yield as the yield spread widens, the resulting capital loss would be avoided because the TBS-T-bond would have been liquidated in the swap.

2. If the low-coupon 5 percent TBP-T-bond experienced a 10-basis-point decrease in its yield as the yield spread widens, then a significant capital gain would occur for the benefit of the swapper who acquired the bond.

3. If some combination of both (1) and (2) occurs, then the swap yields some blend of each of the benefits.

In the example of the intermarket swap the swapper suffers by earning the lower yield of only 6.60 percent on the TBP-T-bond rather than the higher 7.0 percent yield on the TBS-T-bond. However, if the workout time for this swap is short, then the bond swapper only suffers this reduced yield for a short time. After the workout time, the swap can be reversed (that is, the TBS-T-bond can be repurchased and the TBP-T-bond sold) and two benefits will thereby occur: (a) the swap will have realized a "pickup" of about 1.0 percent of the value of the bonds because of the realized capital gain on the TBP-T-bond and/or the capital loss that was avoided on the TBS-T-bond, and also (b) the higher yield to maturity offered by the TBS-T-bond will be regained when the swap is reversed and the TBS-T-bond is repurchased.[29]

Rate Anticipation Swap   A bond investor who foresees a change in the level of interest rates may consider a **rate anticipation swap.** For example, if the national economy is advancing toward a boom, the rate of inflation and all interest rates should increase. Therefore, long-term bonds should be sold and swapped for holdings of cash or short-term bonds in order to avoid capital losses from the anticipated increase in the level of interest rates. The risks associated with these bond swaps are inversely proportional to the ability of the bond swapper to forecast market interest rates.

Pure Yield-Pickup Swap   The fourth category of bond swaps is the **pure yield-spread-pickup swap;** it is a simple transaction based on no expectation of market changes, so the risks associated with erroneous forecasts are absent. This swap is accomplished by selling a bond that has a given YTM and simultaneously buying a similar bond which offers a higher YTM. Unfortunately, the TBP-T-bond with the higher YTM may expose the bond swapper to more default risk.

---

[29]Most bond swap suggestions are offered, as might be expected, by bond brokers who hope to earn trading commissions if the swaps occur. Since a bond broker gains commission income regardless of whether the swap is profitable for the bond investor, advice from brokers should be scrutinized.

Appendix 12B

Alternative Formulations of the Yield Curve[30]

The present value P_0 of a bond may be represented in terms of the bond's yield-to-maturity (YTM), spot rates of interest (S), or forward rates (F), respectively, as shown in Equation (12B-1).

$$P_0 = \sum_{t=1}^{n} \frac{C_t}{(1 + \text{YTM})^t} = \sum_{t=1}^{n} \frac{C_t}{(1 + S_t)^t} = \sum_{t=1}^{n} \frac{C_t}{\prod_{i=1}^{t} (1 + F_i)^t} \qquad (12B\text{-}1)$$

Equation (12B-1) makes the same statement in three different ways. Expanding each of the three bond price formulas in Equation (12B-1) to the first two periods' terms results in Equations (12B-2), (12B-3), and (12B-4).

$$P_0 = \frac{C_1}{1 + \text{YTM}} + \frac{C_2}{(1 + \text{YTM})^2} + \cdots \qquad (12B\text{-}2)$$

$$P_0 = \frac{C_1}{1 + S_1} + \frac{C_2}{(1 + S_2)^2} + \cdots \qquad (12B\text{-}3)$$

$$P_0 = \frac{C_1}{1 + F} + \frac{C_2}{(1 + F_1)(1 + F_2)} + \cdots \qquad (12B\text{-}4)$$

where
P_0 = present value
C_t = cashflow occurring at time t
YTM = yield-to-maturity (or internal rate of return, or dollar-weighted rate of return)
S_t = discount rate applied to payment received t periods from now, that is, the spot or current interest rate on bond that matures t periods in future
F_t = discount rate implicitly applied at $t - 1$ to payment receivable at time t, that is, the forward or future interest rate on a *one-period bond*

[30]This appendix originated as a teaching note written by Professor Jonathan E. Ingersoll at Yale. Professor David F. Babbel at Wharton added some examples. Professor Francis is indebted to them for their permission to alter and reprint it.

Spot and Forward Rates   To begin with, let us ignore dollar quantities and instead focus on the relationships between the three interest (or discount) rates denoted F_t, S_t, and YTM. The spot rate is the geometric mean of the forward rates (F). Equation (12B-5), and the equivalent formulas numbered (12B-6) and (12B-7), shows relationships between the spot and forward rates.

$$(1 + S_t)^t = (1 + F_1)(1 + F_2) \cdots (1 + F_t) \tag{12B-5}$$

$$S_t = \sqrt[t]{(1 + F_1)(1 + F_2) \cdots (1 + F_t)} - 1.0 \tag{12B-6}$$

$$(1 + F_t) = \frac{(1 + S_t)^t}{(1 + S_{t-1})^{t-1}} \tag{12B-7}$$

Compare and contrast the spot and forward rates with the YTM. A bond's YTM is the weighted average of forward rates where weights are determined in accordance with the size of the cashflows occurring at each point. Consider an arithmetic example.

Assume the existence of a bond with 3 years remaining to maturity, with an annual coupon of $100. The bond's cashflows are $C_1 = \$100$, $C_2 = \$100$, and $C_3 = \$1100$. Suppose that the forward rate term structure is $F_1 = 0.10$, $F_2 = 0.11$, and $F_3 = 0.15$ for the three periods. Given these assumed numerical values, we can calculate the spot rates of interest as shown in Table 12B-1.

After computing the price of the bond, the YTM can be determined to be the discount rate that equates the present values of all the cashflows to the bond's price. That value in this case is YTM $= 0.11817851 \times 100 = 11.817851$ percent. The present value of the same bond is calculated below using the various discount rates discussed above.

Table 12B-1
CALCULATIONS FOR THE SPOT RATES

In the first time period the spot rate and future rate are the same.

$$1.0 + F_1 = 1.0 + S_1 = 1.10$$

or, after subtracting 1,

$$F_1 = S_1 = 0.10 \times 100 = 10.0\%$$

For the second period's spot rate,

$$\sqrt{(1 + F_1)(1 + F_2)} - 1.0 = S_2$$

or substituting in values

$$\sqrt{(1.10)(1.11)} - 1.0 = S_2 = 0.104988688 \times 100 = 10.4988688\%$$

For the third period,

$$\sqrt[3]{(1 + F_1)(1 + F_2)(1 + F_3)} - 1.0 = S_3$$

or

$$\sqrt[3]{(1.10)(1.11)(1.15)} - 1.0 = S_3 = 0.119793223 \times 100 = 11.9793223\%$$

Table 12B-2
CALCULATIONS FOR THE PRESENT VALUE AND THE ASSOCIATED YTM FOR $100 COUPON 3-YEAR BOND

$$P_0 = \frac{\$100}{1.10} + \frac{\$100}{(1.1)(1.11)} + \frac{\$1100}{(1.1)(1.11)(1.15)}$$

$$= \frac{\$100}{1.1} + \frac{\$100}{(1.104988688)^2} + \frac{\$1100}{(1.119793223)^3}$$

$$= \$90.9091 + \$81.9001 + \$783.32921 = \$956.2031$$

The YTM that is derived from the price of $956.2031 is calculated and found to be YTM $= 0.1182 \times 100 = 11.82$ percent after rounding off, as shown below.

$$P_0 = \frac{\$100}{1.11817851} + \frac{\$100}{1.11817851^2} + \frac{\$1100}{1.11817851^3}$$

$$= \$89.4312 + 78.9793 + 786.7908 = \$956.2031$$

Calculating Present Values

Using the spot or forward rates of interest from the numerical example in Table 12B-1, the present value of the bond paying a coupon of $100 per year for 3 years is computed in Table 12B-2. The YTM associated with that price is also calculated in Table 12B-2.

Tables 12B-3 and 12B-4 show how the present value and the associated YTM was calculated for 2-year and 1-year bonds, respectively. Next, let's examine the different yield curves that are embedded in the numerical examples above.

Table 12B-3
CALCULATIONS FOR THE PRESENT VALUE AND THE ASSOCIATED YTM FOR $100 COUPON 2-YEAR BOND

$$P_0 = \frac{\$100}{1.1} + \frac{\$1100}{(1.1)(1.11)}$$

$$= \frac{\$100}{1.1} + \frac{\$1100}{(1.104988688)^2}$$

$$= \$90.9091 + \$900.90090 = \$991.801$$

The YTM that is derived from the price of $991.801 is calculated and found to be YTM $= 0.104754 \times 100 = 10.4754$ percent, as shown below.

$$P_0 = \frac{\$100}{1.104754} + \frac{\$1100}{1.104754^2}$$

$$= \$90.51788 + \$901.2837 = \$991.801$$

Table 12B-4

CALCULATIONS FOR THE PRESENT VALUE AND THE ASSOCIATED YTM FOR $100 COUPON 1-YEAR BOND

$$P_0 = \frac{\$1100}{1.1} = \$1000$$

The YTM that is derived from the price of $1000 is easily seen to be YTM = 0.10 × 100 = 10.0%.

The Term Structure of Interest Rates

Using completely general terms, the "term structure of interest rates" is a relationship between time and interest rates. The interest rates used in portraying the term structure of interest may be YTMs, spot rates, or forward rates.

Term structures of interest should be formulated in terms of spot rates or forward rates of interest, since the YTM changes if the size of the coupon changes. As Carleton and Cooper pointed out:

> As many people have shown, the concept of yield-to-maturity . . . is an ambiguous concept. For a conventional bond (if not for some hybrid financial contracts or real asset purchase), the expected cash flow pattern implies a unique yield-to-maturity as a solving—or internal— rate of return. Its economic meaning is moot, however, inasmuch as reinvestment of intermediate cash flows at the solving rate is implied. To borrow a concept from capital budgeting literature, the price of an asset equals its present value only in the sense that its cash flows have been discounted at the market's return requirements. It is true that associated with each bond is a derived yield-to-maturity, but that does not give us license to say that yield-to-maturity is a market-required rate, exogenous to the individual bond in question.[31]

The term structures of interest under three different formulations are graphed below in Figures 12B-1, 12B-2, and 12B-3. *The most commonly graphed term structure is the third, but this is the least informative of the three term structures and is ambiguous as well.* In Figure 12B-1 the term structure is independent of the timing of cashflows. In Figure 12B-2 the term structure is independent of the timing of cashflows. But, in Figure 12B-3 the term structure depends on the cashflow stream. For different bonds that have coupons of $100 and $500, the calculations are shown below in Table 12B-5.

Consider a bond selling for $1932.3078 and having an annual coupon of $500. The YTM on this $500 coupon bond will be 11.51 percent if it matures in 3 years. However, the bond maturing in 3 years with $100 per year coupons which was analyzed above with spot and forward rates has a YTM of 11.82 percent. Table 12B-5 shows other YTMs for these two hypothetical bonds with varying terms to maturity. This contrast between 3-year bonds with different coupons illustrates why we cannot determine the correct "market yield-to-maturity" independent of a particular bond and why the YTM is not unique over dates. On the other hand, the term structure of interest using either

[31]W. T. Carleton and Ian A. Cooper, "Estimation and Uses of the Term Structure of Interest Rates," *Journal of Finance*, Sept. 1976, vol. XXXI, no. 4, pp. 1067–1083.

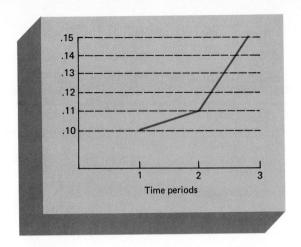

Figure 12B-1 Forward interest rate term structure.

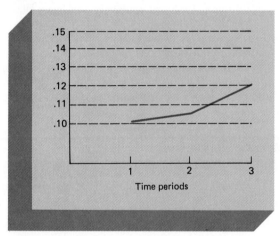

Figure 12B-2 Spot interest rate term structure.

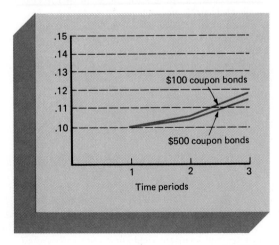

Figure 12B-3 Term structure in terms of YTMs.

Table 12B-5
DIFFERENT YTMs FOR DIFFERING MATURITIES WITH TWO DIFFERENT BONDS

Time periods until maturity	1	2	3
Present value of $100 coupon bond given future rates	$1000.00	$991.80	$956.19
YTM of $100 coupon bond	0.10	0.1047	0.1182
Present value of $500 coupon bond given future rates	$1363.64	$1683.05	$1932.31
YTM of $500 coupon bond	0.10	0.1042	0.1151

the spot or forward rates of interest applies to any financial instrument, regardless of the size or timing of the cashflows.[32]

The key to the differences highlighted in this discussion is the differences in the implicit reinvestment rate assumptions that underlie each different formulation of the problem. *The YTM calculations assume that all cashflows are immediately reinvested at the YTM until the bond's maturity—a highly dubious assumption. It is more realistic to assume that any cashflows are reinvested at the future rates.*

Selected Appendix References

Bierwag, G. O., *Duration Analysis* (Cambridge, Mass.: Ballinger Press, 1987).

Carleton, W., and Ian A. Cooper, "Estimation and Uses of the Term Structure of Interest Rates," *Journal of Finance,* Sept. 1976, vol. XXXI, no. 4, especially pp. 1067–1068.

Fisher, L., and R. L. Weil, "Coping with the Risk of Interest Rate Fluctuations," *Journal of Business,* Oct. 1971, vol. 44, pp. 408–431.

Caks, John, "The Coupon Effect on Yield to Maturity," *Journal of Finance,* March 1977, pp. 103–115.

[32]For a numerical example of how to construct a spot rate yield curve see Frank J. Fabozzi and T. Dessa Fabozzi, *Bond Markets, Analysis and Strategies* (Englewood Cliffs, N.J.: Prentice-Hall, 1989), chap. 6. Spot rates and spot rate yield curves are widely used at the investment banking firms and large commercial banks on Wall Street.

Chapter 13

Interest Rate Risk

Of all the bonds in existence, U.S. Treasury bonds are the easiest to value because they are default-free. There is no chance that the U.S. Treasury will go bankrupt. Bonds issued by corporations, which might go bankrupt, are a little more complicated. Corporate bonds are discussed in Chapter 14. Let us begin by reviewing the present value model.

13-1 THE PRESENT VALUE OF A BOND

The *present value* formula for a bond is given in Equation (13-1).

$$\text{Present value} = \frac{\text{coupon}_1}{(1 + \text{interest rate}_1)^1} + \frac{\text{coupon}_2}{(1 + \text{interest rate}_2)^2}$$

$$+ \cdots + \frac{\text{coupon}_T + \text{face value}}{(1 + \text{interest rate}_T)^T} \qquad (13\text{-}1)$$

The terms on the right-hand side of Equation (13-1) are defined as follows:

Interest rate: The interest (or discount) rate is specific for each particular bond; it is a market rate that fluctuates constantly. Some people use each different period's *spot interest rate* to calculate present values—the time subscripts acknowledge different periods' spot rates. Most people, however, use the yield-to-maturity (YTM).[1] The time subscripts are not needed with

[1]Spot rates are not used by many investors because they do not have a *spot rate yield curve* from which to obtain each period's spot rate. Appendix 12B explains the spot rate yield curve.

the YTM because it has the same value throughout the bond's life; it is a compound average rate of return.

The **yield-to-maturity** is the discount rate that equates the present value of all the bond's expected future cashflows with the current market price of the bond. It is calculated in the same way as the internal rate of return for evaluating capital budgeting projects. Assume the YTM is 10 percent (which may be stated as 10.0% or 0.10).

Face value: A bond's **face value** equals its *principal value*. The face value and the date when it is due to be repaid (its *maturity date*) are printed on the bond and cannot change during the life of the bond. If a $1000 face value bond is to be repaid in 3 years, the bond's terminal period is $T = 3$; we use these values in Equation (13-1).

Coupon: The **coupon** is the product of the coupon rate and the face value. The timing of coupon interest payments is also important. Assume a coupon rate of 6 percent; thus the bond pays $60 (or $1000 times 0.06) on the last day of each year of its 3-year life.

Substituting the values assumed above into Equation (13-1) yields the following:

$$\text{Present value} = \frac{\$60}{(1 + 0.10)^1} + \frac{\$60}{(1 + 0.10)^2} + \frac{\$60 + \$1000}{(1 + 0.10)^3}$$

$$= \$54.545 + \$49.586 + \$796.393 = \$900.52$$

This discounted cashflow calculation tells us that the bond's present value is $900.52.

The information needed to use the present value formula to value a bond is easy to obtain. The bond's principal amount, its coupon interest payments, and the dates of these cashflows are all printed on the bond. The only question in valuing a bond is how to select the appropriate interest rate for discounting the cashflows. Different discount interest rates are appropriate for different bond issues because different bonds have different coupons, maturities, and risks of default. Default risk is an issue we will postpone until the next chapter's discussion of corporate bonds.

13-2   **VALUING A RISKLESS BOND**

There is a large, active market for U.S. Treasury bonds. The prices of these marketable pieces of the national debt vary continuously and are published in many newspapers. Figure 2-1 is an excerpt from a newspaper that shows one day's prices of marketable U.S. Treasury securities.

The coupon interest rate, denoted i in the formulas that follow, applies to the bond's face value. The \$10,000 face value, denoted F hereafter, is a popular denomination. A \$10,000 face value bond with a 3.5 percent coupon rate (namely, $i = 0.035 \times 100 = 3.5\%$) pays \$350 interest ($iF = 3.5\% \times \$10,000$) per year until it matures and repays its \$10,000 principal.

To show how to determine the value of a bond, we analyze a hypothetical \$10,000 U.S. Treasury bond that pays a 3.5 percent annual coupon rate in **semiannual** payments[2] of \$175.00. Therefore, the bond's compounding interval is 6 months. Assume there are exactly twenty 6-month periods until the bond matures and the face value of \$10,000 is received. The bond's market rate of return is the appropriate discount rate to use in valuing the bond. Assume the bond's yield-to-maturity is 6 percent per annum, or 3 percent per 6-month period.[3]

The **discount factor** for cashflows received t periods in the future and discounted at the YTM is the quantity $1/(1 + \text{YTM})^t$. Present value tables contain the discount factors for a wide range of time spans and different rates of discount. The cashflows in each of the nineteen 6-month periods are $c_t = \$175.00$. In addition, $c_{20} = \$10,175.00$ when the bond matures at the end of 10 years (or 20 semiannual periods). The present value of these cashflows, denoted p_0, is calculated in Equation (13-1a).

[2]If a bond is purchased between the dates when the semiannual interest payments occur, the seller receives **accrued interest** from the party purchasing the bond. For example, if the bond is sold 3 months after a semiannual interest payment, the purchaser pays the market price of the bond on that date plus half the \$175 interest earned but not yet received by the party selling the bond.

$$\begin{array}{l} \text{Accrued} \\ \text{interest} \end{array} = \frac{\begin{array}{c}\text{days since last}\\ \text{interest payment}\end{array}}{\begin{array}{c}\text{days between last}\\ \text{and next coupon}\\ \text{payments}\end{array}} \times \begin{array}{l}\text{semiannual}\\ \text{interest}\\ \text{payment}\end{array}$$

The number of "days" is counted from the delivery date instead of the transaction date. Taxation of the income from accrued interest is complicated.

For a more detailed discussion see Robert W. Kolb, *Interest Rate Futures* (Richmond, Va.: Robert F. Dame Publishing, 1982), pp. 76–79. Or, see Sidney Homer and Martin L. Leibowitz, *Inside the Yield Book* (Englewood Cliffs, N.J.: Prentice-Hall, 1972), chap. 13. Or, see Marcia Stigum, *Money Market Calculations: Yields, Break-Evens and Arbitrage* (Homewood, Ill.: Dow Jones–Irwin, 1981), pp. 87–105. Accrued interest will not be discussed further. Ignoring the accrued interest introduces an approximation into the calculations, unless it is assumed that the bond purchase was made on the coupon payment date.

[3]By financial convention, the *annual YTM* is calculated by doubling the semiannual yield. No compounding is taken into consideration, rendering the stated annual YTM less than the effective annual yield of $(1.0 + \text{SA-YTM})^2 - 1.0$, where SA-YTM stands for semiannual YTM.

$$p_0 = \sum_{t=1}^{20 \text{ half years}} \frac{\$175}{(1 + 0.03)^t} + \frac{\$10,000}{(1 + 0.03)^{20}} \qquad (13\text{-}1a)$$

$$= \$8140.32$$

The bond's present value of $8140.32 will be its *asked price*.

13-3   **BONDS' YIELDS-TO-MATURITY**

There are several different ways to calculate a bond's YTM.

Simple Formula for Approximating the YTM

If you are caught without a hand-held calculator, a bond's **approximate yield-to-maturity,** denoted AYTM, can be estimated by hand by using Equation (13-2).

$$\text{AYTM} = \frac{\begin{array}{c}\text{average capital gain} \\ \text{or loss per year}\end{array} + \text{annual coupon interest}}{\text{average investment}} \qquad (13\text{-}2)$$

For a 3.5 percent coupon bond maturing in 10 years and a market price of $8140.32 for a $10,000 face value bond, we obtain:

$$\text{AYTM} = \frac{(\$10,000 - \$8,140.32)/10 + (0.035)(\$10,000)}{(\$8,140.32 + \$10,000)/2}$$

$$= 0.0590 \times 100 = 5.90\% \qquad (13\text{-}2a)$$

The bond's exact YTM is 6.00 percent. Equation (13-2) yields an approximation that is off by ten–one-hundredths of one percentage point. This error of 10 **basis points** is why Equation (13-2) is said to yield only approximations.[4]

Bond Tables

Tables have been prepared to show the correct price for a bond with any given term-to-maturity and any YTM. Figure 13-1 shows the page from a book of bond tables for bonds with 3.5 percent coupon rates.[5] The values in this table

---

[4]See Gabriel A. Hawawini and Ashok Vora, ''Yield Approximations: A Historical Perspective,'' *Journal of Finance,* March 1982, vol. 37, no. 1; eq. (II.5) in table II provides a formula that yields better approximations.

[5]The bond tables for Treasury bills and municipal bonds are not appropriate for Treasury bonds because the number of days in the year is counted differently. Municipals, T-bills, and money market securities assume a 360-day year, while T-bonds assume there are 365 days in the year (if it is not leap year, when 366 days are used) for the purpose of calculating bond interest. See Marcia Stigum, *Money Market Calculations: Yields, Break-Evens and Arbitrage* (Homewood, Ill.: Dow Jones–Irwin, 1981).

Yield	8-3	8-6	8-9	9-0	9-3	9-6	9-9	10-0
2.00	111.35	111.67	111.98	112.30	112.61	112.92	113.23	113.53
2.20	109.76	110.03	110.29	110.56	110.82	111.09	111.35	111.61
2.40	108.19	108.41	108.63	108.86	109.07	109.29	109.51	109.73
2.60	106.64	106.82	107.00	107.18	107.35	107.53	107.70	107.88
2.80	105.12	105.26	105.40	105.53	105.67	105.80	105.93	106.07
3.00	103.63	103.73	103.82	103.92	104.01	104.11	104.20	104.29
3.20	102.16	102.22	102.27	102.33	102.38	102.44	102.49	102.55
3.40	100.71	100.73	100.75	100.77	100.78	100.81	100.82	100.84
3.60	99.29	99.27	99.25	99.24	99.22	99.20	99.18	99.17
3.80	97.89	97.84	97.78	97.73	97.67	97.63	97.57	97.52
4.00	96.51	96.43	96.33	96.25	96.16	96.08	95.99	95.91
4.20	95.16	95.04	94.91	94.80	94.68	94.56	94.44	94.33
4.40	93.82	93.67	93.52	93.37	93.22	93.07	92.92	92.78
4.60	92.51	92.33	92.14	91.97	91.78	91.61	91.43	91.26
4.80	91.22	91.01	90.79	90.59	90.38	90.18	89.97	89.77
5.00	89.96	89.72	89.47	89.23	88.99	88.77	88.53	88.31
5.10	89.33	89.08	88.81	88.57	88.31	88.07	87.82	87.59
5.20	88.71	88.44	88.16	87.90	87.64	87.38	87.12	86.87
5.30	88.09	87.81	87.52	87.25	86.97	86.70	86.43	86.17
5.40	87.48	87.18	86.88	86.60	86.30	86.02	85.74	85.47
5.50	86.87	86.56	86.25	85.95	85.64	85.35	85.06	84.77
5.60	86.27	85.95	85.62	85.31	84.99	84.69	84.38	84.09
5.70	85.67	85.34	85.00	84.68	84.35	84.03	83.71	83.41
5.80	85.08	84.74	84.38	84.05	83.71	83.38	83.05	82.73
5.90	84.49	84.14	83.77	83.43	83.07	82.74	82.39	82.06
6.00	83.91	83.54	83.17	82.81	82.44	82.10	81.74	81.40
6.10	83.33	82.95	82.56	82.20	81.82	81.46	81.10	80.75
6.20	82.76	82.37	81.97	81.59	81.20	80.83	80.46	80.10
6.30	82.19	81.79	81.38	80.99	80.59	80.21	79.82	79.46
6.40	81.63	81.21	80.79	80.39	79.98	79.59	79.20	78.82
6.50	81.07	80.64	80.21	79.80	79.38	78.98	78.58	78.19
6.60	80.51	80.08	79.63	79.21	78.78	78.38	77.96	77.57
6.70	79.96	79.52	79.06	78.63	78.19	77.78	77.35	76.95
6.80	79.42	78.96	78.50	78.06	77.61	77.18	76.75	76.34
6.90	78.87	78.41	77.93	77.48	77.03	76.59	76.15	75.73
7.00	78.34	77.86	77.38	76.92	76.45	76.01	75.56	75.13
7.10	77.80	77.32	76.83	76.36	75.88	75.43	74.97	74.53
7.20	77.27	76.78	76.28	75.80	75.32	74.86	74.39	73.94
7.30	76.75	76.24	75.73	75.25	74.76	74.29	73.81	73.36
7.40	76.23	75.72	75.20	74.70	74.20	73.72	73.24	72.28
7.50	75.71	75.19	74.66	74.16	73.65	73.17	72.67	72.21
7.60	75.20	74.67	74.13	73.62	73.10	72.61	72.11	71.64
7.70	74.69	74.15	73.61	73.09	72.56	72.06	71.56	71.08
7.80	74.19	73.64	73.09	72.56	72.03	71.52	71.01	70.52
7.90	73.69	73.13	72.57	72.04	71.50	70.98	70.46	69.97
8.00	73.19	72.63	72.06	71.52	70.97	70.45	69.92	69.42
8.10	72.70	72.13	71.55	71.00	70.45	69.92	69.39	68.88
8.20	72.21	71.63	71.05	70.49	69.93	69.40	68.86	68.34
8.30	71.73	71.14	70.55	69.98	69.42	68.88	68.33	67.81
8.40	71.24	70.65	70.05	69.48	68.91	68.36	67.81	67.29
8.50	70.77	70.17	69.56	68.99	68.40	67.85	67.29	66.76
8.60	70.29	69.69	69.07	68.49	67.90	67.35	66.78	66.25
8.70	69.83	69.21	68.59	68.00	67.41	66.84	66.27	65.74
8.80	69.36	68.74	68.11	67.52	66.92	66.35	65.77	65.23
8.90	68.90	68.27	67.64	67.04	66.43	65.86	65.28	64.73
9.00	68.44	67.81	67.17	66.56	65.95	65.37	64.78	64.23
9.20	67.53	66.89	66.24	65.62	65.00	64.41	63.81	63.25
9.40	66.64	65.98	65.32	64.69	64.06	63.46	62.85	62.28
9.60	65.76	65.09	64.42	63.78	63.14	62.53	61.92	61.34
9.80	64.90	64.22	63.54	62.89	62.24	61.62	61.00	60.41
10.00	64.05	63.36	62.67	62.01	61.35	60.72	60.09	59.50

Figure 13-1 A page from the bond table for 3.5 percent coupon bonds.

show the percentage of face value for which bonds with a 3.5 percent coupon rate should sell if they are to have the YTM shown in the left column. Books of bond tables have a separate page for every plausible rate of coupon interest. These books of bond tables have provided a popular way to find a bond's yield-to-maturity for decades. However, inexpensive hand-held calculators are now available that can calculate exact YTMs instantly.

The values in Figure 13-1 were calculated using Equation (13-1) so that tedious present value calculations can be avoided. The bond tables may be used to solve two kinds of problems. If the term-to-maturity is known, the bond tables can be used to look up (1) the bond price if the YTM is known or (2) the YTM if the market price is known.

Solving for a Bond's YTM

To determine the YTM of a bond, three methods may be used. First, the approximate YTM can be calculated with Equation (13-2). Second, the YTM may be found for a given price and maturity if a bond table is available. The third way to determine yields is more cumbersome. We have defined the YTM as the discount rate that equates the present value of all *promised* cashflows to the cost of the investment. Since the face value F, the coupon rate i, the annual coupon interest payment iF, and the purchase price p_0 are fixed quantities that are printed in newspapers, Equation (13-3) may be solved for the only unknown value in the equation—the YTM.

$$p_0 = \sum_{t=1}^{T} \frac{\text{cashflow}_t}{(1 + \text{YTM})^t} = \sum_{t=1}^{T} \frac{iF}{(1 + \text{YTM})^t} + \frac{F}{(1 + \text{YTM})^T} \qquad (13\text{-}3)$$

It is difficult to evaluate a polynomial equation of degree T, like Equations (13-1) and (13-3). Polynomials of degree T are usually solved by laboriously trying different values of the YTM until one is found that produces the desired mathematical equality. Such computations may be expedited by using a calculator or a computer.

Investors in a coupon-paying bond will earn the YTM promised on the purchase date if and only if all of the following three conditions are fulfilled.

1. The bond is held until it matures rather than being sold before it reaches maturity.

2. The bond does not default on any of its cashflows. That is, the bond issuer pays all coupons and the principal in full at the scheduled times.

3. All cashflows (namely, the coupon payments) are immediately reinvested at an interest rate equal to the promised YTM.

In view of these three conditions, a bond's YTM may be correctly viewed as an *expected* yield-to-maturity because it may differ from the compound rate of return that is actually earned if any of the three conditions are not fulfilled.

Reinvestment Rate Affects the YTM

As mentioned above, a bond's yield to maturity is based on the dubious assumption that all cashflows throughout the bond's life (namely, the coupon interest) are reinvested immediately upon receipt in something that earns the YTM. This assumption is frequently untrue because the coupon interest income might be consumed, for example, rather than reinvested. This is equivalent to

Table 13-1

DIFFERENT REINVESTMENT RATE ASSUMPTIONS FOR AN 8% COUPON BOND PURCHASED AT PAR

Reinvest-ment rate	Interest on interest		Coupon income	Capital gain or discount	Total return	Total realized compound yield
	% of total return	Amount				
0%	0	$ 0	$1600	0	$1600	4.84%
5	41	1096	1600	0	2696	6.64
6	47	1416	1600	0	3016	7.07
7	53	1782	1600	0	3382	7.53
8†	58†	2201†	1600†	0	3801†	8.00†
9	63	2681	1600	0	4281	8.50
10	67	3232	1600	0	4832	9.01

†Yield from yield book.

reinvesting the funds at a zero rate of return; the YTM realized over the life of the bond will be reduced accordingly.

Table 13-1 illustrates the effects of different reinvestment rates on a bond's realized YTM. Table 13-1 shows the total compounded rate of return that is realized (that is, the effective YTM) for a bond bought at face value 20 years before it matured and that pays an 8 percent coupon rate. As you can see, only 4.84 percent total YTM is realized if the coupon interest is consumed instead of being reinvested. Essentially, the bond's YTM is reduced by consuming the coupons rather than reinvesting them because the investor will not get to earn the **interest-on-the-interest.** But the same bond has a realized total yield of 9.01 percent if the coupons are reinvested at 10 percent. This shows the importance of the reinvestment opportunities and highlights an often-ignored source of bond risk: *the reinvestment rate risk can cause a bond's realized yield to deviate from its promised YTM.*

Contrasting Various Bond Yield and Return Measures

Discussions about bonds are complicated by the fact that there are different ways to measure the yield of a particular bond. Consider these four different bond yield concepts:

1. *Coupon rate:* The coupon rate or nominal rate is the fixed rate of interest printed on the bond certificate. Coupon rates are contractual rates that cannot be changed after the bond is issued. (Coupon rates are zero for T-bills and other zero coupon bonds.)

2. *One-period rate of return:* The single-period (for example, the 1-month or 1-year period) rate-of-return formula for a coupon bond is as follows:

$$r_t = \frac{\text{capital gain or loss + coupons, if any}}{\text{purchase price}} \qquad (13\text{-}4)$$

The one-period rate of return varies from higher to lower in each period as the bond's price rises and falls, respectively.

3. *Current yield:* Every bond that pays coupon interest has a positive current yield, or, synonymously, coupon yield, defined as follows:

$$\text{Current yield} = \frac{\text{dollars of coupon interest per year}}{\text{current market price}}$$

   For example, a 6.0 percent coupon bond with $1000 face value that is
   selling at the discounted price of $900 has a current yield of $60/$900 =
   0.0666, or 6.66%. The current yield is an annual cashflow measure
   based on current market prices.

4. *Yield-to-maturity:* A bond's YTM is the discount rate that equates the
   present value of a bond's promised cashflows to the bond's current
   market price.

Figure 13-2 illustrates how three of the four different interest rate measures
interact with the market price of a default-free bond with $1000 face value, 6.0

Figure 13-2 The relationships between different measures of the yield from a 6%
coupon bond with 25 years to maturity.

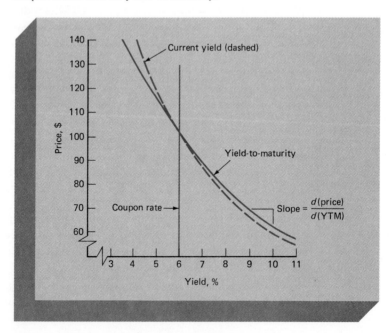

percent coupon rate, and 25 years until maturity. The one-period rate of return is not shown in this figure because it depends on the beginning- and end-of-period prices of the bond, which are both absent from the figure. The coupon rate is invariant in Figure 13-2. The YTM and the current yield are positively related and both vary inversely with the bond's price because they both involve fixed cashflows that are divided by the price of the bond. In passing, it is worthwhile to note that the price-yield curves in Figure 13-2 are **convex** to the origin. The negative slope and the *convexity of the price-YTM curve* provide explanations for the intricate bond price movements that are discussed later in this chapter.[6]

Yield-to-Call (YTC)

An investor who owns a callable bond should calculate its yield two different ways: (1) assume the bond is held to maturity and calculate the YTM and (2) assume the issuer calls the bond before it matures and calculate the yield-to-call (YTC). The conservative approach is to use whichever of these two yields is the lowest for investment decision-making, because this is the minimum yield that may be expected. The YTC is calculated similarly to the YTM. Equation (13-3) can be solved for the YTC by setting the terminal period T equal to the time-to-call instead of the time-to-maturity.[7] If only an approximate YTC is needed, Equation (13-2) may be adapted to that purpose by using the time-to-call instead of the time-to-maturity.

To see how to evaluate a callable bond, reconsider the $10,000 bond that paid a 3.5 percent coupon rate semiannually for 10 years. Equation (13-1a) indicates that this bond had a present value of $8140.32 when its YTM was 6.0 percent. If the bond were callable at 107 percent of its face value in 5 years (which equals 10 semiannual periods), its yield to first call would be YTC = 9.4 percent. Set $T = 10$ semiannual periods and $p_0 = \$10,700$, and solve for

---

[6]Convexity is measured by the second derivative:

$$\frac{d^2(\text{price})}{d(\text{YTM})^2} = \text{convexity} = \text{the derivative of the slope in Figure 13-2}$$

For more information about the financial implications of convexity, see Frank J. Fabozzi and T. Dessa Fabozzi, *Bond Markets, Analysis and Strategies* (Englewood Cliffs, N.J.: Prentice-Hall, 1989), chap. 4. Also see Mark L. Dunetz and James M. Mahoney, "Using Duration and Convexity in the Analysis of Callable Bonds," *Financial Analysts Journal*, May–June 1988, pp. 53–72. Appendix 13B in this book provides a detailed investigation of convexity.

[7]For a detailed discussion of callable bonds, see Sidney Homer and Martin L. Leibowitz, *Inside the Yield Book* (Englewood Cliffs, N.J.: Prentice-Hall, 1972), chaps. 4 and 14. Also see John Finnerty, "Evaluating the Economics of Refunding High-Coupon Sinking Fund Debt," *Financial Management*, Spring 1983, pp. 5–10.

the unknown yield, which is YTC = 4.7 percent × 2 = 9.4 percent at an annual rate in this case.

$$\$8140.32 = \sum_{t=1}^{T=10} \frac{\$175}{(1 + 0.047)^t} + \frac{\$10,700}{(1 + 0.047)^{10}}$$

It would cost the issuer 9.4 percent to call this bond—that is too much. The conservative way to view this bond for investment decision-making purposes is to assume that the bond will earn only its yield-to-maturity YTM = 6.0 percent if held for 10 years instead of YTC = 9.4 percent if held for 5 years.

Investment Characteristics of Different Types of Bonds

Every bond has interest rate risk. Nevertheless, bonds are very dissimilar in a number of significant respects. Table 1-6 lists empirical average rate of return and risk statistics for different types of equity, real estate, precious metal, and bond investments. The statistics on debt securities include long-term, inter-mediate-term, and short-term domestic corporate bonds; T-bills, T-notes, T-bonds, and federal agency bonds; foreign corporate bonds; foreign government bonds; and money market securities. Table 7-4 provides the correlation coef-ficients between these investments. The statistics that describe debt investing are remarkably dissimilar. Table 5-3 in the tax chapter gives the taxable-equiv-alent YTMs for tax-exempt municipal bonds. These statistics are supplemented by detailed definitions of different debt securities in Chapter 2. Figure 6-1 illustrates how market interest rates fluctuate together over the business cycle but are nevertheless kept apart by varying yield spreads. Chapter 12 examines determinants of the level and structure of interest rates. Chapter 14 investigates *default risk* and reviews the various *protective provisions* that may or may not govern each corporate bond issue. These facts are all useful for formulating long-run investment policies that might involve debt securities; they cover a wide range of investment opportunities.

How to Calculate the YTM for a Portfolio of Bonds

The simplest way to estimate the YTM for a portfolio of diversified bonds is to calculate a *weighted average* that uses as weights the market value of each bond issue stated as a fraction of the portfolio's total value. Unfortunately, this simple result provides a poor approximation because it might average together the YTMs from vastly different types of bonds (such as 3-month and 30-year bonds).

The exact YTM for a bond portfolio is sometimes called the *internal rate of return* (IRR). The IRR considers the amount and timing of every different cashflow from each bond in the portfolio. The problem with the IRR is that it is cumbersome to calculate. Equation (13-3) must be set up to include all the portfolio's different cashflows and then solved for the discount rate that equates the present value of all those cashflows to the portfolio's market value.[8]

13-4   **MACAULAY'S DURATION (MD)**

Thus far we have only discussed one measure of a bond's *time dimension*—its time to maturity. As we shall see next, bonds have another important time dimension—the bond's "duration."

In 1938 F. R. Macaulay suggested studying the *time structure* of a bond by measuring its *average term to maturity*—or duration, as it is more commonly called.[9] A bond's **duration** may be defined as the weighted average number of years until the cashflows occur, with the relative present values of each cashflow used as the weights. **Macaulay's duration** (MD) is defined mathematically in Equation (13-5).

$$MD = \frac{\sum_{t=1}^{T}\left(\dfrac{tc_t}{(1+YTM)^t}\right) + \dfrac{FT}{(1+YTM)^T}}{p_0} \tag{13-5}$$

$$MD = \frac{\sum_{t=1}^{T} t\left(\dfrac{c_t}{(1+YTM)^t}\right)}{p_0} + \frac{T\left(\dfrac{F}{(1+YTM)^T}\right)}{p_0} \tag{13-5a}$$

time periods of payments

relative value accounted for by the cashflow

---

[8]The "best" way to calculate a portfolio's YTM employs "Macaulay's duration," which is defined in Equation (13-5). A bond's **dollar duration** is defined in terms of its Macaulay's duration, as shown below.

$$\frac{dp}{d(YTM)} = \text{dollar duration} = \left(\frac{\text{bond's price}}{1.0 + YTM}\right)(-\text{Macaulay's duration})$$

Dollar duration should be used to calculate a portfolio's YTM. The portfolio's **dollar-duration-weighted YTM** is an average YTM of the bonds that is weighted by both the market value and the dollar duration of each bond holding. The dollar-duration-weighted YTM offers the advantages that it is easier to calculate than the IRR and more accurate than the approximations provided by the simple market-value-weighted YTM.

[9]F. R. Macaulay, *Some Theoretical Problems Suggested by the Movement of Interest Rates, Bond Yields and Stock Prices in the United States Since 1856,* National Bureau of Economic Research (New York: Columbia Univ. Press, 1938). See also J. R. Hicks, *Value and Capital,* 2d ed. (New York: Oxford, 1965), p. 186. Hicks discovered duration independently of Macaulay at a later date.

Equation (13-5) may be used to calculate the duration of a single bond, a diversified portfolio of bonds, or any other asset or liability that has predictable cashflows.

Calculating Macaulay's Duration: A Numerical Example

Consider a bond with a face value F of $1000, a YTM of 6.0 percent, a coupon rate i of 7.0 percent that is paid annually, 3 years until maturity ($T = 3.0$), which is selling for a price of $1026.73. The present value of this bond is calculated with Equation (13-1) to obtain the value of $1026.73 shown below.

(1) Year, t	(2) Cashflow	(3) $1/(1 + \text{YTM})^t$	(4) = (2) × (3)
1	$ 70	$0.9434 = 1/(1.06)^1$	$ 66.04
2	70	$0.8900 = 1/(1.06)^2$	62.30
3	1070	$0.8396 = 1/(1.06)^3$	898.39
			$1026.73 = p_0$

This bond's duration is calculated by using the numerical values from the present value calculations above. The 3-year bond's duration is 2.8107 years, as shown below.[10]

(1) Year, t	(2) Present value of cashflow from column (4) above	(3) Cashflow's present value as a fraction of p_0	(4) (3) × (1)
1	$ 66.04	0.0643	0.0643
2	62.30	0.0607	0.1214
3	898.39	0.8750	2.6250
		1.0	2.8107 = MD

Contrasting Time-Until-Maturity and Duration

A *coupon-paying* bond's duration is always less than or equal to its term-to-maturity; concisely, MD ≤ T. If a bond's only cashflow is made to repay the principal and interest at the bond's maturity, the bond's term-to-maturity is identical to its duration. More succinctly, MD = T for a zero coupon bond. For a bond that has any coupon payments left to pay, however, MD for the

[10]For a computationally simple MD formula, see Gabriel Hawawini, "On the Mathematics of Macaulay's Duration," in *Bond Duration and Immunization Early Developments and Recent Contributions* (New York and London: Garland Publishing, 1982), chap. 2. See also Jess H. Chua, "A Closed Form Formula for Calculating Bond Duration," *Financial Analysts Journal*, May–June 1984, pp. 76–78.

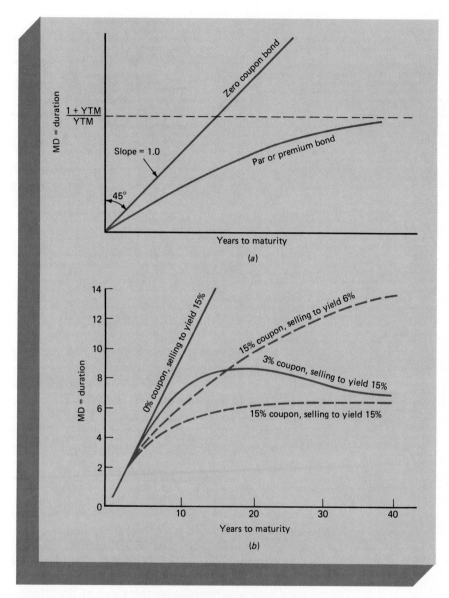

Figure 13-3 Various relationships between time-to-maturity and duration. (*Source:* Panel *b* is reprinted by permission from *The Revolution in Techniques for Managing Bond Portfolios,* The Institute of Chartered Financial Analysts, 1983, p. 42. All rights reserved.)

Table 13-2
BOND DURATION FOR A BOND WITH 6% YTM AT
VARIOUS TIMES UNTIL ITS MATURITY

Years-to-maturity	Various coupon rates			
	0.02	**0.04**	**0.06**	**0.08**
1	0.995	0.990	0.985	0.981
5	4.756	4.558	4.393	4.254
10	8.891	8.169	7.662	7.286
20	14.981	12.980	11.904	11.232
50	19.452	17.129	16.273	15.829
100	17.567	17.232	17.120	17.064
∞	17.667	17.667	17.667	17.667

Source: L. Fisher and R. L. Weil, "Coping with the Risk of Interest Rate Fluctuations: Returns to Bondholders from Naive and Optimal Strategies," *Journal of Business,* Oct. 1971, p. 418.

bond will be less than the bond's term-to-maturity. In the numerical example above, for instance, the annual coupons of $70 caused the 3-year bond to have an average term-to-maturity or duration of 2.8107 years. Earlier and/or larger cashflows shorten the duration of a bond investment. These patterns can be perceived in Figure 13-3 and Table 13-2. Figure 13-3 illustrates relationships between the term-to-maturity and duration of different bonds. Table 13-2 shows the duration of different bonds that have a YTM of 6.0 percent.

The algebraic quantity below, denoted LVMD, calculates the limiting value of MD; it is represented by the horizontal dashed line in Figure 13-3*a*.

$$\text{LVMD} = \frac{1.0 + \text{YTM}}{\text{YTM}} = \frac{1.0}{\text{YTM}} + 1.0$$

LVMD equals 11 years if YTM = $0.1 \times 100 = 10$ percent, for instance. When analyzing duration, the value of LVMD is noteworthy for several reasons. First, the duration of a perpetual bond (such as a British Consul) is equal to LVMD, irrespective of its coupon rate. Second, the duration of a coupon-bearing bond selling at or above its face value increases monotonically with its term-to-maturity and approaches the value of LVMD as its term-to-maturity approaches infinity, as illustrated in Figure 13-3*a*. Third, the duration of a coupon-bearing bond selling at a market price below its face value reaches a maximum before its maturity date reaches infinity and then recedes toward the limiting value of LVMD.

A bond's duration is considered to be a better measure of its time structure than its years-to-maturity because MD reflects the amount and timing of every cashflow rather than merely the length of time until the final payment occurs. Furthermore, MD measures the bond's interest rate risk.

13-5   INTEREST RATE RISK

A bond's **interest rate risk** can be measured by its **elasticity,** denoted EL in Equation (13-7).[11]

$$EL = \frac{\text{percent change in bond's price}}{\text{percent change in } 1.0 + \text{YTM}} \qquad (13\text{-}7)$$

$$EL = \frac{\Delta p/p}{\Delta \text{YTM}/(1.0 + \text{YTM})} < 0 \qquad (13\text{-}7a)$$

For noncallable bonds, a bond's price elasticity with respect to a change in interest rates (EL) will always be a negative number since a bond's price and its YTM always move inversely.

Numerical Example of a Bond's EL Measurement

Consider a 2-year bond that has a 10 percent coupon rate and sells at its face value of $1000.

$$\$1000 = \frac{\$100}{1.10} + \frac{\$1100}{(1.10)^2} = \$90.909 + \$909.091 = \text{present value}$$

Assume that this $1000 bond experiences an increase in its YTM from 10 to 11 percent. As a result, the bond's price drops from $1000 to $982.87.

$$\$982.87 = \frac{\$100}{1.11} + \frac{\$1100}{(1.11)^2} = \$90.09 + \$892.78$$

The bond's price decrease of $17.13 ($1000 − $982.87) equals a 1.713 percent fall from its $1000 price.

$$\text{Percent price change} = \frac{\Delta p}{\text{beginning price}} = \frac{-\$17.13}{\$1000}$$

$$= -0.01713 \times 100 = -1.713\%$$

The increase in the bond's YTM from 10 to 11 percentage points is a rise of approximately nine-tenths of 1 percent, as shown below.

---

[11]The Greek letter delta, Δ, in Equation (13-7) denotes a finite change. If we analyze infinitesimally small changes, then differential calculus can be used to show that:

$$\text{MD} = \frac{dp}{p} \times \frac{1.0 + \text{YTM}}{d(\text{YTM})} = \frac{dp}{p} \bigg/ \frac{d(\text{YTM})}{1 + \text{YTM}} = \text{elasticity} < 0 \qquad (13\text{-}6)$$

See M. H. Hopewell and G. G. Kaufman, ''Bond Price Volatility and Term to Maturity: A Generalized Respecification,'' *American Economic Review,* Sept. 1973, pp. 749–753. See also R. Haugen and D. W. Wichern, ''The Elasticity of Financial Assets,'' *Journal of Finance,* Sept. 1974, pp. 1229–1240.

$$\text{Percent change in YTM} = \frac{\Delta \text{YTM}}{1 + \text{YTM}} = \frac{+0.01}{1.10} = +0.0090909 \doteq \tfrac{9}{10} \text{ of } 1.0\%$$

Equation (13-7) tells us that the bond's interest rate elasticity (EL) is a negative 1.90.

$$\text{EL} = \frac{\Delta p/p}{\Delta \text{YTM}/(1 + \text{YTM})} = \frac{-0.01713}{0.00909} = -1.90 \qquad (13\text{-}7b)$$

An elasticity measure of -1.90 means that a change in the bond's YTM of about nine-tenths of 1 percent will cause an inverse percentage change in the bond's price that is 1.90 times as large. In other words, the bond's price decline of 1.713 percent $(-1.90 \times \tfrac{9}{10} \text{ of } 1\% = 0.01713)$ was exactly what we expected.

MD Equals EL   A bond's price elasticity with respect to a change in its YTM can be calculated with Equation (13-7). Alternatively, the formula for MD, Equation (13-5), can be used to calculate the bond's elasticity. The two formulas produce the same numerical answer. To convince yourself of this convenient coincidence, re-consider a numerical example.

MD for the 2-year bond that has a 10 percent coupon rate and sells at its face value of $1000 (from the preceding elasticity example) is calculated below with Equation (13-5).

$$\text{MD} = [(1)(\$90.909/\$1000)] + [(2)(\$909.091/\$1000)]$$
$$= 0.090909 + (2)(0.909091) = 1.90 \text{ years} \qquad (13\text{-}5b)$$

Notice that this 2-year bond's duration of 1.90 years equals its price elasticity of 1.90 that was calculated in Equation (13-7b). It can be shown that, in general, MD = EL.

To show how a bond's percentage price fluctuations from any change in its yield are inexorably determined by the bond's elasticity, we can rewrite Equation (13-7) as Equation (13-8) below.

$$\left[\frac{\Delta p}{p} \right] = \text{EL} \left[\frac{\Delta \text{YTM}}{1 + \text{YTM}} \right] \qquad (13\text{-}8)$$

$$= \text{MD} \left[\frac{\Delta \text{YTM}}{1 + \text{YTM}} \right] \qquad (13\text{-}8a)$$

Equation (13-8) is derived simply by solving Equation (13-7) for the percentage price change, denoted $\Delta p/p$. Equation (13-8a) is derived from Equation (13-8) by substituting MD in place of EL. Equations (13-8) and (13-8a) show that a bond's elasticity, or, equivalently, its duration, determines the size of the per-centage price change that occurs when a bond's YTM changes. MD and EL are conceptually and numerically equivalent measures of a bond's interest rate risk.[12] They are both good benchmarks of *interest rate risk* because they measure the sensitivity of a bond's price to changes in the market interest rates. In addition, they are also fairly good measures of a bond's total risk because the *systematic fluctuations* in market interest rates that affect all bonds are the main source of risk in high-quality bonds.[13]

Bond Price Theorems

It is possible to state bond price theorems that summarize the relationships among a bond's term to maturity, its duration, its elasticity, and its interest rate risk. These theorems can also be discerned from the mathematical formulas for MD and elasticity [namely, Equations (13-6), (13-7), and (13-8)] and from Figures 13-2, 13-3, and 13-4. Figure 13-4 illustrates various prices for a bond with a 3 percent coupon rate. The infinite number of different prices that a 3 percent coupon bond can assume when the bond's YTM is 2, 3, or 4 percent are graphed over all possible terms to maturity.[14]

Theorem 1   *Bonds' prices move inversely to bonds' YTMs.* More concisely, $\partial p/\partial(\text{YTM}) < 0$.[15]

[12]MD and EL will give slightly different numerical values under two conditions. (1) Equation (13-7) is a *point elasticity* formula. Substantial changes in the interest rate will be explained a little better with a formula for *arc elasticity*. (2) MD assumes that the *yield curve is flat,* since the same YTM is used to discount each period's cashflow. If the slope of the yield curve shifts substantially, this change can have a small effect on the MD calculation.

Some analysts prefer to use **modified duration,** denoted MMD, which is defined below.

$$\text{MMD} = \frac{\text{MD}}{1.0 + \text{YTM}}$$

For an intuitive discussion, see Robert W. Kopprasch, "Understanding Duration and Volatility," in Frank J. Fabozzi and Irving M. Pollack, eds., *The Handbook of Fixed Income Securities,* 2d ed. (Homewood, Ill.: Dow Jones–Irwin, 1987), chap. 5.

[13]Default risk, which affects low-grade bonds, is the topic of Chapter 14.

[14]The basis for the theorems was derived formally by B. G. Malkiel, "Expectations, Bond Prices, and the Term Structure of Interest Rates," *Quarterly Journal of Economics,* May 1962, pp. 197–218. The relationship between term-to-maturity and duration was analyzed by Gabriel Hawawini, "On the Relationship between Macaulay's Bond Duration and the Term to Maturity," *Economics Letters,* 1984, vol. 12.

[15]Using Equations (13-1) or (13-3) and taking the partial derivative of the present value with respect to the YTM furnishes mathematical proof of theorem 1.

$$\frac{\partial p_0}{\partial(\text{YTM})} = \sum_{t=1}^{T} \frac{-tc_t}{(1 + \text{YTM})^{t+1}} < 0$$

where c_t represents the cashflow in period t. This partial derivative must be negative in sign, because all the numerical quantities are positive and thus the negative sign determines the derivative's sign. Similar differential calculus analysis of Equation (13-3) can provide proof of some of the other bond price theorems. Note that the first derivative is illustrated as the slope of the solid price-YTM curve in Figure 13-2.

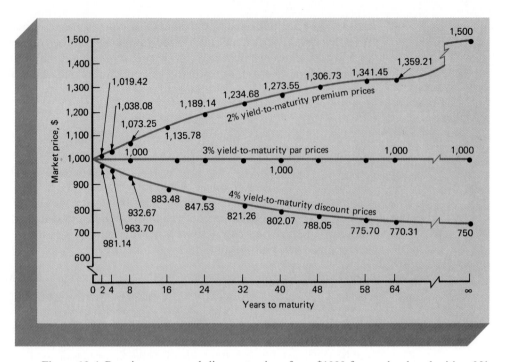

Figure 13-4 Premium, par, and discount prices for a $1000 face value bond with a 3% coupon rate for various maturities at YTMs of 2%, 3%, and 4% (compounded annually).

Theorem 1 reflects the fact that the solid curve in Figure 13-2 is negatively sloped. It also explains why the top curve in Figure 13-4 traces out *premium prices* that occur when the YTMs fall and the bottom curve traces out *discount prices* that occur when the YTMs rise.

Theorem 2 *If all other factors are held constant, a bond's interest rate risk increases with the length of time remaining until it matures.*[16]

The prevalence of positive relationships between the interest rate risk measure MD and the time until the bond matures, shown in Figure 13-3, provides some support for theorem 2. Theorem 2 also explains why the price changes (measured by the difference between the premium and the discount curves) in Figure 13-4 are greater at the longer maturities.

Theorem 3 *A bond's interest rate risk increases at a diminishing rate as the time remaining until its maturity increases.*

Theorem 3 is illustrated in Figure 13-4; notice how the slopes of the curves

---

[16]Theorem 2 is not true for very long-term bonds that are selling at a discount. However, it is true for all other bonds, and it is not far off the mark for long-term discounted bonds.

for premium-priced and discount-priced bonds grow flatter at the longer maturities. As these slopes get flatter, the price fluctuations stop increasing and at the same time the interest rate stops increasing. The way the positive relationships between MD and years until the bond's maturity tend to flatten at the longer maturities in Figure 13-3 also supports Theorem 3.

Theorem 4 *The price change that results from an equal-sized increase or decrease in a bond's YTM is asymmetrical. More specifically, for any given maturity, a decrease in yields causes a price rise that is larger than the price loss that results from an equal increase in yields.*[17]

Theorem 4 can be discerned from the solid curve in Figure 13-2. The fact that the *convexity* of the price-YTM curve decreases (that is, the price-YTM curve gets flatter) as the YTM increases indicates that the bond's price declines are smaller at the higher YTMs.[18]

Theorem 5 *A bond's interest rate risk varies inversely with its coupon rate.*

Numerical evaluation of Equation (13-5) reveals that a bond's MD varies inversely with the size of that bond's coupons. Since MD is an interest rate risk measure, this proves that theorem 5 is true. Figure 13-3*b* illustrates a few examples that support the same conclusion.

The market prices of U.S. Treasury bonds vary significantly from their face values during their lives. The five bond price theorems above explain why these default-free bonds experience this interest rate risk.

13-6   **IMMUNIZING INTEREST RATE RISK**

Immunizing to eliminate interest rate risk is a useful application of the MD measure.[19] **Immunization** will provide a compound rate of return over the im-

---

[17]Theorem 4 assumes yields change from the same starting value whether they move up or down.

[18]Taking the second derivative of present value Equation (13-3) results in the formula for a bond's **convexity:**

$$\frac{d^2p}{d(\text{YTM})^2} = \sum_{t=1}^{T} \frac{t(t+1)c_t}{(1+\text{YTM})^{t+2}} > 0$$

where c_t represents the cashflow in period t. The numerical value of this derivative decreases as the YTM increases; this explains the asymmetric price movements mathematically. Convexity is useful in explaining the bond price theorems and in achieving better immunizations.

[19]In addition to the duration strategies discussed in this chapter, put and call options (Chapters 22 and 23), interest rate futures (Chapter 24), and options on futures (Appendix 24A) provide useful ways of managing interest rate risk. In addition, see Frank J. Fabozzi and T. Dessa Fabozzi, *Bond Markets, Analysis and Strategies* (Englewood Cliffs, N.J.: Prentice-Hall, 1989), chaps. 11, 12, 13, and 14.

munized period that equals the YTM, regardless of the fluctuations in market interest rates during this period. An example is instructive.

Immunization with One Bond—A Simple Example

Suppose that the Palmer Corporation wants to invest $1000 of its cash in a U.S. Treasury bond with a 9 percent coupon rate and face value of $1000 that matures in 10 years. The corporation wants to buy this bond because it will need $1000 to pay a bill coming due in precisely 10 years. An investor in this situation faces interest rate risk as a result of the "reinvestment problem."

A **reinvestment problem** arises when coupon interest must be reinvested at future market interest rates that are below the original YTM. For example, Table 13-3 shows calculations that assume market interest rates shift and then remain fixed at any of four different levels; these new levels are the future *reinvestment rates*. The initial effect of any change in market interest rates is the change in value of the asset; a price gain (loss) occurs immediately when the level of rates is assumed to fall (rise). At each of the four different reinvestment rates assumed for the rest of the bond's 10-year life, the total holding period return from the 10-year 9 percent bond works out differently.

After an initial change in interest rates that is presumed to occur right after the Palmer Corporation buys the $1000 T-bond, the remainder of the decade portrayed in Table 13-3 proceeds without further changes in market interest rates. But, as the decade progresses, the **interest-on-interest** component of a bond's total return exerts an increasing influence. By the end of the decade, Table 13-3 shows that the interest-on-interest dominates the capital gain (or loss) in determining the bonds' total return over the decade. This outcome makes sense. Capital gains occur quickly, whereas changes in reinvestment rates take time to exert their effect on the bond's total return gradually over the decade.[20]

Two opposing forces operate on the total return of a bond—first, interest-on-interest and, second, the bond's market price fluctuations. Considering these opposing forces, the natural question to ask is: At some point in the future do the opposing forces of capital gain and reinvestment returns exactly offset one another? More specifically, if market interest rates jump from, say, 9 to 11 percent and a capital loss occurs right after the $1000 T-bond is purchased, at what point in the future will that capital loss be made up by reinvesting the coupon income payments at the higher future interest rate of 11 percent? The offsetting effects of price change and reinvestment return exactly offset each other when the bond investment has been continuously maintained for the *duration* of the bond. In this case the 10-year T-bond's MD happens to be 6.79 years. The key to immunization is MD.

Table 13-3 shows four sets of calculations worked out for interest rates as

[20]To be more precise, the interest-on-interest equals the interest-on-reinvested-coupons plus interest-on-interest from interest on reinvested coupons.

Table 13-3
TOTAL RETURN FROM A 9% BOND DUE IN 10 YEARS THAT IS HELD THROUGH VARIOUS REINVESTMENT RATES*

Three income or loss sources	Four different reinvestment rates	Holding period in years					
		1	3	5	6.79†	9	10
Coupon income	5%	$90	$270	$450	$611	$810	$900
Capital gain		$287	$234	$175	$100	$39	0
Interest on interest		$1.25	$17	$54	$105	$191	$241
Total return		$378	$521	$679	$816	$1040	$1141
Total yield		37.0%	15.0%	11.0%	9.0%	8.5%	8.2%
Coupon income	7%	$90	$270	$450	$611	$810	$900
Capital gain		$132	$109	$83	$56	$19	0
Interest on interest		$2	$25	$78	$149	$279	$355
Total return		$224	$404	$611	$816	$1108	$1255
Total yield		22.0%	12.0%	10.0%	9.0%	8.6%	8.5%
Coupon income	9%	$90	$270	$450	$611	$810	$900
Capital gain or loss		0	0	0	0	0	0
Interest on interest		$2	$32	$103	$205	$387	$495
Total return		$92	$302	$554	$816	$1197	$1395
Total yield		9.0%	9.0%	9.0%	9.0%	9.0%	9.0%
Coupon income	11%	$90	$270	$450	$611	$810	$900
Capital loss		−$112	−$95	−$75	−$56	−$18	0
Interest on interest		$2	$40	$129	$261	$502	$647
Total return		$20	$215	$504	$816	$1294	$1547
Total yield		2.0%	6.7%	8.5%	9.0%	9.7%	9.8%

*Most of the dollar quantities in the table have been rounded to the nearest whole dollar.
†Duration of a 9% bond bought at par and due in 10 years.
Source: Adapted from Frank J. Fabozzi and Irving M. Pollack, eds., *The Handbook of Fixed Income Securities*, 2d ed. (Homewood, Ill.: Dow Jones–Irwin, 1987), p. 679, exhibit 1.

high as 11 percent and as low as 5 percent. Note that as interest rates fluctuate from 5 to 11 percent, the Palmer Corporation is still able to earn the 9 percent total return through a simple immunization strategy. The firm merely maintains its investment position unchanged for 6.79 years—which happens to be this 10-year T-bond's MD.

Another immunization strategy could also be employed to solve Palmer's

10-year investment problem. To guarantee itself a YTM of 9 percent for a 10-year period during which the reinvestment rates fluctuated, Palmer could invest its money in a bond with a *duration* of 10 years. Some calculations will reveal that the time-to-maturity for a par bond with an MD of 10 years is approximately 23 years.

Investors only need to immunize to lock in a desired rate of return when future market interest rates are expected to change. As Table 13-3 shows, it is easy for Palmer to earn a YTM of 9.0 percent if the level of interest rates stays fixed at 9.0 percent, but that is very unlikely in a dynamic economy.

Investors' desires to immunize (or lock in) an interest rate increase as market interest rates approach what are perceived to be peak levels. Bond investors who expect market interest rates to fall in the future will want to buy bonds at peak interest rates for two reasons. First, bonds will enjoy capital gains if their market interest rates decline. Second, locking in a high YTM is most rewarding to investors at a time when market rates are high.

Immunizing a Portfolio of Bonds

The objective of a portfolio manager who immunizes is to eliminate the portfolio's interest rate risk. Even when corporate bonds are included in the portfolio, immunization does not attempt to reduce any risk other than interest rate risk.

Immunization is said to exist if the total value of a portfolio of bonds at the end of some specified planning horizon is equal to the value of the portfolio based on the YTMs that existed when it was purchased. Stated differently, if the portfolio is immunized, the returns from it will be no less than the returns promised over the planned holding period at the time the investment was made. An example of a company that owns a portfolio containing only two positions will clarify this definition.

Consider again the Palmer Corporation with its loan to be repaid in one lump sum 10 years in the future. However, let us change some of the assumptions. Now assume the Palmer Corporation has a $20,000 debt coming due in 10 years that it wishes to immunize. Call this $20,000 liability the first item in the Palmer portfolio. Palmer is considering the purchase of default-free bonds that have 10-year maturities and face values totaling $20,000. Call the Palmer Corporation's cash set aside to purchase these bonds the second item in the company's portfolio of only two items. To invest this cash without taking any *reinvestment rate risks,* the firm considers purchasing a $20,000 *zero coupon* default-free bond that matures in 10 years. If this asset can be selected so that its maturity date falls on the due date of the outstanding $20,000 debt, it will be very convenient for the Palmer Corporation. By matching the maturity dates of an asset and a liability that are of the same size and that involve no intermediate cashflow problems, the interest rate risk in Palmer's two-item portfolio can be eliminated. This **maturity matching strategy** is the simplest kind of protection against interest-rate risk.

Unfortunately, this example of the Palmer Corporation's portfolio containing a $20,000 liability is unrealistic in three respects. (1) The zero coupon bonds with the specific maturity date needed may not exist. (2) It is typically impossible to find fixed-income assets *of any kind* with maturity dates that synchronize exactly with the due dates of the existing liabilities. And if the asset is a coupon bond, its duration will be less than its term-to-maturity. (3) Assets do not typically come in the exact denomination (such as $20,000) that equals the liability to be paid with the proceeds. Solving the problems created by these three realities leads to the *duration matching immunization strategy* described below.

Duration Matching—A Better Immunization Strategy   A portfolio of bonds can be immunized by selecting the bonds in the portfolio so that their *weighted average* MD equals the MD of an offsetting liability that has the same dollar value. For instance, if the Palmer Corporation had a $20,000 liability that was coming due in 10 years and had to be repaid in one lump sum, this liability would have a MD of 10 years (since the intermediate cashflows are zero). The Palmer Corporation might immunize this $20,000 liability by purchasing two different bonds that had a weighted average duration of 10 years and an aggregate value of $20,000 at their duration (as differentiated from their maturity). This *duration matching* transaction would fully immunize the $20,000 portfolio. The duration of a portfolio equals the dollar-weighted average of the durations of the bonds that make up the portfolio, as shown in Equation (13-9).[21]

$$\text{MD}_p = \frac{V_1(\text{MD}_1) + V_2(\text{MD}_2)}{V_1 + V_2} \tag{13-9}$$

where V_1 and V_2 = dollar values of two bonds in portfolio
     MD_1 and MD_2 = two bonds' respective durations
        MD_p = weighted average duration of the portfolio containing two bonds[22]

[21]Equation (13-9) might lead to an approximation if the YTMs change by different amounts, $\Delta \text{YTM}_1 \neq \Delta \text{YTM}_2$. Since the YTMs are an input to the duration calculations, every asset that has a different YTM will have its duration affected differently by a change in the market interest rates. (See section entitled "How to Calculate the YTM for a Portfolio of Bonds.") To be accurate in calculating the duration for a portfolio, the aggregate cashflows for the entire portfolio must be used in Equation (13-5) to calculate the portfolio's duration.
[22]Redington first showed how Macaulay's duration worked for the assets and liabilities of a firm and invented the expression "immunization." See F. M. Redington, "Review of the Principle of Life Office Valuations," *Journal of the Institute of Actuaries*, 1952, vol. 78, pp. 286–340. Fisher and Weil showed that a duration matching strategy would almost perfectly immunize the value of a portfolio even though market interest rates fluctuated; see Lawrence Fisher and Roman L. Weil, "Coping with the Risk of Market Interest Rate Fluctuations: Returns to Bondholders from Naive and Optimal Strategies," *Journal of Business*, Oct. 1971, pp. 408–431.

LP Formulation of the Duration Matching Strategy   The duration matching immunization strategy endeavors to keep the weighted average duration of the assets in a diversified portfolio of bonds equal to some desired time horizon, denoted H. The following *linear programming (LP)* formulation is the simplest way to solve the duration matching immunization problem when N different assets are being considered as candidates for the portfolio.[23]

$$\text{Maximize: YTM}_p = \sum_{i=1}^{N} x_i \text{ YTM}_i$$

subject to the following constraints:

$$\sum_{i=1}^{N} x_i \text{ MD}_i = H \text{ years}$$

$$\sum_{i=1}^{N} x_i = 1.0 \qquad \text{where } x_i > 0 \text{ for all } i$$

The proportion of the portfolio invested in asset i is denoted x_i. The LP evaluates N different assets and solves to find the x_i values that maximize the portfolio's weighted average YTM. Additional constraints could be added if desired.

"Duration Wandering" and Rebalancing   The duration of a bond will not move in one-to-one correspondence with the passage of time—as shown above in Figure 13-3. Therefore, the manager of a portfolio of bonds that is immunizing must "rebalance" the bonds in the portfolio on a periodic basis to maintain the portfolio's duration at the value that will eliminate its interest rate risk. Annual or semiannual rebalancing may be sufficient. To illustrate, suppose the remaining life in the planning period for the Palmer portfolio has declined by 1 year—from a decade to 9 years. The duration of the original bonds in the portfolio may have declined by less than 1 year—say, to a weighted average of 9.2 years. To neutralize the risky effects of this *duration-wandering* tendency, the manager of the bond portfolio should rebalance the portfolio in order to match the duration of the bond assets with the remaining time in the planning horizon. *Rebalancing* the portfolio may be done on dates when cash is received or by selling off some or all of the original bonds and buying bonds that have a shorter duration. Care should be taken to avoid liquidating bonds that have temporarily depressed prices and/or generating other trading costs that do not provide benefits of commensurate value. Left unchecked, unavoidable duration wandering will cause the market value of the portfolio to fluctuate in a fashion

[23]An LP program to solve this problem has been published in BASIC for an IBM-PC or compatible. See Richard Bookstaber, *The Complete Investment Book* (Glenview, Ill.: Scott, Foresman, 1985). See chap. 8, entitled "Immunization: Risk Management Strategies for Bond Portfolios," for a detailed explanation of the computer program. The program is also available through Appendix D of this book.

that will almost always diminish the effectiveness of the immunization. But by monitoring and adjusting the portfolio's duration, the manager of a portfolio of bonds can reimmunize it in the face of continual shifts in the market interest rates.[24]

13-7 PROBLEMS WITH DURATION AND IMMUNIZATION

Various criticisms have been aimed at the MD measure of duration and at immunization, as we shall see next.

Changes in the Term Structure of Interest Rates

Since the YTM is one of the determinants in the duration formula, fluctuating market interest rates cause changes in bonds' durations. These changes in the durations of the assets and liabilities in a portfolio are another source of risk. **Stochastic process risk** refers to uncertainty arising from shifts in the term structure of interest rates. Portfolio managers can deal with stochastic process risk by mathematically deriving duration measures that depend explicitly on the movement in the term structure of interest rates. However, if the shift in the yield curve incorporated into the duration measure is inappropriate, the supposedly immunized portfolio can be exposed to interest rate risk.[25] Analysts have developed duration measures, discussed in the following section, to deal with various types of stochastic process risk.

Alternative Duration Measures

Fisher-Weil Duration Professors Fisher and Weil suggested the duration measure defined in Equation (13-10).[26]

[24]For a discussion of various bond portfolio management techniques, see H. Gifford Fong and Frank J. Fabozzi, *Fixed Income Portfolio Management* (Homewood, Ill.: Dow Jones–Irwin, 1985). Also see Michael R. Granito, *Bond Portfolio Immunization* (Lexington, Mass.: Lexington Books, 1984). See also George G. Kaufman, G. O. Bierwag, and Alden Toevs, eds., *Innovations in Bond Portfolio Management* (Greenwich, Conn.: JAI Press, 1983). In addition, see Gerald O. Bierwag, *Duration Analysis* (Cambridge, Mass.: Ballinger Press, 1987).

[25]Immunization, rebalancing immunized portfolios, and dealing with the stochastic process risk that results from changes in the yield curve which affect bonds' durations are all discussed in G. O. Bierwag, George G. Kaufman, and Alden Toevs, "Duration: Its Development and Use in Bond Portfolio Management," *Financial Analysts Journal*, July–Aug. 1983, pp. 15–35.

[26]Lawrence Fisher and Roman L. Weil, "Coping with the Risk of Market Interest Rate Fluctuations: Returns to Bondholders from Naive and Optimal Strategies," *Journal of Business*, Oct. 1971, pp. 408–431.

$$\text{FWD} = 1 \left(\frac{c_1/(1 + r_1)}{p_0} \right) + 2 \left(\frac{c_2/(1 + r_1)(1 + r_2)}{p_0} \right)$$

$$+ \cdots + T \left(\frac{c_T/(1 + r_1)(1 + r_2) \cdots (1 + r_T)}{p_0} \right) \qquad (13\text{-}10)$$

The FWD measure is conceptually similar to MD; for most bonds the two measures produce similar duration values. However, the *Fisher-Weil duration* (*FWD*) measure might be superior to Macaulay's measure because FWD considers the single-period interest rate (represented by the r_t symbols) during the period when each cashflow occurs. In contrast, the MD formula uses the invariant YTM as a discount rate. Essentially, the FWD brings the term structure of interest rates into the analysis, while the simpler MD measure implicitly assumes that the yield curve is horizontal at the value of YTM.

CIR Duration   Cox, Ingersoll, and Ross (CIR) proposed a third duration measure. CIR used stochastic calculus to formulate an interest rate generating function and then derived a complex duration measure.[27]

Testing MD, FWD, and CIR   Financial researchers have tested the competing measures of duration referred to as MD, FWD, and CIR. One published study reported that:

> the evidence suggests that the Macaulay measure of duration performs reasonably well in comparison to its more sophisticated counterparts and, because of its simplicity, appears to be cost-effective.[28]

Other researchers have reached the same conclusion.

Babbel Duration   David Babbel has developed a duration measure that is based on what he calls a "term structure of interest rates volatility" measure. Babbel's duration measure (BD hereafter) is similar in some ways to MD, but it is also significantly different. For example, his measure is valid for nonparallel shifts in the yield curve, whereas MD is strictly valid only for parallel shifts.

---

[27]J. C. Cox, J. E. Ingersoll, and S. Ross, "Duration and the Measurement of Basis Risk," *Journal of Business,* Jan. 1971.

[28]Competing measures of duration are discussed by G. O. Bierwag, George G. Kaufman, and Alden Toevs, "Duration: Its Development and Use in Bond Portfolio Management," *Financial Analysts Journal,* July–Aug. 1983, pp. 15–35.

Also see Patrick W. Lau, "An Empirical Examination of Alternative Interest Rate Risk Immunization Strategies," unpublished Ph.D. dissertation, University of Wisconsin, 1983. Lau conducts empirical tests of immunization strategies that are based on different definitions of duration and also concludes that Macaulay's duration is more cost-effective than the FWD or CIR measures.

Babbel has tested empirically the ability of his BD measure to immunize risk and reported encouraging test results.[29]

Other Models MD, FWD, CIR, BD, and many other measures are called *one-factor models* because they are based on fluctuations in one interest rate. Other authors are developing more complex immunization strategies.[30]

Various researchers have been active in the development of *two-factor interest rate risk models*. The two-factor models usually use a short-term and a long-term interest rate as their two factors.[31]

Each of the alternative duration measures mentioned above implies a different duration strategy. No single model is superior under all circumstances; each one is good in the environment it is modeled to reflect.[32]

13-8   SUMMARY AND CONCLUSIONS

We began by showing how to calculate the present value of a default-free bond. Then the YTM was defined as the discount rate that equates the present value of all a bond's promised cashflows with its current market price. The YTM was contrasted with other bond return and bond yield measurements.

[29]David F. Babbel, "Duration and the Term Structure of Interest Rate Volatility," in G. G. Kaufman, G. O. Bierwag, and A. Toevs, eds., *Innovations in Bond Portfolio Management* (Greenwich, Conn.: JAI Press, 1983), pp. 239–265. More complete test results can be obtained from Professor Babbel, Finance Department, Wharton School, University of Pennsylvania, Philadelphia, Penn.

[30]Babbel's model is a one-factor model in which the 1-year spot rate is the factor. All other rates are modeled based on how they move relative to changes in the 1-year rate. A one-factor model like Babbel's and two-factor models are derived and tested by Jeffrey Nelson and Stephen Schaefer, "The Dynamics of the Term Structure and Alternative Portfolio Immunization Strategies," in G. G. Kaufman, G. O. Bierwag, and A. Toevs, eds., *Innovations in Bond Portfolio Management* (Greenwich, Conn.: JAI Press, 1983), pp. 61–102.

[31]See M. J. Brennan and E. S. Schwartz, "A Continuous Time Approach to the Pricing of Bonds," *Journal of Banking and Finance*, 1979, vol. 3, pp. 133–155. Also see M. J. Brennan and E. S. Schwartz, "Conditional Predictions of Bond Prices and Returns," *Journal of Finance*, May 1980, vol. 35, no. 2, pp. 405–416. See also M. J. Brennan and E. S. Schwartz, "An Equilibrium Model of Bond Pricing and a Test of Market Efficiency," *Journal of Financial and Quantitative Analysis*, Sept. 1982, pp. 301–329. For a discrete time two-factor model, see G. O. Bierwag, G. G. Kaufman, and Cynthia M. Latta, "Bond Portfolio Immunization: Tests of Maturity, One- and Two-Factor Duration Matching Strategies," *Financial Review*, May 1987, pp. 203–220.

[32]To see how duration can be used to analyze interest rate risk in preferred stock, see Patrick Casabona, Frank J. Fabozzi, and J. C. Francis, "The Why's and the How's of Applying Macaulay and Hicks Duration to Analyze Financial Riskiness," *Journal of Portfolio Management*, Winter 1984.

Macaulay's duration was defined as the average length of time that the funds remain tied up in an investment. The MD formula revealed that a bond's duration is the weighted average length of time until each cashflow is received, using the relative present values of the cashflows as the weights. MD was shown to be a different measure of the time structure of a bond's cashflows than was the bond's term-to-maturity. Then a bond's price elasticity with respect to a change in interest rates was defined and shown to be (1) equal to MD and (2) a measure of a bond investment's interest rate risk. MD and EL were used to derive five bond pricing theorems that are insightful for bond investors.

Immunization strategies were introduced to eliminate the interest rate risk in a portfolio of bonds. The discussion revealed that duration was not only (1) an insightful measure of the time structure of a bond's cashflows and (2) a measure of a bond's interest rate risk, it was also (3) useful in the development of strategies for managing the interest rate risk in a portfolio of bonds.

Essay Questions

13-1 What is the duration of a bond that has a YTM of 6 percent and a perpetual maturity? Show your calculations. *Hint: There is a short-cut formula for perpetuities in Chapter 13* (Figure 13-3 and Table 13-2).

13-2 What is the relationship between a bond's coupon rate and its duration? Explain.

13-3 "It is possible for a bond portfolio manager to immunize the portfolio against any interest rate risk." True, false, or uncertain? Explain.

13-4 What happens to a bond's duration if the bond's YTM rises?

13-5 "Duration does not correspond with the exact date of any particular cashflow that a default-free bond may experience. Therefore duration is a worthless measure of the time structure of a bond's cashflows." True, false, or uncertain? Explain.

13-6 Check a newspaper listing for Treasury securities that is more complete than Figure 2-1. Do some Treasury bonds ever have more than one year for their maturity date? Why?

13-7 Under what conditions would a bond's coupon rate be larger than its current yield? Explain.

13-8 What is the bid-asked spread for the 3½'s of 1998 listed in Figure 2-1? Does anyone profit from this spread? Explain.

Problems

13-9 Calculate the present value and MD for a bond paying an 8.0 percent coupon rate annually on its $1000 face value if it has 8 years until its maturity and a YTM of 9.0 percent. Show your computations. What is this bond's interest rate elasticity? *Hint: Check footnote 10 in Chapter 13 for a simple formula to ease your computational work.*

13-10 Reconsider the bond described in Question 13-9. Assume the bond's YTM was 8.0 percent and recalculate its present value, MD, and EL. What can you conclude from this problem about the relationship between (*a*) the level of market interest rates and (*b*) interest rate risk?

13-11 Would you prefer to invest in (*a*) a 10-year bond with a 4.5 percent coupon rate which is selling at 89.89 percent of its face value or (*b*) a similar 10-year bond which is selling at par and has a 5.85 percent coupon rate? Assume both bonds are issued by the same firm and have the same provisions in every respect except that their coupon rates differ. Explain why you prefer one bond over the other.

13-12 Consider the tombstone from Salomon Brothers in Figure 13-5. Assume that Salomon's average commission rate on the common stock was one-fourth of 1 percent to sell the stock and the previously owned bonds plus another one-fourth of 1 percent for all new securities purchased. How much commission did the Chrysler Corporation pay to dedicate its pension fund? *Hint: Read Appendix 13A to learn about dedicated-pension strategies.*

13-13 (*a*) Calculate the duration of the following three U.S. Treasury bonds assuming coupons are paid semiannually.

Figure 13-5 Tombstone from *The New York Times* announcing that Salomon dedicated Chrysler's pension portfolio. (*Source:* August 16, 1984, *The New York Times*, p. D19.)

Bond	Coupon rate	Years until maturity	Yield-to-maturity	Macaulay's duration
A	10.0%	2.0	10.0%	?
B	10.0	3.0	10.0	?
C	0	3.0	10.0	?

(b) Explain why the three bonds above have different durations using intuitive verbal economics rather than pure mathematics.

13-14 Assume that the U.S. Treasury issued a bond that pays coupons of 10.0 percent semiannually for 15 years. (a) What will be the price of the bond 2 years after its issue date if the market rate of interest is 12 percent? (b) What will this bond's Macaulay's duration be 2 years after it is issued?

13-15 Assume that the U.S. Treasury issued a bond that pays coupons of 10.0 percent semiannually for 15 years. (a) What will be the price of the bond 5 years after its issue date if the market rate of interest is 8.0 percent? (b) What will this bond's Macaulay's duration be 5 years after it is issued?

13-16 A U.S. Treasury bond that has a $1000 face value and pays a 12.0 percent coupon semiannually currently is selling for $856. (a) If the bond issue has 14 years until maturity, what is its YTM? (b) What is this bond's YTM if it is selling for $1150?

13-17 Calculate the YTM and Macaulay's duration for the two Treasury bonds below.

Year	Bond 1 cashflows	Bond 2 cashflows	
0	−$1000	−$1000	←Purchase price
1	100	0	
2	100	0	
3	100	0	
4	100	0	
5	100	0	
6	1100	1700	←Selling price

13-18 Gerald Jones purchased a 10 percent coupon semiannual bond of the Farr Corporation at par value which had 10 years to maturity. Immediately after Jones purchased the bond, interest rates on bonds of this risk level rose to 12 percent and remained there until the bond was sold at the end of the fifth year. If the yield curve remained flat during the 5-year period that Jones owned the bond and he reinvested all of his coupon interest, what rate of return did he earn on his 5-year investment? Ignore taxes and commissions.

13-19 Using the information in Problem 13-18, what return would Mr. Jones earn if he sold the bond in 3 years?

13-20 Using the information in Problem 13-18, what return would Jones earn if the interest rate fell to 8 percent right after he purchased the bond and then remained there for the 5 years he invested in the bond?

13-21 Determine the duration of the bond in Problem 13-18 just after it was purchased so that it had 10 years until it matured. Find the duration both (a) before the bond's YTM rose above 10 percent and (*b*) after the interest rate changed to 12 percent.

13-22 A 3.0 percent coupon Treasury bond that has 16 years until its maturity date yields 3.0 percent so that it is priced to sell at its par value of $10,000. (*a*) If the market interest rate rises by 100 basis points from a starting point where the YTM equals 3.0 percent, how much will the bond's price change? (*b*) If the market interest rate falls by 100 basis points from a starting point where the YTM equals 3.0 percent, how much will the bond's price change? (*c*) Which of the bond pricing theorems describes what your calculations have documented? *Hint: See Figure 13-4.*

Selected References

Bierwag, G. O., *Duration Analysis, Managing Interest Rate Risk* (Cambridge, Mass.: Ballinger Press, 1987).

   This mathematical monograph discusses interest rate risk in a comprehensive manner. The book begins by defining the YTM and proceeds logically to explain interest rate risk and increasingly sophisticated methods for managing interest rate risk.

Bierwag, G. O., George G. Kaufman, and Alden Toevs, "Duration: Its Development and Use in Bond Portfolio Management," *Financial Analysts Journal*, July–Aug. 1983, pp. 15–35.

   An easy-to-read survey of the research that led to duration as a useful tool for bond portfolio managers. Only a little elementary algebra is used.

Fabozzi, Frank J., and T. Dessa Fabozzi, *Bond Markets, Analysis and Strategies* (Englewood Cliffs, N.J.: Prentice-Hall, 1989).

   This college finance textbook describes bond markets and surveys modern interest rate theory. A little differential calculus is used.

Fisher, Lawrence, and Roman L. Weil, "Coping with the Risk of Market-Rate Fluctuations: Returns to Bondholders from Naive and Optimal Strategies," *Journal of Business*, Oct. 1977, pp. 408–431.

   This study investigates the effectiveness of immunization in reducing interest rate risk. Portfolio management with a shifting term structure of interest rates is simulated. Only elementary algebra is used.

Haugen, R. A., and D. W. Wichern, "The Elasticity of Financial Assets," *Journal of Finance*, Sept. 1974, pp. 1229–1240.

   Algebra and differential calculus are used to derive both the duration and elasticity measures of interest rate risk from the present value model of security valuation. Bankruptcy risk is also considered in the analysis so that it is relevant for both stock and bond valuation.

Hopewell, M. H., and G. G. Kaufman, "Bond Price Volatility and Term to Maturity: A Generalized Respecification," *American Economic Review*, Sept. 1973, pp. 749–753.

   Differential calculus is used to show that Macaulay's duration is a measure of interest risk for bonds.

Appendix 13A

Dedicated Pension Strategies

Pension funds are the largest investors in the United States. **Defined-benefit pension plans** are usually the biggest pensions; they are funded by employers that have voluntarily granted their employees a fringe benefit that takes the form of a legally enforceable liability to pay specified pension benefits. The typical defined-benefit pension plan promises monthly payments until the retired employees and their beneficiaries die.

Dedicated pension plans are a sophisticated new kind of portfolio strategy that is used to fund some of the largest defined-benefit pension plans. A **dedicated pension plan** is a formal strategy for bond investing that minimizes the risk that the portfolio manager will be unable to meet a *series* of scheduled pension payments because of interest rate risk.[33]

Dedicated pension plans use duration and immunization, and go on to address a broader range of portfolio objectives that concern pension fund managers. Dedicating part of a pension fund involves endeavoring to synchronize a pension fund's cash inflows and outflows, analyzing the pension fund's actuarially determined future liabilities, and attempting to reduce the corporation's cost of funding its pension obligations. A 1982 case involving the pension fund of the hypothetical Palmer Corporation will be used as a vehicle for discussion.

There are two techniques for dedicating a portfolio: (1) multiple liability (or multiperiod) immunization and (2) cashflow matching. The second method is more popular because it is the simpler of the two techniques.[34] The Palmer case discussed below is a case of cashflow matching.[35]

[33]For an explanation of the various types of pension plans and different bond portfolio management procedures, see J. L. Maginn and Donald L. Tuttle, eds., *Managing Investment Portfolios,* sponsored by The Institute of Chartered Financial Analysts (Boston, Mass.: Warren, Gorham & Lamont, 1983), pp. 63–85 of chap. 4 and chap. 9.

[34]For a more in-depth discussion of immunization see H. Gifford Fong and Frank J. Fabozzi, *Fixed Income Portfolio Management* (Homewood, Ill.: Dow Jones–Irwin, 1985). For a discussion of multiple liability (or multiperiod) immunization, see pp. 138–142. Also see G. O. Bierwag, G. K. Kaufman, and Alden Toevs, "Immunization Strategies for Funding Multiple Liabilities," *Journal of Financial and Quantitative Analysis,* March 1983, pp. 113–124.

[35]The Palmer Corporation's dedicated pension portfolio case is adapted from Peter E. Christensen,

(continues)

Determining the Employer's Pension Liabilities

The *first step* taken to establish a dedicated strategy for a pension fund is to forecast the employer's benefit payout obligations. Table 13A-1 shows the year-by-year schedule of annual nominal dollar payments that the Palmer Corporation is legally obligated to make to its retirees over a 30-year period. Schedules of expected benefit payouts like Table 13A-1 are prepared by actuaries who consider the retirees' mortality projections, spousal benefits, and cost-of-living adjustments that may reasonably be expected in the future. Such schedules of expected pension obligations should be reviewed by external actuarial consultants to determine if the assumptions on which the projections are based remain accurate and to extend the projections as a basis for new plans.

Most employers' not-yet-retired workers comprise a larger potential pension fund liability than do their already-retired workers. However, the employer's obligation to its not-yet-retired workers is usually not funded by a dedicated bond portfolio because of various unknowns. Uncertainty about the workers' turnover rate, mortality rate, retirement age, future layoffs and hirings, and other factors makes it difficult to estimate the employer's retirement obligation to its not-yet-retired workers. For these reasons, only that $328,586,813 portion of the Palmer Corporation's total pension funding obligation that is easy to assess actuarially because it is made up of known retirees is being committed to a dedicated pension strategy. A different corporation's management might have decided to dedicate more or less of its total pension obligation.

Selecting the Optimum Portfolio of Assets

After the actuaries have provided the employer with an estimate of its expected benefit payout obligations, like the one shown in Table 13A-1, the *second step* in the dedication procedure is to delineate whatever constraints the pension fund manager wants to place on the dedicated bond portfolio. That is, the pension fund manager must specify what quality of bonds from what sector of the bond market are to be purchased and dedicated to meeting the expected annual liabilities. The financial managers of the Palmer Corporation stipulated that they wanted only U.S. Treasury obligations in their dedicated bond portfolio.[36]

Finally, the *third step* in establishing a dedicated pension portfolio plan is to specify the *reinvestment rate assumption* to be used in planning for the cash inflows and outflows. *This third step is much more important than it may seem because the timing of cash receipts and disbursements frequently cannot be synchronized.* In particular, if

---

(continued)

Sylvan G. Feldstein, and Frank J. Fabozzi, ''Dealing with High Corporate, State, and Municipal Pension Costs by 'Dedicating' a Bond Portfolio,'' in Frank J. Fabozzi and Irving M. Pollack, eds., *The Handbook of Fixed Income Securities* (Homewood, Ill.: Dow Jones–Irwin, 1983), chap. 37, exhibit 4, p. 823.

[36]If the pension fund's managers were seeking higher rates of return, they might have stipulated a more complicated constraint. For example, more aggressive pension fund managers might stipulate that corporate bonds of AA grade or better be selected, with a maximum of 20 percent of the portfolio to be invested in the bonds of foreign corporations. Pragmatically speaking, the optimum portfolio is selected using a mathematical programming algorithm called linear programming (LP). The investment constraints thus determine what bonds the LP computer program is given from which to make its selection and what inequality or equality constraints are placed on the LP selection algorithm.

Table 13A-1

**PALMER CORPORATION'S
SCHEDULE OF EXPECTED BENEFIT
PAYOUTS, 1982**

Year	Payout amounts
1982	$ 8,067,461
1983	23,225,960
1984	22,444,547
1985	21,626,503
1986	20,776,913
1987	19,897,961
1988	18,994,617
1989	18,062,762
1990	17,117,618
1991	16,147,201
1992	15,163,588
1993	14,177,133
1994	13,188,631
1995	12,192,553
1996	11,224,388
1997	10,266,058
1998	9,338,069
1999	8,433,031
2000	7,575,599
2001	6,767,880
2002	5,996,468
2003	5,278,810
2004	4,604,799
2005	3,939,332
2006	3,439,599
2007	2,934,052
2008	2,497,460
2009	2,093,629
2010	1,748,721
2011	1,447,570
Total liability	$328,568,813

the selected reinvestment rate that the actuary approves is high enough, it may be advantageous for the pension fund manager to purchase bonds with high yields that mature before the date of the liability they were purchased to fund and then to reinvest the maturing principal at the reinvestment rate for the short time until the liability comes due. Thus, we see how the reinvestment rate can affect the optimum pension fund investment decisions.

High market interest rates of over 13 percent were available from U.S. Treasury bonds in 1982 when the Palmer pension portfolio was dedicated. After considering those investment opportunities, Palmer's actuaries and auditors selected 13.08 percent as the reinvestment rate that was appropriate.

After the schedule of expected benefit payouts has been actuarially estimated in step 1, the portfolio constraints have been laid down by the financial managers of the sponsoring corporation in step 2, and the reinvestment rate has been selected in step 3, the pension fund manager can set about structuring the least-cost dedicated pension portfolio. Structuring a least-cost pension portfolio that will fully fund (or **defease**) the expected benefit payouts is a complicated task for which the pension fund manager will usually retain a financial consultant.

The financial consultant that structures the dedicated pension portfolio will probably formulate the portfolio selection problem as a *linear programming (LP)* problem that is solved via computer. An LP is a mathematical programming technique that employs linear equations and inequalities as constraints while it either maximizes or minimizes some objective that is also a linear equation—such as finding the minimum-cost funding plan for a pension obligation over 30 years. For each year this LP program must select from among the numerous bond issues available the appropriate quantities of each issue that have maturity dates that precede the dates when the estimated pension payments must be made and also have the least cost when the income from the reinvestments is considered.[37] Table 13A-2 shows the dedicated pension portfolio selected to meet the needs of the Palmer Corporation by purchasing only round lots of bonds.[38]

Comparing the Cash Inflows and the Cash Outflows

Table 13A-3 lists and compares the annual cash receipts and disbursements for the Palmer Corporation's dedicated pension portfolio over the 30-year planning horizon. In every year the cash receipts from maturing principal and coupon interest income almost exactly equals the cash outflow requirements forecasted by the actuary in Table 13A-1.[39] Since most of the portfolio's coupon income is being paid out shortly after it is received, the portfolio is assuming very little reinvestment risk.[40] This also allowed the portfolio to lock in the high interest rates of over 13 percent that existed in 1982 and thereby reduce the employer's pension costs.

Table 13A-3 contains no bond price information because bond prices have nothing to do with the Palmer portfolio's annual cash inflows and outflows. The portfolio's default-free Treasury bonds are held until their maturity so that all coupon income and principal payments can be assumed to occur as expected when formulating the portfolio's LP problem. However, even if corporate bonds that suffered deteriorating quality ratings and the associated declines in their market prices were included in the portfolio, these price declines would not affect the cashflows in Table 13A-3 as long as the bonds' issuers punctually met all their scheduled coupon and principal payments.

[37]Most colleges offer courses in operations research, management science, or applied mathematics that explain how to formulate and solve linear programming (LP) problems.

[38]Structuring a dedicated pension portfolio that has a high probability of meeting all the pensions' funding needs in every year usually requires that low-quality bonds that might default in the years ahead not be considered as potential investments. Callable bond issues and issues that are backed by large sinking funds should also not be included in the portfolio because they may be redeemed before their maturity dates. After a dedicated pension portfolio is established, the quality of its assets should be reviewed and the portfolio should be rebalanced at least once per year.

[39]A large surplus of $17,446,270 was selected by the linear program (LP) for the year 2002 because there were no desirable Treasury bond issues available in the subsequent years.

[40]The linear program (LP) was formulated with a reinvestment rate assumption of 13.08 percent while the market yields on U.S. Treasury bonds were over 13 percent in 1982 when the Palmer portfolio was dedicated. As a result, the LP determined that the least-cost way to fund Palmer's pension liabilities was to lock in the high current rates rather than earn the lower reinvestment rate of 13.08 percent.

Table 13A-2

THE PALMER CORPORATION'S DEDICATED PENSION PORTFOLIO OF U.S. TREASURY BONDS SELECTED IN 1982

Par amount, 000	Coupon rate	Maturity date
$ 673	11.125%	8/31/82
3,000	12.125	10/31/82
3,000	14.125	4/30/83
3,000	15.500	10/31/83
2,600	13.875	4/30/84
3,200	12.125	9/30/84
3,000	13.375	3/31/85
3,100	15.875	9/30/85
2,600	14.000	3/31/86
3,200	14.875	6/30/86
3,900	16.125	11/15/86
2,900	13.750	8/15/87
3,100	12.375	1/15/88
3,200	14.000	7/15/88
3,000	14.625	1/15/89
7,800	14.500	7/15/89
2,000	10.750	8/15/90
3,000	13.000	11/15/90
4,600	14.500	5/15/91
9,400	14.625	2/15/92
3,100	8.625	8/15/93
2,900	9.000	2/15/94
2,000	8.750	8/15/94
2,700	10.125	11/15/94
5,300	10.375	5/15/95
2,400	12.625	5/15/95
12,000	11.500	11/15/95
2,900	8.500	5/15/99
3,300	7.875	2/15/00
3,800	11.750	2/15/01
12,000	15.750	11/15/01
8,700	14.250	2/15/02
2,500	11.750	2/15/10

Savings to the Palmer Corporation

Table 13A-4 lists the market prices that existed on August 2, 1982 for all the bonds listed in Table 13A-2. Note that on that date the aggregate market value of all the bonds in the Palmer portfolio was $135,271,091. This amount was adequate to fully fund the total benefit payouts of $328,586,813 that are listed in Table 13A-1. The YTM for the

Table 13A-3
SUMMARY OF THE PALMER PORTFOLIO'S CASHFLOW MATCH

Year	Maturing principal	Coupon income	Rein-vestment income	Liability payments	Surplus or deficits	Cumulative surplus
1982	$ 673,000	$ 2,503,309	$ 8,049	$ −1,991,886	$ 1,192,471	$ 1,192,471
1983	6,000,001	17,225,743	136,890	−23,395,126	−32,493	1,159,979
1984	5,600,001	16,376,368	115,092	−22,639,894	−548,433	611,546
1985	6,200,001	15,589,118	125,441	−21,831,010	83,551	695,097
1986	8,900,001	14,747,806	139,292	−20,989,299	2,797,800	3,492,897
1987	6,800,001	13,347,306	223,511	−20,117,685	253,133	3,746,030
1988	6,300,001	12,442,307	181,143	−19,220,445	−296,995	3,449,036
1989	10,800,002	11,583,120	203,721	−18,295,716	4,291,127	7,740,162
1990	2,000,000	10,232,745	303,141	−17,353,893	−4,818,006	2,922,156
1991	7,600,001	9,822,745	240,129	−16,389,795	1,273,081	4,195,237
1992	9,400,002	8,273,371	419,266	−15,409,479	2,683,160	6,878,397
1993	3,100,001	7,585,997	266,296	−14,423,738	−3,471,445	3,406,952
1994	4,900,001	7,188,122	151,788	−13,435,751	−1,195,841	2,211,111
1995	10,400,002	6,745,935	282,143	−12,441,571	4,986,508	7,197,619
1996	12,000,002	5,066,373	980,330	−11,466,433	6,580,272	13,777,891
1997		4,376,373	763,687	−10,505,644	−5,365,585	8,412,306
1998		4,376,373	411,971	−9,570,064	−4,781,721	3,630,586
1999	2,900,000	4,376,373	161,191	−8,659,294	−1,221,730	2,408,856
2000	3,300,001	3,999,935	158,856	−7,789,960	−331,167	2,077,688
2001	3,800,001	3,646,748	174,601	−6,969,810	651,539	2,729,227
2002	20,700,003	1,858,624	1,076,967	−6,189,324	17,446,270	20,175,497
2003		293,750	1,261,810	−5,458,227	−3,902,667	16,272,830
2004		293,750	1,009,177	−4,773,300	−3,470,373	12,802,457
2005		293,750	780,738	−4,105,701	−3,031,213	9,771,244
2006		293,750	583,442	−3,564,531	−2,687,339	7,083,904
2007		293,750	408,293	−3,060,435	−2,358,391	4,725,513
2008		293,750	256,204	−2,606,610	−2,056,656	2,668,857
2009		293,750	122,502	−2,194,587	−1,778,335	890,522
2010	2,500,000	146,875	102,462	−1,834,878	914,459	1,804,981
2011			77,319	−1,522,835	−1,445,517	359,465
2012		4,150		−361,893	−357,743	1,721
Totals:	$133,873,022	$183,567,913	$11,129,600	−$328,568,813	$1,721	

Palmer portfolio was 13.21 percent on August 2, 1982, reflecting the high yields available in the market on that date.

Table 13A-5 summarizes the potential benefits to the Palmer Corporation from dedicating part of its pension portfolio. These savings are predicated upon the willingness of Palmer's actuaries to raise their reinvestment rate assumption from the old 7.0 percent rate to the new rate of 13.08 that was appropriate on August 2, 1982. The portfolio's internal rate of return of 13.08 percent on August 2, 1982 was the appropriate reinvestment rate assumption based on the current market investment opportunities that

Table 13A-4

PRICING OF THE BONDS IN THE PALMER DEDICATED BOND PORTFOLIO

Bond name	Face value, $000	Coupon rate	Maturity date	Yield to maturity or call	Price	Market value
Treasury	673	11.125%	8/31/82	9.86%	$100.065	$ 704,842
Treasury	3,000	12.125	10/31/82	10.49	100.317	3,101,458
Treasury	3,000	14.500	4/30/83	12.07	101.626	3,159,946
Treasury	3,000	15.500	10/31/83	12.65	103.129	3,211,411
Treasury	2,600	13.875	4/30/84	12.97	101.313	2,726,329
Treasury	3,200	12.125	9/30/84	12.85	98.623	3,287,422
Treasury	3,000	13.375	3/31/85	13.07	100.624	3,153,582
Treasury	3,100	15.875	9/30/85	13.41	106.126	3,456,679
Treasury	2,600	13.875	4/30/84	12.97	101.313	2,726,329
Treasury	3,200	12.125	9/30/84	12.85	98.623	3,287,422
Treasury	3,000	13.375	3/31/85	13.07	100.624	3,153,582
Treasury	3,100	15.875	9/30/85	13.41	106.126	3,456,679
Treasury	2,600	14.000	3/31/86	13.36	101.748	2,767,790
Treasury	3,200	14.875	6/30/86	13.39	104.374	3,382,276
Treasury	3,900	16.125	11/15/86	13.69	107.624	4,331,851
Treasury	2,900	13.750	8/15/87	13.40	101.250	3,121,229
Treasury	3,100	12.375	1/15/88	13.29	96.501	3,009,648
Treasury	3,200	14.000	7/15/88	13.40	102.378	3,297,253
Treasury	3,000	14.625	1/15/89	13.55	104.501	3,155,750
Treasury	7,800	14.500	7/15/89	13.50	104.379	8,194,975
Treasury	2,000	10.750	8/15/90	13.22	88.002	1,859,778
Treasury	3,000	13.000	11/15/90	13.29	98.498	3,038,360
Treasury	4,600	14.500	5/15/91	13.55	104.747	4,961,032
Treasury	9,400	14.625	2/15/92	13.55	105.624	10,566,399
Treasury	3,100	8.625	8/15/93	13.15	74.001	2,418,066
Treasury	2,900	9.000	2/15/94	13.09	76.002	2,325,135
Treasury	2,000	8.750	8/15/94	13.05	74.251	1,566,202
Treasury	2,700	10.125	11/15/94	13.15	81.747	2,265,643
Treasury	5,300	10.375	5/15/95	13.23	82.563	4,493,456
Treasury	2,400	12.625	5/15/95	13.21	96.373	2,377,763
Treasury	12,000	11.500	11/15/95	13.19	89.501	11,035,299
Treasury	2,900	8.500	5/15/99	12.91	70.001	2,082,755
Treasury	3,300	7.875	2/15/00	13.15	64.187	2,238,726
Treasury	3,800	11.750	2/15/01	13.28	89.499	3,608,092
Treasury	12,000	15.750	11/15/01	13.58	115.000	14,204,267
Treasury	8,700	14.250	2/15/02	13.38	105.999	9,797,030
Treasury	2,500	11.750	2/15/10	13.19	89.375	2,370,645

*Prices as of August 2, 1982: market value, $135,271,091; average maturity, 1/15/93; average coupon, 13.059%; average yield, 13.21%; internal rate of return, 13.08%.

Table 13A-5

REPORT OF THE PALMER PORTFOLIO'S REDUCED FUNDING REQUIREMENTS

Total expected benefit payments from Table 13A-1	$328,568,813
Present value of total benefit payments using 7% discount rate	$190,184,656
Portfolio cost (market value in 1982)	$135,271,091*
Savings (28.8% of $190,184,656)	$ 54,913,565

*This equals the present value of total expected benefit payments using 13.08 percent discount rate.

could be locked in on that date. The actuaries had adopted the 7.0 percent reinvestment rate assumption in the years before the Palmer pension's funding risk was reduced by the portfolio dedication strategy.[41]

At the old reinvestment rate of 7.0 percent the present discounted value of the Palmer Corporation's expected benefit payouts is shown in Table 13A-5 to be $190,184,656. Stated differently, Palmer's pension fund could have been fully funded in 1982 by putting $190,184,656 into the fund and reinvesting all cash inflows at 7.0 percent until they were disbursed. If the reinvestment rate were increased from 7.0 to 13.08 percent in 1982, however, only $135,271,091 would have been needed to fully fund the same expected payments. This 28.8 percent reduction from $190,184,656 to $135,271,565 is how much the Palmer Corporation saved by adopting the portfolio dedication strategy. The decrease of $54,913,565 is additional income for the Palmer Corporation that was attained by dedicating a portion of its pension fund in order to convince its actuaries to raise their reinvestment rate assumption from 7.0 to 13.08 percent.

Why Should the Actuaries Change Their Minds?

It may appear as if the only reason why the Palmer Corporation was able to save $54 million was merely because its actuaries *arbitrarily* changed their minds about the reinvestment rate assumption. This is an oversimplification. In truth, the higher reinvestment rate resulted from the Palmer Corporation's switch to a dedicated pension strategy that reduced its funding risk by locking in the lucrative high market rates that were available in 1982. The actuaries were willing to raise their reinvestment rate assumption to 13.08 percent because it was clear that the dedicated pension fund had obtained 30-year default-free investments that safely yielded 13.08 percent.

Prior to adopting the dedicated pension strategy in 1982, the Palmer Corporation had invested its pension funds in actively managed common stock investments. While the Palmer actuaries acknowledged that common stock investments average significantly higher rates of return than bond investments, they also knew that the common stock investments typically suffer more variability of return from year to year than do the bond investments (as shown in Table 1-6, for instance). As a result of the high risks associated with common stock investing, the actuaries decided that 7.0 percent was the average rate of return they should select in their conservative judgment to use as a reinvestment rate assumption for whatever portion of the Palmer pension portfolio was

[41]Financial Accounting Standards Board Statement 87 sets out the guidelines that the accounting profession is supposed to use in approving discount rates that are appropriate for dedicating defined-benefit pensions in order to defease the pension liability.

invested in common stocks. However, in 1982 when a $328,568,813 portion of the Palmer pension was committed to a dedicated pension strategy that locked in market yields of 13.08 percent for the next 30 years, the actuaries understandably saw fit to adopt the higher 13.08 percent reinvestment rate assumption for the dedicated portion of Palmer's pension funds. The only investment risk that might deter the dedicated pension funds from earning 13.08 percent return over the next 30 years was that the small portion of total portfolio income from reinvestment income might decrease if future market interest rates fell. But, even if this unfortunate outcome did occur, the reinvestment income was such a small portion of the dedicated pension portfolio's total income that the portfolio's long-run goals would not be greatly reduced.

Benefits for the Palmer Corporation

Because the adoption of a dedicated pension strategy allows the Palmer Corporation to fund its legal obligations to its retired workers with greater precision, the corporation is able to enjoy the following five benefits.

1. Conservative low reinvestment rate assumptions (of 7.0 percent) can be replaced with conservative reinvestment rate assumptions that are much higher (in this case, 13.08 percent).

2. Increasing the reinvestment rate assumption greatly reduces the present value of scheduled benefit payouts listed in Table 13A-1.

3. The Palmer Corporation can enjoy new options, such as reducing its annual payments into the pension fund or increasing the employees' retirement benefits.

4. Reduced pension funding requirements can relieve pressure on management to raise the income of the Palmer Corporation.

5. Dedication of the portion of its pension obligation owed to retired employees almost entirely eliminates the funding risk associated with that large segment of Palmer's overall pension obligation. As a result, Palmer's future income and expense statements will probably not need to report large and disconcerting fluctuations in its unfunded liabilities.

The benefits listed above are available to any company or governmental agency that has pension funding obligations if the sponsor of the pension plan is willing to adopt a well-conceived dedicated pension strategy.[42] Furthermore, all dedicated pension strategies need not be exactly like the Palmer Corporation's plan. Provision for more active portfolio management can be provided. Cost-of-living benefits can be included in the pension plans. The number of retired workers in the dedicated pension fund can be increased or decreased. And, financial futures contracts can be employed to immunize the dedicated pension portfolio against interest rate risk.[43]

[42]For a nonmathematical critique of dedicating defined-benefit pension plans, see K. P. Ambachtsheer, "Pension Fund Asset Allocation: In Defense of a 60/40 Equity/Debt Asset Mix," *Financial Analysts Journal*, Sept.–Oct. 1987.

[43]Computer programs are available to do the LP to immunize a bond portfolio. A program written in BASIC on a floppy disk that will run on an IBM-PC may be purchased for $70 from Dr. Richard Bookstaber. Dr. Bookstaber's address and information about other programs that he generously offers for sale at prices that barely cover the shipping charges can be obtained from Richard Bookstaber, *The Complete Investment Book*, (Glenview, Ill.: Scott, Foresman, 1985).

Appendix 13B

Using Convexity
to Get Better
Immunizations

This appendix shows how to extend the duration matching strategy to ensure that interest rate risk does not become a problem when market interest rates fluctuate. The explanation will be phrased in terms of the dashed curve that is convex toward the origin in Figure 13B-1 and the present value model.

**Price-YTM
Relationships**

Consider a bond with 18 years until it matures that pays a 12 percent coupon rate. The curve of dashes that is convex toward the origin of Figure 13B-1 can be generated by solving Equation (13-3) repeatedly at enough of the YTMs between 5 and 14 percent to trace out the illustrated locus of prices and their associated YTMs. The resulting curve is called the **price-YTM curve;** some people also call a curve like this the asset's **present value profile.** The first and third columns of Table 13B-1 list the pairs of YTMs and prices used to draw the price-YTM curve made up of dashes in Figure 13B-1. A similar price-YTM curve can be generated to represent any bond or any diversified portfolio of bonds. The other two curves in Figure 13B-1 are estimates of the price-YTM curve; they will be explained below.

The duration matching approach to immunization involves, essentially, the matching of an asset and a liability with equal present values and the same duration. Consider price-YTM curves that resemble the dashed curve in Figure 13B-1. More specifically, consider how the present values of an asset and a liability that are supposed to be immunized move together along their price-YTM curve as the YTM used to discount their cashflows varies. It is unlikely that just because an asset and a liability have the same pair of values for their present values and durations at some particular discount rate that they will continue to have identical values at different discount rates. That is, as various discount rates are used to trace out the remainder of their price-YTM curves, their present values and/or durations will probably diverge. Stated differently, when the YTM changes, *duration wandering* occurs and the portfolio must be *rebalanced* to keep it fully immunized. Only if the price-YTM curves of the asset and the liability match perfectly over a wide range of YTM values will they remain immunized at different market interest rates.

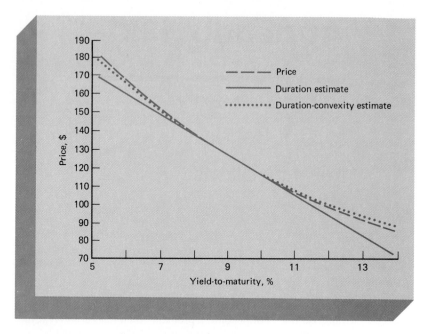

Figure 13B-1 Price-YTM relationships for 12 percent coupon bond with 18 years until maturity. (*Source:* Mark L. Dunetz and James M. Mahoney, "Using Duration and Convexity in the Analysis of Callable Bonds," *Financial Analysts Journal,* May–June 1988, fig. E.)

Table 13B-1

NUMERICAL COMPARISON OF ACTUAL AND PROJECTED PRICE-YTM CURVES FOR 12% COUPON BOND WITH 18 YEARS UNTIL MATURITY

(1) YTM	(2) YTM change, B.P.	(3) Present value or price	(4) Duration-projected price*	(5) Price − projected = difference	(6) MMD-and-convexity-projected price†	(7) Price − projected = difference
5.00%	−400	$182.446	$168.899	$13.547	$179.800	$2.646
6.00	−300	165.496	158.299	7.197	164.430	1.066
7.00	−200	150.726	147.699	3.027	150.424	0.302
8.00	−100	137.816	137.099	0.717	137.780	0.036
9.00	0	126.499	126.499	0.000	126.499	0.000
10.00	+100	116.546	115.899	0.647	116.580	0.034
11.00	+200	107.768	105.299	2.469	108.024	0.256
12.00	+300	100.000	94.699	5.301	100.830	0.830
13.00	+400	93.104	84.099	9.005	94.999	1.895
14.00	+500	86.964	73.499	13.465	90.529	3.565

*Calculated with Equation (13B-6).
†Calculated with Equation (13B-7).

Slope and Convexity of the Price-YTM Curve

The slope and convexity of the price-YTM curves can be analyzed to achieve more perfect immunizations and thus eliminate interest rate risk.

Slope In an effort to find an asset and a liability with price-YTM curves that match perfectly over a wide range of YTM values, that is, that will remain immunized as market interest rates vary, both the slope and the convexity of the price-YTM curves should be considered. Convexity can be analyzed with differential calculus. First, the formula for the *slope of the price-YTM curve* can be determined mathematically from Equation (13-3) by taking the first derivative of p_0 with respect to YTM to obtain Equation (13B-1).

$$\frac{dp_0}{d(\text{YTM})} = \sum_{t=1}^{T} \frac{-tc_t}{(1 + \text{YTM})^{t+1}} = \text{slope of price-YTM curve} \qquad \text{(13B-1)}$$

where c_t denotes the cashflow from coupons and/or principal in period t.

Modified Duration The derivative in Equation (13B-1), $dp/d(\text{YTM})$, can be easily converted into a measure of modified duration by dividing the derivative by p as shown in Equation (13B-2).

$$\text{MMD} = \frac{dp}{d(\text{YTM})} \Big/ p$$

$$= \frac{\sum_{t=1}^{T} -tc_t \Big/ (1 + \text{YTM})^{t+1}}{p_0} \qquad \text{(13B-2)}$$

Substituting the values for the 12 percent coupon bond with 18 years until its maturity into Equation (13B-2) will reveal that the bond's MMD is 8.38 years when YTM = 9.0 percent.

Convexity Taking the derivative of $dp_0/d(\text{YTM})$ in Equation (13B-1) with respect to $d(\text{YTM})$ yields the second-order derivative shown in Equation (13B-3).

$$\frac{d^2p_0}{d(\text{YTM})^2} = \left(\frac{1.0}{(1 + \text{YTM})^2}\right) \sum_{t=1}^{T} (t^2 + t) \frac{c_t}{(1 + \text{YTM})^t} \qquad \text{(13B-3)}$$

Equation (13B-3) is divided by the asset's present value to obtain the **convexity** measure defined in Equation (13B-4).

$$\text{Convexity} = \left(\frac{1.0}{p(1 + \text{YTM})^2}\right) \sum_{t=1}^{T} (t^2 + t) \frac{c_t}{(1 + \text{YTM})^t} \qquad \text{(13B-4)}$$

The convexity of the price-YTM curve for an asset or a liability can be calculated for the values of the YTM and time-to-maturity that are substituted into Equation (13B-4). For example, the 12 percent coupon bond with 18 years until its maturity has a convexity value of 107 when the bond's YTM equals 9.0 percent.

If an asset and a liability have price-YTM curves with equal slopes (or equivalently, MMDs) and the same convexity, then their prices will move together as their discount rates vary in response to changes in the market YTMs. In other words, the prices of the asset and the liability will move together, and in so doing they immunize each other.[44]

Numerical Comparison of Immunization Techniques

If a *duration matching immunization strategy* that ignores convexity is used, the projected market value of a bond can be computed with Equation (13B-6).

$$
\begin{array}{l}\text{Projected} \\ \text{market} \\ \text{value}\end{array} = \begin{array}{l}\text{current} \\ \text{market} \\ \text{value}\end{array} + \left(\begin{bmatrix}\text{current} \\ \text{market} \\ \text{value}\end{bmatrix} \times \begin{bmatrix}\text{modified} \\ \text{duration,} \\ \text{MMD}\end{bmatrix} \times \begin{bmatrix}\text{change} \\ \text{in} \\ \text{yield}\end{bmatrix} \right) \qquad (13B\text{-}6)
$$

Column (4) of Table 13B-1 shows the duration-based projected market value of the 12 percent coupon bond with 18 years to maturity. The solid line in Figure 13B-1 illustrates these duration-based projected market values so that they can be visually compared with the actual values. Column (5) of Table 13B-1 shows the difference between the bond's actual market value and its projected market value at differing YTMs. This difference represents the size of the imperfection in the duration matching immunization strategy.

If a *duration and convexity matching immunization strategy* is used, the projected market value of a bond can be computed with Equation (13B-7)

$$
\begin{array}{l}\text{Projected} \\ \text{market} \\ \text{value}\end{array} = \begin{array}{l}\text{current} \\ \text{market} \\ \text{value}\end{array} + \left(\begin{bmatrix}\text{current} \\ \text{market} \\ \text{value}\end{bmatrix} \times \begin{bmatrix}\text{modified} \\ \text{duration,} \\ \text{MMD}\end{bmatrix} \times \begin{bmatrix}\text{change} \\ \text{in} \\ \text{yield}\end{bmatrix} \right)
$$

$$
+ \left(\begin{bmatrix}\text{one-} \\ \text{half}\end{bmatrix} \times \begin{bmatrix}\text{current} \\ \text{market} \\ \text{value}\end{bmatrix} \times [\text{convexity}] \times \begin{bmatrix}\text{change} \\ \text{in YTM} \\ \text{squared}\end{bmatrix} \right) \qquad (13B\text{-}7)
$$

Column (6) of Table 13B-1 shows the duration-and-convexity-based projected market value of the 12 percent coupon bond with 18 years to maturity over a range of different YTM values. The dotted curve in Figure 13B-1 traces out the duration-and-convexity-based projected market values so that they can be compared visually with the duration-based projections and the actual values. Column (7) of Table 13B-1 shows the difference between the bond's actual market value and its duration-and-convexity-based projected market value. This difference represents the size of the imperfection in the duration and convexity matching immunization strategy.

By comparing the sizes of the imperfections in the two immunization strategies, the duration matching imperfections from column (5) of Table 13B-1, and the duration and convexity matching imperfections in column (7), we show that the more complex du-

---

[44]To see the generality of the immunization statements, consider the bond price change, denoted Δp. By taking a Taylor series expansion of this bond price change we can show that it can be approximated in terms of the sum of the differentials shown below.

$$
\Delta p = \frac{dp_0}{d(\text{YTM})} + \frac{1}{2} \frac{d^2 p_0}{d(\text{YTM})^2} + \cdots + \frac{1}{n!} \frac{d^n p_0}{d(\text{YTM})^n} \qquad (13B\text{-}5)
$$

By confining our attention to the first two derivatives in the Taylor series, we show that if we restrict our attention to (1) the slope, as measured by the first derivative of Equation (13B-1), [or MMD from Equation (13B-2)] and (2) the convexity, as measured by the second derivative of Equations (13B-3) and (13B-4), then the asset and the liability will have prices that are immunized.

ration and convexity matching immunization strategy provides more protection against interest rate risk.

It is possible for callable bonds to have price-YTM curves that are concave instead of convex. Advanced procedures for calculating call-adjusted convexity have been suggested to deal with these cases.[45]

[45]This appendix draws from Mark L. Dunetz and James M. Mahoney, "Using Duration and Convexity in the Analysis of Callable Bonds," *Financial Analysts Journal*, May–June 1988, pp. 53–72. This article delves into the convexity problems that can accompany callable bonds. Also see Frank J. Fabozzi and T. Dessa Fabozzi, *Bond Markets, Analysis and Strategies* (Englewood Cliffs, N.J.: Prentice-Hall, 1989), chap. 4.

Chapter 14

Default Risk and

Purchasing-Power Risk

Chapter 13 discussed *interest rate risk;* it affects all investors. *Purchasing-power risk* also affects all investors; it is the subject of the last half of this chapter. But first, we will consider the *default risk* faced by those who invest in securities issued by corporations.

Default risk *is that portion of a security's total variability of return that results from changes in the issuer's financial condition.* The reason that security prices react to changes in the issuer's financial condition stems from the U.S. legal framework. In particular, stockholders' *limited liability* and the *legal bankruptcy procedures* have major influences.

DEFAULT RISK

A company that is unable to meet its obligatory debt payments because its checking account is overdrawn is said to be technically **insolvent.** Highly profitable companies can be technically insolvent from time to time. If the value of a firm's assets falls below its liabilities, it is said to be *insolvent in the bankruptcy sense;* this is a more serious kind of insolvency. If an insolvent company fails to make a scheduled payment of interest or principal on a debt, the firm is said to be in **default.** If payment is not made fairly quickly, lawsuits usually follow. While details differ from case to case, the typical bankruptcy situation begins with attempts at out-of-court negotiations. If agreements with creditors cannot be obtained, either the insolvent company files for bankruptcy or the company's creditors sue it in the bankruptcy courts. Very few unpaid debts are simply forgotten.

The question addressed in most bankruptcy hearings is whether the firm should be declared bankrupt and have its assets *liquidated* at a public *bankruptcy auction,* with the proceeds divided among the creditors. A liquidation occurs if the bankruptcy court feels the resulting value would exceed that likely to be obtained if the firm were to continue in operation.

Bankruptcy Law Establishes the Priority for Claims

If the firm's assets are liquidated at a bankruptcy auction, the proceeds are paid out to creditors according to the following list of established legal priorities.

1. The attorney's fees and court costs associated with the bankruptcy proceeding are paid off first.

2. Any remaining proceeds from the bankruptcy go to pay back wages due to workers, up to a maximum of $2000 per worker.

3. Any remaining proceeds are used to pay back taxes to any federal, state, and/or local governments.

4. If any auction proceeds are left (and sometimes none are left at this stage), creditors holding *secured* loans are paid. For example, mortgage lenders and the holders of collateralized loans made to the company would be paid. This class of creditors typically receives only about 30 percent of the money owed to them by the bankrupt firm.

5. If any funds remain, the company's general, or *unsecured,* creditors are paid. It is commonplace for general creditors to receive about 10 cents on every dollar the bankrupt company owed them; but even this paltry sum will not be paid unless all higher priority claims have been paid in full.

6. Preferred stockholders are paid if any auction proceeds are still left. A normal liquidation receipt is 2 cents on each dollar paid for preferred stock.

7. Common stockholders are paid last; they usually receive nothing from their investment.[1]

Chrysler's Dance Along the Precipice of Bankruptcy

The default risks that lead to bankruptcy are faced by all firms at all times. Interestingly, it is this *possibility of default,* rather than the actual bankruptcy, that causes most investor losses. Consider the classic case of the Chrysler Corporation, the large automobile manufacturer, when it nearly went bankrupt in 1980.

[1]For more details about bankruptcy see Edward I. Altman, *Corporate Financial Distress* (New York: Wiley, 1983).

Table 14-1
CHRYSLER CORPORATION'S FINANCIAL DATA, 1979–1985

Year/ month		Bond rating	Bond price	Bonds' yield-to- maturity	Common stock price	Quarterly earnings per share	Quarterly cash dividend
1979	Jan.	BBB	$67⅝	13.97%	$10½		
	Feb.	BBB	78	11.99	9½		
	Mar.	BBB	75⅛	12.50	10¼	(0.95)	$0.10
	Apr.	BBB	76	12.35	9¾		
	May	BB	73⅜	12.84	8⅜		
	Jun.	BB	69½	13.62	9⅛	(3.31)	0.10
	Jul.	BB	71½	13.23	8¼		
	Aug.	B	67¼	14.12	8½		
	Sep.	B	63½	15.00	8⅜	(7.15)	0
	Oct.	B	58¼	16.37	7⅜		
	Nov.	B	52	18.30	6½		
	Dec.	B	51½	18.49	6¾	(5.77)	-0
1980	Jan.	B	54	17.68	10⅛		
	Feb.	B	55½	17.23	9		
	Mar.	B	50⅛	19.03	6⅛	(6.84)	0
	Apr.	B	37⅜	25.02	7⅛		
	May	B	49	19.48	6⅝		
	Jun.	B	45½	20.91	6¾	(8.13)	0
	Jul.	B	46¾	20.41	7⅜		
	Aug.	B	44	21.62	9¼		
	Sep.	B	49⅝	19.33	9⅛	(7.42)	0
	Oct.	B	50	19.21	8¼		
	Nov.	B	50	19.24	7		
	Dec.	B	43	22.18	4⅞	(3.61)	0
1981	Jan.	CCC	34½	27.16	5⅝		
	Feb.	CCC	37⅞	24.97	5⅜		
	Mar.	CCC	41½	23	6¾	(4.56)	0
	Apr.	CCC	44⅛	21.76	6½		
	May	CCC	42½	22.55	6⅜		
	Jun.	CCC	45⅞	21.04	6⅝	0.06	0
	Jul.	CCC	51	19.06	6¼		
	Aug.	CCC	46⅝	20.77	5⅛		
	Sep.	CCC	44⅛	21.89	4⅝	(2.14)	0
	Oct.	CCC	45	21.53	4⅛		
	Nov.	CCC	40	24.02	4		
	Dec.	CCC	40⅞	23.58	3⅜	(0.54)	0
1982	Jan.	CCC	38⅛	25.16	4¼		
	Feb.	CCC	41½	23.32	4¾		
	Mar.	CCC	39⅜	24.50	4⅞	(1.31)	0
	Apr.	CCC	41⅛	23.59	5¾		
	May	CCC	45½	21.52	6		

Table 14-1
CHRYSLER CORPORATION'S FINANCIAL DATA, 1979–1985 (continued)

Year/month		Bond rating	Bond price	Bonds' yield-to-maturity	Common stock price	Quarterly earnings per share	Quarterly cash dividend
	Jun.	CCC	45	21.77	6⅞	1.30	0
	Jul.	CCC	47⅛	20.89	7⅜		
	Aug.	CCC	52	19.05	8⅛		
	Sep.	CCC	55⅜	17.85	8¾	(0.23)	0
	Oct.	CCC	57⅛	17.41	10⅞		
	Nov.	CCC	57½	17.32	11½		
1983	Dec.	CCC	58¾	16.98	17¾	(1.04)	0
	Jan.	CCC	65¾	15.11	17¾		
	Feb.	CCC	70¼	14.06	14⅞		
	Mar.	CCC	74	13.26	17	1.03	0
	Apr.	CCC	77¾	12.51	26⅛		
	May	CCC	79	12.28	25⅝		
	Jun.	B	76	12.89	32	1.28	0
	Jul.	B	75	13.11	28⅛		
	Aug.	B	72¾	13.61	27¾		
	Sep.	B	72⅝	13.66	29½	0.34	0
	Oct.	B	75¼	13.11	27½		
	Nov.	B	75	13.18	26½		
1984	Dec.	B	75	13.20	27⅝	1.64	0
	Jan.	B	73	13.65	30⅜		
	Feb.	B	75	13.23	27¼		
	Mar.	B	74½	13.36	25⅜	3.08	0.15
	Apr.	B	73⅛	13.68	25¼		
	May	B	72⅞	13.76	22¾		
	Jun.	BB	69½	14.57	25	3.62	0.15
	Jul.	BB	72⅛	13.98	27¾		
	Aug.	BB	71⅞	14.06	29		
	Sep.	BB	72¼	13.99	30½	0.97	0.20
	Oct.	BB	71¾	14.13	31⅛		
	Nov.	BB	76⅜	13.11	27½		
	Dec.	BBB	78	12.78	32	4.08	0.25
1985	Jan.	BBB	79⅝	12.46	32		
	Feb.	BBB	79¾	12.45	33		
	Mar.	BBB	80½	12.31	33⅜	4.10	0.25

Table 14-1 documents some effects of Chrysler's close call with bankruptcy. Table 14-1 lists Chrysler's monthly bond ratings, bond prices, stock prices, quarterly earnings (or losses) per share, and cash dividend data for the years 1979 through 1985. The data show clearly that the firm's earnings and bond quality ratings deteriorated precipitously during the 1979–1981 period.

Chrysler was able to avert bankruptcy only by obtaining a special $1.5 billion loan from Congress in 1980.[2] This federal loan enabled Chrysler to borrow another $2 billion from private sources and narrowly avert bankruptcy.

As is usual in these cases, there were some easily observable warning signs of Chrysler's financial failure. Table 14-1 shows that the corporation completely discontinued its already slashed common stock cash dividend in mid-1979. Preferred stock cash dividends were also canceled. Chrysler's bonds were downgraded from BBB to BB in May of 1979 and further downgraded to B in August of the same year. The firm had been reporting losses since 1978. The losses took on alarming proportions in 1979–1980. The company's name was in the headlines of newspapers around the world and details about its grim financial condition were public knowledge.

Note how Chrysler's stock and bond prices collapsed month by month. The decline of the common stock's price from over $20 per share in 1977 to less than $4 in 1981 indicates that investors were aware of the weakening condition of the firm for some time before it arrived on the brink of disaster.[3]

14-2   **SECURITIES QUALITY RATINGS**

The second column of Table 14-1 lists the quality ratings of Chrysler's bonds. Comparing these quality ratings with the other financial information shown in Table 14-1 suggests that **bond ratings** indicate the likelihood that a bond issue will fall into bankruptcy. Chrysler's bond ratings, for instance, dropped steadily from BBB in 1979 deep into the **junk bond** category of CCC-grade by 1982 as the firm neared bankruptcy. **Junk bonds** are any bonds rated below the BBB category by Standard & Poor's, or equivalently, below Baa by Moody's. Securities brokers euphemistically refer to junk bonds as **high-yield bonds** because they promise high yields-to-maturity.

Definitions of Quality Ratings

Financial services such as Standard & Poor's and Moody's study thousands of different corporations, analyze their financial situations, and assign quality ratings to each issue of marketable securities. Table 14-2 explains the quality ratings that Moody's and Standard & Poor's assign to bond issues. The different

---

[2]Federal officials explained that Chrysler's unusual federal government loan was made for two reasons. First, Chrysler was a major defense contractor for the U.S. government. Chrysler had a subsidiary that manufactured tanks (later sold to raise cash) and thus contributed to the national defense. And, second, the firm provided employment for thousands of U.S. citizens.

[3]Steven Katz, Steven Lillien, and Bert Nelson, ''Stock Market Behavior Around Bankruptcy Model Distress and Recovery Predictions,'' *Financial Analysts Journal*, Jan.–Feb. 1985, pp. 70–74.

Table 14-2

MOODY'S AND S&P'S BOND QUALITY RATINGS

Category	Moody's	Standard & Poor's	Definition of rating
High grade	Aaa	AAA	The AAA rating is the highest rating assigned to a debt instrument. It indicates extremely strong capacity to pay principal and interest. Bonds in this category are often referred to as "blue-chip."
	Aa	AA	These are high-quality bonds by all standards. They are rated lower primarily because the margins of protection are not quite as strong as those of Aaa and AAA.
Medium grade	A	A	These bonds possess many favorable investment attributes, but may be susceptible to impairment if adverse economic changes occur.
	Baa	BBB	Issuers of these bonds are regarded as having adequate capacity to pay principal and interest. The bonds are rated BBB if the bond issue lacks certain protective elements so that adverse economic conditions could lead to a weakened capacity for payment.
Speculative	Ba	BB	These are bonds regarded as having minimum protection for principal and interest payments during both good and bad times. Bonds in this or any lower category are called **junk bonds.**
	B	B	These bonds lack characteristics of other more desirable investments. Assurance of interest and principal payments over any long period may be very weak.
Default	Caa	CCC	These are poor-quality issues that may be in default or in danger of default.
	Ca	CC	These are highly speculative issues, often in default or possessing other marked shortcomings.
	C		This is the lowest-rated class of bonds. These issues can be regarded as extremely poor in investment quality; they might go bankrupt, in Moody's opinion.
		C	Income bonds on which no interest is being paid are rated C by Standard & Poor's.
		D	A bond issue rated D by Standard & Poor's is in default, with principal and/or interest payments in arrears.

rating agencies seldom give different ratings for the same security. If two financial services do give the same security different ratings, it is referred to as a **split rating.** The few split ratings that do occur are rarely more than one rating grade level apart.

Financial analysts have studied hundreds of different bonds and their quality

Table 14-3
DEFAULT RATES AND THE ISSUERS' BOND
RATINGS

Period	AAA	AA	A	BBB
1920–1929	0.12%	0.17%	0.20%	0.80%
1930–1939*	0.42	0.44	1.94	3.78
1920–1939	0.30	0.30	1.1	2.3
1950–1979	0	0	0	0

Sources: W. B. Hickman, *Corporate Bond Quality and Investor Experience* (Washington, D.C.: National Bureau of Economic Research, 1958); Gordon Pye, "Gauging the Default Premium," *Financial Analysts Journal,* Jan.–Feb. 1974, pp. 49–52; J. H. Wood and N. L. Wood, *Financial Markets* (Orlando, Fla.: Harcourt Brace Jovanovich, 1985), table 10.8, p. 293.
*Depression years.

ratings over several decades and computed the percentage of firms in each bond quality rating category that defaulted. Table 14-3 summarizes some of their research findings; it shows only moderate rates of default. Firms defaulted at all quality levels in the 1920s and 1930s, however. The default rates were the highest during the decade that included the Depression of the early 1930s. More important, in each period sampled, a larger percentage of poorly rated firms defaulted than firms that were highly rated.[4] This finding suggests that the quality ratings the financial services sell to their subscribers can be helpful in assessing the probability that a firm will default or be declared bankrupt.

Average Returns Vary with the Quality Ratings

It would seem that investors should require issuers of high-risk securities to pay higher rates of return than issuers of low-risk securities; otherwise, why should investors assume the greater risk of loss? The historical returns that bond investors have experienced should furnish evidence of a positive risk-return relationship.

Although there are exceptions, bond investors usually hold their positions longer than stock investors. This lower turnover means that bond markets are *less liquid* than the stock markets. In particular, bonds with low quality ratings and small bond issues are usually illiquid. Liquidity problems in the bond markets make it difficult to obtain and interpret bond market data. By focusing on long-term returns, however, the bond market's general equilibrium tendencies can be discerned.

[4]There are cases in which corporations with high quality ratings have turned up in bankruptcy court, but the corporations' bond quality ratings were not lowered far enough in advance to allow investors to liquidate their holdings and avoid the ensuing losses, for example, Penn Central in the 1970s and Texaco in the 1980s.

Table 14-4

AVERAGE YIELDS-TO-MATURITY FOR BONDS WITH DIFFERENT QUALITY RATINGS OVER VARIOUS PERIODS

Bond index	1955–1967 yield	1968–1979 yield	1981–1985 yield
Long-term Treasury bonds	3.88%	7.01%	12.98%
AAA corporate bonds	4.25	7.88	13.51
AA corporate bonds	4.36	8.12	14.14
A corporate bonds	4.52	8.34	14.68
BBB corporate bonds	4.97	8.90	15.43

Source: Standard & Poor's Trade and Securities Statistics, 1986; author's averages of the data.

Table 14-4 shows average bond yields during the periods 1955–1967, 1968–1979, and 1981–1985. The fact that market yields increase with the riskiness of the ratings provides evidence that investors dislike risk. Figure 14-1 shows the relationship between risk and corporate bond yields at different times. Corporate bonds yield progressively higher interest rates as their ratings deteriorate. In addition, Federal Reserve Board policy; fiscal policy; the supply of and demand for loanable funds; and other factors that constantly change cause the relationship between market interest rates and bond ratings to shift minute by minute every day. But, *high-risk bonds must always pay the highest returns in order to attract investors.*[5]

Junk Bond Investing

Prior to 1977 the most prestigious investment banking firms typically refused to underwrite junk bond issues. When an issuer of investment grade bonds fell on hard times and its bond ratings dropped to the BB or lower levels, the bonds were called **fallen angels.** A bond trader at Drexel Burnham Lambert (DBL) named Michael Milken and some others changed things. Mr. Milken started underwriting **original-issue junk;** more than any other single person, he created the junk bond industry. Milken's junk bond initial public offerings (IPOs) were so profitable that, almost single-handedly, his operations financed the growth of DBL from a lackluster brokerage in the 1970s to a respectable investment banking firm in the 1980s. DBL was paying Milken millions of dollars per week before they fired him in 1989, when he got into trouble with the SEC. By that time even the most elite investment banking firms were underwriting *original-issue junk.* The total dollar value of all junk bond IPOs in 1986 was about 20

---

[5]For a classic empirical investigation of the determinants of the yield spreads between different issues of bonds, see Lawrence Fisher, "Determinants of Risk Premiums on Corporate Bonds," *Journal of Political Economy,* June 1959, vol. LXVII, no. 3, pp. 217–237.

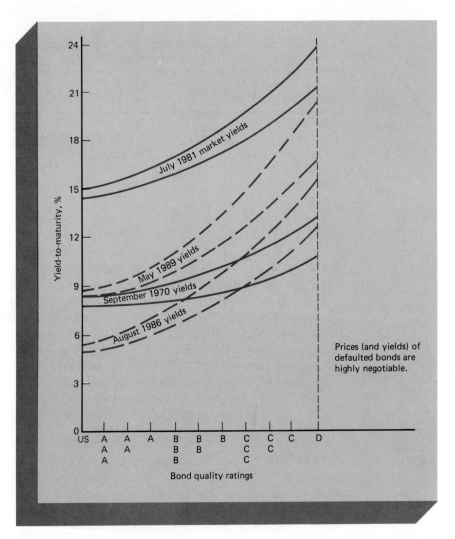

Figure 14-1 The risk structure of bond yields on (*a*) September 1970, (*b*) July 1981, (*c*) August 1986, and (*d*) May 1989.

percent of the aggregate value of all corporate bond issues underwritten that year.[6]

It was futile to research junk bond investment returns during the early 1980s because the new industry had generated very little empirical data to investigate. However, as time passed, more data became available and researchers started comparing the high yields promised by junk bonds to the yields that were

[6]Edward I. Altman, ''The Anatomy of the High-Yield Bond Market,'' *Financial Analysts Journal,* July–Aug. 1987, p. 13, table I.

simultaneously offered by the default-free Treasury bonds of comparable maturity. The junk bonds rated BB with 10 years to maturity promised approximately 250 basis points more than comparable Treasuries, averaged over several years. CCC-rated bonds with 20 years to maturity promised over 500 basis points more than the Treasuries. The annual yields varied considerably from year to year. Nevertheless, early researchers concluded that even after a small percent of the junk bond issuers defaulted and/or went bankrupt each year, the *net returns* from junk bond investing were attractive.[7]

By the late 1980s enough data had been accumulated to allow researchers to delineate unattractive features about junk bond investing. First, in an effort to procure more lucrative junk bond IPOs, aggressive investment bankers were underwriting issues of smaller firms. These smaller firms were sometimes riskier, and in addition, financial analysts found it was harder to obtain information about them. Sometimes analysts were able to get the least information about the riskiest issuers. Second, when aged junk bonds were investigated, their default rates turned out to be worse than originally believed.

Billions of dollars worth of new junk bonds were issued each year, and most of these new issues did not default in their first 2 years. The resulting low default rates on each year's growing number of junk bond IPOs biased the average annual default rates downward, because the older issues were not considered separately. A few percent of all outstanding, junk bonds continued to default each year, as reported in earlier years. However, *when a sample of aged junk bonds were analyzed, the cumulative default rates were high.* Over one-third of the junk bonds that were more than 11 years old had defaulted. Furthermore, many of the junk bond issues that did not default were exchanged for other securities that defaulted later. The cumulative default rates that a buy-and-hold investor could expect were far higher than the default rates calculated without aging.[8]

---

[7]See Edward I. Altman and Scott A. Nammacher, *Investing in Junk Bonds* (New York: Wiley, 1987). Also see M. S. Fridson, F. Wahl, and S. B. Jones of Morgan Stanley's Credit Research Department for reports of low default rates in the March 1988 issue of the firm's monthly junk bond publication entitled *High Performance,* and also in Morgan's *The Anatomy of the High Yield Debt Market: 1987.* See also Douglas Hallet (*The Wall Street Journal,* March 30, 1987), who cites a junk bond default rate of 1.6 percent per year.

[8]For details see Edward I. Altman and Scott A. Nammacher, "The Default Rate Experience on High-Yield Corporate Debt," *Financial Analysts Journal,* July–Aug. 1985, vol. 41, no. 4, pp. 25–41. Also see M. E. Blume and D. B. Keim, "Lower-Grade Bonds: Their Risks and Returns," *Financial Analysts Journal,* July–Aug. 1987, vol. 43, no. 4, pp. 26–33. The Altman-Nammacher and Blume-Keim studies impart a pleasant view of junk bond investing. For a less positive view see M. I. Weinstein, "A Curmudgeon's View of Junk Bonds," *Journal of Portfolio Management,* Spring 1987, pp. 76–80. For negative information see Paul Asquith, David W. Mullins, and E. D. Wolff, "Original Issue High-Yield Bonds: Aging Analysis of Defaults, Exchanges and Calls," *Journal of Finance,* Sept. 1989, pp. 923–952. This latter study is the most informative.

A third negative consideration that weighs against junk bond investing is the future outlook. The progressively larger number of new junk bond IPOs that were issued by smaller and riskier issuers suggested that perhaps both the annual and the cumulative default rates would be higher in the 1990s than they were in the 1980s. The final nail in the junk bond coffin involves Drexel Burnham Lambert (DBL) and Michael Milken. DBL was forced by the SEC to fire Michael Milken. As explained above, Milken was the "backbone" of the junk bond market. DBL's rise to power during the 1980s ended with its bankruptcy in 1990. Thereafter the junk bond market shrank and became less liquid.

In view of the important role default risk plays in determining the desirability of an investment, the factors that influence an issuer's default risk are reviewed in the section below.[9]

Using Multiple Discriminant Analysis to Discriminate among Default Risk Categories

Discriminant analysis is a statistical procedure used to classify an observation on the basis of a set of associated independent variables. A linear *multiple discriminant analysis* (MDA) function takes the form:

$$z_i = b_1 x_{1i} + b_2 x_{2i} + b_3 x_{3i} + b_4 x_{4i} + b_5 x_{5i} \qquad \text{where } i = 1, 2, \ldots, n$$

The data consist of observations on, say, n different companies. The dependent variable z can take on discrete values that symbolize *qualititive categories*. For example, let a bankrupt firm be represented by $z = 0$ and a nonbankrupt firm be indicated by $z = 1.0$.

Edward Altman was able to discriminate between failed and nonfailed companies using the following MDA function.[10]

$$z_i = 0.033 \left(\frac{\text{EBIT}}{\text{total assets}} \right)_i + 0.999 \left(\frac{\text{sales}}{\text{assets}} \right)_i + 0.006 \left(\frac{\text{aggregate market value of all equity}}{\text{book value of debt}} \right)_i$$

$$+ 0.014 \left(\frac{\text{retained earnings}}{\text{total assets}} \right)_i + 0.012 \left(\frac{\text{working capital}}{\text{total assets}} \right)_i$$

where EBIT stands for earnings before interest and taxes. Using a sample of 66 firms (33 bankrupt and 33 nonbankrupt), Altman was able to correctly predict 52 firms (or 79 percent of the sample).

Based on each firm's financial ratios, the MDA function determines a z-score. The average z-score for the bankrupt firms was $z = -0.29$. The average value was $z = 5.02$ for the nonbankrupt firms. Figure 14-2 suggests two normal

---

[9]For details about municipal bond analysis consult Sylvan G. Feldstein, Frank J. Fabozzi, Irving M. Pollack, and Frank G. Zarb, *The Municipal Bond Handbook*, vol. I and II (Homewood, Ill.: Dow Jones–Irwin, 1983).

[10]Edward I. Altman, "Financial Ratios, Discriminant Analysis, and the Prediction of Corporate Bankruptcy," *Journal of Finance*, Sept. 1968, pp. 589–609. Also see E. I. Altman, *Corporate Financial Distress* (New York: Wiley, 1983).

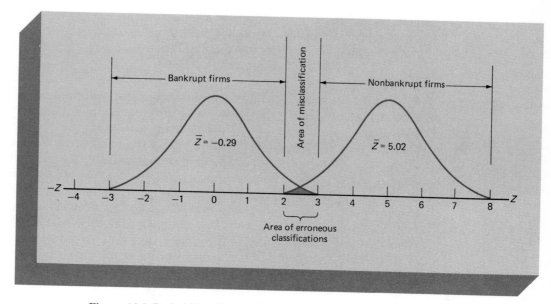

Figure 14-2 Probability distributions of z-scores for bankrupt and nonbankrupt firms.

probability distributions of z-scores for bankrupt and nonbankrupt firms. The MDA cannot discriminate in the area where these two probability distributions overlap, and some firms are misclassified.

MDA has also been used successfully to predict the quality ratings of different bond issues. However, the purveyors of bond quality ratings typically use nonstatistical classification procedures.

14-3   **DETERMINING CORPORATE BOND QUALITY RATINGS**

When a securities analysis firm assigns a quality rating to a bond issue, the most important pieces of financial information considered are (1) the level and trend of the issuer's financial ratios and (2) the issuer's significance and size.[11]

---

[11]G. E. Pinches and K. A. Mingo, "A Multivariate Analysis of Industrial Bond Ratings," *Journal of Finance,* March 1973, pp. 1–32. Pinches and Mingo showed how to use factor analysis and multiple discriminant analysis to assign bond quality ratings with a high degree of accuracy. See also Robert S. Kaplan and Gabriel Urwitz, "Statistical Models of Bond Rating: A Methodological Inquiry," *Journal of Business,* April 1979, vol. 52, no. 2, pp. 231–262. Kaplan and Urwitz developed a model to estimate bond ratings which works very well. However, they found that a common multiple regression model is nearly as accurate at classifying bond issue ratings as their more sophisticated model.

This section reviews the coverage ratios, financial-leverage ratios, liquidity ratios, and profitability ratios that bond analysts study when assessing the quality of an issue. Section 14-4 discusses the issuer's significance and size.

Coverage Ratios

Some securities analysts believe that the single most important financial ratio determining the quality rating of a bond issue is the "coverage ratio." A **coverage ratio** is a measure of how many times the issuing company's earned income *covers* the interest charges and other costs related to a bond issue. In other words, coverage ratios divide the earnings available for the payment of bond charges by the bond charges themselves. A coverage ratio of 1 indicates that the issuing firm has just enough income to pay its interest expense. This is important because it reflects the probability that the firm will default on its interest payments. Table 14-5 summarizes some guidelines used in evaluating coverage ratios to see what quality ratings should be assigned to bond issues.

As Table 14-5 indicates, bond analysts consider not only the issuer's coverage ratios but also the *stability* of the earnings. The *trend* of the ratios is also evaluated. An upward trend suggests that better times lie ahead, assuming the ratios will continue to rise. A flat trend portends little change. A downward trend usually causes bond raters to lower quality ratings for the bond issuer as a warning to potential investors that troubled times may lie ahead.

The coverage ratios may be calculated on before-tax or after-tax earnings. Some bond analysts include lease payments and sinking fund payments with interest payments and calculate a coverage ratio called the *times-fixed-charges-earned ratio*. This ratio would tend to have values below the ratios in Table 14-5, for example, since deducting fixed charges like lease and/or sinking fund payments would lower the ratios.

The **pretax fixed-charge coverage** ratio defines income as the firm's net income plus income taxes plus gross interest charges (this includes any rental income too). The debt-service charges in the denominator are defined to include gross

Table 14-5
COVERAGE RATIOS AND QUALITY RATINGS

Coverage ratio	Stability of earnings	Quality rating
6 and over	Cyclical	Investment grade
4 and over	Stable	Investment grade
3 to 6	Cyclical	Medium grade
2 to 4	Stable	Medium grade
Under 3	Cyclical	Speculative grade
Under 2	Stable	Speculative grade

Source: Jerome B. Cohen, Edward D. Zinbarg, and Arthur Zeikel, *Investment Analysis and Portfolio Management*, 4th ed. (Homewood, Ill.: R. D. Irwin Inc., 1982), p. 481.

interest expenses. This coverage ratio is

Pretax fixed-charge coverage

$$= \frac{\text{pretax income} + \text{gross interest expense}}{\text{gross interest expense}} \quad (14\text{-}1)$$

When different versions of a ratio are encountered, do not rashly judge them to be erroneous. Sometimes several different variations of the same ratio are all useful for slightly different purposes. The important point to remember, however, is that only **consistently defined** ratios should be compared with each other.

A fixed-charges coverage ratio that is lower than the industry average values may have two causes. First, earnings may be too low. If so, the firm's poor profitability would also show up as rates of return on assets that are low and as rates of return on equity that are below those of most other firms. Second, the firm may be too deeply in debt and thus incur too much interest expense. If so, this will also show up as high financial-leverage ratios, as we shall see next.

Financial-Leverage Ratios

Companies that use borrowed funds to supplement the capital provided by their owner's equity are said to be using **financial leverage.** Ideally, money will be borrowed at a low interest rate and reinvested within the firm at a rate of return that exceeds the interest rate on the debt—the difference is profit. However, a firm can get too deeply into debt. If a firm uses too much financial leverage, its fixed interest expense will be so high that if profits fall even slightly the firm will not be earning enough to pay its contractual interest expense. This can quickly lead to bankruptcy; that is why bond investors are interested in evaluating the indebtedness of issuing firms.

Three of the most popular ratios used to measure financial leverage are the *total-debt-to-equity ratio,* the *long-term-debt-to-capitalization ratio,* and the *long-term-debt-to-equity ratio.* The terms used in these three ratios are standard items from a firm's balance sheet, except for **capitalization,** a financial term that accountants no longer use in their statements.

The **long-term-debt-to-capitalization** ratio is calculated to determine what fraction of the firm's permanent capital is from debt.

$$\text{Long-term-debt-to-capitalization} = \frac{\text{long-term debt}}{\text{capitalization}} \quad (14\text{-}2)$$

Capitalization refers to a firm's permanently committed capital funds. A firm's capitalization is the sum of its permanently maintained current liabilities, long-term debt, preferred stock, and stockholders' equity. A firm's capitalization is also called its *permanent capital.*

Problems can arise when defining financial-leverage ratios. Some of these problems relate to what is called *off-balance-sheet debt.* Unfunded pension liabilities (that is, the amount by which the pension fund's liabilities exceed the fund's assets), leases, and product guarantees are common sources of off-balance-sheet liabilities. The financial statement items used to calculate the ratios above may ignore these long-term liabilities since they do not normally appear on balance sheets. This results in understated leverage ratios. Some financial analysts simply ignore this problem. The more conscientious analysts, however, insert into the firm's liabilities an amount equal to any pension fund deficit, the present value of future lease payments, the present value of servicing contractual guarantees, and/or other off-balance-sheet liabilities. Since different bond analysts may make different estimates of these values, they come up with different leverage ratios for the same firm. This complicates ratio comparisons.

Another problem in calculating financial-leverage ratios is deciding whether to use *book values* or *market values*. When the book value and market value methods produce significantly different ratios, the financial analyst should calculate the leverage ratios using both methods. The different ratios may help the bond analyst get a clearer idea about whether the firm is too deeply in debt and to discern the trend of its indebtedness over time.

Liquidity Ratios   **Liquidity ratios** are used to evaluate the solvency of a firm and thus to determine if the firm will be able to pay its bills on time. The two most common liquidity ratios are the *current ratio* and the *quick ratio*.

$$\text{Current ratio} = \frac{\text{current assets}}{\text{current liabilities}} \tag{14-3}$$

$$\text{Quick ratio} = \frac{\text{current assets} - \text{inventories}}{\text{current liabilities}} \tag{14-4}$$

Current liabilities are bills due to be paid within 1 year. *Current assets* include cash, marketable securities, accounts receivable, inventory, and any other asset that should in the normal course of business turn into cash within 1 year. Some analysts say that a healthy firm should have a current ratio of 2, that is, two dollars of current assets for every dollar of current liabilities. However, other values are commonly considered safe; the norm varies from industry to industry.

Critics of the current ratio point out that the portion of current assets held in inventory is not liquid unless customers are eagerly waiting to buy it and pay cash for it. These analysts prefer to use the quick ratio. A quick ratio of 1 is sometimes suggested as a minimum standard because it means there is one dollar of cash, marketable securities, and accounts receivable (all of which are more liquid than inventory) for each dollar of bills due to be paid in the current year. Other ratios measure liquidity indirectly; they are called turnover ratios.

Turnover Ratios   **Turnover ratios** are used to measure the *activity* within a firm. Use of these ratios is based on the premise that assets not being actively employed must not be very useful and are therefore probably neither liquid nor profitable. There are four ratios that measure asset turnover and thus give an indirect indication of the liquidity and profitability of the assets:

$$\text{Accounts receivable turnover} = \frac{\text{annual sales}}{\text{average accounts receivable}} \qquad (14\text{-}5)$$

$$\text{Collection-period-in-days} = \frac{360 \text{ days}}{\text{accounts receivable turnover}} \qquad (14\text{-}6)$$

$$\text{Collection-period-in-days} = \frac{\text{accounts receivable}}{\text{average day's sales}} \qquad (14\text{-}6a)$$

$$\text{Inventory-turnover ratio} = \frac{\text{annual sales}}{\text{average inventory}} \qquad (14\text{-}7)$$

$$\text{Total-asset turnover} = \frac{\text{annual sales}}{\text{total assets}} \qquad (14\text{-}8)$$

For example, the *accounts-receivable-turnover ratio* for a company that has annual sales of $1,500,000 and beginning- and end-of-year receivables of $450,000 and $550,000, respectively, is 3.

$$\frac{\text{Annual sales}}{\text{Average accounts receivable}} = \frac{\$1,500,000}{(\$450,000 + \$550,000)/2} = \frac{\$1,500,000}{\$500,000} = 3$$

This firm's *collection period* averages 120 days.

$$\frac{360 \text{ days}}{\text{Accounts receivable turnover}} = \frac{360}{3 \text{ times}} = 120 \text{ days} \qquad (14\text{-}6)$$

The collection-period-in-days is the same however it is calculated.

$$\frac{\text{Average accounts receivable}}{\text{Average day's sales}} = \frac{\$500,000}{\$1,500,000/360} = \frac{\$1,500,000}{\$4,166.66} = 120 \text{ days}$$

The accounts-receivable-turnover ratio and the collection-period-in-days give some indication of the liquidity of the current asset called "accounts receivable." Similarly, the *inventory-turnover ratio* measures how rapidly a firm sells out and replaces its inventory. The *total-asset-turnover ratio* is designed to gauge whether all the assets owned by a firm are being used or if some are lying dormant. Bond rating agencies, bond investors, and others who have loaned the firm money can get different perspectives on the firm's liquidity and how well managed the firm is by studying the turnover ratios.

Cashflow Ratios   Firms generate the following kinds of **cashflows:**

1. *Adjusted income* is the firm's normal operating income before taxes.
2. *Interest expense on long-term debt* is added back into the firm's income-after-interest-expense because the resulting income-before-

interest-expense is a cashflow that may be used to pay interest expense.

3. *Depreciation* is an expense item deducted from the firm's revenue to allow for the replacement of plant and equipment that declines in value because of wear and tear. But the replacements and/or repairs need not actually be made simply because the bookkeeping entry deducting depreciation expense is made. Thus, depreciation is a noncash expense that financial analysts view as a cashflow that can be used for interest expense or to repair the firm's physical assets, whichever is most needed.[12]

One cashflow ratio is found by calculating the total of the three cashflow items listed above and then dividing this total cashflow by the total interest expense on the firm's long-term debt. Solvency cannot be maintained in the long run unless this cashflow ratio has a value in excess of 1.[13]

$$\text{Cashflow-to-long-term-debt ratio} = \frac{\text{total annual cashflow}}{\text{long-term debt}} \qquad (14\text{-}9)$$

If the **cashflow-to-long-term-debt ratio** indicates that a firm's cashflow, stated as a percent of its debt, is less than the firm's interest rate paid on total long-term debt, the firm may default on its interest payments.

Profitability Ratios   An increase in the profitability of a bond issuer does not directly imply capital gains for the firm's bond investors. Nevertheless, bond raters and investors track the profitability of firms issuing bonds because profitability is an excellent indicator of a firm's financial health. One of the more useful **profitability ratios** is the *rate-of-return-on-total-assets,* which is useful in measuring the profitability of the total firm.

$$\text{Rate-of-return-on-total-assets} = \frac{\text{net profit before taxes}}{\text{total assets}} \qquad (14\text{-}10)$$

The rate of return on assets will be lowest for firms that have too many assets, high debt levels, low earnings, or some combination of these problems.

A profitability ratio that can reveal more about earnings weakness is the *operating-margin ratio.*

---

[12]Stated differently, **depreciation** is an allocation of the cost of the asset over its useful productive life, not a deduction for any repairs.
[13]Financial Accounting Standards Board Statement Number 95 went into effect in 1988 and, for the first time, required businesses to include a Statement of Cash Flows (rather than merely a Statement of Changes in Financial Position) when issuing a complete set of financial statements. See J. J. Mahoney, M. V. Sever, and J. A. Theis, "Cash Flow: FASB Opens the Floodgates," *Journal of Accountancy,* May 1988, pp. 27–38.

$$\text{Operating margin} = \frac{\text{operating income}}{\text{sales}} \qquad (14\text{-}11)$$

Operating income is a firm's pretax earnings before depreciation and interest expense (that is, before nonoperating expenses) are deducted to obtain the firm's taxable income. Dividing operating income by sales gives the percentage of every sales dollar available to pay overhead expenses and contribute toward profits. If this ratio is too low, it means the firm should either raise its sales price per unit, cut its direct manufacturing (or operating) costs, or both.

Another popular profitability ratio is the *pretax-rate-of-return-on-long-term-capital ratio*.

Pretax rate-of-return on long-term capital =

$$\frac{\text{pretax income} + \text{interest}}{\text{long-term capital}} \qquad (14\text{-}12)$$

The sum of pretax income and interest is the total amount a firm has available to pay its interest expenses.

The pretax-rate-of-return-on-permanent-capital ratio states the firm's income as a percent of its permanent capitalization. It is useful for comparison with current interest rates. If the ratio does not exceed current interest rates, the company is probably not earning enough to pay its interest expense—this condition will result in low bond quality ratings.

Profitability ratios are useful both for historical (or *time-series*) comparisons with the firm's own ratios in order to discern trends within the firm and for *cross-sectional* comparisons with the firm's competitors in order to find strengths or weaknesses.

Financial Ratios and Bond Quality Ratings

In explaining how it rates industrial bonds, Standard & Poor's (S&P) prefaces the data in Table 14-6 with the following statement.[14]

> Of all the financial ratios and measures that have been discussed, the ones that usually carry the most weight in rating determinations are pretax fixed-charge coverage, cash flow to long-term debt, pretax return on total capital invested, and long-term debt to capitalization. *Table 14-6* provides five-year average values of those financial measures for a representative sample of industrial companies with long-term debt ratings in each of the rating categories considered to be investment grade.

When examining Table 14-6, remember that different ratios are favored by each bond analyst and each bond rating agency, and that for any given set of ratios, different values are appropriate for each industry. Also, don't forget

---

[14]*Standard & Poor's Rating Guide* (New York: McGraw-Hill, 1979), p. 42; italicized words added.

Table 14-6

AVERAGE RELATIONSHIPS BETWEEN RATIOS AND BOND RATINGS, 1983–1985

Rating category	Pretax fixed-charge coverage	Cashflow to long-term debt	Pretax return on long-term capital	Long-term debt to capitalization
Equation	(14-1)	(14-9)	(14-12)	(14-2)
AAA	7.48 times	309.0%	25.6%	8.9%
AA	4.43	118.4	22.0	18.9
A	2.93	75.4	18.0	24.5
BBB	2.30	45.7	12.1	31.5
BB	2.04	27.0	13.8	45.5
B	1.51	18.9	12.0	52.0
CCC	0.75	15.1	2.7	69.3

Source: Standard & Poor's, *Debt Rating Criteria* (New York: McGraw-Hill, 1986), p. 51.

that through the ups and downs of the normal business cycle, the values of every firm's ratios vary in a cyclical fashion.[15]

14-4   ECONOMIC SIGNIFICANCE AND SIZE OF THE ISSUER

When bond raters and other financial analysts assess the financial condition of a security issuer, they must consider more than the company's financial ratios. The issuing firm's competition, its size, its importance in its industry, and related factors must also be considered before assigning a quality rating or making an investment in a bond. This analysis of factors external to the bond-issuing firm should start with the firm's competitors.

Issuer's Industry

To discern important facts about the industry in which a bond issuer operates, S&P bond analysts study seven key points.[16]

   1. *Position in the economy:* Is the firm in the capital-goods sector (such as machinery production), the consumer-durables sector (such as auto-

[15]For detailed numerical examples of financial ratio calculations, consult a book about that topic, such as Leopold A. Bernstein, *Financial Statement Analysis,* 4th ed. (Homewood, Ill.: Irwin, 1989). Also see George Foster, *Financial Statement Analysis,* 2d ed. (Englewood Cliffs, N.J.: Prentice-Hall, 1986.)

[16]*Standard & Poor's Rating Guide* (New York: McGraw-Hill, 1979), p. 28.

mobile production), or the consumer-nondurables sector (such as food manufacturing)?

2. *Life cycle of industry:* Is the industry in a growth, stable, or declining phase?

3. *Competitive nature:* What is the nature and intensity of the competition in the industry? Is it on a regional, national, or international basis? Is it based on price, quality of product, distribution capabilities, image, or some other factor? Is the industry regulated (as in broadcasting), which provides some competitive protection?

4. *Labor situation:* Is the industry unionized? If so, are labor contracts negotiated on an industrywide basis, and what is the recent negotiating history?

5. *Supply factors:* Does the industry generally have good control of key raw materials, or is it dependent upon questionable sources?

6. *Volatility:* Is there an involvement with rapidly developing or changing technologies? Is there a dependence on a relatively small number of major contracts (as is sometimes the case in the aerospace industry, for example)?

7. *Major vulnerabilities:* Is the industry likely to be a prime target for some form of political pressure? Are substantial environmental expenditures likely to be mandated? Are near-term energy shortages possible? What is the ease-of-entry into the industry?

Answers to these questions inform the bond analyst about the industry's growth potential, problems that may plague the industry, and the stability of the industry's sales. After these questions are answered, the analyst can move on to consider the issuer's competitive situation within its industry.

Issuer's Competitors

The key questions that S&P raters consider when evaluating an issuer's competition are listed below.[17] The questions are primarily about the firm whose bonds are being rated in order to keep the research from becoming an aimless and costly inquiry into each of the bond issuer's competitors. The cost of this research can be limited by inquiring only into how the competition affects the bond issuer.

1. *Market share:* Does the company have a large enough portion of the market share (be it regional, national, or international) to significantly influence industry dynamics? This may be especially important in a market dominated by only a few producers. Does the company have the opportunity to exercise price leadership? Does the company offer a

[17]*Standard & Poor's Rating Guide* (New York: McGraw-Hill, 1979), pp. 29–30.

full range of products or have proprietary products or a special niche in the market?

2. *Technological leadership:* Is the company usually among the first with new developments, or is it typically a follower? How do research and development expenditures compare with the industry average?

3. *Production efficiency:* Is the company a relatively low-cost producer? Are its facilities newer or more advanced than the average? Is it more or less vertically integrated than the average? If mandated expenditures (such as for pollution control) are required, has the company already complied to a greater or lesser extent than its competitors? Does the company face a more onerous labor situation than its competitors?

4. *Financial structure:* How does a company's use of leverage and various types of financing vehicles compare with that of others in the industry?

After the bond raters have answered these questions to their satisfaction, they focus on the last phase of bond rating: studying the new issue's indenture contract.

14-5   **PROTECTIVE PROVISIONS IN THE ISSUER'S INDENTURE**

The bond owners' rights are spelled out in the legal instrument called the **indenture.** The protective provisions spelled out in the indenture can raise the quality rating for an issue by one or two grades if a strong issuer grants liberal provisions. In spite of the importance of these provisions, however, they are less important than the issuer's earning power. All the liberal protective provisions in the world will not get a high-quality rating for a firm that faces a future of continuing losses.

Bond issuers commonly provide the following types of protective provisions to ensure the safety of the bondholder's investment.

1. The issuer pledges specific assets as collateral.

2. The issuer subordinates other legal claims on its assets or income.

3. The issuer provides for a sinking fund with which to pay off the bonds even if the issuer defaults on its other debts.

4. The issuing firm's management promises to operate the firm in certain ways to protect the bondholders.

Let us consider these provisions in more detail.

**Collateral
Provisions**

A paragraph in a bond indenture which specifies that certain assets of the issuing company become the property of the bond investors if the issuer defaults on the interest or principal payments of the bond issue is called a *collateral provision*. Many bond issues have no collateral provision, but those that do are rated somewhat higher.

Debentures are bonds that have no assets pledged as collateral to help guarantee the bondholders that they will be repaid in case of bankruptcy. If the issuer does go bankrupt, the debenture owners will find themselves placed in the undesirable category of ''general creditors'' by the bankruptcy court. *General creditors* include the public utilities, suppliers of raw materials who sold on credit, and other junior-level creditors. To avoid this default risk, bond investors can buy mortgage bonds, for example, in order to obtain a collateral provision. Mortgage bonds have a prior claim in bankruptcy on the specific asset that was pledged as collateral.

Bondholders don't get a collateral provision for nothing. Such a provision increases the bond issue's price per bond slightly, and it lowers the interest income yield. By buying collateralized bonds, the investor gives up some cash in order to get a safer investment; this is a risk-return trade-off.

**Subordination
Provisions**

To make safety-conscious investors more willing to buy bonds, the indenture can include clauses that subordinate certain claims or assets. A *subordination clause* places other bond issues or specified creditors in an inferior or secondary legal position with respect to claims on the issuer's assets if the issuer defaults on the interest or principal payments.

The so-called *after-acquired property clause* is an example of a subordination clause. Such a clause states that if an issuer acquires additional assets after a first mortgage bond (or other type of collateralized bond, as specified) is outstanding, these new assets will automatically become part of this first mortgage bond's collateral. Such a clause protects the first mortgage bondholders from having the firm acquire newer assets with later mortgage bond issues against which the first mortgage bond owners would hold no claim. In effect, this clause subordinates the claim of any later mortgage bond buyers to the first mortgage bondholders' claim: first mortgage bondholders can claim their old assets and all the newer assets as collateral, too.

Another fairly common subordination is called the *dividend test clause*. Such a clause limits the claim of the common stockholders (who essentially run the corporation through their voting power at annual stockholders' meetings) on corporate profits. Profits might be used to pay either cash dividends to stockholders or interest to bondholders. The dividend test clause specifies that the issuer cannot pay annual cash dividends in excess of annual earnings. Such a clause helps ensure that if the firm suffers losses, its borrowing power and liquid assets will be retained to pay bondholders rather than used to pay cash dividends to the common stockholders.[18] There are several other similar clauses that subordinate maximization of common stockholders' profit to bondholders' safety.

Sinking Fund Provisions

A sinking fund provision requires the issuer to make payments into a **sinking fund** every year. Sinking fund provisions typically require that the issuer's sinking fund deposits be held by a third party (for example, a bank) that uses the funds to repurchase the issuer's outstanding sinking fund bonds.

A sinking fund provides safety of repayment for bondholders that can increase through the years. After a number of years' payments to the sinking fund have been used to retire more of the issuer's outstanding bonds each year, bond rating agencies may acknowledge this progressive retirement ahead of the bonds' maturity date by raising the issue's quality rating. An improved quality rating will increase the bond's market price and thus enrich the bondholders. Well-funded sinking funds provide price supports for their bonds, but sinking funds can also work to the detriment of bondholders in two significant respects.

First, some sinking fund provisions provide that bonds may be redeemed at stipulated dates or by random selection before the issue matures. Thus, an investor may have gone to the trouble of evaluating a bond issue and purchasing a bond at what is considered to be an attractive yield-to-maturity only to have the investment called away by a sinking fund prematurity-date purchase. Second, issues with sinking funds pay lower yields because they offer their bondholders greater safety. This is another example of the *risk-return trade-off*— the lower-risk investments can attract buyers at lower rates of return.

Other Protective Provisions

Some indenture contracts forbid the issuer to sell off its own assets in order to lease the same assets back again. The purpose of **sale-and-leaseback** arrangements is to free capital invested in plant and equipment so that it may be spent for other purposes. Meanwhile, the use of the asset is assured because the seller of the asset contracts to lease it back as part of the sales agreement. Bondholders want provisions against sale-and-leaseback transactions because they deplete the issuer's collateral assets; a leased asset cannot be part of the firm's collateral.

Debt-test clauses are common in issues of speculative grade bonds. Such provisions limit the issuer's ability to create additional debt and thereby protect bondholders in two ways. First, they limit the issuer's ability to undertake rapid expansion, which is usually risky. Second, if the issuer should go bankrupt, such clauses limit the number of creditors competing for the remaining assets.

Negative pledge clauses limit the issuer's ability to pledge assets as collateral

[18]For more details see Avner Kalay, "Stockholder-Bondholder Conflict and Dividend Constraints," *Journal of Financial Economics,* July 1982, vol. 10, pp. 211–233.

for any future borrowings. This protects existing bondholders from having to face senior bankruptcy claims that might have arisen with later issues of other collateralized bonds.

Prohibitions against the sale of subsidiary corporations are common. Such provisions allow the issuer to sell major subsidiaries only if they immediately repay the previously outstanding debt. This protects bondholders from losing important sources of income or collateral assets that the issuer owns through its subsidiaries.

New Protective Provisions

The high and volatile interest rate environment of the 1970s and 1980s spawned a wide variety of new protective provisions. They include the following bonds: (1) **Zero coupon bonds** have provisions to protect bond investors from reinvestment risk. (2) **Put bonds** contain embedded put options allowing the bond investor to put the bond back onto the issuer at a preset price if advantageous for the investor. (3) **Foreign-currency bonds** are issued in the United States, but their coupons and/or principal are paid in a foreign currency so as to protect international investors from foreign exchange risk. (4) **Adjustable-rate bonds,** also called **floating-rate bonds,** pay a coupon that is indexed to some economic benchmark. For instance, a commercial bank that issued AA-rated floating-rate bonds might index these bonds to pay a coupon rate that is reset to 30 basis points above the 3-month T-bill rate every 6 months. This is an interesting example because if the financial condition of the issuing bank deteriorated sufficiently for its floating-rate bonds to be downgraded to A-grade, then the bond market might want 50 basis points over the 3-month T-bill rate from this issue. As a result, the A-rated bonds would sell at a discount unless the bank's financial condition improved.[19] (5) **Inflation-linked bonds** first emerged in the United States during the 1980s. The coupons and/or principal of these bonds is linked to some index of the general price level (like the consumer price index) to protect the investors from purchasing power risk.

It should now be apparent that an almost unlimited variety of provisions can be inserted in an indenture.[20] The ingenuity with which safety-seeking bondholders encumber issuers' managements is refreshing—but do not forget that nothing is granted for free. Every protective provision bondholders obtain reduces the rate of return they can expect to earn from their bonds. There are

---

[19]For details about adjustable-rate bonds see Frank J. Fabozzi, *Floating Rate Instruments* (Chicago, Ill.: Probus, 1986).

[20]For more detailed analysis of bond indentures and protective provisions, see Mitchell Berlin and Jan Loeys, "Bond Covenants and Delegated Monitoring," *Journal of Finance,* June 1988, vol. 43, no. 2, pp. 397–412. See also T. H. Ho and R. F. Singer, "Bond Indenture Provisions and the Risk of Corporate Debt," *Journal of Financial Economics,* Dec. 1982, vol. 10, pp. 375–406. Also see C. W. Smith and J. B. Warner, "On Financial Contracting: An Analysis of Bond Covenants," *Journal of Financial Economics,* June 1979, vol. 7, pp. 117–161.

rare exceptions to this rule, but generally the natural economic order of things requires a trade-off of risk for return.

Bond and Stock Prices Anticipate Quality Rating Changes

Bond Price Reactions Table 14-1 showed how Chrysler Corporation's bond quality ratings, bond prices, and stock prices all declined as that firm moved toward bankruptcy during the 1979–1981 period. This section reports on two separate studies designed to discern more information about the timing of bond and stock price movements for corporations that experience bond rating changes.

Public Bond Ratings The data in Table 14-1 suggest that bond and stock investors in a deteriorating corporation, like Chrysler in the 1979–1981 period, should be able to sell their securities before the firm goes bankrupt and thus avoid catastrophic losses. Scrutiny of the data in Table 14-1 raises an important question in this regard, however. Did Chrysler's bond and stock prices fall in *reaction* to the falling quality ratings, or did prices fall first? That is, did astute investors foresee the oncoming bankruptcy before the bond rating agencies? Stated more generally: When the financial condition of an issuing company deteriorates (or just the opposite, grows in profitability and liquidity and has its rating raised), do the public announcements of bond rating changes contain any information of value to investors?

Empirical Analysis of Bond Rating Changes Dr. Mark Weinstein analyzed the monthly market price changes of 132 different bond rating changes.[21] Weinstein investigated to discover if bond prices reacted to quality rating changes with a lead, a lag, simultaneously, or if they did not react at all.

Weinstein reported that (1) bond prices experienced a statistically insignificant price reaction during the month in which their rating was changed and (2) bond prices accomplished most of their price reaction to a rating change during the year *preceding* the announcement of the rating change. Stated differently, it appears that Standard & Poor's and Moody's quality rating changes are *following rather than leading* the movements in market prices. The implication of this finding is that bond investors should do their own bond analysis rather than spend their time and money on Moody's and/or S&P bond quality rating publications.

Stock Price Reactions to Bond Rating Changes Professors Paul A. Griffin and Antonio Z. Sanvicente (GS hereafter) analyzed 63 downgradings and 65 upgradings of bond ratings in order to estimate the effect of these changes on

[21]Mark I. Weinstein, "The Effect of a Rating Change Announcement on Bond Prices," *Journal of Financial Economics*, Dec. 1977, vol. 5, no. 3, pp. 329–350.

the market prices of the issuing corporations' common stock.[22] GS analyzed the stocks' monthly rates of return in order to detect any unusual or abnormal common stock returns that might be associated with the change in the corporations' bond ratings.

GS Findings About Stock Prices   GS reported stock price findings that were similar to Weinstein's conclusions about bond price reactions. GS reported that (1) corporations' stock prices did experience statistically significant price reactions to quality rating changes in bonds issued by the same corporation, (2) most of the stock price reaction occurred in the 11 months *prior* to the announcement of the bond rating change, and (3) the stock price reactions in the month that the rating change occurred were only marginally significant. The GS results suggest that people who wish to speculate on the effects that bond rating changes will have on the same corporation's common stock should do their own research.

Anticipatory Prices   Weinstein and GS both reported that most of the movements in the prices of bonds and stocks issued by companies experiencing bond quality rating changes occurred *before* the rating change occurred. Stated differently, the security prices anticipated the forthcoming announcement of a change in the quality rating. This anticipatory price behavior is the result of aggressive security analysis by many investors.

The remainder of this chapter moves beyond the investment implications of default risk to consider purchasing-power risk.

14-6   PURCHASING-POWER RISK

Bonds, savings accounts, life insurance policies, and many other **monetary instruments** are called **dollar-denominated assets** because they promise to make their payments in dollars rather than in real goods such as food or clothing. This means that the coupon interest payments and principal repayment contractually promised to bonds' owners are *fixed dollar quantities that do not increase with inflation.* As a result, if any inflation occurs, bondholders are repaid in dollars that have less purchasing power over real (physical) goods than the dollars that were originally invested in the bonds. This possible loss

---

[22]P. A. Griffin and A. Z. Sanvicente, "Common Stock Returns and Rating Changes: A Methodological Comparison," *Journal of Finance,* March 1982, vol. XXXVII, no. 1, pp. 103–119. The study actually employed three different methods to gauge the effects of a bond rating change on the issuer's stock. See also G. Pinches and C. Singleton, "The Adjustment of Stock Prices to Bond Rating Changes," *Journal of Finance,* March 1978, vol. XXXIII, no. 1, pp. 29–44.

in purchasing power over real goods is **purchasing-power risk.** Purchasing-power risk is often larger than investors realize because they are unaware of inflation and its implications.

Measuring the Inflation Rate

The consumer price index (CPI), tabulated monthly by the U.S. government's Bureau of Labor Statistics, measures the cost of a representative basket of consumer goods. The basket contains specified quantities and qualities of various items of food, clothing, housing, and health care products bought by the average urban household. The price of this hypothetical basket of goods at a particular point in time determines the value of the CPI. The percentage change in the CPI over time measures the **rate of inflation,** as shown below in Equation (14-13). The inflation rate is denoted q.

$$q = \frac{(\text{CPI for month } t + 1) - (\text{CPI for month } t)}{\text{CPI for month } t} \qquad (14\text{-}13)$$

For example, if the cost of the market basket goes from $200 to $202 in 1 month, the rate of inflation would be 1.0 percent.

$$q = \frac{\$202 - \$200}{\$200} = \frac{\$2}{\$200} = 0.01 \times 100 = 1.0\%$$

If the CPI increases 1 percent in some month, this monthly rate of 1 percent should be *annualized* as shown below to get the annual rate of inflation of 12.68 percent.

$$[1.0 + (1.0\% \text{ per month})]^{12} = (1.01)^{12} = 1.1268 = (1.0 + 0.1268)$$

Investors should compare interest rates to the inflation rate to control their purchasing-power risk.

Nominal Returns Exceed Real Returns

When you read in a newspaper that a savings account pays an interest rate of 6 percent, for example, that is the investment's "nominal" rate of return. **Nominal rates of return** are money rates of return that are not adjusted for the effects of inflation.

An investment's **real rate of return** during some period is calculated by removing the rate of inflation from the nominal return, as shown in Equation (14-14). The *real return* is denoted rr.

$$1.0 + rr = \frac{1.0 + r}{1.0 + q} \qquad (14\text{-}14)$$

For example, if a common stock earns a 10 percent nominal rate of return, $r = 0.1 \times 100 = 10\%$, for a year when the inflation rate is 8 percent, $q =$

$0.08 \times 100 = 8\%$, the stock's real rate of return is less than 2 percent that year.

$$1.0 + rr = \frac{1.10}{1.08} = 1.0185 \qquad \text{or } rr = 1.85\% \qquad (14\text{-}14a)$$

This common stock investment resulted in a 1.85 percent increase in real purchasing power. The rest of the investment's nominal rate of return is lost to inflation. Stated differently, the only portion of an investment's nominal rate of return that results in increased consumption opportunities for an investor is the real rate of return. Investors who suffer from **money illusion** fail to realize this; they naively believe that the investment in this example yields more than a 1.85 percent real gain.[23]

A Handy Formula for Approximations

Equation (14-14) can be simplified by multiplying both sides of the equation by the quantity $(1.0 + q)$ and rearranging to obtain the mathematically equivalent equations (14-15) and (14-15a).

$$1.0 + r = (1.0 + rr)(1.0 + q) \qquad (14\text{-}15)$$

$$r = rr + q + (q)(rr) \qquad (14\text{-}15a)$$

People looking for a quick way to calculate the nominal rate of return have reasoned that the product of q times rr in Equation (14-15a) will often be a tiny value that can usually be ignored with little loss of accuracy. Therefore, they restate Equation (14-15a) in the simplified form shown in Equation (14-16).[24]

$$r \doteq rr + q \qquad (14\text{-}16)$$

Equation (14-16a) shows how to find rr after r and q are known.

$$rr \doteq r - q \qquad (14\text{-}16a)$$

When the inflation rate is low, Equations (14-16) and (14-16a) provide an easy way to closely approximate the nominal and real rates of return.

Next, let us compare the nominal and the real rates of return from different types of investments.

---

[23]Some detailed studies on the effect of inflation on stock prices include J. Hasbrouck, "Stock Returns, Inflation, and Economic Activity: The Survey Evidence," *Journal of Finance,* Dec. 1983, vol. 39, pp. 1293–1310. Also see G. W. Schwert, "The Adjustment of Stock Prices to Information about Inflation," *Journal of Finance,* March 1981, vol. 36, pp. 15–29. See also R. Stulz, "Asset Pricing and Expected Inflation," *Journal of Finance,* March 1986, vol. 41, pp. 209–224.

[24]Equation (14-16) is equivalent to Irving Fisher's theory, Equation (12-1), about the relationship that should exist between nominal interest rates and the rate of inflation.

14-7   COMPARING NOMINAL AND REAL INVESTMENT RETURNS EMPIRICALLY

Table 1-6 summarizes investors' average rates of return over more than two decades. The statistics in Table 1-6 are stated in nominal terms; these nominal values can be diminished by the rate of inflation shown in that table to obtain real returns.

The remainder of this section reviews the findings of various financial analysts who studied investments in various kinds of securities to discern the impact of inflation on the securities' nominal returns.

Findings of Early Researchers

Pioneering thinking by Fisher and Williams during the 1930s provided compelling logic which suggested that the returns from securities should vary directly with the rate of inflation.[25]

But during the 1970s, Bodie, Jaffe and Mandelker, and Nelson all published empirical studies that challenged the received theory of Fisher and Williams.[26] Using empirical data from the 1953 to 1974 period, they all found that both the nominal and the real returns from common stocks were negatively correlated with the inflation rate.

Fama and Schwert examined the returns from T-bills, T-bonds, corporate bonds, real estate, labor income, and common stocks.[27] They concluded that only T-bills and both types of bonds provided investors with complete hedges against both expected inflation and unexpected inflation. Moosa, Hasbrouck, and Gultekin used more recent data to investigate the ability of common stocks to provide a hedge against inflation.[28] Their conclusions agreed with the research mentioned above.

Stulz developed a model in which real returns are negatively related to the

---

[25]See Irving Fisher, *The Theory of Interest* (New York: Macmillan, 1930). Also see John Williams, *The Theory of Investment Value* (Amsterdam: North Holland, 1938).

[26]Z. Bodie, "Common Stocks as a Hedge against Inflation," *Journal of Finance*, May 1976, vol. 31, pp. 459–470; Z. Bodie and V. I. Rosansky, "Risk and Return in Commodity Futures," *Financial Analysts Journal*, May–June 1980, pp. 27–39; J. Jaffe and G. Mandelker, "The Fisher Effect for Risky Assets: An Empirical Investigation," *Journal of Finance*, May 1976, vol. 31, pp. 447–458; C. R. Nelson, "Inflation and Rates of Return on Common Stocks," *Journal of Finance*, May 1976, vol. 31, pp. 471–483.

[27]E. F. Fama and G. W. Schwert, "Asset Returns and Inflation," *Journal of Financial Economics*, 1977, vol. 5, pp. 115–146.

[28]N. Gultekin, "Stock Market Returns and Inflation," *Journal of Finance*, June 1983, vol. 38, pp. 663–674; J. Hasbrouck, "Stock Returns, Inflation, and Economic Activity: The Survey Evidence," *Journal of Finance*, Dec. 1983, vol. 39, pp. 1293–1310; S. A. Moosa, "Inflation and Common Stock Prices," *Journal of Financial Research*, Fall 1980, vol. 3, pp. 115–128.

Table 14-7
AVERAGE REAL RATE OF RETURNS FOR DIFFERENT CATEGORIES OF INVESTMENTS,
1926–1987

Inflation-adjusted series	Summary statistics of annual returns (1926–1987)			
	Geometric mean	Arithmetic mean	Standard deviation	First-order auto-correlation
Inflation-adjusted common stocks	6.6%	8.8%	21.2%	.00
Inflation-adjusted small stocks	8.8	14.2	35.2	.07
Inflation-adjusted long-term corporate bonds	1.8	2.3	10.0	.29
Inflation-adjusted long-term government bonds	1.2	1.7	10.2	.18
Inflation-adjusted intermediate-term government bonds	1.7	1.9	7.1	.34
Inflation-adjusted U.S. Treasury bills (real interest rates)	0.4	0.5	4.4	.66

Source: Stocks, Bonds, Bills and Inflation (SBBI): 1985 ed., updated in *SBBI 1988 Yearbook* (Chicago, Ill.: Ibbotson Associates, 1988), exhibit 27, p. 77.

inflation rate and the money stock.[29] And, as we shall see next, Roger Ibbotson has investigated the effects of inflation on various investment returns using empirical data spanning the years from 1926 to 1987.

Ibbotson's Empirical Work

Ibbotson prepared various portfolios to facilitate the comparison of both nominal and real investment returns from different categories of assets.[30] Ibbotson set up diversified portfolios of common stocks, U.S. Treasury bills, U.S. Treas-

[29]R. Stulz, "Asset Pricing and Expected Inflation," *Journal of Finance,* March 1986, vol. 41, pp. 209–224.
[30]Roger Ibbotson, *Stocks, Bonds, Bills and Inflation (SBBI):* 1985 ed., updated by *SBBI 1988 Yearbook* (Chicago, Ill.: Ibbotson Associates, 1988). Ibbotson, a finance professor at Yale's School of Organization, has published many empirical studies of investment returns.

ury bonds, and corporate bonds by selecting a representative sample of each of these types of securities. Equations (7-1), (7-2), and (7-3) show how Ibbotson calculated the one-period rates of return. The portfolios were formed without any attempt to pick either the best or the worst securities in each category. The portfolios thus represented indexes of *average* investment performance. A *naive buy-and-hold* investment strategy should produce results like those of Ibbotson's hypothetical portfolios.

Figure 14-3 Nominal and real common stock returns, 1926–1987. (*Source: Stocks, Bonds, Bills and Inflation, SBBI:* 1985 ed., updated by the *SBBI 1988 Yearbook,* Chicago, Ill.: Ibbotson Associates, 1988, exhibit 18, p. 59.)

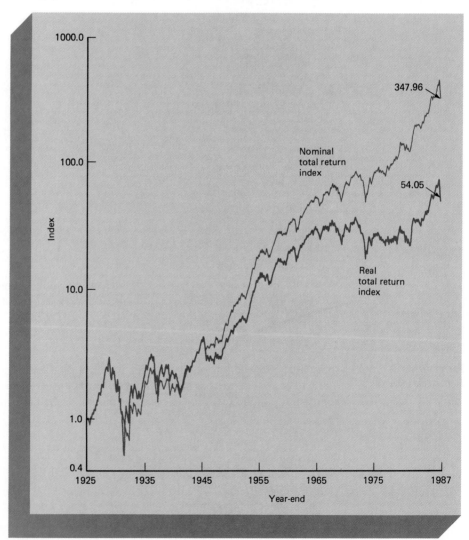

Figure 7-2 on page 199 shows how one dollar invested at the end of 1925 would probably have grown if it had been invested in each different type of investment portfolio and then continually reinvested for the next 62 years. Table 14-4 summarizes the investment performances illustrated in Figures 7-2 and 14-3 to aid in comparing the risk and return from the various investments. These results are all stated on a before-commission and before-tax basis. Comparing the annual yields from the T-bills with the annual rates of inflation reveals

Figure 14-4 Risk and average return statistics for major categories of investment assets. (*Source: Stocks, Bonds, Bills and Inflation, SBBI:* 1985 ed., updated by the *SBBI 1988 Yearbook,* Chicago, Ill.: Ibbotson Associates, 1988, exhibit 8, p. 25.)

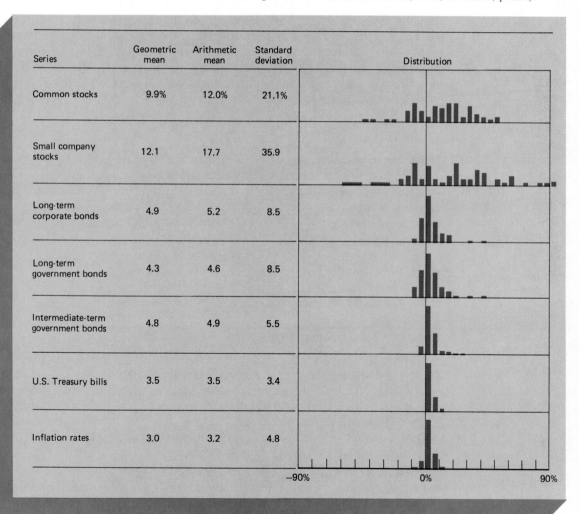

Series	Geometric mean	Arithmetic mean	Standard deviation	Distribution
Common stocks	9.9%	12.0%	21.1%	
Small company stocks	12.1	17.7	35.9	
Long-term corporate bonds	4.9	5.2	8.5	
Long-term government bonds	4.3	4.6	8.5	
Intermediate-term government bonds	4.8	4.9	5.5	
U.S. Treasury bills	3.5	3.5	3.4	
Inflation rates	3.0	3.2	4.8	

that the Treasury bill investment's nominal returns approximated the rate of inflation—T-bills yielded almost no real return.

To provide more perspective on the bond returns, we present both real and nominal returns from several investment indexes in Table 14-7 and Figure 14-4, respectively. A comparison of these summary statistics shows that, on average, the common stocks (represented by the S&P 500 index) earned much greater returns than any of the bond investments. Do not hastily conclude from this difference, however, that common stock investments are better than bond investments. Common stocks must pay higher returns to compensate their investors for assuming the greater risks associated with common stock investing.

Comparing the risk statistics in Table 14-7 and Figure 14-4 for common stocks with the bonds' risk statistics is informative. Investment risk is measured by the *standard deviation* of returns. Comparing the bond risk statistics with the common stock statistics shows that, in both the *nominal* and the *real* sense, stock is a far more risky investment than any of the bond portfolios. Common stock investors suffer more anxiety, lose more sleep, and endure a greater possibility of bankruptcy to get their higher average returns. However, do not forget that a poorly diversified stock investor can have an experience that diverges substantially from the averages.

Real versus Nominal Returns Year by Year

The real rate of return measures the percentage increase in purchasing power over physical goods that an investment yielded. Table 14-7 and Figures 7-2, 14-3, and 14-4 summarize the nominal and real returns from various investment averages. Scrutinizing the year-by-year returns reveals that occasionally most investments had a positive nominal return, $r_t > 0$, and a negative real return, $rr_t < 0$, meaning that the asset's nominal return was less than the inflation rate, $r_t < q_t$. Stated differently, this means that none of the assets shown in Figures 7-2, 14-3 and 14-4 is a *consistently* good inflation hedge.

14-8   **SUMMARY AND CONCLUSIONS**

The present value model is used to value bonds. Sometimes the most difficult part of the bond valuation process is determining the appropriate market interest rate to use as the discount rate—this is where default risk analysis and bond quality ratings can be useful.

Standard & Poor's and other bond rating services use financial ratio guidelines such as those in Table 14-6 to aid them in assigning a quality rating to a bond issue. This tentative rating is reexamined in light of the protective provisions in the issue's indenture and the issuer's economic significance and competitive position, and the tentative rating may be moved upward or downward as deemed appropriate.

The relationship between the appropriate discount rate and a bond's quality rating changes continuously through time, as shown in Figure 14-1. Federal Reserve Board policy, fiscal policy, the supply of and demand for loanable funds, and many other factors cause this relationship to vary. However, *the risk-return relationship is always positive.*

The difference between default-free Treasury bonds and corporate bonds is that corporate bonds must pay higher rates of interest in order to induce investors to assume the default risk. Since all interest rates tend to rise and fall together, as shown in Figure 6-1 at page 165, corporate bond interest rates merely fluctuate at a slightly higher level than do Treasury bond interest rates.

Bond rating agencies like Fitch's, Standard & Poor's, and Moody's, spend considerable resources assessing the quality of bond issues. The bond ratings they purvey seem to have some validity because the highest grade bonds offer the lowest market interest rates available on any given date, the bond quality ratings are written into the investment guidelines handed down by most state governments, and bond issuers pay thousands of dollars annually merely to have their bond issues given current ratings. Empirical evidence compiled by Weinstein, and Griffin and Sanvicente, however, raised serious questions about whether the bond ratings determined the market yields or whether the reverse was true. The stock and bond price movements anticipate the quality rating changes by so many months that it seems as if the market prices might be guiding the rating agencies in making their rating changes.

Purchasing-power risk is like a hidden tax that transfers wealth from creditors and subsidizes debtors. If the debtors pay a nominal interest rate that is below the rate of inflation, inflation benefits debtors at the expense of their lender. Therefore, bond investors, who are essentially lenders, cannot afford to overlook the purchasing-power risk that accompanies inflation.

The default risk is greatest on low-grade corporate bonds. And the purchasing-power risk is highest in the high-inflation economies of the world. But, in the final analysis, one of the nicest things about long-term bond investing is that investors can be relatively free from worry about interest income fluctuations if they so desire. By simply buying a high-grade bond with little risk of default which offers contractual interest payments and repayment of the principal at specified times, the investor can have peace of mind and earn nominal cashflows that are known in advance. In contrast, for security analysts who do default risk analysis and monetary economists who forecast interest rates, the bond markets also offer opportunities to speculate for breathtaking profits.

Essay Questions

14-1   Look up information on two companies that both drill oil wells—Exxon and Zapata. Both corporations' bonds are traded on the NYSE and both have bond issues maturing in 1997. Compare and contrast the Exxon 6s of 1997 with Zapata Corporation's 10¼s of 1997. If you had to make a choice between these two bonds, in which bond issue would you prefer to invest? Explain the reasons for your choice.

14-2   Compare and contrast investing in home mortgages to investing in collateralized bonds with a sinking fund.

14-3   Weinstein's study of bond price movements showed that gains could be earned by buying corporate bonds on the day their quality rating was upgraded. True, false, or uncertain? Explain.

14-4   Why might you (or Professors Griffin and Sanvicente) suspect that when a corporation has its bond rating changed, this event might affect the market price of its common stock?

14-5   Do you think that bond rating agencies like Standard & Poor's and Moody's give any heed to the monetary policies of the Federal Reserve when they assign quality ratings to outstanding issues?

14-6   An investor named Kerri Kumar who lived in the country of Exotica doubled her net worth in 1 year. During that year the cost of living, as measured by Exotica's CPI, quadrupled. Has Ms. Kumar's financial condition improved or become worse during this remarkable year? Explain.

Cases

14-7   (CFA exam question) Georgia-Pacific Corporation, a large forest products manufacturer, had two AA-rated, $150 million par amount, intermediate-term debt issues outstanding in 1985.

	10.10% notes	Floating-rate notes
Maturity	1990	1987
Issued	6/12/80	9/27/79
At par to yield	10.10%	12.00%
Callable: (beginning on)	6/15/86	10/01/84
At	100	100
Sinking fund	None	None
Current coupon	10.10%	16.90%
Changes	Fixed	Every 6 months 0.75% above 6-month Treasury bill rate
Range since issued	—	16.90–12.00%
Current price	73⅜	97
Current yield	13.77%	17.42%
Yield-to-maturity	15.87%	—
Price range since issue	100–72	102–93

Assume it is 1985. Based on the above data answer the following questions. (*a*) *State* the minimum coupon rate of interest at which the company could sell a fixed-rate issue at par due in 1990. Assume the same indenture provisions as the 10.10% notes and disregard any tax considerations. (*b*) *Give* two reasons why the floating-rate notes are not selling at par (offering price). (*c*) *State* and *justify* whether the risk of call is high, moderate, or low for the fixed-rate issue. (*d*) Assuming a decline in interest rates is anticipated, *identify* and *justify* which issue would be most appropriate for an actively managed bond portfolio where total return is the primary objective. (*e*) *Explain* why yield-to-maturity is not valid for the floating-rate note. (*f*) If interest rates remain stable or increase prior to maturity, *identify* which issue will have the higher realized compound yield and *give* the reason.

14-8   The Apex Tobacco Corporation has produced and sold snuff and chewing tobacco for over 100 years. But dipping snuff and chewing tobacco have fallen in popularity. Declines in sales and rising production costs resulted in a large deficit at the end of 19X8. Apex's financial statements document the dire circumstances into which the firm has fallen.

Apex Tobacco, Balance Sheet, December 31, 19X8 (in thousands, $)

Current assets	$375	Current liabilities	$450
Fixed assets	375	Long-term debt (unsecured)	225
		Capital stock	150
		Retained earning (deficit)	(75)
Total assets	$750	Total liabilities and NW	$750

Apex Tobacco—Selected Financial Data: 19X5–19X8

Year	Sales	Net profit after tax, before fixed charges
19X5	$2625	$262.5
19X6	2400	225.0
19X7	1425	(75.0)
19X8	1350	(112.5)

External appraisers suggested that the company would have a liquidation value of about $600,000. Management concluded that, as an alternative, a reorganization was possible with additional investment of $300,000. Management was confident that the firm could undertake the manufacture of new smoking products, such as long, slim cigars for women; cigarette papers of varying colors for the roll-your-own market; Turkish water pipes (or hookahs); and stylish small pipes for customers who wish to smoke less than the normal full bowl. Outside consultants concluded that this broadened product line could be produced and marketed readily through Apex's existing marketing channels and that new investment of $300,000 was needed. The consultants also forecast that the additional investment would restore earnings to $125,000 a year after taxes and before fixed charges. Apex's common stock sells at about 8 times its earnings per share. Management is negotiating with a local investment group to obtain the additional equity investment of $300,000. If the funds are obtained, the holders of the long-term debt would be issued one-half of the common stock in the reorganized firm in place of their present debt claims. New shares of stock would also be issued to sell to the new investors in Apex so that the old stockholders' voting power and potential earnings per share would be diluted or "watered down" after the reorganization.

Should the stockholders and creditors agree to the reorganization, or should they force bankruptcy and liquidation of the firm's assets at auction?

Matching Question

14-9   Match names of the financial ratios below with the proper definition from the list of brief definitions.

Name of ratio		Definition of ratio
1. Current ratio	A.	$\dfrac{\text{Earnings available for bond servicing charges}}{\text{Bond servicing charges}}$
2. Operating margin	B.	$\dfrac{\text{Annual sales}}{\text{Average inventory}}$
3. Coverage ratio	C.	$\dfrac{\text{Operating income}}{\text{Sales}}$
4. Return on assets	D.	$\dfrac{\text{Current assets}}{\text{Current liabilities}}$
5. Inventory turnover	E.	$\dfrac{\text{Taxable income}}{\text{Total assets}}$

Problems

14-10   If CPI_t was 222 and 5 years later CPI_{t+5} was 357.5, what was the average annual rate of inflation? Show your computations.

14-11   Compute each year's *real* rate of return for a savings account from the data below.

Year	Rate of interest	CPI	Inflation rate, q	Real rate of return, rr
19X1	5.0%	180	Undetermined	Undetermined
19X2	5.0	190		
19X3	6.0	202		
19X4	6.0	210		
19X5	6.0	220		

14-12 Reconsider the interest income from the savings account in Problem 14-11. In addition, assume the saver is in the 30 percent income tax bracket. What is the saver's real after-tax rate of return each year?

14-13 As he reached his thirtieth birthday, Carl McGowan started to consider how much he would need to retire comfortably when he reached age 65. Carl began preparing his estimates by trying to evaluate the effects that two different inflation rates would have on the cost of living 35 years in the future. How much more will it cost Carl to live if the inflation rates average (*a*) 3 percent per year for 35 years? (*b*) 6 percent per year for 35 years?

14-14 Charlotte Halpern bought a 10-year zero coupon STRIP for $6139.13 on December 31, 1977 and received the bond's $10,000 face value when it matured on December 31, 1987. (*a*) What was Charlotte's compounded effective rate of return from this bond? (*b*) If inflation averaged 6 percent per year during the decade that Charlotte had her money invested in the zero, what was her real rate of return from the bond?

14-15 Lucinda Baines bought 100 shares of ABC stock for $40 per share. Nine years later the stock was selling for $60 per share. During Lucy's 9-year investment the consumer price index rose from $CPI_0 = 110$ to $CPI_9 = 190$. ABC pays zero cash dividends. Has the real value of Ms. Baines's investment in ABC increased?

14-16 In 1978 Ralph Raneri bought a 1965 Ford Mustang for $1200 and spent $2800 restoring it to like-new condition. He kept the car in his garage where he and his friends could admire it; it was rarely driven. Ten years later a personal hardship forced Ralph to sell his beloved Mustang for $12,000. The consumer price index had risen from 190 in 1978 when Ralph invested the $4000 in the car to 280 when he sold it in 1988. Was Ralph's car a good financial investment?

Selected References

Bernstein, Leopold A., *Financial Statement Analysis,* 4th ed. (Homewood, Ill.: Irwin, 1989).

   This textbook stresses fundamental analysis of financial statements using ratios. Problems that inflation causes for the financial analyst are also considered.

Cottle, Sidney, Roger F. Murray, and Frank E. Block, *Security Analysis* (New York: McGraw-Hill, 1988).

   This book teaches fundamental analysis of stocks and bonds with an eye toward ratio analysis and assessing bankruptcy risks.

Stocks, Bonds, Bills and Inflation: The Past and the Future, 1989 ed. (Chicago, Ill.: Ibbotson Associates, 1989).

   An easy-to-read empirical analysis of market premiums for default risk and purchasing-power risk in stock and bond indexes. The empirical work is well grounded in the theory of financial economics. An updated edition is published every year.

Part 4

Equity Valuation

Chapter 15

Stock Valuation

Securities analysts study companies' earnings and their managements, the economic outlook, the firms' competition, market conditions, and many other factors. Then their research findings are used in the models explained in this chapter to form estimates of the value of an equity share. If the security's price is less than its estimated value, then it appears to be a good buy—or at least worthy of further investigation.

15-1   SOME VALUATION CONVENTIONS

An investor who buys a share of the Avery Corporation's stock for $50 and then sells it for $55 a year later, after collecting a cash dividend of $2.50, earned a rate of return of 15 percent.

$$r = \frac{(p_1 - p_0) + d_1}{p_1} = \frac{(\$55 - \$50) + \$2.50}{\$50} = \frac{\$7.50}{\$50} = 15\%$$

If the stock market is efficient, then 15 percent is an equilibrium rate of return for Avery's stock.

Single-Period Valuation Model

Solving the one-period rate-of-return equation above for the purchase price yields the single-period valuation model of Equation (15-1).

$$p_0 = \frac{p_1 + d_1}{1 + r} \tag{15-1}$$

453

Figuring out the risk-adjusted discount rate to use in the valuation model is an important part of the valuation process.

A **fundamental principle of valuation** says that *in perfectly efficient markets all securities in an equivalent risk class should be priced to yield the same rate of return*. This principle implies that Avery's equilibrium rate of return of 15 percent should be used as the risk-adjusted discount rate to find the present value of Avery's stock.

If Avery's stock is expected to pay a cash dividend of $2.50 and then sell for $55 per share a year later and 15 percent is the appropriate **capitalization rate,** the valuation model suggests the stock has a present value of $50.

$$p_0 = \frac{p_1 + d_1}{1 + r} = \frac{\$55 + \$2.50}{1 + 0.15} = \frac{\$57.50}{1.15} = \$50$$

Stated differently, the *intrinsic value* of Avery's stock is estimated to be $50 per share.

Models are *simplified* versions of reality. The models with which this chapter deals are mathematical models, like Equation (15-1), that relate certain independent variables, such as dividends and earnings, to the value of the stock. The models are simplified versions of the financial processes that actually determine asset prices. The innumerable complications encountered in real life are assumed away to allow us to build models that are easy to work with.

Definitions of the Symbols

The mathematical models in this chapter use conventions that are defined here for easy reference.

p_t = market price of a security at period t

v_t = present value of one share of common stock at period t

e_t = earnings per share at period t

d_t = dividends per share at period t paid to stockholders of record at the start of period t

r_t = *average* internal rate of return of all investments within the firm during period t

k_t = appropriate discount rate at time t = firm's risk-adjusted cost of capital

f = retention ratio (which is assumed constant) = fraction of earnings per share that is retained inside the firm

$1 - f$ = payout ratio = dividends/earnings = fraction of earnings per share paid to investors as a cash dividend

g = fr = rate of growth in earnings, which is assumed to remain constant

t = a counting index that indicates the time period, for example, a quarter or a year count

15-2   **CAPITALIZING CASH DIVIDENDS**

J. B. Williams and M. J. Gordon have developed a model relating the value of an equity share to its cash dividends.[1] They hypothesized that the value v_0 of a share of stock equals the present value of the infinite ($t = \infty$) stream of dividends d to be received by that stock's owner.

$$v_0 = \sum_{t=1}^{\infty} \frac{d_t}{(1 + k)^t} = \frac{d_1}{(1 + k)^1} + \frac{d_2}{(1 + k)^2} + \cdots + \frac{d_\infty}{(1 + k)^\infty} \qquad (15\text{-}2)$$

In Equation (15-2), k is the capitalization rate which is appropriate for the firm's risk class. Riskier streams of income are discounted at higher capitalization rates. More specifically, the capital asset pricing model (CAPM) of Figure 10-3 and Equation (10-12) tells us what capitalization rate to use after we assess the stock's beta, or systematic risk coefficient.

The logic of the dividend model is undeniable. Cash dividends are the only income from a share of stock which is held forever. Therefore, the value of a share of stock held to perpetuity can only be the present value of its stream of cash dividends from now until perpetuity. But, you may ask, what if the share is sold after the investor owns it for only a few years? The model includes this possibility.

What Happens If the Shares Are Sold?

If an investor sells a share after, say, three periods, the present value of the share is shown in Equation (15-3).

$$v_0 = \sum_{t=1}^{3} \frac{d_t}{(1 + k)^t} + \frac{v_3}{(1 + k)^3} \qquad (15\text{-}3)$$

$$v_0 = \frac{d_1}{(1 + k)^1} + \frac{d_2}{(1 + k)^2} + \frac{d_3 + v_3}{(1 + k)^3} \qquad (15\text{-}3a)$$

The v_3 term represents the present value of the share in period $t = 3$ when it is sold. Let us consider v_3.

According to the logic of Equation (15-2), v_3 is the present value of all dividends from period $t = 4$ to infinity, as shown in Equation (15-4).

$$v_3 = \sum_{t=1}^{\infty} \frac{d_{t+3}}{(1 + k)^t} \qquad (15\text{-}4)$$

$$= \frac{d_4}{(1 + k)^1} + \frac{d_5}{(1 + k)^2} + \frac{d_6}{(1 + k)^3} + \cdots + \frac{d_\infty}{(1 + k)^\infty} \qquad (15\text{-}4a)$$

[1] These books are classics. See J. B. Williams, *The Theory of Investment Value* (Cambridge, Mass.: Harvard, 1938). Also see M. J. Gordon, *The Investment, Financing and Valuation of the Corporation* (Homewood, Ill.: Irwin, 1962).

To show how the dividend model encompasses situations in which a share is sold before infinity, Equation (15-4a) is substituted into Equation (15-3a) to obtain Equation (15-3b).

$$v_0 = \frac{d_1}{(1 + k)^1} + \frac{d_2}{(1 + k)^2} + \frac{d_3}{(1 + k)^3}$$

$$+ \frac{d_4/(1 + k)^1 + \cdots + d_\infty/(1 + k)^\infty}{(1 + k)^3} \qquad (15\text{-}3b)$$

The following algebraic identity is useful.

$$\frac{d_{n+3}/(1 + k)^n}{(1 + k)^3} = \frac{d_{n+3}}{(1 + k)^n(1 + k)^3} = \frac{d_{n+3}}{(1 + k)^{n+3}}$$

With the aid of the identity above, Equation (15-3b) can be equivalently rewritten as Equation (15-3c).

$$v_0 = \frac{d_1}{(1 + k)^1} + \frac{d_2}{(1 + k)^2} + \frac{d_3}{(1 + k)^3}$$

$$+ \frac{d_4}{(1 + k)^{3+1}} + \frac{d_5}{(1 + k)^{3+2}} + \cdots + \frac{d_\infty}{(1 + k)^\infty} \qquad (15\text{-}3c)$$

Comparison of Equations (15-3c) and (15-2) will reveal that they are equal. This shows the indirect manner in which the dividend model considers retained earnings and capital gains. That is, v_0 includes v_3, the value of the share in the future. And v_3 includes capital gains which result from retained earnings. Thus, the dividend model does not ignore the effects of capital gains or retained earnings.

Definitions and Relationships in the Dividend Model

In order to show the interaction of earnings, dividends, retained earnings, and the growth rate of the firm, the model can be reformulated to treat these variables explicitly. Dividends are related to earnings by defining dividends to be equal to the payout ratio of $1 - f$ times earnings, as shown in Equations (15-5) and (15-5a).

$$D_t = (1 - f)E_t = \text{corporation's total cash dividends} \qquad (15\text{-}5)$$

$$d_t = (1 - f)e_t = \text{cash dividends per share} \qquad (15\text{-}5a)$$

Total corporate retained earnings of fE dollars are assumed to be reinvested within the all-equity firm to earn a rate of return of r. Since the firm we are discussing here has borrowed no money, it can only grow from retained earnings. This allows earnings to grow at the rate of $g = fr$ per period, as shown in Equation (15-6), assuming no external capital is invested in the firm.

$$E_t = E_0(1 + g)^t = E_0(1 + fr)^t \qquad (15\text{-}6)$$

$$e_t = e_0(1 + g)^t = e_0(1 + fr)^t \qquad (15\text{-}6a)$$

As long as the retention ratio is a positive number, $f > 0$, dividends per share will change each period as indicated in Equation (15-7) if no new shares are issued.

$$d_t = (1 - f)(1 + fr)^t(e_0) \tag{15-7}$$

$$d_t = (1 - f)(1 + g)^t(e_0) \tag{15-7a}$$

$$d_t = (1 - f)(e_t) \tag{15-7b}$$

In the case where some fraction f of earnings is retained and earns a return of r within the firm, the present value of a share of stock is determined by substituting Equation (15-7) into (15-2) to obtain (15-8). In Equation (15-8) the beginning cash dividend per share is restated in terms of the beginning earnings per share by substituting $e_0(1 - f)$ in place of d_0.

$$v_0 = \sum_{t=1}^{\infty} \frac{e_0(1 - f)(1 + fr)^t}{(1 + k)^t} \tag{15-8}$$

Equation (15-8) may be rewritten equivalently as (15-9) by using Equation (15-7).[2]

$$v_0 = \sum_{t=1}^{\infty} \frac{d_0(1 + fr)^t}{(1 + k)^t} = \sum_{t=1}^{\infty} \frac{d_0(1 + g)^t}{(1 + k)^t} = \frac{d_1}{k - g} \tag{15-9}$$

---

[2]If dividends grow at some constant rate, denoted g, then future dividends are related to current dividends as shown below. First note that Equation (15-8) can be equivalently rewritten as Equation (F1).

$$p = \sum_{t=1}^{\infty} \frac{d_0(1 + g)^t}{(1 + k)^t} \tag{F1}$$

$\Sigma\, d_0 x = d_0 \Sigma\, x$ because d_0 is a constant. This relation means that Equation (15-8) or (F1) may be rewritten as shown below.

$$p_0 = d_0 \sum_{t=1}^{\infty} \frac{(1 + g)^t}{(1 + k)^t} \tag{F2}$$

$$p_0 = d_0 \left(\frac{(1 + g)^1}{(1 + k)^1} + \frac{(1 + g)^2}{(1 + k)^2} + \frac{(1 + g)^3}{(1 + k)^3} + \cdots \right) \tag{F3}$$

Multiplying (F3) by $(1 + k)/(1 + g)$ yields (F4).

$$p_0 \left(\frac{1 + k}{1 + g} \right) = d_0 \left(1.0 + \frac{(1 + g)^1}{(1 + k)^1} + \frac{(1 + g)^2}{(1 + k)^2} + \cdots \right) \tag{F4}$$

Subtracting (F3) from the preceding equation yields Equation (F5).

$$\left(\frac{1 + k}{1 + g} - 1.0 \right) p_0 = d_0 \tag{F5}$$

By assuming that $k > g$, the preceding equation can be rearranged as shown below.

$$\left[\frac{(1 + k) - (1 + g)}{1 + g} \right] p_0 = \left(\frac{k - g}{1 + g} \right) p_0 = d_0 \tag{F6}$$

(continues)

Equation (15-8) may be rewritten equivalently as (15-8a) since $g = fr$. By substituting $e_1(1 - f)$ for d_1 in Equation (15-9) below, we get Equation (15-9a).

$$v_0 = \sum_{t=1}^{\infty} \frac{e_0(1 - f)(1 + g)^t}{(1 + k)^t} \tag{15-8a}$$

$$v_0 = \frac{d_1}{k - g} \tag{15-9}$$

$$v_0 = \frac{e_1(1 - f)}{k - g} \tag{15-9a}$$

One advantage of the dividend valuation model is that it may be rewritten equivalently in different forms. For example, Equations (15-2), (15-8), (15-9), and (15-9a) are all useful representations of the same model. Equation (15-8) explicitly shows the relationship of earnings e, dividend policy f, internal profitability r, the firm's cost of capital k, and the firm's growth rate g in the determination of the value of the stock. This model may be used to determine the value per share by defining all the variables on a per-share basis as shown, or the model may be used to value the entire firm by using the total quantities represented by the variables in capital letters in Equations (15-5) and (15-6).

Effects of Dividend Policy

Equation (15-9b) is particularly useful for studying the effects of dividend policy on value. A corporation's cash dividend policy is represented by the variable f. First, consider a firm that is expected to endure forever; thus, it can be valued with Equation (15-9b). Assume this is a typical firm in which the internal rate of return on new investments just equals the discount rate (that is, $r = k$).

$$v_0 = \frac{e_1(1 - f)}{k - fr} = \frac{e_1(1 - f)}{k - g} \qquad \text{since } g = fr \tag{15-9b}$$

$$= \frac{e_1(1 - f)}{k(1 - f)} \qquad \text{if } r = k$$

$$v_0 = \frac{e_1}{k} \tag{15-10}$$

(continued)

Multiplying the right-hand side of (F6) by $1 + g$ yields (F7).

$$p_0(k - g) = d_0(1 + g) = d_1 \tag{F7}$$

where $d_0(1 + g)^1 = d_1$ denotes next period's dividends per share. Equation (F8), which is identical to Equation (15-9), can be obtained by rearranging the preceding equation as follows.

$$p_0 = \frac{d_1}{k - g} \tag{F8}$$

Equation (15-10) shows that regardless of the firm's initial earnings e_0 or riskiness (which determines k), *the firm's value is not affected by dividend policy.* That is, *when $r = k$, dividend policy is irrelevant* since f, which represents the firm's dividend policy, cancels completely out of Equation (15-10).[3]

Realistically, cash dividend payments can affect stock prices when they convey to investors valuable information about the expectations and intentions of the corporation's board of directors or give outsiders some other valuable *signal.*[4] However, when we constructed this model, we assumed stock markets were perfectly efficient; therefore, all information is public knowledge in this simplified version of reality. In such a model it is impossible (by definition) for cash dividend policy to convey information about which investors were not already informed.

Equation (15-10) is also proof that capitalizing earnings is equivalent to capitalizing dividends when $r = k$. Equation (15-10), which capitalizes only earnings, was derived from Equation (15-8). Equation (15-9), which capitalizes dividends, was also derived from Equation (15-8). This shows mathematical proof of *the equivalence of capitalizing dividends and capitalizing earnings when $r = k$.* When $r = k$, the quantity $1/k$ is the same as the price-earnings ratio (or earnings multiplier).

Table 15-1 uses the dividend model equation (15-9*b*) to show the effects of various dividend policies, as represented by the value assigned to f, on the value of a hypothetical share. The values in Table 15-1 are computed on the assumption that earnings per share are $e_0 = \$5$, the firm's cost of capital is constant at $k = 15$ percent, and the internal profitability of the firm varies between 5 and 15 percent, that is, $r = 5$, 10, and 15 percent.

Table 15-1 shows the effect of various values of r, k, d, and e in determining v. Inspection of Equation (15-9*b*) and Table 15-1 reveals that the optimal dividend policy depends on the relationship between the firm's internal rate of profit r and its discount rate k as explained below.

Growth Stocks Should Not Pay Cash Dividends

Firms that earn a return on invested funds that is higher than their cost of capital (or discount rate) are growth firms. **Growth firms** have $r > k$ and maximize their value by retaining all earnings for internal investment. For example,

---

[3]This section draws from the classic article by M. H. Miller and F. Modigliani, "Dividend Policy, Growth and the Valuation of Shares," *Journal of Business,* Oct. 1961, pp. 411–433.

[4]See P. Asquith and D. W. Mullins, "The Impact of Initiating Dividend Payments on Shareholders' Wealth," *Journal of Business,* Jan. 1983, pp. 77–96. Also see J. A. Brickley, "Shareholder Wealth, Information Signalling and the Specially Designated Dividend," *Journal of Financial Economics,* Aug. 1983, pp. 187–209. See also T. E. Dielman and H. R. Oppenheimer, "An Examination of Investor Behavior during Periods of Large Dividend Changes," *Journal of Financial and Quantitative Analysis,* June 1984, pp. 197–216. All of these studies document statistically significant cash dividend announcement effects that resulted from **signals** the market perceived to be implied by unusual cash dividend payments.

Table 15-1

NUMERICAL VALUES FOR A CORPORATION'S STOCK UNDER DIFFERENT ASSUMPTIONS ABOUT GROWTH OPPORTUNITIES WITHIN THE FIRM

Growth firm, $r > k$	Declining firm, $r < k$	Normal firm, $r = k$
$r = 20\%$	$r = 10\%$	$r = 15\%$
$k = 15\%$	$k = 15\%$	$k = 15\%$
$e_1 = \$7.50$	$e_1 = \$7.50$	$e_1 = \$7.50$

Valuation model: $v_0 = \dfrac{e_1(1 - f)}{k - fr}$ (15-9b)

Consider three cases with high payout ratios:

If $f = 33.3\%$, $v = \$60$	If $f = 33.3\%$, $v = \$42.86$	If $f = 33.3\%$, $v = \$50$
$v = \dfrac{(7.50)(0.666)}{0.15 - (0.333)(0.20)}$	$v = \dfrac{(\$7.50)(0.666)}{0.15 - (0.333)(0.10)}$	$v = \dfrac{(\$7.50)(0.666)}{0.15 - (0.333)(0.15)}$
$v = \dfrac{\$5}{0.0833} = \$60$	$v = \dfrac{\$5}{0.1166} = \$42.86$	$v = \dfrac{\$5}{0.10} = \$50$

Consider three cases with high retention rates:

If $f = 66.6\%$, $v = \$150$	If $f = 66.6\%$, $v = \$30$	If $f = 66.6\%$, $v = \$50$
$v = \dfrac{(\$7.50)(0.333)}{0.15 - (0.666)(0.20)}$	$v = \dfrac{(\$7.50)(0.333)}{0.15 - (0.666)(0.10)}$	$v = \dfrac{(\$7.50)(0.333)}{0.15 - (0.666)(0.15)}$
$v = \dfrac{\$2.50}{0.0166} = \$150$	$v = \dfrac{\$2.50}{0.0833} = \$30$	$v = \dfrac{\$2.50}{0.05} = \$50^*$
Conclusion: v increases with the retention rate for firms with growth opportunities, $r > k$.	Conclusion: v increases with the payout ratio $(1 - f)$ for declining firms, $r < k$.	Conclusion: v is not affected by dividend policy when $r = k$.

*This case is like the Avery Corporation on pages 453–454.

in past decades Polaroid and IBM were growth stocks because of technological breakthroughs that gave those corporations profitable market-penetrating powers. During the 1950s and 1960s their enviable positions allowed Polaroid and IBM to raise capital at a cost of k percent per year and reinvest it internally at a higher rate of r percent per year. Firms with such profitable investments available would be foolish not to reinvest all their earnings if they could not raise capital externally. The model accurately depicts this situation and shows that paying dividends would decrease the value of such a firm.

Declining Firms Should Pay Cash Dividends

Firms that do not have profitable opportunities to invest may be called **declining firms.** A firm typically declines because its product becomes obsolete, its sales continue to decline, and no further investment within the firm is profitable. Examples of declining firms include the buggy-whip industry after the automobile became popular in the 1930s. Manufacturers of home-movie cameras suffered similar obsolescence problems during the 1980s when VCR machines became popular. Declining firms have so few, if any, profitable investment opportunities that their return on investment r remains below their cost of capital or discount rate k. In this case, the optimal cash dividend policy is for the firm to pay out everything it earns to its shareholders. Stated differently, the firm will maximize its value to its shareholders by liquidating itself and paying one big final cash dividend as soon as it becomes clear that r will remain below k for the foreseeable future.

Dividend Policy Is Irrelevant for Normal Firms

The vast majority of firms have precious few growth opportunities; they have few investments with $r > k$. These **normal firms** *operate in a static equilibrium where their internal rate of return from their investments just equals their cost of capital or discount rate, $r = k$. For these firms, dividend policy has no effect on the value of an equity share.* That is, the value of the corporation's shares is unchanged whether it pays out 10 percent of its earnings as dividends, or 90 percent, or any other percentage. The numerical example in the lower right-hand column of Table 15-1 portrays this case. In addition, Table 15-2 shows that the Avery Corporation's stock price grows 10 percent every year but still has a present value of $50 every year into the foreseeable future if we assume (*a*) the cash dividends grow at $fr = 0.666 \times 0.15 = g = 10$ percent per year because two-thirds ($f = 0.666$) of each year's earnings per share are retained for internal investment, (*b*) the internal rate of return is 15 percent, $r = 15\%$, and (*c*) the capitalization rate is also 15 percent, $k = 15\%$. Table 15-2 shows

Table 15-2

MULTIPERIOD FINANCIAL ANALYSIS OF AVERY CORPORATION'S FUTURE STOCK PRICES

Terminal period, T	Future value at $g = 10\%$		Present value at $k = 15\%$			
	Cash dividend	Market price†	Cumulative cash dividend	+	Future price	= Year's total
0	NA*	$50	NA		$50	$50
1	$2.50	55	$2.18		47.82	50
2	2.75	60.50	4.26		45.74	50
3	3.03	66.55	6.25		43.76	50
4	3.33	73.20	8.15		41.85	50
5	3.66	80.53	9.97		40.03	50
10	5.89	129.68	17.94		32.06	50
20	15.29	336.37	29.44		20.56	50
50	266.80	5,869.55	44.58		5.42	50
100	31,319.57	689,030.62	49.41		.59	50
∞	∞	∞	50.00		0	50

*NA means not applicable.
†Note that $k = d_1/p + g = 5\% + 10\% = 15\%$ every year.

that under these circumstances the Avery Corporation's stock yields its investors (or, synonymously, its cost of capital is) $k = d_1/p + g = 5$ percent $+ 10$ percent $= 15$ percent in each year.

Growth in Size Not Equivalent to Growth in Value

It is easy to be deceived into thinking that a firm which is getting bigger in a physical sense is a growth firm. For example, suppose the Avery Corporation increases its total sales, its labor force, and its profits, and sees its stock price rise. Does this make Avery a growth stock? Not necessarily. The Avery Corporation may be getting physically larger by retaining earnings and/or selling new issues of common stock to the public. These funds are raised at a weighted average cost of capital of k. Then they are reinvested and earn a rate of return of r. But if $r = k$, the *discounted present value* of the dollars invested does not grow. The value of funds invested in the Avery Corporation tends to increase only enough to compensate investors for bearing the risk and inconvenience of postponing consumption in order to invest.

Increases in Avery's share prices are due to earnings retention. The retained earnings earn a rate of r, causing earnings and dividends per share to grow. But future dividends and capital gains must be discounted at the appropriate discount rate k to find their present value. As long as $r = k$, the *present value* of future dividends and capital gains just equals the present value of the earnings which were retained to finance this expansion. Thus, the Avery Corporation gets physically bigger in size and the price of its shares rises, but the *present value* of an investment in it does not. If it paid out 100 percent of its earnings in dividends, the firm could still continue to get bigger by issuing new securities instead of retaining earnings. Either way, the present value of the benefits received from a dollar invested would be unchanged because $r = k$.

Simplifications in the Dividend Model

The present value of cash dividends model shows the effects of dividend policy on an all-equity firm under different assumptions about profitability. However, the simplified nature of the model can lead to conclusions that are true for the model but not true in practice. Consider the simplifying assumptions that underlie the dividend valuation model.

1. There is *no external financing*. The dividend model contains no debt and interest expense variables or allowance for new shares to be issued. And since retained earnings are the only source of funds with which the firm may expand, dividend policy and investment must compete for the firm's earnings.

2. *The internal rate of return r for the firm is constant*. This ignores the diminishing marginal efficiency of investment which would normally reduce r as a firm's investment is increased.

3. The appropriate *discount rate k remains constant.* Thus, the model ignores the possibility of a change in the firm's risk class and the resulting change in k.

4. The firm and its stream of *earnings are perpetual,* so T goes to infinity.

5. *No income taxes exist.*

6. *The growth rate g = fr is constant forever.*

7. The following *growth constraint* must not be violated:

$$k > fr = g$$

   If $g > k$, the value of a share would be infinite.

8. The firm's *dividend policy f remains fixed* to infinity.

Consider the problems introduced by these eight assumptions. We begin with a review of capital budgeting and financing and how such matters affect dividend policy and the value of the firm.

No Outside Financing   The present value of all future cash dividends model confounds dividend policy with the investment program of the firm. Since the model excludes funds from external financing, every dollar of dividends takes away a dollar from earnings retained for investment. When such a situation exists, either the firm's investment program, its dividend policy, or both will be suboptimal. This problem is represented graphically in Figure 15-1. A review of the optimum investment program shows the result of ignoring external financing.

Figure 15-1 has the values of r and k on its vertical axis. The figure depicts a hypothetical firm's investment opportunities as the firm makes its financial

Figure 15-1 A firm's investment opportunities.

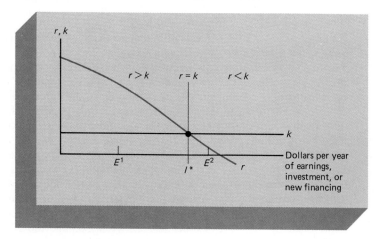

plans for the next year. Both the corporation's total profit and its total investment are measured on the horizontal axis in dollars per year. The firm's marginal
cost of capital equals its average cost of capital k, as represented by the horizontal line at k percent per year.[5]

The rates of return r on each investment open to the firm are shown as
decreasing as more investment occurs; this reflects the assumption that the
most profitable investments will be made first and the poorer investments made
last. The total dollar value of the annual investments is also measured along
the horizontal axis. In Figure 15-1, I^* dollars of investment occurs where
$r = k$. I^* is the optimal investment regardless of whether the capital to finance
this investment is raised by selling stock, bonds, or preferred stock; by retaining
earnings; or by obtaining a loan—as long as k does not change.

To the left of I^* dollars of investment, the internal rate of return is larger
than the firm's cost of capital $r > k$, and the firm could increase its value by
expanding investment to I^*. If earnings are only E^1, an investment of I^* is still
the amount that will maximize the firm's value. The firm should invest I^* if it
has to sell new securities to raise the needed funds. However, the dividend
model excludes outside financing. Thus, for this situation, the model would
show that the owner's wealth (that is, the present value v) is maximized by
retaining and investing the firm's total earnings of E^1 and paying no dividends.
In a model that allowed for outside financing, the firm should sell new securities
to finance investment of I^*; only this investment would truly maximize the
owner's wealth.

Constancy of r   Assuming that the most profitable investments are made first,
common sense indicates that eventually no more profitable investments will be
left. This is correctly represented graphically in Figure 15-1 by a declining
investment r curve. But the dividend model assumes that r is constant (an
assumption which is true, if ever, only over a tiny range of investments).

If total earnings in Figure 15-1 were E^2 dollars, for example, the dividend

---

[5]Capital budgeting students will notice that investments up to I^* have positive net present
values, but investments over I^* (for example, E^2) have negative net present values.
Figure 15-1 is oversimplified; actually, because of corporate income taxes, the real
firm's cost of capital decreases if debt capital is used. Also, the average rate of return
on investment is not shown. The discussion omits the difference between the marginal
return and the average return, but some writers have shown the importance of this
distinction in terms of such models. The assertions made in this chapter that firms which
have $r = k$ are not growth firms is true only if r is the average rate of return. If $r' =
k$, where r' is the marginal rate of return, then $r > r' = k$, and the firm is a growth firm.
Strictly speaking, $r' = k$ is the optimum condition. If $r = k$, this implies $r' < k$, which
is suboptimal because some investments have been undertaken which have marginal
returns less than the marginal cost of capital. See E. Lerner and W. Carleton, "The
Integration of Capital Budgeting and Stock Valuation," *American Economic Review*,
Sept. 1964, pp. 683–702. Lerner and Carleton examine the effects of a diminishing
marginal efficiency of investment on the dividend model.

model indicates that they should all be paid out in dividends because $r < k$ at E^2. In a model which recognizes that r declines, the optimal policy would be to retain earnings of I^* for investment and pay dividends of $(E^2 - I^*)$ dollars. Since the simple model always indicates that the optimal dividend payout is either zero, 100 percent, or irrelevant, the dividend policy which actually maximizes the owner's wealth will rarely be indicated by this oversimplified model.

Constancy of k A firm's cost of capital, or equivalently, the appropriate discount rate k varies directly with the risk of the firm. Figure 10-3 is a graph of the capital asset pricing model (CAPM), or security market line (SML) as it is also called. The CAPM shows that as the risk of a firm (or any asset) increases, the appropriate discount rises too. The present value of the firm's income moves inversely with the discount rate. By assuming that the discount rate k is constant, the model excludes these effects of risk on the value of the firm. Risk measurement and the appropriate discount rate were discussed in Chapters 1, 10, and 11.

Infinite Life It is fairly realistic to assume that a modern corporation endures perpetually. It will have new managements, and probably new products, and maybe even a new name, too, as time passes. But, in principle, the legal corporate shell can live forever.

Even the demise of the firm after a few decades will have little effect on the firm's present value. A few computations will show that the present value of money received a few decades in the future is modest indeed. For example, after 40 years a dollar is worth very little; $\$1/(1 + 10\%)^{40} = 2.2$ cents. As a result, errors in forecasting events in the far future have little impact on the present value of an equity share.

No Taxes This unrealistic simplification ignores income taxes. Furthermore, at those times in the United States when it is legislated, the differential tax rates on dividends and capital gains income should be considered.

Constant Growth Rate This assumption is a modest simplification of reality. It can be easily changed without changing the conclusions. The assumption that g does not change is made merely to simplify the mathematics.

Cost of Capital Exceeds the Growth Rate, $k > g$ This assumption is realistic. Although a firm could sustain very high growth rates for a few years, no firm could double or triple its earnings every year indefinitely. If a firm's earnings doubled annually for a few decades, its total profit would grow to exceed the gross national product (GNP) of the United States.

Constant Dividend Payout Ratio, $(1 - f)$ The assumption that the firm has a constant retention rate f is merely another effort to simplify the mathematical form of the model. If f did change far in the future, the conclusions of the model would probably not be changed because the present value of future dollars is smaller. Furthermore, this assumption is fairly realistic. Most firms do tend to maintain a fixed retention rate when it is averaged over a complete business cycle.

Beginning social scientists should not become discouraged about the dividend model because it is built on eight less-than-realistic assumptions. Remember, this model is designed to be a simplified version of reality, for good reasons: to keep the mathematics as simple as possible and to focus on the main issues in the valuation theory of equity shares. And the model yields some fascinating insights; for example, would you have believed that dividend policy does not affect the value of most normal firms? Let us analyze this issue further.

15-3   **EFFECTS OF CASH DIVIDEND PAYMENTS AND NONPAYMENTS**

Although the *dividend policy* of the normal corporation has no long-term effect on the price of its shares, stock prices do react to *cash dividend payments* in a significant and predictable manner. This *price dropoff* does not conflict with the findings above that dividend policy is irrelevant.

Price Dropoff   The board of directors of most large corporations meet quarterly to decide how
when a Stock   much, if any, cash dividend to pay. If they decide to pay a cash dividend, the
Goes Ex-Dividend   directors must then also stipulate the stockholders' "record date" and the
"payment date" for the cash dividend. Every stockholder who owned the stock on the **record date** is legally entitled to receive whatever cash dividend is declared, even if they sell their shares before the dividend is actually paid. Investors who buy a stock after the record date are not entitled to receive the cash dividend. On the first trading day after the record date the stock is said to be **trading ex-dividend.** The **payment date** when the cash dividend is actually paid usually comes a few weeks after the record date.

Since the value of a common stock equals its present value, the market price of a share of stock should drop when cash dividends are paid by an amount equal to the present value of the dividend. This is a logical stock price reaction to cash dividend payments. This **dropoff** in market price when the stock starts trading ex-dividend, denoted DO, is defined in Equation (15-11).

$$\text{DO} = \frac{\text{closing price}}{\text{before dividend}} - \frac{\text{ex-dividend opening price}}{\text{on the next trading day}} \qquad (15\text{-}11)$$

The market price of every share of stock almost always experiences a price

Table 15-3

CORPORATIONS THAT PAID ZERO CASH DIVIDENDS FOR A DECADE, 1970–1980

Stocks that paid zero cash dividends	Average annual rate of return, 1970–1980
NVF	41.7%
National Semiconductor*	33.3
Teledyne*	32.2
Tosco*	28.9
Data General*	25.3
Penn Central	19.9
Digital Equipment*	17.4
Lockheed	13.9
Median for 500 stocks	9.4
Crown Cork & Seal	4.6
DPF*	−5.7
Memorex*	−13.9

*This corporation has never paid any cash dividends.
Source: Fortune, May 4, 1981, p. 351.

dropoff DO that is within a few cents of the value of the cash dividend payment.[6] These price dropoffs do not conflict with the fact that the cash dividend policy of a normal corporation, as measured by the value of the fraction f, has no effect on the value of the stock.

How Do You Handle Cash Dividend Payouts of Zero?

Companies seeking rapid growth sometimes reinvest all earnings within the firm. Such corporations pay no cash dividends; their payout ratio is zero, $(1 - f) = 0$. As Table 15-1 shows, paying zero cash dividends is an optimal dividend policy if the firm has profitable internal investment opportunities such that $r > k$.

A dozen common stocks that paid no cash dividends and the average annual rate of return that an investor would have earned on these stocks are listed in Table 15-3. Some of these stocks did very well, while a few at the bottom of

[6]For a review of recent investigations of cash dividend dropoffs and an analysis of this phenomenon, see Kenneth M. Eades, Patrick J. Hess, and E. Han Kim, "On Interpreting Security Returns during the Ex-Dividend Period," *Journal of Financial Economics,* March 1984, vol. 13, no. 1, p. 34. Also see Theoharry Grammatikos, "Dividend Stripping, Risk Exposure, and the Effect of the 1984 Tax Reform Act on Ex-Dividend Day Behavior," *Journal of Business,* April 1989, pp. 157–174.

the list did poorly. The bottom stocks presumably experienced price declines because most investors believed that these firms had no profitable internal investment opportunities. Alternatively, maybe these firms were paying no dividends because they were experiencing losses instead of profits year after year. Either of these circumstances dictates that investors should sell the stock. In contrast to the few firms that investors viewed disdainfully, most of the firms listed in Table 15-3 enjoyed high rates of price appreciation even though they paid no cash dividends for at least a decade. Investors apparently viewed these firms as having valuable growth opportunities and assessed their value per share using "price-earnings ratios," which are the topic of the next section.

How to Value Declining Firms That Nevertheless Pay Cash Dividends

In addition to corporations paying no cash dividends, there are other cases for which the present value of cash dividends model is *inappropriate* for valuation work. For example, some declining corporations continue to pay cash dividends with borrowed money. (In fact, some declining corporations have actually continued to pay cash dividends right up to the time they filed for bankruptcy.) In such financially perverse cases, security analysts may use the corporation's past "earnings multipliers" to value the stock.

Earnings multipliers are also called *price-earnings ratios*—the phrases are synonymous. The next section explains the theory that underlies the price-earnings ratios that are widely discussed in the financial press.

15-4   FUNDAMENTAL ANALYSTS' PRICE-EARNINGS RATIO

Fundamental analysts prepare their estimates of a common stock's **intrinsic value** per share by multiplying the ith stock's normalized earnings per share, denoted $e_{i,t}$ for the tth period, times the share's earnings multiplier $m_{i,t}$ as shown in Equation (15-12).

$$p_{i,t} = e_{i,t} m_{i,t} \tag{15-12}$$

Theory Underlying the Price-Earnings Ratio

The theory that underlies the price-earnings ratio, or earnings multiplier, stems from the present value of cash dividends model of Equation (15-9).

$$v_0 = \sum_{t=1}^{\infty} \frac{d_0(1 + fr)^t}{(1 + k)^t} = \sum_{t=1}^{\infty} \frac{d_0(1 + g)^t}{(1 + k)^t} = \frac{d_1}{k - g} \tag{15-9}$$

The **price-earnings ratio** is derived by dividing both sides of Equation (15-9) by earnings per share, as shown in Equations (15-13), (15-13a), and (15-13b).

$$m_{i,0} = \frac{p_{i,0}}{e_{i,0}} = \sum_{t=1}^{\infty} \frac{(d/e)(1 + g)^t}{(1 + k)^t} \tag{15-13}$$

Table 15-4

CAPITALIZATION RATES AND THEIR EQUIVALENT MULTIPLIERS WHEN INCOME IS CONSTANT

Capitalization rate, k	Riskiness	Equivalent multiplier, $1/k$
2	Negligible risk	50 times
4		25
6		16.7
8		12.5
10	Medium risk	10
12		8.3
15		6.7
20		5
25		4
33		3
50	High risk	2

$$m_{i,0} = \frac{p_{i,0}}{e_{i,0}} = \frac{d}{e} \sum_{t=1}^{\infty} \frac{(1 + g)^t}{(1 + k)^t} \qquad (15\text{-}13a)$$

$$m_{i,0} = \frac{d_{i,1}/e_{i,0}}{k_i - g_i} \qquad (15\text{-}13b)$$

The ratio $d_{i,t}/e_{i,t}$ in Equations (15-13) and (15-13a) is called the **dividend payout ratio.**[7] Averaged over all corporations in the United States, about 50 percent of aggregate corporate earnings are paid out in cash dividends. Small new corporations typically pay less than 50 percent and blue-chip stocks pay more.

Determining an Appropriate P/E Ratio

Much of a fundamental security analyst's work centers on determining the appropriate earnings multiplier. The main factors to consider when estimating what price-earnings ratio to use to value an equity share are (1) the risk of the security, which determines the capitalization rate k, (2) the growth rate of the dividend stream g, (3) the duration of any expected growth, and (4) the dividend payout ratio. In addition, as the national economy and credit conditions change, these macroeconomic forces cause interest rates, capitalization rates, and earnings multipliers to fluctuate with the business cycle. Table 15-4 suggests the

[7]The equity share valuation model represented by Equations (15-9) and (15-13) has been developed by B. G. Malkiel. See B. G. Malkiel, "Equity Yields, Growth, and Structure of Share Prices," *American Economic Review,* Dec. 1963, pp. 1004–1031, and "The Valuation of Public Utility Equities," *Bell Journal of Economics and Management Science,* 1970, pp. 143–160, and B. G. Malkiel and J. G. Cragg, "Expectations and the Structure of Share Prices," *American Economic Review,* Sept. 1970, pp. 601–617. These articles present the received theory about price-earnings ratios.

general nature of the relationship between capitalization rates, multipliers, and risk when growth in income is zero. With this general background in mind, we will examine the determinants of price-earnings ratios.

Earnings Multipliers Vary Inversely with the Capitalization Rate in a Cyclical Manner   Figure 15-2a shows that capitalization rates vary with the firm's risk class and the prevailing bull- or bear-market conditions. Figure 15-2b shows how price-earnings ratios fluctuate inversely to the capitalization rates.

A **normal market** is a market in which most security prices are experiencing modest growth and the average price-earnings ratio is in the low- to mid-teens. When **bear-market** selling drives the average earnings multipliers to values below the teens, many market prices will be temporarily deflated below their normal values. In contrast, a **bull market** will bid up average earnings multipliers to levels in the high teens or twenties and most stocks will be temporarily overpriced. These numerical guidelines should not be taken too literally; they differ with the particular stock market index that is being observed. Furthermore, the definitions of bear and bull markets are not based entirely on the level of a stock market index. The *direction of change* and the *volume of shares traded,* as well as the *level of the market,* interact to help differentiate between bull- and bear-market conditions.

The risk-return relationship described by the CAPM (Figure 10-3) illustrates the positive relationship between an asset's undiversifiable risk and the appropriate discount rate (or expected rate of return) for the asset. Fundamental analysts can measure the risk of the company in recent periods, adjust these historical risk statistics for any expected changes, and then use these risk statistics to obtain capitalization rates from their estimate of the CAPM.

Figure 15-2 (*a*) Capitalization rates and (*b*) earnings multipliers are affected by risk and macroeconomic conditions.

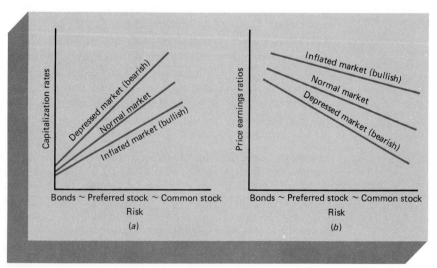

Another Way to Estimate the Appropriate Discount Rate, k   If a stock is efficiently priced, its value and price will be equal, $v_0 = p_0$. Equation (15-14) models the valuation process for a constantly growing, dividend-paying stock that is efficiently priced. Equation (15-14) merely extends Equation (15-9) to include efficient pricing so that $p_0 = v_0$.

$$p_0 = v_0 = \frac{d_1}{k - g} \qquad (15\text{-}14)$$

Solving Equation (15-14) for k as a function of p (instead of v_0) yields Equation (15-15) below.

$$k = \frac{d_1}{p} + g \qquad (15\text{-}15)$$

Equation (15-15) suggests that the discount rate that is appropriate to value a stock equals the stock's cash dividend yield, d/p, plus the stock's average rate of price appreciation g. Since the dividend yield and rate of price appreciation for most stocks are easy to calculate, Equation (15-15) provides an additional way to estimate the appropriate value of k.

Equation (15-15) also provides a double-check on the estimated value of k. The expected rate of return (or, equivalently, k) obtained from the CAPM can be compared to the value of k estimated with Equation (15-15) to discover discrepancies in the two methods of estimating the stock's capitalization rate. Improved estimates of k may result if any discrepancies can be resolved.

The **capitalization rate** is synonymously called the **risk-adjusted cost of capital,** the **risk-adjusted discount rate,** and the **required rate of return.** After the capitalization rate has been determined, the growth rate in dividends per share must be estimated.

Estimated Growth Rates Affect Multipliers   If a security is expected to become more valuable in the future, the anticipated appreciation tends to make it more valuable now. In order to place a current value on future growth in value, growth potential must be assessed before it occurs. The growth rate for dividends or earnings per share is usually a good measure of growth in a firm's earning power.

It is important to develop accurate estimates of the firm's dividend or earnings growth rate and the period of time this growth may be expected to continue.[8] Table 15-5 contains numerical values that need to be multiplied by the common stock's dividend payout ratio, d/e, to obtain the appropriate earnings multiplier. Table 15-5 shows that the growth rate and the expected duration of

[8]See Frank J. Fabozzi, Patrick Casabona, and J. C. Francis, "The Why's and the How's of Applying Macaulay and Hicks Duration to Analyze Financial Riskiness," *Journal of Portfolio Management,* Winter 1984, pp. 52–58. Also see J. B. Gould and E. H. Sorensen, "Duration: A Factor in Equity Pricing," *Journal of Portfolio Management,* Fall 1986, pp. 38–43.

Table 15-5

PRICE-EARNINGS RATIOS FOR STOCKS IN VARIOUS RISK CLASSES AND WITH DIFFERENT GROWTH RATES IN NORMAL MARKET CONDITIONS

Type of risk	Capitalization rate, k, %	Growth rate in dividend, g, %	Appropriate P/E ratio if earnings growth continues for					
			5 years	10 years	15 years	20 years	25 years	Forever
Outcome fairly certain, low risk; example: high-quality preferred stock	2	0	50(d/e)	50(d/e)	50(d/e)	50(d/e)	50(d/e)	50(d/e)
		1	52.4(d/e)	54.8(d/e)	57(d/e)	59.0(d/e)	61.1(d/e)	100(d/e)
	4	0	25(d/e)	25(d/e)	25(d/e)	25(d/e)	25(d/e)	25(d/e)
		1	26.2(d/e)	27.2(d/e)	28(d/e)	28.8(d/e)	29.5(d/e)	33.3(d/e)
		2	27.4(d/e)	29.6(d/e)	31.6(d/e)	33.3(d/e)	35(d/e)	50(d/e)
Some uncertainty, medium risk; example: blue-chip stock	6	0	16.7(d/e)	16.7(d/e)	16.7(d/e)	16.7(d/e)	16.7(d/e)	16.7(d/e)
		2	18.2(d/e)	19.5(d/e)	20.5(d/e)	21.4(d/e)	22.1(d/e)	25(d/e)
		4	19.9(d/e)	22.8(d/e)	25.5(d/e)	27.9(d/e)	30(d/e)	50(d/e)
	10	0	10(d/e)	10(d/e)	10(d/e)	10(d/e)	10(d/e)	10(d/e)
		3	11.3(d/e)	12.3(d/e)	13(d/e)	13.5(d/e)	13.8(d/e)	14.3(d/e)
		6	12.8(d/e)	15.1(d/e)	17(d/e)	18.6(d/e)	20(d/e)	25.0(d/e)
	14	0	7.1(d/e)	7.1(d/e)	7.1(d/e)	7.1(d/e)	7.1(d/e)	7.1(d/e)
		4	8.3(d/e)	9(d/e)	9.6(d/e)	9.8(d/e)	9.9(d/e)	10(d/e)
		8	9.7(d/e)	11.7(d/e)	13.2(d/e)	14.3(d/e)	15.2(d/e)	16.6(d/e)
High degree of risk; example: medium-sized business	20	0	5(d/e)	5(d/e)	5(d/e)	5(d/e)	5(d/e)	5(d/e)
		4	5.8(d/e)	6.1(d/e)	6.3(d/e)	6.3(d/e)	6.3(d/e)	6.3(d/e)
		8	6.6(d/e)	7.6 (d/e)	8.2(d/e)	8.3(d/e)	8.3(d/e)	8.3(d/e)
		12	7.6(d/e)	9.5(d/e)	10.8(d/e)	11.7(d/e)	12.4(d/e)	14.0(d/e)
	26	0	3.8(d/e)	3.8(d/e)	3.8(d/e)	3.8(d/e)	3.8(d/e)	3.8(d/e)
		4	4.4(d/e)	4.6(d/e)	4.6(d/e)	4.6(d/e)	4.6(d/e)	4.6(d/e)
		8	5(d/e)	5.5(d/e)	5.6(d/e)	5.6(d/e)	5.6(d/e)	5.6(d/e)
		12	5.7(d/e)	6.7(d/e)	7.2(d/e)	7.2(d/e)	7.2(d/e)	7.2(d/e)

Formulas to derive multipliers:

$$\frac{d}{e} = \text{payout ratio}$$

$$M = \left(\sum_{t=1}^{p} \frac{(1+g_1)^t}{(1+k)^t} + \sum_{t=p+1}^{\infty} \frac{(1+g_1)^p (1+g_2)^{t-p}}{(1+k)^t} \right) \frac{d}{e} \qquad M = \frac{(d/e)(1+g)}{k-g}$$

growth in dividends have an important influence on the earnings multipliers. In fact, the growth rate is as important as the capitalization rate in preparing estimates of the appropriate earnings multipliers.

Estimating Intrinsic Value with Zero Earnings Growth   To see how the multipliers in Table 15-5 are used to estimate intrinsic values, consider a hypothetical example. Suppose that security markets are normal and a security analyst has estimated the risk and growth statistics for the ABC Corporation. Assume that when ABC's beta systematic risk is traced through an estimate of the CAPM, the appropriate capitalization rate turns out to be $k = 10$ percent.

If no dividend growth is expected for ABC, the appropriate earnings multiplier from Table 15-5 is 10 times the payout ratio. The price-earnings ratio was derived by finding the present value of unity each year to infinity and multiplying this value by the payout ratio, as shown in Equation (15-16).

$$\text{Zero-growth earnings multiplier} = \frac{d_1}{e} \sum_{t=1}^{\infty} \frac{1.0}{(1 + \text{capitalization rate})^t} \qquad (15\text{-}16)$$

$$= \frac{d_1/e}{\text{capitalization rate}} \qquad (15\text{-}16a)$$

Further assume that ABC's normalized earnings per share are currently $4 per year and that its average payout rate is 50 percent of earnings, $d/e = 0.5$. Applying the earnings multiplier to the corporation's earnings per share implies that the intrinsic value of ABC is about $10 \times \$4 \times 0.5 = \$20$ per share.

There are numerous places where errors may creep into estimates of earnings per share, the dividend payout ratio, the capitalization rate, and the dividend growth rate. Therefore, it is not certain that ABC's intrinsic value is exactly $20 per share. A **margin for error** should be included with value estimates. It is possible that an error of plus or minus 10 percent, which is the range from $18 to $22, could occur in a carefully prepared analysis of a common stock. Therefore, if the stock were selling at $15, it would seem to be underpriced and therefore a good buy. But if it were selling at $18.50 or $21.75, it would be within the margin for error and therefore judged to be priced approximately correctly.

Estimating Intrinsic Value with Perpetual Earnings Growth   If it is assumed that ABC's earnings are currently $4 per share but will grow with cash dividends forever at, say, 3 percent per year, the intrinsic value estimate will be quite different from what it was with zero growth. Table 15-5 shows that for a capitalization rate of 10 percent and a growth rate of 3 percent, the correct multiplier is 14.3 times d/e. This multiplier is derived by using a capitalization rate of $k = 10$ percent to find the present value of a stream of numbers starting at unity and growing at a rate of $g = 3$ percent per year to infinity, as shown in Equation (15-17).

$$
\begin{matrix} \text{Earnings} \\ \text{multiplier} \\ \text{for perpet-} \\ \text{ual growth} \end{matrix} = \frac{d_1}{e} \sum_{t=1}^{\infty} \frac{(1 + \text{growth rate})^t}{(1 + \text{capitalization rate})^t} \qquad (15\text{-}17)
$$

$$
= \frac{d_1/e}{(\text{capitalization rate} - \text{growth rate})} = \frac{d_1/e}{k - g} \quad (15\text{-}17a)
$$

Equation (15-17a) is equivalent to (15-17). Note that Equation (15-17a) is also equal to Equation (15-16) when the growth rate is zero.

For beginning earnings of $4 per share, a perpetual growth rate of 3 percent, and a cash dividend payout rate of one-half, the intrinsic value estimate is $14.3 \times \$4 \times 0.5 = \$28.60$ per share. Allowing for errors, the estimate of the intrinsic value is in the range $\$28.60 \pm 10\% = \$25.74$ to $\$31.46$.

Estimating Intrinsic Value with Temporary Growth   It is not likely that a well-managed firm's growth will remain zero nor is it likely that a firm can maintain its dividend growth at a high level forever. Therefore, suppose ABC's dividends are expected to grow at 3 percent for 5 years and then level off. In this case, Table 15-5 indicates that the appropriate price-earnings multiplier is 11.3 times d/e. This implies that a most likely estimate of the intrinsic value is $0.5 \times 11.3 \times \$4 = \$22.60$. But the intrinsic value could range from $\$22.60 \pm 10\% = \$20.34$ to $\$24.86$, allowing for the 10 percent margin for error.

As seen above, the intrinsic value of ABC is highly dependent on its dividend growth. Zero growth implies ABC is worth $20 per share, while perpetual growth at 3 percent implies a value of $28.60. Between these two extremes, a value of $22.60 is implied if dividends grow at 3 percent for 5 years and then level off and have zero growth thereafter.

Payout Ratio Affects the Earnings Multiplier   The preceding examples demonstrated the effect that the size and duration of the growth rate can have on the earnings multiplier.[9] The dividend payout ratio also affects the earnings multiplier. The theoretical analysis that led up to the values shown in Table 15-5 indicates that if other things remain constant, reducing a corporation's dividend payout cuts its multiplier and thus its intrinsic value proportionately.

[9]See Robert A. Haugen and Dean W. Wichern, "The Elasticity of Financial Assets," *Journal of Finance,* Sept. 1974, pp. 1229–1240. Also see C. C. Holt, "The Influence of Growth Duration on Share Prices," *Journal of Finance,* Sept. 1962, pp. 465–475.

An important question related to the payout ratio is how to evaluate it. That is, since corporations' dividends per share are a different percentage of their earnings per share practically every quarter, what is the best estimate of a firm's payout ratio? A glance at the right-hand column of Table 15-6, for example, shows how IBM's payout ratio fluctuated from a high of 66 percent when earnings per share were down in 1979 to a low of 38 percent when the earnings surged upward in 1984. Many corporations' payout ratios fluctuate more than this because the firms endeavor to maintain undiminished cash dividends even though their earnings fluctuate violently at times. And when a corporation incurs a loss (that is, negative earnings per share), its payout ratio is simply undefined for that accounting period.

Estimating the payout ratio that a huge corporation like IBM seeks to maintain is usually not difficult. Table 15-6 shows that no losses were incurred, and the payout ratio fluctuates around 50 percent from year to year. For a more risky company, it is necessary to estimate the corporation's *normalized earnings* per share averaged over the complete business cycle. After a share's normal earnings are estimated, all that need to be done is divide normalized earnings per share into the corporation's regular cash dividend per share to find the payout rate to use in the determination of an earnings multiplier.

For unusual cases—for example, for corporations that have experienced losses—the fundamental security analyst can use the corporation's past earnings multipliers as a starting point. The firm's historical multipliers can be adjusted to derive earnings multipliers with which to estimate a share's future intrinsic value.

Table 15-6
SELECTED FINANCIAL DATA FOR IBM COMMON STOCK ON A PER SHARE BASIS

Year	Per share book value	Range of market price	Per share earnings	Average price-earnings ratio	Per share cash dividend	Cash dividend payout ratio
1988	$62.87	$102–129	$ 8.67	13 times	$4.40	51%
1987	64.09	102–176	8.72	16	4.40	50
1986	56.73	119–161	7.81	18	4.40	56
1985	51.98	117–158	10.67	13	4.40	41
1984	43.23	99–128	10.77	10	4.10	38
1983	38.02	92–134	9.04	12	3.71	41
1982	33.13	55–98	7.39	11	3.44	46
1981	30.66	48–71	5.63	11	3.44	61
1980	28.18	50–72	6.10	10	3.44	56
1979	25.64	61–80	5.16	13	3.44	66
1978	23.14	58–77	5.32	12	2.88	54

**Subjective
Factors Affect
Multipliers**

In estimating a stock's intrinsic economic value, there are many subjective considerations. Care must be taken in weighting the different impacts of these subjective factors on d_t, e_t, g, and k so as not to double-count the effect of one change in d_t, e_t, g, or k unless it truly affects more than one of these variables. Unfortunately, many changes (for example, the addition or deletion of a product line, mergers, or a new competitor) can affect the values of d_t, e_t, g, and k simultaneously. In addition, the firm's management and financial position are important factors; they require subjective evaluations that can affect d_t, e_t, g, and k individually or in unison.

Management Evaluation   In forecasting the risk and earnings of a corporation, fundamental analysts consider the firm's management. The depth and experience of management, the existence of factions or clashing personalities that can cause bottlenecks in an organization, and management's ability to react effectively to changes all affect the firm's risk and its future income.

A firm's research and development (R&D) program should also be considered. If a company has new discoveries or advanced technology which will give it a competitive advantage in the future, the potential benefit usually has a favorable effect on the intrinsic value of its securities by decreasing risk and/or increasing earnings growth.

Analysis of Financial Ratios   In forecasting earnings and their multipliers, the issuing firm's financial statements must be considered. Financial analysis can also shed light on the firm's management, its growth areas, and its risk.[10] These factors affect intrinsic value estimates. Section 14-3 discusses financial ratios.

Factors Affecting Intrinsic Value   Various studies have sought to determine the major factors that determine stock prices. One classic study used a mathematical statistics process called *multivariate analysis*. This study of 63 firms listed on the NYSE found that, on the average, 31 percent of the variation in a stock's price could be attributed to changes in the level of the whole stock market and 20 percent to changes peculiar to each firm which were assumed to come from within the firm. These percentages varied from industry to industry. The average percentages for six industries are shown in Table 15-7. The study suggests that fundamental analysts must be able to forecast many factors that might introduce volatility into stock prices if they are to *time* their trades advantageously.

---

[10]Empirical evidence showing how firms' financial ratios affect their beta systematic risk coefficients is reported in W. H. Beaver, P. Kettler, and M. Scholes, "The Association between Market Determined and Accounting Determined Risk Measures," *Accounting Review*, Oct. 1970, pp. 654–682, and D. J. Thompson II, "Sources of Systematic Risk in Common Stocks," *Journal of Business*, April 1976, vol. 49, no. 2, pp. 173–188.

Table 15-7

PROPORTIONS OF STOCK PRICE VARIATION ATTRIBUTABLE TO VARIOUS RISK FACTORS

Industry	Firm	Market	Industry	Industry subgroups
Tobacco	0.25	0.09	0.17	0.49
Oil	0.15	0.37	0.20	0.28
Metals	0.15	0.46	0.08	0.31
Railroad	0.19	0.47	0.08	0.26
Utilities	0.22	0.23	0.14	0.41
Retail	0.27	0.23	0.08	0.42
Overall	0.20	0.31	0.12	0.37

Source: B. J. King, ''Market and Industry Factors in Stock Price Behavior,'' *Journal of Business,* Jan. 1966, pp. 139–190.

15-5 ATTAINING GOOD TIMING FOR STOCK TRADES

Some investors buy and hold securities to obtain the long-run price appreciation and the dividends normally attained from common stocks. This **buy-and-hold strategy** involves no attempt to ''buy low and sell high'' or otherwise outguess the turns in the market. In contrast to the long-run investors, *traders* try to predict market turns so they will earn more profits by buying at cyclically low prices and selling at cyclically high prices. Portfolio managers who are active **traders** hope to beat the buy-and-hold strategy through what is called good **market timing.**

A trader who buys at market low points and sells at market high points can avoid capital losses and earn larger trading profits than a buy-and-hold strategy would. However, this is easier said than done. Investigations into the investment performance of mutual funds with the published objective of maximizing their investors' income by trading actively reveal that few have been able to earn a significantly higher rate of return than has been earned with a naive buy-and-hold strategy.[11]

Forecasting the National Economy

It is important to be able to predict the course of the national economy because business activity is an important determinant of security prices. Gross national product (GNP), aggregate corporate profits after taxes, and the various stock market averages tend to rise and fall together over time. These economic time

[11]See William F. Sharpe, ''Mutual Fund Performance,'' *Journal of Business,* January 1966, supplement, ''Security Prices,'' pp. 119–138. Later studies have provided additional evidence that mutual funds do not outperform naive buy-and-hold strategies. The investment performance of mutual funds is investigated in Chapter 21.

Table 15-8
ECONOMIC INDICATORS THAT LEAD GNP

Indicator	Typical lead times ahead of GNP, months
Private housing starts	3–34
New durable goods orders	2–28
Average work week	1–18
S&P 500 stock average	4–10

Sources: See Jesse Levin, "Prophetic Leaders," *Financial Analysts Journal,* July–Aug. 1970. For current statistics see the appendixes to *Business Conditions Digest,* published by the U.S. Department of Commerce, updated and published monthly.

series do not move exactly concurrently, however. Several economic variables rise and fall some months ahead of similar changes in the GNP.

Consider the **leading economic indicators** listed in Table 15-8. Note that the stock market *leads* the national economy. Since the stock market is a leading economic indicator, investors are well advised not to bother to forecast the national economy directly. Instead they should follow those indicators which lead stock prices. This provides a valuable forecasting tool. Housing starts, durable goods orders, and the number of hours in the average workweek all tend to turn down several months before a bear market begins.[12]

Since bull and bear markets have preceded the associated turns in the national economy by as much as 13 months, a forecast of the economy must extend more than 13 months into the future if it is to be useful in anticipating turns in the stock market. Furthermore, the forecast should be broken down into a series of quarterly figures to give more insight into the timing of the expected changes.

Pinpointing the Time to Trade

A good economic forecast that discloses the timing of changes and provides some detail about inflation and other matters can be useful to investment decision makers. Ultimately, however, the ability of an economic model to predict exact dollar quantities is not so important to the security analyst as its ability to foretell the *timing and direction of the changes* in the various rates of economic growth. Indications of shifts in the direction of the economy allow

[12]For a detailed economic analysis of the economic indicators that lead the stock market, see Geoffrey H. Moore, "Security Markets and Business Cycles," in *Business Cycles, Inflation, and Forecasting,* National Bureau of Economic Research Study Number 24 (Cambridge, Mass.: Ballinger, 1980), chap. 9. Also see R. D. Arnott and W. A. Copeland, "The Business Cycle and Security Selection," *Financial Analysts Journal,* March–April 1985, pp. 26–32.

portfolio managers to assume a defensive position when bear markets are foreseen and to be aggressive when bullish conditions are expected.

Economic forecasts that extend far into the future and/or show very much detail within the national economy are always based on a set of assumptions about the world situation and its impact on the fiscal and monetary policy of the nation. Assumptions about the particular industry in which a company is located and its competitors are also important to a securities analyst who is estimating the impact of economic developments on a given industry or firm. Figure 15-3 shows the series of decisions that form the basis for any given forecast of the intrinsic value of a corporation's shares.

In forecasting the times when any given security's price will rise above or fall below the intrinsic value that will prevail under normal market conditions,

Figure 15-3 Lattice of assumptions underlying a security analyst's intrinsic value per share forecast.

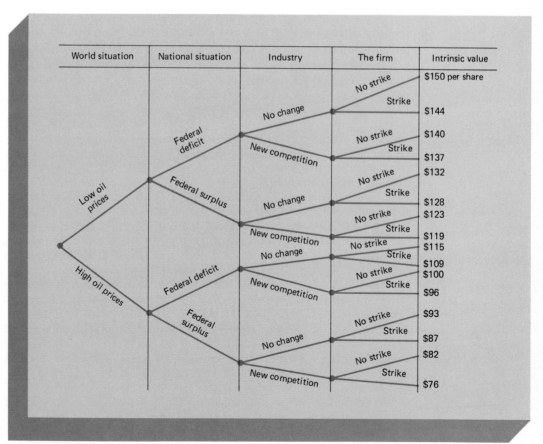

the fundamental analyst must ultimately estimate both (1) what each quarter's earnings per share will be[13] and (2) what the earnings multipliers will be in each quarter.

It is difficult to forecast the quarterly earnings per share and longer-term earnings growth rates for most corporations.[14] Some financial analysts use personal interviews and their intuition to form their forecasts, but this approach is only practical if a few homogeneous securities will be analyzed for an extended period. If numerous heterogeneous corporations are to be forecast, some type of computerized formalized forecasting model is appropriate.[15]

Earnings multipliers fluctuate as much as earnings per share do. These fluctuations can be decomposed into three segments that can be forecast separately. (1) Macroeconomic factors cause the bull-bear market swings. (2) The price-earnings ratios of corporations that have a seasonal earnings pattern also fluctuate seasonally but in an inverse manner that tends to offset whatever earnings seasonality is repetitive. (3) There is an idiosyncratic component in the outlook of every firm. The securities analyst must predict each of these unique changes in earnings multipliers and earnings separately.

For the long run, say for securities which are held over 6 months, forecasting security prices in order to make advantageously timed trades may be an attainable objective. After 6 months, market turns which were soundly forecast will usually come to pass, short-run random security price fluctuations will tend to average out to zero, and fundamental analysis can be profitable for those who are experienced professional fundamental securities analysts.

---

[13]Evidence exists which suggests that earnings per share fluctuate randomly. See J. Lintner and T. Glauber, "Higgledy Piggledy Growth in America," reprinted in J. Lorie and R. Brealey, eds., *Modern Developments in Investment Management,* 2d ed. (Hinsdale, Ill.: Dryden Press, 1978).

[14]See Lawrence Brown and Michael Rozeff, "The Superiority of Analysts' Forecasts as Measures of Expectations: Evidence from Earnings," *Journal of Finance,* March 1978, vol. XXXIII, no. 1, pp. 1–16. Also see J. G. Cragg and B. G. Malkiel, "The Consensus and Accuracy of Some Predictions of Growth of Corporate Earnings," *Journal of Finance,* March 1968, vol. 23, no. 1, pp. 67–84. In addition, see Edwin Elton and Martin H. Gruber, "Earnings Estimates and the Accuracy of Expectational Data," *Management Science,* April 1972, vol. 18, no. 2, pp. 409–424. Also see Edwin Elton, Martin J. Gruber, and Mustafa Gultekin, "Expectations and Share Prices," *Management Science,* Sept. 1981, vol. 27, no. 9.

[15]Single equation econometric models that yield estimates of the earnings per share and price-earnings ratios of individual firms may be found in J. C. Francis, "Analysis of Equity Returns: A Survey with Extensions," *Journal of Economics and Business,* Spring–Summer 1977, vol. 29, no. 3, pp. 181–192.

A more complex econometric model uses a simultaneous equation model of the firm to forecast earnings. See J. C. Francis and D. R. Rowell, "A Simultaneous Equation Model of the Firm for Financial Analysis and Planning," *Financial Management,* Spring 1978, pp. 29–44.

Some Guidelines About When to Buy or Sell

After an extended bull market has pushed the prices of most stocks to high levels, the prevailing optimism will be reflected in certain ratios. The market average price-earnings ratio will be high, and the average stock's cash dividend yield will be remarkably low. Reverse but symmetric statements are true after the market has been through a long bearish period. The tendencies of these market average ratios can be used to delineate guidelines about when it is advisable to consider selling out or buying into the market. Figure 15-4 (shown below and on page 482) illustrates some guidelines that are stated in terms of the Standard & Poor's 500 Composite Stocks Index statistics.

Figure 15-4 S&P 500 market statistics, 1968–1988, for (*a*) P/E ratio on S&P 500, (*b*) S&P 500 market index, (*c*) S&P 500 market index (with different buy and sell signals), and (*d*) cash dividend yield from S&P 500. (*Source:* Trendline, 25 Broadway, New York, N.Y. 10004.)

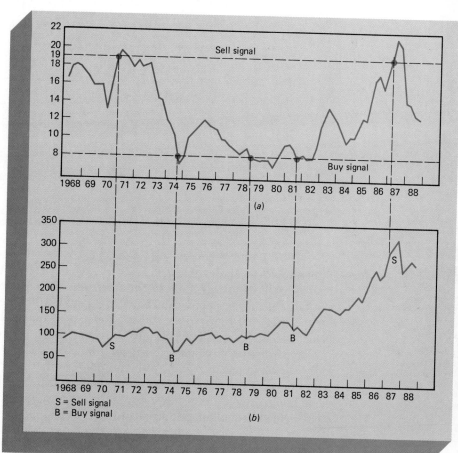

Figure 15-4 *(continued)*

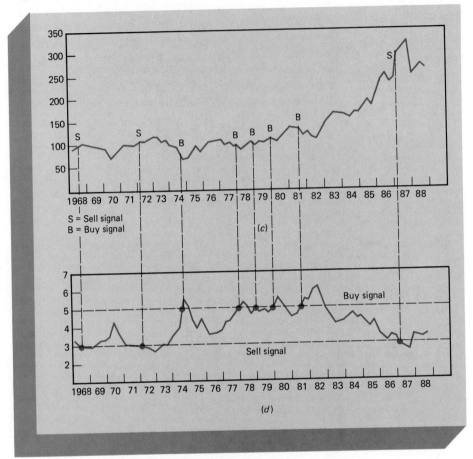

(c)

(d)

Figure 15-4*a* shows that the S&P 500 price-earnings ratio seldom gets as high as 19 or as low as 8; these extremes may therefore be interpreted as sell and buy signals, respectively. Figure 15-4*d* shows that the cash dividend yield for the S&P 500 rarely rises above 5 percent or falls below 3 percent; these values can be used as corroborative buy and a sell signals, respectively.

Comparing the buy and sell signals from panels *a* and *d* with the S&P 500 index shown in panels *b* and *c* of Figure 15-4 shows that the signals given were not optimal. They were useful in providing perspective and in making worth-while trading suggestions, however. In particular, notice that both panels *a* and *d* gave almost simultaneous signals to sell several months before the October 1987 crash. Likewise, both indicators gave a series of buy signals starting in 1974 that would have been profitable to follow.

SUMMARY AND CONCLUSIONS

Dividend discount models are a venerable approach to stock valuation problems. The models provide an explanation of what determines the value of an equity share which is both logical and elegantly simple. Formal analysis of dividend discount models reveals that dividend policy, as measured by the size of a corporation's dividend payout ratio, $1 - f$, has no effect on the value of the stock issued by most corporations. Cash dividend policy only affects the value of shares in growth firms and firms that are declining.

Cash dividend payments cause the market price of the issuer's stock to drop off by an amount equal to the per share cash dividend payment. The price dropoffs caused by the *cash dividend payments* do not contradict the proposition that a firm's *dividend policy* (measured by f) has no effect on the value of most corporations' stock.

The price-earnings ratios used by fundamental analysts can be analyzed by reformulating the discounted cash dividend model in terms of earnings per share. The resulting theoretical model shows that earnings multipliers should vary directly with the issuer's cash dividend payout ratio, the size of the firm's growth rate, and the expected duration of the growth. In addition, the earnings multiplier should vary inversely with the issuer's riskiness. To complicate matters, stock prices and the associated price-earnings ratios fluctuate with bull- and bear-market conditions.

It is not easy to find underpriced and overpriced securities. Professional fundamental analysts usually forecast changes in a corporation's income fairly accurately, and security prices sometimes adjust to the new intrinsic value before the latest earnings are announced to the public.

Fundamental analysis of the relevant facts is a logical way to estimate the true value of a going concern. As a result, fundamental analysis is the most widely used method of estimating security prices. Errors in intrinsic value estimates can be attributed to (1) the analyst not having all the relevant information, (2) the analyst not thoroughly analyzing the available information, or (3) the market being in a state of temporary disequilibrium—for instance, the stock market dropped one-fourth of its value in October 1987 although the fundamental facts were unchanged. Forecasting the forces that shape stock prices is a difficult task. Even under ideal conditions, fundamental analysis can suggest only a price range rather than a specific value.

Selecting advantageous times to buy and sell is risky. Since the stock market is a strong leading indicator of general business activity, a good economic forecast that extends at least 1 year ahead can be helpful in predicting the stock market. In addition, considering the buy-sell guidelines that are implicit when (1) the market average price-earnings ratios get low or high, respectively, and (2) the market average dividend yield gets high or low, respectively, can result in some good investment timing decisions.

Essay Questions

15-1 "A fundamental analyst's estimate of the intrinsic value of a share of stock is different from the present value of all that share's income from cash dividends." Is this statement true, false, or uncertain? Explain.

15-2 Discuss the simplifying assumptions that underlie the discounted cash dividends valuation models. Can any problems arise from using such simplifications?

15-3 Do investors capitalize dividends or earnings when estimating the value of a stock?

15-4 "Dividend policy is irrelevant in spite of the fact that cash dividend payments nevertheless cause stock price dropoffs." True, false, or uncertain? Explain.

15-5 Does an increase in a firm's growth rate g always mean an increase in its intrinsic value? Explain.

15-6 Can factors which are external to the firm, such as national economic conditions, affect the intrinsic value of a share of stock? Explain why or why not.

15-7 "An increase in a firm's liquidity ratios means the firm is well managed and safe. This invariably increases its earnings multipliers." Is this statement true, false, or uncertain? Explain why or why not. *Hint: See Section 14-3.*

15-8 Can fundamental analysis be used for quick, short-range value forecasts, or is it useful only for determining long-run equilibrium values? Explain.

Problems

15-9 The Blume Company is a small, growing manufacturer of lawn equipment which is planning to go public for the first time. Assume that Mr. Blume, the president of the firm, has hired you as a financial consultant to estimate the price per share at which the stock should be sold. The Westerfield Corporation and the Pettit Corporation are also young lawn equipment manufacturers that have recently gone public and have similar product lines (they even have the same accountant). Data on these three corporations are:

Earnings per share	Westerfield	Pettit	Blume's totals
Earnings per share, 19X5	$5	$11	$1,000,000
Average EPS, 19X0–19X5	$5	$8	$780,000
Median market price, 19X5	$29	$145	?
Average price, 19X0–19X5	$27	$110	—
Dividends per share, 19X5	$3	$7.20	$500,000
Average dividends, 19X0–19X5	$2.80	$6.50	$390,000

(Table continues on page 485.)

Earnings per share	Westerfield	Pettit	Blume's totals
Book value per share, 19X0	$81.23	$112.10	$131,500
Growth in EPS, 19X0–19X5	0	5%	6%
Debt-equity ratio, 19X0	9%	42%	45%
Current assets-current liabilities ratio	3.1	1.9	2.0
Employees	180	90	80
Sales	$17,000,000	$9,800,000	$8,800,000

The sales, earnings, and stock prices of all lawn equipment manufacturers have followed rates of change in national income (that is, GNP) in the past few years. Historical data show that the two public firms have beta coefficients (of systematic risk) of about one. The future for the lawn equipment industry is bright. Because of increased suburban living and rising affluence, it is expected that the market for lawn equipment will continue to expand. The economic outlook promises steady growth, and securities markets are normal. What data above will you ignore in pricing Blume's stock? If Blume issues 1 million shares, what price per share will you recommend?

15-10 The Archer Corporation has a beta volatility coefficient of 1.0. Assume that the CAPM (or SML) assigns a capitalization rate of $k = 10$ percent to an asset with a beta of 1.0. Archer's normalized earnings of $2 per share are all paid as cash dividends. Per-share earnings have been growing at 3 percent per annum for some time, and the current market price of $28.60 reflects this growth experience. However, because of a technological breakthrough, Archer's earnings are expected to grow at the increased rate of 6 percent per year for the foreseeable future. What effect do you think this technological innovation will have on Archer's market price per share when the news becomes public?

15-11 For a firm with earnings per share of $10, dividends per share of $6, a cost of equity capital of 10 percent, and an internal rate of return of 15 percent, calculate its value by using the dividend model of Equation (15-9).

15-12 Compare and contrast the importance of dividend policy (a) with and (b) without the preferential tax rates on capital gains by using any dividend valuation model you prefer. Assume that the internal rate of return equals the firm's cost of capital, $r = k$, and that the capital gains tax rate, denoted t, is half the tax rate for ordinary income, $0.5T = t$.

15-13 Three automotive analysts, George Gross, David Deter, and Nancy Necter, are all analyzing the Biloxi Corporation's common stock. They learned that Mr. Desmond Biloxi, who founded the firm, laid down a no-debt financing policy that the firm adheres to even though Mr. Biloxi passed away years ago. All three analysts agree that (a) Biloxi has a beta that indicates that a capitalization rate of $k = 12$ percent is appropriate for the stock, (b) next year's earnings per share are expected to be $7.50, and (c) Biloxi is expected to retain one-third of its earnings to finance its expansion. However, the three analysts foresee different profit prospects for Biloxi. George forecasts that Biloxi will earn an internal rate of return of 20 percent for the foreseeable future. David's forecast is more dire;

he predicts a 10 percent rate of return. Nancy projects a 12 percent rate of return on Biloxi's internal investments. Do the facts and assumptions that the three analysts are using imply significantly different intrinsic values for Biloxi's stock? Explain.

15-14 Susan Tarkington is a common stock analyst who is trying to figure out what capitalization rate to use to value a growing firm named the Duluth Corporation. Since Duluth is only a few years old, there are not enough market price data to judiciously estimate a beta systematic risk coefficient for the corporation's stock. Duluth has been paying a small cash dividend yield of 2 percent for the past 2 years. Several analysts with whom Susan has discussed Duluth expect the stock to continue the 15 percent per year rate of price appreciation it has been experiencing for the past 2 years. Can you suggest how Susan might obtain a capitalization rate for valuing Duluth's stock?

15-15 John Simpson's father Ralph is displeased. Father and son are arguing about whether the mammoth United Telephone and Telegraph (UTT) Corporation, for which Ralph has worked for 28 years, is a growth company. The father is working hard to send his son to college for a business degree. But, he thinks his son does not know what he is talking about when the young business student claims that UTT is not a growth firm and its stock is not a growth stock.

   Ralph is sure UTT is a growth stock for several reasons. He reminds John that when Hawaii and Alaska became states, UTT quickly acquired the Hawaiian Telephone and Telegraph Corporation and the Alaskan Telephone and Communications Corporation so UTT's services extend into all 50 states. In addition, Ralph points to the following statistics from UTT's most recent annual report, calling them "growth statistics." UTT retains one-third of its earnings and the cash dividends are growing at $g = 4$ percent.

Year	Per share cash dividend	UTT's stock price per share	Number of employees
19X0	$4.00	$50.00	30,730
19X1	4.20	52.10	31,331
19X2	4.35	54.01	31,763
19X3	4.50	56.22	35,720 (merger occurred)
19X4	4.70	58.51	36,302
19X5	4.85	60.82	36,900

Is UTT a growth stock? Explain.

15-16 Jack Mitchell is trying to estimate the intrinsic value per share for a growth stock issued by the Falzone Corporation. Mitchell estimates that Falzone will grow at 8 percent per year for 10 years and then level off. During this growth period the corporation will be more risky than the average company, and Jack thinks 14 percent would be an appropriate capitalization rate. Falzone's earnings per share are currently $3.00 and the corporation is paying 50 cents per share cash dividend. What do you think its stock is worth?

Selected References

Cottle, Sidney, R. F. Murray, and F. E. Block, *Security Analysis*, 5th ed. (New York: McGraw-Hill, 1988).

>   This nonmathematical book should be read by anyone who aspires to be a fundamental analyst.

Gordon, M. J., *The Investment, Financing, and Valuation of the Corporation* (Homewood, Ill.: Irwin, 1962).

>   This classic book discusses Gordon's model for capitalizing dividends. Some calculus is used, but mostly algebra.

Malkiel, B. G., "The Valuation of Public Utility Equities," *The Bell Journal of Economics and Management Science*, 1970.

>   This classic article provides an empirical test of the price-earnings valuation model of Equation (15-13). Regression analysis is used.

Miller, M. H., and F. Modigliani, "Dividend Policy, Growth and the Valuation of Shares," *Journal of Business*, Oct. 1961, pp. 411–433.

>   This classic article provides the theory of valuation for shares in an all-equity corporation and is presented with some analysis and review of relevant theories. Freshman college algebra used.

Modigliani, F., and M. H. Miller, "The Cost of Capital, Corporation Finance and the Theory of Investment; Corporate Income Taxes, and the Cost of Capital: A Correction," *American Economic Review*, June 1958, pp. 433–443. More recently, see Miller's "Debt and Taxes," *Journal of Finance*, May 1977, vol. XXXIII, no. 2, pp. 261–276.

>   This classic article shows how to value a corporation that uses debt financing. Freshman college algebra is used.

Whitbeck, V., and M. Kisor, "A New Tool in Investment Decision Making," *Financial Analysts Journal*, May–June 1963.

>   A classic easy-to-read empirical study of earnings per share and multipliers.

Appendix 15A

Econometric Models for Determining Earnings Multipliers

The discussion of fundamental analysis has touched on numerous factors that a security analyst should consider in forming intrinsic-value estimates. The factors that affect estimates of the price-earnings ratio may be quantified and estimated econometrically using multiple regression analysis.

General Form of a Model

The following variables are the determinants of the earnings multiplier, denoted M, that are usually considered:

X_1 = risk of the firm

X_2 = forecasted earnings

X_3 = growth rate for earnings

X_4 = sponsorship—the number of institutional investors

X_5 = competitive position and management ability

X_6 = economic and credit conditions

Through some complex but partially unspecified process, represented in mathematical notation by Equation (A15-1), all these variables are considered simultaneously in determining the earnings and dividends multipliers.

$$M = f(X_1, X_2, X_3, X_4, X_5, X_6) \qquad \text{(A15-1)}$$

In words, Equation (A15-1) says the multiplier is some unspecified mathematical function f with X_1, X_2, X_3, X_4, X_5, and X_6 as the determinants.

A multiple regression of the form shown in Equation (A15-2) can be fit with recent data.

$$M = b_0 + b_1X_1 + b_2X_2 + b_3X_3 + b_4X_4 + b_5X_5 + b_6X_6 + u \qquad \text{(A15-2)}$$

Table A15-1
Statistical Estimates of the Econometric Model

Year	Multiple regression model	Correlation
1961	$M_i = 15.52 + 1.82g_i - 1.75(d/e)_i - 1.53b_i$	.70
1962	$M_i = 12.42 + 1.02g_i + 4.28(d/e)_i - 2.87b_i$	.73
1963	$M_i = 9.20 + 1.28g_i + 6.84(d/e)_i - 1.21b_i$	.69
1964	$M_i = 14.37 + 0.96g_i + 3.29(d/e)_i - 3.54b_i$	.66
1965	$M_i = 7.47 + 1.52g_i + 5.58(d/e)_i - 0.95b_i$	.80

Source: B. G. Malkiel and J. G. Cragg, "Expectations and the Structure of Share Prices," *American Economic Review*, Sept. 1970, p. 610, table 3.

where b_0 = regression intercept
      b_i = multiple regression coefficient of X_i
   X_i's = independent variables listed above
      u_i = unexplained error, $E(u) = 0$

Econometric Model in Three Variables

One published study suggested that three independent variables largely determine the price-earnings multiplier. The variables used in this study are defined as follows:

M_i = ith firm's price-earnings multiplier, dependent variable to be predicted by model

g = historical growth rate of firm = X_{1i}

d/e = ith firm's average dividend payout ratio = X_{2i}

b = ith firm's beta coefficient, measuring its systematic risk = X_{3i}

A sample of over 150 firms was employed to estimate the cross-sectional multiple regression model shown in Equation (A15-2). An examination of the statistical estimates of this econometric model are shown in Table A15-1. These statistics reveal several things. First, as indicated by the correlation coefficients which are all significantly greater than zero, the statistics were able to predict fairly well. Second, earnings growth (as measured by g_i) always tends to have a positive effect on the multipliers. The effect of the dividend payout is not clear [since the coefficient of $(d/e)_i$ erratically changed signs in 1961]. Third, systematic risk, as measured by ith firm's beta, has a negative effect on the multiplier. And finally, the model is not perfectly stationary over time. This last finding means that the changing regression coefficients should be reestimated if the model is to be kept current and useful for prediction.[16] The statistics in Table A15-1 are informative; they support the theory presented in Chapter 15.

[16]B. G. Malkiel and J. G. Cragg, "Expectations and the Structure of Share Prices," *American Economic Review*, Sept. 1970, pp. 615–616.

Chapter 16

Earnings and Stock Prices

The discussion of stock valuation in Chapter 15 made one thing clear—prices are dependent on the earning power that underlies the stock. This conclusion is the same if the valuation model is formulated in terms of cash dividends instead of earnings, because a share's cash dividends must ultimately come from its earnings per share. Therefore, we will delve deeper into the relationship between stock prices and earnings per share. Fundamental analysts' stock valuation techniques will be investigated in this chapter, and some stock selection techniques will be evaluated.

16-1 FORECASTED EARNINGS, ACTUAL EARNINGS, AND STOCK PRICES

Niederhoffer and Reagan (NR) gathered data on 150 NYSE-listed common stocks—50 that enjoyed the greatest price gains, 50 that suffered the greatest price declines, and 50 stocks that were picked randomly.[1] The 50 randomly selected stocks were a *control group* used as a benchmark against which to compare the biggest gainers and the biggest losers. NR observed more than merely the prices of these stocks.

NR calculated three percentage changes for each of their 150 stocks: (1) the percentage change in the stocks' prices, (2) the percentage change in the earnings per share that professional financial analysts *forecasted* for each of the

---

[1]See Victor Niederhoffer and Patrick Reagan, "Earnings Changes, Analysts Forecasts, and Stock Prices," *Financial Analysts Journal*, May–June 1972, vol. 28, no. 3, pp. 65–71.

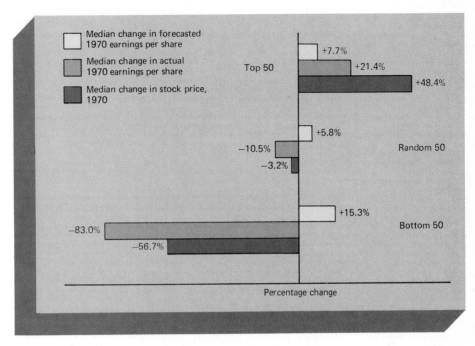

Figure 16-1 One-year median changes in forecasted earnings, actual earnings, and stock prices. (*a*) Returns over (− 60, 0) period; (*b*) returns over (− 1, 0) period; (*c*) returns over (1, 60) period. (*Source:* Victor Niederhoffer and Patrick Reagan, ''Earnings Changes, Analysts Forecasts, and Stock Prices,'' *Financial Analysts Journal,* May–June 1972, vol. 28, no. 3, fig. 1, p. 67.)

150 stocks,[2] and (3) the percentage change in the stocks' *actual* earnings per share. These were all 1-year changes from the same year. Figure 16-1 summarizes NR's findings.

NR determined nine median percentage changes—the change in the actual earnings, the change in earnings that was forecasted, and the concurrent price change—for the three groups. Figure 16-1 shows what valuation theory taught us to expect; the stocks that had the largest gains in price experienced the greatest increases in their earnings. Likewise, the stocks with the largest price declines also experienced the greatest decreases in their earnings. In contrast to the two extreme groups, the representative random sample of stocks in the control group suffered a modest 3.2 percent price decline as their actual earnings dropped the median amount of 10.5 percent.

[2]The earnings forecasts were obtained from a Standard & Poor's monthly publication, *Earnings Forecaster,* which polls security analysts every month and publishes their earnings forecasts for hundreds of stocks.

Although the relationship we expected between the percentage changes in the stock prices and their actual earnings is easily observable in Figure 16-1, it is impossible to discern any meaningful relationship between the *forecasted* earnings and the stocks' price changes. The only conclusions we can draw about the earnings forecasts is that, first, they are all biased. The earnings forecasters seem to underestimate the big changes in earnings. Second, the earnings forecasts do not seem to have any impact on the stocks' prices. This second conclusion is evaluated further in the next section.

16-2   **SURPRISING CHANGES IN EARNINGS AFFECT STOCKS' PRICES**

Professors Latané and Jones (LJ) doubted that the investors' expectations about future earnings prospects had no effect on stock prices. Instead, they suggested that *surprisingly good* or *surprisingly bad* changes in earnings should have a significant impact on stock prices.[3] They even developed a way to measure surprisingly good and bad earnings changes. Equation (16-1) defines what LJ called **standardized unexpected earnings** (SUE) for the common stock of corporation i during quarterly period t.

$$SUE_{i,t} = \frac{\text{(actual quarterly EPS)}_{i,t} - \text{(forecasted quarterly EPS)}_{i,t}}{\text{standard deviation of the forecasting error}_i} \quad (16\text{-}1)$$

The numerator of Equation (16-1) is the **forecasting error** for corporation i that occurs when the tth quarter's earnings are publicly announced. This forecasting error is a measure of the size of the "surprise" that occurs when the earnings per share are announced. If the forecasting error was zero, there was presumably zero surprise.

After the forecasting errors are determined, the denominator of Equation (16-1) was calculated; it is the standard deviation of the forecasting errors. Dividing each forecasting error by that stock's standard deviation makes the SUEs dimensionless index numbers that can be used for intercompany comparisons. If corporations A and B both had forecasted earnings of $2.00 and actual earnings of $3.00, for example, they would have identical forecasting errors of $1.00. But, if corporation A was a predictable firm whose forecasting errors had a small standard deviation of 50 cents and, in contrast, corporation B was a firm with volatile earnings and a standard deviation of $2.00, the SUE values of the two firms would differ substantially.

[3]H. Latané and C. Jones, "Standardized Unexpected Earnings—1971–77," *Journal of Finance*, June 1979, vol. 34, pp. 717–724.

$$SUE_{A,t} = \frac{(actual\ EPS)_t - (forecasted\ EPS)_t}{standard\ deviation\ of\ errors_A} = \frac{\$3.00 - \$2.00}{0.50} = 2.0$$

$$SUE_{B,t} = \frac{(actual\ EPS)_t - (forecasted\ EPS)_t}{standard\ deviation\ of\ errors_B} = \frac{\$3.00 - \$2.00}{\$2.00} = 0.5$$

The computations above show that investors in stock A were much more pleasantly surprised by its earnings than were the investors who followed stock B, even though both securities had identical forecasting errors of +$1.00.

Foster, Olsen, and Shevlin (FOS) used Equation (16-1) to compute the SUE values from the prices of 2053 corporations' stocks over 32 consecutive quarters of earnings announcements.[4] After the (2053 stocks × 32 quarters) 65,696 SUE values were calculated, they were arrayed and assigned to one of ten "surprise decile" portfolios. Portfolio 1 contained the 10 percent (either 6569 or 6570) most negative SUE values—a portfolio full of the "worst news." Portfolio 10 contained the 10 percent largest positive SUE values—a portfolio of the "best surprises." The SUE values in decile portfolios 2 through 9 were arrayed accordingly. Abnormal returns from the stocks measured over three different periods are shown in Figure 16-2.

Figure 16-2a illustrates the decile portfolio returns measured over the [−60, 0] period; it begins 60 days before the earnings were announced in *The Wall Street Journal* and includes the announcement date (time $t = 0$). Figure 16-2b shows the decile portfolios' returns measured over the [−1, 0] period, which runs from 1 day before the earnings announcement through the announcement date. Figure 16-2c displays the 10 portfolios' returns measured over the [1, 60] period—from the day after the earnings announcement through the following 60 days.

Figure 16-2a, b, and c illustrates similar direct relationships between the size and sign of the unexpected earnings surprise and the size and sign of the stocks' abnormal returns. In addition, Figure 16-2a shows that when corporations announce unexpectedly good earnings (such as portfolios 9 or 10), their stock prices tend to increase *prior* to the announcement date. When corporations announce unexpectedly poor earnings (such as portfolios 1 or 2), their stocks' prices tend to decrease *prior* to the announcement date, as indicated by Figure 16-2a. Essentially, Figure 16-2a provides evidence that, *on average, the stock market correctly anticipates earnings changes before they are announced* and responds to them in the way valuation theory suggests.

During the 2-day period surrounding the announcement date, Figure 16-2b

---

[4]See George Foster, Chris Olsen, and Terry Shevlin, "Earnings Releases, Anomalies and the Behavior of Security Returns," *Accounting Review,* Oct. 1984, vol. 59, no. 4, pp. 574–603. The study is also discussed by George Foster, *Financial Statement Analysis* (Englewood Cliffs, N.J.: Prentice-Hall, 1986), see chaps. 8 and 11, especially pp. 383–384, 392, and 396–397.

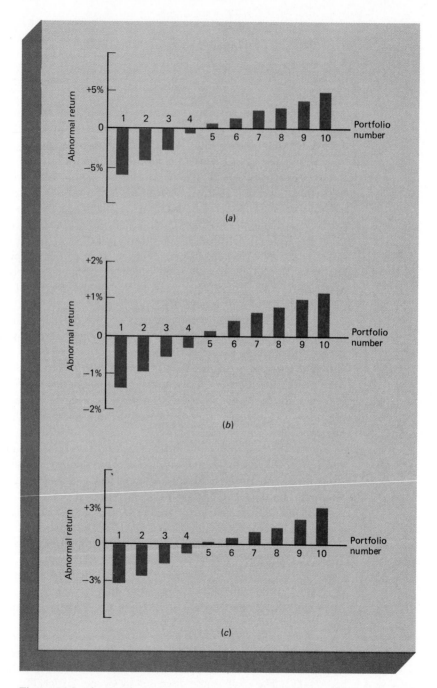

Figure 16-2 Abnormal common stock returns during three periods surrounding earnings announcement dates. (*Source:* George Foster, Chris Olsen, and Terry Shevlin, "Earnings Releases, Anomalies and the Behavior of Security Returns," *Accounting Review,* Oct. 1984, vol. 59, no. 4, pp. 574–603.)

shows that larger earnings surprises in either direction result, on average, in larger price reactions in the same direction. Stated differently, the market typically reacts rationally to new information.[5]

Figure 16-2c documents a *market inefficiency*[6]; it indicates that the direct relationship between the unexpected earnings surprises and the abnormal stock returns that was documented in Figure 16-2a and b continues for 2 months *after the earnings are announced*. For instance, an investor in decile portfolio 10 can expect to accumulate abnormal gains of 3.23 percent for 2 months after the unexpectedly good earnings news is made public. This finding suggests that an investor could earn abnormal returns simply by looking at the quarterly earnings announcements in *The Wall Street Journal* and, based on the sign and size of the SUE, then taking either a long or a short position in portfolio 10 or 1, respectively.

The studies of stock price reactions to earnings announcements reviewed above suggest two observations. First, the studies leave little doubt that earnings are an important determinant of stock prices. Second, it is highly probable that even more compelling results could have been attained if more and better earnings measures had been utilized. The studies above were all based on the earnings reported by the corporation's own accountants. The next section discusses ways to obtain better estimates of a company's earning power in those cases when the reported accounting earnings are not a true reflection of what actually occurred.

16-3   **ACCOUNTING EARNINGS ARE AMBIGUOUS**

Unfortunately, earnings per share cannot be measured very precisely. Table 5-7 on page 158 contains an outline of the model underlying the accounting profession's income and expense statements. Despite the model's seeming simplicity, many questions arise concerning the definitions and measurements of the various items determining income. Stated differently, the **generally accepted accounting principles** *(GAAP hereafter) leave room for interpretation.*

Also note the quotation beneath Table 5-7; it is reproduced from a respected intermediate accounting textbook. Although the uncertainty voiced in the quo-

---

[5]For evidence that ''good news'' tends to be announced earlier than expected, while ''bad news'' tends to be announced later than expected, see V. V. Chari, R. Jagannathan, and A. Ofer, ''Seasonality in Security Returns: The Case of Earnings Announcements,'' *Journal of Financial Economics,* May 1988, vol. 21, no. 1, pp. 101–121. In addition, the ''timeliness'' of the announcement (defined to be the difference between the expected announcement date and the actual announcement date) tends to affect the size of the abnormal return. Furthermore, around earnings announcement dates, trading volume tends to pick up and security prices become more volatile. Also see G. Foster, *Financial Statement Analysis* (Englewood Cliffs, N.J.: Prentice-Hall, 1986), pp. 377–386.
[6]The concept of efficient markets was introduced in Section 8-6.

tation may come as a shock to neophytes, experienced accountants and analysts have long recognized the problems involved in preparing income estimates.

The latitude of alternative GAAPs that the accountant may follow in deriving a firm's income is often not the cause of skewed accounting income reports. The accountant needs some leeway to select an accounting procedure that most clearly reports the true economic consequence of a business transaction. Yet accountants regularly produce income statements that financial analysts must alter significantly in order to obtain estimates of a firm's true economic income. Distorted income statements often result from (1) the accountant's use of an accounting procedure that is inappropriate for the relevant economic transaction and/or (2) pressure on the accountant from top management to minimize the firm's income taxes and/or (3) pressure on the accountant from top management to "window-dress" the corporation's financial statements. A numerical example is analyzed below.

Contrast of Two Income Statements for the Same Firm

Table 16-1 shows two income and expense statements for the same company. These two statements are identical in every way except for some of the accounting procedures used to prepare them. Income statement B tends to minimize taxable income. Income statement A is a true representation of the firm's economic income. The divergent accounting procedures followed in developing income statements A and B both conform with the GAAP. Both income statements are correct on the basis of accounting practices, but only income statement A provides a true picture of the economic results of the firm's operations.

The five items where statements A and B differ are keyed at the right margin of Table 16-1; they indicate some of the points where confusion and deception can enter into accountants' measurements of a business's earnings.

Sales (1)   Statement A includes under sales revenue both cash sales and current sales made on installment contracts. The firm factors its accounts receivable as soon as they arise and thus realizes the cash proceeds of the installment contract sales immediately. But the firm's statement B does not recognize the credit sales until the customer's final cash payment is actually received and the factoring company has no potential bad debt claims against the firm. Both practices of installment sales recognition are GAAP. However, the procedure shown in statement A is the true reflection of the actual sales revenues.[7]

---

[7]The SEC responded to problems like this with *Accounting Series Release No. 95.* ASR 95 has the descriptive title: "Accounting for Real Estate Transactions Where Circumstances Indicate That Profits Were Not Earned at the Time the Transactions Were Recorded." In a related matter, APB Opinion No. 21 required companies to record transactions resulting in notes receivable at the fair market value instead of the face value of the note. See APB Opinion No. 21, "Interest on Receivables and Payables," AICPA, New York, 1971.

For additional GAAP opinions about how sales should be recognized, see Statements of Financial Accounting Standards (SFAS) 66 and 67, Financial Accounting Standards Board, Stamford, Conn.

Table 16-1

TWO INCOME STATEMENTS FOR THE SAME COMPANY IN THE SAME YEAR PREPARED WITH GAAP

	Statement B, $, 000s omitted		Statement A, $, 000s omitted		Key, see text
Sales revenue		$9200		$11,000	(1)
less: Returns and allowances		− 1000		− 1000	
Net sales		$8200		$10,000	
Beginning inventory	$2000		2000		
Purchases and freight in	6000		6000		
Net purchases	$8000		8000		
less: Ending inventory	− 2000		− 3000		(2)
Cost of goods sold		6000		5000	
Gross margin		2200		5000	
Operating expenses					
Selling costs	1500		1500		
Depreciation	500		300		(3)
Pension	100		20		(4)
Other expenses	200		50		(5)
Salaries	200		200		
Bonuses	100		100		
Total operating expenses		− 2600		− 2170	
Net operating expenses		(400)		2830	
less: Interest		− 100		− 100	
Income (loss) before taxes		(500)		2730	
less: Federal taxes (33%) (refund)		(166)		− 909	
Net income (loss) from operations		(334)		1821	

Inventory (2) Statement A used the first-in-first-out (FIFO) method of inventory valuation while B used the last-in-first-out (LIFO) method. During periods of inflation the FIFO method tends to result in higher reported profits.

Consider contrasting numerical examples of LIFO and FIFO. Imagine that 1-ton widgets are the inventory items and that one widget is always carried in inventory. Assume that, early in the accounting year represented in Table 16-1, the cost of widgets rose from $2000 a piece to $3000. The inventory is valued at cost, so the beginning inventory value of the one-widget inventory is $2000 whether LIFO or FIFO is used. This value is shown in Tables 16-1 and 16-2.

If we assume the newest widgets are used in production first, then the LIFO method is appropriate to value the inventory. Thus, during the inflationary accounting period when widget prices rose 50 percent, the value of the inventory was constant; that is, the value of the widget in ending inventory is assumed

Table 16-2
LIFO INVENTORY ACCOUNTING DURING INFLATION (Statement B)

	Inventory value
Beginning inventory (one widget at $2000)	$2000
plus: Purchases (two widgets at $3000 each)	+ $6000
Cost of goods available for sale	$8000
less: Ending inventory (one widget at $2000)	− $2000 (undervalued)
Cost of goods sold	$6000 (overvalued)

to remain unchanged. This means that relative to the year's ending market prices of $3000 per widget, LIFO undervalues ending inventory, overestimates the cost of goods sold, and accordingly underestimates profit during inflation. Table 16-2 depicts this LIFO process. If FIFO had been used, the ending inventory (of one widget purchased for $3000) would be valued at $3000 and the cost of goods sold in Table 16-2 would be $5000.

Some consideration of these methods reveals that FIFO incorporates inventory capital gains or losses into regular income, while LIFO does not. Thus, FIFO often causes profit to be more volatile than LIFO. FIFO is assumed to be the most realistic method of inventory valuation in this case (although the least advantageous for tax purposes) for two main reasons. First, it was initially assumed that the manufacturer sold the oldest items in inventory first. Second, profits and losses on the inventory are reflected in reported income as they occur.

Not only does the LIFO versus FIFO decision have different effects on income, switching from one of these inventory valuation techniques to the other can also result in some spectacular earnings modifications. Comparing the federal income taxes a company reports in its published financial statements to the appropriate proportion of its reported pretax income is a good way to detect if the company keeps "two sets of books."[8]

Depreciation (3)   Assuming that no new technology or unusually heavy use is likely to depreciate the value of the firm's assets before they are worn out, the straight-line depreciation used in statement A is more honest (but less desirable for tax purposes) than the accelerated sum-of-the-digits depreciation procedure employed in statement B.

---

[8]Some companies keep one set of books for management decision-making purposes and a different set of books to show to the Internal Revenue Service (IRS). Presumably the books for management reflect the firm's true economic earnings. For a detailed explanation of a multimillion-dollar inventory valuation switch that the Chrysler Corporation used in 1970, see Abraham Briloff, *Unaccountable Accounting* (New York: Harper & Row, 1972), pp. 36–39.

Several depreciation techniques may be used in the financial statements that a firm presents to the public.

1. Straight-line method
2. Units of production method
3. Double declining balance method
4. Sum-of-the-digits method

The third and fourth methods are accelerated methods of depreciation. The second method may be used to accelerate depreciation during a period of rapid production. To understand how depreciation affects profit, a numerical example using the first and fourth methods will be used.

Imagine an asset that costs $1000 with an expected life T of 3 years and no salvage value. By use of the straight-line method, depreciation is constant at $333.33 ($1000/3 = cost/T) for each of the 3 years. With the sum-of-the-digits method, the annual depreciation starts large and diminishes each year because a decreasing fraction is multiplied by the cost of the asset (a stable amount) to determine each year's depreciation, as shown in Table 16-3. The numerator of this fraction decreases by one each year. As shown in Table 16-3, the numerator represents the number of years left in the life of the asset. The denominator of the fraction remains stable; if the life expectancy of an asset is T years, the denominator would be $T(T + 1)/2$. In this case, $T = 3$ works out to be a denominator of $3(4)/2 = 6$.

Accelerated depreciation increases depreciation costs in the early years of a new asset's life; it thereby decreases the firm's reported accounting income and net taxable profit when the asset is new. Stated differently, accelerated depreciation postpones taxes on income. Postponing taxes provides the taxpayer an interest-free loan from the federal government. The total depreciation

Table 16-3

**SUM-OF-THE-DIGITS DEPRECIATION CALCULATIONS FOR
AN ASSET WITH A 3-YEAR LIFE**

Year, t	Depreciation as fraction of cost	Sum-of-the-digits annual dollar depreciation
1	$\dfrac{T}{T(T + 1)/2} = \dfrac{3}{6}$	$500.00
2	$\dfrac{T - 1}{T(T + 1)/2} = \dfrac{2}{6}$	$333.33
3	$\dfrac{T - 2}{T(T + 1)/2} = \dfrac{1}{6}$	$166.66
Totals	1	$1000.00

expense is unchanged; only its timing is altered. As Table 16-1 shows, however, it can affect any particular year's reported accounting income significantly.

As a result of various rulings, the IRS has *increased the disparity* between the two depreciation techniques it requires for tax reporting (namely, ACRS and MACRS) and the depreciation techniques used most frequently in publicly reported accounting statements. Today the IRS *requires* firms to depreciate their assets for tax purposes using the *accelerated cost recovery system (ACRS)* if the asset was acquired between 1980 and 1987. For assets acquired after 1986 either the straight-line method or the *modified accelerated cost recovery system (MACRS)* is required. In most cases, the ACRS and MACRS depreciation techniques will differ markedly from the traditional techniques.

For tax accounting, the IRS requires firms to explicitly assign all depreciable assets to one of several different categories that are based on the life of the asset and whether it is residential or nonresidential real estate. Depreciation for each category of assets is narrowly defined under the accelerated cost recovery system (ACRS). The ACRS guidelines give the accountant little leeway in tax accounting for depreciation. In almost every case the ACRS guidelines result in unrealistically rapid write-offs, and also, more rapid write-offs than would be allowed under the traditional accelerated depreciation techniques. The ACRS was not created by the IRS or the accounting profession. ACRS was developed by the U.S. Treasury as a fiscal measure, designed to renew American technology by providing firms with cash for accelerated asset renewal. The ACRS rules can also make depreciation accounting a more complex problem for the financial analyst to unravel in an effort to discern the firm's true economic income.

Pension Costs (4)   Pension funds are legally divided into two categories— *defined contribution* plans and *defined benefit* plans.[9] **Defined contribution plans** require the employer to contribute a specified amount (such as a percentage of every employee's wages) into a segregated fund that is for the employees' retirement benefits. Defined contribution plans are also called **profit-sharing plans.** Accounting for these defined contribution plans is simple; the employer's cost is deducted as a current business expense from each year's income and expense statement. No liabilities for unfunded pension obligations appear on the employer's balance sheet.

The *defined benefit* plans are more complicated than the *defined contribution* plans. A **defined benefit plan** arises when the employer promises to pay each qualified employee a specified pension when they retire. The employer's pension cost is based on estimates that determine which employees are qualified for pension benefits. Factors such as the employee's years of service with the employer and the employee's age at retirement determine whether an employee

---

[9]The Employee Retirement Income Security Act (ERISA) of 1974 governs pension funds; it was discussed in Chapter 4.

is qualified for a pension; they also determine the amount of the sponsoring employer's liability for pension fund payments.

Actuaries estimate the dollar value of the employer's legal liability to its retirees under a defined benefit pension plan. But to prepare their estimates, the actuaries must make assumptions about the number of employees who will work long enough to reach retirement age and the number of retirees who will qualify for a pension. Further assumptions must be made about the retirees' salary levels when they retire, the number of employees who will have legally *vested* pension claims against the employer but will quit before they reach retirement age, how many years the retired employees will collect pension benefits before they die, how many qualified spouses will live after the worker who earned the pension dies, and how long the qualified spouses will continue to collect the pension.[10]

After the actuarial assumptions are established, the actuaries work with the firm's management to select a discount rate that can be used to calculate the *discounted present value of the future pension liabilities.* When the present value of the employer's pension liability has been estimated, the employer must determine how much of its earnings to set aside in a segregated account to fund this pension liability.

In an extraordinarily controversial 1985 ruling, FASB Statement No. 87 greatly limited the latitude that employers have when reporting their pension fund's assets, liabilities, costs, and policies. FASB 87 requires employing firms to disclose in a footnote to their financial statements the firm's pension accounting and funding policy, the pension charge for the year, and any unfunded pension liability of the company.

If a pension fund's assets are less than (exceed) its liabilities, the fund has a deficit (surplus). FASB 87 requires that the firm must show a balance sheet liability if it has a pension deficit that exceeds 10 percent of its pension assets; a liability of this size cannot merely be reported in a footnote.[11] These pension liabilities must be paid for out of the employer's earnings as soon as possible.[12]

---

[10]For a discussion of estimating an employer's pension liabilities see D. Don Ezra, "How Actuaries Determine the Unfunded Pension Liability," *Financial Analysts Journal,* July–Aug. 1980. See also Richard A. Ippolito, "The Economic Burden of Corporate Pension Liabilities," *Financial Analysts Journal,* Jan.–Feb. 1986.

[11]More specifically, an additional liability must be created if the accumulated employee benefit obligations of the pension fund sponsor exceed the fair value of the pension fund's assets. These accumulated benefit obligations ignore future salary progression and, as a result, underestimate the sponsoring corporation's legal liability by that amount.

[12]If the rate of return that the actuary uses to calculate the present value of the firm's pension liability is unrealistically high, then the pension plan's liabilities will be reduced to unrealistically low levels, and the firm's pension costs can be reduced on the income statement. However, the company may then have to make large cash contributions in the future to make up any pension funding deficits that materialize later. See Appendix 13A for an example of how pension liabilities are calculated.

Let us assume that the company shown in Table 16-1 has a defined benefit pension plan. Statement B reflects a large pension expense deduction, and statement A reports a small deduction. The large deduction in statement B might result because the employer wants to make a larger than necessary pension fund contribution to accomplish one or more of the following goals: (1) to minimize its income tax payments, (2) to smooth (or average down) unusually large earnings for that particular year, and/or (3) to accumulate surplus assets in its pension fund to minimize the chance of being underfunded if a bear market diminishes the market value of the pension assets.[13] To accomplish any of these objectives, the employer could urge its actuaries to make high pension cost estimates to make the large deductions shown in statement B appear necessary. However, if the firm has a youthful labor force with few workers near retirement age, statement A's treatment of pension costs is the more forthright approach.[14]

Expensing versus Capitalizing (5)   There are many items which the accountant may either write off as current expenses or capitalize and then amortize over a period of years. For example, motion-picture production costs, oil well exploration costs, advertising campaign costs, and many other items are not clearly either an expense or an asset purchase. Such outlays represent matters of managerial discretion that the fundamental analyst should scrutinize. Prior to the issuance of FASB Statement No. 2, companies were entitled to either capitalize research and development (R&D) outlays or expense them. The rules now prohibit capitalizing R&D outlays.[15]

Statements A and B differ because some outlays that were expensed on statement B were capitalized on statement A. The fundamental analyst should scrutinize these entries in comparing the two income statements to see if either GAAP or the accountant handled the transaction inappropriately. A securities analyst who believes that the outlays should be capitalized, should adjust downward the item entitled "Other expenses" in statement B.

---

[13]FASB 87 does not permit a corporation sponsoring a pension fund to show any pension surpluses as assets on the balance sheet. Shrewd corporate raiders will nevertheless ferret out such pools of corporate wealth when they select corporations as targets for leveraged buyouts. As a result, pension fund surpluses exert upward pressure on the price of the sponsoring corporation's stock.

[14]For discussion of pension funds see Jay Vawter, "Determination of Portfolio Policies: Institutional Investors," in John L. Maginn and Donald L. Tuttle, eds., *Managing Investment Portfolios,* sponsored by The Institute of Chartered Financial Analysts (Boston, Mass.: Warren, Gorham & Lamont, 1983), chap. 4, pp. 67–84.

[15]FASB No. 2, "Accounting for Research and Development Costs," Stamford, Conn., Oct. 1974. An exception to the rule is material, equipment, or facilities that have "alternative future uses." For a list of activities that should be included in R&D and examples of activities that should be excluded, see paragraphs 9 and 10 of FASB 2.

Effects on Accounting Income   Table 16-1 summarizes the five differences in accounting procedures discussed above and shows their effects on accounting income.[16] Statement B indicates the firm has zero income tax liability; instead, the firm received a $166,000 federal income tax refund to partially offset its losses. In contrast, Firm A paid $909,000 in federal income taxes. This difference in the income taxes makes it easy to forget that the two statements were both computed for the same firm and that the underlying business transactions were identical. Nevertheless, the firm could find several certified public accountants to certify either one of the income statements shown in Table 16-1.

As our example suggests, unethical financial managers can manipulate accounting procedures to make the reported earnings of their firm come out to be any number they wish within a wide range. Therefore, financial analysts should read firms' reported income figures with care and a degree of skepticism. As we will see later in this chapter, financial analysts may obtain more relevant information by focusing on a firm's cashflows instead of its reported earnings.

After a financial analyst has ferreted out and resolved the various ambiguities that may creep into a firm's income and expense statements, the analyst should go on to examine the firm's earnings per share (EPS).

Additional Vagaries Creep into Reported EPS	Estimates of the intrinsic value of an equity share usually focus on **earnings per share** (EPS) because EPS measures the dollar amount of earning power available to support the stock's price.[17] But when studying EPS, common stock analysts quickly discover that a corporation's EPS can be affected by several accounting conventions that are open to interpretation. More than one measure of EPS may be reported, for example, if a company has convertible securities, warrants, stock options, or other contracts that permit the number of shares of common stock outstanding to be increased in future periods. Moreover, income or losses caused by extraordinary events will result in additional EPS measures being reported. The complications caused by these alternative measures of EPS are discussed next.

[16]FASB No. 96, ''Accounting for Income Taxes,'' Dec. 1987, provides guidelines for reporting income taxes and tax liabilities.

[17]Technically speaking, EPS on the common stock is net income after *reported* taxes (but reported taxes can differ from the amount of taxes that must be paid) less preferred stock dividend payments divided by the weighted average number of shares of common stock outstanding. To compute the weighted average number of shares outstanding, determine the weights by the length of time the shares have been outstanding. For example, if there were 1.2 million shares outstanding for the first 8 months of the reporting year and 1.5 million shares in the last 4 months, then the weighted average number of shares is 1.3 million, as shown below.

$$(1.2 \text{ million shares}) \times (8/12) + (1.5 \text{ million shares}) \times (4/12) = 1.3 \text{ million shares}$$

Potential Dilution of Earnings per Share[18] An increase in the number of shares of common stock outstanding may dilute a corporation's EPS. Such an increase in the outstanding shares can occur (1) because management elects to sell more shares, (2) if contracts give various parties the option to purchase common stock from the corporation, and/or (3) if a corporation exchanges common stock for debt in order to reduce its debt-equity ratio.

Examples of contracts that grant investors the option to purchase common stock from the corporation include convertible bonds, convertible preferred stock, executive stock options, and warrants to purchase common stock.

If the potential dilution attributable to the existence of convertible security contracts may result in an EPS decline of less than 3 percent, the potential dilution need not be reported. However, for those corporations in which the diluting impact on EPS is greater than 3 percent, EPS must be presented two ways. First, dilution that considers only *common stock equivalents* is used to determine EPS.[19] This first required measure is called **primary EPS**. Second, the maximum potential dilution of EPS must be reported. This second measure is termed **fully diluted EPS**.[20]

Extraordinary Gains and Losses Analysts attempt to estimate the future "normal" earnings of the companies they investigate. However, certain events may disrupt or distort the "normal" stream of income. For example, a company might take a considerable loss by closing down an unprofitable division or a firm may win a legal judgment in which a substantial award is received. How should such unusual events be reported?

Accountants have debated how to treat extraordinary items on the income statement. Some accountants held that extraordinary items should be reported on the income statement for the current period. The opposing view was that extraordinary items would distort income, and hence such gains or losses should simply be added to or subtracted from retained earnings. In 1966, the controversy was virtually ended with the issuance of APB Opinion No. 9, "Reporting the Results of Operations." This opinion requires that extraordinary items be

---

[18]Based on APB Opinion No. 15, "Earnings per Share," AICPA, New York, 1969.

[19]*Common stock equivalents* are defined as options or warrants to purchase common stock and certain convertible securities. For a convertible security to be considered a common stock equivalent, the current yield of the security at the time of issuance has to be less than two-thirds of the prime interest rate when the security was issued. Common stock equivalents may be used when the result will be a decline in a loss per share.

[20]A study of the impact on financial statement users of the requirement in APB Opinion 15 calling for reporting of fully diluted earnings per share indicates that investors do react to information on potential dilution. See Steven J. Rice, "The Information Content of Fully Diluted Earnings per Share," *The Accounting Review*, April 1978, vol. LIII, no. 2, pp. 429–438.

reported separately in the income statement, net of taxes. The exception to this reporting rule is *prior period adjustments,* which the opinion defines as[21]:

> those material adjustments which (a) can be specifically identified with and directly related to the business activities of particular prior periods, and (b) are not attributable to economic events occurring subsequent to the date of the financial statements for the prior period, and (c) depend primarily on determinations by persons other than management, and (d) were not susceptible to reasonable estimation prior to such determination. Such adjustments are rare in modern financial accounting.

FASB No. 16 went on to limit prior period adjustments to (1) the correction of an error in a published statement and (2) adjustments that result from income realized as tax benefits from preacquisition loss carryforwards of a purchased subsidiary.

Stringent requirements for an item to be classified as *extraordinary* were established in APB Opinion No. 30 issued in 1973.[22] The opinion requires that the item be both unusual in nature and not expected to recur in the foreseeable future.[23]

Two examples of extraordinary items are (1) losses due to a major casualty, such as a flood, and (2) losses due to an expropriation of business assets by foreign governments. Three examples of transactions or events that are not included as extraordinary items are (1) the write-down of inventory, (2) gains or losses due to foreign exchange fluctuations, and (3) gains or losses from the disposition of a segment of the business.[24]

---

[21]APB Opinion No. 9, paragraph 23.

[22]APB Opinion No. 30, "Reporting the Results of Operations," AICPA, New York, 1973.

[23]The SEC requires a company to file Report Form 8-K within 10 days after the close of any month in which any significant problem arises; extraordinary items can fall under this requirement. The SEC requirements were extended in 1982. Now the 8-K must also be filed promptly to report the following: (1) changes in control of the corporation and how these changes occurred, (2) information about mergers, acquisitions, and dispositions, (3) bankruptcy or receivership judgments affecting the corporation, (4) changes in the corporation's certifying accountant, (5) resignation of a corporate director, and (6) additional financial information, to include pro forma financial information on acquired subsidiaries.

[24]The accounting rules for reporting the impact of foreign exchange fluctuations on earnings were set forth in FASB Statement No. 8, "Accounting for the Translation of Foreign Currency Transactions and Foreign Currency Statement," AICPA, Stamford, Conn., 1975. For a summary of the statement see David Norr, "Currency Translation and the Analyst," *Financial Analysts Journal,* July–Aug. 1976, pp. 46–54. In the article immediately following David Norr's, John K. Shank discusses the pitfalls of FASB

(continues)

How Can We See the Forest through the Trees?

We have seen that the accountants' neatly formatted income and expense statements can be misleading. Experienced fundamental common stock analysts learn that the different EPS numbers that accountants can report under GAAPs force them to come to grips with an array of "footnotes to accounting statements" and FASBs. Analysis of these perplexities can obscure the fundamental question: "Exactly what is this stock's EPS?"

The new cashflow statements that the Financial Accounting Standards Board began to require as of July 15, 1988 can help common stock analysts "see the forest through the trees." Section 16-4 describes the new cashflow statements required by FASB No. 95.

16-4   CASHFLOW STATEMENTS FURNISH AN INCOME MEASURE

The cashflows that can be taken out of a business enterprise during a given period without diminishing the firm's future profitability provide a tangible quantity on whch the financial analyst can focus. Measuring a firm's cashflow is a good way to estimate economic income. "Cash flow from operations (CFO)," for example, is a well-known measure that many accounting textbooks explain.[25] After CFO is explained, a newer cashflow measure called "free cashflow (FCF)" will be introduced.

(continued)

Statement No. 8. See John K. Shank, "FASB Statement 8 Resolved Foreign Currency Accounting—or Did It?," *Financial Analysts Journal,* July–Aug. 1976. Rita M. Rodriquez has examined the impact of FASB No. 8 on a sample of large U.S. multinationals; see her "FASB No. 8: What Has It Done to Us," *Financial Analysts Journal,* March–April 1977, pp. 40–47. She found that there was no significant impact on the earnings of the companies in her sample. More recently, FASB No. 52 has been issued to modify FASB No. 8. FASB Statement No. 52 revises the accounting requirements for translation of foreign currency transactions and foreign currency financial statements. Speaking very simply, FASB No. 52 adopts the functional currency approach and requires each financial statement to be stated in its functional foreign currency before being translated into dollars. In contrast, FASB No. 8 specified the dollar as the measuring unit for all entities.

[25]See Leopold A. Bernstein, *Financial Statement Analysis,* 3d ed. (Homewood, Ill.: Irwin, 1983), chap. 13 and its appendices, especially Appendix A. Chapter 14 suggests ways to deal with the effects of inflation. Or see chapter 14 in the fourth edition, published in 1989. Also see L. A. Bernstein and M. M. Makay, "Again Now: How Do We Measure Cashflows from Operations?," *Financial Analysts Journal,* vol. 41, no. 4, pp. 74–77.

Alternatively, see George Foster, *Financial Statement Analysis,* 2d ed. (Englewood Cliffs, N.J.: Prentice-Hall, 1986), table 3.4, p. 63. See also A. C. Sondhi, G. H. Sorter, and G. I. White, "Transactional Analysis," *Financial Analysts Journal,* Sept.–Oct. 1987, pp. 57–64.

Cashflow from Operations (CFO)

A firm's **cashflow from operations (CFO)** can be computed directly from the sources and uses statements prepared by the company's accountants. The simplest way to compute CFO is to list the elements of revenue that generate cash and the expenses that use cash; this approach focuses on the cash inflows and outflows. The framework outlined in Table 16-4 can also be used to calculate CFO indirectly from a company's income and expense statement.

The three columns on the right-hand side of Table 16-4 explain the differences between the two different income and expense statements for the same firm

Table 16-4

CONVERTING ACCRUAL ACCOUNTING FOR INCOME TO CASHFLOW ACCOUNTING
(in thousands)

	Statement B	Statement A	Key
Determine cash inflows			
Starting with sales	$9,200	$11,000	(1)
plus: Decrease (−increase) in accounts receivable	+1,800	0	
equals: Cash collections on sales	$11,000	$11,000	
plus: Other revenues (+ or − adjustment for noncash items)	−1,000	−1,000	
equals: Total cash collections from operations	$10,000	$10,000	
Deduct cash outflows			
Cost of goods sold* (excluding depreciation, amortization, etc.)	−$6,000	−$5,000	
less: Operating expenses (including depreciation)	−2,600	−2,170	
plus: Depreciation (add back since it is not a cash outlay)	+500	+300	(3)
Other expenses (including interest)			
plus: Increase (−decrease) in inventories	+1,000	0	(2)
plus: Decrease (−increase) in trade payables			
plus: Increase (−decrease) in prepaid expenses			
Pension expense adjustment	+80	0	(4)
Other expenses adjustment	+150	0	(5)
plus: Decrease (−increase) in accrued liabilities			
Income tax expense* (excluding deferred taxes— it is noncurrent)			
plus: Decrease (−increase) in accrued taxes			
equals: Total cash outflows for operations	−$6,870	−$6,870	
Net result: Cashflow from operations (CFO)	$3,130	$3,130	

*This number should exclude items that do not affect cash. Statement of Financial Accounting Standards 95 discusses taxes; if taxes were included the two CFOs would differ.
Source: L. A. Bernstein, *Financial Statement Analysis,* 3d ed. (Homewood, Ill.: Irwin, 1983, pp. 412–413. Also see Bernstein's fourth edition, 1989, p. 448.

that were shown in Table 16-1. Table 16-4 unravels the apparent disparities between the two income statements and shows (1) that the firm earned $3,130,000 cashflow from operations and (2) that this same amount of CFO can be obtained from either of the income statements in Table 16-1.[26]

The Financial Accounting Standards Board (FASB), noting the inadequacy of information provided by the traditional income and expense statements and the value of additional information provided by cashflow analysis, issued FASB No. 95, which requires all firms to include cashflow statements in their publicly disclosed financial statements after 1988.[27]

Free Cashflow (FCF)

Free cashflow (FCF) is a comprehensive measure of cashflow that includes cashflow from operations (CFO) as well as cash dividends; purchases of treasury stock; changes in certain (on and off) balance sheet items; some sources and uses items; and some footnote items such as changes in the firm's pension surplus, reserves, and accruals. To ferret out the firm's FCF, a complete set of financial statements must be analyzed. The analyst must unravel various gimmicks that accountants can use to smooth the firm's accounting profit from year to year; conceal cash "stored" in reserve accounts, surpluses, and/or accruals for future use by the firm's management; and report accounting income that diverges from the firm's economic income.

Focusing on a single share of stock instead of the entire corporation allows us to formulate a definition of a firm's economic income on a per share basis. The **economic income,** *or earnings, on a per share basis during a given period equals the maximum amount of consumption opportunities that can be withdrawn from the share during that period without diminishing the consumption opportunities that can be obtained from the share in future periods.*[28] Cash dividends provide a crude estimate of the average amount of FCF for many corporations. However, the FCF numbers contain more current information because they vary every year to reflect the firm's current activities, while cash

---

[26]For an enlightening story about the vast differences between reported earnings and book values of companies like Alcoa, Affiliated Publishing, First Boston, Merrill Lynch, Union Carbide, and Capital Cities/ABC see "The Many Ways of Figuring Financial Results," *Business Week,* April 11, 1988, p. 131. The article also compares and contrasts the accounting philosophies of the Value Line and the Standard & Poor's financial service corporations.

[27]For a discussion of how accountants initially viewed FASB 95 and how they recommend implementing it, see J. J. Mahoney, M. V. Sever, and J. A. Theis, "Cash Flow: FASB Opens the Floodgates," *Journal of Accountancy,* May 1988, pp. 27–38.

[28]Milton Friedman, *A Theory of the Consumption Function* (Princeton, N.J.: Princeton, 1957). For a deeper discussion of many of the problems raised here, see R. K. Jaedicke and R. T. Sprouse, *Accounting Flows: Income, Funds and Cash,* Prentice-Hall Foundations of Finance Series (Englewood Cliffs, N.J.: Prentice-Hall, 1965).

dividends are usually only changed every few years (*after* a sustainable change in the firm's earning power has been established).[29]

FCF can be defined in accounting-oriented terms, as shown in Equation (16-2).[30]

$$
\begin{array}{l}
\text{Free} \\
\text{cash-} \\
\text{flow}
\end{array}
=
\begin{array}{l}
\text{revenue} \\
\text{to the} \\
\text{firm}
\end{array}
-
\begin{array}{l}
\text{firm's} \\
\text{operating} \\
\text{costs}
\end{array}
-
\begin{array}{l}
\text{investments} \\
\text{to sustain} \\
\text{earnings}
\end{array}
\qquad (16\text{-}2)
$$

Ten different financial analysts will probably develop ten different estimates of the FCF for a given firm in a particular year. These differences can be

[29]For a classic investigation into the information content of cash dividend payments see John Lintner, "Distribution of Income of Corporations," *American Economic Review,* May 1956, vol. 46, pp. 97–113. Also see John Lintner, "Dividends, Earnings, Leverage, Stock Prices, and the Supply of Capital to Corporations," *Review of Economics and Statistics,* Aug. 1962. The theory of cash dividend policy was advanced significantly by E. F. Fama and H. Babiak, "Dividend Policy: An Empirical Analysis," *Journal of the American Statistical Association,* Dec. 1968, vol. 63, pp. 1132–1161.

The following empirical studies mostly reach the conclusion that cash dividends have a positive but marginally significant effect on the market value of equity shares. (1) F. Black and M. Scholes, "The Effects of Dividend Yield and Dividend Policy on Common Stock Prices and Returns," *Journal of Financial Economics,* May 1974, vol. 1, pp. 1–22. Insignificant cash dividend effects are reported. (2) M. Blume, "Stock Returns and Dividend Yields: Some More Empirical Evidence," *Review of Economics and Statistics,* Nov. 1980, pp. 567–577. Stocks that pay zero cash dividends are reported to earn abnormally high returns. (3) M. J. Brennan, "Taxes, Market Valuation and Corporate Financial Policy," *National Tax Journal,* 1970, vol. 23, pp. 417–427. (3) E. J. Elton and M. J. Gruber, "Marginal Stockholder Tax Rates and the Clientele Effect," *Review of Economics and Statistics,* Feb. 1970, vol. 52, pp. 68–74. The effects of income taxes on cash dividends are estimated empirically. (4) R. H. Litzenberger and K. Ramaswamy, "Dividends, Short Selling Restrictions, Tax-Induced Investor Clienteles and Market Equilibrium," *Journal of Finance,* May 1980, vol. 35, pp. 469–481. (5) R. H. Litzenberger and K. Ramaswamy, "The Effect of Personal Taxes and Dividends on Capital Asset Prices," *Journal of Financial Economics,* June 1979, vol. 7, pp. 163–195. A positive and significant relationship between dividend yield and common stock returns is reported. (6) M. H. Miller and M. Scholes, "Dividends and Taxes," *Journal of Financial Economics,* Dec. 1978, vol. 6, pp. 333–364. Also see M. H. Miller and M. Scholes, "Dividends and Taxes: Some Empirical Evidence," *Journal of Political Economy,* 1982, vol. 90, pp. 1118–1141. Insignificant empirical results are reported in the latter article. (7) A. R. Ofer and D. R. Siegel, "Corporate Financial Policy, Information, and Market Expectations: An Empirical Investigation of Dividends," *Journal of Finance,* Sept. 1987, vol. 42, pp. 889–911. (8) W. F. Sharpe and H. B. Sosin, "Risk, Return and Yield, New York Stock Exchange Common Stocks, 1928–1969," *Financial Analysts Journal,* March–April 1976, vol. 32, pp. 33–42.

[30]The Equation (16-2) definition of FCF is from M. H. Miller and F. Modigliani, "Dividend Policy, Growth and the Valuation of Shares," *Journal of Business,* Oct. 1961, pp. 411–433.

attributed to differences in the sophistication of the financial analysts. An accomplished financial analyst will thoroughly understand accounting, will know all the FASBs, and will analyze the Notes to the Financial Statements in order to develop refined estimates of the FCF. In contrast, unsophisticated financial analysts will develop oversimplified FCF estimates that overlook cashflow sources that are subtle but can nevertheless be substantial.[31]

A corporation's FCFs are an excellent measure of its economic income. The present value of the FCF on a per share basis, Equation (16-3), is as logical and acceptable a measure of the share's value as is the venerable present value of cash dividends model.

$$\text{Present value per share} = \sum_{t=1}^{\infty} \frac{\text{FCF per share}_t}{(1 + k)^t} \qquad (16\text{-}3)$$

where k is a risk-adjusted discount rate.

Sections 16-3 and 16-4 of this chapter delineated ambiguities in the way accounting earnings are derived and suggested guidelines to derive more meaningful income measurements. But these suggestions are not meant to indicate that accounting earnings per share are worthless information. Research has shown that, in spite of the ambiguities, accountants' earnings per share can be used to calculate price-earnings ratios, array stocks on the basis of these earnings multipliers, and select a portfolio of stocks with low price-earnings ratios that outperforms a naive buy-and-hold strategy.

16-5   **BASU'S PORTFOLIOS OF STOCKS WITH LOW P/E RATIOS**

The theory of price-earnings ratios (called simply P/E ratios hereafter) was spelled out in Chapter 15. This section presents empirical evidence about a well-known investment strategy based on P/E ratios. The strategy is easy to apply: Buy stocks that have low P/E ratios in order to earn high risk-adjusted rates of return. Respected investment advisors use low P/E ratios as one of

---

[31]The use of free cashflow (FCF) and related cashflow measures is becoming increasingly popular with professional investors. See J. M. Laderman, "The Savviest Investors Are Going with the Flow," *Business Week,* Sept. 7, 1987, p. 92. See also J. M. Laderman, "A Divining Rod for Deal Stocks Is Striking Gold," *Business Week,* March 21, 1988, p. 120.

Two related investment advisory firms in Fort Lee, N.J. [Cash Flow Investors, Inc. (CFI) and Systematic Financial Management] manage money by investing in those firms that generate the highest rates of FCF. The CFI common stock portfolio, for example, is always fully invested in common stocks; no attempt is made to outguess the market's ups and downs. Stocks are selected by proprietary software that analyzes the FCF of thousands of stocks daily. The CFI common stock portfolios earn higher rates of return than the S&P 500.

their investment criteria, with significant success.[32] A classic study that advocates the selection of low P/E stocks and thoroughly documents the results of the strategy was done by Dr. S. Basu.[33]

Dr. Basu analyzed market data on over 750 NYSE listed stocks from the 14-year period between September 1956 and August 1971. The first step in his analysis was to array all these stocks based on the values of their year-end P/Es. Second, Basu formed five equal-sized portfolios from the quintiles of each year's array of the stocks' P/E's. Third, the monthly rates of return for the five P/E quintile portfolios were calculated using the stocks' returns from the following year. Returns from the *following year* were used because this simulates selecting an investment portfolio on the basis of historical P/E ratios. Fourth, Basu computed the characteristic line in risk-premium form, Equation (16-4), for the quintile portfolios formed each year using the following year's returns.

$$r_{p,t} - R_t = A_p + B_p(r_{m,t} - R_t) + e_{p,t} \qquad (16\text{-}4)$$

where $r_{p,t} - R_t$ = risk premium on the pth P/E quintile portfolio in tth month

$r_{m,t} - R_t$ = rate of return risk premium in the tth month from Lorie-Fisher market index

A_p = alpha regression intercept coefficient or Jensen's portfolio performance measure (explained in Chapter 21) for pth quintile portfolio

[32]The ability of investment advice published in the *Value Line Investment Survey* to outperform the market has been documented by several studies. See Fischer Black, "Yes Virginia, There Is Hope: Tests of the Value Line Ranking System," *Financial Analysts Journal,* Sept.–Oct. 1973. Also see T. E. Copeland and D. Mayers, "The Value Line Enigma, 1965–1978: A Case Study of Performance Evaluation Issues," *Journal of Financial Economics,* 1982, vol. 1, no. 3. See also L. Brown and M. Rozeff, "The Superiority of Analysts Forecasts as Measures of Expectations: Evidence from Earnings," *Journal of Finance,* March 1978, pp. 1–16. Also see C. Holloway, "A Note on Testing an Aggressive Strategy Using Value Line Ranks," *Journal of Finance,* June 1981, pp. 711–719.

[33]S. Basu, "The Investment Performance of Common Stocks in Relation to Their Price-Earnings Ratios: A Test of the Efficient Markets Hypothesis," *Journal of Finance,* June 1977, vol. XXXII, no. 3, pp. 663–682. More recently, assertions that the P/E ratio subsumes the "size effect" are made by S. Basu, "The Relationship between Earnings Yield, Market Value, and the Return for NYSE Stocks: Further Evidence," *Journal of Financial Economics,* 1983, vol. 12, no. 1.

Evidence that sample selection bias affected Basu's statistics has been published by R. Banz and W. Breen, "Sample-Dependent Results Using Accounting and Market Data: Some Evidence," *Journal of Finance,* Sept. 1986, vol. 41, no. 4, pp. 779–793. For a more recent empirical test of Basu's hypothesis that finds different results see R. Stafford Johnson, Lyle C. Fiore, and Richard Zuber, "The Investment Performance of Common Stocks in Relation to Their Price-Earnings Ratios: An Update of the Basu Study," *The Financial Review,* Aug. 1989, vol. 24, no. 3, pp. 499–505.

B_p = beta regression slope coefficient for portfolio p or index of pth portfolio's systematic risk

$e_{p,t}$ = residual return for portfolio p in month t which was left unexplained by regression

Basu replicated the four steps outlined above using Equation (16-4) for each of the 14 years. Table 16-5 contains summary statistics. Quintile portfolio 5 contains the 20 percent of the stocks with the highest P/E's. Portfolio 1 contains the one-fifth of the stocks with the lowest P/E's and, purportedly, the highest risk-adjusted rates of return. Essentially, each quintile portfolio in Table 16-5 may be viewed as a mutual fund that acquires many NYSE stocks in a given P/E quintile (but no others) on April 1, holds the portfolio 1 year, and then

Table 16-5

BASU'S PERFORMANCE MEASURES AND RELATED STATISTICS FOR QUINTILE PORTFOLIOS ARRAYED ON P/E RATIOS, 1957–1971

Performance	Quintile P/E portfolio[a]					Market portfolio[a]	
	5	4	3	2	1	S	F
Median P/E ratio[b]	35.8	19.1	15.0	12.8	9.8	15.1	
Average annual rate of return r_p^c	0.0934	0.0928	0.1165	0.1355	0.1563	0.1211	0.1174
Average annual excess return $r_p'^d$	0.0565	0.0558	0.0796	0.0985	0.2260	0.0841	0.0804
Systematic beta risk B_p	1.1121	1.0387	0.9678	0.9401	0.9866	1.0085	1.0000
Treynor's reward-to-volatility measure[e]	0.0508	0.0537	0.0822	0.1047	0.1237	0.0834	0.0804
Sharpe's reward-to-variability measure[f]	0.0903	0.0967	0.1475	0.1886	0.2264	0.1526	0.1481
Jensen's measure of average excess return[g] and	−0.0330	−0.0277	0.0017	0.0228	0.0467	0.0030	
t value in parentheses	(−2.62)	(−2.85)	(0.18)	(2.73)	(3.98)	(0.62)	

[a]5 = highest P/E quintile, 1 = lowest P/E quintile, S = total sample, and F = Fisher stock market index.
[b]Based on 1957–1971 pooled data.
[c]$\overline{r}_p = (\sum_{t=1}^{168} r'_{pt})/14$, where r'_{pt} is the continuously compounded return of portfolio p in month t (April 1957 to March 1971).
[d]$\overline{r}_p = (\sum_{t=1}^{168} r'_{pt})/14$, where r'_{pt} is the continuously compounded excess return ($r'_{pt} - r_{ft}$) of portfolio p in month t (April 1957 to March 1971).
[e]Mean excess return on portfolio p divided by its systematic risk, Eq. (21-4).
[f]Mean excess return on portfolio p divided by its standard deviation, Eq. (21-2).
[g]The regression intercept term in Eq. (21-6).
Source: S. Basu, "The Investment Performance of Common Stocks Relative to Their Price-Earnings Ratios: A Test of the Efficient Markets Hypothesis," *Journal of Finance,* June 1977, table 1.

liquidates it and reinvests the proceeds in a similar P/E quintile portfolio on April 1 of each year thereafter.

The top three lines of Table 16-5 support the theory about P/E's. The first and second quintile portfolios, with their low P/E's, earned much higher average rates of return and had higher average risk premiums than the quintile portfolios with higher P/E's. The inverse relationship between P/E and average return is clearly visible in the top three lines. However, these statistics in the top three lines *ignore the effects of differences in risk*.

The fourth line of Table 16-5 lists the five quintile portfolios' beta systematic risk coefficients. There is no obvious relationship between the P/E's of the five portfolios and their betas. Thus, it appears that the differences in returns documented in the second and third lines of Table 16-5 are purely the result of P/E's.

The fifth, sixth, and seventh lines in Table 16-5 present Treynor's, Sharpe's, and Jensen's risk-adjusted investment performance measures.[34] All three measures vary inversely with the P/E of the quintile portfolio, providing further evidence to support the idea that, on average, low P/E stocks earn better *risk-adjusted rates of return* than high P/E stocks. These results from three different investment performance measures (that all measure return per unit of risk borne) are even more impressive than the simple return data shown in the first three lines of Table 16-5.

The resounding success of simply buying stocks with low P/E's gave Dr. Basu some pause; it appeared too easy to earn superior rates of return. Furthermore, the superior risk-adjusted rates of return from low P/E stocks seemed to violate the efficient market hypothesis (introduced in Section 8-6). Therefore, Dr. Basu pressed his inquiry further to be certain that the low P/E ratio investment strategy was advisable.

Basu deducted an allowance for the security analysis and portfolio management expenses that are appropriate for a large portfolio in order to determine the returns net of these costs. More specifically, he deducted (1) the NYSE commissions that existed during his sample period, (2) a research fee of ¼ of 1 percent each year, and (3) federal income taxes appropriate for an investor in the 50 percent tax bracket. After these costs were deducted from the quintile portfolio with the lowest P/E, Dr. Basu found that the portfolio earned from 0.5 to 2.5 percent per annum more than a randomly selected portfolio (that is, without regard to the stocks' P/E's) in the same risk class.

Basu's after-costs results are well worth considering when selecting common stocks. The one or two percentage points per year additional rate of return that an investor who must pay commissions and income taxes could hope to attain

---

[34]Treynor's investment performance measure is defined in Equation (21-4) and illustrated in Figure 21-5. Sharpe's portfolio performance measure is defined in Equation (21-2) and illustrated in Figure 21-2. Equations (21-5) and (21-6) define the Jensen measure and Figure 21-6 illustrates it.

from the lowest P/E portfolio is a statistically significant additional annual return. Stated differently, selecting low P/E stocks appears to be a slow but fairly steady way to outperform the naive buy-and-hold strategy.

16-6   SUMMARY AND CONCLUSIONS

A company's assets are only worth their auction value if they cannot be used to generate earnings. The empirical results summarized in Figures 16-1 and 16-2 furnish compelling evidence that earning power is the engine that drives the stock prices of corporations that are going concerns.

Fundamental common stock analysis requires many skills. Patience is needed to sift through a company's income and expense statement and find the places where the GAAP failed to produce reports that reflect the economic realities of the transaction. Familiarity with the Financial Accounting Standards Board (FASB) rulings is needed to supplement the basic accounting skills, and a "detective's nose for the unusual" is essential when endeavoring to unscramble a set of accounting statements. When punctilious financial analysis reveals income and expense statements that are deceptive, an entirely new earnings estimate must be prepared.

The financial analyst must exercise additional care when the corporation's earnings estimate is reduced to a per share basis. Extraordinary income and loss items must be handled according to narrow FASB guidelines, and the potential for EPS dilution must be fully reported.

Cashflow measurements offer the financial analyst an alternative route to obtaining unbiased estimates of a company's earnings. FASB No. 95 went into effect in 1988; it dictates that the accounting profession provide cashflow statements to supplement the traditional set of financial statements. Sophisticated financial analysts can go a step farther and estimate the firm's free cashflow (FCF).

$$\begin{matrix} \text{Free} \\ \text{cash-} \\ \text{flow} \end{matrix} = \begin{matrix} \text{revenue} \\ \text{to the} \\ \text{firm} \end{matrix} - \begin{matrix} \text{the firm's} \\ \text{operating} \\ \text{costs} \end{matrix} - \begin{matrix} \text{investments} \\ \text{to sustain} \\ \text{earnings} \end{matrix} \qquad (16\text{-}2)$$

The present value of the FCF on a per share basis, Equation (16-3), is a logical and acceptable measure of the intrinsic value of an equity share.

In spite of the ambiguities that can detract from the information value of a corporation's reported earnings, the accounting statements nevertheless provide valuable earnings information. Dr. Basu showed how the price-earnings ratio that is computed from reported accounting earnings can be used to select stocks that have good price-appreciation potential. His analysis showed that stocks with low P/E ratios earned risk-adjusted rates of return that beat the returns earned by a naive buy-and-hold strategy.

Essay Questions

16-1   Why are fundamental common stock analysts concerned with the level and trend of a corporation's earnings? Explain.

16-2   How would reported assets, expenses, and accounting income be affected by a switch from LIFO to FIFO inventory valuation during an inflationary period? Explain.

16-3   Explain three ways in which a company can manipulate its earnings within the framework of generally accepted accounting principles. Give examples of each.

16-4   Answer the following question that appeared on the 1980 Level One Chartered Financial Analysts (CFA) exam. (*a*) Generally accepted accounting principles require the presentation of corporate earnings per share data on the face of the income statement. (1) Explain the meaning of "primary earnings per share." (2) Explain how "fully diluted earnings per share" differs from "primary earnings per share." (*b*) Comment on the probable reason(s) why an industrial company might choose to use straight-line depreciation for financial reporting purposes while using accelerated depreciation for tax purposes. (*c*) Briefly discuss the impact of the accounting recognition of deferred income taxes on a company's cashflow.

16-5   Distinguish between (*a*) an extraordinary item and (*b*) a prior period adjustment.

16-6   What are some *accounting factors* which could cause a firm's historical average growth rate to decrease in future years? To increase?

16-7   Answer the following questions from the 1982 exam for Chartered Financial Analysts (CFA).

>   There are certain accounting signals that might be viewed as tipoffs to deteriorating earnings capacity and financial position. While these signals are not prima facie evidence of trouble, they are at least an indication that further analysis is in order by an analyst. For each of the following, discuss why deterioration might be implied: (*a*) increase in receivables, (*b*) changes in accounting policies, (*c*) intangible assets increase, (*d*) increases in non-recurring income, (*e*) reserve manipulations.

16-8   Compare and contrast the following pairs of words and phrases: (*a*) accelerated depreciation, straight-line depreciation, (*b*) FIFO, LIFO, (*c*) balance sheet, income statement, (*d*) cashflow from operations (CFO), accountant's net income, (*e*) capitalizing, expensing, (*f*) accrual accounting, cash accounting, (*g*) special items, extraordinary items.

16-9   Consider the empirical studies of earnings announcements discussed in Section 16-1. The Niederhoffer and Reagan (NR) study discerned no rational relationship between forecasted earnings and stock prices. In view of the NR findings, how was the study by Foster, Olsen, and Shevlin (FOS) able to use earnings forecasts to rationalize stock prices?

Problems

16-10 The Alpha Corporation purchased a $100 asset and depreciated it straight-line over 4 years. The Omega Corporation purchased a $100 asset and depreciated it using the sum-of-the-digits method over 4 years. Assume that both the Alpha and the Omega Corporations had sales of $10,000 per year, had total expenses (with the exception of the new depreciation expense) of $9000 per year, and are in the 40 percent income tax bracket every year for at least the next 4 years. What is the after-tax income for the Alpha and the Omega Corporations every year for each of the next 4 years? Show your computations.

16-11 Compare and contrast the price-earnings (P/E) ratio with its reciprocal, the earnings ratio (E/P). (*a*) Do the two ratios convey the same information? (*b*) Is one of the two ratios preferable for the purpose of doing numerical analysis?

16-12 Two financial analysts named Whitbeck and Kisor (W&K) are analyzing the common stock issued by the Roist Corporation. The stock is selling at a price of $p = \$130$ per share, earnings per share are EPS $= \$7.00$, and the cash dividend is $d = \$3.50$ per share. W&K projected a $g = 6$ percent growth rate for Roist with a standard deviation for the growth rate of 5 percent. In an effort to ascertain if the Roist stock was undervalued, W&K estimated the following cross-sectional regression model to explain the P/E ratios of stocks.[35]

$$\text{P/E} = 8.2 + 1.5(g, \%) + 0.067[(d/\text{EPS}), \%] - 0.20(\text{S.D.}, \%)$$

(*a*) What P/E ratio do you think is appropriate for the Roist stock? (*b*) Is the Roist stock undervalued at its market price of $p = \$130$ per share?

16-13 Reconsider the Roist stock from the preceding question. Suppose that W&K revise their growth rate estimate upward from 6 to 10 percent while all other values remain unchanged. (*a*) What theoretical P/E ratio is appropriate for Roist under the new growth assumption? (*b*) What is Roist's intrinsic value per share with the higher growth rate?

16-14 Compare and contrast Whitbeck and Kisor's cross-sectional regression model to evaluate price-earnings ratios, from Problem 16-12, with the theoretically derived formula for the price-earnings ratio from Chapter 15 and Equation (15-13*b*). Are the two models compatible?

$$m_{i,0} = \frac{p_i}{\text{EPS}_{i,0}} = \frac{d_{i,1}/\text{EPS}_{i,0}}{k_i - g_i} \qquad (15\text{-}13b)$$

Compare the two models with respect to the effects that (*a*) the growth rate, (*b*) the riskiness of the stock, and (*c*) the stock's cash dividend payout ratio have on the price-earnings ratio.

[35]V. Whitbeck and M. Kisor, "A New Tool in Investment Decision-Making," *Financial Analysts Journal*, May–June 1963, pp. 55–62. Many estimates of this classic model have been prepared since W&K first suggested the model.

16-15 Consider the IBM data in Table 15-6. Why do you think IBM's price-earnings ratio fluctuated from a low of 10 in 1984 to a high of 18 in 1986?

Selected References

Bernstein, Leopold A., *Financial Statement Analysis,* 4th ed. (Homewood, Ill.: Irwin, 1989).

Chapters 10 through 14 delve into analysis of earnings, cashflows, and suggestions for dealing with the effects of inflation on financial statements.

Bildersee, John S., "Some Aspects of the Performance of Nonconvertible Preferred Stocks," *Journal of Finance,* Dec. 1973, vol. XXVIII, no. 5, pp. 1187–1201.

A risk-return analysis of the nonconvertible preferred stock investment security. Simple correlation and regression analysis are used. This article distills Bildersee's unpublished doctoral dissertation entitled "Risk and Return on Preferred Stocks," University of Chicago, 1971.

Briloff, Abraham, *Unaccountable Accounting* (New York: Harper & Row, 1972).

A nonmathematical, case-by-case discussion, giving names of large corporations and large CPA firms, dates, and numerous actual examples of accounting entries which do not reflect the economic realities.

Cottle, Sidney, Roger F. Murray, and Frank E. Block, *Security Analysis* (New York: McGraw-Hill, 1988).

Chapters 10 through 17 inclusive present a detailed explanation of the traditional approach to analyzing an income statement. Chapters 18 and 19 address the balance sheet.

Foster, George, *Financial Statement Analysis,* 2d ed. (Englewood Cliffs, N.J.: Prentice-Hall, 1986).

An approach to financial analysis that relies heavily on economic theory and uses simple econometric analysis of empirical data is explained in this book. The accounting aspects of financial statement analysis are not stressed.

Part 5

Movements of Stock Prices

Chapter 17

Technical Analysis

There are two main approaches to analyzing securities—technical analysis and fundamental analysis. This chapter explains the philosophy of technical analysis and presents tools used by technical analysts.

A **technical analyst,** or **technician,** is a security analyst who believes it is not productive to work through all the fundamental facts about the issuing corporation—the company's earnings, its products, forthcoming legislation that might affect the firm, ad infinitum. Instead, technical analysts believe that these innumerable fundamental facts are summarized and represented by the market prices of a security. Technical analysts focus most of their attention on *charts of security market prices* and on related summary statistics about security transactions. As a result, technical analysts are sometimes called **chartists.** Most technical analysts prepare and study charts of various financial variables in order to make forecasts about security prices, but an increasing number use quantitative rather than graphical tools. Dozens of different techniques are used by professional technical analysts.[1] In this chapter, we will explore some of the more prominent technical analysis tools. But first, we will review the concepts that are at the core of technical analysis.

17-1   **THEORETICAL FOUNDATION OF TECHNICAL ANALYSIS**

Technical analysis is based on the widely accepted premise that security prices are determined by the supply of, and the demand for, securities. The tools of technical analysis are therefore designed to measure certain aspects of supply

---

[1]Dr. Richard Bookstaber has proposed a modern, computer-based quantitative approach to technical analysis; see Richard Bookstaber, *The Complete Investment Book* (Glenview, Ill.: Scott, Foresman, 1985), chaps. 14–20.

and demand. Typically, technical analysts record historical financial data on charts, study these charts in search of patterns that they find meaningful, and endeavor to use the patterns to predict future prices. Some charts are used to predict the movements of a single security, others are used to predict the movements of a market index, and, still others are used to predict the action of both individual assets and the market. Some of these same charts are also used to predict the fluctuations in the price of a commodity, a foreign exchange, or a rate of interest.

A classic book by Edwards and Magee[2] articulated the basic assumptions underlying technical analysis as follows:

1. Market value is determined by the interaction of supply and demand.

2. Supply and demand are governed by numerous factors, both rational and irrational.

3. Security prices tend to move in trends that persist for an appreciable length of time, despite minor fluctuations in the market.

4. Changes in a trend are caused by the shifts in supply and demand.

5. Shifts in supply and demand, no matter why they occur, can be detected sooner or later in charts of market transactions.

6. Some chart patterns tend to repeat themselves.

In essence, technical analysts believe that past patterns of market action will recur in the future and can therefore be used for predictive purposes.

Chapters 15 and 16 explained how fundamental analysts estimate the *value* of shares of stock. In contrast, technical analysts estimate *prices* instead of values. They tend to ignore fundamental valuation facts such as the firms' risks and earnings growth rates in favor of various barometers of supply and demand they have devised. A classic technical analysis book lyrically asserts that[3]:

> It is futile to assign an intrinsic value to a stock certificate. One share of United States Steel, for example, was worth $261 in the early fall of 1929, but you could buy it for only $22 in June 1932. By March 1937, it was selling for $126 and just one year later for $38 . . . . This sort of thing, this wide divergence between presumed value and actual value, is not the exception; it is the rule; it is going on all the time. The fact is that the real value of a share of U.S. Steel common is determined at any given time solely, definitely and inexorably by supply and demand, which are accurately reflected in the transactions consummated on the floor of the . . . Exchange.
>
> Of course, the statistics which the fundamentalists study play a part in the supply and demand equation—that is freely admitted. But there are many other

---

[2]R. D. Edwards and John Magee, Jr., *Technical Analysis of Stock Trends,* 4th ed. (Springfield, Mass.: John Magee, 1958), p. 86.
[3]R. D. Edwards and John Magee, Jr., *Technical Analysis of Stock Trends,* 4th ed. (Springfield, Mass.: John Magee, 1958), p. 3.

factors affecting it. The market price reflects not only the differing fears and guesses and moods, rational and irrational, of hundreds of potential buyers and sellers, as well as their needs and their resources—in total, factors which defy analysis and for which no statistics are obtainable, but which are nevertheless all synthesized, weighted and finally expressed in one precise figure at which a buyer and seller get together and make a deal (through their agents, their respective brokers). This is the only figure that counts.

   In brief, the going price as established by the market itself comprehends all the fundamental information which the statistical analyst can hope to learn (plus some which is perhaps secret to him, known only to a few insiders) and much else besides of equal or even greater importance.

This quotation makes some strong assertions and articulates the spirit of technical analysis.

In defending their practices, most technical analysts do not accuse fundamental analysts of being illogical. In fact, some security analysts use both fundamental and technical security analysis tools. However, the technical analysis purists assert the superiority of their methods over fundamental analysis by pointing out that technical analysis is easier, faster, and can be simultaneously applied to more stocks than fundamental analysis. This latter claim is true. However, if technical analysis cannot predict security prices very well, the fact that it is easier to learn or simpler to use is inadequate justification.

Many technical analysts would say that fundamental analysis is not worthless, but it is just too troublesome to bother with. First, they point out that even if a fundamental analyst does find an underpriced security, they must wait and hope that the rest of the market recognizes the security's true value and bids its price up. Second, fundamental analysis is hard work. Third, technical analysts cite the inadequacy of the income statements produced by accountants (as discussed in Chapter 16) which form the basis for much fundamental analysis. Finally, technical analysts point out the subjective aspects of the earnings multipliers used by fundamental analysts. In view of these undesirable aspects of fundamental analysis, consider some of the tools used by technical analysts to measure supply and demand and to forecast securities prices.[4]

17-2   **THE VENERABLE DOW THEORY**
_____

The Dow theory is one of the oldest and most famous technical tools; it was originated by Charles Dow, founder of the Dow Jones Company and editor of *The Wall Street Journal* around 1900. Mr. Dow died in 1902, and the Dow

---

[4]Although this chapter focuses on charting of common stock prices, technical analysis of other market indicators and other types of financial instruments is also widely practiced. For an admiring report about the profitability of one group's technical analysis in commodity trading, see Shawn Tully, "Princeton's Rich Commodity Scholars," *Fortune,* Feb. 9, 1981, pp. 94–98.

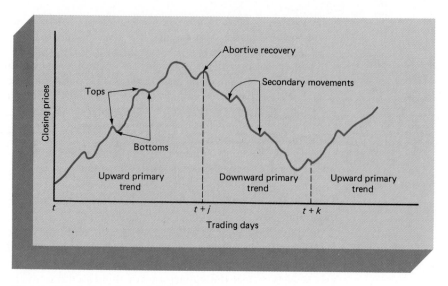

Figure 17-1 A line chart of daily prices annotated with Dow theory signals.

theory was developed further and given its name by staff members at *The Wall Street Journal.* Today, many versions of the theory exist and are used; it is the basis for much of the work done by technical analysts. The Dow theory is used to delineate trends in the market as a whole or in individual securities. According to Mr. Dow[5]:

> The market is always considered as having three movements, all going at the same time. The first is the narrow movement from day to day. The second is the short swing, running from two weeks to a month or more; the third is the main movement, covering at least 4 years in duration.

Dow theory practitioners refer to these three components as:

1. **Primary trends** are commonly called bear or bull markets. Delineating primary trends is the primary goal of the Dow theorists.
2. **Secondary movements** last only a few months. Secondary movements are sometimes called *corrections.*
3. **Tertiary moves** are simply the daily fluctuations. The Dow theory asserts that daily fluctuations are essentially meaningless random wiggles. Nonetheless, the chartist should plot the asset's price or the mar-

---

[5]*The Wall Street Journal,* Dec. 19, 1900.

ket average each day in order to trace out the primary and secondary trends.[6]

Figure 17-1 is a **line chart** that a Dow theorist might develop. Line charts are constructed by plotting each day's closing (or opening, or high, or low) prices and connecting them with a piecewise continuous line. Figure 17-1 shows a primary uptrend existing from period t to the peak price, which occurred just before day $t + j$. On trading day $t + j$, an "abortive recovery" occurs, signaling a change in the direction of the market's primary movement. An **abortive recovery** occurs when a secondary movement fails to rise above the preceding top. Before $t + j$, all the tops are ascending; but after the abortive recovery, the tops are descending until just before day $t + k$. At $t + k$, a secondary movement fails to reach a new bottom, signaling the start of a bull market. Most Dow theorists do not believe that the emergence of a new primary trend has been truly *confirmed* until the pattern of ascending or descending tops occurs in both the industrial and railroad averages.[7]

17-3　　　　　**BAR CHARTS**

Technical analysts employ different charting techniques. Figure 17-1 is an example of a line chart. Figure 17-2 is a bar chart. **Bar charts** have vertical bars representing each day's price movement. Each bar spans the distance from the day's highest price to the day's lowest price, and a small cross on each bar marks that day's closing price.

Line charts and bar charts usually have bar graphs along the bottoms of the charts showing the **volume of shares traded** at each date. Figure 17-2 shows such volume data. Next to the prices, trading volume is the second most important statistic technicians follow. As an example of how technical analysts try to relate stock price moves and the volume of shares traded, consider a pattern called the "head and shoulders" formation.

---

[6]For a discussion of how to measure trends via computer see Richard Bookstaber, *The Complete Investment Book* (Glenview, Ill.: Scott, Foresman, 1985), chap. 19.

[7]A supportive empirical test of the Dow theory is reported by David A. Glickstein and Rolf E. Wubbels, "Dow Theory Is Alive and Well," *Journal of Portfolio Management*, April 1983, pp. 28–31. Statistically speaking, the Dow theory is based on trends that can be measured by serial correlation (or autocorrelation) coefficients that are significantly different from zero. In 1988 Fama and French reported statistically significant trends in security prices measured over 3- to 5-year periods. The longer-term serial correlations they reported measure the type trends on which the Dow theory and some other technical analysis theories are based. See E. F. Fama and K. R. French, "Permanent and Temporary Components of Stock Prices," *Journal of Political Economy*, April 1988, vol. 96, no. 2, pp. 246–273.

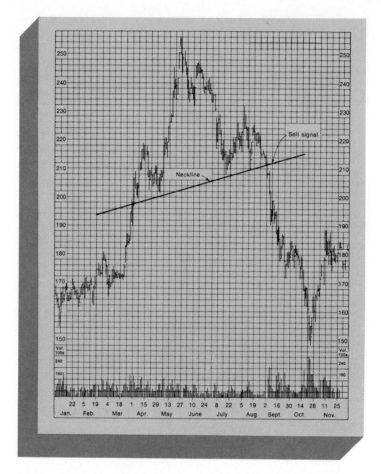

Figure 17-2 A bar chart of a head and shoulders top formation.

Head and Shoulders Top on a Bar Chart

A head and shoulders top (HST) is a formation which is supposed to signal that the security's price has reached a top and will decline in the future. Figure 17-2 shows a HST; the market action that forms a HST can be broken down into four phases.

1. *Left shoulder:* A period of heavy buying followed by a lull in trading pushes the price up to a new peak before the price begins to slide down.

2. *Head:* A spurt of heavy buying raises prices to a new high and then allows the price to fall back below the top of the left shoulder.

3. *Right shoulder:* A moderate rally lifts the price somewhat but fails to push prices as high as the top of the head before a decline begins.

4. *Confirmation or breakout:* Prices fall below the neckline, that is, the line drawn tangent to the bottoms of the left and right shoulders.

This breakout is supposed to precede a price drop and is a signal to sell. The chart in Figure 17-2 could be for either a market index or an individual asset.

Many Other Patterns Exist

Technical analysts have described numerous patterns that they believe will indicate the direction of future price movements. Triangles, pennants, flags, channels, rectangles, double tops, triple tops, wedge formations, and diamonds are only some of the patterns for which chartists search. A minority of chartists employ very complex charts and/or search for very intricate patterns. *Point-and-figure charts* and the *Elliot wave theory* are the names of some of these more elaborate charting techniques. In addition, someone with a rich imagination can conceive new patterns and interpret them as they see fit at any time.

17-4   **CONTRARY OPINION THEORIES**

Theories of contrary opinion advocate doing the opposite of what some particular group of investors are doing. The **odd-lot theory,** for instance, assumes that small investors are usually wrong, and it is therefore advantageous to pursue strategies that are the opposite of what the odd-lotters are doing.

The Odd-Lot Theory

Round lots are transactions involving multiples of 100 shares. **Odd lots** are transactions of less than 100 shares. Since the sales commissions on odd lots are higher than the commissions on round lots, professional investors rarely trade odd lots. Most odd-lot purchases are made by amateur investors with limited resources—''the man in the street.''

Odd-lot trading volume is reported in the financial section of many large newspapers. The odd-lot statistics are broken down into the number of shares purchased, sold, and sold short. Most odd-lot theorists chart the ratio of odd-lot sales to odd-lot purchases week by week. Some odd-lot chartists, however, chart only the odd-lot statistics from Mondays since odd-lot traders are believed to transact most of their trading on Mondays. The odd-lot purchases-sales index is typically plotted concurrently with some market index—it is used by some chartists as a leading indicator of market prices. High odd-lot purchases-sales ratios are presumed to forecast falls in market prices, and low purchases-sales ratios are presumed to occur toward the end of bear markets.

Figure 17-3 shows the S&P 500 Composite Stock Index and the Dow Jones Industrial Average in the top two panels. The concurrent odd-lotter purchases-sales ratio is shown in the bottom panel of Figure 17-3. The October 1987 international stock market crash is noteworthy; let us focus on that event and see how well the technical indicators forecasted it. During the weeks prior to October 1987, contrary to the odd-lot theory of contrary opinion, the odd-lotters were increasingly selling more shares than they bought as the market rose to its pre-October high. After the October 1987 crash the odd-lotters

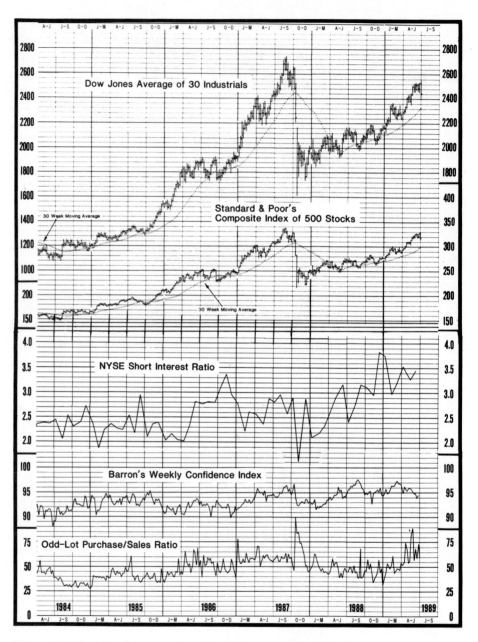

Figure 17-3 Graphs of two stock market indicators, the NYSE Short Interest Ratio, *Barron's* confidence index, and the odd-lotters purchases-sales ratio. (*Source: Daily Action Stock Charts,* June 16, 1989, pp. 4 and 5; Trendline, a Division of Standard & Poor's, New York.)

became big buyers when stock prices were near their lows—the best time to buy. These rational trading patterns by odd-lotters defy the contrary opinion theory about them.[8] In order to avoid being hurt by technical trading rules that do not perform as they should, technical analysts typically look for **confirmation** by searching for other indicators that are issuing the same signal as the indicator they are following. As more confirmations are found from other technical indicators that are all simultaneously issuing the same signal to buy or sell, the technical analyst grows more confident that it is time to consummate a trade.

Two Different Theories About Short Sellers

Several chartists follow short-sales trading statistics. (Short sales are defined in Section 8-3.) Some short-sales followers use aggregate statistics as an indicator of overall market sentiment, and some follow the short sales for individual securities in search of information about that security. However, both groups interpret a high level of **outstanding short sales** (or **uncovered short positions** or **short interest,** as it is variously called) as a sign of increased future demand for securities with which to cover outstanding short positions. Thus, rising short sales is believed to foretell future demand for securities that will bid up their prices. This is the **short-sales contrary opinion** theory.

Figure 17-3 illustrates the **NYSE Short Interest Ratio,** which measures the total amount of short sales, stated as a percentage of the total volume of shares traded, measured over the 30 trading days around the tenth of each month. A ratio above 1.5 percent is considered bullish, and below 1.0 percent is bearish. The empirical data graphed in the middle panel of Figure 17-3 contradict this contrary opinion theory at the time the October 1987 stock market crash occurred. The NYSE Short Interest Ratio varied at high levels above 2.5 for months prior to October 1987. However, all of this short interest did not create enough demand for purchases to cover the short sales to prevent the October crash. The NYSE Short Interest Ratio gave the wrong signal. Instead of giving the warnings the contrary opinion theory suggests, the NYSE Short Interest Ratio seems to indicate that short sellers were trading rationally before the October 1987 crash.

In startling contrast to the followers of the short-sales contrary opinion theory, another group of technical analysts believes that short sellers tend to be *more sophisticated* than the average investor. This second group asserts that when short sales for the market as a whole or for an individual security are high, sophisticated investors expect a price decline, and it should therefore follow shortly. Around October of 1987 the center panel in Figure 17-3 provides evidence in support of this second short-sales theory. However, it is not clear that either of the two short-sales technical theories that we considered here

---

[8]For another view, see T. J. Kewley and R. A. Stevenson, "The Odd-Lot Theory for Individual Stocks," *Financial Analysts Journal,* Jan.–Feb. 1969. There is much conflicting evidence about technical analysis. This study, for example, suggests that the odd-lot theory gives good buy signals but not good sell signals.

give reliable insights.[9] That is why most technical analysts follow more than one technical indicator.[10]

The confidence index is defined as the ratio of high-grade bond yields divided by low-grade bond yields. The ratio is supposed to reveal how willing investors are to take investment risks. When bond investors grow more confident about the strength of the national economy, they shift their holdings from high-grade to lower-grade bonds in order to obtain the higher yields. This change bids up the prices of low-grade bonds, lowers their yields relative to high-grade bonds, and increases the confidence index.

Calculating the Confidence Index

Barron's, the weekly financial newspaper, publishes figures on the confidence index regularly in its *Market Laboratory* section. The **Barron's confidence index** is the ratio of the average yield from *Barron's* list of the 10 highest-grade bonds over the average yield of the Dow Jones 40 bond index. The equation below defines the *Barron's* confidence index (BCI).

$$\text{BCI} = \frac{\text{average yield of } Barron's \text{ 10 highest-grade bonds at time } t}{\text{average yield of Dow Jones 40 bonds at period } t \text{ (lesser grade)}}$$

The *Barron's* definition of the confidence index is widely used because it is published each week, but it has no intrinsic superiority over another confidence index (CI) that is defined somewhat similarly.

Interpretation of the Confidence Index

The confidence index has an upper limit of positive unity (CI < +1.0) since the yields on high-quality bonds can never be as high as the yields on similar low-quality bonds. In periods of economic boom, as investors grow optimistic

---

[9]For an empirical report that strongly supports the idea that a high (low) level of short interest is a reliable bullish (bearish) market indicator, see Thomas J. Kerrigan, ''The Short Interest Ratio and Its Component Parts,'' *Financial Analysts Journal,* Nov.–Dec. 1974, pp. 45–49. Kerrigan's study also cites other studies of the short interest that, as he points out, contradict his findings.

[10]Investors Intelligence of Larchmont, New York, publishes a Sentiment Index (SI) that is a ratio. The SI ratio is defined as the number of investment advisers who are bearish divided by the total number of investment advisers. The SI is promoted as a contrary opinion tool. For an empirical study that reports the SI is worthless, see Michael E. Solt and Meir Statman, ''How Useful Is the Sentiment Index?,'' *Financial Analysts Journal,* Sept.–Oct. 1988, pp. 45–55.

and their risk aversion diminishes, the yield spread between high- and low-quality bonds narrows and the confidence index rises. A rising confidence index is interpreted by chartists as an indication that the managers of the "smart money" are optimistic. On the assumption that the wisdom of these investors will be borne out, confidence index technicians predict that the stock market will *follow* the leadership of the "smart" money managers. Some confidence index technicians claim that the confidence index leads the stock market by 2 to 11 months. Thus, an upturn in the confidence index is supposed to foretell rising optimism and rising prices in the stock market. Conversely, a fall in the index is expected to precede a drop in stock prices.

The next-to-the-bottom panel of Figure 17-3 displays the *Barron's* confidence index (BCI). The BCI was at historically high levels and rising prior to the October 1987 crash. This buy signal was very costly for those technicians who followed it.

There is no question that the confidence index tends to be positively correlated with the stock market over the complete business cycle. This is not unique, however; numerous economic series are correlated with the stock market. The confidence index is usually, but not always, a leading indication. Like most other technical indicators, the confidence index sometimes issues erroneous signals and should therefore not be used without confirming evidence from other indicators.

17-6	**BREADTH OF MARKET**

Breadth-of-market indicators are used to measure the underlying strength of market advances or declines. For example, it is possible that the Dow Jones Industrial Average of 30 blue-chip stocks would still be rising for some time after the market for the majority of lesser-known stocks had already turned down. This occurred for several weeks prior to the October 1987 international stock market crash, for example. To gauge the real underlying strength of the market, analysts need tools to measure the breadth of the market's moves.

Calculating Breadth-of-Market Statistics

Several methods exist for measuring the breadth of the market. One of the easiest is to compare the number of issues that advanced in price and the number that declined in some particular market, such as the NYSE. More specifically, subtract the number of issues whose prices declined from the number of issues whose prices advanced each day to get *daily net advances or declines*. The data on advances and declines are published daily in most financial and national newspapers. Although the number of net advances or declines is calculated daily in the example below, many technicians also calculate it weekly.

Day	Advances	−	Declines	=	Daily net advances and declines	Breadth
Tuesday	745		634		+111	111—Begin
Wednesday	994		391		+603	714
Thursday	468		914		−446	268
Friday	255		1118		−863	−595
Monday	669		589		+ 80	−515
Tuesday	582		657		− 75	−590

The breadth-of-market statistic is obtained by simply cumulating the daily net advances and declines. The *breadth statistic* may become negative during a bear market, as it did in the example above. This is no cause for alarm since the breadth level is entirely arbitrary; it depends on the date when the cumulative breadth series was begun. Only the direction, not the level, of the breadth-of-market statistics is relevant.

Interpretation of Breadth Data

Figure 17-4 shows breadth-of-market data for the NYSE. The Trendline Division of Standard & Poor's prepared the chart; the breadth data are labeled the **advance-decline line.** Technical analysts compare the breadth of market with one of the market averages or, as in Figure 17-4, with two market indicators. The breadth and market indicators usually move in tandem. Technical analysts watch for the trend in breadth to diverge from the trend in the market.

Figure 17-4 shows that before the October 1987 international stock market crash, the advance-decline line had been declining for almost 2 months. The decline indicated that many small stocks were turning down. This indicator of weakening market demand was giving technical analysts good warnings about the forthcoming October 1987 downturn.

17-7   **RELATIVE STRENGTH ANALYSIS**

The relative strength approach to technical analysis suggests that the prices of some securities rise relatively faster in a bull market or decline relatively more slowly in a bear market than other securities—that is, some securities exhibit **relative strength.** Relative strength technicians believe that by investing in securities that have demonstrated relative strength in the past, an investor will earn higher returns because the relative strength of a security sometimes continues for some time.

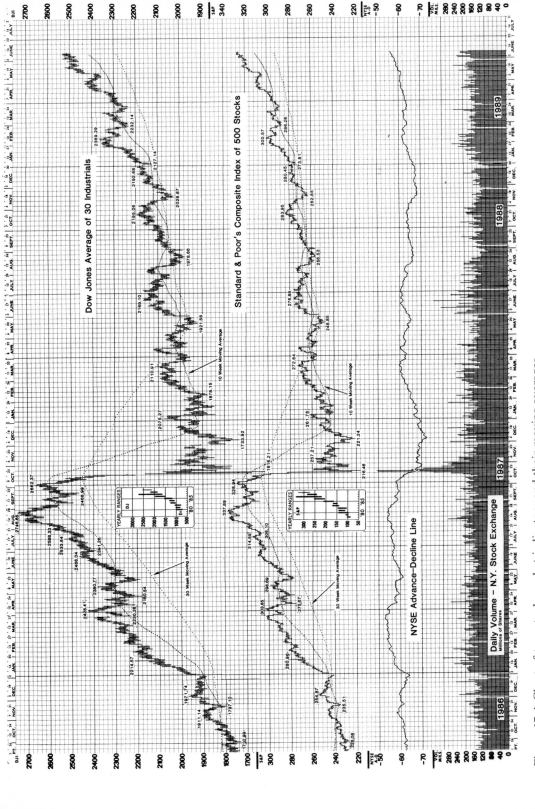

Figure 17-4 Chart of two stock market indicators and their moving averages, advance-decline line, and trading volume, 1986–1989. (*Source: Daily Action Stock Charts*, June 16, 1989, cover page, published by Trendline, a Division of Standard & Poor's, New York.)

Table 17-1
RELATIVE STRENGTH DATA FOR ANONYMOUS CORP

Year	Price of A*	Price of EIA†	Price of MIA‡	P_A/P_{EIA}	P_A/P_{MIA}	P_{EIA}/P_{MIA}
19X3	$30	$17	$210	30/17 = 1.78	30/210 = 0.144	17/210 = 0.081
19X4	36	18	250	36/18 = 2	36/250 = 0.144	18/250 = 0.072
19X5	72	20	285	72/20 = 3.6	72/285 = 0.253	20/285 = 0.070

*P_A is the average price of Anonymous Corporation for the year.
†P_{EIA} is S&P electronics industry average for the year.
‡P_{MIA} represents S&P 500 average for the year.

Measuring Relative Strength

The relative strength concept may be applied to individual securities or industries. Technicians measure relative strength in several ways. Some simply calculate rates of return and classify those securities with historically high average returns as securities with high relative strength. More frequently, technicians observe certain ratios to detect relative strength in a security or an industry. For example, consider the data for Anonymous Corporation (denoted A), a hypothetical growth firm in the electronics industry (EI), shown in Table 17-1.

From 19X3 to 19X4 Anonymous did slightly better than most of the firms in the electronics industry, as evidenced by the fact that its price grew relatively more than the electronics industry average; the ratio P_A/P_{EIA} rose from 1.78 to 2. Moreover, from 19X3 to 19X4 the electronics industry showed weakness relative to all industrial stocks: the ratio P_{EIA}/P_{MIA} declined from 0.081 to 0.072. From 19X3 to 19X4 Anonymous showed no increased strength relative to its market average: the ratio P_A/P_{MIA} was invariant at 0.144. But from 19X4 to 19X5 Anonymous showed considerable strength relative both to its industry and to the market.[11]

Interpretation of Relative Strength Data

A relative strength technician would typically plot the ratios of (1) the security relative to its industry and (2) the security relative to the market. A chart like the one shown in Figure 17-5 might result for the Anonymous Corp.

Figure 17-5 shows that although the electronics industry is failing to keep pace with the market, the Anonymous Corporation is developing relative strength both in its industry and in the market. After preparing charts like this for numerous firms from different industries over a length of time, the technician would select certain industries and firms which demonstrated relative strength

---

[11]For a discussion of computing relative strength by computer, see Richard Bookstaber, *The Complete Investment Book* (Glenview, Ill.: Scott, Foresman, 1985), chap. 18. For further discussion of relative strength computations see J. W. Wilder, *New Concepts in Technical Trading Systems* (Greensboro, N.C.: Trend Research, 1978), sec. VI.

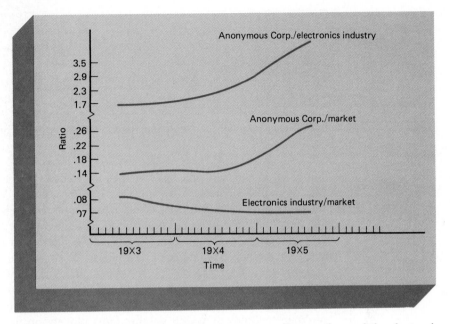

Figure 17-5 Relative strength data for Anonymous Corporation and the electronics industry.

to be the most promising investment opportunities. A number of empirical studies supporting relative strength have been published.[12]

17-8   **CHARTING VOLUME OF SHARES TRADED DATA**

The daily national newspapers and the financial newspapers across the United States publish the total volume of shares traded in various security markets during the previous day—if it was a trading day. Some financial newspapers also publish the number of shares traded in selected individual issues. For example, Figure 17-6 shows an excerpt from a typical financial newspaper giving the volume of shares traded data on the NYSE.

[12]See J. Brush, "Eight Relative Strength Models Compared," *Journal of Portfolio Management,* Fall 1986, pp. 21–28. Also see M. Greene and B. Fielitz, "Long-Term Dependence of Common Stock Returns," *Journal of Financial Economics,* May 1977, pp. 339–349. Furthermore, see R. Arnott, "Relative Strength Revisited," *Journal of Portfolio Management,* Spring 1979, pp. 19–23. And see J. Bohan, "Relative Strength: Further Positive Evidence," *Journal of Portfolio Management,* Fall 1981, pp. 36–39. Also see J. Brush and K. Boles, "The Predictive Power in Relative Strength and CAPM," *Journal of Portfolio Management,* Summer 1983, pp. 20–23.

MARKET DIARY   N.Y.S.E.

	Yesterday	Prev. Day
Advanced	926	966
Declined	579	523
Unchanged	500	493
Total Issues	2005	1982
New Highs	210	149
New Lows	12	13

Figure 17-6 Data about the volume of shares traded on the NYSE.

Many technical analysts believe they can get a better idea of whether a market is bullish or bearish by studying trading volume. Volume is supposed to be a measure of the intensity of investors' emotions. There is a Wall Street adage that "it takes volume to move a stock," either up or down in price. And, a large amount of trading volume is often associated with large price changes. Thus it is reasonable for stock price chartists to study volume data in an effort to discern what might cause specific stock price movements. But the cause-and-effect relationship between the volume of shares traded and the price change in the traded security is vague and hard to unravel.[13]

Volume technicians watch volume most closely on days when supply and demand appear to be moving to a new equilibrium. If high volume occurs on days when prices move up, the market is considered to be bullish. High volume on days when prices are falling is a bearish sign. If the same price changes occurred on low trading volume, they would be considered less significant.

There is one occasion when falling prices and high volume are considered bullish. When technicians feel the end of a bear market is near, they watch for a high volume of selling as the last of the bearish investors liquidate their holdings—this is called a "selling climax." A **selling climax** is supposed to eliminate the last of the bears who drive prices down by selling, clearing the way for the market to turn up.

Some technicians also look for a "speculative blowoff" to mark the end of a bull market. A **speculative blowoff** is a high volume of buying that pushes prices up to a peak; it is supposed to exhaust the enthusiasm of bullish speculators and make way for a bear market to begin. Technicians who believe that

---

[13]Security transactions are sometimes grouped into two categories: (a) *information trading* and (b) *liquidity trading*. Sometimes a large volume of liquidity (or noise) trading can take place without causing any price change. Research into the implications of the volume of shares traded includes Prem C. Jain and Gun-Ho Joh, "The Dependence between Hourly Prices and Trading Volume," *Journal of Financial and Quantitative Analysis*, Sept. 1988, vol. 23, no. 3, pp. 269–284. Also see J. M. Karpoff, "The Relation between Price Changes and Trading Volume: A Survey," *Journal of Financial and Quantitative Analysis,* March 1987, vol. 22, no. 1, pp. 109–126. See also G. E. Tauchen and M. Pitts, "The Price Variability-Volume Relationship on Speculative Markets," *Econometrica*, March 1983, vol. 51, pp. 485–505.

a speculative blowoff marks the end of a bull market say "the market must die with a bang, not a whimper."

Figure 17-4 shows bar charts of the DJIA and the Standard & Poor's 500 composite stocks index plotted with the daily volume on the NYSE along the bottom of the chart.

17-9   **MOVING-AVERAGE ANALYSIS**

Moving-average technicians, or rate-of-change technicians, as they are also called, like to watch a moving average of the price of the security they follow. The *moving average* is used to provide a smoothed, stable reference point against which the daily fluctuations can be gauged. *Rate-of-change analysis* is used for individual securities or market indexes.[14]

Construction of a Moving-Average Chart

Selecting the span of time over which to calculate the moving average affects the volatility of the moving average. Some technicians who perform rate-of-change analysis use a 200-day moving average of closing prices. The moving average changes each day as the most recent day is added and the two-hundred-and-first day is dropped. To calculate a 200-day moving average (MA_t) of the DJIA on day t, the formula below is employed.

$$MA_t = \frac{1}{200} \sum_{j=1}^{200} DJIA_{t-j}$$

$$= \frac{1}{200} (DJIA_{t-1} + DJIA_{t-2} + \cdots + DJIA_{t-200})$$

Figure 17-4 shows the 30-week moving average of the DJIA and Standard & Poor's index of 500 composite stocks as dotted lines. It is from this relationship between the market prices and the moving average that technicians obtain their information.

Interpreting Charts with a Moving Average

When the daily prices penetrate the moving-average line, technicians interpret this penetration as a signal. When the daily prices move downward through the moving average, they frequently fail to rise again for many months. Thus, a downward penetration of a flattened moving average suggests selling. When actual prices are above the moving average but the difference is narrowing,

[14]For an enlightening in-depth discussion of various moving-average techniques see Richard Bookstaber, *The Complete Investment Book* (Glenview, Ill.: Scott, Foresman, 1985), chapter 15.

this is a signal that a bull market may be ending. Several buy and sell signals followed by moving-average chartists are given below.

Moving-average analysts recommend buying a stock when (1) the moving average flattens out and the stock's price rises through the moving average, (2) the price of a stock falls below a moving-average line that is rising, and (3) a stock's price that is above the moving-average line falls but turns around and begins to rise again before it ever reaches the moving-average line.

Moving-average chartists recommend selling a stock when (1) the moving-average line flattens out and the stock's price drops downward through the moving-average line, (2) a stock's price rises above a moving-average line which is declining, and (3) a stock's price falls downward through the moving-average line and turns around to rise but then falls again before getting above the moving-average line.

The buy and sell signals initiated by a moving-average trading system vary with the length of time over which the moving-average is calculated. Moving averages calculated over short time spans tend to touch off many unfruitful trades.

Adherence to the moving-average trading rules over many months and many different stocks shows that sometimes profitable trades are signaled. But the rules touch off unprofitable trades, too. This is why most technical analysts use more than one technique of technical analysis and compare the buy and sell signals issued by these different technical tools before they actually trade.

17-10   **SUMMARY AND CONCLUSIONS**

This chapter provides a sampling of technical analysis tools. All the technical analysis tools have one common characteristic—they attempt to measure supply and demand. Technical analysis assumes that at least some of the *shifts in supply and demand occur gradually over time,* rather than instantaneously. When shifting prices are detected, they are presumed to be the result of gradual shifts in supply and demand rather than a series of instantaneous shifts that all coincidentally happened to be moving in the same direction. Since these *shifts are expected to continue as the price gradually reacts* to news or other factors, the price change pattern is extrapolated to predict further price changes.

Some economists believe that technical analysis does not adequately measure supply and demand conditions or predict prices. These disbelievers suggest that security markets are *efficient markets* that impact new information into security prices instantaneously.[15] As a result, these financial economists believe that security *price changes* are a series of random numbers which occur in reaction to the random arrival of news. When a security's price moves in the

[15]Eugene F. Fama, "Efficient Capital Markets: A Review of Theory and Empirical Work," *Journal of Finance,* May 1970, pp. 383–417 and "The Behavior of Stock Market Prices," *Journal of Business,* Jan. 1965, pp. 34–105.

same direction for several days, those who believe that securities markets are efficient interpret these moves as a series of independent changes in supply or demand, which coincidentally happen to move the price in the same direction. They assert that technical analysts are wrong in believing that supply and/or demand adjust gradually, causing trends that may be used for predicting future prices. The evidence provided by economists to support their efficient markets hypothesis will be examined in Chapter 18.

Essay Questions

17-1   According to the Dow theory, what is the significance of an *abortive recovery* that follows a series of ascending tops?

17-2   How is the moving average used in analyzing stock prices? Can the moving average be meaningfully calculated in different ways? Explain.

17-3   Which of the technical indicators discussed in Chapter 17 gave the clearest and most unambiguous forewarning of the October 1987 international stock market crash? Explain.

17-4   What significance do technical analysts attribute to the volume of odd-lot trading? Explain.

17-5   (*a*) What is the confidence index supposed to measure? (*b*) Does the confidence index have any limit on its upper value? Why or why not? (*c*) What relevance does this measure of bond investors' confidence have for common stock investors?

17-6   (*a*) How are data on the number of shares that advance and decline on a given trading day used by technical analysts? (*b*) Does knowing the number of advances or declines for only one day convey meaningful information? Explain.

17-7   Compare and contrast the concepts of relative strength and undiversifiable systematic risk. If a stock has high relative strength, what is the implication for that stock's rates of return?

17-8   Define the phrases (*a*) speculative blowoff and (*b*) selling climax. (*c*) What do these concepts have in common?

17-9   Are the technical analysis tools presented in the chapter useful for analyzing individual securities, market indexes, or both? Explain.

17-10 ''Experienced technical analysts usually have one favorite tool that they follow closely.'' Is the statement true, false, or uncertain? Explain.

Problems

17-11 Consider the following 14 days of data for the Hemmel Corporation's common stock. On which day do you think the market received important new information that affects the value of Hemmel's stock?

Day	Closing price	Volume of shares traded
1	$29.25	1,000
2	$31.125	11,000
3	$32.50	3,000
4	$33.125	2,000
5	$33.75	500
6	$32.875	2,000
7	$32.125	1,000
8	$31.50	1,000
9	$31.75	12,000
10	$33.125	500
11	$34.50	2,000
12	$34.00	3,000
13	$33.75	2,000
14	$32.625	500

17-12 (*a*) Calculate a 5-day moving average from the Hemmel Corporation's closing price data from Problem 17-11. *Note: You will only be able to calculate nine moving-average prices since it is impossible to calculate the average for the first four days.* (*b*) Over what range does Hemmel's price vary? (*c*) Over what range do the moving-average values of Hemmel's prices vary?

17-13 Consider the spectacular stock market crash of October 1987 and answer the questions pertaining to the following data.

1987 Monthly Average Financial Data

	Jan.	Feb.	Mar.	Apr.	May	June	July	Aug.	Sept.	Oct.	Nov.	Dec.
Yields-to-maturity												
T-bond	6.97	7.12	7.05	7.80	8.52	8.29	8.24	8.47	9.16	9.30	8.65	8.72
AA	8.86	8.82	8.78	9.31	9.81	9.70	9.64	9.83	10.48	10.62	9.97	10.08
A	9.07	8.94	8.91	9.39	9.91	9.89	9.90	10.16	10.77	10.98	10.51	10.59
BBB	9.47	9.50	9.42	9.55	10.44	10.38	10.42	10.61	11.25	11.55	10.99	11.06
Standard & Poor's 500 Composite Stocks Index												
S&P 500	265	281	293	289	289	301	310	329	319	280	245	241

(*a*) Do you think the Federal Reserve's monetary policy might have played a role in the October 1987 crash? (*b*) Construct a confidence index (CI) from the interest rate data above. (*c*) Did the CI you constructed give any indication of the October 1987 stock market crash? (*d*) If your CI gave any indications of the October 1987 crash, were they leading, coincident, or lagging indications? (*e*) If your CI failed to give a clear-cut leading indication of the October 1987 market crash, should you abandon technical analysis?

Selected References

Bookstaber, Richard, *The Complete Investment Book* (Glenview, Ill.: Scott, Foresman, 1985).

> Chapters 14 through 20 inclusive explain various technical analysis tools. A computer program written in BASIC language that is ready to run on a personal computer is printed at the end of each chapter.

Edwards, R. D., and John Magee, Jr., *Technical Analysis of Stock Trends,* 5th revised ed. (Springfield, Mass.: Stock Trends Service, 1966).

> This classic book has been used for years by technical analysts. It is easy to read and many different techniques are explained.

Jiler, William L., *How Charts Can Help You in the Stock Market* (New York: Trendline, 1962).

> This popular book on charting explains many techniques and gives examples.

Levy, R. A., *The Relative Strength Concept of Common Stock Forecasting* (Larchmont, N.Y.: Investors Intelligence, 1968).

> This book explains some of the nonchart-oriented quantitative technical tools.

Pring, Martin J., *Technical Analysis Explained,* 2d ed. (New York: McGraw-Hill, 1985).

> This comprehensive book elucidates a large number of technical analysis techniques that are used with individual stocks, bonds, commodities, and market averages. Helpful illustrations are provided.

Trendline, A Division of Standard & Poor's, New York.

> In addition to its weekly and monthly books of charts, Trendline also purveys computer software for technical analysis. See Trendline's software packages named Trendline-II and Trendline-PRO.

Wilder, J. Welles, *New Concepts in Technical Trading Systems* (Greensboro, N.C.: Trend Research, 1978).

> This book explains precisely how to execute different technical analysis trading rules. Computer programs written by the author may also be purchased.

Chapter 18

Behavior of Stock
Market Prices

People have been studying the way security prices fluctuate for over a century. In 1841 Charles Mackay assembled a book of readings about Tulip-mania and some equally famous market "bubbles" which had a self-explanatory title: *Extraordinary Popular Delusions and the Madness of Crowds*.[1] In contrast to Mackay's astonishing stories, in 1900 a French mathematician named Louis Bachelier set forth formal models in which security prices were random outcomes that had probabilities attached to them.[2] Bachelier was one of the first to study security price movements mathematically. Then, in 1936 the famous economist John Maynard Keynes suggested the following scenario.[3]

> . . . most of these persons are, in fact, largely concerned, not with making superior long-range forecasts of the probable yield of an investment over its whole life, but with forecasting changes in the conventional basis of valuation a short time ahead of the general public. They are concerned, not with what an investment is really worth to a man who buys it "for keeps," but with what the market will value it at, under the influence of mass psychology, three months or a year hence. . . . For it is not sensible to pay 25 for an investment of which you believe the prospective yield to justify a value of 30, if you also believe that the market will value it at 20 three months hence.

[1]Charles Mackay, *Extraordinary Popular Delusions and the Madness of Crowds* (London: Richard Bentley, 1841). Reprinted by Harmony Books, a division of Crown Books, New York, 1980.
[2]Louis Bachelier, "Theory of Speculation," a doctoral dissertation that was translated to English and published by Paul H. Cootner, ed., *The Random Character of Stock Market Prices* (Cambridge, Mass.: M.I.T. Press, 1964).
[3]John Maynard Keynes, *The General Theory of Employment, Interest and Money* (New York: Harcourt Brace Jovanovich, 1936), pp. 154–155.

Thus the professional investor is forced to concern himself with the anticipation of impending changes, in the news or in the atmosphere, of the kind by which experience shows that the mass psychology of the market is most influenced.

Thinking took another turn during the 1950s when an econometrician named Holbrook Working and his colleagues articulated the notion that security prices fluctuated around their intrinsic values.[4] Over the decades many financial economists have suggested models to describe the behavior of security prices. But, until massive security price data could be statistically analyzed with computers, the various theories about security price movements were largely conjectures.

18-1   COMPUTERIZED RESEARCH METHODOLOGY ACCELERATED THE STUDY OF SECURITY PRICE FLUCTUATIONS

Professor Eugene Fama published an empirical study in 1965 that analyzed the stock price movements of all the stocks that make up the Dow Jones Industrial Average.[5] Fama investigated daily price changes for 30 stocks over a 5-year period. The computations were formidable; Fama's classic study could not have been done without an electronic database and a computer. Fama analyzed the differences between the natural logarithms of the stocks' prices, because those differences are the **continuously compounded rate of price change.**

$$\dot{r}_{i,t} = \ln (1 + r_{i,t}) = \ln \frac{p_{i,t}}{p_{i,t-1}} = \ln p_{i,t} - \ln p_{i,t-1} \qquad (18\text{-}1)$$

Fama, like many other researchers, studied rates of price change instead of the raw stock prices because the average *rate of price change* for most stocks does not change from year to year if it is measured over a representative sample period. In contrast, the *price* of the typical common stock increases about 6 percent per year. It is easier to make comparisons between average *rates of change* since the typical stock's average rate of price change remains constant.

Fama's study was designed to measure the degree of randomness with which stock prices fluctuated. He thought that financial information arrived randomly and, assuming that prices responded efficiently to the new information, the prices should fluctuate randomly too. Fama delineated three levels of market efficiency.

The first hypothesis is the **weakly efficient market hypothesis.** The weakly efficient hypothesis stipulates that *historical* price and volume data for securities contain no information which can be used to earn a trading profit above what

[4]Holbrook Working, "A Theory of Anticipatory Prices," *American Economic Review,* May 1958, pp. 188–199.
[5]Eugene F. Fama, "The Behavior of Stock Market Prices," *Journal of Business,* Jan. 1965, pp. 34–105.

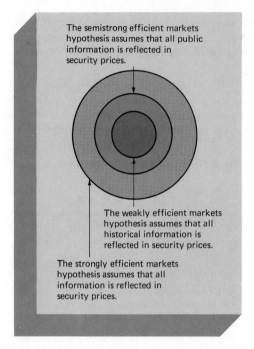

The semistrong efficient markets hypothesis assumes that all public information is reflected in security prices.

The weakly efficient markets hypothesis assumes that all historical information is reflected in security prices.

The strongly efficient markets hypothesis assumes that all information is reflected in security prices.

Figure 18-1 A Venn diagram of the three levels of information that might be reflected in stock prices.

could be attained with a naive buy-and-hold investment strategy.[6] This hypothesis suggests that technical analysis is well-recorded but worthless folklore.

Fama's **semistrong efficient market hypothesis** specifies that markets are efficient enough for prices to reflect *all publicly available* information. Consequently, only those insiders who have access to valuable information could earn a profit larger than what could be earned by using a naive buy-and-hold strategy in a semistrong efficient market.

Fama's third hypothesis is called the **strongly efficient market hypothesis;** it claims that *no one* can earn a profit larger than what could be earned with a naive buy-and-hold strategy by trading on short-term security price movements. Security markets can be strongly efficient if the rates of stock price changes are independent random variables and none of the market participants use inside information.

Different levels of security price efficiency are contrasted in Figure 18-1. The three hypotheses about pricing efficiency overlap—they differ only in the

[6]As explained in the sub-section of Section 7-5 entitled "The Naive Buy-and-Hold Strategy," the investment policy of randomly selecting securities (for example, with an unaimed dart), buying them, and holding them while reinvesting all dividends yielded about 10 percent per annum before taxes over the past half century (see Table 7-3).

degree of market efficiency. Our review of evidence about pricing efficiency begins with the weakest hypothesis and ends with evidence about the strongest.[7] Evidence about imperfections in the efficient markets hypotheses is reviewed midway through this chapter. The closing pages present the results of empirical tests of anomalies in the efficient markets theory.

18-2   **EVIDENCE SUPPORTING THE WEAKLY EFFICIENT HYPOTHESIS**

Weakly efficient markets were defined as markets where past prices provide no information that would allow a trader to earn a return above what could be attained with a naive buy-and-hold strategy. This definition means that while traders and speculators may earn positive rates of return, they will not beat a naive buy-and-hold strategy with *information obtained from historical data.*

Of course, some lucky people sometimes manage to beat the naive buy-and-hold strategy—and some unlucky ones lose everything. But we should not try to reach general conclusions from specific cases. Instead, we will consider scientific analyses of massive empirical data in an effort to reach general conclusions.

**Filter Rules
Execute Trades
Mechanically**

Eugene Fama and Marshall Blume programmed their computer to trade through a mechanical security trading strategy called an **x percent filter rule** that operates as follows[8]:

> If the price of a security rises at least *x* percent, buy and hold the security until its price drops at least *x* percent from a subsequent high. Then, liquidate the long position and assume a short position until the price rises *x* percent.

By varying the value of *x*, one can test an infinite number of filter rules. The filter rules might enable an investor to earn significant profits if some of the patterns used by technical analysts are reliable indicators.

Various studies have been conducted using different stocks, different filter rules, and different sample periods. Filters as small as one-half of 1 percent (that is, $x = 0.005$), as large as 50 percent ($x = 0.5$), and many values between these extremes have been tested. Some filter rules using small values of *x* can

---

[7]Fama's suggestion that three categorizations be used for empirical tests of market efficiency was outlined in Eugene F. Fama, ''Efficient Capital Markets: A Review of Theory and Empirical Work,'' *Journal of Finance,* May 1970, pp. 383–417.

[8]See E. F. Fama and M. E. Blume, ''Filter Rules and Stock Market Trading,'' *Journal of Business,* Jan. 1966, pp. 226–241. For an earlier work, see Sidney Alexander, ''Price Movements in Speculative Markets: Trends or Random Walks,'' *Industrial Management Review,* May 1961, pp. 7–26.

earn the investor a return above the naive buy-and-hold strategy if the commissions incurred in buying and selling are ignored. The one-half of 1 percent filter rules tend to be the most profitable. However, after commissions are deducted, Fama and Blume reported that none of the 30 DJIA stocks that they investigated outperformed the naive strategy. In fact, some ran up considerable net losses.

More recently, Sweeney developed a filter rule that was able to earn modest profits.[9] Sweeney replicated Fama and Blume's tests and found that the part of their filter rule that resulted in the short positions usually generated the trading losses. In contrast, Sweeney found that the long positions were often profitable. So, Sweeney programmed his computer to trade an x percent filter rule with no short positions, as follows:

> If the price of a security rises at least x percent, buy and hold the security until its price drops at least x percent from a subsequent high. Then, liquidate the long position and invest the proceeds in risk-free short-term bonds until the price reaches its next trough and then rises x percent.

Sweeney also found that filter rule trading tended to be fairly consistently profitable in some stocks while being fairly consistently unprofitable year after year in other stocks. After delineating and eliminating these problems in Fama and Blume's filter rule, Sweeney's filter rules could mechanically trade some stocks and earn a statistically significant rate of profit after the tiny trading costs incurred by NYSE floor traders were deducted. If the higher commission rates that most investors pay are deducted, however, Sweeney's filter rule was not profitable.

In conclusion, it seems that some patterns do exist that can be used as basis for a profitable trading strategy. But these patterns are so complex or so weak that filter rules are unable to generate profits from every stock, or even substantial profits from the stocks that are profitable to trade. This research finding furnishes some support for the weakly efficient markets hypothesis.

Serial Correlation   Security price changes do not appear to have significant momentum or inertia to cause changes of a given sign to be followed by changes of that same sign; the filter rules probably would have detected such trends if they existed. However, security prices might follow some pattern of **reversals** in which price

---

[9]See Richard J. Sweeney, "Some New Filter Rule Tests: Methods and Results," *Journal of Financial and Quantitative Analysis,* Sept. 1988, vol. 23, no. 3, pp. 285–300. Or see P. D. Praetz, "Rates of Return and Filter Rules," *Journal of Finance,* March 1976, vol. 31, pp. 71–75.

Readers interested in commodities trading may study the application of filter rules and other tests explained in this chapter to commodity prices. See Richard A. Stevenson and Robert M. Bear, "Commodity Futures: Trends or Random Walks?" *Journal of Finance,* March 1970, pp. 65–81. The filter rules can be profitable in the commodity markets.

changes of one sign tend to be followed by changes of the opposite sign. Serial correlation might detect a pattern of reversals that filter rules overlooked.

Serial correlation (or, synonymously, **autocorrelation**) measures the correlation coefficient between a series of numbers with lagged numbers in the same series. A significant positive serial correlation indicates the presence of trends. The presence of negative serial correlation documents the existence of more reversals than might occur randomly. Numbers that are truly random will have zero serial correlation. Figure 18-2 illustrates various serial correlations.

Financial analysts typically measure serial correlation in a sample of security prices by estimating the correlation between the rate of security price changes in period t (denoted r_t) and price changes in the same security that occur k periods earlier (denoted r_{t+k}); k is the number of periods of lag. The correlation coefficient from regression equation (18-2) measures the serial correlation coefficient for asset i with a lag of k periods.

$$r_{i,t+k} = c_{0,i} + c_{1,i} r_{i,t} + e_{i,t} \qquad E(e_{i,t}) = 0 \qquad (18\text{-}2)$$

Figure 18-2 Price fluctuations for five hypothetical stocks with different serial correlation coefficients.

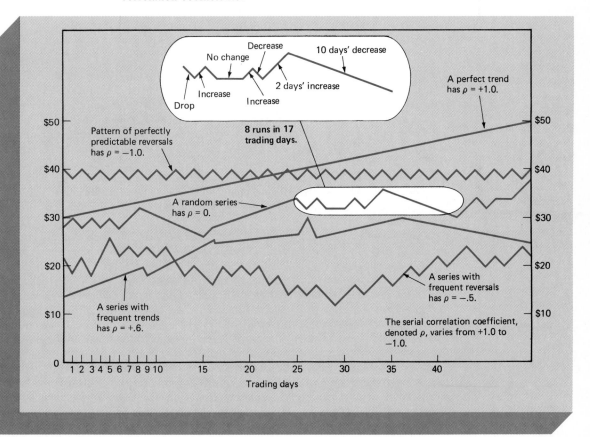

where $c_{0,i}$ and $c_{1,i}$ are the regression intercept and slope statistics, respectively, and $e_{i,t}$ is the unexplained residual.

There is a long-term upward trend of about 6 percent per year in the prices of common stocks. So if the period over which the returns are measured spans several years, a positive serial correlation will probably be observed. If the period over which the returns are measured is short (such as monthly) and the lag spans a substantial fraction of the length of the business cycle (say, 3 years) then a significant negative serial correlation will be found as the stock market rises and falls with the business cycle.[10] But these business cycle gyrations and rising long-run trends are not of primary interest here. Studies of security price behavior have focused on the *short-term patterns* used by technical analysts. Therefore, let us search for patterns in short-term (daily, weekly, or monthly) stock price returns that might net us a larger profit after commissions from aggressive trading than a naive buy-and-hold strategy would yield. If such patterns exist, they would indicate that security prices do not fluctuate randomly.

Various serial correlation studies about security prices have been published. Many different securities, many different lags (that is, different values of k), and many different sample periods have been used. The serial correlation studies failed to detect any significant patterns (that is, any highly significant serial correlation coefficients).[11] Stated differently, the serial correlation tests furnish some support for the weakly efficient markets hypothesis.

[10]See E. Fama and K. R. French, "Permanent and Temporary Components of Stock Prices," *Journal of Political Economy,* April 1988, vol. 96, no. 21, pp. 246–273. Fama and French report highly significant negative serial correlations in stock price returns that are lagged 3, 4, or 5 years. Also see Geoffrey H. Moore, *Business Cycles, Inflation, and Forecasting,* National Bureau of Economic Research Study Number 24 (Cambridge, Mass.: Ballinger, 1980). Chapter 9, entitled "Security Markets and Business Cycles," explains that the stock market is correlated with the real sector of the U.S. economy. See also J. C. Francis, "The Market Risk Factor," in *Management of Investments,* 2d ed. (New York: McGraw-Hill, 1988), chap. 13. These sources all document the well-known impact of the business cycle on stock price movements; this relationship can generate certain serial correlations in stock price changes.

[11]For serial correlations see Eugene F. Fama, "The Behavior of Stock Market Prices," op. cit.; S. Alexander, op. cit.; M. G. Kendall, "The Analysis of Economic Time Series, Part I," *Journal of the Royal Statistical Society,* 1953, vol. 96, pp. 11–25.

More recent studies which embrace a more heterogeneous sample of stocks and extend the previous serial correlation studies may be found in Gabriel A. Hawawini, "On the Time Behavior of Financial Parameters: An Investigation of the Intervaling Effect," unpublished doctoral dissertation, New York University, 1977. Hawawini reports moderately significant positive serial correlations for 1-day trends in some stocks that are less liquid. See also Robert A. Schwartz and David K. Whitcomb, "Evidence on the Presence and Causes of Serial Correlation in Market Model Residuals," *Journal of Financial and Quantitative Analysis,* June 1977, pp. 291–315. Schwartz and Whitcomb report significant negative serial correlations in the residual returns from the characteristic line regressions, denoted $e_{i,t}$ for the ith stock in period t. See also Victor

(continues)

Table 18-1

COUNTING THE RUNS IN STOCK PRICE CHANGES

Price

$35⅞	change 1: ¼ price rise	run 1 is a positive run
$36⅛	change 2: ⅛ price rise	
$36¼	change 3: zero price change	run 2 is a zero run
$36¼	change 4: zero price change	
$36¼	change 5: ⅛ price rise	run 3 is a positive run
$36⅜	change 6: ¼ price fall	
$36⅛	change 7: ⅛ price fall	run 4 is a negative run
$36	change 8: ¼ price fall	
$35¾		

Runs Tests

It is possible that security prices might fluctuate randomly but, in addition, they sometimes follow trends that filter rules and serial correlation could not detect. That is, price changes may be random most of the time but *occasionally* become serially correlated for *varying periods*. To examine this possibility, runs tests may be used to determine if there are runs in the price changes. A **run** occurs in a series of numbers whenever the *changes in the numbers reverse sign*. For instance, eight price *changes* are listed in Table 18-1. These eight price changes generate four runs.

As illustrated in Table 18-1, runs can include any number of transactions. For example, in a bear market a security price that declines for 100 consecutive transactions will generate 100 negative price changes but only one negative run.

Mathematical statisticians are able to determine how many positive, negative, zero, or total runs may be expected to occur in a series of truly random numbers of any size. Therefore, if a consecutive series of security price changes has a positive, negative, zero, or total number of runs that occurs either more frequently or less frequently than would be expected in a series of random numbers, this is evidence of nonrandomness. Published runs tests suggest that

---

(continued)

Niederhoffer and M. F. M. Osborne, ''Market Making and Reversal on the Stock Exchange,'' *Journal of the American Statistical Association*, Dec. 1966, vol. 61, pp. 897–916. Niederhoffer and Osborne report a number of departures from randomness. Most interestingly, they reported that reversals are 3 times more likely to happen than positive price changes. Niederhoffer and Osborne attributed these daily reversals to the way NYSE specialists handled limit and market orders. Unfortunately, these nonrandom patterns are incapable of generating profitable trading schemes. Thus, they are noteworthy academically but of dubious trading value.

the runs in the price changes of various securities are not significantly different from the runs in a table of random numbers.[12] These findings suggest that active traders who search for various types of nonrandom trends from which to earn a profit will not be able to beat a naive buy-and-hold strategy, on average.

Weakly Efficient Markets Hypothesis Is Acceptable

We have reviewed certain empirical filter rule tests, serial correlation tests, and runs tests to see whether they support the weakly efficient markets hypothesis.[13] The results from these scientific studies support the weakly efficient hypothesis. Before considering some anomalous findings, we will review the evidence that supports higher levels of market efficiency.

18-3   **THE SEMISTRONG EFFICIENT MARKETS HYPOTHESIS**

The semistrong efficient markets hypothesis requires more evidence of market efficiency than the weakly efficient markets hypothesis. Weak efficiency only requires that security prices tend not to follow repetitive patterns. The more

---

[12]Eugene F. Fama, op. cit.; S. Alexander, op. cit. The effectiveness of random number tests reviewed here is called into question by Robert Savitt, "When Random Is Not Random: An Introduction to Chaos in Market Prices," *Journal of Futures Markets,* 1988, vol. 8, no. 3, pp. 271–289. This article shows that numbers generated by a deterministic formula can resemble random numbers.

[13]A. B. Larson reports that corn futures prices appear to fluctuate randomly; see A. B. Larson, "Measurement of a Random Process in Futures Prices," in Paul Cootner, ed., *The Random Character of Stock Market Prices* (Cambridge, Mass.: MIT Press, 1964) pp. 219–230. Benoit Mandelbrot reports that spot cotton prices fluctuate randomly; see Benoit Mandelbrot, "The Variation in Certain Speculative Prices," in Paul Cootner, ed., *The Random Character of Stock Market Prices* (Cambridge, Mass.: MIT Press, 1964), pp. 307–332. Richard Roll documents random Treasury bill rates; see Richard Roll, *The Behavior of Interest Rates* (New York: Basic Books, 1970). W. Schwert finds that the prices of seats on the NYSE fluctuate randomly; see W. Schwert, "Stock Exchange Seats as Capital Assets," *Journal of Financial Economics,* Jan. 1977, pp. 51–78. J. P. Stein's research uncovers randomly fluctuating prices for art; see J. P. Stein, "The Monetary Appreciation of Paintings," *Journal of Political Economy,* Oct. 1977, pp. 1021–1036. Richard Stevenson and Robert Bear have found that several different commodity prices fluctuate with little deviation from randomness; see Richard Stevenson and Robert Bear, "Commodity Futures: Trends or Random Walks?" *Journal of Finance,* March 1970. Brad Cornell and David Mayers report that foreign exchange prices fluctuate randomly; see Brad Cornell and David Mayers, "The Efficiency of the Market for Foreign Exchange under Floating Rates," *Review of Economics and Statistics,* Feb. 1978.

demanding **semistrong efficient markets hypothesis** requires that *all public information* be fully reflected in security prices. This means that information in *The Wall Street Journal, Moody's,* and *Standard & Poor's* publications, for example, contains nothing of value to professional investors. In order to see the impact of important public information announcements, consider the stock market's reaction to sudden changes in a government-controlled interest rate that are announced after secret meetings.

Announcement Effects from Changes in the Federal Reserve's Discount Rate

Interest rates affect security prices because market interest rates determine the discount rates that are appropriate to use in determining present values. Therefore, changes in the **Federal Reserve discount rate,** announced after the Federal Reserve Board decides to change this monetary policy variable in confidential meetings, may be expected to affect security prices. This is especially true since announcements of changes in the discount rate are so widely publicized in the financial press.

Research into the effects of discount rate changes has shown that the average common stock's price changes a small but statistically significant amount (never exceeding one-half of 1 percent) on the first trading day following the public announcement by the Federal Reserve of a change in the discount rate.[14] This change is not enough to yield a trading profit. Most of the price change associated with the announcement seems to occur *before* the actual announcement—the market anticipates changes in the Fed's discount rate policy. The semistrong hypothesis tends to be supported by this empirical finding.

Effects of Stock Splits and Stock Dividends

Stock splits and stock dividends are essentially paper-shuffling operations that do not change the total value of the firm or investors' wealth. For example, a 100 percent stock dividend, or equivalently, a 2-for-1 stock split, means that twice as many shares will be outstanding and that each share will be worth half as much.[15] If security markets efficiently equate security prices with security values, the *total value of all the firm's outstanding shares* will not be affected

---

[14]R. N. Waud, "Public Interpretation of Discount Rate Changes: Evidence on the 'Announcement Effect,'" *Econometrica,* 1971.

[15]To accountants and attorneys, stock splits are different from stock dividends; the difference is related to the treatment of the equity section of the balance sheet. With a stock split, the par value per share is decreased to reflect the split; the number of shares outstanding is simultaneously increased so as to leave the total amount in the capital account unchanged. With stock dividends, a portion of retained earnings equal to the value of the stock dividend is transferred from retained earnings to the capital account. Both adjustments are pure bookkeeping entries that leave total equity and total assets unchanged and hence have no real economic significance.

by these mere changes in the unit of account.[16] Stock splits and stock dividends are publicly announced events that furnish a good vehicle with which to test the semistrong efficient markets hypothesis.

The study discussed here was conducted by Professors Fama, Fisher, Jensen, and Roll (FFJR hereafter); it is based on a sample of 940 stock splits and stock dividends that occurred on the NYSE between 1927 and 1959.[17] In essence, the study asked if stock splits or stock dividends had any influence on investors' one-period rates of return, defined in Equation (18-3).

$$r_t = \frac{\text{capital gains or loss} + \text{cash dividend, if any}}{\text{purchase price}} \tag{18-3}$$

All the shares were adjusted for the stock splits and stock dividends before the rates of return were calculated. This adjustment ensured that only actual changes in the investor's wealth would be measured rather than the meaningless price changes associated with a stock dividend or split. For example, when a 2-for-1 split or 100 percent stock dividend occurs, the share's price before the stock dividend or split should be halved so that no changes in the investor's wealth would be attributed to it in calculating rates of return.

The following numerical example shows how a share of stock selling for $100 per share can fall to $50 per share as the result of a 2-for-1 split or 100 percent stock dividend without changing the owner's 5 percent rate of return. The stock dividend or split occurred between periods 2 and 3. Since the investor owns twice as many shares after the split but each share has half the previous market price, the investor's wealth is unchanged. And the investor's income in this simple example is $5 of cash dividends per period per $100 of investment

---

[16]Some firms occasionally have stock splits to broaden the market for their shares. For example, in the second quarter of 1979 IBM shares were selling for $300 each and IBM declared a 4-for-1 stock split (or, equivalently, a 300 percent stock dividend). This 4-for-1 split reduced the cost of a round lot (100 shares) from $30,000 to $7500. Splitting high-priced shares may be advisable if a firm is seeking to broaden its shareholder group to include families that may not have $30,000 to invest but do have $7500. However, the additional small investors gained by such actions cannot be expected to control enough investing power to raise the price of the shares. The stock split changed nothing of any significance.

[17]E. Fama, L. Fisher, M. Jensen, and R. Roll, ''The Adjustment of Stock Prices to New Information,'' *International Economic Review,* Feb. 1969, vol. 20, no. 2, pp. 1–21. The FFJR study was replicated with allowance for shifting beta statistics, and similar results were obtained; see Sasson Bar-Yosef and Lawrence D. Brown, ''A Re-examination of Stock Splits Using Moving Betas,'' *Journal of Finance,* Sept. 1977, vol. XXXII, no. 4, pp. 1069–1080.

Changes in the unit of account increase the volatility of a stock's price, but this does not translate into any change in the value of the shares. See James A. Ohlson and Stephen H. Pennman, ''Volatility Increases Subsequent to Stock Splits: An Empirical Aberration,'' *Journal of Financial Economics,* June 1985, vol. 14, no. 2, pp. 251–266.

before and after the change in the unit of account. The stock yields a constant 5 percent rate of return each period.

Time period, t	$t = 1$	$t = 2$	$t = 3$	$t = 4$
Market price per share	$100	$100	$50	$50
Cash dividend per share	$5	$5	$2.50	$2.50
Earnings per share	$10	$10	$5	$5
Number of shares held per $100 original investment	1	1	2	2
Rate of return, Equation (18-3)	5%	5%	5%	5%

Characteristic Line Used   In order to have a standard of comparison against which the rates of return may be evaluated, it is necessary to make adjustments for the differences in returns resulting from bull-market or bear-market price swings. The characteristic line, defined in Equation (10-3), was calculated for each security studied in order to make adjustment for these changes in the market conditions.

$$r_{i,t} = a_i + b_i r_{m,t} + e_{i,t} \qquad (10\text{-}3)$$

Each stock's characteristic line was fitted using a total of 60 monthly returns from the 30 months before and 30 months after the change in its unit of account.

Residual Errors   The residual errors e_t around the time of the stock split or stock dividend are the focus of this study of stock dividends and splits (and a number of other studies reviewed in this chapter). Since these unexplained residual returns are important in this and other studies, we will delve into their measurement and interpretation in some detail. Figure 18-3 illustrates a hypothetical characteristic line.

   If the residual error at the time of the stock split or stock dividend was zero ($e_{i,t} = 0$), then the security's actual rate of return equaled exactly what the characteristic line predicted and the change had no positive or negative effects on investors' returns. If the residual error was positive ($e_{i,t} > 0$), the asset's return was above the characteristic line and the stock split or stock dividend was apparently boosting returns above normal. A negative residual error ($e_{i,t} < 0$) occurs when the actual rate of return is below the characteristic line because some negative influence is affecting that period's rate of return. If the belief that stock splits and stock dividends created something of value is true, the residual errors will tend to be positive after the stock dividend or split because the value of the firm should increase.

Monthly Residual Errors Averaged   The residual errors about the characteristic line are the results of many influences other than stock splits and stock dividends. Therefore, it is not reasonable to examine the residuals of *individual*

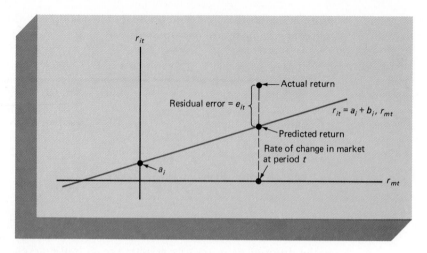

Figure 18-3 A stock's characteristic line with residual error.

firms following a split or dividend and draw conclusions. To overcome this problem, the residual errors averaged over 940 stocks were calculated for each month before and after the stock split or dividend. In effect, this approach averages to zero the influences that are not due to the stock dividend or split. If the average residuals are significantly different from zero in the months after the change, this indicates that the change affected the value of the firm. Equation (18-4) defines the average residuals $\bar{e}_t$ for the tth month before or after the month in which the stock dividend or split occurred.

$$\bar{e}_t = \frac{1}{940} \sum_{e=1}^{940} e_{i,t} = \frac{1}{940} (e_{1,t} + e_{2,t} + e_{3,t} + \cdots + e_{940,t}) \qquad (18\text{-}4)$$

For example, the average residual 6 months before the split month would be denoted $\bar{e}_{-6}$.

Figure 18-4 shows that the residual error averaged over 940 stocks tended to be increasingly positive in the 30 months preceding the stock dividend or split. But after the change in the unit of account, the average residuals fluctuate around zero for the next 30 months. These findings require clarification.

Cumulative Average Residuals (CARs) To measure the cumulative month-by-month effect that the stock dividend or split may have, sum the average monthly residuals from Equation (18-4) chronologically over $(30 + 1 + 30 =)$ 61 months. Equation (18-5) defines these cumulative abnormal average monthly residual returns, denoted CARs.

$$\text{CAR} = \sum_{t=-30}^{30} \bar{e}_t = \sum_{t=-30}^{30} \sum_{i=1}^{940} e_{i,t} \qquad (18\text{-}5)$$

Note that the CARs graphed in Figure 18-5a, b, and c all increase in the months *preceding* the stock split or stock dividend. This rise in returns in the

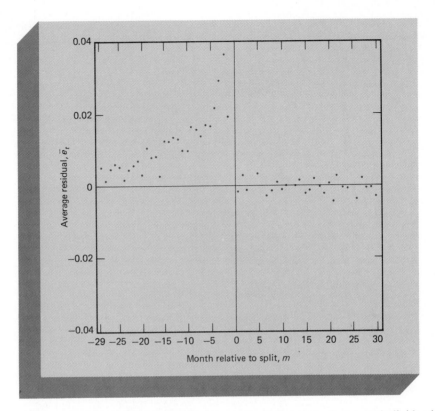

Figure 18-4 The residual errors in the months before and after a stock dividend or split averaged over 940 stocks. (*Source:* E. Fama, L. Fisher, M. Jensen, and R. Roll, ''The Adjustment of Stock Prices to New Information,'' *International Economic Review*, Feb. 1969, vol. 20, no. 2, fig. 2a.)

months prior to the change can be attributed to an increase in the firm's earning power that (correctly or incorrectly) is *anticipated by the market*. The thinking of investors in the market works as follows. A stock dividend or split is often accompanied by an increase in the *cash* dividend. Thus, the stock split or dividend is interpreted by the market as evidence of an upcoming increase in cash dividends. Cash dividend payments often *contain information about the internal workings of a corporation*. When a board of directors declares an increased cash dividend, for instance, this suggests that the directors are confident that the earnings power of the firm has risen enough to maintain a higher level of future dividends. This anticipated increase in earnings provides the basis for the higher returns preceding the stock split or stock dividend.

Interpreting the Results   If a firm that declares a stock dividend or split subsequently fails to raise its cash dividend, it will disappoint the market. As a result, its price and returns can be expected to rise in anticipation of the stock split or dividend and then fall if its cash dividends and earnings fail to rise.

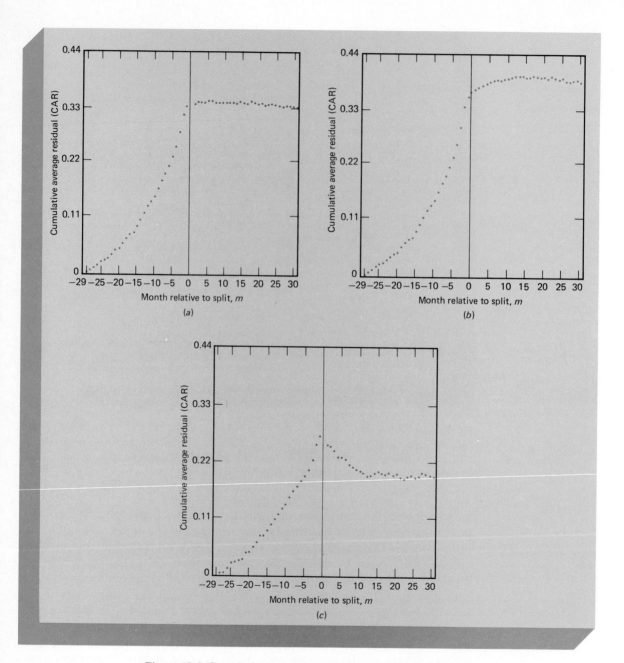

Figure 18-5 Cumulative average residual errors (CARs) in the months before and after a stock dividend or split for (*a*) 940 total splits, (*b*) 672 splits followed by cash dividend increases, and (*c*) 268 splits followed by cash dividend decreases. (*Source:* E. Fama, L. Fisher, M. Jensen, and R. Roll, ''The Adjustment of Stock Prices to New Information,'' *International Economic Review,* Feb. 1969, vol. 20, no. 2, Figs. 2b, 3c, and 3d.)

Figure 18-5*a* shows the cumulative average residuals (CARs) aggregated over all 940 changes in the unit of account. Figure 18-5*b* and *c* shows graphs of the CARs for firms that had stock dividends or splits and then either increased or decreased their cash dividend.

Figure 18-5*b* shows that firms which had stock dividends or splits and subsequently raised cash dividends had small positive residuals in the months *after* the stock dividend or split because the market had *correctly* anticipated the increase. That is, the earnings rise that paid for the increased cash dividend was anticipated and most of the capital gains occurred before the rise in the firm's earnings and cash dividends was announced. Thus, owners of securities that split and also increased their earning power enjoyed abnormally high returns, on average, during the months surrounding the stock dividend or split.

Figure 18-5*c* tells a different story. The firms that had stock dividends or splits and then *decreased* their cash dividends experienced high returns (that is, positive residuals, on average) until the cash dividend declined. Then the value of the stock fell, causing negative residuals ($e_{i,t} < 0$) *after* the cash dividend reduction, which was presumably the result of lower earning power. Thus, investors who bought stocks that had stock dividends or splits followed by *decreases* in their cash dividends were worse off because the stocks experienced capital losses, on average, after the split month, as shown in Figure 18-5*c*.

Conclusions about Stock Splits   This evidence indicates that stock dividends and splits by themselves are worthless—but might convey valuable information about a firm's earning power. Earning power is the basic source of stock values. Stock dividends and splits alone cause high returns for several months before cash dividends are paid because the market expects an increase in the firm's earnings. If the expected increase in the cash dividend does not materialize, the information content of the stock dividend or split is rejected, and returns fall below normal for a while before resuming their pattern along the characteristic line. In the long run, neither the market value of the firm nor the investor returns are changed by stock splits and dividends. Thus, any price changes that occur near the time of stock dividends and splits can be attributed to their implicit information content.

If an investor can correctly anticipate stock dividends and stock splits, the data suggest that it is possible to earn abnormal gains ($e_{i,t} > 0$). However, further studies of the average residuals show they tend to be zero *after* the announcement date of the stock dividend or split.[18] Therefore, speculation on the announcement of stock dividends or splits should *precede the public announcement* if it is to be profitable. This probably requires considerable investment in research to detect the probability of forthcoming stock dividends

---

[18]W. H. Hausman, R. R. West, and J. A. Largay, "Stock Splits, Price Changes, and Trading Profits: A Synthesis," *Journal of Business,* Jan. 1971, pp. 69–77.

and splits before they are announced. The average investor would probably be better off ignoring stock dividends and splits and forecasting earnings instead.

Conclusions about the Semistrong Markets Hypothesis

Moody's manuals, Standard & Poor's reports, and audited financial information filed with the Securities and Exchange Commission are readily available to investors around the world. This background information about corporations provides the perspective needed to evaluate new information. Financial newspapers and news services compete to deliver new information as quickly as possible so that investors can obtain the latest news quickly at minimal cost. The evidence above suggests that, on average, investors interpret this news correctly. When news affects the value of a security, it causes reevaluations— and security trading that *begins immediately and affects prices at once.* The studies reviewed above show that security prices not only react immediately and rationally to news, they often *anticipate* it. In short, security prices seem to reflect publicly available information, as the semistrong hypothesis suggests.

18-4   EVIDENCE THAT SUPPORTS THE STRONGLY EFFICIENT MARKETS HYPOTHESIS

The **strongly efficient markets hypothesis** suggests that *all information,* public or not, is fully reflected in security prices. This idealistic economic situation results in a *perfectly efficient market* where prices and values are always equal as they fluctuate randomly together in response to the arrival of new information.

One obvious way to check the validity of the strongly efficient markets hypothesis is to examine the profitability of trades in securities made by insiders to see if the insiders' access to valuable information allows them to earn statistically significant trading profits.

Trading on Inside Information

Federal law defines **insiders** as the directors, officers, consultants, significant shareholders, and any other persons who have access to material nonpublic information about a firm. (Sections 4-1 and 4-3 discuss the law that pertains to insiders.) This section examines the rates of return earned by business executives who trade the stock of the corporation that employs them.

Jaffe's Study   Federal law requires all insiders to notify within 1 month the Securities and Exchange Commission (SEC) in writing of all trades they have made in their corporation's stock. The SEC then publishes these insider trades in its monthly pamphlet, *Official Summary of Insider Trading,* available to the public through the U.S. Government Printing Office. Professor Jeffrey F. Jaffe

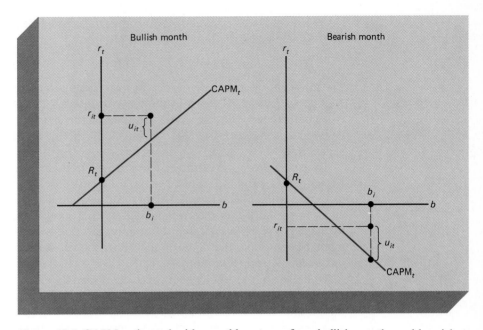

Figure 18-6 CAPM estimated with monthly returns from bullish months and bearish months.

analyzed the *Official Summary* over 6 years to measure insiders' trading profits.[19] The capital asset pricing model (CAPM) furnished the engine for Dr. Jaffe's analysis.

Using the CAPM for empirical work is complicated by the discontinuity encountered in going from the ex ante (future-oriented) theoretical CAPM to the ex post (historically observable) CAPM. When dealing with the ex post data, the CAPM model must be recast to reflect adjustments to disequilibrium situations. As shown in Figure 18-6, the high beta stocks have the highest returns in bull markets and the lowest returns in bear markets.

Jaffe estimated the CAPMs for different months by first estimating the characteristic regression lines of all NYSE stocks; he used the time-series regression equation (10-3) on page 267 to estimate the betas. Each stock's beta systematic risk coefficient and monthly returns were then taken from these first-pass regressions and used for the second-pass regression estimates of each month's

[19]J. F. Jaffe, "Special Information and Insider Trading," *Journal of Business,* July 1974, pp. 410–428. Another study of the profitability of insider trading is J. H. Lorie and V. Niederhoffer, "Predictive and Statistical Properties of Insider Trading," *Journal of Law and Economics,* April 1968, pp. 35–51.

CAPM. Regression equation (18-6) shows the cross-sectional regression model used to estimate the tth month's CAPM.

$$r_{i,t} = c_{0,t} + c_{1,t}(\text{beta}_i) + u_{i,t} \quad \text{for } i = \text{i}, \ldots, n \text{ stocks at time } t \quad (18\text{-}6)$$

The intercept $c_{0,t}$ and slope $c_{1,t}$ coefficients for month t were found by regressing each stock's rate of return in month t, denoted $r_{i,t}$, on their beta systematic risk coefficients. The ith stock's residual error from the CAPM in month t, denoted $u_{i,t}$, measures whether the stock did better or worse than the CAPM suggested.

To assess the value of the insiders' trades in their own corporation's stock, Dr. Jaffe measured the residual errors for the ith stock in month t, as illustrated in Figure 18-6. These residual errors are positive if the return from the trade exceeds the expected return indicated by that month's CAPM, or vice versa for negative residuals. Stated differently, after allowing for bullish or bearish market conditions, the $u_{i,t}$ term measures the ith stock's positive or negative unsystematic return in month t.

To delineate the stocks being actively traded by insiders, Jaffe studied each month's *Official Summary of Insider Trading*. He selected the stocks in each month that had three more inside sellers than buyers—Jaffe labeled this event a *selling plurality* by insiders. Three more insiders buying than selling in the same month was called a *buying plurality*. Jaffe then recorded the monthly residual errors $u_{i,t}$ for each of the stocks that showed an insiders' plurality. After compiling such facts for many stocks and for many years, Jaffe summed up the residual errors for all stocks traded actively by a plurality of insiders in the tth month. Equations (18-7) and (18-8) define the average residual error from the CAPM in month t for stocks that the plurality of insiders bought or sold, respectively. The upper limits of summation, B and S, refer to the number of stocks bought and sold, respectively, by the plurality of insiders in month t.

$$\begin{array}{l}\text{Average buyers'} \\ \text{plurality residual}\end{array} = bu_t = \frac{1}{B}\sum_{i=1}^{B} u_{i,t} \qquad (18\text{-}7)$$

$$\begin{array}{l}\text{Average sellers'} \\ \text{plurality residual}\end{array} = su_t = \frac{1}{S}\sum_{i=1}^{S} u_{i,t} \qquad (18\text{-}8)$$

Combining the *absolute values* of the sums in Equations (18-7) and (18-8) as shown in Equation (18-9) yields the average residual for all insiders' trades in month t; it is denoted U_t.

$$U_t = |bu_t| + |su_t| \qquad (18\text{-}9)$$

The average residual from the CAPM for all insider plurality trading in month t is a measure of extra returns earned by the average insider.

Appropriate buying and selling commissions were subtracted from each insider's trade to obtain net profit. Then the average residuals after commissions

Table 18-2

**CUMULATIVE AVERAGE RESIDUAL MEASURES OF
INSIDERS PROFIT RATES, NET OF 1% COMMISSIONS**

Months cumulated	Cumulative average residual
$C = 1$	$U_{t1} = -0.0102$
$C = 2$	$U_{t2} = 0.0009$
$C = 8$	$U_{t8} = 0.0307$

Source: J. F. Jaffe, "Special Information and Insider Trading," *Journal of Business,* July 1974, pp. 410–428.

were cumulated over $C = 1, 2,$ and 8 months after the month in which the plurality of insiders originally made its trades. This yielded the cumulative average residuals that are defined in Equation (18-10) and shown in Table 18-2.

$$\overline{U}_c = \sum_{m=1}^{C=1,2,8} U_{t+m} \qquad (18\text{-}10)$$

Table 18-2 shows that 1 month ($C = 1$) after a plurality of insider buying or selling, the insiders' net profit after commissions averaged ($-0.0102 \times 100 =$) -1.02 percent of the value of the stock. This negative cumulative average residual indicates the average insider lost money on the trade after 1 month. After the stock was held 2 months ($C = 2$), the insiders broke about even, $U_2 = 0.0009$. Only after 8 months did the plurality of insiders' stocks experience enough price change to pay the commissions and yield ($0.0307 \times 100 =$) 3.07 percent net profit. Statistically speaking, this rate of insiders' trading profit is significantly above zero. Practically speaking, the average insider certainly is not getting rich by making investments based on their information.

Seyhun's Study   Dr. H. N. Seyhun analyzed insiders' trading between 1975 and 1981 using a larger sample and a different research methodology than Jaffe.[20] Seyhun, like Jaffe, reported that insiders earned trading profits. But Seyhun suggested that Jaffe's estimates of the insiders' modest profits were upward biased.

In addition, Seyhun extended Jaffe's study by examining *outsiders* who traded on inside information purchased from one of the financial services that purveys data about insiders' trading activities. Seyhun found that, on average, outsiders who traded on the latest available information reported by insiders to the SEC were unable to earn positive profits from their trades.

---

[20]H. N. Seyhun, "Insiders' Profits, Costs of Trading, and Market Efficiency," *Journal of Financial Economics,* June 1986, vol. 16, no. 1, pp. 189–212.

Monopolistic Access to Valuable Inside Information Appears To Be Limited

The fact that insiders, on average, can earn trading profits from their information refutes the strongly efficient markets hypothesis. Discovery of such flaws in the perfect markets hypothesis prompts one to wonder how many people have monopolistic access to valuable information. Seyhun addressed this question when he reported that *outsiders* who followed the insiders' trades a few weeks later could not earn returns that beat the naive buy-and-hold strategy.[21]

After probing corporate insiders, who undeniably have monopolistic access to valuable information, it seems appropriate to examine another well-informed group—professional portfolio managers. These managers are the individuals that are next most likely to be able to obtain and profit from valuable investment information before it fully affects market prices. Since mutual funds are a highly visible group of professionally managed portfolios, we will briefly consider their ability to outperform the market averages.

In Chapter 21 various aspects of mutual fund performance are analyzed. Rankings of the annual returns achieved by 30 funds for which data could be obtained show (in Table 21-1) that over a 10-year period no individual fund was able to earn a *consistently* better-than-average rate of return. This finding suggests that no individual fund had any relative advantage in obtaining valuable information. A plot of the performance of a sample of 23 mutual funds relative to the efficient frontier in risk-return space (in Figure 21-1) showed that none of the funds was an efficient investment. These and other unbiased mutual fund studies prepared by professors of finance at various colleges, all point to the conclusion that no funds possess any knowledge that has not already been fully reflected in securities prices.[22]

Sections 18-2, 18-3 and 18-4 outlined the three hypotheses that comprise the efficient markets theory. Implications of this theory suggest important investment policies. For instance, those who accept all three hypotheses of the efficient markets theory without reservation will think technical analysis is worthless; they will also favor passive investing over active investment management. In view of the investment consequences that depend on the credibility an investor attaches to the efficient markets theory, Sections 18-5 and 18-6 review empirically observed anomalies in the theory. In Section 18-7 we reconsider the efficient markets theory in light of the anomalies.

[21]During 1988 many newspapers published stories about the millions of dollars Ivan Boesky made by trading on inside information and manipulating security prices. While we have no reason to doubt these sensational accounts, their importance was exaggerated by overenthusiastic newspaper reporters. Scientific studies place the importance of such market imperfections in a better perspective.

[22]Numerous studies published by brokerage houses and others regularly show the great rates of return some mutual fund earned over a flattering but unrepresentative sample period. However, these studies are self-serving advertisements, not unbiased assessments. Chapter 21 reports various unbiased, scientifically prepared empirical studies showing that mutual funds do not outperform a naive buy-and-hold strategy.

18-5   SHILLER'S EMPIRICAL EVIDENCE AGAINST THE EFFICIENT MARKETS THEORY

The efficient markets theory grew in popularity during the late 1960s and early 1970s, and a large body of empirical evidence supporting the theory was published. However, respectable evidence that weighed against the efficient markets theory was also published.[23] In 1981, for example, the research findings of Professor Robert J. Shiller dealt a blow to the efficient markets theory.

Shiller used empirical data for (1) the 1871 through 1979 Standard & Poor's 500 Composite Stocks (S&P 500) Index and (2) the 1928 through 1979 Dow Jones Industrial Average (DJIA).[24] He used per share cash dividends and stock price data, denoted d and p, respectively, that had been adjusted to remove inflationary effects and other factors that might confound his tests. Shiller compared the market prices of these two stock market indexes with their present values. The present values v were calculated using Equation (18-11).

$$v_t = \sum_{f=t+1}^{T} \frac{d_f}{(1+k)^{f-t}} + \frac{p_T}{(1+k)^{T-t}} \qquad (18\text{-}11)$$

where v_t = present value at time t for $t = 1871, 1872, \ldots , 1979$ for S&P
$\quad\ T$ = terminal period, $T = 1979$
$\quad\ f$ = period counter of periods when cash dividends occur; for instance, in 1871, $f = 1872$

Essentially, Equation (18-11) calculates the present value at time t of all future cash dividend income. Period t is incremented year by year to calculate a new present value for each year. Shiller used both constant and time-varying real interest rates for the discount rate k in different applications of Equation (18-11). Figure 18-7 illustrates some representative findings about the divergence Shiller

---

[23]For a collection of security price movement studies, see "Symposium on Some Anomalous Evidence on Capital Market Efficiency," *Journal of Financial Economics,* June–Sept. 1978. These studies presented evidence against the efficient markets theory. Another argument against efficient markets was made by Sanford Grossman and Joseph Stiglitz, "On the Impossibility of Informationally Efficient Markets," *American Economic Review,* June 1980, vol. 3, pp. 393–408.

[24]Several papers presenting evidence against the efficient markets theory have been published by R. J. Shiller. See, for example, R. J. Shiller, "Do Stock Prices Move Too Much to Be Justified by Subsequent Changes in Dividends?," *American Economic Review,* June 1981, vol. 71, pp. 421–436 and R. J. Schiller, "The Use of Volatility Measures in Assessing Market Efficiency," *Journal of Finance,* May 1981, vol. 36, pp. 291–311. For a supporting study see S. LeRoy and M. Porter, "The Present Value Relation: Tests Based on Implied Variance Bounds," *Econometrica,* May 1981, vol. 49, pp. 555–574. See also Lawrence H. Summers, "Does the Stock Market Rationally Reflect Fundamental Values?," *Journal of Finance,* July 1986, vol. 41, no. 3, pp. 591–602.

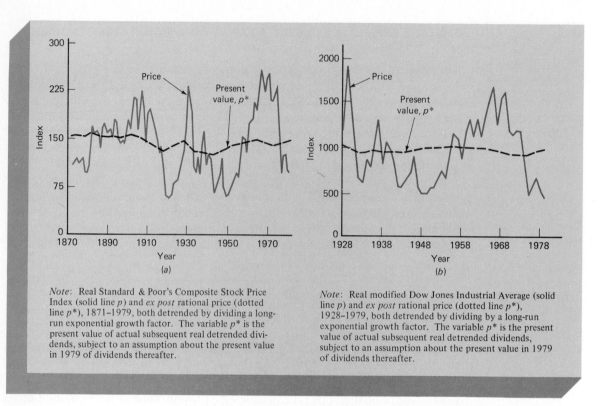

Note: Real Standard & Poor's Composite Stock Price Index (solid line *p*) and *ex post* rational price (dotted line *p**), 1871–1979, both detrended by dividing a long-run exponential growth factor. The variable *p** is the present value of actual subsequent real detrended dividends, subject to an assumption about the present value in 1979 of dividends thereafter.

Note: Real modified Dow Jones Industrial Average (solid line *p*) and *ex post* rational price (dotted line *p**), 1928–1979, both detrended by dividing by a long-run exponential growth factor. The variable *p** is the present value of actual subsequent real detrended dividends, subject to an assumption about the present value in 1979 of dividends thereafter.

Figure 18-7 Time series graphs of market prices and their concurrent present values for (*a*) Standard & Poor's 500 Composite Stocks and (*b*) Dow Jones Industrial Average. (*Source:* R. J. Shiller, "Do Stock Prices Move Too Much to Be Justified by Subsequent Changes in Dividends?" *American Economic Review,* June 1981, vol. 71, figs. 1 and 2, p. 422.)

found between the market prices and the present values of the two portfolio-like stock market indexes he analyzed.

As explained in earlier chapters [see Equation (15-2)], the theory of finance suggests that the true economic value of a security equals the present value of its cash dividend income. However, Figure 18-7*a* and *b* illustrates significant differences between the present value of the two stock indexes' cash dividends and their market prices.

Professors Marsh and Merton faulted Shiller by poining out that the fluctuations in earnings are smoothed out of cash dividend payments.[25] They showed

[25]See T. A. Marsh and R. C. Merton, "Dividend Variability and Variance Bounds Tests for the Rationality of Stock Prices," *American Economic Review,* June 1986, pp. 483–498. Statistical refinements in Shiller's model, Equation (18-11), have been suggested. See R. Flood and R. Hodick, "Asset Price Volatility, Bubbles, and Process Switching,"

(continues)

that the present value of cash dividend payments, which is recalculated each year, must necessarily fluctuate less than market prices do because the year-to-year cash dividend payments are a series of fairly smooth payments. Shiller replied that some of the disparities shown in Figure 18-7 are so large that at least part of the over- and underpricing must be caused by more than the smoothing of cash dividend payments.[26] Shiller's initial insightful study and his reply to Marsh and Merton raise questions about imperfections in the efficient markets theory.

18-6   **ANOMALOUS EMPIRICAL EVIDENCE ABOUT PRICING EFFICIENCY**

Many researchers have discovered anomalies in the efficient markets theory.[27]

Anomalies in the Efficient Markets Hypothesis Discovered before the 1980s

The return regularities in stock prices that were reported before the 1980s are reviewed first. Each of these flaws in the efficient markets theory is described before attempting to reach any conclusions about their effects on the theory.

Low-Priced Stocks   One of the first anomalies in the efficient pricing of common stocks was reported in 1936 by L. H. Fritzemeier. Fritzemeier worked through numerous hand calculations to show that low-priced common stocks

---

(continued)
Journal of Finance, March 1986, vol. 41, pp. 831–843. Also see James Hamilton, ''On Testing for Self-Fulfilling Speculative Price Bubbles,'' *International Economic Review,* Oct. 1986, vol. 27, pp. 545–552. Furthermore, see Allan Kleidon, ''Variance Bounds Tests and Stock Price Valuation Models,'' *Journal of Political Economy,* Oct. 1986, vol. 94, pp. 953–1001. And see Kenneth West, ''A Specification Test for Speculative Bubbles,'' *Quarterly Journal of Economics,* Aug. 1987, vol. 102, pp. 553–580. See also Wayne Joerding, ''Excess Stock Price Volatility as a Misspecified Euler Equation,'' *Journal of Financial and Quantitative Analysis,* Sept. 1986, vol. 23, no. 3, pp. 253–267. The refinements suggested by these studies are designed to delineate the source of the price-value disparity.

[26]For Shiller's reply to Kleidon (and also Marsh and Merton), see R. J. Shiller, ''The Probability of Gross Violations of a Present Value Variance Inequality,'' *Journal of Political Economy,* 1988, vol. 96, pp. 1089–1092.

[27]Other studies in the same vein as Shiller's include O. Blanchard and M. Watson, ''Bubbles, Rational Expectations, and Financial Markets,'' in P. Wachtel, ed., *Crises in the Economic and Financial Structure* (Lexington: Lexington Books, 1982). Also see J. Y. Campbell and R. J. Shiller, ''Stock Prices, Earnings, and Expected Dividends,'' *Journal of Finance,* July 1988, vol. XLIII, no. 3, pp. 661–676. And, see G. Evans, ''Expectational Stability and the Multiple Equilibria Problem in Linear Rational Expectations Models,'' *Quarterly Journal of Economics,* Nov. 1985, vol. 100, pp. 1218–1233.

(continues)

tended to earn higher rates of return than high-priced stocks.[28] More recent research using massive computerized databases, however, suggests that the low-priced stocks which earn the highest rates of return may be significantly positively correlated with the size and riskiness of the issuing corporation. Thus, even though the low-priced stocks do perform differently than the medium- and high-priced stocks, on average, the price level of the stock may really only be a proxy (or, stated differently, a redundant measure) for the size and/or the riskiness of the issuing firm.

Price-Earnings Ratio Effects Basu's study of stocks with low P/E ratios documents another anomaly to the efficient markets theory.[29] Other studies have since confirmed the popular old belief that common stocks selling at low multiples of their earnings per share earn abnormally high rates of return. The P/E ratio effect remains a robust and statistically significant determinant of common stock returns (see Table 16-5). No one has been able to explain why this return regularity exists. In fact, the causes for most of the return regularities in stock prices reported here remain undetermined—but they are nevertheless flaws in the efficient markets theory.

Cash Dividend Yield The effects of cash dividends have been the subject of study for decades because dividend policy is important to students of both managerial finance and investments.

(*continued*)
In addition, see R. Flood and P. Garber, "Market Fundamentals versus Price Level Bubbles: The First Tests," *Journal of Political Economy,* Aug. 1980, vol. 88, pp. 645–670. Furthermore, see C. Granger and R. Engle, "Dynamic Model Specification with Equilibrium Constraints: Cointegration and Error-Correction," *Econometrica,* March 1987, vol. 55, pp. 251–276. Also see L. Summers, "Does the Stock Market Rationally Reflect Fundamental Values?," *Journal of Finance,* July 1986, vol. 41, no. 3, pp. 591–602. And, see J. Poterba and L. Summers, "The Persistence of Volatility and Stock Market Fluctuations," *American Economic Review,* 1986, vol. 76, pp. 1142–1151.

[28]See L. H. Fritzemeier, "Relative Price Fluctuation of Industrial Stocks in Different Price Groups," *Journal of Business,* April 1936, pp. 113–154. Also see M. E. Blume and F. Husic, "Price, Beta, and Exchange Listing," *Journal of Finance,* May 1973, vol. 28, no. 2, pp. 283–299. See also Dan Galai and Benjamin Bachrach, "The Risk-Return Relationship and Stock Prices," *Journal of Financial and Quantitative Analysis,* June 1979. And see R. Edmister and J. Greene, "Performance of Super-Low-Price Stocks," *Journal of Portfolio Management,* Fall 1980, pp. 36–41. More recently, see Hans R. Stoll and R. E. Whaley, "Transactions Costs and the Small Firm Effect," *Journal of Financial Economics,* vol. 12, pp. 57–79.

[29]S. Basu, "The Investment Performance of Common Stocks in Relation to Their Price-Earnings Ratios: A Test of the Efficient Markets Hypothesis," *Journal of Finance,* June 1977, vol. XXXII, no. 3, pp. 663–682. Also see S. Basu, "The Relationship between Earnings Yield, Market Value and Return for NYSE Common Stocks: Further Evidence," *Journal of Financial Economics,* June 1983, vol. 12, no. 1, pp. 129–156.

Income tax laws in most countries encourage investing by taxing capital gains income at a lower tax rate than ordinary income. (Even the U.S. Tax Reform Act of 1986, which taxes capital gains and cash dividend income at the same rate, allows the capital gains tax to be postponed until the gain is realized.) Such tax laws lead us to suspect that investors might prefer a dollar of capital gains income over a dollar of cash dividend income, if all other factors are equal.

In contrast, it has been suggested that some investors prefer the cash dividend income because it involves less uncertainty than the gains from price fluctuations. In hopes of resolving the two different viewpoints, many researchers have studied the relation between common stock returns and cash dividend yields to determine if it is positive, not significantly different from zero, or negative.[30] The various studies do not reach a consensus, but most of them suggest that cash dividend yields have a positive but marginally significant effect on the market value of equity shares. Cash dividend effects of any kind can be considered another anomaly in the efficient markets theory.

January Effect   Another return regularity that has been observed for decades is the tendency for stock prices to decline slightly during the last few trading days of December and then move up smartly during January. Much of a year's price appreciation typically occurs in January. Observers have hypothesized that tax-loss selling in December followed by reinvesting during the next few weeks might cause the January effect. But, no one has scientifically isolated the cause.[31] The well-known January effect has also been linked to various

---

[30]The following empirical studies suggest the range of results obtained. See F. Black and M. Scholes, "The Effects of Dividend Yield and Dividend Policy on Common Stock Prices and Returns," *Journal of Financial Economics,* May 1974, vol. 1, pp. 1–22. Insignificant cash dividend effects are reported. Also see M. Blume, "Stock Returns and Dividend Yields: Some More Empirical Evidence," *Review of Economics and Statistics,* Nov. 1980, pp. 567–577. Stocks that pay zero cash dividends are reported to earn abnormally high returns. And, see R. Litzenberger and K. Ramaswamy, "The Effect of Personal Taxes and Dividends on Capital Asset Prices," *Journal of Financial Economics,* June 1979, vol. 7, pp. 163–195. A positive and significant relationship between dividend yield and common stock returns is reported. Furthermore, see M. H. Miller and M. Scholes, "Dividends and Taxes," *Journal of Financial Economics,* Dec. 1978, vol. 6, pp. 333–364. Also see M. Miller and M. Scholes, "Dividends and Taxes: Some Empirical Evidence," *Journal of Political Economy,* 1982, vol. 90, pp. 1118–1141. Insignificant empirical results are reported in the latter article. More recently, see A. R. Ofer and D. R. Siegel, "Corporate Financial Policy, Information, and Market Expectations: An Empirical Investigation of Dividends," *Journal of Finance,* Sept. 1987, vol. 42, pp. 889–911.

[31]See E. Dyl, "Capital Gains Taxation and Year End Stock Market Behavior," *Journal of Finance,* March 1977, pp. 165–175. Also see B. Branch, "A Tax Loss Trading Rule," *Journal of Business,* April 1977, pp. 198–207. In addition, see C. Jones, D. Pearce, and

(continues)

other effects, and it has been shown that significant portions of the other effects often occur in January.[32] The persistence of the January effect as it reappears in many different studies is an imperfection in the weakly efficient markets hypothesis.

Business Cycle Effects   Many years ago the National Bureau of Economic Research (NBER) pinpointed the stock market averages as the best leading indicator of business activity in the United States.[33] The stock market always declines months before the economy enters a recession. Unfortunately, the stock market is not a flawless leading indicator of business activity; it sometimes

------

(continued)

J. Wilson, ''Can Tax Loss Selling Explain the January Effect? A Note,'' *Journal of Finance,* June 1987, pp. 453–461.

Many studies that analyze the efficacy of various motives for selling stocks have been published; the action is often categorized as irrational behavior. See, for example, J. Lakonishok and S. Smidt, ''Volume of Winners and Losers: Taxation and Other Motives for Stock Selling,'' *Journal of Finance,* Sept. 1986. pp. 951–974. Also see W. DeBondt and R. Thaler, ''Further Evidence of Investor Overreaction and Stock Market Seasonality,'' *Journal of Finance,* July 1987, pp. 557–581.

[32]The combined effects of the firm's size, January, and neglect by institutional investors are discussed by C. Barry and S. Brown, ''Limited Information as a Source of Risk,'' *Journal of Portfolio Management,* Winter 1986, pp. 66–72.

The size and January effects are evaluated together by D. Keim, ''Size-Related Anomalies and Stock Return Seasonality: Further Empirical Evidence,'' *Journal of Financial Economics,* June 1983, pp. 13–32.

The firm's size, January, and yield effects are investigated by D. Keim, ''The Interrelation between Dividend Yields, Equity Values and Stock Returns: Implications of Abnormal January Returns'' (Ph.D. dissertation, University of Chicago, 1983). Also see D. Keim, ''Dividend Yields and Stock Returns: Implications of Abnormal January Returns,'' *Journal of Financial Economics,* 1985, vol. 14, pp. 473–489. In addition, see D. Keim, ''Dividend Yields and the January Effect,'' *Journal of Portfolio Management,* Winter 1986, pp. 54–60.

Firm size, neglect, and the price-earnings ratio are the topics of R. Dowen and S. Bauman, ''The Relative Importance of Size, P/E and Neglect,'' *Journal of Portfolio Management,* Spring 1986, pp. 30–34.

Firm size, neglect, price-earnings ratio, and January are effects that are evaluated by A. Arbel, ''Generic Stocks: An Old Product in a New Package,'' *Journal of Portfolio Management,* Summer 1985, pp. 4–13.

[33]For a detailed and expert discussion, see Geoffrey H. Moore, ''Security Markets and Business Cycles,'' in *Business Cycles, Inflation and Forecasting,* National Bureau of Economic Research Studies in Business Cycle Number 24 (Cambridge, Mass.: Ballinger, 1980), chap. 9.

Business cycle–related fluctuations may be what caused the 3- to 5-year reversals reported by E. F. Fama and K. R. French, ''Permanent and Temporary Components of Stock Prices,'' *Journal of Political Economy,* April 1988, vol. 96, no. 2, pp. 246–273.

crashes when no recession follows—for instance, in October 1987.[34] Presumably, the market anticipates a recession that never fully materializes after the warnings of a downturn occur. Nevertheless, the business cycle has an undeniable effect on stock prices. This relationship between stock prices and business activity can introduce trends, business cycle fluctuations, and other patterns that might be considered blemishes on the efficient markets theory.

Beta Effects The capital asset pricing model (Chapter 10) and the arbitrage pricing theory (Chapter 11) are the premier theoretical models about investment behavior. Both models indicate that systematic risk should be the main determinant of common stocks' expected returns. Therefore, it would be incorrect to call beta effects anomalous to the efficient markets theory. Instead, the effects of beta risk should be filtered out of the returns being examined in order to isolate those portions of the unexplained residual returns that are anomalous. The study of stock dividends and splits by Fama, Fisher, Jensen, and Roll (Section 18-3) provides an example of how to filter out beta effects when searching for a return regularity. Multivariate statistical tests of anomalies in the efficient markets theory that are reviewed at the end of this chapter incorporate another statistical adjustment to hold beta effects constant. These statistical refinements are essential if *unbiased conclusions* are desired.

Anomalies in the Efficient Markets Hypothesis Discovered during the 1980s

Many additional return regularities were discovered by researchers in the 1980s. This section briefly describes more recent anomalies in the efficient markets theory.

Within-the-Month Effects Research has shown that stock price returns tend to be positive during the first half of the month; then they typically average zero from midmonth until the last few days of the month, and finally they tend to become positive again on the last few days of the month.[35] Any particular month may deviate substantially from this pattern. But this return regularity is a flaw in the weakly efficient markets hypothesis.

The Sales:Price Effect Professors Senchack and Martin suggested that the ratio of sales, on a per share basis, divided by price per share was a better indicator of superior returns than the venerable price-earnings ratio. Senchack

---

[34]See A. Arbel, S. Carvell, and E. Postnieks, "The Smart Crash of October 19th," *Harvard Business Review,* May–June 1988, pp. 124–136. The authors present empirical evidence that the stock market crashed in October 1987 because most stocks were overpriced.

[35]See Robert A. Ariel, "A Monthly Effect in Stock Returns," *Journal of Financial Economics,* March 1987, vol. 18, no. 1, pp. 161–174.

and Martin provide credible empirical evidence that documents another imperfection in the efficient markets theory (since some sales could be unprofitable).[36]

Effect of Cashflows Because accounting earnings are so vaguely defined (see Table 16-1), because the Financial Accounting Standards Board ruling number 95 requires cashflow accounting statements starting in 1988, and because corporate raiders tend to focus on cashflows when planning their takeovers, it has been suggested that the cashflow per share has more influence on a stock's price than earnings per share.[37] Since a corporation's cashflows can be obtained from its publicly reported financial statements, this return regularity might be interpreted as an efficient markets imperfection.

Unsystematic (or Diversifiable) Risk Effects Measurements of diversifiable risk are usually made with a regression statistic called the *residual variance* (or its square root, the standard error) around the characteristic line. The CAPM and APT, which are the received asset pricing theories, explicitly assign zero influence to diversifiable (or unsystematic) risk in the determination of assets' prices. In spite of the importance of these theories, some empirical studies nevertheless report that diversifiable risk has significant explanatory power over stock prices.[38]

Effects of Skewness or Coskewness Skewness is usually equated with the third statistical moment. Skewness is a statistic that measures lopsidedness in a probability distribution. Coskewness measures an asset's systematic skewness with the market portfolio. Theoretical and empirical research has suggested that assets which can contribute positive skewness to an investor's portfolio are more desirable than assets that contribute negative skewness or have sym-

---

[36]See A. Senchack and J. Martin, "The Relative Performance of the PSR and PER Investment Strategies," *Financial Analysts Journal,* March–April 1987, pp. 46–56.

[37]See J. J. Mahoney, M. V. Sever, and J. A. Theis, "Cash Flow: FASB Opens the Floodgates," *Journal of Accountancy,* May 1988, pp. 27–38. See also J. M. Laderman, "The Savviest Investors Are Going with the Flow," *Business Week,* Sept. 7, 1987, p. 92. See also J. M. Laderman, "A Divining Rod for Deal Stocks Is Striking Gold," *Business Week,* March 21, 1988, p. 120.

[38]G. Douglas, "Risk in the Equity Markets: An Empirical Appraisal of Market Efficiency," *Yale Economic Essays,* Spring 1969, pp. 3–45. Also see I. Friend, R. Westerfield, and M. Granito, "New Evidence on the CAPM," *Journal of Finance,* June 1978, pp. 903–920.

In this context, it should be noted that portfolio theory does not presume that diversifiable risk should be ignored by undiversified investors. Diversifiable risk can harm **undiversified investors,** and they should minimize it too.

metric probability distributions of returns, if all other factors are equal.[39] Co-skewness represents another shortcoming in the efficient markets theory that could be used profitably by active investments analysts.

Agency Effects   Jensen and Meckling suggested that corporate executives, in their roles as agents for the stockholders, may not always try to make decisions that maximize the value of the firm for the owners of the firm.[40] Empirical evidence suggests that such *agency costs* tend to cause the average rate of return from common stocks to vary directly with the percentage of the corporation's stock owned by the managers of the corporation.[41] This finding implies that firms managed by executives who are also owners (at least partially) will tend to be better investments than firms managed by executives who are merely employees. This return regularity provides another loophole in the efficient markets theory from which investments analysts can hope to profit.

Earnings Controversy Effects   Professors Carvel and Strebel have suggested a return regularity that stems from difficulties in forecasting a firm's earnings. Carvel and Strebel reported that a stock's future returns may be positively related to controversy (or uncertainty) about the stock's future earnings per share.[42] The degree of controversy is usually measured with the coefficient of variation of the earnings forecasts prepared by professional securities analysts which are published by the financial services.[43]

Effects of Earnings Surprises   "Earnings surprises" can be defined in various ways. One way, for example, is a relatively large deviation from an earnings forecast. Stocks that have surprisingly good or bad earnings tend to experience

---

[39]See A. Kraus and R. Litzenberger, "Skewness Preference and the Valuation of Risk Assets," *Journal of Finance,* Sept. 1976, pp. 1085–1100. Also see I. Friend and R. Westerfield, "Co-skewness and Capital Asset Pricing," *Journal of Finance,* Sept. 1980, pp. 897–913. And see G. Barone-Adesi, "Arbitrage Equilibrium with Skewed Asset Returns," *Journal of Financial and Quantitative Analysis,* Sept. 1985, vol. 20, pp. 299–313.

[40]Michael C. Jensen and William H. Meckling, "Theory of the Firm: Managerial Behavior, Agency Costs and Ownership Structure," *Journal of Financial Economics,* 1976, vol. 3, pp. 305–360.

[41]Wi Saeng Kim, Jae Won Lee, and Jack Clark Francis, "Investment Performance of Common Stocks in Relation to Inside Ownership," *Financial Review,* Feb. 1988, vol. 23, no. 1, pp. 53–64.

[42]See S. Carvel and P. Strebel, "A New Beta Incorporating Analysts' Forecasts," *Journal of Portfolio Management,* Fall 1984, pp. 81–85.

[43]Two companies collect and publish earnings forecasts from professional security analysts: I/B/E/S, or Institutional Brokers Estimate System, owned by Lynch Jones and Ryan, and Zacks Investment Service, both in New York City. I/B/E/S makes its service available at no charge to academic researchers.

abnormal price appreciations or declines, respectively.[44] The abnormal price moves are apparently the market's reaction to important financial information that was not anticipated. Abnormal price reactions violate the perfectly efficient markets hypothesis.

Effects of Trends in Analysts' Earnings Forecasts Trends in a corporation's forecasted earnings per share can be measured. One possible measure is the percentage change from the most current consensus earnings forecast to the 1-year-ahead consensus earnings forecast. Empirical evidence suggests that stock prices are affected by such trends in earnings forecasts.[45] The efficient markets hypotheses provide no rationale for such price reactions.

Effect of an "Earnings Torpedo" When the market has high expectations for a stock's earnings and as a result has bid up that stock's price in anticipation of high future earnings, the stock's price can sink as if it were torpedoed if the actual earnings turn out to be significantly worse than expected.[46] Such price reactions can reach proportions that represent anomalies in an efficient pricing mechanism.

Effects of Relative Strength Relative strength is a *technical analysis* tool that was explained in Section 17-7. The ability of relative strength measures to pinpoint return regularities has been supported by several different empirical studies.[47] These studies document another anomaly in the efficient markets theory.

[44]See Sections 16-1 and 16-2 for statistics measuring stock price reactions to earnings surprises.

[45]See T. Kerrigan, "When Forecasting Earnings It Pays to Watch Forecasts," *Journal of Portfolio Management,* Summer 1984. Furthermore, see R. Arnott, "The Use and Misuse of Consensus Earnings," *Journal of Portfolio Management,* Spring 1985, pp. 18–27. And see G. Benesh and P. Peterson, "On the Relation between Earnings Changes, Analysts' Forecasts and Stock Price Fluctuations," *Financial Analysts Journal,* Nov.–Dec. 1986, pp. 29–39.

[46]See G. Benesh and P. Peterson, "On the Relation between Earnings Changes, Analysts' Forecasts and Stock Price Fluctuations," *Financial Analysts Journal,* Nov.–Dec. 1986, pp. 29–39.

[47]See J. Brush, "Eight Relative Strength Models Compared," *Journal of Portfolio Management,* Fall 1986, pp. 21–28. Also see M. Greene and B. Fielitz, "Long-Term Dependence of Common Stock Returns," *Journal of Financial Economics,* May 1977, pp. 339–349. Furthermore, see R. Arnott, "Relative Strength Revisited," *Journal of Portfolio Management,* Spring 1979, pp. 19–23. And see J. Bohan, "Relative Strength: Further Positive Evidence," *Journal of Portfolio Management,* Fall 1981, pp. 36–39. Also see J. Brush and K. Boles, "The Predictive Power in Relative Strength and CAPM," *Journal of Portfolio Management,* Summer 1983, pp. 20–23.

Residual Reversal Effects Residual reversals can be measured by observing the residual errors, denoted $e_{i,t}$ for the ith asset in period t, from the characteristic line of Equation (10-3). Reversals refer to the sign changes (positive to negative, or vice versa) in these residuals. Empirical evidence has documented the tendency for the residuals to reverse sign more than would occur randomly.[48] This nonrandom price behavior flaws efficient markets theory again.

Firm's Size Effect Small firms tend to earn better rates of return than large firms.[49] Various research studies using the total dollar value of all outstanding common stock as a measure of the firm's size have substantiated the size effect. There is also considerable research about the interaction of the size effect and other return regularities.[50] However, no cause-and-effect reason has been delineated to explain this and most of the other observed return regularities.

[48]See R. Schwartz and D. Whitcomb, "Evidence on the Presence and Causes of Serial Correlation in the Market Model Residuals," *Journal of Financial and Quantitative Analysis,* June 1977, pp. 291–313. Also see Barr Rosenberg and Andrew Rudd, "Factor-Related and Specific Returns on Common Stocks: Serial Correlation and Market Inefficiency," *Journal of Finance,* May 1982, pp. 543–554. See also B. Rosenberg, K. Reid, and R. Lanstein, "Persuasive Evidence of Market Inefficiency," *Journal of Portfolio Management,* Spring 1985, pp. 9–16. In a similar vein, evidence that stocks that enjoy price appreciation in one week decline in price the next week, and vice versa, has been presented in Bruce N. Lehman, "Fads, Martingales, and Market Efficiency," unpublished manuscript, April 1989.

[49]See R. Banz, "The Relationship between Return and Market Value of the Common Stock," *Journal of Financial Economics,* March 1981, pp. 3–18. For an overview of size-related issues see W. Schwert, "Size and Stock Returns, and Other Empirical Regularities," *Journal of Financial Economics,* June 1983, pp. 3–12.

[50]The combined effects of size and other factors are examined in T. Cook and M. Rozeff, "Size and Earnings/Price Ratio Anomalies: One Effect or Two?" *Journal of Financial and Quantitative Analysis,* Dec. 1984, pp. 449–466. In addition, see R. Banz and W. Breen, "Sample-Dependent Results Using Accounting and Market Data: Some Evidence," *Journal of Finance,* Sept. 1986, pp. 779–793. And, see D. Goodman and J. Peavy, "The Interaction of Firm Size and Price-Earnings Ratio on Portfolio Performance," *Financial Analysts Journal,* Jan.–Feb. 1986, pp. 9–12.

The size and January effects are evaluated together by D. Keim, "Size-Related Anomalies and Stock Return Seasonality: Further Empirical Evidence," *Journal of Financial Economics,* June 1983, pp. 13–32. And, see R. Roll, "Vas Ist Das? The Turn of the Year Effect and the Return Premia of Small Firms," *Journal of Portfolio Management,* Winter 1983, pp. 18–28. And, see G. Constantinides, "Optimal Stock Trading with Personal Taxes: Implications for Prices and the Abnormal January Returns," *Journal of Financial Economics,* March 1984, pp. 65–90. Also read J. Lakonishok and S. Smidt, "Trading Bargains in Small Firms at Year-End," *Journal of Portfolio Management,* Spring 1986, pp. 24–29. And read P. Schultz, "Personal Income Taxes and the January Effect: Small Firm Stock Returns before the War Revenue Act of 1917: A Note," *Journal of Finance,* March 1985, pp. 333–343. Read also D. Keim and R.

(continues)

Effect of Neglect Neglected stocks are variously defined as stocks that lack popularity with the large institutional investors, stocks not followed by many professional security analysts, or stocks about which it is difficult to get information. Research has suggested that these neglected stocks tend to earn better than average returns; it represents another anomaly in the efficient markets theory.[51]

Day-of-the-Week and Time-of-the-Day Effects Stock prices tend to rise on Fridays more often than any other day of the week and have risen least often on Mondays. This day-of-the-week pattern is without economic rationale.[52] Not only do an inordinate number of losses occur on Mondays, most of these

---

(continued)

Stambaugh, "Predicting Returns in the Stock and Bond Markets," *Journal of Financial Economics,* 1986, vol. 17, pp. 357–390. And, consult R. Rogalski and S. Tinic, "The January Size Effect: Anomaly or Risk Mismeasurement?" *Financial Analysts Journal,* Nov.–Dec. 1986, pp. 63–70.

The size and residual risk effects are the topics of J. Lakonishok and A. Shapiro, "Stock Returns, Beta, Variance and Size: An Empirical Analysis," *Financial Analysts Journal,* July–Aug. 1984, pp. 36–41. Also see S. Tinic and R. West, "Risk, Return and Equilibrium: A Revisit," *Journal of Political Economy,* Feb. 1986, pp. 127–147.

A combination of the size, January, and day-of-the-week effects are the topic of R. Rogalski, "New Findings Regarding Day-of-the-Week Returns over Trading and Non-Trading Periods: A Note," *Journal of Finance,* Dec. 1984, pp. 1603–1614. See also D. Keim, "Daily Returns and Size-Related Premiums: One More Time," *Journal of Portfolio Management,* Winter 1987, pp. 41–47. Size and January effects are the topics of C. Barry and S. Brown, "Limited Information as a Source of Risk," *Journal of Portfolio Management,* Winter 1986, pp. 66–72. D. Keim, "Dividend Yields and Stocks Returns: Implications of Abnormal January Returns," *Journal of Financial Economics,* 1985, vol. 14, pp. 473–489. D. Keim, "Dividend Yields and the January Effect," *Journal of Portfolio Management,* Winter 1986, pp. 54–60.

Size, neglect, and the P/E ratio are studied by R. Dowen and S. Bauman, "The Relative Importance of Size, P/E and Neglect," *Journal of Portfolio Management,* Spring 1986, pp. 30–34.

The firm's size, neglect, the P/E ratio, and January effects are the topics of A. Arbel, "Generic Stocks: An Old Product in a New Package," *Journal of Portfolio Management,* Summer 1985, pp. 4–13.

[51]See A. Arbel and P. Strebel, "The Neglected and Small Firm Effects," *Financial Review,* Nov. 1982, pp. 201–218. Also see A. Arbel, S. Carvel, and P. Strebel, "Giraffes, Institutions and Neglected Firms," *Financial Analysts Journal,* May–June 1983, pp. 57–62. For a theoretical model that embraces size effects and the effects of neglect, see Robert Merton, "A Simple Model of Capital Market Equilibrium with Incomplete Information," *Journal of Finance,* July 1987, pp. 483–510.

[52]See Frank Cross, "The Behavior of Stock Prices on Fridays and Mondays," *Financial Analysts Journal,* Nov.–Dec. 1973, pp. 67–69. Also see Kenneth R. French, "Stock Returns and the Weekend Effect," *Journal of Financial Economics,* March 1980. More

(continues)

losses take place before lunch. On the other four trading days of the week, prices tend to rise throughout the day. Both the day-of-the-week and the time-of-the-day have stock price implications that recur too frequently to be ignored.[53] These statistically significant return regularities represent another defect in the weakly efficient markets hypothesis.

Effects of the Book-Value-to-Price Ratio Empirical evidence has been published showing that stocks having high book values per share relative to their per share market price tend to perform well.[54] In particular, when a stock's price falls below its book value, the stock is judged to be a potential good buy. The reason for this relationship between book value and market price is unknown, but it could be because accountants sometimes make depreciation deductions when an asset is appreciating. In addition, the use of depreciation techniques that accelerate the writeoffs excessively might contribute to this effect. In any event, an efficient market should see through this effect instead of reacting to it.

How to Place Bets on the Return Regularities

Some managers of common stock portfolios have taken note of the return regularities and jumped on the anomaly bandwagon in hopes of capturing some extraordinary returns.[55] Some who have placed their bets on one or more anomalies have done so in an ad hoc manner. Before they use the findings about nonefficient pricing effects, money managers should pause to determine which return regularities are merely proxies for other effects and therefore redundant and which are sufficiently independent to recur by themselves.

Multivariate Statistics Jacobs and Levy used multivariate statistical techniques to analyze simultaneously 25 different return regularities.[56] Their re-

---

(*continued*)

recently, see R. A. Connolly, ''An Examination of the Robustness of the Weekend Effect,'' *Journal of Financial and Quantitative Analysis,* June 1989, pp. 133–169. Connolly's findings suggest that the weekend effect ended about 1975.

[53]Day-of-the-week and time-of-the-day effects are investigated by L. Harris, ''A Transaction Data Study of Weekly and Intradaily Patterns in Stock Returns,'' *Journal of Financial Economics,* 1986, vol. 16, pp. 99–117. Also see L. Harris, ''How to Profit from Intradaily Stock Returns,'' *Journal of Portfolio Management,* Winter 1986, pp. 61–64. See also M. Smirlock and L. Starks, ''Day-of-the-Week and Intraday Effects in Stock Returns,'' *Journal of Financial Economics,* 1986, vol. 17, pp. 197–210.

[54]B. Rosenberg, K. Reid, and R. Lanstein, ''Persuasive Evidence of Market Inefficiency,'' *Journal of Portfolio Management,* Spring 1985, pages 9–16.

[55]*Pensions and Investment Age,* Nov. 10, 1986, p. 92.

[56]See Bruce I. Jacobs and Kenneth N. Levy, ''Disentangling Equity Return Regularities: New Insights and Investment Opportunities,'' *Financial Analysts Journal,* May–June 1988, pp. 18–43.

search methodology "purified" the results and disentangled the return regularities so that the true anomalies could be separated from the anomalies that were merely redundant proxies. Table 18-3 shows some summary statistics.

Table 18-3 shows the average monthly rate of return and t-statistics attributed to each of 25 different anomalies that were investigated by Jacobs and Levy. The t-statistic is a well-known indicator of statistical significance; it is explained in many statistics textbooks. As a rule-of-thumb, a t-statistic that has an ab-

Table 18-3
MONTHLY AVERAGE RETURNS TO ANOMALIES

Anomaly	Naive anomaly		Pure anomaly		Differential (pure − naive)	
	Monthly average	t-statistic	Monthly average	t-statistic	Monthly average	t-statistic
Low P/E	0.59%	3.4†	0.46%	4.7†	−0.13%	−1.4
Small size	0.15	2.3*	0.12	2.7†	−0.03	−0.7
Yield	−0.01	−0.1	0.03	0.5	0.04	0.4
Zero yield	0.00	0.0	0.15	1.3	0.15	0.6
Neglect	0.14	1.9*	0.10	1.7*	−0.04	−0.7
Low price	−0.01	−0.1	0.01	0.2	0.02	0.3
Book/price	0.17	1.4	0.09	1.2	−0.08	−0.7
Sales/price	0.17	3.1†	0.17	3.7†	−0.01	−0.2
Cash/price	0.36	2.7†	0.04	0.6	−0.32	−2.3*
Sigma	0.16	0.6	0.07	0.6	−0.09	−0.4
Beta	−0.01	−0.0	0.04	0.3	0.05	0.4
Coskewness	0.09	0.6	0.04	0.7	−0.05	−0.3
Controversy	−0.33	−2.1*	−0.05	−0.8	0.27	2.0*
Trend in estimates (−1)‡	0.48	4.8†	0.51	8.1†	0.03	0.3
Trend in estimates (−2)‡	0.40	4.4†	0.28	4.9†	−0.12	−1.3
Trend in estimates (−3)‡	0.29	3.0†	0.19	3.8†	−0.10	−1.3
Earnings surprise (−1)‡	0.44	2.1*	0.48	3.7†	0.04	0.2
Earnings surprise (−2)‡	0.47	1.8*	0.18	0.8	−0.28	−1.8*
Earnings surprise (−3)‡	−0.03	−0.1	−0.21	−1.1	−0.18	−1.0
Earnings torpedo	−0.00	−0.0	−0.10	−1.7*	−0.10	−1.2
Relative strength	0.30	1.4	0.34	3.5†	0.04	0.3
Residual reversal (−1)‡	−0.54	−4.9†	−1.08	−17.8†	−0.54	−7.3†
Residual reversal (−2)‡	−0.13	−1.4	−0.37	−8.1†	−0.23	−3.3†
Short-term tax	−0.08	−0.4	−0.04	−0.4	0.04	0.3
Long-term tax	−0.29	−1.6	−0.00	−0.1	0.28	1.7*

*Significant at the 10 percent level.
†Significant at the 1 percent level.
‡Parenthetical integers refer to months of lagged responses.
Source: Bruce I. Jacobs and Kenneth N. Levy, "Disentangling Equity Return Regularities: New Insights and Investment Opportunities," *Financial Analysts Journal,* May–June 1988, table II, p. 25.

solute value in excess of 2.0 indicates the presence of a statistically significant result rather than a random sampling error. Two sets of returns and t-statistics are shown for each of the 25 anomalies in the table.

The two columns of statistics under the heading "Naive anomaly" in Table 18-3 were estimated on a one-anomaly-at-a-time basis without trying to control for statistical confounding from other effects. The columns under the heading "Pure anomaly," were prepared using a multivariate regression that considered 25 anomalies and 38 industry effects jointly. The purified anomaly results differ from the naive anomaly results because when two or more anomalies measure the same thing, the multivariate regression controlled for (or purified) each effect so that it is independent of the other effects. The last two columns in Table 18-3 show the results of the statistical purification by presenting statistics about the differences between the naive and the purified sets of anomaly statistics.

Insightful Findings Table 18-3 contains some insights. First, note that even though other researchers previously reported significant findings, 10 of the 25 return regularities analyzed by Jacobs and Levy were statistically insignificant (namely, $-2.0 < t$-statistic < 2.0) in both their naive and pure forms. These insignificant return regularities do not mean that the original research was flawed. More likely, the cause for differing statistics is **sampling error.** Statistics are dependent on their underlying samples. As a result, a different sample can yield different statistics. In addition, if the statistical test is formulated in a slightly different manner, the test can yield different results.

Second, even though some of the pure anomaly effects are smaller than the naively measured effects, the statistical significance of the pure effects may nevertheless be greater. Each effect behaves differently and must be evaluated separately when it is purged of confounding effects. The residual reversal effect, for example, is unusual because it is stronger in its purified form than in its naive form.

Third, the significance of some anomalies (such as the cashflow effect) disappears when the confounding effects of the other variables are statistically removed. Fourth, the strength and persistence of several of the anomalies are sufficient to constitute flaws in the efficient markets hypothesis. For example, note that residual reversals, forecasted trends in earnings, and earnings surprises continue to show statistically significant effects for 2 to 3 months. Fifth, the lack of statistical significance attached to the beta systematic risk variable detracts from the validity of the CAPM. Furthermore, it indirectly detracts from the arbitrage pricing theory because the CAPM beta can be decomposed into APT betas.

Profiting from Return Anomalies Estimates prepared by Jacobs and Levy indicated that only 11 of the 25 pure anomalies that they investigated paid statistically significant abnormal returns. Stated differently, this means that chasing return regularities can be a futile exercise for anyone who is not good at econometrics and does not have access to massive empirical stock market data and substantial computing power. Table 18-3 shows the additional abnormal returns that could be obtained by investing in stocks with return regularities in basis points (that is, one one-hundredth of 1 percent). Earning incremental gains that are measured in basis points is not a way to get rich quick.

Anyone attempting to profit from some of the abnormal returns associated with return regularities should remember that the idiot of chance will doubtlessly sprinkle their results with sampling errors. Only diversified portfolios of many stocks can expect to attain the average results reported by Jacobs and Levy. A portfolio made up of only a modest number of different stocks would be likely to experience sampling errors and thus be highly sample dependent. In summary, all of this means that only diversified portfolios that employ consultants like Jacobs and Levy and are able to spread the costs of these consultants over a portfolio worth millions of dollars should attempt to profit from return regularities.

18-7   **SUMMARY AND CONCLUSIONS**

Despite a century-and-a-half of thinking about the way security prices fluctuate, it was not until the 1960s that the power of the computer allowed financial analysts to test their theories and hunches with massive empirical data.

Much of the research during the 1960s and 1970s was devoted to substantiating the theory of efficient markets. The efficient markets theory makes statements about what information is reflected in security prices. The efficient markets theory can be broken down into the following three hypotheses:

1. The *weakly efficient markets hypothesis* states that security prices reflect all *historical* information. If this hypothesis is true, then technical analysis, which is practiced by thousands of people, would not be a worthwhile activity.

2. The *semistrong efficient markets hypothesis* stipulates that all *public* information has its effect on market prices. No valuable investment information could be gained from reading such sources as *The Wall Street Journal* or Standard & Poor's publications if this second hypothesis is accurate.

3. The *strongly efficient markets hypothesis* requires that security prices reflect *all information*. If the markets are strongly efficient, even those who possess inside information would not have investment information of any value.

Numerous scientific empirical studies confirmed a surprisingly large number of implications of the three hypotheses above. However, some anomalies in the efficient markets theory also emerged.

Professor Shiller published a study suggesting that the NYSE alternated between being bullishly overpriced for a few years and then bearishly under-priced for a while, relative to the present value of the market's cash dividend income. In addition, various price patterns and rate of return regularities emerged from scientific investigations. Buying low-priced stocks, buying stocks with low price-earnings ratios, buying in January, and other investment tactics tested yielded abnormally high rates of return. These findings violated the efficient markets theory. In addition, many new anomalies were uncovered during the 1980s. Within-the-month return patterns, sales:price ratio effects, cashflow: price ratio effects, agency effects, earnings controversy effects, earnings sur-prise effects, forecasted trends in earnings effects, earnings torpedo effects, relative strength effects, residual reversal effects, firm-size effects, neglect effects, day-of-the-week effects, time-of-day effects, book-value-to-price ratio effects, and other anomalies were reported. These studies did not uncover any get-rich-quick opportunities. The anomalies yielded additional rates of return that, if they were statistically significant, could be measured in basis points. These anomalies are difficult for investors to capture because of computational problems. Nevertheless, the number of persistent anomalies that have been uncovered blemishes the efficient markets theory as a description of reality.

As a result of empirical research we know that it is possible to gain insights from some forms of technical analysis, that there are certain times when it is slightly more advantageous to buy or sell common stocks, and that it is possible, on average, to enhance an investment's rate of return somewhat by noting the information content of particular return regularities that a stock might possess. These findings, however, do not negate the value of the efficient markets model. It is costly to implement trading strategies that are designed to benefit from the anomalies in the efficient markets theory. Without the sophisticated and costly resources needed to implement these strategies, investors are well ad-vised to *act as if the efficient markets theory were descriptive of reality*. In the final analysis, the efficient markets theory simply documents the well-known adage that "you cannot expect to get something for nothing." Who would disagree with that?

Essay Questions

18-1   Consider the statement that Keynes made in 1936 (reproduced in the introductory section of this chapter) in light of the more recent scientific empirical studies of stock prices. Do you think the view that Keynes espoused has any validity today? Explain.

18-2   Heidi Rorschach claims to have become an expert technical analyst. Ms. Ror-schach asserts that she has been able to make a long series of profitable invest-ments by using the head and shoulders (H&S) pattern (see Figure 17-2). Evaluate her claims in light of the efficient markets research.

18-3   Mr. Wieley Faux just came into possession of an after-tax inheritance of $200,000 and is eager to invest it. For 2 years he has been collecting articles from newspapers and popular magazines that describe the January effect, the day-of-the-week effect, the time-of-the-day effect, and the within-the-month effects. Mr. Faux hopes to be able to earn his living by actively trading $200,000 worth of common stocks at the advantageous times suggested by the articles he has saved that describe return regularities. What advice would you give Wieley?

18-4   Why should anyone be interested in the unexplained residual terms, denoted $e_{i,t}$, in the simple linear regression model of Equation (10-3) for the one-period rates of return from the ith security for periods $t = 1, 2, \ldots, T$?

18-5   Executives and other insiders have access to valuable inside information that should enable them to buy stock in the corporation that employs them when the stock's market price is depressed and sell the stock when the price is elevated and thus make substantial profits. Is this statement true, false, or uncertain? Explain.

18-6   Professor Robert J. Shiller's market study of over- and underpricing of stock market indexes demolished the efficient markets theory and showed that it should be easy to earn large trading profits. Is this statement true, false, or uncertain? Explain.

18-7   If you were given the investment management responsibility for a portfolio of common stocks that had a $100 million market value, would you establish a passive or an active investment management system? What are the arguments in favor of each approach? *Hint: Review Section 8-7.*

18-8   Many empirical tests of the efficient markets theory use the characteristic line, CAPM, or some other explicit model from financial theory. Do you see any methodological contradiction in using such theoretical asset pricing models to test the efficient markets theory? Explain.

18-9   What implications does the efficient markets theory and the empirical evidence that supports it have for each of the following phenomena? (*a*) The S&P 500 dropped more than 20 percent in less than a month during the October 1987 international stock market crash (see Figures 1-1 and 17-4). (*b*) A common stock mutual fund named Mutual Shares has low risk (its beta is only 0.49), low management fees, zero load fees, and earns a higher rate of return than the S&P 500. (*c*) Scientific empirical studies of mutual funds' performance (reviewed in Chapter 21) show that many mutual funds do not earn risk-adjusted rates of return that are as good as could be obtained by picking stocks with a dart. (*d*) Data reviewed in Sections 16-1 and 16-2 (see Figure 16-2 on page 494) indicate that when a corporation announces earnings that are surprisingly good (bad), the stock's price experiences abnormally high (low) returns for 60 days *after* the surprising announcement. (*e*) Data reviewed in Sections 16-1 and 16-2 (see Figure 16-2) indicate that when a corporation announces earnings that are surprisingly good (bad), the stock's price experiences abnormally high (low) returns for 60 days *before* the surprising announcement.

18-10 A man from Mars asked an earthling what kind of bird was in front of them. The earthling said it was a crow. As a matter of fact, the bird was an *albino* crow. The martian sketched a drawing of the crow to take back to Mars. The martian wrote the following comment at the bottom of its pencil sketch: "A type of white bird they call a crow." (*a*) How would a statistician describe this misconception? (*b*) What would a statistician suggest to avoid such misconceptions?

Problems

18-11 Reconsider the 14 days of price data on the Hemmel Corporation's stock that are listed with Problem 17-11. Analyze these data using an *x* percent filter rule like the one Fama and Blume used. On what days would you buy and sell Hemmel stock if you used (*a*) an $x = 4$ percent filter rule? (*b*) an $x = 8$ percent filter rule?

18-12 Reconsider the 14 days of price data on the Hemmel Corporation's stock that are listed with Problem 17-11. Analyze these data using an *x* percent filter rule like the one Sweeney developed. On what days would you buy and sell Hemmel stock if you used (*a*) an $x = 4$ percent filter rule? (*b*) an $x = 8$ percent filter rule?

18-13 Reconsider the 14 days of price data on the Hemmel Corporation's stock that are listed with Problem 17-11. Analyze these data and determine the number of (*a*) positive, (*b*) zero, and (*c*) negative runs that are present.

18-14 The Jaring Corporation declared a 200 percent stock dividend between the second and third quarters. (*a*) How many shares of stock could be purchased for $150 in each quarter? (*b*) Calculate the stockholders' one-period rates of return for the second and third quarters from the data below.

Quarters of the year, Q	$Q = 1$	$Q = 2$	A 200% stock dividend $Q = 3$	$Q = 4$	$Q = 1$
Beginning market price per share	$150	$150	$50	$50	$50
Cash dividend per share	$ 7.50	$ 7.50	$ 2.50	$ 2.50	$ 2.50
Earnings per share	$ 15	$ 15	$ 5	$ 5	$ 5
Number of shares for $150 of investment	??	??	??	??	??
One-period rate of return	??	??	??	??	??

18-15 If the price of a stock rises from $50 to $55 per share during a month in which no cash dividends are paid, what is the stock's (*a*) simple noncompounded rate of price change during the month? (*b*) continuously compounded rate of price change during the month? (*c*) Why do the two rates of price change differ? *Hint: See Equation (18-1).*

18-16 The statistics in Table 10-2 and Figure 10-2 indicate that IBM's characteristic line
is $r_{I,t} = -1.04 + 1.021 r_{M,t} + e_{I,t}$. (a) Use this characteristic line, the S&P 500
returns below, and the IBM returns in Table 10-1 to calculate IBM's four quarterly
predicted returns and residual returns for 1979.

Year and quarter	IBM's quarterly rate of return, %	S&P 500 quarterly rate of return, %	IBM's predicted rate of return, %	Unexplained rate of return residual, %
1979-1	6.660	7.075	8.2565	−1.5965
1979-2	−5.883	2.559	?	?
A 4-for-1 stock split on June 11, 1979				
1979-3	−6.494	7.490	?	?
1979-4	−3.712	−0.110	?	?

(b) Based on your calculations, did IBM's 4-for-1 stock split tend to raise the
price of IBM stock?

Selected References

Fama, Eugene F., "Efficient Capital Markets: A Review of Theory and Empirical
Work," *Journal of Finance,* May 1970, pp. 383–417.

This classic paper articulates the efficient markets theory. The paper espouses a
worthwhile and insightful way to view security prices.

Jacobs, Bruce I., and Kenneth N. Levy, "Disentangling Equity Return Regularities:
New Insights and Investment Opportunities," *Financial Analysts Journal,* May–June
1988, pp. 18–43.

This paper provides an easy-to-read review of the previous research and reports
some insightful findings from a multivariate statistics investigation of 25 anomalies
in the efficient markets hypothesis.

Shiller, R. J., "Do Stock Prices Move Too Much to Be Justified by Subsequent
Changes in Dividends?," *American Economic Review,* June 1981, vol. 71, pp.
421–436.

This classic paper presents empirical evidence that stock market prices vary so far
out of line with their estimated values that the deviations cannot reasonably be
attributed to sampling error.

Part 6

Portfolio Selection

Chapter 19

Investment Decision Theory

Investment decision theory, which analyzes how to get from investors' preferences to the optimal investment decisions, is reviewed in this chapter. First, *time preference theory* examines how individual investors decide whether to invest or consume their income. A second segment of decision theory deals with *choices that must be made under conditions of uncertainty*. Essentially, the latter half of this chapter shows the advantages of making decisions that maximize an investor's expected utility.

19-1　　　**TWO-PERIOD TIME PREFERENCE MODEL**

Irving Fisher developed time preference theory during the early 1900s.[1] Fisher's time preference model analyzes how to decide whether to (1) consume now or (2) invest now in order to consume more later. The model assumes that all the alternatives being considered are *known with certainty*. Let us study Fisher's consumption-investment decision model as it relates to a fellow we will refer to as Mr. Average.

Mr. Average is a consumer who will earn $20,000 both this year and next.

[1]Irving Fisher published three books that form the basis for the theory of choice: (1) *The Rate of Interest* (New York: Macmillan, 1907), (2) *The Nature of Capital and Income* (New York: Macmillan, 1912), and (3) *The Theory of Interest* (New York: Macmillan, 1930). Fisher's classic work has been summarized, supplemented with related developments, and published with one consistent set of notation in J. Hirshleifer, *Investment, Interest, and Capital* (Englewood Cliffs, N.J.: Prentice-Hall, 1970), see chaps. 1, 2, 3, and 4.

Point A in Figure 19-1 illustrates these **initial endowments** in a two-period time preference model. This model will be used to analyze whether Mr. Average should invest part of his income for the future or borrow against his future income to finance current consumption in excess of his current income.

Mr. Average could consume all his first year's income and save nothing. If he saved nothing in year 1, that would make it impossible for his second year's consumption to exceed his income in the second year. Point A represents the alternative of earning $Y_1 = \$20,000$ in year 1 and $Y_2 = \$20,000$ in year 2 and consuming it all in the year in which it was earned.

Consumption-Investment Opportunities

If Mr. Average is given only the simplest kind of investment opportunities, they will provide an infinite number of consumption-investment alternatives from which he may choose. Mr. Average could splurge his money, for instance, by going to a bank or consumer finance company and applying for a 5 percent, $r = 5\%$, loan against his second year's income of $Y_2 = \$20,000$.

$$\frac{Y_2}{1 + r} = \frac{\$20,000}{1 + 0.05} = \frac{\$20,000}{1.05} = \$19,047.61905$$

By combining the present value of his second year's income discounted at 5

Figure 19-1 Income and consumption opportunities in a two-period time preference model for Mr. Average.

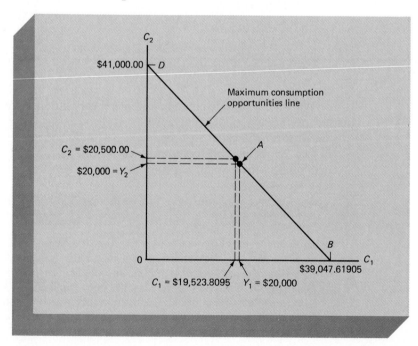

percent, $19,047.62, with his first year's income of $Y_1 = \$20,000$, Mr. Average could potentially splurge as much as $39,047.62 in year 1.

$19,047.62	present value of second year's income $= Y_2/(1 + r)$
+ 20,000.00	first year's income, Y_1
$39,047.62	maximum consumption opportunity in year 1

Point B in Figure 19-1 represents Mr. Average's opportunity to borrow as much as possible against his second year's income in order to consume everything in the first year. If Mr. Average splurges at point B, he will be forced into the painful frugality of zero consumption in year 2. Point B is an irrational consumption opportunity, of course, because starvation in year 2 is not a desirable alternative.

In contrast to the total splurge, Mr. Average could pursue the opposite extreme of starving himself in year 1 in order to maximize his investment opportunities. In order to invest the maximum amount, Mr. Average could consume nothing in year 1, $C_1 = 0$, and invest his entire first year's income in a bank account that paid 5 percent interest, $r = 5\% = 0.05 \times 100$.

$$(Y_1)(1 + r) = (\$20,000)(1 + r) = (\$20,000)(1.05) = \$21,000.00$$

Investing his entire first year's income Y_1 would permit Mr. Average to have a total of $41,000.00 available for consumption in year 2.

$21,000	investment of first year's income $= (Y_1)(1 + r)$
+ 20,000	second year's income, Y_2
$41,000	maximum possible consumption in year 2

This possibility is represented by point D in Figure 19-1.

We can calculate Mr. Average's year 2 consumption opportunities by using Equation (19-1).

$$\begin{pmatrix} \text{Year 1's} \\ \text{investment} \end{pmatrix} \times \begin{pmatrix} 1.0 + \text{rate} \\ \text{of interest} \end{pmatrix} + \begin{matrix} \text{year 2's} \\ \text{income} \end{matrix} = \begin{matrix} \text{year 2's} \\ \text{consumption} \end{matrix}$$

$$(Y_1 - C_1)(1 + r) + Y_2 = C_2 \tag{19-1}$$

$$(\$20,000 - C_1)(1 + r) + \$20,000 = C_2$$

$$\$41,000 - (1.05)(C_1) = C_2 \tag{19-1a}$$

Equation (19-1a) is graphed as the *maximum consumption opportunity line* in Figure 19-1. The intercept is $41,000 and the slope is $-(1 + r) = -1.05$. The negative slope of -1.05 represents the fact that every dollar Mr. Average consumes in the first year will reduce his second year's consumption opportunities by $1.05. Since the consumption opportunity line is a continuous line, Mr. Average has an infinite number of consumption-investment alternatives from which to select in this two-period time preference model. Economists analyze decisions made by consumers like Mr. Average by using *indifference curves*.

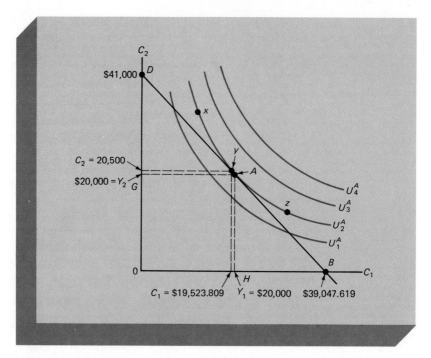

Figure 19-2 A set of indifference curves and a consumption opportunity line for Mr. Average.

Indifference Curves

The words "utility" and "happiness" have similar meanings in economics. Essentially, *utility theory* is an economic theory about how people maximize their happiness. Consumers' consumption-investment decisions can be analyzed using *utility isoquants* or happiness isoquants that are called **indifference curves.** The four indifference curves shown in Figure 19-2 are imposed over Mr. Average's consumption opportunity line from Figure 19-1.[2]

Mr. Average's preference orderings are represented by the indifference map in Figure 19-2. Each indifference curve represents a combination of consumption-investment choices that provide the same amount of happiness for one particular consumer. For example, points x, y, and z on indifference curve U_2 in Figure 19-2 all provide Mr. Average with the same amount of happiness or utility. These curves are synonymously called **utility isoquants** because the investor's utility is equal at every point on any given indifference curve.

The higher numbered indifference curves in Figure 19-2 represent higher levels of happiness, or higher utility, for the consumer. Thus, all the points

---

[2]Mr. Average's utility function is a multiplicative two-period utility of consumption function of the following form: $u = U(C_1, C_2) = C_1 C_2$, where u indicates the number of utils derived. Mathematically speaking, functions of this form are called rectangular hyperbolas. The resulting indifference curves approach both axes asymptotically.

along indifference curve U_4 are more desirable than any point on curve U_3. Likewise, every point on curve U_3 makes the consumer happier than any point on curve U_2. Logically, therefore, consumers will maximize their utility by selecting a *feasible* (or affordable) choice that lies on their highest attainable indifference curve.

Utility-Maximizing Choice

The indifference map in Figure 19-2 integrates the preferences of Mr. Average with his consumption opportunity line to determine how many dollars he must consume and invest in each year to maximize his happiness.

Figure 19-2 indicates that Mr. Average will maximize his utility by consuming $19,523.81 of his $20,000 income and investing the remaining $476.19 in the first year. Mr. Average's $476.19 investment will grow at 5 percent to be worth $500 in the second year.

$$
\begin{aligned}
(\$476.19)(1.05) &= \$\ \ \ 500 \qquad \text{investment's value} = (Y_1 - C_1)(1.0 + r) \\
&\quad \ \ \underline{20{,}000} \qquad \text{income in year 2} = Y_2 \\
&\quad \ \ \$20{,}500 \qquad \text{consumption in year 2} = C_2 \\
&\qquad\qquad\qquad\qquad\quad\ \ = Y_2 + (Y_1 - C_1)(1.0 + r)
\end{aligned}
$$

Combining Mr. Average's $500 future investment value with his $20,000 of second-year income indicates that Mr. Average's utility-maximizing decision will result in $20,500 of consumption in year 2. Point Y on indifference curve U_2 illustrates Mr. Average's point of maximum attainable happiness in this Fisherian two-period decision context.

Mr. Average would be happier at the higher levels of utility represented by indifference curves U_3 or U_4 in Figure 19-2. But Mr. Average cannot afford the higher consumption levels required to attain these higher-level indifference curves. Mr. Average's highest level of attainable expenditures lies along the consumption opportunity line *DAB*, and this much money cannot purchase more than the level of utility attained at tangency point y on indifference curve U_2. Small changes in the shape of the utility function affect the decisions the investor makes.

Mr. Spendthrift's Indifference Map

Figure 19-3 illustrates a different set of utility-maximizing consumption-investment decisions. The personality represented in Figure 19-3 has less patience than Mr. Average.[3] The indifference curves in Figure 19-3 represent the preference orderings of Mr. Spendthrift, who chooses to consume $C_1 = \$23,809.52$ in the first year. On a $Y_1 = \$20,000$ annual income, Mr. Spendthrift must borrow $3809.52 to finance this high level of first-year consumption.

---

[3]Mr. Spendthrift's utility function is a two-period utility of consumption function of the following form: $u = U(C_1, C_2) = 9000C_1 + C_1C_2$, where u indicates the number of utils that Mr. Spendthrift derived from the consumption.

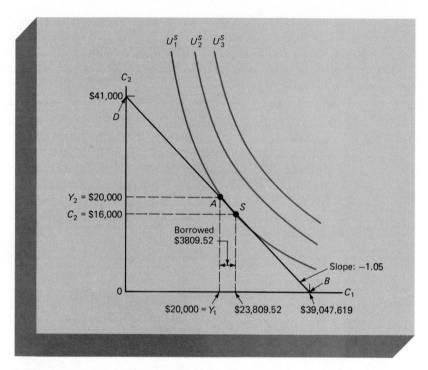

Figure 19-3 Applying Mr. Spendthrift's indifference curves to consumption opportunities that equal Mr. Average's.

In the second year Mr. Spendthrift needs to repay the $3809.52381 debt plus 5 percent interest for a total of $4000.00.

$$(C_1 - Y_1)(1.0 + r) = (\$3809.52381)(1.05) = \$4000.00$$

As a result of the debt repayment only $16,000 of his $20,000 income is left for Mr. Spendthrift to consume in the second year. Point S in Figure 19-3 indicates Mr. Spendthrift's utility-maximizing decision.

Changing the Interest Rate

Equation (19-1) would be equally appropriate to analyze someone's consumption opportunities if the interest rate changed. For example, if the interest rate increases from $r = 5\%$ to $r = 10\%$, the numerical values for Mr. Average would have to be modified as shown in Equation (19-1b).

$$(Y_1 - C_1)(1 + r) + Y_2 = C_2 \tag{19-1}$$

$$(\$20,000 - C_1)(1.10) + \$20,000 = C_2 \tag{19-1b}$$

Given Mr. Average's same $20,000 income in years 1 and 2, the consumption-investment line PAM for $r = 10\%$ is illustrated in Figure 19-4. The consumption-

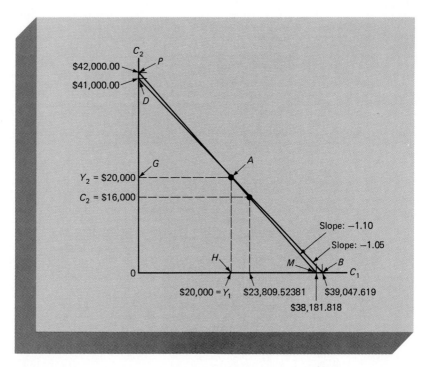

Figure 19-4 Mr. Average's income, consumption, and investment opportunities for interest rates of $r = 5\%$ and $r = 10\%$.

investment line *DAB* from Figure 19-1 is also reproduced in Figure 19-4 to illustrate the different consumption-investment decisions that occur when interest rates change.

When the interest rate is 10 percent, $r = 10\%$, Mr. Average's maximum possible consumption in year 2 increases to \$42,000, because his interest income increases above what it was when the interest rate was lower.

$$(Y_1)(1 + r) = (\$20,000)(1 + r) = (\$20,000)(1.10) = \$22,000$$

Increasing the interest rate from $r = 5\%$ to $r = 10\%$ reduces Mr. Average's consumption opportunities in year 1 to a maximum of \$38,181.81818, as shown below.

$$(\$20,000)/(1.10) = \quad \begin{matrix} \$18,181.81818 \\ + \$20,000.00000 \\ \hline \$38,181.81818 \end{matrix} \quad \begin{matrix} \text{present value of } Y_2 \\ \text{year 1's income} = Y_1 \\ \text{total year 1 consumption} = C_1 \end{matrix}$$

The maximum year 1 consumption opportunity at point *M* in Figure 19-4 is less than point *B* because increasing the interest rate from 5 to 10 percent reduced the discounted present value of year 2's income. These new con-

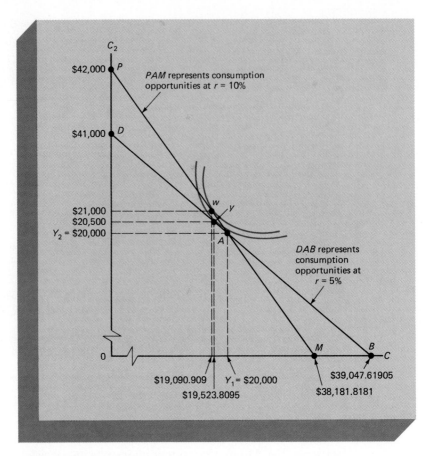

Figure 19-5 Consumption lines for $r = 5\%$ and $r = 10\%$ and Mr. Average's indifference map.

sumption possibilities result in new utility-maximizing investment-consumption decisions.

Changing Interest Rates Change the Optimal Decisions

Mr. Average's maximum consumption opportunity lines for $r = 5\%$ and $r = 10\%$ from Figure 19-4 are both reproduced in Figure 19-5. In addition, the indifference maps for Mr. Average from Figure 19-2 are superimposed over the consumption opportunity lines in Figure 19-5.

Raising the interest rate changes Mr. Average's utility-maximizing decision from point y on consumption line DAB to point w on line PAM. Since point w is on a higher indifference curve than point y, Mr. Average will be happier after the increase in the interest rate. Point w provides Mr. Average with the first-year consumption opportunities of $C_1^w = \$19,090.90909$ and second-year consumption opportunities of $C_2^w = \$21,000$. Mr. Average is happier in a high interest rate environment because the resulting increased interest income rewards the self-denial and savings tendencies that are part of Mr. Average's personality.[4]

DECISION-MAKING UNDER UNCERTAINTY

We have seen how utility is related to consumption, wealth, investing, and the rate of return, and how an indifference map in risk-return space may be used to maximize investor utility. However, the discussion focused on two-period utility maximization under conditions of *certainty*. Now we will analyze single-period decision-making under *uncertainty;* risk is an explicit part of the decision model discussed in this section.[5]

Utility of Wealth   A **utility-of-wealth function** is a formula or a graph of a formula which shows how much utility, or how many utils, or how much happiness, a person derives from different levels of wealth. A utility-of-wealth function might be symbolically written as $u = U(W)$, which means that utils, denoted u, are some unspecified mathematical utility function, represented by the symbol U, of W dollars of wealth. Intuitively, a utility-of-wealth function means that money can be used to buy things that make someone happy. Figure 19-6 shows a graph of a utility-of-wealth function.

Utility theory is useful for analyzing the logic of decisions involving risk. The analysis of such decisions is based on the expected utility principle. The

[4]It is possible to trace out the supply and demand curves for loanable funds and find an equilibrium market interest rate that will equate supply and demand within the context of the two-period time preference model. In Figure 19-2 Mr. Average responded to the 5 percent interest rate by consuming $19,523.81 of his $20,000 first year's income and saving the remaining $476.19048. If we added up the *savings* at $r = 5\%$ for all consumers who wish to save, we would have one point on the *supply of savings curve*.

In Figure 19-3 we saw that Mr. Spendthrift responded to an interest rate of $r = 5\%$ by borrowing $3809.52 to increase his consumption above his $20,000 annual income. By summing across all consumers who wish to *borrow* at $r = 5\%$, we can obtain one point on the *demand for loan funds curve*.

By changing the interest rates again and again, we can determine more and more points on the supply and demand curves, until we have enough points to trace out the entire demand and supply curves. The market equilibrium interest rate is then determined to be at the intersection point of the supply and demand curves. This equilibrium rate of interest will cause all savers to save enough to precisely meet the demand for loanable funds from all borrowers.

[5]This section draws on Milton Friedman and Leonard J. Savage, "The Utility Analysis of Choices Involving Risk," *Journal of Political Economy,* Aug. 1948, vol. LVI, no. 4, pp. 279–304. Reprinted in Stephen H. Archer and Charles A. D'Ambrosio, eds., *The Theory of Busines Finance,* 2d ed. (New York: Macmillan, 1976).

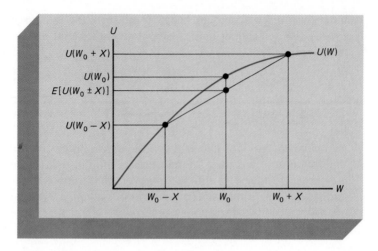

Figure 19-6 A diminishing marginal-utility-of-wealth function rationalizes risk-averse decision-making.

expected utility principle says that decision makers make decisions which maximize their *expected utility*.

Maximizing *expected utility* is different from simply maximizing the utility of the expected value of the possible outcomes. To understand the difference, consider the definition of expected utility: a decision to undertake some risky course of action is the weighted average of the utils from the possible outcomes that are calculated by using the probabilities of each outcome for the weights.

Consider a concrete example of how to calculate the expected utility from a fair bet for one dollar. If you decide to enter into a coin-tossing gamble, you have made a decision to undertake a risky course of action. There are two possible outcomes—heads you win $1 or tails you lose $1. The probability of getting heads and winning the dollar is denoted $P(\text{head})$. $P(\text{tail})$ represents the probability of getting tails and losing $1. The utility from the gamble that results if heads turns up and you win the dollar is represented by $U(\text{head})$ and the disutility of getting tails and losing a dollar is $U(\text{tail})$. Thus, the *expected utility* of the gamble is written symbolically as:

$$E[U(\text{coin toss})] = P(\text{head}) \times U(+\$1 \text{ head}) + P(\text{tail}) \times U(-\$1 \text{ tail})$$
$$= (.5) \times U(+\$1 \text{ head}) + (.5) \times U(-\$1 \text{ tail})$$

In contrast to the expected utility, the *utility of the expected outcome* of the gamble is calculated as follows:

$$U[E(\text{coin toss})] = U\{[P(\text{head}) \times +\$1 \text{ head}] + [P(\text{tail}) \times -\$1 \text{ tail}]\}$$

$$U[E(\text{dollar outcome})] = U[(.5)(+\$1) + (.5)(-\$1)] = U[0]$$

Consider a more general explanation of how to apply the expected utility principle to analyze decisions involving risky outcomes.

Diminishing Marginal Utility and Risk Aversion

Marginal utility of wealth may be defined as the additional utility a person gets from a small change in their wealth. To determine whether marginal utility is rising or falling, the slope of the utility function must be observed. **Decreasing marginal utility** is present when the utility function rises at a less steep rate—that is, the curve is progressively flatter at higher dollar amounts. **Increasing marginal utility** exists when the utility function rises at an increasingly steep rate—the curve keeps getting steeper at higher levels of wealth.

Risk-averse behavior will result if the investor has diminishing marginal utility of wealth or returns. Diminishing marginal utility-of-wealth and utility-of-returns functions are graphed in Figures 19-6 and 19-7, respectively. They are both concave to (bulge away from) the horizontal axis. Any function U is **concave** if and only if $U(x) > (P)U(x - y) + (1 - P)U(x + y)$ for a value of P that is a positive fraction, $+1.0 > P > 0$. In the context of expected utility computations, you can think of P and $(1 - P)$ as being the probabilities of the two uncertain outcomes.

Utility functions that are concave to the wealth axis are particularly interesting because they always result in risk-averse decisions, that is, rational decisions. Irrational decisions are interesting only as pathological cases that are intellectual curiosities.

Diminishing marginal utility of wealth or of returns leads to risk-avoiding behavior since, from any point on the utility-of-wealth or utility-of-returns curve, a risky investment has a lower expected utility than a safe investment with the same expected outcome. That is, if an investment offers a 50-50 chance of increasing or decreasing a given level of starting wealth by X dollars, the loss of utility from the bad outcome is larger than the gain in utility from the

Figure 19-7 Using a diminishing marginal-utility-of-returns function to analyze risk-averse decisions.

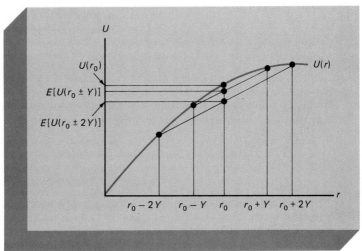

favorable outcome if the utility diminishes. Symbolically, $[.5U(W_0 - X)]$ + $[.5U(W_0 + X)] < U(W_0)$. Thus, the person with diminishing utility of wealth would prefer to keep W_0 rather than make a risky investment or bet to attain $(W_0 + X)$ or $(W_0 - X)$ with equal probability. Figure 19-6 represents this situation graphically.

Since the utility of the certain starting wealth $U(W_0)$ is larger than the expected utility of an equal amount of uncertain wealth $E[U(W_0)]$, the risk-averter prefers not to assume the risk, $U(W_0) > E[U(W_0)]$. The risk-averter prefers simply to hold W_0 cash rather than assume risks in an effort to increase this wealth. If the chance for gains from the risky investment were large enough, the risk-averse investor might find it sufficient compensation to assume the risk. Thus, risk-averters may accept risky investments, but only if they perceive the odds to be in their favor.

People everywhere commonly exhibit behavior that indicates they have diminishing marginal utility of wealth. People typically require higher hourly wages to persuade them to work overtime. Millionaires are not willing to work as hard to make their second million as they were to make their first million. Examples like these suggest that most people have the kind of marginal utility of wealth (namely, diminishing marginal utility) that makes them risk-averse.[6]

Equivalence of the Utility of Wealth and Return Functions

Utility preference orderings are invariant under a positive **linear transformation** of the utility function. Graphically speaking, this means that any utility curve (such as the ones in Figures 19-6 and 19-7) can be raised or lowered (that is, can have a constant added or subtracted), can be scaled down without having its shape changed (that is, can be divided by a positive constant), or can be expanded without changing its curvature (that is, can be multiplied by a positive constant) without changing the way the utility function would *rank the desirability* of a set of investment opportunities. Any of the preceding transformations would change the number of utils assigned to any given outcome, but *the decision-maker's preference rankings would be invariant under a positive linear transformation.*

Since the one-period rate of return is a positive linear transformation of the investor's wealth, this implies that a given investor's utility-of-returns function is simply a linear transformation of that investor's utility-of-wealth function, and the two will yield the same preference orderings for any given group of investment opportunities. Thus, the investor's utility curves shown in Figures 19-6 and 19-7 are merely linear transformations of each other and result in

---

[6]Risk-averters may make a trip to Las Vegas, buy a lottery ticket, or do some other type of gambling. However, this is presumably done to obtain entertainment and does not represent a genuine preference for risk-taking.

identical preferences for single-period changes in wealth or equivalent one-period rates of return. The positive linear transformation between wealth and the one-period rate of return is shown below.

$$r_t = \frac{W_t - W_{t-1}}{W_{t-1}} \tag{19-2}$$

where W_{t-1} denotes beginning-of-period wealth (a positive constant). The symbol W_t represents end-of-period wealth, and r_t is the one-period rate of return—W_t and r_t are random variables that are linear transformations of each other.

The *invariance* of a set of preference rankings under a positive linear transformation has important implications for utility analysis. This invariance means that if investors are shown to be risk-averse (or risk-loving) in an analysis of their wealth, they will also be risk-averse (or risk-loving) when choosing among investments that have their outcomes measured in terms of one-period rates of return. Being able to impute risk-averse (or risk-loving) behavior to investors because of their preferences toward monetary outcomes expedites and generalizes the application of utility theory.

Graphical Utility Analysis of Investment Returns

Suppose an investor can earn a rate of return of r_0 with certainty. Alternative two is that the investor can invest in a risky investment which will return $(r_0 + y)$ or $(r_0 - y)$ with equal probability. Symbolically, the probabilities are: $P(r_0 - y) = (P_1) = P(r_0 + y) = (P_1) = \frac{1}{2}$. Both the riskless and the risky investment have the same expected return of r_0.

$$E(r) = (P_0)(r_0 + y) + (P_2)(r_0 - y)$$
$$= \frac{1}{2}(r_0 + y) + \frac{1}{2}(r_0 - y) = r_0$$

Since the expected returns are the same, a risk-averse investor will prefer the sure return because the risk-averter's diminishing marginal utility will cause the disutility from a return of $(r_0 - y)$ to exceed the gain in utility from a return of $(r_0 + y)$.

Furthermore, suppose that this risk-averter has a third investment alternative in an even riskier investment which is expected to yield either $(r_0 - 2y)$ or $(r_0 + 2y)$ with equal probability. This latter investment is riskier (that is, has more variability of return) than the other risky investment, but it offers the same expected return. The calculations below show that the two risky investment alternatives have equal expected returns. But the second alternative involves small risk.

$$E(r) = (P_1)(r_0 - y) + (P_2)(r_0 + y)$$
$$= \frac{1}{2}(r_0 - y) + \frac{1}{2}(r_0 + y) = r_0$$

The third has the largest variability of return.

$$E(r) = (P_1)(r_0 + 2y) + (P_2)(r_0 + 2y)$$
$$= \frac{1}{2}(r_0 - 2y) + \frac{1}{2}(r_0 + 2y) = r_0$$

A risk-averse investor will rank the desirability of the riskiest investment last since its expected return is the same as the other investment, but it entails more risk. Therefore, the riskiest investment will have the least expected utility. Symbolically, $U(r_0) > E[U(r_0 \pm y)] > E[U(r_0 \pm 2y)]$. This is shown graphically in Figure 19-7. The preceding examples demonstrate that expected utility is determined by both the expected return and the risk statistics.

Expected Utility, Expected Return, and Risk Formulas

Expected utility is determined by expected return *and* risk.[7] Symbolically, this is summarized in Equation (19-3).

$$E(U) = f[E(r), \text{risk}] \qquad (19\text{-}3)$$

$$= f[E(r), \sigma] \qquad (19\text{-}3a)$$

where $E(U)$ = expected utility
$E(r)$ = expected return
risk = variability of returns and is measued by standard deviation of returns, denoted σ
f = some mathematical function

An increase in expected return will increase the investor's expected utility if risk does not also increase. Or a decrease in risk will increase expected utility if expected return does not decrease simultaneously.[8] Concise definitions of expected utility, expected return, and risk are below.

The **expected utility** of some event that involves probabilistic outcomes $E(U)$ is defined in Equation (19-4).

$$E(U) = \sum_{i=1}^{N} P_i U_i \qquad (19\text{-}4)$$

where U_i = utility of outcome i
P_i = probability of ith outcome
N = number of possible outcomes, $i = 1, 2, \ldots, N$

[7]Strictly speaking, the standard deviation of returns is only a risk surrogate rather than an absolute risk measure. See Sections 1-4, 1-5, and 1-6 for a more complete discussion of risk. Throughout this book, standard deviation σ and variance σ^2 are used interchangeably as measures of *total* risk.

[8]Technically, it can be shown that expected utility is a function of $E(r)$ and σ only if the utility function is quadratic or if the distribution of rates of return is a two-parameter distribution (such as a normal distribution) or if both of these conditions are true.

Equation (19-5) defines the expected rate of return $E(r)$.

$$E(r) = \sum_{i=1}^{N} P_i \, r_i \qquad (19\text{-}5)$$

where r_i represents the ith possible rate of return. The expected value is like a weighted average of the possible rates of return where the probabilities are the weights.

Equation (19-6) shows the formula used to calculate the standard deviation of returns for the ith security from expected rates of return.

$$\sigma = \sqrt{\sum_{t=1}^{T} (P_t) \, [r_{i,t} - E(r_i)]^2} \qquad (19\text{-}6)$$

When calculating the standard deviation of returns from historical rates of return, the *ex ante probabilities* must be replaced by *ex post relative frequencies*. In such cases it is common to assume that each of the T different historical outcomes is equally likely to occur, more concisely, $P = 1/T$. Thus, ex post equation (19-6) is rewritten as the equivalent ex ante equation (19-6a).

$$\sigma = \sqrt{\sum_{t=1}^{T} \frac{1}{T} [r_{i,t} - \bar{r}_i]^2} \qquad (19\text{-}6a)$$

Before the utility analysis of risky investment alternatives can be performed, the investment analyst must be supplied with (1) probability distributions of outcomes and (2) a utility function in order to find the expected utility for each outcome. For example, in selecting among N alternative investments, N probability distributions of return representing each different investment and its probabilistic return is required. And a utility function assigning utils to each possible rate of return the investment might generate is also needed. Only after the utility function and the probability distributions are known can utility analysis proceed.

Numerical Example—Making Investment Decisions

Consider three objects of choice, say, investments A, B, and C; their probability distributions of returns are defined in Table 19-1.

Figures 19-8 through 19-10 represent the utility functions for a risk-averting, a risk-indifferent, and a risk-seeking investor, respectively. Since investments A, B, and C all offer the same expected return of 3 percent, it is clear that the three investors will rank these three investments differently *purely because of their differences in risks*.

Table 19-1
PROBABILITY DISTRIBUTIONS OF RETURNS FOR THREE INVESTMENTS

| Investments | Investment outcomes and their probabilities | | | | | | | Characteristics | |
	Outcomes	−3%	0	3%	6%	9%	$\Sigma p = 1$	$E(r)$	σ
A	↑	.5		+		.5	1	$E(r_A) = 3\%$	$\sigma_A = 6\%$
B	Probabilities		.5	+	.5		1	$E(r_B) = 3\%$	$\sigma_B = 3\%$
C	↓			1			1	$E(r_C) = 3\%$	$\sigma_C = 0$

Risk-Averter's Computations The risk-averter's expected utility from A, B, and C is calculated as shown in equation series (19-7) below.

$$E[U(A)] = \sum_{i=1}^{2} (P_i)\,[U(r_i)] \qquad (19\text{-}7a)$$
$$= \tfrac{1}{2}[U(-0.03)] + \tfrac{1}{2}[U(0.09)]$$
$$= \tfrac{1}{2}(-3.045) + \tfrac{1}{2}(8.595)$$
$$= 2.785 \text{ utils}$$

Figure 19-8 Risk-averter's concave quadratic utility-of-returns function.

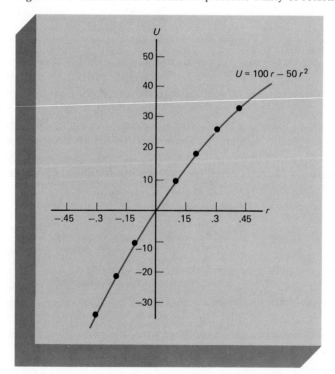

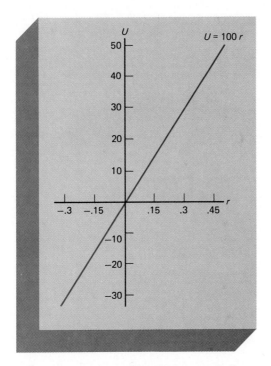

Figure 19-9 A risk-indifferent investor's linear utility-of-returns function.

$$E[U(B)] = \tfrac{1}{2}[U(0)] + \tfrac{1}{2}[U(0.06)] \qquad (19\text{-}7b)$$
$$= 0 + \tfrac{1}{2}(5.82)$$
$$= 2.91 \text{ utils}$$

$$E[U(C)] = 1[U(0.03)] \qquad (19\text{-}7c)$$
$$= 1\,(2.955)$$
$$= 2.955 \text{ utils}$$

The computations above indicate that the risk-averter derives the most satisfaction from investment C, which has the least variability of return.

Risk-Indifferent Investor's Computations The risk-indifferent investor's expected utils from the same three investments are calculated with equation series (19-8).

$$E[U(A)] = \tfrac{1}{2}[U(-0.03)] + \tfrac{1}{2}[U(0.09)] \qquad (19\text{-}8a)$$
$$= \tfrac{1}{2}(-3) + \tfrac{1}{2}(9)$$
$$= 3 \text{ utils}$$

$$E[U(B)] = \tfrac{1}{2}[U(0)] + \tfrac{1}{2}[U(0.06)] \qquad (19\text{-}8b)$$
$$= 0 + \tfrac{1}{2}(6)$$
$$= 3 \text{ utils}$$

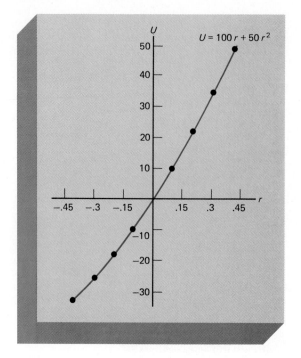

Figure 19-10 A risk-lover's convex-shaped quadratic utility-of-returns function.

$$E[U(C)] = 1[U(0.03)] \qquad (19\text{-}8c)$$
$$= 1(3)$$
$$= 3 \text{ utils}$$

Since investments A, B, and C differ only with respect to their risk, the risk-indifferent investor assigns the same utility to all three. Symbolically, $E[U(A)] = E[U(B)] = E[U(C)]$ for the risk-indifferent investor.

Risk-Lover's Computations   The risk-lover's utility calculations are performed with equation series (19-9).

$$E[U(A)] = \tfrac{1}{2}[U(-0.03)] + \tfrac{1}{2}[U(0.09)] \qquad (19\text{-}9a)$$
$$= \tfrac{1}{2}(-2.055) + \tfrac{1}{2}(9.405)$$
$$= 3.225 \text{ utils}$$

$$E[U(B)] = \tfrac{1}{2}[U(0)] + \tfrac{1}{2}[U(0.06)] \qquad (19\text{-}9b)$$
$$= 0 + \tfrac{1}{2}(6.18)$$
$$= 3.09 \text{ utils}$$

$$E[U(C)] = 1[U(0.03)] \qquad (19\text{-}9c)$$
$$= 1(3.045)$$
$$= 3.045 \text{ utils}$$

The risk-lover prefers the large variability of return exhibited by investment A. The three investors' expected utilities are summarized in Table 19-2.

Table 19-2

DIFFERENT INVESTMENT PREFERENCES FOR RISKY INVESTMENTS

Investor	Asset A, most risky $E(r_A) = 3\%$ $\sigma_A = 6\%$	Asset B, medium risk $E(r_B) = 3\%$ $\sigma_B = 3\%$	Asset C, least risky $E(r_C) = 3\%$ $\sigma_C = 0$
Risk-averter	$E[U(A)] = 2.785$	$E[U(B)] = 2.91$	$E[U(C)] = 2.955$
Risk-indifferent	$E[U(A)] = 3$	$E[U(B)] = 3$	$E[U(C)] = 3$
Risk-lover	$E[U(A)] = 3.225$	$E[U(B)] = 3.09$	$E[U(C)] = 3.045$

Investments A, B, and C all have identical expected returns of 3 percent, $E(r) = 3\%$; only their variability of return differs. The lower expected utilities assigned to A and B by the risk-averse investor are due to distaste for their larger variability of returns. And the larger expected utility the risk-lover associates with investments A and B reflects this investor's preference for risk. Thus, the *two parameters*—mean and variance of returns—are both reflected in expected utility. In all cases, expected utility measures the effects of both $E(r)$ and σ. Symbolically, $E(U) = f[E(r), \sigma]$.

The preceding numerical example showed how a rational, risk-averse, wealth-seeking investor will select investments that minimize risk at any given level of expected return in order to maximize expected utility in a world of uncertainty.

Selecting Investments in Terms of Risk and Return

Given the investor's utility function, we have seen how an individual will be able to select investment assets (either consciously or subconsciously) in terms of the investments' expected returns and risks. Figure 19-11 shows graphically how an investor will select between investments by examining only their expected returns and risk. The exhibit is a graph in risk-return space of the seven hypothetical securities listed in Table 19-3.

Figure 19-11 also shows a utility map in risk-return space representing the preference of some risk-averse investor (like the one whose utility-of-return curves were shown in Figs. 19-7 and 19-8). In this indifference map, the investor's utility is equal all along each indifference curve. The graph is called an **indifference map in risk-return space.** Since investments S, TB, and FR are all on the same indifference curve (that is, U_2), the investor obtains equal expected utility from them although their expected returns and risk differ considerably.

An infinite number of indifference curves could be drawn for the risk-averter depicted in Figure 19-11, but they would all be similar in shape and would all possess the following characteristics:

1. Higher indifference curves represent more investor satisfaction. Symbolically, $U_5 > U_4 > U_3 > U_2 > U_1$ because the investor likes higher expected return and dislikes higher risk.

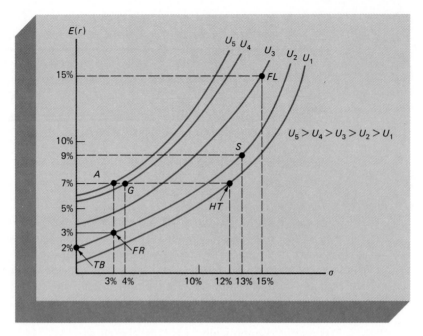

Figure 19-11 Opportunity set and an investor's preferences in risk-return space.

2. All indifference curves slope upward. This is because the investor requires higher expected returns as an inducement to assume larger risks. Consider, for example, the investor's indifference among FR, TB, and S, which is a result of S's expected return being just enough above the expected return of FR to compensate the risk-averse investor for assuming the additional risk incurred in going from FR to S. The difference in risk between investment TB and investment FR is just enough to compensate the investor for accepting TB's lower rate of return and still be as happy as with FR or S. Investment TB is

Table 19-3
RISK-RETURN STATISTICS FOR SEVEN INVESTMENTS

Name of security	Expected return, $E(r)$, %	Risk, σ, %
Acme Corporation (A)	7	3
General Technology Inc. (G)	7	4
Franklin Limited Company (FL)	15	15
Fairfield Rubber (FR)	3	3
Hadley Tire Corporation (HT)	7	12
Sawmill Corp. (S)	9	13
Treasury bills (TB)	2	0

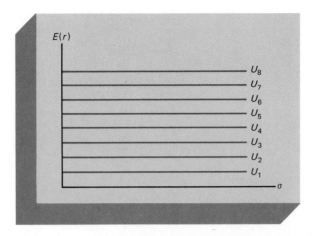

Figure 19-12 Risk-indifferent wealth maximizer's risk preferences in risk-return space.

        called the **certainty equivalent** of investments FR and S because it involves no risk.

3. The indifference curves grow steeper at higher levels of risk. This reflects the investor's diminishing willingness to assume risk as the returns become higher.

    Given the investment opportunities and the investor preferences shown in Figure 19-11, we see that the investor prefers asset A over any of the other investments since A lies on a higher indifference curve than any other investment. In fact, Figure 19-11 delineates the following explicit preference ordering.[9]

$$U(A) > U(G) > U(FL) > U(TB) = U(S) = U(FR) > U(HT)$$

Two Remarkable Sets of Preferences

The indifference map graphed in Figure 19-11 represents a set of rational, wealth-seeking, risk-averse preferences. Figure 19-11 is implied by a utility-of-returns function like the ones in Figures 19-7 and 19-8. Figures 19-9 and 19-10 represent radically different investment preferences: the preferences of a risk-indifferent investor and of a risk-loving investor, respectively.

    Figure 19-12 is simply another way of representing the linear utility-of-returns

[9]Classic theories of investing that grew out of the one-period utility analysis of decision-making under uncertainty are James Tobin, "Liquidity Preference as Behavior towards Risk," *Review of Economic Studies,* Feb. 1958, vol. XXVI, no. 1, pp. 65–86. Sharpe's capital asset pricing model (CAPM) is an extension of Tobin's model. See William F. Sharpe, "Capital Asset Prices: A Theory of Market Equilibrium under Conditions of Risk," *Journal of Finance,* Sept. 1964, vol. XIX, no. 3, pp. 425–442.

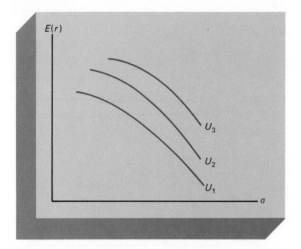

Figure 19-13 Risk-lover's risk preferences in risk-return space.

function graphed in Figure 19-9. Some people have suggested, for example, that large corporations which make decisions via committees may be appropriately modeled as having linear utility functions. In contrast, Figure 19-13 results from a risk-lover's utility function; it is derived from the underlying utility function illustrated in Figure 19-10. These two cases of investment preferences are presented as intellectual curiosities. They do not represent behavior that is risk-averse. They are worth studying, however, so that if we encounter the types of behavior they imply, we will be able to recognize and understand it.

19-3   **SUMMARY AND CONCLUSIONS**

This chapter reviewed several classic economic decision models. The concepts of utility, indifference curves, and intertemporal investment decision-making were introduced via Irving Fisher's two-period income-consumption-savings model. It was shown that investing could be used to increase the investor's happiness—or level of utility.

Then it was shown that investors who have positive but diminishing marginal utility of wealth and/or returns prefer (1) more wealth to less wealth, if all other factors are held constant, and (2) also prefer less risk to more risk. In a risky and uncertain world, these investors will maximize the expected utility from their investment activities by selecting assets that have the maximum expected return in their risk class, or the minimum risk at any particular level of expected return.

The objective of rational investment management, then, is to delineate and select those investments which have the maximum expected return within the risk class the investor prefers over whatever single-period planning horizon is appropriate for the investor. The investor need not select an individual asset. A portfolio can usually be selected that will yield higher expected utility than any individual asset.

Essay Questions

19-1 Is the following statement true, false, or uncertain? To a large extent, your personal happiness depends on your financial position. Explain.

19-2 According to Fisher's two-period time preference model, how should an increase in market interest rates affect an individual investor if all other factors remain unchanged?

19-3 What are the characteristics of a risk-averse person's indifference curves?

19-4 If an investor sets out to maximize their wealth, would this person ever have any use for the one-period rate of return measure? Explain.

19-5 Is utility theory useful for modeling the decision-making processes used by large corporations and governments? Explain.

19-6 Does the probability distribution of returns that describes an investment have any effect on the utility an investor can expect to obtain from the investment?

19-7 Do investors face any constraints that keep them from maximizing the happiness they can hope to derive from their investments? Explain.

Problems

19-8 Draw a graph of the utility-of-wealth function for a risk-lover. What are the characteristics of a risk-lover's marginal utility of wealth?

19-9 If their risk is the same, is investment A or B better? Show how you could rationally choose between them. *Hint: Show how one asset dominates the other asset in the same risk class.*

	A	B
Cost at time $t = 0$	$W_0 = \$500$	$W_0 = \$40$
Sale proceeds at time $t > 0$	$W_T = \$800$	$W_T = \$95$

19-10 How does risk affect utility? Be as explicit as possible in your explanation. A mathematical proof would be the best possible answer.

19-11 Rank the desirability of the following four investments to you. Use your own personal preferences and show your work graphically.

Investment	$E(r)$	σ
A	10%	5%
B	10	10
C	5	5
D	12	10

19-12 Write down your social security number. Assume that you can purchase a risky investment which will pay one of two equally likely rates of return. This investment will pay the rate of return indicated by the last digit in your social security number with a .5 probability and the rate of return indicated by the next-to-the last digit with a .5 probability. Calculate the expected return of this investment. For example, for the social security number 307-38-3152, the expected return is .5(5%) + .5(2%) = 3.5% = $E(r)$. If you were the risk-averse investor shown in Figure 19-8, would you rather have a certain (that is, one riskless) investment paying the expected return calculated from the last two digits of your social security number or the risky investment based on the equal probability of the last two digits? Explain. Use graphs or mathematics. *Hint: Appendix 19A explains the mathematical solution to this problem.*

19-13 Nat Logger and Hal Power are security analysts who are such close friends that they frequently discuss their personal views on various investment opportunities, compare their conclusions, and offer each other suggestions on how to improve their investment decision-making skills. Nat has the following logarithmic utility-of-wealth function based on natural (or napierian) logarithms: $u = \ln r$. In contrast to Nat, his friend Hal has the following square root utility-of-wealth function: $u = r^5 = \sqrt{r}$. Nat and Hal have been arguing over whether the White Corporation's stock or Zebra Inc.'s stock is the most desirable investment. Hal and Nat have agreed on the following probability distributions of returns for White and Zebra, but they disagree about which is the better investment: White or Zebra. Explain your choice.

	Rate of return, r	Probability	Nat's $u = \ln r$	Hal's $u = \sqrt{r}$
White	5.0%	.25	$\ln 5 = 1.609$	$\sqrt{5} = 2.236$
	10.0	.50	$\ln 10 = 2.303$	$\sqrt{10} = 3.162$
	20.0	.25	$\ln 20 = 2.996$	$\sqrt{20} = 4.472$
		1.0		
Zebra	10.0%	.25	$\ln 10 = 2.303$	$\sqrt{10} = 3.162$
	20.0	.50	$\ln 20 = 2.996$	$\sqrt{20} = 4.472$
	40.0	.25	$\ln 40 = 3.689$	$\sqrt{40} = 6.325$
		1.0		

19-14 Reconsider the difference in investment choices that existed between security analysts Nat Logger and Hal Power in the preceding question. As it turns out,

Pat Logger and Val Power are friends who frequently discuss, among other things, their husbands' work. In particular, the discussion that Nat and Hal have been having about whether White Corporation's or Zebra Inc.'s stock is the most desirable investment has spread to their wives. The wives are in complete agreement with the probability distributions of returns for White and Zebra that their husbands set forth. But both wives have preference structures that differ from their husbands'. Pat Logger has the following logarithmic utility of wealth function based on natural (or napierian) logarithms: $u = 88 + 4 \ln r$. Val Power has the following square root (or power of one-half) utility of wealth function: $u = -2 + 10r^{.5} = -2 + 10\sqrt{r}$. Not surprisingly, since their utility functions are intrinsically different, the two women disagree about whether the White or the Zebra will maximize their expected utility. They are considering discussing the problem with their husbands to see if, perhaps, they are missing something. However, they are afraid that they may only wind up with four different opinions instead of obtaining any kind of resolution to the difference. Do you think more differences of opinion will emerge if the two married couples discuss the White-Zebra choice together? Explain.

	Rate of return, r	Probability	Mrs. L's $u = 88 + 4 \ln r$	Mrs. P's $u = 2 + 10\sqrt{r}$
White	5.0%	.25		
	10.0	.50		
	20.0	.25		
		1.0		
Zebra	10.0%	.25		
	20.0	.50		
	40.0	.25		
		1.0		

Problems (Appendix 19A)

19-15 Analyze the following utility function: $U(w) = -w^{-.5}$. (a) Draw a graph of the function. (b) Is marginal utility increasing, constant, decreasing? (c) What is the function's absolute risk aversion (ARA)? (d) What is the function's relative risk aversion (RRA)? (e) As the investor's wealth increases, will more, the same, or less dollars be invested in risky assets? (f) As the investor's wealth increases, will a larger, the same, or a smaller proportion of the investor's total wealth be invested in risky assets?

Selected References

Fisher, Irving, *The Theory of Interest* (New York: Macmillan Company, 1930).

   This classic book introduces economic decision-making and establishes the foundations for the modern theories of economic decision-making in uncertainty.

Friedman, M., and L. J. Savage, "The Utility Analysis of Choices Involving Risk," *The Journal of Political Economy,* Aug. 1948, pp. 279–304.

> A classic paper rationalizing choice under uncertainty with the expected utility hypothesis. Only algebra is used.

Hirshleifer, J., *Investment, Interest, and Capital* (Englewood Cliffs, N.J.: Prentice-Hall, 1970).

> This book traces the development of decision theory, as it applies to financial economics, from the early certainty models of Irving Fisher through the modern risk-return models of Harry Markowitz.

Markowitz, Harry, *Portfolio Selection* (New York: Wiley, 1959).

> Chapters 10 through 13 discuss the utility theory underlying the selection of efficient assets. Most of the mathematics is freshman college algebra.

Neumann, John Von, and Oskar Morgenstern, *Theory of Games and Economic Behavior,* 3d ed. (Princeton, N.J.: Princeton, 1953).

> This book provides a seminal explanation of utility theory.

Appendix 19A

Mathematical
Utility Analysis

A utility-of-wealth function can be written as $U = f(W)$ or $U(W)$. Figure 19-6 shows a graph of one particular utility-of-wealth function. The notion of marginal utility is a little more complex; it involves segments of the utility-of-wealth function. In words, **marginal utility** of wealth may be defined as the additional utility a person gets from a change in wealth. Mathematically, marginal utility is the first derivative of the utility function—that is, $dU/dW = U'(W)$. The sign of the second derivative of the utility function determines whether marginal utility is rising or falling.

Decision-makers act so as to maximize their *expected utility*. As explained in Chapter 19 and defined in Equation (19-4), the expected utility from a decision to undertake some risky course of action is the weighted average of the utils from the possible outcomes which are calculated using as the weights the probability of each outcome.[10]

Marginal Utility

Decreasing marginal utility is present when the utility function rises at a less steep rate, namely, when the second derivative of the utility function is negative, $d^2U/dW^2 < 0$ or equivalently $U''(W) < 0$. *Constant marginal utility* is present when the utility function is linear and thus rises at a constant rate. Constant marginal utility occurs when the second derivative of the utility function is zero, $d^2U/dW^2 = U''(W) = 0$. When the utility function rises at an increasingly steep rate or, equivalently, when the second derivative of the utility function is positive, $d^2U/dW^2 = U''(W) > 0$, *increasing marginal utility* exists.

Risk-averse behavior will result if the investor has diminishing marginal utility of wealth or returns. Diminishing marginal utility-of-wealth and utility-of-returns functions

---

[10]Some of the important literature is in the following books: S. Archer and C. D'Ambrosio, *The Theory of Business Finance: A Book of Readings* (New York: Macmillan, 1967), readings 2–4, 39, and 40; Harry Markowitz, *Portfolio Selection,* Cowles Foundation Monograph 16 (New York: Wiley, 1959), chaps. 10–13; and J. L. Bicksler and P. A. Samuelson, *Investment Portfolio Decision-Making* (Lexington, Mass.: Lexington Books, 1974), readings 1–8 and 14–18.

Table 19A-1

THREE CATEGORIES OF ATTITUDES ABOUT RISK-TAKING

Second derivative	Behavioral implication	Gambling decisions
1. $U''(W) < 0$	Risk averse	Reject fair gamble
2. $U''(W) = 0$	Risk neutral	Indifferent to fair gamble
3. $U''(W) > 0$	Risk lover	Accept a gamble, even if it is slightly unfair

are graphed in Figures 19-6 and 19-7, respectively. They are both concave from the horizontal axis. Table 19A-1 summarizes the behavioral implications that can be discerned from the sign of the second derivative of a utility function.

Analysis of Quadratic Utility Functions

For **quadratic utility functions** it may be shown that expected utility is completely determined by expected return $E(r)$ and risk.

$$E(U) = Q[E(r), \text{risk}] \qquad (19A\text{-}1)$$
$$= Q[E(r), \sigma^2] \qquad (19A\text{-}1a)$$

where $E(U)$ = expected utility

$E(r)$ = expected return, risk is measured by variance of returns

Q = quadratic function

Consider the quadratic utility-of-wealth and -return functions (19A-2) and (19A-3).

$$u = U(W) = W - aW^2 \qquad \text{iff } W < \frac{1}{2a} \text{ for } a > 0 \qquad (19A\text{-}2)$$

$$u = U(r) = r - br^2 \qquad \text{iff } r < \frac{1}{2b} \text{ for } b > 0 \qquad (19A\text{-}3)$$

Equations (19A-2) and (19A-3) are graphed in Figures 19A-1 and 19A-2, respectively. Figures 19A-1 and 19A-2 also show the marginal utility curves. Note that the marginal utility curves begin at 1.0, diminish continuously, and, perversely, become negative as larger returns are obtained.

The preference orderings of a utility function are invariant under a positive linear transformation of the basic random variable.[11] This implies that the diminishing quadratic utility-of-wealth function (19A-2) is equivalent to the diminishing quadratic utility-of-returns function (19A-3), since one variable is a positive linear transformation of the other. Stated differently, the behavioral implications of Equations (19A-2) and (19A-3) are similar.

[11]J. Von Neumann and O. Morgenstern, *Theory of Games and Economic Behavior,* 3d ed. (Princeton, N.J.: Princeton, 1953), pp. 22–24. Equation (19-2) above displays the particular positive linear function that transforms changes in wealth into rates of return.

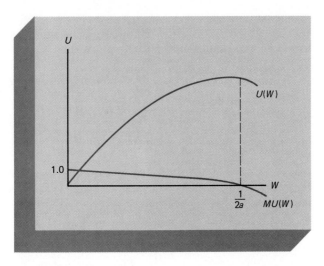

Figure 19A-1 Quadratic utility-of-wealth function with continuously diminishing marginal utility.

Taking the expected value of Equation (19A-3) yields (19A-4).

$$E(U) = E(r - br^2) \qquad\qquad\qquad\qquad (19A\text{-}4)$$
$$= E(r) - bE(r^2)$$
$$= E(r) - b\sigma^2 - bE(r)^2 \qquad \text{since } E(r^2) = \sigma^2 + E(r)^2$$
$$= Q[E(r), \sigma^2] \qquad\qquad\qquad\qquad (19A\text{-}4a)$$

Figure 19A-2 Quadratic utility-of-returns function with continuously diminishing marginal utility.

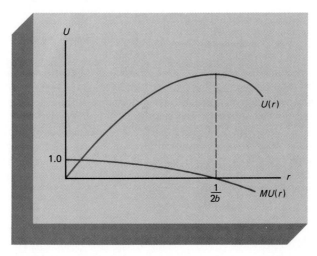

Equation (19A-4a) shows that expected utility is a function of expected return and risk as measured by the variance of returns. Expected utility varies directly with $E(r)$ and inversely with risk in the quadratic utility function.

$$\frac{\partial E(U)}{\partial E(r)} = 1 - 2bE(r) > 0 \qquad E(U) \text{ increases directly with } E(r)$$

and

$$\frac{\partial E(U)}{\partial \sigma^2} = -2b < 0 \qquad E(U) \text{ varies inversely with risk, Var}(r)$$

for the values to which b and r are constrained in Equation (19A-3). Thus, investors with diminishing quadratic utility of wealth or returns desire more $E(r)$ and less risk.

Solving Equation (19A-4a) for σ^2 yields Equation (19A-5).

$$\sigma^2 = \frac{E(r)}{b} - E(r)^2 - \frac{E(U)}{b} \qquad\qquad (19A\text{-}5)$$

$$= \frac{E(r)}{b} - E(r)^2 - \text{a constant} \qquad\qquad (19A\text{-}5a)$$

Varying the constant term in Equation (19A-5a) generates the quadratic indifference map in $[E(r), \sigma^2]$ space shown in Figure 19-11. Figure 19-11 shows that investors whose utility is well approximated by Equation (19A-3) will maximize their expected utility by selecting investments with the maximum return in some risk class, that is, by *selecting efficient portfolios*.

Two-Parameter Distribution of Returns Can Be Sufficient for $[E(r), \sigma^2]$ Analysis

It can be shown that if the probability distribution of rates of return is a two-parameter distribution (such as the normal distribution) and the investor has a diminishing single-period utility function, the investor can maximize expected utility by selecting investments with the minimum risk at each rate of return (or, conversely, the maximum return at each risk class).[12]

$$E[U(r)] = \int U(r)f(r|m_1,m_2)\, dr \qquad\qquad (19A\text{-}6)$$

$$= F(r|m_1,m_2) \qquad\qquad (19A\text{-}6a)$$

where $f(r|m_1,m_2)$ is a two-parameter probability distribution of returns which is completely specified by m_1 and m_2. For example, if Ms. Investor had a logarithmic utility function (that is, diminishing marginal utility) and if the probability distribution was a two-parameter distribution (such as a normal distribution), she would maximize her expected utility by maximizing returns at any given risk class since $\partial E(U)/\partial E(r) = \partial F/\partial m_1 > 0$ and $\partial E(U)/\partial \sigma^2 = \partial F/\partial m_2 < 0$. Thus, selection of investments in terms of $E(r)$ and σ does not necessarily imply a quadratic utility function. A logarithmic or other utility function or others that have positive but diminishing marginal utility also imply that mean-variance efficient portfolios are optimal *if* the probability distribution of returns is a two-parameter distribution.

---

[12]Equation (19A-6) only sketches the outlines of the proof. For the complete proof see J. Tobin, "Liquidity Preference as Behavior towards Risk," *Review of Economic Studies*, Feb. 1958, pp. 65–86.

Pratt and Arrow developed measures of absolute and relative risk aversion to help analyze the behavior implied by a particular utility function.[13]

Absolute Risk Aversion (ARA)

Consider an investor who is given the choice of either (1) keeping W_c dollars of wealth with certainty or (2) entering into a risky investment with an expected value of $E(W)$ = W and outcomes described by the additive random variable Z where $E(Z) = 0$ and $\text{Var}(Z) > 0$. Further assume that the choice has been constructed so the investor is indifferent between (1) having W_c for certain and (2) the uncertain amount equal to $W + Z$. Since $U(W_c) = E[U(W_c)]$ it can be said, more concisely,

$$U(W_c) = E[U(W_c)] = E[U(W + Z)] \qquad \text{(19A-7)}$$

The dollar difference between W and W_c is the maximum amount the investor would be willing to pay to have W_c with certainty rather than face the uncertain investment outcome. The quantity $\Pi = W - W_c$ is a measure of **absolute risk aversion;** it equals the amount the investor would be willing to pay for an insurance policy that would make the actuarial expectation of the risky investment equal to W_c.

Taylor Series Expansion   The investor's utility from the risky investment, $U(W + Z)$, can be analyzed further by using Taylor series expansions.[14] Taking the Taylor series expansion of $U(W + Z)$ around W results in the expression below.

$$U(W + Z) = U(W) + U'(W)\,[(W + Z) - W] + [1/(2!)]U''(W)\,[(W + Z) - W]^2$$
$$+ [1/(3!)]U'''(W)[(W + Z) - W]^3 + \cdots \qquad \text{(19A-8)}$$

By taking the expected value of this Taylor series expansion and ignoring all terms that involve the third- and higher-order derivatives, we can rewrite the equation above as follows.

$$E[U(W + Z)] = E[U(W)] + U'(W)E(Z) + \tfrac{1}{2}U''(W)E(Z - 0)^2 \qquad \text{(19A-9)}$$

Since $E(Z - 0)^2 = E[Z - E(Z)]^2 = \text{Var}(Z)$ and $U(W)$ is a constant, the preceding equation can be restated as shown below.

$$E[U(W + Z)] = U(W) + \tfrac{1}{2}U''(W)\text{Var}(Z) \qquad \text{(19A-10)}$$

Recall that the investor's certain wealth can be restated as $W_c = W - \Pi$. Expand-

---

[13]See John W. Pratt, ''Risk Aversion in the Large and in the Small,'' *Econometrica,* Jan.–April 1964. Also see Kenneth J. Arrow, *Essays in the Theory of Risk Bearing* (Amsterdam: North Holland Press, 1971).

[14]The **Taylor series expansion** is used to approximate the value of the continuous function f at the point x (1) if the function exists over an interval that includes the values of both point x and point a in the formula below and (2) if the relevant derivatives of the function exist.

$$f(x) = f(a) + f'(a)\,(x - a) + \frac{f''(a)}{2!}\,(x - a)^2 + \frac{f'''(a)}{3!}\,(x - a)^3 + \cdots$$

Taylor series expansions are typically covered in the second semester of freshman calculus. Many elementary calculus and mathematical economics textbooks discuss the Taylor series expansion in more detail.

ing the quantity $U(W - \Pi)$ in a Taylor series expansion around W results in Equation (19A-11).

$$U(W_c) = U(W - \Pi) = U(W) + U'(W)[(W - \Pi) - W] + \cdots \quad \text{(19A-11)}$$

Equation (19-11) can be simplified by ignoring terms above the first derivative in order to obtain the approximation below.

$$U(W_c) = U(W) + U'(W)(-\Pi) \quad \text{(19A-12)}$$

We know from Equation (19A-7) that $U(W_c) = E[U(W + Z)]$; this implies that Equations (19A-12) and (19A-10) are equal. These facts allow us to substitute and thereby derive Equation (19A-13).

$$U(W) + \tfrac{1}{2}U''(W)\text{Var}(Z) = U(W) + U'(W)(-\Pi) \quad \text{(19A-13)}$$

Solving Equation (19A-13) for Π yields

$$\Pi = -\tfrac{1}{2}\text{Var}(Z)\,\frac{U''(W)}{U'(W)} \quad \text{(19A-14)}$$

Since the quantity $\tfrac{1}{2}\text{Var}(Z)$ is a constant, the quantity $-U''(W)/U'(W)$ measures the amount of risk aversion in the utility function U evaluated at point W. Thus, Equation (19A-15) defines a measure of *absolute risk aversion (ARA)*.

$$\text{ARA}(W) = \frac{-U''(W)}{U'(W)} \quad \text{(19A-15)}$$

Properties of Absolute Risk Aversion   ARA has several interesting properties. First, assuming that no one dislikes being wealthier, that is, $U'(W) > 0$, it follows that the sign of ARA is determined by the sign of $U''(W)$. Second, if ARA consistently has the same sign over all positive values of W, it is said that the utility function reveals *global* risk preferences. More specifically, a utility function is said to be **globally risk-averse** if the sign of ARA is positive over all values of W, **globally risk-neutral** if it is zero, or **globally risk-loving** if it is negative. As mentioned above, if two utility functions differ by a positive linear transformation, they will rank investments the same way. Third, this invariant ranking extends to another noteworthy ARA characteristic. If two utility functions differ by a positive linear transformation, their ARA will be the same.

The first derivative of ARA(W) is the appropriate measure of how absolute risk aversion behaves when the investor's wealth changes. Table 19A-2 shows how to interpret the first derivative of ARA(W).

Relative Risk Aversion (RRA)

The absolute risk-aversion (ARA) measure can be adapted to be a measure of proportional or **relative risk aversion** (RRA). This redefinition begins by rescaling the ARA quantity $\Pi = W - W_c$ to be the *percent* of wealth (rather than an absolute dollar amount) that an investor would give up in order to avoid the risky investment alternative laid out above. More specifically, let Π_R be defined to be equal to $(W - W_c)/W$. Solving the definition of Π_R for W_c yields $W_c = W(1.0 - \Pi_R)$. Next, the stochastic component must also be similarly rescaled so that $z = (Z + W)/W$. Thus, z is the stochastic element

Table 19A-2
HOW TO INTERPRET THE FIRST DERIVATIVE OF ARA(W)

Condition	Definition
1. Increasing absolute risk aversion, ARA$'(W) > 0$	Investor holds fewer dollars in risky assets as W increases.
2. Constant absolute risk aversion, ARA$'(W) = 0$	Investor holds same number of dollars in risky assets as W increases.
3. Decreasing absolute risk aversion, ARA$'(W) < 0$	Investor holds more dollars in risky assets as W increases.

stated as a percent of the invested wealth. Thus, $E(z) = 1.0$. Intuitively, the quantity Wz is the dollar gain or loss from the risky investment.

Taylor Series Expansion RRA can be analyzed by expanding Wz in a Taylor series around the point W to obtain Equation (19-16).

$$U(Wz) = U(W) + U'(W)E(Wz - W) + \frac{U''(W)}{2!}E(Wz - W)^2 + \cdots \quad (19A\text{-}16)$$

The third- and all higher-order derivatives are ignored. Taking the expected value of both sides of Equation (19A-16) and rearranging results in Equation (19-17):

$$E[U(W)] = U(W) + 0 + \frac{U''(W)}{2!} W^2 \text{Var}(z) \quad (19A\text{-}17)$$

Recalling the rescaled definition of W_c and taking a Taylor series expansion of it around W yields the following equations:

$$U(W_c) = U[W(1.0 - \Pi_R)]$$
$$= U(W) + U'(W)[W(1.0 - \Pi) - W] + \cdots \quad (19A\text{-}18)$$

Ignoring all terms with a second- or higher-order derivative and rearranging Equation (19A-18) results in Equation (19A-19).

$$U(W_c) = U(W) + U'(W)(-\Pi_R W) \quad (19A\text{-}19)$$

Equating the quantity $E[U(W)]$ from Equation (19A-17) to $U(W_c)$ in Equation (19A-19) results in Equation (19A-20) below.

$$\Pi_R = \frac{-\text{Var}(z)}{2} \frac{WU''(W)}{U'(W)} \quad (19A\text{-}20)$$

Interpretation of RRA Since the quantity $\text{Var}(z)/2$ in Equation (19A-20) is a constant, it can be ignored and Π_R can be restated without this constant as shown in Equation (19A-21). The RRA(W) measure in Equation (19A-21) can be interpreted as a measure

Table 19A-3

HOW TO INTERPRET THE FIRST DERIVATIVE OF RRA(W)

Condition	Definition
1. Increasing relative risk aversion, RRA$'(W) > 0$	Investor holds a smaller proportion in risky assets as W increases.
2. Constant relative risk aversion, RRA$'(W) = 0$	Investor holds same proportion in risky assets as W increases.
3. Decreasing relative risk aversion, RRA$'(W) < 0$	Investor holds larger proportion in risky assets as W increases.

of the percentage change in the risk premium that the investor would pay to avoid the risky investment alternative.[15]

$$\text{RRA}(W) = \frac{-WU''(W)}{U'(W)} \qquad (19A\text{-}21)$$

Stated differently, RRA(W) is an approximate measure of relative (or proportional) risk aversion evaluated at wealth level W.[16]

[15]In the derivations of the ARA(W) and RRA(W) some higher-order terms were dropped after taking the Taylor series expansions. For this reason the ARA(W) and RRA(W) measures are approximations rather than exact measures. However, they are good approximations because the coefficients of the terms involved, first, Π_R (and Π), and second, the moments of z (or Z), have similar sizes. Therefore, when these roughly similar terms are dropped, the approximations that are introduced into ARA(W) and RRA(W) can be safely overlooked.

[16]Jan Mossin, *Theory of Financial Markets* (Englewood Cliffs, N.J.: Prentice-Hall, 1973). Mossin shows how to derive the definitions of ARA(w) and RRA(w) in an exact, but less intuitive, fashion.

Table 19A-4

RISK-AVERSION CHARACTERISTICS OF DIFFERENT UTILITY-OF-WEALTH FUNCTIONS

Utility function	Absolute risk aversion	Relative risk aversion	Conditions
Quadratic	Increasing	Increasing	$a > 0$
$u = W - aW^2$	ARA $= 2a/(1.0 - 2aW) > 0$	RRA $= 2aW/(1.0 - 2aW) > 0$	$W < 1 - 2aW$
Logarithmic	Decreasing	Constant	
$u = \ln W$	ARA $= 1.0/W$	RRA $= 1.0$	None
Positive power	Decreasing	Constant	
$u = W^b$	ARA $= (1.0 - b)/W$	RRA $= 1.0 - b$	$0 < b < 1.0$
Exponential	Constant	Positive	
$U = -e^{-bW}$	ARA $= b$	RRA $= bW$	$b > 0$

The first derivative of RRA(W) with respect to W, denoted RRA$'(W)$, is the appropriate measure of how relative risk aversion behaves when the investor's wealth changes. Table 19A-3 shows how to interpret the first derivative of RRA(W). It is informative to compare Tables 19A-2 and 19A-3.

Note the implications of ARA(W) and RRA(W) for stock price volatility if all investors have logarithmic utility, for example. A significant drop in stock prices (such as occurred in October 1987) reduces investors' aggregate wealth. Since ARA$'(W)$ is negative for the logarithmic utility function, the decrease in wealth increases investors' absolute risk aversion. As a result, the more stock prices fall, the more risky assets (namely, stock shares) will be sold as investors "flee for safety." The reverse is also true; an increase in wealth diminishes absolute risk aversion, and investors buy more risky assets in a bull market. Summarizing, a negative ARA$'(W)$ increases stock price volatility. This implication for stock price volatility applies to any utility function that has constant relative risk aversion RRA$'(W) = 0$.

Analysis of Different Utility Functions   Table 19A-4 lists the risk-aversion characteristics of various common types of utility-of-wealth functions.[17] The logarithmic utility function is the most logical representation of rational, risk-averse economic behavior.[18]

---

[17]For a more detailed discussion of utility analysis in an investment setting, see Gordon J. Alexander and Jack Clark Francis, *Portfolio Analysis,* 3d ed. (Englewood Cliffs, N.J.: Prentice-Hall, 1986), chaps. 2 and 3.

[18]See Mark Rubinstein, "The Strong Case for the Generalized Logarithmic Utility Models as the Premier Model of Financial Markets," *Journal of Finance,* May 1976, vol. XXXI, no. 2, pp. 551–571.

Chapter 20

Capital Market
Theory: A Closer Look

Capital market theory draws the asset pricing implications out of a model of economic equilibrium. The theory simultaneously considers all marketable investments—every stock, bond, option, commodity future contract, warrant, educational investment, work of art, real estate, as well as other assets. Parts of the theory have already been introduced. The concept of risk measurement was defined in Chapter 1. The discussion of portfolio analysis in Chapter 9 culminated in the introduction of a portfolio pricing model, the capital market line (CML). The distinction between total risk, systematic risk, and unsystematic risk was explained and the capital asset pricing model (CAPM), also called the security market line (SML), was presented in Chapter 10. Arbitrage pricing theory (APT) was the topic of Chapter 11. This chapter pulls all of these models together and shows how they form a unified economic theory.

20-1 **INVESTMENT OPPORTUNITIES IN RISK-RETURN SPACE**

By using a powerful computer and advanced mathematics, we can portfolio analyze thousands of assets at once and determine the efficient frontier. Figure 20-1 shows the investment opportunities that portfolio analysis might show to exist if all capital assets in the world were considered.

The Efficient Frontier

All the investment opportunities in the world are assumed to be represented by the scalloped quarter-moon-shaped drawing in Figure 20-1. *Individual assets lie along the lower right portion of the scalloped quarter-moon-shaped set of investment opportunities;* they are represented by the dots.

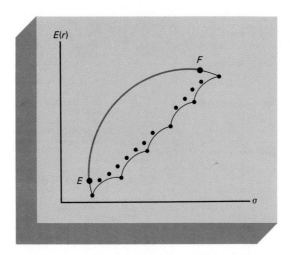

Figure 20-1 A set of investment opportunities without borrowing and lending.

Individual assets like stocks and bonds contain both systematic risk and unsystematic risk and are not efficient investments. Only *portfolios derived via Markowitz diversification* have had the unsystematic risk reduced to zero and can attain the efficient frontier. The efficient frontier is represented by the heavy dark curve from *E* to *F* in Figure 20-1. The portfolios lying on the efficient frontier contain only systematic risk caused by variations in the economic, political, and sociological environment that simultaneously affect nearly every asset in some way. As a result, the efficient assets along the curve *EF* in Figure 20-1 are highly positively correlated.[1]

Borrowing and Lending at a Riskless Rate

The investment opportunities shown in Figure 20-1 may be extended by considering the possibilities of borrowing and lending. To keep the model simple, suppose that all investors can borrow or lend at one riskless rate of return, denoted R. By definition, *the* **riskless asset** *has zero variability of return,* $\text{Var}(R) = 0$.

Figure 20-2 represents the investment opportunities that would exist in equilibrium if all investors were Markowitz portfolio analysts, could borrow or lend at rate *R,* and had "homogeneous expectations." The term **homogeneous expectations** indicates that all investors visualize the same expected return, risk,

---

[1]Figure 9-4 shows that only risky assets that lie along a straight line in risk-return space can be perfectly positively correlated. The assets on the curved efficient frontier in Figure 20-1 are highly positively correlated because they all move together systematically. But they are not perfectly positively correlated because the curve *EF* is not a straight line.

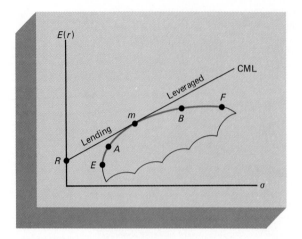

Figure 20-2 The capital market line (CML) is the efficient frontier when borrowing and lending at the riskless rate are considered.

and correlation statistics for any specific asset in the world.[2] Different assets can and will be perceived differently. But any particular asset will be perceived homogeneously. Assuming homogeneous expectations allows us to represent the investment opportunities visualized by every investor with just one graph, rather than with separate graphs that represent differences of opinion over the risk and return statistics of specific assets. The *capital market line* (CML) shown in Figure 20-2 is specified mathematically in Equation (20-1).

$$E(r_i) = R + \left(\frac{E(r_m) - R}{\sigma_m} \right) \sigma_i \qquad (20\text{-}1)$$

$$\frac{\text{Total}}{\text{return}} = \frac{\text{reward for}}{\text{waiting}} + \frac{\text{reward for}}{\text{risk bearing}} \qquad (20\text{-}1a)$$

where $E(r_i)$ = expected rate of return from ith portfolio, whose total risk is
measured by standard deviation σ_i
   R = riskless rate of interest

---

[2]Assuming homogeneous expectations is an inadequate assumption to assure a unique equilibrium. What economists call *common knowledge* must be assumed to guarantee a unique equilibrium. Common knowledge has been defined by Aumann as the ultimate equilibrium emerging from a DeGroot-type convergence of posterior beliefs. See Morris H. DeGroot, "Reaching a Consensus," *Journal of the American Statistical Association,* 1974, vol. 60, pp. 118–121. Also see Robert J. Aumann, "Agreeing to Disagree," *Annals of Statistics,* 1976, vol. 4, pp. 1236–1239. **Common knowledge** is said to exist between agents B and C when both agents know that an event has occurred, B knows that C knows the event has occurred, C knows that B knows the event has occurred, ad infinitum.

$E(r_m)$ = expected rate of return from market portfolio, denoted m

σ_m = market portfolio's standard deviation of returns.

Market Portfolio Portfolio m in Figure 20-2 is a huge portfolio containing all assets in the world in the proportions x_i^*, where

$$x_i^* = \frac{\text{total value of the } i\text{th security}}{\text{total value of all securities in the market}}$$

Asset m is called the **market portfolio.** The market portfolio contains all securities in exactly the proportions they are supplied in equilibrium because it is the one unique portfolio that all investors want to buy. The return on the market portfolio is the weighted average return on all capital assets.[3] The market portfolio is a useful theoretical construct because the return on m is the return that the Dow Jones, Standard & Poor's, and NYSE averages are approximating.

20-2 **ASSUMPTIONS UNDERLYING CAPITAL MARKET THEORY**

Capital market theory is based on the assumptions underlying portfolio analysis.

Portfolio Analysis Assumptions Four assumptions form the basis for performing Markowitz portfolio analysis in order to delineate the efficient frontier:

1. The rate of return from an investment is its most important outcome. Investors conceptualize the various possible rates of return from an investment as a probability distribution of rates of return—either consciously or subconsciously.
2. Investors' risk estimates are proportional to the variability of return

---

[3]The market portfolio was Professor Eugene Fama's concept. See Eugene Fama, "Risk, Return and Equilibrium: Some Clarifying Comments," *Journal of Finance,* March 1968, pp. 32–33. For empirical estimates of the market portfolio see R. G. Ibbotson and Carol L. Fall, "The United States Market Wealth Portfolio," *Journal of Portfolio Management,* Fall 1979. See also R. G. Ibbotson and Laurence B. Siegel, "The World Market Wealth Portfolio," *Journal of Portfolio Management,* Winter 1983.

For an explanation of the critical role of the market portfolio in empirical tests of the capital market theory, see Richard Roll, "A Critique of the Asset Pricing Theory's Tests," *Journal of Financial Economics,* March 1977, pp. 129–176. Roll's critique, made in a general equilibrium context, does not diminish the usefulness of empirical characteristic line statistics that are based on some narrowly defined market index. Such partial equilibrium analysis can usefully supplement general equilibrium analysis.

(namely, the standard deviation or variance) they perceive for a security or portfolio.

3. Investors are willing to base their decisions on only two parameters of the probability distribution of returns, the expected return and the variance (or its square root, the standard deviation) of returns. Symbolically, $U = f\{E(r), \sigma\}$, where U denotes the investors' utility.

4. For any risk class, investors prefer a higher rate of return to a lower one. Symbolically, $dU/dE(r) > 0$. Conversely, among all securities with the same rate of return, investors prefer less rather than more risk. Symbolically, $dU/d\sigma < 0$.

Investors who conform to the preceding assumptions will prefer efficient portfolios.[4] Such investors are **Markowitz diversifiers.**

Capital Market Theory Assumptions

Capital market theory consists of the logical, mathematical, and economic implications of portfolio analysis. The additional assumptions necessary to generate the capital market theory are as follows:

1. All investors are Markowitz-efficient diversifiers who delineate and seek to attain the efficient frontier. Thus, the four assumptions above are among those on which the capital market theory is constructed.

2. An infinite amount of money can be borrowed or lent at the risk-free rate of interest R. The return on short-term U.S. Treasury bills may be used as a proxy for R. Essentially, this assumption allows investors to have idealized margin accounts. No other borrowing is permitted.

3. *Idealized uncertainty* prevails so that all investors visualize the same probability distributions for the future rates of return from a particular asset. Stated differently, investors have *homogeneous expectations*. This assumption does not imply that different assets are not perceived to have different risk and/or rate of return statistics.

4. All investors have the same "one-period" investment horizon.

5. All investments are infinitely divisible; fractional shares may be purchased in any portfolio or any individual asset.

6. No taxes and no transaction costs for buying and selling securities exist. Thus, trading is said to be "frictionless."

7. No inflation and no change in the level of interest rates exist (or all changes are fully anticipated).

8. The capital markets are in equilibrium.

---

[4]Figures 19-8 and 19-11 use utility theory to illustrate the investment preferences of an investor who is characterized by the four preceding assumptions.

Readers unaccustomed to economic analysis are sometimes disappointed by a theory that is based on a list of unrealistic assumptions, but they should not be. The assumptions provide a concrete foundation on which a theory can be derived by applying the forces of logic, intuition, and mathematics. Without these assumptions, the analysis would degenerate into a polemical discussion of which historical facts, folklore, and institutions are significant, which are insignificant, what their relationships are, and what conclusions might be reached by a "reasonable person." Such discussions are seldom productive.

Traditionally, economists have based their analyses on as few and as simple assumptions as possible. Then a theory is derived with conclusions and implications which are incontestable, given the assumptions. Next, the assumptions are relaxed to determine what can be expected in more realistic circumstances. Thus, the final test of a theory should not be the realism of its assumptions but rather the predictive power of the resulting model. Later in this chapter, the assumptions underlying the capital market theory will be aligned more closely with reality. But first, capital market theory will be examined in a unified presentation.

20-3   **CAPITAL ASSET PRICING MODEL (CAPM)**

The expected returns for *portfolios* (but not individual assets) depend on their standard deviations and a linear function called the CML. In contrast, the equilibrium rate of return for *individual assets* such as individual stocks and bonds is given by the CAPM. The prices of portfolios can be determined with the CAPM too. Reconsider the rationale lying behind the CAPM to understand how the prices of the individual assets are determined.[5]

The variance of a two-security portfolio is given by Equation (20-2).

$$\text{Var}(r_p) = x_1^2 \, \text{Var}(r_1) + x_2^2 \, \text{Var}(r_2) + 2x_1 x_2 \, \text{Cov}(r_1, r_2) \qquad (20\text{-}2)$$

For an *n*-security portfolio, the variance is given by Equation (20-2a).

$$\text{Var}(r_p) = \sum_{i=1}^{n} x_i^2 \, \text{Var}(r_i) + \sum_{i=1}^{n} \sum_{j=1}^{n} x_i x_j \sigma_{ij} \qquad (20\text{-}2a)$$

Note that within the expression for the risk of a portfolio of any size are covariance terms between all possible pairs of assets that are candidates for the portfolio. The essence of Markowitz diversification is to find securities with the lowest covariances. If all other factors are equal, demand will be high for investments that have a low covariance of returns with the market portfolio.

[5]The CAPM was introduced in Chapter 10, where the CAPM is explained in terms of the beta coefficient, obtained from the characteristic line, Equation (10-3). This chapter rationalizes the CAPM without referring to the characteristic line.

Securities that have high covariance with the market portfolio have high systematic risk and will experience low demand. As a result, the prices of securities with high systematic risk will fall and prices of securities with low systematic risk will be bid up. Since equilibrium rates of return move inversely with the price of the security, securities having a high covariance with the market will have *relatively low prices* (that is, low relative to their income but not necessarily low in dollar amounts) and high expected returns. Conversely, securities with low or negative covariances will have relatively high prices and therefore experience low expected rates of return in equilibrium. The resulting relationship is depicted in Figure 20-3. Equation (20-3) is a mathematical statement of the CAPM in terms of the covariance.[6]

$$E(r_i) = R + \frac{E(r_m) - R}{\text{Var}(r_m)} \text{Cov}(r_i, r_m) \qquad (20\text{-}3)$$

where $\dfrac{E(r_m) - R}{\text{Var}(r_m)}$ = slope of CAPM = market price of risk

R = riskless rate of interest, or the reward for waiting

$\text{Cov}(r_i, r_m)$ = ith asset's covariance of returns with market

$E(r_i)$ = equilibrium expected return for ith asset

The expected return $E(r_i)$ is the appropriate discount rate to use in valuing the ith security's income. Stated differently, $E(r_i)$ is the **cost of capital** or **capitalization rate** that should be used to find the present value of an asset with whatever amount of systematic risk the ith asset has.

Figure 20-3 and Equation (20-3) say, in words, that at equilibrium every asset should be priced so that its expected return is a linear function of its covariance of return with the market. Stated differently, the expected return from any market asset is an increasing function of its systematic risk. Since systematic risk is the portion of a security's total risk that cannot be reduced

---

[6]The intuitive discussion of covariance effects above assumes that all expected returns are fixed and equal, and all variances are equal and constant too. For an early mathematical derivation of the CAPM, see W. F. Sharpe, "Capital Asset Prices: A Theory of Market Equilibrium under Conditions of Risk," *Journal of Finance,* Sept. 1964, vol. XIX, no. 3, footnote 22. For a review of several different mathematical derivations of the CAPM, see J. C. Francis and S. H. Archer, *Portfolio Analysis,* 2d ed. (Englewood Cliffs, N.J.: Prentice-Hall, 1979), appendix to chap. 8. Jack L. Treynor also developed the CAPM in an unpublished paper. Treynor was working alone and mailed copies of his paper to various interested people; W. F. Sharpe acknowledges Treynor's paper in the sixth footnote of "Capital Asset Prices. . . ." Unfortunately, Treynor never did publish his paper. Later developments of the CAPM can be found in John Lintner, "The Valuation of Risk Assets and the Selection of Risky Investments in Stock Portfolios and Capital Budgets," *The Review of Economics and Statistics,* Feb. 1965, pp. 13–27. For a different formulation of the same model, see Jan Mossin, "Equilibrium in a Capital Asset Market," *Econometrica,* Oct. 1966, pp. 768–783.

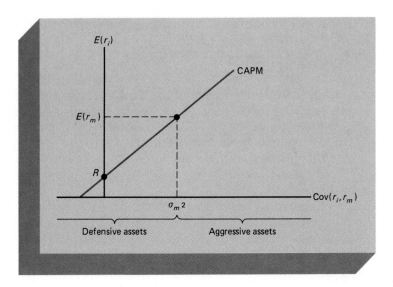

Figure 20-3 The CAPM formulated in terms of covariance with the market.

by diversification, the CAPM is intuitively appealing. The more risk a security has that cannot be eliminated by diversification, the more return investors will require to induce them to hold that risky security in their portfolios.

The expected rate of return that the CAPM suggests for an asset is made up of two separate components:

1. The CAPM's intercept R represents the **price of time.** This component of the ith asset's expected rate of return compensates the investor for delaying consumption in order to invest.

2. The CAPM's second component is the market **price of risk**—it is measured by the slope of the CAPM, $[E(r_m) - R]/\text{Var}(r_m)$. The market price of risk is multiplied by the ith asset's covariance. This second component compensates the investor for taking undiversifiable risks.

The locus of equilibrium expected returns shown in Figure 20-3 is the CAPM. The CAPM is a separate and distinct relation to the CML shown in Figure 20-2. In equilibrium, an *individual* security's expected return and risk statistics will lie *on the CAPM and below the CML.* In equilibrium, only *efficient portfolio* $[E(r), \sigma]$ pairs will lie *on* the CML. Portfolio $[E(r), \text{Cov}(r_i, r_m)]$ pairs will also lie on the CAPM. Thus, even under idealistic assumptions and at static equilibrium, the CML will not include all points if portfolios and individual securities are plotted together on one graph.

The economic process that determines the expected returns of individual securities held in diversified portfolios *does not consider total risk.* Unsystematic risk is not particularly undesirable since it can be diversified away to zero in a diversified portfolio.[7]

Defensive and Aggressive Securities

In Figure 20-3, the portion of the horizontal axis representing below-average and negative covariances is marked as including **defensive securities.** These securities are defensive because they offer the opportunity to reduce a portfolio's total risk by including them in a portfolio that is positively correlated with the market portfolio (as nearly all portfolios will be). Defensive assets covary with the market less than average; they have betas that are less than positive unity.

Aggressive securities offer opportunities for speculation; their price reactions to changes in market conditions are more volatile than the reactions of defensive securities. Aggressive assets have more than average positive covariance with the market; they have betas that exceed $+1$.

CAPM Restated

Chapter 10 suggested that the beta regression coefficient from Equations (10-3) and (10-6) was a *measure of systematic risk*. This chapter suggested that an asset's covariance of returns with m was a *measure of systematic risk*. These two measures of undiversifiable risk are mathematically equivalent, which means that two methods of defining the CAPM are available. In Figures 10-3 and 20-4a the CAPM is defined in terms of the beta regression coefficient b_i. The CAPM in terms of the $Cov(r_i, r_m)$ is shown in Figure 20-4b. The two presentations of the CAPM in Figure 20-4 are mathematically and economically equivalent. The only difference between the two CAPM graphs is that the horizontal scale of the CAPM in terms of the beta coefficient is $[1/Var(r_m)]$ times the length of the horizontal scale of the other graph. This is a result of the definition of the beta coefficient shown in Equation (20-4).

$$b_i = \frac{Cov(r_i, r_m)}{Var(r_m)}$$

$$= Cov(r_i, r_m) \frac{1}{Var(r_m)} \qquad \text{where } \frac{1}{Var(r_m)} \text{ is constant for all assets} \qquad (20\text{-}4)$$

Equation (20-3) may be equivalently restated in terms of the beta coefficient as shown in Equation (20-5).

[7]Total risk is the relevant risk measure for investors who do not diversify. For example, if Mom and Pop have all their wealth invested in a grocery store, the *total risk* of that investment is relevant to its owners because the diversifiable risk has not been diversified away.

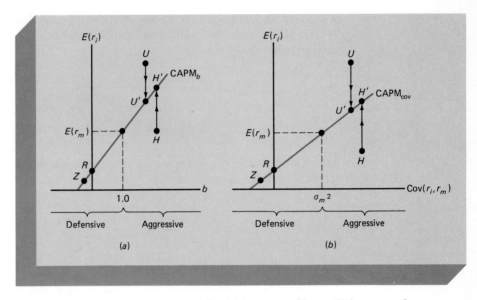

Figure 20-4 Equivalent CAPM models: (*a*) in terms of beta; (*b*) in terms of covariance.

$$E(r_i) = R + \frac{E(r_m) - R}{\text{Var}(r_m)} \text{Cov}(r_i, r_m) \qquad (20\text{-}3)$$

$$= R + [E(R) - R] \frac{\text{Cov}(r_i, r_m)}{\text{Var}(r_m)}$$

$$= R + [E(r_m) - R]b_i \qquad (20\text{-}5)$$

. Equation (20-5) represents the CAPM graphed in Figure 20-4*a*. But, Figure 20-4*a* is equivalent to the graph in Figure 20-4*b*, which represents Equation (20-3).

Overpriced and Underpriced Indications

The CAPM has asset pricing implications for both portfolios and individual securities. Points between the CAPM and the $E(r)$ axis, like point U in Figure 20-4, represent **underpriced** securities. Since points like U represent securities with unusually high returns for the amount of systematic risk they bear, these securities will enjoy strong demand that will bid their prices up until their equilibrium rate of return is driven back onto the CAPM at point U'.

Assets lying between the CAPM and the systematic risk axis have prices that are *too high*—**overpriced.** The asset at point H in Figure 20-4, for instance, does not offer sufficient return to induce rational investors to accept the amount of systematic risk it bears. As a result, the asset's price will fall owing to lack of demand and will continue to fall until the denominator of the rate-of-return formula is low enough to allow the expected return to reach the CAPM at a point like H'.

$$\uparrow\!E(r_H) = \frac{E(\text{capital gains or losses} + \text{dividends})}{\downarrow \text{purchase price}} \qquad (20\text{-}6)$$

$$E(r_H) = \frac{E\{p_t - p_{t-1} + d_t\}}{\downarrow p_{t-1}} \qquad (20\text{-}6a)$$

Then the capital loss will cease and an equilibrium purchase price will remain constant until a change in the firm's systematic risk, a change in R, or some other change causes a disequilibrium.

Negative Correlation with Portfolio *m*

Consider point Z in Figure 20-4; it represents a security that has an equilibrium rate of return *below the return on riskless asset R*. Capital market theory explains that the price of Z is maintained at high levels by the Markowitz diversification benefits it offers. Homestake Mining and the other low-beta gold mining stocks listed on the NYSE provide examples of assets like asset Z in Figure 20-4.

Discontinuity between Ex Ante Theory and Ex Post Data

Portfolio theory asserts that equilibrium *expected* returns are determined by *expected* risk—this is an **ex ante** or expectations-oriented theory. Although investor expectations are affected by **ex post** data, these historical returns are not used directly by investors as a basis for their decisions about the future. Plans for the future are based on their *expectations about the future*. Thus, a "jump" is made in going from the capital market theory, which is stated in terms of expectations, to actual historical data. If the probability distribution of historical returns has remained stable over time, then historical average return and variance statistics can be used to estimate expected returns and expected variances. However, historical data play no role in the capital market theory.

To perform a complete test of the capital market theory, we must observe expectations—a task that is practically impossible. Expectations may be formed from historical observations, but unless investors' past expectations were always correct, historical data cannot satisfactorily validate or deny the ex ante capital market theory.

20-4   **RELAXING THE ASSUMPTIONS**

This section aligns the assumptions underlying capital market theory more closely with reality. First, the assumption that one riskless interest rate exists

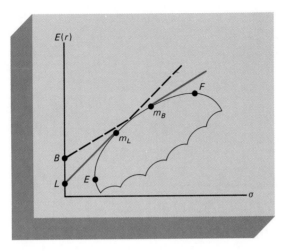

Figure 20-5 The capital market line when borrowing (*B*) and lending (*L*) rates differ.

at which everyone may borrow or lend without limit will be relaxed to determine the effects.

Multiple Interest Rates

Realistically, the **borrowing rate** B is higher than the **lending rate** L. In Figure 20-5 this is represented by two riskless interest rates at points L and B—these points represent lending and borrowing opportunities, respectively. The dashed portions of the two lines emerging from points L and B do not represent investment opportunities; they are included merely to delineate the construction. Two tangency portfolios, denoted m_L and m_B, are shown for lenders and borrowers, respectively. They replace the single market portfolio m. The kinked line formed by the solid sections of the two lines and a section of the opportunity locus is the relevant efficient frontier when the borrowing and lending rates differ. As a result, the CML has a curved section between m_L and m_B in Figure 20-5.[8]

In Figure 20-5 points m_L and m_B are two separate tangency portfolios for lending and borrowing, respectively. The existence of multiple tangency portfolios modifies things. Reconsider the mathematical representation of the CAPM

---

[8]See K. L. Hastie, ''The Determination of Optimal Investment Policy,'' *Management Science,* Aug. 1967, pp. B757–B774. Hastie was the first analyst to study relaxing the assumptions. See also M. J. Brennan, ''Capital Market Equilibrium with Divergent Borrowing and Lending Rates,'' *Journal of Financial and Quantitative Analysis,* Dec. 1971, vol. 6, no. 5, pp. 1197–1205. Brennan shows that, under certain assumptions, a weighted average of the borrowing and lending rates could emerge as a single rate.

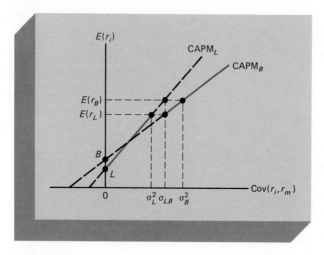

Figure 20-6 The CAPM for borrowing does not align perfectly with the CAPM for lending.

in terms of the covariance, Equation (20-3). If separate borrowing and lending rates are assumed, then two different CAPM's emerge.

$$E(r_i) = B + \frac{E(r_{mB}) - R}{\text{Var}(r_{mB})} \text{Cov}(r_i, r_{mB}) \qquad \text{for } E(r_i) > E(r_{mB}) \qquad (20\text{-}3a)$$

$$E(r_i) = L + \frac{E(r_{mL}) - R}{\text{Var}(r_{mL})} \text{Cov}(r_i, r_{mL}) \qquad \text{for } E(r_i) < E(r_{mL}) \qquad (20\text{-}3b)$$

Since $B > L$, the two CAPMs above will have different vertical axis intercepts.

Figure 20-7 Transactions costs blur the capital market line (CML).

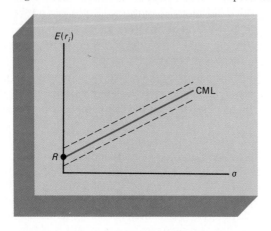

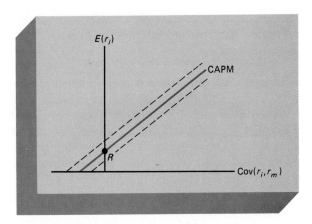

Figure 20-8 The capital asset pricing model (CAPM) is obscured slightly when transactions costs are considered.

The two CAPMs will also have different slopes because $Var(r_{mB})$ and $Var(r_{mL})$ will diverge. Since the CAPMs' covariances are measured with respect to two different tangency portfolios, the covariances also differ. Figure 20-6 illustrates $CAPM_L$ and $CAPM_B$ of Equations (20-3a) and (20-3b).

Transaction Costs   If transaction costs (such as brokerage commissions, search costs, etc.) are considered, these realities can be modeled as "bands" on the sides of the CML and the CAPM, as shown in Figures 20-7 and 20-8. The top and bottom transaction cost bands can be thought of as being a few percentage points apart. It would not be profitable for investors to buy and sell securities located between these two bands because transaction costs would consume the potential profit that induces such trading. As a result, the markets would never quite reach the theoretical equilibrium, even if all the other assumptions were retained.[9]

General Uncertainty or Heterogeneous Expectations   Eliminating the assumptions about *homogeneous expectations* and/or a *common investment horizon* would require drawing an efficient frontier, CML, and CAPM composed of "fuzzy" curves and lines. The more investors' expectations differed, the fuzzier and more blurred all lines and curves would become. In effect, the lines would become bands. Because of the resulting uncertainty,

[9]See Mark B. Garman and James A. Ohlson, "Valuation of Risky Assets in Arbitrage-Free Economies with Transactions Costs," *Journal of Financial Economics,* Sept. 1981, vol. 9, no. 3, pp. 271–280.

the analysis becomes determinate only within limits. Only major disequilibriums will be corrected. Statements could not be made with certainty.[10]

Different Tax Rates for Capital Gains

Many countries in the world have legislated lower income tax rates on capital gains (or price appreciation) income than on ordinary (or earned wage and rent and cash dividend) income to encourage investment. The U.S. tax laws offered such preferential capital gains tax rates until the law was changed in 1986. Recognizing the existence of tax rates on ordinary income that differ from the tax rates on capital gains income blurs the picture of economic equilibrium.

The after-tax rate of return r^{at} is defined below.

$$r^{at} = \frac{(\text{capital gains})(1 - T_G) + (\text{dividends})(1 - T_O)}{\text{price at beginning of holding period}} \tag{20-7}$$

where T_G is the capital gains tax rate and T_O is the tax rate applicable to ordinary income. If capital gains are taxed at a different rate than ordinary income, every investor would see a slightly different CML and CAPM in terms of after-tax returns that depended on their particular tax situation. As a result, a static equilibrium could never emerge, even if all the other assumptions were rigorously maintained.[11]

If capital gains are taxed at a lower tax rate than the ordinary income from cash dividends, a dollar of cash dividends will be worth less than a dollar of capital gains on an after-tax basis. Figure 20-9 illustrates an extended CAPM hypothesized by Professor Brennan that allows for this tax effect. The **cash dividend yield** from a share of stock is defined as the cash dividend per share stated as a percentage of the current market price of the stock. Brennan's extended CAPM includes the cash dividend yield as an explanatory variable, in addition to the beta coefficient, to capture the effects of a preferential income tax rate on capital gains income. The three-dimensional CAPM plane of Figure

[10]See N. Gressis, G. C. Philippatos, and J. Hayya, "Multiperiod Portfolio Analysis and the Inefficiency of the Market Portfolio," *Journal of Finance,* Sept. 1976, vol. 31, no. 4, pp. 1115–1126. For an extension see John E. Gilster, Jr., "Capital Market Equilibrium with Divergent Investment Horizon Length Assumptions," *Journal of Financial and Quantitative Analysis,* June 1983, vol. 18, no. 2, pp. 257–268. Several people have analyzed the homogeneous expectations assumption. More recently, see A. R. Admati, "A Noisy Rational Expectations Equilibrium for Multi-Asset Securities Markets," *Econometrica,* May 1985, vol. 53, no. 3, pp. 629–657.

[11]See M. J. Brennan, "Taxes, Market Valuation and Corporate Financial Policy," *National Tax Journal,* Dec. 1970, vol. 23, no. 4, pp. 417–427. Brennan's model was extended by R. H. Litzenberger and K. Ramaswamy, "The Effect of Personal Taxes and Dividends on Capital Asset Prices: Theory and Empirical Evidence," *Journal of Financial Economics,* June 1979, vol. 7, no. 2, pp. 163–195. Also see Ronald F. Singer, "Endogenous Marginal Income Tax Rates, Investor Behavior and the Capital Asset Pricing Model," *Journal of Finance,* June 1979, vol. 34, no. 3, pp. 609–616.

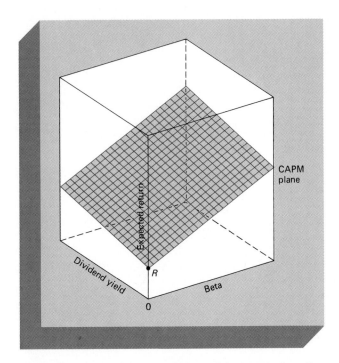

Figure 20-9 Brennan's three-dimensional CAPM that allows for lower capital gains tax rates.

20-9 should explain securities returns better than a model that ignores taxes if capital gains are taxed at a preferential tax rate.

Indivisibilities

If we drop the assumption that all assets are infinitely divisible, the CAPM would degenerate into a dotted line. Each dot would represent an opportunity attainable with an integral number of shares—but little would be gained from examining this blurry scenario.

Varying Rates of Inflation

The most easily observed interest rates are *nominal interest rates*. Equation (12-1), which represents Irving Fisher's classic theory about what determines the level of nominal interest rates, is repeated below.

$$
\begin{array}{lll}
\text{Nominal} & \text{real} & \text{expected} \\
\text{interest} = & \text{interest} + & \text{rate of} \qquad\qquad (12\text{-}1) \\
\text{rate, } r_t & \text{rate, } rr_t & \text{inflation, } q_t
\end{array}
$$

Equation (12-1) shows that the primary factor that moves all market interest rates is changes in the rate of inflation. The rate of inflation fluctuates with the

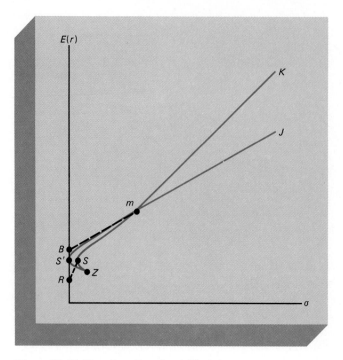

Figure 20-10 The absence of a riskless interest rate complicates the CML model.

growth rate in the money supply, the level of investment, monetary policy, fiscal policy, and other factors.

Relaxing the assumption that the level of interest rates never varies means that the market interest rate on default-free securities must vary in both the nominal and the real sense, $Var(R) > 0$ and $Var(rr) > 0$. The realism of this is seen by noting, for instance, the way that the Treasury bill rate varies. Stated differently, a riskless asset does not exist.

Acknowledging that the level of interest rates can change means point R in Figure 20-10 ceases to exist as a possibility and is replaced by a risky nominal interest rate at a point like Z. The efficient frontier is now the curve from S to K, or from S' to K, assuming all money is borrowed at rate Z. Portfolio S or S' is the minimum-risk portfolio—it may or may not contain default-free securities, and it may not actually have zero risk, as S' does. A point like S will be the minimum-variance portfolio if returns on Z and m are uncorrelated but not perfectly negatively correlated.[12]

---

[12]See Figure 9-4 and the accompanying discussion of how the correlation coefficient determines the degree of convexity.

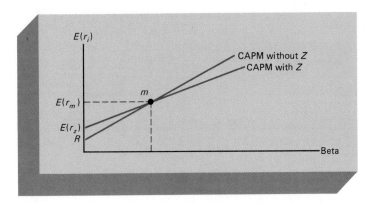

Figure 20-11 Utilizing the zero beta portfolio shifts the CAPM.

If borrowing at rate B instead of rate R is considered, the efficient frontier becomes SmJ or $S'mJ$, depending on whether S or S' is the minimum-variance portfolio. If it is assumed that funds may be lent (but not borrowed) at rate R, then the efficient frontier becomes the nonlinear set of opportunities through points $RSmK$.

Point Z in Figure 20-10 has a beta of zero, in spite of its small positive variance, because its variability of return is all unsystematic risk that is uncorrelated with the returns from the market portfolio. The existence of portfolio Z may cause the CML to have curvature. The CML can still be shown to be linear when Z is considered, however, because borrowing, lending, and short sales can be used to create linear portfolio possibility lines.[13]

The CAPM derived with portfolio Z is a slightly different asset-pricing model. The CAPM remains linear when the zero-systematic-risk portfolio with an expected return of $E(r_Z)$ is employed (in place of the riskless rate R), because the expected return and beta risk of all portfolios are *linear* weighted averages of the expected returns and betas from assets m and Z.

---

[13]See K. L. Hastie, "The Determination of Optimal Investment Policy," *Management Science,* Aug. 1967, pp. B-771 and B-772. More recently, Black developed the **zero-beta portfolio** (ZBP) that is free of systematic risk. Black derived the ZBP mathematically and derived some theorems about it. See Fischer Black, "Capital Market Equilibrium with Restricted Borrowing," *Journal of Business,* 1972, vol. 45, pp. 444–445. Empirical estimates of the returns on the ZBP were also prepared. See F. Black, M. C. Jensen, and M. Scholes, "The Capital Asset Pricing Model: Some Empirical Tests," in M. C. Jensen, ed., *Studies in the Theory of Capital Markets* (New York: Praeger, 1972). Essentially, the ZBP is an all-equity portfolio that has positive variance but zero correlation with the market portfolio. Borrowing and lending at some riskless interest is an unneeded assumption if it is instead assumed that funds may be borrowed (for example, by short selling) and lent (that is, invested) at the ZBP rates.

$$E(r_p) = x_m E(r_m) + x_Z E(r_Z) \qquad \text{where } x_Z = 1.0 - x_m \qquad (20\text{-}8)$$

For a two-asset portfolio made up of assets denoted Z and m, the portfolio's beta can be written as Equation (20-9).

$$b_p = x_m b_m + x_Z b_Z \qquad \text{where } x_Z = 1.0 - x_m \qquad (20\text{-}9)$$

If it is assumed that funds may be raised by selling portfolio Z short (that is, negative values for x_Z), then the new linear CAPM with a flatter slope that is illustrated in Figure 20-11 emerges.

20-5   **INTEGRATING THE CAPM AND APT MODELS**

Burmeister and McElroy prepared empirical estimates of a linear factor model under various suppositions.[14] Their work suggests that under reasonable assumptions *the CAPM can be found nested inside of the APT*. Working independently, Wei analyzed the CAPM and APT models theoretically and showed their equivalency under plausible assumptions.[15] Wei went on to extend the CAPM and APT models by showing how to include the CAPM's market portfolio in an integrated APT model.

Figure 11-4 depicts a three-dimensional APT plane. Figure 20-9 illustrates a CAPM that was extended to be three-dimensional. The findings of Burmeister and McElroy and Wei suggest that these seemingly different two-factor models may actually be quite similar. Furthermore, the work done by Burmeister and McElroy and by Wei supports extending the CAPM to include 4, 5, . . ., K risk factors. The CAPM's market portfolio might or might not be one of the risk factors in this more general K-factor model. In short, Burmeister and McElroy and Wei have extended the CAPM and APT models and shown how to merge them.

If more than two risk factors were involved, the asset pricing model becomes a K-dimensional hyperplane that is impossible to illustrate graphically. Equation (11-35) on page 313 represents such a K-factor model. Future empirical research should document the superiority of the merged theories over the independent CAPM or APT models.

---

[14]See Edwin Burmeister and Marjorie B. McElroy, "Joint Estimation of Factor Sensitivities and Risk Premia for the Arbitrage Pricing Theory," *Journal of Finance,* July 1988, pp. 721–733.

[15]See K. C. John Wei, "An Asset-Pricing Theory Unifying the CAPM and APT," *Journal of Finance,* Sept. 1988, pp. 881–892.

20-6   **ROLE OF THE CHARACTERISTIC LINE**

The formula for the characteristic line, Equation (10-3), was not employed in this chapter's review of capital market theory. The beta slope coefficient from the characteristic line was used in Chapter 10 to derive the CAPM shown in Figure 10-3. However, instead of using beta, the CAPM was discussed in terms of the covariance in this chapter. Figure 20-4 and Equations (20-3), (20-4), and (20-5) show that the CAPMs developed in terms of the beta and the covariance were mathematically and economically equivalent.

Because of a mere coincidence, the characteristic line is closely related to the capital market theory. The characteristic line is a statistically significant relationship that has intuitive appeal and corroborates the theory. But, the CAPM and CML models stand alone and do not rely on the characteristic line.

20-7   **SUMMARY AND CONCLUSIONS**

Capital market theory begins with an efficient portfolio model called the CML. The CAPM is an implication of risk reduction that is derived from the CML. The CAPM has wide applications in finding over- and underpriced assets. Additional applications for the CML and CAPM will be developed in the chapters that follow.

The simplifying assumptions underlying capital market theory were relaxed one at a time. Each time, the implications of the model were slightly obscured. If all were relaxed simultaneously, the result would be even less determinate. However, the fact that the analysis is not derivable under realistic assumptions does not mean it has no value. The analysis still rationalizes complex behavior that is observed in the financial markets (such as diversification) and offers realistic suggestions about the directions that prices and returns should follow when they deviate significantly from equilibrium. The theory is a powerful engine for analysis.[16]

[16]Capital market theory has been extended into the international securities markets by Bruno H. Solnik, "An International Market Model of Security Price Behavior," *Journal of Financial and Quantitative Analysis,* Sept. 1974, pp. 537–554. See also the book of readings: E. J. Elton and M. J. Gruber, eds., *International Capital Markets* (Amsterdam: North-Holland, 1975). In particular, see Rene Stulz, "On the Effects of Barriers to International Investment," *Journal of Finance,* Sept. 1981, vol. 36, no. 4, pp. 923–934.

Essay Questions

20-1 Which of the two graphs in Figure 20-12 is incorrect? Explain.

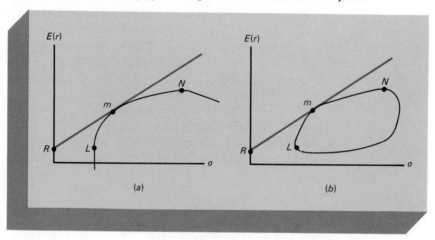

Figure 20-12 Plausible and impossible efficient frontiers.

20-2 Compare and contrast your conception of the characteristic lines for the common stock issued by a highly leveraged steel company that manufactures a cyclical product and the common stock of a profitable, countercyclical red ink manufacturer.

20-3 Compare and contrast the CML and the CAPM. (*a*) What assets lie on both lines in equilibrium? (*b*) What assets should never lie on the CML?

20-4 Explain how you would find the beta coefficient for some firm using historical data. (*a*) What data would you need? (*b*) What would you do with the data? (*c*) What can you use this beta for?

20-5 Given the assumptions underlying capital market theory, rationalize the following separability theorem: The investment decision of which asset to buy is a separate and independent decision from the financing decision of whether to borrow or lend.

20-6 Basic Scientific Research, Inc. (BSRI) employs a group of scientists working to develop new products that can be patented, manufactured, and sold to obtain large monopolistic profits until the products' patents expire. Investors in BSRI stock are told that the corporation has a small chance of inventing a highly lucrative product like Xerox or Polaroid. They are also told that, quite frankly, it is entirely possible that BSRI will simply consume its original capital with no payoff at all. The best possible outcome is the long shot that BSRI's research will be fruitful and thus will turn their investment into a multimillion-dollar capital gain. Use risk-return analysis to evaluate this investment opportunity.

20-7 How do you rationalize the CAPM illustrated in Figure 18-6 of Chapter 18 in view of the fact that economic theory asserts the CAPM should *always be a positive relationship* between risk and return?

Problems

20-8   Assume that the return on the market is 14 percent and the risk-free rate is 8 percent. (*a*) What is the formula for the CAPM? (*b*) Use the CAPM to determine whether the following stocks are overpriced or underpriced.

Stock	Expected return, %	Beta
A	17	1.2
B	14	0.8
C	15	1.5
D	16	0.75

20-9   A diversified portfolio is composed of the following five stocks. (*a*) What is the portfolio's beta? (*b*) What does the CAPM suggest the expected return for this portfolio should be?

Stock	Price	Number held	Estimated beta
Z	$20	1000	0.8
AB	30	2000	0.9
QZ	15	4000	1.25
DB	10	1000	1.05
RST	8	5000	1.15

Assume that the expected market return is 16 percent and the expected risk-free rate is 9 percent.

20-10   If a portfolio was composed of the first four stocks of Problem 20-9 above, what should its expected return be?

20-11   If a portfolio was composed of the last three stocks of Problem 20-9, what should its expected return be?

20-12   Assume that the return on the market is 14 percent and the risk-free rate is 8 percent. Use this information and the CAPM to determine which of the following stocks is overpriced or underpriced.

Stock	Expected return, %	Beta
A	17	1.4
B	14	1.2
C	15	1.1
D	16	1.3

20-13 Determine which stocks in Problem 20-12 would be overpriced if the market return were 16 percent and the risk-free rate 9 percent.

20-14 Edward Hawkins is an astute investor who has estimated a beta coefficient of 1.25 for the Gibson Computer Corporation. Hawkins believes the expected market return will be 14 percent. The risk-free rate is currently 9 percent. What return does Hawkins expect an investor to receive from Gibson Computer's stock?

20-15 What return would Ed Hawkins expect to receive on Gibson Computer Corporation of Problem 20-14 if the risk-free rate and market return are 8 and 16 percent, respectively?

20-16 The market portfolio has an expected return of 14 percent and a standard deviation of returns of 10 percent. If the risk-free rate is 8 percent, what return would you make if you invested 50 percent of your funds in market portfolio m and 50 percent of your funds at the risk-free rate? What is the risk of your portfolio?

20-17 Use the information given in Problem 20-16 and determine the expected return and risk of a portfolio composed of 75 percent market portfolio and 25 percent risk-free rate.

20-18 Use the information given in Problem 20-16 and determine the risk and return of a portfolio that borrowed 30 percent of the portfolio's equity and then invested all of the borrowed funds and equity funds in the market portfolio m.

20-19 Using the information given in Problem 20-16, determine the risk and return of a leveraged portfolio that has 160 percent of the owner's equity invested in the market portfolio m.

20-20 Assume that the standard deviation of the returns on the market portfolio m is 0.1, the standard deviation of returns from asset B is 0.2, and the correlation between the returns from assets m and B is .5. (a) What is the value of the covariance between the returns from m and B? (b) What is asset B's beta coefficient?

20-21 A finance professor named Dr. Rita Mandenaro established a reputation as a respectable financial analyst by publishing empirical estimates of the following CAPM.

$$E(r_i) = R + [E(r_m) - R](\text{beta}_i) \qquad (20\text{-}5)$$

The Edison Electric Utility Corporation (EEUC) has requested a rate increase from its state Public Utility Rate Setting Commission (PURSC) because the corporation's executives feel the 8.5 percent average annual rate of return EEUC's common stock has been earning in recent years is inadequate. Financial executives at EEUC have heard of the professor's reputation and retained her to provide the PURSC with expert testimony about why the EEUC should be granted permission to raise its electricity prices. Professor Mandenaro estimates the riskless rate of interest to be 7 percent, the average return on the S&P 500 stock market index to be 11 percent, and the EEUC's beta coefficient to be 0.61. How can the professor use her skills to argue that the EEUC should be granted a rate increase by the PURSC? Show your calculations.

Selected References

Alexander, G. J., and J. C. Francis, *Portfolio Analysis,* 3d ed. (Englewood Cliffs, N.J.: Prentice-Hall, 1986).

This monograph reviews the capital market theory in Chapters 7 through 10. Algebra, calculus, and statistics are used.

Fama, Eugene F., ''Risk, Return and Equilibrium: Some Clarifying Comments,'' *Journal of Finance,* March 1968, pp. 29–40.

Fama introduced the market portfolio concept and clarified some early questions about the capital market theory.

Markowitz, Harry, *Portfolio Selection,* Cowles Foundation Monograph 16 (New York: Wiley, 1959).

See the footnote on p. 100 for the first published capital market theory work.

Sharpe, William F., ''A Simplified Model for Portfolio Analysis,'' *Management Science,* Jan. 1963, pp. 277–293. See especially part 4 on the diagonal model.

This published condensation of Sharpe's doctoral dissertation extends the footnote on p. 100 of Harry Markowitz's 1959 book.

Sharpe, William F., ''Capital Asset Prices: A Theory of Market Equilibrium under Conditions of Risk,'' *Journal of Finance,* Sept. 1964, pp. 425–552.

This article pulls together the findings of Markowitz, Treynor, and Tobin into a unified formulation of the capital market theory.

Tobin, James, ''Liquidity Preference as Behavior towards Risk,'' *The Review of Economic Studies,* Feb. 1958, vol. XXVI, no. 1, pp. 65–86.

This classic article developed the asset pricing implications of borrowing and lending at the riskless interest rate.

Treynor, Jack L., ''Toward a Theory of Market Value of Risky Assets,'' unpublished manuscript, 1961.

This unpublished manuscript is cited in W. Sharpe's 1964 paper. Treynor appears to be one of the first to contribute to the capital market theory.

Chapter 21

Investment

Performance

Evaluation

Trillions of dollars are invested in marketable securities in the United States. Most of these funds are managed by professional investment management services that earn their living by providing portfolio management services for fees. The largest and most popular types of publicly available portfolio management services are provided by the **institutional investors** below.

1. The trust departments of large, big-city commercial banks
2. Investment advisory services (which are often subsidiaries of mutual fund management companies, security brokerage firms, or investment newsletter services)
3. The investment management departments of large life insurance companies
4. Investment companies (primarily the open-end investment companies called mutual funds)

The publicly available portfolio management services receive the funds they manage from the following major sources of investable wealth:

1. Pension funds
2. Wealthy individuals
3. College endowments
4. Charitable foundations

These investors own and ultimately control the funds, but they frequently entrust their investment decisions to some portfolio management service. Before delegating the investment management function to a hired consultant, however, they have asked themselves two questions. First, should they try to manage the funds themselves? Let us focus on those investors that have decided to seek investment management services externally. This leads to the second question: Which portfolio management service should be selected?

This chapter addresses the question of how to select the ''best'' portfolio management service. The tools introduced in this chapter are also useful to portfolio managers who wish to evaluate and improve their own money management skills. The remainder of the chapter explains both good and bad ways to evaluate the portfolio performances of bank trust departments, investment advisors, investment management departments of life insurance companies, mutual funds, and other money managers. Tools that can be used to rank the historical performance of all these different portfolios will be explained. Some naive methods and some logical methods of portfolio performance evaluation will be considered and compared.

All the logical methods are derived from various parts of the risk-return analysis presented in Chapters 9 and 10. Whether the old, naive methods or the newer, more logical methods of portfolio performance are used, however, one common problem exists: data availability. Historical rate-of-return data are required in order to evaluate the investment performance of any portfolio. Not all portfolio management services make adequate data about their past performance available to the public.

The performances of dozens of mutual funds that had enough data available to meaningfully investigate are evaluated in this chapter. Mutual funds are examined rather than other portfolios because, by law, mutual funds must publicly disclose their operating results. Also, provisions of the Investment Company Act of 1940 limit mutual funds' use of leverage (that is, issuing debt), buying on margin, taking more than 9 percent of the proceeds from the sale of new shares for sales commissions, selling the funds' shares on margin, and short selling. These requirements ensure a certain amount of similarity among mutual funds. Because of these similarities, the tax-exempt income status that mutual funds can attain, the requirements that they disclose their holdings and income, and the popularity they have with investors, mutual funds make an interesting subject for study. Before evaluating the investment performances of the mutual fund managers, however, let's first investigate the organizations and objectives of mutual funds.

21-1   **INVESTMENT COMPANIES DEFINED**

Investors with modest amounts to invest may be well advised to buy shares in a mutual fund because they have insufficient funds to buy a diversified portfolio. Since investors should buy stock in round lots (multiples of 100 shares) to incur the lower stockbroker commissions on round lots, and since the average New York Stock Exchange (NYSE) stock costs about $30 per share, it takes, on average, $3000 per issue (100 shares times an average price of $30 per share) to buy one round lot of stock. Multiplication of $3000 per stock issue by, say, 15 different stock issues needed to obtain diversification suggests $45,000 (15 issues times $3000 per issue) as the minimum needed to begin investing in individual securities in a diversified manner.[1]

Millions of aspiring investors lack sufficient capital to buy a diversified portfolio. Furthermore, even if they have enough money, most people do not have the expertise and time to manage a portfolio. As a result, enterprising portfolio managers have created public portfolios of diversified securities in which even small investors can afford to buy shares. These public portfolios, called investment companies, typically assume one of two basic forms: (1) the open-end investment company, usually called a **mutual fund,** and (2) the closed-end investment fund.

Mutual Funds

More than 54 million persons, companies, and other organizations have accounts in over 2700 open-end investment companies in the United States.[2] The size of these individual accounts ranges from a child's single share, valued at only a few dollars, to a large pension fund's multimillion-dollar interests in several different mutual funds. The total asset holdings of individual mutual funds range from only a few million dollars to billions.

Mutual funds are conduits from savings to investment. The funds pool the savings of many people by commingling them into one large, diversified investment portfolio. Many mutual funds own over 100 different issues of stocks and/or bonds. But no single investor owns any particular asset. Instead, an investor who has purchased a certain percentage of the mutual fund's total shares outstanding owns that percentage of every asset the fund has. Investors can cash in their shares in the fund whenever they wish at the net asset value per share on that day. The **net asset value per share** equals the value of the fund's total net assets after liabilities are deducted, with the net total value being divided by the total number of shares outstanding on that day. Thus, the net asset value per share fluctuates every time any asset experiences a change in its market price.

According to Subchapter M of the Internal Revenue Code, all income earned by a mutual fund is tax-exempt if the fund (1) distributes at least 90 percent of its cash dividend and interest income in the same year it is received, (2) diversifies by placing no more than 5 percent of its total assets in any one security issue, and (3) is registered with the Securities and Exchange Commission under

[1]Selection of 15 as the minimum number of stock issues needed to obtain diversification is somewhat arbitrary; this problem is analyzed in Figure 9-1 of Chapter 9. Consult that figure and then select whatever number between 10 and 20 you think is appropriate.
[2]Investment Company Institute, *Mutual Fund Fact Book,* 1989. A copy of this annual booklet can be obtained for $9.95 by writing to Publications Department, Investment Company Institute, 1600 M Street NW, Suite 600, Washington, DC 20036.

the provisions of the Investment Company Act of 1940. Since practically every mutual fund meets these provisions, there is virtually no double taxation (that is, taxation paid by both the fund and the shareholder on the fund's earnings).

By law, open-end investment companies are required to publish a one- or two-paragraph statement of the fund's investment objectives. These objectives can be grouped into the following main categories. The stock and bond funds include:

1. *Growth funds:* These funds tend to invest only in common stock and plan to assume significant risks to obtain stocks that are expected to provide substantial price appreciation. Over 500 growth-oriented funds operated in 1988—this is the second largest category.

2. *Income funds:* Investment in stocks and bonds that pay high cash dividends and coupon interest is the objective of income funds. Risky stocks offering higher potential capital gains tend to be avoided in favor of ''blue-chip'' stocks.

3. *Balanced funds:* These funds divide their holdings between fixed-income securities and low-risk common stocks in order to avoid the risk of loss. These highly risk-averse funds have low rates of return.

4. *High-yield corporate bond funds:* These mutual funds invest in the bonds of business corporations that have low bond quality ratings to earn interest rates higher than the U.S. Treasury bonds pay while taking less bankruptcy risk than common stock investors. These high-yield mutual funds are often called **junk bond funds.**

5. *Municipal bond funds:* These funds buy only municipal bonds to obtain their tax-exempt coupon income. Only substantial individuals (a stockbroker's euphemism for rich people) who are in high income tax brackets regularly buy shares in municipal bond funds. Within the major category of municipal bond funds are two subcategories of funds—(a) short-term municipal bond funds and (b) long-term municipal bond funds.

6. *Treasury bond funds:* Investors that are extremely averse to the possibility of bond default losses can purchase shares in these mutual funds, which only invest in default-free U.S. Treasury bonds.

7. *Global funds:* These funds invest in foreign securities; they can be divided into two subcategories: (a) global equity funds and (b) global bond funds.

8. *Liquid asset funds:* These mutual funds are also called **money market funds** because they invest in money market instruments such as Treasury bills. One of the main assets of some liquid asset funds is bank deposits (called certificates of deposit or CDs) of over $100,000 that are left with the bank for a specified number of days. The 90-day or 180-day CDs sometimes pay high rates of interest with practically no

risk. The investment objective of the liquid asset funds is to earn high rates of interest from liquid, low-risk, short-term bonds, bank deposits, and other money market instruments. Some money market funds specialize in short-term tax-exempt municipal bonds (see 5a above). With about 600 funds, there are more mutual funds that invest in money market securities than in any other category. This is also the most rapidly growing category of mutual funds.

Investor's Return from Mutual Fund Investing

Investors obtain three types of income from owning mutual fund shares: (1) cash dividend or interest disbursements, denoted d, (2) capital gains disbursements, denoted c, and (3) change in the fund's net asset value (nav) per share from capital gains and cash dividends that were not distributed to the owners, denoted by $\mathrm{nav}_{t+1} - \mathrm{nav}_t$ for the tth period. The one-period rate of return for a mutual fund share is defined in Equation (21-1).

$$r_t = \frac{c_t + d_t + (\mathrm{nav}_{t+1} - \mathrm{nav}_t)}{\mathrm{nav}_t} \tag{21-1}$$

Mutual fund investors do not receive the entire amount of income in the numerator of Equation (21-1) because of three deductions. First, the fund's management fee of from 0.4 to 1.5 percent per year of the net asset value is deducted to pay the portfolio's management expenses. And second, some mutual funds, called **load funds,** deduct from 4 to 8.5 percent (usually the latter) of the mutual fund owner's original investment to pay a commission to the mutual fund salesperson. **No-load funds** are mutual funds that sell their shares primarily by mail and telephone and charge their investors no sales commission. Finally, some mutual funds deduct **12b-1 fees** from shareholders' assets. If a mutual fund deducts the 12b-1 fees, the deduction typically equals a few percent of the fund's total assets per year; these monies go to pay sales commissions and related promotional expenses that do not benefit the investors.

All mutual funds are called open-end because they can keep selling more shares, and thus keep growing larger, as long as investors will buy more shares. Fund managers want their funds to grow larger so they can charge their management-fee percentage on a larger amount of total assets and thus pay themselves larger fees.

Closed-End Funds

Closed-end investment companies are like mutual funds in that both are publicly owned investment portfolios. But closed-end funds differ from open-end funds in several important respects. First, as the name implies, a closed-end fund cannot sell more shares after its initial offering—the size of the portfolio is legally constrained. Second, the shares of closed-end funds are not redeemable at their net asset value, as are mutual fund shares. The shares of the closed-end funds trade on stock exchanges at market prices that are usually at a discount, but are sometimes at a premium, relative to their net asset values.[3] Third, the Investment Company Act allows closed-end funds to borrow money, trade options and futures contracts, and speculate aggressively. Fourth, the law allows closed-end funds to pursue diversification and investment objectives that cover a wider range than the open-end funds; this makes them more difficult to categorize than mutual funds. Closed-end funds have never been as popular as mutual funds.

Closed-end funds are essentially marketable shares of common stock. As a result, their one-period rates of return are calculated like common stock returns—with Equation (1-2). The rest of this chapter analyzes mutual fund returns data to show how investment performance analysis is done and to see if mutual fund managers can earn returns for their investors that exceed the returns available from other investments.

21-2	**RANKING FUNDS' RATES OF RETURN**

When an investor considers the purchase of shares in mutual funds, the first question to be asked is: "Can the mutual funds earn a higher return for me than I can earn for myself?" To help answer this question, Table 21-1 shows data on the performances of 30 randomly selected mutual funds over a decade.

Column 1 of Table 21-1 shows average rates of return over the whole decade. These average annual returns are what would have been earned if a tax-exempt investor had purchased shares on January 1, 1970, held them 10 years while reinvesting the dividends, and sold the shares at the end of December 1979. Note that only *one* of the 30 mutual funds earned a rate of return above the 20.14 percent that an investor could have earned by picking stocks listed on the NYSE with a dart or using some other naive buy-and-hold strategy.[4]

Of the 30 funds, the best performance exceeded the average by only 1.1

[3]For a discussion of the prices of closed-end shares, see Rex Thompson, "The Information Content of Discounts and Premiums on Closed-End Fund Shares," *Journal of Financial Economics,* 1978, vol. 6, p. 151.

[4]As explained on page 195, a naive buy-and-hold strategy means randomly selecting securities, buying them, and holding them regardless of what information becomes available about them or the market. The naive buy-and-hold strategy is used as a standard of comparison because it represents an investment that someone with no skill should be able to earn with no good luck or bad luck. The actual returns from a naive buyand-hold strategy have been estimated by different researchers. See Ibbotson Associates, *Stocks, Bonds, Bills and Inflation: 1985 Yearbook* (Chicago, Ill.: Capital Market Research Center, 1985). See also Roger G. Ibbotson, Laurence Siegel, and Kathryn S. Love, "World Wealth: Market Values and Returns," *Journal of Portfolio Management,* Fall 1985. Also see R. G. Ibbotson, R. C. Carr and A. W. Robinson, "International Equity and Bond Returns," *Financial Analysts Journal,* July–Aug. 1982.

Table 21-1
RANKINGS OF THE ANNUAL RETURNS FROM 30 MUTUAL FUNDS*

Fund	Average annual return† (1)	1970 (2)	1971 (3)	1972 (4)	1973 (5)	1974 (6)	1975 (7)	1976 (8)	1977 (9)	1978 (10)	1979 (11)
Templeton Growth Fund	21.24	14	1	16	1	6	1	1	1	9	22
Standard & Poor's 500 index‡	20.14	6.5	1.5	8.5	10.5	1.5	3.5	6.5	1.5	4.5	3.5
Pioneer Fund	13.99	15	16	5	13	3	3	8	8	6	12
T. Rowe Price New Era Fund	12.89	27	8	3	22	28	18	19	13	1	3
T. Rowe Price New Horizons Fund	12.27	1	7	30	26	7	27	2	2	4	2
Putnam Investors Fund	11.30	2	3	22	20	14	21	25	21	14	4
American Mutual Fund	11.19	17	21	10	9	11	6	11	7	16	18
Affiliated Fund	11.05	28	17	6	7	5	5	24	29	7	21
Keystone Aggressive Stock Fund	10.71	3	15	29	30	8	7	3	3	2	1
Franklin Custodian Fund	10.31	18	30	4	5	21	16	4	17	10	27
Investment Co. of America	9.94	13	12	17	12	10	8	15	4	21	23
Putnam Growth Fund	9.92	10	14	13	16	20	25	10	5	25	8
Dreyfus Leverage Fund	9.60	5	23	15	23	25	26	9	14	3	13
Chemical Fund Inc.	9.57	9	2	14	19	22	30	28	9	13	10
Fidelity Fund, Inc.	9.51	7	13	20	11	16	12	16	18	23	6
Windsor Fund	9.46	30	25	25	8	1	2	14	25	12	19
National Investors Corp.	9.04	6	5	28	25	2	24	21	12	5	9
Fidelity Puritan Fund	8.99	21	29	7	6	18	9	12	22	26	26
Dreyfus Fund	8.60	16	22	23	17	19	11	20	10	15	14
Delaware Fund	8.50	22	28	24	10	9	4	18	27	11	15
Keystone Discount Bond Fund	8.20	11	20	8	3	26	10	5	23	28	28
Hamilton Funds, Inc., Series H-DA	7.56	25	6	21	18	4	20	27	19	22	17
Massachusetts Investors Trust	7.06	29	9	9	21	17	14	30	15	17	16
Fidelity Trend Fund	6.77	12	11	26	27	13	19	17	11	19	7
Massachusetts Investors Growth	6.51	8	10	18	29	27	29	26	6	8	5
Wellington Fund	6.38	26	26	11	14	24	15	22	20	24	20
Keystone Growth Fund	6.36	4	4	27	28	15	28	23	16	20	11
Investors Stock Fund	5.75	19	19	19	24	12	13	29	24	18	24
Investors Mutual	5.55	24	18	12	15	23	17	13	30	27	25
Investors Selective Fund	5.51	23	27	1	2	30	22	7	26	29	29
Colonial Income Fund	5.25	20	24	2	4	29	23	6	28	30	30

*Raw data from *Investment Companies,* Wiesenberger Investment Services, 1981.
†The average annual rate of return is the geometric mean rate of return from 1970 through 1979.
‡Fractional rankings show where the index ranks between the ranks of mutual funds in a given year, e.g., in 1971, S&P ranked between the first and second mutual funds.

percentage points. The data indicate that, on the average, the 30 mutual funds did not earn returns for investors that a naive investor could not attain alone at less cost.

Columns 2 through 11 of Table 21-1 show the rankings of the 30 funds' yearly rates of return. The most striking feature of the rankings is their lack of consistency. None of the 30 funds was able to consistently outperform the naive buy-and-hold strategy over the decade. In fact, none of the 30 funds is even able to reach the top half of the rankings consistently throughout the decade.

21-3   **EFFICIENCY AND RELIABILITY OF THE FUNDS' PERFORMANCES**

Are mutual funds really as poor at managing investments as the data in Table 21-1 indicate? After all, they might be maximizing their returns in a very low risk class where high returns were not available. This would mean the funds were efficient investments along the bottom portion of the efficient frontier. Figure 21-1 shows the actual performance of 23 mutual funds in risk-return space relative to the efficient frontier (that is, the curve *EF*) which existed at that time.

Farrar's Portfolio Analysis of Mutual Funds

Figure 21-1 is from an award-winning doctoral dissertation written by Donald Farrar; it is based on monthly data from 23 mutual funds. It shows that none of the funds was efficient; only a few had average returns that were within one percentage point of the efficient frontier. Note, however, that the funds tended to cluster into homogeneous groups. The funds that sought growth and were

Figure 21-1 The performance of 23 mutual funds graphed in risk-return space. (*Source:* Donald E. Farrar, *The Investment Decision under Uncertainty,* Englewood Cliffs, N.J.: Prentice-Hall, 1962, p. 73.)

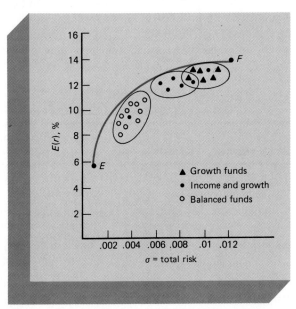

willing to assume risk to attain it formed a cluster which tends to lie above the cluster of less aggressive income-growth funds. The highly risk-averse balanced funds cluster at the lower rates of return.

The Investment Company Act of 1940 requires mutual funds to publish a written statement of their investment objectives and make it available to their shareholders. A fund's objective can be changed only if the majority of the shareholders consent in advance to the new objective. Farrar classified the 23 funds he analyzed into three categories of investment objectives. The three categories Farrar used are listed below in descending order with respect to the aggressiveness with which the fund's management implies it will seek a high average rate of return and assume the corresponding risks.

1. Growth

2. Growth and income

3. Income, growth, and stability (called a balanced fund)

The stated objectives that mutual funds issue to their shareholders are not always dependable. Stated differently, there is sometimes no relation between the stated investment objectives and the actual performance of some mutual funds. Although the 23 funds Farrar analyzed in Figure 21-1 tended to remain in fairly consistent risk-return groupings over time, the risk-return groupings did not always match the funds' stated objectives. In fact, quantitative risk measures give a clearer picture of the funds' investment objectives than the published statements of the funds' managers.

Portfolios' Risk Classes

Portfolios' average rates of return vary as bullish and bearish periods push the prices of securities up and down. As a result, average rates of return are not satisfactory measures with which to classify mutual funds' risk and return. Certain quantitative risk measures, however, tend to be more stationary. Fur-

Table 21-2
PORTFOLIO SYSTEMATIC RISK MEASURES DEFINED

Range of beta	Level of the portfolio's risk	Description of price volatility
0.5 to 0.7	Low	Share prices vary about half the rate of the market index
0.7 to 0.9	Medium	Share prices rise about 80% of the rate of the market index
0.9 to 1.3	High	Share prices vary directly with the rate of change in the market index

Table 21-3
RISK-RETURN RELATIONSHIPS FOR MUTUAL FUNDS

Risk class	Range of betas	Number of funds	Average beta	Average variance, σ^2	Average rate of return
Low	0.5 to 0.7	28	0.619	.000877	9.1%
Medium	0.7 to 0.9	53	0.786	.001543	10.6%
High	0.9 to 1.1	22	0.992	.002304	13.5%

Source: Irwin Friend, Marshall E. Blume, and Jean Crockett, *Mutual Funds and Other Institutional Investors: A New Perspective* (New York: McGraw-Hill, 1970), p. 150.

thermore, since risk and return are positively related, the quantitative risk measures also indicate whether the portfolio can be expected to earn a high, medium, or low rate of return over a complete business cycle.

Two quantitative risk surrogates are appropriate for measuring the historical risk of portfolios. First, the standard deviation of historical rates of return may be used to measure total risk. Second, portfolios' beta coefficients, obtained from their characteristic lines (which were fit with historical data), may be used to measure systematic or undiversifiable risk. Either of these risk surrogates is satisfactory for categorizing portfolio risk. Examples of both will be given later in this chapter.

Mutual funds' beta coefficients may be classified as explained in Table 21-2. Table 21-3 shows the relationship between the two risk surrogates and the average rates of return for 103 mutual funds; the two risk surrogates are highly positively related to each other and to the portfolios' average rates of return.

Table 21-4 compares the published investment objectives of the portfolios

Table 21-4
COMPARISON OF THE PERFORMANCES OF THE MUTUAL FUNDS WITH THEIR PUBLISHED OBJECTIVES*

Beta coefficient	Number of funds in category				Average rate of return, %			
	Growth	Growth and income	Income and growth	Income, growth, and stability	Growth	Growth and income	Income and growth	Income, growth, and stability
0.5 to 0.7	3	5	4	16	6.9	10.1	9.7	9.1
0.7 to 0.9	15	24	7	7	11.2	10.0	10.0	12.2
0.9 to 1.1	20	1	0	1	13.8	9.5		13.5

*Investment objectives as classified by Arthur Wiesenberger Services in 1967.
Source: Irwin Friend, Marshall E. Blume, and Jean Crockett, *Mutual Funds and Other Institutional Investors: A New Perspective* (New York: McGraw-Hill, 1970), p. 150.

with their quantitative risk and average return statistics. It shows that the standard deviations and beta coefficients of the portfolios were much better indicators of the actual performance of the portfolios than their published statements. The data in the table also show that the betas and standard deviations for the portfolio vary together positively.[5]

21-4   **SHARPE'S PORTFOLIO PERFORMANCE MEASURE**

In assessing the performance of a portfolio, *it is necessary to consider both risk and return.* Ranking portfolios' average returns ignores the skill with which they minimize risk and therefore presents an oversimplified picture. Determining the relative efficiency of a portfolio, as done in Figure 21-1, is a more comprehensive analysis of a portfolio's performance. However, it is often desirable to be able to *rank* portfolios' performances. The real need is for an index of portfolio performance that is determined by *both* the return and the risk of a portfolio. Equation (21-2) defines a *single-parameter portfolio performance index* that is calculated from both the risk and return statistics. William F. Sharpe devised an index of portfolio performance, denoted S_i, that is defined in Equation (21-2) for portfolio i.

$$S_i = \frac{\text{risk premium}}{\text{total risk}} = \frac{\bar{r}_i - R}{\sigma_i} \tag{21-2}$$

where $\bar{r}_i$ = average return from portfolio i
σ_i = standard deviation of returns for portfolio i
R = riskless rate of interest

The numerator of Equation (21-2), $\bar{r}_i - R$, is called the risk premium for portfolio i. The **risk premium** is the additional return over and above the riskless rate that is paid to induce investors to assume risk.

Sharpe's index of performance generates one (ordinal) number that is determined by both the risk and the return of the portfolio or other investment being evaluated. Figure 21-2 graphically depicts Sharpe's index. S_i measures the slope of the line starting at the riskless rate R in Figure 21-2 and running

---

[5]There is a mathematical reason we would expect the betas and standard deviations to be highly positively correlated. The beta is defined as

$$b_i = \frac{\text{Cov}[(r_{i,t}, r_{m,t})]}{\text{Var}(r_{m,t})} = \frac{\rho_{i,m}\sigma_i\sigma_m}{\text{Var}(r_m)} = \frac{\rho_{i,m}\sigma_i}{\sigma_m}$$

Note that as the correlation in the numerator in the far right-hand definition of beta approaches +1.0, the beta becomes a positive linear transformation of the asset's standard deviation, σ_i. In fact, most mutual funds are highly positively correlated, for instance, $\rho_{i,m} = .9$.

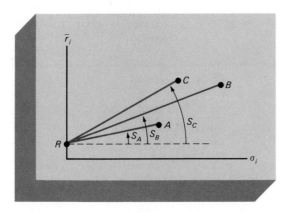

Figure 21-2 Sharpe's index of portfolio performance.

out to asset i. Thus $S_C > S_B > S_A$ indicates that asset C is a better performer than asset B and B is better than A. The fact that the portfolios have different average returns or are in different risk classes does not hinder a direct comparison or ranking with Sharpe's performance index.[6]

Sharpe gathered data on the risk and return of 34 mutual funds for a decade and ranked their performances. Table 21-5 lists each fund's average return, standard deviation, and Sharpe's performance measure. The Dow Jones Industrial Average (DJIA) was used as a standard of comparison in evaluating the performance of the funds. Figure 21-3 shows a frequency distribution of the S_i values for the 34 mutual funds listed in Table 21-5 and the DJIA.

Of the 34 funds shown in Figure 21-3, 12 had risk-premium-to-risk ratios above the 0.667 of the DJIA. The average of the 34 mutual funds' ratios is 0.633, which is below the DJIA's 0.667. This means that the DJIA was a more efficient portfolio than the average mutual fund in the sample. Moreover, the annual fees and sales commissions charged by mutual funds can exceed the commissions incurred in purchasing securities directly if you create your own portfolio. Clearly, the efficiency of the average mutual fund investment is below that of the DJIA. It follows that many investors would be better off creating their own portfolios of randomly selected stocks instead of buying mutual funds.[7]

[6]I. Friend and M. Blume, "Measurement of Portfolio Performance under Uncertainty," *American Economic Review,* Sept. 1970, pp. 561–575. This study questions portfolio performance measures.

[7]Another study of 38 mutual funds from 1958 to 1967 showed similar but not identical results. This study showed that only 18 out of the 38 mutual funds outperformed the S&P 500 stocks average, but the average risk-premium-to-risk ratio for the 38 funds was slightly above the S&P 500 ratio. K. V. Smith and D. A. Tito, "Risk Return Measures of Ex Post Portfolio Performance," *Journal of Financial and Quantitative Analysis,* Dec. 1969, pp. 464–465.

Table 21-5

PERFORMANCES OF 34 MUTUAL FUNDS 1954–1963

Mutual fund	Average annual return, %	Standard deviation of annual return, %	Risk premium* to standard deviation ratio = S_i
Affiliated Fund	14.6	15.3	0.75896
American Business Shares	10.0	9.2	0.75876
Axe-Houghton, Fund A	10.5	13.5	0.55551
Axe-Houghton, Fund B	12.0	16.3	0.55183
Axe-Houghton, Stock Fund	11.9	15.6	0.56991
Boston Fund	12.4	12.1	0.77842
Broad Street Investing	14.8	16.8	0.70329
Bullock Fund	15.7	19.3	0.65845
Commonwealth Investment Company	10.9	13.7	0.57841
Delaware Fund	14.4	21.4	0.53253
Dividend Shares	14.4	15.9	0.71807
Dow Jones Industrial Average (DJIA)	16.3	19.9	0.66700†
Eaton and Howard, Balanced Funds	11.0	11.9	0.67399
Eaton and Howard, Stock Fund	15.2	19.2	0.63486
Equity Fund	14.6	18.7	0.61902
Fidelity Fund	16.4	23.5	0.57020
Financial Industrial Fund	14.5	23.0	0.49971
Fundamental Investors	16.0	21.7	0.59894
Group Securities, Common Stock Fund	15.1	19.1	0.63316
Group Securities, Fully Administered Fund	11.4	14.1	0.59490
Incorporated Investors	14.0	25.5	0.43116
Investment Company of America	17.4	21.8	0.66169
Investors Mutual	11.3	12.5	0.66451
Loomis-Sales Mutual Fund	10.0	10.4	0.67358
Massachusetts Investors Trust	16.2	20.8	0.63398
Massachusetts Investors—Growth Stock	18.6	22.7	0.68687
National Investors Corporation	18.3	19.9	0.76798
National Securities—Income Series	12.4	17.8	0.52950
New England Fund	10.4	10.2	0.72703
Putnam Fund of Boston	13.1	16.0	0.63222
Scudder, Stevens & Clark Balanced Fund	10.7	13.3	0.57893
Selected American Shares	14.4	19.4	0.58788
United Funds—Income Funds	16.1	20.9	0.62698
Wellington Fund	11.3	12.0	0.69057
Wisconsin Fund	13.8	16.9	0.64091

*S_i = (average return − 3 percent)/std. dev. The ratios shown were computed from original data and thus differ slightly from the ratios obtained from the rounded data shown in the table.

†This is a market average, not a mutual fund.

Source: William F. Sharpe, "Mutual Fund Performances," *Journal of Business,* Supplement, January 1966, p. 125.

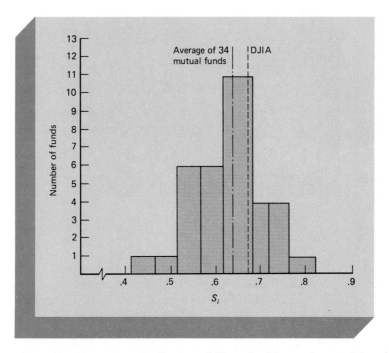

Figure 21-3 Frequency distribution of Sharpe's risk-premium-to-risk ratio for 34 mutual funds.

In calculating the data in Table 21-5, which are shown in Figure 21-3, the management expenses of the mutual funds were deducted to determine net returns to the funds' investors. If the management expenses of the 34 funds are ignored, 19 of them had better performance index scores than the DJIA. The sample data indicate that before management expenses, the average mutual fund performs about as well as a market average such as the DJIA. But the returns to the funds' shareholders, after the funds' operating expenses are deducted but ignoring the sales commission paid by fund investors, were less than those of the DJIA. It seems that mutual fund managers' salaries and other professional management expenses lowered the net returns to shareholders because these costs were larger than the increased returns they generated.

21-5   **TREYNOR'S PORTFOLIO PERFORMANCE MEASURE**

Jack Treynor conceived an index of portfolio performance that is based on systematic risk, as measured by portfolios' beta coefficients. To use Treynor's measure, the characteristic regression lines of the portfolios must be estimated with Equation (21-3).

$$r_{p,t} = a_p + b_p(r_{m,t}) + e_{p,t} \qquad t = 1, 2, \ldots, T \qquad (21\text{-}3)$$

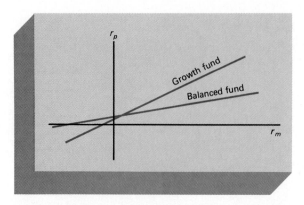

Figure 21-4 Characteristic regression lines for portfolios.

where $r_{p,t}$ = rate of return on portfolio p in period t
  $r_{m,t}$ = return on market index in period t
  $e_{p,t}$ = random error term for portfolio p in period t
  a_p = intercept coefficient for portfolio p
  b_p = portfolio's beta coefficient

Figure 21-4 shows typical characteristic lines for two portfolios with different management policies toward risk.

   As discussed in Chapter 10, the beta coefficient from a characteristic line is a measure of an asset's systematic or undiversifiable risk. Treynor suggests measuring a portfolio's return relative to its systematic risk rather than relative to its total risk, as does the Sharpe measure.

Figure 21-5 Treynor's investment performance measure in $[b, E(r)]$ space.

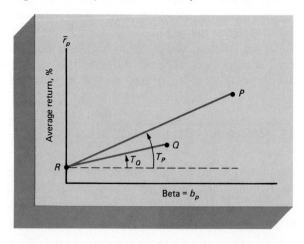

Equation (21-4) defines Treynor's index of portfolio performance, denoted T_p for the pth portfolio.[8]

$$T_p = \frac{\text{risk premium}}{\text{systematic risk index}} = \frac{\bar{r}_p - R}{b_p} \tag{21-4}$$

where $\bar{r}_p$ and b_p are the average rate of return and beta coefficient, respectively, for portfolio p. Graphically, T_p is a measure of the slope of the line from R to the pth portfolio as shown in Figure 21-5. As this figure demonstrates, portfolio P is more desirable than portfolio Q because P earned more risk premium per unit of systematic risk; that is, $T_P > T_Q$.

21-6   **JENSEN'S PORTFOLIO PERFORMANCE MEASURE**

Dr. Michael C. Jensen has modified the characteristic regression line to make it useful as a one-parameter investment performance measure.[9] The basic random variables in Jensen's model are risk premiums, as defined in Equation (21-5).

$$rp_{i,t} = r_{i,t} - R_t \tag{21-5}$$

where $rp_{i,t}$ = risk premium for asset i in period t
$r_{i,t}$ = one-period rate of return from asset i in period t
R_t = riskless rate observed in period t

Jensen restates the original characteristic line of Equation (10-3) in risk premiums instead of returns. Equation (21-6) defines Jensen's characteristic line in risk-premium form.

$$r_{i,t} - R_t = A_i + B_i(r_{m,t} - R_t) + u_{i,t} \tag{21-6}$$

$$rp_{i,t} = A_i + B_i(rp_{m,t}) + u_{i,t} \tag{21-6a}$$

$$B_i = \frac{\text{Cov}[(r_{i,t} - R_t)(r_{m,t} - R_t)]}{\text{Var}(r_{m,t} - R_t)} \tag{21-7}$$

where $rp_{m,t} = r_{m,t} - R_t$ = risk premium for market index for period t; the regression's explanatory variable

---

[8]J. Treynor, "How to Rate Management of Investment Funds," *Harvard Business Review,* Jan.–Feb. 1965, pp. 63–75.

[9]M. C. Jensen, "Risk, the Pricing of Capital Assets, and the Evaluation of Investment Portfolios," Ph.D. dissertation, University of Chicago, 1968. M. C. Jensen, "The Performance of Mutual Funds in the Period 1945–64," *Journal of Finance,* May 1968, vol. XXIII, no. 2, pp. 389–416. M. C. Jensen, "Risk, the Pricing of Capital Assets, and the Evaluation of Investment Portfolios," *Journal of Business,* April 1969, vol. 42, pp. 167–247.

A_i = alpha = this ordinary least squares (OLS) regression intercept is Jensen's investment performance measure for ith asset

B_i = regression slope coefficient = beta systematic risk index

$u_{i,t}$ = residual risk premium for ith asset in tth period which is left unexplained by the regression; it has an expected value of zero, $E(u_{i,t}) = 0$

As illustrated in Figure 21-6, the capital asset pricing model (CAPM) may be restated in terms of Jensen's beta. And even though Jensen's beta, Equation (21-7), is different from the original beta systematic risk coefficient of Equation (10-6), these two different betas will have very similar numerical values for the same assets.

Taking the mathematical expectation of Equation (21-6) or (21-6a) results in Equation (21-8).

$$E(r_{i,t} - R_t) = A_i + B_i E(r_{m,t} - R_t) \tag{21-8}$$

since $E(u_{i,t}) = 0$. Equation (21-8) is represented graphically in Figure 21-6 as the capital asset pricing model (CAPM) reformulated in risk premiums.

Explanation of Jensen's Alpha Measure

The alpha intercept in Jensen's characteristic line in risk-premium form is a (positive, zero, or negative) regression estimate of the excess returns from the ith asset. This alpha estimates the excess returns averaged over the sample

Figure 21-6 Capital asset pricing model restated in risk-premium form with several assets' investment performance statistics indicated.

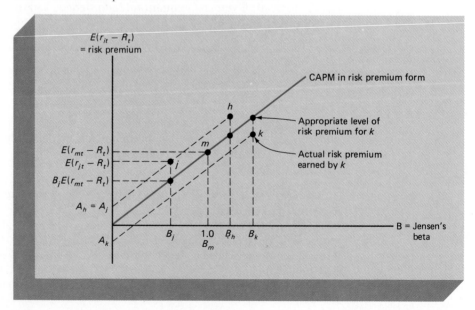

period used to estimate the characteristic line regression. If the ith asset was correctly priced so that it yielded no returns that were either more or less than that of the appropriate risk premium, $E(r_{i,t} - R_t) = 0$, then the alpha intercept will have a value of zero, $A = 0$. But if the jth asset has rates of return in excess of its appropriate risk premium, so that inequality (21-9) is true, then this jth asset's alpha intercept will be positive and will provide an empirical estimate of these excess returns averaged over the sample period used to estimate the regression.

$$\text{If} \qquad E(r_{j,t} - R_t) > B_j(r_{m,t} - R_t) \qquad \text{then } A_j > 0 \qquad (21\text{-}9)$$

The positive excess return, $A_j > 0$, shown in inequality (21-9) measures a vertical distance above the CAPM reformulated in risk-premium form. This quantity is the jth asset's excess returns; it is depicted graphically in Figure 21-6. Essentially, any individual asset or portfolio that has a positive alpha over the sampled period has earned an average rate of return that exceeds what is appropriate for the asset's level of systematic risk.

If the kth asset is overpriced, so that it yields risk premiums that are inappropriately low for its level of systematic risk over some sample period, this asset's alpha will be negative, $A_k < 0$, for a regression estimated over that sample period. This situation is mathematically specified by inequality (21-10).

$$\text{If} \qquad E(r_{k,t} - R_t) < B_k E(r_{m,t} - R_t) \qquad \text{then } A_k < 0 \qquad (21\text{-}10)$$

The inadequate return situation represented by inequality (21-10) is also illustrated in Figure 21-6.

The alpha regression intercept term in Jensen's characteristic line reformulated in risk premiums can be used to evaluate the investment performance of assets. For example, if the jth asset outperformed the market, this is represented by $A_j > 0$. If asset m earned returns that were exactly appropriate for its level of systematic risk, $A_m = 0$. If the kth asset performed poorly, then $A_k < 0$. The three assets' investment performances could be ranked as shown in inequality (21-11).

$$A_j > 0 = A_m > A_k \qquad (21\text{-}11)$$

Three Caveats About Using Jensen's Alpha Measures

Consider two assets named h and j. Suppose these two assets' excess returns measured over the same sample period are identical, that is, $A_h = A_j$. Further suppose that asset h has more systematic risk than asset j, $B_h > B_j$, as shown in Figure 21-6. Could it be concluded that these two assets performed equally well simply because their alphas are identical? The answer is negative. To see why, reconsider Treynor's investment performance ranking device, defined in Equation (21-12).

$$T_j = \frac{E(r_{j,t} - R_t)}{B_j} > \frac{E(r_{h,t} - R_t)}{B_h} = T_h \qquad (21\text{-}12)$$

Inequality (21-12) utilizes Treynor's performance ranking device to show that asset j's performance surpassed asset h's performance, although their Jensen alpha measures were identical, $A_j = A_h$. The point is that Jensen's alpha cannot be used to *rank* the performance of different assets unless it is risk adjusted by dividing it by beta.

$$\text{Risk-adjusted alphas: } \frac{A_j}{B_j} > \frac{A_h}{B_h} \tag{21-13}$$

Thus the first caveat is that Jensen's alpha should not be used for ranking purposes. It does have asset-pricing implications, and it measures excess returns empirically. But it is not suitable for ranking purposes until it has been divided by beta.[10]

The second caveat concerns the interpretation of the alpha intercept term from the original characteristic line that is estimated with rates of return rather than risk premium, that is, a_i in Equation (10-3). This original alpha is different from Jensen's alpha, $a_i \neq A_i$. More important, the original alpha should not be used for investment performance evaluation; it has no direct asset-pricing implications.

A third caveat is that Jensen's alpha is merely a sample statistic that is subject to sampling errors. In fact, the alphas of many stocks are, statistically speaking, not significantly different from zero.

21-7   **McDONALD'S EMPIRICAL RESULTS**

Using 120 monthly rates of return from a decade, John G. McDonald analyzed the performance of 123 mutual funds. The Sharpe and Treynor performance measures were used in the slightly reformulated manner shown in Equations (21-2a) and (21-4a).

$$S_p = \frac{E(r_{p,t} - R_t)}{\sigma_p} \tag{21-2a}$$

$$T_p = \frac{E(r_{p,t} - R_t)}{b_p} \tag{21-4a}$$

Dr. McDonald used *monthly observations* of the 30-day commercial paper rate as a surrogate for the riskless rate; this is why the riskless rates in Equations (21-2a) and (21-4a) have time subscripts for $t = 1, 2, \ldots, 120$ months. These monthly observations of R_t were subtracted from each portfolio's monthly rate of return to obtain monthly risk premiums, denoted $r_{p,t} - R_t$. Then the average

---

[10]Keith Smith and Dennis Tito were the first researchers to suggest that Jensen's performance measure should be modified by dividing it by beta; see Keith V. Smith and Dennis A. Tito, ''Risk-Return Measures of Ex-Post Portfolio Performance,'' *Journal of Financial and Quantitative Analysis*, Dec. 1969, vol. IV, p. 466.

Table 21-6

PORTFOLIO PERFORMANCE STATISTICS FOR 123 MUTUAL FUNDS

Fund's stated objective (sample size)	Average beta	Average standard deviation	Average $E(r - R)$	Average Sharpe	Average Treynor	Average Jensen
Maximum capital gain (18)	1.22	5.90	0.693	0.117	0.568	0.122
Growth (33)	1.01	4.57	0.565	0.124	0.560	0.099
Growth-income (36)	0.90	3.93	0.476	0.121	0.529	0.058
Income-growth (12)	0.86	3.80	0.398	0.105	0.463	0.004
Balanced (12)	0.68	3.05	0.214	0.070	0.314	−0.099
Income (12)	0.55	2.67	0.252	0.094	0.458	−0.002
Total sample (123)	0.92	4.17	0.477	0.133	0.510	0
Market average				0.133	0.510	

Source: John G. McDonald, "Objectives and Performance of Mutual Funds," *Journal of Financial and Quantitative Analysis,* June 1974, table 1, p. 319.

risk premium, denoted $E(r_{i,t} - R_t)$, over the 120 months was divided by the appropriate risk measure to compare the portfolios' performances. Table 21-6 shows a summary of the statistics.

McDonald found that, on average, the funds with more aggressive objectives took more risk and earned higher returns, as was found in the Friend-Blume-Crockett study (see Table 21-3). The McDonald study also found that a few funds departed from their stated objective; similar results were reported (see Table 21-4) in the Friend-Blume-Crockett study and elsewhere (Figure 21-1).

Concerning the investment performance of the 123 funds, McDonald's study reported that slightly over half the 123 mutual funds (that is, 67 out of 123) had values for Treynor's performance index that exceeded the stock market average. Use of Sharpe's performance measure shows that about 31.7 percent (that is, 39 out of 123) of the funds outperformed the stock market average. Thus, using a slightly different specification of the Sharpe and Treynor portfolio performance measures and a different sample did not yield any significantly different conclusions. On average, *mutual funds perform about as well as a naive buy-and-hold strategy*. All the scientific studies of mutual fund performance reach essentially the same conclusions.

21-8   **COMPARING INVESTMENT PERFORMANCE MEASURES**

The Treynor, Sharpe, and Jensen investment performance measures may be compared and contrasted from several perspectives. The Sharpe measure is suitable for evaluating portfolios; it is less appropriate for evaluating the performance of individual assets because it measures *total risk* instead of systematic risk. Stated differently, Sharpe's measure evaluates assets relative to the capital market line (CML), which is a portfolio pricing model, while the Treynor and Jensen measures are formulated in the capital asset pricing model (CAPM) context and analyze both portfolios and individual assets. Thus, the Treynor and Jensen measures are more suitable for a wider range of performance evaluation problems than the Sharpe measure.

Algebraic Relationships

Jensen's characteristic line in risk-premium form, Equation (21-6), is suitable for evaluating the performance of both portfolios and individual assets. If the asset is priced correctly, then the $[B_i, E(r_i - R)]$ pairs from Equation (21-6) for all assets should fit on the CAPM of Equation (21-8). Jensen's alpha can be viewed as a measure of disequilibrium in Equation (21-8).

Treynor's single-parameter performance measure can be derived from the CAPM of Equation (21-8) by dividing both sides of that equation by its beta to obtain Equation (21-14).

$$T_i = \frac{E(r_i - R)}{B_i} = \frac{A_i}{B_i} + E(r_m - R) \qquad (21\text{-}14)$$

Equation (21-14) shows mathematical proof that the Treynor is simply a positive linear transformation of Jensen's measure since the $E(r_m - R)$ term is a constant over all assets. Sharpe's portfolio performance measure may also be derived from Equation (21-8) by substituting the definition of the beta coefficient from Equation (21-15) into the CAPM of Equation (21-8) as shown below in Equation (21-8a).

$$B_i = \frac{\sigma_m \sigma_i \rho_{i,m}}{\sigma_m^2} \qquad \text{by definition} \qquad (21\text{-}15)$$

$$E(r_i - R) = A_i + \frac{\sigma_m \sigma_i \rho_{i,m}}{\sigma_m^2} E(r_m - R) \qquad (21\text{-}8a)$$

For portfolios that are well diversified, $\rho_{i,m} = +1.0$. Therefore we can drop the correlation coefficient from Equation (21-8a) for well-diversified portfolios. Then, after dividing by σ_i, we obtain Sharpe's portfolio performance measure, Equation (21-16).

$$S_i = \frac{E(r_i - R)}{\sigma_i} = \frac{A_i}{\sigma_i} + \frac{E(r_m - R)}{\sigma_m} \qquad (21\text{-}16)$$

Since the $E(r_m - R)/\sigma_m$ term in Equation (21-16) is constant over all assets, Sharpe's portfolio performance measure is shown to be an approximately positive linear transformation of Jensen's alpha measure. Explicitly, Sharpe's $S_i = $ Jensen's $A_i/\sigma_m + $ constant.

A final comparison can be made between T_i and S_i by remembering that Treynor's measure can be defined as $T_i = E(r_i - R)/B_i$ and substituting $(\sigma_m \sigma_i \rho_{i,m})/\sigma_m^2 = B_i$. This manipulation results in $T_i = E(r_i - R)/[(\sigma_i \rho_{i,m})/\sigma_m]$; so for well-diversified portfolios that have $\rho_{i,m} = +1.0$, we have the approximation shown in Equation (21-17).

$$T_i = S_i \sigma_m \qquad (21\text{-}17)$$

Equation (21-17) shows that S_i and T_i are also approximately linear transformations of each other. This theoretical result was confirmed by an empirical study that reported the rankings obtained from using S_i and T_i were .97 correlated.[11]

General Discussion of the Performance Measurement Tools

When analyzing and comparing the merits of alternative investments, two classes of problems are usually considered[12]: (1) selectivity problems and (2) timing problems.

Selectivity Problems This asset-specific category of problems focuses on information that is idiosyncratic to individual assets. The Sharpe, Treynor, and Jensen evaluation tools are well suited to analyzing this class of problems.

Timing Problems This category of problems focuses on how particular investment assets react or adapt to changes in the state of nature. These problems cannot be analyzed within the framework provided by the Treynor, Sharpe, and Jensen evaluation tools unless the underlying theoretical framework (namely, the CML and/or CAPM) is extended.[13]

---

[11]William F. Sharpe, "Mutual Fund Performances," *Journal of Business*, Supplement, Jan. 1966, p. 125.

[12]A third class of problems that is considered less frequently is how to evaluate the performance of returns from a nonlinear model (such as a call option that is deep in the money) using linear tools (such as the CAPM). Some intractable problems arise with this third class of investment evaluations.

[13]The arbitrage pricing theory (APT) model is more suitable for analyzing timing-oriented problems than the CAPM because the APT admits multiple explanatory variables. The APT can thus analyze new states of nature as one of the explanatory variables. The APT is discussed in Chapter 11.

For a highly pro-CAPM discussion, see David Mayers and Edward Rice, "Measuring Portfolio Performance and the Empirical Content of Asset Pricing Models," *Journal of Financial Economics*, March 1979, pp. 3–28. For an extremely anti-CAPM discussion see Richard Roll, "A Critique of the Asset Theories Tests, Part I: On Past and Potential Testability of the Theory," *Journal of Financial Economics*, March 1977, pp. 129–176. For an analysis that reports both shortcomings and strengths of the CAPM, see Philip H. Dybvig and Stephen A. Ross, "Differential Information and Performance Measurement Using a Security Market Line (aka CAPM)," *Journal of Finance*, June 1985, vol. XL, no. 2, pp. 383–399.

For details about market timing studies see Roy D. Henriksson and Robert C. Merton, "On Market Timing and Investment Performance, II. Statistical Procedure for Evaluating Forecasting Skills," *Journal of Business*, Oct. 1981, vol. 54, pp. 513–533. See also Roy D. Henriksson, "Market Timing and Mutual Fund Performance: An Empirical Investigation," *Journal of Business*, Jan. 1984, vol. 57, pp. 73–96. Also see Ravi Jagannathan and Robert A. Korajczyk, "Assessing the Market Timing Performance of Managed Portfolios," *Journal of Business*, April 1986, vol. 59, no. 2, part 1, pp. 217–235. And see A. R. Admati, S. Bhat Tacharya, P. Pfleiderer, and S. A. Ross, "On Timing and Selectivity," *Journal of Finance*, July 1986, vol. 41, no. 3, pp. 715–732.

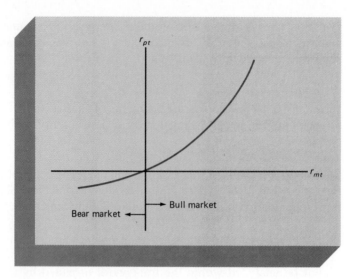

Figure 21-7 Curvilinear characteristic line for a portfolio that outguesses the market's turning points.

21-9   **EVALUATING INVESTMENT TIMING DECISIONS**

In an effort to discern whether some portfolio managers were able to foresee the market's bullish upturns and bearish downturns, Treynor and Mazuy[14] reformulated the characteristic regression line by adding a second-order term, as shown in Equation (21-18). The equation is a time-series multiple regression model estimated over $t = 1, 2, \ldots, T$ periods.

$$r_{i,t} = a_i + b_{1,i}(r_{m,t}) + b_{2,i}(r_{m,t}^2) + e_{i,t} \qquad (21\text{-}18)$$

where $r_{i,t}$ = rate of return from investment i in tth period
$r_{m,t}$ = return on market index in period t
$e_{i,t}$ = random error term for investment i in period t
a_i = intercept coefficient for investment i
$b_{1,i}$ = beta coefficient for market returns from investment i
$b_{2,i}$ = beta coefficient for squared-market-returns from investment i

Figure 21-7 illustrates the Treynor-Mazuy model for the case when the second-order term contributes positively to the return of asset i, $b_{2,i} > 0$.

---

[14]Jack L. Treynor and Kay K. Mazuy, "Can Mutual Funds Outguess the Market?," *Harvard Business Review,* July–Aug. 1966, vol. 44, no. 4, pp. 131–136. Also see F. J. Fabozzi and J. C. Francis, "Mutual Fund Systematic Risk for Bull and Bear Markets: An Empirical Examination," *Journal of Finance,* Dec. 1979, vol. XXXIV, no. 5, pp. 1243–1250.

Suppose that the ith asset is a mutual fund managed by a person who is able to predict bull- and/or bear-market conditions. To maximize this portfolio's gains, this omniscient portfolio manager shifts the portfolio into high beta securities as bull markets begin. Then when the bullish advance is complete and a bearish decline is starting, the manager will liquidate the high beta assets and buy low beta securities (and/or sell high beta assets short). As a result of such adept *market timing* decisions, the portfolio would have $b_{2,i} > 0$, as illustrated in Figure 21-7. In contrast, if a portfolio manager could not outguess the market turns, $b_{2,i}$ would equal zero (and not be significantly different from zero, statistically speaking).

Treynor and Mazuy estimated Equation (21-18) for 57 mutual funds (more specifically, 32 balanced funds and 25 growth funds) over 10 annual returns. After finding that 56 of these mutual funds had $b_{2,i} = 0$ and only one had a slightly positive value for $b_{2,i}$, Treynor and Mazuy concluded that none of the mutual funds in their sample had the ability to foresee either bull- or bear-market conditions. Essentially, all 57 of the mutual funds appeared to have linear characteristic regression lines that fit their data better than the curvilinear model shown in Equation (21-18).

21-10   **SUMMARY AND CONCLUSIONS**

This chapter's discussion of portfolio performance tools used mutual funds to provide examples. Some conclusions can be drawn regarding mutual funds and the tools used to evaluate portfolio performance.

**Conclusions
About Mutual
Fund Investing**

The portfolio performance analysis of mutual funds suggests that many investors who own or are considering buying mutual fund shares could expect higher rates of return and less risk if they invest their own funds by selecting securities randomly and then simply holding them. This statement does not mean that all mutual fund shares represent poor investment decisions. Mutual funds can perform some valuable investment services.

Consider an average, amateur investor who has $6000 or less to invest. Assume that this small investor will purchase only round lots (to avoid paying the higher odd-lot trading cost) and that the securities have an average cost of $30 per share. Such an investor would be able to buy only two securities, because $30 times 100 shares equals $3000 per round lot. Since two round lots are too few securities to minimize the portfolio's unsystematic portion of total risk, this investor should probably look for a mutual fund.

Although mutual funds do not typically earn high rates of return, they are usually able to reduce their risk to the systematic level of the market fluctuations. So, the fortunes of a mutual fund investor are not tied to the fortunes of only a few individual securities. Therefore, unless investors have the resources to perform Markowitz diversification (namely, access to a computer, a database for many securities, and the ability to analyze data with the computer), they might be better off investing in a mutual fund.

The majority of mutual funds earn long-run average rates of return that exceed the returns paid by insured savings accounts. Thus, investors receive some added return for assuming risk unless some misfortune forces them to liquidate their holdings in a period of depressed prices.

Finally, mutual funds can help an investor stay in some preferred risk class (although that risk class is not necessarily the one the fund says it will pursue in its statement of investment objectives). By examining mutual funds' quantitative risk coefficients, an investor can find a fund that will fairly consistently maintain a given level of risk. Table 21-3 explains the risk implications of various portfolio risk measures. As mentioned before, mutual funds do tend to stay in a given risk class and select assets that earn an average return for that level of risk. This is a valuable service that amateur or part-time investors might not be able to provide for themselves.

Conclusions about Portfolio Performance Measures

Ranking portfolios' yearly rates of return reveals whether any of them are consistently able to outperform their competitors. However, such rankings may make an efficient low-risk portfolio appear to be doing poorly. To evaluate a portfolio adequately, the level of risk it assumes must be *considered simultaneously* with its rate of return. Unfortunately, the statements of a few portfolio managers about the degree of risk (and concurrent expected returns) they will seek are misleading. In contrast, portfolios' empirically measured risk coefficients furnish more stationary indexes of the level of risk the portfolios undertake. If the standard deviation is used, portfolios' standard deviations and average rates of return may be plotted in $[\sigma, E(r)]$ space and compared with the efficient frontier. Sharpe's index of portfolio performance measures the risk premium per unit of risk borne by individual portfolios. This index considers both risk and return and yields one index number for each portfolio; these index numbers may be used to rank the performances of a group of portfolios or individual assets.

Some analysts prefer Treynor's portfolio performance measure because systematic risk is more relevant than total risk in certain applications and because Treynor's measure can be used to compare both individual assets and portfolios. But Treynor's performance measure has the disadvantage that it is sensitive to the market index used, and it is not clear which market index is most appropriate. The Treynor index uses portfolios' beta systematic risk coefficients and average returns to compare portfolios' performance in $[b, E(r)]$ space. The Treynor, Jensen, and Sharpe investment performance measures all tend to rank mutual funds similarly.

Conclusions about Portfolio Management Practices

There are several common traps a portfolio manager may fall into which can shackle the portfolio's performance. If the securities markets are highly efficient, a search for undervalued securities is not likely to yield returns that exceed those that could be attained by using a naive buy-and-hold strategy. If markets are judged to be highly efficient, a passive portfolio management practice like *indexing the portfolio* to some market index may be the most cost-effective approach. *Active portfolio management* practices are only appropriate if there are significant market inefficiencies that can be exploited legally and profitably.

To be efficient, a portfolio's funds should be allocated among various unrelated securities (such as domestic and foreign stocks, bonds, options, and commodities) in order to take full advantage of Markowitz diversification and to maximize the expected return. Judging from the performance statistics reviewed above, all mutual fund managers have room for improvement.[15]

Performance Evaluation of Other Portfolios

Many billions of dollars of investment capital in the United States are being moved about from one investment manager to another. A number of Fortune 500 corporations, for example, have pension fund assets worth tens of billions of dollars being managed by various investment advisors in separately managed pools of capital.[16] The financial managers who control these mobile investment funds are continually searching for and evaluating places to invest their funds productively. But their studies of bank trust departments, investment advisers, mutual funds, life insurance companies' funds management programs, and other institutional investment management organizations are not reported to the general public. Furthermore, since the institutional investment management organizations are not required by law to disclose their performance results (as are mutual funds), they may keep their results secret. This is why the studies of mutual fund performance are much richer and more widely available than similar studies of other institutional investors.

Publicly disseminated scientific studies of various institutional investment management organizations[17] are not sufficiently plentiful to justify detailed conclusions about the relative investment management skills of the various organizations. However, the limited material available suggests that mutual

---

[15]For an analysis of the principal-agent sharing rule problems that arise when portfolio managers are hired to manage investments, see Sudipto Bhattacharya, "Delegated Portfolio Management," *Journal of Economic Theory,* 1985, vol. 36, pp. 1–25.

[16]Details about the pension funds of hundreds of large corporations are published annually by *Institutional Investor;* see the Pensions Directory published in the January issue each year.

For an analysis of the investment performance of 120 pension funds over the 1968–1983 sample period, see Stephen A. Berkowitz, Louis D. Finney, and Dennis E. Logue, *The Investment Performance of Corporate Pension Funds: Why They Do Not Beat the Market Regularly* (New York: Quorum Books, 1988). The title of this 130-page book provides a clue about its conclusions.

[17]W. G. Burns and R. H. Klemm, "Performance of Bank Managers of Trust Funds," R. L. White Center for Financial Research, unpublished manuscript, August 1973. Edward Malca, *Bank-Administered Co-mingled Pension Funds* (Lexington, Mass.: Lexington Books, 1973). I. Friend, M. Blume, and J. Crockett, op. cit.

funds do not tend to do significantly better or worse than the trust departments of commercial banks or life insurance companies.

Essay Questions

21-1   "Closed-end investment companies redeem their shares at the current net asset value." Is this statement true, false, or uncertain? Explain.

21-2   How is the income of an open-end investment company taxed?

21-3   "Rankings of portfolios' average returns show that, although the average mutual fund does not outperform the market, a few truly superior funds consistently beat the market." Is this statement true, false, or uncertain? Explain.

21-4   Read *Institutional Investor* magazine's June 1989 article entitled "Can Phony Performance Numbers Be Policed?" What does this article suggest that a portfolio manager do to avoid being duped by investment advisers who show deceptive investment performance statistics?

21-5   How well does the mutual fund industry perform relative to a naive buy-and-hold investment strategy?

21-6   Assume you have been put in charge of a mutual fund with a large staff of fundamental analysts and millions of dollars of assets spread over more than 100 different securities. The fund's gross return is about average for the industry, but its management expenses are high, so its net yield to its investors is slightly below average. The previous management did not try to specialize as a growth or safety fund but ran the firm as a general-purpose fund. What do you plan to do with your fund? Explain why.

Problems

21-7   Consider the following summary statistics about five investment portfolios.

Portfolio	Average return	Standard deviation	Beta	Correlation, ρ
Alpha (A)	7%	3	0.4	.89
Beta (B)	10	8	1.0	.91
Gamma (Γ)	13	6	1.1	.90
Delta (Δ)	15	13	1.2	.95
Epsilon (E)	18	15	1.4	.88

Assume that the riskless rate of interest is 3.0 percent. (*a*) Which of the portfolios performed the best according to Sharpe's measure? The worst? (*b*) Which performed the best according to Treynor's performance measure? The worst? (*c*) Assume that the riskless rate of interest was 6.0 percent. Under this new assumption, which portfolio ranks the best according to Sharpe's measure? According to Treynor's measure? Show your calculations and draw graphs to illustrate the work. Label all variables in your calculations and graphs.

The information below will be used with Problems 21-8 through 21-13. A regression was run for the five mutual funds using the following model:

$$rp_{p,t} = A_p + B_p rp_{m,t} + u_{p,t} \quad \text{for } t = 1, 2, \ldots, T$$

where $rp_{p,t}$ = quarterly excess fund return = rate of return from mutual fund p − T-bill rate

$rp_{m,t}$ = quarterly excess market return = rate of return from market portfolio − T-bill rate

A_p = alpha coefficient (Jensen's performance measure) for portfolio p

B_p = beta coefficient for portfolio p

$u_{p,t}$ = error term for portfolio p in period t

Fund	Alpha coefficient, %	Alpha's standard deviation, %	Beta coefficient	Beta's standard deviation, %	R^2	Mean return, %	Mean standard deviation, %
A	−0.24	0.4143	1.08	0.06	.94	1.71	7.42
B	2.03	0.9200	1.62	0.14	.89	3.68	11.71
C	4.27	1.3400	1.45	0.20	.75	6.02	11.25
D	3.46	1.2700	1.36	0.19	.74	5.26	10.78
E	1.18	1.4100	1.30	0.21	.68	3.00	10.64
S&P 500						1.99	6.74
T-bill						2.52	0.76

21-8   Rank the five funds using the Jensen performance measure.

21-9   Rank the five funds with the Sharpe performance measure.

21-10 Rank the five funds using Treynor's performance measure.

21-11 Which of the five funds had the most systematic risk?

21-12 Which of the five funds is the least correlated with the market?

21-13 Which of the five funds' returns moved more closely with the market's returns?

The following data will be used for Problems 21-14 through 21-17.

Year and quarter	Guardian Fund return, %	Acorn Fund return, %	S&P 500 return, %	T-bill return, %
1983—2	9.42	13.17	11.10	2.04
1983—3	−1.28	−2.72	−0.10	2.14
1983—4	2.70	0.00	0.40	2.13
1984—1	−4.53	−5.78	−2.40	2.14
1984—2	−2.64	−1.09	−2.61	2.50
1984—3	10.13	10.45	9.68	2.50
1984—4	4.95	1.51	1.76	2.63

(*Table continues on page 672.*)

Year and quarter	Guardian Fund return, %	Acorn Fund return, %	S&P 500 return, %	T-bill return, %
1985—1	8.23	11.95	9.18	2.29
1985—2	6.33	7.35	7.34	2.15
1985—3	−2.04	−3.70	−4.10	1.78
1985—4	11.15	13.57	17.19	1.90
1986—1	11.64	13.95	14.02	1.79
1986—2	5.48	6.59	5.85	1.61
1986—3	−6.44	−6.66	−6.94	1.33
1986—4	1.58	3.62	5.58	1.46

21-14 Calculate the Treynor and Sharpe performance measures for the Guardian Fund.

21-15 Calculate the Treynor and Sharpe performance measures for the Acorn Fund.

21-16 Calculate the Jensen performance measure for the Guardian Fund and the Acorn Fund.

21-17 Is the Guardian Fund or the Acorn Fund the most aggressive?

Selected References

Alexander, Gordon, and Jack Clark Francis, *Portfolio Analysis,* 3d ed. (Englewood Cliffs, N.J.: Prentice-Hall, 1986).

 Chapter 13 uses advanced statistics and discusses different investment performance evaluation techniques and problems.

Berkowitz, Stephen A., Louis D. Finney, and Dennis E. Logue, *The Investment Performance of Corporate Pension Funds: Why They Do Not Beat the Market Regularly* (New York: Quorum Books, 1988).

 This 130-page book is rich with empirical data that suggests pension fund managers do not manage money quite as well as the mutual fund managers.

Fama, E. F., "Components of Investment Performance," *Journal of Finance,* June 1972, pp. 551–568.

 This paper uses mathematical statistics to analyze the Sharpe and Treynor portfolio performance evaluation tools.

Jensen, Michael C., "The Performance of Mutual Funds in the Period 1945–64," *Journal of Finance,* May 1968, pp. 389–416.

 An analysis of the performance of mutual funds that uses regression analysis.

Sharpe, William F., "Mutual Fund Performance," *Journal of Business,* Supplement on Security Prices, January 1966, pp. 119–138.

 This risk-return analysis of mutual fund performance uses correlation, regression, and statistical inference.

Part 7

Other Investments

Chapter 22

Puts and Calls

Generally, **options** are legal contracts giving their owner the right, but *not the obligation,* to buy or sell something at a predetermined price. In the securities industry, options are marketable contracts entitling their owner to buy or sell a specific quantity of a particular security at a fixed price within a predetermined period. There are two basic types of options on securities—calls and puts.

A **call** is an option to buy, that is, an option to call in shares for purchase. Every call is a marketable contract giving its owner (or holder or buyer) the option of buying 100 shares of some specific stock at a predetermined price within some designated interval of time. The prespecified price at which an option can be exercised is called the **exercise price** or **contract price** or **striking price.**

A **put** is an option to sell, that is, an option to "put" shares to someone else. Each put is a marketable contract giving its owner (or holder or buyer) the option to sell 100 shares of some stock within a fixed period at a prespecified exercise price.

Calls and puts are marketable securities that are separate from their underlying assets. An option is created whenever an option writer sells a new option to an option buyer. Three things can be done with an option after it is created: (1) trade it in active secondary markets, (2) exercise it to buy or sell the underlying asset, or (3) hold it until it matures. The calls and puts traded on listed *option exchanges* have various maturities that extend to a maximum of almost 1 year from the day of their origination. Tailor-made options covering different periods can be obtained in the *over-the-counter options market*. If an option is not exercised before its expiration date, it matures and is useless and worthless thereafter.

An option buyer pays an option writer a **premium** for granting the option. After options have been created, they can be traded at market-determined premiums (or prices) that fluctuate continuously. The party who buys an option is **long the option.** Option writers are said to be **short the option.**[1] An option writer who owns the security on which a call was written is **writing calls covered,** instead of **writing uncovered** (or naked). Writing calls covered is a less risky strategy than writing uncovered—details of both strategies are explained below.

American options may be exercised by their owner any time before they reach their maturity date. **European options** can be exercised only on the day they expire. These two names refer to two different categories of exercise dates for calls and puts—they have nothing to do with the country in which the option is originated or traded. For example, some options traded in Europe can be exercised at any time during their life; thus they are American options. Investors that buy American options get all the same benefits as investors that buy the similar European options, plus those who buy American options are provided with more opportunities to exercise their options. As a result, American options are always worth at least as much as the analogous European options.

Options owners usually do not exercise their options. Two other choices are available. The party who owns the option can continue to hold it while awaiting further developments or unexpired options can be sold in the secondary market. In the secondary market an option might pass through the hands of many different owners before it reaches maturity. It is easy to buy and sell options; just call a brokerage house, open an account, and give the broker your order.

22-1   **POSITION GRAPHS FOR CALL OPTIONS**

An investor who thinks a security's price will rise may **buy a call;** such investors are said to have a **long call position.** If the security's price falls, *no more than the premium can be lost.* Losing the premium is not as bad as losing the value of the underlying asset since call premiums are typically only about 10 to 15 percent of the value of the optioned securities. But if the security's price rises, the call buyer must decide whether to exercise the call and reap the gains from selling the stock, capture the gains by selling the option, or retain the call and hope for further price rises.

Explanation of the Position Graphs   Figure 22-1*a* is a graph of a call buyer's position. Profit or loss is measured along the vertical axis. The profitable upper segment of the vertical axis is separated from the unprofitable lower segment by the horizontal axis. The market price of the optioned security is measured along the horizontal axis.

First, let us consider the potential profits and losses for the call depicted in

[1]Long and short positions were defined in Section 8-3.

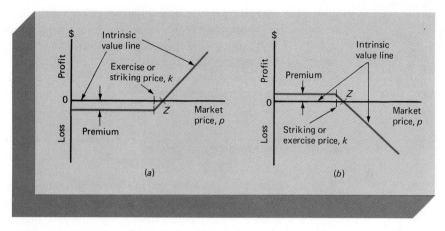

Figure 22-1 Position graphs for a call option: (*a*) profit and loss of call buyer; (*b*) profit and loss of uncovered call writer.

Figure 22-1*a*. The line that is below and parallel to the horizontal axis traces out a loss; this loss equals the premium that was paid for the call. The loss continues up to the point where the market price of the optioned security rises above the option's exercise price. When the market price exceeds the exercise price by precisely enough to cover the premium paid, the option buyer's profit would be zero if the call was exercised. This is the **break-even point;** it is denoted as point *z* in the figure. If the market price of the optioned security rises above the break-even point, then the buyer reaps a net profit after the cost of the premium is deducted (ignoring commissions and taxes) if the call is either exercised or sold.

Intrinsic Value of a Call   Let *p* stand for the market price of the optioned security and *k* denote the call's exercise price. Equation (22-1) defines the **intrinsic value of a call.**

$$\text{Intrinsic value of a call} = \text{Max}(0, p - k) \qquad (22\text{-}1)$$

Equation (22-1) shows that a call's intrinsic value is either zero or the quantity *p − k,* whichever is greater. This quantity is delineated by the kinked *intrinsic value lines* in Figure 22-1. The intrinsic value of a call is important because it defines the call's value at expiration (when it has no time value left) and it sets a floor under the call's value any time before the expiration date.

Figure 22-1*b* portrays the position of the **call writer.** The call's intrinsic value to the person who wrote it (or sold it, or is **short the call**) is traced out by the kinked intrinsic value line in Figure 22-1*b*. The parallel line above the horizontal axis in Figure 22-1*b* shows profits for the call seller, who gets to keep the premium for doing nothing as long as the price of the optioned security does not rise above the exercise price. If the price of the optioned security rises above the exercise price, call buyers can either minimize losses when the price of the security is between k and k + premium or maximize profits when p exceeds the quantity k + premium by exercising the call. As a result, call sellers should assume that the calls they wrote might be exercised whenever p exceeds k. The point where $p = k$ + premium is the *break-even point*, denoted z in Figure 22-1, for both the call writer and the call buyer.

22-2   **POSITION GRAPHS FOR A PUT OPTION**

Position graphs for the writer and the buyer of a put option are shown in Figure 22-2. The put buyer hopes the optioned security's price will fall, for instance, as would a short seller. But unlike a short seller, the put buyer's *losses are limited to the premium* if the security experiences a price rise. If the security's market price falls below the exercise price of the put ($p < k$), the put owner's profit equals the excess of the exercise price over the market price of the optioned security less the premium paid, symbolically, $k - p$ − premium.

If the price of the security rises above its exercise price, the put writer gets to keep the premium for doing nothing because it is not profitable for the put buyer to exercise. *The gains to the writers of both put and call options can never exceed the premiums they receive.*

22-3   **SHOULD BEARS SELL SHORT OR BUY A PUT?**

An investor who wants to speculate that the price of some security will fall can choose among buying a put on the security, selling the asset short, or

Figure 22-2 Position graphs for put option: (*a*) put buyer; (*b*) put writer

writing a call. We will compare and contrast buying a put on the security with shorting it, because those two positions are somewhat similar.

The purchase of a put is usually more desirable than taking a short position for several reasons. First, the investment in a put is limited to the premium, whereas a short seller usually must put up a larger sum. This means that *the put option offers more financial leverage* than the short position. Second, *the put option buyer can lose no more than the premium* if the price of the optioned security rises. In contrast, a short seller's losses are unlimited if the security's price should keep rising. A third reason that buying a put may be more desirable than selling short derives from the way cash dividends are handled. Short sellers must make up for any cash dividends paid on the securities they borrowed. That is, short sellers must take from their pockets an amount of cash equal to any cash dividends and pay it to the party who lent them the securities.

Although the put option is a useful security, it is not always the preferred choice over a short sale. *One big disadvantage of buying options is that they expire and become worthless.* Therefore, if the speculator is not confident that the price of the security will decline before the put expires, then a short position may be more advisable. Paying a series of put premiums while waiting for the price of the optioned security to decline can be a costly strategy.

Put and call options can be used for three different types of financial activities: (1) speculations on short-run price changes, (2) long-run investments involving either long-term options or continuous reinvestment in a series of short-term options,[2] and (3) forming more complex options. Before examining complex option strategies, let us look at the markets where options are traded.

22-4   **OPTIONS MARKETS**

Options are traded on several organized options exchanges and in an over-the-counter (OTC) market for options.

OTC Market for Puts and Calls

The over-the-counter (OTC) markets for equity options and debt options have developed differently. The market for equity options has dwindled to a handful of firms in recent years. The exchanges where standardized options are listed have taken most of the volume in equity options away from the OTC market.

The OTC dealers in debt options are large banks and investment banking firms. They provide quotations of current prices for the debt options in which

---

[2]See Richard M. Bookstaber, *Option Pricing and Investment Strategies* (Chicago, Ill.: Probus, 1987), chap. 7, for a discussion of how a portfolio manager can use options to reshape the probability distribution of returns from the portfolio. See figures 7-8 and 7-9.

they deal in response to telephone inquiries. Potential option buyers call an OTC dealer to settle on an exercise price, determine what length of time they want the option contract to cover, and negotiate a mutually satisfactory premium.

Organized Options Exchanges

In 1973 the Chicago Board of Options Exchange (CBOE) began trading call options on about two dozen stocks; no puts were traded initially. The CBOE was America's first options exchange and organized secondary market for options. Trading volume flourished, and by 1990 the CBOE had increased the number of option contracts listed to include both puts and calls on about 160 different stocks that each have several different exercise prices and various maturities. Both the number and the volume of option contracts traded keeps growing.

The CBOE's rapid success encouraged other options exchanges to open. Today organized markets for listed options thrive on the trading floors of the following four securities exchanges:

1. The Chicago Board of Options Exchange (CBOE)
2. American Stock Exchange (AMEX)
3. Philadelphia Stock Exchange (PHLX)
4. Pacific Stock Exchange (PSE)

Trading Listed Options   Members of each exchange meet during trading hours on the floor of their exchange to buy and sell options. Clandestine deals are not part of the price determination process. Buyers and sellers come together and buy and sell options openly. The exchanges employ clerks who observe the options trading and instantly transmit the price of every trade to other options exchanges and news services around the world. Most trades that members of the option exchanges transact are done for clients of securities brokerages—the members of the exchanges are essentially brokers for the larger brokerage firms that handle different kinds of securities.

The Options Clearing Corporation (OCC)   The four security exchanges that make markets in listed options all clear their option transactions through the Options Clearing Corporation (OCC). The OCC has its headquarters in Chicago, but it is owned by the four security exchanges. The OCC is regulated by the SEC, as are all option markets in the United States.

The options traded at all four exchanges are issued by the OCC, but the OCC does not write them. Instead, the OCC serves as the intermediary between every option writer and every option buyer. The OCC is also a clearing house and a guarantor for the options, substituting its ability to deliver for the option writer's ability to deliver. As a result, the options issued at the four organized options exchanges are *highly marketable securities;* buyers need not check the integrity of the party who wrote an option before purchasing it.

Efficiency of the Organized Options Market Having the OCC's guarantee of financial integrity on every option lowers transaction costs. For instance, it eliminates the credit investigation that would be necessary if the OCC did not stand behind every contract. Owners of options can close out their positions at any time before the option expires by selling the option at its current market price. Having the OCC as the centralized clearing agent is fundamental to the maintenance of smoothly functioning secondary markets where options can be traded actively at any time before they expire.

The four organized options markets record all their trades in the memories of computers that are operated by the OCC and by those brokerage firms that are clearing members of the OCC. Since the OCC puts its own name on every option contract, it essentially becomes the seller in every option purchase and the buyer in every option sale. This procedure removes the need for any contact between buyers and sellers of OCC options. This expedites the clearing process because the OCC's computers need only bring together the final buyer and seller in order to consummate each option contract. All intermediate buyers and sellers that owned or sold the option prior to its delivery are erased from the computer's memory when their positions are closed.

Published Option Prices Figure 22-3 shows the prices of put and call options on common stocks that are listed on the CBOE. Table 22-1 lists various mar-

Figure 22-3 Newspaper listing of one day's premiums for put and call options.

The value of both put and call options increases with the length of time until they expire.

Option & NY Close	Strike Price	Calls—Last Apr	Calls—Last May	Calls—Last Jul	Puts—Last Apr	Puts—Last May	Puts—Last Jul
I B M	120	29	s	s	r	s	s
149⅝	125	25¼	s	s	r	s	s
149⅝	130	20¼	s	21¼	r	s	1
149⅝	135	15	s	16⅜	1-16	s	1¾
149⅝	140	10⅜	11	15½	¼	1½	3¼
149⅝	145	6⅛	8⅛	11½	15-16	3⅛	5¼
149⅝	150	2⅞	5⅜	9	2¾	5	7
149⅝	155	1 3-16	3½	6¾	6¼	8¾	9⅞
149⅝	160	7-16	1⅞	4¾	10½	13	13¼
149⅝	165	1-16	s	3⅛	15½	s	r
In Pap	55	3¾	r	6	1-16	r	r
58	60	⅝	1¾	2¾	3	3½	4½
58	65	⅛	¾	1¾	6¾	r	r
58	70	r	s	¾	r	s	r
Pepsi	55	26	s	s	r	s	s
81¾	60	21¼	s	r	r	s	r
81¾	65	16¼	s	r	r	s	r
81¾	75	7¾	s	9	1-16	s	1½
81¾	80	3¼	5	6¾	¾	2½	3½

"s" means that no July put options on IBM with an exercise price of $120 were offered for sale.

As the exercise price decreases, the calls become more valuable and the puts become less valuable.

"r" indicates that no put options with expirations in July were traded on IBM stock for the exercise price of $160 per share.

The closing price of Pepsi's common stock on the NYSE was $81.75 per share.

Put options on Pepsi stock with an exercise price of $80 per share that have April, May, and July expirations sold for 75¢, $2.50, and $3.50, respectively, on a per share basis.

Call options that had an $80 exercise price on Pepsi stock sold for $3.25, $5.00, and $6.75 for options expiring in April, May, and July, respectively.

Table 22-1

MARKETABLE ASSETS ON WHICH OPTIONS MAY BE OBTAINED AND THE ORGANIZED EXCHANGES WHERE THE OPTIONS ARE TRADED*

Optionable Assets

Common stocks AMEX, CBOE, PSE, PHLX
Stock market indexes and subindexes AMEX, CBOE, IMM f, NASDAQ, NYFE f, NYSE, PSE, PHLX

U.S. Treasury bonds and notes CBT f
Eurodollar deposits IMM f, LIFFE f

Australian dollars SFE f
Canadian dollars CBOE,† ME, PHLX, VSE
Deutsche marks CBOE,† IMM f, EOE, LSE, ME, PHLX
Dutch florin EOE
ECU (European currency unit) EOE
French franc CBOE,† PHLX
Pound sterling CBOE,† IMM f, EOE, LIFFE, LSE, ME, PHLX
Swiss franc CBOE,† IMM f, ME, PHLX
Yen CBOE,† PHLX

Gold COMEX f, EOE, MCE f, ME, VSE
Silver CBT f, COMEX f, EOE, TFE, VSE
Gold and silver index PHLX

Cattle CME f
Corn CBT f
Cotton NYCE f
Hogs CME f
Soybeans CBT f, MCE f
Sugar CSCE f
Wheat KC f, MCE f, MPLS f

Organized Option Exchanges

AMEX American Stock Exchange, in New York
CBOE Chicago Board of Options Exchange
CBT Chicago Board of Trade
CME Chicago Mercantile Exchange
COMEX Commodity Exchange, in New York
CSCE Coffee, Sugar, and Cocoa Exchange, in New York
EOE European Options Exchange
IMM International Monetary Market (at CME)
KC Kansas City Board of Trade
LIFFE London International Financial Futures Exchange
LSE London Stock Exchange
MCE MidAmerica Commodity Exchange, in Chicago
MPLS Minneapolis Grain Exchange
ME Montreal Exchange
NASDAQ National Association of Securities Dealers Automated Quotations
NYCE New York Cotton Exchange

(Table 22-1 continues on the next page.)

Table 22-1

MARKETABLE ASSETS ON WHICH OPTIONS MAY BE OBTAINED AND THE ORGANIZED EXCHANGES WHERE THE OPTIONS ARE TRADED* (continued)

Organized Option Exchanges

NYFE New York Futures Exchange
NYSE New York Stock Exchange
PSE Pacific Stock Exchange, in California
PHLX Philadelphia Stock Exchange
SFE Sydney Futures Exchange
TFE Toronto Futures Exchange
VSE Vancouver Stock Exchange

*f indicates that an option on a futures contract is also traded. Futures contracts are orders to buy an asset at a future date. They are described in Chapter 24.
†Denotes a European option.

ketable assets on which options may be obtained, and the organized exchanges where these options are traded actively. It should be noted that Table 22-1 was out-of-date as soon as it was in print. Old options that do not generate enough trading volume to pay the cost of listing them are delisted and new options are listed by the exchanges; these changes are continuous.

22-5   **INTRODUCTION TO BINOMIAL OPTION PRICING MODELS**

This section derives a simple valuation model for determining the premium for a call option. The binomial option pricing model that is derived assumes that the optioned security will experience one of two possible rates of return over the period that is analyzed. Over the single-period (such as a month) planning horizon the optioned security's price can go either up by $u = 1 + r_u$ with probability $P(\text{up})$ or down by $d = 1 + r_d$ with probability $P(\text{down}) = 1.0 - P(\text{up})$. To keep the mathematics simple, we assume that the optioned securities pay out zero cashflows. Cash dividends, for example, are presumed to be zero during the life of an optioned stock. Income taxes, brokerage commissions, transfer taxes, and margin requirements also are ignored. The convention used to represent the risk-free interest rate is $RR = 1 + R$. Finally, it is assumed that the investor can sell short and gain full and immediate use of the proceeds from any short sale. Figure 22-4 illustrates a hypothetical example that assumes the initial price of the optioned security is \$45.45 and that this price fluctuates up or down by 10 percent.[3]

[3]To prevent profitable arbitrage opportunities, the following inequality must not be violated: $u > RR > d$. If $RR < d < u$, for example, an investor could borrow at RR and purchase the security in order to make a riskless profit with zero equity investment. Conversely, if $RR > u > d$, the riskless investment would dominate two risky assets.

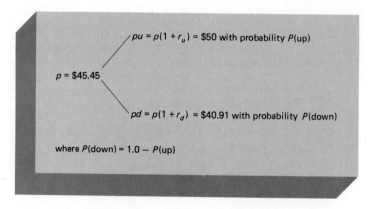

Figure 22-4 Binomial price moves for an optioned security.

One-Period Binomial Call Pricing Formula

The terms of the call option contract and rational economic decision-making combine to imply that at expiration a call is worth either zero or the excess of the optioned security's price over the exercise price, whichever is greater. More concisely, if the price of the optioned security rises, the call will be worth Cc_u when it is exercised. To continue the concrete numerical example, assume the option's exercise price is $k = \$40$.

$$Cc_u = \text{Max}[0, pu - k] \qquad (22\text{-}1a)$$

$$\$10 = \text{Max}[0, \$45.45(1.1) - \$40]$$

But, if the price of the optioned security falls, the exercised call will be worth Cc_d.

$$Cc_d = \text{Max}[0, pd - k] \qquad (22\text{-}1b)$$

$$\$0.91 = \text{Max}[0, \$45.45(0.9) - \$40]$$

Figure 22-5 illustrates the two possible call premiums.

Suppose that we create a portfolio with h shares of the optioned security that is financed by borrowing B dollars at a riskless rate of $RR = 1.0 + 0.05$. This portfolio will be worth $ph - B$ dollars initially. The portfolio will have one of the two values illustrated in Figure 22-6 at the end of the period.[4]

We now have enough information to determine what the call is worth. To find out what the call's premium should be, we must find values for B and h that will equate the end-of-period values of the call for each possible state of nature. Mathematically, this means that the two formulas below must be solved simultaneously.

[4]See Mark Rubinstein and Hayne E. Leland, "Replicating Options with Positions in Stock and Cash," *Financial Analysts Journal*, July–Aug. 1981, pp. 63–74.

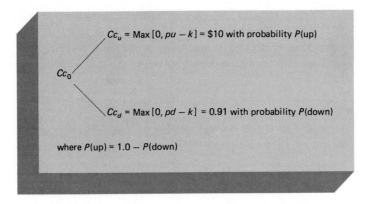

Figure 22-5 Call premiums fluctuate directly with the price of the optioned security.

$$Cc_u = uhp - RRB = (1.1)\$45.45h - (1.05)B$$

$$Cc_d = dhp - RRB = (0.9)\$45.45h - (1.05)B$$

It is simple to solve two linear equations in two unknowns. Their solutions are shown below. The value of h^* is called the **hedge ratio.**

$$h^* = \frac{Cc_u - Cc_d}{(u - d)p} \tag{22-2}$$

$$= \frac{[(1.1)\$45.45h - (1.05)B] - [(0.9)\$45.45h - (1.05)B]}{(1.1 - 0.9)\$45.45} = 0.92$$

$$B^* = \frac{uCc_d - dCc_u}{(u - d)RR} \tag{22-3}$$

$$= \frac{(1.1)[(0.9)\$45.45h - (1.05)B] - (0.9)[(1.1)\$45.45h - (1.05)B]}{(1.1 - 0.9)(1.05)}$$

$$= \$32.30$$

Figure 22-6 The portfolio's end-of-period value varies directly with the price of the optioned security.

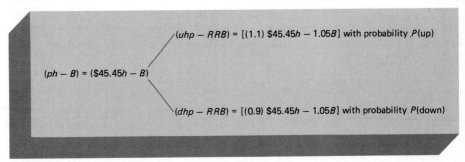

A portfolio containing $h^* = 0.92$ of one share that is financed by borrowing $B^* = \$32.30$ must have the same initial cost as the call in order to prevent arbitrage. Stated differently, the condition described in Equation (22-4) will prevent profitable arbitrage between the call and the portfolio containing the call.

$$Cc_0 = h^*p - B^* \qquad (22\text{-}4)$$

Equation (22-4) is a **call pricing model;** let us restate it in a more useful form. Equation (22-4) can be simplified by substituting for h^* and B^* to obtain:

$$Cc_0 = \frac{Cc_u - Cc_d}{u - d} + \frac{uCc_d - dCc_u}{(u - d)RR} \qquad (22\text{-}4a)$$

It is also useful to rearrange Equation (22-4a) as shown below.

$$Cc_0 = \left. \frac{r - d}{u - d} Cc_u + \frac{u - RR}{u - d} Cc_d \right/ RR \qquad (22\text{-}4b)$$

Equation (22-4b) can be simplified by using known values to define the quantities q and $1 - q$.

$$q = \frac{RR - d}{u - d} = \frac{1.05 - 0.9}{1.1 - 0.9} = 0.75$$

$$1 - q = \frac{u - r}{u - d} = \frac{1.1 - 1.05}{1.1 - 0.9} = 0.25$$

Substituting in the quantities q and $1 - q$ results in Equation (22-4c).

$$
\begin{aligned}
Cc_0 &= \frac{qCc_u + (1 - q)Cc_d}{RR} \qquad\qquad\qquad\qquad\qquad (22\text{-}4c)\\[2mm]
&= \frac{(0.75)[(1.1)\$45.45h - (1.05)B] + (0.25)[(0.9)\$45.45h - (1.05)B]}{1.05}\\[2mm]
&= \$9.35
\end{aligned}
$$

The Equation (22-4) series of formulas all yield exact estimates of the premium for a call that spans one period. This equation and similar formulas are widely used at investment banking firms around the world. The binomial option pricing model is applied to value common stocks, mortgages, and numerous other investments.[5]

---

[5]See David P. Jacob, Graham Lord, and James A. Tilley, "A Generalized Framework for Pricing Contingent Cash Flows," *Financial Management*, Autumn 1987, vol. 16, no. 3, pp. 5–14. The article shows how investment bankers use the binomial option pricing model to value GNMA mortgage-backed securities.

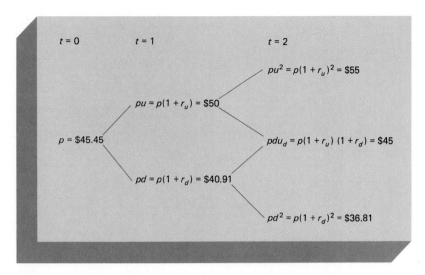

Figure 22-7 Binomial security price moves over two periods.

MultiPeriod Binomial Call Pricing Formula

The same procedure used above can be employed to derive a call pricing formula for an option that has two periods remaining before its expiration. Figure 22-7 shows the three possible prices that the optioned security might attain at the end of period $t = 2$. Figure 22-8 illustrates the call prices implied by the security prices in Figure 22-7. The symbol Cc_{du} indicates the call premium that results when the price of the optioned stock goes down in the first period and

Figure 22-8 Call premium fluctuations over two periods.

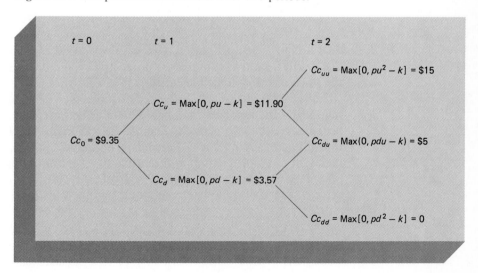

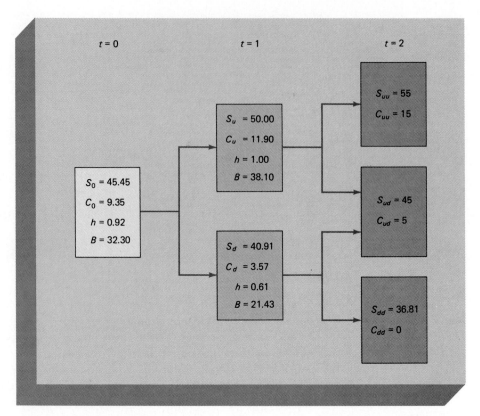

Figure 22-9 Lattice of call option values that follow price changes in the optioned security over two periods. (*Source*: Peter Ritchken, *Options,* Glenview, Ill., Scott, Foresman, 1987, exhibit 9.6, p. 196.)

then up in the second period. Likewise, Cc_{uu} and Cc_{dd} are the call premiums that result from two consecutive price upticks and downticks, respectively, in the price of the optioned security.

Figure 22-9 illustrates all the security prices, associated call prices, hedge ratios, and the amounts that would have to be borrowed to establish riskless hedges over the two periods. The example in Figure 22-9 can be extended to four, five, or any number of periods. The model can also be enriched by the inclusion of branches that represent the payment or nonpayment of cashflows (like cash dividends or coupons) and other events that affect the security's price.[6] Essentially, the binomial model can be transformed into a multiperiod

---

[6]For a discussion of valuing options on stocks that pay cash dividends within a lattice framework, see John Hull, *Options, Futures, and Other Derivative Securities* (Englewood Cliffs, N.J.: Prentice-Hall, 1989), see secs. 9.5 and 9.6, pp. 226–233.

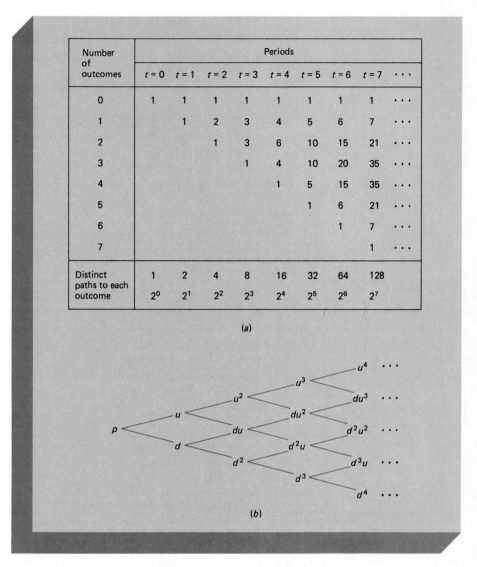

Number of outcomes	Periods							
	$t=0$	$t=1$	$t=2$	$t=3$	$t=4$	$t=5$	$t=6$	$t=7$ $\cdots$
0	1	1	1	1	1	1	1	1 $\cdots$
1		1	2	3	4	5	6	7 $\cdots$
2			1	3	6	10	15	21 $\cdots$
3				1	4	10	20	35 $\cdots$
4					1	5	15	35 $\cdots$
5						1	6	21 $\cdots$
6							1	7 $\cdots$
7								1 $\cdots$
Distinct paths to each outcome	1 2^0	2 2^1	4 2^2	8 2^3	16 2^4	32 2^5	64 2^6	128 2^7

(a)

(b)

Figure 22-10 A binomial random walk generates more outcomes and they tend to become increasingly normally distributed as t increases. (a) Pascal's triangle; (b) lattice showing paths to outcomes (or tree diagram).

option pricing model that yields exact option pricing formulas. When the binomial call pricing model is used to span a finite period (such as a month or a year) with a very large number of very small time intervals, the branches in the lattice proliferate and take an interesting form.

Figure 22-10*a* is called **Pascal's triangle;** it was derived in the 1600s.[7] Figure 22-10*b* illustrates the number of possible outcomes that result when the price movements of a market asset follow a **binomial random walk,** like the one introduced in this section. The integers in Figure 22-10*a* give the number of outcomes that will occur at each different branch in a binomial random walk after *t* periods. Note the form of the frequency distribution that the outcomes are converging upon as the number of periods increases—it is the well-known *normal probability distribution.* We can anticipate that after many periods have passed, the outcomes from a binomial random walk evolve into a continuous time model that has normally distributed outcomes. This result forms the basis for the Black-Scholes option pricing model.[8]

22-6   **BLACK-SCHOLES CALL OPTION PRICING MODEL**

By assuming that assets' continuous rates of return were normally distributed, Fischer Black and Myron Scholes were able to derive mathematical formulas for the values of put and call options.[9] The previous section's discussion of the lattice of outcomes resulting from a binomial random walk suggests the intuition they used to formulate their model. The stochastic calculus used to derive the Black-Scholes option valuation formulas is beyond the scope of this book. However, their call valuation formula is explained below.

---

[7]Many statistics textbooks explain *Pascal's rule* in conjunction with the binomial model. Pascal's rule is used to generate Pascal's triangle of Figure 22-10*a*, to count the number of *combinations* from binomial models, and for other important applications.

[8]See John C. Cox, Stephen A. Ross, and Mark Rubinstein, "Option Pricing: A Simplified Approach," *Journal of Financial Economics,* Sept. 1979, vol. 7, pp. 229–263. Also see Richard J. Rendelman, Jr., and Brit J. Barter, "Two-State Option Pricing," *Journal of Finance,* Dec. 1979, vol. 34, no. 5, pp. 1093–1110. See also P. P. Boyle, "A Lattice Framework for Option Pricing with Two State Variables," *Journal of Financial and Quantitative Analysis,* March 1988, vol. 23, pp. 1–12.

[9]F. Black and M. Scholes, "The Pricing of Options and Corporate Liabilities," *Journal of Political Economy,* May–June 1973, pp. 637–654. The Black-Scholes model was derived by assuming the optioned security's prices are log-normally distributed so that the continuously compounded one-period rates of return $r_{i,t} = \ln(p_{i,t}/p_{i,t-1})$ are normally distributed with a constant known variance.

Gary L. Gastineau and Albert Mandansky developed a competing option valuation model that does not assume stock prices are log-normally distributed. This model is described briefly in "An Index of Listed Option Premiums," *Financial Analysts Journal,* May–June 1977, pp. 3–8; see especially the Appendix. Or, see G. L. Gastineau, *The Options Manual,* 3d ed. (New York: McGraw-Hill, 1988), chap. 7.

Black-Scholes Call Valuation Formula

Equation (22-5) defines the Black-Scholes call option pricing formula.

$$Cc = pN(x) - k[e^{(-Rd)}]N(y) \qquad (22\text{-}5)$$

where x and y are defined in Equations (22-6) and (22-7).

$$x = \frac{\ln(p/k) + [R + 0.5 \text{ Var}(r)]d}{[\text{Var}(r)]^{1/2}d^{1/2}} \qquad (22\text{-}6)$$

$$y = x - [\text{Var}(r)]^{1/2}d_i^{1/2} \qquad (22\text{-}7)$$

In the Black-Scholes formula, Cc denotes the call premium; p denotes the market price of the optioned stock; k stands for the exercise; ln denotes the natural (base e) logarithm; e represents the number 2.7183; the convention $\text{Var}(r_i)$ denotes the variance of the rates of price change for the ith optioned asset, a risk measure; and R denotes the riskless rate of interest. The symbol d_i denotes the fraction of 1 year until expiration of the ith call (for example, 1 month means $d = \frac{1}{12}$). $N(x)$ represents a **cumulative normal-density function** of the argument x (see Table 22-2). $N(x)$ gives the probability that a value of less than x will occur in a normal probability distribution which has a mean of zero and a standard deviation equal to unity. Sample values of $N(x)$ are given below.

$$N(-\infty) = 0 \qquad N(0) = .5 \qquad N(+\infty) = 1.0$$

The call prices suggested by the Black-Scholes model are illustrated by the curves in Figures 22-12c and 22-13a.

Numerical Example of Pricing a Call

All that is needed to use the Black-Scholes model are (1) a table of natural (or Napierian or base e) logarithms and (2) a table of cumulative normal distribution probabilities. The cumulative normal distribution values for $N(x)$ and $N(y)$ are shown in Table 22-2. Many algebra and statistics books and hand calculators contain natural logarithms.

For a numerical example of the Black-Scholes call model, the following data are used: $p = \$60.00$, $k = \$50.00$, $d = 0.333$, $R = 0.07$, and $\text{Var}(r_i) = 0.144$. The convention $d = 0.333$ represents the fraction of 1 year spanned by the option—in this case, 121.54 days out of a 365-day year. The riskless rate (stated at an annual rate) is assumed to be 7 percent, $R = 0.07$. The riskiness of the optioned asset is measured by the variance of its returns, $\text{Var}(r_i) = 0.144$. Estimating the risk statistic is a topic discussed further below. The quantity x is calculated by substituting the numerical values into Equation (22-6) to obtain Equation (22-8).

$$x_i = \frac{\ln(60/50) + [0.07 + 0.5(0.144)](0.333)}{(0.144)^{1/2}(0.333)^{1/2}} \qquad (22\text{-}8)$$

$$= \frac{0.182 + 0.142(0.333)}{0.379(0.577)} = \frac{0.229}{0.219} = 1.046$$

Table 22-2
VALUES OF N(x) FOR GIVEN VALUES OF x FOR A CUMULATIVE NORMAL PROBABILITY DISTRIBUTION FUNCTION WITH ZERO MEAN AND UNIT VARIANCE

x	N(x)	x	N(x)	x	N(x)	x	N(x)	x	N(x)	x	N(x)
		−2.00	.0228	−1.00	.1587	.00	.5000	1.00	.8413	2.00	.9773
−2.95	.0016	−1.95	.0256	−.95	.1711	.05	.5199	1.05	.8531	2.05	.9798
−2.90	.0019	−1.90	.0287	−.90	.1841	.10	.5398	1.10	.8643	2.10	.9821
−2.85	.0022	−1.85	.0322	−.85	.1977	.15	.5596	1.15	.8749	2.15	.9842
−2.80	.0026	−1.80	.0359	−.80	.2119	.20	.5793	1.20	.8849	2.20	.9861
−2.75	.0030	−1.75	.0401	−.75	.2266	.25	.5987	1.25	.8944	2.25	.9878
−2.70	.0035	−1.70	.0446	−.70	.2420	.30	.6179	1.30	.9032	2.30	.9893
−2.65	.0040	−1.65	.0495	−.65	.2578	.35	.6368	1.35	.9115	2.35	.9906
−2.60	.0047	−1.60	.0548	−.60	.2743	.40	.6554	1.40	.9192	2.40	.9918
−2.55	.0054	−1.55	.0606	−.55	.2912	.45	.6736	1.45	.9265	2.45	.9929
−2.50	.0062	−1.50	.0668	−.50	.3085	.50	.6915	1.50	.9332	2.50	.9938
−2.45	.0071	−1.45	.0735	−.45	.3264	.55	.7088	1.55	.9394	2.55	.9946
−2.40	.0082	−1.40	.0808	−.40	.3446	.60	.7257	1.60	.9452	2.60	.9953
−2.35	.0094	−1.35	.0885	−.35	.3632	.65	.7422	1.65	.9505	2.65	.9960
−2.30	.0107	−1.30	.0968	−.30	.3821	.70	.7580	1.70	.9554	2.70	.9965
−2.25	.0122	−1.25	.1057	−.25	.4013	.75	.7734	1.75	.9599	2.75	.9970
−2.20	.0139	−1.20	.1151	−.20	.4207	.80	.7881	1.80	.9641	2.80	.9974
−2.15	.0158	−1.15	.1251	−.15	.4404	.85	.8023	1.85	.9678	2.85	.9978
−2.10	.0179	−1.10	.1357	−.10	.4602	.90	.8159	1.90	.9713	2.90	.9981
−2.05	.0202	−1.05	.1469	−.05	.4801	.95	.8289	1.95	.9744	2.95	.9984

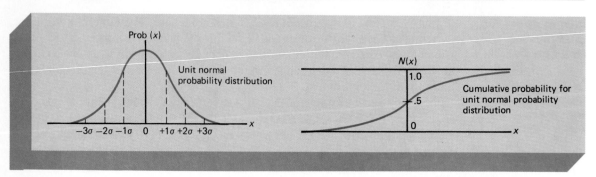

The value of y is evaluated in Equation (22-9).

$$y = x_i - \sqrt{(0.144)} \sqrt{(0.33)} = 1.046 - 0.219 = 0.827 \qquad (22\text{-}9)$$

Substituting the values from above into Equation (22-5) yields Equation (22-10).

$$Cc = \$60.00[N(1.046)] - \$50.00(\text{antiln}[-0.070(0.333)][N(0.827)]) \qquad (22\text{-}10)$$

Looking up the values of the antilog for natural logs and the cumulative normal distribution in tables and completing the calculations indicates that the call is worth \$12.29.

$$Cc = \$60.00(0.853) - \$50.00(0.977)\,(0.796)$$

$$= \$51.18 - \$38.89 = \$12.29$$

Slight differences in interpolating between the values in Table 22-2 will lead to slightly different answers. Components of the Black-Scholes option pricing model are discussed below.

Hedge Ratio

The **hedge ratio** of an option may be defined as the ratio of a dollar change in the option's premium divided by a one-dollar change in the price of the optioned asset. The hedge ratio is also called the **delta factor,** the **neutral hedge ratio,** the **elasticity,** and the **equivalence ratio.** Graphically speaking, the hedge ratio equals the slope of the dashed call price curves in Figures 22-13a and 22-14. These figures illustrate that calls and puts have positive and negative hedge ratios, respectively.

Risk-averse investors seek the hedge ratio that will totally eliminate changes in the value of their position. Mathematically, this *hedge ratio* is given by the value of the quantity $N(x)$ in the Black-Scholes call equation (22-5); it is repeated below in Equation (22-11).

$$N(x) = \frac{d(Cc)}{dp} = \text{slope of call price curve in Figure 22-13a} \qquad (22\text{-}11)$$

$$= \text{hedge ratio}$$

The hedge ratio is used in the mathematical derivation of option pricing models. It is the ratio of the value of the stock held in a long position divided by the size of the debt needed to finance that long position. [See the discussion of h in Equation (22-2).] In the Black-Scholes call pricing model the value of the stock is represented by the first term in Equation (22-5), $pN(x)$, and the second term represents the amount borrowed, $k[e(-Rd)]N(y)$.

Investors can use the hedge ratio to translate the option (either a call or a put) into a fractional equivalent of the underlying instrument. For example, the investor can create a hedged portfolio that has the fraction $(-1)N(x)$ times as many shares of the underlying security as the option is worth, so for small price changes, movements in the value of the stock position will be exactly offset by an opposite and equal movement in the value of the option. For instance, if a call option for 100 shares of ABC stock is in a long position and the hedge ratio based on the current price of ABC is $N(1.65) = 0.9505$, then 95 shares of ABC should be sold short in order to establish a **perfect hedge.**[10]

[10]The hedge ratio is discussed by Richard M. Bookstaber, *Option Pricing and Investment Strategies,* rev. ed. (Chicago, Ill.: Probus, 1987), pp. 54–58.

Conversely, someone who is short a 100-share call on ABC would be perfectly hedged with a long position of 95 ABC shares.

Unfortunately, the hedges formed using the hedge ratio are perfect only as long as the price of the optioned stock doesn't change. As soon as the stock's price changes, the value of $N(x)$ changes, the hedge has to be recomputed, and the hedged portfolio of optioned securities and the option must be correspondingly **rebalanced.**

Risk Statistics and Option Values

Figure 22-11a shows that the standard deviation of returns implied by working backward through the Black-Scholes option pricing model varies over time. The actual market premiums of options were substituted into the Black-Scholes model, and then the equation was solved for the **implied risk statistics** shown

Figure 22-11 Actual historical risk statistics differ from the risk statistics implied by options' market premiums, 1989. (*a*) Actual historical risk statistics, 1989; (*b*) implied risk statistics. (*Source: CBOT Financial Update,* July 21, 1989, p. 35, Major Market Index Options, published by the Chicago Board of Trade, Chicago, Ill.)

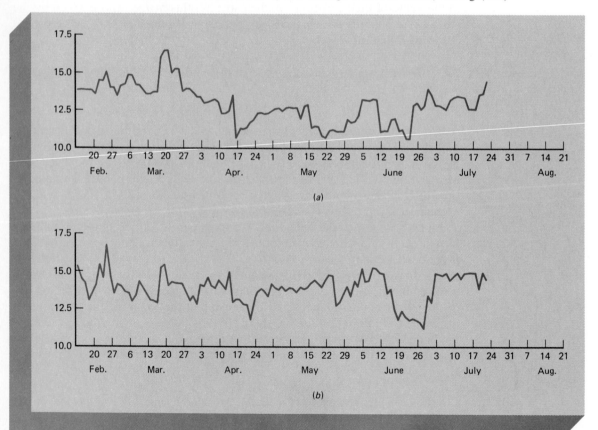

in Figure 22-11*b*.[11] Note that the implied volatility statistics differ from the actual risk statistics in Figure 22-11*a*. Fluctuations in the risk statistics cause option premiums to fluctuate even if all other factors are held constant.

As the riskiness of the underlying security increases, the values of both calls and puts on that asset increase, because they are both more likely to become profitable to exercise. Figure 22-12 illustrates the cause-and-effect relationship between risk and the premiums for calls on the ABC and XYZ corporations.

Figure 22-12*a* and *b* shows the probability distribution of stock prices for the ABC and XYZ corporations, respectively. The different widths of the two symmetric probability distributions indicate that XYZ is a riskier stock than ABC. The exercise prices of the calls on ABC and XYZ stocks have been set equal to their expected stock prices, $E(p) = k$; these two equalities imply that both calls have about a 50-50 chance of ending up either out of the money (if $p < k$) or in the money (if $p > k$).

Figure 22-12*a* and *b* indicates that the probability of exercising the call on XYZ for a large profit is greater than the probability of exercising the call on ABC for an equally large profit. The call on XYZ is worth more than the call on ABC because XYZ is riskier. The premium on XYZ's call is worth more than the premium on ABC's call even if the two stocks and the calls on them are identical in every way except risk.[12] Figure 22-12*c* illustrates how these facts are reflected in various premiums that are appropriate for calls on ABC and XYZ.[13]

Table 22-3 presents some annualized variances for optioned assets that can be used as a guideline. Figure 22-11 showed how these risk statistics can change with the passage of time.[14] One way to obtain current risk statistics is to estimate

[11]See H. Latane and R. J. Rendelman, Jr., "Standard Deviation of Stock Price Ratios Implied in Option Prices," *Journal of Finance*, May 1976, pp. 369–381.

Computer programs for the Black-Scholes model are published by Richard Bookstaber, *The Complete Investment Book* (Glenview, Ill.: Scott, Foresman, 1985). A program to compute the risk statistics implied by option prices is in the book, along with other investment analysis programs that are explained there. The book also explains that the programs in it may be purchased from the author on floppy disks (at a fraction of what it would cost to get them keypunched).

[12]For more details about how a security's volatility affects call option premiums on that security, see Ravi Jagannathan, "Call Options and the Risk of the Underlying Security," *Journal of Financial Economics*, Sept. 1984, vol. 13.

[13]The Black-Scholes model was derived using a normal distribution of continuously compounded returns. Therefore, the variance (or standard deviation) of continuously compounded rates of return should be the risk measure used with the Black-Scholes model. Although systematic (or beta or covariance) risk is relevant in analyzing individual assets with the CAPM and APT, only total risk is relevant in option models.

[14]For a discussion of estimating risk statistics, see Michael Parkinson, "The Extreme Value Method for Estimating the Variance of the Rate of Return," *Journal of Business*, Jan. 1980, vol. 53, no. 1, pp. 61–67. See also Mark B. Garman and Michael J. Klass, "On the Estimation of Security Price Volatilities from Historical Data," *Journal of Business*, Jan. 1980, vol. 53, no. 1, pp. 67–78.

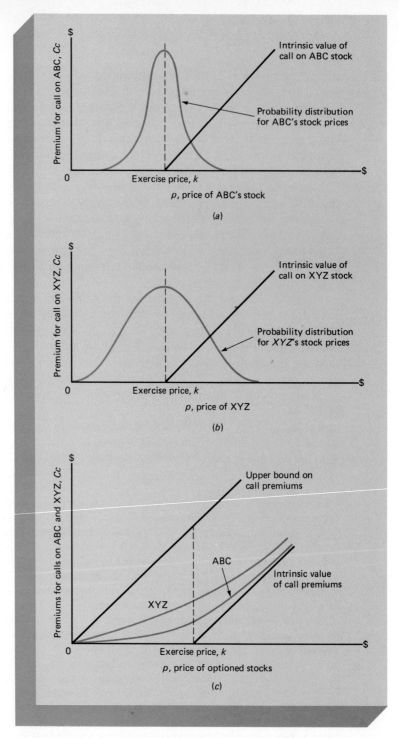

Figure 22-12 Call premiums are affected by risk. (*a*) Call model and probability distribution for ABC's stock price; (*b*) call model and probability distribution for XYZ's stock price; (*c*) determining the premiums for calls on ABC and XYZ.

Table 22-3

**HISTORICAL ESTIMATES OF ANNUALIZED
VARIANCE OF RETURN STATISTICS**

Optioned asset	Annual variances
S&P 500 index	0.18
Gold	0.25
$/yen exchange rate	0.12
30-year T-bond yield	0.18
T-bill interest rate	0.20

Source: Richard M. Bookstaber, Morgan Stanley, New York City. Also see R. M. Bookstaber, *Option Pricing and Strategies in Investing* (Reading, Mass.: Addison-Wesley, 1981). Appendix B lists the risk statistics for stocks on which options were traded in March 1980. These 1980 statistics are out-of-date, but their values are suggestive.

the variance using recent empirical returns and then to subjectively adjust the empirically estimated variance to reflect expected changes in the optioned security's risk.

22-7   **DETERMINANTS OF PUT AND CALL PREMIUMS**

As we have seen, option owners need not exercise their options in order to realize gains. Options are usually sold in the secondary market before they mature in order for the investor to take profits. To understand how to profit from buying and selling unexpired options, consider the determinants of option premiums. The same six factors determine the premiums of both calls and puts:

1. *The price of the underlying asset, p:* It takes a larger premium to induce option sellers to write an option on a high-priced security than on a low-priced security, if all other things are equal. This is because the potential dollar losses from an x percent adverse price move are larger with an option on a high-priced security than they are for a low-priced security.

2. *The length of time the option remains open:* Writers of 6-month options typically charge about 15 percent larger premiums (if all other factors are held constant) than they would to write 3-month options on the same security. The premium they charge is higher because the probability that either a put or a call will be exercised and the option

writer will lose money increases with the time the option remains open.

3. *The riskiness (or price volatility) of the underlying asset:* Advantageous price changes are what make it profitable for investors to exercise options. Buying options on securities that have volatile prices therefore tends to be more profitable than buying options on securities whose prices fluctuate very little. Since the option buyer's gain equals the writer's loss, option writers charge larger premiums to write puts and calls on riskier assets (with more volatile prices).

4. *The exercise price, k:* As the exercise price of a call is increased (decreased), while holding all other factors constant, the option's intrinsic value and premium both decline (increase) because the probability that the call will ever become profitable to exercise is thereby diminished (increased). Changing the exercise price has the reverse effect on puts.

5. The riskless interest rate R has a small positive (negative) effect on call (put) premiums.

6. Cash dividend payments cause the optioned stock to have price drop-offs. These reductions in the price of the optioned stock decrease call premiums and increase put premiums.

Call Option's Premium, Cc

Figure 22-13 illustrates how various factors determine the prices for which call options may be purchased. The dashed curves represent the prices for calls.

In the space below the horizontal stock price axis in Figure 22-13*a* some phrases popular in the option industry are annotated. The phrases refer to the value of the call and are defined as follows:

1. A call is said to be **out of the money** when the market price of the optioned security is less than the exercise price, $k > p$. A call that is out of the money usually has a small positive premium if much time remains before its maturity date, because some chance exists that the price of the optioned security might rise before the option expires.

2. A call that is **at the market** has a market price for the optioned security that is close to the call's exercise price, $k \sim p$.

3. A call that is **in the money** has a market price for its optioned securities that has risen above the call's exercise price, $p > k$.

Call Option's Premium over Intrinsic Value   In Figure 22-13*a* the vertical distance between the intrinsic value line and the dashed curve tracing out the cost of a call option (Cc) measures that **call's premium over intrinsic value,** or the **call's time value,** as it is sometimes called.

$$\text{Premium over intrinsic value of a call} = Cc - \text{Max}(0, p - k) \quad (22\text{-}12)$$

Figure 22-13*a* shows that the premium over intrinsic value of a call is greatest

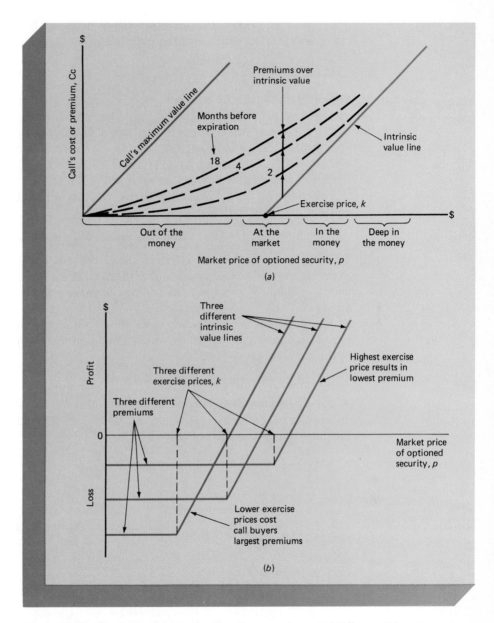

Figure 22-13 The determinants of call option premiums. (*a*) Effects of time-to-maturity; (*b*) effects of differing exercise prices.

when the market price of the optioned asset equals the exercise price of the option, $p = k$. The premium over intrinsic value of a call option: (1) increases with the length of time remaining until the call expires, (2) increases with the riskiness of the optioned security, (3) varies inversely with the absolute value of the difference between the market price of the optioned asset and the exercise price, $|p - k|$, (4) tends to increase slightly with the level of market interest rates, and (5) decreases with the payment of cash dividends by the optioned stock.

Premium for Put Options, Pp

Figure 22-14 illustrates how put prices are determined by (1) the price of the optioned security, (2) the length of time the option remains open, and (3) the option's exercise price. Put premiums are also affected by (4) the riskiness (or volatility) of the optioned security's price, (5) the level of market interest rates, and (6) the cash dividend payouts made by common stocks. The effects of these last three factors cannot be seen in Figure 22-14.

Equation (22-13) defines the **intrinsic value of a put;** this is what a put is worth if it is held until it matures.

$$\text{Intrinsic value of a put} = \text{Max}(0, k - p) \qquad (22\text{-}13)$$

The formula says that the intrinsic value of a put equals either zero or the excess of the put's exercise price over the price of the optioned security, whichever is greater. When a put has positive intrinsic value, it is said to be **in the money.**

The **premium over intrinsic value** for a put is calculated with Equation (22-14); it equals the amount by which a put's premium (Pp) exceeds that put's intrinsic value.

$$\text{Premium over intrinsic value for a put} = Pp - \text{Max}(0, k - p) \qquad (22\text{-}14)$$

A put's premium over intrinsic value can also be measured by the vertical distance between the dashed price curves and the kinked line that traces out the put's intrinsic value in Figure 22-14.

Figure 22-14 The determinants of put premiums.

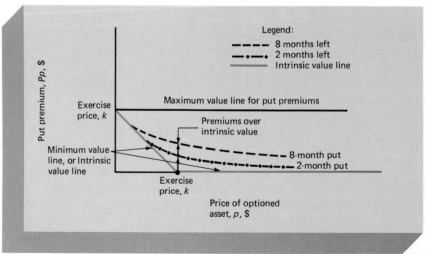

A put's premium over intrinsic value (1) increases directly with the riskiness or price volatility of the optioned asset, (2) increases with the length of time remaining until the put expires, (3) varies inversely with the absolute value of the difference between the market price of the optioned asset and the exercise price, $|p - k|$, and (4) moves inversely with the level of market interest rates. A put's premium over intrinsic value is largest at the point where the market price of the optioned asset is equal to the option's exercise price, $p = k$.

22-8   **SHORT-CUT FOR VALUING PUT OPTIONS**

Black and Scholes derived a formula for pricing European puts. No one has been able to analytically derive a formula for valuing American puts that is as accurate as the numerical approximation techniques, however.[15] Therefore, *the put-call parity formula is sometimes used to estimate the approximate value of a put after the value of a call on the same security has been determined.*[16] Table 22-4 traces the logical derivation of the put-call parity formula.

Table 22-4
DERIVATION OF THE PUT-CALL PARITY FORMULA

Consider the following portfolio: Buy a share of stock for p, sell a call on the share of stock, and buy a put on the same share of stock that has the same exercise price as the call. The value of each one of these positions depends on whether the price of the optioned stock is above or below the options' exercise price.

	Value of portfolio at options' expiration	
	$p < k$	$p > k$
Common stocks	p	p
Short (or write) a call option	0	$k - p$
Long put	$k - p$	0
Totals	k	k

(Table 22-4 continues on the next page)

[15]See M. Parkinson, "Option Pricing: The American Put," *Journal of Business,* Jan. 1977, pp. 21–36. See also M. Brennan and E. Schwartz, "The Valuation of American Put Options," *Journal of Finance,* May 1977, pp. 449–462.

[16]The parity between put and call premiums is explained by Hans R. Stoll, "The Relationship between Put and Call Option Prices," *Journal of Finance,* Dec. 1969, pp. 801–824. See also Robert A. Jarrow and Andrew Rudd, *Option Pricing* (Homewood, Ill.: Irwin, 1983), chaps. 4–6. Or see E. J. Elton and M. J. Gruber, *Modern Portfolio Theory and Investment Analysis,* 2d ed. (New York: Wiley, 1984), pp. 534–537. The Black-Scholes model values European calls and can be used to accurately value Eu-

(continues)

Table 22-4

DERIVATION OF THE PUT-CALL PARITY FORMULA (continued)

Results: The portfolio turns out to be worth k regardless of whether p exceeds k, or vice versa. Therefore, before the portfolio is purchased, it must be worth the present value of k. At that same time, the portfolio must also be worth another sum that equals the value of the share of optioned stock, plus the value of the put, less the value of the short call, or more concisely, $p + Pp - Cc$. Equating the two sums described above results in the *put-call partity formula*.

$$p + Pp - Cc = \frac{k}{(1 + R)^d} \qquad (22\text{-}15)$$

where R is the riskless rate per annum and d is the fraction of 1 year covered by the hypothetical portfolio.

The **put-call parity formula** is restated as follows:

$$\text{Premium on put, } Pp = \text{premium on call, } Cc + \frac{\text{exercise price, } k}{(1 + R)^d} - \text{stock's price, } p \qquad (22\text{-}15a)$$

The same values from the numerical example of how to apply the Black-Scholes call valuation model are employed to determine the value of a put option on the same stock: $p = \$60.00$, which is the price of the optioned stock; $k = \$50.00$, which is the exercise price; $d = 0.333$, which represents 121.54 days out of a 365-day year; $R = 0.07$, which represents 7 percent per annum; and $\text{Var}(r_i) = 0.144$. The Black-Scholes model placed a value on this 4-month call of $Cc = \$12.29$. The value of the put can be calculated by substituting the appropriate values into Equation (22-15):

$$\$12.29 + \frac{\$50}{(1.0 + 0.07)^{0.333}} - \$60 = \$12.29 + \frac{\$50}{1.0226} - \$60$$

$$= \$12.29 + \$48.89 - \$60 = \$1.18 = Pp$$

Applying the put-call parity model to the call price suggested by the Black-Scholes European call pricing model, we find that the put on the same stock is worth at least $1.18.

(continued)

ropean puts by working through the put-call parity formula. However, this procedure will yield only approximate values for American puts.

If American options are being priced, the following research can be useful. See R. Geske, "A Note on an Analytic Valuation Formula for Unprotected American Call Options on Stocks with Known Dividends," *Journal of Financial Economics,* 1979, vol. 7, pp. 375–380. See also R. Whaley, "On the Valuation of American Call Options on Stocks with Known Dividends," *Journal of Financial Economics,* 1981, vol. 9, pp. 207–211. In addition, see R. Geske, "Comments on Whaley's Note," *Journal of Financial Economics,* June 1981, vol. 9, pp. 213–215.

22-9   **THE EFFECTS OF CASH DIVIDEND PAYMENTS**

When a corporation's board of directors declares that the stockholders of a certain date are to receive a cash dividend, that designated date is called the **date of record.** Stocks start **trading ex-dividend** five business days before the date of record. Buyers of stock that is trading ex-dividend are not entitled to receive the cash dividend.

Cash dividend payments usually occur about 2 weeks after the date of record. When a stock begins trading on the ex-dividend date, its market price drops by an amount approximately equal to the cash dividend per share. This **ex-dividend price drop-off** decreases (increases) the value of any call (put) options against the stock, unless the option is "payout protected."

Payout-protected options have their contractual terms adjusted so their value is unaffected by cash dividends.[17] Some over-the-counter options partially protect the option owner from losses resulting from cash dividend payments by reducing the option's exercise price by the amount of the cash dividend per share whenever a cash dividend is paid. Most options listed on organized exchanges are not payout protected.

Since dividend payments affect option prices, they should be considered in determining when to sell or exercise an American option. In contrast, European calls can be exercised only on their maturity date, so *when* they should be exercised is a moot question.

Figures 22-13*a* and 22-15 illustrate the minimum call boundary and the Black-Scholes value curve for an American call option that has not yet expired. The option's kinked intrinsic value line establishes the *minimum value* of the call if it is exercised before its expiration or what it will be worth at expiration. At its expiration the call is said to be "dead." The dashed curves trace out the option's value if it is still "alive" (that is, not exercised). An American call is always worth at least as much or more when it is alive than when it is dead. The vertical distance between the minimum value (or intrinsic value) line and the live value curve measures the *premium over intrinsic value* or *time value* remaining in the option. Figure 22-15 is useful in illustrating some key considerations involved in deciding whether to exercise an American call before the stock starts trading ex-dividend.

If a call on an optioned stock with a pre-cash-dividend market price of p^d is exercised, the call's intrinsic value of Cc^d is given by reference to the minimum value boundary OkZ in Figure 22-15. When the optioned stock starts trading ex-dividend, its price should drop off from p^d to p^e. But the option's premium will not usually fall as much as the price of the optioned stock if the option is alive. At an ex-dividend market price for the optioned stock of p^e, the value of the live call is Cc^e. The Black-Scholes formula can be used to find

---

[17]Specialists at many stock exchanges and brokerage houses automatically reduce open orders for stock by the amount of the dividend on the ex-dividend date.

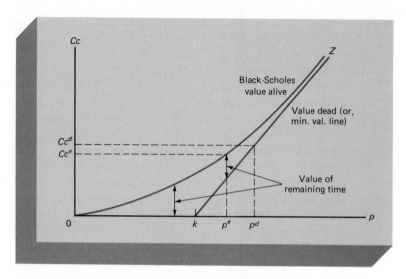

Figure 22-15 The optioned stock's ex-dividend price drop-off affects the value of a call on the stock.

the value of live calls. If the option's live value before it trades ex-dividend Cc^d is greater than its value ex-dividend Cc^e, then the call should be exercised before it trades ex-dividend in order to capture the cash dividend and thus maximize the option owner's wealth.[18] This is the particular case illustrated in Figure 22-15.

22-10   SUMMARY AND CONCLUSIONS

Puts and calls are **contingent claims** on risky underlying financial instruments. Puts and calls can be more desirable than their comparable short and long positions, respectively, because the options provide more financial leverage and limited liability. Figure 22-16 illustrates the leverage effects. *Limited lia-*

[18]Rational call premium adjustments to reflect the payment of cash dividends and other factors were analyzed in Robert C. Merton, "The Theory of Rational Option Pricing," *Bell Journal of Economics and Management Science,* Spring 1973, pp. 141–183. More recently, an exact method was suggested in Richard Roll, "An Analytic Valuation Formula for Unprotected American Call Options on Stocks with Known Dividends," *Journal of Financial Economics,* 1977, vol. 5, no. 2. A practical method that can be iterated to obtain solutions that are as precise as desired is suggested in John C. Cox, Stephen A. Ross, and Mark Rubinstein, "Options Pricing: A Simplified Approach," *Journal of Financial Economics,* Sept. 1979, vol. 7, no. 3.

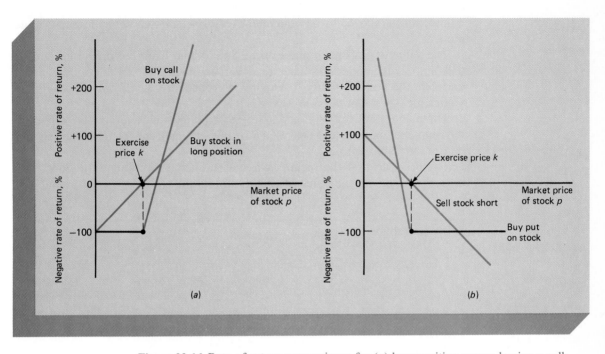

Figure 22-16 Rate-of-return comparisons for (*a*) long position versus buying a call; (*b*) short position versus buying a put.

bility refers to the fact that option buyers cannot lose more than the premiums they paid, which are a small fraction of the price of the optioned security.

Since the first organized options exchanges opened in 1973, the number of new options and the volume of option trading has surpassed all expectations. Option theory also enjoyed a major advance in 1973 when the Black-Scholes model was published. The development of options markets and option pricing models has been symbiotic.

Today the Chicago Board of Options Exchange (CBOE), American Stock Exchange (AMEX), Philadelphia Stock Exchange (PHLX), and Pacific Stock Exchange (PSE) all operate active organized options exchanges. They all clear their trades through the Options Clearing Corporation (OCC). The OCC makes the exchange-listed options liquid by guaranteeing that every option will be executed even if its writer defaults.

Option pricing theory can be divided into two parts. Binomial option pricing models have been developed to deal with a broad class of valuation problems that include options, stocks, bonds, and other risky financial claims. The Black-Scholes call pricing model was the first closed-form option pricing model that provided good estimates. The credibility of both models is enhanced by the fact that in the limiting case of an infinite number of tiny periods, the binomial model can be shown to be equivalent to the Black-Scholes continuous time model.

The value of European puts can be determined from the price of a similar call on the same underlying asset by using the Black-Scholes call pricing model and then the put-call parity formula. This procedure yields only approximate values for American puts, however.

The riskiness of the optioned asset has an important and positive effect on the premiums of puts and calls. As a result, only current risk statistics should be used to value options.

The price dropoff that occurs when a stock starts trading ex-dividend decreases (increases) the value of calls (puts) on the stock.

Essay Questions

22-1   What are the main factors determining put and call premiums?

22-2   Compare and contrast writing a call naked and selling a common stock short.

22-3   Does the Chicago Board of Options Exchange ever trade call options that have the same expiration date but different exercise prices? Why?

22-4   Is there any kind of basic relation between the prices of puts and calls on the same security that might be expected to exist permanently? Explain.

22-5   Compare and contrast the intrinsic value with the time value for (a) a call option and (b) a put option.

22-6   If the XYZ Corporation was confronted with tough new foreign competition that reduced its profit margins and sales, what effect do you expect this would have on the premiums charged for (a) calls and (b) puts on XYZ's stock?

22-7   Consider the following statement: "The OCC is a clearing house that performs administrative functions expeditiously but contributes nothing to the value of the options it handles." Is this statement true, false, or uncertain? Explain.

Problems

22-8   Determine the value of (a) a call and (b) a put on a common stock with the following characteristics:

Standard deviation of returns $= 0.16$

Exercise price $= \$40$

Risk-free rate $= 0.10$

Current price $= \$42$

Time to maturity $= 6$ months

22-9 Use the Black-Scholes call option pricing formula to find the value of (a) call options and (b) put options on the following optioned stocks.

Stock	ABC	XYZ
Time to maturity	4 months	88 days
Standard deviation	0.30	0.40
Exercise price	$40	$60
Price of optioned stock	$40	$68
Interest rate	12%	6%

22-10 George Evans is currently bearish on the common stock of the Franklin Corporation. Franklin's current price is $75 and a 3-month put with an exercise price of $75 is selling for $2. Ignore commissions and taxes. (a) If Evans purchases the put and the price of the stock falls to $71 after 3 months, what kind of return will he make? (b) What kind of return would he make if the price rose to $80?

22-11 As an investor you are bullish on the stock of the XYZ Company. Consequently, you purchase ten 6-month XYZ calls with an exercise price of $50 for $2600. The current price of XYZ stock is $50. How much would the price of XYZ stock need to increase in 6 months for you to make a 10 percent annual rate of return on your investment? Ignore commission charges and taxes.

22-12 As an owner of 500 shares of QEB Company stock, you are considering writing call options on your shares which would have the following terms: strike price = $50, premium = $3, maturity = 3 months. If you did write the options, what return would you make on your investment over the 3 months if the price of the stock rose from its current price of $45 to $50?

22-13 Jean Samples recently purchased a 3-month European call on the stock of the Miller Corporation for $5. This call has an exercise price of $80, and the current price of its stock is $83. (a) For Samples to break even, what price must Miller's stock sell for at the call's maturity? (b) Determine the price at which Miller's stock must sell when the call matures in order for Samples to earn a 20 percent *annual* rate of return on *money invested in call premiums.*

22-14 Using the information given in Problem 22-13, determine the value of the call if a $1.00 cash dividend is paid 1 month after the stock is purchased and the price of the stock stays at $83. Assume the riskiness of Miller's stock is Var(r) = 0.16, and the riskless rate is R = 0.10.

22-15 The current price of Alison Engine Corporation common stock is $50. A call on Alison's stock has a $3 premium and an exercise price of $50. If the call has 3 months until maturity, what standard deviation of returns on the firm's stock is consistent with the above values? Assume the risk-free rate is 9.0 percent.

22-16 The stock of the BBB Company is currently selling for $65. A 3-month call option on the stock with an exercise price of $60 has a premium of $6.20. The standard deviation of returns on BBB stock has been estimated to be 0.18. Currently, the 3-month T-bill rate is 10 percent. (a) Is the option overvalued, undervalued, or priced correctly? (b) If you have confidence in your analysis, how would you react to your findings in (a)?

22-17 The common stock of the ZBZ Corporation has a current price of $40 and a standard deviation of returns of 0.40. Assume a risk-free rate of 8 percent. (*a*) Using the Black-Scholes model, determine the price of a 4-month call option that has a strike price of $35. (*b*) Determine the value of a put on ZBZ's stock that also has a striking price of $35.

22-18 After a quarterly cash dividend of $1.00 per share is paid the market price of an optioned stock drops off $1.00 when it starts trading ex-dividend. The T-bill rate is 10 percent, the hedge ratio (or delta) is $N(x) = .9$, and the standard deviation of the optioned stock is .12. How will the premium for a call option on this stock react to the cash dividend price dropoff? *Hint: Beware of sophistry.*
   a. *Cc* will decline $1.00.
   b. *Cc* will increase $1.00.
   c. *Cc* will decline $0.90.
   d. *Cc* will increase $0.90.

Selected References

Black, F., and M. Scholes, "The Pricing of Options and Corporate Liabilities," *Journal of Political Economy,* June 1973, pp. 637–654.

   The seminal mathematical paper that developed a static equilibrium closed-form pricing model for options.

Bookstaber, Richard M., *Option Pricing and Strategies in Investing* (Reading, Mass.: Addison-Wesley, 1981).

   A well-written discussion using mathematics which explains call options and various option strategies.

Bookstaber, Richard, *The Complete Investment Book* (Glenview, Ill.: Scott, Foresman, 1985).

   Chapters 21 through 27 discuss various aspects of option analysis. Most chapters list a computer program written in BASIC language that is ready to run. Chapter 22 has a binomial option pricing program. Chapter 23 has a program that uses the Black-Scholes model to value options under different assumptions. Chapter 23 has a program to value options on futures. Chapter 23 has a program to estimate risk statistics from historical market prices. Chapter 26 contains a program to derive risk statistics implied by the price of an optioned security. Chapter 27 contains a program to analyze the impact of various selected variables on different option investing strategies.

Gastineau, Gary L., *The Options Manual,* 3d ed. (New York: McGraw-Hill, 1988).

   The first six chapters contain easy-to-read descriptions of options and option markets. Chapters 7 through 11 discuss various call pricing models, options on bonds and commodities, and other topics. The mathematics is moderate.

Hull, John, *Options, Futures, and Other Derivative Securities* (Englewood Cliffs, N.J.: Prentice-Hall, 1989).

   This finance textbook contains some information about futures and a comprehensive coverage of options. Graphs are used to supplement the stochastic calculus in the book.

Jarrow, Robert A., and Andrew Rudd, *Option Pricing* (Homewood, Ill.: Irwin, 1983).

A comprehensive and rigorous mathematical review of the option pricing theory.

McMillan, Lawrence G., *Options as a Strategic Investment,* 2d ed. (New York: New York Institute of Finance, 1986).

This nonmathematical book presents a comprehensive discussion about which option position is appropriate for each investment circumstance and how to manage the position as the option(s) decay with time.

Strong, Robert A., *Speculative Assets* (Chicago, Ill.: Longman Financial Services, 1989).

Chapters 1, 2, 3, and 4 of this finance textbook discuss options in an easy-to-read manner. Only a slight amount of elementary algebra is used, and there are plenty of graphical illustrations.

Chapter 23

Options Applications

While they are interesting investments in their own right, puts and calls are also used to alter existing investments or construct more complex investments. Option theory is also a tool that financial analysts can use to obtain valuable insights. This chapter extends option theory to include examples of these and other applications.

　　　　WRITING COVERED CALLS

Sometimes investors write options against securities that they own. When they do so, they are said to have written **covered options.** For example, an investor might own 100 shares of a stock and also write a call against the shares. If the price of this optioned stock rises and the call is exercised, the covered call writer can simply deliver the shares that were already owned and thus avoid any loss. Assuming the covered call writer's interest expense and commissions incurred in covering the position are less than the premiums received for writing the call, both the call writer and the buyer who exercised the call may be able to gain from the price rise. If the call writer is covered with securities purchased on margin, a handsome rate of return on invested capital may be earned. But, if the price of the optioned security falls, then the call buyer pays the premium for nothing and the covered call writer loses on the long position in the optioned stock. However, the call writer's security price losses are at least partially offset by the call premium income.[1] Figure 23-1 compares writing covered calls with writing uncovered calls.

---

[1]For an extended discussion of covered call writing, see Lawrence G. McMillan, ''Covered Call Writing,'' in *Options as a Strategic Investment,* 2d ed. (New York: New York Institute of Finance, 1986), chap. 2.

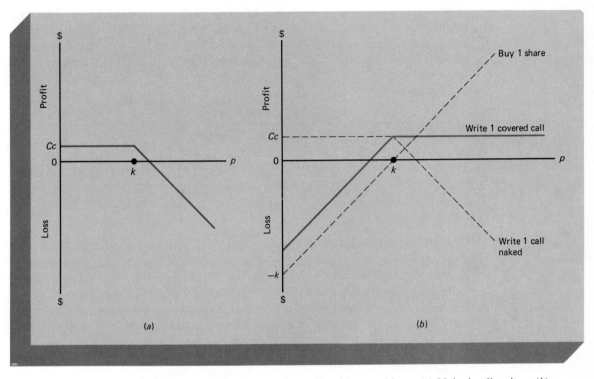

Figure 23-1 Graphs contrasting call writing positions. (*a*) Naked call writer; (*b*) covered call writer.

An option writer who writes a call against some security without owning that security is said to be **writing naked, writing against cash,** or **writing uncovered.** Figure 23-1*a* shows the profit position for a naked call writer. The naked call buyer's profits equal the naked call writer's losses. A comparison of the call writer's exposure to loss in Figure 23-1*a* and *b* shows that writing calls naked is risky if the price of the optioned security rises and writing calls covered is risky if the price of the optioned security falls.

Federal law requires that uncovered option writers put up 15 percent initial margin.[2] In contrast, covered call writers who have the optioned securities at their broker's office are not required to put up additional margin when they write a covered call. Covered call writers must have some money invested in their covering positions, however—their leverage is not infinite.

Covered call writers gain from their call writing only if the price of their optioned stock remains almost unchanged so that the option is not exercised before it expires. If the price of the stock advances significantly, the covered

[2]For a discussion of the margin requirements on options, see Gary L. Gastineau, *The Options Manual,* 3d ed. (New York: McGraw-Hill, 1988), appendix A, pp. 319–324.

call writer would have been better off not having written the option because the appreciating securities are called away at the option's low exercise price. In contrast, if the price of the optioned stock declines, the covered call writer suffers a loss in market value which is at least partially offset by the premium income.[3]

23-2   **SYNTHETIC POSITIONS THAT CAN BE CREATED FROM OPTIONS**

As part of a conscious plan or through a series of transactions that result in a surprising outcome, option traders can attain investment positions that differ from their initial situation.

Synthetic Long Position

An options trader who simultaneously writes (or, synonymously, sells or shorts) a put and buys (or takes a long position in) a call on the same underlying security at about the same exercise prices creates a position that is like owning a long position in the underlying stock. Stated differently, buying a call and selling a put on the same security creates a **synthetic long position** in the optioned security that is similar to an ordinary buy-and-hold position. Consider what happens when Figures 22-1*a* and 22-2*b* are combined at about the same exercise price and you will see that the resulting synthetic long position has the same profit and loss potentials as the long position in Figure 23-2.

The synthetic long position can be more desirable than a straightforward long position because the synthetic position requires less margin investment and thus furnishes more financial leverage.[4] Undesirable features include the margin money required to write the put. Furthermore, the owner of a synthetic long position does not collect cash dividends or coupon interest from the underlying securities. The final undesirable feature of the synthetic long position is that when the options expire, additional option premiums must be paid to recreate the synthetic position.

Synthetic Short Position

A position that is equivalent to the short position can be created by selling (or, synonymously, shorting or writing) a call and simultaneously buying (or, equiv-

---

[3]For a discussion of how the manager of an options portfolio can reshape the probability distribution of returns attainable from the various options, see Richard M. Bookstaber and Roger G. Clarke, *Option Strategies for Institutional Investment Management* (Reading, Mass.: Addison-Wesley, 1983). See figures 5-13, 5-14, and 5-15 on writing covered calls, for instance.

[4]The premium paid for the call that is purchased will normally exceed the premium income from selling the put so that, ignoring margin requirements, there is a negative net cashflow to establish a synthetic long position. For a numerical example, see L. G. McMillan, *Options as a Strategic Investment*, 2d ed. (New York: New York Institute of Finance, 1986), pp. 308–310.

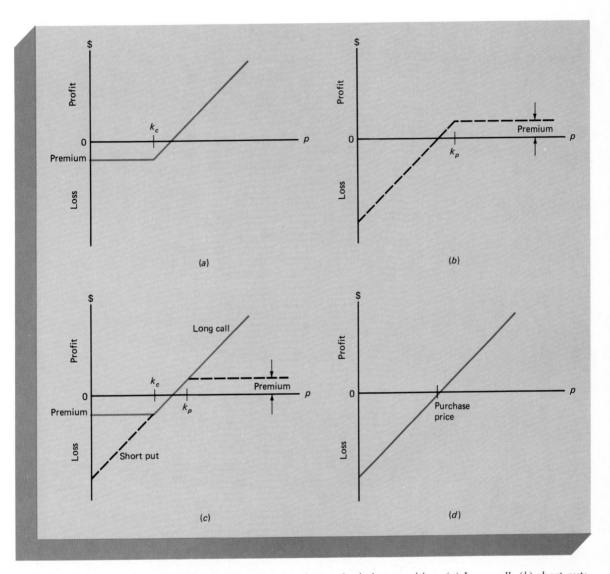

Figure 23-2 The components of a synthetic long position. (*a*) Long call; (*b*) short put; (*c*) synthetic long [see L. G. McMillan, *Options as a Strategic Investment*, 2d ed. (New York: New York Institute of Finance, 1986), pp. 308–310 for more details]; (*d*) ordinary long position in the stock.

alently, getting long) a put with similar exercise prices on the same underlying stock. This can be seen by combining Figures 22-1*b* and 22-2*a*. The resulting **synthetic short position** is illustrated in Figure 23-3.

A synthetic short position is often more desirable than a traditional short position for three reasons. First, the option position is superior because the call that was sold should bring in more income from its premium than is spent

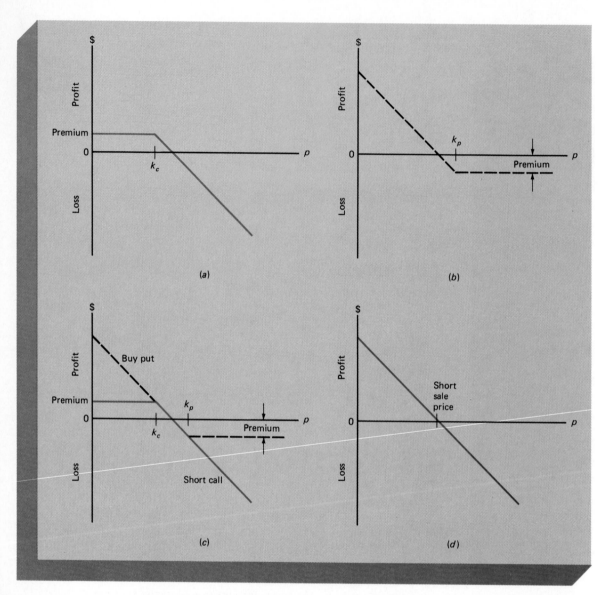

Figure 23-3 The components of a synthetic short position. (*a*) Short call; (*b*) buy put; (*c*) synthetic short position [see L. G. McMillan, *Options as a Strategic Investment*, 2d ed. (New York: New York Institute of Finance, 1986), pp. 310–311 for more details]; (*d*) normal short position in the stock.

to pay for the premium on the long put.[5] Second, the synthetic short sale offers more leverage. Short sales require an initial margin of about 50 percent. The synthetic short position involves a smaller initial investment, as shown below.

Deposit: 15 percent of the optioned stock's price

   plus: the call premium received

   minus: the put premium paid

   Total: An amount that is less than 50 percent of the short position

The third benefit is that the synthetic short seller does not have to pay cash dividends on the optioned stock as the short seller would on the borrowed stock. The disadvantage inherent in any option position is that options expire and more money must be spent for option premiums to reestablish the position.

Other Synthetic Positions

Numerous investment positions can be created synthetically by combining options. Some of these synthetic positions may be more desirable than the position that could have been obtained directly. However, the synthetic position may entail some undesirable aspects. Therefore, the option trader should be aware of the investment implications of synthetic positions.

23-3   STRADDLES

Straddles are created by simultaneously purchasing an equal number of puts and calls that have the same exercise price, with the same times until expiration, all on the same underlying security. The straddle buyer pays a total premium that equals the sum of the premiums for puts and calls that are purchased separately. Straddle buyers are willing to pay the large combined premium because they believe that the price of the optioned security will fluctuate. A price speculator who buys a **long straddle position** gains if the price of the optioned asset makes either a large upward price move, a large downward move, or some combination of large upward and downward moves. Straddles are a useful strategy with highly volatile securities and the stocks of takeover candidates.

The **short straddle position** is opposite but symmetric to the long straddle

---

[5]The premium paid for the put that is purchased will normally be less than the premium income from selling the call; therefore, ignoring margin requirements, there is a positive net cashflow to establish a synthetic short position. For a numerical example, see L. G. McMillan, *Options as a Strategic Investment*, 2d ed. (New York: New York Institute of Finance, 1986), pp. 310–311.

position. Straddle writers are sufficiently confident that the optioned security's price will not vary significantly before the options mature that, with the premium as an inducement, they are willing to write a contract effectively guaranteeing price invariance for the optioned security.

The profit positions of the buyer and the writer of a straddle are depicted in Figure 23-4. Since a straddle is equivalent to a put and call at the same

Figure 23-4 Position graphs for a straddle. (*a*) Straddle buyer; (*b*) straddle writer.

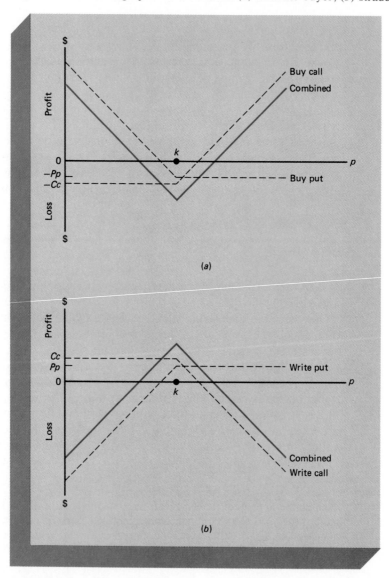

exercise price, the position graphs in Figure 23-4 are merely combinations of Figures 22-1 and 22-2 for the case when the exercise prices of the put and the call are equal.

There may be two writers for a straddle—a put writer and a call writer. This could occur if the party desiring the long straddle buys a put and a call on the same security at different times, for example.

23-4   **SPREADS**

Any investment composed of both long options and similar short options on the same underlying security is a **spread.**[6] The long and short options may have either differing lengths of time until they expire or different exercise prices. Note that a given spread uses either *all* puts or *all* calls—instead of puts and calls together, like a straddle. The way the option prices are listed in the newspaper quotations influences the names given to option spreads.

Some Spreading Vocabulary

As Figure 22-3 shows, newspapers list all options with the same expiration dates in vertical columns. As a result, spreads involving options that have different exercise prices but the same expiration date are called **vertical spreads.** **Horizontal spreads** include those combinations of options having different expiration dates but the same exercise price, because different options that all have the same exercise prices are listed in horizontal rows in the newspapers. Horizontal spreads are also called **time spreads** and **calendar spreads. Diagonal spreads** include mixtures of vertical and horizontal spreads and may also include options in which both the expiration dates and the exercise prices differ. Regardless of whether they were bought or written, all option spreads fit into one of the three categories—vertical spreads, horizontal spreads, or diagonal spreads.

A different way to categorize spreads is based on whether the total price of the spread generates net cash inflows or outflows for the spreader. Spreads which generate premium income that exceeds their related costs are called **credit spreads. Debit spreads** cost the option strategist a net cash outflow to initiate. Various kinds of spreading positions are defined below.

Strangles

A **strangle** is like a straddle with exercise prices that are ''points away'' from the market. Figure 23-5 represents the profit position of the buyer and the writer of a strangle; note the similarity to the straddle illustrated in Figure 23-4. The

---

[6]Spreads may also be created by using options, futures contracts, and/or options on futures contracts. Futures contracts are used to create intercommodity-spreads, intracommodity-spreads, intermarket-spreads, cross-spreads, and other types of spreads. Futures contracts are the topic of Chapter 24.

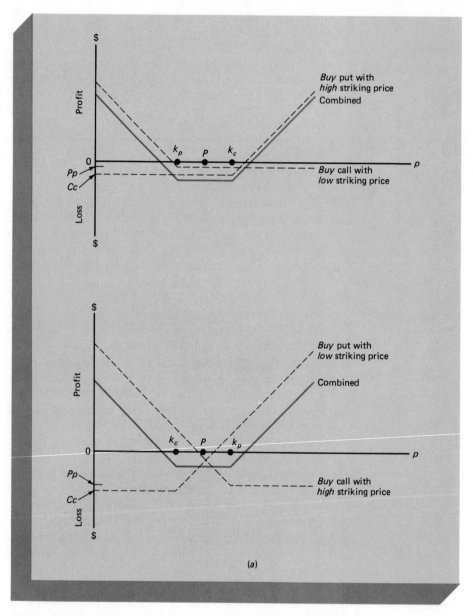

Figure 23-5 Position graphs for a strangle. (*a*) Two long strangles (above); (*b*) two short strangles (on next page).

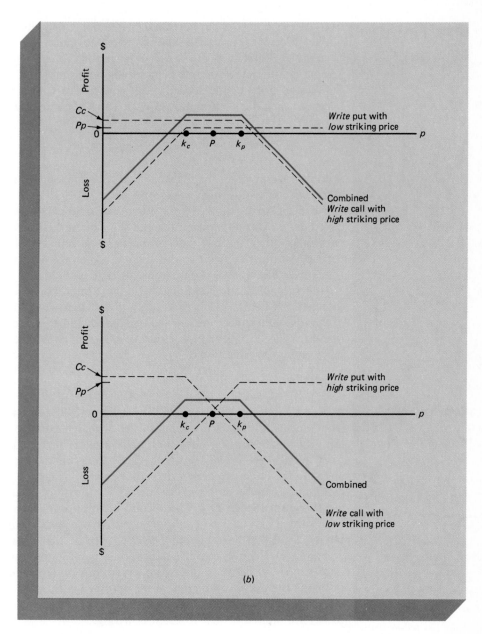

Figure 23-5 *(continued)*

exercise price for the put portion of the strangle is point k_p in Figure 23-5. The market price of the optioned security when the option was written is represented by point P. Point k_c is the exercise price for the call portion of the strangle. The premium on the strangle is less than the premium on the straddle because the market price of the security that is optioned with a strangle must rise or fall more than if it were optioned with a straddle in order for the option buyer to profit.

Bull Spread

A **bull spread** involves buying a call at a certain exercise price while also selling a similar call with a higher exercise price. *Bull spreads* are vertical spreads because the two calls have the same expiration date. Bull spreads are also called *debit transactions* because the sell side of the transaction generates less cash inflow than the buy side of the position requires; as a result, there is a net cash outflow or debit to the client's brokerage account. Figure 23-6 illustrates two different position graphs for bull spreads.

Bull spreads are for optimists who have only moderate confidence in their forecast. As Figure 23-6 shows, only upward (downward) moves in the price of the optioned stock between the two associated exercise prices are profitable (incur losses). Profits and losses are nonexistent above the highest (k_2) exercise price and below the lowest (k_1) exercise price.

Bear Spreads

A **bear spread** can be established by selling a call at some exercise price and simultaneously buying a similar call at a higher exercise price. Bear spreads are *vertical spreads* because both calls usually have the same exercise date. They are also *net credit spreads* because the premium income from selling the call with the lower exercise price will never be as large as the cost of the long call that has the higher exercise price. Two position graphs for bear spreads are shown in Figure 23-7. The second illustration in Figure 23-7 shows that a bear spread can also be established by writing a call and, at the same time, buying a put that has a higher exercise price on the same security.

Figure 23-7 shows that the bear spread is profitable (unprofitable) for price declines (rises) between the two exercise prices. However, no further profits or losses can occur if the price of the optioned security moves below the lower (k_1) exercise price. Cautiously bearish investors like bear spreads because their losses are limited if their forecast is wrong.[7]

---

[7]For an extended discussion of bear spreads, see Lawrence G. McMillan, "Bear Spreads Using Call Options," in *Options as a Strategic Investment,* 2d ed. (New York: New York Institute of Finance, 1986), chap. 8. See pp. 315–318 for a discussion of bear spreads created from put options.

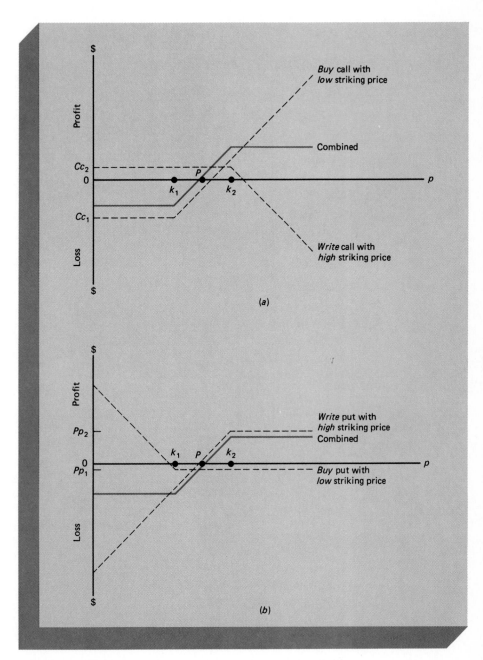

Figure 23-6 Two position graphs for bull spreads. (*a*) With 2 calls; (*b*) with 2 puts.

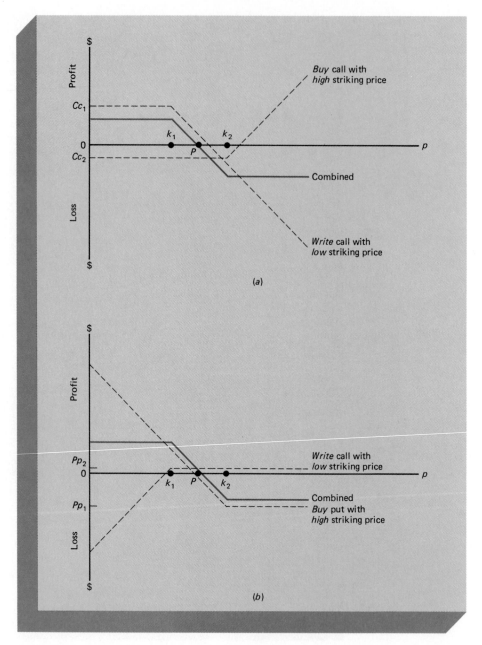

Figure 23-7 Two position graphs for a bear spread. (*a*) With 2 calls; (*b*) with a put and a call.

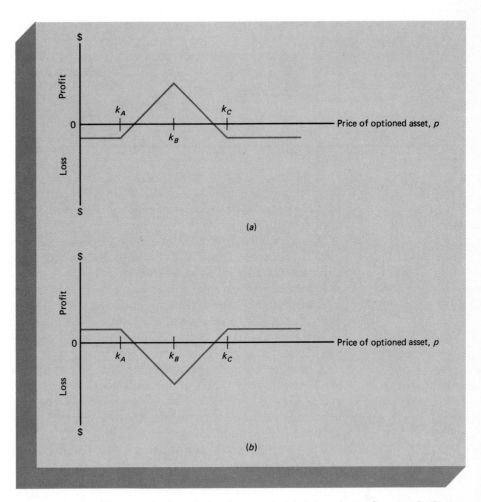

Figure 23-8 Position graphs for a butterfly spread. (*a*) A long butterfly spread; (*b*) a short butterfly spread.

Butterfly Spreads   The **butterfly spread** is a combination of a bull spread and a bear spread on the same underlying security. Figure 23-8 depicts the profit profiles for the long and short butterfly spreads. The long butterfly spread will be profitable if the price of the optioned asset does not fluctuate either up or down. The worst possible outcome for a long butterfly spread occurs if the price moves both up and down. The short butterfly spread is profitable if the price of the optioned asset does fluctuate either up or down, or both. Butterfly spreads can be created in different ways, from various combinations of puts and calls. It is left as an exercise for the reader to determine the construction of long and short butterfly spreads.[8]

Combinations include any position created by buying and selling puts and calls which is not a straddle. The spreads presented in this section are all various kinds of combinations.[9]

23-5   **WARRANTS**

Warrants are like call options. A warrant is an option to buy a fixed quantity of some specific financial instrument at a predetermined price during some prespecified time period.

Warrants differ from calls in certain respects. Stock purchase warrants are the most common type of warrant; let us discuss them for concreteness.[10] **Stock purchase warrants** are written by the corporation that issued the optioned stock rather than by an external option writer. Warrants are given as attachments to the corporation's issue of bonds or preferred stock. They are viewed as "sweeteners," attached to an issue of fixed income securities in order to increase the proceeds of the issue. Warrants may expire at a certain date or they may be perpetual.

A warrant's exercise price k indicates how much the warrant's owner must pay to purchase N shares of common stock. The *minimum value of a warrant* equals $\text{Max}[0, (p - k)]N$. The market price of a warrant that is marketable is indicated by the dashed curves in Figure 22-13a; the call pricing model is directly applicable to warrants.[11]

The terms governing a warrant are specified in detail in the *warrant agreement*. Most warrants are like long-term American call options; they may be exercised anytime within their life of, say, 5 to 10 years. A few warrants have

---

[8]See Lawrence G. McMillan, *Options as a Strategic Investment,* 2d ed. (New York: New York Institute of Finance, 1986), chaps. 10 and 23, or other options books.

[9]Combinations and spreads are not presented here because they have any particular investment aura. Rather, they are presented because (1) they are in sufficiently common use to justify learning their names and (2) sometimes an initial investment position that becomes disappointing can be converted into a more desirable position if the investor is aware of how options can be used to transform positions.

[10]Oil warrants, security market index warrants, and gold warrants exist. And, some bond issues have bond warrants included. These more esoteric types of warrants are not discussed further. However, all warrants resemble calls.

[11]See D. Leabo and R. L. Rogalski, "Warrant Price Movements and the Efficient Market Model," *Journal of Finance,* March 1975. See also A. H. Y. Chen, "A Model of Warrant Pricing in a Dynamic Market," *Journal of Finance,* Dec. 1970. See also D. Emanuel, "Warrant Valuation and Exercise Strategy," *Journal of Financial Economics,* Aug. 1983, vol. 12, pp. 211–236.

perpetual lives, and a few, like European calls, may be exercised only at specific expiration dates.

Most warrants are protected against stock splits and stock dividends, but most are not protected against cash dividend payouts. Some warrants are non-detachable. *Detachable warrants* may be separated from the securities to which they were attached as sweeteners and traded separately.

23-6	**CONVERTIBLE SECURITIES**

Under certain conducive conditions, **convertible bonds** or **convertible preferred stock** may be converted into a stipulated number of shares of common stock in the corporation that issued the convertibles, as explained in Section 2-8.

Latent Warrants   Convertible fixed-income securities can be analyzed as if they were a package of two securities, both issued by the same corporation. The first security in the package is a *nonconvertible fixed-income security* that is noncallable—it can be either a bond or a preferred stock. The second security in the package is a *nonmarketable warrant* containing the restriction that only the associated fixed-income security can be used to pay the exercise price. These nonmarketable warrants are sometimes called **latent warrants.** Since warrants have nonnegative values, convertible securities will always be worth at least as much as nonconvertible securities from the same issuer. Viewed as a two-part package, a convertible security offers (1) periodic fixed income payments until such time as the issuer defaults, or the convertible securities are called by the issuer, or the securities are converted, (2) price fluctuations that result from changes in market interest rates, (3) price fluctuations that result from changes in the price of the common stock into which the convertible securities may be converted (these are actually changes in the value of the latent warrant which is viewed as being "attached" to the convertibles), (4) some downside protection provided by a "floor" price or "safety net" under the investment's price, equal to the present value of the nonconvertible security's fixed income payments, and (5) cashflows from the fixed income payments, which would normally exceed the cash dividends from a common stock investment of equal size. Calculating a value for such a complicated package is not simple. And, to make matters worse, most convertible issues are callable at the issuer's discretion.[12]

[12]This discussion draws on Peter Ritchken, *Options: Theory, Strategy, and Applications* (Glenview, Ill.: Scott, Foresman, 1987), pp. 351–354. Also see M. Harris and A. Raviv, "A Sequential Signaling Model for Convertible Debt Policy," *Journal of Finance*, 1985, vol. 40, pp. 1263–1281. Furthermore, see W. H. Mikkelson, "Convertible Calls and Security Returns," *Journal of Financial Economics*, 1981, vol. 9, pp. 237–264. Also

(continues)

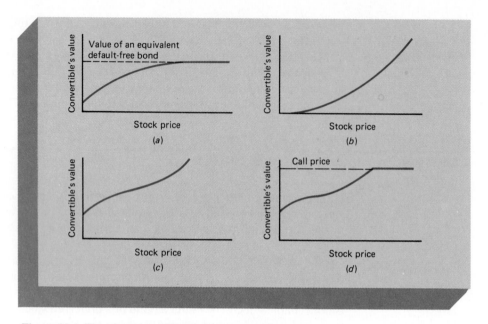

Figure 23-9 The elements of value in a convertible security: (*a*) present value of fixed income; (*b*) value of latent warrants; (*c*) value of a noncallable convertible; (*d*) value of a callable convertible.

Illustrated Analysis Figure 23-9*a* illustrates how the *present value of a non-callable, nonconvertible fixed-income security* tends to increase directly with the value of the issuing corporation's common stock price. This relationship is derived from the fact that as the corporation prospers and the value of its common stock rises, the probability that other securities issued by the same corporation might fall into default decreases. However, an upper limit or "ceiling" on the fixed-income security's price is established by the fact that it can never be worth more than a default-free bond with similar income and maturity provisions.

Figure 23-9*b* shows that the value of the *latent warrant* that is implicit in every convertible security package rises in value directly with the value of the common stock into which it might be converted (since warrants are like the

(continued)

see Jonathan E. Ingersoll, "A Contingent-Claims Valuation of Convertible Securities," *Journal of Financial Economics,* 1977, vol. 4, pp. 289–321. In addition, see Jonathan E. Ingersoll, "An Examination of Corporate Call Policies on Convertible Securities," *Journal of Finance,* 1977, vol. 32, pp. 463–478. See also M. J. Brennan and E. S. Schwartz, "Convertible Bonds: Valuation and Optimal Strategies for Call and Conversion," *Journal of Finance,* Dec. 1977, vol. XXXII, no. 5, pp. 1699–1716.

call options illustrated in Figure 22-13*a*). Adding together the values indicated in Figure 23-9*a* and *b* results in the series of values illustrated in Figure 23-9*c*. Figure 23-9*c* indicates how the value of a noncallable convertible security varies directly with the price of the underlying common stock. However, things are usually more complicated than Figure 23-9*c* reveals.

Most convertible bonds are callable by the issuer at some prespecified call price. This call price imposes a ''ceiling'' that limits the convertible security's price rise. To see how this ''ceiling'' works, consider a hypothetical corporation that enjoys steadily rising earnings. Prosperity will push up the prices of the corporation's common stock, preferred stock, and bonds. The corporation will then call any outstanding convertibles it may have in order to force their owners to convert them into common stock. This is done because corporations do not want an *overhanging issue* of convertibles that limits their ability to issue new securities. So, when the market price of convertible bonds rises relative to their call price, the issuing corporation usually calls the issue. Figure 23-9*d* summarizes all of this—it is merely Figure 23-9*c* with a constraint equal to the price that the market thinks will cause the bonds to be called inserted as a ''ceiling'' on the price of the callable convertible security.

23-7   CALLABLE AND PUTTABLE BONDS

As explained in Chapter 2, many bond issues are callable by the issuing corporation. **Callable bonds** may be conceptually decomposed into two parts: (1) an ordinary bond that is noncallable and (2) a call option that is outstanding against the bond. Investors that buy callable bonds pay a lower price for them than they would have to pay for a noncallable bond. The price reduction on callable bonds equals the premium for a call option that is *embedded* in the bond. Conceptually, the callable bond investor buys a bond and simultaneously sells back a call option on that bond to the issuer of the bond.[13]

Figure 23-10 contains a solid curve that is the **price-yield curve** for a bond that illustrates how the call option affects the price of a callable bond in two ways. First, the call price imposes a ceiling on the callable bond's price. Second,

[13]Call provisions embedded in bonds have been analyzed by several researchers. See P. P. Boyle, ''A Lattice Framework for Option Pricing with Two State Variables,'' *Journal of Financial and Quantitative Analysis,* March 1988, vol. 23, pp. 1–12. Also see T. S. Y. Ho and S. Lee, ''Term Structure Movements and Pricing Interest Rate Contingent Claims,'' *Journal of Finance,* March 1988, vol. 16, no. 5, pp. 1011–1029. And see S. M. Schaefer and E. Schwartz, ''Time-Dependent Variance and the Pricing of Options,'' *Journal of Finance,* Dec. 1987, vol. 17, no. 5, pp. 1113–1128. See also Amir Barnea, Robert A. Haugen, and Lemma W. Senbet, ''A Rationale for Debt Maturity and Call Provisions in the Agency Theoretic Framework,'' *Journal of Finance,* Dec. 1980, vol. 35, pp. 1223–1224.

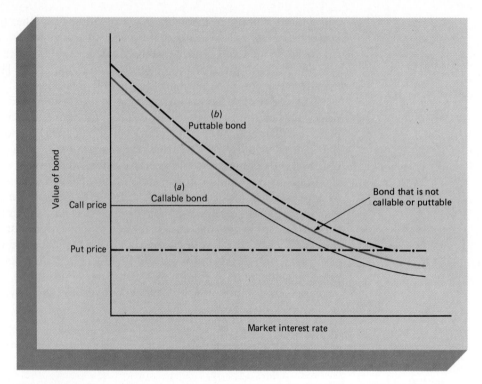

Figure 23-10 The market price of a bond can be constrained by (*a*) the issuer's call option; (*b*) the investor's put option.

the callable bond's price is lower at all levels of market interest rates than that of an identical bond that is not callable. This is because the bond might be called in by the issuer, thus reducing its value.

Some bonds are *puttable*. **Put bonds** are sold with an embedded put option that allows the bond investor to put the bond back to its issuer if its price gets too low. In effect, the put option places a "floor" beneath the market price of the put bond, as shown in Figure 23-10. At all levels of market interest rates, put bonds are worth more than similar bonds that are not puttable because the put option adds positive value to the investor's position.

23-8   OTHER KINDS OF OPTIONS

In addition to puts and calls, we have seen that **embedded options** are contained within warrants, convertible securities, callable securities, and puttable securities. The menu of options also includes puts and calls on foreign exchange, gold, silver, futures contracts, debt securities, economic indexes, and other economic quantities. Some of the more popular options are introduced below.

Executive Stock Options

Some corporations offer **executive stock option** plans as part of their compensation package. These plans typically grant managers call options to purchase the employer's stock at favorable terms. The options usually do not expire as long as the executive remains with the firm. Executive options are supposed to provide an added incentive for managers to work to raise the price of the employing corporation's stock. Most executive stock options cannot be traded.[14]

Options on Economic Indexes

Put and call options can be obtained on various economic indexes. Options can be purchased on stock market indexes like the S&P 500 Composite Stocks Index, S&P 100 Stocks Index, NYSE Index, Major Market Index, Value Line Index, Nikkei Japanese Index, and others.[15] Baskets of common stocks are not delivered; the economic index options are **cash settlement options.** The Black-Scholes model can be used to obtain good estimates of the premiums for index options.

Market index options are sometimes used to earn arbitrage profits from slight pricing disparities between some stock market index and the options on it. More often these arbitragers use futures contracts. Therefore, *index arbitrage* is discussed in Section 24-7 in terms of futures contracts.

Options on market indexes are also useful for hedging systematic market risks, taking a position by paying only the premium instead of investing as much money as a direct position would require (financial leverage), moving into and out of large positions without disrupting the market (market liquidity), and betting on the market's direction. Consider an example of the latter activity that involves the S&P 100 stocks market index—the most heavily traded option in the United States.

---

[14]Executive stock options have been proposed as a way to deal with agency problems within the firm. See R. A. Haugen and L. W. Senbet, "Resolving the Agency Problems of External Capital through Options," *Journal of Finance,* June 1981, pp. 569–581. Furthermore, see D. W. Diamond and R. Verrecchia, "Optimal Managerial Contracts and Equilibrium Security Prices," *Journal of Finance,* May 1982, vol. 37, pp. 225–288. And see Bengt Holstrom, "Moral Hazard in Teams," *Bell Journal of Economics,* Autumn 1982, vol. 12, pp. 324–340. In addition, see Steven Shavell, "Risk Sharing and Incentives in the Principal and Agent Relationship," *Bell Journal of Economics,* Spring 1979, vol. 10, pp. 55–73. And, see Eugene F. Fama and Michael C. Jensen, "Separation of Ownership and Control," *Journal of Law and Economics,* June 1983, vol. 26.

[15]See Frank J. Fabozzi and Gregory M. Kipnis, *The Handbook of Stock Index Futures and Options* (Homewood, Ill.: Dow Jones–Irwin, 1989). See also Donald T. Mesler, *Stock Index Options* (Chicago, Ill.: Probus, 1985).

Nathan Gorbacheb was bearish about the U.S. stock markets. So Nathan called his broker and ordered a put option on the S&P 100 stocks index (ticker symbol: OEX) that expired in July and had an exercise price of 300. The S&P 100 index had a value of 310 at the time of Nathan's purchase. The value of the OEX option is defined to be $100 times the S&P 100 index, which means its market value was 310 times $100, or $31,000. Mr. Gorbacheb made a $3000 initial margin deposit and also paid a put premium of $2.50 × $100, or $250 plus commissions for his out of the money put. Ten days later, when the OEX index was at 295, Nathan could either exercise his put for a cash settlement or sell it. He sold his OEX put for $1300. Nathan made a gross gain of $1300 − $250, or $1050 in 10 days. Nathan's option broker sent him a check for ($1300 gross gain + $300 margin refund, or) $1600. Commission costs and income taxes will have to be deducted to determine Gorbacheb's net gain.

In addition to the stock market indexes, options are also traded on other economic indexes. An option on the Consumer Price Index, for example, is available for those who want to hedge purchasing-power risks.

Interest Rate Options

Options on U.S. Treasury bills, T-notes, T-bonds, Eurodollar deposits, mortgage-backed securities, and other interest rate sensitive instruments are available. They are not cash settlement options; the underlying instruments are delivered.[16]

Interest rate options can be valued with the Black-Scholes option pricing model. However, the Black-Scholes model does not work as well with debt securities as it does with equities for two reasons. The first problem with the Black-Scholes model is that it assumes that the riskiness (or price volatility) of the optioned security is constant throughout the option's life. This assumption is inappropriate for bonds because their price volatility tends to decrease as the bond's maturity date draws nearer. A second problem is that the Black-Scholes model assumes that the riskless interest rate stays constant. Since bond prices and interest rates always move inversely, this second assumption contradicts the positive variance that the Black-Scholes model presumes the bond to have. In spite of these problems, the Black-Scholes model is still useful in valuing interest rate options, unless the debt security is very near maturity.[17]

[16]For more details about interest rate options see John Hull, *Options, Futures, and Other Derivative Securities* (Englewood Cliffs, N.J.: Prentice-Hall, 1989), chap. 10. In addition, interest rate futures contracts are the topic of Sections 24-5 and 24-6 of this book.

[17]For a model in which a bond's price volatility is related to its duration, see S. M. Schaefer and E. S. Schwartz, "Time-Dependent Variance and the Pricing of Bonds," *Journal of Finance,* Dec. 1987, vol. 42, pp. 1113–1128.

Foreign Exchange Options   The Philadelphia Exchange (PHLX), London Stock Exchange (LSE), London International Financial Futures Exchange (LIFFE), and the CBOE trade options on the foreign currencies listed below.

1. Australian dollar
2. British pound
3. Canadian dollar
4. West German mark
5. Japanese yen
6. French franc
7. Swiss franc
8. European Currency Unit (ECU)

The actual currencies are tendered for delivery with foreign exchange options. Since foreign exchange rates fluctuate similarly to stock prices, the Black-Scholes model can be readily adapted to value foreign exchange options.[18]

Options on Futures   Futures contracts on commodities are defined in Chapter 24. Complex financial instruments called **commodity options,** or **options on futures** or **futures options,** are available to place the option strategist two levels away from the physical commodity on which they wish to speculate. Options on futures contracts are the topic of the appendix to Chapter 24.

23-9   **PORTFOLIO INSURANCE**

Portfolio insurance is an investment strategy designed to keep the invested portfolio from losing value in a downturn while maintaining the portfolio's ability to benefit from a market upturn. Most portfolio insurers employ various kinds of hedges to protect a portfolio's value. Before we consider these more sophisticated forms of portfolio insurance, however, let us review a very simple approach to portfolio insurance.

---

[18]For a discussion of foreign exchange options, see John Hull, *Options, Futures, and Other Derivative Securities* (Englewood Cliffs, N.J.: Prentice-Hall, 1989), sec. 6.3. Also see Peter Ritchken, *Options: Theory, Strategy, and Applications* (Glenview, Ill.: Scott, Foresman, 1987), chap. 15.

Stop-Loss Orders: A Simple Form of Portfolio Insurance

The stop-loss order provides a simple but imperfect form of portfolio insurance. Stop-loss orders were designed to guarantee that stipulated marketable securities would never fall below the value their owner specifies in the stop-loss order. For example, an investor's holdings of a common stock could be insured by placing a stop-loss order with the broker stating the price at which the shares should be sold. If the market price of the shares falls to the level specified in the stop-loss order, the broker should immediately liquidate the shares without consulting the client. Stop-loss orders permit the portfolio to appreciate and earn cash dividend income if the position does not get stopped-out in a market downturn. However, the problem with using stop-loss orders is that it is a "path-dependent strategy."

Stop-loss orders result in a **path-dependent strategy** because if the value of the insured portfolio temporarily falls below the price set in the stop-loss order, the portfolio will be liquidated and will earn no more returns until it is reinvested. Selecting the moment when it is advantageous to buy back into the market is a timing question that is beyond the realm of portfolio insurance. Reinvesting at the wrong time can cause the insurance-seeking investor to be "whipsawed." An investor gets **whipsawed** when the security prices move disadvantageously, causing the investor to buy high and sell low—an outcome that is clearly undesirable. After all, if someone knows how to unerringly "buy low and sell high," they would not need portfolio insurance. Another problem with using stop-loss orders is that they may go unexercised just at the time when they are needed the most (such as October 1987). Market makers occasionally suspend all stop-loss orders to correct a temporary imbalance in the order flow reaching the trading floor.

Buying a Protective Put for Insurance

A more dependable form of portfolio insurance is a securities position made up of (1) an underlying portfolio of securities that is to be insured and (2) the "insurance," which is designed to protect the insured portfolio from suffering losses during some specific period. Consider an example of portfolio insurance that guarantees there will be no chance that the insured portfolio will experience any losses from price fluctuations during the life of the insurance program.

Protective Puts   Let us call some diversified portfolio of stocks that is *indexed* to the S&P 500 the *insured portfolio*. Suppose that the portfolio manager of our S&P 500–indexed portfolio purchased put options on the S&P 500 index that had 1 year until expiration and that also had an exercise price exactly equal to the cost of the indexed portfolio. These puts on the S&P 500 comprise the *insurance* needed to guarantee that the portfolio of stocks can suffer no losses from price fluctuations before they expire. The combination of (1) the insured portfolio of stocks and (2) the insurance provided by the **protective put options** on the S&P 500 index comprise a perfectly insured aggregate position. This is a highly desirable portfolio insurance plan. If the market declines in value, the losses on the insured S&P 500 portfolio will be exactly offset by the gains on the insurance provided by the *protective put options* on the S&P 500. Figure 23-11c illustrates the components of this partially hedged position. Figure 23-11 shows that the hedge is partial because it allows the overall position to profit if the market rises; only the losses from adverse market fluctuations are hedged away.

Note that the insured portfolio illustrated in Figure 23-11a resembles a call option buyer's position. Portfolio insurance added a *protective put* to the indexed portfolio's long position and converted the combined position into a **synthetic call option position.**

Table 23-1 shows the dollar value of the overall insured portfolio position if a $100 investment in the S&P 500 indexed portfolio is insured by the initial expenditure of $3.33 for the premium to buy a protective put option on the S&P 500 with an exercise price of $100. Since the $3.33 for the put premium is deducted when the portfolio is originated, only $100 − $3.33, or $96.67, actually gets invested in the S&P 500 indexed portfolio. As a result, if the S&P index is at 125, for instance, the insured portfolio's **upside capture** is 0.9667 times 125, or $120.84 (instead of the entire $125). If the S&P index drops below 100 to a value of $100 − z$, the protective put option will yield a cash settlement of z dollars to ensure that the portfolio has a *guaranteed minimum value* of $100 (even after the cost of the put premium is deducted).

Results from Buying Insurance   There are several noteworthy characteristics of the insured position illustrated in Figure 23-11 and Table 23-1. (1) Once the insurance program is established, it need never be substantially restructured. The insured portfolio will need to be *rebalanced* if its market value increases or decreases during the insurance period (by buying another put with an exercise price equal to the S&P index's new value) to completely foreclose the possibility of any losses from price fluctuations. But, rebalancing is simple; a clerk can periodically rebalance the portfolio's insurance. (2) The results of the insurance plan are independent of the path of the market's price fluctuations. (3) The insured portfolio will never suffer losses from adverse price fluctuations (if puts with exercise prices that equal the market value of the insured portfolio are always used). (4) Nothing limits or inhibits the insured portfolio from appreciating in value and collecting cash dividends to increase its value. (5) The insured portfolio earns a predictable proportion of the rate of return earned on the underlying portfolio. A good portfolio insurance plan should possess all of these qualities.

A Better Alternative Is Needed   Alternative forms of portfolio insurance must be considered because the attractive example of portfolio insurance outlined above is too idealistic. The portfolio insurance plan above cannot actually be attained for several reasons. (1) The protective put options on the relevant market index that have the exercise price desired may not exist. Index options or combinations of individual options that perfectly mimic a particular underlying portfolio may not be listed at the organized option exchanges. Perfect

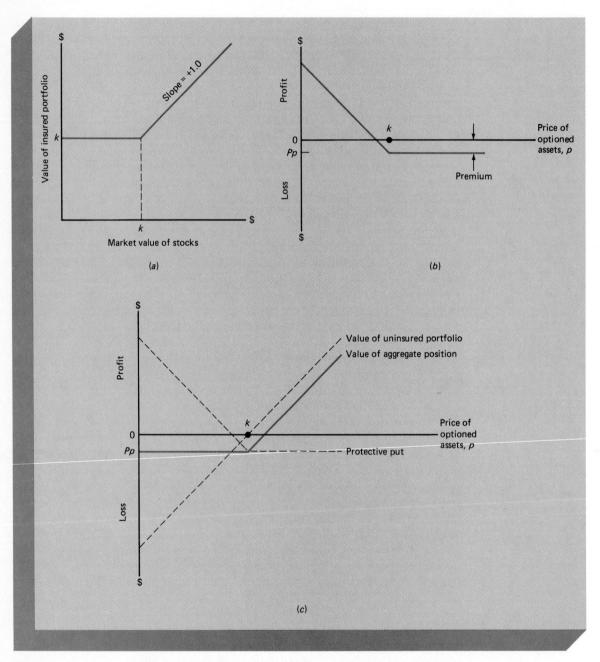

Figure 23-11 Gain-loss graphs for (*a*) an insured portfolio that is indexed to the S&P 500; (*b*) the protective puts on the S&P 500, and (*c*) components of the insured aggregate position.

Table 23-1

**POSSIBLE OUTCOMES FROM PORTFOLIO INSURANCE
PROGRAM USING S&P 500 INDEX AND PROTECTIVE
PUTS WITH EXERCISE PRICE OF $100**

Value of S&P 500–indexed stock portfolio with cash dividends reinvested	Corresponding value of the insured portfolio
$ 75	$100
80	100
85	100
90	100
95	100
100	100
105	$101.50 = .9667 \times 105$
110	$106.34 = .9667 \times 110$
115	$111.17 = .9667 \times 115$
120	$116 \quad = .9667 \times 120$
125	$120.84 = .9667 \times 125$
130	$125.67 = .9667 \times 130$

Source: Mark Rubinstein, "Alternative Paths to Portfolio Insurance," *Financial Analysts Journal,* July–Aug. 1985, p. 43, table 1.

arrangements like those hypothesized in the S&P 500 example are easier to imagine than to find. (2) Usually only short-term options (namely, those with 2 to 3 months until their expiration) are traded in sufficiently liquid markets to make them useful for hedging a large (multimillion-dollar) insured portfolio. (3) The transactions costs associated with some rebalancing plans can be substantial. Still other problems exist and will be discussed below.

Creating a Synthetic Protective Put

When it is impossible to buy a protective put at an option exchange, *a tailor-made protective put can be created synthetically.*[19] Let us consider this approach in depth.

Possible States of Nature   Assume an investor wants to invest $100 in a portfolio of common stocks and obtain portfolio insurance to protect the investment

[19]This section draws on Mark Rubinstein and Hayne Leland, "Replicating Options with Positions in Stock and Cash," *Financial Analysts Journal,* July–Aug. 1981, vol. 37, no. 4, pp. 63–72. Also see Mark Rubinstein, "Alternative Paths to Portfolio Insurance," *Financial Analysts Journal,* July–Aug. 1985, vol. 41, no. 4, pp. 42–52. See also Robert Ferguson, "How to Beat the S&P 500 (without Losing Sleep)," *Financial Analysts Journal,* March–April 1986, vol. 42, no. 2, pp. 37–46.

from a market downturn. This initial investment situation is designated state I in Figure 23-12. Furthermore, assume the investor believes the market value of the portfolio will go either up $20 (denoted u) or down $20 (represented by d) during each of the next two periods, as illustrated in Figure 23-12a. If the portfolio's value goes up $20 in the first period, that event is labeled state u. If the portfolio's value goes up $20 in the first period and then down $20 in the

Figure 23-12 The assumptions underlying a synthetic put on a $100 portfolio. ($a$) Hypothesized market values; (b) asset allocations needed to create a synthetic protective put.

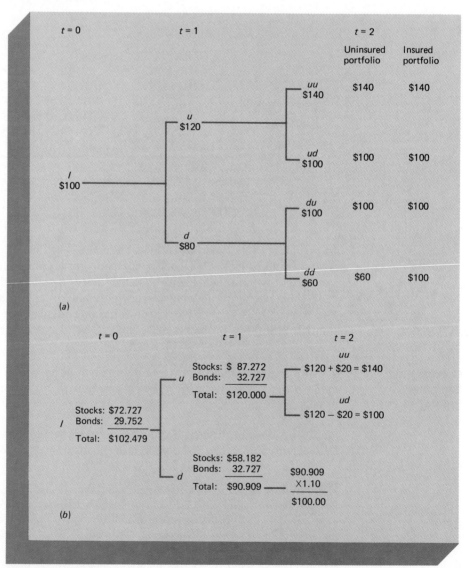

second period, that path leads to state *ud*. Note that state *ud* and state *du* both wind up at the value of $100 after two periods of operation without portfolio insurance. The worst possible outcome in Figure 23-12*a*, state *dd*, is achieved after the portfolio's value goes down in both the first and second periods to reach a terminal value of $60, because it has no portfolio insurance to protect it.

Results With and Without Insurance The two columns of values at the right in Figure 23-12*a* show the market value of the investor's terminal position if the portfolio operates two periods uninsured and two periods insured. Assume the investor wants to be sure that the portfolio's value never falls below $100. In addition, the investor does not want to give up the possibility of attaining the terminal value of $140 if state *uu* should occur. Portfolio insurance can provide the desired results. But, what if the investor cannot buy a protective put to insure the portfolio because it is uncorrelated with any listed put options? The investor can nevertheless create a **synthetic put** by supplementing the portfolio of stocks (denoted *S*) with an investment in risk-free bonds (denoted *B*).

Evaluating the Alternatives Figure 23-12*b* outlines the creation of a synthetic put to insure the portfolio. Assume the investor can borrow at a riskless rate of interest of 10 percent, $R = 0.10$. Begin by considering the four terminal states of nature that are possible—states *uu*, *ud*, *du*, and *dd*. The two most desirable terminal states of nature will be considered first—they are illustrated by the top branches of Figure 23-12*a*. If the investor wants to arrive at state *uu* or state *ud* or a synthetically contrived position that is financially equivalent to state *uu* or *ud*, Equation (23-1) suggests how to achieve that goal.

$$1.2S + 1.1B = \$120 \qquad (23\text{-}1)$$

Equation (23-1) says that in state I if the investor wants to create a position worth $120 at the end of the first period, the investor should (1) invest *S* dollars in a portfolio of stocks that we assume will grow to 1.2 times its initial value or (2) invest *B* dollars in a bond that will grow to $1 + R = 1.1$ times its initial value, or (3) invest in some combination of these two alternatives. After attaining a position worth $120 at the end of the first period, the investor can invest that $120 in common stocks and let nature take its course to state *uu* or state *ud*, either of which the investor considers acceptable.

Next, let us consider the two least desirable outcomes shown in Figure 23-12*a*—states *du* and *dd*. State *dd* is unacceptable because it is worth less than $100. The investor can avoid state *dd* by having $90.909 to invest at the end of the first period. If the investor has $90.909 to invest in a riskless bond that yields $R = 10$ percent per period, it will grow to reach a terminal value of $100 at the end of the second period. Equation (23-2) suggests how to start at state I and reach state *d* with $90.909 to invest in the final period.

$$0.8S + 1.1B = \$90.909 \qquad (23\text{-}2)$$

Equation (23-2) says that in order to create a position worth at least $100 at the end of the second period, the investor can begin by choosing from the following alternatives at state I: (1) Invest S dollars in a portfolio of stocks that we assumed will decline to 0.8 times its initial value, (2) invest B dollars in a bond that will grow to $1 + R = 1.1$ times its initial value, or (3) invest in some weighted average of the two preceding alternatives. After attaining a position worth $90.909 to invest at $R = 10$ percent at the start of period 2, the investor's terminal goal of having at least $100 at the end of period 2 will be guaranteed.

Simultaneous Equation Solution   Equations (23-1) and (23-2) are two linear equations in two unknowns which may be solved simultaneously to find the values of S and B. The mathematical solution is that the investor should begin at state I by investing $S = \$72.727$ in the common stock portfolio and $B = \$29.752$ in riskless bonds. The total cost of this strategy is $72.727 + $29.752, or $102.479. This total may be interpreted to mean the investor is paying $102.479 - $100, or $2.479, more than the uninsured portfolio would cost to attain the desired portfolio insurance. Stated differently, the investor has created a *synthetic put option* that cost a premium of $2.479. This insurance guarantees that the portfolio never arrives at state *dd*. The investor could have achieved the same position by purchasing a $100 portfolio of common stocks and (if one were available) buying a protective put on the portfolio for a premium of $2.479.

Strategy Dynamics   Creating portfolio insurance is not an aggressive investment strategy, like endeavoring to buy undervalued securities or trading actively. However, it is not a totally passive strategy either; it requires that certain investments be bought and sold if various states of nature occur.

In the example illustrated in Figure 23-12, if state u occurs, for instance, Figure 23-12*b* shows that the stock portfolio will be worth $1.2 \times \$72.727$, or $87.272. The bonds will be worth 29.752×1.1, or $32.727, and the total value of the position will have attained an intermediate value of $87.272 + $32.727, or $120, at state u. At that time the $32.727 worth of bonds must be sold, and the proceeds used to make an additional investment in stock so the portfolio is completely invested in stock during the second period.

If state d occurs, Figure 23-12*b* shows that the stock will fall in value to 72.727×0.8, or $58.1816, and the bonds will grow to be worth 29.752×1.1, or $32.727, so the position's total value is $90.909 at the end of the first period. If the investor is to avoid state *dd*, the $58.1816 worth of stock must be liquidated at state d and the proceeds used to increase the bond investment to $90.909. This bond value will then grow to a terminal value of 90.909×1.1, or $100; thus, the unacceptable outcome of having the portfolio's terminal value fall below $100 has been averted.

The example in Figure 23-12 is simple. A more realistic model could be created by decomposing the two-period model into many smaller periods that together span the same time interval with more price changes occurring in smaller increments. The results would be more intermediate steps and more investment decisions to be made, but the dynamic rebalancing strategy would be the same. In essence, dynamic rebalancing of portfolio insurance dictates that:

1. When stock prices fall, sell some stocks and buy more bonds.
2. When stock prices rise, sell some bonds and buy more stock. A computer can be programmed to issue the buy and sell orders needed to execute these mechanical trading rules as the states of nature occur. Thus, portfolio insurance can result in what is called **program trading,** because a computer program generates the trading orders.[20]

Comparing Portfolio Insurance Alternatives   Compare the results of investing $100 in the insured portfolio that is shown in Figure 23-12*a* with the results for the portfolio shown in Table 23-1. The portfolio insured with the purchased put experienced almost exactly the same outcomes as the portfolio insured with the synthetic put. The minor differences between the two approaches to insuring the portfolios result from the fact that the two puts have different premiums. The synthetic put provides portfolio insurance that is similar to what could be obtained with a genuine protective put.

Selecting the Best Portfolio Insurance Strategy

If we wanted to spend the time, we could devise alternative portfolio insurance strategies.[21] Then we could evaluate the alternatives via computer simulation (or some other tool) and choose the best one. Unfortunately, there are so many variations of the portfolio insurance plans discussed above that it is impossible to evaluate them all. However, the examples above provide an adequate introduction to what is achievable with portfolio insurance.

To select the most desirable form of portfolio insurance, the following factors should be considered: (1) What is realistically feasible? For example, put options on the S&P 500 with the desired exercise price and in the denominations needed may not exist. (2) What sort of rebalancing procedure is optimal to implement the portfolio insurance? Stated differently, which form of rebalancing discipline is effective but not too costly?[22]

[20]There are various forms of program trading. Sometimes newspapers discuss the kind of program trading that grows out of "stock index arbitrage." Stock index arbitrage is discussed in Section 24-7.

[21]Another dynamic strategy could be used to create portfolio insurance that compares favorably with the examples outlined in Figures 23-11 and 23-12. Instead of combining the stock portfolio with a protective put, we could create an insured portfolio by combining the stock portfolio with a short position in index futures, which are examined in Chapter 24.

[22]Transaction costs are discussed by Hayne E. Leland, "Option Pricing and Replication with Transactions Costs," *Journal of Finance,* Dec. 1985, vol. 40, no. 5, pp. 1283–1301.

For classroom cases and additional readings dealing with protective puts and portfolio
(continues)

Three categories of rebalancing disciplines have been suggested: (1) timed strategies—rebalancing once each month is an example of a timed strategy, (2) market move disciplines—such as rebalancing every time the market moves a certain percent in either direction, (3) lag strategies—for example, wait until the portfolio is at least *y* percent suboptimal and then rebalance partially toward the optimal rebalancing value but never revise all the way to the optimal level. This lagged adjustments strategy results in continual revisions in the correct direction. But, the revisions never fully attain the optimal and thus reduce the revision costs. Such partial revisions diminish the chance that rebalancing causes the insured portfolio to be whipsawed.[23]

The biggest users of portfolio insurance—pension funds—have become disillusioned with it. Since the October 1987 international stock market crash, the bad publicity given by the press to programmed trading and portfolio insurance caused many pension funds to abandon it. Some users were also discouraged because portfolio insurance cost more to implement and maintain than they had anticipated when they began using it in the mid-1980s.

23-10   **VALUING COMMON STOCK AS A CALL OPTION**

One of the more ingenious applications for the call option model is to use it to value the debt and equity of a leveraged company. Bankruptcy law provides some basic framework for this application of option theory.

According to U.S. law, the stockholders of a bankrupt corporation are entitled to whatever assets the corporation has left after all debts incurred by the corporation are paid. If the liabilities of a bankrupt corporation exceed the value of the firm's assets, the creditors get to keep all the assets and the stockholders get nothing. This *legal framework conforms to an option model in which the corporation's creditors own the company and sell a call option on its assets to the common stockholders.* The value of the debt that must be repaid is equivalent to the exercise price of this call option. If the stockholders

---

(continued)
insurance see K. V. Smith, *Case Problems and Readings: A Supplement for Investments and Portfolio Management* (New York: McGraw-Hill, 1990); in particular, see case problems 15 and 24 and readings 12 and 18. Alternatively, see M. A. Berry and S. D. Young, *Managing Investments: A Case Approach* (Hinsdale, Illinois: Dryden Press, 1990), especially case 26 and technical note 8.
[23]See E. S. Etzioni, "Rebalance Disciplines for Portfolio Insurance," *Journal of Portfolio Management,* Fall 1986, pp. 59–62. Also see C. B. Garcia and F. J. Gould, "An Empirical Study of Portfolio Insurance," *Financial Analysts Journal,* July–Aug. 1987, vol. 43, no. 4, pp. 44–54. In addition, see Robert Ferguson, "A Comparison of the Mean-Variance and Long-Term Return Characteristics of Three Investment Strategies," *Financial Analysts Journal,* July–Aug. 1987, vol. 43, no. 4, pp. 55–66.

take the firm's assets and use them to pay off all the corporation's liabilities, then they can call in the firm's remaining assets. If all the debts cannot be repaid when they come due, the common stockholders' call option expires worthless and the stockholders forfeit all future claims on the corporation. Within this framework, bankruptcy can be viewed as a decision by the stockholders not to pay the money needed to exercise their call on the corporate assets.

There are inherent conflicts of interest between those who own a company and those who loan the company money. One case of such divergent economic motivations can be demonstrated when the protective provisions in a bond issue's indenture contract are analyzed in terms of option theory.

Bond investors typically benefit from a provision stipulated in the bond issue's indenture requiring that coupon interest payments be paid to them at scheduled dates. If a scheduled coupon payment is missed, the bond owners can sue the corporation in bankruptcy court and force the stockholders to pay the firm's debts and thereby exercise their option to call in the company's assets ahead of time—that is, before the principal payment comes due. If the stockholders cannot make a scheduled coupon payment, essentially, the bond-holders can take over the corporation. Thus, provisions for coupon payments may be interpreted as evidence that the stockholders have a call option on the corporation which is not a European option. This paragraph outlined one of the inherent conflicts of interest between a corporation's owners and its creditors; other similar conflicts emerge in the remainder of this section.

An example of how to use option theory to value the debt and equity of a company is provided below.

A Hypothetical Corporate Example

Consider a corporation that has two classes of debt. The corporation's plant and equipment was financed with an issue of discount bonds which has a principal value of D_1 dollars; the corporation's total assets were pledged as *collateral* for this issue of zero coupon bonds. In addition, the corporation has unsecured debts owed to suppliers with a total value of D_2 dollars. The suppliers include public utilities and firms that sell raw materials; the law calls these uncollateralized lenders **general creditors.** Assume the debts all have the same maturity date and that protective provisions in the indenture prohibit the corporation from paying any cash dividends until the debt is all paid off.[24]

The owners of the mortgage bonds have the most *senior claim* on the assets of the corporation. Stated differently, the law subordinates the claims of the general creditors to those of the collateralized bond investors. The common stockholders have the most *junior claim* on the corporate assets if the firm goes

[24]The prohibition against cash dividend payments before all debts are paid grows out of another conflict of interest between the firm's owners and its creditors. This prohibition prevents stockholders from draining the assets out of the corporation via cash dividend payments for themselves if they anticipate that the corporation might go bankrupt.

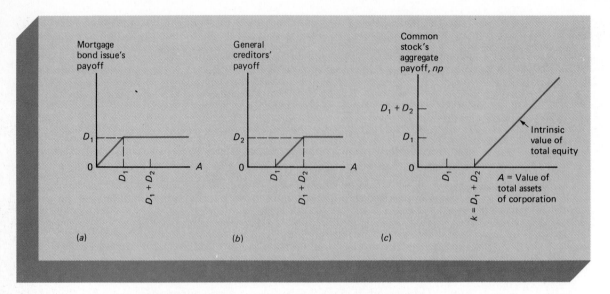

Figure 23-13 Using option theory to estimate the intrinsic value of different types of claims against a hypothetical corporation. (*a*) Mortgage bond investors are like call writers who are likely to receive their premium of D_1; (*b*) general creditors are like call writers whose premium of D_2 is less likely to be paid; (*c*) equity owners are like someone who bought a call with an exercise price of $D_1 + D_2$.

bankrupt. Figure 23-13 shows how, when the options expire, *the intrinsic values of these claims on the corporation depend on the market value of the corporation's total assets, denoted A.*

Compare the situation of the covered call writer of Figure 23-1*b* with the solution shown in Figure 23-13. Figure 23-13*a* illustrates how the mortgage bond owners are like covered call writers; they have a position that is equivalent to holding the company's assets in a long position and simultaneously writing a call with an exercise price that equals the debt of D_1, which must be paid at maturity. Figure 23-13*b* shows that the general creditors' position is the sum of the following contingent items:

1. Holding the corporate assets with a market value of A dollars in a long position, plus,
2. Being liable for a collateralized debt of D_1 against the company's assets (thus, the company's assets have a net asset value of $A - D_1$, which is a limited liability in the event that $A < D_1$), plus,
3. Simultaneously writing a call option with an exercise price equal to the total debt that must be paid at maturity, $D_1 + D_2$.

The total value of all outstanding stock is illustrated in Figure 23-13*c*. Because common stockholders have limited liability, their total equity is worth zero until the market value of the corporation's total assets exceeds the corporation's total debts, $A > D_1 + D_2$. The corporation is presumed to have n shares of common stock selling at a price of p dollars per share. When the debts come due (or, equivalently, when the stockholders' options expire), the total value of the three classes of claims against the corporation's total assets of A dollars will be divided up as shown in Equation (23-3).

$$A = D_1 + D_2 + np \qquad (23\text{-}3)$$

When the debts mature, if $A < D_1 + D_2$, then the common stock is worthless, $p = 0$. But if $A > D_1 + D_2$, the value of a share of common stock is positive. Summarizing, Equation (23-4) is the model suggested by option theory for calculating the intrinsic value per share of the common stock when the firm's debts come due.

$$p = \frac{\text{Max}[0, (A - D_1 - D_2)]}{n} \qquad (23\text{-}4)$$

At maturity, the total value of the mortgage bond issue is defined in Equation (23-5) to be equal to either the principal amount of the issue of mortgage bonds D_1 or the total value of the corporation's assets A, whichever is less.

$$\text{Total value of mortgage bond issue} = \text{Min}[D_1, A] \qquad (23\text{-}5)$$

When the general creditors' claim comes due, Equation (23-6) shows that its intrinsic value is either the total value of the claims of the general creditors D_2 or the value of the corporation's assets that are left after the collateralized debt is paid, $A - D_1$, whichever is less.

$$\begin{array}{l}\text{Intrinsic value of} \\ \text{aggregate general} \\ \text{creditors' claims}\end{array} = \text{Min}[D_2, (A - D_1)] \qquad (23\text{-}6)$$

Equation (23-6) should be rewritten as Equation (23-6a) to recognize the fact that the general creditors are not liable for the bankrupt corporation's debts if these debts exceed the value of the corporate assets, $(D_1 + D_2) > A$.

$$\begin{array}{l}\text{Intrinsic value of} \\ \text{aggregate general} \\ \text{creditors' claims,} \\ \text{with limited} \\ \text{liability}\end{array} = \text{Max}\{0, \text{Min}[D_2, (A - D_1)]\} \qquad (23\text{-}6a)$$

All the options on this hypothetical corporation are European options since they cannot be exercised before the expiration date of the debt.

Option Theory and the Prices of Corporate Securities

Figure 23-13 delineates intrinsic values. Option theory tells us that when we consider the riskiness of the optioned assets (as shown in Figure 22-12) and the different times until the expiration of the option (as shown in Figure 22-13a), options are usually worth premiums that exceed their intrinsic values. This section considers these additional considerations and shows how to develop estimates of the worth of the debt and equity of a corporation which are more definitive than the intrinsic values shown in Figure 23-13.[25]

If common stock is valued as a call option on the corporation's assets, Figure 23-14 provides the model for valuing the debt and equity securities of the hypothetical corporation defined by Equations (23-3) through (23-6). The 45-degree line out of the origin in Figure 23-14 traces the maximum aggregate value boundary for all the corporation's outstanding debt and equity. This maximum value limit for the call simply means that the call on a corporation's assets cannot be worth more than the corporation's total assets themselves. The corporation's total debt is equivalent to the exercise price of the stockholders' call option. The 45-degree line rising out of the exercise price on the horizontal axis, $k = D_1 + D_2$, traces out the intrinsic (or minimum) value of the stockholder's call on the corporation's assets. The curve in Figure 23-14 equals the aggregate market value of the corporation's outstanding common stock, denoted np; it can be computed with the Black-Scholes call pricing formula.[26]

The model shown in Figure 23-14 indicates that if the value of the firm's total assets A remains constant, any change in the value of the corporation's equity is offset by an opposite but equal change in the value of the corporation's debt securities. For instance, for total assets valued at A^*, the following balance sheet identity is appropriate.

$$\text{Total assets} - \text{total debt} = \text{total equity}$$

$$A^* - (D_1^* + D_2^*) = np^*$$

Consider the Salem Corporation's contemplated acquisition of the Walsh Corporation. After the acquisition, the Salem Corporation would have total assets that are estimated to be worth $A = \$50$ million, and one $D = \$30$ million bond issue that must be repaid in one year ($d = 1.0$) with a $R = 6$ percent rate of interest. After the acquisition, the risk of the enlarged Salem Corporation's total assets is expected to be: Variance $= 0.04$. Will Salem's total net worth be simply $A - D = \$50 - \$30 = \$20$ million after the acquisition? Or are there additional considerations? The Black-Scholes call option model suggests that

---

[25]The implications of option theory for the prices of corporate securities have been investigated by F. Black and J. Cox, "Valuing Corporate Securities: Some Effects of Bond Indenture Provisions," *Journal of Finance,* May 1976, vol. 31, pp. 351–378. Also see T. Ho and R. Singer, "Bond Indenture Provisions and the Risk of Corporate Debt," *Journal of Financial Economics,* March 1982, vol. 10, pp. 375–406.

[26]To review several numerical examples of how to price corporate securities using the Black-Scholes call pricing model, see S. A. Ross and R. W. Westerfield, *Corporate Finance* (St. Louis, Mo.: Times Mirror/Mosby College Publishing, 1988), pp. 521–528. Or see R. A. Brealey and S. C. Myers, *Principles of Corporate Finance,* 3d ed. (New York: McGraw-Hill, 1988), pp. 484–489.

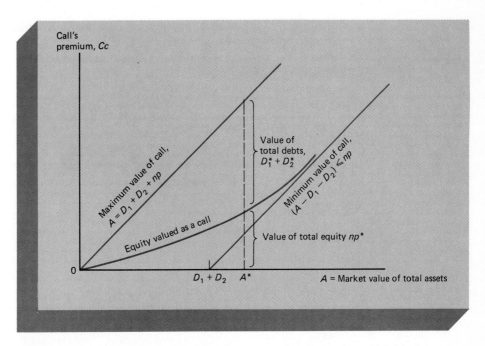

Figure 23-14 Using call option pricing theory to value the equity and debt of a corporation at expiration of the debt.

Salem's total equity will be worth $21.75 million because Salem's growth potential after the merger adds $1.75 million additional value to the book value of $20 million. (See Problem 23-19 and its solution for another insightful application of the Black-Scholes model in valuing a corporation's equity.)

The call option valuation model illustrated in Figure 23-14 can be used to analyze bond and common stock investments. For instance, changing the riskiness of the endeavor in which the corporate assets are being employed, changing the amount of corporate debt, changing the maturity date of the firm's debt, and other considerations can be explicitly analyzed with this application of the Black-Scholes call pricing model. These factors will change the value of the corporations' outstanding debt and equity in a predictable manner that is illustrated in Figure 23-14.[27]

Option theory can be as appropriate as, or more so than, the venerable present value of future income models from Chapters 15 and 16 for analyzing certain investment opportunities. Valuable and subtle investment insights into

[27]Robert Merton, ''On the Pricing of Corporate Debt,'' *Journal of Finance*, May 1974, pp. 449–470. Section 22-7 discusses the factors that affect option values in the Black-Scholes model. When the Black-Scholes model is used to value debt and/or equity, changes in any of these variables have investment implications.

firms that are teetering on the edge of bankruptcy, troubled companies that are reorganized by the bankruptcy court, leveraged buyouts, merged firms, new firms that are in the planning stages, and other special situations càn be obtained by applying option theory.

23-11   **SUMMARY AND CONCLUSIONS**

Puts and calls can be viewed as fundamental elements that can be combined to form more complex investments. For example, Figures 23-2 and 23-3 show how synthetic long and short positions could be created by combining put and call options. It is useful to think of puts and calls this way in order to be able to decompose, analyze, combine, and alter investment positions. In addition, such conceptualization contributes to the ability to create new positions.

By combining puts and calls in various ways, one can create investment positions that will be profitable if the price of the underlying asset rises, falls, rises and falls, or does not change at all. The number of different straddles, spreads, and other combinations that can be created from puts and calls is almost infinite.

Puts and calls are also useful security analysis tools. By delineating the implicit (or hidden) options embedded in complex securities, it is possible to determine their value more accurately. By viewing bonds that are callable or puttable as a combination of a noncallable bond and an option, as illustrated in Figure 23-10, we can evaluate the complex security as a combination of more fundamental elements that are easier to value individually. The option pricing models are useful in this valuation work.

Option theory can also provide tools with which to estimate the value of common stock, bonds, and other corporate securities. Analyzing these investments with option theory can yield insights. As shown in Figure 23-14, for example, the inherent conflict between a corporation's stockholders and its bond investors is revealed by call pricing theory. This model can also be used to estimate the value of a firm's securities.

Essay Questions

23-1   List the factors that determine (a) call prices and (b) put prices. (c) Indicate whether each of these factors has a positive, zero, or negative effect on the option's premium.

23-2   Evaluate the following claim: By writing calls against a long position in the underlying stock, it is possible to both reduce the portfolio's risk and increase its expected rate of return. Is this statement true, false, or uncertain? Explain.

23-3   (a) Explain how to create the economic equivalent of a short position (called a synthetic short position) by combining options. (b) Is the synthetic short position as desirable as the genuine short position? Explain.

23-4   Compare the following two investments in the Sportee Kayak Boat Company (SKBC). (a) Buy 10 shares of SKBC common stock at $100 per share (a $1000 total investment). (b) Buy a call option on SKBC stock which has a $100 exercise price for $10 per share. This 100-share call option's total price is $1000 ($10 per share × 100 shares.) Which investment do you prefer? Why? Under what conditions would you prefer the other investment?

23-5   What are the differences between a warrant and a call option on the same corporation's stock?

23-6   (a) If an issue of bonds is callable, what effect (if any) will this have on the market price of the bonds? (b) If an issue of bonds is puttable, what effect (if any) will this have on the market price of the bonds?

23-7   What is the "latent warrant" in a convertible security?

Problems

23-8   The cash market price of gold bullion advanced rapidly from $345 per ounce on July 7, 1986 to $387 on August 14, 1986. As a result, the prices of options on gold futures contracts changed, too, as the following prices for options expiring in October 1986 indicate. For instance, one October call with an exercise price of $340 per ounce on 100 troy ounces of gold at Comex cost $1250 on July 7, 1986 and that call could be sold for $5010 on August 14, 1986.

Date	Oct 340 call	Oct 350 call	Oct 360 call	Oct 340 put	Oct 350 put	Oct 360 put
7-7-86	$1250	$ 650	$ 350	$430	$770	$1450
8-14-86	5010	4040	3090	40	60	120
Gain (loss)	$3260	$3390	$2740	($390)	($710)	($1330)
Commission	− 50	− 50	− 50	− 50	− 50	− 50
Net gain	$3210	$3340	$2690	($440)	($760)	($1380)

Which one of the six options above would have been the best one to buy on July 7, 1986 if you had known what the price of gold was going to be on August 14, 1986? Show your calculations and explain how you selected the best one.

23-9   Before 1986, when capital gains on investments held over 6 months were taxed at a lower income tax rate than ordinary income, I. M. Bullish bought 100 shares of GM stock at $40 per share on February 1, 19X1. Ms. Bullish held the shares for price appreciation, which she expected to occur over the next 6 months. Five months after purchasing the shares, on July 4, 19X1, the price of GM reached $80 per share. Then, Bullish turned bearish about GM and wanted to sell the stock. Her accountant reminded her that if she held the 100 shares for one more month, her ($80 − $40) × 100 shares, or $4000, total gain would be taxed at the long-term capital gains tax rate of 20 percent rather than at the 40 percent ordinary income tax rate. Ima Bullish wanted to pay the lower capital gains tax rate, but she was convinced that GM's stock price peaked at $80 per share and would fall drastically before August. (*a*) What would you have recommended for her? (*b*) How could she have kept her $40 per share gain and still have it taxed at the more desirable long-term capital gains tax rate?

23-10 On July 6, 1973, the only call on the common stock of Texas Instruments (TI) that was being traded on the CBOE was a July call with a $90 exercise price. The optioned stock's price had just fallen to $83 per share. The TI call was out of the money. It was selling for only $1⅜, or $1.375, per optioned share of stock. Assume you had purchased this July call on July 6, 1973 for 1⅜. On July 27, in the short time before the option expired, the price of TI stock shot up to $108.75. (*a*) What do you estimate the July call of TI's stock was worth when the optioned stock price hit $108.75? (*b*) What is the percentage gain in the price of the call from $1⅜ to the July 27 price (or premium) that you estimated? (*Note: This situation actually occurred.*)

23-11 The price of GM common stock had been hovering around $50 per share for a long time, and Avner Goldstein thought the stock was poised for a big move. So, Mr. Goldstein considered purchasing a July call with a $50 exercise price for a premium of $3 per share in case the stock's price rose. He also purchased a July put with an exercise price of $50 for a premium of $2 in case the stock's price fell. (*a*) What is the name of the position Avner is considering? (*b*) What would be the total cost of Avner's aggregate position? (*c*) Construct a table showing Avner's gains and losses from his put and call options at $10 stock price intervals for GM prices from $30 to $70 inclusive. (*d*) At what stock prices would Mr. Goldstein break even on his combination of options?

23-12 As explained in the preceding problem, the price of GM common stock had been hovering around $50 per share for a long time, and Avner Goldstein thought the stock was poised for a big move. Mr. Goldstein considered the position outlined in the preceding problem and rejected it because it required too much initial investment. Then GM's price dropped to $47 and Mr. Goldstein became impatient. He purchased a June call with a $50 exercise price for a premium of $2 per share in case the stock's price rose. In addition, he purchased a June put with an exercise price of $45 for a premium of $2 in case the stock's price fell. (*a*) What is the name of the position Avner has accumulated? (*b*) What was the total cost of Avner's aggregate position? (*c*) Construct a table showing Avner's gains and losses from his put and call options at $5 stock price intervals for GM prices from $25 to $70 inclusive. (*d*) At what stock prices would Mr. Goldstein break even on his combination of options?

23-13 On July 1 the price of AT&T common stock was $32 and Charlynn Maniatis paid a premium of $3 per share for an October call with a $30 exercise price on it. At the same time she accepted a $1 per share premium to write an October call on AT&T with a $35 exercise price. (*a*) What is the name of the position Charlynn has acquired? (*b*) How much did Charlynn pay for this portfolio of two calls? (*c*)

Construct a table showing Charlynn's gains and losses from her two call options at $5 stock price intervals for AT&T prices from $25 to $45 inclusive. (*d*) At what AT&T stock price would Charlynn Maniatis break even on her portfolio of two options?

23-14   Ralph Tomacino was mildly pessimistic about the Orwell Corporation so he established a *bear spread* when its stock was at $32 per share. Ralph paid $3 per share for an October call on Orwell with a $30 exercise price. He also wrote an October call on Orwell with a $35 exercise price for a premium of $1 per share. (*a*) How much did Ralph pay for his bear spread? (*b*) Construct a table showing Ralph's gains and losses from the bear spread at $5 stock price intervals for Orwell's stock prices from $25 to $40 inclusive. (*c*) At what stock price would Ralph Tomacino break even on his bear spread?

23-15   Jonathon Livingston bought a July call on GM stock that had a $50 exercise price, bought a July call on GM stock that had a $70 exercise price, and wrote two July calls on GM stock that both had $60 exercise prices. (*a*) What is the name of the position Jonathon has acquired? (*b*) How much did Jonathon pay for these options? (*c*) Construct a table showing Jonathon's gains and losses from his options at $10 stock price intervals for GM prices from $40 to $80 inclusive. (*d*) At what stock price would Jonathon break even on his portfolio of options?

23-16   The total market value of the Azore Corporation's total assets is $90,000. Azore has a $110,000 issue of zero coupon bonds maturing in 1 year. The riskless rate of interest is 9.5 percent. The standard deviation of returns on Azore's stock is 0.4, or equivalently, the variance is 0.16. (*a*) Calculate the value of all common stock shares outstanding in the Azore Corporation using the Black-Scholes call option pricing model. (*b*) Why might Azore's stock have a positive value when the firm's debts of $110,000 exceed its total market value?

23-17   Draw graphs showing how (*a*) the long butterfly spread and (*b*) the short butterfly spread positions can be constructed from puts and/or calls.

23-18   Draw two well-labeled probability distributions. (*a*) Draw a normal bell-shaped curve and assume it delineates the probabilities attached to the terminal values from a long position in the 500 stocks that comprise the S&P 500 stock index. Next, assume you buy put options on the S&P 500 index to insure your portfolio of 500 stocks. (*b*) Now, draw a probability distribution of stock prices that delineates the probabilities.

23-19   The Star Corporation is being sued in bankruptcy court by its bond trustee because it failed to make a scheduled coupon interest payment on its outstanding bond issue; its bankruptcy hearing is to be held in 90 days, $d = 0.25$. The corporation has total assets valued at $A = \$40$ million, but its liabilities exceed its total assets. The defaulted issue of collateralized bonds has a face value of $D_1 = \$25$ million and matures in 10 years. Star's general creditors have claims with a total value of $D_2 = \$20$ million, and the riskless interest rate is $R = 7.0$ percent. The corporation's bond indenture provisions have forced it to cease paying cash dividends until its coupon interest payments are current, and the firm's assets are being used in a manner that generates the risk statistic: Var(assets) = 0.25. You are the chief executive officer of General Motors (GM), and you are considering making a tender offer to acquire the troubled Star Corporation. You instruct your Executive Vice President/Treasurer to use the Black-Scholes call valuation model to analyze the Star Corporation. (*a*) What is the exercise price of the Star stockholders' call option of firm's assets? (*b*) How long is it until this option expires? (*c*) What is the aggregate value of Star's common stock while the troubled corporation is in bankruptcy court? (*d*) What is the market value of Star's two categories of liabilities?

Selected References

Bookstaber, Richard M., *Option Pricing and Investment Strategies,* rev. ed. (Chicago, Ill.: Probus, 1987).

A well-written discussion that explains call options and various option strategies. Mathematics is used.

Cox, John C., and Mark Rubinstein, *Options Markets* (Englewood Cliffs, N.J.: Prentice-Hall, 1985).

A comprehensive review of option theory and the mathematics of options.

Fabozzi, Frank J., ed., *The Handbook of Fixed Income Options: Pricing, Strategies and Applications* (Chicago, Ill.: Probus, 1989).

The book explains options on fixed-income securities, option pricing models, option premium dynamics (such as delta, gamma, and theta), valuing callable bonds, compound options, and options on interest rate swaps.

Ritchken, Peter, *Options: Theory, Strategy, and Applications* (Glenview, Ill.: Scott, Foresman, 1987).

An easy-to-read book that uses mathematics to analyze and explain options, option theory, and option strategies.

Turnbull, Stuart M., *Option Valuation* (Toronto, Ontario, Canada: Holt, Rinehart and Winston of Canada, Ltd., Dryden Press, 1987).

This booklet and the accompanying floppy diskette for a personal computer show how to evaluate various options and option statistics.

Chapter 24

Futures Contracts

Futures contracts are legal contracts that stipulate the type of commodity covered by the contract, the future date when the commodity will be delivered, the price per unit for the commodity, the quantity of the commodity that is to be delivered, the quality specifications for the commodity, and related details. These details cannot be changed once a contract is executed.

Futures contracts offer commodity traders two possibilities. The first possibility is the right to initiate a **long position** that entitles them to *take physical delivery* of the specific commodity on the date stipulated and at the place designated in the contract. Alternatively, the commodity trader can initiate a **short position** that gives the right to *make delivery* of the commodity as contracted. Together, a long and a short position on the same commodity, delivery month, delivery place, and at the same price create one futures contract.

A trader who takes a **long speculative position** does so in the belief that the price of the underlying commodity will rise so that between the date the long position is initiated and the date that delivery must be made, the long position can be resold to someone else at the *commodity futures exchange* for a gain. Conversely, a trader who initiates a **speculative short position** does so in the belief that the price of the commodity will come down before the delivery date arrives. If the price does decline, the sale of the right to deliver (or effectively, the buying of a similar short sale contract at a lower unit price than the price at which the short sale was initiated) results in a gain for the short seller. If the price forecast of either the long or short speculator is in error, the erroneous party will suffer a loss that is the other party's gain.

Speculators are not the only people who trade futures contracts. Risk-averters and arbitragers also use futures contracts in their hedges.

The futures contracts traded at commodity exchanges are standardized contracts that vary only with respect to the price and maturity date for each transaction. The *uniformity* of futures contracts expedites rapid trading in a *homogeneous commodity*. The successive buyers of each futures contract usually pay a different price than was agreed upon for the initial sale, or any other sales that might have preceded it.

Futures contracts are traded by transferring the contract through a third party called the "clearing house." Every commodity exchange has a **clearing house** that inserts itself between every buyer and seller. The clearing house pays the seller the contracted price for the agreed-upon quantity and simultaneously sells a new but identical futures contract to the buyer at whatever price the seller and the buyer agreed on. That price can be either the same or different than was arranged in any preceding or succeeding transaction. The clearing house keeps track of the details of each transaction and communicates directly with each buyer and seller separately. The responsibility to make delivery is reassigned by the clearing house each time the contract is resold.

Commodity futures contracts are usually called **futures.** Futures are one type of **financial instrument;** stocks, bonds, and options are other types. In the United States, futures markets are governed by the Commodity Futures Trading Commission (CFTC).

24-1   **COMMODITIES TRADING**

Commodities include farm products like cotton, soybeans, hogs, and their derivatives, such as soybean meal, soybean oil, and pork bellies (unsliced bacon). Other homogeneous raw materials, such as silver, gold, copper, and heating oil, are also actively traded commodities. Financial futures on various bonds, stock market indexes, foreign currencies, and other financial quantities are also traded.

The physical commodities are traded in what are synonymously called **cash, physicals,** or **actuals markets.** Grain elevators and stockyards where farmers sell their products are examples of *cash markets*. The NYSE and foreign exchange dealers are examples of the cash markets for financial commodities. Commodity futures contracts are traded at organized markets called **futures exchanges.**

Futures contracts that do not fall due for delivery within the current month are called *futures contracts*. Futures contracts that are to be delivered within the current month are usually called **spot contracts** instead of futures contracts. Both spot and futures contracts are traded at commodity exchanges, but physical commodities are not traded there. The commodity exchanges in the United States are listed at the bottom of Figure 24-1.

Most commodity exchanges have one or two large trading rooms; each room contains several "trading rings." Trading occurs in the **trading rings,** or **trading pits,** within a **trading room.** Exchange members who want to buy or sell futures go to the appropriate trading room, step into the trading pit, and indicate by

Futures

Financial

WEST GERMAN MARK (IMM)
125,000 marks; $ per mark

—Season— High	Low		High	Low	Close	Chg.	Open Interest
.5975	.4918	Jun	.5018	.4885	.5004	+83	52,204
.5977	.4946	Sep	.5065	.4910	.5035	+87	42,286
.5825	.4962	Dec	.5082	.4925	.5056	+89	1,578
.5083	.5000	Mar	.5110	.5015	.5077	+91	23

Last spot .5002, up 84.
Est. sales 61,671. Wed.'s sales 29,009.
Wed.'s open int 96,091; off 1,904.

3-MONTH EURODOLLAR DEPOSITS (IMM)
$1 million; pts of 100%, add on

92.12	88.76	Jun	90.80	90.66	90.66	—.08	155,616
91.92	88.70	Sep	91.37	91.03	91.05	—.21	246,397
91.76	88.84	Dec	91.52	91.20	91.22	—.18	129,294
91.73	88.90	Mar	91.65	91.38	91.40	—.15	71,902
91.63	88.82	Jun	91.56	91.29	91.32	—.14	38,728
91.56	88.74	Sep	91.48	91.26	91.34	—.14	31,290
91.43	89.85	Dec	91.38	91.14	91.16	—.14	25,478
91.42	89.96	Mar	91.38	91.17	91.17	—.14	18,814

Est. sales 348,415. Wed.'s sales 116,020.
Wed.'s open int 775,212, off 3,931.

U.S. TREASURY BILLS (IMM)
$1 million; pts of 100%

93.48	90.48	Jun	92.80	92.70	92.73	—.11	89
93.13	90.41	Sep	92.67	92.42	92.43	—.12	15,892
92.98	90.50	Dec	92.94	92.65	92.68	—.12	3,781
93.07	90.75	Mar	92.97	92.81	92.84	—.10	370
92.90	91.28	Sep	92.63	92.63	92.58	—.06	7

Est. sales 7,148. Wed.'s sales 2,307.
Wed.'s open int 20,139, up 526.

U.S. TREASURY BONDS (CBT)
8%-$100,000 prin.; pts. and 32d's of 100%

97-25	73-11	Jun	97-6	95-14	95-15	—1-1	33,346
97-25	72-26	Sep	97-6	95-13	95-14	—1-2	238,083
97-19	72-18	Dec	97	95-8	95-9	—1-1	22,132
97-8	72-1	Mar	96-20	95-3	95-3	—1	7,350
96-30	75	Jun	96-5	94-28	94-28	—31	3,932
96-24	79-1	Sep	96	94-20	94-20	—30	4,135
95-26	80	Dec			94-12	—29	298
95-17	79-21	Mar			94-4	—28	150

Est. sales 450,000. Wed.'s sales 240,059.
Wed.'s open int 309,568, off 259.

10-YEAR U.S. TREASURY NOTES (CBT)
$100,000; pts and 32d's of 100%

98-26	89-9	Jun	98-23	97-17	97-18	—22	6,521
99-16	89-13	Sep	98-30	97-22	97-24	—22	69,386
99-18	91-17	Dec	99	97-28	97-29	—22	3,456

Est. sales 33,000. Wed.'s sales 30,010.
Wed.'s open int 79,364, up 3,048.

MUNI BOND INDEX (CBT)
1000x index, pts & 32nds of 100%

95-16	77-6	Jun	95-9	94-15	94-16	—17	4,607
95-10	78-6	Sep	95-6	94-4	94-5	—20	12,187
94-17	81-10	Dec	94-6	93-18	93-18	—20	927
94-2	85-19	Mar	93-9	93-1	93-1	—20	227

Last index 94-18, off 05.
Est. sales 7,000. Wed.'s sales 3,311.
Wed.'s open int 18,034, off 71.

Key to the exchanges:

CBOE	Chicago Board Options Exchange
CBT	Chicago Board of Trade
CME	Chicago Mercantile Exchange
COMEX	Commodity Exchange Inc., N.Y.
IMM	International Monetary Market of the Chicago Mercantile Exchange
KCBT	Kansas City Board of Trade
NYCSCE	New York Coffee, Sugar and Cocoa Exchange
NYCTN	New York Cotton Exchange
NYCTN.CA	New York Cotton Exchange, Citrus Associates
NYFE	New York Futures Exchange
NYM	New York Mercantile Exchange
PHIL	Philadelphia Exchange

Industrials

CRUDE OIL (NYM)
42,000 gallons; $ per barrel

20.12	12.68	Sep	18.50	18.18	18.21	—.07	48,632
19.50	12.75	Oct	18.21	17.88	17.91	—.17	49,159
19.23	15.00	Nov	18.09	17.80	17.87	—.13	27,061
19.05	12.87	Dec	18.00	17.73	17.80	—.14	23,048
18.93	15.67	Jan	17.84	17.65	17.73	—.12	12,789
18.84	15.74	Feb	17.78	17.55	17.68	—.12	11,391
18.80	16.10	Mar	17.74	17.51	17.65	—.11	11,383
18.71	16.30	Apr	17.75	17.50	17.63	—.11	11,107

Est. sales 16,639. Wed.'s sales 82,753.
Wed.'s open int 62,025, off 1,938,479.

HEATING OIL No. 2 (NYM)
42,000 gallons; cents per gallon

54.50	36.25	Sep	49.85	49.00	49.12	—.42	19,717
54.90	37.20	Oct	50.50	49.60	49.66	—.47	12,616
55.50	38.00	Nov	51.10	50.30	50.36	—.38	8,723
56.05	39.00	Dec	51.80	51.10	51.11	—.43	11,102
54.50	46.60	Jan	51.95	51.30	51.31	—.38	4,488
53.50	48.00	Feb	51.40	50.80	50.56	—.38	3,163
51.35	46.40	Mar	49.14	48.80	48.66	—.43	1,375
49.76	45.00	Apr	47.40	47.40	46.76	—.48	694
48.00	44.50	May	46.10	46.10	45.76	—.48	130
50.95	44.90	Jun	47.00	46.30	45.21	—.48	17

Est. sales 13,942. Wed.'s sales 16,399.
Wed.'s open int n.a.

LUMBER (CME)
150,000 bd. ft.; $ per 1,000 bd.ft.

196.00	167.10	Jul	183.00	181.90	182.90	+.20	2,844
194.70	175.10	Sep	186.60	185.70	186.40	—.30	1,691
190.60	176.30	Nov	184.00	182.90	183.70	—.40	1,828
192.00	181.20	Jan	189.20	188.50	189.50	....	276
191.80	185.00	Mar	191.20	191.00	191.20	—.30	255
194.20	188.00	May	193.20	193.00	193.20	—.80	848
196.00	177.50	Jul	195.00	195.00	196.00	....	200

Est. sales 717. Wed.'s sales 775.
Wed.'s open int 7,942, up 22.

Foods and Fiber

COCOA (NYCSCE) 10 tons; $ per ton

1895	1120	Jul	1153	1127	1151	+4	5,760
1850	1127	Sep	1193	1165	1192	+6	12,361
1735	1133	Dec	1223	1200	1220	+4	9,276
1535	1133	Mar	1236	1210	1233	+13	6,605
1465	1138	May	1244	1215	1244	+15	5,113
1335	1154	Jul	1232	1231	1259	+12	1,242
1308	1180	Sep	1270	1249	1279	+12	4,589

Est. sales 9,370. Wed.'s sales 6,687.
Wed.'s open int 44,946, up 167.

COFFEE (NYCSCE) 37,500 lb. ¢ per lb.

155.25	112.20	Jul	118.75	116.00	118.62	+1.19	5,902
152.90	108.50	Sep	112.75	110.70	112.70	—.08	10,539
149.50	107.10	Dec	109.50	107.50	109.45	—.51	6,211
146.00	107.00	Mar	110.75	108.75	110.33	—1.67	1,751
124.50	108.00	May	112.50	110.50	111.51	—1.49	294

Est. sales 6,300. Wed.'s sales 10,981.
Wed.'s open int 24,730, up 931.

COTTON (NYCTN) 50,000 lb.; ¢ per lb.

69.35	49.26	Jul	69.10	68.45	68.69	—.65	7,066
70.45	50.35	Oct	70.36	69.75	69.96	—.43	6,903
70.40	50.75	Dec	70.20	69.61	69.77	—.58	18,316
71.10	53.60	Mar	70.75	70.40	70.40	—.70	2,936
71.50	55.90	May	71.29	70.80	70.75	—.73	1,958

Est. sales 5,000. Wed.'s sales 8,285.
Wed.'s open int 37,835, up 1,009.

Livestock

HOGS, Live (CME) 30,000 lb. ¢ per lb.

51.00	43.25	Aug	46.70	46.12	46.52	+.17	4,445
47.00	38.55	Oct	41.15	40.55	40.95	+.55	9,802
47.25	38.75	Dec	42.75	42.02	42.42	+.40	6,536
45.40	41.75	Feb	43.45	42.82	43.20	+.35	2,742
45.10	39.40	Apr	40.60	40.10	40.37	+.25	1,276
48.70	44.25	Jun	45.50	44.95	45.45	+.28	347
48.95	44.95	Jul	45.72	45.72	45.85	+.28	140
45.60	43.85	Aug	44.20	44.20	44.25	+.20	11

Est. sales 9,131. Wed.'s sales 7,964.
Wed.'s open int 25,299, up 804.

PORK BELLIES (CME)
40,000 lb; ¢ per lb.

58.20	24.27	Aug	26.82	25.55	26.20	+.28	5,404
61.60	38.70	Feb	40.15	39.25	39.25	—.47	7,284
60.00	38.65	Mar	39.80	39.00	39.12	—.55	938
60.90	39.70	May	40.65	40.40	40.40	—.37	213
60.90	40.50	Jul	41.00	40.70	40.70	—.35	77
55.80	39.85	Aug	40.60	39.20	39.30	—1.05	48

Est. sales 4,047. Wed.'s sales 4,045.
Wed.'s open int 13,964, up 8.

Metals

COPPER (COMEX) 25,000 lb.; ¢ per lb.

116.55	110.20	Aug	112.60	112.60	112.85	—.45	336
131.50	76.00	Sep	114.20	112.40	112.65	—.45	15,194
		Oct			111.70	—.30	
126.00	77.45	Dec	110.80	108.20	109.25	+.05	6,293

Est. sales 5,000. Wed.'s sales 5,342.
Wed.'s open int 21,823, up 89.

GOLD (COMEX) 100 troy oz., $ per troy oz.

575.00	360.50	Aug	375.00	369.20	373.70	+3.60	6,570
382.00	369.50	Sep			375.40	+3.60	514
575.50	365.00	Oct	379.00	373.00	377.40	+3.60	12,321
574.50	367.50	Dec	382.50	376.80	381.40	+3.60	68,635
516.00	374.50	Feb	386.00	380.50	385.10	+3.60	8,404
525.80	377.50	Apr	385.10	384.70	388.80	+3.50	11,554
497.00	381.00	Jun	392.50	388.50	392.60	+3.50	10,864
487.00	384.50	Aug			396.40	+3.50	8,211
472.00	391.00	Oct			400.20	+3.50	2,681
455.50	394.00	Dec	401.50	401.50	404.10	+3.60	6,847
450.00	397.50	Feb			408.10	+3.60	9,804
415.50	402.00	Apr	413.00	413.00	412.10	+3.70	1,715
		Jun	414.00	414.00	416.10	+3.70	

Est. sales 35,000. Wed.'s sales 15,837.
Wed.'s open int 148,120, off 2,219.

Grains and Oilseeds

CORN (CBT) 5,000 bu.; $ per bu.

3.60	2.33	Jul	2.59¾	2.55¾	2.59¼	+.02½	57,338
3.17¼	2.34¾	Sep	2.48	2.45½	2.47¼	+.00¾	22,826
2.95	2.30¾	Dec	2.45¾	2.43¼	2.45¼	+.00½	67,142
2.86½	2.38½	Mar	2.53¾	2.51¼	2.53½	+.00½	10,920
2.89½	2.43½	May	2.58¼	2.56¼	2.58¼		3,168
2.84	2.44½	Jul	2.60	2.57¾	2.59¼	+.00¾	1,845
2.55	2.34	Sep			2.47		72

Est. sales 40,000. Wed.'s sales 56,434.
Wed.'s open int 163,863, up 3,148.

OATS (CBT) 5,000 bu.; $ per bu.

2.77	1.58	Jul	1.68¾	1.65¼	1.66½	—.00¾	4,156
2.43	1.65	Sep	1.75½	1.72	1.73½	—.00¼	2,714
2.47	1.74	Dec	1.84¾	1.81½	1.82½	—.00½	2,499
2.24	1.82	Mar	1.92½	1.90	1.90½	—.00½	293
2.00	1.86	May			2.04¼		54

Est. sales 1,000. Wed.'s sales 1,954.
Wed.'s open int 9,716, up 4.

Figure 24-1 Newspaper excerpt showing one day's futures prices.

open outcry and/or by standardized hand signals their intention to transact business.[1] When the buyer and the seller settle on the contract terms, clerks immediately post the latest price to the electronic *commodity board* on the trading room wall. Transaction prices are also sent out immediately by wire to the board rooms of brokerage houses and other exchanges around the world.

Floor brokers are independent members of the commodity exchange who do most of the trading. For a commission, they buy and sell futures for their customers. Orders to buy and sell come into the exchange by phone calls or telegraph messages to the floor brokers from their customers. The floor brokers walk to the appropriate pit, execute the trades, and then notify their customers.

The **independents,** as these floor brokers are called, execute orders for the public and for their own accounts as well—this is called **dual trading.** Dual trading involves an inherent conflict of interest. For example, it is illegal for floor brokers to trade for their own account while they are preparing to execute for one of their clients an order that might change the price of the commodity.[2]

The independents on the trading floors of commodities exchanges assume different roles. Most of them are **brokers** who execute trades for those who do not own exchange seats. Some are **speculators** who provide market liquidity by interpreting market information and bridging the gaps between outside orders that vary in size and timing by taking positions for their own account. **Spreaders** are arbitragers who earn their living by enforcing the *law of one price* on the exchange floor. Spreaders execute *intertemporal spreads* between different delivery months, *intermarket spreads* between different exchanges, and *intercommodity spreads* between different commodities. Some independents are **hedgers** that help clients manage their risk exposure. Finally, some independents are brokers, hedgers, and speculators—all at the same time.

Futures Contracts	Futures contracts are not actually traded on the floor of the exchange—**trading cards** that represent them are traded. There is a different color card for each commodity, and all exchange members carry an assortment of different colored trading cards with their names preprinted on them. Transactions are completed

---

[1]The after-hours computerized trading system named **Globex,** started in 1989 by Chicago Mercantile Exchange and Reuters, might replace trading pits in the years ahead—if it succeeds. For details see Saul Hansell, ''The Computer that Ate Chicago,'' *Institutional Investor,* Feb. 1989, pp. 181–188.

[2]For details about commodity markets, see the following books on the subject. R. W. Kolb, *Understanding Futures Markets,* 2d ed. (Glenview, Ill.: Scott, Foresman, 1988). Also see J. F. Marshall, *Futures and Option Contracting* (Cincinnati, Ohio: South-Western, 1989). See also E. W. Schwartz, J. M. Hill, and T. Schneeweis, *Financial Futures* (Homewood, Ill.: Irwin, 1986). And see Robert A. Strong, *Speculative Markets* (Chicago, Ill.: Longman Financial Services, 1989). In addition, see Raymond M. Leuthold, Joan C. Junkus, and Jean E. Cordier, *The Theory and Practice of Futures Markets* (Lexington, Mass.: Lexington Books, D. C. Heath, 1989).

whenever a buyer and a seller get together in the pit and agree to jot down the same prices, delivery months, and quantities on their appropriate trading cards; then they hand the cards to one of the clerks on the trading floor. *Modern futures contracts* are really a set of legal contract provisions, rules, regulations, and exchange bylaws that govern every transaction flowing through a futures exchange.

Commodity Board Prices

For any given commodity, different futures contracts that have varying **delivery months** are available. The *delivery months* for futures are determined by the commodity exchange with the approval of the Commodity Futures Trading Commission (CFTC). The prices of the futures contracts on a given commodity are different for each delivery month. Commodity futures prices are listed for each delivery month on a **commodity board** like the one shown in Table 24-1; these prices are in cents per bushel. The commodity board is kept current by exchange clerks.

Floor traders get their trading information from several sources—they watch the commodity board, they observe the action in the pits where they trade, and they read the news coming out of the wire service news machines when they are not engaged in trades. Depending on the individual, they also use fundamental analysis, technical analysis, and other sources of information.

Price Fluctuation Limits

Each commodity futures contract has **minimum price fluctuation limits** that are determined and enforced by its commodity exchange. New bids must be higher than the existing bids, and new asked (or offering) prices must be less than the existing asked prices by at least the amount of the minimum fluctuation. The minimum price limit fluctuations are designed to prevent haggling over **ticks** (minimum price changes) that are insignificant. However, trades can always be executed at the existing prices.

Commodity exchanges also enforce **maximum daily price fluctuation** rules on futures contracts to prohibit large and potentially destabilizing price increases or decreases. If a commodity's price changes by the daily limit, trading

Table 24-1
COMMODITY BOARD FOR CHICAGO WHEAT

Delivery month	December	March	May	July	September
High and low	490-311	499-350	491-366	479-344	484-360
Previous close	370	377¼	379	355	363¾
Opening today	371½	377	378¾	353	362
Today's high	371	379	379	353	362
Today's low	368¾	377¼	377	350½	361
Ticker	369	379	378	350	361¼

in that commodity for the remainder of the day cannot occur at prices above that day's maximum or below the minimum limit price. **Limit price moves** usually stop trading for the rest of that day. The next day trading resumes, but the price cannot change more than the daily limit or trading will be halted again.

The maximum price fluctuation limits seldom halt trading. But when the Soviet Union made massive wheat purchases in 1972, when the Hunt brothers tried to corner the silver market in 1980, and at other less noteworthy times, several consecutive days of price limit moves occurred and locked many traders into their positions while prices moved against them and caused them substantial losses. Some economists suggest that price fluctuation restrictions distort natural supply and demand relationships and thus misallocate resources when they do come into play. There is a perennial debate about whether the price change limits do more harm than good.[3]

Clearing House's Guarantee Provides Liquidity

As explained above, the clearing house becomes the seller from whom all buyers obtain delivery and the buyer to whom all sellers make delivery.[4] In addition to acting as an intermediate for expediting the flow of transactions, the *clearing house guarantees that every futures contract will be fulfilled* even if one of the parties defaults.[5] When one party to a futures contract defaults, the clearing house pays whatever costs are necessary to fulfill the contract. This provision frees futures traders from checking each other's credit every time they trade and thus *makes the futures contract liquid*. The clearing house sues the defaulted party to collect damages after it executes the contract for them.

Mechanics of Trading Commodity Futures

Commodity traders usually start by opening a trading account with a **futures commission merchant,** or, synonymously, **commodities broker,** at a brokerage firm that deals in commodities. The brokerage firm may employ an individual who owns a *membership* at a commodity exchange, or the brokerage may arrange with one or more floor traders who are members of a commodity exchange to execute their trades.

The major full-service brokerage firms (like Merrill Lynch, Pierce, Fenner & Smith, for instance) assist the general public in trading futures. Some firms

---

[3]See M. J. Brennan, "A Theory of Price Limits in Futures Markets," *Journal of Financial Economics,* 1988, vol. 16, no. 2, pp. 213–233.

[4]The traders on the floor of a commodity exchange make it a point to know the names of the other sides of all of their trades in order to expeditiously clear up any mistakes—called **out trades**—before the clearing house steps in to intermediate. By knowing the other party to an *out trade,* the trader can negotiate a settlement. Such direct negotiation avoids inconvenient arbitration of the *out trade,* which can be costly.

[5]The members of a commodity exchange are required to buy stock in their clearing house and support its guarantee fund by making large deposits into it.

like Morgan Stanley and Goldman, Sachs specialize in assisting the larger buyers of commodities.[6] In addition, there are discount brokers in the commodity futures business who do not provide free research and other amenities that are superfluous to executing trades. As a result, the discount brokers charge their clients commissions that are about one-third as much as one of the full-service brokerages would charge for the same transaction. Lind-Waldock, Macro-Source, Murias Commodities Inc., and Jack Carl Associates are all discount commodities brokerages.

Contract Units Futures contracts for each commodity are only available in *standardized quantities*. For example, on the Chicago Board of Trade one contract of soybean meal specifies 100 tons as the **unit,** the T-bond contract calls for one Treasury bond that has a $100,000 face value and an 8 percent coupon rate, and the wheat contract specifies 5000 bushels as the standard unit. To trade futures contracts, the trader tells the broker to **short futures** (which means sell futures) or to buy a **long position,** and gives the number of units, the asked or bid price, and the desired delivery month. When trading futures, a customer must either pay cash in advance or pay the **initial margin requirement** of 3 to 15 percent when the order is initiated. Margined traders do not have to pay for the remainder of their transaction until they take delivery—which they rarely do; they usually sell the contract before the delivery date.

For example, if the customer wanted to short 200 tons of soybean meal for delivery in November, the broker would notify the floor trader at the soybean trading pit of the Chicago Board of Trade to "sell two November soy meals." The floor trader would execute the order immediately and report back to the broker that the transaction had been consummated. Brokers usually notify their clients of the price at which their transaction was executed within 5 to 30 min after the order was placed.

Reversing Out of a Position Very few futures buyers and sellers actually take or make delivery, respectively, on their futures contracts. Sometime before the delivery date arrives, about 97 percent of the contracts are closed out (or eliminated). A contract can be closed out by **reversing out** of the position; the seller buys back a contract like the one they previously sold from a seller who simultaneously wants out of their obligation to accept delivery. Alternatively,

---

[6]A few large prestigious banks (such as Morgan Guaranty) and brokerage houses (like Salomon, Morgan Stanley, and Goldman, Sachs) refuse to let any client open an account with less than a $1 million initial deposit. In contrast, Merrill Lynch, Pierce, Fenner & Smith will open new accounts worth only a few thousand dollars. As a result of these policies, Merrill Lynch has thousands of small clients, while the more prestigious firms have fewer clients, but with greater wealth.

a trader can **roll out** the position by trading their position for a similar position that has a later delivery date.[7]

Market Liquidity   Active futures traders want **liquid markets,** in which a large volume of contracts are traded. This is desirable because it allows those who are trading large positions to buy or sell at any time without causing a significant price change.[8]

Open Interest

Prices are determined by buyers' and sellers' expectations. Thus, one key to profitable speculation is fast and accurate information processing.

One of the more widely watched commodity futures statistics is called the **open interest.** Several large, national newspapers publish the commodity futures prices and the open interest for futures contracts. On the day when a new futures contract starts trading and the first contract is sold, the open interest advances from zero to one. During the early months of a contract's trading life (of 1 year for most commodities), many more contracts are opened than are closed and the net open interest accumulates daily to become a total of thousands of contracts within a few months. Later, as the contract's delivery date draws nearer, more positions are closed out with reversing trades than are opened. As a result, the open interest declines back to zero on the contract's delivery date. Only a small percent of all the futures contracts that are opened are ever actually delivered; the rest are wiped out by reversing trades. The typical pattern of a futures contract's lifetime open interest is shown in Figure 24-2. The daily **volume of contracts traded** during the life of any particular futures contract is highly positively correlated with the daily open interest in that contract.

Convergence of Spot and Futures Prices

During the life of a futures contract, its futures price (and during the delivery month, its spot price) tends to rise and fall with the underlying commodity's cash (or physicals) price. Through these price fluctuations the correlation coefficients between futures and the underlying physical commodity vary but remain positive. However, the futures price remains above the spot price by the amount of the carrying charges under normal market conditions.

As the delivery date nears, the futures price tends to converge with the spot and cash prices because as the futures contract approaches its delivery date,

[7]For an informative discussion of the trading rules and market-making in a futures market and an explanation of some of the rules, see William J. Silber, "Marketmaker Behavior in an Auction Market: An Analysis of Scalpers in Futures Markets," *Journal of Finance,* Sept. 1984, vol. xxxix, no. 4, pp. 937–954.

[8]For a discussion of the factors that determine the volume of contracts traded in a given commodity, see Lester Telser and Harlow Higginbotham, "Organized Futures Markets: Costs and Benefits," *Journal of Political Economy,* Oct. 1977, pp. 969–1000.

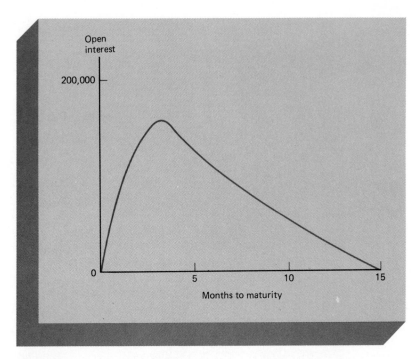

Figure 24-2 Graph of the open interest over the life of a hypothetical futures contract.

it eventually turns into a spot contract and also becomes an increasingly good substitute for the physical commodity. Even after the contract expires and the commodity is delivered, however, the futures prices and the cash prices are still affected by carrying costs because many futures traders "roll their hedges forward" again and again rather than take delivery on them. In market vernacular, the "basis strengthens" (that is, it approaches zero) in a normal market as the delivery date draws nearer, and the cash and the futures prices move closer together but do not quite converge. Finally, on the last permissible delivery date (when the contract will cease to exist), the futures price converges with the spot price as the basis shrinks to zero, as illustrated in Figure 24-3. Futures prices do not usually converge with the cash (or physicals) price (1) because of the transportation costs between physicals markets and futures markets and (2) because the physical commodities that are available for immediate delivery are of different quality than the commodities delivered to fulfill futures contracts.[9]

---

[9]The futures prices for financial futures are usually about the same as the cash prices because (1) transportation costs are close to zero for financial instruments and (2) there are no quality differences between the financial instruments delivered against futures contracts and those traded in the cash markets.

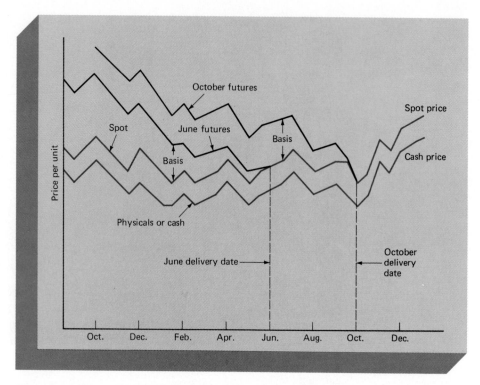

Figure 24-3 The prices of spot and futures covary and converge at the contract's maturity, while the prices of cash and futures covary together but do not converge for storable physical commodities.

24-2   **PRICE RELATIONSHIPS, MARKET CONDITIONS, AND RETURNS**

The relationship between the spot price and futures price for a commodity at any given instant may be determined by different factors.

Normal and Inverted Markets

The futures price is normally higher than the spot price for **storable commodities.** The excess of futures price over spot price in **normal markets** is sufficient to cover the **carrying charges** incurred while holding a commodity for future delivery. This *normal carrying charge relationship* induces profit-seeking speculators to buy commodities when their prices are low (such as grain at harvest time) and store them for future delivery. Essentially, speculative greed helps allocate consumption smoothly over time.

More generally, the difference between futures and spot prices on the same commodity at a given moment is called the **basis.**

$$\text{Basis}_t = \text{futures price}_t - \text{spot price}_t \qquad (24\text{-}1)$$

If futures exceed spot prices, the difference is called a **premium.** If the spot price exceeds the futures price, the future is said to be at a **discount** to the spot price.[10]

The premium of futures prices over spot prices may be slightly less than the cost of carrying the commodity in inventory if a "convenience yield" exists.[11]

> The **convenience yield** can be defined as the sum of extra advantages (other than appreciation in the market value) which a manufacturer may derive from carrying stocks above his immediate requirements rather than holding the equivalent value in cash and buying stocks at a later date.

When the futures price (fp) is less than the spot price (sp), namely, $fp < sp$, an **inverted market** is said to have occurred. A grain market may get inverted, for example, when the current supply of a commodity is very low, keeping spot prices high, but the current crop is expected to yield a large harvest, so futures prices are low.[12]

Relationship between Spot and Futures Prices for Storable Commodities

Many commodities can be stored for future delivery. The market prices for storable commodities conform to Equation (24-2) when market conditions are normal.

$$fp_t \leq sp_t + tC \qquad (24\text{-}2)$$

where C denotes the total cost of carrying the commodity for 1 month minus the commodity's convenience yield (if any exists) and t represents the number of months until the delivery date. For financial commodities, interest expense represents almost the entire carrying cost, essentially, $C = (r)(sp)$.

Note the inequality sign in Equation (24-2). The inequality implies that fu-

---

[10]If the basis is restated as shown in Equation (24-1a), then the basis is negative and has an *absolute value* equal to the carrying costs in normal markets.

$$\text{Basis} = \text{spot price} - \text{futures price} \qquad (24\text{-}1a)$$

[11]The convenience yield concept was first introduced in Nicholas Kaldor, "Speculation and Economic Stability," *Review of Economic Studies,* 1939–1940, vol. 7.

[12]Commodities like fresh eggs, fresh potatoes, live cattle, and, some people would say, Treasury bills, are unstorable. (Futures contracts on fresh eggs and fresh potatoes are no longer traded.) For these *nonstorable commodities* the theory of carrying costs is irrelevant, and, as a result, spot prices often exceed futures prices. For *storable commodities,* just before harvest time when current supplies are short but a bumper crop is forthcoming, inverted markets occur sometimes. See Holbrook Working, "Theory of the Inverse Carrying Charge in Futures Markets," *Journal of Farm Economics,* Feb. 1948, vol. XXX. To read classic theory about the relationship between spot and futures prices, see Holbrook Working, "The Theory of Price of Storage," *American Economic Review,* Dec. 1949, pp. 1254–1262. For empirical evidence also see M. J. Brennan, "The Supply of Storage," *American Economic Review,* March 1958.

tures prices cannot normally rise above the combination of spot prices plus the carrying costs. This inequality results from the fact that current inventories can be carried into future months for consumption at a later date merely by paying the carrying cost. But the reverse is impossible. Future harvests or debt securities that are scheduled for future delivery cannot be consumed or utilized before they are delivered. Therefore, futures prices for storable commodities increase by the amount of the monthly carrying costs each month under normal market conditions.

Inequality (24-2) can be extended to explain the difference between the prices of two futures contracts on the same storable commodity that have different delivery dates. Inequality (24-3) can be used to estimate the **price spread** between the near-futures and the distant-futures contracts.

$$fp_2 \leq fp_1 + C(t_2 - t_1) \qquad (24\text{-}3)$$

The time subscript t_2 represents the *distant future* and the subscript t_1 represents the *near future*. The quantity $t_2 - t_1$ is the time difference between the expiration dates of the two futures contracts.

If inequality (24-3) ever became temporarily reversed, profit-seekers would quickly restore it by simultaneously performing the following transactions as soon as the violated inequality is observed: (1) Buy a long position in the near-futures contract that provides for delivery fairly soon, at time t_1; (2) take a short position in the distant-futures contract for delivery much later, at time t_2; (3) take delivery at time t_1 at price fp_1 and store the commodity for C cents per month; (4) at time t_2 deliver the stored commodity at a price of fp_2 to reap a profit with certainty; (5) keep doing this transaction as many times as you can because you will earn a riskless profit until inequality (24-3) is restored. This five-step **arbitrage** process is such an easy ''money pump'' that Equation (24-3) is rarely violated.[13]

One-Period Returns from Futures

The one-period rate of return from purchasing a futures contract in period t and selling it in period $t + 1$ is defined in Equation (24-4). The price of the futures contract in period t is denoted fp_t.

$$r_t = \frac{fp_{t+1} - fp_t}{fp_t} \qquad (24\text{-}4)$$

Equation (24-4) ignores the broker's commission—commissions should be deducted from the numerator to reduce the effective holding period return.[14]

[13]Stock index arbitrage with futures contracts is discussed in Section 24-7. Stock index arbitrage provides a new application of this arbitrage.
[14]Dusak defines the return as in Equation (24-4); see Katherine Dusak, ''Futures Trading and Investor Returns: An Investigation of Commodity Market Risk Premiums,'' *Journal of Political Economy,* Dec. 1973, pp. 1387–1406. Fischer Black, in contrast, argues that

(continues)

Margin Requirements

Most futures traders do not invest the full amount of the denominator in Equation (24-4); they only make small down payments called the **initial margin.**[15] Margin requirements are set and enforced by the commodity exchanges to accomplish several objectives. First, margin requirements are supposed to help maintain the financial integrity of futures contracts and futures traders by limiting their risk exposure. Second, margins are supposed to control pyramiding of debt that could contribute to a market crash. Third, margins are supposed to provide financial leverage so that traders who desire to do so may take larger positions.

Initial margin requirements of 3 to 15 percent are common.[16] If the margined commodity's price falls too much on a long position (or rises too much on a short position), the trader receives a **margin call** to put up additional margin money, which is called the "maintenance margin."

Maintenance margin or **variation margin** requirements call for additional money that margin traders may be required to pay to their brokerage to ensure their performance of the futures contract if the price of their commodity position fluctuates adversely. For example, if a speculator buys a futures contract long on 10 percent initial margin and then the commodity's price falls 5 percent, half the speculator's initial margin (or equity in the position) gets wiped out. In this case the broker will ask the futures trader to meet the maintenance margin requirement. If the trader does not quickly put up the maintenance margin money, the broker will liquidate the futures contract being held as collateral for the loan that was used to buy the contract. *To avoid the losses and ill-feelings that can result from a margin call, the clearing house requires its broker-members to make all of their accounts "mark to the market" each*

(continued)
it is not possible to define the rate of return for a highly leveraged futures contract; see Fischer Black, "The Pricing of Commodity Contracts," *Journal of Financial Economics,* Jan. 1976. Returns on margined futures contracts are defined in Zvi Bodie and Victor Rosansky, "Risk and Return in Commodity Futures," *Financial Analysts Journal,* May–June 1980, pp. 38–39. Professor Lester Telser argues that margins affect the rates of return but does not explicitly show how he thinks they should be measured. See L. Telser, "Margins and Futures Contracts," *Journal of Futures Markets,* 1981, vol. 11, no. 2.

[15]Commodity brokerages define a client's **margin** to be equal to the equity value in the client's account. The equity equals the sum of the following amounts: (1) cash, (2) cashlike securities (namely, U.S. Treasury bills that are left on deposit at the broker's office), and (3) the net total of the unrealized gains on open positions less the unrealized losses (that is, net "paper profits" that may be positive or negative).

[16]Common stock initial margin requirements, set by the Federal Reserve Board, are currently 50 percent—they have varied from 50 to 75 percent. It is not appropriate to compare the sizes of stock market margins and commodity margins, however, because stock traders do not usually have to "mark to the market" daily as do commodity traders.

trading day. A futures account is **marked to the market** when it meets the maintenance margin requirement based on the current unit price and resulting contract value.[17]

Marking to the Market Daily with Cash and/or T-Bills

The requirement that every futures account be marked to the market every trading day means that futures traders must stand ready to make cash contributions to their account on the days when adverse price fluctuations diminish the value of their account. The good news is that clients can make cash withdrawals from their account on days when their holdings benefit from advantageous price moves. Some futures traders prefer to leave excess margin in their accounts in the form of interest-bearing Treasury bills, rather than deal with daily cash inflows and outflows as the market value of their account fluctuates.

Futures traders are allowed to give their brokerage firm cash or interest-bearing U.S. Treasury bills or some combination of both to meet their margin requirement. It can be to the trader's advantage to use income-producing T-bills for margin deposits. While T-bill returns may not be high, even a small return exceeds a return of zero on cash deposits that are left with the brokerage. Leaving excess margin in an account also helps avoid a margin call. It has been estimated that the effective cost of using T-bills to mark to the market is small.[18]

24-3   **HEDGING**

Losses from an adverse price move in a long or short commodity futures position may be reduced, and perhaps even eliminated, by hedging. However, hedging also reduces the potential gains. **Hedging** may be defined as arranging for a short position to come due at about the same time that an offsetting long position matures. The closer in size that the dollar values of the long and short positions are, the closer the maturity dates of the long and short positions, and the higher the correlation between the long and short positions, the more perfect

---

[17]Maintenance margins are approximately 75 percent of the initial margins at most commodity brokerage firms, but this relationship varies from broker to broker. However, any time the customer's equity falls below the required maintenance margin, the customer receives a margin call. Margins are discussed in Raymond M. Leuthold, Joan C. Junkus, and Jean E. Cordier, *The Theory and Practice of Futures Markets* (Lexington, Mass.: Lexington Books, D. C. Heath, 1989). In chap. 2 see pp. 38–41 for detailed numerical examples of how maintenance margins are calculated.

[18]See E. Elton, M. Gruber, and J. Rentzler, "Intra-Day Tests of the Efficiency of the Treasury Bill Futures Market," *Journal of Business,* 1989. The paper analyzes T-bill futures and finds that the cost of marking to the market stated as a percentage of the interest income from the position is trivial.

the hedge will be. Consider three basic types of hedges: the perfect hedge, a buying hedge, and a selling hedge.

Perfect Hedges

Hedges are made by combining long and short positions (shown in Figure 8-1a and b, respectively). Someone who owns identical long and short positions on the same asset has a position that is **perfectly hedged** (see Figure 8-5). Price fluctuations cannot affect the market value of a perfectly hedged position. The owner of a perfectly hedged position is contractually bound to earn a profit of zero and losses of the same amount.

In actuality very few commodity futures hedges are truly perfect. Unavoidable "basis risks" introduce elements of risk into every commodity hedge. These "basis risks" are investigated later in this chapter.

Buying Hedges

A **buying hedge** is a purchase of futures to protect the buyer against price rises. Many people call a buying hedge a **long hedge** because the hedger is long the futures contract. Breakfast cereal manufacturers who buy grain commodities, shoe manufacturers who buy hides, and other commodity users employ buying hedges to protect themselves from price increases in their raw material. For example, consider a manufacturer of breakfast cereals that has contracted to deliver fixed quantities of breakfast cereals to supermarkets at a fixed price every month for a year. Essentially, this cereal manufacturer has contracted to be *short physical cereal*. If the price of the grain used to make the cereal rises above the price for which the cereal manufacturer has contracted to sell, the cereal manufacturer will be legally obligated to perform under a contract that entails losses and may even result in the firm's bankruptcy. To avoid this risk, the cereal manufacturer can buy grain futures providing for delivery of the quantity of grain needed to fill the orders at a cost that allows a margin for profit. The cereal manufacturer has thus hedged away the buying risks and can concentrate on manufacturing good cereal efficiently. The speculator who sells the grain futures contract to the cereal manufacturer will bear all the risks of an increase in the price of the grain.[19]

Selling Hedge

A **selling hedge** or **short hedge,** as it is also called, involves shorting futures to avoid losses from possible price declines on a commodity that is in inventory. Consider, for example, a **mortgage banking** firm that originates home mortgages (which are collateralized long-term bonds) and then carries them in inventory

[19]For a theoretical analysis of hedging, see L. L. Johnson, "The Theory of Hedging and Speculation in Commodity Futures," *Review of Economic Studies,* 1960, vol. 27, no. 3, pp. 139–151. More recently, see Ron W. Anderson and Jean-Pierre Danthine, "Hedging and Joint Production: Theory and Illustrations," *Journal of Finance,* May 1980, vol. 35, no. 2, pp. 487–497.

until such time as they can be resold to a mortgage investor—like Ginnie Mae (GNMA). Suppose the mortgage banker reads that the Federal Reserve will continue to raise interest rates for the foreseeable future. To protect the mortgage banking firm from losses if its inventory of mortgages falls in value as a result of increases in market rates of interest, the mortgage banker can sell GNMA futures to hedge its inventory of mortgages. By selling GNMA futures equal in value to the inventory, the mortgage banker has hedged its selling risks. The speculator who buys the GNMA futures assumes the risks of a price drop.[20]

If the mortgage banker introduced in the preceding paragraph is wrong and market interest rates decline, then the market prices of the broker's mortgages will rise. If this happens, the hedged seller may not profit from the rising value of the inventory. A selling hedge decreases the profit from a price rise as well as the possibility of loss from a price fall. But, many people and many firms are so risk-averse that they use hedges regularly.[21]

Basis Risks

Although a selling hedge may reduce the commodity processor's losses from declines in the market value of its inventory, there are other risks inherent in every hedge. These **basis risks** are listed and defined below. As a result of any of these four different basis risks, a commodity's basis may become larger or smaller rather than remain fixed. If the basis changes, the hedger can suffer losses or reap gains. These losses or gains can be substantial over several units of commodity futures.

1. *Quantity risk:* The unit of measurement used in a futures contract may not correspond precisely to the amount of commodity that is to be hedged. Because the futures contracts are all uniform and cannot be tailormade, the unhedged portion of the deal is at risk.

2. *Quality risk:* An undesirable grade of the commodity may be all that is available or **cheapest to deliver.** If so, the party who sold the futures contract will deliver the undesirable grade. Even if the desired grade is available, the party that makes delivery on the futures contract may find it more profitable to deliver a lower grade than the futures contract specifies and pay to the buyer the penalty fee that is provided in every futures contract to discourage such incidents. This basis risk could cost the futures buyer who received the unsatisfactory grade of the commodity additional expense.

[20]For more details about hedging with financial futures, see Stephen Figlewski, Kose John, and John Merrick, *Hedging with Financial Futures for Institutional Investors* (Cambridge, Mass.: Ballinger, 1986).

[21]All the incentive to hedge is not a result of risk aversion; some imperfect hedges are undertaken purely for profit. Imperfect hedges that are entered to earn profits are called *arbitrages.* Arbitrage was explained in Section 8-9.

3. *Location risk:* The only futures contracts that are available to be purchased may provide for delivery at an undesirable location. Thus, the buyer could incur shipping costs that constitute a basis risk.

4. *Expiration date risk:* A futures contract that offers delivery in the month the goods are needed may not exist. Thus, the hedger could be forced to buy or sell a futures contract that provided for delivery in a month that differed from the desired month. Such a contract could result in additional storage expenses for the frustrated hedger. The possibility of incurring such costs is another basis risk.[22]

As a result of these basis risks, perfect hedges are a rarity. The truth is that hedging can reduce the large risks associated with a price level change. But the basis risks can be so substantial that some speculators earn their livings by "trading on the basis."

Trading on the basis occurs when a futures trader attempts to profit by trading on anticipated changes in the basis. Stated differently, basis traders are speculating on the changes in the *difference between prices* that they expect, rather than on the price of a single position. Seen thusly, trading on the basis is a modest form of price speculation that focuses on the small differences in the prices between two partially offsetting positions, rather than on the more substantial price fluctuations in a totally unhedged position.

Spreading with Futures

Those who *trade on the basis* frequently use various kinds of "spreads." If a trader thinks the basis is larger than the actual carrying cost between two futures contracts that are identical in every way except their delivery dates, for example, that trader may acquire the two **legs** necessary to form a **calendar spread.** The trader will **leg into the spread** by buying the near futures contract for one leg and selling short the distant futures contract for the other leg. If the basis between these two futures narrows, as the trader expected, the spread would yield a profit. The profitability of the spread is unaffected by price level changes, only the basis matters.

The Treasury-bill–Eurodollar spread, called a **TED-spread,** is an example of an **intercommodity spread.** The TED-spread uses offsetting positions in Treasury bill futures and Eurodollar futures to gain from interest rate differentials between the two contracts that appear to be temporarily out of line.

Soybean traders use another intercommodity spread, called the **crush spread,** to speculate on misaligned prices between soybeans and the soybean derivatives, since there is a mathematical relationship between how much soybean

[22]In order to invest in commodity futures indirectly, some people buy shares in commodity funds. Evidence suggesting that commodity funds tend to be bad investments has been published in E. J. Elton, M. J. Gruber, and J. Rentzler, "New Public Offerings, Information and Investor Rationality: The Case of Publicly Offered Commodity Funds," *Journal of Business,* Jan. 1989, vol. 62, no. 1, pp. 1–16.

meal and soybean oil can be produced when a unit of soybeans is crushed. The crush spread can be formulated in several different ways. For example, there may be as many as three legs to a crush spread if the trader buys long positions in both meal and oil and shorts the beans.[23]

Economic Effects of Hedging and Spreading

Considering the implications of the hedges and spreads outlined above reveals that these activities help shape market prices. Spreading tends to align the forward interest rates that are implicit in various futures contracts with the rates in the yield curve, maintains the basis between spot and futures at levels that correspond to realistic carrying costs, and supports the law of one price.

The risk-reducing benefits of hedging and spreading are acknowledged by the margin requirements. Commodity brokerages require margins on hedged positions and spreads that are substantially below what they require for an uncovered position.

24-4   THEORIES ABOUT HOW SPOT AND FUTURES PRICES CONVERGE

Financial economists are not in agreement about precisely how large the basis should be in normal market conditions with storable commodities.

Keynes-Hicks Theory of Normal Backwardation

Two English economists named Keynes and Hicks argued that the futures price (fp) for storable commodities should normally be slightly less than the expected spot prices $E(sp)$ by the amount of an insurance premium they called **normal backwardation.** The Keynes-Hicks viewpoint is formalized as Equation (24-5).

$$fp_t = E(sp_t) + \text{(a tiny positive insurance premium)}(T - t) \qquad (24\text{-}5)$$

where t denotes the point in time when the prices are observed and T is the terminal period when the futures contract is due for delivery. The differences between $[fp - E(sp)]$ and $T - t$ are expected to converge on zero as the delivery date approaches. Unfortunately, since the **expected spot price** can never really be observed and measured, the Keynes-Hicks hypothesis does not readily yield to direct empirical testing. Keynes and Hicks hypothesized that speculators provide a valuable insurance function for hedgers, and thus hedgers should pay what they called *normal backwardation* to induce speculators to assume the risks associated with providing this insurance.[24]

---

[23]For more details about spreading, see Courtney Smith, *Commodity Spreads* (New York: Wiley, 1982).

[24]For an early explanation of normal backwardation, see J. M. Keynes, *A Treatise on Money,* Vol. II, and also *The Applied Theory of Money* (London: Macmillan, 1924). Also see J. R. Hicks, *Value and Capital,* 2d ed. (Oxford: Clarendon Press, 1946), chaps. IX and X, especially pp. 136–139.

Hardy's Hypothesis about Gamblers

C. O. Hardy suggested that the Keynes-Hicks theory is wrong. Hardy argued that futures prices should normally be at a slight premium over the expected spot prices. He hypothesized that special types of "speculative insurance" have been developed to meet the need for[25]

> protection against various types of loss where no proper distribution of risk can be obtained. In this type of contract, a large group of private insurers enters into a contract by which they agree to recompense the insured for his loss, dividing the cost between themselves. If the individual insurer writes many policies, and none are large, he secures a combination of risks which protect him against excessive loss. But there is a large speculative element involved in fixing the premium rates.

Hardy's speculators are like gamblers who are willing to pay for the opportunity to gamble. As a result, Hardy hypothesizes that speculators will bid futures prices up above what they actually expect the spot prices to be in the future. Hardy's hypothesis is summed up by Equation (24-6).

$$fp_t = E(sp_t) - (\text{a tiny ``gamblers fee''})(T - t) \qquad (24\text{-}6)$$

Hardy's "gamblers fee" $[fp_t - E(sp_t)]$ is sometimes called **contango** or **forwardation.**

Some of Hardy's opponents argue that Hardy's view is inappropriate for futures prices because diversification is not very useful for reducing the insurer's risk exposure against *systematic fluctuations* in futures prices. Thus, the situation envisioned by Hardy is not economically self-perpetuating.

Unbiased Expectations Hypothesis

The debate about whether futures prices normally lie a little above or a little below their expected spot price raged on for decades without resolve. More recent empirical tests, however, indicate that the ideas of Keynes and Hicks and Hardy are all wrong. Hartzmark has published a comprehensive test suggesting that spot prices are *unbiased estimates* of futures prices.[26] Equation (24-7) formalizes the **unbiased expectations hypothesis.**

$$fp_t = E(sp_t) \qquad (24\text{-}7)$$

Equation (24-7) defines a situation in which futures prices are unbiased estimates of the spot prices expected to emerge in the future. Abstracting from the continuous fluctuations that characterize actual market prices, we illustrate in Figure 24-4 the essential differences between the Keynes-Hicks theory of normal backwardation, Hardy's theory about people who will pay to gamble,

[25]C. O. Hardy, *Risk and Risk Bearing* (Chicago: University of Chicago Press, 1940), pp. 67–69. Also see C. O. Hardy and L. S. Lyon, "The Theory of Hedging," *Journal of Political Economy,* April 1923, vol. 31, no. 2, pp. 276–287.
[26]Michael L. Hartzmark, "Returns to Individual Traders of Futures: Aggregate Results," *Journal of Political Economy,* 1987, vol. 95, no. 6, pp. 1292–1306.

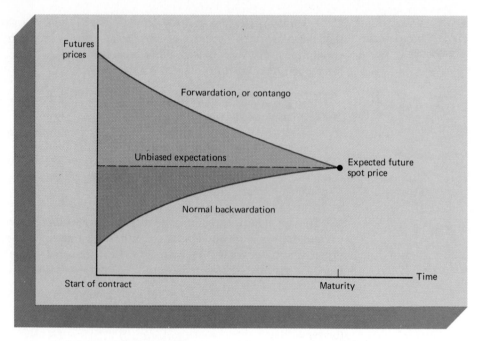

Figure 24-4 Three competing hypotheses about the way futures prices converge on spot prices, assuming spot prices remain constant.

and the unbiased expectations hypothesis. Until more compelling research emerges, Hartzmark's empirical findings cast considerable doubt over both the Keynes-Hicks theory of normal backwardation and Hardy's hypothesis about forwardation.

24-5   **VALUING FUTURES ON TREASURY BILLS**

Several specific financial futures contracts are reviewed next to consider the factors that shape futures prices. The futures contracts on U.S. Treasury bills are analyzed first because T-bills are the simplest.

The International Monetary Market (a subsidiary of the Chicago Mercantile Exchange) and the MidAmerica Commodity Exchange (a subsidiary of the Chicago Board of Trade) both trade 90-day futures contracts on U.S. Treasury bills that have units of $1,000,000 and $500,000, respectively.

A T-Bill Example   Suppose a large corporation wanted to invest enough money to ensure it would have $1 million available to pay a bill that comes due 180 days in the future. Consider two different transactions that could earn the corporation a riskless rate of return on the funds over the 180 days.

Arrangement 1—Buy T-bill: Pay C dollars of cash for a $1,000,000 U.S. Treasury bill that matures in 180 days.

Arrangement 2—Buy a forward contract on T-bills: Buy two items: (1) Pay cash for a T-bill that matures in 90 days with a face value of F and (2) purchase a *forward contract* that 90 days in the future will deliver a second 90-day T-bill that has a $1 million maturity value. Let F represent the dollar price that must be paid for this forward contract when the second T-bill is delivered 90 days in the future. The present value of this forward contract is $F/(1 + R)$.

Table 24-2 shows the cashflows from the two different 180-day investment arrangements. Consideration of these two cashflow arrangements reveals that they are identical. Since the arrangements have identical cashflows, the **law of one price** tells us they should have the same value, as indicated in Equation (24-8).

$$\frac{F}{1 + R} = C \qquad (24\text{-}8)$$

Economic Processes That Align Prices

If Equation (24-8) is violated, one or more of the economic processes listed below will be set in motion to restore it.

1. *Arbitrage:* Riskless profits can be earned from selling short the more expensive arrangement and using the proceeds from that short sale to buy the cheaper arrangement. This arbitrage will continue to be profitable until the two arrangements have identical costs, as represented by Equation (24-8).
2. *Buy the cheapest arrangement:* Since the two arrangements listed in Table 24-2 produce identical cashflows, investors will purchase whichever arrangement costs the least. The demand pressures should bid up the price of the cheapest alternative and bring the costs of the two arrangements together.

Table 24-2
CASHFLOWS FROM TWO ALTERNATIVE 180-DAY INVESTMENTS

Days in the future	$t = 0$	$t = 90$	$t = 180$
Arrangement 1; Buy genuine 180-day T-bill			
Buy 180-day T-bill for cash	C		$1,000,000
Arrangement 2; Buy "homemade 180-day T-bill"			
Buy 90-day T-bill in cash market	$F/(1 + R)$	F	
Purchase 90-day forward contract		$-F$	$1,000,000
Sums from arrangement 2	$F/(1 + R)$	0	$1,000,000

3. *Switch arrangements:* At some point in time, if the cost of one of the arrangements listed in Table 24-2 differs from the cost of the other, investors will liquidate the more expensive alternative and simultaneously replace it by purchasing the less costly alternative. This switching activity will tend to enforce Equation (24-8).

Transactions costs can slow up the economic processes described above. The costs of gathering information, telephone expenses, postal fees, brokerage commissions, taxes, and the time and effort expended by the investments manager are costs that should be considered before undertaking one of the economic processes listed above. After considering these costs, investors will sometimes find it advantageous to permit small deviations from Equation (24-8) to go unattended. Transactions costs are small enough, however, that any significant deviations from Equation (24-8) should be profitable to correct.

It matters not which combination of the three economic processes listed above realigns the prices of the two arrangements in Table 24-2 to bring them into equilibrium. Equation (24-8) can be used to price T-bill forward contracts in all three cases. Furthermore, an equation that is analogous to Equation (24-8) can be used to price T-bill *futures contracts* since futures are similar to forward contracts. A **forward contract** occurs when a seller agrees to deliver a specific commodity to a buyer at some future date that the two parties agree upon. Forward contracts are privately negotiated and are not standardized or publicly traded like futures contracts.

A 90-day futures contract on the T-bill could have been used in Table 24-2 instead of the 90-day forward contract. The futures contract was not used because the initial margin and the requirement to mark to the market on the future would have caused the two alternative patterns of cashflows to differ. These differences are small enough, however, that Equation (24-8) is useful for pricing the futures contract. More importantly, even though the costs of using forward contracts and futures contracts differ, the economic pressures that form the prices are the same.[27]

Cost of Marking to the Market on T-Bill Futures

The cost differences between a forward contract and a futures contract are less than might be imagined. To estimate the cost of marking to the market, consider a $1 million Treasury-bill future that is priced to yield 9 percent interest over a 60-day period for a total of $1 million $\times$ 60/360 $\times$ 9.0%, or $15,000 interest income. Elton, Gruber, and Rentzler estimated the cost of marking to the market for this futures contract at an average of only $4 per contract. Stated

[27]There are several ways to calculate the yield and the price on Treasury bills. For a comprehensive discussion see Marcia Stigum, *Money Market Calculations* (Homewood, Ill.: Dow Jones–Irwin, 1981).

as a fraction of the $15,000 interest income, the cost of marking to the market is insignificant.[28]

As explained in Chapter 2, Treasury bonds have maturities that range from 10 to 30 years when issued, and they pay coupon interest semiannually. T-bond futures are traded at the MidAmerica Commodity Exchange and the Chicago Board of Trade in denominations of $50,000 and $100,000, respectively. The $100,000 Treasury-note future traded at the Chicago Board of Trade is like the T-bond future on a similar bond that simply has a shorter maturity.

The T-bond future specifies that the deliverable instruments include any one of a large number of T-bonds that has over 15 years to maturity and is not callable within the next 15 years. The T-bond contract calls for a bond with an 8 percent coupon, but other coupon rates can be delivered if appropriate price adjustments are made according to "conversion factors." Tables of "conversion factors," prepared by the futures exchanges, consider each issue's coupon rate and its time until maturity. **Conversion factors** for T-bonds with coupons that differ from 8 percent are used by T-bond futures traders so they can determine the **cheapest deliverable instrument.** T-bonds with coupons greater than 8 percent are worth more and therefore have conversion factors in excess of one, while T-bonds with coupons of less than 8 percent are worth less and have conversion factors of less than one.

Valuing a T-Bond Future

Consider two different ways a trader could purchase a T-bond that would be worth F dollars when it matured.

> *Arrangement A—cash market:* A T-bond with E dollars of face (or ending) value could be purchased for C dollars of cash.

> *Arrangement B—futures and cash markets:* Buy two items: (1) Purchase a T-bond future that for F dollars will deliver a bond with a face value of E dollars and (2) simultaneously buy a T-bill with a maturity value of F dollars that expires on the future contract's delivery date. If the T-bill yields a rate of return of R, its cost will be $F/(1 + R)$.

If the T-bond does not pay any coupons before it is delivered under the

---

[28]See E. Elton, M. Gruber, and J. Rentzler, "Intra-Day Tests of the Efficiency of the Treasury Bill Futures Market," *Journal of Business,* 1989.

futures contract, the *law of one price* suggests that arrangements A and B should have the same value since they yield identical cashflow patterns (of C dollars initial investment followed by E dollars of ending repayment).

$$\frac{F}{1 + R} = C \tag{24-9}$$

Next, consider the slightly more complex case that occurs when coupon payments occur. If the T-bond pays coupon interest with a present value of v, the cost of buying the bond in the cash market should be reduced to the amount $C - v$. After this adjustment for the coupon payments, arrangements A and B are still equivalent. Therefore, the *law of one price* implies that Equation (24-10) should not be violated.

$$\frac{F}{1 + R} = C - v \tag{24-10}$$

If we know exactly which T-bond is the *cheapest deliverable instrument,* Equation (24-10) can be used to value T-bond futures contracts. It is realistic to assume that we can tell in advance exactly which T-bond will be the cheapest deliverable instrument and will therefore be delivered. However, since the model developed ignores *marking to the market,* Equation (24-10) will only furnish good approximations instead of exact answers. The economic processes listed in the preceding section will ensure that Equation (24-10) will not be substantially violated.

Other Interest Rate Futures

Futures contracts on other riskless debt securities can also be valued with Equation (24-10). The futures contracts on bank certificates of deposit (CDs) and Eurodollars, which are traded at the International Monetary Market, and the Municipal Bond Index contract and the two GNMA contracts traded at the Chicago Board of Trade can all be valued with a model like Equation (24-10).

24-7   **FUTURES CONTRACTS ON STOCK MARKET INDEXES**

Figure 24-5 shows the price quotations for several futures contracts on different stock market indexes and refers to the futures exchanges that trade them. The prices of all these contracts except one are determined by multiplying 500 times the value of the underlying index. The future on the Major Market Index (MMI) is the deviant; it is priced at 250 times its index.

All stock index futures are **cash settlement** contracts. The fact that the underlying securities never change hands reduces the commission and transfer costs to much less than what would be incurred if similar transactions were carried out, for example, by exercising options.

Futures on stock market indexes are used for three different functions that

FUTURES

S&P 500 INDEX (CME) 500 times index

	Open	High	Low	Settle	Chg	High	Low	Open Interest
June	323.45	323.75	318.80	319.80	− 4.15	328.45	263.80	55,177
Sept	327.90	328.30	323.20	324.25	− 4.20	332.95	271.50	90,615
Dec	332.00	332.00	327.30	328.30	− 4.25	336.80	298.90	3,299

Est vol 87,127; vol Wed 57,434; open int 149,092, −362.
Indx prelim High 323.80; Low 319.21; Close 320.08 −3.75

NYSE COMPOSITE INDEX (NYFE) 500 times index

	Open	High	Low	Settle	Chg	High	Low	Open Interest
June	180.40	180.65	178.35	179.00	− 1.90	183.40	149.60	2,042
Sept	182.85	183.15	180.30	181.00	− 2.30	185.55	153.90	4,750
Dec	184.60	184.60	182.40	183.10	− 2.45	187.30	161.10	765
Mr90	184.80	184.80	184.80	185.20	− 2.60	189.00	170.20	234

Est vol 10,463; vol Wed 6,259; open int 7,791, +164.
The index: High 180.82; Low 178.57; Close 178.97 −1.86

MAJOR MKT INDEX (CBT) $250 times index

	Open	High	Low	Settle	Chg	High	Low	Open Interest
June	490.80	490.80	481.80	484.25	− 6.00	496.50	442.50	3,981
July	493.40	493.40	485.50	487.55	− 6.15	500.00	469.10	1,612

Est vol 8,700; vol Wed 3,990; open int 5,681, +470.
The index: High 489.76; Low 482.20; Close 483.70

KC VALUE LINE INDEX (KC) 500 times index

	Open	High	Low	Settle	Chg	High	Low	Open Interest
June	287.95	287.95	285.10	285.60	− 2.60	290.10	245.65	661
Sept	292.50	292.80	289.70	290.00	− 3.00	294.70	267.40	1,079

Est vol 450; vol Wed 238; open int 1,746, +12.
The index: High 288.00; Low 285.59; Close 285.96 −2.03

CRB INDEX (NYFE) 500 times index

	Open	High	Low	Settle	Chg	High	Low	Open Interest
July	230.50	231.90	229.80	231.30	+ .40	250.50	227.05	1,242
Sept	231.90	233.15	231.70	232.80	+ .50	249.10	228.60	532
Dec	232.25	232.25	232.25	233.30	+ .60	245.25	229.45	299

Est vol 1,055; vol Wed 694; open int 2,124, −8.
The index: High 232.00; Low 230.41; Close 231.92 +.98

—OTHER INDEX FUTURE—

Settlement price of selected contract. Volume and open interest of all contract months.

KC Mini Value Line (KC) 100 times index
Sep 290.00 −3.00; Est. vol. 25; Open Int. 81

CBT—Chicago Board of Trade. CME—Chicago Mercantile Exchange. KC—Kansas City Board of Trade. NYFE—New York Futures Exchange, a unit of the New York Stock Exchange.

Figure 24-5 Newspaper excerpt showing one day's price quotations for futures contracts on indexes of financial markets.

are explained next: (1) speculating on the market, (2) hedging, and (3) index arbitrage.

Using Stock Market Index Futures to Speculate

Frieda Pareto was optimistic about the stock market, so she called her broker and gave him a market order to buy a long position of one September futures contract on the Standard & Poor's 500 Stocks Composite Index (S&P 500), traded at the Index and Option Division of the Chicago Mercantile Exchange. The S&P 500 index was at 296 when Frieda bought it. The contract cost her $148,000 (296 times 500), but she had enough T-bills in her account to cover the initial 10 percent margin requirement. After lunch Frieda phoned a sell order to her broker. The S&P 500 was at 297.5 when her sell order was executed, so she made $750 [or (297.5 − 296) × 500]. Essentially, Frieda *bet on the market* and won. If she had bearishly shorted the S&P 500 contract at 296 and after lunch reversed out of the position at 297.5, she would have suffered a loss of $750 [(296 − 297.5) × 500] plus the commission costs.

Hedging with
Stock Market
Index Futures

Investors may want to hedge a long position in the stock market by selling short stock market index futures. Such a hedge would be useful if the stock market takes a bearish plunge, because the investor's gains on the short futures position will offset the losses on the long stock market position. Conversely, if the investor has a short position in the stock market, a compensating long position in stock market index futures would hedge the losses that would occur if the market appreciates. (See Figures 8-5 and 8-6.) Futures on stock market indexes are very useful for hedging because they are liquid and the commission costs are much less than taking the offsetting position directly in common stocks.

Large brokerage houses frequently find themselves with inventories of millions of dollars of diversified common stock holdings at the end of a trading day. When such a situation reaches precarious proportions, management may hedge the firm's position overnight (or over the weekend) until the size of the inventory can be cut back. If (1) the stock holdings are perfectly correlated with the stock market index used to form the hedge,[29] and (2) the dollar values of the long and short positions are equal,[30] the hedge will be perfect. More realistically, (1) if the stock market position is not perfectly correlated with the stock market index futures and/or (2) the dollar values of the long and short positions are not equal, the hedge will be imperfect and some gains or losses are possible.[31] An imperfect hedge will nevertheless reduce the risk from fluctuations in the market value of the position.

Some brokerage houses, index funds, pension funds, arbitragers, and other traders knowingly set up imperfect stock market hedges in order to profit from them. One approach to this activity is called "index arbitrage."

Index Arbitrage

Index arbitrage can be done on any security market index. Most index arbitrage, however, is done using the S&P 500 index and the futures contract on the S&P 500 index. The S&P 500 and the maturing S&P 500 futures contract will

[29]Correlation coefficients between different stock market indicators are shown in Table 7-2. The table shows that all U.S. stock market indexes are highly positively correlated.
[30]The offsetting long and short positions need not be of equal dollar value to form a perfect hedge if leverage is used to alter the beta (or price elasticities) of either the long position or the short position or both. A perfect hedge can be formed with long and short positions of differing amounts if one or both positions are leveraged so that their simultaneous gains and losses are precisely offsetting. The price elasticities can also be changed by using put and/or call options.
[31]For a discussion of different techniques to establish the optimal hedge ratio, see Edward W. Schwartz, Joanne M. Hill, and Thomas Schneeweis, *Financial Futures* (Homewood, Ill.: Irwin, 1986), chap. 7. More recently, significant improvements have been suggested in the simple regression method used to determine hedge ratios. See Mark Castelino, "Basis Volatility: Implications for Hedging," *Journal of Financial Research,* Summer 1989. Also see Mark Castelino, "Futures Markets: Minimum Variance Hedging Revisited," *Journal of Portfolio Management,* Spring 1990.

have the same price at the contract's maturity, because the futures contract's cash settlement is based on the closing market value of the S&P 500. However, prior to the contract's maturity date the values of the S&P 500 and the futures contract on it fluctuate continuously and usually differ a little. In particular, a strong bull market can cause the stock market futures price to rise significantly above the index on which its price is based. Such disparities violate the *law of one price*. **Index arbitragers** earn profits by correcting deviations from the law of one price. Consider an example.

Stock Index Arbitrage: An Example Suppose the S&P 500 index is at 290 and at the same time a S&P 500 futures contract that matures in 3 months is trading at 293. In order to profit from this price disparity, index arbitragers buy the 500 stocks that make up the index in the same proportions as they are in the S&P 500 index and sell short the S&P 500 index futures. This imperfect hedge locks in profits equal to the three-point spread between the S&P 500 future at 293 and the basket of 500 stocks at 290.[32] In addition, the arbitragers get to keep whatever cash dividends may be paid by the 500 stocks they hold. Professional arbitragers typically create hedges like this that are worth $10 million or more—usually more.

Any fluctuations in the S&P 500 that may occur after the "index arb" establishes the arbitrage position cannot affect the three-point profit—it is locked in. For instance, if all 500 stocks somehow went bankrupt at once, the 290 loss on the basket of 500 stocks would be more than earned back from the short position in the S&P 500 futures contract as it plunged from 293 to zero. And, if the S&P 500 doubled its 290 value, the huge gain from the long position in the 500 stocks would be three points larger than the huge loss on the associated short position in the futures contract.

Index Arbitrage Algebraic Analysis There are different ways to synthesize stock market index arbitrage in order to derive a formula to value the futures contract. One possible scenario involves considering the following two investment arrangements.

Arrangement 1—buy the stocks in the index: Assume that at time $t = 0$ the investor can buy all the stocks that comprise the chosen stock market index (or shares in an index fund) for C dollars. Further assume that the investor wants to hold these securities until time T and that total cash dividends with a present value of v are paid during that holding period. If the investor sells the rights to all these cash dividends to a collection agent for v dollars when the stocks are purchased, the total initial outlay at time $t = 0$ for the basket

---

[32]The construction of the S&P 500 index is analyzed in Chap. 7. For a more detailed explanation of hedging and arbitrage see Sections 8-3, 8-8, and 8-9.

of stocks is $C - v$. Assume that at time T the terminal value (TV) of the basket of stocks turns out to be TV1 dollars.

Arrangement 2—buy the index futures: Assume that at time $t = 0$ the investor buys for F dollars a futures contract on the stock market index that represents the same value as the portfolio of indexed stocks. Assume the terminal value of the index futures contract turns out to be TV2 dollars. Thus, at terminal time $t = T$, this futures contract will be worth TV2 $- F$ dollars. Assume that also at time $t = 0$ the investor buys a T-bill that will also mature at time $t = T$ with a face value of F dollars. The T-bill pays zero coupons and yields riskless rate R so that it can be purchased for $F/(1 + R)$. The T-bill is left on deposit at the brokerage house to meet the margin requirements on the futures contract so that $F/(1 + R)$ is the total initial outlay for this arrangement. When the T-bill matures at time $t = T$, its proceeds of F dollars are returned so the arbitrager gets to keep a net total of TV2 dollars.

Table 24-3 summarizes the cashflows associated with arrangements 1 and 2 above. Stock index futures contracts are written so that the terminal value of the contract equals the terminal value of the underlying basket of stocks. Therefore, arrangements 1 and 2 in Table 24-3 must both be worth the same terminal values, TV1 = TV2. Since the two arrangements have identical terminal values at time $t = T$, the law of one price should cause their initial costs at time $t = 0$ to be equal. The initial costs at time $t = 0$ are equated in Equation (24-11) to gain some insights into what determines the futures price.

$$v - C = \frac{-F}{1 + R} \qquad (24\text{-}11)$$

Solving Equation (24-11) for the ratio F/C provides an equation that tells us how to value stock index futures contracts.

$$\frac{F}{C} = (1 + R) - \frac{v}{C}(1 + R) \qquad (24\text{-}11a)$$

$$= f\left(R, \frac{v}{C}\right)$$

The quantity v/C is the average cash dividend yield for the basket of stocks over the holding period. Equation (24-11a) says that the ratio F/C should (1) vary inversely with the average cash dividend yield from the basket of stocks, $d(F/C)/d(v/C) < 0$, and (2) vary directly with the riskless interest rate, $d(F/C)/dR > 0$. Note that as the delivery date approaches, the values of v and R both approach zero so that on the delivery date of $t = T$, the ratio reaches a value of $F/C = 1$. This intuitively pleasing terminal value is reassuring.

The stock market index futures valuation model of Equation (24-11a) was derived without considering whether the cash dividends could be forecast accurately or what the commission costs would do to the index arbitrage profits. Both problems are minor. Cash dividends can be forecast for a few months with great accuracy because most corporations make the same periodic cash

Table 24-3

CASHFLOWS FROM TWO ALTERNATIVE STOCK MARKET ARRANGEMENTS

Time in the future	$t = 0$	$t = T$
Arrangement 1—buy the stocks in the index		
Buy stocks	$-C$	TV1
Sell present value of cash dividends	v	
Totals	$v - C$	TV1
Arrangement 2—buy T-bill and index futures		
Buy stock index futures on margin		$TV2 - F$
Buy T-bill	$-F/(1 + R)$	F
Totals	$-F/(1 + R)$	TV2

dividend payments consistently. And the commission costs for large trades are tiny—10 cents per share is not unusual. Sometimes block traders will do large transactions for only 6 cents a share. As a result, Equation (24-11a) provides a fairly accurate guideline for pricing stock market index futures.

Using Futures Can Yield Substantial Savings in Commissions

The savings to a portfolio in commission costs alone can justify using futures contracts to hedge a common stock position rather than using the common stock itself to form an offsetting position. Consider the round-turn (buy and the sell) commissions for a $40 million portfolio.

If $40 million of common stock can be sold and bought back at a total round-turn commission cost of 1 percent, this transaction would involve $400,000 in commission costs. In contrast, the round-turn commission cost for a futures contract on the Standard & Poor's Index is only about $25 per contract. Since 500 of these futures contracts would hedge the $40 million portfolio, the total commission cost of using the futures contracts would be 500 contracts × $25 commission, or $12,500. The estimated commission savings is $400,000 − $12,500, or $387,500. The disadvantage of hedging with futures contracts is that after some months the futures contracts will expire; a new hedge must be established and the $12,500 commission cost must be incurred again if the need for the hedge remains. However, the futures commissions expenses in the example above could be repaid 32 times ($12,500 × 32 = $400,000) before they added up to the commissions on one round-turn in the stocks themselves.

24-8   **DO PROGRAM TRADING AND TRIPLE WITCHING HOURS DESTABILIZE THE MARKETS?**

Before financial futures contracts existed, **program trading** referred to purchases or sales of large blocks of securities in the secondary market that were ordered by a computer. The phrase still means the same thing, but financial futures have given program trading increased importance.

Portfolio insurance, examined in Section 23-9, causes portfolio managers to sell stock market index futures short and/or buy protective put options when market prices decline. If the trend reverses, the portfolio insurers buy futures and write puts. Large transactions need to be executed hurriedly because a large number of sell or buy orders are executed at about the same time. Portfolio insurance has increased the incidence of program trading.

Index funds include mutual funds, pension funds, and other diversified portfolios that buy and hold the securities that comprise some security market index. Index funds usually follow indexes on which liquid futures contracts are traded so that they can supplement their buy-and-hold investment returns with additional gains from *index arbitrage.* If their market index drops below the market value of the securities on which that index is based, some index funds sell a portion or all of their relatively overpriced securities. If their market index rises above the market value of the underlying securities, program trades are quickly executed to acquire underpriced stocks.

The large transactions executed by portfolio insurers and index arbitragers often generate hastily executed *program trades.* Such program trading of common stocks is usually routed through the NYSE Designated Order Turnaround (DOT) system in order to obtain executions almost instantaneously. It is claimed by some that these DOT trades and other programmed trades destabilize securities markets.[33]

The critics of program trading point out that the large transactions it creates tend to exacerbate fluctuations in the market. However, a report prepared by the U.S. Commodity Futures Trading Commission argues that program trading of futures contracts is not destabilizing.[34] In particular, this federal government study reports that program trading did not contribute to the October 1987 securities market crash.

Program trading is not the only potentially destabilizing influence in the stock markets. The financial markets were typically disrupted on those quarterly days when many options and futures contracts on stock market indexes all matured on the same day. The closing hour of trading on those days when the

---

[33]See Ira G. Kawaller, Paul D. Koch, and Timothy W. Koch, "The Temporal Price Relationship between S&P 500 Futures and the S&P 500 Index," *Journal of Finance,* Dec. 1987, pp. 185–217. Also see this book's discussion of the October 1987 securities market crash and the Brady report.

[34]U.S. Commodity Futures Trading Commission, *Final Report on Stock Index Futures and Cash Market Activity during October 1987,* published by the CFTC in January 1988. Also see Dean Furbush, "Program Trading and Price Movement: Evidence from the October 1987 Stock Market Crash," *Financial Management,* Autumn 1989, vol. 18, no. 3, pp. 68–83. Mr. Furbush is an SEC economist; his study concludes that portfolio insurance and other forms of program trading did not contribute to the October 1987 market crash.

options on many individual stocks expire, the options on stock market indexes expire, and the futures contracts on the stock market index mature is called a **triple witching hour.** The volatility of the affected markets increases noticeably during the last hour of trading when many large blocks of stock are liquidated.[35] To make matters even worse, the hasty block trades touched off by these program traders tend to involve selling into bearish markets and buying into bullish markets. In 1989 the exchanges varied the expiration times of the financial instruments in hopes of reducing the impact of the triple witching hour.

24-9   **SUMMARY AND CONCLUSIONS**

Commodities are homogeneous raw materials traded in large volumes every day. To protect themselves against the risk of adverse price fluctuations in these commodities, business people have developed financial instruments called commodity futures contracts. Futures contracts are bought and sold at commodity exchanges in trading rings where buyers and sellers who are members of the exchange come together. The bid prices of potential buyers and the asked prices of potential sellers are proclaimed in *open outcry* as trades are consummated.

Commodity price *speculators* buy futures contracts with the intention of buying (selling short) them at a lower (higher) price than the price for which they sell (buy to cover their short position). Speculators rarely take delivery on their futures contracts. In contrast, *hedgers* use futures contracts to reduce their risk exposure rather than as a way to earn speculative profits. Speculators and hedgers buy and sell futures contracts among themselves as they pursue their speculative profits and risk-averting hedges, respectively.

Futures prices normally exceed spot prices by the amount of the carrying charges. However, *inverted markets* occur when futures prices are less than spot prices. The difference between the *spot price* and the *futures price* is called the *basis.* The spot and futures prices converge and force the basis to zero when the contract's delivery date arrives.

Interest rate futures have bonds or other interest-rate-sensitive assets as the deliverable commodity. Futures contracts on Treasury bills, notes, and bonds

---

[35]For a study of the effects of triple witching hours, see H. R. Stoll and R. Whaley, "Program Trading and Expiration Day Effects," *Financial Analysts Journal,* March–April 1987, vol. 43, no. 2, pp. 16–28. Also see Arnold King, "How the Stock Market Can Learn to Live with Index Futures and Options," *Financial Analysts Journal,* Sept.–Oct. 1987, vol. 43, no. 5, pp. 33–39. And, see G. J. Santoni, "Has Program Trading Made Stock Prices More Volatile?" *Review,* published by the Federal Reserve Bank of St. Louis, vol. 69, no. 5, pp. 18–29. More recently, see Raymond M. Leuthold, Joan C. Junkus, and Jean E. Cordier, *The Theory and Practice of Futures Markets* (Lexington, Mass.: Lexington Books, D. C. Heath, 1989), pp. 267–268, 355, 379.

are examples of some of the financial instruments used by both speculators and hedgers. The factors that shape the prices of futures contracts on Treasury securities were reviewed. *Swaps, arbitrage,* and the desire to deliver the *cheapest available instrument* were shown to provide support for the *law of one price*.

Chapter 7 explained that stock market averages and indexes are indicators that track the average price of the securities in particular markets. Chapter 24 introduces futures contracts on stock market indexes; the explanation uses the Standard & Poor's 500 Stocks Composite Index as an indicator for a *cash settlement* futures contract rather than as a deliverable commodity. *Initial margins, variation (or maintenance) margins,* and the requirement of all commodity exchanges to *mark to the market* at the close of each day's trading were all reviewed. Then various strategies available to those who foresee either bull or bear markets and want to speculate accordingly were presented. Hedging strategies for risk-averters were investigated. Finally, index arbitrage, which is a source of *program trades,* was examined.

Financial futures contracts are still a fairly new product; new products are still rapidly emerging, and much growth in the futures industry lies ahead.

Essay Questions

24-1 Compare and contrast selling a futures contract without owning an inventory in the commodity and selling a common stock short.

24-2 What functions are performed by the clearing house at a commodity exchange?

24-3 Define an inverted market and suggest what might cause one to occur.

24-4 "Futures prices are determined after spot prices are known. Adding carrying costs to spot prices yields futures prices." Is this statement true, false, or uncertain? Explain.

24-5 "Speculation is an evil pastime for wealthy playboys. It destabilizes prices and misallocates resources, and it should be made illegal." Is the quotation true, false, or uncertain? Explain.

24-6 Why do you think there are no futures markets for commodities like coal, raisins, and salt? Does the absence of futures markets mean that no speculation in these commodities occurs?

24-7 Assume you are hired by the Chicago Board of Trade (CBT) to be a consultant to its New Products Committee. You are directed to do research to discern commodities on which the CBT might advantageously trade futures contracts. List and explain six criteria you would adopt for screening commodities in order to select high-volume candidates in which the CBT might initiate trading.

24-8 What determines the size and sign of the basis for (*a*) an agricultural commodity? (*b*) a financial future?

24-9   What factors prevent hedges from being a perfect hedge? Explain.

24-10 Suppose that long-term Treasury bonds are currently yielding higher interest rates than Treasury notes—that is, the yield curve is sloping upward. Further assume that you have done economic research that makes you confident that the yield curve will flatten out, causing the yield spread between T-notes and T-bonds to narrow. How can you profit from this flattening of the yield curve if your expectations are borne out?

24-11 "The existence of two almost identical T-bill futures contracts which are traded at competing commodity exchanges is economically undesirable because it fragments the market." Is the preceding sentence true, false, or uncertain? Explain.

24-12 If someone buys a Treasury bond in a long position and then realizes that the T-bond's price is going to decline because of a previously unforeseen turn in interest rates, what can they do to avoid losses? Describe more than one way to avoid the imminent loss.

24-13 Compare and contrast a long position in futures contracts with owning a call option position of the same size on the same asset. *Hint: Refer to the chapter about call options.*

Problems

24-14 Define the one-period rate of return for a commodity investor who purchased a futures contract on margin and gave the commodity broker a U.S. Treasury bill to hold as the margin.

24-15 (*a*) Jim Jones expects to harvest 40,000 bushels of soybeans from his farm in September 19XX. On May 1, 19XX the September futures price of soybeans is $6.00 per bushel. If Jim believes this is a good price, what should he do to lock in the $6.00 price? (*b*) Show Jim's position at the September harvest if the futures price of soybeans falls to $5.00 a bushel and the basis is zero. Ignore commission charges and taxes.

24-16 Elaine Franklin grows cotton. As of June 19XX Elaine expects to produce 300,000 pounds of cotton for her September 19XX harvest. The September futures price for cotton is $0.80 per pound. (*a*) If Elaine decides to hedge one-half of her production, what should she do? (*b*) What would Elaine's price gain or loss on her cotton be if the futures price of cotton falls to $0.60 per pound at harvest time and the basis is zero? Ignore commission charges and taxes.

24-17 In July 19XX Mrs. Sample's Syrup Company signed a contract with several food distributors to deliver several truckloads of syrup in November 19XX at the price agreed on in July. A Vice President of Mrs. Sample's Syrup is concerned about the rising price of sugar between now and November. (*a*) What should the company do to hedge its profit on the syrup sale? Assume that 672,000 pounds of sugar will be needed to produce the syrup and that the current price of sugar is $0.23 per pound. (*b*) If the price of sugar goes to $0.35 per pound and if Mrs.

Sample's Syrup Company does not hedge its position, how much would they lose? Ignore commission costs.

24-18 The Taylor Construction Company recently signed a contract to construct several condos at a fixed price. J. G. Taylor, owner of the company, is fearful of rising lumber prices. (*a*) What should Taylor do to hedge the firm's lumber position? Assume that 1.5 million board feet of lumber will be necessary and that the current price per 1000 board feet is $178. The condos are scheduled to be completed in about 8 months. *Hint: Outside research into lumber contract units is needed.* (*b*) What would be the loss for Taylor Construction Company if the company did not hedge its position and the price of lumber rose to $190 per 1000 board feet? Ignore commission costs.

24-19 Assume it is June 1, 19XX, you expect the price of wheat to increase over the next 3 months, initial margin requirements call for a minimum of 10 percent down, and the current price of wheat is $3 per bushel. (*a*) If you have $10,000 to invest, what should you do? Assume a $40 commission per contract. (*b*) Assume you purchased six wheat contracts on June 1, 19XX and then the price of wheat goes to $3.50 per bushel over the next 3 months. What is your rate of return after commission costs? (*c*) How much will you earn or lose net of commission costs if you take the long position on June 1, 19XX and the price of wheat goes to $2.25 per bushel over the next 3 months?

24-20 In March 19XX you are bearish on the price of gold over the next 6 months. If you sell 10 gold futures contracts short at the price of $450 per troy ounce, what will you earn if the price of gold goes to $400 per troy ounce over this period? Assume a $1500 margin and $35 commission per contract.

24-21 Assume you were managing a $7.5 million portfolio of common stock and were bearish about the next 6 months. (*a*) If 6-month futures contracts on the S&P 500 are available and the S&P 500 index is currently at 150, how can you advantageously use your bearish expectations to hedge your long position in the stock market? (*b*) What will happen to the overall value of the portfolio if it has been fully hedged and the common stock portfolio declines in value by $1.5 million to a total value of $6 million and the S&P 500 index simultaneously falls to 120?

24-22 Today Joe Speculator is bearish on the stock market. (*a*) What return will Joe make if the S&P 500 index is currently at 130 and Joe sells 10 S&P 500 futures contracts short? Assume that 6 months from now the S&P 500 has fallen to 100. (*b*) What return will Joe earn if the S&P 500 index increases to 150 over 6 months? (*c*) Calculate Joe's rate of return in part (*b*) if he had invested on a 10 percent margin.

Selected References

Anderson, Ronald W., ed., *The Industrial Organization of Futures Markets* (Lexington, Mass.: Lexington Books, 1984).

   A collection of scholarly articles about futures markets. Several chapters analyze price manipulation.

Duffie, Darrell, *Futures Markets* (Englewood Cliffs, N.J.: Prentice-Hall, 1989).

This MBA-level textbook presents a rigorous and concise discussion of futures contracts, futures markets, futures options, hedging, and the federal regulatory framework. Mathematical statistics is used. The book also lists some helpful Fortran computer codes.

Fabozzi, Frank J., and Gregory M. Kipnis, eds., *Handbook of Stock Index Futures and Options* (Homewood, Ill.: Dow Jones–Irwin, 1989).

A collection of articles about different aspects of stock index futures and options written by experts in their respective segments of the subject.

Kaufman, Perry J., *Handbook of Futures Markets* (New York: Wiley-Interscience, 1984).

A thick nonmathematical volume of facts about commodities, futures contracts (including financial futures), and options.

Leuthold, Raymond M., Joan C. Junkus, and Jean E. Cordier, *The Theory and Practice of Futures Markets* (Lexington, Mass.: Lexington Books, D. C. Heath, 1989).

This comprehensive college textbook analyzes every aspect of futures markets, futures trading, and options on futures. Calculus and statistics are used.

Samuelson, Paul, "Intertemporal Price Equilibrium: A Prologue to the Theory of Speculation," *Weltwirtschaftliches Archiv,* 1957, vol. 79, pp. 181–219; reprinted in J. E. Stiglitz, ed., *Collected Scientific Papers of Paul A. Samuelson,* Vol. II (Cambridge, Mass.: MIT Press, 1966), chap. 73, pp. 946–984.

This classic article by the Nobel laureate analyzes the price determinants for storable agricultural commodities.

Siegel, Daniel R., and Diane F. Siegel, *Futures Markets* (Orlando, Florida: Dryden Press, 1990).

A textbook for advanced undergraduates or masters students that covers financial futures, agricultural futures, options, and options on futures.

Appendix 24A

Options on Futures

Chapters 22 and 23 introduced options and Chapter 24 introduced futures contracts. This appendix considers options and futures together and discusses a financial instrument called a **futures option,** or an **option on a futures contract,** or a **commodity futures option.** Figure 24A-1 is a newspaper excerpt that shows one day's price quotations for some actively traded futures options.

Characteristics of Futures Options

All options on futures are two steps removed from the underlying asset. First, there is the futures contract on the underlying asset. Second, there is the put or call option on the futures contract. This seems complicated. But options on futures are actually like ordinary futures contracts that have only limited liability and different margin procedures.

Buying a Futures Option   The *buyer* of one futures option may exercise the option to assume a position in one future. But the position which will be assumed depends on whether the option buyer purchased a put or a call. If a *call option was purchased,* the buyer has the right to exercise the call option by purchasing a long (but not a short) position in the specified future at the exercise price that was stipulated in the option contract. In contrast, if a *put option was purchased,* the buyer has the option to exercise that put by establishing a short (not a long) position in the specific future at the exercise price which was stipulated in the put option contract. Put and call options must be exercised or sold before their maturity dates, or they will expire and become worthless. The buyers of put and call options on futures have the right, but not an obligation, to exercise the options that they have purchased. Options need not be exercised to be profitable, however. Options are marketable financial instruments. The owners of profitable put and call options on futures usually choose to realize their profits by selling the option for a higher price than they paid for it instead of exercising it and entering a futures market position.

Writing a Futures Option   Consider the responsibility of the seller of the futures option. Unlike the option buyer, the option writer has a *legal obligation* to perform.

OPTIONS ON FUTURES

Financial

3-MO. EURODOLLAR DEPOSITS (IMM)
$1 million; pts of 100%

Strike	Calls-Last			Puts-Last		
Price	Jun	Sep	Dec	Jun	Sep	Dec
9025	0.41	0.87	1.09	r	0:10	0.16
9050	0.17	0.68	0.91	0.01	0.14	0.22
9075	0.02	0.50	0.74	0.11	0.21	0.29
9100	0.01	0.35	0.60	0.34	0.30	0.38
9125	r	0.23	0.45	0.59	0.43	0.48
9150	r	0.14	0.34	0.84	0.58	0.61
9175	r	0.08	0.25	s	0.77	0.76

Prev.day calls vol: 9,599 Open int. 199,356
Prev.day puts vol. 8,056 Open int. 250,395

10-YR. U.S. TREASURY NOTES (CBT)
$100,000 prin, pts & 64ths of 100%

Strike	Calls-Last			Puts-Last		
Price	Sep	Dec	Mar	Sep	Dec	Mar
96	2-25	3-05	s	0-41	1-14	s
97	1-47	2-29	s	1-00	1-37	s
98	1-13	1-61	s	1-27	2-01	s
99	0-50	r	s	2-02	r	s
100	0-33	1-13	s	2-47	s	s
101	0-19	r	s	s	s	s
102	0-12	r	s	s	s	s

Estimated volume 2,800
Prev.day calls vol. 1,863 Open int. 20,713
Prev.day puts vol. 877 Open int. 24,835

U.S. TREASURY BONDS (CBT)
$100,000, pts & 64ths of 100%

Strike	Calls-Last			Puts-Last		
Price	Sep	Dec	Mar	Sep	Dec	Mar
90	5-43	6-00	r	0-20	0-57	1-33
92	3-63	4-32	4-60	0-39	1-24	2-00
94	2-36	3-18	3-46	1-10	2-02	2-50
96	1-31	2-18	2-50	2-02	2-59	3-46
98	0-51	1-33	2-07	3-21	s	s
100	0-26	0-62	1-30	4-59	s	s
102	0-13	0-39	1-06	6-45	s	s

Estimated volume 105,000
Prev.day calls vol. 42,770 Open int. 278,590
Prev.day puts vol. 26,388 Open int. 229,639

MUNICIPAL BOND INDEX (CBT)
1,000 x index, pts & 32ds of 100%

Strike	Calls-Last			Puts-Last		
Price	Jun	Sep	Dec	Jun	Sep	Dec
86	8-32	s	r	0-01	s	r
88	6-32	s	r	0-01	s	r
90	4-32	s	s	0-01	0-21	s
92	2-32	2-58	3-08	0-01	0-50	1-40
94	0-41	1-44	s	0-09	1-34	s
96	0-02	0-59	1-23	1-33	s	3-42
98	s	0-26	s	r	s	s

Estimated volume 12,000
Prev.day calls vol. 1,145 Open int. 3,910
Prev.day puts vol. 1,100 Open int. 5,057

BRITISH POUND (IMM)
62,500 pounds, cents per pound

Strike	Calls-Last			Puts-Last		
Price	Jul	Aug	Sep	Jul	Aug	Sep
1475	5.76	r	r	0.82	1.40	2.12
1500	3.96	4.70	5.40	1.52	2.24	2.96
1525	2.56	3.34	4.08	2.58	3.36	4.06
1550	1.42	2.28	3.00	4.02	4.80	5.40
1575	0.84	1.50	2.14	5.84	6.44	7.00
1600	0.42	0.94	1.50	7.90	8.38	8.84
1625	0.26	0.60	1.06	10.16	10.50	10.80

Prev.day calls vol. 1,147 Open int. 10,034
Prev.day puts vol. 592 Open int. 9,733

CANADIAN DOLLAR (IMM)
100,000 dollars, cents per dollar

Strike	Calls-Last			Puts-Last		
Price	Jul	Aug	Sep	Jul	Aug	Sep
825	0.52	0.74	0.87	0.25	0.41	0.54
830	0.27	0.50	0.63	0.46	0.69	0.84
835	0.13	r	0.42	0.82	r	1.11
840	0.06	0.18	0.30	1.25	r	1.46
845	0.02	r	0.19	r	r	r
850	0.01	r	0.12	r	r	r
855	r	r	0.08	r	r	r

Prev.day calls vol. 74 Open int. 6,789
Prev.day puts vol. 228 Open int. 9,608

WEST GERMAN MARK (IMM)
125,000 marks, cents per mark

Strike	Calls-Last			Puts-Last		
Price	Jul	Aug	Sep	Jul	Aug	Sep
47	3.38	s	r	0.06	0.14	0.27
48	2.47	r	2.77	0.14	0.27	0.45
49	1.65	1.86	2.07	0.31	0.52	0.73
50	0.98	1.24	1.48	0.63	0.89	1.13
51	0.52	0.78	1.03	1.17	1.42	1.66
52	0.25	0.47	0.68	1.90	2.12	2.30
53	0.12	0.27	0.43	2.76	2.90	3.03

Prev.day calls vol. 3,105 Open int. 72,988
Prev.day puts vol. 8,672 Open int. 87,929

Figure 24A-1 Newspaper quotations for futures options.

What option writers are obligated to perform, however, depends on whether they sold a put or a call option.

If the *writer of one call option* on a futures contract is notified that the buyer is exercising the option, the call seller must instantly deliver the specified futures contract. More precisely, the call seller must deliver the optioned futures contract at the stipulated exercise price and the delivered contract must be fully marked to the market at the time it is delivered. If the writer of the option does not have a long position in the deliverable instrument, the writer must pay the initial margin and assume a short position in the futures contract.

Next, let's consider the position of someone who wrote a put option on a future. If the *writer of one put option on a futures contract* is notified that the buyer is exercising the option, the put seller is obliged to instantly assume a long position. That is, the put writer must accept delivery by letting the option buyer put the optioned futures contract to them at the exercise price.

Rights versus Obligations for the Option Parties

Options are *unilateral* contracts. In contrast, futures contracts are *bilateral* contracts. Anyone who buys a futures option acquires the right—but not the obligation—to assume a long or a short position in one futures contract at the prearranged exercise price at any time during the life of the option, assuming it is an American option. (European options are usually written on forward contracts.) Since option buyers have no obligation to perform after their premium is paid, they are not required to mark to the market as are the sellers of futures options.

In contrast to option buyers, anyone who writes a futures option is committed to assume a long or a short position (for a call or a put, respectively) in the futures market at the striking price if the buyer exercises the option. Since option writers are required to perform, these writers are required to deposit an initial margin when a position is opened. Furthermore, this margin is marked to the market daily to reflect changes in the market value of the futures option.

The buyer of an American option on a futures contract may exercise the option at any time before it expires. All this takes is a phone call to the buyer's broker, who then notifies the clearing house. The clearing house will proceed to establish a futures position for the buyer—a long position for a call option writer or a short position for a put option writer. At the same time, the seller of the option is obliged to instantly assume the opposite futures position at the prearranged exercise price.

Assigning a particular option writer to respond to a buyer exercising an option is done on a first-in-first-out basis at the exchanges. Typically, the clearing house member that has the largest number of positions in an option that expires in the relevant month is first selected by the clearing house's computer, which keeps an inventory of writers. Then, the oldest outstanding written option within that clearing house member's inventory is selected to fulfill the demands of the exercising option buyer.

Futures Options Specifications: A T-Bond Example

As might be expected, the expiration months for options on T-bond futures are identical to the delivery months on T-bond futures—March, June, September, and December of each year.

The market prices of both T-bonds and T-bond futures are quoted in terms of percentage points followed by thirty-seconds of a percentage point. For example, a T-bond quoted at 99-16 would be worth $99\frac{16}{32}$ or 99.5 percent of the bond's face value. Thus, a $100,000 T-bond quoted at 99-16 would be worth $99,500. Each thirty-second of a point is worth $31.25 for a $100,000 bond.

Unlike T-bond futures, options on T-bond futures are quoted in sixty-fourths of a percentage point. A premium of 2-32, for instance, represents a premium of $2500.

Determinants of Premiums for a Call on a T-Bond Future

Consider a futures option on a T-bond future that has an exercise price of 60 percent of face value. Figure 24A-2 illustrates the determination of this option's price. When the underlying T-bond

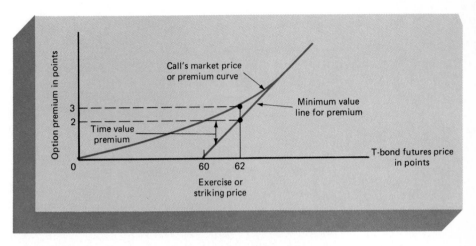

Figure 24A-2 Premium breakdown for call on T-bond future.

futures contracts are trading at 62-00, the call option on these contracts has a *minimum value* or *intrinsic value* of two points, denoted 2-00. However, the price on this call is 3-00 points (that is, $3000) because the premium is one point above its intrinsic value when the T-bond future's price is 62-00. The *premium over intrinsic value* for a call option is calculated as follows:

$$
\begin{matrix}
\text{Premium over} & \text{call} & & & \text{market price} \\
\text{intrinsic} & = \text{option's} & + \text{exercise} & - \text{of underlying} \\
\text{value} & \text{premium} & \text{price} & \text{asset} \\
\\
1 & = \quad 3 & + \quad 60 & - \quad 62
\end{matrix}
$$

Determinants of Premiums for a Put on a T-Bond Future   Figure 24A-3 illustrates the primary determinants that influence premiums for a put option on a T-bond future when the exercise price is 60-00. If the underlying T-bond future is trading at 58-00 (that is, $58,000 for a $100,000 T-bond), the put option's premium is 3-00 points (namely, $3000). This 3-00 point market price is made up of an intrinsic value of 2-00 plus a **premium over intrinsic value** (or **time value premium**) of one point.

$$
\begin{matrix}
\text{Premium} & & & \\
\text{over} & \text{put's} & \text{put's} & \text{put's} \\
\text{intrinsic} & = \text{premium} & + \text{market} & - \text{exercise} \\
\text{value} & \text{or price} & \text{price} & \text{price} \\
\\
1 & = \quad 3 & + \quad 58 & - \quad 60
\end{matrix}
$$

Advantages and Disadvantages of Options on Futures

Are there any advantages to buying options on futures instead of simply buying the same futures contract directly? The answer is yes, there are two advantages. First, speculators who buy options on futures enjoy *limited liability;* the buyer of an option on a futures contract cannot lose more than the premium paid for the option. In contrast, those who buy futures contracts directly must put down an initial margin and then mark to the market based on each day's settlement price. As a result, the owner of a futures contract could lose much more than the cost of an option's premium. Option buyers

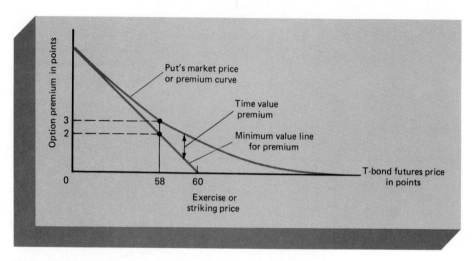

Figure 24A-3 Premium breakdown for put on T-bond future.

do not obtain this limited liability for nothing. Options do not become profitable until the price of the underlying asset moves far enough in the appropriate direction to cover the cost of the option's premium. As a result, speculators who forecast the market's move correctly will always make a larger gain from a futures contract than from a futures option on the same contract.

The second advantage of futures options is that they probably require *less cash* than may be needed to buy the option on the underlying commodity directly. This advantage becomes evident when comparing the exercise cost of the two different options. When a direct option is exercised on the underlying asset, the underlying asset must be purchased with cash—this is a large outlay.[36] In contrast, someone who exercised an option on a futures contract need only pay the *initial margin* on the future. However, the low-cost exercise advantage may be worthless to some speculators. After all, the options need not be exercised to be profitable. Futures options that have appreciated over their initial premium can simply be sold to another speculator in order to realize the gain. Therefore, buying the option on a future is an advantage over buying the option directly to buyers who may want to exercise the option instead of simply selling it to recognize a gain.

Selected Appendix References

Black, Fischer, "The Pricing of Commodity Contracts," *Journal of Financial Economics,* vol. 3, nos. 1 and 2, pp. 167–179.

[36]Options on most physical commodities are not available in the United States. Thus, the discussion of acquiring optioned physical commodities must be taken within a limited context. Over-the-counter (OTC) options on any commodity can be tailor-made and their prices determined by negotiation. But OTC options are less liquid than listed options, and their price determination process can be difficult.

Moriarity, Eugene, Susan Phillips, and Paula Tosini, "A Comparison of Options and Futures in the Management of Portfolio Risk," *Financial Analysts Journal,* Jan.–Feb. 1981, pp. 61–67.

Turnbull, Stuart M., *Option Valuation* (Toronto, Ontario: Holt, Rinehart and Winston of Canada, Ltd., 1987). Chapter 8 explains a computer program that can be useful in evaluating options on futures.

Wolf, Avner, "Fundamentals of Commodity Options on Futures," *Journal of Futures Market,* 1982, vol. 2, no. 4, pp. 391–408.

Chapter 25

International Investing

Figure 1-1 illustrates how markets around the world reacted to the **international stock market crash of October 1987.**[1] This simultaneous multinational collapse occurred in spite of the plethora of disparate institutional arrangements that characterize international stock markets. (Table 3-9 summarizes the institutional arrangements in 23 different countries.) Systematic market movements like the ones that occurred simultaneously in October of 1987 around the world result from similar beliefs about what determines investment values combined with telecommunication networks that disseminate economic news instantly. Essentially, fast and far-reaching information processing has fostered an international stock market that transcends the boundaries of any single country.

New York, Tokyo, and London are the three most important financial markets in the world.[2] Substantial international financial markets exist in other cities too. One of these stock markets is open almost every hour of the day. Figure 25-1 lists stock market indexes from these markets as they are published

---

[1]See Richard Roll, "The International Crash of 1987," *Financial Analysts Journal,* Sept.–Oct. 1988, pp. 19–35. Also see Avner Arbel and Albert E. Kaff, *Crash: Ten Days in October . . . Will It Strike Again* (Chicago, Ill.: Longman Financial Services, 1989). See also A. Arbel, S. Carvell, and E. Postnieks, "The Smart Crash of October 19th," *Harvard Business Review,* May–June 1988, pp. 124–136.

[2]For empirical estimates of the value of worldwide invested wealth and the rates of return it yields, see R. G. Ibbotson, L. B. Siegel, and K. S. Love, "World Wealth: Market Values and Returns," *Journal of Portfolio Management,* Fall 1985, vol. 12, no. 1, pp. 1–11. Also see R. G. Ibbotson, R. C. Carr, and A. W. Robinson, "International Equity and Bond Returns," *Financial Analysts Journal,* July–Aug. 1982, vol. 38, no. 4, pp. 61–83. Some of this material is in Chapter 7 of this book, see Table 7-4. For empirical bond return data, see M. Adler, "Global Fixed-Income Management," *Financial Analysts Journal,* Sept.–Oct. 1983.

EXCHANGE	8/7/89 CLOSE	NET CHG	PCT CHG
Tokyo Nikkei Average	34630.38	− 111.61	− 0.32
Tokyo Topix Index	2615.48	+ 2.21	+ 0.08
London FT 30-share	1957.0	+ 16.2	+ 0.83
London 100-share	2341.5	+ 14.0	+ 0.60
London Gold Mines	202.4	− 0.5	− 0.25
Frankfurt DAX	1592.03	+ 1.73	+ 0.11
Zurich Credit Suisse	651.6	+ 4.3	+ 0.66
Paris CAC General	502.6	− 2.2	− 0.44
Milan Stock Index	1180	+ 7	+ 0.60
Amsterdam ANP-CBS General	204.5	+ 0.8	+ 0.39
Stockholm Affarsvarlden	1312.4	− 4.4	− 0.33
Brussels Stock Index	6287.64	+ 15.34	+ 0.24
Australia All Ordinaries	1680.0	+ 9.1	+ 0.54
Hong Kong Hang Seng	2563.77	− 15.3	− 0.59
Singapore Straits Times	1351.74	+ 2.56	+ 0.19
Johannesburg J'burg Gold	1656	− 22	− 1.31
Toronto 300 Composite	closed		
Euro, Aust, Far East MSCI-p	979.8	− 11.7	− 1.18
p-Preliminary			

	Aug 4	Aug 3	% This Year
U.S.	316.7	317.4	+ 23.7
Britain	702.8	697.5	+ 28.7
Canada	433.0	433.2	+ 17.9
Japan	1546.5	1549.1	+ 8.9
France	523.2	526.9	+ 18.2
Germany	249.0	247.5	+ 19.8
Hong Kong	1922.3	1970.7	− 5.3
Switzerland	228.4	228.4	+ 15.6
Australia	335.7	335.1	+ 15.6
World Index	542.0	545.4	+ 9.6

(a) (b)

Figure 25-1 Newspaper excerpt showing daily values of stock market indexes from around the world: (a) foreign stock market indexes; (b) Morgan Stanley indexes.

regularly in the financial press. Informative and timely financial indicators like these help keep geographically segregated financial markets economically intertwined. Nevertheless, the cultures and institutions of the countries of the world differ sufficiently to maintain some significant disparities between their capital markets. This chapter explores the varied investment opportunities that are evolving in today's complicated and dynamic global financial market.

25-1   MULTINATIONAL DIVERSIFICATION

Portfolio theory is a useful tool with which to analyze the possibilities made available through multinational investing.

Grubel's Classic Analysis

The initial application of portfolio theory in an international context was by Professor Herb Grubel.[3] Grubel's model assumes two countries that are economically isolated. In each of these countries, there are three types of wealth: real assets, money, and marketable bonds. The model explores what happens when the initial economic barriers are removed, assuming that only marketable bonds and consumer goods are traded. Neither money nor real assets may be traded. The consumer goods are assumed to be consumed immediately rather than becoming objects of international trade. In this model a portfolio of marketable bonds from both countries would have an expected return that is de-

[3]Herbert Grubel, "Internationally Diversified Portfolios: Welfare Gains and Capital Flows," *American Economic Review*, Dec. 1968, pp. 1299–1314.

Table 25-1

IMPACT OF INTERCOUNTRY RETURN CORRELATIONS ON THE VARIANCE FROM AN INTERNATIONAL PORTFOLIO

$E(r_1) = E(r_2) = 10\% = $ expected returns in the two countries

$\sigma_1^2 = \sigma_2^2 = 16\% = $ variance of expected returns

$x = 1 - x = 0.50 = $ proportion of assets invested in each country

$$E(r_p) = (x)E(r_1) + (1 - x)E(r_2) \tag{25-1}$$

$$E(r_p) = (0.5)(0.1) + (1.0 - 0.5)(0.1) = 0.1 = 10.0\% \tag{25-1a}$$

$$\text{Var}(r_p) = x^2 \text{ Var}(r_1) + (1 - x)^2 \text{ Var}(r_2) + 2x(1 - x)\sigma_1\sigma_2\rho_{1,2} \tag{25-2}$$

$$= (0.5)^2(0.16) + (1.0 - 0.5)^2(0.16)$$
$$+ 2(0.5)(1.0 - 0.5)\sqrt{0.16}\sqrt{0.16}\ \rho_{1,2} \tag{25-2a}$$

$$\text{Var}(r_p) = 0.08 + 0.08\rho_{1,2} \tag{25-2b}$$

Numerical illustration of the variance reduction:

If the correlation is:	+1.0	+.50	0.0	−.50	−1.0
$\text{Var}(r_p)$ will be:	0.16	0.12	0.08	0.04	0

termined by the expected returns in each country and the proportion of assets invested in each country, as specified in Equation (25-1).

$$E(r_p) = (x)E(r_1) + (1 - x)E(r_2) \tag{25-1}$$

The conventions employed in Equation (25-1) are defined in terms of someone who lives in country 1 and are listed below. These terms are all presumed to be adjusted to reflect foreign exchange risk, or else it is assumed that the foreign exchange rates are pegged.

$E(r_p) = $ expected return from an international portfolio of marketable bonds from countries 1 and 2

$E(r_i) = $ expected return on bonds in country i

$x = $ proportion of the international portfolio's assets invested in country 1, $1.0 > x > 0$

$1 - x = $ proportion of assets invested in country 2

The variance of this two-country bond portfolio, $\text{Var}(r_p)$, would be determined by the variances of returns in each country, the proportion of assets invested in each country, x and $1 - x$, and the correlation of returns between both countries' bonds, as shown in Equation (25-2).

$$\text{Var}(r_p) = x^2 \, \text{Var}(r_1) + (1 - x)^2 \, \text{Var}(r_2) + 2x(1 - x)\sigma_1\sigma_2\rho_{1,2} \qquad (25\text{-}2)$$

where $\text{Var}(r_1) = \sigma_1^2 = $ variance of returns in country 1

$\quad\quad \text{Var}(r_2) = \sigma_2^2 = $ variance of returns in country 2 as seen from country 1
and adjusted for any changes in foreign exchange rate

$\quad\quad\quad\quad \rho_{1,2} = $ correlation coefficient between two countries' investment returns

Table 25-1 illustrates the risk-reduction benefits available to the international investor as the correlation between the two countries' rates of return varies. The intercountry correlation is seen to be important to risk reduction through **multinational diversification.** Table 25-2 presents empirical estimates of the correlations between common stock portfolios in the United States and various foreign countries which can be used to estimate the potential benefits of risk reduction. Table 7-4 shows the intercountry correlations between various categories of investments in different countries.

Table 25-2 shows that estimates of the correlation between the U.S. stock market and foreign stock markets have ranged from as high as .8598 with the

Table 25-2
SUMMARY OF INTERCOUNTRY CORRELATIONS WITH THE UNITED STATES

Sources*	(1)	(2)	(3)	(4)	(5)	(6)
United States	1.000					
Canada	.7025		.8598	.4895		.263
United Kingdom	.2414	.578	.5836	.6420	.26	.225
West Germany	.3008	.335	.4062	.4337	.43	.141
France	.1938	.542	.4139	.1820	.34	.196
Italy	.1465				.09	
Belgium	.1080	.621			.83	
Netherlands	.2107	.583			.53	.189
Japan	.1149		.1796	.5279	−.26	.107
Australia	.0584		.4311	.6626		.225
South Africa	−.1620				.08	
Switzerland		.68				.201
Spain			.0098	.3230		
Venezuela					−.17	
Austria					.26	
Denmark					.19	
Mexico					.02	
New Zealand					.08	

Sources: (1) H. Grubel, 1959–1966 annual, 1968 AER; (2) B. Jacquillat and B. Solnik, 1974–1976 monthly, 1978 JPM; (3) A. M. Rugman, 1951–1975 annual, 1977 JEB; (4) A. M. Rugman, 1970–1975 monthly, 1977 JEB; (5) H. Levy and M. Sarnat, 1951–1967 annual, 1970 AER; (6) D.C. Cho, C.S. Eun, and L.W. Senbet, 1973–1983 monthly, 1986 JF.

Canadian market to as low as $-.26$ with the Japanese market.[4] The use of the correlations from Table 25-2 in the risk analysis model shown in Table 25-1 shows that equal investments in Canada and the United States, for example, would produce a portfolio variance of only 14.88 percent versus 16.0 percent for an investment that was totally in the United States. Equal investments in the United States and Japan could have lowered the portfolio's variance to only 5.92 percent. These results suggest that international diversification could have benefited U.S. investors—and foreign investors as well.[5]

International Investors' Efficient Frontier

It is possible to analyze the effect of multinational diversification on the Markowitz efficient frontier. Not surprisingly, as the number of countries in which investments are made increases, more desirable efficient frontiers become attainable.

Point F in Figure 25-2 indicates the risk level and rate of return for the U.S. stock market alone. Efficient frontier E shows the risk and return combinations which are available from investing only in developing countries; this option is dominated by all the other investment alternatives illustrated in Figure 25-2. Even though point F in the figure represents a portfolio that is fully diversified within the United States, this portfolio is not efficient in an international context. Efficient frontier D indicates the efficient frontier if investments are limited to the five countries that were members of the European Economic Community (EEC) in 1970. If the investment universe is expanded beyond the EEC to include all western European countries, efficient frontier C become attainable. When all high-income countries are considered, the possibilities expand to efficient frontier B. Finally, when all countries, including the developing countries, are allowed into the solution, efficient frontier A is reached. **International efficient frontier A dominates all other investment opportunities in Figure 25-2.** This analysis suggests that the portfolio with the highest rate of return in whatever risk class tends to be composed of investments from many different

---

[4]Unfortunately, the correlation coefficients in Table 25-2 contain considerable sampling error. For example, the correlations between the United States and Belgium range from .1080 to .83, and the correlations between the United States and Japan range from $-.26$ to .5279. We expect these statistics to change intertemporally.

[5]Monthly rates of return from foreign investments in common stocks can be calculated with the equation below after the prices are preprocessed to reflect changes in the foreign exchange rates.

$$\text{Effective monthly rate of return} = \left(\frac{\left(\dfrac{\text{annual cash dividend}}{12 \text{ months}} \right) + p_t}{p_{t-1}} \right) - 1.0$$

where p_t is the market price of the foreign security (or foreign stock market index) existing at the end of period t.

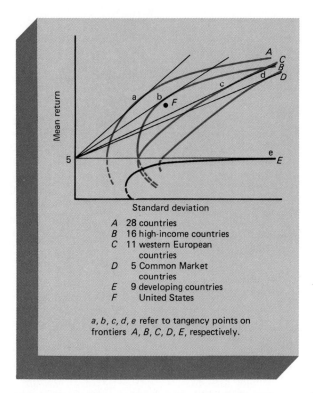

A   28 countries
B   16 high-income countries
C   11 western European
    countries
D   5 Common Market
    countries
E   9 developing countries
F   United States

a, b, c, d, e refer to tangency points on
frontiers A, B, C, D, E, respectively.

Figure 25-2 Different efficient frontiers derived from various investment opportunities. (*Source:* H. Levy and M. Sarnat, "International Diversification of Investment Portfolios," *American Economic Review,* Sept. 1970, pp. 668–675.)

countries.[6] However, barriers to capital flows (which are discussed later) may make the theoretically optimal portfolio unfeasible.

Correlations for the Multinational Investor

Viewed in a risk-return context, the key factor that improves the investment opportunities available in the international capital market is the low correlations between the different countries' securities markets. Viewed differently, international diversification changes the market index that is relevant for assessing undiversifiable risk—a domestic market index should be replaced by a world market index. The correlation of each security with the broader worldwide index is usually lower. Table 25-3 shows empirical statistics about what percent of each domestic portfolio's variance is explained by a worldwide investment

[6]For readings about international investing, see Carl Beidleman, ed., *Handbook of International Investing* (Chicago, Ill.: Probus, 1987); in particular, see Raj Aggarwal, "Alternatives for International Portfolio Diversification," pp. 57–96. For a multiperiod study of the benefits of international diversification, see Robert R. Grauer and Nils H. Hakansson, "Gains from International Diversification: 1968–85 Returns on Portfolios of Stocks and Bonds," *Journal of Finance,* July 1987, vol. 42, no. 3, pp. 721–739.

Table 25-3

**PERCENTAGE OF THE VARIANCE OF DIFFERENT
COUNTRIES' STOCK MARKET INDEXES EXPLAINED BY A
WORLDWIDE INDEX**

Country	R-squared for a market value weighted index	R-squared for an equally weighted index
Australia	11.1%	20.2%
Austria	4.5	20.1
Belgium	26.2	50.1
Canada	66.7	38.2
Denmark	0.8	11.6
France	9.6	40.2
Germany	22.3	49.0
Italy	6.2	25.6
Japan	7.9	15.5
Netherlands	45.4	52.7
Norway	2.0	22.2
Spain	0.4	8.9
Sweden	13.1	28.5
Switzerland	29.5	54.5
United Kingdom	16.9	22.6
United States	88.0	30.0
Simple average	21.9	30.6

Source: Donald R. Lessard, "World, Country and Industry Relationships in Equity Returns: Implications for Risk Reduction through International Diversification," *Financial Analysts Journal,* Jan.–Feb. 1976, pp. 2–8.

index. The statistics in Table 25-3 are the coefficient of determination (that is, the correlation squared, or the R-squared) for the **international characteristic line** shown in Equation (25-3).[7]

$$r_{c,t} = a_c + b_c r_{w,t} + e_{c,t} \qquad (25\text{-}3)$$

In Equation (25-3), the symbol $r_{c,t}$ is the dependent variable in this simple linear regression model—it is the one-period rate of return from country c in

---

[7]For a study that pinpoints flaws in the returns generated by the international markets, see R. A. Cohn and J. J. Pringle, "Imperfections in International Financial Markets: Implications for Risk Premia and the Cost of Capital to Firms," *Journal of Finance,* March 1973, pp. 59–66. Anomalies in the efficient markets hypothesis as it applies to European markets are published by Gabriel Hawawini, *European Equity Markets: Price Behavior and Efficiency* (New York: Salomon Brothers Center for the Study of Financial Institutions, 1984). For a more recent study of international market efficiency, see J. Wilcox, "Practice and Theory in International Equity Investment," *Financial Analysts Journal,* Jan.–Feb. 1986.

period t. The independent variable is $r_{w,t}$, the one-period rate of return in period t from a portfolio that is diversified worldwide and is therefore not highly correlated with the portfolio from any one individual country. The regression intercept for country c is denoted a_c and its regression slope (or beta) coefficient is b_c. This regression slope coefficient is a country-world beta. The unexplained residual return for country c in period t is denoted $e_{c,t}$.

The coefficient of determination for regression Equation (25-3) is inversely related to the desirability of diversifying in each country. Stated differently, the countries with the lowest R-squared statistics are the most desirable for the purposes of obtaining beneficial diversification.

Fundamental Reasons for Low Intercountry Correlations

The intercountry correlations between securities markets are low because different countries and their economic prospects are not closely tied. Different countries have different political systems (for example, capitalism versus socialism), different currencies (such as French francs, Japanese yen, etc.), different foreign exchange regulations (for example, fixed versus floating exchange rates), different trade restrictions (such as import and export limitations and tariffs), different political alliances (such as the communist nations and the democratic nations), and various other barriers to international trade. Furthermore, different countries may be at different phases in their business cycle (for example, the United States might be starting a recovery just when some other countries are in the trough of a recession), undergoing foreign exchange rate changes (because of different intercountry inflation rates, interest rates, monetary policies, and/or fiscal policies), or in differing military postures (such as peace versus cold war versus active aggression) at any given time. As a result of all of these important differences, different countries' security markets are seldom highly synchronized or highly positively correlated with each other.[8]

25-2 **DIVERSIFICATION IN DIFFERENT COUNTRIES**

The benefits that can be obtained from multinational diversification are typically enhanced by barriers to investment, such as restrictions on currency flows, lack of English translations of foreign financial statements, lack of information about local accounting conventions, lack of information about social and cultural differences, government restrictions on foreign ownership, markets where insider trading significantly affects security prices, and markets that are thin

---

[8]For empirical risk and return statistics from various investments in foreign countries, see Yasushi Hamao, "Japanese Stocks, Bonds, Bills and Inflation, 1973–1987," *Journal of Portfolio Management,* Winter 1989, pp. 20–26. Also see Daniel Wydler, "Swiss Stocks, Bonds and Inflation, 1926–1987," *Journal of Portfolio Management,* Winter 1989, pp. 27–32.

with respect to volume of trading or number of traders.[9] When such barriers exist, they cause **international market segmentation,** and diversification tends to be more beneficial. If such barriers to international diversification did not exist, we would have **homogeneous markets.** Multinational diversification will not offer any beneficial risk-reducing opportunities if the international markets are perfectly homogeneous.

The diversification possibilities are bounded because investors have limited funds. Consequently, it is worthwhile to have guidelines about how best to diversify in foreign countries. Using weekly returns from eight different countries over five consecutive years, Professor Bruno Solnik calculated the proportion of variance that could be eliminated from portfolios by increasing the number of assets included in the portfolio. For each country, portfolios of various sizes were constructed from randomly selected stocks from that country and the variance of these portfolios was calculated. These variances were averaged for each portfolio size.[10]

In each country, average portfolio variance declined rapidly until portfolios of approximately 20 randomly selected securities were attained; after that, little additional reduction in the average portfolio's variance was achieved by adding more securities to the portfolio. Table 25-4 shows that the proportion of the average common stock's total variance for each country which was undiversifiable ranged from a low of 19 percent in Belgium to a high of 43.8 percent in West Germany. Stated differently, the average portfolio of domestic stocks achieved with only random diversification in Belgium had 19.0 percent as much risk as the typical individual stock traded in Belgium.

Table 25-4 shows that an internationally diversified portfolio of randomly selected stocks had only 11.7 percent as much variance as the typical individual stock. This statistic implies that we can reduce a portfolio's domestic systematic risk by multinational diversification. Panels *a* through *c* of Figure 25-3 illustrate some risk-reduction possibilities. Unfortunately, the benefits from Solnik's study cannot be taken too literally because the study did not make adjustments to hold the rates of return equivalent from country to country as diversification was employed to reduce the risk. The study implicitly assumed international investors were willing to suffer whatever low rates of return were necessary to achieve variance reductions.

---

[9]For more details about international investment risks, see Bruno Solnik, *International Investments* (Reading, Mass.: Addison-Wesley, 1988). Also see Gunter Dufey and Ian Giddy, *The International Money Market* (Englewood Cliffs, N.J.: Prentice-Hall, 1978). See also Vihang Errunza and Etienne Losq, "International Asset Pricing under Mild Segmentation: Theory and Text," *Journal of Finance,* March 1985, pp. 105–124. In addition, see F. Black, "International Capital Market Equilibrium with Investment Barriers," *Journal of Financial Economics,* Dec. 1974, pp. 337–352.

[10]Professor Solnik was, essentially, extending the methodology developed in John L. Evans and Stephen H. Archer, "Diversification and the Reduction of Dispersion: Empirical Analysis," *Journal of Finance,* Dec. 1968. The Evans-Archer results were presented in Section 9-1; see Figure 9-1.

Table 25-4

RANDOMLY DIVERSIFIED PORTFOLIO'S VARIANCE STATED AS A PERCENT OF THE VARIANCE OF THE AVERAGE INDIVIDUAL STOCK WITHIN A COUNTRY

Belgium	19.0%
France	32.7
West Germany	43.8
Italy	38.0
Netherlands	24.1
Switzerland	44.0
United States	27.0
United Kingdom	34.5
International	11.7%

Source: Bruno H. Solnik, "Why Not Diversify Internationally?" *Financial Analysts Journal,* July–Aug. 1974, pp. 48–54.

To determine how best to diversify, Dr. Solnik examined three strategies of selecting different numbers of randomly selected common stocks. Stocks were selected (1) across countries, (2) across industries, and (3) across both countries and industries. Panels *a*, *b*, and *c* of Figure 25-3 illustrate that selection across countries and across countries and industries are both superior strategies to only selecting across industries. These experiments with random diversification suggest that the optimal portfolio should contain 20 or more common stocks diversified across countries.[11]

An important consideration for investors in foreign securities is foreign exchange risk. Panel *c* of Figure 25-3 indicates that a substantial portion of the risk reduction from multinational diversification occurs whether or not international portfolios are hedged against foreign exchange losses. The hedged portfolio does have lower risk than the unhedged portfolio, but not surprisingly, the rate of return from the hedged portfolio is also reduced. In short, the value of international diversification exists both with and without a concurrent cur-

---

[11]One simple way to diversify internationally without bumping into problems with foreign languages and foreign accounting conventions is to buy shares in one large corporation that is active multinationally. Ford Motor Company has over 30 percent of its sales outside the United States, for instance. And Sony is a Japanese corporation that has 35 percent of its sales in the United States. Unfortunately, research suggests that this approach is not a powerful way to reduce risk; see Bertrand Jacquillat and Bruno Solnik, "Multinationals Are Poor Tools for Diversification," *Journal of Portfolio Management,* Winter 1978, vol. 4, no. 2, pp. 8–11.

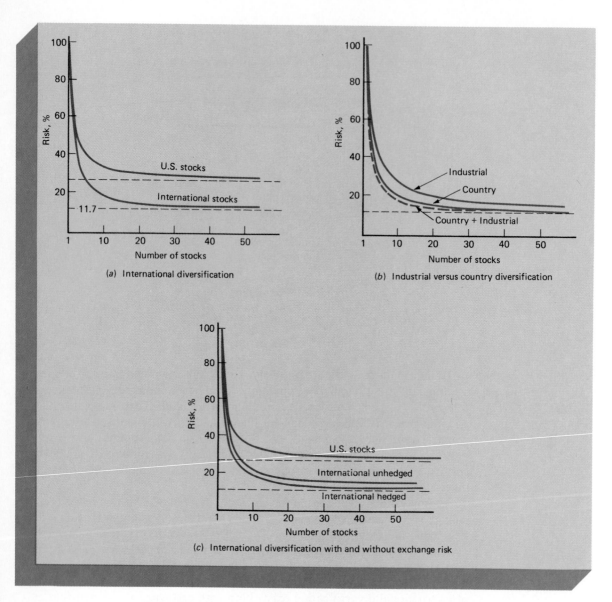

Figure 25-3 Illustrated results of different diversification strategies. (*Source:* Bruno H. Solnik, "Why Not Diversify Internationally?" *Financial Analysts Journal,* July–Aug. 1974, pp. 48–54.)

rency hedge.[12] Foreign exchange risk is considered more closely in the next section.

FOREIGN EXCHANGE RISK

If a domestic investor and a foreign investor invest the same amounts in the same security at the same time, they will earn different rates of return over identical holding periods if the foreign exchange rate fluctuates.

Domestic Investor's Return

Let r_d denote the single-period rate of return that a domestic investor earns after paying for a domestic security with the local currency. The familiar single-period rate of return of Equation (1-2) is restated equivalently as Equation (25-4) to formally define a **domestic investor's return.**

$$r_d = \frac{p_t - p_{t-1} + c_t}{p_{t-1}} \tag{25-4}$$

If a German invests 50 deutsche marks (DM) in a German security that pays no cash dividends or coupon interest and then sells it one period later for DM55, the German earns r_d = (DM55 − DM50 + 0)/DM50 = 10 percent. If an American made the same investment, it would be a different story.

Foreign Investor's Return

If an American invested U.S. dollars in the German security, the American would be a foreign investor. A **foreign investor's return** is measured with Equation (25-5).

$$r_f = \frac{x_t p_t - x_{t-1} p_{t-1} + x_t c_t}{x_{t-1} p_{t-1}} \tag{25-5}$$

If the foreign exchange rate is x = 2DM/\$1 at time $t − 1$, then an American investor must pay \$0.50 for 1 DM. This translates into a purchase price of $x_{t-1} p_{t-1}$ = (0.50)(DM50) = \$25 for the German security. If the exchange rate is invariant, the American will earn the same 10 percent rate of return from the German security that the German investor earned.

Suppose that between time $t − 1$ and time t, the dollar appreciates relative to the DM so that when the American investor sells the German security, the exchange rate is x_t = 0.55. Stated differently, the American made a 10 percent gain on the *investment in the German currency.*

---

[12]The implications for the capital asset pricing model (CAPM) for the international investor have been worked out in Rene Stulz, "On the Effects of Barriers to International Investment," *Journal of Finance,* Sept. 1981, vol. 36, no. 4, pp. 923–934.

$$r_c = \frac{x_t - x_{t-1}}{x_{t-1}} = \frac{0.55 - 0.50}{0.50} = 10\% \tag{25-6}$$

Under these more favorable circumstances, the American investor can sell the German security for $x_t p_t = (0.55)(DM55) = \$30.25$. Equation (25-5) suggests that in this case the American investor's total rate of return is 21%, or $[(0.55)(DM55) - (0.50)(DM50) + 0]/(0.50)(DM50)$, before commissions, fees, and taxes.

Components of Total Return

Manipulating Equations (25-4), (25-5), and (25-6) can result in Equation (25-7).

$$1 + r_f = (1 + r_d)(1 + r_c) \tag{25-7}$$

Equation (25-7) is equivalent to Equation (25-7a).

$$r_f = r_d + r_c + r_d r_c \tag{25-7a}$$

Equation (25-7a) allows us to decompose the American investor's 21 percent total return from the foreign investment into a pure gain in the German market of $r_d = 10\%$ plus a foreign exchange gain of $r_f = 10\%$ plus a cross-product of $(r_d)(r_f) = (0.1)(0.1) = 1\%$.

Foreign Investor's Risk

Investors who undertake a foreign investment face the three risk factors shown in Equation (25-8).

$$\text{Var}(r_f) = \text{Var}(r_c) + \text{Var}(r_d) + \sqrt{\text{Var}(r_c)}\sqrt{\text{Var}(r_d)}\,\rho_{cd} \tag{25-8}$$

$$\text{Var}(r_f) = \text{Var}(r_c) + \text{Var}(r_d) + \text{Cov}(r_c, r_d) \tag{25-8a}$$

$\text{Var}(r_f)$ is the foreign investor's total risk. This *total risk* is the sum of the risk the investor takes in the foreign country's securities market, $\text{Var}(r_d)$, and the **foreign exchange risk,** $\text{Var}(r_c)$, plus the covariance between the foreign security's return and the foreign currency's return, $\text{Cov}(r_c, r_d) = \sigma_c \sigma_d \rho_{cd}$. The covariance can be negative if the value of the foreign investment and the foreign exchange rate fluctuate inversely.

The correlation between the returns from the foreign investment and the foreign exchange rate determines the sign of the covariance term in Equation (25-8). Table 25-5 provides historical estimates of the foreign investor's total risk, the foreign country's securities market, and the foreign exchange risk from investments in selected countries. The fourth column of Table 25-5 lists the ratios of the U.S. investor's (namely, the foreign) risk divided by the risk that a domestic investor in the same country would encounter. Whenever the foreign exchange risk is positively correlated with the investment's returns, that might increase the U.S. investor's risk above a domestic investor's risk

Table 25-5

ESTIMATES OF THE RISKS UNDERTAKEN BY U.S. AND DOMESTIC
INVESTORS IN SELECTED COUNTRIES, BASED ON HISTORICAL DATA,
1970–1980

	(1)	(2)	(3)	(4)
				Foreign/
	Domestic	Currency	Foreign	domestic
	risk	risk	risk	risk
Stocks				
Canada	18.92	4.16	20.29	1.07
France	22.00	10.24	25.81	1.17
Germany	13.87	11.87	18.39	1.33
Japan	16.39	10.42	19.55	1.19
Netherlands	16.37	10.97	18.91	1.16
Switzerland	16.80	14.67	21.40	1.27
United Kingdom	28.94	8.84	31.61	1.09
United States	16.00	0.00	16.00	1.00
Bonds				
Canada	6.16	4.16	7.93	1.29
France	4.39	10.24	11.80	2.69
Germany	6.91	11.87	14.35	2.08
Japan	6.53	10.42	14.36	2.20
Netherlands	7.16	10.97	13.61	1.90
Switzerland	4.33	14.67	15.33	3.54
United Kingdom	12.30	8.84	16.29	1.32
United States	8.96	0.00	8.96	1.00

Source: Bruno Solnik and Bernard Noetzlin, "Optimal International Asset Allocation," *Journal of Portfolio Management,* Fall 1982, vol. 9, no. 1, p. 13.

and cause the ratio to exceed one. Table 25-5 indicates that unfortunate case
is the prevalent outcome.[13]

Hedging Foreign   Research indicates that many foreign exchange rates fluctuate randomly.[14] Steps
Exchange Risk   can be taken to diminish or even eliminate the resulting foreign exchange risk.

[13]For additional discussion of foreign exchange risk, see David K. Eiteman and Arthur
I. Stonehill, "Measuring Foreign Exchange Exposure," in *Multinational Business Finance,* 3d ed. (Reading, Mass.: Addison-Wesley, 1982), chap. 14. See also Gunter Dufey
and S. L. Srinivasuler, "The Case for Corporate Management of Foreign Exchange
Risk," *Financial Management,* Fall 1983.
[14]Gunter Dufey and Ian Giddy, "The Random Behavior of Flexible Exchange Rates:
Implications for Forecasting," *Journal of International Business Studies,* Spring 1975,
vol. 6, no. 1, pp. 1–32.

Some foreign investors hedge their foreign exchange positions by using **foreign exchange options** and/or **foreign exchange futures contracts.**

In 1983 the Philadelphia Stock Exchange (PHLX) started trading listed options on the major foreign currencies. The PHLX lists put and call options on Australian dollars, British pounds, Canadian dollars, West German deutsche marks (DM), Japanese yen, European currency units (ECUs), and Swiss francs. More recently, the Chicago Board of Options Exchange (CBOE) also started listing currency options.[15]

For decades before currency options were traded at an exchange, large banks that wished to hedge their foreign exchange risks bought forward contracts in an *informal interbank market.* This informal forward market in large, tailor-made foreign exchange contracts still exists, but only large banks and selected clients have access to it. In 1972 hedgers were presented with an alternative to the illiquid forward contracts; the International Monetary Market (IMM) in Chicago started trading futures contracts at a commodity exchange. The IMM trades futures on British pounds, Canadian dollars, West German deutsche marks (DM), Japanese yen, and Swiss francs. The MidAmerica Commodity Exchange in Chicago lists futures contracts on some of the same currencies, but the units are smaller.[16]

25-4   **BROKERAGE COMMISSIONS FOR INTERNATIONAL TRANSACTIONS**

To transact international security trades, some brokerage houses charge double the commission rate they charge to transact buy and sell orders in domestic markets. Other brokers simply refuse to deal in multinational transactions. In essence, there are two types of places to trade multinational securities.

1. Large, full-service brokerage houses (Merrill Lynch, Pierce, Fenner & Smith, for instance) that charge full-service commission rates.

2. Major banks that have large international departments (like Citibank and Morgan Guaranty) which issue **American depository receipts** (ADRs

---

[15]A pamphlet about the PHLX may be obtained free by writing to the Federal Reserve Bank of Philadelphia, Research Dept., Ten Independence Mall, Philadelphia, Pa. 19106 and asking for Brian Gendreau, "New Markets in Foreign Currency Options," *Business Review,* July–Aug. 1984, pp. 3–12. Or contact the PHLX and/or the CBOE directly for free information.

[16]For more details about currency futures, see John F. Marshall, *Futures and Options Contracting* (Cincinnati, Ohio: South-Western, 1989), chap. 11. See also R. W. Kolb, *Understanding Futures Markets,* 2d ed. (Glenview, Ill.: Scott, Foresman, 1988), chap. 10. Also see E. W. Schwartz, Joanne M. Hill, and T. Schneeweis, *Financial Futures* (Homewood, Ill.: Irwin, 1986), pp. 320–322 and elsewhere.

hereafter) at commission rates that compare favorably with the rates charged for ordinary domestic transactions.

Large banks with a network of foreign banking offices issue ADRs by purchasing securities in a foreign corporation for their domestic U.S. clients. The bank keeps these securities in the vault of its foreign branch registered in the bank's name. The client is issued an ADR stating that the bank is holding securities for the client. For example, you might purchase an ADR evidencing the fact that Morgan Guaranty Bank is holding 100 shares of Sony common stock for you in the vault of the bank's Tokyo branch. The bank collects cash dividends or coupon interest for you and either reinvests the money or converts it into U.S. dollars and pays it to you—whichever you request. ADRs are available for a modest fee of a penny or two out of each security's cash payment—and they are as liquid as the underlying security.

Although most of the corporations represented by bank ADRs are large and reputable, these issuers enjoy a kind of diplomatic immunity from most of the rules and regulations of the Securities and Exchange Commission (SEC). But this immunity has not hurt the marketability of these foreign securities. Every day hundreds of thousands of foreign shares represented by ADRs are traded in the organized security exchanges and over-the-counter in the United States. In fact, sometimes more shares of a popular stock (like Sony) are traded using ADRs in the United States than are traded in the issuer's homeland.[17]

ADR holders receive all the benefits that someone who owned the underlying security would receive without paying any additional brokerage commission, without losing any marketability, and without the bother of collecting cash dividends in a foreign currency.

25-5   **DIFFERENT APPROACHES TO INTERNATIONAL INVESTING**

There are four approaches to investing multinationally: investing in foreign stocks, investing in ADRs, investing in multinational corporations, and investing in global investment companies; each offers unique benefits. The first three were discussed earlier in this chapter.

Analyzing the performance of investments was the topic of Chapter 21; that chapter provided mutual fund examples. U.S.-based global investment com-

---

[17]For more details about ADRs, see D. T. Officer and J. R. Hoffmeister, ''ADRs: A Substitute for the Real Thing?'' *Journal of Portfolio Management,* Winter 1987, vol. 13, no. 2, pp. 61–67. Also see Leonard Rosenthal et al., ''An Empirical Test of the Efficiency of the ADR Market,'' *Journal of Banking and Finance,* March 1983, vol. 7, no. 1, pp. 17–29.

pany shares are analyzed like mutual fund shares.[18] However, the shares of foreign investment companies require some additional analysis to include foreign exchange risks.[19]

The investment strategies of global investment companies fit into three main categories—investing only in stocks, only in bonds, and/or only in specific countries. The Korea Fund and the Taiwan Fund, for instance, are closed-end common stock investment companies that invest in Korean and Taiwan enterprises, respectively. These portfolios are called **country funds.** An international investor can construct a portfolio of investment company shares to achieve whatever goal they seek.

25-6   **SUMMARY AND CONCLUSIONS**

International investors face all the same risks that domestic investors face plus some additional risks—international marketability risk, international political risk, foreign exchange risk, and information risk (that is, the risk of being forced to work with inferior investment information).

Virtually no foreign markets are as honest, efficient and liquid as the securities markets in the United States. Dealing with the marketability risks in a foreign market can be an unpleasant experience. Furthermore, there is the added marketability risk in some foreign countries—security price manipulation that is illegal in the United States may be permitted in some foreign markets.

International political risk and foreign exchange risk are usually interrelated. Many of the foreign exchange rates in the world are fixed by the governments of the countries that issue the currencies, rather than being freely floating exchange rates determined by supply and demand. However, foreign investors can use currency options and foreign exchange futures contracts to reduce their foreign exchange risk via hedging.

The risk of being forced to compete against foreign investors who may have inside information and faster access to information about their country, and who may even be able to manipulate security prices in their country, places

---

[18]See Ramesh P. Rao and Raj Aggarwal, "Performance of U.S.-Based International Mutual Funds," *Akron Business and Economic Review,* Winter 1987, pp. 98–107.

[19]Alternatives to international common stock investing are international bonds, real estate, and gold, which are discussed in the following articles. See H. Levy and Zvi Lerman, "The Benefits of International Diversification in Bonds," *Financial Analysts Journal,* Sept.–Oct. 1988, pp. 56–64. Also see R. Ibbotson, L. Siegel, and K. Love, "World Wealth: Market Values and Returns," *Journal of Portfolio Management,* Fall 1985. Further, see J. R. Webb and J. H. Rubens, "Portfolio Considerations in the Valuation of Real Estate," *AREUEA Journal,* Fall 1986. Also see R. Aggarwal and Luc A. Soenen, "The Nature and Efficiency of the Gold Market," *Journal of Portfolio Management,* 1988.

the outside investor at a disadvantage. Some large international banks (like Morgan Guaranty, Citibank, and Bank of America) and other institutional investors have foreign offices that manage investments in the host country and are partly staffed by the local citizens of the foreign country. Such foreign nationals not only make low-cost employees, they may also be able to gather valuable information for their employer. Or a foreign investor can simply purchase a highly diversified portfolio of securities in the foreign country without doing intensive investments research—buying shares in a mutual fund that only invests in foreign securities is an example of this passive kind of investment management.

The risk-reducing benefits from international investing may more than offset the disadvantages. The correlations between the securities markets in different countries are usually lower than the correlations available to domestic investors. As a result, multinational investing opportunities offer a more dominant efficient frontier of investment opportunities from which to choose.

Essay Questions

25-1   How might a multinational investor based in the United States use foreign exchange futures to hedge against the risk that the foreign exchange rate changes? *Hint: Some of the material about financial futures in Chapter 24 may be helpful.*

25-2   Are there any risks which are peculiar to international investing? Stated differently, what factors in addition to the usual investment risks should be of particular concern to the multinational investor?

25-3   What induces investors to invest internationally when they face additional risks that are peculiar to multinational investing?

25-4   Does every international investment opportunity provide the investor with new investment opportunities that dominate the old opportunities in a risk-return analysis? Explain.

25-5   What factors explain why the intercountry correlations between securities markets are low? *Hint: You may benefit from consulting an international economics or an international finance textbook.*

25-6   Myron Budnick just bought a Nissan 300Z Turbo and loves the car so much that he wants to invest in the Nissan Corporation's stock. But Nissan is a Japanese company, and Myron does not want to get involved in foreign exchange and the other administrative problems that might arise from a foreign investment. How can Myron buy shares in Nissan without getting involved with any international complications?

25-7   Ralph Jones is interested in multinational diversification but does not have the time or expertise to select individual foreign assets in which to invest. Is there some way he can diversify internationally?

25-8 Since the intercountry correlation between securities markets plays such an important role in international diversification, consider the trend in these statistics. Do you think that, in general, these correlations should increase, stay the same, or decrease with the passage of time? Explain why.

Problems

25-9 Francoise LeClerq is a fashion designer in New York City who follows the investment advice of her twin brother Francois, an automotive engineer in Paris. Francoise and Francois both simultaneously bought stock in Michelin Tire at the price of 180 French francs (FF) per share. At the time of the purchase the exchange ratio was $x_o = \$1/FF6 = \$0.1666$ per franc. (a) How many dollars per share did Francoise pay for her stock? How many FF per share did Francois pay for his?

The expert advice of Francois enabled them to sell their Michelin stock for FF200 2 months later; they received no cash dividends. At the time of the sale the dollar had depreciated relative to the FF; the exchange ratio was $x_1 = \$1/FF5 = \$0.20$ per franc. (b) What rates of return did Francoise and her brother earn over the 2 months they owned Michelin? (c) How did the change in the exchange rate affect Francoise?

25-10 Assume the expected rate of return and standard deviation of returns from investing British pounds in the common stock of Barclays Bank, which is headquartered in England, are 10 percent and 0.2, respectively. The pound has been appreciating relative to the dollar at a rate of 5 percent per year with a standard deviation of 0.1. Also assume that the correlation coefficient between the returns from Barclays stock and the British pound is .5. How much return and total risk should a U.S. investor who pays British pounds for stock in Barclays Bank expect?

25-11 While working as a chemist at a laboratory in New York, Rolf Kierulf won $100,000 in the state lottery and decided he wanted to invest in the common stock of his previous employer, Hoffman LaRoche, a large pharmaceutical corporation headquartered in Switzerland. Rolf bought Swiss francs (SF) in the United States at the rate of $x_o = \$1/SF1.5 = \$0.666$ per franc. He purchased Hoffman LaRoche stock at a price of SF150,000 per share. (a) How many dollars per share did Rolf pay for one share of the stock? (b) Rolf sold the stock for SF160,000 3 months later without receiving any cash dividends. He converted the proceeds of the sale to dollars at a rate of $x_1 = \$1/1.6 = \$0.625$ per SF. What rate of return did Rolf earn over the 3-month holding period? (c) How did the dollar/SF exchange rate affect Rolf's return?

25-12 QUZ is a Public Limited Corporation (PLC) whose stock is currently selling for 30 pounds per share on the London Stock Exchange. A year earlier the stock sold for 25 pounds. During the past year the stock paid no dividend. The current exchange rate between the pound and the dollar is $1.25 per pound. However, a year earlier, it was $1.15 per pound. (a) Determine the rate of return from QUZ during the past year for a U.S. investor; (b) for a British investor.

25-13 Currently, the Japanese yen is trading at \$0.0076923 per yen. A year ago the yen was trading at \$0.0083333 per yen. If the return on Japanese stocks had been 25 percent last year, what would be the net return to a U.S. investor?

The following international security market returns are to be used with Problems 25-14 through 25-18.

Year	United Kingdom	Japan	Canada	Australia	United States
1971	47.99%	46.55%	14.13%	-1.54%	18.16%
1972	3.93	126.56	33.12	21.06	17.71
1973	-23.44	-20.13	-3.11	-12.06	-18.68
1974	-50.33	-15.65	-26.52	-32.97	-27.77
1975	115.06	19.84	15.07	50.71	37.49
1976	-12.55	25.8	9.71	-10.00	26.68
1977	56.49	15.7	-1.37	11.25	-3.03
1978	14.63	53.33	20.55	22.24	8.53
1979	22.2	-11.69	52.55	43.44	24.18
1980	38.8	29.7	22.00	52.20	33.22

25-14 Determine the correlation of returns for the United States, United Kingdom, and Japan over the 10-year period. In addition, determine the standard deviation of returns for the three countries over the same period of time. *Hint: You might want to use a computer program for the statistics.*

25-15 Determine the correlation between the returns from Australia and Canada over the 10-year period. Also determine the standard deviation of returns over the same period.

25-16 With the information generated in Problem 25-14, determine the expected return and risk (as measured by the standard deviation) for a portfolio of 25 percent United Kingdom, 25 percent Japanese, and 50 percent U.S. stocks. Assume the historical means, standard deviations, and correlation coefficients are the expected values.

25-17 Using the information generated in Problem 25-15, determine the expected return and standard deviation of return for a portfolio of 40 percent Australian and 60 percent Canadian stocks. Again, assume the historical statistics are the expected values.

25-18 Using the information generated in Problems 25-14 and 25-15, determine the standard deviation of returns for a portfolio of 50 percent U.S. and 50 percent Canadian stocks.

Selected References

de Caires, Bryan, *The Guide to World Equity Markets,* A Euromoney Publication, 1989.

The volume provides information about common stock investing in 38 foreign countries. The book is rich in market statistics and institutional arrangements.

Fabozzi, Frank J., and Irving M. Pollack, *The Handbook of Fixed Income Securities,* 2d ed. (Homewood, Ill.: Dow Jones–Irwin, 1987).

Chapters 49 through 52 inclusive present insightful information about managing different types of international bond portfolios.

Grabbe, J. Orlin, *International Financial Markets* (Amsterdam, Netherlands: Elsevier, 1986).

This MBA-level textbook explores foreign currencies, currency futures, currency options, currency markets, interest rate and currency swaps, and the Eurobond and other international bond markets using no mathematics beyond algebra.

Hawawini, Gabriel, *European Equity Markets: Price Behavior and Efficiency* (New York: Salomon Brothers Center for the Study of Financial Institutions, 1984).

This scholarly monograph explains the European stock markets in terms of the modern investments theories. The book also reviews empirical research about anomalies in the efficient markets theory as it relates to the European markets. Mathematics beyond algebra is not used.

Institute of Chartered Financial Analysts, *International Bonds and Currencies* (Homewood, Ill.: Dow Jones–Irwin, 1986).

This book is helpful to those who are trying to pass the **Chartered Financial Analysts (CFA)** exams.

Solnik, Bruno, *International Investments* (Reading, Mass.: Addison-Wesley, 1988).

This 12-chapter textbook about international investing introduces the relevant topics and provides good references for additional detailed studies. Elementary algebra and statistics are used.

Answers to End-of-Chapter Problems

The answers to the essay questions are in the Instructors Manual; you should consult your instructor to review them. The detailed calculations used to derive the following numerical answers to the problems are also in the Instructors Manual. If you desire a more detailed explanation, make an appointment with your instructor to see the Instructors Manual.

Chapter 1

1-9 10.0%

1-10 (*a*) 10.0%; (*b*) 21%

1-11 20%, 50%, −50%, −10%, 90%, 20%

1-12 A graph is required.

1-13 $E(r) = 20.0\%$; $Var(r) = 0.1933$; std.dev. $= 0.439696$

1-14 Energy and Diamond are dominated.

1-15 (*a*) 7.0%; (*b*) 1.9%; (*c*) $38

1-16 Municipal's 8% return is highest.

1-17 (*a*) f; (*b*) stock is riskiest; and (*c*) has highest $E(r)$.

1-18 Big earners like tax exempts.

Chapter 2

2-12 After-tax: preferred $= 7.7\% >$ corporate bond $= 7.5\%$

2-13 (*a*) Diluted from $2.06 to $1.67; (*b*) stock price will probably fall, but interest expense is reduced.

2-14 4.17% over 65 days

2-15 13.375%

2-16 (a) 7.0%; (b) 8.0% after tax is higher.

2-17 15.38%

2-18 −4.4%

2-19 Returns are unchanged by splits: −38% and 55%

2-20 20 × $40 = $800

2-21 $950 − $800 = $150

2-22 (a) 40% before tax; (b) 26% after tax

2-23 Annualized equivalent: 23.077%, or 25.76% per 365 days.

2-24 Annualized equivalent: 12.48%, or 13.44% per 365 days.

Chapter 3

3-6 500 sh. × $40 × 0.6 = $12,000

3-7 500 sh. × $40 × 0.75 = $15,000

3-8 100 sh. × $50 × 0.65 = $3250

3-9 r = $95.50/$55 = 173.6%

3-10 $23.08 decline

3-11 $3576.92 addition

3-12 $22.90/$32.50 = 70.46%

3-13 $25/$50 = 50%

3-14 $26.90/$32.50 = 82.77%

3-15 The four columns represent: column 1, thin and shallow market; column 2, thin and deep; column 3, broad and shallow; column 4, broad and deep.

3-16 (a) The bid-asked spread equals the difference between the lowest asked (or offered) price and the highest bid price. (b) Bid-asked spreads are determined by (i) the volume of shares traded, (ii) the continuity with which a security trades, (iii) the riskiness of the security, (iv) the number of institutional investors buying the stock, (v) the average price level of the stock, (vi) the number of markets (such as NYSE, AMEX, OTC) in which the stock is traded, and (vii) the number of different stocks handled by the specialist.

3-17 More securities and more markets will tend to raise the level of social welfare by providing investors (i) more opportunities to reduce their risks by hedging, (ii) more ways to correct mispriced assets via arbitrage, (iii) more different securities over which to diversify, (iv) more instruments with which to create profitable investment positions tailored to different situations, (v) more pathways on which to move closer to an optimal allocation of resources, and/or (vi) more complete markets in which to develop unambiguous security prices.

Chapter 4

Solutions to the matching questions are below:

4-9 1. c; 2. e; 3. f; 4. d; 5. g; 6. a; 7. b

4-10 1. H; 2. I; 3. J; 4. K; 5. L; 6. A; 7. B; 8. C; 9. D; 10. E; 11. F; 12. G

Solutions to the multiple choice questions are below:

4-11 e

4-12 d

4-13 a

4-14 d

4-15 d

4-16 d

4-17 b

4-18 c

4-19 e

Chapter 5

5-10 Taylor's income $10,000 less $1500 is $8500 after taxes.

5-11 The municipal's 6% exceeds 5.3% after taxes.

5-12 Mary's taxable estate, $240,000; zero taxes due. John's taxable estate, $2,240,000; estate taxes due, $705,600.

5-13 (*a*) 14.4%; (*b*) 16.64%

Chapter 6

Solution to case: Smith can subscribe to the needed information services at a price his bank can afford.

Chapter 7

7-9 (*a*) 1.4268; (*b*) 1.75; (*c*) 110.999%; (*d*) the values differ because the weightings differ.

7-10 Price-weighting often causes misleading results, e.g., DJIA.

7-11 (*a*) 11.5%; (*b*) 13.154847%; (*c*) 10.72%

7-12 10.5925%

7-13 7.191%

7-14 (*a*) 6.31667%; (*b*) 7.7798%

7-15 6.028%

Chapter 8

8-10 No action; no action; buy; buy; sell

8-11 (*a*) + 10.0%; (*b*) − 10.0%

8-12 $68,108.80

8-13 (*a*) $48.08; (*b*) sell short.

8-14 $51.71

8-15 $265.26

8-16 (*a*) 14.87%; (*b*) 10.76% after tax

8-17 9.05%

8-18 1. b; 2. c; 3. e; 4. a; 5. d

Chapter 9

9-8   50-50 portfolio's variance = 0.024

9-9   Cor(*AB*) = .243; Cor(*AC*) = .781; Cor(*BC*) = .626

9-10 S.D. A = 16.048%; S.D. B = 2.6573%; S.D. C = 21.044%

9-11 20-40-40 portfolio's $E(r_p)$: 13.6%

9-12 20-40-40 portfolio's S.D.: 11.7257%

9-13 50-50 portfolio's $E(r_p)$: 5.7143%

9-14 50-50 portfolio's S.D.: 8.46%

9-15 Cov(*ab*) = 10.386

9-16 $E(r_p)$ = 10.85%   S1B 11.39 %

9-17 (*a*) R = 8.0% and zero risk; (*b*) $E(r)$ = 11.5% and S.D. = 10%; (*c*) $E(r)$ = 18.5% and S.D. = 30%

9-18 Slope: 0.35

9-19

$E(r_p)$	S.D.$_p$	Weight com. st.	Weight LT bond	Weight T-bills
12.0%	21.1%	100.0%	0	0
9.04	13.4	61.0	32.1	6.9
6.08	6.5	28.0	17.5	54.5
3.5	3.4	0	0	100.0

Chapter 10

10-7 Beta = 1.975 is aggressive and $R^2 = 0.4$.

10-8 GM's beta of 0.94 is defensive with $R^2 = 0.4$.

10-9 IBM's beta is 1.278.

10-10 $\text{Var}(r_{\text{IBM}}) = \text{beta}^2 \, \text{Var}(r_m) + \text{Var}(e)$
$103.5 = (1.27817)^2(42.37242) + 34.2753$
$69.22467/103.5 = R^2 = 0.66883$

10-11 Beta is 1.4961.

10-12 $\text{Var}(r) = \text{beta}^2 \, \text{Var}(r_m) + \text{Var}(e)$
$105.1925 = (1.4961)^2(42.37242) + 10.3503$
$94.8422/105.1925 = 0.9016 = R^2$—diversification

10-13 (a) S.D. A $= 0.5 < 0.6 =$ S.D. B; (b) beta(A) $= 0.447227 < 1.0063 =$ beta(B)

10-14 Defensive beta(GM) $= 0.73127 < 1.10907 =$ beta(DuP)

10-15 AZZ is underpriced; the others are overpriced.

10-16 (a) All three are overpriced. (b) CAPM is market sensitive.

10-17 Cor(XY) $= .91858$

10-18 beta(Q) $= 0.7736$

10-19 $\text{Var}(r_{\text{QZR}}) = 110.08$

Chapter 11

11-9 $E(r_i) = 4.0339 + 3.3898b_{i1} + 2.3729b_{i2}$

11-10 Let $0.5D + 0.5E = g$; then buy i long and sell g short.

11-11 $E(r_i) = 5.857142 + 3.428571b_{i1} + 2.857142b_{i2}$

11-12 Let $0.5R + 0.5Z = ss$, then buy q long and sell ss short.

11-13 Let $0.1A + 0.9B = Z$; sell Z short and buy Q long for a $20 gain.

11-14 OBC value $= \text{Div}_1/(k - g) = [\$2/(1.05)]/(0.165 - 0.05) = \$18.26$

11-15 OBC value $= \text{Div}_1/(k - g) = [\$2/(1.05)]/(0.118 - 0.05) = \$30.88$

11-16 (PV of 1–5 Divs.) + (PV of 6–∞ Divs.) = \$1.64 + \$4.278 = \$5.92*

11-17 (PV of 1–5 Divs.) + (PV of 6–∞ Divs.) = \$1.77 + \$12.12 = \$13.89*

11-18 $E(r_{GEC}) = 4.0\% + 0.9(10\%) + 1.1(2\%) = 15.2\%$

Chapter 12

12-7   10.0% in the third year

12-8   2.59% yield-to-maturity

12-9   \$10,520.64

12-10 10.0%

12-11 13.56%

12-12 13.37%

12-13 13.52%

12-14 14.0%

12-15 (a) $YTM_1 = 6.95\%$; $YTM_2 = 7.21\%$; $YTM_3 = 7.72\%$; $YTM_4 = 7.46\%$; (b) 8.75%

12-16 Buy 3-year bond long and sell the 2-year bond short.

12-17 7.63%

12-18 $q_1 = 3.835$; $q_2 = 4.08$; $q_3 = 4.58$; $q_4 = 4.33$

12-19 7.924%

12-20 12.776%

12-21 12.188%

Chapter 13

13-9   PV = \$944.72, and MD = 6.149 years = EL = elasticity

13-10 PV = \$999.68, and MD = 6.2036 years = EL. YTM and MD move inversely.

13-11 Both bonds have YTM = 5.85%; therefore, taxation is crucial.

13-12 \$3,875,000 aggregate commissions

13-13 (a) $MD_A = 1.86$, $MD_B = 2.66$, $MD_C = 3.0$ years. (b) C has the longest duration because no cashflows precede the principal repayment.

13-14 (a) \$869.97; (b) MD = 7.15 years

13-15 (a) \$1135.90, (b) MD = 6.77 years

13-16 (a) 14.94% = YTM, (b) 10.23% = YTM at \$1150.

13-17 $YTM_1 = 10.0\%$ and $MD_1 = 4.79$ years; $YTM_2 = 9.25\%$ and $MD_2 = 6.0$ years.

*Cumulative rounding errors can create discrepancies of several cents.

13-18 ($659.04 = FV$_5$ of coupons) + ($926.40 = price$_5$) = $1585.44 implies 9.66% rate of return.

13-19 ($348.77 = FV$_3$ of coupons) + ($950.83 = price$_3$) = $1299.60 implies 9.13% rate of return.

13-20 ($600.31 = FV$_5$ of coupons) + ($1081.11 = price$_5$) = $1681.42 implies 10.95% rate of return.

13-21 (a) MD = 6.54 years at YTM = 10%; (b) MD = 6.31 at 12%

13-22 (a) $1170 loss; (b) $1136 gain; (c) Theorems 1 and 4

Chapter 14

14-9 1. D; 2. C; 3. A; 4. E; 5. B

14-10 q = 10.0% per year

14-11 q_2 = 5.55%; rr_2 = −.5 of 1%; q_3 = 6.31%; rr_3 = −.3 of 1%; q_4 = 3.96%; rr_4 = 1.9%, q_5 = 4.76%, rr_5 = 1.18%

14-12 After-tax rr: − 1.9%; −2.0%; +2/10 of 1%; −5/10 of 1%

14-13 (a) 1.03^{35} = 2.81 times more; (b) 1.06^{35} = 7.69 times

14-14 (a) YTM = 5.0%; (b) YTM − 6% = − 1.0% per year = rr

14-15 (4.6% per year gain) − (6.3% per year inflation) = − 1.7% = rr; $(1.0 − 1.7\%)^9$ = .857 → − 14.3% loss of purchasing power.

14-16 (Auto appreciation rate per year 11.6%) − (inflation rate 3.95% per year) = 7.65% real rate of purchasing power increase per year.

Chapter 15

15-9 Value = (C. Div)/(k − g) = 0.50/(0.1 − 0.06) = $12.50 per share

15-10 Increasing g from 3% to 6% should increase the P/E ratio from 14.3 to 25; this increased price value from $28.60 to $50 per share.

15-11 Value = [e(1 − f)]/(k − fr) = [($10)0.6]/[0.1 − (0.4)(0.15)] = $150 per share.

15-12 (a) Ignoring differential tax rates, if r = k: v = [e(1 − f)]/(k − fr) = [e(1 − f)]/[k(1 − f)] = e/k; dividend policy is irrelevant. (b) If t = 0.5T: v = [d_1(1 − T)]/(1 + k) + [d_2(1 − T) + (1 − 0.5T)(v_2 − v_0) + v_0]/[(1 + k)^2]

15-13 Assume: v = [e(1 − f)]/(k − fr). (a) If r = 0.20, then [$7.50(0.666)]/[0.12 − (0.333)(0.2)] = $93.74; (b) if r = 0.12: [$7.50(0.666)]/[0.12 − (0.333)(0.12)] = $62.50; (c) if r = 0.10: [$7.50(0.666)]/[0.12 − (0.333)(0.10)] = $57.67.

15-14 Solving v = d/(k − g) for k yields k = g + (d/p) = 15% + 2% = 17%.

15-15 At UTT v = [e(1 − f)]/(k − fr) = [$6(1 − 0.333)]/[0.12 − (0.333)(0.12)] = $50 and physical expansion occurs. But r = k = 12% is not investment growth.

15-16 Table 15-5 suggests Falzone is only worth P/E = (11.7)(1 − f) = (11.7)(0.1666) = 1.95 times its earnings per share, a $5.85 value.

Chapter 16   16-10 Alpha's after-tax income is $585 every year. Omega's is $576, $582, $588, and
                             $594.

                      16-11 P/E is discontinuous, but E/P is continuous and conveys the same information.

                      16-12 (a) the W&K model suggests P/E = 19.55; (b) yes, it is slightly underpriced.

                      16-13 (a) The W&K model now suggests P/E = 25.55; (b) Roist is now far underpriced—
                             buy it.

                      16-14 The two models are more similar than different, but the W&K model is based
                             on sample-dependent statistics.

                      16-15 Equation (15-9b) suggests P/E = $(1 - f)/(k - fr)$; the IBM data in Table 15-6
                             on page 475 align with this model fairly well.

Chapter 17   17-11 The $1.875 price change with the high volume on day 2 indicates significant new
                             information. The higher volume on day 9 appears to be only a liquidity trade.

                      17-12 (a) 5-day moving averages for days 5–14 are: $31.95, 32.675, 32.875, 32.675,
                             32.40, 32.275, 32.60, 32.975, 33.425, and 33.60; (b) price range: $5.25; (c) the
                             moving average's range: $1.65.

                      17-13 (a) Yes; (b) monthly CI is 0.935, 0.928, 0.932, 0.975, 0.939, 0.934, 0.925, 0.926,
                             0.932, 0.919, 0.907, 0.911; (c) yes, it dropped to 0.919 in October; (d) coincident;
                             (e) not necessarily, seek confirmations from other indicators.

Chapter 18   18-11 (a) The 4% filter issued buy signals on days 1-2, 2-3, 9-10, and 10-11; (b) the 8%
                             filter issued no signals.

                      18-12 (a) and (b) are identical to 18-11(a) and (b) because no short sales were indicated
                             in 18-11.

                      18-13 (a) No zero runs; (b) two positive runs; (c) two negative runs.

                      18-14 (a) Shares purchased for $150 in each month are: 1, 1, 3, and 3; (b) the one-period
                             returns are 5.0% every period.

                      18-15 (a) 10.0%: (b) 9.53%; (c) $[\ln(1 + r)]$ = (continuously compounded return)

                      18-16 (a) Quarterly returns: 8.2565%, 3.65018, 8.6798, and 0.9278; the unexplained
                             residuals are -1.5965, -9.53318, -15.1738, and -4.6398. (b) The 1979-III quar-
                             ter's negative residual of -15.1738% indicates a meaningless 15.1738% unsys-
                             tematic price decline after IBM's split; these market data suggest that IBM's split
                             did nothing to help IBM investors.

Chapter 19   19-8   Marginal utility curve should be positively sloped and increasingly steep.

                      19-9   Asset B is more desirable since r_A = 60% $< r_B$ = 137.5%.

19-10 If an investor has positive but diminishing (or constant, or increasing) marginal utility, risk will have a negative (or zero, or positive) effect on happiness, ceteris paribus. See Equations (19-7), (19-8), and (19-9).

19-11 Construct an indifference map in risk-return space to illustrate your preference ordering. Figure 19-11 is suggestive.

19-12 Risk-averters get more utils from riskless assets. See Instructors Manual for computations.

19-13 Zebra is the expected utility maximizing choice for both men.

19-14 Zebra is also the expected utility maximizing choice for both women because their utility functions are positive linear transformations of their husbands'.

19-15 (a) and (b) Marginal utility is positive and diminishing; (c) ARA $= 1.5/w > 0$; (d) RRA $= 3/2 > 0$; (e) ARA$'(w) < 0$ is decreasing ARA, so more risky investing will occur. (f) RRA$'(w) = 0$ is constant RRA, so the percent at risk will not change.

Chapter 20

20-8   (a) $E(r) = 8\% + [(6\%) \text{ (beta)}]$; (b) $E(r_A) = 15.2\% < 17\%$ implies underpricing; $E(r_B) = 12.8\% < 14\%$ implies underpricing; $E(r_C) = 17\% > 15\%$ implies overpricing; $E(r_D) = 12.5\% < 16\%$ implies underpricing.

20-9   (a) Portfolio's beta $= 1.061$; (b) $E(r_p) = 16.427\%$.

20-10 (a) Portfolio's beta $= 1.0364$; (b) $E(r_p) = 16.255\%$.

20-11 (a) Portfolio's beta $= 1.195$; (b) $E(r_p) = 17.367\%$.

20-12 The CAPM $E(r) = 8\% + [(6\%) \text{ (beta)}]$ implies $E(r_A) = 16.4\% < 17\%$ and underpricing; $E(r_B) = 15.2\% > 14\%$ and overpricing; $E(r_C) = 14.6\% < 15\%$ and underpricing; $E(r_D) = 15.8\% < 16\%$ and underpricing.

20-13 The CAPM $E(r) = 9\% + [(7\%) \text{ (beta)}]$ implies $E(r_A) = 17.4\% > 17\%$ and overpricing; $E(r_B) = 14.6\% > 14\%$ and overpricing; $E(r_C) = 19.5\% > 15\%$ and overpricing; $E(r_D) = 14.25\% < 16\%$ and underpricing.

20-14 A CAPM $E(r) = 9\% + [(5\%)(1.25 = \text{beta})]$ implies $E(r_A) = 15.25\%$.

20-15 A CAPM $E(r) = 8\% + [(8\%)(1.25 = \text{beta})]$ implies $E(r_A) = 18\%$.

20-16 $E(r_p) = (0.5)(8\%) + (0.5)(14\%) = 11\%$, beta $= 0.5$, and standard deviation $= 0.05 = 5\%$.

20-17 $E(r_p) = (0.75)(0.14) + (0.25)(0.08) = 0.125 = 12.5\%$ and the beta is 0.75.

20-18 $E(r_p) = (1 + 0.3)(0.14) + (-0.3)(0.08) = 0.158 = 15.8\%$ and beta is 1.3.

20-19 $E(r_p) = (1 + 0.6)(0.14) + (-0.6)(0.08) = 0.176 = 17.6\%$ and beta is 1.6.

20-20 (a) Cov $= (0.1)(0.2)(0.5) = .01$; (b) beta $= (.01)/(0.1)^2 = 1.0$.

20-21 CAPM estimates suggest $E(r_E) = R + [E(r_E - R)] [\text{beta}_E] = 7\% + [11\% - 4\%] [0.61] = 9.44\% > 8.5\%$; therefore, increase rates.

Chapter 21   21-7   (*a*) Gamma is best and Beta is worst at $R = 3\%$. (*b*) Epsilon is best and Beta is worst at $R = 3\%$. (*c*) Using Sharpe, Gamma is best and Alpha is worst at $R = 6\%$. Using Treynor, Epsilon is best and Alpha is worst at $R = 6\%$.

21-8   From best to worst: C, D, B, E, A.

21-9   From best to worst: C, D, B, E, A.

21-10 From best to worst: C, D, B, E, A.

21-11 Beta Fund has beta $= 1.62$.

21-12 Fund E has the lowest R^2.

21-13 Alpha has highest $R^2 = 0.94$.

21-14 $S_G = 0.272$ and $T_G = 2.03$

21-15 $S_A = 0.29$ and $T_A = 2.124$

21-16 Jensen's alpha for Acorn's is -0.252 and Guardian's is -0.253.

21-17 Acorn's beta is more aggressive.

Chapter 22   22-8   (*a*) $Cc = \$4.427$; (*b*) $Pp = \$0.476$

22-9   (*a*) $Cc_{ABC} = \$3.55$ and $Cc_{XYZ} = \$10.60$; (*b*) $Pp_{ABC} = \$1.99$ and $Pp_{XYZ} = \$1.74$

22-10 (*a*) 100% over 3 months; (*b*) the put would be worthless.

22-11 Almost 26/100 of 1.0 percent stock price increase; that is, slightly less than 13¢ per $50 share.

22-12 $11.11\% + 6.66\% = 17.77\%$

22-13 (*a*) Break-even price $= \$85$; (*b*) stock price rise almost .27 of 1% to $85.23.

22-14 $Cc = \$6.968$

22-15 Standard deviation $= 0.243857$

22-16 (*a*) $6.814 > $6.20, call is undervalued; (*b*) buy calls

22-17 (*a*) $Cc = \$7.146$, (*b*) $Pp = \$1.225$

22-18 C

Chapter 23   23-8   October call with $360 exercise price is best.

23-9   (*a*) Sell short or buy a put on GM while owning the stock; (*b*) hold either hedge for over 6 months.

23-10 (*a*) $Cc = \$18.75$; (*b*) 1363.6% gain on the TI call.

23-11 (*a*) A long straddle; (*b*) $300 + $200 = $500 plus commissions;

(*c*)

GM price	Call profit	Put profit	Straddle profit
$30	− $300	+ $1800	+ $1500
40	− 300	+ 800	+ 500
50	− 300	− 200	− 500
60	+ 700	− 200	+ 500
70	+ 1700	− 200	+ 1500

(*d*) Break-even at $45 and $55.

23-12 (*a*) A long straddle; (*b*) $200 + $200 = $400 plus commissions;

(*c*)

GM price	Put profit	Call profit	Strangle profit
$25	+ $1800	− $200	+ $1600
35	+ 800	− 200	+ 600
41	+ 200	− 200	0
54	− 200	+ 200	0
60	− 200	+ 800	+ 600

(*d*) Break-even at $41 and $54.

23-13 (*a*) Bull spread; (*b*) $300 − $100 = $200;

(*c*)

AT&T price	Long $30 call	Short $35 call	Total profit
$25	− $300	+ $100	− $200
32	− 100	+ 100	0
35	+ 200	+ 100	+ 300
40	+ 700	− 400	+ 300

(*d*) Break-even at $32 per share.

23-14 (*a*) $200;

(*b*)

AT&T price	Long $30 call	Short $35 call	Total profit
$25	+ $300	− $100	+ $200
32	+ 100	− 100	0
40	− 700	+ 400	− 300

(*d*) Break-even at $32 per share.

23-15 (*a*) Long butterfly spread; (*b*) the cost is a net debit of only $300 plus commissions:

Buy 1 July $50 call	− $1200
Buy 1 July $70 call	− 300
Sell 2 July $60 calls	+ 1200

Total cost	− $300 plus commissions

(c) Jonathon's gains and losses are

GM price	July 50 call	July 60 puts	July 70 call	Net profit
$40	− $1200	+ $1200	− $300	− $300
53	− 900	+ 1200	− 300	0
60	− 200	+ 1200	− 300	+ 700
67	+ 500	− 200	− 300	0
80	+ 1800	− 2800	+ 700	− 300

(d) Break-even at $53 or $67 per share.

23-16 (a) Total net worth = $10,570; (b) Black-Scholes values the bonds at only $110,000 − $10,570 = $99,430.

23-17 See Instructors Manual.

23-18 See Instructors Manual.

23-19 (a) k = $45 million; (b) 90 days; (c) total net worth is (0.61625580) ($1 mill.) = $616,255.80 while in court;

(d) $40,000,000.00 = market value of total assets
less: 616,255.80 = value of Star's total equity
         $39,383,744.20 = value of total liabilities
less: 25,000,000.00 = value of senior debt = D_1
         $14,383,744.20 = general creditors' claim = D_2

Chapter 24

24-14   Using T-bills to cover the margin requirement:

$$r = \frac{p_{t+1} - p_t}{p_t} + R\left(\frac{p_t + p_{t+1}}{2}\right) = \begin{array}{l} \text{percent} \\ \text{price} \\ \text{change} \end{array} + \begin{array}{l} \text{interest income} \\ \text{on average} \\ \text{T-bill investment} \end{array}$$

24-15 (a) Sell short eight soybean futures contracts; (b) this perfect hedge permits zero gains and zero losses.

24-16 (a) Sell short three cotton futures contracts; (b) physicals had a [($0.80 × 300,000 = $240,000) less ($0.60 × 300,000 = $180,000) equals] $60,000 loss, plus a gain of $0.20 per pound on the futures (equals $0.20 × 3 contracts × 50,000 = $30,000) for a net total loss of $30,000.

24-17 (a) Buy six sugar futures contracts; (b) unhedged losses would be ($0.12 per pound × 672,000 pounds equals) $80,640.

24-18 (a) Buy 10 lumber futures contracts with 8 months until delivery; (b) unhedged losses would be ($12 per 1000 board feet × 1500 equals) $18,000.

24-19 (a) Buy six wheat contracts for $9000 plus $240; (b) net gain is 50 cents per bushel × 6 contracts × 5000 equals $15,000 less $240 for a 159.74% gain (= $14,760/$9240); (c) losses would be ($0.75 per bushel × 6 contracts × 5000 bushels =) $22,500 plus $240 commissions.

24-20 A \$15,350 investment will reap a profit of (\$50 per ounce $\times$ 10 $\times$ 1000 =) \$50,000 minus \$350 commissions equals \$47,650.

24-21 (a) Sell short 100 S&P contracts; (b) \$1.5 gain on the short position plus \$1.5 loss on the stocks equals zero net gain and zero net loss.

24-22 (a) A short sale of 10 S&P contracts will yield a \$150,000 profit; or, (\$150,000/ \$650,000 = .231 =) 23.1% gain; (b) \$100,000 loss; (c) loss of 153.8% over 6 months.

Chapter 25

25-9 (a) Francois paid FF180 per share. At \$1/FF6 = 0.1666, Francoise paid (FF180) (0.1666) = \$30 per share. (b) Francois earned a return of 11.1%; Francoise earned 33.3%. (c) Francoise made a 20% gain on foreign exchange.

25-10 An American investor in English stock could expect to earn 15.5%, calculated as follows: $r_f = r_d + r_c + r_d r_c = 10\% + 5\% + (10\%)(5\%) = 15.5\%$. The American investor's total risk would be: $\text{Var}(r_f) = \text{Var}(r_c) + \text{Var}(r_d) + \text{S.D.}(r_c)\text{S.D.}(r_d)P_{cd} = 0.04 + 0.01 + 0.02 = 0.07$.

25-11 (a) Rolf Kierulf paid \$100,000 for one share of Hoffman-LaRoche stock; (b) Rolf's return is zero; (c) Rolf made (1.0 + H-L rate of return) (1.0 + currency return) = (1.0666666) (0.9375) = 1.0 = (1.0 + zero total return).

25-12 (a) For an American investor \$24/\$21.73913 = 1.104, or 10.4%; (b) 30 pounds/25 pounds = 1.2, or 20% return for a British investor.

25-13 (1 + market return) (1 + currency percent change) = (1.25)(1.10) = 1.375 or 37.5% return

25-14

	\multicolumn{3}{c}{Correlation matrix}	Standard
	U.S.	U.K.	Japan	deviations
U.S.	1.00			21.843%
U.K.	.659	1.00		46.754
Japan	.389	.152	1.00	43.092

25-15 The correlation is .747. The standard deviations of Australia and Canada are 28.867 and 21.407%, respectively.

25-16 $E(r) = 17.895\%$; the standard deviation is 25.88%.

25-17 $E(r) = 13.92\%$ and the standard deviation is 22.80361%.

25-18 The standard deviation is 20.08931%.

Part 8

Appendixes

Appendices

Appendix A

Future and Present Value Tables

FUTURE VALUE OF $1 AT THE END OF n PERIODS $(1 + k)^n$

Period	1%	2%	3%	4%	5%	6%	7%	8%	9%	10%	12%	14%	15%	16%	18%	20%	24%	28%	32%
1	1.0100	1.0200	1.0300	1.0400	1.0500	1.0600	1.0700	1.0800	1.0900	1.1000	1.1200	1.1400	1.1500	1.1600	1.1800	1.2000	1.2400	1.2800	1.3200
2	1.0201	1.0404	1.0609	1.0816	1.1025	1.1236	1.1449	1.1664	1.1881	1.2100	1.2544	1.2996	1.3225	1.3456	1.3924	1.4400	1.5376	1.6384	1.7424
3	1.0303	1.0612	1.0927	1.1249	1.1576	1.1910	1.2250	1.2597	1.2950	1.3310	1.4049	1.4815	1.5209	1.5609	1.6430	1.7280	1.9066	2.0972	2.3000
4	1.0406	1.0824	1.1255	1.1699	1.2155	1.2625	1.3108	1.3605	1.4116	1.4641	1.5735	1.6890	1.7490	1.8106	1.9388	2.0736	2.3642	2.6844	3.0360
5	1.0510	1.1041	1.1593	1.2167	1.2763	1.3382	1.4026	1.4693	1.5386	1.6105	1.7623	1.9254	2.0114	2.1003	2.2878	2.4883	2.9316	3.4360	4.0075
6	1.0615	1.1262	1.1941	1.2653	1.3401	1.4185	1.5007	1.5869	1.6771	1.7716	1.9738	2.1950	2.3131	2.4364	2.6996	2.9860	3.6352	4.3980	5.2899
7	1.0721	1.1487	1.2299	1.3159	1.4071	1.5036	1.6058	1.7138	1.8280	1.9487	2.2107	2.5023	2.6600	2.8262	3.1855	3.5832	4.5077	5.6295	6.9826
8	1.0829	1.1717	1.2668	1.3686	1.4775	1.5938	1.7182	1.8509	1.9926	2.1436	2.4760	2.8526	3.0590	3.2784	3.7589	4.2998	5.5895	7.2058	9.2170
9	1.0937	1.1951	1.3048	1.4233	1.5513	1.6895	1.8385	1.9990	2.1719	2.3579	2.7731	3.2519	3.5179	3.8030	4.4355	5.1598	6.9310	9.2234	12.166
10	1.1046	1.2190	1.3439	1.4802	1.6289	1.7908	1.9672	2.1589	2.3674	2.5937	3.1058	3.7072	4.0456	4.4114	5.2338	6.1917	8.5944	11.805	16.059
11	1.1157	1.2434	1.3842	1.5395	1.7103	1.8983	2.1049	2.3316	2.5804	2.8531	3.4785	4.2262	4.6524	5.1173	6.1759	7.4301	10.657	15.111	21.198
12	1.1268	1.2682	1.4258	1.6010	1.7959	2.0122	2.2522	2.5182	2.8127	3.1384	3.8960	4.8179	5.3502	5.9360	7.2876	8.9161	13.214	19.342	27.982
13	1.1381	1.2936	1.4685	1.6651	1.8856	2.1329	2.4098	2.7196	3.0658	3.4523	4.3635	5.4924	6.1528	6.8858	8.5994	10.699	16.386	24.758	36.937
14	1.1495	1.3195	1.5126	1.7317	1.9799	2.2609	2.5785	2.9372	3.3417	3.7975	4.8871	6.2613	7.0757	7.9875	10.147	12.839	20.319	31.691	48.756
15	1.1610	1.3459	1.5580	1.8009	2.0789	2.3966	2.7590	3.1722	3.6425	4.1772	5.4736	7.1379	8.1371	9.2655	11.973	15.407	25.195	40.564	64.358
16	1.1726	1.3728	1.6047	1.8730	2.1829	2.5404	2.9522	3.4259	3.9703	4.5950	6.1304	8.1372	9.3576	10.748	14.129	18.488	31.242	51.923	84.953
17	1.1843	1.4002	1.6528	1.9479	2.2920	2.6928	3.1588	3.7000	4.3276	5.0545	6.8660	9.2765	10.761	12.467	16.672	22.186	38.740	66.461	112.13
18	1.1961	1.4282	1.7024	2.0258	2.4066	2.8543	3.3799	3.9960	4.7171	5.5599	7.6900	10.575	12.375	14.462	19.673	26.623	48.038	85.070	148.02
19	1.2081	1.4568	1.7535	2.1068	2.5270	3.0256	3.6165	4.3157	5.1417	6.1159	8.6128	12.055	14.231	16.776	23.214	31.948	59.567	108.89	195.39
20	1.2202	1.4859	1.8061	2.1911	2.6533	3.2071	3.8697	4.6610	5.6044	6.7275	9.6463	13.743	16.366	19.460	27.393	38.337	73.864	139.37	257.91
21	1.2324	1.5157	1.8603	2.2788	2.7860	3.3996	4.1406	5.0338	6.1088	7.4002	10.803	15.667	18.821	22.574	32.323	46.005	91.591	178.40	340.44
22	1.2447	1.5460	1.9161	2.3699	2.9253	3.6035	4.4304	5.4365	6.6586	8.1403	12.100	17.861	21.644	26.186	38.142	55.206	113.57	228.35	449.39
23	1.2572	1.5769	1.9736	2.4647	3.0715	3.8197	4.7405	5.8715	7.2579	8.9543	13.552	20.361	24.891	30.376	45.007	66.247	140.83	292.30	593.19
24	1.2697	1.6084	2.0328	2.5633	3.2251	4.0489	5.0724	6.3412	7.9111	9.8497	15.178	23.212	28.625	35.236	53.108	79.496	174.63	374.14	783.02
25	1.2824	1.6406	2.0938	2.6658	3.3864	4.2919	5.4274	6.8485	8.6231	10.834	17.000	26.461	32.918	40.874	62.668	95.396	216.54	478.90	1033.5
26	1.2953	1.6734	2.1566	2.7725	3.5557	4.5494	5.8074	7.3964	9.3992	11.918	19.040	30.166	37.856	47.414	73.948	114.47	268.51	612.99	1364.3
27	1.3082	1.7069	2.2213	2.8834	3.7335	4.8223	6.2139	7.9881	10.245	13.110	21.324	34.389	43.535	55.000	87.259	137.37	332.95	784.63	1800.9
28	1.3213	1.7410	2.2879	2.9987	3.9201	5.1117	6.6488	8.6271	11.167	14.421	23.883	39.204	50.065	63.800	102.96	164.84	412.86	1004.3	2377.2
29	1.3345	1.7758	2.3566	3.1187	4.1161	5.4184	7.1143	9.3173	12.172	15.863	26.749	44.693	57.575	74.008	121.50	197.81	511.95	1285.5	3137.9
30	1.3478	1.8114	2.4273	3.2434	4.3219	5.7435	7.6123	10.062	13.267	17.449	29.959	50.950	66.211	85.849	143.37	237.37	634.81	1645.5	4142.0
40	1.4889	2.2080	3.2620	4.8010	7.0400	10.285	14.974	21.724	31.409	45.259	93.050	188.88	267.86	378.72	750.37	1469.7	5455.9	19427.	66521.
50	1.6446	2.6919	4.3839	7.1067	11.467	18.420	29.457	46.901	74.357	117.39	289.00	700.23	1083.6	1670.7	3927.4	9100.4	46890.	.	

SUM OF AN ANNUITY OF $1 PER PERIOD FOR n PERIODS $\sum_{t=1}^{n}(1+K)^{n-t} = \frac{(1+K)^n - 1}{k}$

Number of periods	1%	2%	3%	4%	5%	6%	7%	8%	9%	10%	12%	14%	15%	16%	18%	20%	24%	28%	32%
1	1.0000	1.0000	1.0000	1.0000	1.0000	1.0000	1.0000	1.0000	1.0000	1.0000	1.0000	1.0000	1.0000	1.0000	1.0000	1.0000	1.0000	1.0000	1.0000
2	2.0100	2.0200	2.0300	2.0400	2.0500	2.0600	2.0700	2.0800	2.0900	2.1000	2.1200	2.1400	2.1500	2.1600	2.1800	2.2000	2.2400	2.2800	2.3200
3	3.0301	3.0604	3.0909	3.1216	3.1525	3.1836	3.2149	3.2464	3.2781	3.3100	3.3744	3.4396	3.4725	3.5056	3.5724	3.6400	3.7776	3.9184	4.0624
4	4.0604	4.1216	4.1836	4.2465	4.3101	4.3746	4.4399	4.5061	4.5731	4.6410	4.7793	4.9211	4.9934	5.0665	5.2154	5.3680	5.6842	6.0156	6.3624
5	5.1010	5.2040	5.3091	5.4163	5.5256	5.6371	5.7507	5.8666	5.9847	6.1051	6.3528	6.6101	6.7424	6.8771	7.1542	7.4416	8.0484	8.6999	9.3983
6	6.1520	6.3081	6.4684	6.6330	6.8019	6.9753	7.1533	7.3359	7.5233	7.7156	8.1152	8.5355	8.7537	8.9775	9.4420	9.9299	10.980	12.135	13.405
7	7.2135	7.4343	7.6625	7.8983	8.1420	8.3938	8.6540	8.9228	9.2004	9.4872	10.089	10.730	11.066	11.413	12.141	12.915	14.615	16.533	18.695
8	8.2857	8.5830	8.8923	9.2142	9.5491	9.8975	10.259	10.636	11.028	11.435	12.299	13.232	13.726	14.240	15.327	16.499	19.122	22.163	25.678
9	9.3685	9.7546	10.159	10.582	11.026	11.491	11.978	12.487	13.021	13.579	14.775	16.085	16.785	17.518	19.085	20.798	24.712	29.369	34.895
10	10.462	10.949	11.463	12.006	12.577	13.180	13.816	14.486	15.192	15.937	17.548	19.337	20.303	21.321	23.521	25.958	31.643	38.592	47.061
11	11.566	12.168	12.807	13.486	14.206	14.971	15.783	16.645	17.560	18.531	20.654	23.044	24.349	25.732	28.755	32.150	40.237	50.398	63.121
12	12.682	13.412	14.192	15.025	15.917	16.869	17.888	18.977	20.140	21.384	24.133	27.270	29.001	30.850	34.931	39.580	50.894	65.510	84.320
13	13.809	14.680	15.617	16.626	17.713	18.882	20.140	21.495	22.953	24.522	28.029	32.088	34.351	36.786	42.218	48.496	64.109	84.852	112.30
14	14.947	15.973	17.086	18.291	19.598	21.015	22.550	24.214	26.019	27.975	32.392	37.581	40.504	43.672	50.818	59.195	80.496	109.61	149.23
15	16.096	17.293	18.598	20.023	21.578	23.276	25.129	27.152	29.360	31.772	37.279	43.842	47.580	51.659	60.965	72.035	100.81	141.30	197.99
16	17.257	18.639	20.156	21.824	23.657	25.672	27.888	30.324	33.003	35.949	42.753	50.980	55.717	60.925	72.939	87.442	126.01	181.86	262.35
17	18.430	20.012	21.761	23.697	25.840	28.212	30.840	33.750	36.973	40.544	48.883	59.117	65.075	71.673	87.068	105.93	157.25	233.79	347.30
18	19.614	21.412	23.414	25.645	28.132	30.905	33.999	37.450	41.301	45.599	55.749	68.394	75.836	84.140	103.74	128.11	195.99	300.25	459.44
19	20.810	22.840	25.116	27.671	30.539	33.760	37.379	41.446	46.018	51.159	63.439	78.969	88.211	98.603	123.41	154.74	244.03	385.32	607.47
20	22.019	24.297	26.870	29.778	33.066	36.785	40.995	45.762	51.160	57.275	72.052	91.024	102.44	115.37	146.62	186.68	303.60	494.21	802.86
21	23.239	25.783	28.676	31.969	35.719	39.992	44.865	50.422	56.764	64.002	81.698	104.76	118.81	134.84	174.02	225.02	377.46	633.59	1060.7
22	24.471	27.299	30.536	34.248	38.505	43.392	49.005	55.456	62.873	71.402	92.502	120.43	137.63	157.41	206.34	271.03	469.05	811.99	1401.2
23	25.716	28.845	32.452	36.617	41.430	46.995	53.436	60.893	69.531	79.543	104.60	138.29	159.27	183.60	244.48	326.23	582.62	1040.3	1850.6
24	26.973	30.421	34.426	39.082	44.502	50.815	58.176	66.764	76.789	88.497	118.15	158.65	184.16	213.97	289.49	392.48	723.46	1332.6	2443.8
25	28.243	32.030	36.459	41.645	47.727	54.864	63.249	73.105	84.700	98.347	133.33	181.87	212.79	249.21	342.60	471.98	898.09	1706.8	3226.8
26	29.525	33.670	38.553	44.311	51.113	59.156	68.676	79.954	93.323	109.18	150.33	208.33	245.71	290.08	405.27	567.38	1114.6	2185.7	4260.4
27	30.820	35.344	40.709	47.084	54.669	63.705	74.483	87.350	102.72	121.09	169.37	238.49	283.56	337.50	479.22	681.85	1383.1	2798.7	5624.8
28	32.129	37.051	42.930	49.967	58.402	68.528	80.697	95.338	112.96	134.20	190.69	272.88	327.10	392.50	566.48	819.22	1716.0	3583.3	7425.7
29	33.450	38.792	45.218	52.966	62.322	73.639	87.346	103.96	124.13	148.63	214.58	312.09	377.16	456.30	669.44	984.06	2128.9	4587.6	9802.9
30	34.784	40.568	47.575	56.084	66.438	79.058	94.460	113.28	136.30	164.49	241.33	356.78	434.74	530.31	790.94	1181.8	2640.9	5873.2	12941.
40	48.886	60.402	75.401	95.025	120.79	154.76	199.63	259.06	337.88	442.59	767.09	1342.0	1779.1	2360.8	4163.2	7343.9	22729.	69377.	.
50	64.463	84.579	112.79	152.66	209.34	290.33	406.52	573.76	815.08	1163.9	2400.0	4994.5	7217.7	10435.	21813.	45497.	.	.	.

PRESENT VALUE OF $1 $1/(1 + k)^t$

Period	1%	2%	3%	4%	5%	6%	7%	8%	9%	10%	12%	14%	15%	16%	18%	20%	24%	28%	32%
1	0.9901	0.9804	0.9709	0.9615	0.9524	0.9434	0.9346	0.9259	0.9174	0.9091	0.8929	0.8772	0.8696	0.8621	0.8475	0.8333	0.8065	0.7813	0.7576
2	0.9803	0.9612	0.9426	0.9246	0.9070	0.8900	0.8734	0.8573	0.8417	0.8264	0.7972	0.7695	0.7561	0.7432	0.7182	0.6944	0.6504	0.6104	0.5739
3	0.9706	0.9423	0.9151	0.8890	0.8638	0.8396	0.8163	0.7938	0.7722	0.7513	0.7118	0.6750	0.6575	0.6407	0.6086	0.5787	0.5245	0.4768	0.4348
4	0.9610	0.9238	0.8885	0.8548	0.8227	0.7921	0.7629	0.7350	0.7084	0.6830	0.6355	0.5921	0.5718	0.5523	0.5158	0.4823	0.4230	0.3725	0.3294
5	0.9515	0.9057	0.8626	0.8219	0.7835	0.7473	0.7130	0.6806	0.6499	0.6209	0.5674	0.5194	0.4972	0.4761	0.4371	0.4019	0.3411	0.2910	0.2495
6	0.9420	0.8880	0.8375	0.7903	0.7462	0.7050	0.6663	0.6302	0.5963	0.5645	0.5066	0.4556	0.4323	0.4104	0.3704	0.3349	0.2751	0.2274	0.1890
7	0.9327	0.8706	0.8131	0.7599	0.7107	0.6651	0.6227	0.5835	0.5470	0.5132	0.4523	0.3996	0.3759	0.3538	0.3139	0.2791	0.2218	0.1776	0.1432
8	0.9235	0.8535	0.7894	0.7307	0.6768	0.6274	0.5820	0.5403	0.5019	0.4665	0.4039	0.3506	0.3269	0.3050	0.2660	0.2326	0.1789	0.1388	0.1085
9	0.9143	0.8368	0.7664	0.7026	0.6446	0.5919	0.5439	0.5002	0.4604	0.4241	0.3606	0.3075	0.2843	0.2630	0.2255	0.1938	0.1443	0.1084	0.0822
10	0.9053	0.8203	0.7441	0.6756	0.6139	0.5584	0.5083	0.4632	0.4224	0.3855	0.3220	0.2697	0.2472	0.2267	0.1911	0.1615	0.1164	0.0847	0.0623
11	0.8963	0.8043	0.7224	0.6496	0.5847	0.5268	0.4751	0.4289	0.3875	0.3505	0.2875	0.2366	0.2149	0.1954	0.1619	0.1346	0.0938	0.0662	0.0472
12	0.8874	0.7885	0.7014	0.6246	0.5568	0.4970	0.4440	0.3971	0.3555	0.3186	0.2567	0.2076	0.1869	0.1685	0.1372	0.1122	0.0757	0.0517	0.0357
13	0.8787	0.7730	0.6810	0.6006	0.5303	0.4688	0.4150	0.3677	0.3262	0.2897	0.2292	0.1821	0.1625	0.1452	0.1163	0.0935	0.0610	0.0404	0.0271
14	0.8700	0.7579	0.6611	0.5775	0.5051	0.4423	0.3878	0.3405	0.2992	0.2633	0.2046	0.1597	0.1413	0.1252	0.0985	0.0779	0.0492	0.0316	0.0205
15	0.8613	0.7430	0.6419	0.5553	0.4810	0.4173	0.3624	0.3152	0.2745	0.2394	0.1827	0.1401	0.1229	0.1079	0.0835	0.0649	0.0397	0.0247	0.0155
16	0.8528	0.7284	0.6232	0.5339	0.4581	0.3936	0.3387	0.2919	0.2519	0.2176	0.1631	0.1229	0.1069	0.0930	0.0708	0.0541	0.0320	0.0193	0.0118
17	0.8444	0.7142	0.6050	0.5134	0.4363	0.3714	0.3166	0.2703	0.2311	0.1978	0.1456	0.1078	0.0929	0.0802	0.0600	0.0451	0.0258	0.0150	0.0089
18	0.8360	0.7002	0.5874	0.4936	0.4155	0.3503	0.2959	0.2502	0.2120	0.1799	0.1300	0.0946	0.0808	0.0691	0.0508	0.0376	0.0208	0.0118	0.0068
19	0.8277	0.6864	0.5703	0.4746	0.3957	0.3305	0.2765	0.2317	0.1945	0.1635	0.1161	0.0829	0.0703	0.0596	0.0431	0.0313	0.0168	0.0092	0.0051
20	0.8195	0.6730	0.5537	0.4564	0.3769	0.3118	0.2584	0.2145	0.1784	0.1486	0.1037	0.0728	0.0611	0.0514	0.0365	0.0261	0.0135	0.0072	0.0039
25	0.7798	0.6095	0.4776	0.3751	0.2953	0.2330	0.1842	0.1460	0.1160	0.0923	0.0588	0.0378	0.0304	0.0245	0.0160	0.0105	0.0046	0.0021	0.0010
30	0.7419	0.5521	0.4120	0.3083	0.2314	0.1741	0.1314	0.0994	0.0754	0.0573	0.0334	0.0196	0.0151	0.0116	0.0070	0.0042	0.0016	0.0006	0.0002
40	0.6717	0.4529	0.3066	0.2083	0.1420	0.0972	0.0668	0.0460	0.0318	0.0221	0.0107	0.0053	0.0037	0.0026	0.0013	0.0007	0.0002	0.0001	
50	0.6080	0.3715	0.2281	0.1407	0.0872	0.0543	0.0339	0.0213	0.0134	0.0085	0.0035	0.0014	0.0009	0.0006	0.0003	0.0001			

PRESENT VALUE OF AN ANNUITY OF $1 PER PERIOD FOR n PERIODS

$$= \sum_{t=1}^{n} \frac{1}{(1+k)^t} = \frac{1 - \frac{1}{(1+k)^n}}{k}$$

Number of payments	1%	2%	3%	4%	5%	6%	7%	8%	9%	10%	12%	14%	15%	16%	18%	20%	24%	28%	32%
1	0.9901	0.9804	0.9709	0.9615	0.9524	0.9434	0.9346	0.9259	0.9174	0.9091	0.8929	0.8772	0.8696	0.8621	0.8475	0.8333	0.8065	0.7813	0.7576
2	1.9704	1.9416	1.9135	1.8861	1.8594	1.8334	1.8080	1.7833	1.7591	1.7355	1.6901	1.6467	1.6257	1.6052	1.5656	1.5278	1.4568	1.3916	1.3315
3	2.9410	2.8839	2.8286	2.7751	2.7232	2.6730	2.6243	2.5771	2.5313	2.4869	2.4018	2.3216	2.2832	2.2459	2.1743	2.1065	1.9813	1.8684	1.7663
4	3.9020	3.8077	3.7171	3.6299	3.5460	3.4651	3.3872	3.3121	3.2397	3.1699	3.0373	2.9137	2.8550	2.7982	2.6901	2.5887	2.4043	2.2410	2.0957
5	4.8534	4.7135	4.5797	4.4518	4.3295	4.2124	4.1002	3.9927	3.8897	3.7908	3.6048	3.4331	3.3522	3.2743	3.1272	2.9906	2.7454	2.5320	2.3452
6	5.7955	5.6014	5.4172	5.2421	5.0757	4.9173	4.7665	4.6229	4.4859	4.3553	4.1114	3.8887	3.7845	3.6847	3.4976	3.3255	3.0205	2.7594	2.5342
7	6.7282	6.4720	6.2303	6.0021	5.7864	5.5824	5.3893	5.2064	5.0330	4.8684	4.5638	4.2883	4.1604	4.0386	3.8115	3.6046	3.2423	2.9370	2.6775
8	7.6517	7.3255	7.0197	6.7327	6.4632	6.2098	5.9713	5.7466	5.5348	5.3349	4.9676	4.6389	4.4873	4.3436	4.0776	3.8372	3.4212	3.0758	2.7860
9	8.5660	8.1622	7.7861	7.4353	7.1078	6.8017	6.5152	6.2469	5.9952	5.7590	5.3282	4.9464	4.7716	4.6065	4.3030	4.0310	3.5655	3.1842	2.8681
10	9.4713	8.9826	8.5302	8.1109	7.7217	7.3601	7.0236	6.7101	6.4177	6.1446	5.6502	5.2161	5.0188	4.8332	4.4941	4.1925	3.6819	3.2689	2.9304
11	10.3676	9.7868	9.2526	8.7605	8.3064	7.8869	7.4987	7.1390	6.8052	6.4951	5.9377	5.4527	5.2337	5.0286	4.6560	4.3271	3.7757	3.3351	2.9776
12	11.2551	10.5753	9.9540	9.3851	8.8633	8.3838	7.9427	7.5361	7.1607	6.8137	6.1944	5.6603	5.4206	5.1971	4.7932	4.4392	3.8514	3.3868	3.0133
13	12.1337	11.3484	10.6350	9.9856	9.3936	8.8527	8.3577	7.9038	7.4869	7.1034	6.4235	5.8424	5.5831	5.3423	4.9095	4.5327	3.9124	3.4272	3.0404
14	13.0037	12.1062	11.2961	10.5631	9.8986	9.2950	8.7455	8.2442	7.7862	7.3667	6.6282	6.0021	5.7245	5.4675	5.0081	4.6106	3.9616	3.4587	3.0609
15	13.8651	12.8493	11.9379	11.1184	10.3797	9.7122	9.1079	8.5595	8.0607	7.6061	6.8109	6.1422	5.8474	5.5755	5.0916	4.6755	4.0013	3.4834	3.0764
16	14.7179	13.5777	12.5611	11.6523	10.8378	10.1059	9.4466	8.8514	8.3126	7.8237	6.9740	6.2651	5.9542	5.6685	5.1624	4.7296	4.0333	3.5026	3.0882
17	15.5623	14.2919	13.1661	12.1657	11.2741	10.4773	9.7632	9.1216	8.5436	8.0216	7.1196	6.3729	6.0472	5.7487	5.2223	4.7746	4.0591	3.5177	3.0971
18	16.3983	14.9920	13.7535	12.6593	11.6896	10.8276	10.0591	9.3719	8.7556	8.2014	7.2497	6.4674	6.1280	5.8178	5.2732	4.8122	4.0799	3.5294	3.1039
19	17.2260	15.6785	14.3238	13.1339	12.0853	11.1581	10.3356	9.6036	8.9501	8.3649	7.3658	6.5504	6.1982	5.8775	5.3162	4.8435	4.0967	3.5386	3.1090
20	18.0456	16.3514	14.8775	13.5903	12.4622	11.4699	10.5940	9.8181	9.1285	8.5136	7.4694	6.6231	6.2593	5.9288	5.3527	4.8696	4.1103	3.5458	3.1129
25	22.0232	19.5235	17.4131	15.6221	14.0939	12.7834	11.6536	10.6748	9.8226	9.0770	7.8431	6.8729	6.4641	6.0971	5.4669	4.9476	4.1474	3.5640	3.1220
30	25.8077	22.3965	19.6004	17.2920	15.3725	13.7648	12.4090	11.2578	10.2737	9.4269	8.0552	7.0027	6.5660	6.1772	5.5168	4.9789	4.1601	3.5693	3.1242
40	32.8347	27.3555	23.1148	19.7928	17.1591	15.0463	13.3317	11.9246	10.7574	9.7791	8.2438	7.1050	6.6418	6.2335	5.5482	4.9966	4.1659	3.5712	3.1250
50	39.1961	31.4236	25.7298	21.4822	18.2559	15.7619	13.8007	12.2335	10.9617	9.9148	8.3045	7.1327	6.6605	6.2463	5.5541	4.9995	4.1666	3.5714	3.1250
∞	100.0000	50.0000	33.3333	25.0000	20.0000	16.6666	14.2857	12.5000	11.1100	10.0000	8.3333	7.1428	6.6666	6.2500	5.5555	5.0000	4.1666	3.5714	3.1250

Appendix B

Mathematical

Statistical Concepts

Used in Investments

Analysis

Concept 1

The **expected value** of a random variable denoted r is the weighted average of the values that r might assume using the probability assigned to each possible value as its weight.

$$E(r) = \sum_{i=1}^{T} P_i r_i = P_1 r_1 + P_2 r_2 + \cdots + P_T r_T \qquad \text{where } \sum_{i=1}^{T} P_i = 1.0$$

The expected value of a constant denoted c is the constant, $E(c) = c$. The expected value of a constant c times a random variable equals the constant times the expected value of the random variable, $E(cr) = cE(r)$. The expected value of a sum of random variables is the sum of the expectations of the random variables, $E(r + s) = E(r) + E(s)$.

Concept question: Compare and contrast a stock's average return with its expected return.

Concept 2

The **variance** *of a random variable* equals the expected value of the squared random variable less the expected value of the random variable squared, $\text{Var}(r) = E(r^2) - [E(r)]^2$. It follows that: $[E(r)]^2 = E(r^2) - \text{Var}(r)$.

Concept questions: What is the second statistical moment? How do the first two moments about the origin affect the second statistical moment?

Concept 3

The **expected value of the product** *of two random variables* equals the product of their expectations, $E(rs) = E(r)E(s)$, if and only if the two random variables are statistically independent (uncorrelated, for instance).

Concept question: If we expect GM to have an earnings per share of $5 and a price-earnings ratio of 10 times, does that imply that the intrinsic value per share for GM is $50?

Concept 4

The **covariance** *of two random variables* equals the expected value of their product less the product of their expectations, $\text{Cov}(r, s) = E(rs) - E(r)E(s)$. It follows that the expected value of the product of two random variables equals the product of their expectations plus their covariance, $E(rs) = E(r)E(s) + \text{Cov}(r, s)$, if the two random variables are statistically dependent (that is, not zero correlated). The covariance of a random variable with a constant c equals zero, $\text{Cov}(r, c) = 0$.

Concept question: What is the covariance between the riskless rate R and the return from a risky asset r?

Concept 5

The **covariance of linear transformations** *of two random variables* is unaffected by adding or subtracting constants (like a, b, c, and d) to one or both of the variables. However, this covariance is increased by a multiple of any constants that are multiplied by the random variables. Symbolically, $\text{Cov}(a + br, c + ds) = bd\,\text{Cov}(r, s)$.

Concept question: If a law were passed requiring all mutual funds to reduce their management fees to zero, would this affect the riskiness of mutual fund investing?

Concept 6

If two random variables undergo linear transformations, their **correlation** is invariant, $\rho(a + br, c + ds) = \rho(r, s)$.

Concept question: If stock A is split 2-for-1 and stock B pays a 10 percent stock dividend, how should these changes in the unit of account affect the correlation between the returns from these two assets?

Concept 7

The **covariance of the sum** *of two random variables with a third random variable* equals the sum of their covariances, $\text{Cov}(r + s, m) = \text{Cov}(r, m) + \text{Cov}(s, m)$.

Concept question: When a portfolio is created to reduce risk by diversifying, are there any stocks that might increase (rather than decrease) the portfolio's risk? If so, what are the characteristics of the stocks?

Concept 8

The **variance** *of a weighted average of N random variables* equals the weighted sum of all their covariances. Symbolically,

$$\text{Var}\left(\sum_{i=1}^{N} x_i r_i\right) = \sum_{i=1}^{N}\sum_{j=1}^{N} x_i x_j \text{Cov}(r_i, r_j) \qquad \text{where } \text{Cov}(r_i, r_i) = \text{Var}(r_i)$$

where the N weights all sum to positive unity. The variance of an unweighted sum of N random variables equals the sum of all their covariances. Symbolically,

$$\text{Var}\left(\sum_{i=1}^{N} r_i\right) = \sum_{i=1}^{N}\sum_{j=1}^{N} \text{Cov}(r_i, r_j)$$

Concept question: Why isn't the variance of a portfolio equal to the sum of the variances of the assets in the portfolio?

Concept 9

The **third statistical moment,** denoted M_3, is the linear sum of the first three moments about the origin. Symbolically,

$$M_3 = \sum_{t=1}^{T} [r_t - E(r)]^3 = E(r^3) - 3E(r^2)E(r) + 2[E(r)]^3$$

The third statistical moment can be normalized by dividing it by the standard deviation cubed to obtain a **skewness** statistic that is void of any dimension, skew $= M_3/\sigma^3$. *Concept question:* If all other factors were held constant, would you rather have your portfolio of investments have positive skewness, zero skewness, or negative skewness?

Concept 10*

The **conditional probability** that r occurs given some value of x is defined as $P(r|x) = P(r$ and $x)/P(x)$.

The **conditional expectation** of the random variable r given that some value for x has occurred is defined as the expected value of all values of r that occur jointly with the specified value of x, divided by $P(x)$.

$$E(r|x) = \sum r \cdot P(r|x) = \frac{\sum r \cdot P(r \text{ and } x)}{P(x)}$$

Concept question: After determining that you expect GM stock to earn an $E(r_{GM}) = 10\%$ over the next few years, why should you revise your forecast if you subsequently learn that a recession is likely to start soon?

Concept 11*

A **linear regression** *model* of the form $r = a + bm + e$, $E(e) = 0$, may be thought of as being a conditional expectation, $E(r|m) = a + bm$, where a and b are constants. If r is a constant k, then $E(r|m) = k$. If m is a constant, then $E(r|m) = E(r)$. The expected value of a linear regression model of the form $r = a + bm + e$, $E(e) = 0$, equals a linear combination of the expected value of the explanatory variable, $E(r) = a + bE(m)$. *Concept question:* If you had to estimate the expected rates of return for 500 stocks, suggest a short-cut procedure that might be easier than estimating the probability distributions for 500 different stocks.

Concept 12†

The variance of a random variable may be **partitioned** if it can be divided up into mutually exclusive and exhaustive segments. For instance, the variance of a linear regression model of the form $r = a + bm + e$, $E(e) = 0$, may be partitioned into a segment that

---

*For more details about conditional expectations, see Robert B. Ash, *Real Analysis and Probability* (New York: Academic, 1972), chap. 6.
†For more details about the investment applications of the characteristic line model, $r = a + bm + e$, see Kalman J. Cohen and Gerald A. Pogue, "An Empirical Evaluation of Alternative Portfolio-Selection Models," *Journal of Business,* April 1967, vol. XL, no. 2, pp. 166–193.

is explained by the regression and a mutually exclusive residual that is unexplained by the regression. Symbolically,

$$\text{Var}(r) = \text{Var}(a + bm + e)$$
$$= b^2 \, \text{Var}(m) + \text{Var}(e)$$
$$= \text{explained variance} + \text{unexplained variance}$$

Concept question: Why should a diversified investor be more interested in a stock's beta than in its total variance?

Concept 13†

The **covariance of two linear sums** of the same explanatory variable can be stated in terms of their slope coefficients and the variance of their common explanatory variable. Symbolically, $\text{Cov}[(a + bm + e), (c + dm + u)] = bd \, \text{Var}(m)$.

Concept question: Given that there are $(n^2 - n)/2$ covariances between n risky assets, can you think of an easy way to obtain statistical estimates of all of these covariances?

---

†For more details about the investment applications of the characteristic line model, $r = a + bm + e$, see Kalman J. Cohen and Gerald A. Pogue, "An Empirical Evaluation of Alternative Portfolio-Selection Models," *Journal of Business*, April 1967, vol. XL, no. 2, pp. 166–193.

Appendix C

Mathematical

Theorems

**Theorem 1
Jensen's
Inequality**

Let C represent a real-valued function of the form $u = C(w)$; assume that w is a random variable and that $E(w)$ and $E[C(w)]$ exist and are finite.

The expected value of a *convex* function C of the random variable w is larger than or equal to a function C of the expected value of w. Symbolically, $E[C(w)] \geq C[E(w)]$.

Conversely, a *concave* function C of the expected value of w is larger than or equal to the expected value of the function C of w. Symbolically, $C[E(w)] \geq E[C(w)]$.

Concept question: Is the expected utility of returns from a risky investment equal to the utility of the expected return from the same investment?

**Theorem 2
The Law of Large
Numbers**

Let r_1, r_2, r_3, . . . be independent random variables that each have finite means and variances. Let S_n define the sum: $S_n = r_1 + r_2 + r_3 + \cdots + r_n$. The sum S_n approaches $E(S_n)$ as n increases. Symbolically, let e be some tiny positive value; then the limit below approaches zero as n approaches positive infinity.

$$\lim_{n \to \infty} \{[S_n - E(S_n)] > e\} \to 0 \qquad \text{for any tiny value of } e$$

After we divide S_n by n, this theorem tells us that as the sample gets larger *the sample mean asymptotically approaches the population mean.*
Concept question: Do you think that the Dow Jones Industrial Average (of 30 stocks) or the S&P 500 Stocks Composite Index is a better indicator of stock market conditions in the United States?

**Theorem 3
The Central Limit
Theorem**

Let r_1, r_2, r_3, . . . be independent random variables that are drawn from a population that has a finite mean u and constant variance σ^2. Let S_n represent the sum of a sample of size n: $S_n = r_1 + r_2 + r_3 + \cdots + r_n$. The sample mean is: $\bar{r} = S_n/n$. The sampling distribution of the random variable z approaches a normal distribution with mean zero and variance of $+1$ as n increases. Symbolically,

$$z = \frac{\bar{r} - u}{\sigma\sqrt{n}} \sim N(0,1)$$

The random variable z is called the **unit normal variable** in probability tables.

Concept question: If an investor selected a portfolio of heterogeneous assets that included options with highly skewed returns, real estate, common stocks, bonds, futures contracts, and foreign exchange, what sort of probability distribution of returns do you expect this investor's diversified portfolio should have?

Appendix D

Computer Software

Many instructors place a high priority on covering the investments material in the chapters of this book. These instructors believe that their students' best interests would not be well served if they took time away from the textbook material to discuss computers. As a result, *Investments: Analysis and Management,* 5th ed., was written to be used without computers. However, some instructors have a different view. A second group of investments instructors have requested computer software and investments data to accompany this book. This appendix addresses the requests of this latter group without forcing members of the first group to deal with computer applications.

This appendix describes several 5.25-inch floppy diskettes for an IBM-PC or compatible that will be given away free to those who adopt this book *if the instructor requests it.* Using the book is in no way tied to or dependent on the use of these computer applications. However, at the request of an adopting instructor, the local McGraw-Hill salesperson will supply free copies of the floppy disks described below.

The package of investments analysis data and software is large, comprehensive, and professionally prepared. If one of the pieces of software fails to work, it is because of system-level differences between your personal computer and the standard IBM-PC. Such incompatibilities are typically easy to circumvent by someone who is knowledgeable about personal computers. All of the software is designed to do different kinds of investments analysis. The disks contain:

1. Lotus 1-2-3 templates
2. BASIC language programs
3. Mutual fund data and programs
4. Trendline technical analysis data and programs
5. Sophisticated Quadratic Program (QP)

These disks will produce color displays if the user's computer has color capabilities. None of the software is copy protected, so users can make copies for everyone in the class. All the programs are menu-driven and require no previous computer experience.

If an instructor adopts *Investments: Analysis and Management,* 5th ed., and wants the computer software, that instructor should contact the McGraw-Hill salesperson for your college.

The diskette on which the programs come may be read directly into an IBM-PC or compatible personal computer, or uploaded to a mainframe computer for use there.

Diskette of Mutual Fund Data and Investment Analysis Programs

A diskette containing data on hundreds of different mutual funds provides data and a computer program to supply answers to questions that mutual fund investors ask.

1. *Easy to use:* The user need know absolutely nothing about computers to be able to use the mutual fund diskette. The user merely needs to type the letters "MFS-EQ" and the diskette's internal program starts itself. Once it starts, the diskette is menu-driven, so the user need only select which mutual fund or category of mutual funds is of interest. The mutual fund diskette then automatically presents the user with another menu from which to select the type of analysis desired. Most of the computations a mutual fund investor might want (such as average rates of return, beta coefficients, statements of the fund's investment objective, etc.) are stored on the mutual fund diskette. The hundreds of mutual funds on the diskette can be examined on-screen for one or more characteristics that interest the mutual fund analyst.

2. *Business Week's Mutual Fund Scoreboard: Business Week* magazine prepared the mutual fund disk and has sold thousands of subscriptions at $199 per year. *Business Week* calls the diskette its Mutual Fund Scoreboard. Two different Mutual Fund Scoreboard subscriptions are available—one covers the mutual funds that invest only in common stocks and the other one covers those mutual funds that invest only in fixed-income securities. A subscription to either Mutual Fund Scoreboard costs $199 per annum, a subscription to both the Fixed and Equity diskettes costs $229 per annum. For subscription information please write to:

   Business Week Mutual Fund Diskettes
   P.O. Box 1597
   Fort Lee, New Jersey 07024
   Fax: (201) 461-9808

   The free diskette provided by McGraw-Hill Book Company is the Mutual Fund Scoreboard for common stocks. The sample of portfolios on the diskette contains almost every common stock mutual fund in existence in the United States. Most of the facts on the diskette (such as the load fee, the total assets, etc.) are from a recent year. In addition, some historical data about each fund (such as average rates of return) are on the disk too. Up-to-date disks are prepared monthly by *Business Week* for those who wish to pay the Mutual Fund Scoreboard subscription fee to obtain current data. Current updates cannot be obtained for free.

3. *Data:* The mutual fund diskette has several monitor screens full of data on each of its mutual funds. Data about each fund's management fee, load fee,

redemption fee, total assets, year-to-year change in total assets, address, phone number, principal holdings, performance ranking, investment recommendation, and other facts are available for every fund. Average rates of return over different periods for both the fund and the S&P 500 stock market average are presented for direct comparison. Beta systematic risk statistics, the portfolio's turnover rate, average rates of return over various years, and other data are available too.

4. *Screening:* The mutual fund diskette contains a screening program that can be used to call up either an individual fund or all mutual funds that meet selected criteria. Any funds meeting the desired screening criteria will instantly be listed on the screen.

5. *Downloading data:* Data on the mutual fund disk can be transferred (or exported or downloaded) to Lotus 1-2-3 or other computer programs for further analysis. Menu-driven programs are provided on the diskette to download the mutual fund data.

6. *Color monitors:* This diskette operates with either a monochrome or color monitor (that is, viewing screen).

7. *Textbook supplement:* The mutual fund diskette supplements Chapter 21 of *Investments: Analysis and Management,* 5th ed., by providing empirical data about numerous mutual funds. Chapter 21 defines technical terms used on the diskette.

8. *Copying the diskette:* The *Business Week* Mutual Fund Scoreboard is not copy protected. The diskette may be duplicated and used for educational purposes by those who adopt *Investments: Analysis and Management,* 5th ed.

Diskette of BASIC Language Programs for Investments Analysis

A diskette containing BASIC language programs to do the following kinds of financial computations is available. The diskette is entirely menu-driven and requires no computer programming skills in order for the user to perform the financial analysis.

Program 1

Program 1 can be used to generate a page out of a bond table (or bond price book) for any combination of coupon rate and years-to-maturity that the user requests. Different tables for annual and semiannual compounding can be tabulated.

Programs 2 to 6

Programs 2 to 6 include the following computations for analysis of an individual bond: Program 2—present value, Program 3—yield-to-maturity, Program 4—duration, Program 5—realized compound yields, and Program 6—bond-price volatility analysis.*

*Most of the programs were written by Richard Bookstaber, Ph.D., currently a vice president at the Morgan Stanley investment banking firm. The asterisked programs were previously published in Richard Bookstaber, *The Complete Investment Book* (Chicago, Ill.: Scott, Foresman, 1985) and are reproduced here with copyright permission.

Program 7 Program 7 calculates an interest rate risk immunized portfolio of bonds. It uses linear programming to simultaneously analyze the durations of different potential bond investments and determine exactly which bonds and in what proportions should be included in a portfolio to immunize it against interest rate risk.*

Program 8 Program 8 calculates the present value of future cash dividends.

Program 9 Program 9 reads in the market prices of one or more common stocks and the simultaneous observations on some market index and calculates statistics such as the period-by-period rates of return, beta coefficients, average rates of return, standard deviations, correlations with the market, and other statistics.

Program 10 Program 10 does put and call computations based on the Black-Scholes option pricing model to include: (*a*) call premiums (or prices) and (*b*) put premiums (or prices).*

Program 11 Program 11 does Markowitz portfolio analysis. The risk, return, and weights of the assets in efficient portfolios are calculated and displayed. This is a quadratic programming (QP) program.*

Diskette of Lotus 1-2-3 Templates for Investments Analysis

A diskette containing Lotus 1-2-3 templates for investments analysis is provided. You need not know how to use Lotus 1-2-3 to use these templates; they are all menu-driven, so you need only select the calculation you want from a menu and then interactively supply the needed values as they are requested. Each diskette contains templates to do the following kinds of investments analysis.

Template 1 BONDTAB generates a page out of a bond table (or bond price book) for any combination of coupon rate and years-to-maturity that the user requests. Different tables for annual and semiannual compounding are available.

Template 2 BOND1 analyzes an individual bond, including the following computations for either annual or semiannual compounding: (*a*) present value, (*b*) yield-to-maturity, and (*c*) duration. Special consideration is given to convertible bonds and after-tax results.

*Most of the programs were written by Richard Bookstaber, Ph.D., currently a vice president at the Morgan Stanley investment banking firm. The asterisked programs were previously published in Richard Bookstaber, *The Complete Investment Book* (Chicago, Ill.: Scott, Foresman, 1985) and are reproduced here with copyright permission.

Template 3   BOND2 analyzes an individual bond with semiannual compounding, including the following computations: (*a*) present value, (*b*) yield-to-maturity, and/or (*c*) duration. BOND2 is a simplified version of BOND1.

Template 4   STKVAL analyzes common stock that has a constant perpetual growth rate, including calculation of (*a*) the present value of future dividends, (*b*) the required rate of return (or discount rate) implicit in a given stock price, and/or (*c*) the growth rate implicit in any given stock price.

Template 5   2STAGE analyzes a common stock that has two different stages of growth, including calculation of (*a*) the present value of future dividends, (*b*) the required rate of return (or discount rate) implicit in a given stock price, and/or (*c*) the growth rate implicit in any given stock price.

Template 6   3PHASE analyzes a common stock that has three different stages of growth, including calculation of (*a*) the present value of future dividends, (*b*) the required rate of return (or discount rate) implicit in a given stock price, and/or (*c*) the growth rate implicit in any given stock price.*

Template 7   OPTION1 performs simple put and call computations based on the Black-Scholes option pricing model, including (*a*) call premiums (or prices) and (*b*) put premiums (or prices).

Template 8   OPTION2 performs detailed put and call computations based on the Black-Scholes option pricing model, including (*a*) call premiums (or prices) and (*b*) put premiums (or prices). Specific expiration times and cash dividend payments may also be analyzed. OPTION2 is a sophisticated version of OPTION1.

Template 9   MARKPRT performs Markowitz portfolio analysis of a two-asset portfolio. The risk, return, and weights of the assets in portfolios are calculated, and the resulting efficient frontier can be displayed graphically. Either efficient or inefficient portfolios can be analyzed.

Template 10   PEMODEL calculates price-earnings ratios for any risk-adjusted discount rate k, growth rate g, and a number of years n of growth desired.

---

*This three-phase algorithm is not discussed in this book. It was included for comparison purposes and to please Moldovsky aficionados.

Templates 11, 12, ...

These templates contain investments problems that may be solved with the Lotus 1-2-3 templates above. These problem templates have names like PROBMRK for problems to do with Markowitz portfolio analysis, PROBOND for bond problems, PROBOPS for put and call option problems, and PROBSTK for common stock problems.

Each Lotus 1-2-3 template generates either monochrome or color displays, has a one- or two-page introduction, has problems and answers available for students, and generates graphs to illustrate the analysis if desired. The print screen (PrtSc) key can be used to print out the introduction, problems, and/or solutions to the problems on paper, if desired.

A Diskette from Trendline to Do Technical Analysis

The Trendline Division of Standard & Poor's has provided a diskette to supplement Chapter 17, entitled "Technical Analysis." The diskette contains some of the software and data that Trendline purveys to its subscribers. If you would like to obtain current data and/or software to do more kinds of technical analysis, you may subscribe by contacting:

Trendline Division
Standard & Poor's Corporation
25 Broadway
New York, New York 10004

The Trendline disk contains data on 20 well-known stocks (such as GM, IBM, and Exxon) that may be graphed alone or together (for comparison purposes) on different selections of axes. Various moving averages and other indicators are listed on menus and may be selected for calculation and display at the user's command. If your hardware permits, the diskette produces color displays. Additional services such as (*a*) data on additional securities, (*b*) up-to-the-minute data, (*c*) the ability to perform more different kinds of technical analysis, or (*d*) other services from Trendline will not be provided for free, but may be purchased from Trendline.

A Diskette with a Sophisticated Quadratic Program

Professor Douglas McCann has written a sophisticated quadratic programming (QP) computer program in the highly efficient C language. He is graciously making demonstration copies available to us for free. The demonstration copy is compiled and has been constrained so that it will only analyze a maximum of ten assets. McCann's QP handles the full covariance matrix and (unlike simpler QP codes) allows constraints on each variable. Professor McCann sells this QP for $2500 without the constraint that limits it to ten assets.

Appendix E

Investment Analysis
with Hand-Held
Calculators*

Hand-held financial calculators are widely used in financial analysis. This appendix explains some fundamental investment applications with two of the more popular calculators.

A. The Texas Instruments' Student Business Analyst, the BA 35 hereafter, has a list price of $28.

B. The Hewlett Packard Advanced Financial Programmable calculator, the HP 12C, has a list price of $95.

Hand-held financial calculators have built-in financial functions. These financial functions are addressed with five *keys* on both the BA 35 and HP 12C. These five keys and their definitions are:

1. ⬚ or Ⓝ is the number of periods.
2. ⬚ or %i is the rate of return (entered as a percent).
3. PMT is payment (a cashflow, like a bond's coupon).
4. PV is present value, and.
5. FV is future value.

Both the BA 35 and HP 12C have continuous memories. Values stay in the memory of the calculator even when it is turned off (if the battery is charged). The continuous memory feature is helpful, but it can also cause problems if irrelevant values from previous calculations are not cleared out of the memory. The memories are called *registers*. To clear the HP 12C registers, you must use the gold-colored ⬚ key. The ⬚

*This appendix draws heavily on the expertise of Professor Richard Taylor, C.F.A., Ph.D., Arkansas State University.

key permits you to use the gold-lettered functions. For example, when you press [f] clear [REG], you will clear the registers of the HP 12C. In a similar manner, the blue-colored [g] key allows you to use the blue-lettered functions. With the BA 35, pressing the [2nd] key allows you to execute the functions appearing above the keys. For example, pressing [2nd] [FIN] puts you in the finance mode and clears the financial registers.

You may want to control the number of decimal places displayed on your calculator. With the BA 35 you have two choices—either two decimal places or a variable number. Push in sequence [2nd] [STO] to set the level at two. Note that "Dec 2" will appear in the face of the calculator when 2 decimal places are being used. By pushing [2nd] [STO] again, the setting is reversed and you return to the variable decimal mode. With the HP 12C, push [f] followed by the desired number of decimal places; for example, [f] 3 sets the level to 3.

The following pages explain several financial applications for both calculators—time value of money, a bond's yield-to-maturity, stock analysis, geometric mean, arithmetic mean, and standard deviation. The HP 12C features that are available also include simple regression and other forms of analysis.

The Time Value of Money

To begin with, consider four time value of money applications: the present and future values of single sums, and the present and future values of annuities. Some combination of the five financial keys listed above can be used to accomplish any of these calculations. With both calculators, if you know three of the four variables in question, the calculator will solve for the unknown fourth variable. You simply key in the values of the three variables you know and then properly push the button or series of buttons to solve for the value that you do not know. Let's illustrate with examples.

Future Value If you place $100,000 in a savings account that earns 12% for 15 years, how much will you have in the account at the end of 15 years? The solution is:

BA 35	HP 12C
1. [ON/C] [2nd] [STO]	1. [ON] [f] 2
2. [2nd] [FIN] (clears memory)	2. [f] clear [FIN]
3. 100,000 [PV]	3. 100,000 [CHS] [PV]
4. 15 [N]	4. 15 [n]
5. 12 [%i]	5. 12 [i]
6. CPT [FV]	6. [FV]
(answer $547,356.57)	(answer $547,356.58)

The [CHS] means "change sign" and is used on the HP 12C to distinguish between cash and flows and outflows.

Present Value What is the present value of $200,000 to be received in 12 years at an interest rate of 9%?

BA 35	HP 12C
1. 200,000 [FV]	1. 200,000 [CHS] [FV]
2. 12 [N]	2. 12 [n]
3. 9 [%i]	3. 9 [i]
4. CPT [PV]	4. [PV]
(answer $71,106.95)	(answer $71,106.95)

Note that since we are already in the finance mode and have the number of decimal places set to two, it is not necessary to repeat the initialization steps. Also, since the same four keys are being used, it is not necessary to clear the calculator.

Future Value of an Annuity   If you place $2000 at the end of each year for 20 years for retirement purposes in a savings account, how much will you have accumulated at the end of 20 years if the return is assumed to be 10% per year?

BA 35	HP 12C
1. [2nd] [FIN] (clears memory)	1. [f] clear [FIN]
2. 2000 [+/-] [PMT]	2. 2000 [CHS] [PMT]
3. 20 [N]	3. 20 [n]
4. 10 [%i]	4. 10 [i]
5. [CPT] [FV]	5. [FV]
(answer $114,550)	(answer $114,550)

Present Value of an Annuity   Mr. Jay expects to receive $10,000 at the end of each year for the next 10 years. What is the present value of these cashflows if the appropriate rate of return is 14%?

BA 35	HP 12C
1. [2nd] [FIN] (clears memory)	1. [f] clear [FIN]
2. 10,000 [PMT]	2. 10,000 [CHS] [PMT]
3. 14 [%i]	3. 14 [i]
4. 10 [N]	4. 10 [n]
5. [CPT] [PV]	5. [PV]
(answer $52,161.16)	(answer $52,161.16)

Bond Analysis

Calculating a bond's yield-to-maturity will be explained after learning how to find the present value of a bond.

Bond Valuation Determine the present value (or price) of the bonds issued by the Mack Corporation that have 15 years until maturity. The bonds have a coupon rate of 12% (semiannual interest) and a maturity value of $1000. If the yield-to-maturity for bonds of this type is 14%, what is the price of the bond issue?

BA 35	HP 12C
1. [2nd] [FIN]	1. [i] clear [FIN]
2. 1000 [FV]	2. 1000 [FV]
3. 60 [PMT]	3. 60 [PMT]
4. 30 [N]	4. 30 [n]
5. 7 [%i]	5. 7 [i]
6. [CPT] [PV]	6. [PV]
(answer 875.91)	(answer −875.91)

A Bond's Yield-to-Maturity Find the yield-to-maturity of the Mack Corporation bonds given above if the current price is $1100.

BA 35	HP 12C
1. [2nd] [FIN]	1. [i] clear [FIN]
2. 1000 [FV]	2. 1000 [CHS] [FV]
3. 60 [PMT]	3. 60 [CHS] [PMT]
4. 30 [N]	4. 30 [n]
5. 1100 [PV]	5. 1100 [PV]
6. [CPT] [%i]	6. [i]
(5.33 × 2 = 10.65% annual rate)	(5.33 × 2 = 10.65% annual rate)

Since the same five keys are being used, it is not necessary to clear the calculator to solve the next problem. For example, if you wanted to compute the yield-to-maturity that is implied by a different bond price while all other factors remained unchanged, all you would have to do would be to enter a new value for [PV] (the price) and compute [i]. The longer approach was used to show how to compute a yield-to-maturity from the beginning. Also note that for the HP 12C the signs of the cash flows in steps 2, 3, and 5 could all be reversed without changing the solution.

Stock Analysis

The BA 35 and the HP 12C calculators can be used to value stocks and find the investor's rate of return from a stock investment.

Stock Value Suppose investors expect to receive the following stream of cash-flows if they purchase a share of the XYZ Corporation's stock: $2.00, $2.50, and $3.00 in total dividends at the end of years 1, 2, and 3, respectively. The investors also expect to sell the stock for $30 per share at the end of year 3. If the investors require a return of 15%, what price should they pay for the stock?

BA 35	HP 12C
1. ON/C 2nd FIN	1. f clear REG
2. 0 STO	2. f 2
3. 2nd STO	3. 15 i
4. 15 %i	4. 0 g CFo
5. 2 FV	5. 2 g CFj
6. 1 N CPT PV SUM	6. 2.5 g CFj
7. 2.5 FV	7. 33 g CFj
8. 2 N CPT PV SUM	8. f NPV
9. 33 FV	(answer $25.33 per share)
10. 3 N CPT PV SUM	
11. RCL	
(answer $25.33 per share)	

The HP 12C uses its built-in net present value routine that is called by NPV .

A Stock's Return   If the investor in the previous section pays $24 per share for the stock, what return will be earned? The BA 35 has no built-in internal rate of return (IRR) function, so the procedure is like that given in the section entitled ''Bond Valuation,'' except that you should select a return, calculate the present value of the expected cashflows, and compare the calculated present value to the stock's price. Essentially, you find the IRR by trial and error. When you find a discount rate that makes the present value of the expected cashflows equal to the price, you have found the IRR. The HP 12C solution is much easier.

With the HP 12C, the built-in IRR routine is used as follows:

HP 12C
1. f clear REG
2. 24 CHS g CFo
3. 2 g CFj
4. 2.5 g CFj
5. 33 g CFj
6. f IRR
(answer 17.24%)

Means and Standard Deviations

Financial calculators can also be used to calculate common statistics.

Geometric Mean   The geometric mean, arithmetic mean, and standard deviation can easily be calculated with the BA 35 and HP 12C. Suppose the ABC Corporation had the following equally likely annual returns:

Year	Returns, %
1	−5
2	10
3	15

To calculate the geometric mean return, denoted *gr,* the following formula should be used:

$$gr = \{[(1 + r_1)(1 + r_2) \cdots (1 + r_N)]^{1/N} - 1.0\} \times 100$$

The above formula should be applied to the example in the following manner:

$$gr = [(0.95 \times 1.1 \times 1.15)^{1/3} - 1.0] \times 100$$

The two calculators can be used to obtain the following solution:

BA 35	HP 12C
1. ON/C ON/C	1. ON *i* 4
2. .95 ⊠	2. .95 ENTER
3. 1.1 ⊠	3. 1.1 ⊠
4. 1.15 ⊠	4. 1.15 ⊠
5. y^x	5. 3
6. 3	6. 1/x
7. 1/x	7. y^x
8. =	8. 1
9. − 1	9. −
10. =	10. 100
11. ⊠ 100	11. ⊠
12. =	(answer 6.3175%)
(answer 6.32%)	

Standard Deviation   Calculate the standard deviation and arithmetic mean as follows:

BA 35	HP 12C
1. ON/C ON/C	1. *i* 4
2. 2nd STAT	2. *i* clear Σ
3. 5 +/− Σ+	3. 5 CHS Σ+
4. 10 Σ+	4. 10 Σ+
5. 15 Σ+	5. 15 Σ+
6. x̄ (mean)	6. g x̄ (mean)
(answer 6.67%)	(answer 6.6667%)
7. σn−1 (sample standard deviation answer 10.41%)	7. g s (sample standard deviation answer 10.4083%)
8. σn (population standard deviation answer 8.50%)	

To calculate the population standard deviation with the HP 12C, push the following keys in sequence: g x̄ Σ+ g s. The answer is 8.4984%. This sequence should be executed after the sample standard deviation has been determined.

Linear Regression

Simple linear regression can be performed with the HP 12C. One dependent variable (usually called y) and one independent variable (or explanatory variable, usually called x) are used. An example will illustrate this. Suppose you want to calculate the beta coefficient for the returns of the QRT Corporation with the following data:

Year	Stock QRT returns,% (y)	Market returns,% (x)
1	15	17
2	−5	−7
3	9	11
4	12	14

The procedure on the HP 12C is as follows:

1. f clear Σ	This clears statistical registers.
2. 15 ENTER	1st y value
3. 17 Σ+	1st x value
4. 5 CHS ENTER	2nd y value
5. 7 CHS Σ+	2nd x value
6. 9 ENTER	3rd y value
7. 11 Σ+	3rd x value
8. 12 ENTER	4th y value
9. 14 Σ+	4th x value
10. 0 g ŷ,r	Calculates A intercept.
(answer .5806)	
11. STO 0	
12. 0 g x̂,r	
13. CHS	
14. RCL 0 x≷y +	Slope or beta value.
(answer .8194)	

Therefore, the characteristic line is in the form:

$$y = a + bx$$

$$r_i = .5806 + .8194r_M$$

After the regression equation is derived, the correlation can also be easily calculated. To calculate the correlation coefficient, press g ŷ,r x≷y or g x̂,r x≷y. In the above regression, the correlation coefficient is .9987.

Analyzing Bonds Between Interest Payment Dates

One of the most useful built-in finance functions on the HP 12C is the bond function. A present value and yield-to-maturity can be calculated for a bond between interest payment dates. To show how this can be accomplished, we will solve the following two problems.

You are considering purchasing a 9% Jones Corporation bond today (March 30, 1990). If the bond matures on June 4, 2004, what price should you pay for the bond? Assume the appropriate YTM is 12%. The sequence of steps to follow on the HP 12C is as follows:

1.	f 4	Set decimal to 4.
2.	f clear REG	Clears registers.
3.	12 i	Enters yield-to-maturity.
4.	9 PMT	Enters coupon rate.
5.	g M.DY	Set to month-day-year format.
6.	3.301990 ENTER	Purchase date.
7.	6.042004	Maturity date.
8.	f PRICE	Calculate bond's price as a %
	(answer 79.7581)	of par—that is, $797.58.
9.	+	Bond's price plus accrued
	(answer 82.6262)	interest (in dollars, $826.26).

Suppose in the previous problem that you know the price (as a percent of par) but do not know the yield-to-maturity. What is the yield-to-maturity of the Jones Corporation bond if its price is 110 percent of par?

1.	f clear REG
2.	110 PV
3.	9 PMT
4.	3.301990 ENTER
5.	6.042004
6.	f YTM
	(answer 7.8184%)

The above calculations are for semiannual bond coupons and a 365-day year.[1]

[1]For some additional HP 12C programming examples, see Richard Taylor, "Option Valuation for Alternative Instruments with Black-Scholes Model: A Pedagogical Note," *Journal of Financial Education,* Fall 1987, pp. 73–77; and R. Taylor, "Bond Duration Analysis: A Pedagogical Note," *Financial Analysts Journal,* July 3/Aug. 1987, pp. 71–72. See also W. Scott Bauman, Jaroslaw Komarynsky, and John C. Siska Goytre, *Investment Securities Program Guide Using the HP-12C* (New York: McGraw-Hill, 1987). For a good 79-page, double-spaced, typewritten manuscript also see "Quick Acquaint Course for the Hewlett-Packard HP-12C Electronic Calculator," by Professors Stephen D. Messner and Mark H. Goldman, Finance Department, School of Business, University of Connecticut, Storrs, CT.

Name Index

Subject Index

Frequently Used Symbols

$E(x)$ = expected value of x

$E(r)$ = expected rate of return

$Var(r) = \sigma^2$ = variance of returns = total risk

$Cov(x, y) = \sigma_{xy}$ = covariance between x and y

ρ = rho = correlation coefficient

C_t = dollars of consumption at time $t = Y_t - I_t$

Y_t = dollars of income in period t

I_t = dollars invested at time $t = Y_t - C_t$

W = dollars of wealth

$Max(x, y)$ = maximum value of x or y, whichever is greater

$Min(x, y)$ = minimum value of x or y, whichever is less

q_t = rate of inflation in period t

r_t = nominal rate of return in period $t = rr_t + q_t$

rr_t = real rate of return in period $t = r_t - q_t$

R = riskless rate of return, $Var(R) = 0$

$RR = 1 + R = 1$ plus the riskless rate of return

u = number of utils

$U(x)$ = a mathematical utility function

F = bond's face value, or par value

i = coupon rate of interest

c = dollar value of a bond's coupon $= iF$

YTM = yield-to-maturity

AYTM = approximate yield-to-maturity

Δ = delta = finite change

MD = Macaulay's duration